Encyclopedia of
Constitutional Amendments, Proposed Amendments, and Amending Issues,

1789–2002
Second Edition

Encyclopedia of
Constitutional Amendments, Proposed Amendments, and Amending Issues,

1789–2002
Second Edition

John R. Vile

A B C 🝞 C L I O

Santa Barbara, California
Denver, Colorado
Oxford, England

Library of Congress Cataloging-in-Publication Data

Vile, John R.
    Encyclopedia of constitutional amendments, proposed amendments, and amending issues, 1789–2002 / John R. Vile. — 2nd ed.
        p.   cm.
    Includes bibliographical references and index.
    ISBN 1-85109-428-8 (hardcover : alk. paper) — e-book ISBN 1-85109-433-4
    1. Constitutional amendments—United States.   I. Title.

KF4557.V555 2003
342.73'03—dc21   2003001839

07 06 05 04 03   10 9 8 7 6 5 4 3 2 1

This book is also available on the World Wide Web as an e-book. Visit abc-clio.com for details.

ABC-CLIO, Inc.
130 Cremona Drive, P.O. Box 1911
Santa Barbara, California 93116-1911

This book is printed on acid-free paper ∞.
Manufactured in the United States of America

*This book is dedicated to
three great teachers, scholars,
and gentlemen:*

*Henry J. Abraham
Alpheus T. Mason
Walter F. Murphy*

❖ CONTENTS ❖

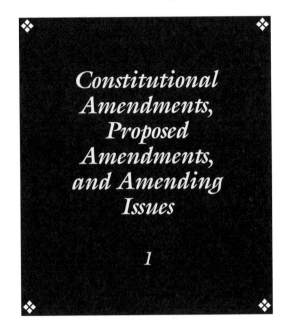

Constitutional
Amendments,
Proposed
Amendments,
and Amending
Issues

1

❖ FOREWORD ❖

I am one of those people who believe that the single most important provision of any constitution is its amending clause. This is not, obviously, to deny the importance of how a given constitution allocates decision-making authority or protects individual rights. But unless one is deluded into believing that a given constitutional text, whether with regard to allocating power or recognizing rights, is doubly perfect—that is, perfect with regard to the issues and contexts within which it was originally written and then perfect throughout time, when both issues and contexts might well be quite different—one must agree that changes even in foundational documents will be necessary. Indeed, I drew the title for a book that I edited, *Responding to Imperfection: The Theory and Practice of Constitutional Amendment,* from a letter written by George Washington to his nephew, Bushrod Washington: "The warmest friends and best supporters the Constitution has do not contend that it is free from imperfections; but they found them unavoidable and are sensible if evil is likely to arise there from, the remedy must come hereafter." Although many have insisted on portraying the founders as "demigods" whose views on constitutional wisdom we are obligated to follow, Washington himself—who was, of course, president of the Constitutional Convention in Philadelphia before becoming the first president of the United States—was becomingly more modest. "I do not think," he wrote, "we are more inspired, have more wisdom, or possess more virtue, than those who will come after us." Fortunately "there is a Constitutional door open" to provide any necessary remedies, as future generations, themselves inspired by their own mixtures of wisdom and experience, will take advantage of Article V. From this perspective, one pays most fealty to the Father of our Country by contemplating the potential presence of imperfections and then working politically to amend the Constitution as a means of truly achieving the "more perfect Union" that is the ultimate aspiration of anyone who joins in our constitutional covenant.

Anyone who shares my—and Washington's!—view of the importance of amendment knows that John Vile is nothing less than a treasure. He is by far our most persistent student of amendment, with unending fascination for everything thought by anyone—whether truly wise or really quite daffy—to be an imperfection and what, therefore, has been proposed as a responsive amendment. But, of course, proposal is quite literally only the beginning of a complex process, and Professor Vile is well aware of every last facet of the process and its implications for the success or failure of proposals for reform.

Professor Vile is also aware of every theoretical debate surrounding amendment. He mentions one of them in his preface: Does Article V set out an exclusive process of amendment per se, or an exclusive procedure only for something we might call "textual" amendments? The very use of this adjective is designed to suggest the possibility that textual amendments are only a subset of a wider set of amendments that include, in their complete description, what can only be described as nontextual amendments that have entered our notion of what the Constitution means even in the absence of a formal Article V process. Another theoretical question, which he addressed in his own contribution to *Responding to Imperfection,* is whether the Constitution is open to limitless change, so long as the formalities of Article V are followed. This allows the possibility that anything might be added to the Constitution should the requisite number of votes be cast in support. That is, the only protection against the reinstitution of slavery, the establishment of the United States as a religious theocracy, or whatever else may be one's worst nightmare is the procedural difficulty established by Article V. But some constitutions, including the German constitution, rule out certain categories of amendments—in Germany's case, any amendment that would undercut the constitution's commitment to protecting "human dignity"—and at least some persons have suggested the same is true of our own Constitution, whether or not it is spelled out clearly.

And, of course, there is the Constitution's wild card, the Article V procedure by which a brand-new convention can be called by Congress on petition of two-thirds of the states. (Presumably, Congress has no discretion in the matter once the states unite in their call.) Although there is little doubt that the generation of the framers anticipated that this would actually become part of the American system of government—after all, most states have experienced constitutional conventions and, indeed, the replacement of an outmoded constitution by one thought more suitable to the times—this part of Article V has, of course, basically become a dead letter. One of the reasons is that the Constitution gives no clue at all as to the procedures that would structure a new convention. For starters, would a second convention be required to adopt the same voting rule—one

state, one vote—as that followed by the framers in Philadelphia? With regard to these issues as well Professor Vile's encyclopedia provides essential guidance for any scholar or layperson trying to wrestle with the truly knotty problems posed by this aspect of our Constitution.

There is little point in going on. It is enough to scan the List of Entries to appreciate the comprehensiveness of Professor Vile's grasp of his subject. Most encyclopedias are the handiwork of an editor who commissions others to write the entries. There was no need to follow that route in this case, for anyone who thinks about constitutional amendment knows that the expert—the possessor of literally encyclopedic knowledge—is John Vile. We are all fortunate to have this absolutely up-to-date second edition in hand even as we can be confident that, if developments warrant, Professor Vile will be busy preparing a third edition for scholars (and others) who depend on him!

Professor Sanford Levinson, W. St. John Garwood and W. St. John Garwood Jr. Regents Chair in Law, University of Texas Law School

❖ ABOUT THIS EDITION ❖

How This Edition Differs from the First and from Works by Other Scholars

This is not the first time that I have published a second edition of a work, but it is the first time that I faced such a formidable obstacle. Recognizing the prominent place that the first edition of this work had come to play in high school, college, and public libraries throughout the nation as well as a resource for individuals with scholarly interest in the subject, my editors at ABC-CLIO insisted that I should not reissue this book until it contained at least one-fourth to one-third new material. As individuals running a business, the editors understandably wanted to be sure that there would be sufficient incentive for those who already owned a first edition of the book to buy the second.

I was just as interested in selling new copies of this book as the editors and just as concerned about giving librarians and scholars a strong incentive to buy the second edition. At least initially, however, the goal of including one-third new material did not seem realistic. How could a volume that initially covered the period from 1789 to 1995 be that significantly expanded if it were only to cover an additional seven years?

What initially appeared to be a formidable obstacle proved ultimately to be a valued opportunity and a spur to deeper scholarship. Although engaged in a number of nonrelated projects since 1996, I have continued to write about and to collect materials on the amending process. In returning to this project, I found that materials on the subjects of the prior edition are significantly richer than I recognized at the time. Moreover, I have continued to locate not only new, but also older, published proposals for new constitutions and amendments with which I was previously unaware, including one by a West Point cadet that was first published in 1815 (see Willard, Simon, Jr.), that appears never to have been explicated by another scholar. Since 1996 several organizations have been formed to pro-

vide for amendment of the U.S. Constitution through initiative and referendum mechanisms like those that have long been established at the state level, and some of these are stirring renewed excitement about the potential of the amending process. They, too, have found a place in this second edition.

The first edition of my *Encyclopedia* was published at a time when others were also turning renewed attention to the amending process. Professor David Kyvig's *Explicit and Authentic Acts* (1996a), another important contribution to our understanding of existing amendments, came out in the same year as the *Encyclopedia*'s first edition. In 2000 Kris Palmer in turn edited another major review of existing amendments in his *Constitutional Amendments, 1789 to the Present*, with Pendergast, Pendergast, and Sousanis subsequently publishing a three-volume survey of amendments under the editorship of Elizabeth Shaw Grunow the following year (2001) entitled *Constitutional Amendments: From Freedom of Speech to Flag Burning*.

Valuable though these other resources are, the second edition of the *Encyclopedia of Constitutional Amendments* is unique on today's market in its central focus on short explanatory essays that group and describe not only existing amendments but also proposed amendments that were not successful and proposed new or revised constitutions. Such proposals continue to multiply and the ability to find them is increasing with technological advances. Once limited to books and pamphlets, proposals for new constitutions and amendments are increasingly finding their way onto the Internet, and they too have been included in this volume.

In this second edition, I have added approximately 100 new entries and revised a majority of the others. I am confident that anyone who fairly compares this second edition with the first will see substantial additions and revisions and that this second edition will remain an indispensable tool for those who are interested in constitutional amendments, proposed amendments, and amending issues.

Previous Works on the Subject

State ratifying conventions and members of Congress began proposing amendments to the Constitution even before all the states had joined the Union, and such proposals have continued at a steady pace ever since. Individual proposals, especially those in the Bill of Rights and later in the post–Civil War period, were often subject to intense dispute and occasional scholarly analysis, but no major compilation of amendments proposed in Congress was prepared until 1896. At this time, Professor Herman Ames, soon to be a historian at the University of Pennsylvania, published a book, which had begun as his Ph.D. dissertation, covering the constitutional amendments that had been proposed in Congress during the nation's first 100 years. The American Historical Association awarded this book its first prestigious Justin Winsor Prize, and the volume's continuing relevance was recognized with its replication in 1970 and again in 2002. In addition to describing the subjects of proposed amendments in his text, Ames included a list of the topics of the 1,736 amendments proposed in the nation's first century. He also included a comprehensive index and bibliography. One hundred years later, his book is still readable and useful.

In 1929 M. A. Musmanno, then a Pennsylvania lawyer and later a judge, analyzed the 1,370 amendments that had been proposed since Ames wrote his book. In part because Musmanno's volume was published as a government document and in part because it covered a shorter time period and was therefore less comprehensive than Ames's, it is less well known but is still a valuable resource.

Although literally hundreds of articles, essays, and books have subsequently addressed the subject of amendments and proposed amendments, no author sought to survey the field in the same comprehensive manner as did Ames and Musmanno until I published the first edition of this *Encyclopedia* in 1996. Once between the time that Ames and Musmanno wrote (Tansill 1926) and several

times afterward, lists of amendments proposed in Congress during designated periods have been published (*Proposed Amendments* 1957, 1963, 1969; Davis 1985; Harris 1992). Just last year, this author edited a set of three volumes that has republished and updated existing listings of these proposed amendments along with Ames's and Musmanno's analyses. I also included a compilation of state petitions to Congress for constitutional conventions that relied largely on a compilation by Michael Stokes Paulsen (1993) (also see Van Sickle and Boughey 1990). These lists and analyses, as well as more recent entries that are now available on the Internet, form the starting point and vital foundation of my study.

From the time that Musmanno wrote to the time that the first edition of this book was published, the number of proposed amendments grew from just over 3,000 to about 10,000; this number has now grown to close to 11,500 (see Number of Proposed Amendments). I was therefore flattered and challenged, as well as a bit intimidated, when Henry Rasof, an editor at ABC-CLIO, called me about the prospect of compiling a book to cover all these proposals, and when Alicia Merritt and I subsequently discussed the possibility of publishing an expanded second edition. No one realizes better than I the impossibility of being an expert on every subject discussed in this volume, as well as the inability of covering everything of importance in essays short enough to be of value for a general reader or high school or college student. My knowledge of the limitations of both editions of this work has been balanced by the realization—verified in my own research by the number of times I relied on Ames and Musmanno—of how useful it is to have a book that provides a starting point for an analysis of individual proposals and issues. I was particularly pleased that the first edition of this book was released in the year marking the hundredth anniversary of the publication of Ames's classic and hope and believe that both my initial volume and this second edition are worthy successors to Ames's and Musmanno's texts.

Current Interest
in the Amending Process

Interest in various scholarly topics waxes and wanes over time, but interest in the amending process had clearly increased in the decade prior to my first edition of this *Encyclopedia,* and it continues to wax today. In addition to my own multiplying works on the subject, the years just before my first edition had witnessed numerous other scholarly treatments of amendments and constitutional change.

Bruce Ackerman's sophisticated theory of constitutional moments, which has now been explicated in two of three anticipated volumes of *We the People* (1991, 1996), had salted discussion of amending issues with terms like "constitutional moments" and "dualist democracy," and has received the most attention (given the number of citations in law reviews, one might indeed refer, with little exaggeration, to "Ackermania"), but many other authors have also addressed the topic. Another Yale professor, Akhil Reed Amar (1988), has advanced the challenging thesis, which he continues to reiterate, that it is possible to amend the Constitution outside of Article V channels, and Walter Murphy (1980) revived interest in the idea that there may be certain implicit limits on the subject of constitutional amendments (also see Suber 1990). Donald Lutz (1994) examined a number of challenging hypotheses about constitutional change in an influential article in the *American Political Science Review* that also compares the U.S. system with that in other nations and points out how much more difficult the American process is in comparison to those of most other nations. In addition to writing several scholarly articles and leading a number of panels at meetings of the American Political Science Association on the subject of constitutional change, Professor Sanford Levinson of the University of Texas (1995) has compiled a book of essays presenting theoretical views of leading scholars on the subject. William Harris II has devoted considerable attention to the amending process in another book (1993), and Stephen Griffin's (1996) book on constitutional interpretation has given significant attention to the subject of constitutional change.

At the time of my first edition of this *Encyclopedia,* the putative ratification of the Twenty-seventh Amendment in 1992, as well as the earlier attempt (since revived) to extend the ratification deadline of the proposed Equal Rights Amendment, had spawned a great deal of commentary on the amending procedure. Much of it had taken its point of departure from an earlier essay by Walter Dellinger (1983) that asked whether such issues should be considered political questions and a response by Laurence Tribe (1983). Both before and after the first edition of this *Encyclopedia,* there has been renewed interest in the still unused Article V constitutional convention mechanism. Russell Caplan's book on the subject (1988) complemented legislation that Orrin Hatch sponsored to deal with such unresolved convention issues (see Vile 1993c, 466–483).

Just prior to the first edition of this *Encyclopedia,* the Republican electoral victories of 1994 and the Contract with America focused considerable attention on specific amending proposals, such as the balanced budget amendment, term limits, flag desecration, prayer in schools, and the item veto. What is therefore so interesting about most current academic works (including some of my own) is that they focus primarily on the *theory* of constitutional amendments and constitutional change.

At the time of my first edition, Bernstein and Agel's (1993) survey of amendments was a notable exception that has since been joined by the Kyvig, Palmer, and Pendergast, Pendergast, and Sousanis volumes identified above. Although adhering to generally high scholarly standards, Bernstein's book, like Kyvig's, succeeded in reaching a popular audience in a fashion that earlier works—most notably the judicious treatment of amendments by Alan P. Grimes (1978), in which he concentrated on congressional debates over amendments—never quite managed. (The Palmer book and the Pendergast, Pendergast, and Sousanis volumes seem more appropriate to reference libraries, with the latter especially appropriate for high schools.) In any case, Bernstein and Agel's work and Kyvig's, as well as other new books—Michael Vorenberg's account of the Thirteenth Amendment in *Final Freedom* (2001) is an especially note-worthy contribution to the literature—have necessarily focused chiefly on amendments that have been adopted rather than those that have been proposed. This second edition of the *Encyclopedia of Constitutional Amendments,* like the first, thus has a unique niche in the literature and on the reference shelf.

Although their short discussion of proposed amendments was lively (Bernstein with Agel 1993, 169–198), it may unintentionally have left many readers with the impression that most proposed amendments have been trivial or ridiculous. If this impression were true, one might well question the value of this book. On such matters, each reader must ultimately make an individual judgment, but I believe that the study of proposed amendments is far from a trivial pursuit. Undoubtedly, there are proposed amendments (just as there are proposed laws) that are naive, unnecessary, or ridiculous—proposals, for example, to outlaw war, to give the president authority over the air force, or to take citizenship away from all nonwhites. Sometimes proposals are wiser than they seem. A recent proposal added for the first time in this book (see Minnesota Boundary) suggested giving back the small portion of Minnesota above the forty-ninth parallel to Canada in an apparently successful attempt to get the attention of U.S. trade representatives negotiating fishing rights between the United States and Canada in the Lake of the Woods. Wise or unwise, however, most proposed amendments have dealt with fairly serious subjects, and the purposes behind amendments that were not adopted have often been accomplished in other ways.

It appears that it is a rare issue indeed that has not been introduced as an amendment. The study of such proposals thus provides a unique window into American history and politics. The fact that the goals of proposed amendments are often achieved by other means testifies not so much to the inadequacy of the amending process as to the dynamics of the U.S. federal system.

As someone who studied political theory before concentrating on U.S. constitutional law, I am probably as fascinated with the the-oretical arguments about constitutional amendments as any other scholars. At the same time, I think that it is important to keep such scholarship anchored in actual practice. I see this book as an effort to do this. I have written both editions of this book so that they address topics of interest to those with theoretical inclinations, while keeping in mind that amendments and proposed amendments should remain the ultimate subjects of a book on the constitutional amending process.

Subjects Covered in this Book

Amendments and Proposed Amendments
Altogether, there are more than 500 entries in this book. The large majority deal with the 27 amendments that have been ratified and with the approximately 11,500 others that have been proposed. Why, then, are there not 11,500 entries? Clearly, the number 11,500 records the approximate number of amendments that have been individually introduced and not the number of subjects that have been addressed. For example, there have been almost 1,000 proposals for the Equal Rights Amendment, and, while this amendment raised related issues, most such proposals can be discussed in a single essay. Similarly, there are hundreds of proposals dealing with reform of the electoral college, abortion, prayer in schools, balanced budgets, term limits, and so on. In most cases, I have grouped the discussion of proposals relating to a single topic in one essay rather than composing separate entries for each proposal. I have also included entries on new proposals, like the one to permit flag salutes (a reaction to a U.S. Circuit Court of Appeals opinion stating that the words "under God" made the salute an impermissible establishment of religion when recited in public schools).

A quick perusal of the Ames and Musmanno volumes, as well as indexes to subsequent lists of amendments, demonstrates that no two authors divide the thousands of proposals in the same manner. Moreover, I cannot guarantee that I have covered all topics. In most cases I had to work from the titles of amendments rather than from the actual texts, and in some cases where I was able to make checks, the titles of amendments turned out to be inaccurate or deceptive. Sometimes, I found it impossible to ascertain the content of a proposal, or I had to make educated guesses about what motivated a particular amendment or which proposals to group in the same essay.

From the second session of the Seventy-fourth Congress to the present, the Legislative Reference Service of the Library of Congress has compiled an annual listing of all proposed laws and amendments and their sponsors. For recent Congresses this information may be further supplemented by my own recently published reprints and update issued by the Law Book Exchange (Vile 2003) and by materials available on the website for the Library of Congress, generally by combing through lists of joint resolutions (which is the way that amending proposals are most generally introduced). Such compilations are extremely helpful, but they are surely far from foolproof. Sometimes the *Congressional Record* was an aid, but this record was often silent about the motivation or meaning of a proposed amendment. In some cases, I have called the staffs of members of Congress who have proposed obscure amendments, but often such members had long since retired, and an educated guess was the best that I could do. In any case, the heart of this book consists of descriptions of the twenty-seven amendments that have been proposed and ratified and the hundreds of other topics that have been proposed as subjects of amendments.

Major Constitutional Reforms Introduced outside Congress

Given the breadth of current musings about the amending process, a book limited to a description of amendments and proposed amendments did not seem adequate to meet the needs of a modern researcher. I therefore included a number of related types of entries.

One class of entry moves outside Congress to consider major reform proposals to rewrite the Constitution or substantially to alter it. This was the subject of my own first book (Vile 1991c). Historian Stephen Boyd (1992) also addressed this topic in a book compiling the texts of ten proposed alternative constitu-

tions. At the time of the first edition of this *Encyclopedia,* my own continuing research revealed that even when these results were combined, our books did not identify all such proposals, and so I included summaries of added proposals I have found from the period that Boyd and I originally covered. In addition, well over a dozen new proposals have been published, or posted on the Internet since the first edition of this book (including a proposed constitution by Jim Davidson for a new nation in the Caribbean to be named "Oceana," but which is clearly designed to influence American thinking on the subject in a more libertarian direction), at which time, to this author's knowledge, there were no such proposals on the Internet. As indicated above, I have continued to locate proposals that were published before the first edition of this work, and I am almost certain that there must be even more that continue to rest in obscurity. Still, the approximately seventy-five such proposals that are known make a fascinating supplement to discussions of more piecemeal reforms and should prove useful for further scholarly comparison and analysis. They also highlight the fact that a new constitution or set of amendments is a potentially viable option to more piecemeal change. Although I do not have comparative data from other nations where formal constitutional change, and even regime changes, are often much more frequent, I have almost concluded that there may be something uniquely American about the idea of private citizens sitting down and deciding to put pen to paper to draft a new constitution or set of amendments; if such proposals continue to multiply at the present rate, they may eventually merit another separate volume, but for now, I have included all that I could find here, including some that are fairly bizarre. It is particularly interesting to see a recent proliferation of proposals by individuals influenced by Ayn Rand, by futurists, and by students of public choice.

When I have been able to identify the authors of proposed constitutions or multiple amendments, I have described them under their authors' names. Where I had no names, as, for example, a proposal under the pseudonym Virginia Vanguard, I used the description of the plan or, in this case, the pseudonym, that the author provided. I have also provided at least a brief biographical sketch of each such individual for whom biographical information was available.

Influential Individuals

I listed two other types of entries under individual names. One type discusses individuals who have had an important impact on how we think about the amending process. Although I have argued elsewhere that American thinkers have been influenced on the subject by previous writers (Vile 1992, 1–21), I limited my focus to Americans, including such individuals as William Penn, George Washington, Thomas Jefferson, John C. Calhoun, Sidney George Fisher, Francis Lieber (a new entry in this edition), and Woodrow Wilson.

In a similar vein, I included entries, several of which are new, on individuals such as Susan B. Anthony, Birch Bayh, John Bingham, Everett McKinley Dirksen, Frederick Douglass, Alexander Hamilton, James Madison, George Mason, George Norris, Elizabeth Cady Stanton, Gregory Watson, and Frances Willard who were especially influential in formulating or pressing for the adoption of various amendments. Where it was appropriate, I mentioned the names and parties of individuals who supported amendments within the entries on proposed amendments. I found a Congressional Quarterly (2000) volume, fortunately updated and expanded since the first edition of this Encyclopedia, to be particularly useful in identifying the political parties of such individuals.

I reserved separate entries for a select number of individuals, including those listed above, whose roles in providing for an individual amendment or set of amendments were extraordinary. I included more entries on the Nineteenth Amendment (including a new one on the Seneca Falls Convention), which provided for women's suffrage, than on others. I did so because this movement was clearly a grassroots effort and because the amendment was advocated so long before it was finally adopted. Support for this amendment thus spanned more than a generation of active supporters.

In this book, I omitted American reformers who were not specifically concerned with constitutional amendments. Researchers interested in such individuals will find Alden Whitman's volume on the subject (1985) to be especially helpful.

Influential Organizations

I included some entries on organizations that were influential in the adoption of amendments—especially the drive for national alcoholic prohibition, which culminated in the Eighteenth Amendment, and the drive for women's suffrage that culminated in the Nineteenth Amendment. I quickly realized, however, that literally hundreds of organizations have labored for or against one or another amendment and that there was no feasible way to discuss all of them here. Readers who are interested in such modern groups should find Clement Vose's magisterial discussion in Constitutional Change (1972) useful. Books focusing on the Eighteenth, Nineteenth, and Twenty-first Amendments often describe such groups and their influences in much greater detail than I do here.

Supreme Court Decisions

Another group of entries in this book consists of Supreme Court decisions. These particularly interest me, because I have long taught American constitutional law. Moreover, as I completed entries on proposed amendments for both editions of this book, I have been frequently struck by the continual interplay between Supreme Court decisions and constitutional amendments, a number of which have overturned such decisions. Even more often, Court decisions have served as catalysts for amending proposals. When I was aware of such connections, I included them in individual entries on proposed amendments. When warranted, I wrote separate essays on such decisions. This second edition includes entries on a number of new decisions. These include Boehner v. Anderson (interpreting the Twenty-seventh Amendment); Clinton v. City of New York (the line-item veto case); City of Boerne v. Flores (striking down the Religious Freedom Restoration Act and thus serving as further impetus for a Religious Equality Amend-

ment); and *United States v. Morrison* (affecting
the scope of federal powers under the commerce clause and thus the scope of the Tenth
Amendment). Other recent opinions relating
to interpretations of the Eighth, Tenth, and
Eleventh Amendments, to the legitimacy of affirmative action programs, and to other modern issues of public policy, like capital punishment and the rights of criminal defendants,
while not treated in separate entries, are incorporated in updates of earlier entries.

I found the information in the *Oxford
Companion to the Supreme Court of the United
States* (Hall 1992) helpful in identifying the
day that Supreme Court decisions were
handed down. I also frequently consulted that
volume when I needed short summaries of
court decisions or information on issues of
law and historical developments. High school
students might also find the companion volume useful (Patrick 1994).

In addition to the Supreme Court decisions
that have prompted amending proposals,
there is another set of important decisions—
namely, those dealing with specific amending
issues. Although the Supreme Court declared
in *Coleman v. Miller* (1939) that issues surrounding the amending process were political
questions for Congress to resolve, it had settled a number of important amending issues
in prior cases. Moreover, several subsequent
court decisions have called into question the
legitimacy of the *Coleman* precedent. I included summaries of such relevant cases, including the 2001 decision in *Cook v. Gralike*
(dealing with constituent instructions regarding proposed amendments).

Unresolved Issues
In addition to the types of entries listed
above, I included essays on key amending issues. These include discussions of the constitutional convention mechanism; whether
there are implicit limits on the amending
process; whether states can rescind ratification
of pending amendments; whether governors
and presidents have a role in the process;
whether there are time limits on such ratifications; whether constituents should be able to
instruct their representatives on introducing
amendments; and so on.

Miscellaneous
From time to time, I included related entries
in this book that seemed useful but did not
really fit into any of the above categories. It
seemed appropriate, for example, to include
an entry on constitutional commissions, even
though this is primarily a mechanism for state
constitutional change. Similarly, I included
notes on the officers that have been designated to certify amendments (I have considerably expanded the essay on the Archivist of
the United States), and essays on such miscellaneous topics as the Articles of Confederation, the Confederate constitution, the Virginia and Kentucky Resolutions, the
Louisiana Purchase, the Hartford Convention, the Peace Convention, the Contract
with America, and critical elections. Because
of their influence on the U.S. Constitution,
the second edition also includes new essays on
the Magna Carta, the English Bill of Rights,
and the Virginia Declaration of Rights.

Since the first edition of the book, a group
known as Citizens for the Constitution has
published a list of guidelines that they think
amendments should meet. This edition includes an essay on these guidelines. This edition also includes a number of new essays that
I thought might help tie various amendments
together. These include a fairly lengthy essay
on the History of Constitutional Amendments suggested by my editors, as well as entries on such subjects as Consensus and the
Amending Process, Constitutional Stupidities
(a title borrowed from a book designed to
have scholars identify the provision in the
Constitution that they think is the least defensible), Deliberation and the Amending
Process, Democracy and Constitutional
Amendments, Enforcement Clauses in
Amendments, Entrenchment Clauses, Federalism and the Amending Process, Implementation Dates of Amendments, the Living
Constitution (which helps explore the links
between constitutional amendment and constitutional interpretation), the Placement of
Constitutional Amendments, Progress and
the Amending Process, the Relevance of Constitutional Amendments, Separation of Powers and the Amending Process, Social and
Economic Rights, Supermajorities, Supreme

Court Decisions Reversed by Constitutional Amendments, Unintended Consequences of Constitutional Amendments (a subject on which David Kyvig has recently edited a book), Voting Rights, and so on.

The Form of This Book

Ames (1896) and Musmanno (1929) discussed proposed amendments in narrative form. Others simply listed the subjects of amendments with their respective resolution numbers, who proposed them, and the dates in which they did so. The publication by the Law Book Exchange of a previously mentioned work reprinting and updating these earlier lists (Vile 2002) should be a boon to scholars of the subject. This *Encyclopedia* should remain a worthy and, for most people, a more accessible accompaniment in that I have organized this book as an encyclopedia of separate entries, each consisting of an essay on an amendment, a proposed amendment, or one of the related themes mentioned above. I chose this format so that the information would be accessible to high school students, college students, and general readers, as well as to advanced researchers in law, political science, and history.

Although such an approach arguably sacrifices some continuity, I have attempted to preserve continuity in four ways. First, I have added a list of entries to the front of this edition of the book to provide readers with an initial overview of all the topics covered. Second, I have grouped multiple entries together under such headings as Congress, the Judiciary, the Presidency, Slavery, States, and Taxation. Third, individual entries are extensively cross-referenced—even more so in this edition than in the first. Fourth, I have included fairly generous references that students and scholars can consult for further information. Individuals interested more generally in the amending process should find the bibliography and index, both of which have been extensively altered for this edition, to be especially useful. Because I make so many references to the Constitution and its amendments, they are also included in an appendix.

As one who has now been studying and teaching the subject for more than twenty-five years, I have long been convinced that the United States Constitution is an important document and that the constitutional amending process is a particularly critical part of it. Students of the subject will know that the governments of a number of American colonies were based on charters, and that Americans, particularly those of a religious bent, often associated such charters not only with written scriptures but also with the idea of a covenant, which was a particularly pervasive scriptural theme. When, after exhausting all legal routes to reform, the colonies collectively declared their independence of Britain, most states began to write their own constitutions. So, too, the Continental Congress began work on the Articles of Confederation. Although it was not ratified until 1781, it proved to be an important, if largely ineffective, prologue to the Constitution that followed.

There were many problems with the Articles, which was a far less democratic document than today's Constitution. There was, for example, no independent executive, and each state had a single vote in Congress. The major problem with the government under the Articles, however, was that it did not secure adequate powers for the national government. States were, for example, responsible for coining their own money and raising the taxes that they paid to the national government, and they began enacting trade barriers against one another that hurt economic development.

These problems were compounded by the fact that when Congress recommended changes, all thirteen state legislatures had to approve. This obstacle was so formidable that despite its many apparent flaws, no amendments were adopted during the time that the Articles were in operation. Moreover, when the founders eventually wrote a new Constitution, they bypassed the mechanism for unanimous state ratification, specifying in Article VII that the new document would go into effect when approved by special constitutional conventions in nine or more states (see Ratification of the U.S. and/or Future U.S. Constitutions), a mechanism subsequently used to ratify the Twenty-first Amendment.

Establishing the Amending Process

The current Constitution was formulated by the fifty-five delegates from twelve states (Rhode Island did not send representatives) who met in Philadelphia from May through September of 1787. Delegates represented a diversity of state interests, most notably those associated with population size and the issue of slavery. The government formulated by the Constitutional Convention differed in significant respects from that under the Articles of Confederation. Although states were retained in a newly devised federal system, congressional powers were significantly expanded. The new government contained three branches of government rather than one. These included a bicameral (rather than a unicameral) Congress that was significantly more representative than the previous Congress in which each state had been represented equally; a single executive, chosen by an independent electoral college, with powers to enforce congressional legislation; and an independent judiciary, whose members would serve "during good behavior."

Although hardly embraced warmly by everyone, the results of the Convention deliberations were generally accepted as an improvement over the Articles of Confederation. Observers also recognized that they embodied imperfect compromises. Moreover, even had the delegates been capable of creating a perfect document, it would likely have required alteration during the course of time. The delegates knew from their experience under British rule that a constitution that could not be altered would likely break, or end up being broken through revolution.

The framers allowed considerable play

within the joints of the instrument that they had created—for example, the judicial system would soon begin exercising the power known as judicial review, by which it interpreted the Constitution and laws made under its authority and declared acts that it considered to be unconstitutional to be void. In addition to providing or allowing for such mechanisms, the framers of the Constitution prudently constructed a process of formal constitutional amendment. This process, which was outlined in Article V of the Constitution, is difficult, but it was considerably easier than the process that was in place under the Articles of Confederation. The new process was to proceed in two steps. Two-thirds majorities of both Houses of Congress would propose amendments (an alternate mechanism for two-thirds of the states to petition Congress to call a constitutional convention has never yet been utilized) and three-fourths of the states would have to ratify them. At congressional specification, states could ratify amendments either through their existing legislatures, or, as in the case of the Constitution itself, through special constitutional conventions called for this purpose. The only permanent stated restriction on the amending process (such restrictions are called entrenchment clauses) was one protecting the Connecticut Compromise by providing that no state could be deprived of its equal suffrage in the U.S. Senate without its consent.

The History of Amendments in America

The constitutional amending process has not been utilized as frequently as might have been anticipated, but this process has been important in updating the document and in keeping it current with popular sentiments. It is possible that the Constitution would not have even been ratified had it not contained an amending mechanism. One of the key arguments of those who opposed ratification of the new Constitution, the Anti-Federalists, was that the document was inadequate without a bill of rights specifying the liberties that individuals would have against the newly created national government. Initially rebuffed by Federalist supporters of the Constitution, such

proponents later recognized that the easiest way to head off a second convention that might attempt to undo the work of the first was to agree to accede to the adoption of such a bill of rights. Significantly, James Madison, who is often identified as the "father" of the U.S. Constitution, went on to shepherd the Bill of Rights through the first Congress.

The ten amendments that were subsequently ratified by the states were appended to the end of the document (see Placement of Constitutional Amendments) and continue to be generally revered by the American people (see Reverence for the Constitution). More importantly, citizens may invoke them in court when they believe that their rights specified there have been violated. These rights, as well as the history of the amending process, will both be described in much greater detail in this book (see Bill of Rights and History of Constitutional Amendments). It is sufficient to note here that these guarantees include protections of religious and political liberty that are established in the First Amendment. They provide for a right to bear arms (Second Amendment); prohibit the government from quartering troops in citizens' homes without their consent (Third Amendment); prohibit "unreasonable searches and seizures" (Fourth Amendment); and provide for a variety of rights for individuals who are accused of crimes, those who are on trial, and even for those who are being punished after being convicted of crimes (Fifth through Eighth Amendments). The Ninth Amendment indicates that the people retain other rights that have not been delegated to the new government, while the tenth and final provision of the Bill of Rights was designed to ease the fear that the new government would destroy the existing states.

The states ratified two amendments from 1791 to 1865, and rejected a third proposal relating to titles of nobility. The Eleventh Amendment reversed an early Supreme Court decision, thus demonstrating that the amending process fit within the newly created system of checks and balances, and protected state sovereignty by clarifying the circumstances in which states could be sued. The Twelfth Amendment was designed to remedy defects in the electoral college, which in the wake of the development of political parties was no longer operating in the manner that the framers had anticipated. In the meantime, many citizens came increasingly to revere the new Constitution, even though it proved incapable of averting the Civil War. A proposal approved by Congress and known as the Corwin Amendment, which might have headed off war, would have done so at the high cost of permanently guaranteeing the existence of slavery in those states that wanted to keep it.

At war's end there was considerable sentiment for attempting to correct the problems that had led to the conflict. Three amendments were eventually ratified with this purpose in mind. The historic Thirteenth Amendment (1865) abolished involuntary servitude except as a punishment for crime. The Fourteenth Amendment (1868) contained a number of provisions. The most important overturned the polarizing *Dred Scott* decision of 1857 by defining citizenship so that it applied to "all persons [including blacks] born or naturalized within the United States," and by guaranteeing "privileges and immunities," "due process," and "equal protection" to all such persons. This amendment later became the vehicle through which the U.S. Supreme Court eventually applied most of the provisions in the Bill of Rights to the states. Initially, the Bill of Rights had applied only to actions by the federal government.

Although it proved far from effective during most of the first century of its existence, the Fifteenth Amendment (1870) prohibited discrimination in voting on the basis of race.

Another hiatus in amendments occurred between 1865 and 1913, but then four amendments were ratified in the next seven years. Usually associated with the Progressive Era in American politics with its increased emphasis on direct democracy, these amendments, respectively, overturned another Supreme Court decision to allow for a national income tax (the Sixteenth Amendment); provided that U.S. Senators would thereafter be selected directly by the voters, rather than by state legislatures (the Seventeenth Amendment); established national alcoholic prohibition (the Eighteenth Amendment); and pro-

hibited discrimination in voting on the basis of sex (the Nineteenth Amendment). The latter amendment was ratified more than seventy years after the Seneca Falls Convention had first brought the issue into the public limelight.

Eight amendments were ratified from 1933 through 1992. These included a number of proposals to deal with what might be considered constitutional housekeeping matters. Thus, the Twentieth Amendment altered the terms under which new presidents and legislators took office with a view of decreasing the power of political "lame ducks." The Twenty-second Amendment (1951) limited the terms that a president could serve. The Twenty-fifth Amendment (1967) provided for cases of presidential disability and for the replacement of vice-presidents. The Twenty-seventh Amendment, originally proposed as part of the Bill of Rights and belatedly ratified in 1992, provided for an intervening election between the time that congressional pay raises were adopted and when they went into effect. In a more substantive development, the Twenty-first Amendment (1933) had in turn provided for the repeal of the Eighteenth Amendment.

Other amendments adopted since the Progressive Era, like the earlier Fifteenth and Nineteenth Amendments, have been designed to increase voting rights. The Twenty-third Amendment (1961) provided for representation in the electoral college for residents of the District of Columbia. The Twenty-fourth Amendment (1964) eliminated poll taxes in federal elections, and the Twenty-sixth Amendment (1971) lowered voting ages to eighteen.

An amendment that Congress proposed to eliminate child labor eventually proved to be unnecessary in light of changing judicial interpretations of the Constitution. Amendments that would have given the District of Columbia voting representation in Congress or mandated equal rights for women were also rejected by the states. However, many of the goals of the second proposal, like the early child labor amendment, were brought about through altered judicial interpretations of the Constitution.

The Importance of Existing Amendments

Many developments have occurred without being incorporated into constitutional amendments, and at least one contemporary scholar has accordingly questioned the importance of this process—a bet that he somewhat hedges by excluding the Bill of Rights from his account (Strauss 2001). I would concede that one clearly could not write a complete account of American constitutional history simply on the basis of the text of the U.S. Constitution and its subsequent amendments. Just as clearly, one could not write such a history without also taking such amendments into account (see Relevance of Constitutional Amendments).

The Preamble of the Constitution begins with the words, "We the People." Through their representatives, the amending process continues to give the people their most direct mechanism for altering or adding provisions that they think are needed. In addition to solving a number of structural problems in the Constitution that have emerged throughout the nation's history, amendments have edged the nation much closer to democracy than when it began (see Democracy and Constitutional Amendments). As the above review has demonstrated, amendments have guaranteed important rights that continue to be expanded and enforced in courts; brought an end to legal chattel slavery, expanded citizenship, and extended equal rights to all; and have significantly expanded voting rights by eliminating barriers based on race, sex, age, and wealth (by eliminating the poll tax).

Although one might quibble with one or another amendment that has been ratified in the nation's history, it is difficult to imagine that many Americans would trade the original unamended Constitution for the one that is in effect today. With or without amendments, we might hope that governments would not abuse freedoms of speech or religion, deny rights to individuals indicted or on trial for crimes, re-impose slavery, or take away voting rights for African Americans, women, or eighteen-year-olds. Still, almost all of us probably feel more secure knowing that there is now specific constitutional language governing such matters.

Significantly, some nations, like Great Britain, that have long relied on an unwritten constitution have been increasingly giving consideration to the adoption of a written document.

The Importance of Amending Proposals

Altogether, Congress has proposed thirty-three amendments (for those not ratified, see Failed Amendments) by the necessary two-thirds majorities. Of these, twenty-seven have been adopted. (Each is described in this book under its number e.g., First Amendment). For every amending proposal that has been adopted, there have been hundreds that have been introduced in Congress and either were never seriously considered or were rejected—a number that is somewhat misleading because many proposals that have been introduced in Congress are duplicative. Despite their lack of success, such proposals not only serve to illumine possible alternatives to existing constitutional provisions but also important constitutional concerns of earlier generations as well as our own.

Between publication of the first edition of this *Encyclopedia* (1996) and the present, scholars have added numerous other books and articles to the subject of constitutional amendments and proposed amendments. The First, Second, Fourth, Tenth, Eleventh, and Fourteenth Amendments are among those that appear currently "hot." Debates continue about the merits of a balanced budget amendment, an amendment providing for congressional term limits, amendments limiting taxes, a religious equality amendment, an anti-flag desecration amendment, and a victims' rights amendment. Debates have resurfaced about the possibility that Congress might still ratify the Equal Rights Amendment. Individuals like Representative Jesse Jackson Jr. (D-IL) have proposed new amendments to provide constitutional protections for social and economic rights like a right to work, to education, to health care, and to a clean environment. Scholars have devoted renewed attention to the issue of whether there should be mandatory retirement ages for members of the judiciary.

Members of Congress have also introduced an amendment that would prohibit states from recognizing gay marriages.

The presidential election of 2000, which produced the first electoral college winner who did not garner a majority of the popular votes in more than 100 years, renewed questions about the desirability of continuing, reforming, or eliminating the current electoral college system by an amendment or through other means. The 11 September 2001 terrorist attack on the World Trade Center in New York and the Pentagon just outside Washington, D.C., has, in turn, led to renewed questions as to whether an amendment needs to be adopted to provide for a situation in which numerous members of the House of Representatives might be simultaneously killed or incapacitated—the Constitution currently permits state governors to make temporary replacements of U.S. Senators but does not have a similar provision for members of the House.

The Author's View of Constitutional Change

In previous books, I have taken positions on most contemporary amending issues. It is my belief that we do not need major constitutional reforms at present and that we should generally be wary of the unintended consequences that such reforms might generate. Because I have viewed both editions of this work as books of summary rather than advocacy, I have tried to write essays on the individual proposals, especially those that are still viable, so that both supporters and opponents of such measures could read these essays and believe that their views have been presented fairly.

In the course of examining so many proposals, I discovered some that I initially thought were worthwhile. In many cases, however, I concluded either that the original constitutional wording was wiser or that proposed changes would require a greater expenditure of effort than was warranted. Moreover, the experience with national alcoholic prohibition serves as a caution: those changes that I would like to see brought about—for example, a federal budget that is kept in relative balance or an end to virtual abortion on demand during the first two trimesters of pregnancy—may prove not to be susceptible to easy constitutional solutions. Many proposed amendments seem ridiculous, not so much because their goals are silly or ignoble, but because certain objectives are simply not amenable to solution by constitutional fiat.

As to existing amendments, I will continue to ponder and explore the meaning of some of the elusive provisions in the Second, Ninth, Tenth, Eleventh, and Fourteenth Amendments, and I doubt that anyone will ever have a complete view of what these amendments were intended to mean in a modern context. I would be hard-pressed, however, if I were to be entrusted with the task of clarifying such amendments with language that was more precise yet as capable of protecting and expanding existing rights as most of the current provisions have proved to be.

When I published the first edition of this book, I indicated that the only amendment that I wish were not part of the Constitution was the Twenty-second Amendment. Rather than an outright repeal of this amendment, however, I then advocated restricting a president to three—rather than two—full terms. Thus I hoped that most presidents elected to a second term would voluntarily continue the two-term tradition established prior to Franklin Roosevelt, but that future presidents would not automatically be regarded as lame ducks in their second terms. Given movements to repeal the Twenty-second Amendment to allow Ronald Reagan (who was soon thereafter diagnosed with Alzheimer's) and Bill Clinton (whose partisans continued to support him even after highly unpresidential behavior) to serve for future terms, although I am still concerned that it was adopted largely for partisan reasons, I am no longer as convinced that the ratification of the Twenty-second Amendment was a mistake. In the aftermath of the terrorist attack on the World Trade Center, I do believe that a constitutional amendment for replacing massive losses of members of the U.S. House of Representatives, and possibly members of the U.S. Supreme Court (along the lines of what the Twenty-fifth Amendment did for presidents and vice-presidents) warrants expedited consideration (see Congress, Emergency Functioning), and this is one of many preexisting proposals to which I have given expanded treatment. I am also fascinated by a "Truth-in-Legislation" Amendment that my friend Brannon Denning and Brooks Smith have recently suggested, essentially requiring that each legislative bill would address one subject and that it would be specified within the bill (see Truth-in-Legislation Amendment). For the most part, however, I often find myself on constitutional matters agreeing with the listener to a congressional speech who noted that "It contained some good things that were not new, and some new things that were not good" (Moore 1925, 15). Scholars have observed that it is possible to approach the Constitution as an instrument or a symbol (Corwin 1981). With this latter function in view, James Madison's reasoning in *Federalist No. 49* has persuaded me that it is often better to forgo minor constitutional changes than to overtinker with the document and thus undermine respect for it (Hamilton, Madison, and Jay 1961, 314–317). I think that the Citizens for the Constitution have done a good job of establishing reasonable considerations to take into account when one considers amending the Constitution. Both legally and symbolically, the Constitution gains value if it is not amended overmuch.

I believe, however, that this argument can easily be carried too far. Governments are dynamic, and constitutions will change over time. Although he has focused on this theme, Bruce Ackerman is certainly not the first to recognize that, under our system, such changes often do not alter the constitutional text. Instead, they are inaugurated by judicial interpretations, and by the development of what the British would call customs and usages (Vile 1994a). I have devoted an entire book to comparisons of the strengths and weaknesses of such changes (Vile 1994a), and I do not by any means think that they have all been for the good, but no book on constitutional amendments can ignore them.

During his debate with Stephen Douglas for the Illinois Senate seat that both were seeking, Abraham Lincoln, who was other-wise strongly committed to the rule of law, opposed the Supreme Court's decision in *Scott v. Sandford* (1857). In so doing, he recognized that if the Supreme Court could decide each issue with finality the first time it came up, then "the people will have ceased to be their own rulers, having, to that extent, practically resigned their government into the hands of that eminent tribunal" (Murphy, Fleming, and Barber 1995, 317).

In a similar fashion, I believe that it is a mistake to argue that the judiciary and other branches of government have the right to bring about drastic changes in our understanding of the Constitution but that the written document that serves as the fundament for such interpretations must somehow remain untouched. Moreover, I believe that there are occasions when the precision of an amendment is preferable to a more ambiguous ruling that is so frequently tied to the specific facts of an individual case.

Thus, I think that Old Glory will always remain a cherished symbol for most Americans, even if it never receives constitutional protection against desecration. However, those who advocate such protection might ultimately do less damage to the Constitution by adopting an amendment providing for such an explicit exception to the First Amendment than if they were to ask the justices to carve out such an exception with no explicit constitutional language to guide them. On other occasions, too, I believe that there would be a distinct advantage in having popular wishes incorporated into the text, which is available for inspection by all, rather than being developed in convoluted case law and in ambiguous understandings and practices that are so often the primary province of academic experts.

Those who worry that any diminution of the Bill of Rights (or other sections of the Constitution) will lead to an avalanche of proposals are, I believe, too fearful. Moreover, if changes in constitutional understandings were actually incorporated into the text, they could serve both as tools of public instruction and as firm bases for judicial decisions. Such arguments, it should be recalled, were among the primary reasons that Thomas Jefferson argued for, and James Madison agreed to, incorporating a bill of rights into the Constitution in the first place.

Acknowledgments

It is impossible to write a book of this length and breadth without accumulating a number of scholarly debts, and I have mustered my share. In writing the first edition, I acknowledged owing special thanks to Henry Rasof of ABC-CLIO for initially contacting me about this project and subsequently providing useful suggestions and editorial help and to Susan McRory, Susan Ficca, Jennifer Job, and Linda Lotz for their work in turning the manuscript into a book. For this edition, I owe primary thanks to Alicia Merritt, acquisitions editor, and Michelle Trader, senior production editor, at ABC-CLIO, as well as to Lauren Arnest, copy editor.

At the outset of the first edition of this project, four individuals read the suggested entries and made helpful suggestions: Professor Barbara Perry of Sweet Briar College, Donna Clilders of Denison University, and Mark Byrnes and Thomas Van Dervort of Middle Tennessee State University (MTSU). At some point in my writing of the two editions of this book, I have called upon most members of the Political Science and History Departments at MTSU for help, including Mark Byrnes, Robb McDaniel, Tyson King-Meadows, Francine Sanders, Jack Turner, Anne Sloan, David Carlton, Everett Cunningham, Lisa Langenbach, and Clyde Willis in the Political Science Department and Jan Leone (who was especially helpful in alerting me to individuals who were influential in the adoption of the Nineteenth Amendment), Bob Hunt, David Rowe, Thad Smith, Fred Rolater, Nancy Rupprecht, Andrew Guilliford, and Lewright Sikes in the History Department. Sarah Peveler, a graduate student at MTSU, and Professor Richard V. Pierard from the History Department at Indiana State University also provided useful information on the Christian Amendment, and Charles Nored gave me access to his files on Christian Reconstructionism. John C. Fortier of the American Enterprise Institute provided information on current plans for an amendment to ensure the continuity of Congress in cases of massive loss of life or incapacitation of members. Gary Freedom at McNeese State University, who has, sadly, passed away since my first edition, directed me to sources on cultural and linguistic rights, and Steve Dillard provided information on the proposed Victims' Rights Amendment and recent court decisions. I also received great encouragement from Henry J. Abraham at the University of Virginia and several helpful bibliographical references from Brannon P. Denning, who since the first edition of this book has completed an additional law degree at Yale and is now a prolific professor of law at Southern Illinois University, and with whom I continue to enjoy corresponding and writing about the amending process.

I have been blessed to teach on a campus that has an especially helpful and friendly library staff. In my first edition I expressed special thanks to Betty McFall and Amy Carr in the MTSU interlibrary loan department, who cheerfully and efficiently handled numerous requests for materials from other libraries. Also, Peggy Colflesh in the Periodicals Department kept me informed as each new issue of *Index to Legal Periodicals* arrived, and Rhonda Armstrong proved helpful in tracking down citations. Library staff members have changed since my first edition, but their willingness to help has not. I have been especially grateful not only for a beautiful new library facility on our campus, but also for an increasing number of indexes on the Internet that have enabled me to access far more journals from my desk than I was once able to do.

On a related note, I am especially grateful to David Huckabee of the Legislative Reference Service at the Library of Congress. Convinced of the value of my project and apparently sympathetic to my own lack of computer savvy, he twice provided written copies of the proposed amendments for my first edition and subsequently taught me how to find such proposals on the Internet on my own for the second edition. I also received help from Mike Gillette in the National Archives and Records Administration and from Michael White in the Federal Register's Office.

Student aides at MTSU did much of the "grunt work" for the first edition of this project. Initially they helped compile twelve long boxes of note cards on which we recorded and labeled the nearly 11,000 proposed amendments that were listed in existing books and reports—a task with which my wife and daughters helped. MTSU student aides subsequently helped by running library errands and by writing and compiling the cards that served as the basis for the entries and bibliography for this book. Aides who helped on the first edition of this project included Kathy Aslinger, Felicia Emery Rasori, Pamela Russell-Short, Clint Petty, Megan Kingree, Jaime Sparks, Robert Fletcher, Jason Reid, and Stephanie Corbin. I am especially indebted to my aide Jenny Picklesimer. In addition to doing more than her share of work transferring amending proposals to note cards, she proved to be an adept and competent proofreader. My former secretary, Clare Christian, also helped coordinate the work of student aides on these and related projects.

Because I have just recently worked with the Law Book Exchange on updating the list of proposed amendments, I did not do additional note cards for this project. I did, however, enlist the help of my secretary, Pam Davis, as well as a temporary secretary, Brooke Hamilton, for typing and web searches. David Dedman, a student aide, helped locate library sources for this second edition, as did my daughter Virginia Vile, who is now a proud student at the Marshall-Wythe Law School at the College of William and Mary. Her twin sister Rebekah did her own part by finishing two degrees in record

time and getting a full-time job, of which my wife and I are also proud. I also owe thanks to Dawn Johnson, who helped me track down source citations for this edition.

Middle Tennessee State University has proved to be a very supportive community in which to work. I appreciate my cooperative colleagues and students, and especially the encouragement I received from students in my constitutional law classes and on the mock trial teams I help coach. I owe special thanks to Dr. John McDaniel, dean of the College of Liberal Arts, and to the Faculty Research Committee at MTSU. Both provided release time for me to work on the first edition of this project, with my dean continuing to give encouragement for this second edition.

I also owe special thanks to my wife, Linda, and to my twin daughters for allowing me to forgo income from one summer of teaching and to devote extensive time from a spring semester and a second summer to speed this project along. More generally, my family made daily sacrifices for a husband and father who sometimes appeared to be more concerned with his scholarship than with their needs. I appreciate their sacrifices and sincerely hope that they can take pride in this volume.

Finally, I relied extensively on the work of previous scholars, especially those who compiled lists and analyses of prior amendments. Despite all my debts, the responsibility for this book is ultimately mine. Any errors in fact or judgment that have crept in must be laid at my own door.

A

❖ *ABINGTON V. SCHEMPP* (1963) ❖

This eight-to-one Supreme Court decision stimulated a number of proposed amendments to restore prayer and Bible reading in public schools. The decision covered both *Abington v. Schempp,* involving a Unitarian family in Pennsylvania, and another case in Baltimore involving an atheistic mother and son *(Murray v. Curlett). Abington* extended the Supreme Court's controversial opinion of the previous year in *Engel v. Vitale,* which had invalidated the recitation of a state-composed prayer in public schools. *Abington* held that, even in the absence of comments, student-led Bible reading and recitation of the Lord's Prayer during school time and under the supervision of public school teachers violated the establishment clause of the First Amendment, as applied to the states through the due process clause of the Fourteenth Amendment.

Justice Tom C. Clark's majority opinion focused on the "wholesome 'neutrality'" that the state was obligated to follow in regard to religion (*Abington* 1963, 222). Denying that his decision was antireligious or secularistic, Clark said that religion must depend for its support on the home, church, and individual conscience (*Abington* 1963, 226). Clark found that the practices in question were devotional rather than simply discussions of historical or literary material or nonsectarian attempts to foster morality. He therefore ruled that they lacked an overriding "secular legislative purpose" and that they had as their "primary effect" the promotion of religion (*Abington* 1963, 222).

Justice William Brennan's extensive concurring opinion is notable for its insistence that establishment clause concerns need to be related to modern historical and educational developments rather than to any narrow view of the framers' original intent. He also denied that the failure to adopt the Blaine amendment in the nineteenth century—itself stimulated in part by judicial decisions (see *The Bible in the Public Schools* 1967)—precluded application of the establishment clause to the states. In addition, Brennan discussed previous unsuccessful attempts to adopt the Christian amendment, recognizing God in the Constitution (*Abington* 1963, 256–258).

Justice Potter Stewart's dissenting opinion extended his earlier dissent in *Engel* by focusing on his paramount concern with religious freedom. Stewart argued that because students were permitted to absent themselves from the devotional practices and because there had been no direct showing of coercion, such practices represented acceptable accommodations of the exercise of the majority's religious beliefs.

Abington indicated that, despite intense criticism and pressure for an amendment to overturn *Engel,* the Court was not going to back away from its earlier opinion. Still, early studies indicated that many public schools ignored the decision. One school superintendent responded to a survey by saying: "I am of the opinion that 99 percent of the people in the United States feel as I do about the Supreme Court's decision—that it was an outrage, and that Congress should have it amended. The remaining 1 percent do not belong in this free world" (Birkby 1973, 117).

Abington arguably increased pressure for an amendment to permit prayer in schools and for other state and congressional legislation to accommodate majority religious practices. Although a six-to-three majority of the Court in *Wallace v. Jaffree* (1985) struck down a state law providing for a moment of silence, it appeared to do so primarily because the law was written to favor prayer over alternative meditative activities and thus left open the possibility that other such laws might be upheld as constitutional. This assumption gained some credence when the Supreme Court refused to review a lower court decision upholding a minute of silence law in Virginia (Masters, October 30, 2001, B01). In *Lee v. Weisman* (1992), however, the Supreme Court extended its ruling in *Abington* to outlaw prayers led by members of the clergy at high school graduations, a decision subsequently extended in *Santa Fe Independent School District v. Doe* (2000) to student-led prayers at football games. Issues like prayer in schools and the posting of the Ten Commandments remain emotional ones that often divide those who believe that schools should be imparting moral values from those who fear any state intervention in matters of religion or conscience. Such issues have reemerged in recent Supreme Court decisions involving the degree of review to give to laws impinging on the practices of religious believers and in the controversy over the need for a Religious Equality Amendment.

See also Blaine Amendment; Christian Amendment; *Engel v. Vitale;* First Amendment; Prayer in Public Schools; Religious Equality Amendment.

For Further Reading:

Abington School District v. Schempp, 374 U.S. 203 (1963).

The Bible in the Public Schools. 1870. Cincinnati, OH: Robert Clarke & Co. Reprint, New York: Da Capo Press, 1967. Introduction by Robert G. McCloskey.

Birkby, Robert H. 1973. "The Supreme Court and the Bible Belt: Tennessee Reaction to the 'Schempp' Decision." In *The Impact of Supreme Court Decisions: Empirical Studies*, 2d ed., ed. Theodore L. Becker and Malcolm M. Feeley. New York: Oxford University Press.

Santa Fe Independent School District v. Doe, 530 U.S. 290 (2000).

Smith, Rodney K. 1987. *Public Prayer and the Constitution: A Case Study in Constitutional Interpretation.* Wilmington, DE: Scholarly Resources.

❖ ABOLITIONISTS ❖

The ratification of the Thirteenth Amendment in 1865 followed more than thirty years of agitation by abolitionists. The transition from widely held antislavery sentiments to pressure for immediate abolition occurred in the 1820s. It coincided both with the elimination of slavery in the British Empire and with American religious revivals led by Charles G. Finney and others (Pease and Pease 1965, xxx–xxxii).

William Lloyd Garrison, editor of the *Liberator,* was probably the best-known abolitionist and advocate of "immediatism" (Pease and Pease 1965, xxix). Garrison founded the New England Anti-Slavery Society. Like the individuals who supported such groups (among them Harriet Beecher Stowe, author of *Uncle Tom's Cabin*), these organizations usually proved better able to denounce slavery than to propose practical plans for its elimination. Like other reform groups, the abolitionists were torn by debates. Controversial issues included how to eliminate slavery, whether violence like that carried out by John Brown was appropriate, whether established religions were friends or foes, how to tie together the rights of blacks and women (many of whom were active in the abolitionist and temperance movements and who, after being disappointed by the Fourteenth and Fifteenth Amendments, lobbied for the Nineteenth Amendment), what role blacks should play in the movement, and what attitude to take toward the U.S. Constitution (Pease and Pease 1965, xlvii–lv).

Some abolitionists. such as Boston's Robert Rantoul, thought that the Constitution was an antislavery document. Some, such as ex-slave Frederick Douglass, argued that the document should be narrowly construed so as not to sanction slavery. Others, such as John Quincy Adams, wanted a constitutional amendment. William Lloyd Garrison saw the Constitution as a slave document (Pease and Pease 1965, lvii–lxii). Ultimately, the doctrine of natural rights, grounded in the language of the Declaration of Independence, appears to have been the strongest argument against slavery (see Douglass's Fourth of July Oration in Storing 1970, 28–38).

Abolitionists helped form the National Liberty Party in 1840, the Free-Soil Party later in the decade, and the Republican Party in 1854. The Republicans nominated Abraham Lincoln in 1860, and his election led to the Civil War. Even those abolitionists who had previously resisted political action supported Lincoln during the war and became strong advocates of the Emancipation Proclamation, of the Thirteenth and Fourteenth Amendments, and of the Union and the Constitution, whose utility many of them had previously doubted (Pease and Pease 1965, lxxxi).

See also Brown, John; Declaration of Independence; Thirteenth Amendment.

For Further Reading:

Dillon, Merton L. 1974. *The Abolitionists: The Growth of a Dissenting Minority.* De Kalb, IL: Northern Illinois University Press.

Pease, William H., and June H. Pease, eds. 1965. *The Antislavery Argument.* Indianapolis, IN: Bobbs-Merrill.

Storing, Herbert, ed. 1970. *What Country Have I? Political Writings by Black Americans.* New York: St. Martin's Press.

TenBroek, Jacobus. 1951. *The Antislavery Origins of the Fourteenth Amendment.* Berkeley, CA: University of California Press.

Wiecek, William M. 1977. *The Sources of Antislavery Constitutionalism in America, 1760–1848.* Ithaca, NY: Cornell University Press.

❖ ABORTION ❖

Long regarded as a matter for state legislative regulation, access to abortion became a major federal issue during the 1970s. Prior to this time, abortion regulations had varied significantly from state to state, allowing the procedure to women in some states (whether residents or those wealthy enough to travel there for that purpose), but effectively denying access to it in other states, causing some women to resort to illegal abortion procedures that often posed threats to their health.

In *Roe v. Wade* (1973), the U.S. Supreme Court upheld a challenge to a restrictive Texas law in a complicated opinion written by Justice Harry Blackmun. Tracing the origin of abortion laws to the nineteenth century, Blackmun noted that such laws had three primary objects—deterring immoral sexual conduct (not raised as an issue in *Roe*), protecting the health of women, and protecting the life of the fetus. Arguing that the Court could no more come to an agreement on when human life began than could philosophers and religious authorities, Blackmun concentrated chiefly on the role of anti-abortion laws in protecting women's health. Relying on the right to privacy that had been articulated in *Griswold v. Connecticut* (1965), Blackmun decided that during the first trimester, or first three months, of pregnancy, the decision as to whether to have an abortion was between a woman and her doctor. During the second trimester, as abortion became riskier, the state could specify appropriate medical precautions to safeguard a woman's health. In the third trimester, when fetuses are generally considered to be "viable" outside their mothers' wombs, the Court allowed states to prohibit abortion, except in cases where the life or health of the mother was at stake. Advocates of abortion strongly supported the opinion in *Roe*, but critics, including some who favored a woman's right to procure an abortion, argued that the Court had usurped the states' lawmaking authority or the right of the people to settle the matter by adopting a constitutional amendment on the subject.

Since *Roe*, the Supreme Court has had to make many other decisions relative to abortion. In recent years, the Court has accepted a number of state laws requiring parental notification for minors seeking abortion (with a judicial bypass for minors shown to be capable of making the decision on their own), waiting periods, and other restrictions—while still keeping the procedure legal. In *Maher v. Roe* (1977), the Court decided that states were not obligated to provide Medicaid funding for abortion but could prefer funding births and not abortion procedures.

There have been numerous proposals to restrict abortion through constitutional amendments. Some proposed amendments would restrict the procedure altogether, while others would leave the matter for decision at the state level where it was prior to 1973. Urged to reconsider its central holding in *Roe,* the Supreme Court ruled in *Planned Parenthood of Southeastern Pennsylvania v. Casey* (1992) that abandoning the decision in *Roe* would destabilize the law and send the wrong signal to those who had lobbied against it. Should the Court ever reverse *Roe,* it is likely that its current supporters would try to overturn the decision through a constitutional amendment.

Debates between self-designated prochoice and prolife advocates (the first favoring and the second disfavoring, or seeking to limit, legal access to abortion) continue to be very emotional, with human life amendments proposed in every session of Congress. To date the necessary majorities for proposing or ratifying such amendments appear to be missing.

See also Right to Life.

For Further Reading:
Maher v. Roe, 432 U.S. 464 (1977).
Planned Parenthood of Southeastern Pennsylvania v. Casey, 500 U.S. 833 (1992).
Roe v. Wade, 410 U.S. 113 (1973).

❖ ACKERMAN, BRUCE (1943–) ❖

Currently Sterling Professor of Law and Political Science at Yale University, Ackerman has written a number of articles and the first two volumes of a projected three-volume set of books designed to explicate processes of change in the United States. Ackerman argues that the United States is a "dualist democracy" in which periods of ordinary democratic politics are interrupted by periods of intense constitutional lawmaking often designed to remove certain

matters of fundamental rights from the reach of ordinary politics. Ackerman is particularly interested in those major regime changes that have occurred outside of the normal politics of ordinary Article V amending processes.

Ackerman argues that there have been three major changes in American history—that inaugurated by the Constitutional Convention of 1787, that brought about by the Civil War, and that which resulted from the New Deal in the 1930s and 1940s. None of these "constitutional moments" have strictly followed the Article V scenario. Moreover, constitutional interpretation often involves the creative synthesis of insights from different constitutional moments.

Typically, successful periods of "higher lawmaking" involve four phases: a signaling phase, a proposal, mobilized popular deliberation, and a period of legal codification by the Supreme Court (Ackerman 1991, 266–267). If any of these phases is short-circuited—as, for example, in Reagan's unsuccessful nomination of Robert Bork to the U.S. Supreme Court—there may be a failed constitutional moment.

Widely critiqued and reviewed, Ackerman's work directs attention to the importance of extraconstitutional changes and to the fact that some such changes are more important than others.

In addition, Ackerman has proposed adding a referendum provision to the Constitution. Under Ackerman's proposal, presidents would be able to propose amendments in their second term. Such proposals would become law if approved by two-thirds of both houses of Congress and subsequently approved by three-fifths of the voters in each of the two succeeding presidential elections (Ackerman 1991, 54–55).

Ackerman has recently suggested that nations seeking to write new constitutions or revise existing ones might want to look to modified parliamentary systems rather than either to the U.S. model or to the more pure parliamentary model used in Great Britain (Ackerman 2000).

Ackerman has also joined another law professor in arguing for a system whereby individuals can anonymously donate "Patriot dollars" to candidates and political organizations that they favor, thereby circumventing some of the perceived problems with current campaign contribution limits (Ayers and Ackerman 2002).

For Further Reading:

Ackerman, Bruce. 2000. "The New Separation of Powers." *Harvard Law Review* 113 (January): 633–729.

———. 1998. *We the People: Transformations.* Cambridge, MA: Harvard University Press.

———. 1989. "Constitutional Politics/Constitutional Law." *Yale Law Journal* 99 (December): 453–547.

———. 1988. "Transformative Appointments." *Harvard Law Review* 101: 1164–1184.

———. 1984. "The Storrs Lectures: Discovering the Constitution." *Yale Law Journal* 93: 1013–1072.

———. 1979. "Unconstitutional Convention." *New Republic* 180 (3 March): 8–9.

Ayers, Ian, and Bruce A. Ackerman. 2002. *Voting with Dollars: A New Paradigm for Campaign Finance.* New Haven, CT: Yale University Press.

Vile, John R. 1993a. *Contemporary Questions Surrounding the Constitutional Amending Process.* Westport, CT: Praeger.

Weiser, Philip J. 1993. "Ackerman's Proposal for Popular Constitutional Lawmaking: Can It Realize His Aspirations for Dualist Democracy?" *New York University Law Review* 68 (October): 907–959.

❖ ADAMS, FREDERICK UPHAM (1859–1921) ❖

An inventor and engineer before becoming labor editor of the *Chicago Tribune*, Adams published a utopian novel, *President John Smith* (1896), that sold more than 750,000 copies. After copious initial chapters analyzing American politics and business cycles, the novel told the story of a one-time federal judge who ran for president as a Populist. After being cheated out of the presidency when he fell one vote short of a majority in the electoral college, the judge called a convention that met in Omaha and wrote a new constitution under which he served as first president. This constitution was based on majority rule and socialism and reflected populist themes that would continue into the Progressive Era.

Adams's proposed constitution, submitted by the Smith character in his novel to popular approval by the people, contained eight articles. The first provided for a president selected by direct popular vote and subject to recall. The plan made no provisions for a vice president; if the president died, he was to be temporarily succeeded by the secretary of state until a special election could be called. (Although Adams constantly referred to a "direct" or "popular" vote throughout his proposed constitution, he continued to use the pronoun "he," and does not appear to have contemplated nationwide voting by women.)

Article II provided for a cabinet of twelve officers—including a superintendent of education—popularly elected and also subject to recall. The Senate was eliminated, with the cabinet taking over some of its functions—ratifying treaties, for example, by a two-thirds vote.

A unicameral Congress of 200 members was described in Article III. Fifty members could submit legislation directly to the people for approval by referendum. All major legislation was to be so approved.

The Supreme Court, outlined in Article IV, would have five members appointed by the president, approved by the people, and subject to retirement by the people's majority vote. Although it would exercise judicial review of state and local laws, the Court would have no power to declare laws adopted by the people to be unconstitutional. Instead, it would be required to give advisory opinions to Congress on ways to make its legislation acceptable.

Article V dealt with currency matters (valuing the dollar on "the average productivity of one hour's work"), and Articles VI and VII provided for the use of the government's power of eminent domain to take over unoccupied land and to socialize basic industries.

Article VIII provided for constitutional repeal, revision, and amendment by majority vote. The constitution contained no bill of rights or definition of citizenship such as that in the Fourteenth Amendment.

At the conclusion of his novel, Adams asked readers to consider forming a "Majority Rule Club" in their vicinity. Adams also advocated his ideas in a socialist magazine that he renamed the *New Times*. Boyd (1992, 96) reports that Adams appears to have abandoned his plans for a new constitution by the turn of the century.

See also Progressive Era.

For Further Reading:
Adams, Frederick U. 1896. *President John Smith: The Story of a Peaceful Revolution*. Chicago: Charles H. Kerr & Company. Reprint New York: Arno Press, 1970.
Boyd, Steven R., ed. 1992. *Alternative Constitutions for the United States: A Documentary History*. Westport, CT: Greenwood Press.

❖ *ADAMSON V. CALIFORNIA* (1947) ❖

Justice Stanley Reed delivered a five-to-four ruling for the U.S. Supreme Court in *Adamson v. California* that had broad implications for the interpretation of the Bill of Rights and the Fourteenth Amendment. In *Adamson,* the Court reaffirmed an earlier decision in *Twining v. New Jersey* (1908) by deciding that the Fifth Amendment guarantee against self-incrimination did not apply to the states through the due process clause of the Fourteenth Amendment. States were thus free, as California had authorized, to permit comment on a defendant's failure to testify in his or her own defense.

Reed thus reaffirmed the doctrine of selective incorporation, which Justice Benjamin Cardozo had articulated in *Palko v. Connecticut* (1937). By this doctrine, the Court did not apply the entire Bill of Rights to the states via the due process clause but only those guarantees that were most fundamental. Similarly, in his concurring opinion in *Adamson*, Justice Felix Frankfurter defended the view that the due process clause was not intended to serve as shorthand for the Bill of Rights and "neither comprehends the specific provisions by which the founders deemed it appropriate to restrict the federal government nor is confined to them" (*Adamson* 1947, 66).

In a dissenting opinion joined by Justice William O. Douglas, Justice Hugo Black, a former U.S. senator from Alabama who believed that his service as a senator had given him spe-

cial understanding of how to read congressional debates, argued that John Bingham and other sponsors (whose views Black analyzed in a thirty-two-page appendix) had designed the first section of the Fourteenth Amendment to overturn the Supreme Court's decision in *Barron v. Baltimore* (1833) and apply the Bill of Rights to the states. Although advocating such total incorporation, which the Court had rejected in the *Slaughterhouse Cases* (1873) and subsequent decisions, Black favored limiting the due process clause to specific guarantees in the Bill of Rights, thus avoiding the "natural-law–due-process formula" (*Adamson* 1947, 90) that Black identified with prior judicial abuses.

Although substantively agreeing with Black, Justices Frank Murphy and Wiley Rutledge argued for "total incorporation plus" (Abraham and Perry 1994, 86), or the view that although the due process clause intended to apply the protections of the Bill of Rights to the states, it might also include additional rights. The Court has followed this philosophy, or the related doctrine that has been called "selective incorporation plus," in cases like *Griswold v. Connecticut* (1965), *Roe v. Wade* (1973), and similar cases when articulating a constitutional right to privacy.

Since *Adamson*, the Court has, by a process of selective incorporation, approached Black's goal of total incorporation by applying all but five guarantees in the Bill of Rights to the states. (The five yet to be incorporated are the Second Amendment's right to bear arms, the Third Amendment's limitation on quartering troops, the Fifth Amendment's right to a grand jury indictment, the Seventh Amendment's right to a petit jury in civil cases, and the Eighth Amendment's right to be free of excessive bails and fines.) In *Griffin v. California* (1965), the Court specifically applied the self-incrimination provision it had rejected in *Adamson*.

See also Incorporation.

For Further Reading:
Abraham, Henry J., and Barbara Perry. 1994. *Freedom and the Court: Civil Rights and Liberties in the United States*, 6th ed. New York: Oxford University Press.
Adamson v. California, 332 U.S. 46 (1947).

❖ ADMINISTRATOR OF THE GENERAL SERVICES ADMINISTRATION ❖

From 1951 to 1984, Congress designated this individual to certify the ratification of constitutional amendments. Prior to this time, the secretary of state performed this function. Since 1984, Congress has entrusted this duty to the archivist of the Library of Congress (Bernstein with Agel 1993, 246–247).

See also Archivist of the United States; Secretary of State.

For Further Reading:
Bernstein, Richard B., with Jerome Agel. 1993. *Amending America: If We Love the Constitution So Much, Why Do We Keep Trying to Change It?* New York: Random House.

❖ AFFIRMATIVE ACTION ❖

Although not specifically mentioning race, the Constitution of 1787 permitted slavery and even counted slaves as three-fifths of a person for purposes of representation in the House of Representatives and direct taxation. In *[Dred] Scott v. Sandford* (1857), Chief Justice Roger Taney declared that blacks were not and could not be American citizens. This decision was overturned by the Fourteenth Amendment, which, in Section 1, assured citizenship to "all persons born or naturalized in the United States and subject to the jurisdiction thereof" and guaranteed basic "privileges and immunities," "due process," and "equal protection" to all such citizens. Section 5 further gave Congress power to enforce these provisions.

Initially giving the amendment a narrow reading in such decisions as the *Slaughterhouse Cases* (1873), the *Civil Rights Cases* (1883), and *Plessy v. Ferguson* (1896), the Supreme Court reversed course in *Brown v. Board of Education* (1954) and outlawed discriminatory Jim Crow laws that had provided for racial segregation. Congress followed with legislation such as the Civil Rights Act of 1964, which used federal commerce powers to outlaw discrimination in places of public accommodation and in hiring.

Questions soon arose as to whether the government could now use racial classifications that had once discriminated against minorities to improve minority representation and compensate for the effects of past discrimination. Generally, liberals approved of such affirmative action plans as effective means of enforcing the Fourteenth Amendment, whereas conservatives opposed them as impositions of "reverse discrimination." The Supreme Court has faced this issue in a large number of cases. In *Regents of the University of California v. Bakke* (1978), Justice Lewis Powell voted with four other members of the Court to strike the use of strict racial quotas at the medical school at the University of California at Davis but joined four other justices in deciding that some consideration of race was appropriate to assure diversity in university admissions. Representative James Collins (R) of Texas introduced an amendment in 1978 that would have prohibited "denial of equal opportunity because of quotas or ratios based on race, color, national origin, religion, or sex" (H.J. Res. 1035). Senator Orrin Hatch (R) of Utah subsequently introduced amendments against affirmative action in 1980 and 1981. The Senate held hearings on the subject in 1981.

Since its decision in *Richmond v. Croson Company* (1989), in which it overturned a 30 percent set-aside program for minority contractors that was established by the Richmond City Council, the U.S. Supreme Court has subjected affirmative action programs to greater scrutiny. In *Adarand Constructors, Inc. v. Pena* (1995), the U.S. Supreme Court announced that it would apply three principles to affirmative action cases. First, it would be "skeptical" of racial classifications, subjecting them to strict scrutiny; second, it would require "consistency" in the treatment of classifications based on race, whether such classifications applied to racial majorities or minorities; and third, it would require "congruence" between what it would permit states and the national government to do (in previous cases the Court has sometimes given the national government greater leeway under the enforcement clauses of the Thirteenth through Fifteenth Amendments).

United States circuit court opinions in *Hopwood v. Texas* (1996) and *Johnson v. Board of Regents of the University of Georgia* (2001) have respectively struck down affirmative action programs at the University of Texas School of Law and the University of Georgia, but a more recent circuit court decision in *Grutter v. Bollinger* (2002) has narrowly upheld such policies (the vote was five to four, and one of the judges registered a strong dissent) at the University of Michigan law school (Schmidt 2002). On December 2, 2002, the U.S. Supreme Court announced that it would review cases involving admissions at the University of Michigan in the 2002–2003 term ("Supreme Court to Weigh In . . ." 2002).

For Further Reading:

Affirmative Action and Equal Protection. 1981. Hearings before the Senate Subcommittee on the Constitution of the Committee on the Judiciary, 97th Cong., 1st sess., on S.J. 41, 4 May, 11, 18 June, and 16 July. Washington, DC: U.S. Government Printing Office.

Eastland, Terry. 1996. *Ending Affirmative Action: The Case for Colorblind Justice*. New York: Basic Books.

Fiscus, Ron. 1992. *The Constitutional Logic of Affirmative Action*. Durham, NC: Duke University Press.

Regents of the University of California v. Bakke, 438 U.S. 265 (1978).

Schmidt, Peter. 2002. "Next Stop, Supreme Court? Appeals Court Upholds Affirmative Action at University of Michigan Law School." *The Chronicle of Higher Education* 48 (24 May): A24–26.

"Supreme Court to Weigh In on Affirmative Action: University of Michigan Cases on Race-Based Admissions to Be Heard." http://www.washingtonpost.com/wp-dyn/articles/A63231-2002Dec2.html.

❖ AGAR, HERBERT (1897–1980) ❖

Herbert Agar was an author, historian, and editor for the *Louisville Courier-Journal*. He also wrote a book, *A Time for Greatness,* during World War II in which he called for national spiritual and political renewal in order to save civilization. He presented his ideas for governmental reform in a chapter entitled "Can We Make Government Accountable and Understandable?" (Vile 1991c, 87–89).

There, as elsewhere in his book, Agar drew a distinction between two types of government. One was a "multiple-agency system" of government like that of the United States, "which seeks to partition and separate the powers of government and to distribute them among various agencies, so that authority will always be subject to checks." The other was a system like that in Great Britain, which "concentrates power in the executive, and sets up a representative body whose sole task is to watch and criticize the executive" (Agar 1942, 83–84). Although Agar's initial critique of the U.S. government appeared to indicate that he favored a parliamentary system of concentrated responsibility, he noted that he was not suggesting "that the Parliamentary form of government is necessarily to be preferred," but rather that it "has much to teach us about the solution of the problem" (Agar 1942, 257).

As one who spent much of his life in England, Agar drew several lessons from the British system. He believed that the executive should be responsible for formulating the budget, with the legislature serving as critic rather than having the authority to add to it. More generally, Agar believed that it was the responsibility of the executive to prepare all needed measures and the function of Congress to act on them, "rejecting them, refining them, proposing alternatives, or accepting them as they are" (Agar 1942, 261).

Agar argued that the American founders intended for the federal system to be closer to this accountability model than it turned out to be in practice. Agar tied the system's failure to achieve this accountability to the Washington administration. He cited the first Senate's unwillingness to serve as a type of privy council in formulating treaties and Congress's refusal to allow Alexander Hamilton to appear on the House floor and "establish direct relations between the heads of Cabinet departments and Congress" (Agar 1942, 265). Agar noted, "if the administration were allowed to bring its bills upon the floor of Congress and there to defend them, the executive could create policy and the Congress, unable to retreat into the darkness itself, would see to it that there was nothing hidden or obscure or unexplained about the measures proposed" (Agar 1942, 277).

Because Agar believed that the American founders had actually intended to have a more accountable system than the one that developed, he held out the possibility that reform might be achieved by "constitutional reinterpretation" rather than by amendment. He indicated, however, that "if the task cannot be done by reinterpretation, it will have to be done by revision, even if that involves a constitutional convention" (Agar 1942, 278).

For Further Reading:

Agar, Herbert. 1942. *A Time for Greatness.* Boston: Little, Brown.

Vile, John R. 1991c. *Rewriting the United States Constitution: An Examination of Proposals from Reconstruction to the Present.* New York: Praeger.

❖ AGRICULTURE ❖

Although the U.S. Constitution was written at a time when the nation was chiefly agricultural, and leading statesmen—including Thomas Jefferson—favored the development of an agrarian republic, the document makes no specific mention of the subject. Undoubtedly, many of the founders anticipated that any agricultural regulations that were needed would be enacted by the states. Although the Supreme Court sometimes struck down such regulations under its interpretation of the due process clause of the Fourteenth Amendment, most nineteenth-century agricultural regulation was exercised at the state level (prices charged by grain elevator operators and railroads were frequent subjects of state concern in the latter half of the century).

Democratic Texas Senator Morris Sheppard, however, proposed an amendment in 1916 and 1917 giving Congress power to purchase, improve, and sell land and make loans for the purpose of promoting farm ownership (S.J. Res. 127; S.J. Res. 76). Similarly, New York's Republican Representative Fiorello La Guardia proposed an amendment in 1917 (probably re-

lated to the U.S. war effort) allowing Congress to regulate "production, conservation, and distribution of foodstuffs and fuel" (H.J. Res. 107). World War I resulted in the War Time Prohibition Act, which went into effect in 1919, more than six months prior to the Eighteenth Amendment (C. May 1989, 66), which constitutionalized the ban on alcohol (but was later overturned by the Twenty-first Amendment).

The Great Depression accented the interdependency between agriculture and other aspects of the economy, and a number of Franklin Roosevelt's New Deal programs were directed toward or included agricultural regulation. Most notable were the National Industrial Recovery Act and the Agricultural Adjustment Act. Initially, the Supreme Court struck down both laws. In *Schechter Poultry Corporation v. United States* (1935), often called the "Sick Chicken" case, the Court declared that the first law, which permitted industries to set codes of fair competition to be approved by the president, was unconstitutional. The Court believed that the law permitted excessive delegation of congressional powers. In *United States v. Butler* (1936), the Court decided that the processing tax on agricultural commodities sanctioned by the Agricultural Adjustment Act invaded state police powers protected by the Tenth Amendment (Kershen 1992, 22). The latter decision especially appears to have sparked a number of proposed amendments giving Congress the power to legislate for agriculture. Democrat Samuel Dickstein of New York proposed one such amendment the day after the decision, and another dozen or so proposals were introduced within the next two years. Some proposals referred only to agriculture, whereas others included regulation of commerce, industry, and labor.

Subsequent Supreme Court decisions in *Mulford v. Smith* (1939) and *Wickard v. Filburn* (1942) upheld a revised Agricultural Adjustment Act under a broad reading of the commerce clause. In the latter case, the Court even recognized congressional authority over crops that were grown for home consumption. With the Supreme Court's broad reading of the commerce clause, less restrictive interpretations of state police powers, and greater judicial deference to governmental regulations in the area of economic policies, congressional proposals for amendments to increase federal powers over agriculture have ceased. Debates continue over desirable farm policies and especially over the wisdom and/or necessity of federal crop supports and subsidies.

For Further Reading:

Kershen, Drew L. 1992. "Agriculture." In *The Oxford Companion to the Supreme Court of the United States,* ed. Kermit L. Hall. New York: Oxford University Press.

May, Christopher N. 1989. *In the Name of War.* Cambridge, MA.: Harvard University Press.

❖ AIR FORCE ❖

Article II, Section 2 of the U.S. Constitution designates the president as "Commander in Chief of the Army and Navy of the United States," as well as of state militias when called to national service. The air force, for which there was no specific warrant in 1787, was subsequently developed and separated from the other two services in 1947. The following January, Republican Representative Claude Bakewill of Missouri introduced an amendment (H.J. Res. 298) designating the president commander in chief of this branch as well. Failure to adopt the amendment does not appear to have lessened presidential powers in this area.

❖ ALBANY PLAN OF UNION ❖

In early America, the colonies were created and governed by royal, corporate, or proprietary charters, which eventually served as models for state and national constitutions. Even during the Articles of Confederation and the early years of the U.S. Constitution, the former colonies continued jealously to guard their rights. It is not therefore surprising that the first real plan proposed for North American union, the Albany Plan of Union, was not ultimately either adopted by the colonies or pushed by the English themselves. This plan, authored chiefly by Benjamin Franklin just be-

fore the French and Indian War in 1754 and proposed by delegates from the northern colonies and from the Iroquois Nations, remains significant in pointing the direction to a possible future union.

The plan had a brief preamble and twenty-five sections. The preamble proposed making "humble application" to the British Parliament for "one general government" in America. The new government was to be "administered by a President-General" appointed by the king and a "Grand Council" chosen by individual colonial assemblies (Section 1). This unicameral council was to have forty-eight representatives from eleven colonies (Section 2), who would meet in Philadelphia when convened by the president-general. Members would serve for three-year terms, with reapportionment to be provided for based on the proportion of taxes paid by each colony, but with the stipulation (somewhat akin to the later Connecticut Compromise) that no state would have more than seven or fewer than two delegates (Section 5).

The Grand Council, like the current House of Representatives, would have had the right to choose its own speaker and could not be arbitrarily dismissed by the president-general. The latter's assent would, however, be required for all acts. The Grand Council was to be given power to make war or peace with Indian tribes, regulate Indian trade, make purchases from the Indians, and found and govern new settlements (Sections 10–15). The Grand Council would also have had power to "make laws, and levy such general duties, imposts, or taxes, as to them shall appear most equal and just" (Section 16). The Grand Council would transmit laws to the king in council in England; in a provision resembling a modern-day legislative veto, such laws were to become effective "if not disapproved within three years after presentation" (Section 21).

The speaker of the Grand Council was designated to succeed the president-general in the case of his death, until the Crown could make a new appointment (Section 22). The president-general was responsible for commissioning all military officers with the consent of the Grand Council, thus establishing civilian control over the military. A final section (Section

25) granted that "the particular military as well as civil establishments in each Colony [will] remain in their present state . . ." The plan does not appear to have provided for a specific amending mechanism.

Although the plan was never adopted, many of the delegates who attended the Congress that established the Articles of Confederation or the subsequent Constitutional Convention (where Benjamin Franklin was the oldest member present) were undoubtedly aware of this proposal. The specific features of both documents diverge in many respects from the Albany Plan of Union, but principles like the division of power between the executive and legislative branches (without, however, specification for an independent judiciary) and civilian control of the military are similar to those in the current Constitution.

For Further Reading:

"Albany Plan of Union," *http://www.constitution. org/bcp/albany.htm.* Accessed 4/27/02.

❖ ALCOHOLIC PROHIBITION ❖

See Eighteenth Amendment.

❖ ALIENS ❖

Article I, Section 8 of the U.S. Constitution entrusts Congress with the power to provide a "uniform Rule of Naturalization." Section 1 of the Fourteenth Amendment further extends citizenship to all persons born in the United States or naturalized. Although the United States is a nation of immigrants, disputes about the status of noncitizens, or aliens, date at least as far back as the Alien Acts of 1798. Federalists adopted the Alien Acts, along with the Sedition Acts, partly because they believed that immigrants (especially those from France and Ireland) were more supportive of the Republican stance against the British than of Federalist Anglophile policies (Urofsky 1988, 171). Since that time, amendments have been introduced both to restrict and to expand the rights of such individuals.

Laws Restricting Aliens

Most proposals would affect states where aliens reside rather than the aliens themselves. Such proposals, especially prominent in the 1930s and 1940s, would exclude aliens from the population count used to apportion representatives in the House (for example, H.J. Res. 263, 1930). Section 2 of the Fourteenth Amendment currently provides that such apportionment be based on "the whole number of persons in each State, excluding Indians not taxed." Excluding aliens from the count would thus reduce representation for states with large immigrant populations, such as California, Florida, and Texas.

Subject to restrictions against discrimination such as those found in the Fifteenth, Nineteenth, Twenty-fourth, and Twenty-sixth Amendments (each of which protects citizens only), states set their own qualifications for voting and officeholding. Thus, there have also been a number of proposals, most prominent from the 1890s to about 1921, that would prevent states from extending either or both privileges to aliens. Many advocates of such restrictions were connected to the Progressive movement and hoped that such restrictions would remove a source of support for corrupt political machines (Welch et al. 1993, 171). This was clearly an objective that could be reached by state law; today, all states include citizenship as a requirement for voting and holding office.

Additional proposals relating to the rights of aliens have sought to allow states to regulate their employment or, as in a proposal introduced by Democratic Representative Thomas Wilson of Mississippi in 1927, to prohibit citizens born overseas from serving as representatives (H.J. Res. 103). Such a proposal would effectively extend the ban on officeholding that now applies, under Article II, Section 1 of the Constitution, only to the presidency.

Laws Protecting Aliens

A New York representative introduced three proposals from 1917 to 1919 that would have prevented states from passing discriminatory laws against aliens. An earlier proposal in 1913 would have granted Congress the "exclusive power to legislate on questions affecting rights and privileges of aliens resident in [the] United States" (H.J. Res. 88). All these proposals appear to have been directed primarily at laws passed by California that discriminated against immigrant Japanese. Laws such as those restricting landholding by Japanese or separating Asian children from those of Anglo-Saxon stock in schools sometimes conflicted with U.S. treaties and embarrassed U.S. foreign policy at a time when Japan was becoming a major world power (Daniels 1968, 31–45).

Related to the question of the treatment of aliens is the question of citizenship. Concerned with providing disincentives for those coming to the United States illegally, advocates of the Birthright Citizenship Amendment have sought to limit the extension of citizenship to individuals born on U.S. soil to those whose mothers are either U.S. citizens or who are, in the least, legally in the United States.

See also Birthright Citizenship Amendment; Fourteenth Amendment.

For Further Reading:

Daniels, Roger. 1968. *The Politics of Prejudice.* New York: Antheneum.

Urofsky, Melvin I. 1988. *A March of Liberty: A Constitutional History of the United States.* New York: Alfred A. Knopf.

Welch, Susan, et al. 1993. *Understanding American Government,* 2d ed. Minneapolis–St. Paul, MN: West.

❖ ALTERNATIVE U.S. CONSTITUTIONS, PROPOSED ❖

The United States is a nation whose founders chose to set forth the fundamental law in a written constitution, which in turn succeeded a previous written document, the Articles of Confederation. In such circumstances, it is not surprising that many reformers have attempted not simply to author individual amendments to the Constitution but that they have also attempted to rewrite the entire document, or to append major revisions to it that often exceeded the length of the original Constitution itself.

Proposals have varied so much that it is difficult to generalize about them. They appear to span most of American history. Then–West Point cadet Simon Willard Jr.'s prolix proposal for reforming and renaming the nation Columbia in 1815 (see Willard, Simon, Jr.) is the earliest such proposal that the author has found. In addition to leading to secession and the writing and implementing of the Confederate Constitution in the South, the period around the U.S. Civil War precipitated at least two proposals for new constitutions, one by the notorious abolitionist John Brown and the other by a lesser-known New York writer named William B. Wedgwood. Since then proposals appear to have been chiefly prompted by "crises (or perceived crises) and constitutional anniversaries" (Vile 1991c, 156). Proposals have been identified from the period of Reconstruction, the Progressive Era, both World Wars, the Great Depression, the 1960s and 1970s, and anniversary celebrations of the Declaration of Independence and the U.S. Constitution. Several proposals over the last decade or so have centered on the fact that the nation has entered a new century and, indeed, a new millennium. Increasingly, such proposals are beginning to appear on the Internet, where their effect is even less easy to measure.

Some proposals can be grouped together. Thus, there are those who favor establishing a parliamentary system of government in place of the existing system based on separation of powers; those who want to strengthen or weaken, or are primarily concerned about, one or another of the existing branches of government; those who want to strengthen the national government against centrifugal state tendencies; those favoring "downsizing" or decentralizing existing powers or even allowing portions of the nation to secede; those who want the United States to recognize more individual political rights; those who want to move the United States in a more socialistic or libertarian direction; those who want the Constitution to guarantee a set of social and economic rights; those who simply string together lists of proposed alterations, often overlapping with popular measures that members of Congress are introducing into that body at the time, etc. There are undoubtedly others who are hoping for more violent revolutionary changes that would fall outside the parameters of this book.

Because of this diversity of perspectives, it is difficult, if not impossible, to identify a "reform" tradition. Not only do proposed alternative U.S. constitutions vary significantly, but most appear to have been written in response to specific crises or with little or no knowledge of the proposals that preceded them. The fact that, after more than a decade of searching, the author of this *Encyclopedia* continues to find proposals from early American history is testament to the obscurity of some of these proposals, and to the scant attention that most of them have received.

It is fascinating to find that, while many proposed major sets of changes or alternative constitutions have been written by academic scholars or practitioners like Woodrow Wilson, William Y. Elliott, Leland Baldwin, Rexford Tugwell, Chester J. Antieau, and Richard Labunski, others have been authored by fairly ordinary citizens, some of whom have preferred to remain anonymous. Some have attempted to rewrite the entire Constitution, while others have preferred to incorporate changes into the existing text. There may, indeed, be something peculiarly American about the idea of sitting down to rewrite the Constitution—one is reminded of Thomas Jefferson's one-time attempt to rewrite (or at least, condense) Holy Scriptures in accord with what he thought Jesus had really said and done—eliminating reports of Jesus's miracles in the process (Jefferson 1989).

Many authors of alternate constitutions have paid little attention to how they might be implemented. Others have proposed liberalizing existing constitutional amending mechanisms; convening, or persuading Congress or the states to convene, constitutional preconventions, conventions, or commissions; convincing states to serve as laboratories for proposed changes; or introducing and/or ratifying proposals by initiative or referendum. The latter mechanisms appear to be increasing in popularity among proponents of new major constitutional alterations; some such advocates believe that the Internet and other forms of modern technology have increased the chances for citizen participation in constitution making and approval.

This author's impression is that there continues to be not only fairly strong support for the existing constitutional document but also fairly widespread fear of, and resistance to, the idea of wholesale constitutional alterations that might threaten existing rights or result in unintended consequences. One indication of such fears is the fact that, to date, the Article V convention mechanism has never been utilized, and only one of twenty-seven amendments adopted (the Twenty-first repealing national alcoholic prohibition) has been ratified through the convention mechanism rather than being ratified by existing state legislatures. Even if never fully adopted, alternate constitutions provide fascinating reading; cast interesting light on their authors; help illumine the nature of earlier historical time periods; point to strengths and weaknesses of existing constitutional structures; explain existing delineations of governmental powers and individual rights and possible alternatives; and serve as storehouses of possible future reforms.

See also Confederate States of America, Constitution of; Constitutional Conventions; Reverence for the Constitution; Unintended Consequences of Constitutional Amendments; or look under individual names of authors for constitutions that they have proposed.

For Further Reading:

Jefferson, Thomas. 1989. *The Jefferson Bible: The Life and Morals of Jesus of Nazareth*. Introduction by F. Forrester Church. Boston: Beacon Press.

Vile, John R. 1991c. *Rewriting the United States Constitution: An Examination of Proposals from Reconstruction to the Present*. New York: Praeger.

❖ AMAR, AKHIL REED (1958–) ❖

Amar is currently a professor of law at Yale University and has written articles analyzing a number of constitutional amendments as well as books on the Bill of Rights (Amar 1997, 1998). Like Bruce Ackerman, Amar argues that the procedures in Article V of the U.S. Constitution are not the exclusive legal mechanisms for amending the Constitution. Unlike Ackerman, who focuses on "constitutional moments," Amar believes either that a majority of voters could petition Congress to call a constitutional convention or that Congress could submit amendments to a popular vote or referendum (Amar 1988, 1994).

Amar bases his argument on the extralegal fashion in which the current Constitution was adopted, on ideas of popular sovereignty current at the nation's founding, and on such constitutional provisions as the Preamble and the First, Ninth, and Tenth Amendments. Amar's argument may also receive some support from experience with amending mechanisms at the state level, although there is one prominent example of such an experiment going awry (*Luther v. Borden* (1849)). If accepted, Amar's view would negate the need for a number of proposed procedural changes in the amending process. Dow (1990), Vile (1990–1991), and Monaghan (1996) have questioned the constitutional support for Amar's views.

Amar's views have served as one of the supports for the National Initiative for Democracy, which met in Williamsburg, Virginia, in February 2002 with hopes of amending the U.S. Constitution through a national referendum.

See also Ackerman, Bruce; National Initiative for Democracy.

For Further Reading:
Amar, Akhil R. 1997. *The Constitution and Criminal Procedure: First Principles.* New Haven, CT: Yale University Press.

———. 1994. "The Consent of the Governed: Constitutional Amendment outside Article V." *Columbia Law Review* 94 (March): 457–508.

———. 1992. "The Bill of Rights as a Constitution." *Yale Law Journal* 100 (Winter): 1131–1210.

———. 1988. "Philadelphia Revisited: Amending the Constitution outside Article V." *University of Chicago Law Review* 55 (Fall): 1043–1104.

Dow, David R. 1990. "When Words Mean What We Believe They Say: The Case of Article V." *Iowa Law Review* 76 (October): 1–66.

Monaghan, Henry P. 1996. "We the People[s], Original Understanding, and Constitutional Amendment." *Columbia Law Review* 96 (January): 121–177.

Vile, John R. 1990–1991. "Legally Amending the United States Constitution: The Exclusivity of Article V's Mechanisms." *Cumberland Law Review* 21: 271–307.

❖ AMENDING PROCESS ❖

See Article V of the U.S. Constitution.

❖ AMENDING PROCESS, PROPOSALS FOR CHANGING ❖

Article V of the U.S. Constitution delineates an amending process. It requires that amendments be proposed by two-thirds majorities of both houses of Congress or by a special convention called by two-thirds of the states. Such proposals then require ratification by three-fourths of the states. About 150 proposals, many redundant, have been introduced in Congress to alter this procedure.

Proposals for Popular Initiative or Referendum

A common proposal appears to have first surfaced around the time of the outbreak of the Civil War as a means of averting conflict by incorporating various slavery compromises into the Constitution. It would provide for some kind of popular initiative or referendum on amendments. Such proposals, which embody a form of direct democracy, were especially common during the Progressive Era, which spanned the first two decades of the twentieth century, at which time there was a great deal of scholarly criticism of the amending process for being too "rigid" (Vile 1992, 135–156). Common variants (for example, S.J. Res. 22, 1919) provided that amendments would be initiated by 500,000 or more voters and ratified by a majority of voters in either a majority of the states or in three-fourths thereof. Similarly, Wisconsin's Republican Senator Robert La Follette proposed in 1912 and 1913 that amendments become effective after being proposed by ten states or a majority of Congress and being ratified by a majority vote of citizens in a majority of the states (Musmanno 1929, 194). In 1923 Senator James W. Wadsworth of New York and Representative Finis J. Garrett of Tennessee proposed a "back to the people" amendment that would allow states to require a popular vote to affirm or overturn a state legislature's ratification of an amendment (Vose 1972, 246). Three years earlier in *Hawke v. Smith (I and II)*, the Court had invalidated such a provision in the Ohio state constitution.

Akhil Reed Amar, a contemporary Yale law professor, has argued that the mechanisms in Article V are not exclusive and that citizens already have the right to propose or ratify amendments by popular majorities (Amar 1988). Similarly, Bruce Ackerman has proposed an alteration to Article V whereby a president could propose an amendment in his second term that could be ratified by a three-fifths vote in the next two elections (Ackerman 1991, 54–55). There have been a number of recent plans, most notably one by the National Initiative for Democracy in 2002, which have called for amending the constitution through referendums.

Proposed Changes in Ratification Procedures

Three sets of changes have been proposed that would alter current ratification procedures. One would limit the power of lame-duck legislatures by requiring that one or both houses of a state legislature ratifying an amendment must have been elected after the amendment was proposed. The House of Representatives actually added such a requirement to the Twentieth Amendment, but it was dropped in conference committee (Grimes 1978, 108). In a related vein, some proposals (for example, H.J. Res. 242, 1919) have attempted to ensure that a certain majority is present when such state ratification votes are taken.

A second set of proposals has attempted to set a time limit, usually five to eight years, during which states must ratify amendments. Currently, the Constitution sets no such limits, and although the Supreme Court decided in *Dillon v. Gloss* (1921) that amendments should be rat-

ified relatively contemporaneously, in *Coleman v. Miller* (1939) the Court suggested that such decisions might be "political questions." In 1992 the archivist of the Library of Congress and a vote in Congress certified the validity of the Twenty-seventh Amendment, even though it was not ratified until more than 200 years after being proposed.

A third set of proposals would tackle another unresolved issue by explicitly providing for state rescission of amendments prior to ratification by the necessary three-fourths majority (Musmanno 1929, 206).

Proposals Offered by the Council of State Governments

A meeting of the Council of State Governments in December 1962 resulted in a number of state petitions to Congress for amendments to liberalize the amending process. The council was clearly shaken by the Supreme Court decision in *Baker v. Carr* (1962) and its implications for judicial review of state legislative apportionment. It proposed eliminating the convention mechanism (and the myriad of questions surrounding it) and allowing three-fourths of the states to ratify identical texts of amendments proposed by two-thirds of the states. A similar amendment was proposed again in 1990 (Tolchin 1990, A12); more recently, some state advocates have proposed allowing three-fourths of the states to propose an amendment that would become valid in two years unless two-thirds majorities of both houses rejected it ("Conference of the States" 1995); a more recent version proposed by Representative Thomas J. Bliley (R-VA) would allow two-thirds of the states to petition for an amendment, which, unless disapproved by two-thirds majorities in Congress, would then be resubmitted to the states for three-fourths approval (Thierer 1999). In two additional proposals offered by the Council of State Governments and severely criticized at the time by scholars (for example, Swindler 1963 and C. Black 1963), the council proposed amendments allowing states to apportion themselves without judicial oversight and setting up a Court of the Union with the power to overturn Supreme Court decisions (Vile 1991c, 98–99).

Although the proposals by the Council of State Governments prompted scholarly attention, a number of similar proposals had been introduced in Congress during the previous decade. They would have enabled states to ratify amendments that had been proposed by two-thirds majorities in both houses of the legislatures of twelve states and transmitted to the U.S. secretary of state and the secretary of state within each state.

Other Proposals

One of the earliest proposed changes affecting the amending process was introduced in 1826 and would have limited the introduction of such proposals to every ten years (H.J. Res. 232, 325); by way of comparison, a proposal introduced by New York's Progressive (and later Republican) Walter Chandler in 1916 (H.J. Res. 315) would have provided for constitutional conventions to meet every thirty years to propose amendments. This embodied an idea advocated by Thomas Jefferson, who thought that a new constitution should be considered each generation. Other proposals have called for making ratification by state conventions (an alternative ratification method specified in Article V and used to ratify the Twenty-first Amendment) the exclusive method of state ratification. Still other members of Congress have proposed making the amending process easier by reducing the required two-thirds majorities in Congress to one-half or three-fifths, by permitting less than two-thirds of the states to call a convention to propose amendments, or by reducing the necessary ratification majority of the states from three-fourths to two-thirds (Musmanno 1929, 192–193). By contrast, an amendment offered by Rhode Island when it ratified the Constitution in 1790 would have required the consent of eleven or more of the original thirteen states for any amendments proposed after 1793 (Ames 1896, 292). Consistent with concerns about the antidemocratic impact of judicial review that were expressed in the Progressive Era, Democrat James Doolittle of Kansas introduced a proposal in February 1914 that would have automatically submitted amendments dealing with U.S. laws invalidated by judicial review to states for their acceptance (H.J. Res. 221).

See also Ackerman, Bruce; Amar, Akhil Reed; Corwin Amendment; Council of State Governments; Crittenden Compromise; Initiative and Referendum; National Initiative for Democracy.

For Further Reading:

Ackerman, Bruce. 1991. *We the People: Foundations.* Cambridge, MA: Belknap.

Amar, Akhil R. 1988. "Philadelphia Revisited: Amending the Constitution outside Article V." *University of Chicago Law Review* 55 (Fall): 1043–1104.

Ames, Herman. 1896. *The Proposed Amendments to the Constitution of the United States during the First Century of Its History.* New York: Burt Franklin; 1970 reprint.

Black, Charles L., Jr. 1963. "The Proposed Amendment of Article V: A Threatened Disaster." *Yale Law Journal* 72 (April): 957–966.

"Conference of the States: An Action Plan to Restore Balance in the Federal System." 1995. Concept paper adopted by the Council of State Governments, the National Governors' Association, and the National Conference of State Legislatures. 1 February.

Grimes, Alan P. 1978. *Democracy and the Amendments to the Constitution.* Lexington, MA: Lexington Books.

Levinson, Sanford. 1996b. "The Political Implications of Amending Clauses." *Constitutional Commentary* 13 (Spring): 107–123.

Musmanno, M. A. 1929. *Proposed Amendments to the Constitution.* Washington, DC: U.S. Government Printing Office.

Swindler, William. 1963. "The Current Challenge to Federalism: The Confederating Proposals." *Georgetown Law Review* 52 (Fall): 1–41.

Thierer, Adam D. March 2, 1999. "The Bliley 'States' Initiative': Empowering States and Protecting Federalism." No. 576. The Heritage Foundation Executive Memorandum.

Tolchin, Mark. 1990. "Fifteen States Rally behind Calls for Amendment to Gain More Powers." *New York Times,* 26 June, A-12, col. 3–6.

Vile, John R. 1992. *The Constitutional Amending Process in American Political Thought.* New York: Praeger.

———. 1991c. *Rewriting the United States Constitution: An Examination of Proposals from Reconstruction to the Present.* New York: Praeger.

Vose, Clement E. 1972. *Constitutional Change: Amendment Politics and Supreme Court Litigation since 1900*. Lexington, MA: D. C. Heath.

❖ AMENDMENT, DEFINITION ❖

The dictionary defines amendment as "1. a change for the better; improvement. 2. a correction of errors, faults, etc. 3. *a*) a revision or addition proposed or made in a bill, law, constitution, etc. *b*) the process of making such changes" (*Webster's New World Dictionary of the American Language* 1970). It has been described as "an extraordinarily rich word" (Levinson 1990a, 25). This richness derives in part from the tension between the first two definitions cited above. An amendment may refer to an improvement suggested by progress in human understanding or the accumulation of greater experience and wisdom. The better understandings of the evils of slavery reflected in the post–Civil War Amendments or in the capacities of women as reflected in the Nineteenth Amendment could serve as examples. The idea of amendment can also refer to a correction of errors that have arisen either because of flaws in the original language or structure or from changes brought about through the course of time. The adoption of the Twelfth Amendment correcting flaws in the original electoral college mechanism would be a good example. In the Bible, the term "amend" is sometimes used to exhort individuals or nations to correct moral faults, as when the prophet Jeremiah tells his countrymen to "amend your ways" (KJV, Jer. 7:3, 5). This usage may be related to the idea of "mending" torn clothes.

Scholars have made periodic attempts to distinguish "constitutional amendment" from "constitutional interpretation" or "revision" and to delineate what kinds of changes require amendments and which can be effected through other means. Historical practice appears to demonstrate that such lines, if they exist at all, are relatively fluid (Vile 1994a, 73–76). The only specific remaining qualification to the existing amending procedures that are delineated within the U.S. Constitution provides that states shall not be deprived of their equal suffrage in the U.S. Senate without their consent. Some advocates of additional substantive limits on amendments base their arguments in part on the idea that the term *amendment* implicitly mandates the adoption of changes consistent with the principles and character of the document being amended.

The Constitutional Convention was originally called essentially to amend the Articles of Confederation and ended up replacing them instead. This example always opens the possibility that another constitutional convention, perhaps one even bypassing the specific mechanisms now outlined in Article V, could use convention or popular ratification of its proposals to bypass existing ratification mechanisms. The fear may well be relatively groundless (see Weber and Perry 1989), but concern that a second convention might become a "runaway" body and throw out the baby with the bathwater appears to be a key reason that this mechanism has yet to be utilized.

See also Constitutional Amendments, Limits on; Progress and the Amending Process.

For Further Reading:
Levinson, Sanford. 1990a. "On the Notion of Amendment: Reflections on David Daube's 'Jehovah the Good.'" *S'vara: A Journal of Philosophy and Judaism* 1 (Winter): 25–31.

Vile, John R. 1994a. *Constitutional Change in the United States: A Comparative Study of the Role of Constitutional Amendments, Judicial Interpretations, and Legislative and Executive Actions*. Westport, CT: Praeger.

Weber, Paul J., and Barbara A. Perry. 1989. *Unfounded Fears: Myths and Realities of a Constitutional Convention*. New York: Praeger.

❖ AMES, HERMAN (1865–1935) ❖

Ames was a historian at the University of Pennsylvania who compiled the first comprehensive list and analysis of proposed amendments to the Constitution. Altogether, Ames compiled 1,736 proposals—many with multiple parts— that had been offered in the first 100 years under the Constitution. The central part of Ames's book, which was honored in 1897 by the American Historical Association, was a narrative analysis of proposed amendments according to subject. An appendix listed the date, subject, and other relevant information about proposed amendments (Ames 1896, 306–422).

In discussing the history of U.S. constitutional amendments, Ames divided the amendments proposed in the first 100 years into four periods: 1789–1803, 1804–1860, 1860–1870, and 1870–1889. He associated the first period with "the perfection of details," the second with "general alterations," the third with "slavery and reconstruction," and the fourth with "general emendations" (Ames 1896, 19). Significantly, Ames's volume was published during the second longest period in U.S. history, from 1871 through 1912 (the first was from 1804 to 1865) during which no amendments were successfully proposed and ratified. Acknowledging that many proposals had failed because they "were suggested as cures for temporary evils, . . . were trivial or impracticable, [or] . . . found a place in that unwritten constitution which has grown up side by side with the written document," Ames identified "insurmountable constitutional obstacles" as the central barriers to amendments (Ames 1896, 301). Although suggesting—like other critics from the Progressive Era (Vile 1992, 140–141)—that "the majorities required are too large," Ames did not specify what majorities he would regard as ideal (Ames 1896, 304).

Ames's work has recently been reprinted, along with all nonoverlapping subsequent collections of amending topics proposed in Congress (Vile 2003).

For Further Reading:

Ames, Herman. 1896. *The Proposed Amendments to the Constitution of the United States during the First Century of Its History.* New York: Burt Franklin; 1970 reprint.

Vile, John R., ed. 2002. *Proposed Amendments to the U.S. Constitution, 1787–2001.* 3 Vols. Union, NJ: The Lawbook Exchange.

❖ ANNAPOLIS CONVENTION ❖

Richard Labunski (2000), a journalism professor at the University of Kentucky, has advocated creating a preconvention as a way of inducing states to call an Article V convention. Although the circumstances were much different, the convention that proposed the U.S. Constitution was itself preceded by a preconvention, albeit a fairly truncated one. In 1785 representatives of Virginia and Maryland met at George Washington's home at Mt. Vernon, Virginia, to discuss conflicts they were having with navigation on the Potomac River at a time when Congress had no power over such interstate commerce. James Madison and others used this meeting as a chance to call a broader meeting of the states on the topic of navigation.

When this new meeting convened in Annapolis, Maryland, on 11 September 1786, there was outward cause for pessimism. Only New York, New Jersey, Pennsylvania, Delaware, and Virginia had sent delegates, and they hardly had authority to act on behalf of all thirteen states. Nonetheless, the twelve delegates, which included New York's Alexander Hamilton and Virginia's Edmund Randolph and James Madison, unanimously chose Delaware's John Dickinson as chair and proceeded to deliberate. They unanimously reported their findings to Congress in a report dated 14 September 1786, apparently in the deft hand of Alexander Hamilton (Solberg 1958, 54).

The genius of Hamilton's prose lay in his effort to use the Annapolis Convention as a springboard for a still broader discussion of problems under the Articles of Confederation. He did so by drawing from the commission of the three delegates from New Jersey whose legislature had authorized them "to consider how far a uniform system in their commercial regulations and *other important matters,* might be necessary to the common interest and permanent harmony of the several States" (Solberg 1958, 56). Hamilton used this commission to suggest that other states, too, might recognize that "regulating trade is of such comprehensive extent, and will enter so far into the general System of the federal government, that to give it efficacy, and to obviate questions and doubts concerning its precise nature and limits, may require a correspondent adjustment of other parts of the Foederal System" (Solberg 1958, 57–58).

Accordingly, the delegates to Annapolis proposed a meeting of commissioners:

to meet at Philadelphia on the second Monday in May next, to take into consideration the situation of the United States, to devise such further provisions as shall appear to them necessary to render the constitution of the Foederal Government adequate to the exigencies of the Union; and to report such an Act for that purpose to the United States in Congress assembled, as when agreed to, by them, and afterwards confirmed by the Legislatures of every State, will effectually provide for the same. (Solberg 1958, 58–59)

Fortunately for this resolution, the winter of 1786–1787 witnessed, among other disturbances, Shay's Rebellion in Massachusetts. The apparent inability of the government under the Articles of Confederation to meet this contingency, as well as the cogency of Hamilton's argument for considering questions of trade within a larger context, persuaded additional states to appoint delegates to the Constitutional Convention. Eventually, delegates from all the states except Rhode Island met in Philadelphia to propose what became the Constitution of the United States. Although passed on to the states for approval by Congress, Article VII of the new Constitution bypassed existing state legislatures by providing that the new Constitution would instead be approved by special conventions called within each state.

See also Constitutional Convention of 1787; Labunski, Richard.

For Further Reading:
Labunski, Richard. 2000. *The Second Constitutional Convention: How the American People Can Take Back Their Government.* Versailles, KY: Marley and Beck Press.

Solberg, Winton, ed. 1958. *The Federal Convention and the Formation of the Union.* Indianapolis: The Bobbs-Merrill Company, Inc.

❖ ANTHONY, SUSAN BROWNELL (1820–1906) ❖

Susan B. Anthony was a schoolteacher who was initially interested in the temperance and antislavery movements. She subsequently devoted her efforts to women's suffrage and has been called "the greatest individual in the American suffrage movement" (Kraditor 1981, 12).

Although she was a friend of Frederick Douglass, like her close friend Elizabeth Cady Stanton, Anthony opposed ratification of the Fourteenth and Fifteenth Amendments when they failed to extend to women the rights accorded to African American men; indeed, Anthony declared that she "would sooner cut off my right hand than ask for the ballot for the black man and not for woman" (quoted in McFeely 1991, 266). Anthony and Stanton subsequently established women's suffrage as an "independent feminist movement" (Dubois 1978, 202) and founded the National Woman Suffrage Association in 1869. The same year, women who had supported the Fourteenth and Fifteenth Amendments founded the rival American Woman Suffrage Association. From 1868 to 1870 Anthony edited *The Revolution*, and in 1872 she was tried and convicted in New York State for voting *(United States v. Anthony)*. The amendment that eventually became the Nineteenth Amendment was first introduced in Congress in 1878 (Kraditor 1981, 206) and is often called the Susan B. Anthony amendment. However, it was not proposed by the necessary majorities in Congress until 1919, and the states ratified it in 1920. In the interim, the two leading suffrage organizations had merged into the National American Woman Suffrage Association (NAWSA), with Stanton serving as its first president from 1890 to 1892 and Anthony serving from 1892 to 1900, at which time Carrie Catt became president.

See also Nineteenth Amendment; Stanton, Elizabeth Cady.

For Further Reading:
Dubois, Ellen C. 1978. *Feminism and Suffrage: The Emergence of an Independent Women's Movement*

in America, 1848–1869. Ithaca, NY: Cornell University Press.

Kraditor, Aileen S. 1981. *The Idea of the Woman's Suffrage Movement, 1890–1920.* New York: W. W. Norton.

McFeely, William S. 1991. *Frederick Douglass.* New York: W. W. Norton.

❖ ANTIEAU, CHESTER (1913–) ❖

In 1995 Chester Antieau, a professor emeritus of constitutional law at Georgetown University, published a book designed to offer changes in the Constitution as the nation approached the year 2000. The book is divided into three parts. The first identifies rights that the Supreme Court already implicitly recognizes that should be recognized explicitly. The second discusses existing constitutional provisions that need amendment. The third discusses additional rights that should be included in the Constitution. In defending his proposals, Antieau makes constant reference to earlier legal theorists and philosophers; to previous historical documents and events; to treaties, international human rights declarations, and conventions; and to provisions in the constitutions of a variety of foreign nations and the fifty states.

The four rights that courts implicitly recognize and that Antieau believes should be added to the Constitution are freedom of association, freedom of enterprise, freedom of movement, and the right of privacy. Antieau does not address the difficulties to which judicial enforcement of economic rights led during the New Deal. He does note, however, that the right of privacy could be in conflict with the right to life, but he does not indicate how he would resolve this issue.

Antieau proposes a number of changes to existing constitutional provisions. He wants to expand the guarantees in the Eighth Amendment specifically to protect "the inherent dignity of the human person," to outlaw torture, and to stipulate a right to bail (Antieau 1995, 37). He advocates changing the grounds for impeachment to "serious misconduct to the harm of the nation" (Antieau 1995, 56) and proposes establishing special nonlegislative tribunals to try such impeachments. Antieau wants to modify the Seventh Amendment to eliminate jury trials in civil cases. He further advocates allowing the president to exercise a line-item veto, eliminating the pocket veto, and allowing Congress to override presidential vetoes by less than a two-thirds majority. Antieau supports allowing the Supreme Court to issue advisory opinions and wants to withdraw federal diversity jurisdiction from the federal courts. He favors state-appointed counsel for indigents in civil as well as criminal cases, giving particular attention to cases of child custody. Antieau would allow naturalized citizens to be eligible for the presidency and favors the introduction of constitutional amendments by popular initiative. He also wants the First Amendment to recognize the right of both the public and the press to have access to information.

Many of the rights that Antieau would add to the Constitution are social and economic rights like those contained in other twentieth-century constitutions, including the right to an education; the right to a healthy environment; and the right to adequate social services, such as housing, health care, employment, food, clothing, and social security. He emphasizes the importance of a number of interrelated rights of movement, including the rights of asylum, departure, emigration, voluntary expatriation, and entry and return and the freedom from exile and deportation. Miscellaneous proposals would establish the people's right to recall members of Congress, the right to conscientious objection to military service, and the right not to be executed.

Although Antieau presents an interesting array of proposals, his overall scheme is fairly piecemeal. He does not discuss in any depth the degree to which the listing of social and economic rights would provide cures for such ills. He also does not discuss at any length the impact that new constitutional guarantees might have on the power of the judiciary and on the current scheme of separation of powers.

For Further Reading:

Antieau, Chester J. 1995. *A U.S. Constitution for the Year 2000.* Chicago: Loyola University Press.

❖ ANTI-FEDERALISTS ❖

Even before the Constitution was written, there were individuals such as Virginia's Patrick Henry and George Mason who feared the new national government. They were concerned that it would result in undue consolidation of the states, accent aristocratic tendencies, and jeopardize individual liberties. After the Constitution was proposed for ratification by the states, these forces opposed to a new government became known as Anti-Federalists. They led a vigorous opposition both in public debates and in the ratifying conventions for the new Constitution, noting that it was not being adopted according to the forms specified under the Articles of Confederation. The Anti-Federalists were hindered in their debate by the superior organization of the Federalists, who were pushing for the Constitution, by the support of George Washington for the new Constitution, and by the general consensus that the existing Articles were inadequate.

The two most important outcomes of the debate between the Federalists and Anti-Federalists were arguably the writing of a series of eighty-five essays in defense of the new Constitution, known as *The Federalist Papers,* and the adoption of the first ten amendments to the Constitution, known as the Bill of Rights. Although the Constitutional Convention had barely touched on this issue, the lack of a bill of rights quickly became an important Anti-Federalist rallying point. Federalists initially responded, in *The Federalist Papers* and elsewhere, by arguing in somewhat contradictory fashion that the Constitution already protected important rights (prohibitions against bills of attainder and ex post facto laws, for example) and that additional rights were unnecessary or inappropriate. Anti-Federalists indicated that they would press the states to either propose a second convention or ratify the new Constitution conditionally. Key Federalists, among them James Madison, indicated that they would support a bill of rights once the new Constitution was adopted. This promise—kept by James Madison, who sponsored the Bill of Rights during the First Congress—undoubtedly aided, and may have been essential to, ratification of the document. Initially applying only to the national government and not to the states, the Bill of Rights had little direct impact on governmental operations until the judicial incorporation of the Bill of Rights into the due process clause of the Fourteenth Amendment, which largely occurred in the twentieth century.

At the state ratifying convention, a number of Anti-Federalists argued that the amending process in Article V of the U.S. Constitution would be too difficult (Vile 1992, 32–33). The weakness of this argument was that the new process requiring proposal by two-thirds of both houses of Congress and ratification by three-fourths of the states appeared considerably easier than the process under the Articles of Confederation. This process had required unanimous state consent to amendments proposed in Congress.

See also Bill of Rights; Federalists; Madison, James; Mason, George.

For Further Reading:

Gillespie, Michael L., and Michael Lienesch, eds. 1989. *Ratifying the Constitution.* Lawrence, KS: University Press of Kansas.

Hamilton, Alexander, James Madison, and John Jay. 1787–1788. *The Federalist Papers.* Reprint, New York: New American Library, 1961.

Kenyon, Cecelia, ed. 1985. *The Antifederalists.* Boston: Northeastern University Press.

Lash, Kurt T. 1994. "Rejecting Conventional Wisdom: Federalist Ambivalence in the Framing and Implementation of Article V." *American Journal of Legal History* 38 (April): 197–231.

Main, Jackson T. 1961. *The Antifederalists: Critics of the Constitution, 1781–1788.* Chicago: Quadrangle Books.

Storing, Herbert, ed. 1981. *The Complete Anti-Federalist.* 7 vols. Chicago: University of Chicago Press.

Vile, John R. 1992. *The Constitutional Amending Process in American Political Thought.* New York: Praeger.

❖ ANTIPOLYGAMY LAWS ❖

See Marriage, Divorce, and Parenting.

❖ ANTI-SALOON LEAGUE ❖

One of the organizations that led the push for adoption of the Eighteenth Amendment and national alcoholic prohibition was the Anti-Saloon League, founded in the 1890s. The league existed in tension with the Prohibition Party, which had been established in 1869 and in many ways had been modeled on the antislavery campaign that had resulted in the Civil War and the eventual adoption of the Thirteenth Amendment. Whereas the Prohibition Party ran its own candidates, the Anti-Saloon League adopted a "balance-of-power policy" (Blocker 1976, 162) that enabled it to ally itself with whatever party was willing to adopt its stance as part of its platform. The Prohibition Party was, for a time at least, tempted by an alliance with the Populist Party and its broad agenda of social reform. By contrast, the Anti-Saloon League "posited the existence of a unified constituency closely associated with the churches, the major political parties, and the free enterprise system" (Blocker 1976, 207). The saloon was often viewed as a center of foreign—and Catholic—influence and machine politics (Grimes 1978, 84). By focusing on this institution, the league was especially successful in appealing to middle- and upper-class white Protestant progressives.

The failure of Prohibition and the adoption of the Twenty-first Amendment led to problems for the league. By 1948, it had split into the National Temperance League and the Temperance Education Foundation (Blocker 1976, 235). The Prohibition Party continues to field candidates but is a minor force in current American politics.

See also Eighteenth Amendment.

For Further Reading:

Blocker, Jack S., Jr. 1976. *Retreat from Reform: The Prohibition Movement in the United States, 1890–1916.* Westport, CT: Greenwood Press.

Grimes, Alan P. 1978. *Democracy and the Amendments to the Constitution.* Lexington, MA: Lexington Books.

Kerr, K. Austin. 1985. *Organized for Prohibition: A New History of the Anti-Saloon League.* New Haven, CT: Yale University Press.

❖ APPROPRIATENESS OF AMENDMENTS ❖

See Citizens for the Constitution, the Constitutional Amendment Initiative.

❖ ARCHIVIST OF THE UNITED STATES ❖

The Archivist of the United States, who heads the National Archives and Records Administration (NARA), is the individual currently responsible for certifying constitutional amendments. The secretary of state performed this function by custom through 1818 and by statute until 1951. Congress then transferred the duty to the administrator of general services, who published the *Federal Register.* Congress transferred both functions to the archivist in 1984. The provision of the code specifying the archivist's authority is relatively brief. It provides that:

> Whenever official notice is received at the National Archives and Records Administration that any amendment proposed to the Constitution of the United States has been adopted, according to the provisions of the Constitution, the Archivist of the United States shall forthwith cause the amendment to be published, with his certificate, specifying the States by which the same may have been adopted, and that the same has become valid, to all intents and purposes, as a part of the Constitution of the United States. (1 U.S.C. § 106(b) (1984))

Under this provision, the archivist is the one who submits amendments that Congress has proposed to state governors, who then submit them to the state legislatures. Sometimes states ratify amendments, however, even before they receive official notice. Whenever they act, they send their proposals to the archivist, who in turn gives them to the Office of the Federal Register (OFR) to check for "facial legal sufficiency and an authenticating signature" ("Constitutional

Amendment Process," archives website). If the necessary three-fourths of the states respond, the archivist then certifies the validity of the amendment, and it is published in the *Federal Register* and in U.S. Statutes at Large ("Constitutional Amendment Process," archives website).

On 18 May 1992, after forty states had ratified it, archivist Don Wilson certified ratification of the Twenty-seventh Amendment and had it published the next day in the *Federal Register*. This was controversial because of the long time that had elapsed between the amendment's proposal in 1789 (as the second of twelve amendments submitted to the states at that time) and its putative ratification in 1992. Senators Robert Byrd and Charles Grassley criticized Wilson for not submitting the issue to Congress, as the secretary of state had done with the controversial Fourteenth Amendment. It is not clear, however, that an amendment must be certified or published before it becomes part of the Constitution. Moreover, although Congress subsequently voted to confirm Wilson's judgment (Bernstein with Agel 1993, 246–247), this too was probably legally unnecessary (Dellinger 1983, 402).

One contemporary scholar has questioned whether it is appropriate for members of the executive branch, like either the secretary of state or the archivist, to certify amendments. Pointing to the Supreme Court's declaration in *Hollingsworth v. Virginia* (1798) that a president's signature was not necessary to the validity of constitutional amendments, this scholar further notes that "the very nature of the powers of the executive branch is to faithfully execute the laws, rather than to pass judgment upon the validity of the constitutional amendment" (Ishikawa 1997, 591). Acknowledging that his solution would not be without problems of its own, most notably the precedent in *Coleman v. Miller* (1939) essentially renouncing such review, this same scholar believes that courts could more fairly and effectively determine matters involving procedural questions surrounding the ratification of amendments (Ishikawa 1997, 592–593).

See also Administrator of the General Services Administration; *Coleman v. Miller;* *Hollingsworth v. Virginia;* Office of the Federal Register; Secretary of State.

For Further Reading:

Bernstein, Richard B., with Jerome Agel. 1993. *Amending America: If We Love the Constitution So Much, Why Do We Keep Trying To Change It?* New York: Random House.

"Constitutional Amendment Process," *http://www.archives.gov/federal_register/constitution/amendment_process.html*.

Dellinger, Walter. 1983. "The Legitimacy of Constitutional Change: Rethinking the Amending Process." *Harvard Law Review* 97 (December): 380–432.

Ishikawa, Brendon T. 1997. "Everything You Always Wanted to Know about How Amendments Are Made, but Were Afraid to Ask." *Hastings Constitutional Law Quarterly* 24 (Winter):545–597.

❖ ARTICLE V OF THE U.S. CONSTITUTION ❖

This is the article that delineates the constitutional amending process. It provides two ways for amendments to be proposed and two ways for them to be ratified. To date, all amendments have been proposed by a two-thirds vote of both houses of Congress, but two-thirds of the states may also petition Congress to call a convention to propose such amendments. Moreover, calls that fall short of a mandate may still serve to exert pressure on Congress to act—as they did, for example, in pressuring Congress to propose the Seventeenth Amendment, which provided for direct election of senators. All but one of the existing twenty-seven amendments have been ratified by the legislatures in three-fourths of the states, but Congress may stipulate that ratification be effected by special conventions called in each of the states. This latter procedure was specified by the delegates to the Constitutional Convention of 1787 with respect to the Constitution itself and by Congress in the case of the Twenty-first Amendment, repealing national alcoholic prohibition.

Limits

Article V delineates two substantive limits on the amending process. One, dealing with slave importation, is no longer relevant. The second prohibits states from being denied their equal vote in the U.S. Senate without their consent. Although a number of Supreme Court decisions have rejected the notion that there are additional limits on the amending process, some contemporary scholars (W. Murphy 1980, for example) believe that the issue is still viable. The argument was raised by those who questioned the legitimacy of amendments proposed in the wake of *Texas v. Johnson* (1989) and *United States v. Eichman* (1990) to prohibit flag desecration.

Origins

Article V is important because it offers a peaceful alternative to the kind of revolution that the colonists were forced to proclaim in the Declaration of Independence. Although philosophers had been discussing the need for constitutional change for centuries, formal amending mechanisms were necessitated by the development of written constitutions and thus originated in colonial charters first granted by William Penn. Such mechanisms also appeared in most of the state constitutions written during the American Revolutionary War period. Early state constitutions provided for amendment by legislative action, by state conventions, or through a council of censors (Vile 1992, 25). The Articles of Confederation provided for amendments to be approved by Congress and ratified by unanimous consent of the state legislatures. The unanimity requirement made this provision ineffective and served to caution the framers of the U.S. Constitution about devising an amending process that was too difficult.

The Constitutional Convention

Delegates to the Constitutional Convention of 1787 generally agreed that a formal amending process was needed. The Virginia plan proposed that congressional consent to such amendments should not be required, and the first formal proposal that emerged at the convention specified that Congress should call a convention to propose amendments at the request of two-thirds of the states (Farrand 1966, 2:159). George Mason expressed concern that this mechanism might be used to subvert the states, Alexander Hamilton thought that Congress should be able to propose amendments on its own, and James Madison argued that the convention mechanism was too vague. Therefore, a new proposal was offered: two-thirds majorities in Congress would propose amendments when Congress so chose or when it was petitioned by two-thirds of the state legislatures. The clause entrenching the slave importation agreement was added at this time (Farrand 1966, 2:559). Two days before the Constitution was signed, the proposed amending provision was altered so that Congress could propose amendments or states could petition Congress to call a convention to propose amendments. The convention mechanism was designed to circumvent Congress. If Congress refused to propose amendments, a convention could do so. The convention adopted this alteration after George Mason expressed fears that amendments would be impossible if Congress proved to be unresponsive (Farrand 1966, 2:559–560). The clause protecting state representation in the Senate was also added then.

Principles of Article V

Article V embodies a number of distinct concerns and principles. Consistent with the desire that the Constitution be paramount to ordinary legislation, the process is intended to be difficult, but not impossible (Ginsburg 1989–1990; Vile 1993a, 101–105). There is no constitutional provision, such as that which Thomas Jefferson advocated, for automatic constitutional revision or review at periodic intervals. Consistent with federalism, the article allows states to initiate, and requires that they ratify, amendments. Consistent with the desire for deliberation, the process involves at least two stages and requires supermajorities for each one. Consistent with suspicions of entrenched power and an emphasis on popular sovereignty, Article V offers a pathway around a recalcitrant Congress.

The History of Article V

Although scholars have praised the amending process throughout most of U.S. history (scholars writing around the Civil War and the Progressive Era sometimes being exceptions), the process has arguably proved more difficult in practice than was anticipated (Berry 1987). This difficulty is particularly evident when the federal process is compared with counterparts at the state level or with processes in most foreign countries (Lutz 1994) or when the history of the amending process is examined (Grimes 1978; Bernstein with Agel 1993). The primary obstacle has been the difficulty of proposing amendments by the requisite majority of both houses of Congress. Although more than 11,000 such proposals have been introduced in Congress—many redundant and centering around a few major issues—only thirty-three have been reported to the states for ratification by the necessary majorities. Of these proposals, twenty-seven have been ratified.

Many of these amendments fall into distinct clusters. The first ten amendments, the Bill of Rights, were ratified in 1791 and were the result of Anti-Federalist criticisms of the new Constitution. The Thirteenth, Fourteenth, and Fifteenth Amendments were ratified in the five-year period after the Civil War. Four amendments were ratified from 1913 to 1920, at the end of the Progressive Era. Many amendments have helped make the U.S. system of government considerably more democratic than it was when it was established. Expansions of the franchise—for example, in the Fifteenth, Nineteenth, and Twenty-sixth Amendments—have been especially important. Proposals for new or substantially altered constitutions have rarely stirred more than passing interest (see Boyd 1992; Vile 1991c).

Alternative Means of Change

The difficulty of the amending process has encouraged other means of change (Lutz 1994). Judicial interpretations of the Constitution have contributed to its flexibility, but congressional practices and presidential initiatives have also proved important (Vile 1994a). An unwritten constitution has, in effect, grown up around and supplemented the words of the written document. Although written constitutional provisions have the capacity to trump conflicting customs and usages, changes can often be effected to fill in constitutional gaps and silences. On at least four occasions (the Eleventh, the Thirteenth and Fourteenth, the Sixteenth, and the Twenty-sixth Amendments), amendments have been adopted to overturn Supreme Court decisions. The Supreme Court, in turn, interprets such amendments. At times, it may construe such provisions more restrictively or more expansively than their authors intended.

Unresolved Issues

In early American history, the Supreme Court resolved some important issues. In *Hollingsworth v. Virginia* (1798), for example, it decided that the president's signature was not needed for a constitutional amendment. In *Dillon v. Gloss* (1921), it ruled that ratification of amendments should reflect a contemporary consensus. In *Coleman v. Miller* (1939), however, the Court decided that such issues were political questions to be resolved by the elected branches of government. Many such issues remain unresolved. A number of them center on the still unused convention mechanism (Caplan 1988). Other unresolved questions involve whether states have the power to rescind ratification of amendments prior to the time a three-fourths majority is mustered, whether states should be permitted to ratify amendments they have previously rejected, and how long states have to ratify amendments. This last issue was prominent in the case of the Twenty-seventh Amendment, which was putatively ratified more than 200 years after it was originally proposed by Congress. Additional issues involve what conditions Congress can place on proposed amendments and whether Congress can extend a previously specified ratification date, as it did in the case of the failed equal rights amendment (Vile 1992, 45–54).

A number of procedural changes in the constitutional amending process have been proposed to clarify these questions or to make the amending process easier. Akhil Reed Amar (1988) suggests that Article V mechanisms may not be the exclusive means by which formal constitutional changes can be effected. He believes that such changes might also be effected by popular initiative or ratified by referendum. Professor Bruce Ackerman (1991) favors adopting an amendment to allow for ratification of amendment by referendum. Perhaps more importantly, Ackerman argues that major changes in constitutional interpretation have been initiated at various times in American history, most notably in the writing and ratification of the Constitution, the post–Civil War period, and the New Deal, without following the letter of Article V amending processes.

See also History of Constitutional Amendments in the United States.

For Further Reading:
Ackerman, Bruce. 1991. *We the People: Foundations.* Cambridge, MA: Belknap.

Amar, Akhil R. 1988. "Philadelphia Revisited: Amending the Constitution outside Article V." *University of Chicago Law Review* 55 (Fall): 1043–1104.

Bernstein, Richard B., with Jerome Agel. 1993. *Amending America: If We Love the Constitution So Much, Why Do We Keep Trying to Change It?* New York: Random House.

Berry, Mary F. 1987. "How Hard It Is to Change." *New York Times Magazine,* 13 September, 93–98.

Boyd, Steven R., ed. 1992. *Alternative Constitutions for the United States: A Documentary History.* Westport, CT: Greenwood Press.

Caplan, Russell L. 1988. *Constitutional Brinkmanship: Amending the Constitution by National Convention.* New York: Oxford University Press.

Farrand, Max, ed. 1966. *The Records of the Federal Convention.* 4 vols. New Haven, CT: Yale University Press.

Ginsburg, Ruth B. 1989–1990. "On Amending the Constitution: A Plea for Patience." *University of Arkansas at Little Rock Law Journal* 12: 677–694.

Grimes, Alan P. 1978. *Democracy and the Amendments to the Constitution.* Lexington, MA: Lexington Books.

Lutz, Donald S. 1994. "Toward a Theory of Constitutional Amendment." *American Political Science Review* 88 (June): 355–370.

Murphy, Walter F. 1980. "An Ordering of Constitutional Values." *Southern California Law Review* 53: 703–760.

Vile, John R. 1994a. *Constitutional Change in the United States: A Comparative Study of the Role of Constitutional Amendments, Judicial Interpretations, and Legislative and Executive Actions.* Westport, CT: Praeger.

———. 1993a. *Contemporary Questions Surrounding the Constitutional Amending Process.* Westport, CT: Praeger.

———. 1993b. *The Theory and Practice of Constitutional Change in America: A Collection of Original Source Materials.* New York: Peter Lang.

———. 1992. *The Constitutional Amending Process in American Political Thought.* New York: Praeger.

———. 1991c. *Rewriting the United States Constitution: An Examination of Proposals from Reconstruction to the Present.* New York: Praeger.

❖ ARTICLES OF CONFEDERATION ❖

After the Revolutionary War and before the Constitution of 1787 the newly liberated states established a league of friendship among themselves governed by a document known as the Articles of Confederation. Pennsylvania's John Dickinson was largely responsible for writing the document, but the Continental Congress, which approved it in 1777, modified his handiwork so as to keep major powers at the state level. Requiring unanimous state approval, the Articles did not go into effect until Maryland, which had been holding out until the larger states renounced their claims to western lands, ratified it in 1781.

Formed at a time when states were extremely jealous of their powers and suspicious of strong executive power, such as that exercised by George III during the colonial period, the Articles embodied the principle of state sovereignty. Article II provided that "each state retains its sovereignty, freedom, and independence, and every Power, Jurisdiction and right, which is not by this confederation expressly delegated to the United States, in Congress assembled" (Solberg 1958, 42). Whereas the current U.S. Constitution is based on the division of power among three branches, the unicameral legislative branch—in which each state has an equal vote—dominated the Articles. This branch, however, was not entrusted with power over interstate commerce, and on key matters, the consent of nine or more states was required. Members of the Confederation Congress were elected by the state legislatures, and they further depended on the states for raising revenue and mustering armies.

Article XIII provided for an amending process. Congress would vote on amendments, which were then to be approved by all thirteen state legislatures. This process ultimately proved too wooden, and despite several attempts, including two that fell but a single state shy of adoption (Bernstein with Agel 1993, 12), no amendments survived the gauntlet of unanimous state ratification.

Although the government under the Articles provided a useful transition from British to American rule and was responsible for such achievements as the Northwest Ordinance of 1787, contemporaries came to agree that it did not provide for an adequate central authority. Accordingly, when the Constitutional Convention of 1787 met, the delegates decided to start with a new plan rather than attempt to revise the existing document. Ignoring the provision of Article XIII, the delegates specified that the new document would go into effect when ratified by nine of the states. The convention delegates further provided that the new document would be ratified not by the existing state legislatures, which would lose power to the new Congress, but by special conventions called within the states. So technically, at least, the new system was adopted illegally (Kay 1987; Ackerman and Katyal 1991). Article V of the U.S. Constitution continued the two-step process for amendment, providing that two-thirds of both houses would propose amendments that three-fourths of the states would have to ratify.

Particularly in early American history, debates arose between individuals who believed that the new Constitution simply added some congressional powers while continuing to reserve key powers to the states that were part of a continuing "compact," and those who thought that the new government was intended to be significantly different and that it had effectively created a new nation of "We the People." Although the outcome of the Civil War put to rest extreme views of state sovereignty, debate continues over the appropriate role for states in the federal system created by the new Constitution.

For Further Reading:

Ackerman, Bruce, and Ned Katyal. 1991. "Our Unconventional Founding." *University of Chicago Law Review* 62 (Spring): 475–573.

Bernstein, Richard B., with Jerome Agel. 1993. *Amending America: If We Love the Constitution So Much, Why Do We Keep Trying to Change It?* New York: Random House.

Jensen, Merrill. 1966. *The Articles of Confederation.* Madison: University of Wisconsin Press.

Kay, Richard S. 1987. "The Illegality of the Constitution." *Constitutional Commentary* 4 (Winter): 57–80.

Solberg, Winton, ed. 1958. *The Federal Convention and the Formation of the Union.* Indianapolis, IN: Bobbs-Merrill.

❖ ASSOCIATION, FREEDOM OF ❖

Although the Constitution does not specifically delineate a right of association, the Supreme Court has recognized it. For example, it declared in a unanimous decision written by John Marshall Harlan II in *National Association for the Advancement of Colored People v. Alabama ex rel. Patterson* (1958, 460) that freedom of association was essential to "effective advocacy" and "an inseparable aspect of the 'liberty' assured by the Due Process Clause of the Fourteenth Amendment, which embraces freedom of speech." The Court accordingly voided an Alabama law requiring that the state chapter of the NAACP disclose the list of its members, who might then be subject to reprisals.

Ironically, when two Florida congressmen (Republican Charles Bennett and Democrat Donald Matthews) introduced amendments designed to preserve freedom of association in 1963 (H.J. Res. 728 and 775), their objective was to insulate the areas of private business, housing, and education from the effects of the Supreme Court's decision in *Brown v. Board of Education* (1954), which had mandated racial desegregation. Such an amendment, which appears to have had little chance of success, would have permitted states to segregate students by race and sex in public schools, subject to the "separate but equal" standard originally established in *Plessy v. Ferguson* (1896) but repudiated in *Brown* (*Congressional Record*, 16909–10, 19449 (1963)).

The freedom of association under the First Amendment was one of the bases cited in *Griswold v. Connecticut* (1965) as a foundation for the right of privacy. This right was expanded in *Roe v. Wade* (1973) to include the right of a woman to obtain an abortion, at least in the first two trimesters of pregnancy.

For Further Reading:

National Association for the Advancement of Colored People v. Alabama ex rel. Patterson, 356 U.S. 449 (1958).

❖ ATTORNEY GENERAL ❖

Although she remained in office throughout both of Bill Clinton's terms, Attorney General Janet Reno, like current Attorney General John Ashcroft, was surrounded by controversy. Most prominent were the disputes surrounding her response to the Branch Davidian religious movement led by David Koresh (he died along with most of his followers when the building burned after being attacked by the F.B.I. in Waco, Texas), and, later, for the handling of the immigration of Elian Gonzales (whose mother had died at sea while bringing him from Cuba to the United States but who was eventually returned, at the insistence of the U.S. and Cuban governments, to his father in Cuba).

Perhaps motivated by the former issue (the latter did not occur until 1999), Democrat Ralph Hall of Texas proposed an amendment in August 1998 that the individual with the responsibilities of the current attorney general be an elected official (see Vile 2003, 3:1692). Currently, the attorney general is a cabinet officer, indeed one of the first so established, appointed by the president with the advice and consent of the U.S. Senate. If the attorney general were to be elected, that individual would presumably be more accountable to the American people, but, similarly, it might be difficult to hold the president personally accountable for enforcing the laws of the United States.

For Further Reading:

Vile, John R., ed. 2003. *Proposed Amendments to the U.S. Constitution, 1787–2001.* 3 Vols. Union, NJ: Law Book Exchange.

B

❖

❖ BACON, SELDEN (1861?–?) ❖

Bacon was the spokesman for a group of New York lawyers in the late 1920s and early 1930s. He argued in a pamphlet and a follow-up article that the Tenth Amendment implied limits on the amending process in addition to those explicitly stated in Article V (see Vile 1992, 169–170). Bacon contended that Roger Sherman had inserted the words "to the United States" in the Tenth Amendment specifically to limit Article V—the amending process being such a power "not delegated to the United States" but given to the states or their people. By this addition, Sherman hoped to close the potential loophole that the delegates to the Constitutional Convention of 1787 had created whereby Article V might strip people of their liberties (S. Bacon 1930, 780).

According to Bacon's interpretation, matters that the Tenth Amendment reserved to the people could be effected only through the use of the convention method of ratification. Bacon cited the Eighteenth Amendment, which provided for national alcoholic prohibition, as an amendment requiring such popular ratification (S. Bacon 1930, 793). He argued that its effects on personal liberty were significantly different from previous amendments that the Supreme Court had recently upheld against similar challenges. Although Henry Taft (1930) attempted to refute his arguments, Bacon reiterated them before the Supreme Court in arguing the case of *United States v. Sprague* (1931). Although the Court rejected Bacon's arguments, similar arguments continue to interest both modern proponents of sub-stantive limits on the amending process and those who favor ratification of amendments by referendum.

See also Constitutional Amendments, Limits On.

For Further Reading:

Bacon, Selden. 1930. "How the Tenth Amendment Affected the Fifth Article of the Constitution." *Virginia Law Review* 16 (June): 771–791.

Taft, Henry. 1930. "Amendment of the Federal Constitution: Is the Power Conferred by Article V Limited by the Tenth Amendment?" *Virginia Law Review* 16 (May): 647–658.

Vile, John R. 1992. *The Constitutional Amending Process in American Political Thought*. New York: Praeger.

❖ BAILEY, MARTIN J. (1927–2000?) ❖

One of the most unusual texts of a new constitution was published posthumously in a book by Martin J. Bailey, a longtime economist (Ph.D. Johns Hopkins University) at Emory University and other institutions who also held a variety of governmental positions. Entitled *Constitution for a Future Country* (2001), the proposed constitution and accompanying text justifying it are among the most detailed and complex ever to be offered.

Bailey, whose views were chiefly influenced by the public choice school of economics, whose proponents concentrate on the ties between economic choices and political institutions, be-lieved that existing governments are riddled by inefficiencies. These largely result from the fact that special interests are able to organize and lobby for legislation to give themselves great benefits at only minimal costs to the public at large, who therefore have less incentive to or-ganize against them. Bailey estimated that close to 50 percent of governmental spending is wasteful and could be sharply reduced if gov-ernments were given fewer monopolies and if individuals could express their true preferences when it came to what programs they were will-ing to support through taxation.

Apart from his analysis and the draft of a new constitution, Bailey does not appear to have taken concrete steps to get his constitution adopted. Although his model serves as a clear alternative to the kind of system that is embod-ied in the United States, he appears to think that a proposal like his own has the best chance in a new nation. Speaking of existing countries and the possibility of initiating change by con-stitutional convention, he notes that:

> Every such country already has too many entrenched interests for such a conven-tion to have an appreciable chance of suc-cess. The only hope for its adoption is in a new country of unusually prudent vot-ers with unusually perspicacious leaders. (Bailey 2001, 168)

Bailey might have added that it would also help if the nation were composed chiefly of economists familiar with, and supportive of, such mechanisms as "a Lindahl tax," the "Thomson Insurance Mechanism," and the "Vickrey-Clarke-Groves, or VCG mechanism," all of which are prominently featured in his book.

Bailey's proposal is far too complicated to be explained in a short essay by a noneconomist, but Bailey himself identified what he consid-ered to be the seven prime characteristics of his proposal. They were:

1. stratified random selection of official legislators [selected by chance rather than through elections];

2. a demand-revealing process [designed to ascertain public will] in each official legislature;
3. estimated Lindahl taxes [designed so that citizens favor taxes that benefit them and oppose those that are overly costly];
4. potentially generous compensation for legislators based on all relevant out-comes, combined with competition among legislatures;
5. protection from bribery and extortion;
6. referenda with combined demand–re-vealing mechanisms; [and]
7. monitoring and enforcement of the performance of approved programs. (Bailey 2001, 51)

Bailey's constitution is rare in its provision that legislators would not only be randomly se-lected but, once chosen, would be sealed off from their constituents and forbidden to corre-spond with them. (This author knows of only one other such proposal, drafted by Jim David-son for a hypothetical country called "Oceana.") Competition would be encouraged in Bailey's system among both courts (which would have to support themselves through user fees) and legislatures, but ultimately the people would settle almost every question through use of referenda. Governments would be strictly limited in their powers. Significantly, Bailey would put strict limits on judicial constructions of his document. He specified in a provision on the judiciary that:

> The courts shall interpret the law as it [was] meant when enacted, and shall not amend or modify the law. The only law, in addition to this constitution, shall be statute law. The courts shall interpret the constitution in terms of the meaning it had at the time it was ratified and simi-larly for the interpretation of each consti-tutional amendment and of each law. (Bailey 2001, 110)

Although Bailey's constitution puts great emphasis on freedom of contract and other property-related rights, he devotes significantly less attention to traditional civil liberties. Perhaps because he was so confident that the mechanisms he had devised would be effective, his section on civil liberties is one of the sketchiest of his constitution:

> Bill of rights. Standard stuff, including strict prohibition of retroactive laws. Strict prohibition of involuntary servitude in any form, except that in the case of foreign invasion or an imminent threat of same, the government may use emergency powers to compel military service for up to a maximum of sixty days by citizens represented in official legislatures and qualified to vote, whose compensation shall be provided by law. Freedom of association and of political expression shall not include freedom to form coalitions or conspiracies by voters having the purpose of misrepresenting the harms to them of legislative proposals on the ballot. (Bailey 2001, 99)

As theories of public choice become increasingly prominent in the academic community, it would not be surprising to see many of Bailey's proposals reflected elsewhere. However, the high degree of economic sophistication that would be required to understand—much less evaluate—Bailey's proposals, and others like them, is likely to serve as a fairly strong obstacle to their adoption.

See also Davidson, Jim.

For Further Reading:
Bailey, Martin J. 2001. *Constitution for a Future Country.* New York: Palgrave.

❖ *BAKER V. CARR* (1962) ❖

Baker v. Carr was the six-to-two decision in which Justice William Brennan declared for the Supreme Court that matters of state legislative apportionment were not political questions unfit for judicial resolution, but were justiciable under the equal protection clause of the Fourteenth Amendment. The decision remanded

for consideration a Tennessee scheme of state legislative apportionment that favored rural counties and had not been altered since 1901, and it appeared to overturn an earlier plurality opinion in an Illinois case, *Colegrove v. Green* (1946). It also prepared the way for the Court to apply a one-person, one-vote standard for apportionment in both houses of a state legislature in *Reynolds v. Sims* (1964).

Focusing on a state matter rather than on a dispute among the three branches of the national government, *Baker v. Carr* does not appear to have overturned the Court's decision in *Luther v. Borden* (1849), which was that the question of whether a state government is republican is a political question. *Baker* also seems to have left standing the decision in *Coleman v. Miller* (1939), entrusting decisions about the ratification of amendments to the elected branches (discussed in *Baker* 1962, 214–215).

In *Baker,* Brennan identified six factors involved in political questions:

> [1.] a textually demonstrable constitutional commitment of the issue to a coordinate political department; [2.] or a lack of judicially discoverable and manageable standards for resolving it; [3.] or the impossibility of deciding without an initial policy determination of a kind clearly for nonjudicial discretion; [4.] or the impossibility of a court's undertaking independent resolution without expressing lack of the respect due coordinate branches of government; [5.] or an unusual need for unquestioning adherence to a political decision already made; [6.] or the potentiality of embarrassment from multifarious pronouncements by various departments on one question. (*Baker* 1962, 217)

Brennan noted that the citizens of Tennessee had no initiative and that the state amending process made it difficult for the people to initiate changes in the apportionment process (*Baker* 1962, 193–194). Justices Douglas and Clark wrote concurring opinions, and Justices Frankfurter and Harlan authored vigorous dissents questioning the wisdom of judicial intervention in this complex area and suggesting that the framers of the equal protection clause had not intended for it to apply to such controversies.

Baker and follow-up opinions stimulated calls for amendments in Congress and increased public opposition to the Warren Court. In a move led by Illinois Senator Everett Dirksen, the states fell but a single vote short of mustering the necessary two-thirds majority needed to force Congress to call a special constitutional convention on the subject. The decision also generated controversial proposals for amendments by the Council of State Governments. Scholars have both praised (Ely 1980) and criticized the Court for its apportionment decisions (Elliott 1974). In recent years, the primary controversies involving apportionment have centered less on the justiciability of the issue (or on subsequent controversies over "one person, one vote") than on the degree to which such districts can be gerrymandered so as to create districts that are composed predominately of minority-race members. Although in decisions such as *Shaw v. Reno* (1993), *Bush v. Vera* (1996), and *Shaw v. Hunt* (1996), the Court has indicated that it looks unfavorably on districts drawn strictly on the basis of race, it has arguably yet to set clear standards in this area, perhaps in part vindicating Frankfurter and Harlan's concern about the complexity of judicial decision making in regard to this issue.

See also Council of State Governments; Dirksen, Everett McKinley; Political Questions; *Reynolds v. Sims*; States, Legislative Apportionment.

For Further Reading:

Baker v. Carr, 369 U.S. 186 (1962).

Elliott, Ward. 1974. *The Rise of Guardian Democracy*. Cambridge, MA: Harvard University Press.

Ely, John Hart. 1980. *Democracy and Distrust*. Cambridge, MA: Harvard University Press.

Irons, Peter, and Stephanie Guitton, eds. 1993. *May It Please the Court*. New York: New Press.

Lee, Calvin B. T. 1967. *One Man One Vote: WMCA and the Struggle for Equal Representation*. New York: Charles Scribner's Sons.

❖ BALANCED BUDGET AMENDMENT ❖

Among the powers the Constitution grants to Congress in Article I, Section 8 is the power "to borrow Money on the credit of the United States." As early as 1798, Thomas Jefferson advocated an amendment to withdraw such authorization. Somewhat ironically, however, when he subsequently became president, he proved willing to borrow the $15 million for the Louisiana Purchase (Savage 1988, 106–107). Similarly, his Republican successor, James Madison, borrowed to finance the War of 1812.

Governmental debt was not uncommon in the eighteenth and nineteenth centuries, especially during wartime. From a modern perspective, in which debt seems almost routine, it seems unusual to discover that amendments were offered in the 1820s and 1830s for spending federal surpluses. Later in the nineteenth century, Section 4 of the Fourteenth Amendment indicated that the United States would honor its own, but not the Confederate, debt.

In the 1870s and 1880s, amendments were introduced to limit the national debt, but the last several decades have been the most active period for such proposed amendments. Hundreds of proposals have been introduced during this time. One commentator noted that, in this respect, "the balanced budget amendment has shown itself to be the constitutional equivalent of the Energizer bunny" (Kyvig 1995, 99). In 1969 the National Taxpayers Union was formed to support the balanced budget amendment. Although generally associated with conservatives, this group has also mustered some support among liberals, including then-Illinois Democratic Senator Paul Simon.

At one time or another, as many as thirty-two of the needed thirty-four states have petitioned Congress to call a convention to address the balanced budget amendment, although some have since withdrawn their petitions. Moreover, on several occasions, a balanced budget amendment has been voted on in Congress. The proposal was especially popular during the Reagan and Bush years, and, after being highlighted in the 1994 Republican Contract with America, the amendment gained renewed attention.

In August 1982 the Senate voted sixty-nine to thirty-one for a balanced budget amendment, but it stalled in the House of Representatives. In 1986 a balanced budget amendment fell a single vote short of the needed majority in the Senate. In 1990 it was seven votes shy of the needed majority in the House, and in 1992 it fell only nine votes short (Kyvig 1995, 114, 118–119). After the Republican gains in the 1994 congressional elections, a balanced budget amendment passed the House of Representatives, but it subsequently came up a single vote shy of adoption in the Senate. One of the amendment's supporters, Republican Senate Majority Leader Robert Dole of Kansas, ultimately cast his vote against the amendment. This parliamentary maneuver allowed him to reintroduce the measure in 1996, just before he retired to run for president. On June 6, 1996, the amendment fell two votes short of the needed majority. The vote in the Senate was even closer on March 4, 1997, when the Senate vote of sixty-six to thirty-four fell a single vote shy of the required two-thirds vote, despite the fact that all fifty-five Senate Republicans voted in favor of the measure. The vote was attributed in part to a last-minute defection by Democrat Robert G. Torricelli of New Jersey, who had advocated such an amendment in his Senate campaign and previously voted three of three occasions for a similar measure (Taylor 1997, 577).

An article published in 2000 has suggested that a Balanced Budget Amendment is likely both to be adopted and (like the Prohibition Amendment) later repealed. The first conclusion, however, is based on the somewhat dubious belief that states do not have power to rescind proposals for constitutional convention because such rescissions are not "statutorily required to be officially recorded and printed in the Federal Register" (see Ishikawa 2000, 357).

Although the idea of a balanced budget appears relatively simple on the surface, its supporters are motivated by different objectives, and these are sometimes in tension. Like earlier supporters of an amendment to limit the percentage of income that could be collected through the income tax that was sanctioned in

the Sixteenth Amendment, many supporters see the balanced budget mechanism primarily as a means of curtailing the increased activities and expenditures of the federal government since the New Deal was introduced in the 1930s and 1940s. Others anticipate that such an amendment would require the government to increase taxes to pay for current programs.

Differences in objectives and approaches are reflected in the variety of amendments that have been introduced in Congress on the subject. These have included proposals to limit governmental expenditures to a fixed percentage of the gross national product; to require Congress to stay in session until it proposes a balanced budget; to prevent expenditures from exceeding revenues except in cases of war or emergency; to require every appropriation measure to be accompanied by a revenue-raising measure; to require the approval of an extraordinary majority of Congress to raise taxes; to require the approval of an extraordinary majority of Congress to raise the ceiling on the debt; to mandate increased taxes in certain deficit situations; to begin paying back the national debt; and to provide for a taxpayer's bill of rights. Some such proposals have been tied to prohibitions against unfunded federal mandates or to proposals for a presidential line-item veto.

Economists vigorously debate the desirability or undesirability of a balanced federal budget. Critics of unbalanced budgets, and of a debt that is now in the trillions of dollars, believe that such budgets contribute to inflationary pressures, lead to higher interest rates, and generally transfer burdens from the current generation to generations yet unborn. Defenders argue that the links between budget deficits and inflation and higher interest rates are problematic and point out that future generations often benefit from current expenditures (contrast J. Davidson 1992 and McIntyre 1992; also see Moore and Penner 1980 and Fink and High 1987). Moreover, the widely accepted economic theory developed by John Maynard Keynes suggests that governmental deficits can help stimulate the economy during times of recession and that balanced budgets can actually prolong such recessions. In the last thirty years or so, however, the federal government has usually run deficits even in years of prosperity—there was no surplus from 1969 until the second term of the Clinton administration. This suggests to some proponents of a balanced budget amendment that the political pressures on members of Congress to reap rewards for current constituents, the price of which is deferred to future taxpayers, may need a constitutional counterweight such as a balanced budget amendment. Critics of the deficit also point to the increasing percentage of the budget that is needed to service such debt and the wealthier members of society who will profit from such payments.

Ironically, Presidents Reagan and George Bush Sr. advocated balanced budget amendments at the very time their own administrations (aided, to be sure, by Democratic Congresses) engaged in massive deficit spending. Historically, deficits often have been connected in the popular mind to various forms of governmental corruption or to providing special privileges for the wealthy. Going all the way back to the conflict between Thomas Jefferson (who generally advocated fiscal austerity) and Alexander Hamilton (who argued that the public debt could be a public blessing), the debate over budget deficits has often been phrased in highly moralistic terms suggestive of conflicts between good and evil and not simply between rival economic views (Savage 1988). The analogy between governmental budgets and individual budgets is also frequently evoked, but the analogy often proves inconclusive because many households do, in fact, engage in deficit financing on a fairly consistent basis, especially on items such as houses or cars. Moreover, this analogy suggests that the federal government should distinguish between expenditures for immediate consumption and those on behalf of capital investments, which it does not do now.

Two questions that dog the balanced budget amendment are those of appropriateness and enforceability. To the extent that the amendment appears to sanction one, possibly transient, economic theory over another, some argue that it has no place in a constitution intended to endure over time ("Balanced Budget Amendment" 1983). Other questions center

on who would have standing to sue under such an amendment, how the amendment would be enforced, and, particularly, what role the courts would play in its enforcement (see J. Bowen 1994). At least since 1937, U.S. courts have generally taken a hands-off approach to economic affairs, and such an amendment might, wisely or unwisely, inject courts back into such controversies. Moreover, legislation designed to achieve balanced budgets—most notably the Balanced Budget and Emergency Deficit Control Act of 1985, better known as the Gramm-Rudman-Hollings law—initially proved relatively unsuccessful in ending deficits. To some, this suggests that stronger medicine is needed; others fear that an amendment might prove similarly unenforceable and that it would ultimately bring disrespect on the Constitution. Certainly, amendments that call for government to project future budgets may enable Congress to engage in some creative predictions. Much of the pressure for a balanced budget amendment eased when the federal government began showing surpluses during the Clinton administration in the 1990s. Some of the focus then shifted to the question as to whether the government should pay down the debt, finance new programs, or provide greater protection for such programs as Social Security (generally the position favored by Democrats) or whether the government should cut taxes (generally the position favored by Republicans). The latter idea was incorporated into President George W. Bush's proposals for a $1.3 trillion tax cut over a ten-year period. In 2002 the national budget is back in the red, in part because of an economic slowdown and in part because of increased expenditures connected to the war against terrorism precipitated by attacks against the United States on 11 September 2001. The Republican congressional victories of 2002 make it likely, however, that Bush's tax cuts will proceed as planned.

A number of recent proposals would limit federal expenditures to a certain percentage of the gross national product, usually pegged at right about 20 percent, or, from a somewhat different perspective, would require supermajorities to enact new taxes. A creative amendment on a related subject was proposed by Republican Representative Doug Ose in July 2001. It would require both Congress and the president to forfeit their salaries at the end of each year until they had agreed to general appropriations bills for the following year.

For Further Reading:

"The Balanced Budget Amendment: An Inquiry into Appropriateness." 1983. *Harvard Law Review* 96 (May): 1600–1620.

Bowen, James W. 1994. "Enforcing the Balanced Budget Amendment." *Constitutional Law Journal* 4 (Spring): 565–620.

Davidson, James D. 1992. "Yes, to Save Congress from Itself." *The World & I* 7 (August): 110, 112–115.

Fink, Richard H., and Jack C. High, eds. 1987. *A Nation in Debt: Economists Debate the Federal Budget Deficit.* Frederick, MD: University Publications of America.

Ishikawa, Brendon T. 2000. "The Stealth Amendment: The Impending Ratification and Repeal of a Federal Budget Amendment." *Tulsa Law Journal* 33 (Winter): 353–381.

Kyvig, David E. 1995. "Reforming or Resisting Modern Government? The Balanced Budget Amendment to the U.S. Constitution." *Akron Law Review* 28 (Fall/Winter): 97–124.

McIntyre, Robert S. 1992. "No, It Would Wreck the Economy." *The World & I* 7 (August): 111, 116–117, 119.

Moore, W. S., and Rudolph G. Penner, eds. 1980. *The Constitution and the Budget: Are Constitutional Limits on Tax, Spending and Budget Powers Desirable at the Federal Level?* Washington, DC: American Enterprise Institute for Public Policy Research.

Savage, James D. 1988. *Balanced Budgets and American Politics.* Ithaca, NY: Cornell University Press.

Taylor, Andrew. 1997. "Senate Again One Vote Short; GOP Says House Will Act," *Congressional Quarterly,* 55 (8 March): 577–578.

❖ BALDWIN, LELAND (1897–1981) ❖

Baldwin was a retired professor of history from the University of Pittsburgh when he proposed a new constitution in a 1972 book entitled *Reframing the Constitution: An Imperative for Modern America.* Identifying the existing system of federalism, separation of powers, and a weak party system as some of the problems in the current government, Baldwin described his plan as "a modified version of the Cabinet or Parliamentary form" (Baldwin 1972, 96).

Baldwin's plan called for the creation of a unicameral Congress consisting of 200 elected members. It would also have up to fifteen congressmen-pro-forma to serve as a type of shadow cabinet and enough appointed congressmen-at-large to give the majority party a 55 percent voting majority of the membership. This constitution would entrust Congress with more explicit powers (the administration of some of which could, however, be delegated to the states), and members would be elected to five-year terms, subject to prior dissolution.

The president, similar to a prime minister, would preside over Congress and be its executive arm. Like members of Congress, the president would serve for a five-year term, subject to a vote of no confidence. The vice presidency would be eliminated. Instead, Congress would elect a successor in case of presidential death or disability.

The courts would be headed by a new body designated as the Senate and consisting of fifty law senators (two from each of the fifteen new states described below and others elected on the basis of population apportionment) and fifty senators-at-large. Senators would be appointed for life but would be required to retire at age seventy. The chief justice, who would be selected by the Senate, would preside over that body and would live in the White House and serve as head of state. The entire Senate would vote on matters of constitutional interpretation. The Senate could suspend the writ of habeas corpus and exercise similar power in times of emergency. It could also dissolve Congress, conduct investigations, and impose reforms on state governments. In cases of conflict between the president and Congress, the chief justice and two-thirds of the Senate could dissolve Congress.

Baldwin provided mechanisms to recognize political parties and for the nomination and selection of the elected branches. He also provided for significant state reorganization. Existing states would be divided into fifteen new states. Alaska would be given the option of becoming a commonwealth or joining a group of northwestern states. Each state would draw up a new constitution consolidating existing governments and providing for a unicameral legislature and an appointive senate.

The Bill of Rights would be modified, in accord with the twentieth-century incorporation process, to apply to both the states and the national government. Baldwin would broaden protections against discrimination to cover "sex, race, color, religion, or birth out of wedlock." He would explicitly vest Congress with power over gun ownership, thus modifying the current Second Amendment.

Baldwin also wanted to liberalize the constitutional amending process. Two-thirds majorities of the Senate or the Congress would be empowered to propose amendments, subject to ratification by either three-fourths of the state legislatures or a majority of the electorate. Alternatively, one-half of the states could propose amendments. Baldwin also specified mechanisms for calling a new constitutional convention.

For Further Reading:

Baldwin, Leland. 1972. *Reframing the Constitution: An Imperative for Modern America.* Santa Barbara, CA: ABC-CLIO.

Boyd, Steven R., ed. 1992. *Alternative Constitutions for the United States: A Documentary History.* Westport, CT: Greenwood Press.

Vile, John R. 1991c. *Rewriting the United States Constitution: An Examination of Proposals from Reconstruction to the Present.* New York: Praeger.

❖ BANKING ❖

The U.S. Constitution neither specifically mentions banking nor authorizes Congress to establish corporations. Congressional authority to establish a national bank was a major issue in the administration of George Washington and contributed to the emerging split between the Federalist and Republican Parties. Secretary of the Treasury Alexander Hamilton, who would soon be a leading Federalist, favored broad federal powers and emphasized the development of commerce and industry; he accordingly argued that the bank was constitutional. Secretary of State Thomas Jefferson, who would soon lead the Republican Party, was wary of broad federal powers and emphasized agricultural development; he, and Attorney General Edmund Randolph, accordingly argued that the bank was unconstitutional. Washington sided with Hamilton, and Congress created a bank with a twenty-year charter. Although this charter lapsed, Congress reestablished the bank in 1816.

Maryland challenged the constitutionality of this bank and attempted to tax its branch in Baltimore. In *McCulloch v. Maryland* (1819), Chief Justice John Marshall decided that the national government had the right to establish the bank under the doctrine of implied powers. He also voided Maryland's tax on the bank. This decision did not, however, prevent Andrew Jackson (who associated banks with eastern monied interests) from vetoing a bank bill that was introduced during his administration. He also had his secretary of the treasury, Roger Taney (later a chief justice of the U.S. Supreme Court), move monies from the national bank to various state institutions.

Three amendments proposed in Congress in 1793 and 1794 would have made bankers ineligible to serve in Congress. Amendments proposed in 1813 and 1814 would have specifically authorized a bank. A spate of proposals made immediately after *McCulloch* and reflecting resolutions voted on in a number of state legislatures would have prohibited branches of the national bank outside the District of Columbia.

At least three proposals from 1837 to 1840, apparently stimulated by the panic of 1837, would have prohibited the issuance of state bank notes. Oklahoma Democratic Senator Thomas Gore introduced a proposal in 1933, probably in response to the Great Depression, that would have required states to get congressional consent before chartering banks (S.J. Res. 18).

See also *McCulloch v. Maryland.*

For Further Reading:

Jefferson, Thomas. 1791. "Opinion of the Constitutionality of a National Bank." In *Documents of American Constitutional and Legal History,* ed. Melvin I. Urofsky. New York: Alfred A. Knopf, 1989, 132–146.

❖ BANKRUPTCY ❖

Although the Constitution grants Congress power in Article I, Section 8 to make "uniform Laws on the subject of Bankruptcies throughout the United States," a lasting system of national legislation was not established until 1898 (Coleman 1992, 61). A proposal introduced in 1822 would have allowed states to adopt legislation in the interim (Ames 1896, 265). With some reservations, this was basically what the Supreme Court agreed to in a four-to-three decision in *Ogden v. Saunders* (1827), in which Chief Justice John Marshall, author of an earlier case on state insolvency laws in *Sturges v. Crowinshield* (1819), dissented.

For Further Reading:

Ames, Herman. 1896. *The Proposed Amendments to the Constitution of the United States during the First Century of Its History.* Reprint, New York: Burt Franklin, 1970.

Coleman, Peter J. 1992. "Bankruptcy and Insolvency Legislation." In *The Oxford Companion to the Supreme Court of the United States,* ed. Kermit L. Hall. New York: Oxford University Press.

———. 1974. *Debtors and Creditors in America: Insolvency, Imprisonment for Debt, and Bankruptcy, 1607–1900.* Madison: State Historical Society of Wisconsin.

❖ *BARRON V. BALTIMORE* (1833) ❖

In this seven-to-zero decision (there were only seven justices at this time) authored by Chief Justice John Marshall, the Supreme Court decided that the first ten amendments to the Constitution, known as the Bill of Rights, applied only to the national government and not to the states. In this case, Baltimore had diverted streams that subsequently filled a wharf owned by Barron and rendered it useless. Citing the takings clause of the Fifth Amendment, Barron argued that the government had illegally deprived him of his property without just compensation. In response, Marshall argued that the Constitution had been designed to limit the national government rather than the state governments. He pointed out that provisions of the Constitution that did limit the states (those found in Article I, Section 10, for example) concerned matters relevant to the national government and had been explicitly applied to the states. Marshall further noted that if individuals had desired alterations in their own state constitutions, they would have called conventions rather than use "the unwieldy and cumbrous machinery of procuring a recommendation from two-thirds of Congress and the assent of three-fourths of their sister states" (*Barron* 1833, 250).

Although Marshall did not say so, when James Madison had introduced his initial version of the Bill of Rights, Madison had favored an amendment limiting the states, but his proposal had failed for lack of congressional support. The Fourteenth Amendment, which was ratified in 1868, provided protections against state deprivations of privileges and immunities, due process rights, and equal protection for U.S. citizens. Some supporters of the amendment, including Congressman John Bingham, knew about *Barron v. Baltimore* and apparently hoped that the Fourteenth Amendment would overturn it. Although Justice John Marshall Harlan I agreed, the rest of the Supreme Court initially rejected this interpretation. In the twentieth century, although never officially embracing the doctrine of total incorporation that Harlan and later Justice Hugo Black advocated, the Court has gradually used the due process clause of that amendment (in a development generally referred to as selective incorporation) to apply almost all the guarantees found in the Bill of Rights to the states as well as to the national government.

See also *Adamson v. California;* Incorporation; *Palko v. Connecticut.*

For Further Reading:

Barron v. Baltimore, 32 U.S. 243 (1833).

Schwartz, Bernard. 1992. *The Great Rights of Mankind: A History of the American Bill of Rights.* Madison, WI: Madison House.

❖ BAYH, BIRCH, JR. (1928–) ❖

Indiana Senator Birch Bayh, a graduate of Purdue University who received his J.D. degree from Indiana University, was influential in the writing of the Twenty-fifth Amendment providing for cases of presidential disability and for replacing vice presidents. He also worked for the adoption of the Twenty-sixth Amendment, successfully lowering the voting age to eighteen, and for the Equal Rights Amendment, which failed to achieve an adequate number of states for ratification.

Born in Terre Haute, Indiana, in 1928, Bayh was elected to the Indiana House of Representatives, where he served as speaker and minority leader before being elected, as a Democrat, to the U.S. Senate in 1962. He was elected to three terms and served on the Judiciary Committee on the Constitution, where he did most of his work on behalf of amending the Constitution. Bayh has written two books on his work in pushing for the Twenty-fifth Amendment. He now practices law in Washington, D.C.

For Further Reading:

Bayh, Birch. 1968. *One Heartbeat Away: President Disability and Succession.* Indianapolis: Bobbs-Merrill.

———. 1966. *The Making of an Amendment.* Indianapolis: Bobbs-Merrill.

"Birch E(vans) Bayh, Jr.," *Contemporary Authors Online.* The Gale Group. 2001. Updated 08/07/2001.

❖ BEASLEY, ROBERT (Dates unknown) ❖

Robert Beasley, a Californian who seems otherwise to have faded into obscurity, proposed a new constitution for the United States in a pamphlet published in 1864 in both English and Spanish and titled *A Plan to Stop the Present and Prevent Future Wars.* His plan, which actually preceded his proposed constitution, called for all persons to vote on whether to continue the Civil War, with nonvoters to be penalized by a $1,000 fine. If the vote was affirmative, all would then be placed in the army and "compelled to assist in prosecuting the war" (Beasley 1864, 3). The constitution, constantly referred to as being for "the sovereign States of North and South America," followed.

Under this scheme, the House of Representatives would be composed of two representatives from each state and the Senate of one from each. The Senate would have to vote on charges of impeachment by three-fifths rather than two-thirds, and members of Congress would receive $5 for each day of service plus expenses. Perhaps in response to Lincoln's forceful actions in prosecuting the war, only Congress would have the power to suspend the writ of habeas corpus.

The president and vice president would not be permitted to serve for consecutive terms. Each voter would write the name of his preferred candidate for president on a ballot, with the Senate deciding tie votes. The president would receive a yearly salary of $40,000. His power to pardon would be restricted in cases of "lying, larceny, and impeachment" (Beasley 1864, 13). He could also be removed from office for "conviction of lying, larceny or other high crimes and misdemeanors" (Beasley 1864, 14).

Most of the provisions of the Bill of Rights would be incorporated. Government officers convicted of stealing were to be fined, with proceeds to go toward the construction of a national cemetery. Those stealing over $10,000 were to be "hung with a rope by the neck until dead" and denied burial in this cemetery (Beasley 1864, 16).

States were to be prohibited from interfering in the domestic affairs of other states and would be expelled from the Union for fifty years for so doing. States could secede and keep government property within their boundaries. Beasley would further provide for the purchase of "white servants" from Europe to become citizens after fifteen years (Beasley 1864, 18). Slaveholders would be able to take their slaves into the territories, thus affirming the 1857 decision in *Scott v. Sandford*, with states subsequently deciding whether to have slavery according to the principle of popular sovereignty. The national government could call on each state for a quota of troops; if the quota were not met, "all the males and half the females in his State" would be drafted (Beasley 1864, 20). Neither slavery nor polygamy would exclude a state from the Union. In language similar to that later used in the Fourteenth Amendment, voting in federal elections and officeholding were to be limited to "white male citizens of the age of twenty-one years and upwards" (Beasley 1864, 20).

Beasley would have officially adopted the Monroe Doctrine and authorized Congress to carry it out. Adjacent islands could be admitted into the Union after 1900, but states in Europe, Asia, and Africa would have to wait until after 2000. States would have the power to prohibit their citizens from interfering in the "domestic concerns" of their neighbors or "lying to their own or their neighbor's dumb brutes [presumably slaves], or unnecessarily abusing them in any way" (Beasley 1864, 21).

Beasley identified himself as one of the "sovereign people" of Rio Vista, California, who doubted that he was "a servant of God" (Beasley 1864, 3) and proposed four scriptures "as admonitions to all people" (Beasley 1864, 21). These dealt with the subjection of wives to husbands, instructions for familial relations, master-slave relations, and the proper allocation of responsibilities between Caesar and God.

Secret political parties were to be outlawed, and political parties could not nominate individuals for office. Amendments were to be ratified by five-sixths (rather than three-fourths) of the states, and ratification by conventions in five states would be sufficient to inaugurate the new government.

In an addendum, Beasley asserted, in apparent reference to slaves, that "whatsoever God has made inferior, man cannot make equal or superior" (Beasley 1864, 23). He further proposed a census for after the war and laws "that will give every one a chance to have a husband

or a wife," and he suggested that the seat of government should be "within one or two hundred miles of the 'Isthmus of Panama'" (Beasley 1864, 24).

A number of subsequent writers picked up on Beasley's idea for a referendum on war. His proslavery constitution was otherwise overtaken by events, and it appears to have quickly faded from public view.

For Further Reading:

Beasley, Robert. 1864. *A Plan to Stop the Present and Prevent Future Wars: Containing a Proposed Constitution for the General Government of the Sovereign States of North and South America*. Rio Vista, CA: Robert Beasley.

❖ BECKER, THEODORE L. (1932–) ❖

In 1976, when he was a professor of law and political science at the University of Hawaii, Becker offered a series of proposed constitutional reforms in a textbook entitled *American Government: Past—Present—Future*. He referred to his plan as a type of *eutopia*—that is, a "good" or "desirable" place—as opposed to a *utopia*, which literally means "no place" (Becker 1976, 432).

In an attempt to increase governmental responsiveness and accountability, Becker favors a national presidential primary (NPP). However, his ultimate aim is to institute a presidential election tournament (PET), whereby candidates would emerge (as in organized athletic contests) first from the states, then from one of four regions, then from either the East or the West, and finally from the contest between those two champions, with campaign costs funded by the government. Becker would also institute a vote of "no confidence" as a means of executive recall and suggests that voting should be a compulsory, perhaps even a paid, activity. Citizens would, however, be given a "no preference" option (Becker 1976, 459).

Becker favors a unicameral rather than bicameral Congress. He would also establish an "executive Committee, Council, or Cabinet" to run its affairs (Becker 1976, 467). He anticipates a legislature of from 500 to 1,000 people in which at least half of the representatives are selected at random. He also favors a national initiative and referendum process that might be effected by home cable television or computer hookups.

Becker would like to see presidents run for office on a ticket that includes members of their cabinet. The president would, in turn, have to get 60 percent approval of Congress to fire a cabinet member (Becker 1976, 474). Greater administrative oversight would be provided by Congress and by ombudsmen, who would form a "countergovernment" (Becker 1976, 509).

Becker also anticipates numerous reforms of the judicial and criminal justice systems. He favors either setting up a national appeals court to ease the Supreme Court's workload or appointing eighteen Supreme Court justices who would work on nine-judge panels. Judges would serve for twelve to fifteen years rather than for life and would retire at age seventy. As in Congress, a good portion of the judges would be chosen by lottery, albeit from members of the bar, with all judges undergoing at least six months' training at a judicial academy. Members of the lay public would preside in many trials, the state's peremptory challenges for jurors would be eliminated, jury pools would be widened, and jury pay would be increased.

Becker favors the repeal of all so-called victimless crime laws, such as those prohibiting consensual sex, gambling, drug use, and the like.

In 1992 Becker—then at Auburn University—was working with Barry Krusch, author of *The 21st Century Constitution* (1992), to develop a national network of individuals interested in a second constitutional convention. As a class project, Becker had previously organized a simulated constitutional convention in Hawaii. Becker is one of the supporters of the National Initiative for Democracy, or Philadelphia II, which is designed to amend the U.S. Constitution by referendum. Becker continues to be an advocate of using modern technology to strengthen direct democracy within the United States.

See also National Initiative for Democracy.

For Further Reading:

Becker, Theodore L. 1976. *American Government: Past—Present—Future*. Boston: Allyn and Bacon.

Becker, Theodore Lewis, and Christa Daryl Slaton. 2000. *The Future of Teledemocracy*. Westport, CT: Praeger.

Krusch, Barry. 1992. *The 21st Century Constitution: A New America for a New Millennium*. New York: Stanhope Press.

❖ BIBLE READING IN SCHOOLS ❖

See *Abington v. Schempp; Engel v. Vitale;* Prayer in Public Schools.

❖ BILL OF RESPONSIBILITIES ❖

Although individual rights and responsibilities are arguably correlative, the Constitution currently provides protection for the former largely without specifying the latter. Rexford Tugwell and Jeremy Miller have been among the proponents of a new constitution that lists such responsibilities in the proposed document. More generally, some commentators have argued that American laws should devote more attention to citizen duties than they currently do (Glendon 1991, 76–108).

As part of its contribution to the Bicentennial of the U.S. Constitution, the Freedoms Foundation in Valley Forge, in consultation with a number of scholars, developed a one-page Bill of Responsibilities. It is based on the presumption, stated in a one-paragraph preamble, that "Freedom and responsibility are mutual and inseparable" and that "we can ensure enjoyment of the one only by exercising the other."

Perhaps as a parallel to the Bill of Rights, the Foundation's Bill of Responsibilities was divided into ten parts. These included the responsibilities: "to be fully responsible for our own actions and for the consequences of those actions; to respect the rights and beliefs of others; to give sympathy, understanding and help to others; to do our best to meet our own and our families' needs; to respect and obey the laws; to respect the property of others, both private and public; to share with others our appreciation of the benefits and obligations of freedom; to participate constructively in the nation's political life; to help freedom survive by assuming personal responsibility for its defense; and to respect the rights and to meet the responsibilities on which our liberty rests and our democracy depends" (Freedoms Foundation 1985, italics omitted).

Each of these responsibilities is followed by a brief explanation. Unlike its counterpart Bill of Rights, the Bill of Responsibilities appears to have been offered for citizen reflection rather than in the hopes that it would be adopted as a set of constitutional amendments.

For Further Reading:

Freedoms Foundation. 1985. "Bill of Responsibilities." Valley Forge, PA: Freedom Foundation.

Glendon, Mary A. 1991. *Rights Talk: The Impoverishment of Political Discourse*. New York: Free Press.

❖ BILL OF RIGHTS ❖

Collectively, the first ten amendments to the U.S. Constitution are designated the Bill of Rights. These amendments are among the most venerated in the entire document. Curiously, the subject of such a bill received little attention at the Constitutional Convention of 1787, although some debate was stirred near the end of the convention when George Mason of Virginia, who had authored his state's pathbreaking declaration of rights in 1776, proposed a motion for such a bill. Similarly, Virginia's Richard Henry Lee tried unsuccessfully to get the Congress under the Articles of Confederation to add a bill of rights before sending the Constitution to the states for approval (Schwartz 1992, 105).

The Federalist–Anti-Federalist Controversy

The absence of such a bill quickly became one of the rallying points for Anti-Federalists opposed to the new Constitution. Federalist proponents of the document initially argued that such a bill was unnecessary and could even prove dangerous in the event that key rights were omitted. Leading proponents of the Constitution subsequently realized that adding a bill of rights would be far less likely to jeopardize the new document than would the prospect of a second convention, which many Anti-Federalists were advocating.

James Madison, who would guide the Bill of Rights through the First Congress, also appears to have been influenced both by the wishes of his Virginia constituents, from whom he was seeking a seat in the new House of Representatives (he had not been appointed by the Virginia legislature to the U.S. Senate), and by correspondence with his close friend and political ally Thomas Jefferson, who was then serving as a minister to France. Ironically, although Jefferson would later criticize the exercise of judicial review by Federalist judges, he argued in his letters to Madison that, with a bill of rights in place, judges would be in a better position to guard civil liberties (Mason and Baker 1985, 276–294).

Actions by Congress

In the process of ratifying the U.S. Constitution, eight states submitted more than 100 substantive amendment proposals (Schwartz 1992, 157). Many in Congress wanted to postpone consideration of a bill of rights until the new Constitution had been more thoroughly tested, but congressional debates indicate that Madison especially believed that such a bill was essential to gaining the confidence of those who had opposed ratification of the document (Vile 1993c, 137–160).

Madison formulated a list of nine amendments with forty-two separate rights for congressional consideration (Lutz 1992, 55); most of Madison's proposals dealt with individual political rights rather than guarantees for state sovereignty, which some Anti-Federalists had sought. In the course of debate and deliberation, Congress deleted four of Madison's proposed amendments. They would have provided a declaration of the people's right to alter the government, applied guarantees of freedom of conscience and the press to the states (thus anticipating the later incorporation controversy), limited certain appeals to the Supreme Court, and explicitly mentioned the doctrine of separation of powers (Schwartz 1992, 169). All twelve amendments that subsequently emerged from House and Senate action (including action by a Committee of Eleven, which included Madison, in the House and conference reports in both houses) were based on Madison's original draft, with changes related "to form rather than substance" (Schwartz 1992, 169). Madison was not successful in incorporating proposals into the constitutional text; instead, the Congress followed Roger Sherman's suggestion that the Bill of Rights be appended to the end of the document. The House voted to accept the Bill of Rights on September 24, 1789, with the Senate concurring the following day (Schwartz 1992, 186).

Donald Lutz has divided commentators on the Bill of Rights into four groups: those who view it as the product of a few creative minds, those who see it as the embodiment of ideas in the Magna Carta and other English precedents, those who view it as distillations of amendments that were offered in state conventions that ratified the Constitution; and those who see it as a summary of rights found within state constitutions of the founding period (Lutz 1992, 50–51). Although each point of view has some evidence to support it, Lutz emphasizes the latter view, demonstrating that twenty-six of the rights on Madison's original list were found in the state constitutions, nine were found in five of seven contemporary constitutions, four were found in six, and thirteen were found in all seven existing state documents (Lutz 1992, 67; also see Conley and Kaminski 1992); many of these rights, in turn, had their origin in colonial charters (Lutz 1992, 68–69). Whereas the first eight amendments contain provisions protecting individual rights (with special attention to the rights of political participation and rights for those accused of criminal behavior), the Ninth and Tenth Amendments are directed toward different concerns and are thus sometimes excluded from discussions of the first eight amendments. Unlike many twentieth-century bills of rights, the U.S. version does not attempt to guarantee social and economic rights.

State Ratification

Of the twelve amendments proposed by Congress, one—dealing with congressional representation and originally listed as the first amendment—fell a single state shy of ratification and thus remains a dead letter (Amar 1992, 1137–1145). The other, dealing with the timing of congressional pay raises and originally the second amendment, putatively became the Twenty-seventh Amendment, with a belated ratification in 1992. Apparently, the first ten amendments became part of the Constitution with their ratification by Virginia in late 1791. Secretary of State Thomas Jefferson notified the state governors of this ratification on March 1, 1792 (Schwartz 1992, 186). In 1939, the sesquicentennial of the adoption of the U.S. Constitution, Connecticut and Georgia added their ratifications in a symbolic display that illustrates the Bill of Rights' grip on the popular mind (Schwartz 1992, 191).

The Incorporation Controversy

For all the attention that this part of the Constitution receives, the Bill of Rights was not the source of frequent judicial decision making in the first 100 years of the republic. In large part, this was because the courts interpreted the Bill of Rights as a limitation only on the actions of the national government and not on the states, where most early legislating took place. The wording of what became the First Amendment—beginning with "Congress shall make no law"—appeared to confirm that the Bill of Rights applied only to actions of the national government. This view was confirmed by Chief Justice John Marshall in *Barron v. Baltimore* (1833), in which he cited the debates over the Bill of Rights as proof.

Among the supporters of the Fourteenth Amendment, which was ratified in 1868, at least some advocates—among them Congressman John Bingham, who was largely responsible for authoring the first section—appear to have been motivated by a desire to overturn *Barron v. Baltimore*. Initially, the Court rejected this incorporation doctrine in the *Slaughterhouse Cases* (1873) and other contemporary decisions. In the early twentieth century, however, the Supreme Court adopted the view of selective incorporation, under which courts applied individual guarantees to the states via the due process clause of the Fourteenth Amendment on a piecemeal basis. Over time, all but five provisions were so applied to the states, with the Warren Court proving particularly active in this area (Hall 1991, 8). The result is that the Bill of Rights has had considerably more influence in the twentieth century than in the nineteenth.

The Bill of Rights Today

Periodically, scholars express fear that a constitutional convention might revise the Constitution in a way that would weaken the Bill of Rights. A review of proposals that have been offered, however, suggests that although there is sometimes stronger support for the concept of a bill of rights than for the individual guarantees listed, few proposed amendments would have directly challenged the rights specifically listed in the first ten amendments. Many such proposals—those attempting to perpetuate slavery, for example—would today be regarded largely as historical curiosities (Vile 1991b). A number of important amendments, including the three adopted after the Civil War, as well as proposals from the Progressive Era, have significantly expanded individual rights and provided for greater democracy (Grimes 1978).

Some scholars argued against proposed amendments to prevent flag desecration on the basis that such an amendment would have constituted the first narrowing of the Bill of Rights in the nation's history. Some of these scholars also argued that there are implicit limits on the amending process that would prevent its use for such purposes.

Whereas the Warren Court generally made liberal rulings on the Bill of Rights, the Burger and Rehnquist Courts have been more cautious about expanding such rights and have, in many cases, narrowed but not abandoned earlier rulings. As a consequence, some liberal scholars now argue that those seeking expanded protections for individual rights should look increasingly to their own state constitutions and their state bills of rights for protection, with the federal Bill of Rights serving more as a floor than a ceiling. A number of individuals who have written and proposed new constitutions in recent years, especially those of libertarian persuasion, have significantly expanded the attention they devote in such documents to rights, often articulating rights like privacy and travel that courts have recognized but that have not been formally added to the existing constitutional text. Consistent with practice in a number of states prior to the adoption of the U.S. Bill of Rights, a number of recent proposals list rights at the beginning of their documents rather than appending them to the end. The current Bill of Rights focuses on political rights, or rights against the government. A number of proponents of new rights, among them Congressman Jesse Jackson Jr., have focused on social and economic rights, which governments would be obligated to provide.

See also Anti-Federalists; *Barron v. Baltimore;* Federalists; Fourteenth Amendment; Incorporation; Jackson, Jesse L., Jr.; Madison, James; Magna Carta; Placement of Constitutional Amendments; Social and Economic Rights; Virginia Declaration of Rights.

For Further Reading:

Alderman, Ellen, and Caroline Kennedy. 1991. *In Our Defense: The Bill of Rights in Action.* New York: William Morrow.

Amar, Akhil R. 1992. "The Bill of Rights as a Constitution." *Yale Law Journal* 100 (Winter): 1131–1210.

"The Bill of Rights." 1991. Bicentennial issue of *Life* (Fall).

Bodenhamer, David J., and James W. Ely Jr., eds. 1993. *The Bill of Rights in Modern America after 200 Years.* Bloomington, IN: Indiana University Press.

Bryant, Irving. 1965. *The Bill of Rights: Its Origin and Meaning.* Indianapolis, IN: Bobbs-Merrill.

Cogan, Neil H., ed. 1997. *The Complete Bill of Rights: The Drafts, Debates, Sources, and Origins.* New York: Oxford University Press.

Conley, Patrick T., and John P. Kaminski, eds. 1992. *The Bill of Rights and the States: The Colonial and Revolutionary Origins of American Liberties.* Madison, WI: Madison House.

Grimes, Alan P. 1978. *Democracy and the Amendments to the Constitution.* Lexington, MA: Lexington Books.

Hall, Kermit L., ed. 1991. *By and for the People: Constitutional Rights in American History.* Arlington Heights, IL: Harlan Davidson.

Kurland, Philip B., and Ralph Lerner, eds. 1987. *The Founders' Constitution.* Vol. 5. Chicago: University of Chicago Press.

Lutz, Donald S. 1992. *A Preface to American Political Theory.* Lawrence, KS: University Press of Kansas.

Mason, Alpheus T., and Gordon E. Baker. 1985. *Free Government in the Making: Readings in American Political Thought.* 4th ed. New York: Oxford University Press.

Peck, Robert S. 1992. *The Bill of Rights and the Politics of Interpretation.* St. Paul, MN: West.

Schwartz, Bernard. 1992. *The Great Rights of Mankind: A History of the American Bill of Rights.* Madison, WI: Madison House.

Schwartz, Bernard, ed. 1980. *The Roots of the Bill of Rights.* 5 vols. New York: Chelsea House.

Stone, Geoffrey R., Richard A. Epstein, and Cass R. Sunstein, eds. 1992. *The Bill of Rights in the Modern State.* Chicago: University of Chicago Press.

Vile, John R. 1993c. "Three Kinds of Constitutional Founding and Change: The Convention Model and Its Alternatives." *Political Research Quarterly* 46: 881–895.

———. 1991b. "Proposals to Amend the Bill of Rights: Are Fundamental Rights in Jeopardy?" *Judicature* 75 (August-September): 62–67.

gument that Bingham specifically intended for the privileges and immunities clause and the due process clause of the Fourteenth Amendment to overturn the Court's decision in *Barron v. Baltimore* (1833) and apply all of the Bill of Rights to the states (a process usually referred to as incorporation). There is no doubt that Bingham, who had been a strong foe of slavery and a defender of the principle of equality announced in the Declaration of Independence, was a strong advocate for the rights of African Americans, whom he hoped to protect through this amendment.

Sometimes called "the Cicero of the House" (Beauregard 1989, 97), Bingham was a special judge advocate who led the successful prosecution of the Lincoln assassins, a leader in the unsuccessful impeachment trial of President Andrew Johnson, chairman of the House Judiciary Committee from 1869 to 1873, and a minister plenipotentiary to Japan from 1873 to 1885.

See also Incorporation.

For Further Reading:

Adamson v. California, 332 U.S. 46 (1947).

Beauregard, Erving E. 1989. *Bingham of the Hills: Politician and Diplomat Extraordinary.* New York: Peter Lang.

❖ BINGHAM, JOHN A. (1815–1900) ❖

John Bingham was a lawyer and Republican congressman from Ohio from 1854 to 1873. Supreme Court Justice Hugo Black once described Bingham as "the [James] Madison of the first section of the Fourteenth Amendment" (*Adamson v. California* 1947, 74). Bingham, who served on the congressional Joint Committee of Fifteen on Reconstruction, drafted all of Section 1 of the Fourteenth Amendment except for the first sentence, which defines citizenship (Thaddeus Stevens appears to have been most responsible for the other sections of the amendment).

Dispute continues about Justice Black's ar-

❖ BIRTHRIGHT CITIZENSHIP AMENDMENT ❖

More than a dozen members of the U.S. House of Representatives have supported an amendment first introduced by California Representative Elton Gallegly in October 1991 and designed to deny citizenship to persons born in the United States whose mothers are not legal residents. If adopted, this amendment, which has received public support from former California Republican Governor Pete Wilson, would modify the first clause of the Fourteenth Amendment, which specifies that "all persons born or naturalized in the United States, and subject to the jurisdiction thereof, are citizens of the United States and of the State wherein they reside." The Fourteenth Amendment originally was adopted to overturn the unpopular decision in *Scott v. Sandford* (1857), wherein Chief Justice Roger Taney and a majority of the Supreme Court had declared that blacks were not and could not be citizens of the United States whether they were born here or not. At least one attorney, who focuses chiefly on the intent of its authors rather than on actual language of the provision, has argued that the Fourteenth Amendment is already subject to an interpretation that excludes children of illegal aliens from citizenship (Wood 1999).

On the surface, Gallegly's amendment resembles proposals that were introduced earlier in the century by members of Congress from the West Coast and designed to limit citizenship to persons born in the United States of parents who were eligible for citizenship. The primary purpose of these earlier proposals appears to have been to restrict property ownership by children born to legal Japanese immigrants living in the United States. At the time, the parents of such children were ineligible for citizenship and were prevented from owning property in the state of California (Musmanno 1929, 180–181).

By contrast, Gallegly's proposal is aimed at the problem of providing government services to illegal immigrants at a time when the nation is facing a rising tide of immigrants. Like earlier Japanese immigrants, most modern immigrants are from non-European nations. Although the topic is hotly debated, it appears that legal immigrants generally pay their own way, but illegal immigrants often cost governments more in spending on social programs than the immigrants contribute in taxes (Welch et al. 1993, 9). The costs of such illegal immigration tend to fall disproportionately on states such as Florida, Texas, and California, which have large immigrant populations.

To the extent that illegal immigrants come to the United States in the expectation that their children born here will become citizens, the birthright citizenship amendment might serve to deter immigration by such aliens and any problems they might bring with them. Those who oppose this amendment fear any erosion of the Fourteenth Amendment. They also note

that the proposed amendment would treat illegal alien fathers and mothers differently and would penalize children for the status of their parents, over which they have no control (see "Birthright Citizenship Amendment" 1994). In *Plyler v. Doe* (1982), the Supreme Court used such an analysis to strike down a Texas law that allowed the public schools to exclude children of illegal aliens. Although the principle may be valid, the Supreme Court might be reluctant to apply such analysis to void an amendment.

One proposed variant of the birthright citizenship amendment, which would have only prospective effect, would deny citizenship to individuals born in the United States who do not have at least one natural parent who is a U.S. citizen or lawful permanent resident. This proposal would classify children of illegal aliens as "permanent lawful residents" who would not be permitted to naturalize until they were eighteen years old, and then only contingent upon have no felony conviction on their records. Congress could further require that they have resided in the United States for at least five years (Hsieh 1998).

In a much different vein, Congress adopted a law, entitled the Child Citizenship Act, that went into effect in February 2001. It provided that most children under eighteen who have been adopted from abroad by an American parent are now automatic citizens ("Children Adopted Abroad" 2001, 12).

For Further Reading:

"Children Adopted Abroad Win Automatic Citizenship," 2001. *Migration World Magazine* 19 (March): 12.

Hsieh, Christine J. 1998. "Note: American Born Legal Permanent Residents? A Constitutional Amendment Proposal." *Georgetown Immigration Law Journal* 12 (Spring): 511–529.

Musmanno, M. A. 1929. *Proposed Amendments to the Constitution*. Washington, DC: U.S. Government Printing Office.

Schuck, Peter H., and Rogers M. Smith. 1985. *Citizenship without Consent: Illegal Aliens in the American Polity*. New Haven, CT: Yale University Press.

Welch, Susan, et al. 1993. *Understanding American Government*. 2d ed. Minneapolis–St. Paul, MN: West.

Wood, Charles. 1999. "Losing Control of America's Future: The Census, Birthright Citizenship, and Illegal Aliens." *Harvard Journal of Law and Public Policy* 22 (Spring): 465–522.

❖ BLACK, HUGO LAFAYETTE (1886–1971) ❖

President Franklin D. Roosevelt appointed Hugo Black, then a second-term senator from Alabama who had supported both the New Deal and FDR's court-packing plan (but whose onetime membership in the Ku Klux Klan was not revealed until after his confirmation), to the Supreme Court in 1937. Black served there for thirty-four years, including the entire tenure of the Warren Court. Many of his decisions significantly influenced thinking about the meaning of key constitutional amendments and the role of the Court in interpreting the Constitution.

In *Coleman v. Miller* (1947), Black wrote a concurring opinion stating that procedural questions surrounding the amending process were "political questions" for Congress to resolve.

In *Adamson v. California* (1947), Black articulated the view, repeated in numerous subsequent cases, that John Bingham and other authors of the first section of the Fourteenth Amendment intended for it to incorporate all the provisions of the Bill of Rights and make them applicable to the states. Black saw these and other guarantees as both a floor and a ceiling for the federal judiciary (Yarbrough 1988, 264); although judges were obliged to apply all the provisions of the Bill of Rights to the states, they should wait for the people to amend the Constitution via Article V before going any further. Despite his otherwise broad interpretation of the Fourteenth Amendment, Black argued in a dissenting opinion in *Connecticut General Life Insurance Co. v Johnson* (1938) that the word "person" in that Amendment did not, as his colleagues believed, include corporations.

In a number of cases, Black accused his brethren of short-circuiting this democratic process by reading their own views into the document. In *Griswold v. Connecticut* (1965), saying that Article V was "good for our Fathers" and "good enough for me" (*Griswold* 1965, 522), Black rejected the Court's expansive reading of privacy rights in striking down a state birth-control law. In *Harper v. Virginia State Board of Elections* (1966), Black also dissented from a Supreme Court decision invalidating a state poll tax on the basis of a judicial reading of the equal protection clause of the Fourteenth Amendment that was unsupported by an act of Congress: "when a 'political theory' embodied in the Constitution becomes outdated . . . a majority of the Supreme Court are not only without constitutional power but are far less qualified to choose a new constitutional political theory than the people of this country proceeding in the manner provided by Article V" (*Harper* 1966, 678).

Similarly, in *Katz v. United States* (1967), Black dissented from the Court's decision using the Fourth Amendment to forbid warrantless electronic searches. Black said that it was not the Court's function to "'keep the Constitution up to date' or 'to bring it into harmony with the times'"; the Court was not intended to be "a continuously functioning constitutional convention" (*Katz* 1967, 373).

Black was also known for his view, articulated in *New York Times Co. v. United States* (1971) and elsewhere, that the freedom of speech guaranteed in the First Amendment is absolute. In his view, however, this amendment did not extend full protection to symbolic speech (see Black's dissent in *Tinker v. Des Moines Independent Community School District* (1969)). On another First Amendment issue, Black was a strong advocate of separation of church and state, and he authored the Court's decision in *Engel v. Vitale* (1962) outlawing prayer in public schools and prompting numerous calls for a constitutional amendment.

In *Oregon v. Mitchell* (1970), Black helped precipitate passage of the Twenty-sixth Amendment by ruling that a provision in the 1970 Voting Rights Act Amendments of 1970 lowering the minimum voting age to eighteen would apply to federal but not to state elections.

For Further Reading:

Black, Hugo L. 1969. *A Constitutional Faith.* New York: Alfred A. Knopf.

Dunne, Gerald T. 1977. *Hugo Black and the Judicial Revolution*. New York: Simon and Schuster.

Freyer, Tony. 1990. *Hugo L. Black and the Dilemma of American Liberalism*. Glenville, IL: Scott, Foresman.

Griswold v. Connecticut, 381 U.S. 479 (1965).

Newman, Roger K. 1994. *Hugo Black: A Biography*. New York: Pantheon Books.

Yarbrough, Tinsley E. 1988. *Mr. Justice Black and His Critics*. Durham, NC: Duke University Press.

❖ BLACK PANTHERS ❖

While the mainline civil rights groups organized during the 1960s followed Dr. Martin Luther King Jr. in pursuing desegregation through nonviolent means, others responded to continuing discrimination and oppression by heeding Malcolm X's exhortation to defend their rights "by any means necessary" (quoted in Bloom 2000, 84).

African American college students Bobby Seale and Huey Newton founded what came to be known as the Black Panther Party in Oakland, California, in October of 1966. Admirers of revolutionary thinkers and leaders (including Karl Marx, Mao Tse-tung, and Che Guevara) from throughout the world, party members, later joined by Eldridge Cleaver, pursued a strategy of "armed self-defense" that led them into frequent and often bloody conflicts with the police. As the party's reputation for militancy spread, new chapters were established in cities throughout the nation.

The Black Panther Party engaged in one of the more bizarre attempts to rewrite the Constitution from September 5 to 7, 1970, when about 6,000 members met at Temple University in Philadelphia in a "Revolutionary People's Convention" (Vile 1991c, 102–104). David Hilliard, the party chief of staff, stated the convention's hope of composing a "constitution that will guarantee and deliver to every American citizen the inviolable human rights to life, liberty and the pursuit of happiness" ("Panthers Plan New Convention" 1971, 503). Clearly, however, the Panthers intended to move beyond these fairly conventional-sounding aims.

The party's founder and minister of defense, Huey Newton, had recently been released from prison, where he had been serving time for the murder of a police officer. His presence at the convention was a drawing card for Easterners to catch a glimpse of him and assess his leadership and speaking abilities (Pearson 1994, 226). However, no new constitution emerged from the Panthers' deliberations, and a subsequent gathering at Howard University in November 1970 was a failure.

Convention discussions centered on a number of subjects, ranging from socialism to women's liberation to human rights (Moore 1970, 1298). A contemporary magazine identified the primary proposals as:

- Abolishment of present political boundaries; creation of independent, self-governing communities from which political power would flow upward.
- A rotating police force of volunteers, under community control, with community councils, instead of courts, to deal with criminals.
- A national defense force of volunteers, trained in guerilla warfare.
- Free housing, health care, education and daycare centers for children.
- U.S. support of the Communist Vietcong in South Vietnam and the Communist Pathet Lao in Cambodia; return of Taiwan to Red China; "liberation" of Palestine from "Zionist colonialism." ("Rising Clamor for Black Separatism" 1970, 82)

With this agenda, it is hardly surprising that the Panthers' convention had little success. Moreover, by the late 1970s the party dissolved (Jeffries 1998, 118). The convention gives some insight, however, into the political turmoil of the era and shows an attempt to use a fairly traditional tool, the constitutional convention, in the hope of achieving fairly radical changes.

For Further Reading:

Bloom, Joshua. 2000. "Black Panther Party." In *Civil Rights in the United States*. 2 vols. Edited by

Waldo E. Maqrtin Jr. and Patricia Sullivan. New York: Macmillan Reference USA., I: 84–85.

Jeffries, Judson L. 1998. "Black Panther Party." In *The Encyclopedia of Civil Rights in America*. Edited by David Bradley and Shelley Fisher Fishkin. Armond, NY: M. E. Sharpe, Inc.

Moore, Trevor W. 1970. "A Rumbling in Babylon: Panthers Host a Parley." *Christian Century* 87 (28 October): 1296–1300.

"Panthers Plan New Convention." 1971. In *Facts on File Yearbook, 1970*. Vol. 30. New York: Facts on File.

Pearson, Hugh. 1994. *The Shadow of the Panther: Huey Newton and the Price of Black Power in America*. Reading, MA: Addison-Wesley.

"Rising Clamor for Black Separatism." 1970. *U.S. News and World Report* 69 (21 September): 82.

Vile, John R. 1991c. *Rewriting the United States Constitution: An Examination of Proposals from Reconstruction to the Present*. New York: Praeger.

❖ BLAINE AMENDMENT ❖

Modern controversies over prayer and Bible reading in schools date back more than a century, to the time when an unofficial Protestant establishment was increasingly challenged by Catholics, Jews, and others. These religious minorities objected both to Protestant religious exercises in public schools (readings, for example, from the King James Bible) and to the unavailability of government funding for nonpublic schools.

In 1875 President Ulysses S. Grant delivered a speech advocating an amendment requiring states to fund a system of free public schools and preventing any public funds from being allocated to parochial schools. Representative and former House Speaker James G. Blaine of Maine (the noted orator and unsuccessful Republican presidential nominee in the election of 1884) subsequently introduced an amendment applying the establishment and free exercise clauses of the First Amendment directly to the states and prohibiting public support of parochial schools (H.R. 1, 1875). Blaine, then seeking the Republican nomination for president, appears to have been motivated largely by political concerns (Green 1992, 40–51).

Some modern scholars cite debates over this amendment as evidence that contemporaries did not believe that the Fourteenth Amendment had intended to incorporate the provisions of the Bill of Rights and apply them to the states (A. Meyer 1951; F. O'Brien 1965). Steven Green (1992) has argued, however, that these debates are inconclusive on this point and that participants were more concerned about contemporary religious controversies.

Blaine's proposal stimulated considerable debate, including a proposed amendment by Democratic Congressman William O'Brien of Maryland in 1876 forbidding all religious tests and prohibiting ministers from holding public office. Democrats in the House Judiciary Committee accepted Blaine's proposal but weakened it by including a provision that "this article shall not vest, enlarge, or diminish legislative power in the Congress," thus making it declaratory only (Green 1992, 58). This amended version passed the House by a vote of 180 to 7. The Senate deleted the Democratic addition to the amendment. This body, however, added a clause providing that the proposed amendment "shall not be construed to prohibit the reading of the Bible in any school or institution" (cited by Green 1992, 60). This provision was added in apparent reaction to a series of decisions by school boards prohibiting religious instruction and Bible reading in public schools. One such decision had been upheld by the Ohio State Supreme Court in 1872 (Green 1992, 46–47). The Senate vote of twenty-eight to sixteen fell four votes shy of the majority needed to send it on to the states (Green 1992, 67), but a number of states adopted versions of the Blaine amendment (E. Larson 1993).

Variations of the Blaine amendment continued to be introduced in Congress throughout the nineteenth and early twentieth centuries; one scholar cited nineteen proposals in addition to Blaine's (F. O'Brien 1965, 210). Such proposals were supported by a group called the National League for the Protection of American Institutions (A. Meyer 1951, 944–945). An amendment introduced by Senator Henry Blair of New Hampshire in 1888, although intended to exclude public school teachings of doctrines "peculiar to any sect," would nonetheless have required states to educate children "in virtue, morality, and the principles of the Christian religion" (F. O'Brien 1965, 196). Proposals intended to permit religious exercises in school were stimulated anew by Supreme Court decisions in *Engel v. Vitale* (1962) and *Abington v. Schempp* (1963) relating to prayer and Bible reading in public schools. Recent discussion of a religious equality amendment has been stimulated by the opinion that religious believers have suffered discrimination and that their free exercise rights have not been fully protected.

See also Prayer in Public Schools; Religious Equality Amendment.

For Further Reading:
Green, Steven K. 1992. "The Blaine Amendment Reconsidered." *American Journal of Legal History* 36 (January): 38–69.

Hamburger, Philip. 2002. *Separation of Church and State.* Cambridge, MA: Harvard University Press.

Klinkhammer, Marie C. 1965. "The Blaine Amendment of 1875." *Catholic Historical Review* 21: 15–49.

Larson, Edward J. 1993. "The 'Blaine Amendment' in State Constitutions." In *The School-Choice Controversy: What Is Constitutional?* ed. James W. Skillen. Grand Rapids, MI: Baker Books.

Meyer, Alfred W. 1951. "The Blaine Amendment and the Bill of Rights." *Harvard Law Review* 64: 939–945.

O'Brien, F. William. 1963. "The Blaine Amendment, 1875–1876." *University of Detroit Law Journal* 41 (December): 137–205.

❖ *BOEHNER V. ANDERSON* ❖

The first, and apparently only, challenge brought under the belatedly ratified "Madison" or Twenty-seventh Amendment, was brought by John Boehner and other members of Congress who were challenging two provisions of the Ethics Reform Act of 1989. The first provision provided for a congressional cost of living increase (COLA) to go into effect at the first of each year. The second modified an earlier provision by establishing a citizen board to recommend quadrennial adjustments to congressional salaries to see that they were consistent with those in the private sector.

The Twenty-seventh Amendment provides that "No law, varying the compensation for services of the Senators and Representatives shall take effect until an election of Representatives shall have intervened." In examining the Ethics Reform Act of 1989, U.S. District Judge Stanley Sporkin lauded the law for limiting outside honoraria that members of Congress could receive and essentially depoliticizing the issue of congressional pay. Judge Sporkin found the contention that Congress would have to enact "a separate law for each and every raise, including a COLA" to be "an extremely strained reading of the 27th amendment—a reading for which the plain language of the amendment provides no support" (*Boehner v. Anderson*, 142). Similarly, he denied that each COLA "constitutes a separate law, which varies Congress' compensation before an election has intervened and which therefore violates the 27th Amendment" (*Boehner v. Anderson*, 143). He noted that "each year the COLA becomes effective by the terms of the 1989 Act; no additional law is necessary. In short, each COLA is not a law and, therefore, is not subject to the requirements of the 27th Amendment" (*Boehner v. Anderson*, 143).

Judge Ruth Bader Ginsburg (now a U.S. Supreme Court justice) wrote the decision for the U.S. Circuit Court for the District of Columbia affirming the lower court opinion. Since the Ethics Reform Law was adopted in 1989 and did not mandate the first COLA increase until 1991, she found that it met the Twenty-seventh Amendment's criterion for an intervening election. She further rejected Boehner's subsequent challenge to the cancellation of the 1994 COLA on the basis that it represented a new argument not considered in the lower court and arguably in conflict with Boehner's stated premise that his pay raise had constituted an "injury" that gave him judicial standing. Because no pay increase had been effected under the quadrennial provision, and none was scheduled prior to 1999, Ginsburg ruled that this provision was not yet ripe for review.

These decisions could arguably call the effectiveness of the Twenty-seventh Amendment into question. They do not directly address the question of the legitimacy of the amendment's belated ratification. First proposed as part of the Bill of Rights in the late eighteenth century, it was not ratified until 1992.

See also Twenty-seventh Amendment.

For Further Reading:

Boehner v. Anderson, 809 F. Supp. 138 (D.D.C. 1992).

Boehner v. Anderson, 30 F.3d 156 (D.C. Cir. 1994).

❖ *BOERNE, CITY OF V. FLORES* (1997) ❖

Momentum has grown in recent years for adoption of a Religious Equality Amendment. Proponents believe that such an amendment has been necessitated by a number of decisions by the U.S. Supreme Court, including *City of Boerne v. Flores* (1997).

In 1990 the U.S. Supreme Court issued a decision in *Employment Division v. Smith* in which it decided that a state could deny unemployment benefits to individuals who had broken a state law criminalizing the use of drugs, including peyote, that Smith and a colleague had ingested as part of their religious exercises as members of a Native American church. In previous cases, the Supreme Court had usually required a state to demonstrate a "compelling governmental interest" when a law of general applicability fell with particular force on a religious exercise, but in *Smith,* the Court distinguished such cases by arguing that they had all involved the exercise not simply of freedom of religion but also of related rights. In *Smith,* the Court ruled that states did not need to show a compelling governmental interest in cases where laws of general applicability incidentally burdened religious practices.

Concerned that this new approach did not

adequately protect the freedom of religious exercise guaranteed in the First Amendment of the U.S. Constitution, Congress adopted the Religious Freedom Restoration Act (RFRA) of 1993. Justified as an exercise of congressional enforcement authority under Section 5 of the Fourteenth Amendment, RFRA sought to reverse *Smith* by reinstituting the "compelling governmental interest" test in such cases.

When St. Peter Catholic Church in Boerne, Texas, subsequently attempted to expand its facilities, it came into conflict with a zoning ordinance designed to preserve the architectural heritage of the city. Archbishop Flores sought an exemption under the provisions of RFRA. In a ruling that illumines the contemporary Supreme Court's understanding of Section 5 of the Fourteenth Amendment and that has led to renewed calls for a constitutional amendment to do what RFRA was unable to do, the Supreme Court, in a decision written by Justice Anthony Kennedy, declared RFRA to be unconstitutional.

Reaffirming the *Smith* decision, Justice Kennedy interpreted Section 5 of the Fourteenth Amendment as a "remedial" rather than as a "substantive" power. Citing John Marshall's opinion in *Marbury v. Madison* (1803), which had established judicial review of congressional legislation, Kennedy noted that, if Congress could use Section 5 of the Fourteenth Amendment to redefine the Constitution, "no longer would the Constitution be 'superior paramount law, unchangeable by ordinary means.' It would be 'on a level with ordinary legislative acts, and, like other acts, . . . alterable when the legislature shall please to alter it" (*Boerne,* 529). Kennedy further argued that remedial legislation must establish both proportionality in addressing problems to which it is directed as well as "congruence between the means adopted and the legitimate end to be achieved" (*Boerne,* 533). By contrast, Kennedy pointed out that the compelling governmental interest test was "the most demanding test known to constitutional law" (*Boerne,* 534). He further noted that:

The substantial costs RFRA exacts, both in practical terms of imposing a heavy litigation burden on the States and in terms of curtailing their general regulatory power, far exceed any pattern or practice of unconstitutional conduct under the Free Exercise Clause as interpreted in Smith. (*Boerne*, 534)

Kennedy's opinion was joined by Chief Justice Rehnquist and by Justices John Paul Stephens, Clarence Thomas, and Ruth Bader Ginsburg. Antonin Scalia wrote a concurring opinion.

Justices Sandra Day O'Connor, Stephen Breyer, and David Souter continued to question the Supreme Court's earlier decision in *Smith*. Unless and until their view becomes the majority view of the Court, a constitutional amendment appears to be the only way that courts could be required to use the "compelling governmental interest" test in cases involving perceived infringements on religious liberty.

See also Religious Equality Amendment.

For Further Reading:
Boerne, City of v. Flores, 521 U.S. 507 (1997).
Employment Division v. Smith, 494 U.S. 872 (1990).

❖ BOUNDARY, U.S. AND CANADA ❖

See Minnesota Boundary.

❖ BRICKER AMENDMENT ❖

In the 1950s Senator John Bricker, a conservative Republican senator from Ohio, spearheaded a drive for a constitutional amendment related to treaties and executive agreements. A substitute for this amendment came only one vote shy of being proposed by the necessary two-thirds majority in the Senate in 1954 (the vote was sixty in favor to thirty-one against). Following its first introduction in 1951, more than sixty-five proposals like Bricker's were offered over the next ten years. By 1954 the issue was described as "a major question of national

policy" (Schubert 1954, 258), and proponents of the amendment continued offering amending resolutions into the 1980s.

Support for such amendments can be traced to a number of developments. A Supreme Court decision in *Missouri v. Holland* (1920) had suggested that Congress could exercise powers under the authority of treaties that it did not have under the Constitution. *United States v. Pink* (1942) appeared to magnify further executive powers under executive agreements. Some individuals expressed concern that the United Nations and a series of conventions it had drawn up might be used to undermine state sovereignty, afford fewer protections than Americans were accustomed to under the Bill of Rights, or interfere with purely domestic concerns. Such fears were, in turn, heightened by a California District Court opinion in *Fujii v. California* (1950) that overruled a portion of the state's Alien Land Law on the basis of a provision in the U.N. Charter (Tananbaum 1988, 5).

Supporters of an amendment emphasized different concerns. With a view toward *Missouri v. Holland*, Bricker's original proposal called for repeal of the supremacy clause in Article VI of the Constitution and substitution of a phrase more clearly indicating that treaties had to be made "in pursuance" of the Constitution and not simply under its authority. Bricker's original proposal would also have limited the reach of treaties and executive agreements with regard to individual rights, the form of government, and matters lacking in "mutuality of interest" or those within the U.S. "domestic jurisdiction." In addition, it called for publication of executive agreements and for their termination within six months of the end of a president's term (Tananbaum 1988, 221).

The American Bar Association supported an alternative proposal directed more toward the protection of states' rights. It provided that "a treaty shall become effective as internal law of the United States only through legislation by Congress which it could enact under its delegated powers in the absence of such treaty" (Tananbaum 1988, 222). The proposal by Georgia Senator Walter George that the Senate came close to proposing provided both that "a provision of a treaty or other international agreement which conflicts with this Constitution shall not be of any force or effect" and that agreements other than treaties "shall become effective as internal law in the United States only by an act of Congress" (Tananbaum 1988, 225).

President Eisenhower worked belatedly and largely behind the scenes against such proposals—although he publicly supported something known as the Knowland-Ferguson Proposal that would have prohibited treaties from violating the Constitution and would have required a roll-call vote on treaties (Garrett 1972, 195)—which he considered unnecessary and thought might tie his hands in foreign negotiations. Supreme Court decisions in *Rice v. Sioux City Memorial Park* (1955) and *Reid v. Covert* (1957) also allayed some of the concerns that had been raised in earlier cases. In the *Reid* case, Justice Hugo Black stated that "no agreement with a foreign nation can confer power . . . which is free from the restraints of the Constitution" (*Reid v. Covert* 1957, 16).

One scholar on the subject believes that the Bricker controversy alerted Eisenhower to the need to consult Congress on foreign policy matters. This scholar also believes that the controversy was a factor in delaying U.S. ratification of the U.N. Genocide Convention until 1986 (Tananbaum 1988, 218–219). Another scholar has noted that the Bricker controversy presaged some of the controversies during the Vietnam War over the respective powers of the legislative and executive branches in the area of foreign policy (Garrett 1972).

Recent years have witnessed increased American participation in such international organizations as the World Trade Organization (WTO) and in agreements with foreign nations such as those involved in the North American Free Trade Agreement (NAFTA). The latter created a free-trade zone within the United States, Canada, and Mexico, which might later be expanded throughout the hemisphere. Under the Trade Act of 1974, such agreements, which sometimes vest considerable discretion in international boards not directly accountable to the American people, have been given expedited review through the so-called fast track mechanism. This mechanism, which some scholars have compared to an informal constitutional amendment (Ackerman and Golove 1995), substitutes approval by a majority vote of both houses of Congress for a treaty requiring a two-thirds vote in the Senate. Under this arrangement, however, congressional floor debate is truncated, and Congress is limited to an up or down vote (Thomas 2000). It is possible that concerns reflected in public demonstrations about the scope of such agreements, the lack of popular input, and the power that such agreements sometimes end up vesting in international bodies, could eventually result in further efforts to amend the constitution similar to those expressed in the Bricker Amendment.

See also *Missouri v. Holland.*

For Further Reading:

Ackerman, Bruce, and David Golove. 1995. "Is NAFTA Constitutional?" *Harvard Law Review* 108 (February): 801–929.

Garrett, Stephen A. 1972. "Foreign Policy and the American Constitution: The Bricker Amendment in Contemporary Perspective." *International Studies Quarterly* 16 (June): 187–220.

Schubert, Glendon. 1954. "Politics and the Constitution: The Bricker Amendment during 1953." *Journal of Politics* 16 (May): 257–298.

Tananbaum, Duane. 1988. *The Bricker Amendment Controversy: A Test of Eisenhower's Political Leadership.* Ithaca, NY: Cornell University Press.

Thomas, Chantal. 2000. "Constitutional Change and International Government." *Hastings Law Journal* 52 (November): 1–46.

❖ BROWN, JOHN (1800–1859) ❖

John Brown was the fervent abolitionist who led a bloody attack on proslavery settlers in Pottawatomie, Kansas, in May 1856 and on the arsenal at Harpers Ferry, Virginia (now West Virginia), in October 1859. Although he had hoped to encourage a slave revolt by the latter action, he was unsuccessful in this endeavor, a number of his sons were killed in the raid, and he was subsequently hanged.

Brown and forty-five followers held a constitutional convention on 8 May 1858 in Chatham, Ontario. There they voted on a provisional constitution Brown had composed consisting of a preamble and forty-eight articles. It was designed to create an initial government for the free state that Brown hoped his attack on Harpers Ferry would create (Oates 1970, 243).

The unicameral Congress was to be composed of five to ten members serving three-year terms and elected by the persons "connected with the organization" (Fogleson and Rubenstein 1969, 48). The president, vice president, and five members of the Supreme Court were to be selected in similar fashion, with the executive also serving a three-year term, and all subject to impeachment and removal. Members of the three branches were to choose the commander in chief for a three-year term, with a treasurer, secretary of state, secretary of war, and secretary of the treasury chosen in a similar manner. The Constitution addressed recruiting for government posts and for the army and dealt with court-martials, the treatment of prisoners and neutrals, deserters, and captured property.

All persons in the organization were responsible for laboring "for the common good," with prohibitions on "profane swearing, filthy conversation, indecent behavior, or indecent exposure of the person, or intoxication or quarreling" and "unlawful intercourse of the sexes" (Fogleson and Rubenstein 1969, 57). The constitution also called for respecting "the marriage relation" (Brown's own two marriages had resulted in twenty children) and for setting aside Sunday for rest and for "moral and religious instruction and improvement, relief of the suffering, instruction of the young and ignorant, and the encouragement of personal cleanliness" (Fogleson and Rubenstein 1969, 57–58).

Article 46 of Brown's constitution proclaimed its intention to "amend and repeal" rather than dissolve the Union. It further specified that "our flag shall be the same that our fathers fought under in the Revolution" (Fogleson and Rubenstein 1969, 59).

Those who signed the document elected Brown as commander in chief, but the office of president was left vacant after two black nominees both declined to serve (Oates 1970, 246).

For Further Reading:

Fogleson, Robert M., and Richard E. Rubenstein. 1969. *Mass Violence in America: Invasion at Harper's Ferry.* New York: Arno Press.

Oates, Stephen B. 1970. *To Purge This Land with Blood: A Biography of John Brown.* New York: Harper and Row.

Renehan, Edward J., Jr. 1995. *The Secret Six: The True Tale of the Men Who Conspired with John Brown.* New York: Crown.

❖ *BROWN V. BOARD OF EDUCATION* (1954) ❖

There are few, if any, twentieth-century cases that better demonstrate the ability of the Supreme Court to alter current understandings of the Constitution—and thus provide a substitute for constitutional amendment—than this case. Here the Court overturned the doctrine of "separate but equal" that had been sanctioned in *Plessy v. Ferguson* (1896) and declared that segregation would have no place in U.S. public education. This opinion, in turn, sparked both support and opposition, including numerous attempts to trim the power of the Court in succeeding decades.

In delivering the unanimous opinion for the Court, Chief Justice Earl Warren recognized that the intention of those who wrote the Fourteenth Amendment could not be fully ascertained. Instead, he chose to focus on the importance of education in the modern context. Relying in part on contemporary psychological studies, Warren argued that racial segregation generated feelings of inferiority that adversely affected the motivation of minority students to learn (*Brown* 1954, 494).

A companion case, *Bolling v. Sharpe* (1954), extended the prohibition on segregation to the District of Columbia under authority of the due process clause of the Fifth Amendment, which, unlike the Fourteenth Amendment, applied to the national rather than the state governments. In the following year, the Court issued *Brown v. Board of Education II,* in which it declared that local school authorities, subject to the supervision of U.S. district courts, were responsible for seeing that desegregation was implemented "with all deliberate speed" (*Brown II* 1955, 301). Other decisions later applied the desegregation decision in *Brown* to areas outside the field of education.

Initially *Brown* stirred both passionate support and passionate opposition, including numerous amending proposals. Subsequent decisions involving race have led to proposed amendments dealing with affirmative action policies, state control of schools, and school busing.

Few contemporary constitutional scholars disagree with what the Court did in the *Brown* decision, and many believe that the case rectified a fundamental error in constitutional interpretation in the *Plessy* decision. *Brown* continues to interest those who study the meaning of constitutional amendments. Many scholars continue to debate whether the decision can be, or needs to be, squared with the "original intent" of those who wrote and ratified the Fourteenth Amendment (McConnell 1995). The decision also raises the issue of the level of generality by which the Constitution, and its amendments, should be interpreted. Should constitutional interpreters be bound by the original intent of the framers regarding segregation generally, or segregation in schools specifically, or by the framers' and ratifiers' wider intent, or perhaps, in plainer language, as regards "equal protection of the laws"?

Brown proclaimed that education had assumed increased importance in American life. Later decisions, most notably *San Antonio Independent School District v. Rodriguez* (1973), however, refused to declare that education was a "fundamental right" that states had to fund equally for all. A number of state courts have subsequently concluded that their own constitutions require stricter funding standards than the U.S. Supreme Court has attributed to the U.S. Constitution, and some proponents of national constitutional amendments have favored adding one specifically guaranteeing the right to an education.

See also Fourteenth Amendment; *Plessy v. Ferguson;* Social and Economic Rights.

For Further Reading:
Kluger, Richard. 1975. *Simple Justice: The History of* Brown v. Board of Education *and Black America's Struggle for Equality.* 2 vols. New York: Alfred A. Knopf.

McConnell, Michael W. 1995. "Originalism and the Desegregation Decisions." *Virginia Law Review* 81 (May): 947–1140.

San Antonio Independent School District v. Rodriguez, 411 U.S. 1 (1973).

Wilkinson, J. Harvie, III. 1979. *From* Brown *to* Bakke: *The Supreme Court and School Integration: 1954–1978.* New York: Oxford University Press.

❖ BUSING ❖

See School Busing.

C

❖

❖ CABINET ❖

The president's cabinet is not specifically mentioned in the U.S. Constitution, but it grew up in the administration of George Washington and consists of those individuals who head the major executive departments. They may also give the president advice, although most modern presidents (and some early presidents like Andrew Jackson who was known for relying upon his "kitchen cabinet") rely more on their personal staffs for the latter function. The cabinet has grown from its original three officers—the secretary of state, secretary of treasury, and attorney general—to fifteen. George W. Bush proposed in June 2002 that the fifteenth cabinet-level department be created for the Secretary of Homeland Security, headed by former Pennsylvania governor Tom Ridge, whose position had been created in the aftermath of the terrorist attacks against the United States of 11 September 2001. Ridge was approved, as the U.S. Constitution requires, by the U.S. Senate, which voted on 22 January 2003.

In April 1818 Democratic Representative William Lewis of Virginia introduced an amendment containing provisions whereby Congress would appoint members of the cabinet and the judiciary, with members of Congress apparently to be excluded from consideration as executive officers. Similarly, Whig Representative Joseph Underwood of Kentucky introduced a proposal in 1842 directed toward depriving the president of the power to select certain cabinet officers.

Article I, Section 6 of the U.S. Constitution prevents members of Congress from simultaneously serving as executive officers, and practice dictates that cabinet officers do not appear on the floor of Congress to answer questions. In the 1890s Gamaliel Bradford argued for a bill introduced by Democratic Representative George H. Pendleton of Ohio to allow the former—since the practice is not forbidden by the Constitution, it would not require an amendment (G. Bradford 1891, 1893; Cobb 1924). At about the same time, Republican Representatives William Barrett and Ernest Roberts of Massachusetts introduced amendments to enable members of Congress to serve as cabinet officers, an idea that Supreme Court Justice and Harvard law professor Joseph Story had previously advocated (Story 1833, 2: 333–337). Curiously, Woodrow Wilson, who had been an early advocate of parliamentary-oriented reforms, nixed an idea proposed by outgoing President William Howard Taft that would have granted cabinet officers nonvoting seats in Congress (Sundquist 1986, 51).

Allowing cabinet officers to hold dual memberships in the cabinet and in Congress would weaken the separation of powers and move the United States closer to a parliamentary system of government, in which cabinet members are regularly selected from the legislature. The parliamentary model has been a favorite of those seeking wholesale reform of the U.S. Constitution (Vile 1991c, 157–158) but has also been subject to intense criticism (see Sargentich 1993). Although enabling members of Congress to serve on the cabinet might improve executive liaison with Congress, the pressures on an individual responsible for heading an executive agency and representing constituents from a district or state would be immense.

In 1998 Texas Representative Ralph Hall (see Attorney General entry) introduced an amendment calling for the election of the attorney general, who is a cabinet officer. Other proposals for a new U.S. Constitution, including a number that want to "downsize" existing government or provide for educational reform, have called for the elimination of one or more cabinet posts.

See also Parliamentary System.

For Further Reading:

Bradford, Gamaliel. 1893. "Congress and the Cabinet—II." *Annals of the American Academy of Political and Social Sciences* 4 (November): 289–299.

———. 1891. "Congress and the Cabinet." *Annals of the American Academy of Political and Social Sciences* 4 (November): 404–424.

Cobb, Frank. 1924. "A Twentieth Amendment." In *Cobb of "The World": A Leader in Liberalism,* ed. John L. Heaton. New York: E. P. Dutton.

Sargentich, Thomas O. 1993. "The Limits of the Parliamentary Critique of the Separation of Powers." *William and Mary Law Review* 34 (Spring): 679–739.

Story, Joseph. 1833. *Commentaries on the Constitution of the United States.* 3 vols. Boston: Hilliard, Gray and Company. Reprint, New York: Da Capo Press 1970.

Sundquist, James L. 1986. *Constitutional Reform and Effective Government.* Washington, DC: Brookings Institution.

Vile, John R. 1991c. *Rewriting the United States Constitution: An Examination of Proposals from Reconstruction to the Present.* New York: Praeger.

❖ CALHOUN, JOHN C. (1782–1850) ❖

Along with Henry Clay and Daniel Webster, John C. Calhoun was one of the congressional giants of the early nineteenth century. Calhoun served as a member of the South Carolina legislature (1808–1809), member of the House of Representatives (1811–1817), secretary of war (1817–1825), vice president (1825–1832), secretary of state (1844–1845), and senator from South Carolina (1832–1844, 1845–1850). Despite his ability, his greatness has been somewhat diminished by his strong defense of slavery and of an extreme form of states' rights.

In addition to defending slavery as a positive good, Calhoun was among the South's strongest advocates of the doctrines of nullification and secession, which eventually led to disunion and civil war. In Calhoun's *Disquisition on Government,* he outlined his theory of concurrent majorities, which, in contrast to a system built simply on numerical majorities, was intended to provide each major interest or portion of the community with "a concurrent voice in making and executing the laws or a veto on their execution," thus preserving the status quo absent a consensus to change it (Calhoun 1953, 20). Calhoun's central concern was protection of regional interests, particularly slavery. But others have noted that the principle could be extended to others, indeed, even to racial minorities (Kuic 1983).

In his *Discourse on the Constitution and Government of the United States,* Calhoun lavishly praised the constitutional amending process, calling it the "*vis medicatrix* of the system" (Calhoun 1851–1856, 295) and describing it (somewhat counter to James Madison's description in *The Federalist Papers*) as a purely federal mechanism that embodied Calhoun's own view of concurrent majorities. Calhoun also gave the amending process a critical role in his theory of nullification, which would have entrusted states with the power to challenge federal legislation. On occasions when a state questioned the legitimacy of federal power, Calhoun called upon the majority exercising such disputed power to validate its view by adopting a constitutional amendment. Even here, however, Calhoun appeared to preserve the states' right to challenge amendments that exceeded implicit limits on the constitutional amending process (Vile 1992, 86).

During the nullification crisis of the 1820s and early 1830s, in which Calhoun opposed higher federal tariffs and challenged President

Andrew Jackson's assertion of federal authority, Calhoun advocated calling a constitutional convention to resolve the controversy. It would appear that he anticipated a body whose power "was much broader than that actually set forth in the exact language of the amending article" (Pullen 1948, 45).

Late in life, Calhoun came to fear that the amending process might be used, as it later would be in the Thirteenth Amendment, to abolish the institution of slavery, which he had defended. Accordingly, in his *Discourse*, Calhoun advocated creating a dual executive representing the North and the South, with each executive required to approve acts of congressional legislation before they became law (Calhoun 1851–1856, 392). Ironically, the very amending supermajorities that Calhoun praised were an obstacle to such a proposal.

A series of proposals introduced by Ohio's Democratic Representative Clement Vallandigham in February 1861 and apparently designed to forestall war appear to share features of Calhoun's thinking. One part of this proposal would have divided the nation into four sections, and another would have required a majority from all sections if a vote were so demanded by one-third or more of the senators.

For Further Reading:

Calhoun, John C. 1953. *A Disquisition on Government and Selections from the Discourse.* Edited by C. Gordon Post. Indianapolis, IN: Bobbs-Merrill. [Originally published as part of *The Works of John C. Calhoun.* Edited by Richard K. Crallé. New York: D. Appleton and Company, 1851–1856.]

———. 1851–1856. *The Works of John C. Calhoun.* Edited by Richard K. Crallé. New York: D. Appleton and Company. Reprint, New York: Russell and Russell, 1968.

Coit, Margaret L. 1961. *John C. Calhoun: American Portrait.* Boston: Houghton Mifflin.

Kuic, Vukan. 1983. "John C. Calhoun's Theory of the 'Concurrent Majority.'" *American Bar Association* 69: 482–486.

Niven, John. 1988. *John C. Calhoun and the Price of Union: A Biography.* Baton Rouge: Louisiana State University Press.

Pullen, William R. 1948. *Applications of State Legislatures to Congress for the Call of a National Constitutional Convention, 1788–1867.* Master's thesis, University of North Carolina at Chapel Hill.

Vile, John R. 1992. *The Constitutional Amending Process in American Political Thought.* New York: Praeger.

❖ CAMPAIGN CONTRIBUTIONS AND EXPENDITURES ❖

Members of Congress introduced a number of amendments calling for congressional regulation of campaign contributions and expenditures in the 1920s. A proposal introduced by Democrat Thomas Rubey of Missouri in 1926 demonstrates the difficulty of overly specific regulation in this ever-changing area. It would have excluded from office senators who had knowingly authorized the expenditure of more than $10,000 or representatives who had authorized more than $5,000 for their nomination and election (H.J. Res. 279).

A number of laws regulating campaign contributions and expenditures were subsequently introduced in Congress in the 1970s, 1980s, and 1990s. Such laws typically call for limits on contributions or campaign expenditures or disclosures of contributions made by individuals or political action committees. The Supreme Court examined provisions of the Federal Election Campaign Act of 1971 (subsequently amended in 1974) in *Buckley v. Valeo* (1976). In this case, the Court upheld congressionally imposed requirements for disclosure of campaign contributions as well as limits on the amount of money that an individual could contribute to another's campaign as reasonable efforts to combat corruption or its appearance. The Court, however, struck down limits on the moneys that wealthy individuals such as Ross Perot and Steve Forbes could contribute to their own campaigns as well as congressionally imposed limits on overall spending. The Court did accept limits on the spending of presidential candidates who had voluntarily accepted such campaign limits in exchange for public funding. The Court ruled that other limits on personal expenditures or campaign spending interfered with free speech rights guaranteed under the First Amendment. The Supreme Court effectively reaffirmed the *Buckley* precedent in *Nixon v. Shrink Missouri Government PAC* (2000), when it ruled that states had similar rights to regulate the size of campaign contributions to candidates. The majority opinion was written by Justice David Souter and joined by five other justices. Justice Anthony Kennedy favored overruling *Buckley*'s distinction between campaign expenditures and contributions to permit the states or Congress to attempt to regulate both (thereby lessening the perceived need for any constitutional amendment permitting this), while Justices Clarence Thomas and Antonin Scalia thought that *Buckley* had provided inadequate reasoning for limiting the contributions of individuals to candidates running for office.

The 1980s and 1990s brought a number of new proposals for constitutional amendments permitting either state or congressional regulation in this area. Some such proposals seemed to be aimed directly at *Buckley v. Valeo*. Thus a House Joint Resolution (No. 11) introduced in 1991 specified that campaign expenditures are not to be considered a form of protected speech under the First Amendment. A more recent proposal introduced by Iowa Republican Representative James A. Leach in February 2001 would specifically restrict monies that an individual could spend on his or her own campaign.

There is frequent criticism of the rising costs of political campaigns, the need for officeholders to engage in constant fund-raising, and the possibility that officeholders are improperly influenced by campaign contributions. Still, previous legislation in this area has often spawned loopholes and proved ineffective. Moreover, expenditure limits might give further advantage to incumbents, who already have significant advantages when running for reelection. President George W. Bush reluctantly signed a campaign spending law, the McCain-Feingold Campaign Reform Act (one of the sponsors, Arizona Senator John McCain had made this one of his major issues in his 1999–2000 quest for the Republican nomination) enacted in April 2002. This law is designed to limit so-called soft money expenditures that are spent on behalf of a candidate but not under the candidate's direction, but questions, which are likely to be taken up in court, remain about its constitutionality and effectiveness.

A proposal for "Amendment 28" has been posted on the Internet by John Francis Lee of Corpus Christi, Texas, who has identified himself in e-mail correspondence as "an ordinary private citizen of the USA, in despair over the present corrupt state of the American political class" (private e-mail correspondence with author dated 25 June 2002). His proposal has eight sections and is aimed, in part, at the decision in *Buckley v. Valeo*. The first, and most important, would prohibit candidates for elected office from accepting or soliciting "campaign funds except individually, from those citizens of the United States eligible to vote for the office in question" (Lee 2002 *http://www.28thamen.org*). A second section would limit the value of any single contribution to the equivalent of forty hours of work at minimum wage or $100. Section 3 would impose similar limits on individuals' contributions to their own campaigns. Section 4 would limit solicitations to the "calendar year of the contested election." Section 5 would require recording and reporting requirements for all contributions, and Section 6 would apply to primary and related elections. Section 7 would distribute all unspent campaign funds to the U.S. Treasury, and Section 8 would provide congressional enforcement power including imprisonment and fines.

Major reforms appear unlikely in the absence of a major scandal or catastrophe or firm control of the government by a party committed to such reform (Sorauf 1988, 382–388).

For Further Reading:

Alexander, Herbert E. 1992. *Financing Politics: Money, Elections and Political Reform,* 4th ed. Washington, DC: Congressional Quarterly Press.

Lee, John Francis. 2002. "Amendment 28," *http://www.28thamen.org/.* Accessed 6/21/02.

Limitations of Expenditures in Elections. 18 February 1990. Printed Hearings. Senate.

Nixon v. Shrink Missouri Government PAC, 528 U.S. 377 (2000).

Sorauf, Frank J. 1988. *Money in American Elections.* Glenview, IL: Scott, Foresman.

❖ CAPITAL PUNISHMENT ❖

The issue of governmentally imposed death penalties is a highly emotional one. Individual attitudes are likely to be shaped by fundamental moral values, by assessments of the deterrent value of such punishments, and by judgments as to whether the death penalty impacts certain groups in a discriminatory fashion.

The Fifth and Fourteenth Amendments specify that no person shall be "deprived of life, liberty, or property, without due process of law." Taken together with the Fifth Amendment requirement of a grand jury in cases of "capital" crimes, such evidence is fairly conclusive that the American founders did not intend to outlaw the death penalty. Still, like other punishments, the death penalty is subject to the provision in the Eighth Amendment against "cruel and unusual punishments." Moreover, some scholars believe that the Eighth Amendment ought to be interpreted in light of evolving moral standards that, throughout most of the world, have led to the abolition of the death penalty (see the 1963 dissent of Justice Goldberg to a denial of certiorari in *Rudolph v. Alabama* in D. O'Brien 2000a, 1123–1125). Still, despite massive efforts to overturn the death penalty (Epstein and Kobylka 1992), prior to 1968 the Supreme Court had never invalidated a death penalty on such grounds (White 1991, 4).

The first proposed constitutional change in the death penalty appears to have been in 1901, when Pennsylvania Republican Congressman Henry Cassel proposed the penalty for destruction of U.S. property; he also proposed deportation or lifetime imprisonment for members of anarchical societies. In the 1940s, Democratic Representative Walter Huber proposed abolishing the death penalty for all crimes other than treason. New York Representative Adam Clayton Powell proposed abolition of the death penalty in 1961, and his proposal was followed later in the decade by a number of others.

By far the largest number of amendments proposed in relation to capital punishment have called for permitting states to impose this penalty. Some proposals have also called for a federal death penalty in cases of treason or air piracy. Most proposals in favor of the death penalty appear to have been prompted by the Supreme Court's decision in *Furman v. Georgia* (1972). In that case, the Court decided that the death penalty, as then administered, was too arbitrary and hence unconstitutional. States rushed to adopt new laws.

By the time the Court rendered its next significant decision on the death penalty in *Gregg v. Georgia* (1976), thirty-five states had passed death penalty laws, and Congress had adopted such a penalty for cases of air piracy. In *Gregg*, the Court upheld the validity of the death penalty in cases in which there was a bifurcated trial that separated the decision on guilt or innocence from the decision on a penalty and when aggravating and mitigating circumstances were considered. In a companion case, *Woodson v. North Carolina*, the Court reversed a mandatory death penalty for first-degree murder cases.

The death penalty remains the subject of intense political debate, heightened by fears that in some states the penalty, which is irrevocable, may have been applied to individuals who were innocent. The Court continues to hear cases involving the degree of discretion to be awarded to juries in death penalty cases and the number of appeals that defendants may file in such cases. Few justices appear inclined to accept the views advocated by former Justices Thurgood Marshall, William Brennan, and Harry Blackmun that such a penalty is necessarily in violation of the cruel and unusual punishment clause, although there is renewed discussion as to whether the penalty should be applied to individuals who are below the age of eighteen (Supreme Court decisions currently allow the execution of individuals who were over the age of sixteen at the time they committed their crimes but not of those who were younger). Analyzing what it believed to be a clear trend in the states against such punishments, the U.S. Supreme Court recently overturned a prior ruling by deciding in *Atkins v. Virginia* (2002) that the death penalty cannot be applied to individuals who are retarded, with the cut-off appearing to be an I.Q of seventy to seventy-five or below. Similarly, in *Ring v. Arizona* (2002), the Court ruled that only a jury could decide whether aggravating factors existed that would warrant the implementation of the death penalty. Recent cases have also arisen about whether current mechanisms are adequate to ensure effective counsel for individuals on death row.

Representative Henry Gonzalez, a Mexican American Democrat representing the San Antonio, Texas, area (Barone and Ujifusa 1994, 1257–1259), has reintroduced amendments designed to abolish the death penalty completely. The chances of such an amendment being adopted in the near future appear to be quite dim.

See also Eighth Amendment.

For Further Reading:
Barone, Michael, and Grant Ujifusa. 1994. *The Almanac of American Politics 1994.* Washington, DC: National Journal.

Epstein, Lee, and Joseph F. Kobylka. 1992. *The Supreme Court and Legal Change: Abortion and the Death Penalty.* Chapel Hill: University of North Carolina Press.

Meltsner, Michael. 1974. *Cruel and Unusual: The Supreme Court and Capital Punishment.* New York: William Morrow.

White, Welsh S. 1991. *The Death Penalty in the Nineties: An Examination of the Modern System of Capital Punishment.* Ann Arbor: University of Michigan Press.

❖ CASCOT SYSTEM FOR SOCIAL CONTROL OF TECHNOLOGY ❖

See Marduke, P. G.

❖ CATT, CARRIE LANE CHAPMAN (1859–1947) ❖

Carrie Lane Chapman Catt was a former teacher and school superintendent who survived the deaths of two husbands and was a major force in the second generation of leadership in the movement for women's suffrage. This movement culminated in the ratification of the Nineteenth Amendment.

In 1889 Catt was elected secretary of the Iowa Woman Suffrage Association; in 1895 she was chair of the National Organization Committee of the National American Woman Suffrage Association (NAWSA); and in 1900 she succeeded Susan B. Anthony as president of that organization, serving until 1904. She also served as president from 1915 to 1920, when the Nineteenth Amendment (also called the Susan B. Anthony amendment) was ratified. Catt was a strong organizer with a determined "faith in God's eternal law for the evolution of the race" (quoted in Fowler 1986, 57). Before her reelection as NAWSA president, Catt was active in the International Woman Suffrage Alliance as well as in the New York State Woman Suffrage Party. Catt's decision as NAWSA president "to concentrate on a constitutional amendment rather than proceeding state by state" (Fowler 1986, 30)—as many southern suffragette advocates who favored states' rights wanted (see Wheeler 1993)—is often credited with resulting in the ratification of the Anthony amendment.

After adoption of the Nineteenth Amendment, Catt continued to be active in a number of concerns, including the League of Women Voters, which she founded in 1920, and several organizations devoted to world peace. Catt also helped organize the Woman's Centennial Congress of 1940.

See also Anthony, Susan Brownell; Nineteenth Amendment.

For Further Reading:
Fowler, Robert B. 1986. *Carrie Catt: Feminist Politician.* Boston: Northeastern University Press.

Wheeler, Margorie S. 1993. *New Women of the New South: The Leaders of the Woman Suffrage Movement in the Southern States.* New York: Oxford University Press.

❖ CENSUS ❖

Although each state is represented equally in the Senate, representation in the U.S. House of Representatives is based on population. Article I, Section 2 of the Constitution provides that representation in the House shall be based on an "enumeration," or census, conducted every ten years. Section 2 of the Fourteenth Amendment, designed to eliminate the notorious three-fifths clause (by which "such other persons," namely slaves, had been counted as three-fifths of a person for purposes of representation and taxation), further specified that "Representatives shall be apportioned among the several States according to their respective numbers, counting the whole number of persons in each State, excluding Indians not taxed."

Congress currently interprets these provisions so as to include both legal and illegal aliens, giving some extra representation to states with large populations of illegal aliens and also making them eligible for federal funds based on population formulas. At least one attorney, who points out that illegal aliens can be legally deported at any time and thus lack the stability of other state residents, has argued that Congress already has the power, which he thinks it should exercise, to authorize the Census Bureau to exclude illegal aliens from census counts. He has further argued that, if the courts do not accept such an interpretation, which is based more on what he considers to be the original intent of the framers of the constitutional provisions than on the word "persons," he favors a constitutional amendment to exclude such illegal aliens from the count (Wood 1999). Several members of Congress have also proposed such an amendment.

See also Birthright Citizenship Amendment; Congress, Representation in; Three-fifths Clause.

For Further Reading:
Wood, Charles. 1999. "Losing Control of America's Future: The Census, Birthright Citizenship, and Illegal Aliens," *Harvard Journal of Law and Public Policy* 22 (Spring): 465–522.

❖ *CHANDLER V. WISE* (1939) ❖

Chandler v. Wise was a companion case to *Coleman v. Miller* (1939). Taxpayers, citizens, and voters had challenged Kentucky's ratification of the child labor amendment. They argued that it should be voided because of its prior rejection by the legislature and a majority of other states and because it had not been ratified within a reasonable time, a requirement seemingly mandated in *Dillon v. Gloss* (1921). They sought a court order requiring that the state governor, who had certified and forwarded the amendment before becoming aware of the suit, notify the secretary of state that Kentucky's ratification was invalid.

The Supreme Court rejected this request by a seven-to–two decision written by Chief Justice Hughes, with Justices Black and Douglas concurring and Justices McReynolds and Butler dissenting. Consistent with the decision in *Coleman v. Miller,* the majority decided that "after the Governor of Kentucky had forwarded the certification of the ratification of the amendment to the Secretary of State of the United States there was no longer a controversy susceptible of judicial determination" (*Chandler v. Wise* 1939, 477–478).

See also Child Labor Amendment; *Coleman v. Miller.*

For Further Reading:
Chandler v. Wise, 307 U.S. 474 (1939).

❖ CHILD LABOR AMENDMENT ❖

Throughout history, children have engaged in labor. Industrialization and the accompanying rise of manufacturing and mining, however, created situations in which children often worked long hours in hazardous and unhealthy circumstances without parental supervision and protection and in circumstances that precluded adequate time for them to receive an education. By 1900 "one child in six between the age of ten and fifteen was gainfully employed, and there were more than 1,750,000 child laborers in America" (S. Wood 1968, 3). Many of the reform organizations associated with the Progressive movement coalesced around opposition to child labor; the most effective organization, the National Child Labor Committee (NCLC), was established in April 1904.

Initially, this committee and other organizations focused on reform at the state level, but despite successes in many states, the resulting legislation was not uniform and was especially weak in the South. There, children were frequently employed in the textile industry, and weak regulations depressed adult wages and gave southern manufacturers a labor advantage. By 1912 the NCLC had concluded that national legislation was needed. A number of Supreme Court decisions, among them *Champion v. Ames* (a 1903 case upholding congressional powers to regulate interstate transportation of lottery tickets), suggested that such powers were within congressional authority. There was at least one proposal introduced in Congress in 1914 to proceed instead by constitutional amendment.

In 1916 Congress passed the Keating-Owen bill, attempting to discourage child labor by prohibiting for thirty days the interstate transportation of goods made by companies employing children under the age of fourteen or violating standards set for the employment of children between ages fourteen and sixteen. President Woodrow Wilson reconsidered his earlier constitutional reservations and encouraged the passage of and signed this bill, which has been described as "the crowning achievement of progressivism" (S. Wood 1968, 78).

Progressive hopes were dashed in *Hammer v. Dagenhart* (1918) when the Supreme Court declared in a five-to-four decision written by Justice William Rufus Day that the Keating Owen bill violated the Fifth and Fourteenth Amendments. With his reasoning called into serious question by Justice Oliver Wendell Holmes's vigorous dissenting opinion, Day attempted to distinguish between the congressional regulation of items that were in themselves harmful and the regulation of those that were not. The Court also viewed the law as an unconstitutional regulation of manufacturing rather than a legitimate exercise of commerce power. The decision has been called "a breach—not a temporary breach—in constitutional interpretation that signaled return, for almost a generation, to conservative jurisprudence" (S. Wood 1968, 182).

Although several congressmen proposed a constitutional amendment to reverse this decision, a majority settled instead on an amendment to the Revenue Act of 1919 that leveled a 10 percent tax on goods produced by child labor. In an eight-to-one decision written by Chief Justice Taft (*Bailey v. Drexel Furniture Company* (1922)), the Court subsequently struck down that law too, arguing that the provisions were designed as a penalty rather than a tax and that they unfairly impinged on state police powers in violation of federal principles, especially the Tenth Amendment.

In response, Congress proposed the child labor amendment in 1924 by a vote of 197 to 69 in the House and 61 to 23 in the Senate. Omitting references to women, which some proposals had included, it read as follows:

> Section 1. The Congress shall have power to limit, regulate, and prohibit the labor of persons under 18 years of age.
> Section 2. The power of the several States is unimpaired by this article except that the operation of state laws shall be suspended to the extent necessary to give effect to legislation enacted by this Congress. (Grimes 1978, 102)

By 1924, however, the American labor movement was weak, Progressive sentiment was waning, and there was widespread disappointment with the Eighteenth Amendment's attempt to enact national alcoholic prohibition. The proposed child labor amendment also faced strong opposition. In what one scholar identified as "an instructive, almost eerie, parallel with the ERA [equal right amendment]" (Mansbridge 1986, 31), this waning commitment to reform was combined with concerns as diverse as states' rights, parental control over children, the rights of private religious schools, and communist influence. Such fears were fanned by opposition groups such as the American Bar Association, the Sentinels of the Republic, a publication known as *Woman Patriot,* which had previously opposed women's suffrage, the *Southern Textile Bulletin* edited by David Clark, and southern industrial leaders (Trattner 1970, 170–174). Textually, some believe that the amendment might have had a better chance of adoption had it set the age for child labor at sixteen rather than at eighteen and that the word "employment" might have seemed less threatening than "labor" to those who were concerned that the amendment might give the federal government undue influence over life on the farm or life within individual households (Aldous 1997).

As 1925 ended, only four states had ratified and nineteen had rejected the proposed amendment (Grimes 1978, 103). The tide seemed to turn with the coming of the New Deal. A number of states that had previously rejected the amendment now reversed themselves, an action that was challenged in the courts. In *Coleman v. Miller* (1939) the Supreme Court ruled that the validity of such appeals, as well as the issue of whether they had come within a reasonable time, were "political questions" for Congress to resolve. Eventually, twenty-eight states ratified the amendment.

In the meantime, child labor provisions were incorporated in regulations adopted through the National Industrial Recovery Act, a law subsequently invalidated in the 1935 decision in *Schechter Poultry Corp. v. United States* (Trattner 1970, 190–200). Child labor provisions were subsequently added to the Fair Labor Standards Act of 1938 and were upheld in *United States v. Darby Lumber Co.* (1941), when the Supreme Court explicitly overturned *Hammer v. Dagenhart* and declared that it would no longer be bound by earlier restrictive interpretations of the Fifth and Tenth Amendments. As an amendment issue, child labor has subsequently been moot.

For Further Reading:

Aldous, Joan. 1997. "The Political Process and the Failure of the Child Labor Amendment." *Journal of Family Issues* 18 (January): 71–92.

Davidson, Elizabeth H. 1939. *Child Labor Legislation in the Southern Textile States*. Chapel Hill: University of North Carolina Press.

Freedman, Russell. 1994. *Lewis Hine and the Crusade against Child Labor*. New York: Clarion Books.

Grimes, Alan P. 1978. *Democracy and the Amendments to the Constitution*. Lexington, MA: Lexington Books.

Mansbridge, Jane J. 1986. *Why We Lost the ERA*. Chicago: University of Chicago Press.

Report on the Condition of Women and Children as Wage Earners. 1910–1913. U.S. Department of Labor. 19 vols. Washington, DC: U.S. Government Printing Office.

Trattner, Walter I. 1970. *Crusade for the Children: A History of the National Child Labor Committee and Child Labor Reform in America*. Chicago: Quadrangle Books.

Wood, Stephen B. 1968. *Constitutional Politics in the Progressive Era: Child Labor and the Law*. Chicago: University of Chicago Press.

❖ *CHISHOLM V. GEORGIA* (1793) ❖

One of the most important cases of the pre-Marshall Supreme Court, this was also the first decision overturned by an amendment, in this case the Eleventh. At issue was whether a citizen of another state—here, the executor of the estate of a Charleston, South Carolina, merchant from whom Georgia had purchased supplies in 1777 but whom it had not paid—could sue a state without its consent. Asserting state sovereignty, Georgia refused even to argue its case.

The decision was a seriatim decision, with each justice writing a separate opinion, in which all the justices (Blair, Wilson, Cushing, and Jay) except Iredell agreed. The majority decided that, under the general principles and structures of the Constitution and the specific language of Article III (which extended judicial power to controversies "between a State and Citizens of another State"), a state was subject, both as a defendant and as a plaintiff, to federal judicial jurisdiction. Justice Wilson's opinion was an especially far-reaching discussion of how the U.S. Constitution recognized the people, rather than rulers or governments, as sovereign. However, the Court's ruling contradicted explicit assurances that the Federalists had given the Anti-Federalists during debates over the ratification of the Constitution (Mason and Stephenson 2002, 157).

Although not dealing directly with the constitutionality of a federal law, this case clearly anticipated the exercise of judicial review prior to John Marshall's decision in *Marbury v. Madison* (1803). Justice Iredell thus noted that an act of Congress exceeding constitutional authority would be void "because it would be inconsistent with the Constitution, which is a fundamental law paramount to all others, which we are not only bound to consult but sworn to observe" (*Chisholm v. Georgia* 1793, 433).

Justice Cushing seemed to anticipate, if not invite, an amendment when he noted that "if the Constitution is found inconvenient in practice in this or any other particular, it is well that a regular mode is pointed out for amendment" (*Chisholm v. Georgia* 1793, 468). Subsequent decisions interpreting the Eleventh Amendment, most notably *Hans v. Louisiana* (1890), appear to have confirmed the understanding of state sovereign immunity advocated by the dissenters in *Chisholm* rather than that advocated by the majority. In recent years the Eleventh Amendment has begun to figure more prominently in U.S. Supreme Court decision making.

See also Eleventh Amendment; Supreme Court Decisions Reversed by Constitutional Amendments.

For Further Reading:

Chisholm v. Georgia, 2 U.S. (2 Dall.) 419 (1793).

Mason, Alpheus T., and Donald G. Stephenson Jr. 2002. *American Constitutional Law: Introductory Essays and Selected Cases*. 13th ed. Englewood Cliffs, NJ: Prentice-Hall.

Mathis, Doyle. 1967. "*Chisholm v. Georgia:* Background and Settlement." *Journal of American History* 54: 19–29.

❖ CHRISTIAN AMENDMENT ❖

Unless one counts the reference to "the Year of our Lord one thousand seven hundred and eighty-seven" that is sometimes appended to Article VII of the U.S. Constitution, the document contains no direct reference to God. The Reformed Presbyterian Church, whose roots were in the Scottish Covenant tradition, considered the absence of such a reference to, and acknowledgment of, God to be a fatal flaw. Members of this denomination accordingly re-

fused to participate in voting or holding office. Some members participated in the War of 1812, however, and a group of "New Side" Reformers (who believed that they should support the government under the Constitution) eventually split from the "Old Side" Reformers in 1833. The Reformed Presbyterian Church remained a small denomination, and it does not appear to have significantly influenced public opinion in the nation's early years.

As the controversy over slavery developed and intensified, however, many abolitionists also began to denounce the Constitution as a flawed document. Although abolitionists typically regarded the Constitution's acquiescence in slavery rather than its failure to acknowledge God as its fatal weakness, the two critiques often merged. Reformed Presbyterians viewed the Constitution's acquiescence in slavery as a logical consequence of its failure to acknowledge the Almighty.

Ironically, when the Confederate states drafted their constitution, they rewrote their preamble specifically to invoke "the favor and guidance of Almighty God" (DeRosa 1991, 135). For their part, in 1859, the Reformed Presbyterians had passed their first resolution specifically calling on the Union to acknowledge God. Typical of many subsequent proposals, their amendment called for:

1. An express acknowledgment of the being and authority of God. 2. An acknowledgment of submission to the authority of Christ. 3. That it should recognize the paramount obligation of God's law, contained in the Scriptures of the Old and New Testaments. 4. That it may be rendered, in all its principles and provisions, clearly and unmistakably adverse to the existence of any form of slavery within the national limits. (Jacoby 1984, 55–56)

In February 1863 a convention composed of members of a number of religious denominations met in Xenia, Ohio. It supported a proposal by Presbyterian layman John Alexander for a constitutional amendment to acknowledge "the rulership of Jesus Christ and the supremacy of the divine law" (Borden 1979,

159). The National Association To Secure the Religious Amendment of the Constitution subsequently chose Alexander as its first president. The *Christian Statesman* was the official journal of this organization, which was later renamed the National Reform Association. One of the association's most prominent members was Judge William Strong, who later served on the Supreme Court from 1870 to 1880.

The National Reform Association held conventions, presented petitions, published and distributed literature, and otherwise pressed for an amendment. The association received a diplomatic but noncommittal reply when it met with President Lincoln in February 1864. The association's mission appears to have been aided both by the soul-searching that the Civil War occasioned and by Lincoln's use of religious concepts in explaining and justifying the war.

The movement for a Christian amendment had its greatest prominence in the period from 1872 to 1875. One historian noted that during this time there were "a striking number of conflicts which raised fears that the historic Protestant basis of American society and government was being lost" (Jacoby 1984, 290). The period was also notable for support for the Blaine amendment, which would have prohibited state aid to parochial schools, often administered by and associated with Roman Catholics.

In 1876 proponents of the Christian amendment presented petitions with over 35,000 signatures to the House of Representatives. In that same year, the National Reform Association succeeded in keeping the Centennial Exposition from opening on Sunday. By then, however, the association faced increasing opposition from individuals who feared that an amendment recognizing God or Jesus might undermine the liberty of non-Christians and nonbelievers that was guaranteed by the establishment clause of the First Amendment. The association also appears to have somewhat diluted its own effectiveness by endorsing other causes with Christian backing, including the rising temperance movement that eventually resulted in the adoption of the Eighteenth Amendment.

Since 1947 there have been more than fifty-five proposals in Congress for variations of the Christian amendment. Sponsors have included Republican congressman, and later independent candidate for president in 1980, John Anderson. Modern proposals may have been stimulated in part by contemporary Supreme Court decisions relative to prayer and Bible reading in the public schools, but there have been far more calls for amendments specifically designed to reverse these decisions than to recognize God in the Constitution.

The National Reform Association dissolved in 1945, but the National Association of Evangelicals (NAE) subsequently took up its cause. The NAE supported an amendment under which "this nation devoutly recognizes the authority and law of Jesus Christ, Savior and Ruler of all nations, through whom are bestowed the blessings of Almighty God" (Borden 1979, 167). The NAE now supports a version of the religious equality amendment that mentions God but is chiefly concerned with guaranteeing religious liberty.

Some individuals, including the Christian Reconstructionists described in the essay that follows, believe that the current U.S. Constitution is already predicated upon Christian principles, a view that seems to be widely shared by Americans who have found it difficult to accept Supreme Court decisions relative to prayer and other religious exercises in public schools. Thus, the 2000 Platform of a group known as the Constitution Party begins its preamble by acknowledging God and solemnly declaring "that the foundation of our political position and moving principle of our political activity is our full submission and unshakable faith in our Savior and Redeemer, our Lord Jesus Christ." Before getting into such particulars as opposition to another constitutional convention, advocacy of gun control, opposition to the New World Order and the like, the platform proceeds to announce that:

> The U.S. Constitution established a Republic under God, rather than democracy; our Republic is a nation governed by a Constitution that is rooted in Biblical law, administered by representatives who are Constitutionally elected by the citizens; [and] in a Republic governed by Constitutional law rooted in Biblical law,

all Life, Liberty and Property are protected because law rules. ("Constitution Party 2000 National Platform")

After the Ninth U.S. Circuit Court of Appeals ruled in *Newdow v. United States Congress* (2002) that it was unconstitutional for school students to recite the pledge of allegiance with the words "under God" (the court, which is likely to be reversed, thought this constituted an impermissible "establishment" of religion contrary to the First Amendment), a number of members of Congress introduced amendments to overturn this ruling. Some specifically contained the words "under God." If adopted, such an amendment would at least indirectly accomplish one of the aims of those who originally favored the Christian Amendment.

See also Blaine Amendment; Flag Salute; Religious Equality Amendment.

For Further Reading:

Borden, Morton. 1979. "The Christian Amendment." *Civil War History* 25 (June): 156–167.

"Constitution Party 2000 National Platform," *http://www.constitutionparty.com/ustp-99pl.html.* Accessed 5/29/02.

DeRosa, Marshall L. 1991. *The Confederate Constitution of 1861: An Inquiry into American Constitutionalism.* Columbia: University of Missouri Press.

Handy, Robert T. 1971. *A Christian America: Protestant Hopes and Historical Realities.* New York: Oxford University Press.

Jacoby, Steward O. 1984. *The Religious Amendment Movement: God, People and Nation in the Gilded Age.* 2 vols. Ph.D. dissertation, University of Michigan.

Kramnick, Isaac, and R. Laurence Moore. 1996. *The Godless Constitution: The Case against Religious Correctness.* New York: W. W. Norton.

Morton, Robert K. 1933. *God in the Constitution.* Nashville, TN: Cokesbury Press.

Proceedings of the National Convention to Secure the Religious Amendment of the Constitution of the United States held in Pittsburgh, February 4, 5, 1874, with an Account of the Origin and Progress of the Movement. 1874. Philadelphia: Christian Statesman Association.

❖ CHRISTIAN RECONSTRUCTIONISM ❖

States and localities are increasingly faced with requests to post the Ten Commandments in public schools—a practice the U.S. Supreme Court invalidated in *Stone v. Graham* (1980)—and in public places, especially courthouses. Advocates of these postings are often motivated by animus against Supreme Court decisions that have outlawed prayer in public schools and the belief that the nation needs to be brought back to what they consider to be its Judeo-Christian moorings. Aware that the Supreme Court is likely to apply the *Lemon* test (first announced in *Lemon v. Kurtzman* (1971)) and require that such actions be justified by a "secular legislative purpose" (the flaw detected in *Stone v. Graham*), these activists often seek to accompany the commandments with other documents and to justify their display as a way of informing the public of America's legal heritage.

This volume contains a constitution written by Bill Strittmatter designed to establish a Christian Constitution for the United States patterned on the Ten Commandments. This intent is similar to that associated with the movement known as Christian Reconstructionism, or Theonomy. The movement was founded by Rousas John Rushdoony (1917–2001), the American son of a family of Armenian immigrants and the founder and president of the Chalcedon Foundation (a name based on an early Christian creed), who was deeply influenced by Professor Cornelius Van Til of the Westminster Theological Seminary, a breakaway from Princeton. Van Til believed strongly that Christians ultimately had to base their arguments on the Bible rather than on human reason.

The Christian Reconstructionist movement, which appears to have had at least some influence on current right-wing politicians, is predicated on the idea that all of government needs to be brought into subjection to the law of God. These would include not only the Ten Commandments, but most of the accompanying law of the Old Testament, or Hebrew Scriptures. Most Christians believe that the Ten Commandments articulate enduring principles but that accompanying Biblical laws are largely irrelevant to daily life and governance. By contrast, Rushdoony believed that most such laws express eternal verities, continue to have validity, and should ideally be enforced by governments.

Rushdoony was a prolific writer. His most detailed views of governance are set forth in *The Institutes of Biblical Law* (1973). Economist Gary North (Rushdoony's son-in-law with whom he was not always on good personal terms) and ethicist Greg Bahnsen are among those who have advocated Rushdoony's views. Unlike earlier proponents who believe the nation needs to adopt a Christian Amendment specifically acknowledging God, most Reconstructionists believe that the American framers intentionally created a Christian constitution in which laws upholding Christianity were to be left, under terms of the First Amendment (which at the time applied only to the national government and thus did not obliterate state religious establishments), to individual states. One scholar notes that, "In Rushdoony's view, the Constitution did not need to include a Christian confession because the states were already a Christian establishment or settlement" (Edgar 2001).

The Reconstructionists see a relatively minor role for the national government, largely limited to administering justice, providing for defense, and allowing for the development of free enterprise. Most government would revert to state and local levels and even to individual families, which would be patriarchal and would especially assume the role of education now largely carried out by the state (Clapp 1990, 12–13). Not surprisingly, Rushdoony was a strong proponent of the home schooling movement. Under Christian reconstructionism, prisons would be abolished and replaced either by restitution, in some cases involving forms of "biblical" slavery, or capital punishment. A scholar of the movement notes that in his *Theonomy in Christian Ethics,* Reconstructionist Greg Bahnsen advocated capital punishment for fifteen crimes including "not only murder and rape, but sodomy, Sabbath breaking, apostasy, witchcraft, blasphemy and incorrigibility in children" (Clapp 1990, 14–15).

Gary North favors stoning, largely because of the widespread availability of rocks and their low cost.

It is not clear that Reconstructionists have, like Strittmatter, actually written a new U.S. Constitution or that they necessarily envision the imposition of Old Testament law in the near future. Most hold what is known as a postmillennialist view of history, under which they believe that a thousand-year rule of Jesus Christ on earth, the millennium, will be ushered in through the increase of God's Kingdom on earth, and many recognize that such a development could take hundreds, if not thousands, of years. Still, it would not be surprising to find that individuals from this movement might increasingly look to the Old Testament for models of laws and constitutions at both state and federal levels.

See also Christian Amendment; Prayer in Public Schools, Strittmatter, Bill.

For Further Reading:

Clapp, Rodney. 1990. *The Reconstructionists.* Downers Grove, IL: Intervarsity Press.

Edgar, William. 2001. "The Passing of R. J. Rushdoony." *First Things: A Monthly Journal of Religion and Public Life* (August): 24.

Rushdoony, Rousas John. 1973. *The Institutes of Biblical Law.* Phillipsburg, NJ: Presbyterian and Reformed Publishing Co.

❖ CHURCH, JOSEPH (1918–) ❖

Psychologist Joseph Church has advanced what the cover of his 1982 book, *America the Possible: Why and How the Constitution Should Be Rewritten,* described as "An Iconoclastic View of the Social, Political, and Economic Order in the U.S.—with Some Startling Suggestions for Change" (Church 1982). Born in Gardner, Massachusetts, in 1918, Church was educated at the New School for Social Research, Cornell University, and Clark University. He subsequently taught at Vassar College and, beginning in 1965, at Brooklyn College of the City University of New York. Church's other books deal largely with topics of childhood and adolescence, but this hardly deterred him from advancing wide-ranging views of contemporary American problems and what he believes to be their solutions. He is particularly disturbed by the continuing influence of what he considers to be myths—especially those generated by religion and Victorian sexual morality—and he expresses his ideas about family organization, the economy, and law and order as well as describes the outlines of what he would include in a new constitution. Acknowledging that he has "no faith in human perfectibility," Church states that he does "have a strong faith in human improvability, and this is enough" (Church 1982, 29).

In outlining what he describes as "the dimensions of a humane society," Church stresses the goals of greater human fulfillment; the need for greater egalitarianism; and the need for the nation to withdraw from foreign military alliances and commitments, to provide for human physical needs, and for democracy. In contrast to those who argue for constitutional brevity, Church notes that such an approach is "dangerously misguided." He explains:

> We have learned a great deal about how societies work in the nearly 200 years that our present Constitution has been in effect. It would be foolish or insane not to incorporate that learning into a new document. We do not want to accord the people in power great flexibility in decision making. They have all too consistently made the wrong decisions, sometimes out of avarice and self-interest, but often out of sheer stupidity. (Church 1982, 81)

Church's ideas on the family are among his most provocative and are based on "the libertarian premise that the state should interfere as little as possible in the private lives of individuals" (Church 1982, 87). He is willing to allow any consensual living arrangements that individuals care to choose, including homosexual marriages and "living together" arrangements. He is not opposed to prostitution or even bestiality "as long as the animals are not made to suffer" (Church 1982, 94). (He did not explain how the presence of such suffering would be as-

certained.) Apart from laws against rape, he is willing to lower the age of consent and to permit "noncoercive sex with children" (Church 1982, 94), as well as abortion on demand—at least early during a pregnancy. He hopes to abolish the stage of adolescence by allowing children to declare themselves to be independent, a decision that would, however, be irrevocable—children so emancipated would be permitted to drive, have access to pornography, consume alcohol or other drugs, decide whether to attend school, and, of course, engage in sexual relations. They would also qualify for his proposed "universal living-allowance program" (Church 1982, 119). High schools and colleges would be replaced by "research institutes staffed by scholars and scientists" (Church 1982, 123). Church's ideas on economic organization, although not quite so shocking to ordinary sensibilities, are equally provocative.

In the chapter of his book entitled "The New Constitution," Church indicates that he has respect for those who framed the Constitution and what they wrote, but that there are "reasons to start again" (Church 1982, 234). He wants the new constitution to stress "the democratic, humanitarian, and idealistic foundations of both the Declaration of Independence and the Constitution" as well as "to reassert the supremacy of the people" (Church 1982, 234–235). Aware of proposals advanced by both Rexford Guy Tugwell and Dwight Macdonald, Church wants to go even further.

Church's first proposal calls for abolishing the presidency. He associates the presidency with war and with aggrandizement of power, and he hopes to replace the office with a chief administrator (CA) selected by Congress. With the CA now becoming a mere administrative arm of the legislative branch, the new "balance of powers" within government would consist of "the legislature, the judiciary, and the electorate" (Church 1982, 244). Church also advocates replacing existing states with new arrangements, perhaps allowing for divisions into an urban and a rural America. Most, if not all, funding of programs like education and health care would be provided from national progressive income taxes on personal (albeit not corporate) income, but local groups would apparently maintain authority over the daily operations of such programs. The people would in turn have broad authority that they would exercise through the referendum, initiative, and recall processes (Church 1982, 248).

The most distinctive aspect of Church's proposal (which does not present actual new constitutional language) is how many principles he squeezes into the preamble of his proposed document. The preamble should, he says, "make explicit that ours is a pluralistic society and that the rule of the majority must not work hardships on any minority or group of minorities" (Church 1982, 249). It should affirm electoral supremacy through the referendum, initiative, and recall, mechanisms that would go so far as to allow voters to accept or reject budgets on a line-by-line basis (Church 1982, 250). The preamble would apparently include provisions for "something approaching full-time voting" and the establishment of "full-time polling sites" (Church 1982, 253). The preamble would "include the basics of our foreign policy," including the guiding principle of "peaceful coexistence," a dissolution of all foreign alliances, a commitment to work through the United Nations, and a commitment to free trade (Church 1982, 254–255). The preamble would also limit arm sales by governments and by private individuals and set a figure for "the maximum desirable population size of the nation," which Church estimates would be "200 million souls" (Church 1982, 257). The preamble should also "establish that the foundation of our society is the rights set forth in the various amendments to the original Constitution" (Church 1982, 258).

After setting forth the principles to be covered in his prolix preamble, Church moves on to other matters. He expresses a near conspiratorial view of existing political parties in the United States but is not altogether clear with what would replace them. Congress would continue to be bicameral, and it would provide health care and a universal living allowance for all. The current Senate would be replaced by a House of Delegates based on the representation of special-interest groups—delegates being selected through a system of "preferential balloting of the kind used in many nongovernmental organizations" (Church 1982, 263).

Members of both houses would serve five-year terms, subject to voter recall.

Although Church would eliminate the states, he provides for "the right of secession to any part of the country, big or small, that wants to go it alone." This provision is coupled with two provisos. The first, intended to avoid idle threats, provides that secession "would be irrevocable for a period of fifty years." The second provides for "free migration into and out of the seceding territory for a period of five years" (Church 1982, 267).

The judiciary would be significantly altered. All courts would operate "with a uniform system of laws" (Church 1982, 268). Church would establish "a second system of courts of legislative review, culminating in a second Supreme Court" (Church 1982, 268). Much like the Council of Revision that had been rejected by the Constitutional Convention of 1787, the new courts would review all acts of legislation at the times of their passage, without waiting for cases to arise. Judges would not only be elected, but they would be permitted, if not expected, to campaign for their offices (Church 1982, 269).

Church hopes to draw a clear line between legality and morality. In reviewing current constitutional provisions, he favors spelling out many current guarantees more concretely. Thus, he favors a constitution that specifies the exclusionary rule, limits the use of grants of immunity, and the like. Church favors the nationalization of many industries and of "our national resources" (Church 1982, 275). Although opposed to capital punishment, he favors a constitutional right to die and specifies that "the means of suicide should always be made available upon request" to prisoners (Church 1982, 279).

Church is particularly concerned about what he considers to be the "antiquated" provisions of the First Amendment. In addition to desiring to eliminate tax exemptions for churches and the government provision of chaplains, Church proposes changing the national motto to "In Humankind We Trust" (Church 1982, 282). He thinks that the Government Printing Office should "grant to every citizen the right to publish, at public expense, a pamphlet of up to ten pages a year, to be distributed through the same channels as other government publications" (Church 1982, 284). He thinks that the Constitution should specify "the right of American citizens to travel abroad" (Church 1982, 285).

Unlike some proponents of new constitutions, Church is relatively vague as to how his own proposals might be put into effect. Noting that he is a "man of thought, not of action," he suggests that his main efforts were devoted to "consciousness raising" (Church 1982, 287). He observes that:

My primary hope lies not in economic, legal, and political revolution, but in a psychocultural revolution, whereby we come to realize that we have built our social institutions in a quicksand of false assumptions and that these ill-founded institutions needlessly deform our humanity. From this sort of awareness, institutional changes could flow quite readily—not necessarily painlessly, but in a manageable way. (Church 1981, 294)

As highly idiosyncratic as Church's proposals are, little evidence exists that they are generally known in the law or political science communities or that they have significantly influenced the future direction of constitutional change.

For Further Reading:
Church, Joseph. 1982. *America the Possible: Why and How the Constitution Should Be Rewritten*. New York: Macmillan and Company.
"Joseph Church," Contemporary Authors Online, Gale, 2002, *http://www.galenet.com*. Updated 02/27/2002.

❖ CITIZENS FOR THE CONSTITUTION, THE CONSTITUTIONAL AMENDMENT INITIATIVE ❖

In 1999 the Century Foundation published a document entitled, "*Great and Extraordinary Occasions: Developing Guidelines for Constitutional Change*. As part of the constitutional amendments initiative cochaired by former Republican congressman Mickey Edwards and former Democratic congressman Abner Mikva and endorsed by a large number of scholars and political figures, the document was designed to lead to reconsideration of what appeared to be excessive resort to the constitutional amendment process in the 104th and 105th Congresses. In these separate Congresses, amendments were proposed to effect a balanced budget, campaign finance reform, congressional term limits, a ban on flag desecration, limits on tax increases, promotion of religious equality, a line-item veto, facilitation of state-proposed amendments, birthright citizenship, electoral college reform, and enhancement of crime victims' rights. They all received serious congressional consideration, with a number of these amendments reaching the floor of one or both houses of Congress. Kathleen Sullivan, a law professor at Stanford University, wrote an article decrying what she regards as "constitutional amendment fever" that was included as an appendix to the Century Foundation report.

The Century Foundation document proposes eight guidelines intended to introduce a modicum of self-restraint into the constitutional amending process. The first five guidelines relate primarily to the content of amendments, while the last three relate chiefly to procedural issues. The guidelines are applied especially negatively to the proposed amendments relating to a federal balanced budget, to victims' rights, to the flag desecration amendment, and to the failed Equal Rights Amendment. The report relies in part on the perception that the Eighteenth Amendment, which had (before being repealed by the Twenty-first) provided for national alcoholic prohibition, was an example of what could happen when the amending process became a tool for enacting temporarily popular, but ultimately unwise, social policies. The report also drew negative lessons from prolix state constitutions that often draw little distinction between legal and political matters.

The Foundation's first consideration is that proposed amendments should "address matters that are of more than immediate concern and that are likely to be recognized as of abiding importance by subsequent generations" (Citizens for the Constitution 1999, 9). Commentary stresses the necessity of casting most constitutional provisions "in general terms" that would provide for future contingencies rather than simply addressing current policy preferences.

The second consideration suggests that amendments should be assessed for whether they "make our system more politically responsive or protect individual rights" (Citizens for the Constitution 1999, 11). The report argues that the rights of some minorities or crime victims, for example, might already be capable of being addressed through ordinary political means. Moreover, the flag-desecration amendment might actually grant "power at the behest of an already dominant majority and at the expense of an extremely unpopular and utterly powerless minority" (Citizens for the Constitution 1999, 14).

On a related note, the third consideration suggests that amendments should not be adopted when the results could be achieved by ordinary political means. The document argues that ordinary political processes generally allow for "greater flexibility" than do constitutional amendments. The Equal Rights Amendment is cited as an example of an amendment that addressed goals that were capable of achievement—often at the state level—without the use of the heavy artillery of constitutional amendment. By contrast—although the report writers do not favor such an amendment—if it were desirable to protect the American flag, previous judicial decisions have indicated that this could not be done through ordinary legislative means.

A fourth consideration asks whether a proposed amendment is "consistent with related constitutional doctrine that the amendment leaves intact" (Citizens for the Constitution 1999, 17). Pointing to the framers' desire for cohesiveness of the Constitution, this consideration is designed to see that an amendment—like the flag desecration or campaign finance reform amendment—is not in conflict with other legal doctrines that give much wider range to First Amendment freedoms.

The fifth consideration asks whether proposed amendments "embody enforceable, and not purely aspirational, standards" (Citizens for

the Constitution 1999, 19). The document expresses particular concern over the enforceability of the balanced budget amendment and the possibility that vague amendments, such as the Equal Rights Amendment, might lead to an undesirable increase in judicial power.

The last three considerations deal primarily with the degree of scrutiny that proponents of amendments give to their proposals. Thus, guideline six suggests that the proponents of amendments need to consider the manner in which their proposals will "interact with other constitutional provisions and principles" (Citizens for the Constitution 1999, 21). The report is particularly critical of proposals like the Equal Rights Amendment, whose proponents were unwilling or unable to address the effects that adoption of such an amendment would have.

Guideline seven centers on the need for "full and fair debate" (Citizens for the Constitution 1999, 22) over the merits of proposed amendments, considering both questions of policy and operation. The report suggests that, in light of the supermajority required to propose amendments, Congress might consider requiring that proposed amendments receive a two-thirds vote in committee before being sent to the floor of Congress. It further suggests that, aside from clarifying language, no substantive changes should be offered to amendments on the floor of Congress that have not been fully vetted in committee.

Guideline eight suggests that amendments should be proposed with "nonextendable deadline[s]" for ratification (Citizens for the Constitution 1999, 24). In cases where extensions are permitted, the report further proposes that they should require two-thirds majority votes in Congress. It also suggests that states that initially ratified should have the right to rescind such ratifications when extensions are given. Again citing the Equal Rights Amendment, the report notes that "The perception that the amendment might be adopted despite the absence of a contemporary consensus supporting it contributed to the divisiveness that characterized the campaign for its adoption" (Citizens for the Constitution 1999, 25).

Although apparently written independently, an article by law professor J. B. Ruhl examining proposals for an Environmental Quality Amendment also seeks to establish two sets of filters through which amendments should pass. The first would "define whether an amendment to dictate a particular social policy generally is socially acceptable and institutionally necessary given conditions in the social and political realms" (Citizens for the Constitution 1999, 254), while the second would "test the implementability of specific proposals to embody the social policy decision" *(Id.)*. Under the first category, Ruhl argues that amendments should be "1. [s]upported by broad social approval [and] 2. [n]ot capable of being fully implemented through other political and legal institutions" *(Id.)*. Under the second category, Ruhl argues that amendments should be "1. [r]educible to legal principles that are binding in effect" 2. sufficiently clear to minimize unanticipated interpretations; [and] 3. [e]nduring even in the face of shifting political climates" (Ruhl 1999, 254).

Taken together, both sets of guidelines are designed to see that the constitutional amending process remains a highly deliberative mechanism and that the Constitution be preserved as fundamental law rather than as a collection of policy choices. It is not altogether clear that the report actually stopped any amendments in their tracks, but it may well have led to greater scrutiny of proposals that had been gaining in popularity.

For Further Reading:
Chemerinsky, Erwin. 2000. "Citizens for the Constitution," *Insights on Law & Society* 1 (Fall): 14–15.

Citizens for the Constitution. 1999. *Great and Extraordinary Occasions*. New York: Century Foundation, Inc.

"The Constitution Project." At *http://www.info@constitutionproject.org/index.html*. Last accessed 11/21/02.

Ruhl, J. B. 1999. "The Metrics of Constitutional Amendments: Why Proposed Environmental Quality Amendments Don't Measure Up," *Notre Dame Law Review* 74 (January): 245–281.

❖ CITIZENSHIP, DEFINITION OF ❖

Although the Constitution of 1787 refers to "citizens" in a number of places (in specifying qualifications for officeholders, for example), nowhere does it specifically define such citizenship. This omission enabled Chief Justice Roger Taney to argue in *Scott v. Sandford* (1857) that blacks were not and could not be citizens and thus had no right to appear in U.S. courts.

Democratic Representative Thomas Florence of Pennsylvania (1861) and Whig Senator Garrett Davis of Kentucky (1864) were subsequently unsuccessful in trying to have Taney's understanding explicitly written into the Constitution. Instead, the first sentence of the Fourteenth Amendment overturned *Scott* and extended citizenship to "all persons born or naturalized in the United States and subject to the jurisdiction thereof."

In *United States v. Wong Kim Ark* (1898), the Supreme Court decided that citizenship extended to children born in the United States to parents who were Chinese citizens. Only children born to diplomatic personnel in the United States, children born to foreigners during hostile occupations, or Indians subject to tribal governance were considered exempt from U.S. jurisdiction and citizenship. Citizenship has subsequently been referred to as a qualification for voting in the Fifteenth, Nineteenth, Twenty-fourth, and Twenty-sixth Amendments, although state laws rather than provisions of the U.S. Constitution currently bar aliens from the franchise.

Justice Harry Blackmun's decision in *Roe v. Wade* (1973) voiding most state abortion regulations rested in part on the view that *citizenship* as used in the Fourteenth Amendment and elsewhere in the Constitution refers only to postnatal life. This decision has prompted numerous calls for a right to life amendment.

A number of proposed amendments related to qualifications for the presidency have sought to repeal the provision in Article II, Section 1 of the U.S. Constitution that limits the presidency to "natural born" citizens. Concerned that some individuals are illegally entering the United

States with the purpose of obtaining citizenship for their children or that, in the least, this is an additional incentive for illegal immigration, proponents of a birthright citizenship amendment have also proposed limiting citizenship to those born in the United States of at least one parent who is either a citizen or is, at the least, legally within the boundaries of the nation.

See also Birthright Citizenship Amendment; Fourteenth Amendment.

❖ CITIZENSHIP, DUAL ❖

In September 1942, in conjunction with a bill to limit anticipated immigration from Europe following the end of World War II, Republican Senator Rufus Holman of Oregon, chair of an ad hoc Committee on Defense (Irons 1983, 51), introduced a resolution that was intended to grant Congress the power to prohibit dual citizenship (S.J. Res. 163). In his speech before the Senate (Holman 1942), Holman referred specifically to Japanese Americans, some of whom held joint citizenship in the United States and Japan. Such dual citizenship arose from the fact that, in addition to the principle of *jus soli* (law of the soil), Japan applied the doctrine of *jus sanguinis* (law of the blood). This latter principle allowed people born abroad of Japanese nationals to maintain joint citizenship—citizenship that could, however, be renounced and did not apply to Japanese born in the United States after 1925 (see Justice Murphy's dissenting opinion, *Korematsu v. United States* (1944), 237 n.4).

Such dual citizenship contributed to suspicions that Japanese Americans constituted a disloyal "fifth column." Such fears were used in *Hirabayashi v. United States* (1943) and *Korematsu v. United States* (1944) to justify curfews for Japanese Americans and their exclusion from certain areas of the West Coast. This exclusion was accompanied by an executive order detaining some 112,000 Japanese American citizens in camps during World War II. During the Reagan administration, Congress passed a law providing monetary compensation for living victims of this detention.

For Further Reading:

Holman, Rufus. 1942. "Restriction of Immigration." *Congressional Record*, 77th Cong., 2d sess, Vol. 88, pt. 6: 7193–7194.

Irons, Peter, ed. 1989. *Justice Delayed: The Record of the Japanese Internment Cases*. Middletown, CT: Wesleyan University Press.

Smith, Page. 1995. *Democracy on Trial: The Japanese American Evacuation and Relocation in World War II*. New York: Simon and Schuster.

❖ CITIZENSHIP, LOSS OF ❖

The Constitution provided no definition of national citizenship prior to the Fourteenth Amendment. This did not stop Congress from proposing an amendment in 1810 that would have provided that a person would "cease to be a citizen" upon accepting, without congressional approval, "any title of nobility or honour . . . from any emperor, king, prince, or foreign power" (Anastaplo 1989, 298–299). The origins of this amendment relative to titles of nobility are obscure. If it had been adopted, it would have provided a sanction for a similar provision already in Article I, Section 9 of the Constitution.

In *Trop v. Dulles* (1958), the Supreme Court struck down as "cruel and unusual punishment" the application of a law providing for forfeiture of citizenship to a native-born American who had deserted during a time of war. On the same day, however, in *Perez v. Brownell* (1958), the Supreme Court, in a five-to-four vote, upheld a provision of the Nationality Act of 1940 whereby Congress provided that individuals voting in foreign elections would forfeit their citizenship. The Court saw this as a reasonable exercise of power under congressional authority to regulate foreign affairs.

In *Afroyim v. Rusk* (1967), the Court reversed itself in another five-to-four decision and ruled that the Fourteenth Amendment protects against loss of citizenship except by voluntary renunciation. Several members of Congress subsequently proposed amendments from 1967 through 1969 that would have given Congress authority to provide by law for loss of nationality and citizenship.

See also Titles of Nobility.

For Further Reading:

Anastaplo, George. 1989. *The Constitution of 1787: A Commentary.* Baltimore, MD: Johns Hopkins University Press.

Gordon, Charles. 1982. "The Power of Congress to Terminate United States Citizenship." *Connecticut Law Review* 4 (Spring): 611–632.

❖ CITIZENSHIP, OFFICEHOLDING RIGHTS ❖

New York's state ratifying convention proposed a resolution, never introduced in Congress, that would have excluded non-native-born citizens not only from the presidency and vice presidency but also from Congress (Ames 1896, 74). Northeastern Federalists reintroduced this idea during debates over the Alien and Sedition Acts (Kuroda 1994, 109), at which time many immigrants were more sympathetic to the Democratic-Republican Party. Federalists introduced similar proposals during the War of 1812.

See also Presidency, Qualifications for.

For Further Reading:

Ames, Herman. 1896. *The Proposed Amendments to the Constitution of the United States during the First Century of Its History.* Washington, DC: U.S. Government Printing Office. Reprint, New York: Burt Franklin, 1970.

Kuroda, Tadahisa. 1994. *The Origins of the Twelfth Amendment: The Electoral College in the Early Republic, 1878–1804.* Westport, CT: Greenwood Press.

❖ CIVIL RIGHTS CASES (1883) ❖

The Supreme Court's eight-to-one decision in the *Civil Rights Cases* (1883) was one of the most important nineteenth-century decisions with respect to the interpretation of the Thirteenth and Fourteenth Amendments. At issue was the constitutionality of the Civil Rights Act of 1875, a law that attempted to guarantee equal access to public accommodations without respect to race.

In his opinion for the Court, Justice Joseph P. Bradley struck down this law on the basis that Section 1 of the Fourteenth Amendment, providing that "no state shall deny" specified individual rights, did not give Congress the power to interfere with actions of private individuals that had the same effect. As he summarized the purposes of the amendment:

> It does not authorize Congress to create a code of municipal law for the regulation of private rights; but to provide modes of redress against the operation of state laws, and the action of state officers executive or judicial, when these are subversive of the fundamental rights specified in the Amendment. (*Civil Rights Cases* 1883, 11)

Bradley further denied that discrimination by private individuals constituted a "badge of servitude" prohibited by the Thirteenth Amendment.

In his dissenting opinion, Justice John Marshall Harlan accused the Court of giving "too narrow and artificial" a reading to the Thirteenth and Fourteenth Amendments. He pointed out that Congress had, in the Civil Rights Act of 1866, exercised similar power under authority of the Thirteenth Amendment. He argued that places of public accommodation ceased to be merely private but were clothed with a public interest. Moreover, rather than reading the Thirteenth and Fourteenth Amendments simply as negative prohibitions, Harlan argued (with particular emphasis on the definition of citizenship in Section 1 of the Fourteenth Amendment and the enforcement provisions of both amendments) that they were intended to be positive grants of power to government to protect individual rights. Not only did Harlan's arguments lose in this case, but in *Plessy v. Ferguson* (1896), the Supreme Court subsequently upheld state-sanctioned racial discrimination.

The Court's distinction between state action and private action has never been repudiated. Largely as a consequence, when Congress adopted the Civil Rights Act of 1964 outlawing discrimination in places of public accommodation, it relied primarily on its power to regulate commerce between the states. The Supreme Court upheld its authority under this provision in *Heart of Atlanta Motel v. United States* (1964) and *Katzenbach v. McClung* (1964). Only in recent years has the U.S. Supreme Court begun to indicate that Congress may have reached the outer limits of its power under the commerce clause and that, especially in exercising power dealing with areas like criminal law that have traditionally been handled by the states, the Court may require Congress to do more than simply indicate that it is evoking its power under the commerce clause.

See also Fourteenth Amendment.

For Further Reading:
Civil Rights Cases, 109 U.S. 3 (1883).

❖ CIVIL SERVICE REFORM ❖

Although the Constitution mentions a number of appointed offices (members of the cabinet and the courts, for example), nowhere does it detail requirements for lesser officeholders. The so-called spoils system ("to the victor belong the spoils") allowed an incoming administration to dismiss such appointed officials and replace them with its own supporters. Such a system was especially associated with the administration of President Andrew Jackson and helped both to keep government fairly responsive to public opinion and to undercut earlier notions that an office was a form of property.

The growth of government during the Civil War led to increasing concern about the corruption and incompetence that sometimes accompanied a system of personal appointment. Several proposed amendments calling for civil service reform were introduced in the 1870s, but legislative action eventually proved effective with the passage of the Pendleton Act in 1883. This act created a system whereby candidates for government jobs qualified by fulfilling objective criteria of employment and taking competitive examinations. Reaction to the as-

sassination of President James Garfield by a disappointed office seeker helped generate support for this act (Rosenbloom 1971, 80).

Initially covering about 10 percent of the federal civilian workforce, today the civil service system applies to about 90 percent. In 1935 an amendment was proposed to establish the civil service merit principle more firmly in the federal government (H.J. Res. 378), but the prior history of civil service reform suggests that if this reform is desirable, it can be accomplished through regular legislative action.

For Further Reading:
Rosenbloom, David H. 1971. *Federal Service and the Constitution: The Development of the Public Employment Relationship.* Ithaca, NY: Cornell University Press.
Van Riper, Paul P. 1958. *History of the United States Civil Service.* Evanston, IL: Row, Peterson.

❖ CLAIMS AGAINST THE UNITED STATES ❖

Despite the doctrine of sovereign immunity (whereby a sovereign cannot be sued), Congress designates certain classes of cases that can be brought against the government. Since 1855 most of these cases have been heard by the U.S. Court of Claims, which was redesignated in 1982 as the U.S. Claims Court. This court relieves Congress of passing special bills to deal with such matters (Abraham 1998, 166).

After the Civil War, there were sixteen proposed amendments to limit claims resulting from the war, most of which sought to deny claims by those who had been disloyal to the Union. One such proposal received a favorable vote of 145 to 61 in the House of Representatives in 1878 but was not voted on in the Senate. Several proposals would have provided a time limit within which war claims could be filed (Ames 1896, 248). On three occasions between 1905 and 1907, Republican Representative Joseph Keifer of Ohio introduced amending resolutions that would have enlarged the power of the Court of Claims and limited Congress to appropriating money for claims settled by this or other authorized commissions (Musmanno 1929, 151–152).

As of 1982, appeals from the U.S. Court of Claims are heard by the U.S. Court of Appeals for the Federal Circuit. It is considered a legislative court created under Article I of the Constitution rather than an Article III constitutional tribunal; judgments of this court are still subject to review by the Supreme Court.

For Further Reading:

Abraham, Henry J. 1998. *The Judicial Process: An Introductory Analysis of the Courts of the United States, England, and France.* 7th ed. New York: Oxford University Press.

Ames, Herman. 1896. *The Proposed Amendments to the Constitution of the United States during the First Century of Its History.* Reprint, New York: Burt Franklin, 1970.

Musmanno, M. A. 1929. *Proposed Amendments to the Constitution.* Washington, DC: U.S. Government Printing Office.

❖ CLARK, WALTER (1846–1924) ❖

Walter Clark, then chief justice of the North Carolina Supreme Court, presented a speech later published as part of his papers (1906), in which he advocated a number of constitutional changes. These proposals reflected his perspective as a progressive Democrat who believed that the Constitution had been a conservative reaction to a more democratic beginning symbolized by the Declaration of Independence (for critique see Smith 1906). Almost all of Clark's proposals, at least one of which he thought would require a constitutional convention, were aimed at increasing the power of the people and reducing the power of plutocrats who he believed exerted control through their selection of federal judges and senators.

Two of Clark's proposals were eventually achieved by constitutional amendments. One, effected by the Seventeenth Amendment, called for direct election of the Senate. Another, later effected by the Twentieth Amendment, was to change the inauguration dates to reduce the lame duck sessions of Congress.

None of Clark's other proposals have yet been adopted. One such proposal—made without reference to the Article V entrenchment clause that appears to make such a change impossible absent state consent—called for eliminating the equality of state representation in the Senate and granting each state one senator for each million inhabitants or fraction thereof over three-quarters of a million. Another proposal called for replacing the current electoral college system with a proportional plan wherein state votes would be divided among candidates according to the proportion of the popular votes each candidate received. Clark's primary objective in making such a change was to take away the advantage of pivotal states and the advantage enjoyed by candidates who come from such large states. Clark also favored changing the term of the president to six years and making him ineligible for reelection. In addition, Clark advocated removing postmasters from presidential patronage and providing that they would be elected from their districts.

As a judge, however, Clark devoted his greatest attention to the federal judiciary. In his speech, he advocated the election of judges to fixed terms—elsewhere he also suggested popular recall, congressional overrides of judicial decisions, abolition of judicial review, or alterations of judicial jurisdiction (Vile 1991c, 60 n.9). Clark did not believe that the framers of the Constitution had intended to vest judges with the power of judicial review, that is, the power to declare laws to be unconstitutional. He believed such power had been abused in a number of ways. He cited the Supreme Court decision invalidating the income tax (later overturned by the Sixteenth Amendment), the Court's opinion in *Lochner v. New York* (1905) striking down a New York wage regulation of bakers, and other judicial interferences with state autonomy. In what might otherwise appear to be a surprising recommendation coming from a progressive spokesman, Clark suggested: "Nothing can save us from the centripetal force but the speedy repeal of the fourteenth amendment, or a recasting of its language in terms that no future court can misinterpret it" (Clark 1906, 565). As a way of eliminating those judges who were then serving life terms, Clark suggested that Congress could abolish all judgeships below the Supreme Court and then have new ones elected. He also suggested that Congress could curb the jurisdiction of the Supreme Court (Clark 1906, 568).

However radical such proposals might appear, they were consistent with Clark's continuing belief that "the remedy for the halting, halfway popular government which we have is more democracy" (Clark 1906, 572).

For Further Reading:

Clark, Walter. 1906. "Some Defects of the Constitution of the United States." In *The Papers of Walter Clark*. Vol. 2, 1902–1924, ed. Aubrey L. Brooks and Hugh T. Lefler. Reprint, Chapel Hill, NC: University of North Carolina Press, 1950.

Smith, Goldwin. 1906. "Chief Justice Clark on the Defects of the American Constitution." *North American Review* 183 (1 November): 845–851.

Vile, John R. 1991c. *Rewriting the United States Constitution: An Examination of Proposals from Reconstruction to the Present*. New York: Praeger.

❖ *CLINTON V. CITY OF NEW YORK* (1998) ❖

In this case, the U.S. Supreme Court voted by a six-to-three majority to invalidate a provision of the Line-Item Veto Act that went into effect on 1 January 1997. This act effectively entrusted the president with a line-item veto of matters relating to taxing and spending. The Court had rejected a challenge to this act in *Byrd v. Raines* (1997) on the basis that the litigants in that case, members of Congress, did not have proper standing to sue. In *Clinton*, the Court majority agreed that the litigants, New York State and hospitals located there, as well as a farmers' cooperative, did have such status, after President Clinton canceled tax exemptions from which each stood to benefit.

The Line-Item Veto Act had allowed the president to cancel items that involved "(1) any dollar amount of discretionary budget authority; (2) any item of new direct spending; or (3) any limited tax benefit" (cited in *Clinton* 1998, 436). In making such a decision, the president was responsible for determining that such can-

cellations would "(i) reduce the Federal budget deficit; (ii) not impair any essential Government functions; and (iii) not harm the national interest" (cited in *Clinton* 1998, 436). If the president exercised such authority, designed to reduce budget deficits, Congress could adopt a "disapproval bill" rejecting the president's actions, although he in turn would have had authority to veto this bill.

Much as in the *Immigration and Naturalization Service v. Chadha* (1983) decision invalidating the legislative veto, the Supreme Court decided that the authority vested in the president under the Line-Item Veto Act was significantly different from that vested in this office under the U.S. Constitution. The Court observed that:

> The constitutional return takes place *before* the bill becomes law; the statutory cancellation occurs *after* the bill becomes law. The constitutional return is of the entire bill; the statutory cancellation is of only a part. Although the Constitution expressly authorizes the President to play a role in the process of enacting statutes, it is silent on the subject of unilateral Presidential action that either repeals or amends part of duly enacted statutes. (*Clinton* 1998, 439)

The majority concluded that this law was an illegal attempt to bypass the "'finely wrought' procedures that the Framers designed" (*Clinton* 1998, 440) and, more specifically, the presentment clause permitting the president to veto laws that have been passed by both houses of Congress. The Court majority further rejected parallels between cases that involved the exercise of presidential discretion in foreign affairs or cases in which presidents decided not to spend monies that were appropriated. As in *U.S. Term Limits, Inc., v. Thornton* (1995), the Supreme Court decided that:

> If there is to be a new procedure in which the President will play a different role in determining the final text of what may "become a law," such change must come about not by legislation but through the

amendment procedures set forth in Article V of the Constitution. (*Clinton* 1998, 449)

In a concurring opinion, Justice Anthony Kennedy placed greater emphasis on the necessity of preserving a system of separation of powers and thereby securing liberty.

Justice Antonin Scalia disputed both the standing of one of the parties (the farmers' cooperative) and the majority's view that the law was unconstitutional. Scalia noted that "there is not a dime's worth of difference between Congress's authorizing the President to *cancel* a spending item, and Congress's authorizing money to be spent on a particular item at the President's discretion" (*Clinton* 1998, 466). Scalia believed the president's item veto authority was much like his authority to impound funds in certain situations.

Justice David Breyer also authored a dissent, denying that the law violated "any specific textual constitutional command" or "any implicit separation-of-powers principle" (*Clinton* 1998, 469–470). Breyer argued that:

> Literally speaking, the President has not "repealed" or "amended" anything. He has simply *executed* a power conferred upon him by Congress, which power is contained in laws that were enacted in compliance with the exclusive method set forth in the Constitution. (*Clinton* 1998, 475)

As long as the majority view of the Court prevails, it would appear that the only way that the President could be given a line-item veto would be through constitutional amendment. Such proposals, which have been advocated for well over a century, continue to be introduced in Congress.

See also Presidency, Veto Power of.

For Further Reading:
Byrd v. Raines, 521 U.S. 811 (1997).
Clinton v. City of New York, 524 U.S. 417 (1998).
U.S. Term Limits, Inc. v. Thornton, 514 U.S. 779 (1995).

❖ COERCIVE USE OF FEDERAL FUNDS ❖

When the national government provides billions of dollars a year in aid to the states, the ability to condition this aid on certain state behaviors can, at least in theory, result in a significant measure of federal control. From 1943 to 1993, six states (Pennsylvania, Nevada, Oklahoma, Tennessee, Arizona, and South Dakota) have petitioned Congress to call for a convention limiting federal coercion through this funding mechanism.

Although some studies suggest that federal conditions on the use of funds more frequently lead to intergovernmental bargaining than to the direct cutoff of funds (O'Toole 1985, 202–203), states sometimes comply with federal policies rather than risk the loss of aid. Thus, just over half of the states accepted small bonuses that the national government offered to states regulating billboards on interstate highways, but the threat to withhold 10 percent of state constructive funds brought the rest into line (O'Toole 1985, 213). The national government enacted similar laws to get states to reduce speed limits to 55 miles per hour at the time of the Arab oil embargo in the early 1970s (laws that were subsequently repealed), to get states to raise the legal drinking age from 18 to 21, and, more recently, to encourage states to lower the level of alcohol in the blood for determining legal intoxication from 0.10 to 0.08.

In *United States v. Butler* (1936), while striking down the Agricultural Adjustment Act on Tenth Amendment grounds (a decision that was later overturned), the Supreme Court ruled that congressional power to tax and spend under Article I, Section 8 was, as Alexander Hamilton had previously argued, an independent power that could be used to advance the general welfare.

In *South Dakota v. Dole* (1987), the Court, in a seven-to-two decision, upheld a law withholding 5 percent of a state's federal funds for road construction when the state sold alcohol to individuals under twenty-one. In so ruling, the Court established four conditions: (1) the exercise of taxing and spending power must be in pursuit of the general welfare, with the Court indicating a general willingness to defer to congressional judgments; (2) Congress must clearly state its intentions; (3) conditions must be related to a federal interest (identified in this case as safe interstate travel); and (4) the behavior rewarded must not violate another constitutional provision (*Dole* 1987, 207–208). In this same case, the Court rejected arguments that the federal conditions were in possible violation of state control of alcohol guaranteed in the Twenty-first Amendment.

For Further Reading:

O'Toole, Lawrence J., Jr., ed. 1985. *American Intergovernmental Relations: Foundations, Perspectives, and Issues.* Washington, DC: Congressional Quarterly.

South Dakota v. Dole, 483 U.S. 203 (1987).

❖ COLEMAN, CHARLES H. (1900–?) ❖

One of the most modest attempts to rewrite the Constitution was offered by Dr. Charles Coleman in a 1938 publication of the National Council for the Social Studies. Divided into nine articles, Coleman's proposal was actually somewhat shorter than the existing U.S. Constitution. Coleman suggested that such a change would not require a convention but could be adopted by Congress as an amendment after a joint committee held hearings on the subject.

Article One of the new constitution dealt with citizenship, basically drawing from the Fourteenth, Fifteenth, and Nineteenth Amendments. Article Two dealt with the legislative branch. Innovations would have included giving the president power to determine the conditions under which appropriate moneys were spent, four-year terms for the House and eight-year terms for the Senate, and a prohibition (similar to that later ratified in the Twenty-seventh Amendment) on salary increases during a term of office. Congress would have been given a number of new enumerated

powers, including the power "to regulate corporations," "to regulate the conditions of labor," "to promote the conservation of natural resources," and "to encourage agriculture" (Coleman 1938, 24–25). Treaties would be approved by a majority of both houses rather than by a two-thirds vote of the Senate.

Article Three described the executive department. The electoral college would be retained, but individual electors would be eliminated. Also, the vice presidency would be eliminated. Article Four, the judicial article, contained few innovations other than prohibiting individuals convicted of treason from serving in public office. Similarly, Article Five basically repeated provisions relative to relations among the states that are currently found in Article IV of the Constitution.

Article Six dealt with prohibitions on the national government, on the states, and on both. Secession was specifically forbidden to the states. The due process clause and equal protection clause, albeit not the entire Bill of Rights, applied to both sets of government.

Article Seven specified that amendments could be ratified by two-thirds of the states, as long as such states contained at least three-fourths of the population. Article Eight contained the supremacy clause, and Article Nine provided that the new constitution would go into effect when ratified by conventions in thirty-six states. Coleman's plan appears to have had little contemporary impact (Vile 1991c, 79).

For Further Reading:

Coleman, Charles. 1938. *The Constitution up to Date.* Bulletin no. 10. Cambridge, MA: National Council for Social Studies.

Vile, John R. 1991c. *Rewriting the United States Constitution: An Examination of Proposals from Reconstruction to the Present.* New York: Praeger.

❖ *COLEMAN V. MILLER* (1939) ❖

This decision involved a suit brought by Kansas legislators questioning the constitutionality of the state's putative ratification of the child labor amendment. At issue was whether the lieutenant governor had the right to cast the deciding vote in the state senate. Litigants also argued that the proposed amendment had lost its validity because state legislatures in Kansas and other states had previously rejected it and because the thirteen-year gap between the amendment's proposal and ratification was unreasonable.

Chief Justice Charles Evans Hughes's opinion for the Court accepted the right of state senators to bring their suit on the basis that the issues they raised were federal rather than state matters. As to the role of the lieutenant governor, the Court pronounced itself "equally divided" (*Coleman* 1939, 447), thus leaving in place the ruling by the Kansas Supreme Court validating his role. Although he did not repudiate language in *Dillon v. Gloss* (1921) to the effect that amendments should be ratified within a reasonable time, Hughes decided that the effect of prior rejection and the lapse of time between proposal and ratification were "political questions" for Congress to resolve. Hughes's decision has been criticized for relying on the anomalous precedent set by congressional promulgation of the disputed Fourteenth Amendment (Dellinger 1983, 389–405).

Four justices, led by Hugo Black, would have stated the political questions doctrine even more broadly. Justice Butler's dissent relied on *Dillon v. Gloss* (1921) to declare that Kansas's ratification was invalid because it was not contemporary with the amendment's proposal.

Coleman has never been overturned and may have been partly confirmed when Congress voted to accept the long-delayed ratification of the Twenty-seventh Amendment (first proposed in 1789) in 1992. Continuing scholarly criticisms of *Coleman,* as well as judicial modifications of the "political questions" doctrine and a district court decision in *Idaho v. Freeman* (1981), however, cast some doubt on *Coleman*'s continuing validity. Although there would be a danger in allowing courts to declare amendments, especially amendments that might be aimed at court decisions themselves, invalid on the basis of their content, some scholars argue that they are generally adept at handling the kinds of procedural issues that amending controversies often pose. (See, for example, Ishikawa 1997, 594.)

See also *Idaho v. Freeman;* Political Questions.

For Further Reading:

Coleman v. Miller, 307 U.S. 433 (1939).

Dellinger, Walter. 1983. "The Legitimacy of Constitutional Change: Rethinking the Amending Process." *Harvard Law Review* 97 (December): 380–432.

Ishikawa, Brendon T. 1997. "Everything You Always Wanted to Know about How Amendments Are Made, but Were Afraid to Ask." *Hastings Constitutional Law Quarterly* 24 (Winter): 545–597.

"Sawing a Justice in Half." 1939. *Yale Law Journal* 48: 1455–1458.

❖ COLONIAL CHARTERS ❖

Although many American states wrote their first constitutions during the Revolutionary War period, most had previously attempted to defend their liberties on the basis of colonial charters that had been issued to them, usually by the king. A scholar who has examined such charters identified eight elements that most had in common:

> the identification of a grantor; the creation or identification of a grantee; a statement of the reason for the grant; a statement of what was being granted; the license or exclusive use given by the grant; a statement of how the grant was to be administered; specific restrictions or limits on the grant; and the reciprocal duties owed the grantor by the grantee. (Lutz 1988, 35)

In the period preceding the outbreak of the Revolutionary War, the fact that most such grants were made directly by or under the authority of the English king enabled the colonists to deny Parliament's claim to legislate for them. The colonists claimed that their rights as English citizens derived from their loyalty to the king rather than from any acceptance of parliamentary authority (Reid 1993). The general structure of the colonial charters was later reflected in the organization of state constitutions as well as in that of the U.S. Constitution itself.

Charters granted by William Penn in 1682 to 1683 to Pennsylvania appear to have been the first to provide explicitly for an amending process. Such changes required extraordinary majorities—namely, a six-sevenths majority of the Assembly. This and a number of subsequent charters also presaged future entrenchment clauses, such as that in Article V, which guarantees that no state shall be deprived of its equal representation in the Senate without its consent. Early charters also reflected concerns for rights, such as those later protected in the U.S. Bill of Rights. In the charter granted to Delaware in 1701, William Penn thus provided, "That the First Article of this Charter relating to Liberty of Conscience, and every Part and Clause therein, according to the true Intent and Meaning thereof, shall be kept and remain, without any Alteration, inviolably for ever" (Thorpe 1909, 560–561).

Whereas early charters were viewed primarily as grants from the king to his people, later constitutions more clearly resembled compacts, or covenants (with especially deep roots in the Calvinist religious tradition), made collectively by the people by virtue of their own authority (Lutz 1988, 37–38). This foundation in popular sovereignty, in turn, provides the theoretical foundation for the people's right to alter their constitution.

See also Penn, William.

For Further Reading:

Covenant, Polity, and Constitutionalism. 1980. Special issue of *Publius: The Journal of Federalism* (Fall).

Lutz, Donald S. 1988. *The Origins of American Constitutionalism.* Baton Rouge, LA: Louisiana State University Press.

Reid, John P. 1993. *Constitutional History of the American Revolution. The Authority of Law.* Madison, WI: University of Wisconsin Press.

Thorpe, Francis N. 1909. *The Federal and State Constitutions Colonial Charters and Other Organic Laws of the States, Territories, and Colonies Now or Heretofore Forming the United States of America.* 7 vols. Washington, DC: U.S. Government Printing Office.

❖ COMMITTEE ON THE CONSTITUTIONAL SYSTEM ❖

The bicentennial of the U.S. Constitution provided a time for reflection about American constitutionalism and the prospect of constitutional change (Vile 1991c, 125). A nonpartisan Committee on the Constitutional System, which had already served as a sounding board for changes (Robinson 1985), issued a report in January 1987 that received considerable attention. The committee, consisting of a number of prominent politicians and scholars, was cochaired by Senator Nancy Landon Kassebaum of Kansas; C. Douglas Dillon, a former secretary of the treasury; and Lloyd N. Cutler, former counsel to President Carter and later to President Clinton.

Noting signs of strain in the system the framers had created, the committee traced such phenomena as divided government, lack of cohesion, lack of accountability, and the inability to replace failed or deadlocked governments to the separation of powers and to a number of developments that had undercut the power of political parties. The committee majority agreed on three proposals to strengthen such parties: to allow party officeholders to serve as uncommitted delegates to national nominating conventions, to require all states to provide an optional straight-ticket voting mechanism, and to permit public funding of political campaigns. It also recommended three proposals to improve legislative-executive collaboration: to change congressional terms so that members of the House of Representatives would serve for four years and members of the Senate for eight, to allow members of Congress to serve in the cabinet, and to allow majorities of both houses of Congress to approve treaties. The committee also favored a constitutional amendment allowing Congress to set limits on campaign spending.

The committee offered a number of other

proposals, which did not have the majority support of its members, for consideration. These included encouraging the president to appear before Congress, allowing the minority party to form a "shadow cabinet," requiring straight-ticket voting, scheduling elections for Congress after the president and vice president were selected, calling for new elections when the government was deadlocked, and convening conventions every ten years to make recommendations on how better to divide state and federal responsibilities.

Although committee reforms fell far short of the wide-ranging changes that some might have hoped for, it stirred considerable debate and diverse criticism. Thus, political scientist Jeanne Hahn (1987) argued that committee reforms would further entrench the status quo and put more power in the hands of elites. Political scientist James Ceaser critiqued those elements of the plan that imitated the parliamentary model. Defending separation of powers, he blamed most modern political problems on "reformism, collectivism, whiggism [congressional dominance of government], and judicial activism" (Ceaser 1986, 187). The widespread veneration for the Constitution that the bicentennial celebrations evoked probably worked against changes at that time (Vile 1991c, 162).

For Further Reading:

Ceaser, James W. 1986. "In Defense of Separation of Powers." In *Separation of Powers—Does It Still Work?* ed. Robert A. Goldwin and Art Kaufman. Washington, DC: American Enterprise Institute.

Hahn, Jeanne. 1987. "Neo-Hamiltonianism: A Democratic Critique." In *The Case against the Constitution from Anti-Federalists to the Present,* ed. John F. Manley and Kenneth M. Dolbeare. New York: M. E. Sharpe.

Robinson, Donald. 1985. *Reforming American Government: The Bicentennial Papers of the Committee on the Constitutional System.* Boulder, CO: Westview Press.

Vile, John R. 1991c. *Rewriting the United States Constitution: An Examination of Proposals from Reconstruction to the Present.* New York: Praeger.

❖ COMMUNISM ❖

On 7 July 1965, Mississippi sent petitions to Congress to call conventions to propose three amendments. One was directed at overturning Supreme Court decisions—most notably *Reynolds v. Sims* (1964) (applying the "one person one vote" standard)—dealing with apportionment of state legislatures. A second petition—most likely a continuing reaction to the Supreme Court's desegregation decision in *Brown v. Board of Education* (1954) and subsequent cases—called for giving states exclusive control over public education. The third proposed an amendment designed to control communism.

Mississippi pointed to "the existence of the world Communist conspiracy and the fact that the Communist Party, U.S.A., operates as an arm of such conspiracy in seeking to bring about the overthrow of the Government of the United States by force and violence." The state further observed that "the Supreme Court of the United States through its various decisions has circumscribed, limited, or invalidated such congressional enactments" ("House Resolution 14" 1965, 15770). Mississippi accordingly asked for an amendment designed to invest Congress with the power to control communism. Among provisions to be legalized were those preventing the dissemination of communist propaganda in the United States and the expulsion of noncitizens engaged in disseminating such propaganda. At the time, many individuals in the deep South associated communists with the civil rights movement.

The concern with Supreme Court decisions relating to communism appears to have been more prevalent in the late 1950s than in the period that Mississippi offered its amendment. In a number of decisions from 1955 to 1957, the Supreme Court overturned convictions of American communists. Thus, in *Pennsylvania v. Nelson* (1956), the Court had invalidated a state antisedition law on the basis that federal legislation, most notably the Smith Act, already occupied this field. Similarly, in *Watkins v. United States* (1957) it overturned a citation for contempt against a labor leader who had refused to answer certain questions before the

House Un-American Activities Committee (HUAC) about possible communist associates. These decisions prompted the unsuccessful Jenner bill, in which Congress attempted to restrict judicial jurisdiction over such cases (W. Murphy 1962). In a number of subsequent decisions, *Barenblatt v. United States* (1959) being the most prominent, the Court appeared to retreat from its earlier rulings (Belknap 1992, 172). In *Barenblatt*, the Court refused to use the First Amendment to extend exemptions for witnesses testifying before congressional committees.

For Further Reading:

Belknap, Michael R. 1992. "Communism and the Cold War." In *The Oxford Companion to the Supreme Court of the United States*, ed. Kermit L. Hall. New York: Oxford University Press.

"House Resolution 14." *Congressional Record* 89th Cong., 1st sess., 1965, Vol. 111, pt. 12: 15770.

Murphy, Walter F. 1962. *Congress and the Court*. Chicago: University of Chicago Press.

❖ CONCURRENT POWERS ❖

Because the United States has a federal system, some powers are exercised exclusively, or predominantly, by the state or national governments. A larger number of powers—for example, taxation—are shared; these are called concurrent powers. Section 2 of the Eighteenth Amendment, which imposed national alcoholic prohibition, entrusted Congress and the states with "concurrent power to enforce this article." The national government interpreted this clause expansively in the *National Prohibition Cases* (1920), even upholding provisions of the Volstead Act that outlawed beer and wine.

Perhaps with such contemporary construction of the Eighteenth Amendment in mind, New York Democratic Representative Frank Oliver (H.J. Res. 42, 5 December 1927) proposed construing "concurrent power" so as to prevent an act of Congress from invalidating an act adopted by a state. Although the Twenty-first Amendment repealed the Eighteenth, the

national government and the states share an increasing number of powers. An expert on federalism has argued that contemporary federalism thus more closely resembles a "marble cake" arrangement than a "layer cake" scheme (Grodzins 1966).

One of the proposals for a constitutional amendment to prevent flag desecration, while not specifically using the term concurrent powers, would have provided for them. It would have specified that "The Congress and the States shall have power to prohibit the physical desecration of the flag of the United States" (cited in Dorsen 2000, 425).

See also Enforcement Clauses.

For Further Reading:

Dorsen, Norman. 2000. "Flag Desecration in Courts, Congress, and Country." *Thomas M. Cooley Law Review* 17 (Michaelmas Term): 417–442.

Grodzins, Morton. 1966. *The American System: A New View of the Government in the United States*. Chicago: Rand McNally.

❖ CONFEDERATE DEBT ❖

In what some delegates to the Constitutional Convention thought to be an unnecessary provision, Article VI of the U.S. Constitution had provided that the new government would accept the validity of debts contracted under the Articles of Confederation. During discussions of the Fourteenth Amendment after the Civil War, members of Congress expressed fears that the former rebels might one day gain office with the intention of either repudiating federal debts that had been used to wage the war or assuming the debts that the Southern states had made to prosecute the conflict. Several proposals were introduced to prevent either contingency (Flack 1908, 133–136). Section 4 of the Fourteenth Amendment subsequently both guaranteed "the validity of the public debt of the United States . . . including debts incurred for payment of pensions and bounties for services in suppressing insurrection or rebellion" and repudiated either federal or state payment of "any debt or obligation incurred in aid of insurrection or rebellion against the United States, or any claim for the loss or emancipation of any slave."

For Further Reading:

Flack, Horace E. 1908. *The Adoption of the Fourteenth Amendment.* Baltimore, MD: Johns Hopkins. Reprint, Gloucester, MA: Peter Smith, 1965.

See also Fourteenth Amendment.

❖ CONFEDERATE STATES OF AMERICA, CONSTITUTION OF ❖

The constitution that bears the greatest similarity to that of the United States was the one the eleven Confederate States of America adopted after deciding to secede from the Union in 1861. Written by a Committee of Twelve and debated by a convention held in Montgomery, Alabama, in March 1861 (C. R. Lee 1963), the document replaced a similar provisional constitution adopted the previous month. The new constitution was subsequently approved by the Confederate Congress and by the Southern states; approval by five states was necessary for the document to go into effect. Reflecting the philosophy of John C. Calhoun and other Southern constitutionalists (DeRosa 1991, 18–37), the Confederate constitution was built on the doctrine of state sovereignty. It also included a number of provisions designed to control federal spending on special interests.

Although the Confederate constitution followed the outline of the U.S. Constitution, several provisions were different. The preamble included an acknowledgment of God. The constitution explicitly referred to slaves rather than using euphemisms. It permitted two-thirds majorities of state legislatures to impeach judicial or other federal officials acting within a state. In imitation of parliamentary systems, it permitted Congress to grant a seat on the floor of Congress for members of the cabinet to discuss measures but did not, like the provisional constitution, allow members of Congress to hold other offices. The permanent constitution gave the president an item veto of appropriations bills and prohibited congressional appropriations for internal improvements other than aids to navigation and harbor improvements. Although slave importation was prohibited, the right to property in the form of slaves was explicitly affirmed. Appropriations required a two-thirds vote of both houses of Congress, with a provision that all appropriations bills "shall specify in federal currency the exact amount of each appropriation, and the purposes for which it is made." Bills were limited to a single subject.

The president and vice president were to serve single six-year terms and were chosen by an electoral college rather than, as under the provisional constitution, by Congress. The constitution granted the chief executive explicit power to remove department heads at his pleasure and others for specified grievances. Although the constitutional arrangement of the courts was not significantly altered, the Confederate states, perhaps remembering the consolidating effect of U.S. Supreme Court decisions, never got around to establishing their own equivalent.

The constitution did not explicitly prohibit membership by free states, but it did require a vote of two-thirds of both houses to admit new states. The constitution also explicitly granted the government the right to acquire new territory where the right to own slaves was protected.

The provisional Confederate constitution had permitted amendments by a two-thirds vote in Congress (Urofsky 1988, 400). The permanent constitution provided no method for Congress to propose amendments but allowed three states to request Congress to summon a convention to propose amendments. These required ratification by two-thirds of the states. No such amendments were adopted during the Confederate States' brief life.

Article VII of the Confederate Constitution largely emulated the U.S. Constitution by providing that the document would go into effect when ratified by "conventions of five States." The U.S. Constitution had required ratification by nine of thirteen, but it was predicated on a Union of all, whereas the Confederate Constitution was premised on the notion that there were now two separate peoples.

The Confederate constitution provided a number of innovations for the consideration of future reformers (see, for example, Schouler 1908). The circumstances surrounding the constitution's adoption also contributed to fears of a runaway revolutionary convention (Jameson 1887, 257). Although their motivations are quite different and are often associated with the idea that the existing American government has become too large and impersonal and needs "downsizing," a number of recent proponents of new constitutions have advocated recognizing a right of states or localities to secede.

For Further Reading:

Davis, William C. 1994. *"A Government of Our Own": The Making of the Confederacy.* New York: Free Press.

DeRosa, Marshall L. 1991. *The Confederate Constitution of 1861: An Inquiry into American Constitutionalism.* Columbia, MO: University of Missouri Press.

Jameson, John A. 1887. *A Treatise on Constitutional Conventions: Their History, Powers, and Modes of Proceeding.* 4th ed. Chicago: Callaghan and Company.

Lee, Charles Robert, Jr. 1963. *The Confederate Constitutions.* Chapel Hill, NC: University of North Carolina Press.

Schouler, James. 1908. "A New Federal Constitution." In *Ideals of the Republic,* ed. James Schouler. Boston: Little, Brown.

Urofsky, Melvin I. 1988. *A March of Liberty: A Constitutional History of the United States.* New York: Alfred A. Knopf.

❖ CONFESSIONS ❖

One of the most prominent symbols of the activist Warren Court was its decision in *Miranda v. Arizona* (1966). In this case, the Court decided by a five-to-four vote that it would no longer accept confessions in cases of custodial police interrogation unless suspects had been informed of their rights. These included notification of their right to remain silent, the fact that any statements could be used against them, their right to an attorney, and the fact that an attorney would be provided if they were too poor to afford one.

This decision was in many ways a logical follow-up to a number of earlier Supreme Court rulings. It was based on the Court's reading of the self-incrimination clause of the Fifth Amendment as applied to the states via the due process clause of the Fourteenth Amendment. *Miranda* prompted "a firestorm of criticism" by those concerned that the decision would hamstring law enforcement (Bodenhamer 1992, 121). Within a month, North Carolina Democratic Senator Sam Ervin (a constitutional expert who would later chair the Senate Watergate Committee) introduced an amendment to permit the use of "voluntary" confessions and withdraw the jurisdiction of federal courts to "reverse, modify, or set aside" determinations by trial courts that such confessions were voluntary (Ervin 1966, 112). Several other such amendments were introduced from 1966 to 1968, including at least one that would have permitted police to question individuals outside the presence of counsel (H.J. Res. 1260, 1966).

Senator Ervin also attempted to limit federal judicial review of state criminal convictions through writs of habeas corpus that could be introduced in any federal court. Ervin proposed that appeals to federal courts should be limited to instances in which such cases had received a final judgment from "the highest court of that State having jurisdiction to review such judgment" (*Congressional Record*, 22 July 1966, 16721).

Although Ervin's amendment was not adopted, disputes continue over both the use of confessions and the appropriate extent of federal habeas corpus review. The Court under Warren Burger and William Rehnquist has allowed a limited number of exceptions to the *Miranda* rules (*New York v. Quarles* (1984), for example, accepted a "public safety" exception and other cases have permitted slight divergences in wording), but most observers have concluded that the *Miranda* warnings did not have the significant negative impact on confessions that many had anticipated (Bodenhamer 1992, 123). Indeed, some scholars think that the kind of "bright-line" rule established in *Miranda* has actually made it easier for police officers to do their jobs effectively by clearly letting them know what is required of them. Lower courts have also tightened up the number of habeas corpus reviews they will accept. Thus, in *Stone v. Powell* (1976), the Supreme Court decided not to accept federal habeas corpus review of Fourth Amendment claims that had already been given a full hearing in state courts. Federal habeas corpus review continues to be controversial, especially in cases involving the death penalty. Habeas corpus review is now granted in about half of such cases, often significantly delaying executions (Hoffman and Stuntz 1994, 119).

For Further Reading:

Bodenhamer, David J. 1992. *Fair Trial: Rights of the Accused in American History.* New York: Oxford University Press.

Ervin, Sam. "Implications of Supreme Court Decision in *Miranda v. Arizona.*" *Congressional Record,* 89th Cong., 2d sess., 1966, Vol. 112, pt. 13: 16721–2e.

Hoffman, Joseph L., and William J. Stuntz. 1994. "Habeas after the Revolution." In *Supreme Court Review.* Chicago: University of Chicago Press.

❖ CONGRESS, AGE OF MEMBERS ❖

As a means of securing a minimal level of maturity, the framers of Article I, Sections 2 and 3 of the U.S. Constitution set age minimums of twenty-five and thirty for members of the House of Representatives and the Senate, respectively. These articles did not establish any maximum or mandatory retirement age.

In 1971 the Twenty-sixth Amendment was ratified. It lowered the national voting age to eighteen—most states had previously set the age at twenty-one. Perhaps stimulated by this change, the rest of the decade witnessed numerous amending proposals to lower the minimum age for members of Congress. The most commonly advocated proposal, most frequently associated with Democratic Representative Robert Drinan of Massachusetts, called for lowering the minimum age of members of the House to twenty-two years and senators to twenty-seven years.

The 1970s also saw the introduction of a number of proposals to set a mandatory retirement age for members of Congress. Proposed retirement ages ranged from sixty-five to seventy-five. Some of these proposals would also have altered the length of congressional terms, set a maximum age for judges, or set limits on the total number of terms or consecutive terms that members of Congress could serve—a proposal that continues to generate a great deal of contemporary interest and discussion. With no such limits in place, South Carolina's Republican Senator Strom Thurmond (a Dixiecrat candidate for president in 1948) assumed chairmanship of the Senate Judiciary Committee after the congressional elections in 1994 at the age of ninety-two, although, after complaints, he subsequently gave in to committee members' desire for greater autonomy (Hook and Cassata 1995, 466). In 1996 Thurmond was elected to another six-year term in the Senate, but he retired in 2003 at the age of 100. If adopted, congressional term limits might tend to reduce the age of members of Congress.

For Further Reading:

Hook, Janet, and Donna Cassata. 1995. "Low-Key Revolt May Spur Thurmond to Give Colleagues Freer Hand." *Congressional Quarterly Weekly Report* 53 (11 February): 466.

❖ CONGRESS, ATTENDANCE OF MEMBERS ❖

The Constitution makes no provision for the attendance of members of Congress, and some have been known to be absent frequently. For example, Adam Clayton Powell, the flamboyant Harlem representative whose expulsion from the House was voided by the Supreme Court in *Powell v. McCormack* (1969), was present for only 30 percent of all roll-call votes in the 82d Congress and only 54 percent when he became chair of the House Education and Labor Committee (Weeks 1971, 4–5).

Amendments were introduced throughout the 1970s to declare the seats of House and Senate members vacant for excessive absences. One of the earliest, introduced by Maine's Republican Senator Margaret Chase Smith, would have declared a vacancy whenever members failed to be present for a total of 200 or at least 60 percent of roll-call votes (S.J. Res. 192, 1972). Some later proposals would have raised this minimum to 70 percent. By the end of the 1970s, some proposals included exemptions for absences due to hospitalization necessitated by illness or accidents. The 11 September 2001 terrorist attacks on the World Trade Center and the Pentagon have centered attention more recently not on members of Congress who are physically able to attend and do not, but on replacing large numbers of members who might be killed or incapacitated in similar incidents.

See also Congress, Emergency Functioning.

For Further Reading:
Weeks, Kent M. 1971. *Adam Clayton Powell and the Supreme Court.* New York: Dunellen.

❖ CONGRESS, COMMERCE POWERS ❖

No provision of the Constitution has been more frequently or effectively used as a basis for the expansion of national powers than the commerce clause. Indeed, between 1789 and 1950, it was the most frequently litigated provision in the Constitution (Steamer 1992, 167). Found in Article I, Section 8 among the powers of Congress, this provision—which was lacking in the Articles of Confederation—grants Congress power "to regulate Commerce with foreign Nations, and among the several States, and with the Indian Tribes." Without this, or an equivalent, provision, it is likely that the expansion of federal powers in the twentieth century would have required adoption of a number of amendments.

Early in U.S. history, Chief Justice John Marshall gave an expansive reading to the commerce clause, using congressional powers to strike down conflicting state regulations—most notably in *Gibbons v. Ogden* (1824) involving a grant of a steamboat monopoly by the state of New York. The question of whether federal power prohibited all state commercial regulations was more difficult. In *Cooley v. Board of Wardens* (1852), the Court adopted the doctrine of "selective exclusiveness," under which it decided whether a particular area of commerce was one that required a single uniform national rule or whether it was one, like the Philadelphia pilotage regulation upheld in *Cooley,* in which some state variation was permissible.

As the United States industrialized, the national government began to turn to the commerce clause for authority to regulate activities not otherwise delineated in the Constitution. The Court found itself picking and choosing among those activities it was willing to allow Congress to regulate. The Court's belief in laissez-faire economics, and its development of the doctrine of substantive due process, often led it to hedge congressional commerce powers through various limiting doctrines. Thus, in *United States v. E.C. Knight Company* (1895), the Court held that Congress could not prevent the acquisition of a near monopoly in the sugar-refining industry. It reasoned that manufacturing and production were distinct from subsequent commerce and that monopoly was a local rather than a national matter. From the 1890s through 1937, the Court also distinguished between the regulation of goods that were harmful and those that were not (see, for example, the decision in *Hammer v. Dagenhart* (1918) invalidating a national child labor law); the control of goods that had a "direct" effect and those that had only an "indirect" effect on commerce; and the regulation of goods that were within the "stream of commerce" and those that were not.

From the 1920s through the 1930s, a number of amendments were introduced to give Congress more explicit authority over areas such as the regulation of coal, oil, and gas; agriculture; minimum wages; child labor; hours of labor; and other such matters that Congress might otherwise have regulated under its commerce powers. President Franklin Roosevelt effectively resurrected the commerce clause with his New Deal programs, but many went down to defeat, prompting his Court-packing plan.

Although Congress rejected Roosevelt's plan, the Court subsequently reversed course in 1937 and began reading the commerce clause quite expansively. By 1964 the Court in *Heart of Atlanta Motel v. United States* and *Katzenbach v. McClung* upheld the public accommodations section of the Civil Rights Act of 1964 under authority of the commerce clause. Although the Court read one implicit restriction into federal commerce powers in *National League of Cities v. Usery* (1976) when it limited the scope of federal wage regulations as applied to state employees, it subsequently reversed course in *Garcia v. San Antonio Metropolitan Transit Authority* (1985), essentially leaving states to the protections provided by the structure of existing governmental institutions, and renewing some calls for strengthening the Tenth Amendment or otherwise strengthening states' rights.

In 1995, in *United States v. Lopez,* the Supreme Court's five-to-four decision written by Chief Justice William Rehnquist struck down the federal Gun-Free School Zones Act, which prohibited possession of a gun within 1,000 feet of a school, as exceeding federal powers under the commerce clause. Citing *National Labor Relations Board v. Jones & Laughlin Steel Corp.* (1937), Rehnquist wrote that "the scope of the interstate commerce power 'must be considered in light of our dual system of government and may not be extended so as to embrace effects upon interstate commerce so indirect and remote that to embrace them, in view of our complex society, would effectively obliterate the distinction between what is national and what is local and to create a completely centralized government'" (*Lopez* 1995, 556). He further ruled that the exercise of congressional power under the commerce clause was limited to the use of the "channels" of interstate commerce; the "instrumentalities" of such commerce, or "those activities having a substantial relation to interstate commerce, those activities that substantially affect interstate commerce" (*Lopez* 1995, 558–559).

Applying similar limitations in *United States*

v. Morrison (2000), the Court decided that a section of the Violence Against Women Act of 1994 interfered with state police powers and had not, despite congressional attempts to do so, been adequately tied to commercial regulation and that it therefore exceeded congressional powers under the commerce clause.

For Further Reading:

Benson, Paul R., Jr. 1970. *The Supreme Court and the Commerce Clause, 1937–1970.* New York: Denellen.

Bittker, Boris I. 1999. *Bittker on the Regulation of Interstate and Foreign Commerce.* Gaithersburg, MD: Aspen Law & Business.

Frankfurter, Felix. 1964. *The Commerce Clause under Marshall, Taney and Waite.* Chicago: Quadrangle Books.

Maltz, Earl. 1995. "The Impact of the Constitutional Revolution of 1937 on the Dormant Commerce Clause—A Case Study in the Decline of State Autonomy." *Harvard Journal of Law and Public Policy* 19 (Fall): 121–145.

Steamer, Robert J. 1992. "Commerce Power." In *The Oxford Companion to the Supreme Court of the United States,* ed. Kermit L. Hall. New York: Oxford University Press.

United States v. Lopez, 514 U.S. 549 (1995).

❖ CONGRESS, COMMITTEE COMPOSITION ❖

Although the role of congressional committees is not specified in the U.S. Constitution, it is difficult to imagine Congress operating without them. Committees allow members to develop their expertise by specializing in areas of particular interest to them.

Committee assignments are made by leaders within each party, with the majority party appointing committee chairs. Seniority is an important but not exclusive factor in such determinations. The majority party may attempt to enhance its control by assigning a greater proportion of its members to key committees. House Republicans complained about such policies in the 1980s and early 1990s, when Democrats held a majority, but Republicans were unsuccessful when they challenged such rules in court (Davidson and Oleszek 1994, 211). A number of amendments were also introduced. One introduced on 1 July 1992 proposed that membership on congressional committees be apportioned either equally or according to the proportion of members each party held in the House (H.J. Res. 522). Each party has some incentive to treat the other fairly in the area because each knows that the party in power today may be out of power after the next election, and that the rules applied by the majority party to the minority party when it is in power will likely be applied to it when it becomes the minority party.

For Further Reading:

Davidson, Roger H., and Walter J. Oleszek. 1994. *Congress and Its Members.* 4th ed. Washington, DC: Congressional Quarterly.

❖ CONGRESS, DISTRICT REPRESENTATION ❖

Article I, Section 2 of the U.S. Constitution requires that members of the House of Representatives be inhabitants of the states that elect them, but it does not require that they live in their districts. Indeed, although the Constitution apportions representatives according to a state's population, nowhere does it require that such representatives be selected by districts.

In the nation's early history, a number of states selected representatives through use of a general ticket (Ames 1896, 56). This situation led to thirty-four resolutions from 1820 through 1826 proposing that the Constitution be amended to require election of representatives by districts. In 1819, 1820, and 1822, these resolutions passed the Senate but were not voted on in the House. In 1842 Congress passed a law accomplishing the same objective, and petitions for such an amendment subsequently ceased (Ames 1896, 56–57).

The single-member district system of representation is generally believed to contribute to the maintenance of a two-party system. To win any seats in the House of Representatives, a political party's candidate must get a plurality of the votes in one or more districts. By contrast, in systems that use a scheme of proportional representation, minor parties may be rewarded with some seats even if they do not capture a plurality of any single district (for a general analysis of electoral systems, see Sartori 1994, 27–79). Most American party reformers have aimed to strengthen political parties (American Political Science Association 1950; however, see also Krusch 1992, 98, who would prohibit members of Congress from being party members). There thus appears to be little current sentiment for altering the method of selecting House members by district.

One of the reasons that the Court in *Colegrove v. Green* (1946) rejected the opportunity to reapportion Illinois congressional districts was the fear that a judicial remedy might require statewide elections. Subsequent decisions accepting justiciability over such questions and mandating approximate equality of districts, most notably *Baker v. Carr* (1962) and *Wesberry v. Sanders* (1964), have worked within the existing single-member district scheme.

For Further Reading:

American Political Science Association, Committee on Political Parties. 1950. *Toward a More Responsible Two-Party System.* New York: Rinehart.

Ames, Herman. 1896. *The Proposed Amendments to the Constitution of the United States during the First Century of Its History.* Reprint, New York: Burt Franklin, 1970.

Krusch, Barry. 1992. *The 21st Century Constitution: A New America for a New Millennium.* New York: Stanhope Press.

Sartori, Giovanni. 1994. *Comparative Constitutional Engineering: An Inquiry into Structures, Incentives and Outcomes.* New York: New York University Press.

❖ CONGRESS, EMERGENCY FUNCTIONING ❖

World War II ended in 1945 after the United States dropped atomic bombs that wiped out the Japanese cities of Hiroshima and Nagasaki.

Shortly thereafter, a protracted cold war developed between the United States and the Soviet Union. In 1949 Russia exploded its first atomic bomb, and hydrogen bombs followed in the next decade. By the 1960s, both powers had enough weapons to destroy each other, and although this precarious balance of terror may actually have served to deter world war, it also raised popular fears of a war-induced apocalypse.

In such an atmosphere, it is not surprising that concerns arose about the possibility that a war might cripple the government. From 1945 through 1962, there were more than thirty proposals to provide for emergencies (Davidson 2002, 4). The problem was most acute in dealing with the House of Representatives. Under terms of Article I, Section 2, Clause 4 of the Constitution, state executives fill vacancies in the House by issuing "Writs of Election," which would require a substantial lapse of time, and could leave some states unrepresented in that body in the interim. By contrast, under terms of Article I, Section 3, Clause 2, vacancies in the U.S. Senate can be temporarily filled by a state governor until the next meeting of the legislature. The Seventeenth Amendment, in turn, provides that "the legislature of any State may empower the executive thereof to make temporary appointments until the people fill the vacancies by election as the legislature may direct." In any event, there is a constitutionally designated mechanism for filling temporary vacancies in the Senate until an election can be held but not in the House (Davidson 2002, 1–3).

The most common proposal allowed for state governors, acting under authority of a presidential proclamation, to make temporary appointments whenever the number of vacancies in the House of Representatives exceeded 145 (this proposal reflects the fact that the nation's federal system of government—with fifty separate centers of power spread throughout the nation—might make it somewhat less vulnerable to catastrophe than unitary systems without such sovereign subunits). Congress has held a number of hearings on the subject, and proposals for providing temporary replacements for House members in the case of massive casualties or incapacities passed the Senate

in 1954 by a vote of seventy to one, and in 1955 by a vote of seventy-six to three. Although a proposal introduced by Tennessee Democratic Senator Estes Kefauver on the subject and adopted by the Senate in 1960 was not ultimately successful, it became the catalyst for an amendment to repeal the poll tax (Bernstein with Agel 1993, 137).

Despite a number of close calls, most notably the Cuban missile crisis of 1962, the nation has not yet faced a disaster involving massive numbers of congressional vacancies. Questions continue to remain about how the nation would function, and how powers would be allocated, if it were ever faced with such a catastrophe. In 1992 there were revelations of a bunker at the Greenbriar Hotel in White Sulphur Springs, West Virginia, that had been built in the 1950s and designed to house members of Congress in such an emergency. Shelters had been built elsewhere for other members of the government ("Congressional Bomb Shelter Revealed" 1992, 681). Other contingencies for governmental operations after a nuclear war make for fascinating, if somewhat macabre, reading (Zuckerman 1984).

After the horrific terrorist attack by two airplanes on the World Trade Center and another on the Pentagon on 11 September 2001, renewed attention was given by the government to operations in case of an attack on the government. Throughout the day of the attack, the federal government attempted to assure citizens that it was still in operation, although the diversion of President Bush's plane to the Midwest, away from its planned itinerary to the nation's capital, led to some concern. In the months immediately following the attack, Vice President Dick Cheney was often reported to be at a secure location so that he and other employees could continue governmental operations in the case of a disaster, and President Bush announced that plans had been made for a "shadow government" of administrators at a location outside Washington, D.C. In December 2001 Representative Brian Baird, a Washington Democrat, proposed an amendment that would vest state governors with the power to appoint members of the House to ninety-day terms when a quarter or more were killed, disabled, or missing ("Thinking the Unthinkable" 2001, 11). Some question has arisen as to whether governors should have to appoint individuals from the same party as the members that they would be replacing, but the requirement for providing for temporary Senate vacancies contains no such provision.

The American Enterprise Institute has created a website specifically devoted to the "Continuity of Congress" that includes a variety of articles on the subject. This Institute, along with the Brookings Institution, launched a blue-ribbon commission composed of prominent officials and scholars that held hearings and proposed a report in the fall of 2002. The Commission has also given renewed attention to the current line of presidential succession and to how members of the U.S. Supreme Court might be replaced in the event of an attack (personal e-mail correspondence with John C. Fortier, American Enterprise Institute, dated 6/11/02).

See also Twenty-fifth Amendment.

For Further Reading:

Bernstein, Richard B., with Jerome Agel. 1993. *Amending America: If We Love the Constitution So Much, Why Do We Keep Trying to Change It?* New York: Random House.

"Continuity of Congress," *http://www.aeipoliticalcorner.org/continuity.htm* and *http://www.continuityofgovernment.org.* Accessed November 21, 2002.

Davidson, Michael. 2002. "Notes on Proposed Constitutional Amendments on Temporary Appointments of Members of the House." Taken from the website: *www.aeipoliticalcorner.org/continuity.htm.* Accessed 05/16/02.

Ornstein, Norman. 2002. "Preparing for the Unthinkable: Bush's 'Shadow Government' Plan Is a Start—But Only a Start." *The Wall Street Journal,* 11 March, A18.

"Thinking the Unthinkable." 2001. *State Legislatures* 27 (December): 11.

Zuckerman, Edward. 1984. *The Day after World War III.* New York: Viking Press.

❖ CONGRESS, FILIBUSTERS IN SENATE ❖

One of the Senate's most hallowed folkways is the filibuster, which has been in use since 1841. This procedure permits individuals to delay or stop action on a pending bill by monopolizing floor debates in the hope that its sponsors will eventually concede. The first limits were imposed on this mechanism in 1917 after Woodrow Wilson called a group of antiwar progressives opposed to his plans to arm merchant ships "a little group of willful men [who] have rendered the government of the United States helpless and contemptible" (Gettlinger 1994, 3198). In 1975 the Senate modified an earlier rule and permitted a cloture vote by three-fifths of the entire membership rather than the previously required two-thirds of those present and voting (S. Smith 1989, 342). Such cloture votes are still quite difficult to achieve, however, and with some other changes in the way filibusters are conducted, their number has actually increased, with one-half of the total occurring since 1975 (Gettlinger 1994, 3198).

At least three proposed amendments would have altered filibuster procedures. Two proposals introduced in 1916 by West Virginia Democratic Senator William Chilton were designed to cut off debate, one after ten days and the other after twenty hours. In 1969 Democratic Senator Mike Mansfield of Montana offered a proposal preventing the Senate from limiting or closing debate by less than three-fifths of those present and voting (S.J. Res. 36). Although filibusters are often associated in the popular mind with racist senators opposed to progressive civil rights legislation (the longest filibuster was one by South Carolina Senator Strom Thurmond that lasted over twenty-four hours opposing the Civil Rights Bill of 1957), the mechanism allows for delay by any senator with strong views. Now, as in 1929 (see Musmanno 1929, 21), the filibuster seems to be a particularly unlikely candidate for amendment.

For Further Reading:

Gettlinger, Stephen. 1994. "New Filibuster Tactics Imperil Next Senate." *Congressional Quarterly* 52 (5 November): 3198.

Musmanno, M. A. 1929. *Proposed Amendments to the Constitution*. Washington, DC: U.S. Government Printing Office.

Smith, Steven. 1989. "Taking It to the Floor." In *Congress Reconsidered*, ed. Lawrence C. Dodd and Bruce I. Oppenheimer. Washington, DC: Congressional Quarterly.

❖ CONGRESS, IMMUNITY OF MEMBERS ❖

In an attempt to insulate them from political reprisals and to ensure free and open debate, Article I, Section 6 of the U.S. Constitution specifies that members of Congress "shall in all Cases, except Treason, Felony and Breach of the Peace, be privileged from Arrest during their Attendance at the Session of their respective Houses." It further provides that "for any Speech or Debate in either House, they shall not be questioned in any other Place." At least seven proposals have been introduced from 1917 to 1983 to alter one or both of these provisions.

The congressional privilege against arrest is not as broad as it may appear, since the Supreme Court has held that it applies only to civil arrests, which are no longer carried out (R. Baker 1992, 175). The Court's interpretation appears to call into question the need for an amendment introduced in 1983 allowing members going to or returning from Congress to be arrested for traffic violations (H.J. Res. 318).

The most common proposals for alterations have focused on the speech and debate clause and have been directed toward preventing members of Congress from using the congressional platform for libeling individuals. Generally, the Court has interpreted the speech and debate clause liberally. It has thus extended protection beyond the floor of Congress to remarks members make before committees. Moreover, in *Gravel v. United States* (1972) the Court extended some collateral protection to congressional aides, who were described as congressional alter egos.

In *Hutchinson v. Proxmire* (1979), however, a case involving Wisconsin Democratic Senator William Proxmire's much-publicized "Golden Fleece" Awards, the Court ruled that members of Congress could be sued if statements in their press releases were libelous. Similarly, in *United States v. Brewster* (1972), the Court held that the speech and debate clause did not provide a defense for a member of Congress convicted of taking a bribe. Also, in *Gravel v. United States* (1972), the Court said that congressional immunity did not extend to contracts that members of Congress made with book companies. It further decided that a grand jury could inquire into how members of Congress got classified information. In that case, Alaska Democratic Senator Mike Gravel had obtained a copy of the Pentagon Papers and read them into the record of a subcommittee he chaired. Two days after he had done so, California Republican Representative Charles Gubser introduced an amendment (H.J. Res. 754) providing that members of Congress could be prosecuted for disclosing classified information.

For Further Reading:

Baker, Richard A. 1992. "Congress, Arrest and Immunity of Members Of." In *The Oxford Companion to the Supreme Court of the United States*, ed. Kermit L. Hall. New York: Oxford University Press.

Betts, James T. 1967. "The Scope of Immunity for Legislators and Their Employees." *Yale Law Journal* 77 (December): 366–389.

❖ CONGRESS, LEGISLATIVE VETO ❖

The doctrine of separation of powers suggests that Congress makes the laws, the president enforces them, and the courts interpret them. The reality is considerably more complex. Sometimes because of inadequate drafting, sometimes because of the complexity of the subject, and sometimes because Congress has made a conscious attempt to avoid or defer controversial decisions, administrative agencies issue numerous rules designed to implement congressional laws. Congress is understandably concerned that such rules do not usurp its own legislative functions. After numerous reports of agency abuse and incompetence, "criticism of agency rulemaking . . . reached a shrill pitch in the 1970s" (L. Fisher 1991, 142). Although several laws and amendments were introduced in Congress to grant itself a veto over all agency regulations, such attempts failed.

Congress increasingly turned to the so-called legislative veto mechanism, whereby one or both houses granted wide rule-making power to a particular agency while reserving the power to veto administrative decisions that Congress did not approve. Although the mechanism had been used for about fifty years and arguably made Congress somewhat more willing to delegate power to administrative agencies than it otherwise would have been, most presidents were on record as challenging the constitutionality of this mechanism. In *Immigration and Naturalization Service v. Chadha* (1983), a case involving congressional revocation of a decision by the INS to grant permanent-resident status to an East Indian from Kenya who held a British passport, the Supreme Court outlawed such vetoes. It declared that they were contrary to the presentment clause, which allows the president the chance to veto all legislation, and, in the immediate case, to the bicameralism requirement specifying that all legislation pass both houses of Congress (Craig 1988). Within days, an amendment was introduced (H.J. Res. 313) to reinstate the legislative veto mechanism. Although such an amendment was not adopted, Congress appears to have developed a number of informal mechanisms, often at the congressional committee level, by which it still maintains oversight of legislative rule making (L. Fisher 1993, 286–288).

For Further Reading:

Craig, Barbara H. 1988. *Chadha: The Story of an Epic Constitutional Struggle*. New York: Oxford University Press.

Fisher, Louis. 1991. *Constitutional Conflicts between Congress and the President,* 3d ed. Lawrence, KS: University Press of Kansas.

❖ CONGRESS, MEMBERS' ELIGIBILITY FOR OTHER OFFICES ❖

Article I, Section 6 of the U.S. Constitution prohibits a member of Congress from being appointed "to any civil Office under the Authority of the United States, which shall have been created, or the Emoluments whereof shall have been encreased *[sic]* during such time." Throughout the nineteenth century, there were over thirty attempts to extend this ban to exclude appointment to any civil office, sometimes making exceptions for appointments to the judiciary and sometimes extending the ban for two years after a member of Congress left office (Ames 1896, 30–33). One such proposal was offered by Andrew Jackson. He may have been influenced by the "corrupt bargain" he alleged had been struck when, after the four-way election of 1824 involving Jackson, Henry Clay, William Crawford, and John Quincy Adams, Clay shifted his support to Adams and was subsequently rewarded by the newly elected Adams with an appointment as secretary of state (Van Deusen 1937, 179–195). At least four amending proposals introduced from 1929 to 1945 have sought a ban similar to that advocated in the nineteenth century.

Controversies have sometimes been raised when members of Congress have been suggested for, or appointed to, judicial posts or cabinet offices for which salaries have been increased during their tenure. As a remedy, Congress generally adopts legislation reducing the pay for the appointee to that in effect at the beginning of the appointee's term. Thus, when President Clinton appointed Texas Senator Lloyd Bentsen as secretary of treasury, Congress passed a law reducing "'the compensation and other emoluments attached to the office of Secretary of the Treasury' to those in effect on January 1, 1989" (Paulsen 1994, 909). Although acknowledging that such legislation meets "the rationale" behind the emoluments clause, a law professor has argued that it actually violates the constitutional "rule" itself (Paulsen 1994, 911). This suggests either that current practices should be altered or that an amendment should be adopted to bring the Constitution in line with current practice.

For Further Reading:

Ames, Herman. 1896. *The Proposed Amendments to the Constitution of the United States during the First Century of Its History.* Reprint, New York: Burt Franklin, 1970.

Paulsen, Michael S. 1994. "Is Lloyd Bentsen Unconstitutional?" *Stanford Law Review* 46 (April): 907–918.

Van Deusen, Glyndon. 1937. *The Life of Henry Clay.* Boston: Little, Brown.

❖ CONGRESS, OVERRIDING JUDICIAL DECISIONS ❖

Of all the powers exercised by the courts, none has been either more important or more controversial than the power of judicial review. This allows courts to strike down state and federal laws or executive orders that they find to be unconstitutional. Not explicitly stated in the Constitution, the power is arguably an important ancillary to the doctrines of separation of powers, federalism (in the case of unconstitutional state laws), and the supremacy of a written constitution. Chief Justice John Marshall first exercised and justified this power to strike down a federal law in *Marbury v. Madison* (1803), a decision that continues to be at the center of scholarly debate (Alfange 1994).

The Court did not exercise its power to strike down another federal law until the notorious decision in *Scott v. Sandford* (1857). By the end of the nineteenth century, however, the Court was increasingly using its power to strike down state and federal legislation, especially in the realm of economic regulation. Shortly after President Franklin D. Roosevelt threatened to "pack" the Court in 1937, it executed a historic turnabout (see *West Coast Hotel v. Parrish* [1937]) and has subsequently given only minimal scrutiny to most economic legislation. Consistent with reasoning expressed by Justice Harlan Fiske Stone in footnote 4 of the *Carolene Products* case the next year, however, the Court has increasingly exercised its power of judicial review over legis-lation thought to violate guarantees in the Bill of Rights or the Fourteenth Amendment, over possible obstacles to the democratic functioning of government, and for the protection of religious, racial, and other minorities.

The power of judicial review is controversial, partly because it is not stated in the Constitution. It also stirs controversy because, in light of the fact that judges are neither elected by nor directly accountable to the people, the exercise of judicial power can serve to thwart democratic wishes. Its exercise thus presents what Alexander Bickel has called "the counter-majoritarian difficulty" (Bickel 1986, 16).

Many proposals have been made with the intention of reining in judicial review. From just before the Court's turnaround in 1937 through the 1980s, at least twenty-five proposals have been advanced that would have allowed Congress to overturn such decisions. Although other majorities have been suggested, the most common proposal would allow Congress to override court decisions by a two-thirds vote. If adopted, this would give Congress power over judicial decisions equivalent to that which it now exercises over presidential vetoes.

Congress already has the power to override decisions of the Court that are based simply on statutory interpretation. In such cases, which are relatively frequent, Congress can simply adopt new laws to clarify its intentions (Eskridge 1991; Paschal 1991). Currently, if Congress wishes to override a constitutional interpretation of the courts, it must proceed by constitutional amendment. Congress so acted in the case of the Eleventh, Fourteenth, Sixteenth, and Twenty-sixth Amendments. An amendment granting Congress power to make such reversals by a two-thirds vote, without subsequent consent of three-fourths of the states, could significantly impact the operation of the current amending process. The impact of a more recent proposal encouraging Congress to draft amendments to overturn specific decisions from seven months to a year after the Supreme Court's yearly term is more difficult to measure (T. Baker 1995b).

See also Supreme Court Decisions Reversed by Constitutional Amendments.

For Further Reading:

Alfange, Dean, Jr. 1994. "*Marbury v. Madison* and Original Understandings of Judicial Review: In Defense of Traditional Wisdom." In *Supreme Court Review, 1993*. Chicago: University of Chicago Press.

Baker, Thomas E. 1995b. "Exercising the Amendment Power to Disapprove of Supreme Court Decisions: A Proposal for a 'Republican Veto.'" *Hastings Constitutional Law Quarterly* 22 (Winter): 325–357.

Bickel, Alexander. 1986. *The Least Dangerous Branch: The Supreme Court at the Bar of Politics*. 2d ed. New Haven, CT: Yale University Press.

Eskridge, William N., Jr. 1991. "Overriding Supreme Court Statutory Interpretations Decisions." *Yale Law Journal* 101 (November): 331–455.

Paschal, Richard A. 1991. "The Continuing Colloquy: Congress and the Finality of the Supreme Court." *Journal of Law and Politics* 8 (Fall): 143–226.

West Coast Hotel v. Parrish, 300 U.S. 379 (1937).

❖ CONGRESS, PRIVATE BILLS ❖

Most laws that Congress passes are public laws that are phrased in general terms and refer to broad classes of individuals. Indeed, the eighteenth-century French philosopher Jean-Jacques Rousseau argued that just laws were necessarily general, always considering "the subjects as a body and actions by their genera or species, never one man in particular or one unique individual action" (Rousseau 1978, 190). Despite such admonitions, Congress sometimes adopts private laws to provide relief for a single individual. From 1989 to 1991, such laws accounted for only 2.4 percent of the total, but the number was as high as 90 percent from 1905 to 1907 (Congressional Quarterly 1991, 359–360), during which time such bills were often the target of the presidential veto power.

Approximately twenty proposals were introduced from 1876 to 1909 to prohibit or limit private bills, but the number of private bills has been reduced both by the adoption of legislation and by the establishment of courts to hear claims that used to occupy congressional atten-

tion. Moreover, members of Congress who have introduced private bills or promised to introduce private bills for personal gain—as in the Abscam investigation—have been successfully prosecuted (Congressional Quarterly 1991, 166–167). No amendments related to private bills have been introduced in recent years. However, as concerns have been raised about the way members of Congress often add special provisions to laws to benefit individual constituents or groups of constituents, there has been some renewed discussion of a "Truth-in-Legislation" Amendment that would limit legislation to a single topic and/or require that the content of legislation match that of its heading. Proponents of an item veto have made similar arguments on its behalf.

See also Truth-in-Legislation Amendment.

For Further Reading:

Congressional Quarterly. 1991. *Guide to Congress*. 4th ed. Washington, DC: Congressional Quarterly.

Morehead, Joe. 1985. "Private Bills and Private Laws: A Guide to the Legislative Process." *Serials Librarian* 9 (Spring): 115–125.

Rousseau, Jean-Jacques. c.1762. *On the Social Contract with Geneva Manuscript and Political Economy*, ed. Roger D. Masters. Reprint, New York: St. Martin's Press, 1978.

❖ CONGRESS, QUORUM ❖

Article I, Section 5 of the Constitution specifies that a majority of each house of Congress constitutes a quorum, or the number of members required to do business. The House can evade this provision by working as a Committee of the Whole, in which case only 100 members must be present (Kravitz 1993, 215). Either house may also operate with less than a quorum as long as no member objects.

Under current law, a quorum is measured on the basis of living members of the House. This means that a House of Representatives decimated by a terrorist attack could continue to operate until elections were held for replacements (state governors can already make temporary appointments in the case of senators), but it could prove highly undesirable to have a large number of states effectively disenfranchised during such a time of crisis when important legislation might be considered (M. Davidson 2002, 6).

In 1883 Democratic Representative Joseph Wheeler of Alabama introduced an amending resolution to reduce the quorum to one-third of the members of each house (Ames 1896, 39). In 1947 and 1949 Republican Representative Charles Plumley of Vermont introduced resolutions that would accept an individual's quorum call only when one-fifth of the members present called for one.

For Further Reading:

Ames, Herman. 1896. *The Proposed Amendments to the Constitution of the United States during the First Century of Its History.* Reprint, New York: Burt Franklin.

Davidson, Michael. January 20, 2002. "Notes on Proposed Constitutional Amendments on Temporary Appointments of Members of the House," *www.aeipoliticalcorner.org/continuity.htm.* Accessed 5/16/02.

Kravitz, Walter, 1993. *American Congressional Dictionary.* Washington, DC: Congressional Quarterly.

❖ CONGRESS, RECALL OF MEMBERS ❖

Although the Constitution provides for the impeachment and conviction of officials guilty of criminal misconduct, it does not provide for the recall of individuals on grounds of incompetence or unrepresentativeness, and the U.S. Supreme Court's decision in *Cook v. Gralike* (2001) has limited the ability of states to attempt to "instruct" members of Congress or penalize them when they fail to heed such directives. There have been a number of proposed amendments to recall members of Congress, a practice that was permitted under Article V of the Articles of Confederation (Solberg 1958, 43).

The first such proposals focused on senators and came from Virginia representatives from 1803 to 1810. Such proposals, which seem to have reflected concerns over states' rights rather than popular democracy, would have allowed the state legislatures to recall and replace senators. Such proposals may have reflected a view—prominent at the time of the American Revolution—that such legislators were subject to instruction by their constituents, in this case, the state legislatures (G. Wood 1969, 188–196). Interestingly, at least three senators, including future president John Tyler, resigned in the nineteenth century when they were unable to follow the wishes of the state legislatures that had selected them (Ames 1896, 65). Similarly, John Quincy Adams resigned his seat after the Massachusetts legislature elected his successor nine months early (Leish 1968, 1:178).

The recall, like the initiative and referendum, was popular with reformers in the Progressive Era. Most twentieth-century proposals would permit voters to recall both senators and members of the House. A 1987 Gallup poll indicated that 67 percent of the people favored such a mechanism (Cronin 1989, 132). Advocates believe that such a mechanism would promote democracy and accountability. Opponents fear that it might undermine representative government.

See also Constituent Instructions for Amending Constitutions; Initiative and Referendum.

For Further Reading:

Ames, Herman. 1896. *The Proposed Amendments to the Constitution of the United States during the First Century of Its History.* Reprint, New York: Burt Franklin, 1970.

Cronin, Thomas E. 1989. *Direct Democracy: The Politics of Initiative, Referendum, and Recall.* Cambridge, MA: Harvard University Press.

Leish, Kenneth W., ed. 1968. *The American Heritage Pictorial History of the Presidents of the United States.* 2 vols. n.p.: American Heritage.

Solberg, Winton, ed. 1958. *The Federal Convention and the Formation of the Union.* Indianapolis, IN: Bobbs-Merrill.

Wood, Gordon S. 1969. *The Creation of the American Republic, 1776–1787.* New York: W. W. Norton.

❖ CONGRESS, REPRESENTATION IN ❖

One of the most difficult issues the delegates to the Constitutional Convention faced was the issue of representation. Advocates of the Virginia plan wanted states to be represented in both houses of Congress according to population. Advocates of the New Jersey plan wanted to preserve the system under the Articles of Confederation whereby states would be represented equally. In the Connecticut, or Great, Compromise, delegates agreed that representation in the House would be by population and that states would be equally represented in the Senate. The only stated substantive limit on the amending process that is in force provides that no state shall be deprived of such representation without its consent. This provision did not deter two members of Congress from introducing resolutions in 1882 and 1892 to increase the number of senators for more populous states.

The Constitutional Convention was also torn by debates between the slave and free states. The former wanted slaves to count for purposes of congressional representation but not for taxation, whereas the free states had opposite interests. In one of the least defensible parts of the Constitution, the delegates settled on a three-fifths formula, which they incorporated into Article I, Section 2. Under this formula, "three-fifths of such other persons [slaves]" were to count for purposes of taxation and representation (Vile 1993a, 27–28). When the Thirteenth Amendment prohibited slavery, the Southern states—dominated by Democrats who had fought against the Union—actually stood to gain representation. When Section 2 of the Fourteenth Amendment subsequently obliterated the three-fifths clause by providing that representation would now be based on "the whole number of persons in each State, excluding Indians not taxed," it also provided a mechanism whereby representation would be reduced for those states that restricted the vote other than to males under the age of twenty-one or those who were guilty of crimes or of participation in rebellion. These provisions followed numerous resolutions for amendments that had been introduced in Congress. In part because it was difficult to ascertain how many people were actually being deprived of the franchise, this provision was never actually put into effect (Congressional Quarterly 1991, 742).

A number of reforms relating to representation have been proposed in the twentieth century. The 1920s witnessed several proposals to require reapportionment after each decennial census. The topic was then of particular concern, because this was the only time in U.S. history that Congress, faced for the first time with an apparent majority of urban residents, failed to reapportion after such a census (Congressional Quarterly 1991, 742–743). Several subsequent proposals would have limited the number of senators from new states. There have been several proposed amendments that would base representation on the number of U.S. citizens and legal resident aliens within each state rather than on a state's total population, which the Census Bureau now tries to record. The current method of apportionment arguably rewards states with large numbers of illegal aliens with extra representation. At least one scholar, who focuses chiefly on the intention he believes lies behind the census provisions in Article I and the Fourteenth Amendment rather than their explicit reference to "persons," already believes Congress has the authority to exclude illegal aliens from existing counts (C. Wood 1999). A proposal has been made for reapportioning representation in the House after each presidential election, based on the number of voters in such elections. Another proposal (perhaps goaded by the large number of lawyers who are elected to Congress) called for apportioning representatives according to vocation. Others proposed increasing the number of members of the Senate.

The Constitution guarantees that each state will have at least one member in the House of Representatives, and law now caps House membership at 435. This has inevitably meant that, however influential Supreme Court decisions such as *Wesberry v. Sanders* (1964) have been in mandating numerical equality among districts in the same state, interstate numerical equality of districts has been impossible to attain. Thus, in 1980, Nevada and Maine both had two seats, although the former had a population of 787,000 and the latter a population of 1,125,000. By contrast, South Dakota, with a population of 690,000, got only one seat (Butler and Cain 1992, 18). Throughout American history, a number of different mechanisms have been used to ascertain representatives for states with a fraction over or under what they would receive simply on the basis of population (Butler and Cain 1992, 19). The method now used is known as the method of equal proportions and was developed in 1921 by Edward V. Huntington of Harvard and adopted by Congress in 1941. After assigning each state a seat,

> "priority numbers" for states to receive second seats, third seats, and so on are calculated by dividing the state's population by the square root of n(n–1) where "n" is the number of seats for that state. The priority numbers are then lined up in order and the seats given to the states with priority numbers until 435 are awarded." (Congressional Quarterly 1991, 745)

This method of apportionment was upheld in *U.S. Department of Commerce v. Montana* (1992), in which Montana protested its loss of a House seat that reduced its representation to one member. Such situations have led to a number of calls to give each state at least two representatives. In any event, potential inequalities of state representation in the House of Representatives are dwarfed by inequities in the U.S. Senate, where states remain represented by two senators regardless of population differences.

In *Department of Commerce v. United States House of Representatives* (1999), the U.S. Supreme Court rejected plans by the Census Bureau to use statistical techniques to adjust census counts so as to estimate undercounts. In a decision written by Justice Sandra Day O'-Connor, the Court concluded that the Census Act as amended in 1976 did not provide authority for such sampling. In *Utah v. Evans* (2002), however, the Court did uphold a method called "hot-deck imputation" whereby census agents fill in information for houses whose residents they cannot find by imputing characteristics of their nearest neighbors.

See also Congress, Size Of.

For Further Reading:
Butler, David, and Bruce Cain. 1992. *Congressional Redistricting: Comparative and Theoretical Perspectives.* New York: Macmillan.

Congressional Quarterly. 1991. *Guide to Congress.* 4th ed. Washington, DC: Congressional Quarterly.

Vile, John R. 1993a. *Contemporary Questions Surrounding the Constitutional Amending Process.* Westport, CT: Praeger.

Wood, Charles. 1999. "Losing Control of America's Future: The Census, Birthright Citizenship, and Illegal Aliens." *Harvard Journal of Law and Public Policy* 22 (Spring): 465–522.

❖ CONGRESS, SENATE REPRESENTATION ❖

The U.S. Senate is one of the institutions of government most frequently subject to criticism. Some of this centers on institutions like seniority (somewhat modified in recent years) and Senate folkways—most notably the filibuster, by which a small number of passionate senators can simply "talk" a measure to death. Far more fundamental, however, is criticism of the way states are represented in that body. Although the Virginia Plan had proposed that states be represented in both houses of the national legislature according to population, the small (or less populous) states objected. They had equal representation in the Congress under the Articles of Confederation and were reluctant to give it up; the New Jersey Plan accordingly proposed that states be equally represented in the Congress. Eventually, the Connecticut Compromise provided that states would be represented according to population in the House of Representatives and equally in the Senate. This was such a fundamental compromise at the Constitutional Convention of 1787 that it was entrenched within Article V, the amending article, by the provision that no state could be denied its equal suffrage within the Senate without its consent.

Today's Senate is arguably more democratic than that of the first Congress. The Seventeenth Amendment, ratified in 1913, provided that senators would be chosen by direct popular election rather than by the state legislatures, as previously was the case. Critics, however, continue to see the equal state representation in the U.S. Senate as undemocratic and undesirable (Dahl 2001, 17–18). Such criticisms relate directly to the amending process, because the only used mechanism specified in this process requires two-thirds majorities of both houses of Congress to propose amendments. Although not focusing on this aspect of this representation, two public choice advocates have recently identified what they consider to be three negative consequences of this arrangement:

> First, the Senate systematically and unjustifiably redistributes wealth from the large population states to the small ones. Second, it systematically and unjustifiably provides racial minorities a voice in the federal lawmaking process which is disproportionately small relative to their numbers. And finally, it systematically and unjustifiably affords large population states disproportionately little power, relative to their shares of the nation's population, to block federal homogenizing legislation that they consider disadvantageous. (Baker and Dinkin 1997, 23)

Having come to these conclusions, the scholars note that the current constitution, and especially the current entrenchment clause within Article V, makes reform very unlikely. They do offer a number of novel suggestions for possible changes. These include the possibility of repealing the entrenchment clause before reconfiguring representation in the Senate (Baker and Dinkin 1997, 68–72) or allowing larger states to divide. In what would be every high school geography student's nightmare, the authors suggest that California might divide into sixty-five new states (Baker and Dinkin 1997, 72). The authors also argue, not altogether convincingly, that the Supreme Court might interpret the Fifth or Fifteenth

Amendments to inaugurate changes (Baker and Dinkin 1997, 74–81) Finally, they suggest that the large-states might simply engage in a "work stoppage" (Baker and Dinkin 1997, 81) or even that the issue could become salient enough to prompt a popular revolt (Baker and Dinkin, 83–84). Seemingly unconvinced that any of these actions are likely to be taken, the authors primarily use their article as a way of warning future constitution makers of the irrationality of agreeing to a plan like that accepted by the American framers.

See also Constitutional Convention of 1787; Entrenchment Clauses.

For Further Reading:
Baker, Lynn A., and Samuel H. Dinkin. 1997. "The Senate: An Institution Whose Time Has Gone?" *Journal of Law & Politics* 13 (Winter): 21–95.

❖ CONGRESS, SIZE OF ❖

Article I, Section 2 of the U.S. Constitution specifies that the membership of the House of Representatives "shall not exceed one for every thirty Thousand [people]," and Article I, Section 3 guarantees that each state will have at least two senators. The first of twelve amendments proposed by Congress in 1789 (ten of which were ratified as the Bill of Rights) would have provided that when membership in the House reached 100, there would be at least one representative for every 40,000 persons. It also would have mandated that when House membership reached 200, it should not fall below this number, nor should there be more than one representative for every 50,000 persons—requirements that, at some population stage, may well have been contradictory (Amar 1992, 1143). Unlike an accompanying provision that was putatively ratified as the Twenty-seventh Amendment in 1992, the congressional representation amendment was not ratified and is today irrelevant.

There were sixty-five members in the first session of the House of Representatives. After the 1800 census, the number grew to 106, and by 1900, it reached 391. This led to concerns that the size of the House might become too unwieldy. Beginning with a proposal introduced by Anti-Democrat–States' Rights Senator James Barbour of Virginia in 1821, there were just over a dozen proposed amendments to cap the size of the House (the proposed size gradually increasing) until 1911, when the number of House members was set by law at 435 (Congressional Quarterly 1991, 741–742).

Since 1911 there have been a few proposals to raise the number of House members to 450, 480, or 500, as well as a number of proposals to reduce such membership to 300, 350, or 400. There have also been some proposals to increase the size of the Senate by equally increasing the number of senators for all states or by increasing the number of senators apportioned to the more populous states. Unless all states approved the latter amendment, it would be in apparent violation of an entrenchment provision now in Article V that prohibits states from being deprived of their equal representation in the Senate without their consent.

See also Constitutional Amendments, Limits on.

For Further Reading:
Amar, Akhil R. 1992. "The Bill of Rights as a Constitution." *Yale Law Journal* 100 (Winter): 1131–1210.

Congressional Quarterly. 1991. *Guide to Congress.* 4th ed. Washington, DC: Congressional Quarterly.

❖ CONGRESS, SPECIAL ELECTIONS ❖

In Great Britain, which is typical of parliamentary systems, the prime minister and members of Parliament are elected to five-year terms, but the prime minister may call an early election when the minister believes that an election will bolster party support. The prime minister may also call a new election after receiving a vote of "no confidence" in Parliament (Rasmussen and Moses 1995, 82). There is no such provision for ad hoc congressional elections (except in the case of individual members who die) in the U.S. Constitution, and such an election would be counter to the fixed terms of office provided therein.

Numerous individuals who favor incorporation of one or more parliamentary features into the U.S. government have advocated allowing Congress or the president to call such special elections. At least two amendments have been introduced in Congress to this effect, one by Populist Senator William Peffer of Kansas in 1895 and another by Republican Representative Charles Potter of Michigan in 1951. The former was directed specifically at issues of finance and foreign relations. The latter resolution would have required Congress to hold a national election if requested to do so by a two-thirds vote of its members.

See also Parliamentary System.

For Further Reading:
Rasmussen, Jorgen S., and Joel C. Moses. 1995. *Major European Governments.* 9th ed. Belmont, CA: Wadsworth.

❖ CONGRESS, TAXATION BY ❖

See Sixteenth Amendment; Taxation entries.

❖ CONGRESS, TERM LENGTHS ❖

The Constitution sets the terms of members of the House of Representatives at two years and the terms of senators at six years. The terms of House members were designed to keep them especially close and accountable to the people; by contrast, the terms of senators were designed to give them greater independence (Vile 2002a, 27, 31–32).

Because all members of the House are elected every two years, there is a chance for a large turnover in presidential election years, and, although this did not happen in 2002, the president's party almost always loses seats in so-called off-year, or midterm, House elections that occur between presidential contests. By contrast, only one-third of senators run for election in presidential election years, and swings in nonpresidential election years tend to be less dramatic than those in the House.

A study completed in 1991 listed just over 200 proposals that had sought to alter House terms and just over 50 more that would have both altered such terms and limited the number of terms that an individual could serve (S. Richardson 1991, 72–80, 87–90). Proposals have ranged from those calling for yearly election of House members to those calling for terms of three, four, or six years. Similarly, from 1789 to 1991 thirteen proposals were introduced to lower the terms of senators to three or four years or to raise them to eight years; another four would also have limited the number of terms (S. Richardson 1991, 91, 100). Some versions of the four- and eight-year terms have been designed so that such terms would be more closely tied to presidential fortunes and thus encourage greater party discipline and coherence.

By far the most common proposal in regard to congressional term lengths has been to raise the terms of members of the House of Representatives to four years. Longer House terms would arguably give members greater independence and allow them to devote more time to legislating and less to fund-raising. Critics argue that such terms would also mean that House members would not stay in close touch with their constituents.

At least one proposal introduced in 1989 to increase House terms to four years would also have required House members running for the Senate to vacate their seats (H.J. Res. 203). Proposals for raising the length of congressional terms have sometimes been made in conjunction with proposals for a recall mechanism; as described above, they are often also tied to proposals for congressional term limits. It is possible that members of the House who are otherwise reluctant to propose term limits might be more willing to do so in exchange for longer terms, but at present, there seems to be much more pressure for the former change than for the latter.

See also Congress, Term Limits.

For Further Reading:

Richardson, Sula. 1991. *Congressional Terms of Office and Tenure: Historical Background and Contemporary Issues.* Washington, DC: Congressional Research Service, Library of Congress.

Vile, John R. 2002a. *A Companion to the United States Constitution and Its Amendments.* 3d ed. Westport, CT: Praeger.

❖ CONGRESS, TERM LIMITS ❖

In 1951 the states ratified the Twenty-second Amendment limiting the service of presidents to two full terms. Ever since proposals have periodically been introduced to limit the terms that members of Congress can serve. Between 1789 and 1991, 141 such proposals were introduced—most of them after 1950 (S. Richardson 1991, 45). Frequently, such proposals have been tied to calls for altering the length of congressional terms, but since the 1970s the focus appears to have shifted from term lengths to term limits (S. Richardson 1991, 39).

Neither idea, however, is new. The Articles of Confederation limited delegates to serving three one-year terms out of a possible six, and in the early history of the Constitution, Anti-Federalists pressed the idea of limiting the number of terms that members of the Senate could serve (Kesler 1990, 21). In recent years, however, the idea appears to have gained momentum. A number of presidents have expressed their support of the idea. Republican presidential candidates supported the idea in 1988 and 1992. In 1990 a lobby group called Americans to Limit Congressional Terms (ALCT) was formed to press for such an amendment, which was incorporated into the Republican Contract with America (S. Richardson 1991, 53). The House of Representatives voted 227 to 204 in March 1995 for a proposal to limit service by members of the House and Senate to twelve years. By larger margins it rejected proposals to limit service in the House to six years, to apply term limits retroactively, or to allow states to impose their own stricter limits. Although term-limit proposals had stronger support among Republicans than among Democrats, Republicans were far from united. Illinois Republican Representative Henry Hyde voted against such limits, saying, "I just can't be an accessory to the dumbing-down of democracy" (Babson 1995, 918).

In large part, the movement for term limits, like the putative ratification of the Twenty-seventh Amendment, is tied to popular frustration with Congress. This has occurred with the increased professionalization of a body that now seems far removed from the idea of "citizen legislators" that the founders originally contemplated. Ironically, reelection rates for members of Congress have been quite high. People appear to like their own representatives while disliking the institution as a whole (Prinz 1992, 150). This may stem in part from members' focus on constituent service rather than on more controversial political issues. Members also gain name recognition and access to the media through their service and have privileges, such as franking (free use of the mails), that are unavailable to other officeholders.

Advocates of term limits believe that they would help overcome such advantages and bring in "new blood" and new ideas—some amending proposals have been designated as the Citizen Representative Reform Act New Blood Provision. Increased turnover would also decrease the role that seniority plays in congressional assignments and might encourage members to devote more time to issues. Opponents argue that voters already have the power to impose term limits by refusing to reelect their representatives and argue that additional limitations are contrary to the spirit of democracy. Some also fear that term limits would weaken Congress as an institution and give greater power to unelected bureaucrats, many of whom would be able to serve longer than congressional representatives (S. Richardson 1991, 39–41; also compare Frenzel 1992 with Mann 1992).

One obvious obstacle to term limits is the fact that those who have achieved leadership positions in Congress (where seniority plays an important, albeit not dispositive, role) can hardly expect to favor a measure that would undercut their own power. It is possible that outside pressure for such an amendment could be exerted by state petitions to call an Article V constitutional convention on the subject, but to date states have preferred to attempt to limit congressional terms through state laws and referendums (S. Richardson 1989). After considerable academic debate (see, for example, Whitaker 1992), the Supreme Court recently declared in *U.S. Term Limits, Inc. v. Thornton* (1995) that the requirements for members of Congress listed in the Constitution are exclusive and that such state attempts were therefore unconstitutional; another decision in *Cook v. Gralike* (2001) has prevented states from including notations on ballots as to how individuals in Congress voted on the subject of proposed term limit amendments.

Another obstacle to terms limits is that proponents have not been united on precisely what limits are appropriate. Supporters of limits for the Senate have typically advocated from one to three terms. Proposals relative to the House of Representatives have varied from three to ten terms; some proposals also advocate increasing House terms from two to four years, with a two- or three-term limit.

Proposals for term limits have frequently been combined with proposals for altering congressional terms, especially in the House of Representatives. Some proposals have sought to limit the total number of terms an individual can serve, whereas others have focused on the total number of consecutive terms or the total number of years an individual can serve within a given time period (for example, ten out of twelve years). Some proponents of term limits have attempted to limit the total number of years that an individual can serve as president, vice president, a member of the cabinet, or a member of Congress—a proposal that could drastically affect the pool of candidates for these offices. Some proposals have also sought to limit the number of years that individuals can serve as ambassadors, judges, and justices. Obviously, each proposal has a different potential effect on how the U.S. government would operate, and inevitably some of the effects could not be fully anticipated.

Some advocates of term limits are now pressing for a constitutional convention. Attempts to get an unprecedented national referendum (there is no constitutional provision for such a measure) on the subject in the 1996 elections failed. Some proponents of congressional term limits want a single, nationwide standard while others simply want to reverse the U.S. Supreme Court decision in *U.S. Term Limits, Inc. v. Thornton* (1995) and allow states to specify limits according to their own judgment.

See also *U.S. Term Limits, Inc. v. Thornton.*

For Further Reading:

Babson, Jennifer. 1995. "House Rejects Term Limits: GOP Blames Democrats." *Congressional Quarterly Weekly Reports* 53 (1 April): 918–919.

Cloud, David S. 1996. "Term Limits Stall in Senate; GOP Blames Democrats." *Congressional Quarterly* 54 (27 April): 1153–1154.

Frenzel, Bill. 1992. "Term Limits and the Immortal Congress." *Brookings Review* 10 (Spring): 18–22.

Kesler, Charles R. 1990. "Bad Housekeeping: The Case against Congressional Term Limits." *Policy Review* 53 (Summer): 20–25.

Mann, Thomas E. 1992. "The Wrong Medicine." *Brookings Review* 10 (Spring): 23–25.

Prinz, Timothy S. 1992. "Term Limitation: A Perilous Panacea." *The World & I* 7 (January): 143–153.

Richardson, Sula. 1991. *Congressional Terms of Office and Tenure: Historical Background and Contemporary Issues.* Washington, DC: Congressional Research Service, Library of Congress.

❖ CONGRESS, TRUTH-IN-LEGISLATION ❖

See Truth-in-Legislation Amendment.

❖ CONGRESS, VACANCIES IN ❖

The Seventeenth Amendment provides that state governors may make appointments to fill vacancies in the U.S. Senate until the next general election. Because the Constitution makes no such provision for the House of Representatives, vacancies there continue to be governed by the provision in Article I, Section 2 that specifies that "when vacancies happen in the Representation from any State, the Executive Authority thereof shall issue Writs of Elections to fill such Vacancies." Thus, such vacancies can be filled only by special election (Clem 1989, 66). When there is less than a year left in a member's term, states may simply leave a House seat vacant until the next term.

Within a decade after ratification of the Seventeenth Amendment, a New Jersey representative proposed that state governors be permitted to make temporary appointments until House vacancies could be filled by election. This proposal came long before later concerns generated by nuclear weapons that have been reflected in more than a score of proposals to provide for the emergency functioning of Congress. Such concerns have been heightened after the terrorist attack of 11 September 2001 on the World Trade Center and the Pentagon and have generated new attention to the subject.

See also Congress, Emergency Functioning.

For Further Reading:

Clem, Alan L. 1989. *Congress: Powers, Processes, and Politics.* Pacific Grove, CA: Brooks/Cole.

❖ CONSENSUS AND THE AMENDING PROCESS ❖

Because it embodies a system of separated powers, the U.S. Constitution requires an unusual consensus for the adoption of legislation. Legislation must be adopted by both houses of Congress and then either approved by the president or adopted by two-thirds congressional majorities over the president's veto. The requirements for the adoption of constitutional amendments, which affect the wording of the fundamental law of the land, are even more onerous and are arguably designed to mimic, at least in part, the extraordinary consensus that was necessary to adopt the original Constitution. Article V requires two-thirds majorities to propose amendments and three-fourths majorities to ratify

them. The framers clearly designed these requirements in part to assure that amendments
are not adopted on behalf of narrow sectional
interests. On a related matter, in *Dillon v. Gloss*
(1921), the U.S. Supreme Court specifically
noted that amendments are designed to reflect
a contemporary consensus.

The later decision in *Coleman v. Miller*
(1939) declaring that issues of timing were to
be left to Congress, and also the belated ratification of the Twenty-seventh Amendment in
1992 (over 200 years after it was first proposed), have somewhat called the issue of contemporary consensus into question. Many critics of both decisions have argued either that the
Court was correct in *Dillon* and that it should
therefore independently examine amendments
to see whether they reflect a contemporary
consensus, or, if the constitution does not assure such a consensus, that there should be
some measure to assure that such amendments
do reflect a consensus. Since the Eighteenth
Amendment (1919), Congress has usually included a time limit on the ratification of
amendments either within the texts, where they
are presumably self-enforcing, or in accompanying authorizing resolutions. During controversy over the ratification of the Equal Rights
Amendment, Congress extended a deadline
that it had included in its authorizing resolution, but this measure is still controversial.

Some critics of the amending process believe
that it is too difficult and that it requires such
an extraordinary consensus that it becomes almost impossible to use or that it invites change
by other means. One concern that is sometimes
raised to proposed alternatives to the amending
process, as well as to existing methods of constitutional alterations through judicial review, is
that they may not always put adequate emphasis on consensus.

See also *Coleman v. Miller; Dillon v. Gloss;*
Equal Rights Amendment; Time Limits on
Amendments; Twenty-seventh Amendment.

❖ CONSTITUENT INSTRUCTIONS FOR AMENDING CONSTITUTIONS ❖

Between 1996 and 1998, ten states adopted
popular initiatives in which they instructed
their congressional representatives to support a
constitutional amendment favoring term limits
(Kobach 1999, 3). In *U.S. Term Limits, Inc. v.
Thornton* (1995), the U.S. Supreme Court
struck down state legislative attempts to limit
the terms of members of Congress and ruled
that such limits could be enacted only through
a constitutional amendment. The states that
provided for instructions to their representatives on the issue of term limits also provided
that ballots would contain the words "Disregarded Voters' Instruction on Term Limits" in
the cases of legislators who failed to comply
(Kobach 1999, 3). In case after case in both
state and lower federal courts, with one exception (the Supreme Court of Idaho), courts
struck down such constituent "instructions" as
unconstitutional infringements of Article V
(Kobach 1999, 7–8).

At least two scholars have analyzed these decisions and their implications for republican, or
representative, government. One scholar, Kris
Kobach, believes that the decisions ignored a
long history of constituent instructions to legislators beginning before the American Revolution, and continuing through demands for independence from England, demands for the
Articles of Confederations, demands for the
Constitution itself, demands for the Bill of
Rights, and demands for the Eleventh Amendment (Kobach 1999, 27–80). Kobach admits
that such instructions began to decline in the
late nineteenth century (and especially after the
Seventeenth Amendment provided for the direct election of Senators—who had previously
been chosen by state legislatures—in 1913),
but believes they were supplanted in part by
popular initiatives during the Populist and Progressive Eras. He further argues that recent
court decisions have been mistaken in ignoring
this long history of instructions and that requiring notice to voters on ballots of candidates' failure to heed such instructions is valid.

A second writer, Vikram Amar (2000), distinguishes between what he considers to be permissible instructions by voters to their state legislators and what might be impermissible instructions to federal legislators. This author not only notes that the authors of the federal Bill of Rights specifically rejected an amendment that would have permitted the people to give instruction to their federal legislators (a point that Kobach takes simply as recognition that such power of instruction already existed), but that it might be inappropriate for voters from an entire state to try to dictate to representatives from specific districts (V. Amar 2000, 1090). Amar also argues that members of Congress have unique responsibilities to the nation as a whole and that such instructions might be seen as adding qualifications to those specified within the Constitution and thus violating the decision in *U.S. Term Limits, Inc. v. Thornton*.

In *Cook v. Gralike* (2001), the Supreme Court settled the issue by ruling that ballot notations were, like the provisions struck down in *U.S. Term Limits,* an unconstitutional attempt to impose additional qualifications on individuals running for Congress and an impermissible intrusion on legislative discretion.

See also *Cook v. Gralike.*

For Further Reading:

Amar, Vikram David. 2000. "The People Made Me Do It: Can the People of the States Instruct and Coerce Their State Legislatures in the Article V Convention Amendment Process?" *William and Mary Law Review* 41 (March): 1037–1092.

Kobach, Kris W. 1999. "May 'We the People' Speak? The Forgotten Role of Constituent Instructions in Amending the Constitution." *University of California Davis Law Review* 33 (Fall): 1–94.

❖ CONSTITUTIONAL AMENDMENTS, LIMITS ON ❖

Article V of the Constitution establishes the formal procedures by which the document may be amended and specifies two explicit limits (sometimes called entrenchment clauses) on the content of amendments. One such provision that has since expired was introduced on 10 September 1787 at the Constitutional Convention by South Carolina's John Rutledge and was designed to guard a compromise between the North and the South regarding slavery. It prohibited any changes in Article I, Section 9 of the Constitution, which allowed for the importation of slaves until 1808 (Farrand 1966, 2:559).

The other provision, introduced at the convention on 15 September by Pennsylvania's Gouverneur Morris and presumably in effect as long as the Constitution stands, provides "that no State, without its Consent, shall be deprived of its equal Suffrage in the Senate" (Farrand 1966, 2:631). This was designed to protect the Connecticut, or Great, Compromise introduced by Connecticut's Roger Sherman at the Constitutional Convention. It was formulated as a way of mediating the desires of the small states, which favored equal state representation, and those of the large states, which wanted representation to be based on population. This compromise provided that representation in the House of Representatives would be based on population and that representation in the upper house would be apportioned equally among the states, each of which would have two senators. The convention had rejected an earlier proposal by Sherman that, in addition to guaranteeing equal state suffrage, would have prevented each state from being affected "in its internal police" without its consent (Farrand 1966, 2:630).

Just before the Civil War, several amendments, including the Corwin amendment, were proposed that would have permanently frozen the institution of slavery within the Constitution in an attempt to reassure the South and avert war. Abraham Lincoln indicated that he did not oppose such a compromise, but it was not adopted. Ironically, if ratified, this, rather than the amendment abolishing involuntary servitude, would have become the Thirteenth Amendment.

From the time of John C. Calhoun to the present, politicians and scholars have speculated as to whether there are any additional unstated limits on the substance of amendments to the Constitution. Conservative spokesmen such as Selden Bacon and William Marbury challenged the validity of the Fifteenth, Eighteenth, and Nineteenth Amendments on the grounds that they exceeded such implicit restraints. The Court ignored or rejected such arguments in *Myers v. Anderson* (1915), the *National Prohibition Cases* (1920), *United States v. Sprague* (1931), and *Leser v. Garnett* (1922).

A number of contemporary scholars, most notably Walter Murphy (1980), have argued that the Constitution embodies certain fundamental values, such as the protection of human dignity, that implicitly limit any conflicting changes. Such scholars have therefore hypothesized that there are a number of conceivable amendments that would be unconstitutional. Similarly, Eric Isaacson (1992) and Jeff Rosen (1991) argued that the proposed amendment designed to prohibit flag burning would be unconstitutional and would be subject to judicial invalidation. Vile (1985) has argued that the explicit prohibitions in Article V were intended to be exclusive and that acceptance of other implicit limits would unduly elevate judicial powers.

See also Bacon, Selden; Corwin Amendment; Entrenchment Clauses; Marbury, William; Murphy, Walter F.

For Further Reading:
Farrand, Max, ed. 1966. *The Records of the Federal Convention.* 4 vols. New Haven, CT: Yale University Press.

Isaacson, Eric A. 1990. "The Flag Burning Issue: A Legal Analysis and Comment." *Loyola of Los Angeles Law Review* 23 (January): 535–600.

Linder, Douglas. 1981. "What in the Constitution Cannot Be Amended?" *Arizona Law Review* 23: 717–731.

Murphy, Walter F. 1980. "An Ordering of Constitutional Values." *Southern California Law Review* 53: 703–760.

Rosen, Jeffrey. 1991. "Was the Flag Burning Amendment Unconstitutional?" *Yale Law Review* 100: 1073–1092.

Vile, John R. 1985. "Limitations on the Constitutional Amending Process." *Constitutional Commentary* 2 (Summer): 373–388.

Wright, R. George. 1991. "Could a Constitutional Amendment Be Unconstitutional?" *Loyola University of Chicago Law Review* 22: 741–764.

❖ CONSTITUTIONAL COMMISSIONS ❖

One of the mechanisms of state constitutional revision that has not been used at the national level is the constitutional commission. Although the legislative or executive branch sometimes creates such commissions individually, they generally have the support of both branches. Such commissions may propose constitutional reforms for legislative consideration and approval, or they may prepare amendments for a constitutional convention (Rich 1960, 89). Often such commissions attract high-caliber individuals, but their work is usually at the mercy of the state legislatures. Because such commissions lack "the strong legal position and the dynamic character and drama of a convention," a student of the commission has concluded that such commissions are "no substitute" for such conventions (Rich 1960, 99).

As the bicentennial of the Declaration of Independence approached, political scientist Conley Dillon (1974) proposed the establishment of a national constitutional commission to recommend needed changes. The Constitution mentions no such mechanism, but there appears to be no legal obstacle to the creation of such a body, as long as it is only advisory.

See also States, Constitutional Revision.

For Further Reading:
Dillon, Conley. 1974. "Recommendation for the Establishment of a Permanent Commission of Constitutional Review." *Bureaucrat* 3 (July): 211–224.

Rich, Bennett M. 1960. *Major Problems in State Constitutional Revision,* ed. W. Brooke Groves. Chicago: Public Administration Service.

❖ CONSTITUTIONAL CONVENTION OF 1787 ❖

The U.S. Constitution was written at a convention that met in Philadelphia from May through September 1787. The idea of a convention emerged from an earlier meeting by representatives of five states to discuss commercial matters, known as the Annapolis Convention. Congress subsequently authorized a convention "for the sole and express purpose of revising the Articles of Confederation and reporting to Congress and the several legislatures such alterations and provisions as shall . . . render the federal constitution adequate to the exigencies of Government and the preservation of the Union" (Solberg 1958, 64). Altogether, fifty-five delegates from twelve states (Rhode Island did not send any delegates) attended the convention, which elected George Washington as chairman and quickly began to focus on alternatives to the Articles of Confederation rather than attempting merely to amend that document. Many states were spurred to send delegates by Shay's Rebellion, a taxpayer revolt centered in Massachusetts in the winter of 1787–1788 that convinced many men of property that civil order was endangered.

Much of the deliberation at the Constitutional Convention centered on conflicts between the large states, whose interests were initially represented in the Virginia Plan, and the small states, whose interests were reflected somewhat later in the New Jersey Plan (Vile 2002a, 15–16). These plans and other proposals and controversies also reflected tension between advocates of expanded national powers and those who wished to retain many of the states' prerogatives under the Articles of Confederation. Compromises were also necessary to reconcile the conflicting interests of the slave and free states; these included the provision for a fugitive slave clause, for counting slaves as three-fifths of a person for purposes of taxation and representation, and forbidding more than a nominal tax on imported slaves for the following twenty years.

The Constitutional Convention initiated major changes in the government that had been existence under the Articles of Confederation. In addition to significantly expanding the powers of the national government vis-à-vis the states, convention delegates divided the legislative branch into two chambers, the House of Representatives and the Senate (the Congress under the Articles of Confederation had been unicameral) and created an independent executive, headed by a unitary executive, and a judicial branch headed by the U.S. Supreme Court, that eventually claimed the power, known as judicial review, to declare state and federal laws to be unconstitutional. In a book entitled *Constitutional Chaff* (1941), Jane Butzner has collected debates over resolutions, like a Council of Revision or alternative ways of selecting the president, that were considered but not included within the resulting document. Like contemporary proposals for a new constitution, such debates help demonstrate some of the alternatives that might have been and, in some cases, still could be adopted in place of current governmental mechanisms.

Most convention delegates, all of whom had lived through the Revolutionary War, appear to have agreed that a constitutional amending process was a necessary alternative to revolution. Thus, Virginia's George Mason reflected that "the plan now to be formed will certainly be defective, as the Confederation has been found on trial to be. Amendments therefore will be necessary, and it will be better to provide for them, in an easy, regular and Constitutional way than to trust to chance and violence" (Farrand 1966, 1:203). Delegates appear to have agreed that the unused provision for amendment under the Articles of Confederation that required unanimous state consent was too onerous.

The Virginia Plan's initial provision for an amending process was more a statement of intent than a viable mechanism, but it did specify that congressional assent should not be required for amendments. At the end of July, a five-member Committee of Detail proposed a scheme under which Congress would call a convention upon receiving petitions from two-thirds of the states (Farrand 1966, 2:159). Delegates debated these proposals during the last week of the convention, beginning on 10 September. Elbridge Gerry of Massachusetts feared that the proposal did not protect minority state interests; Alexander Hamilton of New York thought that Congress should have a role in initiating amendments; and Virginia's James Madison was concerned about the vagueness of the convention mechanism (Vile 1992, 29). The response was a proposal introduced by Madison and seconded by Hamilton, allowing two-thirds majorities of Congress or two-thirds of the states to propose amendments, which would be ratified by three-fourths of the states. After an objection by South Carolina's John Rutledge, a provision was added prohibiting the importation of slaves for twenty years.

The amending issue reemerged on 15 September, with Virginia's George Mason now objecting that the amending mechanism was too much under the control of Congress. This objection resulted in the still unused provision allowing two-thirds of the states to propose a convention for amending the Constitution. One of Pennsylvania's representatives, Gouverneur Morris, apparently shared earlier concerns raised by Connecticut's Roger Sherman; Morris successfully introduced a provision that states could not, without their consent, be deprived of their equal representation in the Senate. This remains the only entrenchment provision within the current amending clause.

When the delegates to the Constitutional Convention reported their work, it was clear that they had exceeded their mandate to revise the Articles of Confederation. Moreover, new Article VII specified that the Constitution would be ratified by conventions rather than by state legislatures. The success of this ratification is attributable to the better organization of the supporters of the Constitution, the Federalists; to the fact that they were advocating a positive remedy to ills that were generally recognized; and to the strength of their arguments. To date, the formal amending process that the convention developed remains unchanged; it has been used to adopt twenty-seven amendments.

One of the most prominent objections that Anti-Federalists made to the Constitution of 1787 was that it did not contain a Bill of Rights—an addition that Virginia's George Mason had advocated at the convention. Many scholars believe that the ability to adopt such a bill of rights (these first ten amendments were ratified in 1791) through the amending process helped head off a second convention that might have either perpetuated the nation's uncertainty or reversed some of the significant gains in federal powers that had been achieved under the new Constitution. The decision to include such amendments at the end of the document, rather than within the existing text, has continued to influence the way the document is read and understood.

See also Annapolis Convention; Articles of Confederation; Bill of Rights; Ratification of the Existing U.S. and/or Future U.S. Constitutions.

For Further Reading:
Butzner, Jane, comp. 1941. *Constitutional Chaff—Rejected Suggestions of the Constitutional Convention of 1787 with Explanatory Argument.* New York: Columbia University Press.

Farrand, Max, ed. 1966. *The Records of the Federal Convention.* 4 vols. New Haven, CT: Yale University Press.

Solberg, Winton, ed. 1958. *The Federal Convention and the Formation of the Union.* Indianapolis, IN: Bobbs-Merrill.

Vile, John R. 2002a. *A Companion to the United States Constitution and Its Amendments.* 3d ed. Westport, CT: Praeger.

———. 1992. *The Constitutional Amending Process in American Political Thought.* New York: Praeger.

❖ CONSTITUTIONAL CONVENTIONS ❖

The U.S. Constitution was drawn up by the delegates meeting at the Constitutional Convention of 1787. Article VII specified that the new Constitution would not go into effect until ratified by conventions in nine or more states. The delegates also delineated two convention mechanisms in Article V, the amending article. One provided that amendments could, at congressional specification, be ratified by conventions in three-fourths of the states. To date, this mechanism has been used only in the case of the Twenty-first Amendment repealing national alcoholic prohibition.

A second convention mechanism outlined in Article V was stimulated by fears of giving Congress a monopoly on the amending process and permitted two-thirds of the state legislatures to petition Congress to call a convention "for proposing Amendments." Although states have submitted hundreds of petitions for such a convention, to date, the necessary two-thirds of the states have not applied for either a general convention or a convention on a single specified topic (but see Van Sickle and Boughey 1990). In part because no Article V convention has ever been called, a host of unanswered questions continue to surround this process.

No question has dominated the discussion of the convention mechanism more than two interrelated issues: whether a convention must be general or whether it can be restricted to a single topic; and if such a convention is not limited, whether it might become a "runaway" body (Vile 1993b, 55–73). Those who believe that a convention cannot be limited believe that any other kind of convention would not be free to propose amendments in the manner that Article V appears to contemplate. Thus, they conclude that any state applications for a convention that are predicated on such limitations are invalid. As one such scholar argued, "Applications asking for something other than what is meant by Article V are nullities, and thirty-four times zero is zero" (C. Black 1979, 628). This position is bolstered by the fact that most nineteenth-century petitions for conventions appeared to contemplate a general convention rather than one limited to a specific topic.

Walter Dellinger has further argued against a limited convention on the basis that such conventions would allow states "to propose and ratify amendments that enhance their power at the expense of the national government" (Dellinger 1979, 1630), something that he believes is contrary to the intentions of those who wrote the Constitution. Dellinger argues:

States were empowered under Article V to *ratify* amendments; the power to *pro-*

pose amendments was lodged in two national bodies, Congress and a convention. The proceedings suggest that the framers did not want to permit enactment of amendments by a process of state proposal followed by state ratification without the substantive involvement of a national forum. (Dellinger 1979, 1630)

By contrast, a number of scholars have argued that an Article V convention could be limited. William Van Alstyne argued:

[A] generous construction of what suffices to present a valid application by a state for consideration of a particular subject or of a particular amendment in convention, is far more responsive to the anticipated use of Article V than a demanding construction that all but eliminates its use in response to specific, limited state dissatisfactions. (Van Alstyne 1978, 1303)

Similarly, Grover Rees III (1986) argued that the convention mechanism was designed to facilitate state amendments, and an interpretation that would force the states to risk all or nothing would not meet such an objective. Reflecting some reservations, the author of a book on the subject concluded that "a national convention is in all likelihood constitutionally limited to proposing amendments described in the state applications that generated the call" (Caplan 1988, 157). From a somewhat different angle, two other authors have concluded that there are various "political" safeguards, including the requirement that any proposed amendments be ratified by three-fourths of the state legislatures, that make a runaway convention unlikely (Weber and Perry 1989, 105–125).

Legislation proposed by Senators Sam Ervin and Orrin Hatch dealing with constitutional conventions has been predicated on the idea that states do have the authority to call limited conventions. Such legislation has also attempted to address a variety of other questions, including the length of time that petitions calling for a convention are valid; whether states have the power to rescind such petitions; how states would be represented at a convention;

whether a convention would vote by a simple majority or whether it would have to muster a two-thirds vote; and—related to whether conventions may be limited—whether Congress could refuse to submit amendments to the states for ratification, or whether courts might invalidate proposed amendments that appeared to exceed a limited convention call. It is likely that many of these issues will not be resolved unless and until an Article V convention is actually called.

Conventions are common at the state level, where they are frequently used to revise constitutions or propose new ones. The lessons of such conventions, some of which are limited by state law, are not, however, necessarily applicable at the national level (F. Heller 1982).

Significantly, in recent years a number of states have been concerned enough that Congress might feel obliged to call a convention upon the acceptance of a given number of state petitions that they have withdrawn their applications to Congress requesting such conventions, either on a specific topic (like the Balanced Budget Amendment) or for more generalized grievances (R. Lee 1999). There does not appear to be a judicial ruling as to whether such rescissions are valid.

See also Constitutional Convention of 1787; Jameson, John A.

For Further Reading:
Black, Charles L., Jr. 1979. "Amendment by a National Constitutional Convention: A Letter to a Senator." *Oklahoma Law Review* 32: 626–644.

Caplan, Russell L. 1988. *Constitutional Brinkmanship: Amending the Constitution by National Convention.* New York: Oxford University Press.

Dellinger, Walter. 1979. "The Recurring Question of the 'Limited' Constitutional Convention." *Yale Law Journal* 88: 1623–1640.

Heller, Francis H. 1982. "Limiting a Constitutional Convention: The State Precedents." *Cardozo Law Review* 3: 563–579.

Lee, Robert W. 1999. "Battling for the Constitution," 15 *The New American* (26 April), at *http://www.thenewamerican.com/tna/1999/04/vol5no09_constitution.htm.* Accessed 4/24/02.

Rees, Grover, III. 1986. "The Amendment Process and Limited Constitutional Conventions." *Benchmark* 2: 67–108.

Van Alstyne, William. 1978. "Does Article V Restrict the States to Calling Unlimited Conventions Only?—A Letter to a Colleague." *Duke Law Journal* 1978 (January): 1295–1306.

Van Sickle, Bruce M., and Lynn M. Boughey. 1990. "Lawful and Peaceful Revolution: Article V and Congress' Present Duty to Call a Convention for Proposing Amendments." *Hamline Law Review* 14 (Fall): 1–115.

Vile, John R. 1993b. *The Theory and Practice of Constitutional Change in America: A Collection of Original Source Materials.* New York: Peter Lang.

Weber, Paul J., and Barbara A. Perry. 1989. *Unfounded Fears: Myths and Realities of a Constitutional Convention.* New York: Praeger.

❖ CONSTITUTIONAL INTERPRETATION ❖

The United States prides itself on a written Constitution that is unchangeable by ordinary acts of legislation. Still, it is clear that far more changes have been effected in constitutional understandings through interpretations, especially by the judicial branch, than by constitutional amendment. This fact has even led one contemporary law professor to question the relevance of the constitutional amending process (Strauss 2001). Few areas have been more frequent or controversial subjects of inquiry in recent years than questions of constitutional interpretation. Some controversies center on the terminology, and others center on the hermeneutical, or interpretive, principles that should guide members of the judiciary or others who are called upon to apply the Constitution.

Terminologically, debate sometimes centers on a distinction between judicial activism and judicial restraint (Halpern and Lamb 1982; Wolfe 1991); at other times, it centers on a distinction between interpretivism and noninterpretivism (J. H. Ely 1980). Neither set of terms is altogether luminous.

When critics accuse judges of being too "activist," judges may well respond that they are simply enforcing the Constitution as they see it. Moreover, a judge might arguably exercise "restraint" by failing to heed constitutional mandates. This caveat noted, "activist" is a term frequently used to describe a judge who reaches out to deliver opinions in uncharted waters and gives little or no deference to past precedents or to legislative judgments. Such a jurist may argue that judicial activism is necessitated by the failure of the other two branches (A. Miller 1982). An advocate of judicial restraint, by contrast, would give issues maximum time to develop and would typically be respectful and deferential toward both precedents and determinations of constitutionality by other branches of the government. When the Warren Court was frequently criticized for being overly activist and, indeed, for judicially amending the Constitution, Justices Felix Frankfurter and John Marshall Harlan often counseled against getting unduly involved in "political questions" or unnecessarily overturning prior judicial or legislative judgments.

Another dimension in constitutional interpretation centers on the dichotomy between interpretivism and noninterpretivism. Interpretivists attempt to limit their decisions to those they can justify from within the confines of the constitutional text, refusing to give judicial solutions to questions that, in their opinion, the Constitution does not address. Frequently, interpretivists advocate the idea of "original intent." Although there are numerous versions of this principle, all ultimately attempt to answer questions of interpretation whenever possible by asking what the authors or ratifiers of a particular phrase in the Constitution understood or intended for it to mean. Noninterpretivists, by contrast, are likely to look beyond the text to considerations of policy, democracy, or justice, or with a view toward keeping the Constitution up to date. During the Reagan administration, there was a serious public debate on this subject between Attorney General Edwin Meese, an advocate of original intent, and Justice William Brennan, who thought that this interpretive principle was too narrow (see Rakove 1990). This debate also figured prominently in the confirmation hearings of Robert Bork, who, like Meese, was a strong advocate

of original intent (Bork 1990; for a critique of original intent, see Levy 1988).

Knowing that an individual is an advocate of judicial activism or restraint, or that such an individual is an interpretivist or a noninterpretivist, does not always allow one to predict how this individual will decide a given case. This is because everyone has supplementary notions about how much weight to give to words and how to interpret them, about what the historical record of given clauses means, about constitutional structures and relationships, about the need to defer to past precedents (the principle of *stare decisis*), and the like (see Bickel 1986; Bobbitt 1992; L. Goldstein 1991; Tribe and Dorf 1991).

The difficulty of the constitutional amending process undoubtedly prods the judiciary to be more creative than it might be if the process were easier. Overly creative interpretations might, in turn, make authors of amendments nervous about including broad or vague language in constitutional additions. At least part of the opposition to the Equal Rights Amendment appears to have been generated about questions as to how the amendment would be interpreted and applied.

See also Living Constitution; Relevance of Constitutional Amendments.

For Further Reading:

Bickel, Alexander. 1986. *The Least Dangerous Branch: The Supreme Court at the Bar of Politics.* 2d ed. New Haven, CT: Yale University Press.

Bobbitt, Philip. 1992. "Constitutional Interpretation." In *The Oxford Companion to the Supreme Court of the United States,* ed. Kermit L. Hall. New York: Oxford University Press.

Bork, Robert H. 1990. *The Tempting of America: The Political Seduction of the Law.* New York: Free Press.

Ely, John Hart. 1980. *Democracy and Distrust.* Cambridge, MA: Harvard University Press.

Fallon, Richard H., Jr. 2001. *Implementing the Constitution.* Cambridge, MA: Harvard University Press.

Goldstein, Leslie F. 1991. *In Defense of the Text: Democracy and Constitutional Theory.* Savage, MD: Rowman and Littlefield.

Halpern, Stephen C., and Charles M. Lamb, eds. 1982. *Supreme Court Activism and Restraint*. Lexington, MA: Lexington Books.

Levy, Leonard W. 1988. *Original Intent and the Framers' Constitution*. New York: Macmillan.

Miller, Arthur S. 1982. *Toward Increased Judicial Activism: The Political Role of the Supreme Court*. Westport, CT: Greenwood Press.

Murphy, Walter F., James E. Fleming, and Sotirios A. Barber. 1995. *American Constitutional Interpretation*. 2d ed. Westbury, NY: Foundation Press.

Rakove, Jack N., ed. 1990. *Interpreting the Constitution: The Debate over Original Intent*. Boston: Northeastern University Press.

Strauss, David A. 2001. "Commentary: The Irrelevance of Constitutional Amendments." *Harvard Law Review* 114 (March): 1457–1505.

Tribe, Laurence H., and Michael C. Dorf. 1991. *On Reading the Constitution*. Cambridge, MA: Harvard University Press.

Wolfe, Christopher. 1991. *Judicial Activism: Bulwark of Freedom or Precarious Security?* Pacific Grove, CA: Brooks/Cole.

❖ CONSTITUTIONAL STUPIDITIES ❖

The phrase "constitutional stupidities" served as the title of a law school forum, later compiled in a book, in which scholars responded to the question of which still active provisions in the U.S. Constitution were the "stupidest" or "most nonsensical" or "harmful" today. The resulting replies by constitutional scholars, who were initially asked to work independently of one another in coming up with their answers, may or may not reflect popular opinions, but they could easily point to areas of the Constitution that might be the subject of future amendments.

Akhil Reed Amar decided that the provisions of the electoral college, and the possibility of a president elected by a minority, were the stupidest. At least two scholars, William N. Eskridge Jr., and Suzanna Sherry pointed to the provision (unamendable, according to Article V, without a state's consent) guaranteeing states equal suffrage in the U.S. Senate regardless of population. Mark Graber pointed to what he considered to be the ambiguity of the necessary and proper clause in Article I, Section 8. Stephen M. Griffin and Mark Tushnet both nominated Article V of the Constitution, on the basis that the constitutional amending process outlined there is too difficult. Randall Kennedy focused on the provision that individuals seeking the presidency must be natural-born citizens. L. H. Larue singled out the provision allowing judges to serve "during good behavior" and thus for life; L. A. Powe Jr., focusing on the same provision, suggested that Supreme Court justices should serve for eighteen-year terms. Sanford Levinson focused on the provision of the Twelfth Amendment that permits elections for president that reach the U.S. House of Representatives to be decided by giving each state delegation, rather than each representative, a vote; he also expressed concern about the gap between the election of a new president and Congress and the time that these individuals actually take office. This issue was only partially addressed by the Twentieth Amendment.

Matthew Michael believed that individuals should not have to be thirty-five years of age to run for president and thought that this provision might serve to suppress interest in presidential elections among younger voters. Michael Stokes Paulsen pointed out that, under provisions of the existing Constitution, a vice president who was impeached by the House of Representatives, unlike a president in similar circumstances, would have the right to preside over his own trial in the U.S. Senate. Jeffrey Rosen focused on provisions that divided responsibility for assuring suffrage between the nation and the states rather than providing for uniformity. Laurence Tribe pointed to the second section of the Twenty-first Amendment repealing prohibition, arguing that it appeared to make an individual's violation of a state's liquor laws (like keeping a slave) an individual constitutional offense rather than simply allowing states to outlaw such importation on their own. A number of other scholars suggested that concepts like separation of powers or provisions protecting the rights of criminal defendants were not working together in the way that they should, that the whole exercise was too much like a parlor game, or that the whole idea of picking out a particular provision for treatment underestimated the postmodern understanding of the role of minimal written provisions within such a document.

Again, the purpose of this study was not to propose amendments, but the multiple answers certainly point to scholarly concerns that might eventually find their way into amending proposals.

For Further Reading:

Eskridge, William N., Jr., and Sanford Levinson. 1998. *Constitutional Stupidities, Constitutional Tragedies.* New York: New York University Press.

❖ CONSTITUTIONS, PROPOSED NEW U.S. ❖

See Alternative U.S. Constitutions, Proposed.

❖ CONTRACT WITH AMERICA ❖

In an attempt to derive a mandate from the 1994 midterm congressional elections, Republican candidates for the House of Representatives, led by Georgia Representative and soon-to-be Speaker of the House Newt Gingrich, drew up a Contract with America that outlined an ambitious program of legislative and constitutional reform (Wilcox 1995, 69–71; Gillespie and Schellhas 1994). Modeling their agenda on Franklin Roosevelt's broad program of an earlier day, the Republicans hoped to adopt many of these reforms within the first 100 days if they proved successful in the general election. Proposals included adoption of a balanced budget amendment, a legislatively mandated line-item presidential veto (rather than a constitutional amendment), and an amendment to provide for congressional term limits. Although not in the contract, Republicans also promised prompt consideration of an amendment to restore prayer in public schools. One critic subsequently noted that Congress faced a "glut of amendments" (Ornstein 1994, 5), and another

referred to "amendment fever" (Sullivan 1995).

Although the 1994 election brought Republican control of the House of Representatives for the first time since 1952 (as well as control of the Senate, which Republicans kept until 2001, and regained in the elections of 2002), there are those who dispute that the Contract with America was responsible for this victory (Wilcox 1995, 211), and Republican victories in the House did not translate into a Republican victory in the subsequent 1996 presidential contest when Bill Clinton was reelected (the Contract with America appeared to have had almost nothing to do with George W. Bush's election in the 2000 presidential contest). Moreover, once in power, Republicans realized that bold legislative initiatives often face considerable opposition and that constitutional amendments are particularly difficult to enact. Although successful in getting the balanced budget amendment through the House in the first 100 days, Republicans were one vote short in the Senate. In the House itself, Republicans split over the appropriate length of time for limited congressional terms and whether the limit should apply to the total number of years or the number of consecutive years in office. The year after the Contract with America, the Christian Coalition proposed a Contract with the American Family (Reed 1995). Among other proposals, it advocated a Religious Equality Amendment. However, it focused on legislation rather than on an amendment as a way of limiting abortion. None of the amendments proposed in the Contract with America have yet been proposed by the requisite congressional majorities.

See also Balanced Budget Amendment; Congress, Term Limits; Prayer in Public Schools; Presidency, Veto Power of.

For Further Reading:

Gillespie, Ed, and Bob Schellhas, eds. 1994. *Contract with America: The Bold Plan by Rep. Newt Gingrich, Rep. Dick Armey, and the House Republicans to Change the Nation.* New York: Random House.

Ornstein, Norman J., and Amy L. Schenkenberg. 1995. "The 1995 Congress: The First Hundred Days and Beyond." *Political Science Quarterly* 110 (Summer): 183–206.

Redinger, Paul. 1996. "The Faltering Revolution." *ABA Journal* 82 (February): 56–59.

Reed, Ralph. 1995. *Contract with the American Family: A Bold Plan by Christian Coalition to Strengthen the Family and Restore Common-Sense Values.* Nashville, TN: Moorings.

Sullivan, Kathleen M. 1995. "Constitutional Constancy: Why Congress Should Cure Itself of Amendment Fever." *Record of the Bar of the City of New York* 50 (November): 724–735.

Wilcox, Clyde. 1995. *The Latest American Revolution? The 1994 Elections and Their Implications for Governance.* New York: St. Martin's Press.

❖ CONTRACTS CLAUSE ❖

Article I, Section 10 of the U.S. Constitution provides that "no State shall . . . pass any Law impairing the Obligations of Contracts." This was a much-litigated clause in early American history (B. Wright 1938) that was strictly construed to restrict state regulatory powers (in, for example, the cases of *Fletcher v. Peck* (1810), preventing a state from renouncing a sale of land that appears to have been influenced by fraud, and *Dartmouth College v. Woodward* (1819), declaring that a college charter granted by an English king prior to U.S. independence was a contract that a state could not abridge. The clause has been interpreted far more liberally in the twentieth century (for example, *Home Building and Loan Association v. Blaisdell* (1934), upholding a Minnesota Mortgage Moratorium Law suspending debt payments during the Great Depression).

From 1884 to 1889, a time during which the Supreme Court was beginning to rely increasingly on the idea of substantive due process rather than on the contracts clause to protect property rights, a Maryland representative, Louis McComas, introduced several proposals to circumvent the contracts clause. His amendment would have voided any promises a state may have made to a corporation exempting it from taxes.

Perhaps because it was thought that the multiplicity of interests at the national level would serve as adequate protection, there is no provision comparable to the contracts clause limiting the national government (Rossum and Tarr 1999, 390). In 1871 New York Democratic Representative Clarkson Potter offered an amendment prohibiting Congress from chartering corporations or impairing the obligation of contracts. Similarly, in 1982, Republican Representative Robert Walker of Pennsylvania offered two resolutions prohibiting Congress from adopting any laws to abridge the right of citizens to enter into contracts, except when this was necessary to preserve vital and pressing governmental interests (H.J. Res. 466).

A number of recent proposals for new constitutions authored by individuals with libertarian beliefs have sought to strengthen the rights of contracting parties.

For Further Reading:

Rossum, Ralph A., and G. Alan Tarr. 1999. *American Constitutional Law: The Structure of Government.* 5th ed. New York: St. Martin's Press.

Wright, Benjamin F. 1938. *The Contract Clause of the Constitution.* Cambridge, MA: Harvard University Press.

❖ *COOK V. GRALIKE* (2001) ❖

This U.S. Supreme Court decision affirmed two lower federal court decisions by invalidating an amendment to the Missouri Constitution, enacted in the wake of the U.S. Supreme Court decision in *U.S. Term Limits, Inc. v. Thornton* (1995). There the Court had invalidated an Arkansas law keeping the names of congressional candidates off the ballot if they had served for two terms in the U.S. Senate or three terms in the U.S. House of Representatives. The contested Missouri amendment instructed its U.S. representatives to press for an amendment to the U.S. Constitution advocating term limits and provided that, in appropriate cases, electoral ballots indicate either that such representatives had disregarded such instructions or that candidates had declined to support such limits. Justice John Paul Stevens wrote the majority decision of the Court on behalf of four other justices and himself (two others concurred in most parts of the opinion), but all other members of the Court concurred in the result in this case, leaving little likelihood of reversal in the near future.

Missouri had justified its actions with a variety of arguments, including the argument that the power it had exercised was reserved to the states under the Tenth Amendment. It also argued that states could exercise under their power in Article I, Section 4, Clause 1, to regulate the "Times, Places and Manner of holding elections for Senators and Representatives." Justice Stevens rejected both arguments.

Acknowledging that states appeared to "instruct" their representatives in early American history, Stevens noted that none of these examples "was coupled with an express legal sanction for disobedience" (*Cook* 2001, 520). Moreover, absent evidence that states had previously exercised such "legally binding" instructions, this could not be a power that was reserved to the states by the Tenth Amendment. Stevens further noted that, in formulating what is today the First Amendment, Congress specifically rejected a proposal that would have allowed states "to instruct their representatives" (*Cook* 2001, 521).

Stevens also rejected the idea that states could exercise their control under their power to regulate the "times, places and manner" of elections. Citing *U.S. Term Limits*, Stevens argued that these provisions were designed to enable states to assure the honesty and integrity of elections and not as a means of dictating electoral outcomes or favoring one class of candidates over another. Further citing lower court decisions that recognized the ballot statements to be "pejorative," Stevens ruled that such attempts to "dictate electoral outcomes" were simply "not authorized by the Elections Clause" (*Cook* 2001, 526).

There were a number of concurring opinions. Justice Anthony Kennedy indicated that legislators were responsible to the people of a state rather than to their state governments. State legislatures had the right to petition the people, but not to "instruct" them. Consistent with his dissent in *U.S. Term Limits, Inc. v. Thornton*, Justice Clarence Thomas indicated that, although Missouri had not rested its case on the issue, he was still not convinced that states could not add to the qualifications of its

representatives. Chief Justice William Rehnquist, in an opinion joined by Sandra Day O'-Connor, would have rested his decision on the First Amendment, claiming that a candidate has the right "to have his name appear [on a ballot] unaccompanied by pejorative language required by the State" (*Cook* 2001, 530–531).

This decision could conceivably weaken some of the pressure on elected representatives to push for adoption of a term limits amendment, or, indeed, for others. Voters, of course, retain their power to use the ballot box to punish legislators who will not sponsor acts of legislation or amendments that the people favor.

See also Constituent Instructions for Amending Constitutions.

For Further Reading:
Cook v. Gralike, 531 U.S. 510 (2001).

❖ CORPORATIONS ❖

It is doubtful that the United States could have developed economically in the same manner as it has without legal recognition for corporations. Nonetheless, there has often been a perceived conflict in American history between the rights and privileges granted to corporations and those granted to ordinary citizens.

Americans have long been wary of privileges accorded to corporations, especially when these involve grants of monopoly power. The U.S. Constitution did not specifically mention corporations. When ratification of the U.S. Constitution was being considered, Thomas Jefferson wrote to James Madison to suggest that one of his concerns about the document was the absence of a bill of rights that would, among other things, provide for "restriction against monopolies" (Mason and Stephenson 2002, 421). No such amendment was adopted. Partly as a consequence, in the controversy that developed during the administration of George Washington over the constitutionality of incorporating a national bank, neither Jefferson nor Madison succeeded in forbidding the national government from creating such corporations.

Persuaded of its constitutionality and utility

by Secretary of the Treasury Alexander Hamilton, President Washington and the Federalist Congress incorporated a national bank. The U.S. Supreme Court upheld the constitutionality of the bank in *McCulloch v. Maryland* (1819). That same year the Court decided *Dartmouth College v. Woodward,* in which it upheld a charter issued to Dartmouth College even before the American nation had been formed and recognized corporations as artificial persons with legal rights. However, in a popular decision in *Gibbons v. Ogden* (1824), the U.S. Supreme Court under John Marshall used the clause giving Congress control over interstate and foreign commerce to strike down a grant of a monopoly that New York had given to a steamboat company that would have impeded such commerce. Moreover, President Andrew Jackson, whose followers viewed him as a representative of the "common man," later renewed concerns over the power of monied interests by challenging the legitimacy of the national bank. Similarly, in *Charles River Bridge v. Warren Bridge* (1837), Chief Justice Roger Taney, a Jackson appointee, issued a majority decision limiting the scope of corporate rights to those explicitly delineated in corporate contracts. Noting the absence of such specific language in the grant to the first bridge company, he thereby refused to prevent Massachusetts from granting a charter to a second bridge company in proximity to a toll bridge, with which it would compete.

Although this was not its primary purpose, the ratification of the Fourteenth Amendment in 1868 appeared to open up the possibility of renewed protection for corporations, which were becoming increasingly large and important to the development of the postbellum economy. In an unsubstantiated assertion, prominent attorney Roscoe Conkling argued in *San Mateo Co. v. Southern Pacific Railroad* (1885) that one of the intentions of the joint committee on which he had served in Congress to draft the amendment was to protect such corporations (Vile 2001, 131–132). Perhaps influenced by his arguments, in a companion case, *Santa Clara County v. Southern Pacific Railroad* (1886), the Supreme Court ruled that "[t]he court does not wish to hear argument on

the question whether . . . the Fourteenth Amendment . . . applies to these corporations. We are all of the opinion that it does" (*Santa Clara County* 1886, 396). Although this position represented the dominant view of the Court, twentieth-century Supreme Court Justices Hugo Lafayette Black and William O. Douglas later challenged it. Black's dissenting opinion in *Connecticut General Life Insurance Co. v. Johnson* (1938) was especially noteworthy.

Initially, most attempts to regulate corporations were initiated at the state level. This changed with the advent of the New Deal in Franklin Roosevelt's first administration. The Securities Act of 1933 and the Securities Exchange Act of 1934 introduced increased federal regulation of corporations, but much regulation also continues at the state level (R. Hamilton 1987, 8–9).

In the years preceding and following the *Santa Clara County* decision, the U.S. Supreme Court often showed greater solicitude for the rights of corporations than for the rights of African Americans who had previously been enslaved. At a time when representatives of the populist and progressive movements were often calling for greater regulation, if not nationalization, of major corporate entities like railroads, the Court was expanding its interpretation of the due process clauses of the Fifth and Fourteenth Amendments so as to limit the scope of state and national regulations of corporate entities. Thus, in *United States v. E.C. Knight Co.* (1895), the Court ruled that the Sherman Antitrust Act of 1890 did not apply to a purchase of sugar refineries that left a single company in almost complete control of the industry—the Court thought that such regulation was a local matter with only an indirect effect on commerce. Similarly, in *Lochner v. New York* (1905), the Court struck down a state regulation of the hours of bakery workers as an interference with "liberty of contract." Moreover, many states were eliminating statutory restrictions to induce corporations to incorporate within their states (R. Hamilton 1987, 6–7).

Four proposals had been offered in the 1880s to enable states to tax corporations, even in cases in which such states had provided tax exemptions when granting corporate charters.

Another proposal would have prohibited state grants or loans to such corporations. Several other amendments were introduced at the turn of the century, most by New Jersey Democratic Representative Allan McDermott, to give Congress control over corporations.

Such control was eventually exercised by the national government in the New Deal period. Although the Supreme Court initially resisted such control, it eventually recognized increased federal powers under the commerce and taxing clauses. With post–New Deal latitudinarian constructions of such congressional powers, the national government has exercised increasing control over corporations. Such powers were increasingly widened to achieve expanded social objectives as diverse as "environmental protection, consumerism, minority employment, women's rights, and health and safety" (Mayer 1990, 601) during President Lyndon Johnson's "Great Society" initiatives in the 1960s and their aftermath. As federal regulations have multiplied, corporations have, in turn, increasingly used their status as legal "persons" to claim protections under the Bill of Rights, most provisions of which have also been applied to the states via the due process clause of the Fourteenth Amendment. The primary focus of existing cases recognizing corporate rights has centered on:

> first amendment guarantees of political speech, commercial speech, and negative free speech rights; fourth amendment safeguards against unreasonable regulatory searches; fifth amendment double jeopardy and liberty rights; and sixth and seventh amendment entitlements to trial by jury. (Lexis/Nexis on-line summary of Mayer 1990 article)

Decrying this trend, which has shielded corporations from much legislation, consumer advocate and later Green Party candidate for president in 2000 Ralph Nader, and Carl J. Mayer, then a Harvard law student, wrote an article in 1988 proposing an amendment to limit corporate use of such rights (Nader and Mayer 1988, 31). As a professor at Hofstra Law School, Mayer later suggested the following language:

> This Amendment enshrines the sanctity of the individual and establishes the presumption that individuals are entitled to a greater measure of constitutional protection than corporations. For purposes of the foregoing amendments, corporations are not considered to be "persons," nor are they entitled to the same Bill of Rights protections as individuals. Such protections may only be conferred by state legislatures or in popular referenda. (Mayer 1990, 661)

A number of recent proposals for new U.S. constitutions have included provisions that seek to trim both large corporations and expanding governments.

For Further Reading:

Goodnow, Frank J. 1911. *Social Reform and the Constitution*. New York: Macmillan Co. Reprint, New York: Burt Franklin, 1970.

Hamilton, Robert W. 1987. *The Law of Corporations*. St. Paul, MN: West.

Mason, Alpheus T., and Donald Grier Stephenson Jr. 2002. *American Constitutional Law: Introductory Essays and Selected Cases*. 13th ed. Upper Saddle River, NJ: Prentice Hall.

Mayer, Carl J. 1990. "Personalizing the Impersonal: Corporations and the Bill of Rights." *Hastings Law Journal* 41 (March): 577–667.

Nader, Ralph, and Carl J. Mayer. 1988. "Corporations Are Not Persons." *The New York Times* (9 April), sect. 1, p. 31.

Vile, John R. 2001. *Great American Lawyers: An Encyclopedia*. 2 vols. Santa Barbara: ABC-CLIO.

❖ CORWIN AMENDMENT ❖

From the election of President Abraham Lincoln in November 1860 through the session of the lame-duck Congress that met from December 1860 to March 1861, a large number of proposals were introduced to preserve the Union and avert war. These included a series of proposals known as the Crittenden Compromise. Also, the Washington Peace Convention met in February 1861 to accomplish the same end. The Corwin Amendment was the only compromise actually approved by the requisite majorities in Congress and is one of six amendments not subsequently ratified by the requisite number of states.

In December 1860 outgoing President James Buchanan proposed an "explanatory amendment" that was actually a series of three proposals. It would give "express recognition of the right of property in slaves in the States where it now exists or may hereafter exist"; recognize the right to own slaves within the territories (thus legitimizing the 1857 decision in *Scott v. Sandford* that the incoming Republican president had opposed); and recognize slave owners' rights to have escaped slaves returned to them (J. Richardson 1908, 5:638).

The House of Representatives subsequently created a committee of thirty-three (one representative from each state), with Republican Thomas Corwin of Ohio as chairman, to address this issue. The Senate created a committee of thirteen, chaired by Democrat Lazarus Powell of Kentucky, with a similar aim (R. Lee 1961, 7–8). The so-called Corwin Amendment actually appears to have originated in the latter committee and was apparently the product of New York Republican William Seward (soon to be Lincoln's secretary of state), who had access to the new president. The amendment was introduced in the House committee by Massachusetts Republican Charles Francis Adams, son of former president John Quincy Adams and a confidant of Seward's (R. Lee 1961, 17). In the final form proposed by Representative Corwin, the amendment provided for an entrenchment clause that would guarantee the existence of slavery within its contemporary limits: "No amendment shall ever be made to the Constitution which will authorize or give to Congress power to abolish or interfere, within any State, with the domestic institutions thereof, including that of persons held to labor or service by the laws of the said State" (R. Lee 1961, 22).

On the first try, on 28 February 1861, the House fell short of the necessary majority, voting 123 to 71 for the measure. The next vote, held the following day, was 133 to 65. The Senate proposed the amendment by a vote of 24 to 12 on 3 March 1861 (R. Lee 1961, 23–24). In a highly unusual move not required

by the U.S. Constitution, outgoing President James Buchanan signed the amendment (Bernstein with Agel 1993, 91).

In his first inaugural address, President Lincoln (who was willing to permit slavery in the South but adamantly opposed to its expansion in the territories, as the Crittenden Compromise would have allowed) indicated his support for the amendment. He said, "Holding such a provision to now be implied constitutional law, I have no objection to its being made express and irrevocable" (J. Richardson 1908, 6:11). One of his central concerns, shared by other congressional supporters of the amendment, appears to have been to keep border states, in which slavery was permitted, within the Union.

Ohio ratified the Corwin amendment in May 1861; Maryland and Illinois followed in January and February 1862. By then, however, it was clear that the compromise had not been enough to keep the South in the Union. The Thirteenth Amendment, which would be ratified after the war, did not protect the institution of slavery but abolished it. The Corwin Amendment continues to raise questions about whether there are any unstated substantive limits on what can be added to the Constitution (Brandon 1995).

See also Crittenden Compromise; Peace Convention.

For Further Reading:

Bernstein, Richard B., with Jerome Agel. 1993. *Amending America: If We Love the Constitution So Much, Why Do We Keep Trying to Change It?* New York: Random House.

Brandon, Mark E. 1995. "The 'Original' Thirteenth Amendment and the Limits to Formal Constitutional Change." In *Responding to Imperfection: The Theory and Practice of Constitutional Amendment,* ed. Sanford Levinson. Princeton, NJ: Princeton University Press.

Keogh, Stephen. 1987. "Formal and Informal Constitutional Lawmaking in the United States in the Winter of 1860–1861." *Journal of Legal History* 8 (December): 275–299.

Lee, R. Alton. 1961. "The Corwin Amendment in the Secession Crisis." *Ohio Historical Quarterly* 70 (January): 1–26.

Richardson, James E., ed. 1908. *A Compilation of the Messages and Papers of the Presidents, 1789–1908.* 11 vols. n.p.: Bureau of National Literature and Art.

❖ COST-OF-LIVING ADJUSTMENTS ❖

Automatic cost-of-living adjustments (COLAs) became popular during the inflationary 1960s and 1970s, and they were added to the Old Age and Survivors Insurance Program in 1972 (Watson 1985, 628). Although they help protect workers and pensioners against inflation, COLAs also contribute to increased prices. Democratic Representative Bill Burlison of Missouri offered a proposal on 13 June 1977 (H.J. Res. 514) to prohibit automatic increases in the prices of goods or services under any law, contract, or other authority. Congress adopted a law in 1989 that extended relatively automatic COLAs to its members. Subsequent U.S. District Court and U.S. Circuit Court decisions in *Boehner v. Anderson* (1992, 1994) have declared that this law did not violate the Twenty-seventh Amendment, which provided that members of Congress could not give themselves a pay raise that applied before an intervening election.

See also *Boehner v. Anderson.*

For Further Reading:

Watson, Richard A. 1985. *Promise and Performance of American Democracy.* 5th ed. New York: John Wiley & Sons.

❖ COUNCIL OF CENSORS ❖

At the time the U.S. Constitution was written, those states that had amending procedures used one of three means—legislative action, conventions, or a council of censors (Traynor 1927, 61–62). Pennsylvania and Vermont employed the third of these mechanisms. Thus, the Pennsylvania state constitution of 1776 called for a council consisting of two persons from each of the state's cities and counties to meet every seventh year "to enquire whether the constitution has been preserved inviolate in every part; and whether the legislative and executive branches of government have performed their duty as guardian of the people" (Meador 1898, 265). The council would also check into other matters of government and have the authority—the only such power specified in the constitution—to call a convention to propose constitutional amendments.

The Pennsylvania Council of Censors met as scheduled in 1783, but its deliberations were torn by partisan controversy *(Records of the Council of Censors, 1783–1784).* A majority recommended establishing a bicameral rather than a unicameral legislature. It also proposed substituting a governor with veto power for the existing president and council, providing independence for state judges, and eliminating the council of censors mechanism (Meador 1898, 288). Because two-thirds of the council did not agree, however, no convention was called to accomplish these purposes.

The second Pennsylvania Council of Censors was scheduled to meet in 1790, but the year before the legislature called for a constitutional convention. It proposed a constitution that incorporated most of the suggestions made by the earlier council. The new constitution, which was subsequently adopted, omitted the council of censors mechanism. A commentator noted that the citizens had "become wearied with so unwieldy a piece of political machinery" (Meador 1898, 298). The provision remained in the Vermont constitution until 1869 (Meador 1898, 266).

In *Federalist* No. 50, James Madison opposed plans for periodic appeals to the people for constitutional change that Thomas Jefferson had advocated, citing the experience of Pennsylvania. He observed that the state's council had been split into violent factions, consisting in part of individuals who had served in the very government they were called upon to assess. He concluded that "this censorial body, therefore, proves at the same time, by its researches, the existence of the disease, and by its example, the inefficacy of the remedy" (Hamilton, Madison, and Jay 1961, 320).

For Further Reading:

Hamilton, Alexander, James Madison, and John Jay. 1787–1788. *The Federalist Papers*. Reprint, New York: New American Library, 1961.

Meador, Lewis H. 1898. "The Council of Censors." *Pennsylvania Magazine of History and Biography* 22: 265–300.

Records of the Council of Censors. 1783–1784. Journal vols. 1–3. Division of Archives and Manuscripts, Pennsylvania Historical and Museum Commission.

Traynor, Roger J. 1927. *The Amending System of the United States Constitution, an Historical and Legal Analysis*. Ph.D. dissertation, University of California.

❖ COUNCIL OF STATE GOVERNMENTS ❖

In *Baker v. Carr* (1962), the Supreme Court declared that it would no longer consider issues of state legislative apportionment to be "political questions." This decision stirred considerable controversy, including a drive for a constitutional convention led by Republican Senator Everett Dirksen of Illinois. The Council of State Governments issued one of the strongest responses when the General Assembly of States, which it sponsored, proposed three amendments at its December 1962 meeting (Committee on Federal State Relations 1963; for further discussion, see Vile 1991c, 97–100).

The first proposal would have made the amending process easier by allowing two-thirds of the state legislatures to propose amendments by submitting identical texts of such amendments to Congress; this proposal would also have eliminated the convention method of ratifying amendments, thus leaving such power exclusively in the hands of state legislatures. The second proposal, clearly aimed at *Baker v. Carr*, would have declared that "no provision of this Constitution, or any amendment thereto, shall restrict or limit any state in the apportionment of representation in its legislature" (Committee 1963, 9). Much along the lines of the Eleventh Amendment, this proposal also would have restricted judicial juris-

diction over this issue. The third proposal would have created a Court of the Union consisting of the chief justice from each state. This court, whose decisions would be final, would hear petitions from state legislatures concerning issues alleged to be reserved to the states.

The scholarly reaction to these proposals was quite negative. William Swindler (1963) of the College of William and Mary saw these proposals as an attempt to return to a government like that under the Articles of Confederation. Focusing on the proposed reform of the amending process, Yale's Charles Black called the amendments "A Threatened Disaster" (1963); Princeton's Alpheus Mason called the amendments the "'Dis-Union' Amendments" (1964, 199). The title of a popular magazine article summarized such sentiments when it proclaimed, "Seventeen States Vote to Destroy Democracy as We Know It" (Morgan 1963).

Although the proposals by the Council of State Governments failed, and the specific issue of state legislative apportionment by population no longer appears to be of great concern (matters arising from racial gerrymandering continue to receive attention), issues of federalism continue to stir controversy. By 1990, largely prompted by decisions in *Garcia v. San Antonio Metropolitan Transit Authority* (1985) and *South Carolina v. Baker* (1988), fifteen states had adopted resolutions proposing amendments to redress the balance between the state and national governments (Tolchin 1990, A12).

In October 1995 states held a States' Federalism Summit in which they gave favorable consideration to a proposal that would have allowed for what are described as "state-initiated amendments." Such amendments would reverse the current amending process. Under this plan three-fourths of the state legislatures, which are currently limited to proposing constitutional conventions, could propose amendments, which would then have to be ratified by two-thirds majorities in Congress. This proposal was discussed again at the 1997 National Conference of State Legislatures but not adopted (Kincaid 2000, 15).

For Further Reading:

Black, Charles L., Jr. 1963. "The Proposed

Amendment of Article V: A Threatened Disaster." *Yale Law Journal* 72 (April): 957–966.

Committee on Federal State Relations. 1963. "Amending the Constitution to Strengthen the States in the Federal System." *State Government* 10 (Winter): 10–15.

Kincaid, John. 2000. "Constitutional Proposals from the States." *Insights on Law & Society* 1 (Fall): 15.

Mason, Alpheus T. 1964. *The States' Rights Debate: Antifederalism and the Constitution.* Englewood Cliffs, NJ: Prentice-Hall.

Morgan, Thomas J. 1963. "Seventeen States Vote to Destroy Democracy as We Know It." *Look* 27 (3 December): 76–88.

Swindler, William. 1963. "The Current Challenge to Federalism: The Confederating Proposals." *Georgetown Law Review* 52 (Fall): 1–41.

Tolchin, Mark. 1990. "Fifteen States Rally behind Calls for Amendment to Gain More Powers." *New York Times,* 26 June, A-12, col. 3–6.

Vile, John R. 1991c. *Rewriting the United States Constitution: An Examination of Proposals from Reconstruction to the Present.* New York: Praeger.

❖ COURT OF GENERATIONS AMENDMENT ❖

See Tonn, Bruce E.

❖ COURT OF THE UNION ❖

See Council of State Governments.

❖ COURT-PACKING PLAN ❖

Proposed constitutional amendments often represent dissatisfaction with judicial decisions, but amendments are certainly not the only way that such dissatisfaction can be expressed. One of the most dramatic confrontations between the presidency and the judiciary took place with the introduction of President Franklin D. Roosevelt's so-called court-packing plan. He announced this plan in a fireside address in February 1937.

Almost from the time he assumed the presi-

dency, Roosevelt realized that the Supreme Court had the power to scuttle many of his New Deal programs. On 27 May 1935, or Black Monday as it came to be called, the Court delivered three unanimous opinions that struck at various New Deal programs. In *Louisville Joint Stock Land Bank v. Radford,* it invalidated a bill providing mortgage relief to farmers; in *Humphrey's Executor v. United States,* it ruled that the president could not remove members of independent regulatory agencies; and in *Schechter Poultry Corporation v. United States,* it invalidated the National Industrial Recovery Act. The next year the Court continued its attack on the New Deal, albeit by much closer votes, by invalidating the Agricultural Adjustment Act, the National Bituminous Coal Act, and a New York minimum-wage law.

Although Roosevelt was increasingly concerned about the Court's ability to stymie the New Deal, he bided his time through the 1936 election, hoping to keep the focus on other issues. After winning this election in a record landslide, Roosevelt and his aides directed significant attention to the Court issue, exploring a number of options before finally settling on the court-packing plan.

One of the most obvious paths that Roosevelt could have taken would have been to propose one or more constitutional amendments to reverse judicial decisions or to curb judicial decision making. There was no shortage of proposals, some of which dated back to the Progressive Era. These included plans to expand congressional powers under the general welfare clause, to require more than a simple majority of the Supreme Court to declare legislation unconstitutional, to require that judges retire at age seventy, and to allow the attorney general to seek early rulings on the constitutionality of congressional legislation and then permit the next session of Congress to override adverse decisions (Kyvig 1989, 471–473).

Such proposals encountered a number of obstacles. These included the difficulty of deciding on satisfactory language that would grant Congress the necessary power without entrusting it with dangerous authority; the anticipated difficulty of ratification and the time that even a successful ratification might take; the fear that the courts could ultimately restrictively interpret any new amendments; and the fact that if Roosevelt supported an amendment to expand federal powers, "it might seem tantamount to conceding that he had been wrong and the Supreme Court right in their dispute over the constitutionality of New Deal measures" (Leuchtenburg 1995, 111). Roosevelt appears to have been especially influenced by the example of the child labor amendment, which had been proposed by Congress but stymied in the state legislatures. Roosevelt was also concerned that the Liberty League would be able to muster effective opposition to any proposed amendments at the state level (Kyvig 1989).

Working with Attorney General Homer Cummings (who, in turn, appears to have been influenced by Princeton political science professor Edwin S. Corwin), Roosevelt came up with a plan. Ironically, the central plank of this plan had been supported by one of the sitting conservative justices, James McReynolds, when he had served as Woodrow Wilson's attorney general (Leuchtenburg 1995, 120). This plan would have allowed the president to add an additional Supreme Court justice, up to fifteen justices, for any justice with ten years or more of service who did not retire at age seventy. It also provided for additions to lower courts and for expediting judicial work.

Roosevelt justified his plan as a means of helping the aging justices (often contemporaneously referred to as "the nine old men") keep up with their work, but the political implications of the plan were too apparent to hide. In a March fireside chat, Roosevelt compared the three branches of the federal government to three horses, one of which was pulling in the wrong direction (R. Jackson 1941, 340–351). Chief Justice Charles Evans Hughes wrote a letter to Congress assuring its members that the Court was not falling behind in its work. The Senate Judiciary Committee subsequently issued a report that was quite critical of the president's plan, but it was probably the unexpected death of Roosevelt's Senate floor leader, Joe Robinson, that doomed it.

Within months of the proposal of the court-packing plan, however, the Court issued several decisions upholding New Deal measures.

Thus, the decision in *West Coast Hotel v. Parrish* (1937) (which may have been written, although not issued, previous to the plan (G. White 2000, 201)), and the one coming two weeks later in *National Labor Relations Board v. Jones & Laughlin Steel Corp.*, appeared to mark a judicial shift—contemporaneously dubbed the "shift in time that saved nine." Justice Owen Roberts, always a swing vote, appears to have deserted the conservative "Four Horsemen of the Apocalypse" on the Court, and thereafter the Supreme Court upheld fairly expansive federal powers. Scholars still dispute whether the court-packing plan led to this shift, with a recent study by G. Edward White suggesting that the story of this incident has been shaped by the winners so as to conflate developments that had been taking place, and that continued to take place over a number of decades into a simpler, if not simplistic, narrative based on the behaviorist view that judges simply decide on what the law is according to their ideologies rather than according to fundamental principles (White 2000, 302–312). He further argues that "[t]he Court-packing crisis was more of a symptom than a cause of the early twentieth-century 'constitutional revolution'" (White 2000, 305). However the events are ultimately interpreted, many scholarly observers at the time thought that Roosevelt lost his court-packing battle but won the war for the soul of the Court.

Scholars continue to debate the consequences of Roosevelt's strategy. The changes signaled, if not inaugurated, by the Court's shift in 1937 and thereafter certainly seem as consequential as many that had previously been made by constitutional amendments. Bruce Ackerman (1996), who favors many of the developments that the New Deal initiated, argues that this shift marks one of three major "constitutional moments" in U.S. history. David Kyvig believes that Roosevelt may have overestimated the difficulty of the amending process and laments the lack of a "specific constitutional sanction" for the New Deal (1989, 481). Changes not incorporated within the constitutional text are generally more malleable than those that are so incorporated.

See also Ackerman, Bruce; Living Constitution.

For Further Reading:

Ackerman, Bruce. 1996. *We the People: Transformation.* Cambridge, MA: Harvard University Press.

Jackson, Robert H. 1941. *The Struggle for Judicial Supremacy.* New York: Vintage Books.

Kyvig, David E. 1989. "The Road Not Taken: FDR, the Supreme Court and Constitutional Amendment." *Political Science Quarterly* 104 (Fall): 463–481.

Leuchtenburg, William E. 1995. *The Supreme Court Reborn: The Constitutional Revolution in the Age of Roosevelt.* New York: Oxford University Press.

White, G. Edward. 2000. *The Constitution and the New Deal.* Cambridge, MA: Harvard University Press.

❖ COURTS ❖

See Judiciary entries.

❖ CRAM, RALPH (1863–1942) ❖

Ralph Cram offered one of the most iconoclastic schemes of constitutional reform to be proposed in the twentieth century (Vile 1992, 75–78) in a book entitled *The End of Democracy* (1937). Cram was a noted architect whose works, often patterned on medieval structures, included the Cathedral Church of St. John the Divine in New York City (Shand-Tucci 1975).

As the title of his book indicates, Cram was a critic of modern, or what he called "low," democracy. In its place he proposed substituting a "high democracy" or an "aristocratic republic" (Cram 1937, 19), which is what he believed the American framers had intended. Indeed, by extending democracy and increasing governmental powers, the Fourteenth through Nineteenth Amendments had elevated the masses over individuals of character who could exercise true leadership. The result was "quite a new world where quantitative have taken the place of qualitative values and the tabloid type of man controls all things" (Cram 1937, 93). In such a situation, the solid middle class on which democracy should be based had become "the Forgotten Class" (Cram 1937, 94).

To restore this middle class, existing "*political* organization" needed to be replaced by a new "*functional* organization, representation and control" (Cram 1937, 120). Cram advocated a corporate state, which he described as "the substitution for professional politicians chosen on a partizan [sic] or territorial basis, of nonpolitical, non-partizan [sic] delegates or representatives made up of voluntary associations of the functional factors in society" (Cram 1937, 122). Elsewhere, Cram described a quaint scheme whereby individuals were associated in largely autonomous units of 500 families, each with their own farms, gardens, town halls, and professional personnel (Cram 1935, 201–222).

Concentrating more directly on the national government in *The End of Democracy,* Cram critiqued universal suffrage. Recognizing that it would now be difficult to abolish, he advocated restrictions for those convicted of crimes and for those applying for naturalization.

Cram favored rearranging Congress along functional representative lines. Although elsewhere in his book he criticized parliamentary systems, he borrowed a number of their features. He proposed that the president and Congress work together on a legislative budget. He would have repealed the Seventeenth Amendment so as to provide for a Senate known as "a body of men of high character, noble intelligence and wide vision; men of mature judgment, of scholarly attainments and of knowledge of the world" (Cram 1937, 166). Cram thought that such a body could best be chosen partly by appointment and partly by indirect election, some appointments being made by the major secular and religious interests in society. Members would serve from ten years to life. All laws would originate in the House of Representatives, a body that would apparently remain largely unchanged.

Cram, who admired Franklin Roosevelt, also liked the strong presidency that had developed in the United States. He would further strengthen this institution by providing that the president would be chosen for life, quite possibly by members of the House from among those in the Senate. Personally preferring that the president be designated as king, Cram settled on "His Highness the Regent of the Republic of the United States" (Cram 1937, 187). As head of state, the regent would appoint a prime minister, who would choose a cabinet. Like William Yandell Elliott, with whom he was familiar, Cram believed that the head of state should be able to dissolve the House of Representatives; unlike Elliott, Cram thought that the regent should appoint a new prime minister if the vote went against him.

Again drawing from Elliott, Cram thought that the Supreme Court should not be able to invalidate federal laws except by an extraordinary majority. Cram favored unanimity. Like Elliott, he also believed that the Supreme Court should issue advisory opinions.

Continuing to draw from Elliott, Cram further advocated dividing the nation into five or six provinces or commonwealths and decentralizing administration. He wanted to create an order of nonhereditary knighthood, with recipients being designated as "Sir" as a means of recognizing the natural aristocracy. He also advocated expansion of the civil service and the creation of a "Civilian West Point" (Cram 1937, 218). Suspicious of the existing exercise of such freedoms as those of speech and the press, Cram nonetheless recognized that the evils of state licensing might prove worse than current abuses. The key here, as elsewhere, was "the placing of men of character, capacity, and intelligence in all positions, social, economic, political" (Cram 1937, 237).

For Further Reading:

Cram, Ralph. 1937. *The End of Democracy.* Boston: Marshall Jones Company.

Shand-Tucci, Douglass. 1995. *Ralph Adams Cram: Life and Architecture.* Vol. I. Amherst: University of Massachusetts Press.

❖ CRIMINALS, EARLY RELEASE ❖

In recent years citizens have been increasingly concerned about the threat of violent crime. Many states have increased the minimum sentences for individuals convicted of violent crimes, while others have adopted recidivism legislation that expands jail terms for individuals who have committed three or more felonies. Such laws, following a baseball analogy, are often referred to as "three strikes and you're out" laws.

Somewhat in tension with such laws are periodic budget shortfalls during which governors and legislators sometimes propose releasing offenders from prison early in order to save state or federal tax dollars. Perhaps alarmed by this development, Florida Democratic Congressman Robert Wexler proposed an amendment in March 1997 that would prohibit such early release of violent criminals.

❖ CRITICAL ELECTIONS ❖

The amending process is often likened to a "safety valve" that provides an alternative to revolution, but elections perform a similar function on a more regularized basis. Just as some amendments—for example, the Fourteenth—are more far-reaching than others, so too are some elections. Political scientists refer to these as critical, or realigning, elections.

There appear to have been at least five critical elections in the United States. They occurred in 1800, 1828, 1860, 1896, and 1932 (Burnham 1970, 1). Such elections are associated with "short-lived but very intense disruptions of traditional patterns of voting behavior"; they exhibit high intensity on the part of voters, are often associated with the rise or demise of minor parties, and tend to occur with fairly "uniform periodicity" (Burnham 1970, 6–10).

Amendments, like realigning elections, often have a generational dimension (Strickland 1989, 48–50). At least a few amendments appear to have resulted from realigning elections. The Twelfth Amendment remedied a flaw in the electoral college that was evident in the election of 1800. The Civil War amendments (Thirteen through Fifteen) were made possible by Republican gains in 1860 and 1864. Although the election of 1896 kept Republicans in control, a number of Progressive Era amendments reflected reform elements from that election. The election of 1932 manifested itself chiefly in changed judicial interpretations rather than in amendments (although the Twentieth and Twenty-first Amendments soon followed), but it is recognized by some as a key "constitutional moment," equivalent to others affirmed by constitutional amendments (Ackerman 1991).

Because U.S. political parties have weakened in recent years, it has been difficult to establish whether there has been another realigning election; the 1994 midterm congressional elections have been the subject of special attention (Burnham 1995; Wilcox 1995). With a view toward recent ambiguity, a number of political scientists refer to a "dealigning" process (Rohde 1994), and other observers caution that apparent realignments are sometimes fairly transitory (Berke 1995, E-3). Whatever the status of such elections, they serve as a reminder that political changes often occur in clusters (Silva 1970), and majorities that are successful in mustering support for one amendment often develop sufficient momentum to initiate others as well.

For Further Reading:

Ackerman, Bruce. 1991. *We the People: Foundations.* Cambridge, MA: Belknap.

Berke, Richard L. 1995. "Epic Political Realignments Often Aren't." *New York Times,* 1 January, E-3.

Burnham, Walter D. 1995. "Realignment Lives: The 1994 Earthquake and Its Implications." In *The Clinton Presidency: First Appraisals,* ed. Colin Campbell and Bert Rockman. Chatham, NJ: Chatham House.

Rohde, David W. 1994. "The Fall Elections: Realignment or Dealignment." *Chronicle of Higher Education* 41 (14 December): B1–B2.

Silva, Edward J. 1970. "State Cohorts and Amendment Clusters in the Process of Federal Constitutional Amendments in the United States, 1869–1931." *Law and Society Review* 4 (February): 445–466.

Strickland, Ruth A. 1989. *The Ratification Process of U.S. Constitutional Amendments: Each State Having One Vote as a Form of Malapportionment.* Ph.D. dissertation, University of South Carolina.

Wilcox, Clyde. 1995. *The Latest American Revolution? The 1994 Elections and Their Implications for Governance.* New York: St. Martin's Press.

❖ CRITTENDEN COMPROMISE ❖

The period between the election and the inauguration of Abraham Lincoln was marked by a series of attempts to introduce compromises that would keep the Southern states from seceding. Among the most prominent, albeit ultimately unsuccessful, attempts was a series of unamendable amendments offered by Kentucky Unionist Senator John J. Crittenden and first introduced in the Senate on 18 December 1861. Crittenden's proposals, if accepted, would have marked the first attempt to settle the slavery issue by amendment rather than by ordinary acts of legislation (Kirwan 1962, 374). This was a logical approach, because the Southern movement for secession was stimulated in part by fears—raised much earlier by John C. Calhoun and accentuated by Lincoln's election and the growth of the free states—that the amending process could one day be used to abolish slavery throughout the nation.

Altogether, Crittenden proposed seven amendments. Tennessee Senator (later president) Andrew Johnson also introduced a series of amendments designed in part to split the presidency, vice presidency, and membership of the Supreme Court between the North and the South (Dumond 1973, 159). Crittenden's proposals would have (1) restricted and extended the Missouri Compromise line to California, prohibiting slavery north and permitting it south of the line, with new states making their own choices as to whether they would be slave or free; (2) prohibited Congress from abolishing slavery on federal property within slave states; (3) prohibited Congress from abolishing slavery in the District of Columbia as long as it existed in Maryland or Virginia, and even if it did not, abolition would require consent of District residents and compensation; (4) prohibited Congress from interfering with interstate slave transit; (5) provided compensation for owners of fugitive slaves rescued by mobs; and (6) prohibited future amendments altering the three-fifths clause or the fugitive slave clause or interfering with slavery in the South (Kirwan 1962, 375). Crittenden's compromise also called on Congress to pass resolutions recognizing that (1) the fugitive slave laws were constitutional and should be enforced, (2) conflicting state laws should be repealed, (3) provisions of fugitive slave laws offensive to Northerners should be repealed, and (4) laws prohibiting the foreign slave trade should be strengthened (Kirwan 1962, 375–376).

Debates about these proposals occupied much of the lame-duck session of Congress. The Peace Convention meeting in February 1861 submitted proposals to Congress much like Crittenden's.

The Crittenden Compromise has been called "a Southern plan in search of Northern support" (Keogh 1987, 283). Outgoing President Buchanan endorsed the plan. It failed because most Republicans, including incoming President Lincoln, balked at the provisions relating to slavery in the territories and decided instead to support the Corwin Amendment, which merely guaranteed that the national government would not interfere with slavery in those states where it already existed. Crittenden eventually allowed a similar set of proposals drafted by the Peace Convention to be substituted for his own. This substitute did not receive the two-thirds vote necessary to be placed on the House agenda and was voted down in the Senate on 4 March 1861 by a vote of seven to twenty-eight (Keogh 1987, 292).

One of the most fascinating aspects of the Crittenden Compromise was that Crittenden hoped to break the congressional logjam of opposition by having the people vote on the plan in a national plebiscite, or referendum. Unlike some modern advocates of such a provision, Crittenden recognized that such a vote would be extraconstitutional and hence nonbinding, but the Senate refused to send it to the people (Keogh 1987, 288).

See also Calhoun, John C.; Corwin Amendment; Peace Convention.

For Further Reading:
Dumond, Dwight L. 1973. *The Secession Movement, 1860–1861.* New York: Octagon Books.
Keogh, Stephen. 1987. "Formal and Informal Constitutional Lawmaking in the United States in the Winter of 1860–1861." *Journal of Legal History* 8 (December): 275–299.
Kirwan, Albert D. 1962. *John J. Crittenden: The Struggle for the Union.* n.p.: University of Kentucky Press.

❖ CROLY, HERBERT (1870–1930) ❖

Herbert Croly published *The Promise of American Life* in 1909 (1965) and went on to become editor of the *New Republic* from 1914 to 1928. Typical of intellectuals in the Progressive Era, Croly critiqued the amending process in *Progressive Democracy* (1914).

Arguing that the constitutional amending process was overly rigid, Croly agreed with Professor Munroe Smith in stating that "the first article of any sincerely intended progressive program must be the amendment of the amending clause of the Constitution" (Croly 1914, 230). Croly suggested that constitutional changes should be made by a majority of voters, with provisions for due "deliberation" and "territorial distribution of the prevailing majority" (Croly 1914, 231). Croly specifically commended Senator Robert La Follette's plan, whereby amendments could be proposed by a majority of both houses of Congress or one-fourth of the states and subsequently ratified by a majority of voters in a majority of states.

Croly perceived that the rigidity of the amending process had contributed to the role that the Supreme Court had assumed in interpreting and adapting the Constitution. Believing that the Court was beginning to defer more readily to legislative bodies, Croly argued that the power of the people was superior to both. The amending process had converted the democracy of the Constitution into "a golden hoard." Croly intended to open this treasure directly to the people (Croly 1914, 237).

For Further Reading:

Croly, Herbert. 1909. *The Promise of American Life*. New York: Macmillan Company. Reprint, Indianapolis: Bobbs-Merrill, 1965.

———. 1914. *Progressive Democracy*. New York: Macmillan. Reprint, New Brunswick, NJ: Transaction Publishers, 1998.

❖ CULTURAL AND LINGUISTIC RIGHTS ❖

At a time when there have been increasing calls for an amendment making English the official language of the United States, Representative Jimmy Hayes and Senator John Breaux, both Democrats from Louisiana (although Hayes has subsequently switched parties), have introduced a different amendment. Designated the Cultural Rights Amendment (Baron 1990, 24), it would enable people "to preserve, foster, and protect their historic, linguistic, and cultural origins" and see that no one is denied equal protection of the law for exercising such a right (H.J. Res. 408, 1989).

These proposals reflect Louisiana's recent interest in reviving and preserving its unique Acadian heritage, including its French language (J. Taylor 1976, 177–178). The 1921 Louisiana state constitution contained a compulsory English provision, and teachers of the day, from both French and English backgrounds, often humiliated children who continued to speak French in school (Estaville 1990, 116; Brasseau 1989, 11–12).

For Further Reading:

Baron, Dennis. 1990. *The English-Only Question: An Official Language for America?* New Haven, CT: Yale University Press.

Brasseau, Carl A. 1989. "Four Hundred Years of Acadian Life in North America." *Journal of Popular Culture* 23 (Summer): 3–22.

Estaville, Lawrence E. 1990. "The Louisiana French Language in the Nineteenth Century." *Southeastern Geographer* 30 (November): 107–120.

Taylor, Joe Gray. 1976. *Louisiana: A Bicentennial History*. New York: W. W. Norton.

❖ CUMMINGS, RICHARD (1938–) ❖

When the U.S. Constitution was created, Anti-Federalist opponents of the document cited the Baron de Montesquieu to argue that democratic government was impossible over a large land area. James Madison countered in *Federalist* No. 10 that representative, or indirect, democracy was not only possible over a large area but that it would serve the additional function of moderating political factions.

Although the new Constitution was adopted, many Americans continued to look to state and local governments for their most immediate needs. In the 1830s, Alexis de Tocqueville especially commended the New England town meetings. Southern states later attempted to preserve the institution of slavery by seceding from the larger union, but found themselves defeated on the battlefield by those who believed that the Union was indissoluble.

In 1980 attorney, professor, and journalist Richard Cummings published a book entitled *Proposition Fourteen: A Secessionist Remedy*. Drawing from critics of American government from both the right and the left as well as from concerns expressed by discontented localities from throughout the nation, Cummings, like earlier Anti-Federalists, perceived the central problems of America to stem from its large size and the high taxes and unresponsive bureaucracies that this size generated. He believed that Americans, like citizens of other nations, needed to consider the idea of decentralization, or devolution of power. Specifically, he suggested that Article IV, Section 4 of the U.S. Constitution might be altered through the amending process so as to guarantee "a democratic" rather than a "republican" form of government (Cummings 1980, 94). Going beyond those who initiated the Civil War, Cummings was willing to allow not only individual states but also individual localities to secede and govern themselves.

Cummings did not go into great detail as to how such governments might function. He did suggest that "an alliance of small, well-disciplined and highly-motivated armies is the best possible defense for the country" (Cummings 1980, 98). He further believed that localities might be better able to provide for their own welfare, education, and social services. He thus observed that "if money were kept within a locality, it is probable that the area's inhabitants would be at least as compassionate as Congress, and probably more astute than civil servant social workers" (Cummings 1980, 99).

Cummings believed that new communities might be formed along the order of communes or New England towns, with "a single local tax" sufficing to meet local needs. Admitting that his idea sounded "utopian," he believed that such new communities might contribute to "life based on spiritual values; full integration of all age groups, with the old given positions of leadership and veneration, and the young, increased responsibility, a kind of continuing 'celebration of life'" (Cummings 1980, 103). Much like the French philosopher Jean-Jacques Rousseau who had suggested that people might have to be "forced" to be free, Cummings further suggested that citizens might be mandated to participate in politics (Cummings 1980, 110).

Cummings realized that his proposals would be resisted by "the handmaidens of Big Business, Big Labor, and Big Government" (Cummings 1980, 118). Cummings, who had himself worked in the Democratic Party, favored abandoning the two major parties.

Not long before Cummings published his book, Howard Jarvis had led the fight for "Proposition 13" in California, an initiative ratified by the people and limiting property tax rates. Cummings thus titled his own proposal Proposition 14. Beginning with a list of grievances against the national government and the two-party system that supported it, Cummings's proposal provided that the people of local communities were reasserting their autonomy:

- To be free from the abuses of ever-increasing "government" in the form of usurpation of said communities' rightful functions;
- To end taxation beyond reasonable tolerance, and expenditures beyond any control;
- To end the imposition of any form of harmful technology without due regard to the consequences. (Cummings 1980, 123)

They therefore "declare themselves to be self-governing by direct democracy, which is the only system to further mankind and to preserve the world" (Cummings 1980, 123).

There is little evidence that Cummings's idea of secessionism has taken root, but pleas for greater state and local autonomy, or devolution, and for national initiatives and referendums continue.

See also Initiative and Referendum; Naylor, Thomas H.

For Further Reading:
Richard Cummings. 1980. *Proposition Fourteen: A Secessionist Remedy.* Sagaponack, New York: The Permanent Press.

❖ CURRENCY ❖

Article I, Section 8 of the U.S. Constitution invests Congress with power "to coin Money, [and] regulate the value thereof." A controversial exercise of this power occurred during the Civil War when the government issued paper bills, known as "greenbacks," and subsequently passed a law, the Legal Tender Act of 1862, requiring that such currency be accepted in payment for debts. When initially challenged in *Hepburn v. Griswold* (1870), the Supreme Court held by a four-to-three vote that this law—at least as applied to preexisting contracts—violated both the due process clause of the Fifth Amendment and the contracts clause (J. W. Ely 1992, 84). The day the opinion was issued, President Grant appointed two new justices, and when the case was reargued the next year, the Court reversed itself in *Knox v. Lee* in a five-to-four vote, again split along partisan lines (J. W. Ely 1992, 84).

Several contemporary amending proposals, some undoubtedly motivated by these developments, would have made gold and silver the exclusive legal tender or would have limited the issuance of paper currency. Some proposals introduced in 1892 provided for issuing paper money in the amount of $20 per person and equalizing its value with that of gold and silver (Musmanno 1929, 110).

In *Norman v. Baltimore & Ohio Railroad Co., Nortz v. United States,* and *Perry v. United States* (the *Gold Clause Cases* of 1935), the Supreme Court endorsed broad congressional powers over currency. In these cases, it decided that the government could annul requirements in private contracts calling for payment in gold.

A number of proposed new constitutions have provided for additional denominations of existing monies or renaming American currency.

For Further Reading:

Ely, James W. 1992. *The Guardian of Every Other Right: A Constitutional History of Property Rights.* New York: Oxford University Press.

Musmanno, M. A. 1929. *Proposed Amendments to the Constitution.* Washington, DC: U.S. Government Printing Office.

❖ CUSTOMS AND USAGES ❖

Although the text of the Constitution can be changed only by constitutional amendment, its interpretation can be altered in a variety of ways, the most common of which is judicial interpretation. Other customs and usages, however, may also develop as the legislative and executive branches make moves that serve as precedents for future actions. Conceptually, then, the "written" Constitution is surrounded by a larger "unwritten" constitution, more familiar in nations such as Great Britain that are not regarded as having a written constitution (Tiedeman 1890; W. Harris 1993; Vile 1994a).

The most authoritative, albeit dated, discussion of U.S. customs and usages is found in a book published by Herbert Horwill, a scholar from Great Britain, in 1925. In describing the "Law of the Constitution," Horwill referred to the Constitution and its amendments, as well as to the "Statute Law" and "Common Law" surrounding it. He described other conventions that grew up around the Constitution as "customs and usages."

Among the customs that Horwill identified were conventions that had democratized the electoral college, the precedent whereby a vice president who takes over for a president who has died takes his title rather than merely serving as an "acting president," the two-term presidential limit (in force when Horwill wrote, broken by Franklin D. Roosevelt, and later reestablished by the Twenty-second Amendment), the role of the president's cabinet, various customs regarding the appearance of cabinet officers before Congress, the appointment and removal powers, and the custom whereby a member of Congress is expected to be a resident of his or her district. Horwill noted that customs and usages may change or may be incorporated into the Constitution. Thus, prior to the adoption of the Seventeenth Amendment, many state legislatures had already agreed to accept the popular choice for U.S. senators (Horwill 1925, 203–205). Similarly, Woodrow Wilson changed a custom that had been in force since Thomas Jefferson when he decided to read a presidential message before Congress (Horwill 1925, 199).

Describing a similar phenomenon, a recent British author noted the existence of certain "abeyances" in government. He describes such abeyances as contrasting with more determinable conventions and as representing "a form of tacit and instinctive agreement to condone, and even cultivate, constitutional ambiguity as an acceptable strategy for resolving conflict" (Foley 1989, xi). Noting that not all constitutional provisions receive equal scrutiny, other scholars have pointed to what they describe as "underenforced constitutional norms" (Sager 1978).

Although advocates of strict construction of the Constitution have frequently accused liberal justices on the Warren and Burger Courts of interpreting the U.S. Constitution by inventing concepts like "privacy" that are not specifically stated there, a recent scholar has noted that the more conservative justices, who proclaim adherence to constitutional literalism, also rely on certain unwritten norms, like state sovereign immunity and the doctrine that the national government cannot conscript state employees when interpreting the Constitution, and especially the Tenth and Eleventh Amendments (Rubenfeld 2001). A respondent notes that it is dangerous "to overestimate the importance of the most recent cases" and that "historically the Court spends most of its time oscillating within a fairly narrow band in the middle of the continuum [of constitutional interpretations that adhere closely to the text and those that rely on unwritten norms]; and there are institutional mechanisms that explain why it does and will continue to do so" (Vermeule 2001, 475).

Like the idea of customs and usages, the concepts of abeyances and underenforced constitutional norms serve as reminders that, even in a nation that professes adherence to a written constitution, the text needs to be interpreted in light of practices, both written and unwritten, that surround it. Reformers who fail to give attention to such surroundings are likely to misunderstand the operation of government, propose amendments that are not needed, or be frustrated by the effects of their own proposals.

For Further Reading:

Foley, Michael. 1989. *The Silence of Constitutions: Gaps, "Abeyances" and Political Temperament in the Maintenance of Government*. London: Routledge.

Harris, William F., II. 1993. *The Interpretable Constitution*. Baltimore, MD: Johns Hopkins University Press.

Horwill, Herbert W. 1925. *The Usages of the American Constitution*. Reprint, Port Washington, NY: Kennikat Press, 1969.

Rubenfeld, Jed. 2001. "The New Unwritten Constitution." *Duke Law Journal* 51 (October): 289–305.

Sager, Lawrence Gene. 1978. "Fair Measure: The Legal Status of Underenforced Constitutional Norms." *Harvard Law Review* 92: 1212–1264.

Tiedeman, Christopher G. 1890. *The Unwritten Constitution of the United States*. New York: G. P. Putnam's Sons.

Vermeule, Adrian. 2001. "The Facts about Unwritten Constitutionalism: A Response to Professor Rubenfeld." *Duke Law Journal* 51 (October): 473–476.

Vile, John R. 1994a. *Constitutional Change in the United States: A Comparative Study of the Role of Constitutional Amendments, Judicial Interpretations, and Legislative and Executive Actions*. Westport, CT: Praeger.

Wilson, James G. 1992. "American Constitutional Conventions: The Judicially Unenforceable Rules That Combine with Judicial Doctrine and Public Opinion to Regulate Political Behavior." *Buffalo Law Review* 40 (Fall): 645–738.

D

❖

❖ DAVIDSON, JIM ❖

From time to time individuals have proposed new constitutions for the United States. Others have proposed utopias, which are not necessarily capable of realization, but which are designed to cast light on how they believe governments should operate. The proposal for a constitution for Oceania, a name based on the fictional totalitarian state described in George Orwell's *1984* (1949), appears midway between these two approaches. Its chief author appears to have been Jim Davidson.

The project was apparently conceived in 1993 after Tamara Clark was defeated in an election for the Nevada legislature. Believing that fraud was involved, Clark and associates began to formulate the idea of establishing a "floating" concrete nation, designed by architect Sten Sjostrand, located somewhere in the Caribbean, and based on libertarian ideals. The constitution they have developed for this would-be nation has been posted on the Internet and is designed to provoke reflection on current American government. It seems unlikely that Oceania will ever become a physical reality, but its ideals could very well influence individuals who are concerned with reforming the U.S. government. In addition to an introduction and a set of definitions, the constitution of Oceania is divided into ten articles.

The introduction likens the new government to that of a "peaceful dolphin" rather than to sharklike governments that use "force and fraud to extract wealth and labor from their citizens." The introduction specifically cites the U.S. Constitution as one that has been so "vague" as "to allow its government to pass laws clearly at odds with the spirit of liberty in which that once-free nation was founded." Unusual definitions in the constitution include a "child," who is identified as less than sixteen years old, a "teen," who is between sixteen and eighteen, and an "adult," who is eighteen or older. All persons are referred to with nongender-specific designations. Oceanians might be either "persons" or "entities."

Unlike the U.S. Constitution, the constitution for Oceania begins with what is described as "A Partial Listing of Rights." It would require a 95 percent vote to remove rights and a 66 percent vote to add new ones. Rights are categorized under the headings of "life," "liberty," "property," and "privacy." The right to life includes the right of a hospital to turn off life support for individuals whose families no longer have money to afford such care. The right to life also encompasses "the Right to keep and bear Weaponry," and even to set booby traps, if proper warnings are posted. The right encompasses a "Right to Self-Sovereignty" that includes what individuals will put into or wear on their bodies, including using drugs and seat belts and helmets, as well as all kinds of consensual sexual conduct and participation in dangerous sports. The right to life also includes broad rights of free speech, employment, and religious freedom.

The right to liberty includes a prohibition of slavery, a right to travel, a right to assemble, a right to associate and discriminate, and a right to knowledge. This latter right includes the right to engage in insider trading. The right to liberty also includes the right to listen. The right to travel would be facilitated by providing that all land in Oceania "Must contain eight-meter-wide and eight-meter-high easements in a grid format of squares with eight kilometer sides on which there is an Entitlement to travel."

The right to property is based on the proposition that "taxation, civil forfeiture, [and] eminent domain" are all "forms of theft." Individuals would be permitted to sell body parts or engage in sex or medical experiments for money. The right to property includes permission for individuals to operate businesses without licenses. The government would be prohibited from requiring "minimum wage, family leave benefits, medical insurance, disability benefits, unemployment insurance, or workers' compensation." The right to property includes a right to negotiate contracts, including marriage, which appears open to combinations of both genders. The right to free enterprise is explicitly affirmed as is the right to free trade, and limited intellectual property rights. The right to privacy includes protections against warrantless searches, the "Right to Self-Identity," the "Right to Financial Privacy," the "Right to Encryption," the "Right to Secure Conversations," and privacy rights on government property and in the workplace. Unlike adults, children would be vested with certain entitlements to be provided by one or more parents, whom children would have a right to sue. Children and teens would have less-restricted rights than adults, and animals would be protected against "cruel and unusual mistreatment."

Having begun with rights, Article II of the Oceania Constitution deals with "Government Agencies and Power Structures." The judicial branch is the first to be outlined. Denying the possibility of "victimless crimes" in Oceania, this Article would abolish the distinction between civil and criminal law. Judges of the Supreme Court and lower bodies would serve two- or four-year terms; judges would not require "lawyer Licenses." To bring suit in an Oceanian court, individuals would have to obtain court membership, which is anticipated to be widespread. Membership would bring the "right to fair prosecution," the right to a jury, "the Right to a Level Playing Field," the

"Right to Fair Bail and Fines," the "Right to Presumption of Innocency," and other rights currently designated within the U.S. Bill of Rights. A statute of limitations for all crimes is set at ten years. Prisoners would work in their prisons to support themselves or be the objects of charity.

The delineation of the Executive Branch begins with a statement specifying that all major laws must "be decided by referendum." Presidents and vice presidents would serve for four-year terms and have the power to put referendums on the ballot and "sign minor Contracts and legislation." The president could sign treaties to which 75 percent or more of Oceania voters have agreed. Directors of the various departments of war would be selected through popular election and would contract for services with private militia. An "Anti-Law Department" would be responsible for helping to repeal unwanted laws.

The Legislative Branch replaces representative bodies with direct popular legislation, thereby eliminating lobbying. The people are given a restricted list of areas in which they might adopt laws. The provision relating to abortion provides for the possibility of restrictions "after three months gestation where the mother's life is not endangered." The Constitution expresses the hope that "Whenever a need or a problem arises, . . . Oceanians will not ask 'What law can we pass?' but 'What Business can we create?' Elections for elected offices would include designations for "None of the Above" and "Remove This Office."

With formal government so restricted, a section focusing on "The Power Structure of Oceania" deals primarily with the rights of restricted and unrestricted businesses. Governments would be stripped of their powers to "issue or control currency," to generate power, to run a postal service, to finance art, to engage in traffic control, to inspect foods, to provide job training, or to finance scientific research or tourism. The constitution tersely notes that "Governmental charities are compassion at gunpoint." Working conditions currently mandated by governments would now be freely negotiated between employers and their employees.

Article III further designates powers that

would be denied to the government. These would include the right of taxation, of establishing businesses, of running embassies, of owning property or streets, of regulating banking, of running schools, of engaging in "Welfare and Humanitarian Activities" including Social Security, of funding scientific research, of funding police, and of providing fire protection, garbage disposal, public transit, and the like.

Article IV deals with national security. Except in cases of attack, wars would generally be declared by referendum. Oceania might join the United Nations, but such membership must be privately funded. The right to free trade would not include the right to export mind-altering drugs or weapons to nations on forbidden lists.

Article V repeats the earlier right of the people to regulate abortion by referendum after the first three months of gestation. Article VI deals with budgeting and requires agencies to publish a list of donors each year. Some budgets would be funded by user fees by losing parties in court cases.

Article VII identifies a Housing Development as "the most powerful government-like structure in Oceania." Such developments must be subdivided once they reach 5,000 persons. Article VIII permits a county or local government to secede with a vote of 75 percent or higher. Article IX provides that the constitution requires ratification "by unanimous consent of the original Land Owners of Oceania." Article X ends with a list of "suggestions" that have "no Force of law." Among the more novel suggestions are these: allowing animal rights groups to be plaintiffs in animal rights' cases; allowing armed forces to challenge one another to games of skill; and for English to be the official language.

The Constitution of Oceania might well be the best attempt to spell out libertarian ideals in a single constitutional document. The project to build a concrete nation in the Caribbean in the near future appears to have dissolved. Indeed, in personal correspondence with the author, the chief architect of the project (who reports that he became a Christian in 1999 but still largely holds to his libertarian ideals) indicates that the author's purchase of *The Atlantis*

Papers, outlining the proposed government, was the first "in about two years" (Davidson 28 May 2002). In this same letter, however, Davidson cites two newly proclaimed independent nations called Sealand, six miles east of Great Britain, and Awdal Free Port, in the Gulf of Aden near the Red Sea, and indicates that futurists Alvin and Heidi Toffler (discussed in an entry later in this volume) anticipated the development of as many as 5,000 new countries in the twenty-first century. He also notes that his constitution could be applied to "countries organized beyond the Earth" and reflects optimism that, "when the resources of our Solar System are at the disposal of our most creative and inventive minds, many of the problems here on Earth will fade to distance memories." In any event, whether ever incorporated into a specific government or not, the principles articulated in the Oceania document will certainly continue to illumine libertarian ideals and may well influence individuals who would like to move the United States in a more libertarian direction.

See also Bailey, Martin J.

For Further Reading:

"Oceania—The Atlantis Project." At *http://www. oceania.org/indexgif.html.* Accessed April 29, 2002. All quoted materials above are taken directly from the website.

Davidson, Jim. May 28, 2002. Personal correspondence with the author.

Davidson, Jim, with Eric Klien, Norm Doering, and Lee Crocker. 1994. *The Atlantis Papers.* Houston, TX: Interglobal Paratronics, Inc.

❖ DECLARATION OF INDEPENDENCE ❖

One of the foremost documents in American history is the one that explains the reasons that the colonies declared their independence from Great Britain. The Second Continental Congress delegated the task of writing this document to a committee of five men consisting of Thomas Jefferson, John Adams, Benjamin

Franklin, Roger Sherman, and Robert Livingston. Jefferson did the initial drafting, and the document was subsequently debated and revised by Congress as a whole. Congress voted to accept the document on 4 July 1776, and it was signed over the next several months.

The Declaration of Independence was firmly based on a philosophy of natural rights. According to this philosophy, men are created equal and are all entitled to the right to "life, liberty, and the pursuit of happiness." Governments are instituted to secure such rights. Accordingly, "whenever any form of government becomes destructive of these ends, it is the right of the people to alter or abolish it, and to institute new government, laying its foundation on such principles, and organizing its powers in such form, as to them shall seem most likely to effect their safety and happiness."

After arguing that humans were generally more inclined to suffer deprivation of rights than to alter their form of government, Jefferson argued that when faced with attempts to set up despotism, the people have both the "right" and the "duty" to "throw off such government, and to provide new guards for their future security." Much of the remainder of the Declaration focuses on specific grievances the colonists had against the English king.

The Declaration of Independence did not create a new government—that was the task accomplished with the writing of the Articles of Confederation and the U.S. Constitution. The Declaration did effectively set forth principles that continue to guide American government and inspire free peoples throughout the world. When delegates met at the Seneca Falls Convention in Seneca Falls, New York, in 1848 to push for women's rights and begin the drive for women's suffrage that did not culminate until the adoption of the Nineteenth Amendment in 1920, they modeled their "Declaration of Sentiments" on that of the Declaration of Independence (Bernhard and Fox-Genovese 1995, 85–89).

The Constitution and the Bill of Rights arguably gave life to many of the principles embodied in the Declaration of Independence. The eventual ratification of the equal protection clause of the Fourteenth Amendment was an especially important step toward governmental protection of equal rights to liberty. The constitutional amending process provides a viable "safety valve" against the necessity for revolution; changes in judicial interpretation and congressional and presidential practices also accommodate changes that may not be written into the constitutional text. In his original draft of the Bill of Rights, James Madison had proposed adding a prefix to the Constitution specifying "that all power is derived from the people, who have a right to reform or change their government whenever it is found inadequate" (Schwartz 1992, 166). In a similar vein, in July 1976, the bicentennial of the Declaration, Representative Robert Michel, a Republican from Illinois, introduced an amendment (H.J. Res. 1016) to incorporate certain principles of the Declaration of Independence into the preamble of the U.S. Constitution.

See also Fourteenth Amendment; Jefferson, Thomas; Seneca Falls Convention; Virginia Declaration of Rights.

For Further Reading:
Adler, Mortimer J. 1987. *We Hold These Truths: Understanding the Ideas and the Ideals of the Constitution.* New York: Macmillan.
Becker, Carl L. 1970. *The Declaration of Independence: A Study in the History of Political Ideas.* New York: Vintage Books.
Bernhard, Virginia, and Elizabeth Fox-Genovese, eds. 1995. *The Birth of American Feminism: The Seneca Falls Woman's Convention of 1848.* St. James, NY: Brandywine Press.
Gerber, Scott D. 1995. *To Secure These Rights: The Declaration of Independence and Constitutional Interpretation.* New York: New York University Press.
Maier, Pauline. 1997. *American Scripture: Making the Declaration of Independence.* New York: Alfred A. Knopf.
Schwartz, Bernard. 1992. *The Great Rights of Mankind: A History of the American Bill of Rights.* Madison, WI: Madison House.
Vile, John R. 2002a. *A Companion to the United States Constitution and Its Amendments.* 3d ed. Westport, CT: Praeger.
Wills, Garry. 1978. *Inventing America: Jefferson's Declaration of Independence.* New York: Doubleday.

❖ DEFAMATION ❖

The First Amendment to the Constitution prohibits the national government from abridging freedom of speech. This protection has been extended via the due process clause of the Fourteenth Amendment to the states as well. The Supreme Court has ruled, however, that some forms of expression do not constitute free speech. These include "fighting words," obscenity, and libel. Libel refers to written communication that "is injurious to the reputation of another" (*Black's Law Dictionary* 1969, 824). Slander is defamation in spoken rather than written form.

Up to 1964, laws against libel were handled by the states. In *New York Times Co. v. Sullivan* (1964), however, it became clear that such laws could be used to stifle criticism of public officials, in this case an Alabama police commissioner who had taken action against civil rights protesters. Accordingly, the Supreme Court ruled that, in proving libel, public officials have a substantial burden of proof. They have to show that libelous statements made about them were made with "actual malice," that is, with knowledge that they were false or with "reckless disregard" to their truth or falsity. Subsequent rulings have extended this standard to other public figures who are not officials, but not to private individuals who are merely caught up in public controversy (*Gertz v. Robert Welch, Inc.* [1974]).

Although some individuals favor further liberalization of libel laws, others fear that current laws allow too much leeway to those who would abuse free speech. In April 1982 Democratic Representative Bill Burlison of Missouri introduced an amendment that would provide that nothing in the First Amendment "shall prevent the recovery by any person, including any person deemed newsworthy, of damages in a civil action, or the imposition of criminal penalties, in cases involving defamation of such persons" (H.J. Res. 1285). Later amending proposals have expressed concern over the fact that members of Congress might use their protection under the "speech and debate" clause to injure the reputations of private individuals.

For Further Reading:

Lewis, Anthony. 1991. *Make No Law: The Sullivan Case and the First Amendment.* New York: Random House.

❖ DELIBERATION AND THE AMENDING PROCESS ❖

The U.S. Constitution was the result of a convention of fifty-five delegates who met between May and September of 1787. The delegates took the task of writing a new constitution very seriously. They adopted a number of rules to enhance deliberation. One, which was rarely breached and which would be almost impossible if such a convention were to be held today, provided that convention deliberations would be held in secret. Another provided that votes would be listed by states rather than under individual names. A third provided that votes could be retaken, giving delegates a chance to change their minds if they came to different understandings during the course of debates.

The document that emerged from convention deliberations provided a number of mechanisms, including a bicameral Congress and a presidential "signature" (or a supermajority congressional override) to assure that legislation was the result of a deliberative process. Because amendments would involve alterations to the fundamental law, the framers rejected the idea of parliamentary, or legislative, sovereignty that had been dominant in Great Britain. The American framers chose to make the amending process more difficult, requiring supermajorities at both the proposal and ratification stages. One of the framers' major goals appears to be that of assuring that amendments would not be adopted without adequate deliberation and without a consensus in their favor. In light of how few amendments have actually been adopted, some critics believe that the framers may have made the process too difficult, although most agree that there should be some distinction between the legislative process and the amending process.

Some proposals for constitutional initiatives and referendums could short-circuit the deliberative process that is currently involved in the amending process, but there are mechanisms (multiple votes, supermajorities, or specified passages of time between stages, for example) that might be adapted to provide for such deliberation. Although citizens and scholars alike may argue as to whether the current amending mechanism involves the ideal balance, there is general agreement that the process should be one that encourages both deliberation and consensus. The Citizens for the Constitution who authored the Constitutional Amendment Initiative have suggested that one criterion for an amendment should be that the amendment has had the opportunity for "full and fair debate." As part of this suggestion, the group proposed that no substantive changes to amendments should be offered on the floor of Congress that had not been fully vetted in committee.

See also Citizens for the Constitution, the Constitutional Amendment Initiative; Consensus and the Amending Process; Initiative and Referendum; Parliamentary Sovereignty.

❖ DEMOCRACY AND CONSTITUTIONAL AMENDMENTS ❖

When it was established, the U.S. Constitution provided for a system that was far more democratic than those of most other nations of the world at the time, but James Madison made it clear in *Federalist* No. 10 that the system being established was a system of republican, or indirect, democracy. In part by such design, and in part because it was the product of compromises among rival interests, the resulting system of government not only moderated direct democracy but also contained a number of undemocratic features. The Constitution did not actually establish voting rights, but left this matter to the states, most of which denied such rights to blacks and women, and, in some cases, to individuals who did not own a specified amount of property. Similarly, although the Constitution did not mention the institution of slavery

by name, it acquiesced in the institution by providing for the continuing importation of slaves for twenty years, by providing for a fugitive slave clause, and by specifying that slaves would be counted as three-fifths of a person for purposes of taxation and representation. In addition, the Constitution contained no definition of citizenship, leaving the status of free blacks and others to the whims of state law.

By requiring supermajorities both to propose and ratify amendments, the amending provisions of the U.S. Constitution did not embody direct democracy, but an overview of the history of the constitutional amending process indicates that it has subsequently done much to democratize this system. The first ten amendments are concerned more with the protection of individual rights than with direct participation in government. Still, they include guarantees in the First Amendment for freedom of speech, press, assembly, and petition that are essential to democratic governance, while provisions in other amendments provide for due process rights and for jury trials. Depending on one's perspective on federalism, one could question whether the last provision of the Bill of Rights, the Tenth Amendment, expands or narrows rights. Similarly, the Eleventh Amendment, and the doctrine of sovereign immunity that it has been said to embody, arguably makes state governments less accountable to citizens. By contrast, in curing one of the obvious defects of (while not eliminating) the electoral college, the Twelfth Amendment made it more likely that the people, and not members of Congress, would make the decision regarding who would be selected as president and vice president.

The three amendments adopted in the aftermath of the Civil War helped rid the nation of slavery, guarantee equal rights to all citizens, and (on paper) prohibit discrimination on the basis of race. The Fourteenth Amendment, in particular, has often been credited with embodying the sentiments of the Declaration of Independence within the Constitution.

The Progressive Era amendments were also largely democratic in character. One could argue that the Sixteenth Amendment (providing for a national income tax) was not per se democratic or undemocratic and that the Eighteenth

Amendment (providing for national alcoholic prohibition) enabled what proved to be a temporary majority the right to limit individual choice over a matter in which the government's role should have been more limited. However the Eighteenth Amendment is interpreted, it was subsequently repealed by the Twenty-first Amendment. The Seventeenth Amendment clearly extended democracy by providing that U.S. senators would be elected directly by the people of the states rather than by state legislatures. Similarly, the Nineteenth Amendment significantly expanded the franchise by prohibiting discrimination in voting on the basis of sex.

A number of other amendments have provided for the expansion of voting rights. Thus, the Twenty-third Amendment provided for electoral votes for the District of Columbia, the Twenty-fourth Amendment eliminated the poll tax in federal elections, and the Twenty-sixth Amendment lowered the voting age to eighteen. Likewise the Twentieth Amendment attempted to make members more accountable by reducing the terms of lame-duck members. The Twenty-second Amendment, limiting the number of terms that presidents may serve, arguably narrowed popular choice of this branch—although only one previous president, Franklin D. Roosevelt, had been chosen to serve more than two terms. Similarly, the Twenty-fifth Amendment, while providing not only for a method for ascertaining presidential disability, but also for replacing vice presidents, embodies a method of indirect, rather than direct, democracy for doing so.

A scholar of the amending process has observed "a pattern of successive extensions of democracy" (Grimes 1978, 163). He argues that "twenty-one amendments may be said to affirm either the principle of democratic rights or that of democratic processes" while "only three amendments—the Tenth, Eleventh, and Twenty-fifth would appear to be indifferent, or irrelevant, to democratic principles" (Grimes 1978, 166). He accordingly concludes that "the record of the twenty-six amendments to the Constitution is in a sense a record of democracy in America" (Grimes 1978, 167).

A number of caveats should be added to this analysis. First, many of the initial limitations on voting rights—for example, those based on property ownership or church membership—were liberalized at the state level, and periods of progress were sometimes punctuated with periods of backsliding (Keyssar 2000, 53).

Second, guarantees on paper were not always put into immediate operation. Most of the guarantees of individual rights that are found in the Bill of Rights were not applied to state governments until well into the twentieth century. In the early years of their operation, the Fourteenth and Fifteenth Amendments were notoriously ineffective in protecting the rights of newly freed slaves.

Third, by requiring supermajorities, the amending process gives a veto to minorities with strong views and is an obstacle to the immediate realization of many proposals that may be favored by mere popular majorities. Even though proposed by the required majorities in Congress, amendments providing for restricting child labor, equal rights for women, and congressional representation for the District of Columbia have all failed to be ratified. Nevertheless, child labor laws are now accepted by the courts, a place where women have also made substantial gains.

Fourth, a number of fairly important constitutional mechanisms remain that are not fully democratic (although many may embody indirect, or republican, democracy). These include the electoral college system that is used to select the president and vice president and that sometimes results in a winner who does not carry the popular vote; the provision for equal state representation in the U.S. Senate; the system of selection of members of the House of Representatives through single member, winner-take-all districts rather than through a system of proportional representation, which is more common in other democratic nations; and the wide-ranging exercise of judicial review by unelected judges and justices (Dahl 2001). Similarly, the national constitution continues to have no provisions for citizen initiatives, referendums, or recalls, which many states have adopted to make their constitutions more directly accountable to the people.

A number of recent proposals for new constitutions have sought to edge the United

States much closer to a system of direct democracy than to the republican democracy established by the framers.

See also Progress and the Amending Process; Voting Rights, Constitutional Amendments Relating to.

For Further Reading:
Dahl, Robert. 2001. *How Democratic Is the American Constitution?* New Haven, CT: Yale University Press.

Keyssar, Alexander. 2000. *The Right to Vote: The Constitutional History of Democracy in the United States.* New York: Basic Books.

❖ DEROGATORY MATERIAL, TEACHING OF ❖

In 1943 and 1945, Democratic Representative Jerry Voorhis of California introduced amendments that would prohibit the teaching of derogatory materials to citizens of the United States. Voorhis had been a member of the Dies Committee on Un-American Activities, but his appointment had come after he expressed opposition to what he considered to be improper investigatory and accusatory tactics that the committee was utilizing (Voorhis 1947, 207–231). Moreover, both on the committee and throughout his service in Congress, his was generally a liberal voice. Voorhis lost the election of 1946 to Richard Nixon, who campaigned against Voorhis's alleged liberalism.

For Further Reading:
Voorhis, Jerry. 1947. *Confessions of a Congressman.* Garden City, NY: Doubleday. Reprint, Westport, CT: Greenwood Press, 1970.

❖ DILLON, CONLEY (1906–1987) ❖

Political scientist Conley Dillon offered a number of proposals to revise the Constitution about the time of the bicentennial of the Dec-

laration of Independence and the Constitution (Vile 1991c, 25–27). His proposals were closely tied to a resolution by the American Society for Public Administration (ASPA) (C. Dillon 1974). It proposed the establishment of a Permanent Commission for Constitutional Review consisting of fifteen members appointed by the president, the president pro tempore of the Senate, and the Speaker of the House of Representatives (C. Dillon 1977, 14).

Following the ASPA report, Dillon suggested nine areas of study for the commission: (1) "the constitutional basis of our federal structure"; (2) the "selection, removal, and succession" of the president and vice president, as well as "executive branch accountability" and the possibility of "a modified parliamentary system"; (3) "the method of selecting and removing members of Congress, their terms of office, and the[ir] organization and procedures"; (4) the selection and removal of judges; (5) the "distribution and sharing" of powers among the three branches; (6) the "constitutional status and role" of political parties; (7) the "scope of individual and group freedoms and rights"; (8) the organization of a constitutional convention; and (9) ways to deal with loss of confidence in government (C. Dillon 1977, 22).

Dillon also discussed other plans for constitutional change, including plans by Rexford Tugwell, the Reuss Resolution, and the proposal by James L. Sundquist to allow Congress to remove the president, dissolve itself, and call a new election. Dillon acknowledged that "a realistic assessment, however, does not promise action on constitutional review in the near future" (C. Dillon 1977, 22).

❖ *DILLON V. GLOSS* (1921) ❖

This case arose from a habeas corpus petition filed by a petitioner who had been convicted of transporting alcohol in violation of the National Prohibition Act (also known as the Volstead Act), adopted pursuant to the Eighteenth Amendment. The petitioner questioned the legitimacy of the seven-year time limit for ratification that had been incorporated into that amendment. He also claimed that the amendment, which contained a one-year implementation delay, had not been in effect when he was arrested because his arrest had been less than a year from the time the secretary of state had certified the amendment.

Noting that Article V of the Constitution did not specify a ratification time period, Justice Willis Van Devanter observed for a unanimous Court that, without such an understanding, four amendments would still be pending. Analyzing Article V, he concluded that because it treated proposal and ratification not "as unrelated acts, but as succeeding steps in a single endeavor, the natural inference" was that "they are not to be widely separated in time" (*Dillon* 1921, 374–375). He further concluded:

[A]s ratification is but the expression of the approbation of the people and is to be effective when had in three-fourths of the states, there is a fair implication that it must be sufficiently contemporaneous in that number of states to reflect the will of the people in all sections at relatively the same period, which, of course, ratification scattered through a long series of years would not do. (*Dillon* 1921, 375)

Although the Constitution does not specify how long the ratification period should be, Van Devanter concluded that the seven-year span that Congress had established in the case of the Eighteenth Amendment was reasonable. Van Devanter further decided that the Eighteenth Amendment became effective when ratified by the requisite number of states and not when such ratification was certified thirteen days later by the secretary of state.

The current status of *Dillon v. Gloss* is not clear. In *Coleman v. Miller* (1939), the Supreme Court ruled that the question of contemporaneousness was a "political question" for Congress to decide. Moreover, although *Dillon* suggested that it would be "quite untenable" (1921, 375) to consider an amendment proposed in 1789 without a specified time limit to be pending, Congress did exactly this when it voted in 1992 to accept ratification of the Twenty-seventh Amendment.

One contemporary author, who is concerned about the institution's failure to mention specific time limits for the ratification of proposed amendments has argued that:

Dillon's conclusion that Article V contains an implicit time limit is wrong, although its premise that such a time limit is necessary is right. Essentially, the Court in *Dillon* makes the mistake of assuming that because it is advisable from a policy perspective for Article V to contain a ratification time limit, that it therefore does contain such a limit." (Hanlon 2000, 674–675)

See also *Coleman v. Miller;* Time Limits on Amendments.

For Further Reading:

Dillon v. Gloss, 256 U.S. 368 (1921).

Hanlon, Michael C. 2000. "Note: The Need for a General Time Limit on Ratification of Proposed Constitutional Amendments." *Journal of Law & Politics* 16 (Summer): 663–698.

❖ DIRECT DEMOCRACY ❖

See Jeffs, Daniel B.; Initiative and Referendum.

❖ DIRKSEN, EVERETT MCKINLEY (1896–1969) ❖

Everett McKinley Dirksen of Illinois served in the U.S. House of Representatives from 1933 to 1949 and in the Senate from 1951 to 1969. In his Senate years, he was the minority leader during the heyday of President Johnson's Great Society years and the activism of the Warren Court. Dirksen often led the opposition to both. He is remembered for his deep, gravelly voice and for advocating making the marigold the national flower (Penney 1968, 91–92).

When first elected to the House, Dirksen was one of the few Republicans who ran on a platform of repeal of the Eighteenth Amendment (Kyvig 1979, 168). He was subsequently a leading advocate of two proposed amendments. One would have overturned the Supreme Court's decision in *Engel v. Vitale* (1962) and permitted "voluntary participation by students and others in prayer." The other was designed to overturn *Baker v. Carr* (1962) and *Reynolds v. Sims* (1964) by allowing states to apportion at least one house of their state legislatures other than by population. After the apportionment amendment failed to pass in the Senate by a vote of fifty-seven to thirty-nine, Dirksen formed a Committee for Government of the People (CGP) to promote the calling of a national constitutional convention on the subject (Schapsmeier and Schapsmeier 1985, 180). This movement apparently came but a single state shy of the necessary two-thirds majority before faltering (*Proposals for a Constitutional Convention* 1979, 2).

See also *Baker v. Carr;* Prayer in Public Schools.

For Further Reading:

Bonfield, Arthur E. 1968. "The Dirksen Amendment and the Article V Convention Process." *Michigan Law Review* 66 (March): 949–1000.

Dirksen, Everett M. 1968. "The Supreme Court and the People." *Michigan Law Review* 66 (March): 837–874.

Proposals for a Constitutional Convention to Require a Balanced Federal Budget. 1979. Washington, DC: American Enterprise Institute for Public Policy Research.

Schapsmeier, Edward L., and Frederick H. Schapsmeier. 1985. *Dirksen of Illinois: Senatorial Statesman.* Urbana, IL: University of Illinois Press.

❖ DISTRICT OF COLUMBIA, REPRESENTATION FOR ❖

Article I, Section 8 of the Constitution entrusts Congress with the power to legislate on behalf of the nation's capital. During the time of the Articles of Confederation, Congress was threatened by militiamen in Philadelphia who wanted to collect back pay (members of Congress temporarily moved to Princeton, New Jersey, during this crisis), and the experience persuaded the framers that the national government should control its own immediate surroundings (Report to the Attorney General 1987, 52–55). The early capital moved from New York to Philadelphia to the current site. The selection of a spot ceded by Virginia and Maryland was one of the first examples of "logrolling": Southerners promoting the site got their wish in exchange for their support for Alexander Hamilton's plan to pay off Revolutionary War debts in full (Bernstein with Agel 1993, 144–145).

In 1802 Congress provided for a charter that allowed for a mayor and a city council for the new District of Columbia, a plan that continued until 1871. At that time, it was replaced by a territorial government. After a scandal, Congress took control in 1874 and governed the District through congressional committees until 1966. At this time, President Lyndon Johnson used an executive order to appoint a mayor—later elected by the District (Schrag 1985, 10–12). In 1971 Congress granted the District a nonvoting member in the House of Representatives, and Democrat Walter Fauntroy was elected to this post.

As early as 1825, Augustus Woodward had proposed that the District be given representation in Congress. More than 150 such proposals were introduced from the 1880s through 1978 (Report to the Attorney General 1987, 11). The Twenty-third Amendment, ratified in 1961, granted the District representation in the electoral college, but it still had no voting members in Congress. After a 289-to-127 vote in the House on 1 March 1978, followed on 22 August by a 67-to-32 vote in the Senate, a proposal was sent to the states to remedy this long-standing issue (Bernstein with Agel 1993, 146).

The amendment consisted of four parts. The first provided that "for purposes of representation in the Congress, election of the President and Vice President, and article V of this Constitution, the District constituting the seat of government of the United States shall be treated as though it were a State." Section 2 somewhat ambiguously provided that "the exercise of the rights and powers conferred under this section shall be by the people of the District constituting the seat of government, as shall be provided by the Congress." Section 3 would have repealed the now redundant, and possibly contradictory, Twenty-third Amendment, and Section 4 provided for a seven-year ratification deadline.

The District of Columbia subsequently held a convention to write a constitution for the state of New Columbia (Schrag 1985). This convention proved to be overly optimistic, and by the 1985 deadline, only sixteen states had ratified. A key problem with the amendment was political—the District of Columbia was predominantly African American and Democratic, thus offering little to the Republican Party (Vose 1979; Horn 1990). Beyond that, some believed that the amendment violated the one remaining limit on Article V in that, by granting an entity that was not a true state representation in the Senate, it would deprive the others of their equal representation therein and would thus require unanimity. Others were uncomfortable with the notion of treating an entity, still somewhat under congressional control, "as though it were a state."

Some have sought to add the District as a state through ordinary legislation, but given the District's constitutional status, there are doubts about the constitutionality of such a move (but see Raven-Hansen 1975). Another possibility is retrocession—giving the District, perhaps exclusive of federal enclaves, back to Maryland; Virginia's portion has already been so retroceded. Yet another possibility is to allow District residents to vote in Maryland elections, but it is by no means clear that Maryland would favor this move, which might also require repeal of the Twenty-third Amendment.

In *Adams v. Clinton* (2000), with one dissenting vote, the United States District Court for the District of Columbia rejected a suit that would have provided for congressional voting representation in Congress. In this decision, later reaffirmed by the U.S. Circuit Court and the U.S. Supreme Court, the judges rejected both the argument that members of the District of Columbia could properly characterize themselves as "state" citizens or the argument that they had the right to vote in Maryland's elections of representatives as "residual" citizens of that state (although district members had been granted a continuing right to vote in state elections until Congress took complete control in 1801, the court found that this right ended with the complete cession of the territory to the United States).

The court also rejected arguments based on the equal protection and privileges and immunities clauses of the Fourteenth Amendment, the due process clause of the Fifth Amendment, and on the guarantee of a "republican" form of government in Article IV. Looking at specific provisions in the Constitution for the District of Columbia and examining the history of these provisions, the court decided that the guarantee of "one person, one vote" did not apply to cases in which the U.S. Constitution had itself made exceptions. The court noted that "many courts have found a contradiction between the democratic ideals upon which this country was founded and the exclusion of District residents from congressional representation. All, however, have concluded that it is the Constitution and judicial precedent that create the contradiction" (*Adams* 2000, 120–121). Given such precedents, it appears unlikely that citizens of the District of Columbia will obtain voting rights short of the adoption of a constitutional amendment.

The District thus remains something of a constitutional anomaly, what some critics consider to be a remnant of colonialism. Although it remains the center of free government and its members pay federal taxes, its inhabitants are denied direct voting representation in the Congress that meets there and that taxes them.

For Further Reading:

Adams v. Clinton, 90 F. Supp. 2d 35 (2000), *appeal dismissed sub nom. Adams v. Bush,* 2001 U.S. App. LEXIS 25877 (D.D.C. 2001), *cert. denied* 2002 U.S. LEXIS 5485 (U.S. Oct. 7, 2002).

Bernstein, Richard B., with Jerome Agel. 1993. *Amending America: If We Love the Constitution So Much, Why Do We Keep Trying to Change It?* New York: Random House.

Best, Judith. 1984b. *National Representation for the District of Columbia.* Frederick, MD: University Publications of America.

Bowling, Kenneth R. 1991. *The Creation of Washington, D.C.: The Idea and Location of the American Capital. Fairfax, VA: George Mason University Press.

Hatch, Orrin G. 1979. "Should the Capital Vote in Congress? A Critical Analysis of the Proposed D.C. Representation Amendment." *Fordham Urban Law Journal* 7: 479–539.

Horn, Dottie. 1990. "Another Star for the Stripes?" *Endeavors* 8 (Fall): 4–6.

Raven-Hansen, Peter. 1975. "Congressional Representation for the District of Columbia: A Constitutional Analysis." *Harvard Journal of Legislation* 12: 167–192.

Report to the Attorney General. 1987. *The Question of Statehood for the District of Columbia*. 3 April. Washington, DC: U.S. Government Printing Office.

Schrag, Philip G. 1985. *Behind the Scenes: The Politics of a Constitutional Convention*. Washington, DC: Georgetown University Press.

Vose, Clement E. 1979. "When District of Columbia Representation Collides with the Constitutional Amendment Institution." *Publius: The Journal of Federalism* 9 (Winter): 105–125.

❖ DIVIDED GOVERNMENT ❖

Few issues have generated more concern among proponents of a parliamentary system alternative to U.S. government than the issue of divided government. Such a divided government occurs when one party captures the presidency and another captures one or both houses of Congress. This situation is made possible by a system of separation of powers. In parliamentary systems, a scheme of fused powers guarantees that the prime minister, who is chosen by parliament, heads the majority party or coalition. In the United States, by contrast, the president and Congress have different electoral bases. Thus, in the forty-four years from 1946 to 1990, control was divided between Democrats and Republicans for twenty-six years (Mayhew 1991, 1). Democratic President Bill Clinton found himself facing both a Republican House and Senate. Republican George W. Bush's party, although it controlled the House, lost control of the Senate during his first year in office, when Republican Senator James Jeffords from Vermont declared himself an independent and began voting with the Democrats. Republicans regained control of the Senate in the 2002 midterm elections.

Critics of separation of powers contend that this system leads to needless controversy and to legislative gridlock. Defenders argue that divided government often reflects a popular unwillingness to invest either party with control over both branches and that such a division helps guard liberty and deter precipitous legislation. The author of an influential study who investigated the progress of lawmaking and the success of congressional investigations since the end of World War II concluded that, "surprisingly, it does not seem to make all that much difference whether party control of American government happens to be unified or divided" (Mayhew 1991, 198). Another author critiquing the parliamentary model of fused powers has argued that legislative-executive party conflict can be healthy (Sargentich 1993, 707).

See also Parliamentary System.

For Further Reading:

Mayhew, David R. 1991. *Divided We Govern: Party Control, Lawmaking, and Investigations, 1946–1990*. New Haven, CT: Yale University Press.

Sargentich, Thomas O. 1993. "The Limits of the Parliamentary Critique of the Separation of Powers." *William and Mary Law Review* 34 (Spring): 679–739.

❖ DODD, WALTER F. (1880–1960) ❖

One of the most important books on the process of amending state constitutions was written by Walter F. Dodd. Dodd, a professor at Johns Hopkins University, published his book on state amendments in 1910. Although many of the specifics of this work are obviously outdated, Dodd's book is still surprisingly relevant, especially in explaining the development and early use of the constitutional convention mechanism and its relation to the state legislature.

Dodd noted that the development of this mechanism followed three steps: establishing "the distinction between the constitution and ordinary legislation"; developing the convention as a body distinct from the legislature; and submitting the constitution "to a vote of the people, after it has been framed by a constitutional convention" (Dodd 1910, 22). Of these steps, he viewed the first as fundamental and the others as "but the elaboration of machinery to carry out more clearly the distinction between constitutions and ordinary legislation" (Dodd 1910, 22).

In his classic work on constitutional conventions, Judge John Jameson (1887) argued that the constitutional convention mechanism was necessarily subject to legislative control. Dodd argued that, in attempting to cut one would-be sovereign down to size, Jameson had elevated another. Believing that "the process of piecemeal amendment of state constitutions is absolutely under the control of the state legislatures except in the states that have adopted the popular initiative," he argued that constitutional conventions were in a somewhat different category:

> The calling of constitutional conventions is also to a large extent subject to legislative control, but the convention method of altering constitutions is the one more independent of the regular legislatures. . . . The convention loses a large part of its usefulness as an organ of the state if it be treated as strictly subject to control by the regular legislative body. (Dodd 1910, 79)

On another issue, Dodd authored an article supporting the decision in the *National Prohibition Cases* (1920), which held that the Eighteenth Amendment was not unconstitutional. Dodd noted that an understanding that would permit the courts to void amendments "would introduce into American constitutional practice a highly undesirable type of judicial control" (Dodd 1921, 334).

See also Jameson, John A.

For Further Reading:

Dodd, Walter F. 1921. "Amending the Federal Constitution." *Yale Law Journal* 30 (February): 321–354.

———. 1910. *The Revision and Amendment of State Constitutions*. Baltimore, MD: Johns Hopkins University Press.

Jameson, John A. 1887. *A Treatise on Constitutional Conventions: Their History, Powers, and Modes of Proceeding*. 4th ed. Chicago: Callaghan and Company.

❖ *DODGE V. WOOLSEY* (1856) ❖

This case involved a suit by a bank stockholder contesting a new tax that Ohio had laid on a bank. This tax violated a prior act under the previous state constitution limiting such taxes on newly chartered banks to 6 percent.

In declaring that the new tax violated the contract clause, Justice James Wayne declared that the U.S. Constitution was supreme "over the people of the United States aggregately and in their separate sovereignties, because they have excluded themselves from any direct or immediate agency in making amendments to it, and have directed that amendments shall be made representatively for them" (*Dodge* 1856, 348) through the Article V amending process. An author has recently cited this decision in attempting to refute Akhil Reed Amar's contention that popular majorities have authority to amend the Constitution outside of Article V provisions (Monaghan 1996, 128).

For Further Reading:

Dodge v. Woolsey, 59 U.S. (18 How.) 331 (1856).

Monaghan, Henry P. 1996. "We the People[s], Original Understanding, and Constitutional Amendment." *Columbia Law Review* 96 (January): 121–177.

❖ DOLBEARE, KENNETH (1930–), AND JANETTE HUBBELL (1948–) ❖

These two authors, self-described as "an eastern iconoclast who teaches politics at a small college and a southwestern populist who left elementary school teaching to launch a successful small business," published a wish list of constitutional reform couched in a fictional narrative set in the year 2012 (Dolbeare and Hubbell 1996, xiv). *USA 2012: After the Middle-Class Revolution* centers around a college student who reviews with his parents the developments that led to a successful middle-class revolution based on the concept of "economic nationalism" (Dolbeare and Hubbell 1996, xiii).

In the book's invented history, this program was instituted as a result of economic deterioration and a sense of middle-class outrage that resulted in the adoption of a new Declaration of Independence on 4 July 2000. Whereas the document of 1776 was directed against the British, the new Declaration aimed at the two-party system, at large corporations and banks (which come in for particularly intensive criticism by the authors), at the media, at special interests, and at the bureaucracy. The book also reflects concern about the effect of free-trade policies, especially the GATT (General Agreement on Tariffs and Trade) and NAFTA (North American Free Trade Agreement) treaties, on workers.

The book describes how, after extensive debate and discussion, the American people of this fictional future decided to adopt four amendments to restore the United States to its prior prosperity. Most important was the first of those amendments, providing for quarterly popular referendums on major issues of public policy. Neither the president nor the Congress could veto such referendums (Dolbeare and Hubbell 1996, 118–119). This referendum mechanism allowed for a more direct democracy than is currently practiced and helped convert members of Congress into delegates of the people rather than independent decision makers.

The second amendment adopted by the people of the novel limited campaign contributions to $100 for any individual or group and mandated that television and radio stations make free time available to candidates. Elections were shortened, with campaigning limited to sixty days prior to a primary election or ninety days prior to a general election.

The third amendment provided for proportional representation, both within the electoral college and within Congress. The intention of this amendment, which also lifted existing restrictions on third parties, was to encourage a

multiparty system. This amendment also lifted voting registration requirements, extended voting to a two-day weekend, and allowed voters to cast their ballots for "None of the Above" (NOTA).

The fourth amendment was aimed at the judicial system and attempted to balance considerations of individual rights against public concerns. It specifically mandated consideration of "comparative liability and contributory negligence," allowed judges to review jury awards, and attempted to reduce litigation (Dolbeare and Hubbell 1996, 134).

The authors aimed their book at an undergraduate audience. Although they believe it important that the changes they propose in their fictional account be adopted by amendments, they offer their proposals as "discussion drafts" rather than as final products.

For Further Reading:
Dolbeare, Kenneth M., and Janette K. Hubbell. 1996. *USA 2012: After the Middle-Class Revolution.* Chatham, NJ: Chatham House Publishers.

❖ DOMESTIC VIOLENCE, PROTECTION AGAINST ❖

Article IV, Section 4 of the Constitution authorizes the United States to protect states against domestic violence when so petitioned by a state. In *Luther v. Borden* (1849), the Supreme Court upheld a congressional law vesting the power to respond to such requests in the president.

Perhaps reacting to a speech in which outgoing President James Buchanan noted that Southern women retire at night "to apprehensions of civil insurrections" (J. Richardson 1908, 637), Democratic Representative Thomas Florence of Pennsylvania introduced a series of proposals in 1861 that were designed to save the Union by recognizing that slavery was a matter of state option. He also provided, however, that the government had an obligation to come to a state's aid in suppressing slave insurrections (Ames 1896, 171).

In 1870, motivated by a far different concern,

Republican Senator Charles Drake of Missouri introduced another resolution that would have entitled the national government to intervene in cases of Ku Klux Klan violence even when not requested to do so by state governments (Ames 1896, 172). Klan violence remained a legislative concern well into the twentieth century, with Southern white leaders successfully resisting national legislation in this area.

Congress attempted to address a much different issue in the Violence Against Women Act of 1994. The U.S. Supreme Court voided a portion of this act in *United States v. Morrison* (2000) when it decided that the federal claim of authority under the law exceeded congressional power under the commerce clause. Some observers viewed this decision as a victory for rights reserved to the states under the Tenth Amendment.

See also *United States v. Morrison.*

For Further Reading:

Ames, Herman. 1896. *The Proposed Amendments to the Constitution of the United States during the First Century of Its History.* Reprint, New York: Burt Franklin, 1970.

Richardson, James E., ed. 1908. *A Compilation of the Messages and Papers of the Presidents, 1789–1908.* 11 vols. n.p.: Bureau of National Literature and Art.

❖ DOUBLE JEOPARDY ❖

The Fifth Amendment provides that no person shall "be subject for the same offense to be twice put in jeopardy of life or limb." Initially, this doctrine applied only to the national government; for a long time, the Supreme Court rejected its application to the states. In *Palko v. Connecticut* (1937), for example, the Court decided that this was not one of the rights implicit in a scheme of ordered liberty. The Court did not reverse course until *Benton v. Maryland* (1968), the last of the contemporary incorporation cases (Abraham and Perry 1994, 81–83). Contemporary understandings of the doctrine, however, do not prevent prosecution of individuals in cases involving the same set of facts in different jurisdictions (an individual de-

clared not guilty of murder in a state court might later be tried and convicted of violating an individual's civil rights under federal law), nor do such understandings prohibit an individual, like O. J. Simpson, who is acquitted of a criminal act from being successfully prosecuted for civil damages.

In 1958 South Carolina Senator Strom Thurmond introduced a resolution to amend the Constitution so that when an individual appealed a criminal conviction and was granted a new trial, that individual "may be convicted of any crime of which he could have been convicted upon his former trial for such offense." In *Trono v. United States* (1905), the Supreme Court had established a similar rule—applied in the historic case of *Palko v. Connecticut* (1937), but it reversed course in *Green v. United States* (1957). In that case, an individual who successfully appealed a conviction for arson and second-degree murder was subsequently retried and convicted of first-degree murder. The Supreme Court voided this conviction, ruling that when an individual files a criminal appeal, conviction of a lesser offense bars subsequent prosecution of a greater offense, even if the conviction is later reversed on appeal (Sigler 1969, 71–72).

For Further Reading:

Abraham, Henry J., and Barbara Perry. 1994. *Freedom and the Court: Civil Rights and Liberties in the United States.* 6th ed. New York: Oxford University Press.

Sigler, Jay A. 1969. *Double Jeopardy: The Development of a Legal and Social Policy.* Ithaca, NY: Cornell University Press.

❖ DOUGLASS, FREDERICK (1817–1895) ❖

Few Americans have had more inspirational lives or so influenced thinking about the American Constitution, and especially about voting rights, as did Frederick Douglass. Born in Maryland in 1817 as a slave (of a white father and African American mother) under the name Frederick Augustus Washington Bailey, Douglass was taught by his slave owner's wife to read as a youth. After being trained as a ship caulker in Baltimore, he escaped in September 1838 to New York City, where he married and proceeded to New Bedford, Connecticut. Initially serving as a laborer, Douglass attended an Antislavery Society meeting in Massachusetts where he was asked to address the group. He had a commanding presence and a powerful story, and he was eventually employed as an agent for the Massachusetts Antislavery Society (Du Bois 1928–1936). In 1845 Douglass published an influential account of his life known as the *Narrative of the Life of Frederick Douglass,* but, having thus identified his origins and put his continuing freedom in jeopardy, he subsequently left for England until he could return with enough money to buy his freedom from his former master.

After his return to the United States, Douglass founded a newspaper entitled the *North Star,* which he edited for seventeen years. Douglass attended the Seneca Falls Convention in New York in 1848, and it was largely through his insistence and that of Elizabeth Cady Stanton that the Convention resolutions included one on behalf of women's suffrage, which at the time was considered to be a novel idea and subject to considerable ridicule. In the years ahead, Douglass often found that American women were in the forefront of the abolitionist movement. Unlike some abolitionists who viewed the U.S. Constitution as a "covenant with death, an agreement with hell," Douglass chose to interpret that document in a more generous manner (McFeely 1991, 204–207) that did not permanently embody slavery and that probably sat better with the majority of American citizens.

Douglass strongly supported the Northern war effort during the Civil War and encouraged African Americans to sign up to support the Union cause; two of his own sons joined the conflict. Initially less concerned with the amendment designed to outlaw slavery (the Thirteenth) or to guarantee equal rights (the Fourteenth), Douglass focused most of his efforts on black suffrage (what became the Fifteenth Amendment), believing, in the words of a current historian, "that only suffrage would provide African Americans with the power necessary to make themselves truly free" (Vorenberg 2001, 85).

Douglass's support for the Fifteenth Amendment led, at least initially, to a rift with some of the key leaders of the women's rights movement, including Susan B. Anthony and Elizabeth Cady Stanton, who were not above appealing to the perceived superiority of white women over black men in arguing that suffrage for the two groups should go hand in hand. The Civil War had been so clearly fought on behalf of African Americans and suffrage for women was still such a novel idea that Douglass and many other supporters of the Fifteenth Amendment did not believe they could take the chance of risking suffrage for black men by coupling it with that for women. Douglass was sympathetic to the plight of both groups, but he thought that the plight of blacks was far worse, and hence their need for the franchise far greater than it was for women. Writing to a supporter of women's suffrage, Douglass thus said:

> I am now devoting myself to a cause [if] not more sacred, certainly more urgent, because it is one of life and death to the long enslaved people of this country, and this is: negro suffrage. While the negro is mobbed, beaten, shot, stabbed, hanged, burnt and is the target of all that is malignant in the North and all that is murderous in the South, his claims may be preferred by me without exposing in any wise myself to the imputation of narrowness or meanness towards the cause of woman. As you well know, woman has a thousand ways to attach herself to the governing power of the land and already exerts an honorable influence on the course of legislation. She is the victim of abuses, to be sure, but it cannot be pretended I think that her cause is as urgent as . . . ours. (Quoted in McFeely 1991, 268–269)

Shortly after adoption of the Fifteenth Amendment, however, Douglass advocated an amendment to enfranchise women (McFeely 1991, 269) and he continued his support for such an amendment thereafter, joining Anthony and Stanton at suffrage events, and even attending a convention for women's suffrage on the day that he died in 1895 (Du Bois 1928–1936).

Given the setbacks to voting rights that African Americans faced in the aftermath of the adoption of the Thirteenth Amendment, Douglass was undoubtedly disappointed that the promise of black suffrage did not become the immediate reality for which he hoped. Douglass himself lived to be an honored figure, serving as secretary of a commission to Santo Domingo, a marshal and recorder of deeds in Washington, D.C., and, finally, as U.S. minister to Haiti (Du Bois 1928–1936). Although not initially enforced with much effectiveness, the Fifteenth Amendment reemerged in the 1960s and thereafter as a means of guaranteeing that African Americans would not simply have to depend on the goodwill of others but that they could use the political process to help themselves.

See also Abolitionists; Anthony, Susan Brownell; Fifteenth Amendment; Fourteenth Amendment; Seneca Falls Convention; Stanton, Elizabeth Cady; Thirteenth Amendment.

For Further Reading:

Du Bois, W. E. Burghardt. 1928–1936. "Frederick Douglass." In *Dictionary of American Biography,* American Council of Learned Societies, at *http://www.galenet.com.* Accessed 11/26/2002.

Douglass, Frederick. 1845. *Narrative of the Life of Frederick Douglass: An American Slave.* Boston: Anti-Slavery Office. Reprint, New York: Signet Books, 1968.

McFeely, William S. 1991. *Frederick Douglass.* New York: W. W. Norton & Company.

Vorenberg, Michael. 2001. *Final Freedom: The Civil War, the Abolition of Slavery, and the Thirteenth Amendment.* Cambridge, UK: Cambridge University Press.

❖ DUELING ❖

In the eighteenth and nineteenth centuries, gentlemen—especially in the South—sometimes resolved matters of personal honor by engaging in duels. These were closely bounded by recognized social norms (Stowe 1987, 5–49; Wyatt-Brown 1948, 350–361). It was in such a duel that Aaron Burr, a vice president, killed Alexander Hamilton, a former secretary of the treasury. Prior to becoming president, Andrew Jackson also engaged in such duels.

In 1828, the year Jackson was elected president, an amendment was introduced to prohibit dueling. In February 1838 William Graves, a Whig congressman from Kentucky, killed Jonathan Cilley, a Democratic congressman from Maine, in such a duel. Graves was censured, but the House rejected a committee report calling for his expulsion (Seitz 1966, 278). Similarly, two resolutions that would have excluded individuals who participated in such duels from holding office came to naught. Over time, state laws and public sentiment combined to eliminate this vestige of feudal aristocracy.

For Further Reading:

Seitz, Don C. 1929. *Famous American Duels: With Some Account of the Causes That Led up to Them and the Men Engaged.* Reprint, Freeport, NY: Books for Libraries Press, 1966.

Stowe, Steven M. 1987. *Intimacy and Power in the Old South: Ritual in the Lives of the Planters.* Baltimore, MD: Johns Hopkins University Press.

Wyatt-Brown, Bertram. 1948. *Southern Honor: Ethics and Behavior in the Old South.* New York: Oxford University Press.

❖ DURST, JACK ❖

Although he does not identify himself on his website, Jack Durst has responded to the author's query by indicating that as of May 2002 he was a "22 year old undergraduate student" at the University of Nevada (Reno) where he is working on a "pre-law criminal justice degree with a minor in casino management." He also indicates that he is active in local Democratic politics, that he became involved in political theory when he saw the movie "People v. Larry Flynt," that he tries to understand things, including languages, "by building models of them," and that his draft of a new constitution entitled a "Constitution of the Republic" was his "seventh and final draft" (e-mail correspondence with the author dated 5/22/02).

On the website, Durst indicates that "the writing of a new constitution" is "perhaps the greatest protest possible against the current organization of one's country," and says that his work, which was not yet completed as of 18 May 2002, was done "over the course of 2000" ("Constitution of the Republic" 2000). The preamble announces the constitution's intention to "establish an entirely new system of self-government" and to establish a law "which is fair, just, and honorable" ("Constitution" 2000). Durst's detailed Table of Contents outlines eight articles, the first five of which appear to have been completed. Durst lists a variety of theorists, including a number of libertarians who have guided his thinking, but it is difficult to put his rather extensive proposal into a single pigeonhole.

Unlike the U.S. Constitution, where most rights are specified as amendments in the Bill of Rights, Durst's first article begins with a declaration of rights. The rights of expression, the first to be listed, include a prohibition on government ownership of any media outlet "with the exception of a single printing office for the printing of laws and records." The article also includes a specific protection for "academic freedom of any institution of higher education, public or private, in the republic except to the extent that it may require certain courses for license to practice some professions, may require that civics and/or political science classes be taught, and shall, by law, insure the requirement that all human experimental subjects give informed consent" ("Constitution" 2000). Durst not only articulates the rights to privacy but includes a provision that states that "the expectation of privacy in the body, the home and its surrounds is absolute." This right also includes confidentiality of conversations with lawyers, doctors, and other professionals, makes provision for "the dignity of all persons," and prohibits the government from denying a passport "without a finding of good cause by a judge of the trial courts." Durst includes "rights of non-interference" ("Constitution" 2000). These include individuals' ownership of their own bodies and the right of

"consenting adults in private" to engage in "their own sexual and reproductive decisions," "the rights to grow, possess in reasonable quantity, and use any psychoactive substance," and the "right to work in any lawful profession" ("Constitution" 2000). Durst also includes "freedom of religion and culture," specifically exempting conscientious objectors from military service and guaranteeing all individuals "the right to participate in their culture and to enjoy and preserve their cultural heritage" ("Constitution" 2000). Property and corporate rights include the right not to have taxes levied against savings, the right to form corporations, and the right to "form unions or employer's associations, bargain collectively, participate in any organization, or strike" ("Constitution" 2000).

Rights in Durst's constitution are balanced by eight duties that include obedience to law, participation in government, voting, seeking to change laws with which they disagree, protecting the republic, being informed, paying taxes, and honoring contracts.

In Article II, Durst outlines the basic form of his proposed government. Like the current government, it has three branches, but they are "a Republic Council who execute the laws, a judiciary which interprets them, and a Parliament [sic] which causes to be made and approves them." The Republic Council has twelve members who serve three-year terms; it is presided over by the prime minister. Parliament will apparently be a unicameral rather than a bicameral body, and will consist of 100 members who are elected yearly; a supreme court of from three to seven members will head the judiciary. The prime minister will be elected by the parliament and will "serve as liaison between the Council, the Parliament, and the ministers." Durst goes into an elaborate description of elections and voting under his system, a right that may be exercised by individuals as young as fifteen who can demonstrate "the ability to make an informed and reasoned political choice" ("Constitution" 2000). Individuals will be limited to national elective offices for no more than ten years, with candidates selected in "partisan caucuses" and subject to election according to systems that take voters' first, second, and third choices into account. States appear to be replaced by a set of twenty geographically contiguous but shifting districts, each of which has five seats in parliament. Trial judges will serve three-year terms, appellate judges ten-year terms, and members of the supreme court during good behavior. The system of lawmaking is as complicated as that for voting. The parliament and the council will have the power to call consensus committees on topics of their own choosing and on topics about which voters have petitioned. Courts will maintain the power of judicial review, but the parliament will be able to overrule decisions dealing with the interpretation of statutes by a three-fifths vote. "Omnibus bills" are forbidden, and provisions are made for legislation by initiative. Laws made by "cities and local cabinets" are mentioned but not by states or by the districts from which members of parliament are elected. The council has the power to impose taxes, but the total tax on any given item or income is limited to 30 percent. A new common currency, designated the "shilling," shall be established, initially to be "worth .07 of a Swiss Franc," a standard for which there is no explanation. The council has the power to declare war, but the parliament will make laws regarding the military; it will also be able to adopt emergency laws when needed. The supreme court will have power to decide on the constitutionality of wars, and the prime minister, with authority from the council, will have power to declare martial law. Cabinet ministers will serve four-year terms. All ministries shall be similar to those like the ministry of justice/police, which Durst describes in detail. Created by the council, it shall be based on "a uniform police force and prosecutor throughout the republic, divided geographically into departments, with oversight by the legislative and judicial branch and control by the executive" ("Constitution" 2000). A chief prosecutor shall head each police department. He and other heads of local ministries may "form a local cabinet, to govern and coordinate the actions of the executive branch in their area of mutual geographical jurisdiction with the advice and consent of the citizen's advisory board" ("Constitution" 2000).

In Article III, Durst discusses the authorization of laws. He lists twenty-four separate powers of the government including the protection of workers and consumers, the regulation of businesses, the protection of property and civil rights, environmental protection, "fair distribution of inheritances," care "for idiots and the insane," education, "access for all citizens to food, housing, and other necessities," etc. ("Constitution" 2000). No crimes, except for a few designated "felonies," will carry a penalty of more than one year in prison.

Article IV is devoted to the judiciary and to due process rights. In what appears to be a rather unusual provision, the first statement provides that "[t]he judiciary shall insure that children within the republic have access to safe, modern schools which provide knowledge relevant to their futures and useful as citizens" ("Constitution" 2000). The judiciary will include both trial and appellate courts, and Durst specifically recognizes the government's obligation to provide counsel for criminal defendants unable to afford it. In addition to a variety of rights of criminal defendants already recognized in the current U.S. Constitution, Durst provides (perhaps as an alternative to the current exclusionary rule) that "the responsible party shall be liable to compensate all persons wrongly or illegally arrested for actual damages" ("Constitution" 2000). He also incorporates the standard of "beyond a reasonable doubt" in criminal cases and specifies that all references to a jury are "to a jury of 12." Durst would outlaw capital punishment and provide each prisoner "with a rulebook . . . which shall be strictly and unerringly enforced, and shall contain all regulations placed on prisoners which are not placed on ordinary citizens" ("Constitution" 2000). Durst provides that "all adults with equal bargaining power have absolute freedom to make any contract except one for illegal acts and/or services" ("Constitution" 2000). He also outlaws discrimination by law or by any organization tied to the government on the basis of "a. Race, color, ethnicity, or genetic makeup; b. Condition of current or former drug use; c. Gender, marital status, gender or sexual preference; d. Religion; e. Political beliefs; [or] f. Physical disability" ("Constitution" 2000). Article IV further provides that "[t]his constitution is to be broadly construed in such a manner that the greatest liberty is afforded the citizen, the least power and the greatest obligation consistent with that power to the government and to incorporate the long-standing traditions developed under it" ("Constitution" 2000).

Article V specifies how the constitution will be amended. Council members may propose amendments after receiving petitions of 10 percent of the voters. A two-thirds majority of the Council will then send the amendment to a consensus committee, which' amendment, if proposed by a two-thirds majority vote of parliament, will be approved by three-fifths of the people. Such an amendment will be in effect for ten years, after which it will be made permanent, or may be extended as a nonpermanent amendment for an additional ten years. Durst specifies, however, that "No amendment may be made to this constitution which substantially alters the form of the government or the powers of its branches except by singular addition or subtraction of powers, nor may any amendment be made which addresses more than one basic topic" ("Constitution" 2000). He specifies a number of provisions that cannot be amended, but also provides that those provisions that can be amended can be altered by convention. In an idea similar to one once advanced by Thomas Jefferson, Durst provides that no constitution shall be adopted without a provision specifying that "After 10 years, all citizens shall vote on whether to retain this constitution or return to the previous constitution as amended. If a majority votes to return to the previous constitution this constitution shall become null and void" ("Constitution" 2000).

Although included in his detailed table of contents, Durst does not elaborate on the gradual implementation of his plan. Neither does he specify the "Name, Flag, and Location" of the new government, nor the names of its signatories.

Far more detailed than the existing plan of government, Durst's plan appears closer to a parliamentary than to the current presidential model of government. Listing more rights than the current document, Durst's proposal does not go as far as some libertarian proposals in limiting governmental powers. Most fascinating is Durst's apparent (and seemingly unexplained) dismissal of existing state governments and their replacement by districts of shifting dimensions. The fact that Durst and others would attempt to express their views on government by attempting to rewrite the nation's fundamental law is another indication of the importance that most citizens attribute to the nation's constitutive document.

For Further Reading:
Durst, Jack. 2000. "Constitution of the Republic." *http://spynx_jd.tripod.com/constitution/CS-1-A. html.* Accessed 5/18/02.

❖ DUTIES ❖

See Tariffs; Taxation, Export.

❖ DYER V. BLAIR (1975) ❖

John Paul Stevens, who subsequently became and continues to serve as a U.S. Supreme Court justice, wrote this U.S. district court decision. The case involved Illinois's ratification of the equal rights amendment. Members of the legislature had sued Robert Blair, Speaker of the Illinois House of Representatives, for declaring state ratification of the amendment dead after it failed to achieve the three-fifths vote that the legislature and the state constitution had mandated for such amendments (Vile 1993b, 28–30).

Despite the Supreme Court's decision in *Coleman v. Miller* (1939), Stevens declared that this particular amending issue was not a "political question." Citing *Powell v. McCormack* (1969), Stevens argued that, however difficult, this case involved "no more than an interpretation of the Constitution" (*Dyer* 1975, 1301). As to the requisite vote for ratification, Stevens concluded that although Article V of the Constitution does not require an extraordinary majority by ratifying state legislatures, it also does not prohibit states from adopting such a majority.

Citing *Hawke v. Smith (I)* (1920) and the *National Prohibition Cases* (1920), which had decided that a state could not require ratification of amendments by popular referendum, Stevens struck down a provision in the Illinois state constitution that required the election of a new legislature before a vote was taken on a constitutional amendment. Stevens further ruled that because states were performing a federal function when they ratified amendments, any language in a state's constitution regarding a supermajority requirement would be "precatory" (*Dyer* 1975, 1308) or recommendatory only.

This case suggests that caution is in order in interpreting earlier cases, such as *Coleman v. Miller* (1939), that seem to withdraw the courts from consideration of key amending issues.

See also *Coleman v. Miller.*

For Further Reading:

Dyer v. Blair, 390 F. Supp. 1291 (1975).

Vile, John R. 1993b. *The Theory and Practice of Constitutional Change in America: A Collection of Original Source Materials.* New York: Peter Lang.

E

❖ EDUCATION, ESTABLISHMENT OF A NATIONAL UNIVERSITY ❖

Each of the first six presidents is on record as favoring a national university to train public servants, but some, including Thomas Jefferson, had reservations about congressional authority to establish such an institution (Ambrose 1966, 11, 17). James Madison, Charles Pinckney, and James Wilson suggested a measure at the Constitutional Convention of 1787 that would have entrusted such power to Congress, but it was not adopted (Eidelberg 1968, 27). As president, both Thomas Jefferson and James Monroe proposed in annual messages that such an amendment be adopted, and one was introduced in Congress in 1825 (Ames 1896, 274–275).

Although Jefferson had argued as a member of Washington's cabinet that Congress had no authority to establish a military academy, he supported the establishment of West Point during his presidency (Ambrose 1966, 18–19). This and other military academies are the only universities currently operated by the national government. Other U.S. universities, including the University of Virginia, which Jefferson founded after leaving the presidency, are either state or privately funded and operated.

Throughout American history, however, the federal government has encouraged the creation of colleges and universities throughout the nation with the Morrill Acts of 1862 and 1890 being especially important in the creation of land-grant institutions—so-called because they were funded by revenues from the sale of federal lands (Carleton 2002, 27–40, 53–62). More recently, the Higher Education Act of 1965 was used to funnel increased federal funds to colleges and universities (Carleton 2002, 147–159).

For Further Reading:

Ambrose, Stephen E. 1966. *Duty, Honor, Country: A History of West Point*. Baltimore, MD: Johns Hopkins University Press.

Ames, Herman. 1896. *The Proposed Amendments to the Constitution of the United States during the First Century of Its History*. Reprint, New York: Burt Franklin, 1970.

Carleton, David. 2002. *Student's Guide to Landmark Congressional Laws on Education*. Westport, CT: Greenwood Press.

Eidelberg, Paul. 1968. *The Philosophy of the American Constitution: A Reinterpretation of the Intentions of the Founding Fathers*. New York: Free Press.

❖ EDUCATION, RIGHT TO ❖

When the U.S. Supreme Court outlawed the system of *de jure* racial segregation in public schools in *Brown v. Board of Education* (1954), it recognized that education was increasingly important to success. However, the Constitution, which confines itself largely to the delineation of political rights, does not specifically list a right to education. Although today's national government continues to give increasing aid to education, Supreme Court decisions since *Brown* have refused to recognize that the right to an education is a "fundamental right," subject to heightened judicial scrutiny.

Whereas in *San Antonio Independent School District v. Rodriguez* (1973) the Court decided not to invalidate a Texas system of education in which funding varied from one district to another depending on local property taxes, some state courts have subsequently ruled that their own constitutions required greater equality in state educational funding. In an article written shortly before the nation would begin amending its constitution for the first time in more than sixty years, journalist E. L. Godkin (editor of *The Nation*) argued that one area in which the U.S. Constitution should be changed was in the area of education. Specifically pointing to the myriad of problems that he thought stemmed from inadequate education, Godkin asked:

> Would it not be wiser, as well as juster and more humane, to give it [the national government] the power, and not only this, but to make it its duty, to establish schools whenever the State governments, through indolence or indifference, false economy or sheer malevolence, fail to do so? If, in short, the safety of the nation depends on the education of the people, ought not the education of the people to be made a national concern? (Godkin 1864, 143)

Although the national government did work to establish schools for freedmen after the Civil War, the Constitution was never specifically amended to mention the right to an education. Court decisions in *Meyer v. Nebraska* (1923) and *Pierce v. Society of Sisters* (1925) did respectively recognize the right of a school to teach a modern foreign language and the right of parents to send their children to parochial schools.

Individuals who believe that the modern Constitution should include social and economic rights often include the right to an education. Congressman Jesse L. Jackson Jr. (D-IL) has proposed an amendment to the Constitution that would guarantee that "[a]ll citizens of the United States shall enjoy the right to a public education of equal high quality" (Jackson with Watkins 2001, 330). Undoubtedly, the devil would be in the details of such a broadly worded right.

See also Jackson, Jesse L., Jr.; Social and Economic Rights.

For Further Reading:
Godkin, E. L. 1864. "The Constitution and Its Defects." *North American Review* 99 (July): 117–143.
Jackson, Jesse L., Jr., with Frank E. Watkins. 2001. *A More Perfect Union: Advancing New American Rights.* New York: Welcome Rain Publishers.

❖ EIGHTEENTH AMENDMENT ❖

The Eighteenth Amendment providing for national alcoholic prohibition is distinctive for two reasons: it represents the only successful attempt to incorporate sumptuary legislation into the Constitution, and it is the only amendment to have been repealed. The first prohibition amendment to be introduced in Congress was offered by Republican Representative Henry Blair of New Hampshire in 1876, with amendments being introduced sporadically thereafter until 1913. That year the Anti-Saloon League decided to focus its energy on a national amendment. After this decision, dozens of proposals were introduced until the amendment was adopted in 1919.

Some of the American founders, most notably Dr. Benjamin Rush, expressed concern over the health effects of alcohol, and both politicians (including Abraham Lincoln, who signed an abstinence pledge) and religious reformers subsequently encouraged temperance. Maine established statewide prohibition in 1851 (Grimes 1978, 83), but the primary waves of prohibition at the state level occurred in 1864–1865, in the 1880s, and beginning in 1907. It was during the last of these waves that the focus of reform moved from the state to the national level. By 1917 twenty-three states had prohibition laws, although only thirteen were completely dry (U.S. Senate 1985).

Scholars continue to debate the weight to assign to various motivations behind Prohibition. Clearly, some supporters (especially those in the influential Women's Christian Temperance Union) were motivated by religious beliefs, some by medical evidence of the detrimental effects of alcohol use, and some by the belief in moral reform and progress so characteristic of the Progressive Era, during which a constitutional amendment was finally adopted (Timberlake 1970).

More negative cultural forces undoubtedly played a part as well. Many people viewed the saloon as "a political brothel in which corrupt liaisons were formed between foreign-born voters and political bosses" (Grimes 1978, 84), and the Anti-Saloon League became a major focus for prohibition. Reformers were disproportionately rural white Protestants of northern European ethnic stock, and such reformers sometimes saw prohibition as a means of controlling or reforming Catholics, immigrants, African Americans, Indians, and poor whites. With the advent of World War I, some reformers also found that prohibition and anti-German sentiment went well together because Germans were frequently associated with breweries.

Many advocates of temperance nevertheless opposed the idea of prohibition as unwarranted state interference in personal decision making and saw national prohibition as an improper interference with states' rights. Others pointed to the injustice of shutting down what had previously been legitimate businesses. Opponents also pointed out that under the amending process, it was possible for a minority of the people to adopt an amendment that the majority did not support.

Proponents nonetheless insisted on the evils of alcohol. A preface to an amending resolution introduced in Congress in 1914 explained their views:

> Exact scientific research has demonstrated that alcohol is a narcotic poison, destructive and degenerating to the human organism, and that its distribution as a beverage or contained in foods lays a staggering economic burden upon the shoulders of the people; lowers to an appalling degree the average standard of character of our citizenship, thereby undermining public morals and the foundations of free institutions; produces widespread crime, pauperism, and insanity; inflicts disease and untimely death upon hundreds of thousands of citizens and blights with degeneracy their children unborn, threatening the future integrity and the very life of the Nation. (U.S. Senate 1985, 50)

As early as 1890 Congress adopted the Wilson Act, subjecting imported liquor to state regulation. But in *Leisy v. Hardin* (1890), the Supreme Court said that such alcohol was not subject to state regulation as long as it remained in its "original package" (Musmanno 1929, 228–229). The Webb-Kenyon Act of 1913 further strengthened federal control over interstate shipment of alcohol, but proponents of prohibition obviously wanted more.

In 1914 the House of Representatives defeated a prohibition amendment, but support for such an amendment increased as war loomed. In 1917 Congress adopted the Lever Food Control Act restricting the importation of alcohol and prohibiting the use of foodstuffs in its production. That same year, Democratic Texas Senator Morris Sheppard reintroduced a prohibition amendment that the House and the Senate subsequently adopted in December.

As amended, the proposal had a number of unique features. The first paragraph provided for a one-year transitional period, probably in the hope of allaying concerns about putting people out of work. Although it prohibited "the manufacture, sale, or transportation of intoxicating liquors within, the importation thereof into, or the exportation thereof for beverage purposes," the amendment left open the possible use of alcohol for medicinal and other purposes; moreover, the amendment did not explicitly outlaw the purchase of alcohol. The second paragraph of the amendment rather ambiguously provided that the state and national governments would have "concurrent power" to enforce the amendment. The third paragraph was the first to contain a seven-year ratification deadline. A somewhat shorter deadline was initially proposed by Republican Senator (later president) Warren G. Harding in the unrealized hope that the provision might undermine the amendment. The amendment was adopted despite arguments by Idaho's Republican Senator William Borah that the deadline provision was unconstitutional (Grimes 1978, 87).

The amendment was ratified in just over a year, and in 1919 Congress overrode President Woodrow Wilson's veto to adopt the Volstead Act. It defined as intoxicating any beverage—including beer and wine—that contained more than 0.5 percent alcohol.

In *Hawke v. Smith (I)* (1920) the Supreme Court ruled that a state could not require approval of this or other amendments by referendum, thus arguably creating the impression in the public mind that the amendment did not have majority support. That decision might also have paved the way for the decision to have the Twenty-first Amendment adopted through state conventions rather than by state legislatures. In the *National Prohibition Cases* (1920) and again in *United States v. Sprague* (1931), the Supreme Court rejected arguments that the Eighteenth Amendment exceeded implicit limitations alleged to inhere in Article V. The *National Prohibition Cases* also defined concurrent powers to allow the state and national governments to enforce their own provisions and upheld the definition of alcohol in the Volstead Act.

The prohibition movement and the Eighteenth Amendment appear to have reduced but not eliminated alcohol consumption (Kyvig 1985, 13). Although it sanctioned increased governmental power over individuals, Prohibition was widely flouted, and the Eighteenth Amendment is generally believed to have contributed to the rise of organized crime by providing it with a profitable source of illegal revenue. In 1932 the Eighteenth Amendment was repealed by the Twenty-first Amendment.

See also Anti-Saloon League; Twenty-first Amendment; Women's Christian Temperance Union.

For Further Reading:

Grimes, Alan P. 1978. *Democracy and the Amendments to the Constitution*. Lexington, MA: Lexington Books.

Kyvig, David E., ed. 1985. *Alcohol and Order: Perspectives on National Prohibition*. Westport, CT: Greenwood Press.

Musmanno, M. A. 1929. *Proposed Amendments to the Constitution*. Washington, DC: U.S. Government Printing Office.

Timberlake, James H. 1970. *Prohibition and the Progressive Movement, 1900–1920*. New York: Atheneum.

U.S. Senate Committee on the Judiciary, Subcommittee on the Constitution 1985. *Amendments to the Constitution: A Brief Legislative History*. Washington DC: U.S. Government Printing Office.

❖ EIGHTH AMENDMENT ❖

The Eighth Amendment was proposed by the First Congress and ratified in 1791 as part of the Bill of Rights. It provides that "excessive bail shall not be required, nor excessive fines imposed, nor cruel and unusual punishments inflicted." The prohibition against excessive fines has roots in the English Magna Carta, whereas the provisions against excessive bails and cruel and unusual punishments originated in the Massachusetts Body of Liberties and the Virginia Declaration of Rights (Lutz 1992, 53). Both the Virginia and the North Carolina ratifying conventions called for amendments against cruel and unusual punishments, and James Madison linked this guarantee to the provisions against excessive bail and fines when he presented his proposal for a bill of rights before Congress.

Debates in Congress were limited but prescient. William Smith of South Carolina thought that the words "cruel and unusual" were "too indefinite" (Kurland and Lerner 1987, 5:377). Samuel Livermore of New Hampshire positively noted that "the clause seems to express a great deal of humanity," but went on to doubt its necessity and raise some questions: "What is meant by the terms excessive bail? Who are to be the judges? What is understood by excessive fines? It lies with the courts to determine. No cruel and unusual punishment is to be inflicted; it is sometimes necessary to hang a man, villains often deserve whipping, and perhaps having their ears cut off; but are we in the future to be prevented from inflicting these punishments because they are cruel?" (Kurland and Lerner 1987, 5:377). Acknowledging that the legislature should adopt as limited a punishment as proved useful, Livermore said, "we ought not to be restrained from making necessary laws by any declaration of this kind" (Kurland and Lerner 1987, 5:377). Despite his objections, the provision passed overwhelmingly.

Generally, the courts have granted legislatures flexibility in deciding whether fines and bail are excessive. Most contemporary controversy about the Eighth Amendment has centered on the provision prohibiting "cruel and unusual punishments." In *Furman v. Georgia* (1972), the Supreme Court declared that the death penalty as then administered was unconstitutional, but subsequent cases have allowed for such punishment when juries consider aggravating and mitigating circumstances and when trials are bifurcated so that the determination of guilt or innocence is separated from the fixing of a penalty. Numerous amendments have been proposed that would either permit or outlaw capital punishment.

On 1 May 2001, Indiana Democratic Representative Julia Carson introduced an amendment that would have modified the Eighth Amendment by inserting a provision after "cruel and unusual punishments" that would have read "(including incarceration, before or after trial, for minor traffic offenses.)" This amendment appears to have been provoked by a U.S. Supreme Court decision in *Atwater v. City of Lago Vista* (2001), in which the Court decided in a five-to-four majority decision written by David Souter that the arrest of a Texas mother in front of her children and her short incarceration at a cell in the police station for the failure of any of them to be wearing seatbelts was not an unreasonable search and seizure in violation of the Fourth Amendment.

On a related matter, a majority of the Supreme Court has apparently reversed course on earlier rulings that declared that the Eighth Amendment was intended, in noncapital cases, to outlaw punishments that are disproportionate to the crimes they are designed to punish. Thus, in a decision authored by Justice Antonin Scalia, the Court refused in *Harmelin v. Michigan* (1991) to overturn a sentence of life without parole for a man convicted of possession of more than 650 grams of cocaine; Scalia argued that if the framers had intended the Eighth Amendment to outlaw disproportionate punishments, they would have specifically said so. Scalia thought that legislators, rather than judges, should determine such mattes.

Scalia was on the losing side in *Atkins v. Virginia* (2002) when six of nine justices led by Justice John Paul Stevens decided that the cruel and unusual provision of the Eighth Amendment prohibited application of the death penalty to individuals who are retarded, but he agreed with the decision in *Ring v. Arizona* (2002) requiring that a jury, rather than a judge, decide whether the aggravating circumstances were such as to warrant the death penalty.

See also Capital Punishment.

For Further Reading:
Atwater v. City of Lago Vista, 532 U.S. 318 (2001).
Hoffmann, Joseph L. 1993. "The 'Cruel and Unusual Punishment' Clause: A Limit on the Power to Punish or Constitutional Rhetoric?" In *The Bill of Rights in Modern America*, ed. David J. Bodenhamer and James W. Ely Jr. Bloomington, IN: Indiana University Press.
Kurland, Philip B., and Ralph Lerner, eds. 1987. *The Founders' Constitution*. 5 vols. Chicago: University of Chicago Press.
Lutz, Donald S. 1992. *A Preface to American Political Theory*. Lawrence, KS: University Press of Kansas.

❖ EISELEN, MALCOLM R. (1902–1965) ❖

Historian Malcolm Eiselen used the sesquicentennial of the U.S. Constitution to argue for a second constitutional convention (Vile 1991c, 74–75). Altogether, he suggested about a dozen changes that should be contemplated, including abolishing the electoral college, changing the president's tenure of office, clarifying the power of judicial review, considering the federal initiative and referendum, allowing cabinet members to be seated in Congress, nominating presidents more democratically, clarifying issues of presidential disability, making the process of constitutional amendment easier (see Eiselen 1941), abandoning the requirement that treaties be ratified by two-thirds majorities, redistributing powers between state and national governments, and providing mechanisms to avoid "national bankruptcy and financial chaos" (Eiselen 1937, 29–33). Eiselen was particularly concerned about federal spending and suggested longer terms for the president and members of Congress and adoption of the item veto and the executive budget as possible remedies (Eiselen 1937, 32).

Eiselen proposed that members of the convention should be a mixture of elected and appointed delegates, with the American Bar Association, the American Political Science Association, and the American Economic Association among the groups making appointments (Eiselen 1937, 34). Eiselen cautioned that delegates should avoid the temptation to create a document too lengthy or detailed. He recognized that, like the document of 1787, any new constitution would have to embody compromises making it acceptable to the people.

For Further Reading:

Eiselen, Malcolm R. 1941. "Can We Amend the Constitution?" *South Atlantic Quarterly* 40 (October): 333–341.

———. 1937. "Dare We Call a Federal Convention?" *North American Review* 244 (Autumn): 27–28.

❖ ELECTIONS, DATES OF ❖

Article II, Section 1 of the Constitution provides that Congress shall determine a uniform day for choosing presidential electors. For a time, Congress merely specified that such elections should be made thirty-four days prior to the first Wednesday in December (Ames 1896, 114). Before Congress acted in 1845 to set the Tuesday after the first Monday in November for such elections, it received a number of petitions for an amendment setting a uniform date or allowing for more than one day during which elections would be held. Two proposals offered in 1888 to prevent state elections on the same day as federal contests were apparently motivated by concerns that political parties were trading votes for the two sets of offices (Ames 1896, 111). Many individuals who are concerned about low voting rates in the United States have proposed that the day for national elections be on a Saturday or be declared a national holiday, but neither action would require a constitutional amendment.

For Further Reading:

Ames, Herman. 1896. *The Proposed Amendments to the Constitution of the United States during the First Century of Its History.* Reprint, New York: Burt Franklin, 1970.

❖ ELECTIONS, DISPUTED ❖

Article I, Section 5 specifies that "each House shall be the Judge of the Elections, Returns, and Qualifications of its own members." Deciding whom to seat in closely contested elections can become a highly partisan decision.

Prompted by the contested election of five New Jersey representatives, States' Rights Democratic Representative Richard Habersham of Georgia introduced an amendment in 1840 to specify the kinds of evidence Congress could consult in deciding which individuals to seat (Ames 1896, 57). To date, Congress still has no specific constitutional guidelines to follow. When the 104th Congress convened in January 1995, Congress seated four members whose seats were contested, pending further investigation (MacPherson 1995, 28).

In the disputed presidential election of 1876, a commission consisting of a number of U.S. Supreme Court justices was ultimately responsible for awarding disputed electoral votes that resulted in the selection of Republican Rutherford B. Hayes over Democrat Samuel B. Tilden (Robinson 1996). The Supreme Court took an even more direct role in the election of 2000 when its decision in *Bush v. Gore* (2000) ultimately halted vote recounting in the pivotal state of Florida (recounting that the Court decided was standardless and thus in violation of the equal protection clause of the Fourteenth Amendment), resulting in a Bush victory.

Scholars continue to debate the merits of this decision (compare Ceaser and Busch 2000 with Gillman 2001).

For Further Reading:

Ames, Herman. 1896. *The Proposed Amendments to the Constitution of the United States during the First Century of Its History.* Reprint, New York: Burt Franklin, 1970.

Bush v. Gore, 531 U.S. 98 (2000).

Ceaser, James W., and Andrew W. Busch. 2001. *The Perfect Tie: The True Story of the 2000 Presidential Election.* Lanham, MD: Rowman & Littlefield.

Gillman, Howard. 2001. *The Votes That Counted: How the Court Decided the 2000 Presidential Election.* Chicago: University of Chicago Press.

MacPherson, Peter. 1995. "Contested Winners Seated; Challengers in Pursuit." *Congressional Quarterly Weekly Report* 53 (7 January): 28.

Robinson, Lloyd. 1996. *The Stolen Election, Hayes versus Tilden—1876.* New York: Forge.

❖ ELECTIONS, PRIMARY ❖

In *Newberry v. United States* (1921), the Supreme Court ruled that Article I, Section 4 did not give Congress power to regulate party primaries. Shortly thereafter, Oklahoma Republican Representative Manuel Herrick introduced an amendment extending federal election laws to primaries as well as to general elections.

Subsequently, in *United States v. Classic* (1941), the Court allowed regulation of state primaries when such primaries were tied to the process of choosing candidates for federal office. In later outlawing the all-white primary in *Smith v. Allwright* (1944), the Court specifically overturned the *Newberry* decision. Significantly, in outlawing poll taxes in federal elections, the Twenty-fourth Amendment specifically mentioned "any primary or other [federal] election."

See also Twenty-fourth Amendment; Voting Rights, Constitutional Amendments Relating to.

❖ ELECTORAL COLLEGE REFORM ❖

No amendment effort has been more consistent than that for reform of the electoral college. More than 850 proposals have been offered in Congress, making this topic second in overall numbers only to the equal rights amendment. Two reforms of the electoral college have been adopted, the Twelfth Amendment and the Twenty-third Amendment. The Twelfth Amendment requires that electors differentiate between their votes for president and vice president (thus eliminating the possibility of a tie, which occurred in the election of 1800). The Twenty-third Amendment provides that the District of Columbia will have representation equivalent to that of the smallest state—currently, three votes.

Operation

The electoral college system is a complicated scheme formulated at the Constitutional Convention of 1787. Under this system, each state is awarded a number of votes equivalent to its representation in the House and the Senate. States then select electors, who meet in the state's capital. Since the Twelfth Amendment, each elector casts one vote for president and another for vice president, at least one such vote going to an out-of-state candidate. Such votes are then reported to Washington, D.C., and opened in a joint session of Congress.

If no candidate receives a majority of the electoral college—currently 270 out of 538 possible votes—the election for the president goes to the House of Representatives and that of the vice president to the Senate. The House chooses from among the top three candidates (prior to adoption of the Twelfth Amendment, it voted from among five candidates in such circumstances), with each state's delegation getting a single vote. Similarly, the Senate, which previously had no role except in the case of a tie between the runners-up, chooses between the top two candidates for vice president. Typically, the electoral college exaggerates the votes of the winner, thus providing the appearance of greater support for an incoming president and arguably making fraud within one or two states less likely to affect the outcome than if all votes were counted (for a more complete discussion of the operation of the electoral system, see Berns 1992).

Foundation and Development

When the Constitutional Convention first considered presidential elections, it contemplated that Congress would choose the president. Members feared, however, that this method would undercut the system of separation of powers and presidential independence. Similarly, a system of direct election would have been difficult to implement at a time when transportation and communications were slow. Moreover, such a system would have effectively stripped the small states of any real influence in presidential selection. The system adopted, by contrast, had the advantage of reinforcing federalism by incorporating the agreement that already lay at the base of the Connecticut, or Great, Compromise (Hardaway 1994, 82). That is, the smallest states would get at least three votes, because each state was guaranteed at least one member in the House of Representatives and two senators. (For an argument questioning the electoral college's effect on federalism, see "Rethinking the Electoral College Debate" 2001.)

Most of the operation of the electoral college has developed by usage rather than by constitutional mandate. Thus, all states now choose their electors by popular vote, but this is not mandated either in the Constitution or by the Twelfth Amendment. Similarly, all but two states (Maine and Nebraska) now use a winner-take-all system that exaggerates the influence of the more populous states, but this has also developed by custom. There is some dispute as to whether electors were or were not originally expected to exercise independent judgment, but with a few flukes (so-called faithless electors), most follow the pledges that the parties now require of them.

Criticism

The use of the electoral college system raises the possibility that the winner of the electoral vote may not be the winner of the popular vote; to many, this departure from direct democracy is unjustifiable. Until recently, the only election in which such a result clearly happened was the election of 1888, in which Benjamin Harrison amassed 230 electoral votes to President Grover Cleveland's 168, even though Cleveland (who would be reelected in the next presidential election) had received about 100,000 more popular votes. In 2000, however, Republican candidate George W. Bush, who did particularly well in less-populated western states, narrowly won the electoral college despite falling approximately half a million votes nationwide behind his Democratic opponent, Albert Gore Jr. Moreover, there continues to be vigorous debate about whether Bush or Gore actually won the greater number of votes in the pivotal state of Florida, where there were problems with voting machines and vote counting. The Supreme Court eventually brought recounts to an end in *Bush v. Gore* (2000), arguing that Florida officials were not utilizing consistent standards that would lead to equal protection of the law under the Fourteenth Amendment. Journalists and scholars continue to chronicle and debate the election and the accompanying court decisions (see Ceaser and Busch 2001; Correspondents of *The New York Times* 2001; Dershowitz 2001; Dionne and Kristol 2001; Gillman 2001; Political Staff of *The Washington Post* 2001).

Some critics would also include the elections of 1824, 1876, and 1960 as examples in which the winner of the electoral college may not have won the popular vote. In the election of 1824, Andrew Jackson received more popular votes than John Quincy Adams, who was selected by the House of Representatives as the winner. However, there were four candidates, and in the initial voting, none gained a majority of either the electoral or the popular vote. Similarly, there is evidence that Samuel Tilden may have captured more votes in the election of 1876 than his opponent, Rutherford B. Hayes. Hayes, however, was declared the eventual winner after an electoral commission, appointed by the House of Representatives to resolve disputed electoral votes in three states, voted along party lines to give all these votes to Hayes. Corruption was so rampant on both sides in this contest that it is not clear that the electoral college system should be held responsible for the outcome (Hardaway 1994, 128–137). The dispute over who won the popular vote in the election of 1960, in which John F. Kennedy received the greater number of electoral votes, centers on whether he should have been credited with the votes cast for unpledged delegates in Alabama.

In addition to attacks for being undemocratic, the electoral college has been criticized along a number of other lines. It has been argued that the system gives an advantage to particular types of states or minority groups that may hold the balance of power. The winner-take-all feature of the system certainly encourages candidates to go for majorities in the most populous states, whereas the three votes cast by the smallest states are more than they would be entitled to judged purely by population. The winner-take-all feature of the current system has also been criticized for effectively "wasting" the votes of minorities within each state and thus decreasing voter turnout. Other features of the system—for example, the possibility of faithless electors, like the Washington, D.C., elector who cast a blank ballot in the 2000 election in protest over the District's failure to have voting representatives in Congress ("Electoral College" 2001), or the resolution of elections in the House of Representatives rather than by popular vote—are issues that are sometimes raised.

The District Plan

In addition to the reforms incorporated in the Twelfth and Twenty-third Amendments, several reforms have dominated discussion of the electoral college system. A popular proposal dating back to 1800 favors modifying the system along the order of a district plan. Some proposals have called for dividing each state into a number of districts equal to its total number of electors and giving each district a single elector. Others call for using existing congressional districts, with each state electing two electors on an at-large basis. Such a plan was proposed by a twenty-two-to-nine vote in the Senate in 1813, and again in 1819 by a vote of twenty-eight to ten. The House did not act

on the first proposal, and in 1820, its vote of ninety-two to fifty-four was just shy of the required two-thirds majority.

Missouri's Senator Thomas Hart Benton supported the district plan, as did Andrew Johnson. In the 1870s Indiana Senator Oliver P. Morton supported the plan, and in the 1940s and 1950s Representative Frederic R. Coudert Jr. of New York and South Dakota Senator Karl E. Mundt supported it. Other supporters of this plan included South Carolina Senator Strom Thurmond, Arizona Senator Barry Goldwater, and President Harry Truman. Democratic Senators Paul Douglas of Illinois and John F. Kennedy of Massachusetts opposed it.

Whatever its merits, the district system still allows a candidate to win a majority of votes within a state and not win a majority of its electoral votes. Indeed, this plan might still have resulted in George W. Bush's election in 2000 ("Electoral College" 2001). The district plan arguably does little to deal with the problem of "wasted" votes within districts, and it still leaves open the possibility that a president would be elected with less than a majority of popular votes (Peirce 1968, 152–168). Such a system might also encourage gerrymandering of individual districts (Hardaway 1994, 144–145).

The Proportional Plan

A second plan frequently introduced is the proportional plan, under which a state's electoral votes would be divided in proportion to its popular votes. First introduced in 1848, the original plan awarded only whole delegates, but subsequent plans have carried this out to the nearest one-thousandth.

Supporters of a proportional plan have included Nebraska Senator George W. Norris, Massachusetts Senator Henry Cabot Lodge, and Texas Representative Ed Gossett. In 1950, the Senate approved such a plan by a vote of 67 to 27, but in the House, the plan was defeated by a vote of 134 for and 210 against. In 1956 the Senate subsequently voted 48 to 37 for a substitute offered by Price Daniel of Texas that would allow states to choose between the direct and the proportional plan.

Although the proportional plan takes care of the "wasted" vote problem, it does not guarantee a president elected by a majority. In the 1940s and 1950s, some opponents also feared that it would give an advantage to noncompetitive one-party states, especially those in the South, where Democrats typically racked up large majorities.

The Automatic Plan

A third alternative to the current electoral college system is often called the automatic system and appears to have been first contemplated by Thomas Jefferson. This system would eliminate the individual electors and give each state's votes to candidates who captured a majority there.

In 1934, the Senate voted 42 to 24 for such a plan, thus falling short of the required two-thirds. President Lyndon Johnson later supported this plan, as did Indiana Democratic Senator Birch Bayh before he became a supporter of the direct popular vote mechanism. The automatic plan would constitute a relatively minor change in the current system, and some may have opposed this scheme for fear that it would be an obstacle to more serious reforms (Peirce 1968, 177–181).

Direct Popular Election

By far the most popular alternative to the current electoral college system is that of the direct popular vote suggested at the Constitutional Convention of 1787 and first proposed in Congress in 1816. Andrew Jackson has been designated "the spiritual godfather of the direct vote movement" (Peirce 1968, 183). Many observers believe that such a plan could lead to participation by an increased number of political parties. Most such plans have accordingly called for a runoff election in the event that no candidates receive 40 percent or more of the votes. Variations of such plans have called for voters to rank candidates, or give "yes" votes to all candidates they think are acceptable, giving the candidate with the highest number of such votes the election ("Electoral College" 2001).

The Chamber of Commerce and the American Bar Association supported a popular election plan in the 1960s, and Senator Birch Bayh, who was a key proponent of the Twenty-fifth Amendment providing for cases of presidential disability and the Twenty-sixth Amendment lowering the voting age to eighteen, became a prominent supporter. The House of Representatives adopted such a proposal in 1969 by a vote of 338 to 70 (Longley and Braun 1972, 152), but the Senate killed it, twice falling short of the number needed to invoke cloture of debates intended to defeat the measure.

Other Proposals

Other plans have been introduced to give electoral representation to Guam, Puerto Rico, or other U.S. possessions; to allow the U.S. Supreme Court to resolve disputed elections; to allow both houses of Congress—rather than the House of Representatives alone—to resolve elections in which no candidate receives a majority; to require a vote of electors; to require a runoff in cases in which no presidential candidate receives a majority of the popular vote; and so forth. Connecticut Federalist Senator James Hillhouse once suggested that U.S. senators should serve for three-year terms, with retiring senators drawing balls from a box, and the one drawing the colored ball to serve as president for a year (Peirce 1968, 194). Other plans have called for alternating presidents between the North and the South or requiring candidates to get a majority of electors in each of four sections of the nation.

Another plan, recently supported by Jesse Jackson's Rainbow Coalition, calls for majority preference voting (MPV). Under such a system, voters rank candidates in their order of preference, with the votes of last-place candidates being redistributed until one candidate has a clear majority (Richie 1995). Such a plan might well encourage third-party candidates.

In the aftermath of the 2000 presidential election, historian Arthur Schlesinger Jr. proposed creating 102 "superelectors," whose votes would go to the winner of the popular vote, but there are questions about how many such delegates would be appropriate ("Electoral College" 2001). If the number is very large, it would simply seem easier to abolish the current system altogether.

Obstacles to Reform

The diversity of reform proposals has served in part as an obstacle to change, because it has made achieving consensus on an alternative difficult. Moreover, whereas critics charge that the current system is archaic, many defenders of the current system believe that it has been vital to achieving governmental consensus by discouraging third parties. Defenders also believe that the current system is a bastion of federalism that has worked remarkably well. It appears that it would take sustained leadership or another election like that of 1800 or 1824 to inaugurate major reform of the current system. A number of Democratic members of Congress, including newly elected New York Senator Hillary Rodham Clinton (the wife of former president Bill Clinton), proposed abolishing or altering the electoral college in the aftermath of the presidential election of 2000. Most Americans, however, appear to have accepted the legitimacy of a president who gained office without winning the popular vote, and some scholars continue to defend this institution (Gregg 2001). Thus, to date, most of the reforms stimulated by the presidential election of 2000 have focused on changing the types of voting machines and ballots used rather than on reform or abolition of the electoral college.

Prior to the adoption of the Seventeenth Amendment providing for direct election of U.S. senators, a number of states helped the process along by pledging to select the popular vote winners in their states; most such senators, in turn, felt obligated to support popular election. Drawing from this experience, a law professor from Northwestern University has recently suggested that a relatively small number of large states could effectively provide for direct election of the president by pledging their electors to cast their votes for the winner of the national electoral vote (Bennett 2001).

See also Twelfth Amendment; Twenty-third Amendment.

For Further Reading:

Bennett, Robert W. 2001 "Popular Election of the President without a Constitutional Amendment." *Green Bag* 2d 4 (Spring): 241–246.

Berns, Walter., ed. 1992. *After the People Vote: A Guide to the Electoral College.* Rev. ed. Washington, DC: AEI Press.

Bush v. Gore, 531 U.S. 98 (2000).

Ceaser, James W., and Andrew E. Busch. 2001. *The Perfect Tie: The True Story of the 2000 Presidential Election.* Lanham, MD: Rowman & Littlefield.

Correspondents of *The New York Times.* 2001. *36 Days: The Complete Chronicle of the 2000 Presidential Election Crisis.* New York: Henry Holt.

Dershowitz, Alan M. 2001. *Supreme Injustice: How the High Court Hijacked Election 2000.* New York: Oxford University Press.

Dionne, E. J., and William Kristol, eds. 2001. *Bush v. Gore: The Court Cases and the Commentary.* Washington, DC: The Brookings Institution.

Gillman, Howard. 2001. *The Votes That Counted: How the Court Decided the 2000 Presidential Election.* Chicago: University of Chicago Press.

Gregg, Gary L., II, ed. 2001. *Securing Democracy: Why We Have an Electoral College.* Wilmington, DE: ISI Books.

Hardaway, Robert M. 1994. *The Electoral College and the Constitution: The Case for Preserving Federalism.* Westport, CT: Praeger.

Longley, Lawrence D., and Alan G. Braun. 1972. *The Politics of Electoral College Reform.* New Haven, CT: Yale University Press.

Peirce, Neal R. 1968. *The People's President: The Electoral College in American History and the Direct-Vote Alternative.* New York: Simon and Schuster.

Political Staff of *The Washington Post.* 2001. *Deadlock: The Inside Story of America's Closest Election.* New York: Public Affairs.

"The Report of the National Symposium on Presidential Selection." 2001. The Center for Governmental Studies at the University of Virginia. *http://www.goodpolitics.org/reform/report/electoral.htm.* Accessed 11/29/02.

"Rethinking the Electoral College Debate: The Framers, Federalism, and One Person, One Vote." 2001. *Harvard Law Review* 114 (June): 2526–2549.

Richie, Robert. 1995. "Democracy and Majority Preference Voting." *Rainbow* 3, no. 30 (27 July).

❖ ELEVENTH AMENDMENT ❖

The Eleventh Amendment was the first amendment adopted to overturn a Supreme Court decision and the only adopted amendment ever directly to address the judicial branch of government. The amendment has spawned numerous cases that have both expanded and narrowed its apparent scope.

Origins

Article III of the Constitution extends judicial power to controversies "between a State and Citizens of another State." In arguing on behalf of the new Constitution, however, leading Federalists responded to Anti-Federalist criticisms by contending that this clause would not undermine the doctrine of sovereign immunity, according to which a sovereign—in this case, a state government—could not be sued without its consent.

Despite such assurances, in *Chisholm v. Georgia* (1793) the Supreme Court upheld a suit brought against Georgia by the executor of the estate of a South Carolina merchant for payment for goods delivered during the Revolutionary War. The success of this suit may have threatened other states with significant debts. The lower house of the Georgia legislature subsequently passed a bill providing that any federal marshal attempting to enforce the Court's judgment would be "hereby declared guilty of felony, and shall suffer death, without the benefit of the clergy, by being hanged" (cited by Jacob 1972, 57).

Congress proposed the Eleventh Amendment in 1794; it was ratified by the necessary number of states in 1795 but was not promulgated by the secretary of state until 1798, a date that is sometimes incorrectly cited as the official ratification date. The amendment provides that "the Judicial power of the United States shall not be construed to extend to any suit in law or equity, commenced or prosecuted against one of the United States by Citizens of another State, or by Citizens or Subjects of any Foreign State." In *Hollingsworth v. Virginia* (1798), the Court ruled that the original congressional resolution did not require the president's signature for the amend-

ment to be valid and gave the amendment retrospective application.

Early History and Reconstruction Period

The Eleventh Amendment does not appear to have barred many suits during its early history. This was largely because Chief Justice John Marshall ruled in *Osborn v. Bank of the United States* (1824) that the Eleventh Amendment did not bar suits against officers of a state. Moreover, in *Cohens v. Virginia* (1821), Marshall ruled that the amendment did not bar appeals to federal courts in cases in which the states themselves initiated the suits.

By the end of Reconstruction, however, a number of Southern states were repudiating debts, and after resolution of the disputed presidential election of 1876, there was little federal will to enforce such debts by force of arms. Thus, in 1883 the Supreme Court ruled in *Louisiana ex rel. Elliott v. Jamel* that shareholders could not sue Louisiana for interest on bonds. In 1890 Justice Joseph P. Bradley, the same justice whose vote on the electoral commission had resulted in the election of fellow Republican Rutherford B. Hayes, authored the decision in *Hans v. Louisiana* (1890) that reinterpreted and extended the scope of the Eleventh Amendment.

Extending the literal language of the Eleventh Amendment to cover suits brought by a state citizen against its own state, Bradley broadly interpreted the Eleventh Amendment as a restatement of what he believed to be the original constitutional understanding that states could not be sued without their consent. *Ex parte New York* (1921) subsequently extended the breadth of the Eleventh Amendment to forbid admiralty cases (not technically considered cases in "law or equity") against a state without its consent. *Monaco v. Mississippi* (1934) applied the same principle to cases brought against a state by foreign governments (Orth 1987, 139–141).

Limitations of Amendment

State immunity has, however, been somewhat modified by *Ex parte Young* (1908), which effectively reaffirmed *Osborn v. Bank of the United States* (1824) by permitting state officials, as opposed to states themselves, to be sued. Moreover, in *Lincoln County v. Luning* (1890), the Court decided that state immunity was not extended to state subdivisions. Other rulings have held that federal jurisdiction in the area of interstate commerce and in enforcement of the Fourteenth Amendment may override traditional state immunities. Ironically, the concept of sovereign immunity has become so much "part of the United States unwritten constitution" that it has often predominated over "the language of the Amendment" (Orth 1987, 152).

There have been at least two attempts to amend the Eleventh Amendment, one introduced in 1883 and the other in 1913. The former provided that Congress could make provision "by appropriate legislation for the enforcement of contracts entered into by any of the States of the Union" (quoted in Orth 1987, 70).

Recent Interpretations

A number of recent cases have called renewed attention to the Eleventh Amendment and affirmed the broad reading of it. In *Seminole Tribe v. Florida* (1996) the Supreme Court reaffirmed the broad reading of the amendment given in *Hans v. Louisiana* (1890) by deciding, in a five-to-four ruling, that the Eleventh Amendment precluded Indian tribes' suing states without their consent for failing to negotiate in good faith over the establishment of gambling casinos on Indian lands (Greenhouse 1996). In *Alden v. Maine* (1999) the Court decided that a group of state probation officers did not have standing to sue Maine without its consent for violations of the Fair Labor Standards Act. Similarly, in *Kimel v. Florida Board of Regents* (2000), the Supreme Court decided that states could not be subjected to provisions of the Age Discrimination in Employment Act of 1967, as amended, without their consent.

A five-to-four majority of the Court decided in *Federal Maritime Commission v. South Carolina State Ports Authority* (2002) that states could not be sued for failure to berth a gambling cruise ship at its ports. The majority decision, written by Justice Clarence Thomas,

specifically noted that "Dual sovereignty is a defining feature of our Nation's constitutional blueprint." Thomas observed that "the Eleventh Amendment does not define the scope of the States' sovereign immunity; it is but one particular exemplification of that immunity." Thomas further cited an earlier case to say that "[w]e have understood the Eleventh Amendment to stand not so much for what it says, but for the presupposition of our constitutional structure."

Taken together with recent rulings regarding states' rights under the Tenth Amendment, contemporary Supreme Court decision making regarding the Eleventh Amendment reveals a desire by a majority of members of the U.S. Supreme Court to allow states to exercise increased prerogatives. This could ultimately prove to be the central legacy of the Rehnquist Court.

See also *Chisholm v. Georgia; Hollingsworth v. Virginia;* Tenth Amendment; Supreme Court Decisions Reversed by Constitutional Amendments.

For Further Reading:
Federal Maritime Commission v. South Carolina State Ports Authority, 535 U.S. 743 (2002).

Greenhouse, Linda. 1996. "Justices Curb Federal Power to Subject States to Lawsuits." *New York Times* 115 (28 March): A1, A12.

Jacob, Clyde E. 1972. *The Eleventh Amendment and Sovereign Immunity.* Westport, CT: Greenwood Press.

Orth, John V. 1987. *The Judicial Power of the United States: The Eleventh Amendment in American History.* New York: Oxford University Press.

❖ ELLIOTT, WILLIAM YANDELL (1896–1979) ❖

Harvard political scientist William Yandell Elliott published a book entitled *The Need for Constitutional Reform* (1935) during Franklin Roosevelt's first term in office. Elliott advocated a number of reforms designed primarily to strengthen both executive and legislative power and to overcome problems that Elliott perceived in the existing system of separated powers (Vile 1991c, 72–74).

Elliott offered a number of small steps that could be taken to achieve this end. These included a presidential item veto and a prohibition of riders that were not germane to the aims of a bill. The linchpin of Elliott's plan, however, was his proposal for a constitutional arrangement, borrowed from parliamentary systems, under which the president would have the power, at least once during a term, to force members of the House of Representatives to stand for election. If such an election upheld Congress over the president, the president could resign (with Congress then choosing his successor), but the president would not, as in most parliamentary systems, be required to do so.

Elliott desired to cut the power of the Senate (which he associated with special interests) and advocated taking from that body "the power over bills appropriating money or raising revenue" (Elliott 1935, 32). Ideally, states would be reorganized into districts designated as "commonwealths," similar to those used for the Federal Reserve System. Elliott suggested that there might be twelve such regions, each electing eight senators. The president would be able to add fifteen prominent individuals to the Senate; losing presidential candidates would also serve in this body. The vote needed to approve treaties would be changed from two-thirds of the Senate to a simple majority of both houses.

Representation in the House would continue to be based on population, but members would be elected from the new commonwealths rather than from existing states. Elliott favored a form of proportional representation for the House, with up to five representatives per district. He believed that this would help overcome the power of existing interest groups. A continuing committee of both houses would be in "perpetual residence" in Washington, D.C. (Elliott 1935, 37).

Elliott favored a new system for selecting the president. Under his plan, a joint House and Senate committee would nominate presidential candidates, and the House would choose two of these to run in a national election. The pres-

ident would be selected by majority popular vote. The president would choose an executive vice president or an assistant president who would also head the administrative cabinet.

Elliott believed that although the system of judicial review was needed in the current system, such power might be modified if the legislative and executive branches were more responsible. In such a situation, he believed that the Supreme Court should be required to vote by a two-thirds vote before invalidating legislation. Generally, battles "over social reform should be fought out in party politics, not in the courts" (Elliott 1935, 179). Elliott feared that existing protections for criminal defendants—such as the prohibition against double jeopardy—were working to "aid gangsters and racketeers" (Elliott 1935, 204). He also suggested that the Supreme Court should choose the attorney general.

Elliott would strengthen the positions of governors in the new commonwealths. Like the president, they would have the power to dissolve the legislature (now to be unicameral) once during their four-year terms. Elliott would also create governors' councils and legislative steering committees. Like the president, state governors would originate the budget and would be subject to override on money bills only by a two-thirds majority.

Elliott advocated a number of administrative reforms. He wanted to create a civil service head for each department and a permanent cabinet secretariat "to propose and document Cabinet meetings" (Elliott 1935, 203). Elliott also proposed adding an advisory committee to each department consisting of "all the great interests with which it comes into normal contact" (Elliott 1935, 203), and he favored allowing cabinet members to have seats in the Senate and to appear before the House.

Elliott recognized that some of his proposals could be implemented on a piecemeal basis, but he believed that the more substantial changes—especially in regard to the Senate—could best be initiated by a constitutional convention.

For Further Reading:
Elliott, William Y. 1935. *The Need for Constitutional Reform: A Program for National Security.* New York: Whittlesey House.

❖ ELLIS, FREDERICK, AND CARL FREDERICK ❖

Generally, individuals with proposals for constitutional change present them in a scholarly format, but Frederick Ellis and Carl Frederick have chosen to present their ideas in *The Oakland Statement,* which they describe as *A Political Adventure Novel.* Ellis, a graduate of Villanova and Armstrong University (MBA) left his brokerage firm to become involved in civil rights and worked for Senator Eugene McCarthy in 1968 and for George McGovern in 1972. He now lives in Costa Rica, where he says "the idea was born to write a political adventure novel presenting a progressive vision for *real solutions* by creating two new constitutional amendments to the Bill of Rights, resulting in a *popular political economy* for all the people" (Ellis and Frederick 2002, inside back cover). Carl Frederick, who earned his MBA at the University of Chicago, also began in business before writing a best-selling book entitled *Est: Playing the Game the New Way* (1975). After traveling the world, he also settled in Costa Rica.

In this author's judgment, *The Oakland Statement,* like similar books with an overriding political agenda, is fairly poor fiction. In the wake of the 11 September 2001 attack on the World Trade Centers and the Pentagon, the book might also suffer from poor timing. Published in 2000, its story line is based on a leaderless revolution that begins with patriotic terrorists blowing up power stations throughout the nation. Rather miraculously, no one ever appears to be actually killed, and the patriotic terrorists are all eventually pardoned for the great good they have done in calling attention to the nation's problems. Moreover, the result is the convening of a second constitutional convention presided over by former vice president Al Gore Jr. that adds amendments twenty-eight and twenty-nine to what is described as the Bill of Rights.

In the novel, all this occurs between October 2000 and March 2005. The story describes the election of president Veronica Lake, who beats out George W. Bush for the Republican nomi-

nation, chooses Senator John McCain as a running mate, and gives Patrick Buchanan a prominent place in her new administration. By 2005 newly elected Democratic President Paul Wellstone (who has since been killed in a 2002 plane crash), who narrowly beats out Lake and Jesse Ventura, issues his amnesty to the patriots whose violence concentrated the nation's attention on the two amendments. In between, Eugene McCarthy, George McGovern, John Anderson, Jesse Jackson, Jerry Brown (in one of the more creative moments of the book appearing complete with an 800 number "2 RATIFY" (Ellis and Frederick 2000, 245)), and other progressives play cameo roles, with Ross Perot commended on a number of occasions for his role in calling attention to existing problems. Former President Jimmy Carter ends up sidelined by a fall from a horse, while former president Clinton, who has become "a total sex hound since Hillary divorced him," apparently largely ignores the reform movement as he travels the world in search of illicit sex (*Id.,* 151).

Three aspects of this book deserve scholarly attention. They are the Oakland Statement, in which the middle-class revolutionaries announce their philosophy; the mechanism chosen for constitutional reform; and the two amendments that are actually adopted in the book.

The Oakland Statement begins by pointing to the fact that "our citizens are voting less and less, while our economic wealth is being concentrated rapidly into the hands of fewer and fewer people" (Ellis and Frederick 2000, 3). Tying itself to earlier movements for the U.S. Constitution, the Bill of Rights, the Civil War, and the battle for "labor rights and civil rights," the statement goes on to announce that extraordinary action is necessary to accomplish two objectives. The first would "guarantee the absolute right of the people to enjoy the most equitable methods of a representative electoral system," including "proportional representation, preference voting, cumulative voting and referendums at every level of government" (*Id.,* 4). The second would "guarantee the absolute right of the people to participate in the *creation of the national wealth,*" which would be achieved "primarily through the establishment of majority employee owned enterprises and progressive labor organizing" (*Id.*, 4). The Oakland Statement goes on to provide a "rationale" for "extraordinary action" including violence. Specifically, it proposes "the formation of other small (3 to 5 people) autonomous ATTACK UNITS, with the specific purpose of inflicting maximum damage on electrical power while minimizing loss of life" (*Id.*, 6).

The Oakland Statement further expresses the hope that this action will lead states, as it does in the novel, to call a limited constitutional convention specifically to consider these and only these amendments. Although many citizens in the novel question the violent methods used to get public attention, the citizens eventually come to a realization of the importance of the two amendments. As a result, two-thirds of the states petition Congress to call a constitutional convention, and the two amendments are subsequently proposed and ratified by the necessary number of state conventions. Afterwards, Puerto Rico, the Virgin Islands, and the District of Columbia join as new states (the last apparently by congressional resolution rather than by constitutional amendment), and overtures are made to other Caribbean and Central American nations, including Haiti and Cuba, to join.

The texts of both amendments that are eventually proposed and adopted are longer than any current constitutional amendments. Both amendments contain some provisions that are quite specific and others that are quite general. This approach appears to be quite deliberate. The revolutionaries note at one point in the book that "the amendments themselves would have to be in very general language" (*Id.*, 93). Referring to a proposal, similar to one later adopted, providing that "[t]he people shall have the absolute right to enjoy the *most equitable methods* of a representative electoral system," they explain, "If the various branches of government failed to change the electoral process to what citizens believed to be 'most equitable,' then suits could be filed in various courts, challenging the process and at the same time, demanding specific remedies" (Ellis and Frederick 2000, 93–94). The authors appear to

have little concern over the fact that members of the judiciary are not directly accountable to voters.

The Twenty-eighth Amendment has eight sections. The first provides for mandatory voting for all, except for those with conscientious objections to the practice. Section 2 contains a provision that elections "shall be conducted using the most equitable methods as determined by each level of state, district, territory, and local governments utilizing the process of referendums" (Ellis and Frederick 2000, 224). Consistent with the discussion mentioned above, this section also gives citizens a right to go to court to obtain this right. Section 3 provides for the election of the president through "preference voting." In the process, existing provisions providing for the electoral college are repealed (*Id.*, 224–225). Section 4 further provides for "an open referendum process" (*Id.*, 225). Section 5 would increase the number of U.S. Representatives by assuring that no district had more than 250,000 individuals, and Section 6 would accordingly guarantee each state at least three votes. Section 7 provides for the public financing of elections, except for individual contributions limited to no more than $250 each. Section 8 concludes by allowing respective entities to limit the length of electoral campaigns, but also gives citizens the right to challenge such time limits in court.

The Twenty-ninth Amendment has seven sections and is designed to institute a system similar to that which Marshall Tito employed in Yugoslovia after World War II. It is difficult to assess whether this amendment can better be considered to be based upon, or whether it is better viewed as a substitute for, utopian principles. In an earlier section of the book discussing this amendment, aspiring revolutionaries refer both to the failure of the world's great religions and of modern ideologies to create a "new man." One revolutionary notes:

> Maybe, in the distant future, if we last that long, men will come to the conclusion that the high ideals of religions and communitarian practices is not only a better way to live, but might be the *only* way to survive, as the world population increases exponentially. But, as material

beings, right now we gotta look at *real* economic systems that are based on both individualism and collectivism. (Ellis and Frederick 2000, 48)

Section 1 guarantees all citizens from age eighteen to sixty or older the right "to participate in the creation of the national wealth" (Ellis and Frederick 2000, 235). Section 2 further indicates that this will be done "by the majority-employee ownership of conditional and certified enterprises," these categories being determined by the number of employees of each. Section 3 provides governmental charters and licenses for all "private, conditional, and certified enterprises as businesses for profit" (*Id.,* 235). Section 4 specifically guarantees the right to organize "democratic labor unions, supervisor and management employee organizations" (*Id.,* 235). Section 5 provides that the federal government "shall be the employer of last resort for able-bodied and mentally capable citizens" under retirement age (*Id.,* 235). Section 6 proceeds to guarantee further social and economic rights by providing for "the right to free education to the highest levels available, based upon scholastic qualifications" (*Id.,* 235). Section 7 further provides all citizens with "the right to free complete medical and mental health insurance coverage." It also provides that "[a]ll prescription drugs and dental costs, except nonaccidental cosmetic, medical, and dental expenses, shall be included" (*Id.,* 236).

In the novel, the ratification of the two amendments by forty states begins a series of additional reforms at state and local levels, including the city of Oakland where the original manifesto was written. To this author, at least, it would appear far more likely that a more popular cause or causes than the proposed visionary, and arguably impractical, amendments would be required to muster the energy necessary for the nation's first Article V convention. Although it is probably important not to overinterpret a book that is present in the form of a novel, this work is among the few books that anticipates or portrays acts of violence as the necessary catalyst to an Article V convention. One might question the effectiveness of such violence in persuading the public to adopt

changes in a world where there is increased concern over terrorism. Just as importantly, one could argue that existing amending processes, which were designed as a substitute for the kinds of violent actions of the Revolutionary War, would have to be declared as failures if they could only be mobilized through political terrorism.

See also Constitutional Conventions; Social and Economic Rights; Voting Rights entries.

For Further Reading:

Ellis, Frederick with Carl Frederick. 2000. *The Oakland Statement: A Political Adventure Novel.* Miami, FL: Synergy International of the Americas, Ltd.

❖ EMANCIPATION PROCLAMATION ❖

Abraham Lincoln often declared that although he opposed slavery, his primary goal in prosecuting the Civil War was to preserve the Union. As the war continued, Lincoln became convinced that it could best be prosecuted and the future of the Union best be guaranteed by abolishing slavery. The Emancipation Proclamation was officially issued on 1 January 1863, but Lincoln had announced his intention to do so in September of 1862 (Anastaplo 1995, 138). A war measure taken under executive authority, this proclamation declared all slaves in states adhering to the Confederacy to be free. This amounted to 74 percent of all slaves in the United States (Paludan 1994, 155).

Although Lincoln also proposed amendments containing plans for more gradual emancipation for other slaves, the momentum generated by the Emancipation Proclamation made this virtually impossible. The proclamation was extended and placed on firmer constitutional authority when, in 1865, the Thirteenth Amendment to the Constitution, which Lincoln also supported, abolished involuntary servitude throughout the nation.

See also Lincoln, Abraham; Thirteenth Amendment.

For Further Reading:

Anastaplo, George. 1995. *The Amendments to the Constitution: A Commentary*. Baltimore: Johns Hopkins University Press.

Paludan, Phillip S. 1994. *The Presidency of Abraham Lincoln*. Lawrence, KS: University Press of Kansas.

❖ EMBARGOES, ARMS, LOANS, AND FOREIGN AID ❖

In 1934 Republican Senator Gerald P. Nye of North Dakota held hearings indicating that bankers and manufacturers of munitions had made huge profits from their sales to the Allies in World War I (Cole 1962, 79–97). These revelations about the so-called merchants of death increased isolationist sentiment in the United States and led many to suspect that U.S. participation in the war had been engineered to continue such profit making.

Even before the hearings, Democratic Representative Ross Collins of Mississippi had introduced a resolution that would have prohibited making or renewing loans to nations engaged in war, unless the United States itself was engaged in such a war as an ally. Collins repeatedly introduced this resolution in the late 1930s, during which time Congress adopted a number of neutrality acts that were designed to prevent the United States from trading with belligerent nations or taking passage on their ships (DeConde 1971, 567). Some such laws had a "cash and carry" exemption or allowed the president some discretion whether to impose the embargo on one or both sides of a conflict. The Japanese attack on Pearl Harbor in 1941 ended U.S. isolationism.

During the Cold War, the United States used foreign aid as a tool of foreign policy making, but critics charged that such aid was wasteful. In 1949 Republican Senator William Langer of North Dakota offered an amendment restricting foreign aid to times of war. Republican Representative Noah Mason of Illinois introduced similar resolutions in 1957 and 1959, extending the prohibition on foreign aid to international organizations as well as to foreign governments.

For Further Reading:

Cole, Wayne S. 1962. *Senator Gerald P. Nye and American Foreign Relations*. Minneapolis: University of Minnesota Press.

DeConde, Alexander. 1971. *A History of American Foreign Policy*. 2d ed. New York: Charles Scribner's Sons.

❖ EMBARGOES, TRADE ❖

When Thomas Jefferson was president, he decided to ask Congress to declare an embargo on trade with Great Britain and France rather than risk war over the seizure of American vessels and the impressment of American seamen. Such power could be justified either as an exercise of congressional power over foreign commerce or as a means of national defense. Initially defensive in nature, in time embargo became a method, albeit a fairly unsuccessful one, of exerting pressure on belligerents (Mayer 1994, 217). The embargo, which lasted from December 1807 to March 1809, was especially resented in the New England states, which were dependent on such commerce. Both during this embargo and later at the Hartford Convention that met during the War of 1812, these states issued calls to limit congressional embargo powers. The Hartford Convention called for a sixty-day limit (Vile 1993c, 186).

In modern times, the United States has declared embargoes against Iraq and Cuba. The United States also boycotted the Olympics after the Russian invasion of Afghanistan. The U.S. Supreme Court ruled in *Crosby v. National Foreign Trade Council* (2000) that states cannot declare embargoes, or other sanctions against foreign nations (in this case Burma, or Myanmar) that are not supported by the national government.

For Further Reading:

Mayer, David N. 1994. *The Constitutional Thought of Thomas Jefferson*. Charlottesville: University Press of Virginia.

Vile, John R. 1993b. *The Theory and Practice of Constitutional Change in America: A Collection of Original Source Materials*. New York: Peter Lang.

❖ EMERGENCY, NATIONAL ❖

See Congress, Emergency Functioning.

❖ EMPLOYMENT OPPORTUNITY ❖

Unemployment continues to be a major problem, prompting governmental intervention in the form of job creation and training programs as well as unemployment insurance. Franklin Roosevelt's New Deal and Lyndon Johnson's War on Poverty stand out as high points in the national government's efforts. There continue to be sharp debates over what role the government—as opposed to private enterprise—should play in reducing unemployment and over the effectiveness of specific governmental programs (Baumer and Van Horn 1985).

At least seven times since 1983, Representative Major Owens, a Democrat from Brooklyn, New York, has introduced an amendment to guarantee the right to employment opportunity to everyone and to give Congress power to enforce the amendment with appropriate legislation. More recently, Representative Jesse Jackson Jr. (D-IL) has proposed a "full-employment" amendment that would guarantee that every citizen "has a right to work"; and assuring that each will get "just and favorable remuneration for themselves and their family, an existence worthy of human dignity, and supplemented, if necessary, by other means of social protection" (Jackson with Watkins 2001, 252). Current legislative trends, especially in the area of welfare reform, point less toward work as a governmentally guaranteed right and more toward work as a duty to be performed in return for welfare and other benefits.

See also Jackson, Jesse L., Jr.; Social and Economic Rights.

For Further Reading:

Baumer, Donald C., and Carl E. Van Horn. 1985. *The Politics of Employment*. Washington, DC: Congressional Quarterly Press.

Jackson, Jesse L., Jr., with Frank E. Watkins. 2001. *A More Perfect Union: Advancing New American Rights*. New York: Welcome Rain Publishers.

❖ ENFORCEMENT CLAUSES IN AMENDMENTS ❖

Most congressional powers are specified, or implied, in Article I, Section 8, of the U.S. Constitution. Many amendments also either directly or indirectly address congressional powers. To take one of the more obvious examples, the First Amendment provides that "Congress shall make no law . . ." related to certain designated matters. In *Barron v. Baltimore* (1833), Chief Justice John Marshall decided that this and subsequent provisions in the Bill of Rights limited only the national government and not the states, although this decision has subsequently been modified by later Supreme Court decisions indicating that most such provisions now apply to the states via the due process clause of the Fourteenth Amendment.

Beginning with the three amendments adopted after the Civil War, many amendments have included specific authorizations for congressional enforcement, that seem, in part, to echo the necessary and proper clause. Found at the end of Article I, Section 8, it grants power to Congress "[t]o make all Laws which shall be necessary and proper for carrying into Execution the foregoing Powers, and all other Powers vested by this Constitution in the Government of the United States, or in any Department or Officer thereof."

The provision in Section 2 of the Thirteenth Amendment specifying that "Congress shall have power to enforce this article by appropriate legislation" is fairly typical. There are similar provisions in Section 5 of the Fourteenth Amendment and in Section 2 of the Fifteenth Amendment. The central text of the Sixteenth Amendment (providing for an income tax) specifically grants Congress "power to lay and collect taxes" so there is no separate enforcement provision. The Eighteenth Amendment, providing for national alcoholic prohibition, is somewhat unique in that its second section vests "concurrent" enforcement power in both

Congress and the states, with the Twenty-first Amendment providing for the Eighteenth Amendment's repeal, reiterating state powers to restrict importation of alcohol. Rather than a separate section, the Nineteenth Amendment, prohibiting denial of voting on the basis of sex, vests Congress with enforcement authority in its second sentence. Section 2 of the Twenty-third Amendment, the amendment granting electoral college representation to the District of Columbia, is another example of an enforcement clause. There is a similar provision in Section 2 of the Twenty-fourth Amendment, which abolished the poll tax in federal elections, and in Section 2 of the Twenty-sixth Amendment, which lowered the voting age to eighteen. Many proposed amendments contain similar enforcement provisions.

Given the existence of the necessary and proper clause, additional enforcement clauses have a kind of "belt-and-suspenders" quality to them (an analogy suggested in e-mail correspondence by Professor Brannon Denning). However, in a number of cases interpreting the Thirteenth, Fourteenth, and Fifteenth Amendments, the Supreme Court has referred to the enforcement clauses to allow Congress to outlaw practices that, while not unconstitutional in and of themselves, might prove to be unconstitutional obstacles to the rights of equality and voting. Thus, in *Jones v. Alfred H. Mayer Co.* (1968), the Court upheld a provision of the Civil Rights Act of 1866 barring private discrimination in the sale of housing on the basis that it fell within congressional enforcement authority in abolishing slavery. Similarly, in *South Carolina v. Katzenbach* (1966), the Court upheld the congressional suspension of literacy tests in states where they appeared to be serving as significant obstacles to voting. In *City of Boerne v. Flores* (1997) and other more recent cases dealing with the free exercise clause of the First Amendment as applied to the states through the due process clause of the Fourteenth Amendment, however, the Court has made it clear that congressional enforcement of amendments does not give Congress free rein to define and expand the content of such amendments, especially in the face of contrary judicial interpretations.

❖ *ENGLE V. VITALE* (1962) ❖

Few decisions have stirred more calls for a constitutional amendment than this ruling by the Supreme Court authored by Justice Hugo L. Black. At issue was a short nondenominational prayer mandated by the New York State Board of Regents for public school children to recite at the beginning of each school day. A number of parents objected on the basis that the prayer constituted an undue establishment of religion in violation of the First Amendment as applied to the states by the due process clause of the Fourteenth Amendment.

Black agreed with the challengers. Viewing the prayer as a distinctively "religious activity" (*Engel* 1962, 424), he noted that England had been torn by controversy over the Book of Common Prayer and that Americans, especially Thomas Jefferson and James Madison, were aware of the dangers of unifying church and state. Black argued that the fact that the prayer was voluntary and that students could be excused from the exercise was irrelevant. The key was the fact that "a union of government and religion tends to destroy government and to degrade religion" (*Engel* 1962, 431).

Justice William O. Douglas's concurrence focused primarily on the fact that because the schools in question were funded by the government, the state would be financing a religious exercise. In his dissent, Justice Potter Stewart argued that the New York exercise fell short of an establishment of religion and cited a variety of other connections between church and state that were accepted in modern America.

The majority decision in *Engel* was vigorously denounced. New York Republican Congressman Frank Becker called it "the most tragic decision in the history of the United States" (Becker and Feeley 1973, 24). The decision prompted fifty-three representatives and twenty-two senators to introduce anti-*Engel* amendments in the 87th Congress, and the Senate Judiciary Committee held hearings on the subject (Becker and Feeley 1973, 25–26). Congressional opposition was even more pronounced after the Court's subsequent decision extending *Engel*'s prohibitions to Bible reading in *Abington School District v. Schempp* (1963).

To date, the Court has not backed down. In *Wallace v. Jaffree* (1985), it struck down an Alabama law specifically designed to designate school prayer as an option during a moment of silence—a decision that may not, however, apply to moment-of-silence laws that do not put prayer in a privileged position. In *Lee v. Weisman* (1992), the Court extended the ban to prayers delivered by members of the clergy at high school graduations, a decision extended in *Santa Fe Independent School District v. Doe* (2000) to student-led prayers at football games. Pressures for an amendment to establish prayer in schools continue. Some, but not all versions of the Religious Equality Amendment, appear aimed at restoring this practice.

See also Prayer in Public Schools; Religious Equality Amendment.

For Further Reading:

Becker, Theodore L., and Malcolm M. Feeley, eds. 1973. *The Impact of Supreme Court Decisions: Empirical Studies.* 2d ed. New York: Oxford University Press.

Engel v. Vitale, 370 U.S. 421 (1962).

❖ ENGLISH BILL OF RIGHTS ❖

The U.S. Bill of Rights was largely modeled on declarations of rights within state constitutions. However, an earlier model was adopted as statutory law by the English Parliament in 1689 and accepted by William of Orange and his wife Mary. They became king and queen in place of James II, who had fled the country after disputes with Parliament over perceived abuses of power.

After a series of indictments against James II that resemble Jefferson's later charges against George III in the Declaration of Independence, the English Bill of Rights proceeded to guarantee thirteen rights. These include: the "right of the subjects to petition the King" (a provision similar to one, *sans* king, later included in the First Amendment of the U.S. Constitution); the prohibition against raising taxes without parliamentary consent; prohibitions against a "standing army"; the right, lim-

ited to Protestants, to "have arms for their defence suitable to their conditions, and as allowed by law" (a provision that may cast light on the U.S. Second Amendment); the right to freedom of speech and debate for members of parliament; a requirement (quite similar to the latter language of the U.S. Eighth Amendment) "that excessive bail ought not to be required, nor excessive fines imposed, nor cruel and unusual punishments inflicted"; and a provision for impaneling jurors (quoted in Kurland and Lerner 1987, 5:2) The English Bill of Rights also outlined the right of future succession, a perpetual problem in monarchies.

The English Bill of Rights has been described as "one of the great constitutional documents of English history and one of the great charters of the rights and liberties of the subjects under English law" (Walker 1980, 132). It differs from the U.S. Bill of Rights in that, being adopted in a nation with an "unwritten constitution," it was enacted by, and could be undone by, statute rather than by constitutional amendment.

See also Bill of Rights.

For Further Reading:

Kurland, Philip B., and Ralph Lerner, eds. 1987. *The Founders' Constitution.* 5 vols. Chicago: University of Chicago Press.

Walker, David M. 1980. *The Oxford Companion to Law.* Oxford, UK: Clarenden Press.

❖ ENGLISH LANGUAGE AMENDMENT ❖

The issue of language is often tied to sentiments connected with nationality and race (Baron 1990, xiv). Moreover, people who speak a primary language other than the dominant one are sometimes regarded as unpatriotic. Since 1981 a score of proposals have been introduced in Congress to make English the official language of the United States. California Republican Senator Samuel I. Hayakawa, a nationally recognized linguist, introduced the first such amendment. Hearings were held in the Senate (*The English Language Amendment* 1985) and in the House (*English Language Constitutional Amendments* 1989). The Senate version of this amendment was fairly general, whereas the House version prohibited the use of languages other than English except as a means of teaching language proficiency. Some believe that such an amendment could be used to restrict "multilingual tests, forms and ballots, as well as translators for legal and emergency services" (Baron 1990, 24–25). Some states have adopted English-language laws (Baron 1990, 201), but the impact of such legislation has varied from state to state.

Laws against teaching foreign languages have sometimes reflected nativist sentiments. In *Meyer v. Nebraska* (1923), the Supreme Court invalidated a Nebraska law prohibiting the teaching of languages other than English; in this case, the law had been enforced against a parochial school teacher teaching from a German text. Similarly, in *Pierce v. Society of Sisters* (1925), the U.S. Supreme Court voided an Oregon law, supported in part by the Ku Klux Klan, that required parents of children between eight and sixteen to send their children to public (and not private or parochial) schools.

In *Katzenbach v. Morgan* (1966), the Supreme Court upheld a provision of the Voting Rights Act of 1965 that struck down literacy tests for otherwise eligible voters who had completed the sixth grade in an accredited school in Puerto Rico. In *Lau v. Nichols* (1974), the Supreme Court ruled that a school system had to provide a program to deal with some 1,800 Chinese students who knew no English. The Court noted that "[t]here is no equality of treatment merely by providing students with the same facilities, textbooks, teachers, and curriculum; for students who do not understand English are effectively foreclosed from any meaningful education" (*Lau* 1974, 566). This decision provoked considerable controversy over bilingual education. However, with California's adoption of initiative 227 in 1998, which shifted the emphasis in that state from bilingual education to programs of English immersion (Carleton 2002, 167), most such programs are now designed to enable students to make a transition to English (Baron 1990, 11).

Since the adoption of the Bilingual Education Act of 1968, Congress has provided local school districts with funds for bilingual education. As of 1990, it is believed that English is now spoken "by more than 97 percent of the people in the nation" (Baron 1990, 177). Although some individuals see the English language amendment as a way of promoting national unity, others fear that it could be used to discriminate against people for whom English is a second language.

For Further Reading:

Baron, Dennis. 1990. *The English-Only Question: An Official Language for America?* New Haven, CT: Yale University Press.

Carleton, David. 2002. *Student's Guide to Landmark Congressional Laws on Education.* Westport, CT: Greenwood Press.

Lau v. Nichols, 414 U.S. 563 (1974).

Tatalovich, Raymond. 1995. *Nativism Reborn? The Official English Language Movement and the American States.* Lexington: University Press of Kentucky.

❖ ENTRENCHMENT CLAUSES ❖

Under the U.S. Constitution, it is more difficult to adopt constitutional amendments than it is to adopt other legal changes. Entrenchment clauses reflect the view that some provisions of a constitution are so important that they should either be put altogether beyond amendment or that such amendment should be made more difficult than that for other provisions. Article V of the U.S. Constitution contains two entrenchment provisions. It provides that "no Amendment which may be made prior to the Year One thousand eight hundred and eight shall in any Manner affect the first and fourth Clauses in the Ninth Section of the first Article; and that no State, without its Consent, shall be deprived of its equal Suffrage in the Senate." The first clause reflected a sectional compromise between the North and South at the Constitutional Convention that limited control of, or taxation of, slaves for twenty years. By specification, this clause had a set termination date. The second clause, reflecting conflicts between the large and small states at the Convention that resulted in the Great Compromise providing for equal state representation in the U.S. Senate, does not establish an absolute prohibition of changing state representation in the Senate, but, by requiring that no state can be deprived of such equal suffrage without its consent, makes it extremely unlikely that such a change is likely to occur.

The Corwin Amendment, proposed just before the beginning of the Civil War, would have served to prohibit constitutional alterations that "would authorize or give to Congress power to abolish or interfere, within any State, with the domestic institutions thereof, including that of persons held to labor or service by the laws of the said State" (R. Lee 1961, 22). Fortunately, an amendment abolishing slavery, and not the Corwin Amendment, was ultimately added to the Constitution.

Advocates of implicit limits on constitutional amendments (based on constitutional structure and/or philosophy) are in a sense arguing that there are implicit entrenchment clauses in the Constitution in addition to the two listed. The constitutions of a number of nations, including those of France and Germany, prohibit certain changes in the fundamental principles of their constitutions, and in India the supreme court has limited the kinds of amendments that can be added. California and Delaware likewise require that major constitutional revisions can be adopted only through the convention mechanism (Katz 1996, 282–285); Spain has a similar provision.

Entrenchment clauses might appear desirable for rights generally regarded as fundamental, but, as the unsuccessful Corwin Amendment suggests, such proposals could also be unwisely used to freeze into place institutions like slavery that should not have a place in civilized society. It can certainly be argued that, however necessary the compromise providing for equal state suffrage was to the ratification of the U.S. Constitution, this compromise remains one of the most undemocratic aspects of the document, giving equal weight in the Senate (and to a lesser extent in the electoral college) to states with drastically different populations.

One scholar has suggested that although the text of Article V does not specifically require it, Congress should distinguish between mere amendments and more important revisions to basic principles. He thus argues that in cases where legislators propose to alter a fundamental part of the Constitution, for example, the First Amendment, they should consider doing this by convention proposal and ratification (Katz 1996, 291). Similarly, he suggests that entrenched provisions should not be absolute, but should "explicitly require that subsequent amendments to the proposed amendment be proposed using the convention method" (Katz 1996, 291–292).

See also Constitutional Amendments, Limits on.

For Further Reading:
Katz, Elai. 1996. "On Amending Constitutions: The Legality and Legitimacy of Constitutional Entrenchment." *Columbia Journal of Law and Social Problems* 29 (Winter): 251–292.
Lee, R. Alton. 1961. "The Corwin Amendment in the Secession Crisis." *Ohio Historical Quarterly* 70 (January): 1–26.

❖ ENVIRONMENTAL PROTECTION ❖

The text of the U.S. Constitution is silent about a number of contemporary concerns, including the right to an education and the right to a clean environment. Increasing concern over the environment in the 1960s led to a number of proposals late in that decade and thereafter to provide environmental protection.

Typical was a proposal introduced by Democratic Representative Richard Ottinger and Republican Representative Theodore Kupferman (both from New York) in 1968. They described their proposal as "a conservation bill of rights" (*Congressional Record* 1968, 17116). The first section of their proposal broadly guaranteed "the right of the people to clean air, pure water, [and] freedom from excessive noise and [that] the natural, scenic, historic and esthetics qualities of their environment shall not be abridged." The second section called on Congress to draw up a national inventory of "the natural, scenic, esthetics and historic resources of the United States." A third section would have prohibited action by state or federal agencies adversely affecting this heritage "without first giving reasonable notice to the public and holding a public hearing thereon" (*Congressional Record*, 17116–17117). Section 1 of this proposal is especially interesting because, whereas most existing constitutional provisions offer "negative protection for individuals from government action" (Hoban and Brooks 1987, 169), this would commit the government to a more affirmative role (also see Schlickeisen 1994). Other proposals, including one by Democratic Representative Morris Udall of Arizona, whose brother served as secretary of the interior in the Kennedy and Johnson administrations, followed language of the Declaration of Independence in proposing to make environmental rights "inalienable" (H.J. Res. 1205, 1970).

Members of thirty-seven state legislatures petitioned Congress in the 1990s to adopt an Environmental Quality Amendment providing that:

> The natural resources of the nation are the heritage of present and future generations. The right of each person to clean and healthful air and water, and to the protection of other natural resources of the nation, shall not be infringed by any person. (Cited in Ruhl 1999, 247)

Environmental concerns were among those listed by futurist Bruce E. Tonn when he wrote an article in 1991 proposing an amendment to create a "Court of Generations" (Tonn, 1991). Similarly, Representative Jesse Jackson Jr. (D-IL) has called for an amendment declaring that "[a]ll citizens of the United States shall enjoy the right to a clean, safe, and sustainable environment" (Jackson with Watkins 2001, 371). In addition to doubting whether there is a democratic consensus on behalf of such an amendment, a law professor has cited this proposal as an example of a symbolic and aspirational amendment that cannot be reducible to binding legal principles and that is not suffi-

ciently clear so as to avoid unanticipated consequences (Ruhl 1999, 254).

In 1970 the National Environmental Policy Act (NEPA) was signed. It heralded an anticipated "environmental decade," in which environmental legislation and litigation both increased immensely (Wenner 1982, 1). Although courts have never recognized a clean and healthy environment as a constitutional right (Rosenberg 1991, 278), they have enforced congressional laws. Such activity suggests that although the Constitution does not affirmatively protect the environment, there are few constitutional obstacles to accomplishing this objective through legislation.

See also Jackson, Jesse L., Jr.

For Further Reading:
"The Conservation Bill of Rights." *Congressional Record*, 90th Cong., 2d sess., 13 June 1968, Vol. 114, pt. 13: 17116–17117.

Hoban, Thomas M., and Richard O. Brooks. 1987. *Green Justice: The Environment and the Courts.* Boulder, CO: Westview Press.

Jackson, Jesse L., Jr., with Frank E. Watkins. 2001. *A More Perfect Union: Advancing New American Rights.* New York: Welcome Rain Publishers.

Rosenberg, Gerald N. 1991. *The Hollow Hope: Can Courts Bring about Social Change?* Chicago: University of Chicago Press.

Ruhl, J. B. 1999. "The Metrics of Constitutional Amendments: And Why Proposed Environmental Quality Amendments Don't Measure Up." *Notre Dame Law Review* 74 (January): 245–281.

Schlickeisen, Rodger. 1994. "Protecting Biodiversity for Future Generations: An Argument for a Constitutional Amendment." *Tulane Environmental Law Journal* 8 (Winter): 181–221.

Tonn, Bruce E. 1991. "A Court of Generations: A Proposed Amendment to the U.S. Constitution." *Futures* 21: 413–431.

Wenner, Lettie M. 1982. *The Environmental Decade in Court.* Bloomington, IN: Indiana University Press.

❖ EQUAL RIGHTS AMENDMENT ❖

No amendment has been introduced in Congress more frequently than the Equal Rights Amendment (ERA). From its first introduction in 1923 three years after ratification of the Nineteenth Amendment, the amendment has been sponsored several hundred times.

Proposals in Congress

The first time the amendment was actually voted on by a house of Congress was in 1946, when it garnered a thirty-eight to thirty-five vote in the Senate. In 1950 the amendment achieved the needed two-thirds majority with a Senate vote of sixty-five to nineteen; in 1953 the Senate proposed it again by a vote of seventy-three to eleven. In both the 1950 and the 1953 votes, the Senate accepted what was known as the Hayden rider, sponsored by Democratic Senator Carl Hayden of Arizona. This rider provided that the amendment "shall not be construed to impair any rights, benefits, or exemptions now or hereafter conferred by law upon members of the female sex" (Boles 1979, 38). In 1970 a discharge petition effectively pried the amendment from the House Judiciary Committee, where Democratic chairman Emanuel Celler had previously kept it bottled up (Boles 1979, 38). That same year, a House majority of 252 to 15 approved the amendment with no riders. In 1972, the House again adopted the amendment, this time by a 354-to-24 vote, and the Senate followed suit in 1972 by a vote of 84 to 8 (Boles 1979, 13–16).

As finally approved, the Equal Rights Amendment contained a seven-year deadline in its authorizing resolution. Although the amendment came out of the congressional starting gate fast, at the end of seven years, it was still three states shy of the thirty-eight needed for ratification. Accordingly, in 1979, the House voted 233 to 189 and the Senate 60 to 36 to extend the deadline until 30 June 1982 (Berry 1986, 70), but at the end of this time, no new states had ratified, and some of these had attempted to rescind their ratifications. In January 1983 the amendment was reintroduced in the House, but the 278-to-147 vote fell shy of the required two-thirds majority (Mansbridge 1986, 187). Subsequently, the amendment has not been voted on by either house.

Content of the ERA

The Equal Rights Amendment proposed by Congress had three sections. Its heart was Section 1, which provided simply that "equality of rights under the Law shall not be denied or abridged by the United States or by any State on account of sex." The second section invested enforcement power in Congress, and the third provided for a transitional period of two years after its ratification. Alice Paul, the original sponsor of the Equal Rights Amendment, worded the second section of the amendment to invest enforcement power jointly in the states and the federal government. She also opposed inclusion of the seven-year ratification deadline (Hoff-Wilson 1986, 8).

A number of versions of the amendment were introduced before Congress finally settled on one. The original proposal provided that "men and women shall have equal rights throughout the United States and every place subject to its jurisdiction." In 1950 Helen Hill Weed suggested a rider (much like Carl Hayden's) that would have specified that "this article shall not be construed to impair any rights, benefits, exemptions, or prohibition conferred upon men and women equally, or conferred upon one sex alone when inapplicable to both sexes." A Senate resolution of 1953 would have provided that "whenever in this Constitution the term 'person, persons, people,' or any other personal pronoun is used the same shall be taken to include both sexes" (Boles 1979, 121–125). After the House proposed the ERA in 1971, North Carolina Democratic Senator Sam Ervin proposed a substitute that provided that "neither the United States nor any State shall make any legal distinction between the rights and responsibilities of male and female persons unless such distinction is based on physiological or functional differences between them." He also proposed amendments relating to such matters as the military draft, family support, privacy, and homosexuality (Mansbridge 1986, 12).

Debates over the ERA

Such differences in wording and proposed alterations indicate some of the tensions that surrounded the Equal Rights Amendment debate. When it was initially proposed, the National Woman's Party, a "militant" wing of the forces that had pushed for the Nineteenth Amendment (Boles 1979, 40), was one of the few organizations that actively supported the amendment. More moderate organizations such as the League of Women Voters opposed it. They had been working for protective legislation such as minimum wage and maximum hour legislation for women and feared that an equal rights amendment might be used to undermine such gains. Over time many more groups joined the cause, but differences in emphasis remained, as did ambiguity about precisely what results the amendment would have.

Once proposed by Congress, the ERA was initially received quite positively; twenty-one of thirty-two legislatures in session in 1972 ratified with hardly any delays (Boles 1979, 61). In time, thirty-five of the needed thirty-eight states would ratify, but by then the anti-ERA forces had effectively mobilized, and some states that had given their approval attempted to rescind their ratifications. Conservative activist Phyllis Schlafly, founder of the Eagle Forum, appears to have been particularly successful with her Committee To Stop ERA, as was Senator Sam Ervin of North Carolina, who achieved prominence during the Senate investigation of the Watergate scandal and was regarded at the time as a constitutional expert.

Scholars still debate why the ERA failed. In part, its failure may have stemmed from disputes about what the amendment would do. Some thought that it would require women to be included in any future military draft; in a 1981 decision in *Rostker v. Goldberg* the U.S. Supreme Court had deferred to Congress in stating that males, but not females, were required to register for possible military service. Others thought that it would affect family law and possibly invalidate statutory rape laws. Still others charged that it might mandate unisex bathroom facilities or homosexual marriages. With recognition of a right to privacy, the latter possibilities were arguably fairly remote, but

given the way that Article V requires something of a national consensus, opponents did not have to prove their position but only raise sufficient doubts to block the amendment in thirteen or more states (Mansbridge 1986).

Judicial Decisions and the ERA

Ironically, progressive judicial decisions on behalf of women's rights may have served to undercut the impetus for the ERA (L. Goldstein 1987). In the nineteenth century, the Court had been unsympathetic to the issue. Thus, in *Bradwell v. Illinois* (1873), it had upheld an Illinois law barring women from the practice of law, and in *Minor v. Happersett* (1875) it had upheld women's exclusion from the ballot. As late as *Goesaert v. Cleary* (1948), the Supreme Court upheld paternalistic laws restricting women. At just about the time that Congress proposed the ERA, however, the Court began to use the equal protection clause of the Fourteenth Amendment to liberalize women's rights. In *Reed v. Reed* (1971), for example, a unanimous Court held that a state could not select the administrator of an estate on the basis that one candidate was a man and the other a woman. Similarly, in *Frontiero v. Richardson* (1973), the Court struck down a military law that presumed that married women depended on their husbands, who were thus automatically entitled to extra monetary allowances, but made women prove that their husbands were dependent on them. Perhaps more importantly, four of the justices declared that they considered gender to be a "suspect category," thus mandating the Court's most stringent level of scrutiny (the majority of the Court later settled on an intermediate standard for gender-based classifications). In the same year as *Frontiero,* the Court declared in *Roe v. Wade* that the right of privacy gave fairly broad leeway to women in obtaining abortions.

These decisions on behalf of women's rights enabled opponents of the ERA to argue that it was no longer needed. At the same time, the abortion decision enabled them to raise fears that the courts might expand interpretations of the amendment in unforeseen directions that might bring about greater changes in social relationships than many Americans, who were committed to equality in theory, actually wanted in practice (Mansbridge 1986). It has been argued that a key reason the ERA failed to muster the required congressional majorities in 1983 stemmed from fears that it might require states to fund abortions (Craig and O'Brien 1993, 148). For their part, the ERA supporters may have played into the hands of such critics by suggesting, in their attempts to get the ERA adopted, that the amendment would bring about greater changes than it actually would have.

Controversies over the ERA Extension

As the seven-year ratification deadline approached, proponents asked for more time, and in 1979 Congress extended the deadline for another three years. This led to controversy over whether the action was legal and whether the vote should have required a two-thirds majority (Freedman and Naughton 1978).

Lower courts addressed ERA issues in two cases, both of which challenged the idea, set forth in *Coleman v. Miller* (1939), that issues concerning the amending process were "political questions" inappropriate for judicial resolution. In *Dyer v. Blair* (1975), Judge—later Supreme Court Justice—John Paul Stevens ruled that the Illinois state legislature had the power to decide that a three-fifths vote was required for ratification of the amendment. In *Idaho v. Freeman* (1981), Judge Marion Callister decided that Idaho had a right to rescind ratification of the ERA, that Congress had no power to extend the ERA deadline, and that, in any case, such a vote would have required a two-thirds majority. Although it was appealed to the Supreme Court, this case was mooted when the ERA failed to be ratified within the extension that Congress had granted.

However, perhaps heartened by the belated ratification of the Twenty-seventh Amendment (which, however, had no designated ratification limit) in 1992, more than 200 years after it was first proposed by Congress, a number of representatives introduced a resolution in May 1995 requiring that the House of Representatives verify ratification of the Equal Rights Amendment if and when it received an additional three ratifications from the states. A number of scholars have since weighed in on the matter. Supporters of such belated ratification

processes, who generally rely on both what they consider to be the desirability of the ERA and on the Twenty-seventh Amendment precedent, have included Held (1997) and Baker (1999). Opponents, who focus chiefly on the two specified deadlines that have already gone unmet, on the ambiguity of what the amendment would do, and on attempts by states that have ratified to withdraw their ratifications, therefore undermining the idea that the amendment represents an ongoing consensus, have included Denning and Vile (2000).

Given the division that the fight over the ERA engendered, attempts by a number of states to rescind their ratifications of the amendment, and continuing dispute as to what effects it would have if adopted, its current prospects appear dim. A number of states have added such amendments to their own constitutions (Gammie 1989). In the meantime, the U.S. Supreme Court continues to expand protections for women's rights. Ruth Bader Ginsburg, who had distinguished herself as a lawyer by defending women's rights before being appointed a judge and a justice, wrote the U.S. Supreme Court decision in *United States v. Virginia* (1996), declaring that gender classifications must be "exceedingly persuasive," and finding that Virginia's defense of its all-male Virginia Military Institute in Lexington, Virginia, failed to meet this standard and the school was thus obligated to admit women if, as it chose, it continued to remain a state institution.

See also *Idaho v. Freeman;* Nineteenth Amendment; Schlafly, Phyllis; Seneca Falls Convention.

For Further Reading:

Baker, Debra. 1999. "The Fight Ain't Over," American Bar Association Journal 85 (August): 52.

Boles, Janet K. 1979. *The Politics of the Equal Rights Amendment: Conflict and the Decision Process.* New York: Longman.

Craig, Barbara H., and David M. O'Brien. 1993. *Abortion and American Politics.* Chatham, NJ: Chatham House.

Denning, Brannon P., and John R. Vile. 2000. "Necromancing the Equal Rights Amendment." *Constitutional Commentary* 17 (Winter): 593–602.

Freedman, Samuel S., and Pamela J. Naughton. 1978. *ERA: May a State Change Its Vote?* Detroit, MI: Wayne State University Press.

Gammie, Beth. 1989. "State ERA's: Problems and Possibilities." *University of Illinois Law Review* 1989: 1123–1159.

Goldstein, Leslie F. 1987. "The ERA and the U.S. Supreme Court." In *Research in Law and Policy Studies,* ed. Stuart S. Nagel. Greenwich, CT: JAI.

Held, Allison L., Sheryl L. Herndon, and Danielle M. Stager. 1997. "The Equal Rights Amendment: Why the ERA Remains Legally Viable and Properly before the States." *William and Mary Journal of Women and Law* 3: 113.

Hoff-Wilson, Joan, ed. 1986. *Rights of Passage: The Past and Future of ERA.* Bloomington, IN: Indiana University Press.

Mansbridge, Jane J. 1986. *Why We Lost the ERA.* Chicago: University of Chicago Press.

❖ ERVIN, SAM J., JR. (1896–1985) ❖

Sam J. Ervin Jr. of North Carolina served in the U.S. House of Representatives from 1946 to 1947 and in the Senate from 1954 to 1974. Ervin's most visible public role occurred when he served as chairman of the Senate Watergate Committee, which held televised hearings about abuses in the Nixon administration. Although he had a law degree from Harvard, Ervin was known for his down-home country charm, and he was passionately devoted to the U.S. Constitution.

Ervin participated in a number of controversies involving the constitutional amending process. Perhaps most notably, in the wake of the attempt led by fellow Senator Everett Dirksen of Illinois to call a convention to overturn Supreme Court decisions involving state legislative apportionment, Ervin introduced legislation to govern such Article V conventions. Ervin did not believe that such a convention would have to be an open, or general, convention. He believed that Congress, faced with the necessary number of applications, had a mandatory obligation to call such a convention. Ervin believed that states should be able

to rescind calls for such a convention prior to a two-thirds majority or to rescind amendment ratifications prior to a three-fourths majority. Ervin proposed that state requests for a convention should be valid for four years. As to representation at a convention, Ervin proposed that a delegate be selected from each congressional district, with two at-large delegates, bringing each state's representation to its strength in the electoral college. Although he originally advocated following the precedent of 1787 by giving each state delegation a single vote, he later modified this view, proposing to allow each delegate to vote individually (Ervin 1968; Kauper 1968). Ervin's legislation was not adopted, but it might still serve as a model if an Article V convention is ever convened.

Especially in the field of criminal justice, Ervin believed that the activist Warren Court had usurped the role of the amending process. He argued that there was a rather clear line between amending and interpreting the Constitution: "The power to amend is the power to change the meaning of the Constitution, and the power to interpret is the power of determining the meaning of the Constitution as established by the Founding Fathers" (Ervin 1984, 123).

As a senator, Ervin supported an amendment that would have permitted voluntary confessions and limited federal habeas corpus review of criminal convictions. A strong proponent of separation of church and state, Ervin opposed the amendment that would have restored voluntary prayer in public schools (Ervin 1984, 237–248). Ervin also opposed the Equal Rights Amendment. His proposed modifications of this amendment, all unsuccessful, reflected his concerns. His proposed revisions would have allowed laws that protected women, kept child-support laws in force, protected personal privacy, maintained existing definitions of sexual offenses, recognized physiological and functional differences between males and females, and exempted women from military service (Ervin 1984, 265–266).

Summarizing his view of the sanctity of the Constitution, Ervin observed:

> Constitutional amendments are "for keeps." Unlike ordinary laws, they cannot be easily repealed. Once adopted, they

can be removed from the Constitution only by means of the amendatory process created by Article V. . . . Congress and the States should act cautiously, advisedly, soberly, and without emotion when they are asked to add an amendment to the Constitution. They should never adopt an amendment unless it is calculated as well as intended to promote the general welfare of the United States. (Ervin 1984, 273)

For Further Reading:

Ervin, Sam J., Jr. 1984. *Preserving the Constitution: The Autobiography of Sam J. Ervin Jr.* Charlottesville, VA: Michie.

———. 1968. "Proposed Legislation to Implement the Convention Method of Amending the Constitution." *Michigan Law Review* 66 (March): 875–902.

Kauper, Paul G. 1968. "The Alternate Amending Process: Some Observations." *Michigan Law Review* 66 (March): 903–920.

❖ EXECUTIVE OFFICES, EXCLUSION FROM ❖

Officials in the executive branch, including members of the cabinet, are selected by the president with the advice and consent of the Senate. The original Virginia Plan that was introduced at the Constitutional Convention of 1787 included a provision specifying that members of Congress would be ineligible for appointments to the executive or judicial branches, but this disqualification was later applied only to offices that were created or whose salaries were increased during the term of a legislator (Sundquist 1986, 37–38). In contrast to many parliamentary systems where individuals may serve in both the legislative and executive branches, the U.S. Constitution specifies that members of Congress appointed to other offices must resign their seats, but they are, in such circumstances, permitted to accept cabinet or other posts.

Especially in the nation's first 100 years, nu-merous amending resolutions were introduced with a view toward minimizing risks that governmental offices would be awarded simply as political favors. Proposals included exclusion of general contractors, members of Congress, relatives of members of Congress, officeholders in general, and individuals who had served as representatives in the electoral college. Periodically, proposals also surfaced to elect postmasters, district attorneys, and other federal functionaries.

A flurry of proposals were introduced after the presidential election of 1824. In that election, there were four candidates: Andrew Jackson, John Quincy Adams, William Crawford, and Henry Clay. None received the majority of electoral votes necessary for election, and under the terms of the Twelfth Amendment, the House of Representatives had to choose among the top three candidates. Although he had come in last in the balloting, Henry Clay had considerable influence in the House of Representatives, where he was Speaker. He used this influence to support John Quincy Adams, who won on the first ballot, despite the fact that he had received fewer popular and electoral votes than Jackson.

Jackson and his followers were furious when, three days after Adams's selection, he appointed Clay as his secretary of state. Jackson charged that a "corrupt bargain" had been struck (Boller 1984, 35–37). It is not surprising that, in his first annual message after being elected president in 1828, one of Jackson's proposed reforms of the electoral college system called for excluding members of the House who had participated in presidential selection from executive offices (J. Richardson 1908, 2:448).

See also Cabinet.

For Further Reading:

Boller, Paul E., Jr. 1984. *Presidential Campaigns.* New York: Oxford University Press.

Richardson, James E., ed. 1908. *A Compilation of the Messages and Papers of the Presidents, 1789–1908.* 11 vols. n.p.: Bureau of National Literature and Art.

Sundquist, James L. 1986. *Constitutional Reform and Effective Government.* Washington, DC: Brookings Institution.

❖ EXTRACONSTITUTIONAL MEANS OF CHANGE ❖

Although the U.S. Constitution was officially ratified in 1789, it has been formally amended only twenty-seven times. In part, the paucity of amendments stems from the fact that, comparatively speaking, the U.S. Constitution is a relatively brief document that deals primarily with matters of governmental structure rather than with day-to-day policies (Lutz 1994, 357). A contemporary scholar has also hypothesized that "a low amendment rate associated with a long average constitutional duration strongly implies the use of some alternate means of revision to supplement the formal amendment process" (Lutz 1994, 358).

In the United States, it is not always easy to decide which issues are "constitutional" and which are not. Clearly, some changes can be made only by constitutional amendments, whereas others may or may not require such amendments, largely depending on the attitude of those who occupy the government. Judicial decisions, especially those by the Supreme Court, have a major impact on constitutional interpretation. Laws and executive orders can also modify constitutional understandings and practices. The constitutional amending process, the legislative process, and executive orders each have advantages and disadvantages and often act synergistically (Vile 1994a, 111).

In recent years, two prominent scholars have directed renewed attention to extraconstitutional changes. Focusing on the founding period, the Civil War, and the New Deal—the last of which was implemented without the use of any constitutional amendments—Bruce Ackerman has argued that periods of "higher lawmaking" may be effected by actions taken by the political branches that are later codified by the Supreme Court (Ackerman 1991, 266–267).

Working from the premise of popular sovereignty, Akhil Reed Amar has argued that an Article V convention could specify that its proposals be ratified by a majority of the people. Alternatively, in a position that is very close to that advocated by supporters of a referendum amendment, Amar has argued "that Congress

would be constitutionally obliged to convene a proposing convention, if a bare majority of American voters so petitioned Congress" (Amar 1988, 1065; for critique, see Vile 1990–1991; also see Torke 1994).

Partly because of the role that extraconstitutional changes have played in U.S. constitutional history, a scholar has recently published an article that questions the continuing "relevancy" of the constitutional amending process (Strauss 2001). There seems little doubt, however, that formal constitutional amendments can reverse constitutional changes, including judicial decisions, that have grown up outside the Constitution (Denning and Vile, 2002–2003), and the rate at which members of Congress continue to propose amendments suggests that they believe such amendments are important.

See also Ackerman, Bruce; Amar, Akhil Reed.

For Further Reading:
Ackerman, Bruce. 1991. *We the People: Foundations.* Cambridge, MA: Belknap.
Amar, Akhil Reed. 1988. "Philadelphia Revisited: Amending the Constitution outside Article V." *University of Chicago Law Review* 55 (Fall): 1043–1104.
Denning, Brannon P., and John R. Vile. 2002. "The Relevance of Constitutional Amendments: A Response to David Strauss." *Tulane Law Review* 77 (November): 247–282.
Lutz, Donald S. 1994. "Toward a Theory of Constitutional Amendment." *American Political Science Review* 88 (June): 355–370.
Strauss, David A. 2001. "Commentary: The Irrelevance of Constitutional Amendments." *Harvard Law Review* 114 (March): 1457–1505.
Torke, James W. 1994. "Assessing the Ackerman and Amar Theses: Notes on Extratextual Constitutional Change." *Widener Journal of Public Law* 4: 229–271.
Vile, John R. 1994a. *Constitutional Change in the United States: A Comparative Study of the Role of Constitutional Amendments, Judicial Interpretations, and Legislative and Executive Actions.* Westport, CT: Praeger.
———. 1990–1991. "Legally Amending the United States Constitution: The Exclusivity of Article V's Mechanisms." *Cumberland Law Review* 21: 271–307.

F

❖

❖ FAILED AMENDMENTS ❖

Only six amendments that Congress has proposed by the necessary majorities have subsequently failed to be ratified by the states (Keller 1987; for texts, see Anastaplo 1989, 298–299).

The Bill of Rights that Congress proposed in its first session originally contained twelve amendments. The second was putatively ratified in 1992 as the Twenty-seventh Amendment. By contrast, the first proposal, dealing with the size of Congress and the ratio of representation to population, was never ratified.

Two amendments proposed by the required congressional majorities in the nineteenth century failed to be adopted. In 1810, the so-called Reed Amendment, or Phantom Amendment, was introduced to strip citizenship from individuals who accepted titles of nobility from foreign governments. Although it was mistakenly printed in one edition of the U.S. Statutes as though it had been ratified, this amendment actually fell two states short of such ratification, before the entry of additional states made the margin even wider. Making far less progress was the Corwin Amendment, proposed in 1861 on the eve of the Civil War. Its intention, which would have led potentially to a very different outcome than the U.S. Civil War eventually did, was to reassure the South to stay in the Union by prohibiting future amendments that might interfere with slavery. There was at least one proposal introduced in Congress to repeal this amendment, which, of course, became a nullity with the adoption of the Thirteenth Amendment.

Three amendments proposed by Congress in the twentieth century failed to be ratified. One was the Child-labor Amendment proposed in 1924; decisions by the Supreme Court now permit the kind of restrictions of child labor that this amendment was designed to approve. A second was the controversial Equal Rights Amendment for women; many of its objectives have also been achieved through legislation and judicial decision making giving stricter scrutiny to sex-based classifications. The third such proposal, adopted by Congress in 1978, would have treated the District of Columbia as a state for purposes of congressional representation, presidential and vice presidential selection, and the amending process; the goals of this amendment remain unfulfilled.

The Equal Rights Amendment contained a ratification deadline, subsequently extended, in the congressional authorizing resolution but not in the text; the amendment dealing with representation for the District of Columbia had an internal deadline of seven years. Although none of the other amendments had internal deadlines, none presently appear to be a likely candidate for an attempt at ratification similar to the one that resulted in the Twenty-seventh Amendment.

See also Child Labor Amendment; Congress, Size of; Corwin Amendment; District of Columbia, Representation for; Equal Rights Amendment; Titles of Nobility.

For Further Reading:
Anastaplo, George. 1995. *The Amendments to the Constitution: A Commentary.* Baltimore, MD: Johns Hopkins University Press.

Keller, Morton. 1987. "Failed Amendments to the Constitution." *The World & I* 9 (September): 87–97.

Lynch, Michael J. 2001. "The Other Amendments: Constitutional Amendments That Failed," *Law Library Journal* 92 (Spring): 303–310.

❖ *FAIRCHILD V. HUGHES* (1922) ❖

In this companion case to *Leser v. Garnett* (1922), the Supreme Court rejected a challenge to the constitutionality of the Nineteenth Amendment by a plaintiff taxpayer and member of the American Constitutional League. The Court declared that a general citizen, in this case one who was not an elected official and who resided in a state (New York) where women already had the right to vote, had no standing "to secure by indirection a determination whether a statute if passed, or a constitutional amendment about to be adopted, will be valid" (*Fairchild* 1922, 130).

See also *Leser v. Garnett.*

For Further Reading:

Fairchild v. Hughes, 258 U.S. 126 (1922).

❖ FAIRMAN, CHARLES (1897–1988) ❖

In *Adamson v. California* (1947) and subsequent cases, Justice Hugo L. Black cited speeches by John Bingham and other supporters of the Fourteenth Amendment to argue that they had intended to overturn *Barron v. Baltimore* (1833) and incorporate all the provisions of the Bill of Rights and apply them to the states.

Fairman, a professor of law and political science at Stanford University, authored a seminal article designed to refute Black's view. Fairman drew on evidence from records of congressional debates over the Fourteenth Amendment and contemporary civil rights legislation, as well as from debates in the states over ratification of this amendment, observations about contemporary state constitutions, and judicial interpretations contemporary with the amendment's ratification (Fairman 1949). Arguing that contemporaries had not been as clear about their intention as Black attempted to portray them, Fairman ultimately concluded that Benjamin Cardozo's interpretation of the due process clause of the Fourteenth Amendment in *Palko v. Connecticut* (1937) came close to the framers' understanding of the privileges and immunities clause. In that case, Cardozo had argued that the due process clause was designed to protect only those provisions of the Bill of Rights "implicit in the concept of ordered liberty," a view often labeled "selective incorporation."

Fairman's study, like Black's own thesis, continues to be the subject of lively scholarly debate (see Yarbrough 1988; Curtis 1986; Morrison 1949). Over the course of time, the U.S. Supreme Court has incorporated most, but not all, provisions of the Bill of Rights into the Fourteenth Amendment.

See also Black, Hugo LaFayette; Incorporation.

For Further Reading:

Curtis, Michael K. 1986. *No State Shall Abridge: The Fourteenth Amendment and the Bill of Rights.* Durham, NC: Duke University Press.

Fairman, Charles. 1949. "Does the Fourteenth Amendment Incorporate the Bill of Rights? The Original Understanding." *Stanford Law Review* 2 (December): 5–139.

Morrison, Stanley. 1949. "Does the Fourteenth Amendment Incorporate the Bill of Rights? The Judicial Interpretation." *Stanford Law Review* 2 (December): 140–173.

Yarbrough, Tinsley E. 1988. *Mr. Justice Black and His Critics.* Durham, NC: Duke University Press.

❖ FAMILIES ❖

See Marriage, Divorce, and Parenting.

❖ FEDERALISM AND THE AMENDING PROCESS ❖

Before it became a nation, the United States started out as thirteen colonies. These colonies retained many of their powers under the Articles of Confederation. Supermajorities of nine of thirteen states were required under that system for Congress to adopt most important pieces of legislation. Constitutional amendments required the unanimous consent of the states. Although the sizes of their delegations varied, states had an equal vote in the Confederation Congress. Aside from Rhode Island, which chose not to send any delegates, states were equally represented at the Constitutional Convention of 1787.

The convention is often described in terms of conflict between large, or more populous, states and small, or less populous, ones. However, there were other divisions between those who favored a stronger national government and those who did not, between states that held large numbers of slaves (especially in the deep South) and those that did not, and between those states that were largely agricultural and those that were more dependent on trade and industry. Although many delegates undoubtedly arrived with the understanding that they would have to give up some powers to the new national government, very few, if any, arrived either with the expectation that they would have to give up their state identities or a willingness to do so.

Political scientists divide governments into three types. A confederal government like that under the Articles of Confederation divides power between a central government and various constituent states, but allows the latter to exercise primary powers. A unitary government, like that which the colonists knew from England, vests all sovereign authority in the national government and does not have states with permanent boundaries that exercise sovereignty. By contrast, the framers of the Constitution chose a middle, and—at the time—new path by devising what is today called a federal government. Under such a government, powers remain divided between the central government and the states, but the national authority exercises greater powers than it would under the Articles of Confederation. Each set of governments has its own constitution, and each can operate directly on its own citizens, as, for example, in collecting taxes.

One of the major compromises at the Constitutional Convention was designed to resolve the conflict between the large and small states. Large states generally favored the Virginia Plan, which proposed that representation be based on population in both houses of Congress. By contrast, the alternative New Jersey Plan favored equal state representation, like that in effect under the Articles of Confederation, and was accordingly generally favored by the small states. Ultimately, the Convention settled on the Connecticut, or Great, Compromise. Under this plan, states would be represented according to population in the lower house and equally represented in the upper house. This provision was one of only a few—the others of which have expired—that was specifically entrenched in the Constitution against future changes by amendment. The Great Compromise is in part reflected in the number of electors in the electoral college system, which chooses the president.

Article IV of the U.S. Constitution provides various protections for the states, as, for example, protection against invasion. It also lists their obligations to one another, as, for example, in extraditing fugitives and providing privileges and immunities to out-of-state citizens. The Tenth Amendment soon thereafter provided that powers not delegated to the national government would be reserved to the states. Many Anti-Federalist proponents of the Bill of Rights had undoubtedly hoped for even stronger guarantees but were largely thwarted by the deft congressional maneuvering of James Madison. Partly as a consequence, state powers were sometimes trumped by the exercise of federal implied powers recognized in *McCulloch v. Maryland* (1819) and other cases. The Eleventh Amendment strengthened the states by seeming to recognize the doctrine of state sovereign immunity. It is noteworthy that the U.S. Supreme Court has given increased attention to both amendments in recent years.

By contrast, the Fourteenth Amendment attempted to secure various rights against state abridgement and eventually became the means by which the U.S. Supreme Court applied most of the provisions in the Bill of Rights to limit the states. Similarly, the Seventeenth Amendment, while democratizing the process by which U.S. senators were selected, may have undercut federalism by making senators more accountable to the needs of their individual constituents than to the states as political and geographical entities, and constructions of federal powers under the commerce clause and other broad provisions of the Constitutions have provided increased sanction for the exercise of powers by the national government.

Still, the original design at the Constitutional Convention continues to have a major effect on the amending process. Article V specifies that two-thirds majorities of both houses of Congress are required to propose amendments, or, in an alternate method never used to date, two-thirds of the states can petition Congress to call a constitutional convention. Once proposed by either mechanism, amendments must then be ratified by three-fourths of the states. Article VII of the new Constitution did not follow the Articles of Confederation in requiring unanimous consent, but it did specify that the new Constitution would not go into effect until nine or more states ratified it, and no states would be bound in the new union until they consented to join.

The Article V requirements related to the constitutional amendment process implicate federalism in a number of ways. By requiring supermajorities in both the proposal and ratification phases, the process gives groups of states, or their representatives in the Senate, the power to block amendments that they do not favor. Thus, it is unlikely that amendments will be adopted that go against the interest of more than one-fourth of the states, whether they be large or small. If the states in opposition are small ones, this effectively means that a small percentage of the population could thwart amendments favored by a much larger majority. Similarly, a relatively small number of states with the majority of the nation's population might be unable to get amendments that their citizens favor adopted.

All kinds of mathematical models can and have been constructed estimating what percentage of the population could, under the most adverse circumstances, conceivably block an amendment, but such models rarely play out in the real world where states often find themselves bound together, or divided by, interests other than size (Livingston 1956, 242). Still, many of the elements (most notably equal state representation in the U.S. Senate) that assure that Congress does not operate completely according to democratic principles, also assure that the amending process is not altogether democratic.

Generally, the supermajorities required in both stages of the amending process are thought to enhance the likelihood that amendments that are adopted will have a broad national consensus. The two-step process is further designed to promote deliberation in more than one forum. Some proposed changes in the amending process, most notably those that call for the adoption of constitutional amendments through a referendum process, could significantly diminish the current effects that the federal structure has on this process, although some such proposals would require ratification by a majority or more of the voters in a majority of the states. States often seek to protect what they consider to be their prerogatives through proposed amendments. The proposal to overturn the Supreme Court's reapportionment decisions in the 1960s, although ultimately unsuccessful, is one such example.

See also Consensus and the Amending Process; Constitutional Convention of 1787; Deliberation and the Amending Process; Eleventh Amendment; Fourteenth Amendment; Initiative and Referendum; Seventeenth Amendment; Supermajorities; Tenth Amendment.

For Further Reading:

Livingston, William S. 1956. *Federalism and Constitutional Change*. Oxford, UK: Clarendon Press.

❖ FEDERALIST PAPERS ❖

See Federalists.

❖ FEDERALISTS ❖

Soon after the U.S. Constitution was written and sent to the states for ratification, the nation split into two camps. Those who supported the document called themselves Federalists and designated their opponents as Anti-Federalists. The respective sides argued their cases in the state ratifying conventions that subsequently approved the new constitution (see Gillespie and Lienesch 1989). The most famous product of the Federalist/Anti-Federalist debates was a series of articles defending the Constitution that were initially published in a New York newspaper and shortly thereafter collected in a book known as *The Federalist Papers*. Alexander Hamilton, James Madison, and John Jay authored these essays under the pen name of Publius. A number of their essays addressed issues related to the constitutional amending process (Vile 1992 34–41).

Federalist No. 40 was devoted primarily to demonstrating that the authors of the Constitution had been justified in proposing a new constitution. Although admitting that the original purpose of the Constitutional Convention had been to revise the Articles of Confederation rather than to propose a new government, Madison noted that the delegates had also been commissioned to make such alterations as were necessary "to render the Constitution of the federal government adequate to the exigencies of the Union" (Hamilton, Madison, and Jay 1961, 247). Such a goal, he argued, had proved impossible to achieve by mere revisions, and the delegates had therefore pursued their higher duty, subject to approval or disapproval by the people.

In *Federalist Nos. 39* and *43*, Madison defended the amending process as a moderate mechanism. *Federalist No. 39* noted that the amending mechanism is "neither wholly federal nor wholly national" (246). Similarly, *Federalist No. 43* argued that the amending mechanism "guards equally against that extreme facility, which would render the Constitution too mutable, and that extreme difficulty, which might perpetuate its discovered faults" (278). Madison further defended the mechanism for allowing either the states or the national government "to originate the amendment of errors" (278).

In *Federalist Nos. 49* and *50*, Madison explained why the Constitution did not embody two contemporary amending proposals. In the first essay, Madison critiqued a proposal advanced by Thomas Jefferson in his *Notes on the State of Virginia* (Jefferson 1964, 204–205) whereby two branches of government could call a constitutional convention. Madison's chief objection was that frequent conventions would prove destabilizing and would undermine faith in the document. He also believed that such conventions would stir popular passions and tend to aggrandize the legislative branch, whose members would be more numerous and better connected within the population. In *Federalist No. 50*, Madison further opposed Pennsylvania's scheme for periodic reviews of the Constitution by a council of censors. His discussion leads into the defense of separation of powers that is found in the subsequent and better-known essay.

A key Anti-Federalist objection to the Constitution was the absence of a bill of rights. Hamilton addressed this issue in *No. 84*, the penultimate *Federalist* essay. Arguing that such a bill of rights was unnecessary and might even prove dangerous, Hamilton followed up in the final essay by suggesting that a second convention would be unwise and that amendment would be much easier and more prudent after adoption of the new Constitution.

Faced with increasing calls for a bill of rights and frightened by the prospect that a second convention might be called that might undo the work of the first (Levinson 1990b; Weber 1989; Lash 1994), key Federalists agreed to push for a bill of rights once the Constitution was ratified. James Madison subsequently led the fight in the First Congress for what became the first ten amendments to the Constitution.

Opposition to the Constitution appears to have dissipated relatively soon after its ratification. Almost everyone supported the new constitution, but newly created political parties quickly divided on how the new document should be interpreted. One of the first two political parties, organized largely by Alexander Hamilton and advocating strong powers for the national government, subsequently took the Federalist label. James Madison, by contrast, identified with the Democratic-Republican Party that he and Thomas Jefferson organized and that (echoing many of the themes of the original Anti-Federalists) was more suspicious of national power.

See also Anti-Federalists; Bill of Rights; Council of Censors.

For Further Reading:

Gillespie, Michael L., and Michael Lienesch, eds. 1989. *Ratifying the Constitution.* Lawrence, KS: University Press of Kansas.

Hamilton, Alexander, James Madison, and John Jay. 1787–1788. *The Federalist Papers.* Reprint, New York: New American Library, 1961.

Jefferson, Thomas. 1861. *Notes on the State of Virginia.* New York: Darby. Originally published as part of Vol. VIII of *The Writings of Thomas Jefferson,* ed. H. A. Washington. Reprint, New York: Harper and Row, 1964.

Lash, Kurt T. 1994. "Rejecting Conventional Wisdom: Federalist Ambivalence in the Framing and Implementation of Article V." *American Journal of Legal History* 38 (April): 197–231.

Levinson, Sanford. 1990b. "'Veneration' and Constitutional Change: James Madison Confronts the Possibility of Constitutional Amendment." *Texas Tech Law Review* 21: 2443–2461.

Vile, John R. 1992. *The Constitutional Amending Process in American Political Thought.* New York: Praeger.

Weber, Paul. 1989. "Madison's Opposition to a Second Convention." *Polity* 20 (Spring): 498–517.

Wills, Garry. 1981. *Explaining America: The Federalist.* Garden City, NY: Doubleday.

❖ FIFTEENTH AMENDMENT ❖

Before the adoption of the Fifteenth Amendment, the matter of suffrage was purely a matter for the states. Once the Fifteenth Amendment prohibited deprivation of voting rights on the basis of "race, color, or previous condition of servitude," however, a number of other amendments—most notably the Nineteenth and Twenty-sixth—have protected the franchise.

The first resolutions in Congress on African American suffrage were introduced in 1860 and 1861 as a way of averting war. In contrast to amendments that would be introduced after the Civil War, these amendments would have excluded blacks from voting or holding office. One of the supporters of such an amendment was Democratic Senator Stephen A. Douglas of Illinois, who had participated in the famous Lincoln-Douglas debates focusing on the issue of slavery.

After the war, there was considerable, albeit far from universal, sentiment among Republicans to guarantee that the franchise would not be denied on the basis of race. In addition to racist sentiment, there were also concerns that a national guarantee of voting rights would erode the American scheme of federalism. Largely as the result of compromise, Section 2 of the Fourteenth Amendment did not actually forbid disenfranchisement of blacks, but it did give Congress the right to reduce representation in states that did so. This provision was never enforced.

After ratification of the Fourteenth Amendment in 1868, there was continuing concern about voting rights for African Americans. Idealistic principles mixed with more partisan Republican concerns that the black vote might be crucial to the party's continuing electoral success. Congress adopted a number of laws granting suffrage to blacks in the District of Columbia and in the federal territories, and it conditioned the admission of Nebraska into the Union and the seating of Southern state congressional delegates on those states' extending the right to vote to African Americans. Ironically, this legislation left the Northern and border states as the only ones in which such suffrage had not been so guaranteed (U.S. Senate 1985, 36).

Radical Republicans preferred the statutory route, because they wanted to assert congressional power over the area of voting rights; more moderate Republicans feared that rights obtained via legislation would lack the security that an amendment could provide (Maltz 1990, 146). Republican electoral victories in the 1868 elections gave special impetus to such efforts, which probably could not have been enacted under other circumstances.

The debates over the Fifteenth Amendment became quite complex. In the House the original proposal introduced by Massachusetts Republican George Boutwell prohibiting abridgment of the right to vote "by reason of race, color, or previous condition of slavery" was met with unsuccessful calls to guarantee universal suffrage, thus invalidating literacy, property, and any other voting qualifications (Maltz 1990, 147–148). At least one proposal was offered to exclude "Chinamen and Indians not taxed" from the provisions of this amendment; another proposal would have prohibited any restriction of the voting rights of anyone twelve years of age or older (cited in Ames 1896, 230).

For its part, the Senate, mindful of Georgia's attempt to exclude black officeholders from the state legislature, voted on a proposal by Nevada Republican Senator William Stewart that would protect both the right to vote and the right to hold office. The Senate also considered limitations on property and literacy requirements. As initially passed, the amendment also sought to guarantee the popular election of electors for president (Maltz 1990, 149).

After the House rejected this plan, a conference committee was established, from which the current language of the Fifteenth Amendment emerged. This dropped all references to officeholding rights and to qualifications other than race, color, or previous condition of servitude and included a separate enforcement section. The House approved this amendment on 25 February 1869 by a vote of 144 to 44 (35 not voting); the Senate followed the next day by a vote of 39 to 13 (U.S. Senate 1985, 37). The amendment was ratified by February 1870. A controversy over New York's attempted rescission of its ratification was nullified by an additional ratification by Nebraska and a number of other states. Georgia, Texas, Virginia, and Mississippi were required to ratify as a condition of readmission into the Union (Grimes 1978, 58).

The Fifteenth Amendment was evaded by numerous strategies, legal and otherwise. These included adoption of grandfather clauses, literacy tests, and understanding clauses (often enforced in a highly arbitrary manner), poll taxes, the all-white primary, and physical intimidation. These mechanisms proved so effective that

Goldwin Smith (1898, 267) suggested at the turn of the century that the amendment had become a dead letter and should be repealed. From a somewhat different vantage point, attorneys Arthur Machen (1910) and William Marbury argued that the Fifteenth Amendment violated implicit limits on the amending process. The Supreme Court ignored such arguments in voiding Maryland's grandfather clauses in *Myers v. Anderson* (1915).

Despite evasion and slack enforcement of the Fifteenth Amendment, an amending proposal was introduced as early as 1877 to restrict its application. Moreover, members of Congress from the South introduced numerous proposals from 1900 to 1915 to repeal the amendment. Perhaps they realized that although it was being narrowly interpreted at the time, it had the potential for expansive interpretation in the future. Some revival of the amendment occurred with the Supreme Court's decision in *Smith v. Allwright* (1944) invalidating the all-white primary. The amendment subsequently served as a justification for expansive voting rights legislation in the 1960s and thereafter. In cases like *South Carolina v. Katzenbach* (1966), the Supreme Court has sometimes allowed Congress to use its enforcement powers in Section 2 of the amendment to invalidate legislation, like literacy tests, that would otherwise be constitutional.

See also Marbury, William.

For Further Reading:

Ames, Herman. 1896. *The Proposed Amendments to the Constitution of the United States during the First Century of Its History.* Reprint, New York: Burt Franklin, 1970.

Grimes, Alan P. 1978. *Democracy and the Amendments to the Constitution.* Lexington, MA: Lexington Books.

Maltz, Earl M. 1990. *Civil Rights, the Constitution, and Congress, 1863–1869.* Lawrence, KS: University Press of Kansas.

Mathews, John M. 1909. *Legislative and Judicial History of the Fifteenth Amendment.* New York: Da Capo Press, 1971 reprint.

Smith, Goldwin. 1898. "Is the Constitution Outworn?" *North American Review* 166 (March): 257–267.

United States Senate, Subcommittee on the Constitution, Committee on the Judiciary. 1985. *Amendments to the Constitution: A Brief Legislative History.* Washington, DC: U.S. Government Printing Office.

❖ FIFTH AMENDMENT ❖

The Fifth Amendment was proposed by the First Congress and ratified in 1791 as part of the Bill of Rights. The amendment outlines a variety of guarantees, most of which are directed toward the rights of individuals who are accused of crimes.

The multiple guarantees of this amendment were found in several different parts of the bill of rights that James Madison originally presented to Congress and remained separated until Senate deliberations, when they were combined. Madison's original proposals specified that no one would be subject "to more than one trial or one punishment" (Kurland and Lerner 1987, 5:262) rather than to be "twice put in jeopardy." Madison's original proposal also had a broader self-incrimination provision; the limitation to criminal cases was made during House debates.

Grand Jury Indictment

The Fifth Amendment contains five basic guarantees. The first such guarantee requires indictment by a grand jury in "capital" (death penalty) or other "infamous" cases, with an exception for personnel in the armed services. The grand jury is distinct from the petit jury guaranteed in the Sixth Amendment. Whereas petit juries award judgments or decide on guilt or innocence and determine penalties in criminal cases, a grand jury simply ascertains whether a prosecutor has sufficient evidence to proceed with a trial. Such juries are designed to guard against prosecutorial vindictiveness. The purpose of the so-called double-jeopardy provision that follows is similar. If an initial finding of innocence were not considered final, a prosecutor could simply wear down a defendant with repeated prosecutions for the same offense.

Grand jury proceedings have traditionally been secret, both in order to encourage witnesses to make free disclosure and in order to protect the innocent. Some concern has been expressed that the USA Patriot Act of 2001 passed in the aftermath of the terrorist attacks of 11 September 2001 might erode such privacy by its provisions for sharing intelligence gathered through grand juries with a wide variety of governmental agencies (Whitehead 2002, 1113–1115).

The Provision against Self-incrimination

No provision in the Fifth Amendment is better known, or more controversial, than the provision against self-incrimination. A similar guarantee was found in a number of early state constitutions and in proposals offered by the Virginia and North Carolina ratifying conventions (Lutz 1992, 160; for earlier origins, see Levy 1968). One scholar has identified three major purposes of this provision: "(1) maintaining a responsible accusatorial system, (2) preventing cruel and inhumane treatment of suspects, and (3) offering protection for personal privacy" (D. O'Brien 2000a, 974).

Modern judicial decisions have extended the meaning of this clause beyond that of prohibiting physical coercion to assuring that mental coercion is forbidden as well. In its famous decision in *Miranda v. Arizona* (1966), the Supreme Court extended this guarantee from the courtroom to the station house by ruling that police have to inform suspects of their right to remain silent. The U.S. Supreme Court recently reaffirmed this decision in *Dickerson v. United States* (2000).

The Due Process Clause

No clause in the Fifth Amendment has been more important than the due process clause. Due process obviously relates to procedural fairness, but there are times when the Court has given this clause, and its companion clause in the Fourteenth Amendment (the primary vehicle through which most limitations in the Bill of Rights, which once applied exclusively to the national government, are now also applied to the states), a substantive content as well. In the late nineteenth and early twentieth century, this provision was sometimes used to void economic regulations. In *Bolling v. Sharpe* (1954) it was used to outlaw forms of racial segregation at the federal as well as at the state level (the latter is covered under the equal protection clause of the Fourteenth Amendment). Although all provisions of the Constitution are subject to judicial interpretation, this one seems to allow greater leeway than many less open-ended clauses.

The Takings Clause

Unlike the other provisions in the amendment, the last provision of the Fifth Amendment, usually dubbed the takings clause, does not deal with the rights of suspected criminals. Instead, it provides that the government cannot take private property without justly compensating its owners. The right of the government to condemn private property for public use, the so-called right of eminent domain, is thus assumed rather than directly stated. Significantly, in *Chicago, Burlington & Quincy Railway Co. v. Chicago* (1897), the takings clause was the first to be applied to the states via the due process clause of the Fourteenth Amendment. All other provisions of the Fifth Amendment, except for the provision providing for grand jury indictments, have also been so "incorporated."

Attempts to Repeal the Fifth Amendment

There have been attempts to repeal various provisions in the Fifth Amendment. In 1958 Senator Strom Thurmond of South Carolina introduced an amendment designed to alter the provision against double jeopardy. In the next year, a book questioned whether courts had properly interpreted the self-incrimination provision of the amendment and suggested that the principle should not apply to pretrial investigations (although there should be protections against police use of "third degree" tactics) and that the right should apply only to an accused and not to other witnesses called to testify at a trial (Mayers 1959, 229–231). Similarly, a federal judge writing in 1968 offered an amendment designed to change a number of judicial interpretations of the self-incrimination clause (Friendly 1968, 721–722). Some amendments have also been offered that would suspend the prohibition against the taking of private property without compensation during times of war.

See also Substantive Due Process.

For Further Reading:

Bodenhamer, David J. 1992. *Fair Trial: Rights of the Accused in American History.* New York: Oxford University Press.

Friendly, Henry J. 1968. "The Fifth Amendment Tomorrow: The Case for Constitutional Change." *University of Cincinnati Law Review* 37 (Fall): 671–726.

Levy, Leonard W. 1968. *Origins of the Fifth Amendment: The Right against Self-Incrimination.* New York: Oxford University Press.

Lutz, Donald S. 1992. *A Preface to American Political Theory.* Lawrence, KS: University Press of Kansas.

Mayers, Lewis. 1959. *Shall We Amend the Fifth Amendment?* New York: Harper and Brothers.

O'Brien, David M. 2000. *Civil Rights and Civil Liberties.* Vol. 2 of *Constitutional Law and Politics.* 4th ed. New York: W. W. Norton.

Whitehead, John W. 2002. "Forfeiting 'Enduring Freedom' for 'Homeland Security': A Constitutional Analysis of the USA Patriot Act and the Justice Department's Anti-Terrorism Initiatives." *American University Law Review* 51 (August): 1081–1133.

Yandle, Bruce. 1995. *Land Rights: The 1990s' Property Rights Rebellion.* Lanham, MD: Rowman & Littlefield.

❖ FINER, HERMAN (1898–1969) ❖

Political scientist Herman Finer offered far-ranging reforms of U.S. government in a book published in 1960. Finer focused primarily on the presidency, believing that the job had become too onerous for one individual to handle, but he also believed that differing terms of office for the president and members of Congress contribute to the problem.

Finer offered nine major reforms of the existing system. His first and most important proposal was that the president would run on a ticket with eleven vice presidents to be named by national nominating conventions without any instructions from primaries. The president and his cabinet would serve four-year terms, and the two-term limit found in the Twenty-second Amendment would be eliminated. Vice presidents would, like current cabinet members, head executive departments, although some would not have such responsibility but "would be available as deputies to the President and concerned with the main lines of policy as well as general counseling" (Finer 1960, 304).

Finer's second proposal called for making the terms of the president, members of the House, and members of the Senate equal. He favored a four-year term but would accept a five-year stint. He believed that if the executive and legislative candidates ran at the same time and for the same term, this would promote a common platform and would serve to strengthen U.S. political parties.

The third aspect of Finer's plan provided that, to be eligible for president or vice president, an individual "must be presently a member of the House of Representatives or the Senate or must have served at least four years in either house" (Finer 1960, 309). Those elected to the cabinet would be replaced through special elections; individuals on the losing ticket "could be regarded as elected to Congress by the fact of their appearance on the presidential ticket; and they could choose in which house they wished to serve" (*Id.*, 312).

Finer's fourth proposal called for the president to name his first vice president and designate an order of succession among the others. His fifth proposal provided that the president would assume the general direction of policy while allowing each vice president to "conduct the business of his department independently and on his own responsibility" (Finer 1960, 314).

Finer's sixth proposal would give the president the authority to dismiss and replace his vice presidents. Finer also indicated that the president and his cabinet would sit in the House of Representatives and "participate in congressional business—through messages, through debates, [and] through answering the questions" (Finer 1960, 315). Finer proposed reducing the powers of the Senate. It would lose its power to confirm appointments and ratify treaties and would no longer share power with the House in overriding presidential vetoes. Finer's seventh proposal called for maintaining the presidential veto but allowing a 55 percent vote of the House of Representatives to override it.

Although Finer did not believe that Congress should be able to oust the president and his cabinet, he did believe that the president and his cabinet should be able to resign, thus necessitating new elections for both the legislative and the executive branches. This was his eighth proposal. His ninth would have eliminated patronage and spoils, allowing civil servants to continue in office regardless of party affiliation as long as they served the government faithfully and competently.

Finer's is one of the few proposals to develop the idea of a plural executive. It does not appear to have garnered much support.

For Further Reading:
Finer, Herman. 1960. *The Presidency, Crisis and Regeneration: An Essay in Possibilities.* Chicago: University of Chicago Press.

❖ FINLETTER, THOMAS (1893–1980) ❖

Thomas Finletter, attorney and special assistant to the secretary of state, authored a book advocating constitutional reform just as World War II was coming to an end (Finletter 1945). Like Alexander Hehmeyer, Finletter was concerned about the government's ability to function effectively once the war was over (Vile 1991c, 91–93). Finletter was especially concerned about what he perceived to be the lack of fit between governmental means under a system of checks and balances and expanded governmental ends.

Finletter dedicated much of his book to a historical overview designed to show that the existing governmental system resulted in excessive legislative-executive conflict and often led to paralysis. He favored the establishment of more executive-legislative bodies; an institution like the British question hour, where representatives of the administration could explain and justify their policies; and reform of the congressional committee system and its use of seniority. He also advocated establishment of "a joint executive-legislative cabinet" (Finletter 1945, 88). Such a cabinet would be composed of nine congressional leaders from the majority party and nine members of the executive cabinet. Finletter also believed that a majority of both houses of Congress should be able to ratify treaties.

Finletter opposed a parliamentary system, largely because he believed that the American people (and not Congress) had a right to choose their chief executive directly. Finletter believed, however, that the system of fixed election dates should be altered. He proposed that the president and members of both houses of Congress be elected for six-year terms. The president would, in turn, have the power to dissolve Congress and call new elections. Finletter believed that such a system would restore unified government, strengthen party discipline, and make parties more responsible. Finletter also believed that the residency requirement for members of Congress should be eliminated so that parties could run candidates for office outside their districts.

Finletter recognized that formidable forces of "inertia and of satisfaction with things as they are" blocked the path to reform, but he thought that without reform, the conflict between the legislative and executive branches would eventually destroy self-government in the United States (Finletter 1945, 145–147).

For Further Reading:

Finletter, Thomas K. 1945. *Can Representative Government Do the Job?* New York: Reynal and Hitchcock.

❖ FIRST AMENDMENT ❖

The First Amendment was proposed by the First Congress and ratified in 1791 as part of the Bill of Rights. The amendment contains two clauses related to religion. One provides that "Congress shall make no law respecting an establishment of religion." The other forbids Congress from "prohibiting the free exercise thereof." The amendment also provides protection for freedom of speech, press, peaceable assembly, and petition. Without the latter rights, a republican, or representative, form of government would be quite precarious. Although it was originally the third of twelve proposed amendments (the first two of which were not initially ratified), there is some rightful symbolism in the fact that this important amendment now heads the Bill of Rights.

Background

The First Amendment is a distillation of proposals that James Madison submitted to Congress after consulting state constitutions and requests from the state ratifying conventions. In the area of religion, Madison proposed that "the civil rights of none shall be abridged on account of religious belief or worship, nor shall any national religion be established, nor shall the full and equal rights of conscience be in any manner, or on any pretext, infringed" (Kurland and Lerner 1987, 5:25). In attempting to protect freedom of speech and the press, Madison proposed that "the people shall not be deprived or abridged of their right to speak, to write, or to publish their sentiments; and the freedom of the press, as one of the great bulwarks of liberty, shall be inviolable." Similarly, Madison proposed that "the people shall not be restrained from peaceably assembling and consulting for their common good; nor from applying to the Legislature by petitions, or remonstrances, for redress of their grievances" (Kurland and Lerner 1987, 5:25). Madison also proposed that "no State shall violate the equal rights of conscience, or the freedom of the press, or the trial by jury in criminal cases" (Kurland and Lerner 1987, 5:25).

It appears that Madison's wording prohibiting Congress from establishing a "national" religion was dropped largely out of concern that it would imply that the new government was "national" rather than "federal" (Kurland and Lerner 1987, 5:93). A similar concern for states' rights apparently led to the deletion of Madison's guarantee against invasions of individual rights by the states.

Religion

No provisions of the First Amendment have provoked greater controversy than the first two clauses dealing with religion. There may well be implicit tension between the idea that government should not establish religion and the guarantee that it should not interfere with its free exercise. Thus, attempts to guarantee free exercise may appear to further religion, whereas attempts to prevent an establishment may appear to infringe on religious exercise. Congress continues to discuss a Religious Equality Amendment that might better clarify this balance.

The most notable cases before the Supreme Court involving the establishment clause have involved public prayer and Bible reading in public schools. In *Engel v. Vitale* (1962), the Supreme Court ruled that the recitation of a prayer composed by the New York State Board of Regents constituted an impermissible establishment of religion that violated the rights of nonbelievers. Similarly, in *Abington v. Schempp* (1963), the Court struck down daily devotional Bible readings and recitations of the Lord's Prayer in school. Although courts appear to be more receptive toward the idea of a moment of silence during which prayer is not mandated but may take place, the earlier Court decisions continue to bring calls for a constitutional amendment. A decision of the U.S. Court of Appeals for the Ninth Circuit in 2002 that the pledge of allegiance could not be recited in public schools because of its inclusion of the words "under God" is being appealed and could well be reversed either by the Supreme Court itself or by constitutional amendment.

Under its interpretations of the establishment clause, the Supreme Court has struck down most forms of direct governmental aid to parochial schools. In so doing, it formulated the three-pronged *Lemon* test, named after the case *Lemon v. Kurtzman* (1971), in which it was first formulated. This test requires that, to pass constitutional muster, a law must have a secular legislative purpose; must not, as its primary effect, either advance or inhibit religion; and must avoid excessive entanglement between church and state. On occasion the Court has decided that government funding that promotes student or parental participation in parochial schools is not unconstitutional. Thus,

the Supreme Court has permitted tax write-offs for parents who send children to parochial schools (*Mueller v. Allen* (1983)); vocational assistance monies for use by a blind student attending a religious college (*Witters v. Washington Department of Services for the Blind* (1986)); use of a publicly funded sign language interpreter for a deaf student attending a Catholic high school (*Zobrest v. Catalina Foothills School District* (1993)); the use of public school teachers to teach remedial classes in parochial school settings (*Agostini v. Felton* (1997)); and, most recently, the use of state vouchers to private schools in *Zelman v. Simmons-Harris* (2002).

Moreover, the Court does not always apply the *Lemon* test. Thus, in *Marsh v. Chambers* (1983), it permitted continuation of the practice of a chaplain leading prayers at the beginning of a state legislative session; in *Lynch v. Donnelly* (1984), it permitted the display of a religious crèche on public property because this crèche was part of a much larger secular display (see Swanson 1990). Such decisions were written by justices who interpreted the establishment clause as permitting accommodation between the government and religion; others have taken a view of strict separation of church and state, and still others attempt to follow a path of complete neutrality (for one view, see Monsma 1993; for another, see Levy 1986).

The free exercise clause was obviously intended to guarantee a wide range of religious freedoms, but there is question as to the degree to which it should exempt religious people from criminal laws. In *Employment Division v. Smith* (1990), the Supreme Court ruled that state employees fired from their jobs for ingesting peyote as part of a Native American religious ceremony were not entitled to unemployment compensation. The outcry over the decision, which appeared to contradict some earlier cases in which the Court had taken a more sympathetic stance toward actions, albeit not typically illegal ones, motivated by religious beliefs, led to the Religious Freedom Restoration Act. It was designed to ensure that the Court did not override free exercise claims except in cases in which the government was able to establish a compelling state interest. The

Supreme Court overturned this law in *City of Boerne v. Flores* (1997), deciding that it exceeded congressional powers under Section 5 of the Fourteenth Amendment, granting power to "enforce" but not to "reinterpret" the provisions of that amendment. This decision has led to renewed calls for a Religious Equality Amendment, some versions of which would require that courts strike down laws with differential impacts on amendments that do not have a "compelling state interest."

Speech

Few freedoms are more essential to the democratic process than the freedom of speech. But speech can be so related to action that the First Amendment's seemingly absolute prohibition on governmental infringement of the former has been subject to numerous judicial qualifications. In an early case, *Schenck v. United States* (1919), Justice Oliver Wendell Holmes noted that even the most stringent protection accorded to speech would not protect an individual falsely shouting "fire" in a crowded theater and causing a panic. Although there has been much subsequent discussion and eventual judicial repudiation of Holmes's "clear and present danger" test, the notion that even speech has limits has remained. In *Brandenburg v. Ohio* (1969), the Court indicated that it would suppress the expression of pure speech only when it was likely to lead to imminent lawless action (Wirenius 1994).

The Court has been willing to accept reasonable restrictions on the time, place, and manner of speech, but it has been wary of laws that single out speech on the basis of its content. In recent years, the Court has also extended protection to symbolic speech. Its two most controversial cases have been *Texas v. Johnson* (1989) and *United States v. Eichman* (1990), wherein the Court respectively struck down a state law and a federal law designed to prohibit desecration of the American flag. Numerous amendments have been introduced to overturn these decisions, and support in the states is strong for such an amendment. During the Cold War, amendments were also introduced to ban certain types of speech thought likely to lead to subversion of the government.

There are a number of special areas related to freedom of speech that the Supreme Court has treated somewhat differently from others. For example, the Supreme Court has never regarded obscenity as speech. In *Miller v. California* (1973), it identified three criteria for defining obscenity. Under these criteria, speech can be judged obscene if the average person applying contemporary community standards would find that a work taken as a whole appeals to a prurient (lustful) interest in sex; if a work depicts or describes in a patently offensive way sexual conduct specifically defined by law; and if such a work lacks serious literary, artistic, political, or scientific value. Not surprisingly, these criteria still leave considerable room for judicial judgment. In a number of recent decisions, the U.S. Supreme Court has struck down laws designed to protect children from obscene materials on the Internet. Although concerned about children, the Court is also concerned that laws designed to protect children are not so broad that they would deny legitimate rights to adults.

Libel, or defamatory writing, is another special area. Since *New York Times Co. v. Sullivan* (1964), the Court has applied the standard of "actual malice" to cases involving "public figures." This is a stringent test designed to encourage robust criticism of such individuals. Under this test, such figures can collect libel awards only when they are able to demonstrate that information was published with knowledge that it was false or with "reckless disregard" for its veracity (see Lewis 1991).

Although it is an extremely narrow category, the Supreme Court also ruled in *Chaplinsky v. New Hampshire* (1942) that so-called fighting words are not protected by the First Amendment. Such words are derogatory words spoken in close proximity to another person and likely to evoke physical violence rather than reasoned discussion.

The U.S. Supreme Court has generally concluded that the First Amendment protects symbolic expression. Thus in *Tinker v. Des Moines Independent Community School District* (1969), it upheld the right of junior high school students to wear black armbands to school in protest of the Vietnam War. In some cases in which speech has been combined with illegal action, the Court has permitted regulation. In *United States v. O'Brien* (1968), for example, it upheld a law prohibiting individuals from burning their draft cards, which were considered to be government property essential to the national selective service system. The Supreme Court has, however, struck down federal legislation designed to prevent flag desecration on the basis that the law was directed at the content of the expression.

Press

Freedom of the press is a corollary to freedom of speech (Powe 1991), and the two rights often overlap, as in the Internet and libel cases mentioned above. Traditionally, the core of freedom of the press was identified as the prohibition against prior restraint of publication. Although it strongly affirmed this core content in *Near v. Minnesota* (1931), the Supreme Court also insisted that the freedom was wider than this. In *New York Times Co. v. United States* (1971), the Pentagon Papers case, the Supreme Court overruled an injunction against the *Times* and other newspapers and permitted them to publish a classified story critical of American participation in the Vietnam conflict (see Unger 1972). Members of the press have used the First Amendment to assert privileges against being called before grand juries, but, to date, they have had more success in receiving protection through legislation (known as shield laws) than through judicial decisions. Courts have been generally wary of extending protections, like exemption from grand jury testimony, to members of the official press that it does not extend to all—see *Branzburg v. Hayes, In re Pappas,* and *United States v. Caldwell* (1972).

Assembly and Petition

The guarantees for peaceable assembly and petition have not been adjudicated as frequently as others in the First Amendment, but like the other guarantees, they are critical to the functioning of democratic institutions, including petitions for desired constitutional amendments. In recent years, the Supreme Court has held that these and related clauses guarantee a constitutional right of association. In *Griswold*

v. Connecticut (1965), Justice William O. Douglas cited the First Amendment, and this right of association, as one of the foundations of the constitutional right to privacy. More recently, in *Boy Scouts of America v. Dale* (2000) the U.S. Supreme Court limited the application to the Boy Scouts of a New Jersey law forbidding discrimination against homosexuals, on the basis that the Scouts composed a private association, whose views were at odds with homosexual behavior.

All the provisions of the First Amendment have been applied to the states via the due process clause of the Fourteenth Amendment. This means that interpretations by the U.S. Supreme Court serve as a floor below which state standards may not fall, although such interpretations do not prevent states from extending a higher degree of protection to First Amendment freedoms under their own individual constitutions.

See also *Engel v. Vitale;* Flag Desecration; Obscenity and Pornography; Religious Equality Amendment.

For Further Reading:
Branzburg v. Hayes, In re Pappas, and *United States v. Caldwell,* 408 U.S. 665 (1972).
Kurland, Philip B., and Ralph Lerner, eds. 1987. *The Founders' Constitution.* 5 vols. Chicago: University of Chicago Press.
Levy, Leonard W. 1986. *The Establishment Clause and the First Amendment.* New York: Macmillan.
Lewis, Anthony. 1991. *Make No Law: The Sullivan Case and the First Amendment.* New York: Random House.
Monsma, Stephen V. 1993. *Positive Neutrality: Letting Religious Freedom Ring.* Westport, CT: Greenwood Press.
Powe, Lucas A., Jr. 1991. *The Fourth Estate and the Constitution: Freedom of Press in America.* Berkeley, CA: University of California Press.
Swanson, Wayne R. 1990. *The Christ Child Goes to Court.* Philadelphia, PA: Temple University Press.
Unger, Sanford J. 1972. *The Paper and the Papers.* New York: E. P. Dutton.
Wirenius, John F. 1994. "The Road to *Brandenburg:* A Look at the Evolving Understanding of the First Amendment." *Drake Law Review* 43: 1–49.

❖ FISHER, SIDNEY GEORGE (1809–1875) ❖

Philadelphia lawyer Sidney George Fisher published a critique of the U.S. Constitution entitled *The Trial of the Constitution* in 1862 (Vile 1992, 97–105). Largely prompted by Fisher's perception that the rigidity of the formal constitutional amending process had been an obstacle to the satisfactory resolution of the issues that led to the Civil War, Fisher's analysis is remarkable for at least two reasons. First, in contrast to almost all previous commentators other than the Anti-Federalists, Fisher questioned the adequacy of the formal amending process. Second, Fisher proposed the British model of legislative sovereignty as an alternative. However, he also associated this model with cautious and incremental change.

Joseph Story, the prominent U.S. Supreme Court justice and constitutional commentator, had praised the amending process in Article V as an effective safety valve. Fisher argued that this safety valve had been ineffective in preventing revolutionary violence and that "the [constitutional] boiler has burst" (S. Fisher 1862, 27). Using another analogy, Fisher proclaimed that Article V had become "an iron fetter" (*Id.*, 33). In Fisher's judgment, the irony of the amending process was that it was most likely to be used at the very time when its operation was likely to be most dangerous: "To put its cumbrous machinery in motion, the people must be roused, and as the most important organic changes are generally connected with the interests of sections or of classes, the people are very likely to be roused by them, to be divided into parties, to be influenced by passion" (*Id.*, 34).

Having concluded that the existing mechanism for constitutional change was essentially unusable, Fisher proceeded to advocate a system whereby Congress would institute constitutional change subject to popular appeal at the ballot box. In this manner, the people of the current generation rather than those of the American founding would govern. Such a scheme required a substantial limitation of judicial power. Fisher would limit federal judicial review to correcting "unintentional" violations of the Constitution, to controlling state courts, and to "criminal usurpations of power by the Executive or Legislative, or a conspiracy by both to overturn the Government" (S. Fisher 1862, 79).

Although the legislative and executive branches both demonstrated by their actions in the Civil War that the Constitution was a grant of power as well as a list of restraints, Fisher's proposal for a system of legislative sovereignty was not accepted. Fisher's book was published toward the end of the longest period in U.S. history (1804–1865) during which no constitutional amendments were adopted. Ironically, the very process that Fisher criticized for its ineffectiveness was successfully utilized three times from 1865 to 1870. This period was, however, followed by more than a generation before another amendment was adopted. This period, especially the early Progressive Era, also witnessed criticism of the adequacy of the constitutional amending process.

For Further Reading:

Fisher, Sidney G. 1862. *A Philadelphia Perspective: The Diary of Sidney George Fisher Covering the Years 1834–1871*. Reprint, Philadelphia, PA: Historical Society of Pennsylvania, 1967.

Riker, William H. 1954. "Sidney George Fisher and the Separation of Powers during the Civil War." *Journal of the History of Ideas* 15 (June): 397–412.

❖ FLAG DESECRATION ❖

Few recent amendment controversies have provided a faster or more intense response than the Supreme Court's 1989 decision in *Texas v. Johnson*. This decision overturned the conviction of Gregory Johnson under the Texas Venerated Objects Law. Johnson had burned an American flag in front of the Dallas City Hall during the Republican National Convention in 1984. In an intensely argued decision, five of nine Supreme Court justices of diverse ideological leanings ruled that Johnson's action was a form of "symbolic speech" protected under the First Amendment. Both the House and the

Senate passed resolutions expressing their concern about and disappointment with this decision, and they subsequently debated a constitutional amendment on the subject.

History of Flag Desecration Laws and Judicial Decisions

Although the decision in *Texas v. Johnson* initiated a firestorm, concern for protecting the flag dates quite far back in U.S. history. The flag's importance as a national symbol appears to have become increasingly important during the U.S. Civil War. Legislation designed to protect the flag was favorably voted on by the House of Representatives in 1890 and by the Senate in 1904 and 1908. Moreover, between 1897 and 1905, thirty-four states adopted flag desecration laws, with most of the remaining states following suit in the period during and immediately after World War I (R. Goldstein 1990, 38). Many of these laws dealt not only with desecration of the flag but also with improper commercial usage. Thus in *Halter v. Nebraska* (1907), the U.S. Supreme Court upheld the conviction of a businessman who sold beer bottled with flag emblems. On a related matter, however, in *Stromberg v. California* (1931), the Court struck down a California law prohibiting the display of red flags on the grounds that the law was too vague.

The next two cases to reach the Supreme Court dealt not with flag desecration but with flag salutes. Before the U.S. entry into World War II, many states adopted compulsory flag-salute laws in an attempt to encourage patriotism. The Court upheld such a law in *Minersville School District v. Gobitis* (1940). These laws were opposed by Jehovah's Witnesses, who interpreted the flag salute as worship of a graven image. In the aftermath of the Court's decision, Jehovah's Witnesses were victimized by mobs, and as many as 2,000 Witness children were expelled from schools (R. Goldstein 1990, 46). Subsequently, the Supreme Court used Flag Day in 1943 to reverse itself in *West Virginia Board of Education v. Barnette*, now declaring that the First Amendment protected individuals' rights not to violate their consciences by mouthing salutes they did not believe. The Ninth Circuit Court of Appeals has subsequently ruled in *Newdow v. U.S. Congress* (2002) that the flag salute cannot be said in public schools because its use of the words "under God" (added by congressional legislation in 1954) constitutes an unlawful establishment of religion contrary to the First Amendment. This ruling applies only to the Ninth Circuit and seems likely to be reversed.

The Vietnam War and a televised incident of flag burning in Central Park in April 1967 brought renewed attention to the flag and precipitated the first federal legislation on the subject. This law, adopted in 1968, provided a penalty of up to $1,000, a year in jail, or both for anyone who "knowingly cast[s] contempt upon any flag of the United States by publicly mutilating, defacing, defiling, burning, or trampling upon it" (cited in R. Goldstein 1990, 49). Shortly thereafter, a number of proposals were introduced in Congress to guard voluntary flag salutes in public schools and buildings and to allow Congress to protect the flag from desecration.

In *Street v. New York* (1969), the Court struck down the conviction of a man who had burned a flag in the aftermath of civil rights leader James Meredith's assassination. But this case was complicated by the fact that it appeared that his conviction might have resulted from what he said when burning the flag rather than from the act itself. In *Spence v. Washington* (1974), the Court overturned the conviction of an individual who had taped a peace symbol to the flag. That same year, in *Smith v. Goguen*, the Supreme Court declared void for vagueness a Massachusetts law that had been applied to an individual who had worn a flag patch on the seat of his pants. The Supreme Court issued no further decisions on the subject between 1974 and 1989 (R. Goldstein 1990, 63).

Reactions to *Texas v. Johnson*

Scores of amendments were introduced in the wake of the Court's 1989 decision in *Texas v. Johnson;* interestingly, a number of these amendments also sought to exclude campaign spending from First Amendment restraints, thus arguably overturning the Supreme Court's 1976 decision in *Buckley v. Valeo.* President George Bush Sr. went to the Iwo Jima

Monument to announce his support for an amendment introduced by Republican Representative Robert Michel of Illinois. This amendment provided that "the Congress and the states shall have power to prohibit the physical desecration of the Flag of the United States" (Vile 1989, 169).

During hearings on the proposed amendment, some members of Congress—relying on some equivocal language in the Court's opinion and on the testimony of some prominent law professors, including Laurence Tribe of the Harvard Law School—concluded that Congress had the power to overturn the decision in *Texas v. Johnson* by legislation. A vote for a flag desecration amendment was thus defeated in the Senate in 1989 by a vote of fifty-one to forty-eight (R. Goldstein 1990, 28). That same year, however, Congress adopted the Flag Protection Act, which was designed to punish anyone who "knowingly mutilates, physically defiles, burns, maintains on the floor or ground, or tramples upon any flag of the United States." The law exempted "any conduct consisting of the disposal of a flag when it has become worn or soiled" (R. Goldstein 1990, 85).

Accepting expedited review of the law, the Supreme Court struck it down in a five-to-four decision in *United States v. Eichman* (1990). As many supporters of the law appeared originally to have hoped, however, both public and congressional sentiment had cooled since the earlier decision. Faced with arguments that an amendment would protect the flag at the cost of sacrificing the principles for which it stood and that it would be unwise to set the first precedent of restricting the Bill of Rights, Congress could not garner the required two-thirds majorities in 1990 (the votes for an amendment were 254 to 177 in the House and 58 to 42 in the Senate), but the issue has refused to die. In June 1995 the House voted 312 to 120 in favor of an anti-flag desecration amendment, but the Senate could muster only 63 (of a needed 67) votes in December of that year. The House achieved the requisite majorities in June 1997, but senators kept the issue from reaching the floor. The House voted 305 to 124 to adopt such an amendment in June

1999, but the Senate again mustered only 63 votes when it voted on the issue in March 2000 (Dorsen 2000, 430–433). The House reapproved a flag desecration amendment in July 2001, but it again seemed unlikely to gain approval by the necessary majority needed in the Senate. Many states are on record as indicating that they will support this amendment if it is proposed by the necessary congressional majorities.

Issues Raised by the Flag Desecration Amendment

One fascinating aspect of the flag desecration amendment is that it has revived arguments that there might be limits on the amending process. Thus, one scholar argued that such an amendment would violate rights protected by the Ninth Amendment and could be adopted only if language were included specifically indicating that the American people no longer considered flag burning to be a natural right (Rosen 1991). Another author argued that because the First Amendment prohibits Congress from making any law abridging the freedom of speech, such an amendment would have to be adopted by the unused convention route (Isaacson 1990; for critiques of Rosen and Isaacson, see Vile 1993, 136–143).

If a constitutional amendment is adopted, the courts could have difficulty deciding precisely what representations are defined as flags. For example, would representations of flags in newspapers or magazines count? There is also the ironic possibility that an amendment specifically prohibiting flag desecration would actually widen protection for other forms of symbolic speech (Vile 1989).

See also Campaign Contributions and Expenditures; Constitutional Amendments, Limits on; First Amendment; *Texas v. Johnson*.

For Further Reading:
Bates, Stephen. 1991. "Deconstructing the Flag-Burning Debate." *This World & I* 7 (July): 523–529.
Curtis, Michael K., ed. 1993. *The Constitution and the Flag.* Vol. 2. *The Flag Burning Cases.* New York: Garland.

Dorsen, Norman. 2000. "Flag Desecration in Courts, Congress, and Country." *Thomas M. Cooley Law Review* 17 (Michaelmas Term): 417–442.

Dry, Murray. 1991. "Flag Burning and the Constitution." In *The Supreme Court Review, 1990*, ed. Gerhard Casper et al. Chicago: University of Chicago Press.

Goldstein, Robert J. 2000. *Flag Burning and Free Speech.* Lawrence, KS: University Press of Kansas.

———. 1996. *The American Flag Desecration Controversy: A Collection of Documents from the Civil War to 1990.* Kent, OH: Kent State University Press.

———. 1995. *Burning the Flag: The Great 1989–1990 American Flag Desecration Controversy.* Kent, OH: Kent State University Press.

———. 1994. *Saving "Old Glory": The History of the American Flag Desecration Controversy.* Boulder, CO: Westview.

Isaacson, Eric A. 1990. "The Flag Burning Issue: A Legal Analysis and Comment." *Loyola of Los Angeles Law Review* 23 (January): 535–600.

Kaplan, Morton A. 1991. "Freedom of Speech: Its Constitutional Scope and Function." *This World & I* 7 (July): 531–541.

McBride, James. 1991. "'Is Nothing Sacred?': Flag Desecration, the Constitution and the Establishment of Religion." *St. John's Law Review* 65: 297–324.

Rosen, Jeff. 1991. "Was the Flag Burning Amendment Unconstitutional?" *Yale Law Review* 100: 1073–1092.

Tushnet, Mark. 1990. "The Flag-Burning Episode: An Essay on the Constitution." *University of Colorado Law Review* 61: 39–53.

Vile, John R. 1993b. *Contemporary Questions Surrounding the Constitutional Amending Process.* Westport, CT: Praeger.

———. 1989. "How a Constitutional Amendment Protecting the Flag Might Widen Protection of Symbolic Expression." *Louisiana Bar Journal* 37 (October): 169–172.

❖ FLAG SALUTE ❖

The words by which individuals salute the American flag were first written in 1892 and were subsequently revised in 1924, when "My Flag" was changed to "the flag of the United States of America," and in 1954, when Congress added the words "under God" (Fineman 2002, 24). In *West Virginia State Board of Education v. Barnette* (1943), the U.S. Supreme Court reversed an earlier decision and ruled that students could not be forced to salute the American flag in public schools if such a salute was in conflict with their convictions. Many Americans were nevertheless stunned when two of three judges on the Ninth U.S. Circuit Court of Appeals (with jurisdiction over California and other western states) handed down a decision in *Newdow v. U.S. Congress* on 26 June 2002 indicating that it was unconstitutional for school children to recite the pledge of allegiance in public schools. The court held that because the pledge contained the words "under God" in a public school setting where students might feel undue compulsion when the salute was led by a teacher, it constituted an impermissible violation of the establishment clause of the First Amendment by sending a message to nonbelievers in monotheistic religion that they were second-class citizens.

The Ninth Circuit has long been much more liberal than the U.S. Supreme Court, which has often overturned it and may well do so in this case. The morning following the ruling members of Congress lined up collectively to repeat the pledge in the legislative chambers. In addition, a number of members of Congress offered amendments on the same day that would specifically state that it is not an establishment of religion for school students to make such a recitation. Some versions of the amendment specifically identify the current pledge, with the words "under God," which were added by congressional legislation in the Eisenhower administration in 1954. If such an amendment is adopted, it would be the first direct mention of a deity in the U.S. Constitution, thus partially fulfilling the wishes of those who advocated what was known as the Christian Amendment. At least one proposed amendment introduced in the Senate relative to the constitutionality of the flag salute would also permit reference to God on U.S. currency; the words "In God We Trust" were added during the U.S. Civil War.

See also Christian Amendment; Flag Desecration; First Amendment.

For Further Reading:
Fineman, Howard. 2002. "One Nation, Under . . . Who?" *Newsweek* 140 (July 8): 20–25.

❖ FORFEITURE OF OFFICE ❖

See Offices, Forfeiture of, or Ineligibility for.

❖ FOURTEENTH AMENDMENT ❖

No provision of the Constitution has been more disputed among scholars or more litigated before courts than the Fourteenth Amendment. It was proposed by the necessary congressional majorities in June 1866 and ratified in July 1868. The Fourteenth Amendment was wedged between two other amendments that were adopted contemporaneously soon after the Civil War, and an understanding of the dilemmas faced after the war does much to explain it.

Background

Under the terms of the Thirteenth Amendment, involuntary servitude was eliminated. Because slaves had previously counted as only three-fifths of a person for determining a state's representation in the House of Representatives and the electoral college, such freedom presented the possibility that the states of the ex-Confederacy might actually gain representation in the government. In such circumstances, those who had led the rebellion might actually increase their political power, gaining in Congress what they had been unable to achieve on the battlefields. Moreover, almost as soon as the slaves were freed, many of the states that had permitted slavery enacted restrictive Black Codes that effectively stripped the former slaves of their freedom.

Congress reacted by adopting the 1866 Civil Rights Bill, which effectively ignored the Supreme Court's decision in *Scott v. Sandford* (1857) by recognizing the citizenship of all native-born Americans (except some Native Americans) and attempting to protect their rights. Congress also adopted the Freedmen's Bureau Bill of 1866, which authorized military trials for those violating civil rights (U.S. Senate 1985, 30). Both bills were adopted over President Andrew Johnson's vetoes and in the face of arguments that they were unconstitutional. Although the Thirteenth Amendment had abolished slavery, doubts remained as to whether it provided adequate authority for the protection of other civil and political rights that had traditionally rested with the states.

Creation and Proposal

In response to this situation, in December 1865 Congress created a Joint Committee on Reconstruction composed of fifteen members—five Republicans and one Democrat from the Senate, and seven Republicans and two Democrats from the House. The committee was chaired by Republicans Thaddeus Stevens (PA) of the House and William P. Fessenden (ME) of the Senate (W. Nelson 1988, 48). On 12 January 1866, Representative John Bingham (R-OH) introduced a proposed amendment to grant Congress power to provide "equal protection" for "all persons in every State within the Union," and eight days later, a subcommittee incorporated this provision into a proposal giving Congress power "to secure to all citizens of the United States, in every State, the same political rights and privileges; and to all persons in every State equal protection in the enjoyment of life, liberty, and property." The subcommittee also proposed that "whenever the elective franchise shall be denied or abridged in any State on account of race, creed or color, all persons of such race, creed or color, shall be excluded from the basis of representation" (W. Nelson 1988, 49).

The joint committee subsequently presented Congress with two amendments, one to reduce the representation of states restricting voting rights and the other designed to protect the rights of the newly freed slaves. The House adopted the first amendment, but it was postponed in the Senate. The other amendment did not make it through either house (W. Nelson 1988, 50).

In the meantime, the joint committee was reworking its proposals and meshing them into a single amendment. In the process, it changed the language of "political rights and privileges" into "privileges and immunities." Moreover, rather than stripping whites of suffrage in states that restricted the franchise, the committee settled on a provision—apparently first suggested by Indiana Democrat Robert Dale Owen Jr.—to reduce representation for such states and to disenfranchise those who had supported the Confederate cause (W. Nelson 1988, 50–57). It also included a provision guaranteeing the Union debt and repudiating the Confederate debt and making it clear that slaveholders would not be compensated for slaves who had been emancipated. The House accepted this revised amendment in May 1866, but the Committee of the Whole in the Senate subsequently made two important modifications. One was to add the definition of citizenship that became the first sentence of Section 1 of this amendment. The second change was to weaken the prohibition against voting by former Confederates; it now banned from office former Confederates who had joined the cause after taking an oath of allegiance to the U.S. Constitution (W. Nelson 1988, 58). The House subsequently concurred in these revisions (for further discussion of congressional actions, see Virginia Commission on Constitutional Government 1967; James 1956; Flack 1908; Maltz 1990).

Content

As adopted, the Fourteenth Amendment is divided into five sections. It is the longest, the most complex, and arguably the most significant amendment to have been added to the Constitution. Congressman Robert Dale Owen has been credited with the idea of binding together a variety of proposals in a single amendment with the idea of increasing the likelihood of congressional adoption and state ratification. In this respect, the Fourteenth Amendment differed from the Bill of Rights where, with some notable exceptions (consider the takings clause of the Fifth Amendment), "various propositions [or groups of propositions] were offered as separate amendments to be decided upon individually" (Kyvig 1996a, 166). It has been noted that:

> Instead of demanding a supermajority committed to a single measure, the Owen

approach brokered inclusion of individual elements for willingness to accept the other parts of the package. Whether because of the difficulty of assembling such a collation, failure to recognize it as an effective strategy, or perceived undesirability of an approach that compromised the terms of amendment, the Owen method of designing an amendment has not been used again, despite its effectiveness when first employed. (Kyvig 1996a, 167)

Section 1 of the Fourteenth Amendment overturned *Scott v. Sandford* (1857) by extending citizenship to all persons "born or naturalized in the United States and subject to the jurisdiction thereof." It also forbade states to abridge the privileges and immunities of such citizens. More broadly, it prohibited states from denying persons "due process of law" or "equal protection of the law."

Section 2 repealed the three-fifths clause and, in a provision that was never enforced, sought to reduce representation for states restricting the franchise "in the proportion which the number of such male citizens shall be to the whole number of citizens twenty-one years of age in such State." This was the section that was so upsetting to advocates of women's rights such as Susan B. Anthony and Elizabeth Cady Stanton, who had hoped that suffrage for women would be granted along with suffrage for African Americans. Disappointed by both the Fourteenth and the Fifteenth Amendments, they had to wait until 1920 for the adoption of the Nineteenth Amendment granting suffrage to women.

The last three sections of the amendment dealt with incidental matters. Section 3 prohibited officeholding by those who, having taken an oath to uphold the U.S. Constitution, subsequently supported the Confederacy, but it provided that a two-thirds vote of Congress could remove such a disability, and it soon did so. Section 4 guaranteed the Union debt while repudiating that of the Confederacy and denied all claims by former slaveholders for compensation for their slaves. Finally, Section 5, like Section 2 of the Thirteenth Amendment, granted Congress power to enforce the amendment.

Ratification

The ratification of the Fourteenth Amendment was almost as controversial as the debates over its proposal (Fernandez 1966; Suthon 1953). Although the amendment met with favor in the North, most Southern states rejected it. In 1867 Congress subsequently adopted the Military Reconstruction Act, providing that states of the former Confederacy could be readmitted to the Union without military rule if they ratified the Fourteenth Amendment. Several subsequently did so. At about that time, New Jersey and Ohio attempted to rescind their ratifications. Secretary of State William Seward presented the facts to Congress, which declared the amendment adopted (James 1984, 288–299). At least one other state appears to have ratified the amendment prior to the congressional votes, and other ratifications followed before any judicial decisions based on the amendment. Moreover, Congress had not previously found it necessary to take a separate step to "promulgate" an amendment.

Interpretation

Ratification of the Fourteenth Amendment was just the beginning of the controversy over its meaning. Especially difficult to resolve is the question of the extent to which the guarantees in the Fourteenth Amendment were designed to harmonize with, or supersede, earlier understandings of federalism (compare W. Nelson 1988 and Richards 1993). Much contemporary debate has also centered on the question whether the due process clause or the privileges and immunities clause in Section 1 of the amendment was designed to overrule *Barron v. Baltimore* (1833) and apply the provisions of the Bill of Rights to the states. Senator Hugo L. Black later advocated this view based on his reading of the congressional debates on the subject.

The Supreme Court majority did not initially take this position. Indeed, its decisions in the nineteenth century gave restrictive readings to most provisions of the amendment. In the *Slaughterhouse Cases* (1873), the Court narrowly read the privileges and immunities of Section 1 of the amendment. In the *Civil Rights Cases* (1883), the Court overturned the Civil Rights Act of 1875, which had attempted to prohibit discrimination in places of public accommodation. In a distinction that has never been repudiated, the Court reasoned that the Fourteenth Amendment applied only to state action and not to actions by individuals. Finally, in *Plessy v. Ferguson* (1896), the Supreme Court upheld racial segregation and Southern Jim Crow laws by formulating the "separate but equal" doctrine, justifying segregation as long as facilities for races were equal.

Although limiting the scope of the Fourteenth Amendment in the area of civil rights, the Court increasingly began to embrace the idea of substantive due process, by which it imposed limits on governmental regulation of businesses (Cortner 1993; Gillman 1993). In 1886 the U.S. Supreme Court unanimously decided in *Santa Clara County v. Southern Pacific Railroad* that corporations were legal "persons," subject to the protections of the Fourteenth Amendment (a judgment later questioned by Justices Hugo Black and William O. Douglas). Indeed, in the late nineteenth and early twentieth centuries, the Fourteenth Amendment was often more successfully utilized to protect corporate rights than to protect the rights of onetime slaves and their descendants. In a case often thought to epitomize judicial thinking during this era, in *Lochner v. New York* (1905), the Supreme Court found that a New York law regulating the hours that bakers could work was an infringement of their "liberty of contract" under the Fourteenth Amendment. Only in 1937, after Roosevelt introduced his "court-packing" plan, did the Supreme Court retreat from this area, but the Court continues to recognize corporations as legal persons entitled to a variety of rights under the Fourteenth Amendment.

Indeed, although the heyday of economic due process ended in 1937, the twentieth century has witnessed the progressive expansion of the civil rights provisions of the Fourteenth Amendment. Through a process of selective incorporation, the Supreme Court has gradually applied most provisions of the Bill of Rights to the states via the due process clause of the Fourteenth Amendment. Indeed, in *Griswold v. Connecticut* (1965) and *Roe v. Wade* (1973), it ruled that additional penumbral rights of privacy not specifically stated in the Bill of Rights also apply to the states through the due process clause. In *Baker v. Carr* (1962), *Reynolds v. Sims* (1964), and subsequent cases, the Court has also expanded the equal protection clause to cover matters of state and congressional legislative apportionment, generating numerous pleas for an amendment to curb the Court's interpretation. In *Brown v. Board of Education* (1954), the Court overturned *Plessy v. Ferguson* (1896) and gave a broad reading to the equal protection clause (D. Jackson 1992). Although such interpretations have recently been narrowed, in past cases the Court has given similarly broad readings to the congressional enforcement provisions in Section 5 of the Fourteenth Amendment. Although this does not appear to have been the intent of the Amendment (Farnsworth 2000), the Supreme Court has also used the Fourteenth Amendment as a basis for limiting discrimination based on gender. In *Romer v. Evans* (1996), the amendment was also used to strike down a Colorado constitutional provision that limited legislation on behalf of homosexuals. The Fourteenth Amendment has also been applied to classifications based on legitimacy and mental retardation but has been applied only loosely to classifications based on wealth (for example, differences in funding of state educational districts) or age, where it continues to allow states to use relatively arbitrary cutoffs for positions such a police officers and judges.

Some of the most controversial areas of modern public policy—including questions about affirmative action and school busing—continue to center on the meaning of the Fourteenth Amendment.

Proposals for Amendment or Repeal

From 1903 to 1920, several proposals were introduced—most by Southern representatives—to eliminate all but the first sentence of Section 2 of the Fourteenth Amendment. Although Congress had never acted to reduce representation for states that restricted voting rights, the threat was apparently still of concern. In 1920 Democratic Senator James Phelan of Cal-

ifornia introduced an amendment restricting citizenship by birth to those who were white, African, or American Indian, presumably with the intention of excluding those of Asian backgrounds. The 1930s witnessed at least three attempts to repeal Section 1 of the Fourteenth Amendment, one by Senator William Borah of Idaho.

In March 1957 the Georgia General Assembly sent a memorializing resolution to Congress to declare both the Fourteenth and Fifteenth Amendments invalid on the basis of alleged irregularities in the procedures by which they were adopted. A supporter of this resolution argued for an amendment repealing the Fourteenth and Fifteenth Amendments, adding the word "expressly" to the Tenth Amendment, and limiting citizenship to whites. This latter provision provided in relevant part:

> No person shall be a citizen of the United States unless he is a non-Hispanic White of the European race, in whom there is no ascertainable trace of Negro blood, nor more than one-eighth Mongolian, Asian, Asia Minor, Middle Eastern, Semitic, Near Eastern, American Indian, Malay or other non-European or non-white blood, provided that Hispanic whites, defined as anyone with an Hispanic ancestor, may be citizens if, in addition to meeting the aforesaid ascertainable trace and percentage tests, they are, in appearance, indistinguishable from Americans whose ancestral home is the British Isles or Northwest Europe. Only citizens shall have the right and privilege to reside permanently in the United States. (Pace 1986, 99)

The most recent attempt to repeal the Fourteenth Amendment appears to have been made by Democratic Representative John Rarick of Louisiana in 1973.

See also Affirmative Action; Bingham, John A.; Corporations; Equal Rights Amendment; Incorporation; Lieber, Francis; Promulgation of Amendments; Thirteenth Amendment.

For Further Reading:

Bryant, Douglas H. 2002. "Unorthodox and Paradox: Revisiting the Ratification of the Fourteenth Amendment." *Alabama Law Review* 53: 555–581.

Cortner, Richard C. 1993. *The Iron Horse and the Constitution: The Railroads and the Transformation of the Fourteenth Amendment.* Westport, CT: Greenwood Press.

Farnsworth, Ward. 2000. "Women under Reconstruction: The Congressional Understanding," *Northwestern University Law Review* 94 (Summer): 1229–1295.

Fernandez, Ferdinand F. 1966. "The Constitutionality of the Fourteenth Amendment." *Southern California Law Review* 39: 378–407.

Flack, Horace E. 1908. *The Adoption of the Fourteenth Amendment.* Baltimore, MD: Johns Hopkins. Reprint, Gloucester, MA: Peter Smith, 1965.

Gillman, Howard. 1993. *The Constitution Besieged: The Rise and Demise of Lochner Era Police Powers Jurisprudence.* Durham, NC: Duke University Press.

James, Joseph B. 1984. *The Ratification of the Fourteenth Amendment.* Macon, GA: Mercer University Press.

———. 1956. *The Framing of the Fourteenth Amendment.* Urbana, IL: University of Illinois Press.

Kyvig, David E. 1996a. *Explicit and Authentic Acts: Amending the Constitution, 1776–1995.* Lawrence, KS: University Press of Kansas.

Maltz, Earl M. 1990. *Civil Rights, the Constitution, and Congress, 1863–1869.* Lawrence, KS: University Press of Kansas.

Nelson, William E. 1988. *The Fourteenth Amendment: From Political Principle to Judicial Doctrine.* Cambridge, MA: Harvard University Press.

Pace, James O. 1986. *Amendment to the Constitution: Averting the Decline and Fall of America.* Los Angeles, CA: Johnson, Pace, Simmons and Fennell.

Perry, Michael J. 1999. *We the People: The Fourteenth Amendment and the Supreme Court.* Oxford, UK: Oxford University Press.

Richards, David A. J. 1993. *Conscience and the Constitution: History, Theory, and Law of the Reconstruction Amendments.* Princeton, NJ: Princeton University Press.

Suthon, Walter J., Jr. 1953. "The Dubious Origin of the Fourteenth Amendment." *Tulane Law Review* 28: 22–44.

United States Senate, Subcommittee on the Constitution, Committee on the Judiciary. 1985. *Amendments to the Constitution: A Brief Legislative History.* Washington, DC: U.S. Government Printing Office.

Virginia Commission on Constitutional Government. 1967. *The Reconstruction Amendments Debates.* Richmond, VA: Virginia Commission on Constitutional Government.

❖ FOURTH AMENDMENT ❖

The Fourth Amendment was proposed by the First Congress and ratified in 1791 as part of the Bill of Rights. It provides that "the right of the people to be secure in their persons, houses, papers, and effects, against unreasonable searches and seizures, shall not be violated, and no Warrants shall issue, but upon probable cause, supported by Oath or affirmation, and particularly describing the place to be searched, and the persons or things to be seized."

Origins

Like the amendment that precedes it, the Fourth Amendment was largely motivated by abuses of the British when they ruled America. They had used general warrants, or so-called writs of assistance, in tracking down customs violations in the colonies. A number of states subsequently adopted provisions against such warrants, and ratifying conventions in Maryland, Virginia, and North Carolina all proposed amendments dealing with the subject (Lutz 1992, 57).

The proposed bill of rights that James Madison submitted to the House of Representatives contained a provision that is quite similar to what became the Fourth Amendment. One difference was that Madison's version referred to "other property" rather than to "effects." Another difference was that Madison's version specified that the people's rights "shall not be violated by warrants issued without probable cause," whereas the text of the current Fourth Amendment leaves a greater disjunction between the prohibition against unreasonable searches and seizures and the warrant requirement (see Kurland and Lerner 1987, 5:25, 237).

The final version of this amendment presents an interpretive ambiguity—namely, that of establishing the relationship between unreasonable searches and seizures and warrants. It is obvious that the amendment outlaws searches conducted pursuant to warrants that are not supported by probable cause, that are not supported by oath or affirmation, or that do not particularly describe the person or place to be seized. What courts have had to flesh out is precisely what, if any, kinds of warrantless searches are considered to be reasonable and what kinds are "unreasonable" and therefore unconstitutional.

Exceptions to Warrant Requirements

Currently, the courts recognize a number of circumstances in which warrantless searches are not considered to be unreasonable. These include cases involving "hot pursuit" of suspects, "exigent circumstances" in which evidence is in imminent danger of destruction, stop-and-frisk searches incident to arrest [an exception created in *Terry v. Ohio* (1968)], and searches of objects in "plain view" or in "open fields" (D. O'Brien 2000a, 2:829–837). Moreover, because automobiles are mobile, giving criminals unique opportunities to escape or destroy evidence, courts have fashioned a whole host of exceptions related to them (D. O'Brien 2000, 2:859–883).

In *Skinner v. Railway Labor Executives' Association* (1989), the Court permitted drug tests of railroad employees involved in accidents and, in *National Treasury Employees Union v. Von Raab* (1989), of customs officials dealing with drugs. As of June 2002, it has also permitted random drug-testing not only of student athletes (searches that had been approved in an earlier 1995 decision in *Vernonia School District 47J v. Acton*) but also of students involved in other extracurricular activities.

Electronic Surveillance

The problems of wiretapping and other forms of electronic surveillance were obviously not contemplated by the framers of the Fourth Amendment. Perhaps just as obviously, such surveillance poses a threat that is equal to or greater than that which the framers did antici-

pate. In *Olmstead v. United States* (1928), the Supreme Court initially decided against applying the Fourth Amendment to this issue, but it subsequently reversed course in *Katz v. United States* (1967) and ruled that such surveillance, like other searches, requires a warrant.

There is ongoing debate about the impact of the Foreign Intelligence Surveillance Act (FISA) of 1978 and the USA Patriot Act of 2001 on the Fourth Amendment. Both acts have made it easier for the government to conduct electronic surveillance of individuals suspected of being foreign agents or conspiring to commit terrorist activities. The former law established a special Foreign Intelligence Surveillance Court to review such surveillance, while the latter provided for roving wiretaps, for installation pen registers that record the number of all outgoing calls from specific sources, and for expanded disclosures of business records (Whitehead 2002, 1101–1109). A group known as the Electronic Privacy Information Center in Washington, D.C., posted an epitaph on its website over the Fourth Amendment, "1789–2001," after passage of the USA Patriot Act, but an article by George Washington University Law Professor Orin S. Kerr scheduled for publication in the February 2003 issue of the *Northwestern Law Review* argues that provisions in the law for obtaining court approval for pen registers actually recognize some protections that were not previously incorporated into the law (Cohen 2002, B9). In a decision dated 18 November 2002, the United States Foreign Intelligence Surveillance Court of Review issued an opinion reversing the Foreign Intelligence Surveillance Court and permitting Attorney General John Ashcroft to proceed under a relatively broad understanding of the laws relating to wiretapping and the sharing of information enacted to combat terrorism (Sealed Case No. 02–001).

The Exclusionary Rule

Although the Fourth Amendment outlaws unreasonable searches and seizures and sets some basic guidelines for issuing warrants, it does not specify what will happen if the government proceeds to conduct illegal searches. Over time, the Court has formulated the exclusionary rule, whereby such illegally obtained evidence is barred from trials. First applied to the national government in *Weeks v. United States* (1914), this rule was subsequently extended to the states in *Mapp v. Ohio* (1961). Recent cases, however, have recognized some exceptions—for example, the "good faith" exception established in *United States v. Leon* (1984) and the "inevitable discovery" exception established in *Nix v. Williams* (1984). Other provisions of the Fourth Amendment have also been extended to the states via the due process clause of the Fourteenth Amendment.

One Basis for a Right to Privacy

In the Connecticut birth control case *Griswold v. Connecticut* (1965), Justice William O. Douglas cited the Fourth Amendment as one of the sources of the right of privacy. No amendments have been introduced in Congress to repeal the Fourth Amendment, but there are continuing criticisms of judicial interpretations of this amendment (Rothwax 1996), and many proposed new constitutions have suggested language to incorporate existing interpretations of it, including the exclusionary rule.

See also Bill of Rights; Privacy, Right to.

For Further Reading:

Cohen, Patricia. 2002. "9/11 Law Means More Snooping? Or Maybe Less?" *The New York Times,* 7 September, B9.

In re: Sealed Case No. 02–001. Consolidated with 02–002. Decision by United States Foreign Intelligence Surveillance Court of Review. Decided November 18, 2002. *http://www.fas.org/irp/agency/doj/fisa/fiscr111802.html.* Accessed 11/29/02.

Kurland, Philip B., and Ralph Lerner, eds. 1987. *The Founders' Constitution.* 5 vols. Chicago: University of Chicago Press.

Lutz, Donald S. 1992. *A Preface to American Political Theory.* Lawrence, KS: University Press of Kansas.

O'Brien, David M. 2000a. *Civil Rights and Civil Liberties.* Vol. 2 of *Constitutional Law and Politics.* 5th ed. New York: W. W. Norton.

Rothwax, Harold J. 1996. *Guilty: The Collapse of Criminal Justice.* New York: Random House.

Whitehead, John W. 2002. "Forfeiting 'Enduring Freedom' for 'Homeland Security': A Constitutional Analysis of the USA Patriot Act and the Justice Department's Anti-Terrorism Initiatives." *American University Law Review* 51 (August): 1081–1133.

❖ FREE ENTERPRISE ❖

The Constitution of the United States contains a number of protections for private property. These include protections for inventors and writers in Article I, Section I; the contracts clause in Article I, Section 10; the takings, or just compensation, clause of the Fifth Amendment; and the due process clauses of the Fifth and Fourteenth Amendments.

The Constitution does not specifically prohibit the government from creating or purchasing private enterprises. Chief Justice John Marshall's decision in *McCulloch v. Maryland* (1819) authorized the establishment of a national bank as a legitimate means of carrying out other constitutional powers—a means consistent with and not elsewhere prohibited by the Constitution. Although socialism has never been especially popular in the United States—with the Socialist Party suffering a significant decline since the 1930s (Shannon 1967, ix)—the national government has occasionally taken on projects, such as the Tennessee Valley Authority, that could be undertaken by private industry. From time to time, reformers have called on the government to take over the operation of one or another industry, railroads being a special concern toward the end of the nineteenth century.

From 1952 to 1978, more than a dozen amending proposals were introduced in Congress to prohibit the national government from engaging in any private business not specified in the Constitution (thus presumably exempting the post office) that would compete with private enterprise. A number of these proposals also called for repeal of the Sixteenth Amendment and estate or gift taxes, an area in which Congress has recently enacted legislation abolishing the so-called death tax.

Constitutions proposed by libertarian advocates often significantly limit the functions that the national government could perform. Some would even turn over such basic services as postal delivery, highway construction and maintenance, and even police protection to private firms, with expenses being paid through user fees and neighborhood associations. Some individuals who have proposed new constitutions have either envisioned significant new ownership by government of industries that are now private, or significantly reduced governmental roles even in such traditional areas as the provision of postal services, police protection, and public roadways.

See also Sixteenth Amendment.

For Further Reading:
Shannon, David A. 1967. *The Socialist Party of America: A History.* Chicago: Quadrangle Books.

❖ FREEDMEN, REDISTRIBUTION OF ❖

Democratic Senator Garrett Davis of Kentucky, who largely blamed New England "Puritans" rather than Southern slaveholders for the Civil War (Vorenberg 2001, 95) offered two of the more bizarre amendment proposals during debates over the Thirteenth Amendment that abolished involuntary servitude, thus creating a large class of former slaves, often called freedmen (one of the federal bureaus designed to help these individuals would later be known as the Freedman's Bureau). The first of Davis's proposals would have required that slaves be removed from slave states before being given their freedom. The second proposed distributing freedmen throughout the country proportionally to the white population.

Davis's proposals are a reminder that, as early as Thomas Jefferson, many observers thought that the past history of black-white relations in America would make it difficult for the two races to coexist if African Americans were granted freedom (Jefferson 1964, 132). Moreover, as late as Abraham Lincoln, politicians advocated slave recolonization, with Lincoln using his second annual address to advocate an amendment proposing such recolonization, albeit one that would have rested on the consent of those being recolonized (J. Richardson 1908, 6:140).

See also Thirteenth Amendment.

For Further Reading:
Richardson, James E., ed. 1908. *A Compilation of the Messages and Papers of the Presidents, 1789–1908.* 11 vols. n.p.: Bureau of National Literature and Art.

❖ FUTURIST PROPOSALS FOR CONSTITUTIONAL REFORM ❖

See Toffler, Alvin and Heidi; Tonn, Bruce E.

G

❖

❖ GARCIA V. SAN ANTONIO METROPOLITAN TRANSIT AUTHORITY (1985) ❖

Garcia v. San Antonio Metropolitan Transit Authority is one of the most important contemporary cases affecting judicial interpretation of the Tenth Amendment. The issue in the case was whether the San Antonio Metropolitan Transit Authority (SAMTA) was subject to the wage and overtime provisions of the Fair Labor Standards Act that Congress enacted under its authority to regulate commerce. *Garcia* overturned *National League of Cities v. Usery* (1976). In that five-to-four decision, written by Justice William Rehnquist, the Supreme Court had cited concerns about federalism, the chief concern of the Tenth Amendment, in exempting traditional state and local governmental activities (as opposed to private enterprises) from such federal regulations.

After reviewing the history that had transpired since *Usery,* Justice Harry Blackmun wrote the five-to-four decision in *Garcia* in which he argued that the Court had been unable to distinguish with any degree of consistency between those governmental functions that were traditional, and should thus be left to state control, and those that were not, and should therefore be subject to federal regulation. He therefore concluded that this judicial attempt to shield states from federal regulation should be abandoned. Blackmun argued that the very fact that the federal government had appropriated grant monies to SAMTA and other state programs demonstrated that the states had clout in influencing federal decisions. He argued that the structure

of the federal system—and especially the guarantee of equal state suffrage in the Senate—rather than judicial oversight would be sufficient to protect state interests.

Justices Lewis Powell, Warren Burger, William Rehnquist, and Sandra Day O'Connor dissented, putting special emphasis on the importance of the Tenth Amendment as a limit on federal power. Justice Powell noted that "the States' role in our system of government is a matter of constitutional law, not of legislative grace" (*Garcia* 1985, 567). Appealing to "the spirit of the Tenth Amendment," Justice O'Connor, a former Arizona state legislator, noted a number of changes, including the direct election of senators, that had increased the need for judicial vigilance in protecting states' rights (*Id.,* 584–585).

Congress reacted to *Garcia* by adopting a bill allowing states to substitute compensatory time off for overtime pay (Rossum and Tarr 1999, 217). To date, however, Congress has not proposed any of several amendments that have been advocated for overturning or limiting *Garcia* (see Advisory Commission on Intergovernmental Relations 1986, 43–48). Recent discussions of unfunded federal mandates and other issues may, however, indicate renewed concern over state power and recent Supreme Court decisions have directed renewed attention to the Tenth Amendment. The constitutional allocation of powers between state and national governments thus continues to be a key concern.

See also Seventeenth Amendment; Tenth Amendment; Unfunded Federal Mandates.

For Further Reading:

Advisory Commission on Intergovernmental Relations. 1986. *Reflections on Garcia and Its Implications for Federalism.* February. Washington, DC: ACIR.

Garcia v. San Antonio Metropolitan Transit Authority, 469 U.S. 528 (1985)

Rossum, Ralph A., and G. Alan Tarr. 1999. *American Constitutional Law: The Structure of Government.* 5th ed. New York: St. Martin's Press.

❖ GARDINER, WILLIAM (1885–?) ❖

Born in Missouri, William Gardiner worked as a teacher and department store credit supervisor before earning an Ed.D. in 1942. Gardiner may well have been the oldest individual ever to offer a new U.S. constitution for consideration when he published *A Proposed Constitution for the United States of America* in 1973. His plan included an odd mix of prescription and commentary, of existing constitutional provisions and innovations.

Under Gardiner's plan, Congress would continue to be bicameral, but the House would have 200 members serving for four-year terms. Moreover, members of the House would be responsible for electing the president and vice presidents, who would also serve as cabinet members. Senators would serve eight-year terms and would be selected, as they were prior to the adoption of the Seventeenth Amendment, by state legislatures. Legislators in such bodies, like members of the House of Representatives when choosing executive officials, would have to pledge not to consult beforehand about such choices. Strict attendance would be kept by page boys and girls (to whom Gardiner's constitutional proposal makes several references), and members could be removed for missing twice in one month or three times in a year.

The president and eight vice presidents would serve for four-year terms, and the Justice Department would be elevated to a more prominent watchdog role. The Supreme Court would consist of eleven members serving to age seventy. Other officials in government would be required to attend special academies.

In contrast to the existing Constitution, Gardiner's goes into great length in describing the organization of state governments. All counties would have to adopt a county commissioner form of government, with the number of commissioners based on each county's population. Gardiner listed specific state officials and their methods of selection. Under his plan, local school boards would be replaced by parent-teacher associations. Schools would work with industries to provide jobs to keep juveniles from delinquency.

Gardiner proposed prohibiting political parties and lobbying. He would also eliminate campaign managers, speechwriters, and most congressional staff.

Constitutional amendments could be proposed in four ways and ratified in five; they would have a five-year deadline. Gardiner further suggested that his plan might be put into place by a president who made himself a temporary dictator.

Gardiner's greatest innovations would have been in the area of civil liberties. He would permit a speaker to lecture or pray in public schools, "provided he does not boost or condemn any church organization, or question the validity of the Bible" (Gardiner 1973, 9). He would eliminate freedom of the press so that "spoken or printed words that have a deteriorating influence on the morals and stability of the people shall be prohibited" (Gardiner 1973, 15). Gardiner specified that "any mawkish person or news medium that criticizes an apprehending officer for a justifiable killing shall be prosecuted" (Gardiner 1973, 17). Gardiner proposed to eliminate both grand and petit juries and to replace trials with "criminal proceedings" without Fifth Amendment guarantees against self-incrimination, confrontation of witnesses, and private defense attorneys. Capital punishment would be prescribed for a litany of offenses. Individuals who had received "free food" or other relief over the past four years would be prohibited from voting (Gardiner 1973, 27). Guns and other concealed weapons would be registered but not prohibited. In place of the current Bill of Rights, people would be assured of being "treated fairly and squarely" (Gardiner 1973, 43).

Apart from this essay, Gardiner's proposal does not appear to have been the subject of other secondary literature.

For Further Reading:

Gardiner, William. 1973. *A Proposed Constitution for the United States of America.* Summerfield, FL: William Gardiner.

❖ GARRISON, WILLIAM LLOYD (1805–1879) ❖

Few individuals were more important to, or more controversial representatives of, the abolitionist movement against slavery than was William Lloyd Garrison. He lived at a time when the views of individuals in the North and South increasingly diverged and hardened on the issue of slavery, and few views were more radical than his own. Born in Massachusetts in 1805, Garrison was apprenticed to a printer and began in 1826 to edit the *Free Press,* which subsequently went bankrupt. He honed his editorial skills at the *National Philanthropist,* where he advocated a variety of reforms, which, after his association with Benjamin Lundy, began to focus chiefly on the evils of slavery.

Garrison began his editorship of the antislavery *Liberator* in 1831 and continued until the end of 1865, after the Thirteenth Amendment was adopted. In his first issue, Garrison announced "I am in earnest—I will not equivocate—I will not excuse—I will not retreat a single inch—and *I will be heard*" (quoted in Fuess, 1928–1936). Garrison advocated the doctrine of "immediatism" by which slavery was to be abolished immediately without any compensation to slaveowners, but he was not a particularly practical man, and he had few ideas about how abolition would take place. He was a pacifist who rarely voted but relied on the moral force of his ideas and writings to bring about change. He did help organize the New England Anti-Slavery Society in 1831, and, after returning from a trip to England in 1833, helped found the American Anti-Slavery Society and

author its declaration of Sentiments. It declared:

> That all those laws which are now in force, admitting the right of slavery, are . . . before God utterly null and void, being an audacious usurpation of the Divine prerogative, a daring infringement on the law of nature, a base overthrow of the very foundations of the social compact, a complete extinction of all the relations, endearments and obligations of mankind, and a presumptuous transgression of all the holy commandments—and that therefore they ought to be instantly abrogated. (Pease and Pease 1965, 68)

Garrison, whose rhetoric was always forceful, was jailed for libel in 1830 and dragged through the streets of Boston with a rope around his neck in 1835. On the latter occasion, he might very well have been lynched had the city mayor not intervened on his behalf (Fuess, 1928–1836). Although the issue of slavery and states' rights eventually led the Southern states to attempt secession, Garrison had long argued that the Northern states should secede rather than tolerate continuing association with slavery (further demonstrating that extreme views of states' rights are not confined to one area of the nation, some Federalist New Englanders had taken a similar stance, albeit over different issues, at the Hartford Convention of 1815).

Unlike individuals like the ex-slave and abolitionist Frederick Douglass who sought to interpret the U.S. Constitution as a document that looked toward the eventual abolition of slavery, Garrison, who admired the sentiments expressed in the Declaration of Independence, publicly declared in 1843 that the U.S. Constitution was "a covenant with death and an agreement with hell" that should be abrogated. Garrison often found himself in conflict with more orthodox religious believers, whom he believed had compromised with slavery. Much like modern-day flag burners, Garrison riveted public attention in 1854 when he publicly burned a copy of the U.S. Constitution at a gathering on 4 July 1854 at Framingham, Massachusetts.

Initially cool toward Abraham Lincoln, Garrison supported him after Lincoln issued the Emancipation Proclamation and later supported the Thirteenth Amendment. In April 1865 Garrison visited Charleston, South Carolina, laid his hand on the gravestone of former senator and slavery advocate John C. Calhoun, and announced that "Down into a deeper grave than this slavery has gone, and for it there is no resurrection" (quoted in Fuess, 1928– 1936). Although the American Anti-Slavery Society did not, as he wanted, dissolve in 1865, Garrison continued to support a variety of reform causes, including alcoholic prohibition and women's rights. Fanatical in his beliefs and sometimes impractical in his plans for carrying them to fruition, Garrison served as a spokesman and as a symbol for the abolitionist movement, which ultimately helped (with equally passionate defenders of slavery in the South) precipitate a war that resulted in the adoption of an amendment permanently putting an end to chattel slavery. Garrison died in 1879.

See also Abolitionists; Calhoun, John C.; Douglass, Frederick; Emancipation Proclamation; Fourteenth Amendment; Hartford Convention.

For Further Reading:
Fuess, Calude Moore. 1928–1936. "William Lloyd Garrison." *Dictionary of American Biography,* Base Set. American Council of Learned Societies. Accessed through *www.galenet.com* on 11/14/02.

❖ GAY MARRIAGES ❖

See Marriage, Divorce, and Parenting.

❖ GENERAL WELFARE ❖

Article I, Section 8 of the Constitution grants Congress power to lay taxes "to pay the Debts and provide for the Common Defense and general Welfare of the United States." Because this general welfare clause is linked to the taxing power, Congress has "no general power" to legislate for the general welfare but only to tax for this purpose (Peltason 1994, 71).

In *United States v. Butler* (1936), however, although it voided the provision of the Agricultural Adjustment Act it was examining through an interpretation of the Tenth Amendment, the Supreme Court ruled that the taxing and spending powers may be exercised in addition to other grants of power in Article I, Section 8. The Court thus upheld the view originally advanced by Alexander Hamilton over the rival view advocated by James Madison, which would have limited taxing and spending powers to carrying out other specific constitutional grants.

Faced with quite restrictive judicial readings of congressional power over economic issues, members of Congress introduced amendments in 1935, 1936, and 1937 that would have expanded congressional power to legislate on behalf of the general welfare. President Franklin Roosevelt considered support of a proposal that had originally been introduced as part of the Virginia plan at the Constitutional Convention of 1787. It would have allowed Congress to "legislate in all cases for the general interests of the union, and also in those in which the states are separately incompetent, or in which the harmony of the United States may be interrupted by the exercise of individual legislation" (cited in Kyvig 1989, 471). Beginning with *West Coast Hotel v. Parrish* (1937), its historic "switch in time that saved nine," the Supreme Court began to interpret congressional powers under the commerce clause more liberally. Proposals to expand such powers via a new general welfare clause subsequently ceased.

For Further Reading:
Engdahl, David E. 1994. "The Spending Power." *Duke Law Journal* 44 (October): 1–109.

Kyvig, David E. 1989. "The Road Not Taken: FDR, the Supreme Court and Constitutional Amendment." *Political Science Quarterly* 104 (Fall): 463–481.

Peltason, Jack W. 1994. *Corwin and Peltason's Understanding the Constitution.* 13th ed. Fort Worth, TX: Harcourt Brace College Publishers.

❖ GOVERNORS, ROLE IN THE AMENDING PROCESS ❖

From time to time, observers have questioned whether the approval of a state's governor is required to legitimize either a state's ratification of an amendment or a state's application for a constitutional convention. Although no Supreme Court decision has addressed this issue directly (in 1939, in *Coleman v. Miller,* the U.S. Supreme Court declared itself "equally divided" as to whether a lieutenant-governor could cast a deciding vote in a state legislature), the answer appears to be negative (Edel 1981, 107–108). This does not, of course, prevent a governor from urging members of his or her state legislature to support or oppose pending amendments.

At the national level, the Supreme Court decided in *Hollingsworth v. Virginia* (1798) that the president's approval was not required for ratification of an amendment. In *Hawke v. Smith (I)* (1920), the Court further indicated that the "legislature" mentioned in Article V was the lawmaking body. Democratic North Carolina Senator Sam Ervin convincingly argued that "the term 'legislature' should have the same meaning in both the application clause and the ratification clause of Article V" (Ervin 1968, 889). Legislation that he and Utah Republican Senator Orrin Hatch proposed to deal with Article V conventions did not require such gubernatorial approval of convention recommendations.

See also *Hollingsworth v. Virginia.*

For Further Reading:

Edel, Wilbur. 1981. *A Constitutional Convention: Threat or Challenge?* New York: Praeger.

Ervin, Sam J., Jr. 1968. "Proposed Legislation to Implement the Convention Method of Amending the Constitution." *Michigan Law Review* 66 (March): 875–902.

❖ GRAND JURY ❖

The Fifth Amendment to the U.S. Constitution specifies that "no person shall be held to answer for a capital, or otherwise infamous crime, unless on a presentment or indictment of a grand jury." This provision remains one of the few in the Bill of Rights that has not been applied to the states as well as to the national government (*Hurtado v. California* (1884); *Gyuro v. Connecticut* (1968)). Today, less than half of the states have grand jury systems. The remaining states rely on a system of indictment by "information" that is offered in an affidavit by a prosecutor to a judge (Abraham 1998, 112–113).

Whereas a petit jury decides on guilt or innocence, a grand jury decides whether there is sufficient evidence for a prosecutor to bring an individual to trial. The grand jury developed in England as a means of shielding individuals from overzealous or vindictive prosecutors who might bring unwarranted indictments. Federal grand juries typically consist of twenty-three individuals, with twelve or more needed for an indictment. Proceedings are held in secret, without many of the due process safeguards required in an actual trial. Given the dominance that prosecutors sometimes exercise over grand juries, law professors often repeat the joke that prosecutors could get an indictment against a ham sandwich if they wished; the protection thus may not always perform the function for which it was instituted.

In 1973 Republican Congressman Charles Wiggins of California introduced an amendment that would have modified the existing Fifth Amendment requirement to allow Congress to specify whether indictments would proceed by grand jury or by use of information. Several such resolutions have subsequently been introduced, and the House of Representatives held hearings on the subject in 1976 and 1977.

In introducing his amendment, Wiggins noted that most grand jury proceedings were "dominated by the prosecutor." He further observed that "in modern society grand jurors do not ordinarily possess either the skills or the training to conduct the complex investigations that a truly independent evaluation would require" (Wiggins 1973, 125).

See also Fifth Amendment.

For Further Reading:

Wiggins, Charles. 1973. "A Constitutional Amendment Concerning Information Proceedings and Grand Jury Indictments." *Congressional Record.* 93rd Cong. 1st sess., 1973, Vol. 119, pt. 25: 32911–32912.

❖ *GRISWOLD V. CONNECTICUT* (1965) ❖

The scope of judicial interpretation influences the degree to which legislative action or constitutional amendment will be needed to strike down unwise laws. Few modern cases have sparked more intense debate on the subject than this case involving a long-standing state law prohibiting the use of prescription of birth control devices.

Justice William O. Douglas's majority opinion striking down the law was apparently strongly influenced by Justice William Brennan (Garrow 1994, 245–249). Douglas argued that although the Constitution did not specifically mention the right to privacy, the First, Third, Fourth, Fifth, and Ninth Amendments all had "penumbras, formed by emanations from those guarantees which help give them life and substance" (*Griswold* 1965, 484). The majority found that such penumbras, as applied to the states by the due process clause of the Fourteenth Amendment, protected the right of marital privacy.

Justice Arthur Goldberg's concurring opinion emphasized the hitherto largely neglected Ninth Amendment, arguing that it provided a textual basis for the judicial protection of unenumerated rights. In his concurring opinion, Justice John Marshall Harlan argued that the due process clause of the Fourteenth Amendment "stands . . . on its own bottom" (*Griswold* 1965, 478) rather than being intended to incorporate one or more specific provisions in the Bill of Rights. In another concurring opinion, Justice Byron White stated that prohibitions on the use of contraceptives by married couples did not deter illicit sexual activity.

In dissent, Justice Hugo Black reiterated his long-held belief, previously articulated in *Adamson v. California* (1947), that the authors of the due process clause of the Fourteenth Amendment intended to apply the specific guarantees of the Bill of Rights to the states, but no more. As such, the amendment did not authorize the Court to strike down legislation simply because it was unwise. Those who desired to keep the Constitution "in tune with the times" needed to use the amending process (*Griswold* 1965, 522). In his dissent, Justice Potter Stewart agreed that the Court had no power to invalidate a law simply because it was silly or unwise.

Griswold prepared the way for the 1973 decision in *Roe v. Wade* invalidating most state laws on abortion. This decision has prompted numerous calls for a right-to-life amendment, which have on occasion prompted countercalls for amendments protecting reproductive freedom.

See also Abortion; Ninth Amendment; Privacy, Right to; Right to Life; *Roe v. Wade.*

For Further Reading:

Garrow, David J. 1994. *Liberty and Sexuality: The Right to Privacy and the Making of* Roe v. Wade. New York: Macmillan.

Griswold v. Connecticut, 381 U.S. 479 (1965).

❖ GUARANTEE CLAUSE ❖

One of the most elusive provisions of the Constitution is the clause in Article IV, Section 4 providing that "the United States shall guarantee to every State in this Union a Republican Form of Government." It further provides that the United States "shall protect each of them against Invasion; and on Application of the Legislature, or of the Executive (when the Legislature cannot be convened) against domestic Violence." The first part of this guarantee is the only specific restriction in the Constitution "on the form or structure of state governments" (Wiecek 1972, 1). A scholar who has examined the history of this clause has noted that "it was designed to allow the states great flexibility to alter their optional characteristics." He further noted that "The first draft of the Clause was rejected precisely because it could be read to freeze existing state forms and laws into the U.S. Constitution" (Natelson 2002, 830). By providing for change, in a sense the guarantee clause thus did for state governments what Article V (the amending article) did for the national government.

Through most of U.S. history, this clause has been what onetime Massachusetts Senator Charles Sumner called "a sleeping giant" (Wiecek 1972, 290). Although some Republicans relied on this clause for authority to reconstruct the South after the Civil War (others had anticipated that its authority might serve as a substitute for a constitutional amendment abolishing slavery), its inherent ambiguity has made it difficult to apply.

Two amending proposals have related to the guarantee clause. A proposal introduced in 1861 to give each state control over slavery within its territories also stipulated that the national government could still aid states faced with slave insurrections. In 1870 a much different proposal aimed at Klan violence against African Americans would have allowed Congress to authorize intervention even when a state did not apply for aid (Ames 1896, 171–172).

In *Luther v. Borden* (1849), the Supreme Court decided that the question of whether a state government was republican or not was a "political question." As such, the matter was one for Congress to resolve when it decided whether to seat a state's representatives. Alternatively, a president might make such a determination when deciding whether to send aid to a government facing domestic violence, as John Tyler had done in the case of Rhode Island.

For many years, the guarantee clause stood as an obstacle to judicial intervention in matters involving state legislative apportionment. When the Supreme Court eventually decided in *Baker v. Carr* (1962) that this issue was justiciable, it did so on the basis of the equal protection clause of the Fourteenth Amendment rather than the guarantee clause.

If either the Supreme Court or Congress were ever to give an expanded meaning to the guarantee clause, the results could be as politically far-reaching as the adoption of any amendment ratified to date.

Natelson has recently argued that the guarantee clause would permit a state to substitute initiative and referendum mechanisms for state legislatures, albeit not for executive and judicial branches (2002), but it is difficult to know how states without a legislative branch could constitutionally ratify federal amendments. In *Hawke v. Smith (I)* (1920) the U.S. Supreme Court required that amendments be approved either through state legislatures or conventions.

See also *Hawke v. Smith (I)*; Political Questions.

For Further Reading:

Ames, Herman. 1896. *The Proposed Amendments to the Constitution of the United States during the First Century of Its History.* Reprint, New York: Burt Franklin, 1970.

Natelson, Robert G. 2002. "A Republic, Not a Democracy? Initiative, Referendum, and the Constitution's Guarantee Clause." *Texas Law Review* 80 (March): 807–857.

Wiecek, William. 1972. *The Guarantee Clause of the U.S. Constitution.* Ithaca, NY: Cornell University Press.

❖ GUN CONTROL ❖

See Second Amendment.

H

❖ HAMILTON, ALEXANDER (1755–1804) ❖

A brilliant and ambitious immigrant from the Leeward Islands, Hamilton was born in 1755 and immigrated to the United States in 1772 where he attended King's College (now Columbia) and quickly became active in the American revolutionary movement. During the war he served as an aide-de-camp to George Washington and commanded an infantry regiment in the battle of Yorktown. After the war, Hamilton went into practice as an attorney. An admirer of the English system of government, Hamilton favored a strong national government with an equally strong executive. He quickly recognized the weaknesses of the Articles of Confederation and was one of the forces behind the Annapolis Convention that led to the Constitutional Convention of 1787, and was selected to this convention as a delegate from New York.

At the convention, Hamilton favored a stronger national government than most other delegates. This, combined with the fact that the New York delegation was split between those who favored change and those who opposed it, meant that Hamilton did not have as important an influence on the document as did some other members of the convention. He did, however, have some input into the amending process. By 10 September 1787 the delegates were considering a proposal whereby Congress would call a convention to propose amendments after receiving requests from two-thirds of the states. After Elbridge Gerry objected

that states might propose amendments that would unfairly bind other states, Hamilton expressed a different concern, namely that "[t]he State Legislatures will not apply for alterations but with a view to increase their own powers" (Farrand 1966, 2:558). He therefore proposed that:

> The National Legislature will be the first to perceive and will be most sensible to the necessity of amendments, and ought also to be empowered, whenever two-thirds of each branch should concur to call a Convention—There could be no danger in giving this power, as the people would finally decide in the case. (Farrand 1966, 2:558)

The substance of Hamilton's proposal is embodied in the current amending provision in Article V of the U.S. Constitution whereby two-thirds majorities of both houses of Congress propose amendments. To date, all amendments that have been adopted have gone through this procedure.

After the Constitution was proposed, Hamilton was one of three authors of *The Federalist Papers* (the other two were James Madison and John Jay), who urged constitutional ratification. Although Hamilton mentioned the subject in *Federalist No. 85,* Madison wrote the chief essays relating to the constitutional amending process. Hamilton was a strong advocate of judicial review, the process by which American courts can strike down legislation they consider to be unconstitutional, and he addressed this subject in *Federalist No. 78* and in other essays. Such judicial interpretations of the document have made the Constitution much more flexible than it otherwise would have been, arguably obviating the need for many amendments that might otherwise be necessary.

As the first secretary of the treasury, Hamilton urged President George Washington to establish a national bank. In so doing he argued for a broad reading of congressional powers under the "necessary and proper clause," a view the general acceptance of which has also made the adoption of new formal amendments less necessary. Hamilton further argued for a restrictive reading of the Tenth Amendment, an amendment that reserved powers to the states. Hamilton's restrictive reading was largely incorporated into Chief Justice John Marshall's decision in *McCulloch v. Maryland* (1819) and has again permitted fairly wide scope to the exercise of federal powers.

A founder of the Federalist Party, Hamilton often quarreled with fellow party members and worked at cross-purposes with Federalist John Adams. Hamilton's programs were often opposed by Thomas Jefferson, a fellow cabinet member (the first secretary of state) and the founder of the Democratic-Republican Party. However, Hamilton supported the selection by the U.S. House of Representatives of Thomas Jefferson when Jefferson and Aaron Burr (Jefferson's putative running mate whom Hamilton trusted even less than Jefferson) tied in the electoral college in the presidential election of 1800. This election eventually led to adoption of the Twelfth Amendment. Burr killed Hamilton in a duel in 1804.

See also Annapolis Convention; Constitutional Convention of 1787; *McCulloch v. Maryland*.

For Further Reading:

Farrand, Max, ed. 1966. *The Records of the Federal Convention*. 4 vols. New Haven, CT: Yale University Press.

McDonald, Forrest. 1979. *Alexander Hamilton: A Biography*. New York: Norton.

❖ HAMILTON, HUGH L. ❖

One of the most thorough and systematic plans for a new constitution was presented in a book published by Hugh L. Hamilton in 1938. Likening the Constitution to a jigsaw puzzle, Hamilton examined it section by section and concluded that "thirty-one pieces are rotted and have to be thrown away; forty-four of them are badly in need of repair; thirty-seven of them have to be repainted; and we have to make eighteen new pieces to complete the picture. Only thirty-seven of the original pieces are left intact" (H. Hamilton 1938, 5).

Hamilton does not appear to have been motivated by a consistent ideology. His goals were fairly conventional, and he suggested that the main goal of contemporaries was "contentment—congenial occupation, adequate leisure, an absorbing hobby, a pleasant home, and wholesome recreation" (H. Hamilton 1938, 102).

Section I of his new constitution addressed general provisions. Innovations included allowing adjustments on state boundaries, with the proviso that the number of states would not be reduced below thirty. Hamilton also proposed a provision—similar to contemporary neutrality legislation—limiting travel on ships of belligerent nations and restricting loans to or trade with such countries. His constitution further specified that most jobs would be filled through a civil service commission.

Section II of the proposed constitution was the bill of rights. It would deny citizenship "to the insane, the criminal, the illiterate, the non-English speaking and those who fail to comprehend the nature of our government" (H. Hamilton 1938, 112). Freedom of the press would include a provision "prohibiting control of the press in any part of the United States by individuals or groups which tends to abridge their freedom" (H. Hamilton 1938, 113). The current Fourth Amendment would have been modified to make government officials responsible for unreasonable searches and seizures or from "publicity, initiated by their order or performed by them" (H. Hamilton 1938, 113). Hamilton would have permitted the use of sworn testimony by dead witnesses, outlawed capital punishment, and eliminated the due process clause, which he considered to be ambiguous.

Section III outlined states' rights and limitations. It would have required state executives to extradite criminals who had fled to their states.

Congress would be renamed the National Assembly and be divided into a Senate and a Congress; members would receive salaries of $9,000 a year and actual travel expenses. Congress would consist of from 100 to 200 members chosen for a maximum of two six-year terms. The Senate would be a similar size. Instead of representing states, senators would be chosen by "representatives of the professions, finance, service, agriculture, manufacturing, construction, trade, communication and transportation, apportioned according to the census" (H. Hamilton 1938, 122). Senators would serve a single twelve-year term. The National Assembly would have power over child labor, with a provision allowing work by those over age thirteen that was not injurious to their health or schooling. The National Assembly would have control over commerce but not over manufacturing. In a measure similar to some modern proposals for a balanced budget amendment, Hamilton would have required all laws mandating expenditures to "specify the method of raising said funds" (H. Hamilton 1938, 120).

The president would be directly elected by the people to a single six-year term and would be paid $75,000 a year. The vice president would be designated as postmaster general and would be a member of the president's cabinet.

The number of Supreme Court justices would be specified at nine. Judges would be required to retire at age eighty. The power of judicial review would be spelled out, but when the Supreme Court declared a law to be unconstitutional, Hamilton provided that it "shall include the wording of a Constitutional Amendment which would validate the legislation" (H. Hamilton 1938, 132). Hamilton would eliminate the provisions of the current Eleventh Amendment and allow a two-thirds majority of the Supreme Court to impeach the president "for non-adherence to this Constitution" (H. Hamilton 1938, 133).

Amendments would be proposed by two-thirds of both houses of the National Assembly and ratified by the electors. Every twenty-five years the president could call a constitutional convention. Hamilton specified that "no amendment which would prohibit the electorate from changing any part of this Constitution by methods prescribed therein shall ever be proposed or ratified" (H. Hamilton 1938, 134).

Hamilton remains an elusive figure. Several academic journals reviewed his work, but otherwise it appears to have "faded into near oblivion" (Boyd 1992, 153).

For Further Reading:

Boyd, Steven R., ed. 1992. *Alternative Constitutions for the United States: A Documentary History.* Westport, CT: Greenwood Press.

Hamilton, Hugh L. 1938. *A Second Constitution for the United States of America.* Richmond, VA: Garrett and Massie.

❖ *HANS V. LOUISIANA* (1890) ❖

Hans v. Louisiana continues to influence interpretation of the Eleventh Amendment. A Louisiana citizen brought suit against that state to recover money due to him on bonds he had purchased that the state refused to honor.

In *Chisholm v. Georgia* (1793), the Supreme Court accepted jurisdiction over a similar case involving a suit brought against a state by a citizen of another state. Congress subsequently proposed and the states ratified the Eleventh Amendment in response. It stated that the judicial power of the United States would not be interpreted to extend to suits "commenced or prosecuted against one of the United States by Citizens of another State, or by Citizens or Subjects of any Foreign State."

Granting that the Eleventh Amendment did not specifically cover the contingency in the case before the Court, Justice Joseph Bradley returned to what he believed to be the popular understanding of the Constitution prior to *Chisholm,* according to which a state, as a sovereign, could not be sued without its consent. He thereby effectively accepted Justice James

Iredell's dissenting opinion in *Chisholm* over the majority ruling. Justice John Marshall Harlan agreed with the result in *Hans* but did not accept the Court's analysis of *Chisholm v. Georgia*.

Hans in effect viewed the Eleventh Amendment as a restatement rather than a true amendment of the original Constitution (Orth 1992, 251). In so doing, it specifically widened the application of the literal words of the amendment. The Court has continued to utilize this approach in recent decisions, most notably *Seminole Tribe v. Florida* (1996) and *Kimel v. Florida Board of Regents* (2000) broadly interpreting the Eleventh Amendment not only as to what it actually says but according to what the Court considers to be its wider purpose.

See also Eleventh Amendment.

For Further Reading:
Hans v. Louisiana, 134 U.S. 1 (1890).
Orth, John V. 1992. "Eleventh Amendment." In *The Oxford Companion to the Supreme Court of the United States,* ed. Kermit L. Hall. New York: Oxford University Press.

❖ HARDIN, CHARLES (1908–1997) ❖

Political scientist Charles Hardin introduced his plans for governmental reform in the midst of the Watergate crisis of the early 1970s. His objective was summarized in the title of his book, *Presidential Power and Accountability,* but he also described his plans as covering "presidential leadership and party government" (Hardin 1974, 2). After an analysis designed to show that existing limits on the president were inadequate and that the bureaucracy was out of control, Hardin advanced nine proposals, each designed to lead to greater governmental accountability and control (Hardin 1974, 183–185).

First, Hardin proposed that the president and members of the House and Senate be elected at the same time to four-year terms,

with this calendar interrupted if the government dissolved and new elections were called.

Second, Hardin proposed supplementing existing single-member House districts with at-large seats—the party winning the presidency to get 100 extra seats and the losing party 50, provided that the winning party retained a majority. Party committees would select the at-large members, with the minority "shadow cabinet" having input into its party's slate of candidates.

Third, Hardin proposed that members of the House would nominate presidential candidates. These members would also replace a president who was disabled. As part of this proposal, Hardin would eliminate the vice presidency. Fourth, Hardin would significantly reduce the power of the Senate. It would neither confirm nominees to office nor ratify treaties. Moreover, if the House of Representatives waited at least sixty days and repassed a bill that the Senate had rejected, it would still go to the president for his signature.

Hardin's fifth proposal allowed for the override of a presidential veto by a majority of House votes and only limited participation by the Senate.

Sixth, Hardin would allow members of Congress to serve in other offices, especially the president's cabinet. Seventh, the defeated presidential candidate would have a seat in the House and other privileges (including an official residence). Like the president, such individuals would be subject to removal by the party committee that nominated them.

Hardin's eighth proposal provided that the presidency would go to the party winning the national plurality of votes.

His ninth called for repeal of all conflicting constitutional provisions as well as of the two-term presidential limit in the Twenty-second Amendment.

Other than his last proposal, Hardin was fairly vague about how to implement his ideas (see Vile 1991c, 117). Indeed, at one point, he suggested that it would be better to allow some features of a new system to "develop by convention than to stipulate them in advance" (Hardin 1974, 182). This vagueness, as well as what many believed to be the successful resolution of the Watergate crisis, probably hindered the impact of Hardin's proposals. Nonetheless, Hardin reissued his call for reform in 1989, at which time he reiterated the need to replace "the separation of powers between the executive and the legislature by a separation between the government and the opposition" (Hardin 1989, 201).

For Further Reading:

Hardin, Charles M. 1974. *Presidential Power and Accountability: Toward a New Constitution.* Chicago: University of Chicago Press.

Vile, John R. 1991c. *Rewriting the United States Constitution: An Examination of Proposals from Reconstruction to the Present.* New York: Praeger.

❖ HARPER V. VIRGINIA STATE BOARD OF ELECTIONS (1966) ❖

In 1964 the states ratified the Twenty-fourth Amendment. Applying to both primary and general elections for national offices, it prohibited the imposition of a poll tax as a condition of voting. In *Harper v. Virginia State Board of Elections,* Justice William O. Douglas wrote an opinion for the Supreme Court extending the poll tax prohibition to state elections. He relied on the equal protection clause of the Fourteenth Amendment and on his judgment that, as a fundamental right, voting should not be dependent on one's ability to pay a fee.

Justice Hugo Black wrote a striking dissenting opinion in which he stated that the Court should have upheld its earlier decisions in *Breedlove v. Suttles* (1937) and *Butler v. Thompson* (1951). Acknowledging his own personal opposition to the imposition of a poll tax, he argued that such a tax could have a rational basis. Moreover, he argued that, in making its decision, the Court was usurping the amending power:

If basic changes as to the respective powers of the state and national government are needed, I prefer to let those changes be made by amendment as Article V of the Constitution provides. For a majority of this Court to undertake the task . . .

amounts . . . to an exercise of power the Constitution makers with foresight and wisdom refused to give to the Judicial Branch of the Government. (*Harper* 1966, 676)

Citing the "concept of a written constitution," Black further suggested that "when a 'political theory' embodied in our Constitution becomes outdated," the Court was less qualified to come up with a new one "than the people of this country proceeding in the manner provided by Article V" (*Harper* 1966, 678). Black believed that Congress could, under its enforcement authority in Section 5 of the Fourteenth Amendment, outlaw the poll tax if it found that this tax was "being used as a device to deny voters equal protection of the laws" (*Harper* 1966, 679).

Justices John Marshall Harlan and Potter Stewart also dissented. They argued that the majority decision was based on "current egalitarian notions of how a modern democracy should be organized" rather than on any constitutional mandates (*Harper* 1966, 686).

See also Black, Hugo Lafayette; Twenty-fourth Amendment.

For Further Reading:

Harper v. Virginia State Board of Elections, 383 U.S. 663 (1966).

❖ HARTFORD CONVENTION ❖

Early American history witnessed numerous disputes about the respective authority of the state and national governments. In the Virginia and Kentucky Resolution of 1798, James Madison and Thomas Jefferson asserted the right of states to "interpose" themselves on behalf of civil liberties, in this case, by opposing the federal Alien and Sedition Acts, the latter of which they believed to be in conflict with the First Amendment. Later, of course, other southerners would develop this doctrine into the doctrines of nullification and secession.

States' rights sentiment was not, however, confined to the South. Such sentiment became especially strong in New England in the years leading up to and including the War of 1812. Jefferson's proclamation of an embargo, as well as the war itself, interfered substantially with New England commerce and led to resentment, culminating in an 1815 meeting of representatives of these states known as the Hartford Convention. This convention, which was not called by Congress under provisions of Article V, proposed seven amendments.

The first two resolutions reflected the continuing split between free and slave states. Convention delegates proposed eliminating the clause whereby slaves were counted as three-fifths of a person; they also favored requiring a two-thirds vote in both houses of Congress for the admission of new states, thus making the admission of additional slave states less likely. The third and fourth resolutions would have limited Congress's power to impose embargoes to sixty days and would have required a two-thirds vote to do so. The fifth proposal would have required a two-thirds vote for Congress to declare war, absent the need for immediate defense. The sixth proposal would have prevented naturalized citizens from serving in Congress or holding other civil offices, and the seventh would have limited the president to one term (Ford 1898, 688–689).

Delegates from the Hartford Convention arrived in Washington, D.C., as residents were celebrating news of the American victory at the Battle of New Orleans and the signing of a peace treaty with Great Britain (Vile 1993b, 186). The close association of the Federalist Party with the Hartford Convention led to its demise, but a number of the convention's ideas continued to be topics of discussion. Abolitionist leader William Lloyd Garrison was among those who later urged Northern states to secede from the Union rather than continuing their association with slave states.

Later conventions of state delegates that met to discuss possible laws and amendments included the Nashville Convention of 1850 and the Peace Convention of 1865. Neither proved successful in averting the eventual secession, albeit not of the states of the North but of those of the South. The idea of Southern secession is generally considered to be a logical extension of earlier ideas of state nullification advanced by South Carolina Senator John C. Calhoun.

See also Nashville Convention; Peace Convention; Virginia and Kentucky Resolutions.

For Further Reading:
Ford, Paul L., ed. 1898. *The Federalist.* New York: Henry Holt.

Vile, John R. 1993b. *The Theory and Practice of Constitutional Change in America: A Collection of Original Source Materials.* New York: Peter Lang.

❖ *HAWKE V. SMITH (I)* (1920) ❖

This case stemmed from a petition to enjoin the Ohio secretary of state from printing ballots for voter approval of the state legislature's ratification of the Eighteenth Amendment, which provided for national alcoholic prohibition. Ohio had added such referendum provisions to its constitution in November 1918. In January 1919 Ohio's governor sent copies of the state's legislative ratification of the Eighteenth Amendment to the U.S. secretary of state, who included Ohio's ratification in his count.

Writing for a unanimous Court, Justice William Day decided that, in specifying legislative ratification of amendments, the Constitution clearly had in mind "the representative body which made the laws of the people," rather than the people themselves (*Hawke (I)* 1920, 227). Referring to the precedent in *Hollingsworth v. Virginia* (1798), Day argued that, when ratifying amendments, states were performing a federal rather than a legislative function. Perhaps partly motivated by concern about the possible rescission of amendments, Day noted that "any other view might lead to endless confusion in the manner of ratification of federal amendments" (*Hawke (I)* 1920, 230).

Hawke leaves open Congress's option to specify that states ratify amendments by conventions, as in the case of the Twenty-first Amendment, which repealed the Eighteenth. Indeed, the decision in *Hawke* appears to have led some observers to believe that the Eighteenth Amendment would never have been enacted had it required popular approval; this view, in turn, encouraged Congress to seek repeal of this amendment by the hitherto untried state convention method.

A U.S. circuit court opinion in *Kimble v. Swackhamer* (1978) permits referendums on constitutional amendments as long as they are purely advisory, but in *Cook v. Gralike* (2001), the U.S. Supreme Court decided that states could not give binding instructions to their representatives as to how they had to vote on amendments or make negative notations on the ballots of those who refused to support such amendments. As long as the Court continues to recognize *Hawke*, however, those who favor actual ratification of amendments by popular referendums will have to seek a constitutional amendment.

See also Initiative and Referendum; *Kimble v. Swackhamer.*

For Further Reading:

Hawke v. Smith (I), 253 U.S. 221 (1920).

Walroff, Jonathan L. 1985. "The Unconstitutionality of Voter Initiative Applications for Federal Constitutional Conventions." *Colorado Law Review* 85: 1525–1545.

❖ HAWKE V. SMITH (II) (1920) ❖

A companion case to *Hawke v. Smith (I)*, this ruling concerned the submission of the Nineteenth Amendment (prohibiting restrictions on women's suffrage) rather than the Eighteenth Amendment (providing for national alcoholic prohibition) to state voters. In a two-paragraph decision, Justice William Day ruled that, in accord with the companion opinion, the provision of Ohio's constitution requiring approval of amendments by referendum was unconstitutional.

❖ HAZLITT, HENRY (1894–1993) ❖

Journalist Henry Hazlitt was long a believer in the need for constitutional reform (Hazlitt 1931). He offered his proposal for a parlia-

mentary system in a book first published in 1942 and subsequently reissued, in somewhat reduced form, in 1974. Throughout this period, Hazlitt continued to believe that the nation's inflexible Constitution was responsible for many of its ills. He favored a parliamentary system whereby the Congress could vote no confidence in a premier who could, in turn, dissolve Congress and call for new elections.

Hazlitt believed that the first step toward change should be reform of the amending process. He favored adoption of a system like that in Australia. Under such a plan, amendments would be proposed by absolute majorities in both houses of Congress and submitted to the people through a referendum. Ratification would require a majority of voters in a majority of states (Hazlitt 1942, 11–12).

The central reform that Hazlitt advocated was to fuse legislative and executive powers. To this end, he favored significantly reducing the power of the Senate, ending the system of fixed terms of office, and eliminating the president's veto and related powers. Hazlitt concentrated on Congress. Among his more novel suggestions was the proposal that officeholders be deprived of voting rights during their tenure; alternatively, their votes could be segregated at separate polling booths so that the public could see how their positions influenced their votes. Hazlitt thought that the House of Representatives should have about 150 members. Their first task would be to choose a premier. The president would make the ultimate selection, but only after congressional balloting. The premier would, in turn, select a cabinet of ten to twelve persons; like the premier, they would not necessarily have to be selected from Congress.

Members of the cabinet would continue to head executive departments, but undersecretaries would be designated as administrators so that cabinet members could focus on policy issues. The cabinet would formulate major bills. These would then be submitted to a legislative council of about a dozen individuals representing the entire legislature. Bills would then go to standing congressional committees (where seniority would have been eliminated), whose power would be that of revising and overseeing rather than formulating legislative measures (Hazlitt 1942, 140). The cabinet would subsequently set the legislative agenda, with the legislature weighted, when needed, to give the largest party a majority.

Rejecting the initiative except for amendments designed to reduce "the powers, terms or number of legislators or changing the method of election" (Hazlitt 1942, 159), Hazlitt favored the referendum mechanism only as a way of ratifying constitutional amendments. House members would serve four-year terms, subject to dissolution and new elections or to individual recall.

Ideally, Hazlitt favored a Senate of two dozen people chosen for eight-year terms by the House of Representatives, but he realized that this would conflict with the Article V provision that no state be deprived of its equal representation without its consent. He was therefore willing to settle for a Senate with a reduced role, enabling it to delay and reconsider but not block House legislation.

Although he would take away the president's power to veto and to execute laws, make treaties, and direct military policy (Hazlitt 1942, 105), Hazlitt wanted to preserve the president as head of state. In such a position, the president could perform ceremonial functions, advise the premier, and, on extraordinary occasions, dissolve the legislature (Hazlitt 1942, 111). The president would be chosen for a five- to ten-year term by both houses of Congress.

Recognizing that such major changes would be difficult to adopt, Hazlitt proposed a number of less drastic expedients. These included amendments to limit the president to two terms (later adopted with the ratification of the Twenty-second Amendment), to give the president an item veto, to eliminate the requirement that members of Congress reside in the states that select them, to specify that judges retire at seventy or seventy-five years of age, to fix the membership of the Supreme Court, and to allow Congress to remove up to one judge a year for usurping congressional functions. Other proposed reforms included allowing both houses of Congress to approve treaties by majority vote, eliminating the vice presidency,

and reforming congressional rules (Vile 1991c, 86). In his 1974 book, Hazlitt also proposed preventing the president from serving consecutive terms and allowing state governors to appoint one member of the Supreme Court (Vile 1991c, 94 n.2). In an essay first published in 1983, Hazlitt reaffirmed his support for a presidential item veto and sought to prevent the Senate from increasing appropriations approved by the House (Hazlitt 1987).

See also Parliamentary System.

For Further Reading:

Hazlitt, Henry. 1987. "A Proposal for Two Constitutional Amendments." In *A Nation in Debt: Economists Debate the Federal Budget Deficit*, ed. Richard H. Fink and Jack H. High. Frederick, MD: University Publications of America.

———. 1974. *A New Constitution Now*. New Rochelle, NY: Arlington House.

———. 1942. *A New Constitution Now*. New York: Whittlesey House.

Vile, John R. 1991c. *Rewriting the United States Constitution: An Examination of Proposals from Reconstruction to the Present*. New York: Praeger.

❖ HEHMEYER, ALEXANDER (1910–1993) ❖

Attorney Alexander Hehmeyer originally prepared his proposals for constitutional revision as part of a study of domestic political reform being made in anticipation of the end of World War II (Hehmeyer 1943). He hoped to use the sense of urgency generated by the war to stimulate interest in reform (Vile 1991c, 90–91). Recognizing that the only authority a convention would have would be to propose changes, Hehmeyer favored convening a constitutional convention by a concurrent resolution of Congress.

Hehmeyer anticipated a convention of ninety-seven members: forty-eight to be named by the states, sixteen by Congress, sixteen by the president, sixteen by the chief justice, and a chair appointed by Congress (Hehmeyer 1943, 38–40). He foresaw four areas where such a convention should concentrate: relations between the president and Congress, the balance between the nation and the states, liberalization of the amending process, and a reexamination of the Bill of Rights.

In reassessing Congress, Hehmeyer concluded that plans for a parliamentary system were impractical and concentrated instead on seeking "to make Congress more responsive to the President and to make the President more responsive to Congress and to do this without departing radically from existing institutional forms" (Hehmeyer 1943, 64). Initially suggesting a three-year presidential term, Hehmeyer instead recommended a plan by which members of the House of Representatives would serve four-year terms.

Hehmeyer advocated extensive cabinet reform. He proposed reorganizing the cabinet so that it would have eight members: a "Secretary Without Portfolio, Secretary for Administration, Secretary for Legislation, Secretary for International Affairs, Secretary for National Defense, Secretary for Law, Secretary of the Economy, [and a] Secretary for National Welfare" (Hehmeyer 1943, 77). Most such secretaries would not have to run departments; that task would be given to full-time administrators. The secretary of legislation would have the power to initiate legislation in Congress and participate in debates. The president could make changes in the cabinet on the basis of midterm elections. Administrators of agencies could be selected through the civil service system.

Hehmeyer proposed a number of congressional reforms, including the establishment of automatic vote recorders, more efficient parliamentary procedures, better staffing, and a joint legislative council. This council would include three presidential representatives to coordinate legislation between the two houses. Hehmeyer would also reduce the number of standing committees, eliminate the seniority rule, and alter the system of appropriations. He further advocated that treaties be proposed by a majority of both houses of Congress rather than by a two-thirds vote of the Senate.

Hehmeyer believed that there was considerable room to develop regional authorities and consolidate local governments. He also favored eliminating tax duplication and resolving conflicts between state and national taxing authorities.

Hehmeyer respected the Bill of Rights and thought that consideration should be given to including economic and social rights. He also favored a more liberalized amending process. He suggested that amendments should be introduced in one of five ways: "by a majority of the elected membership of both Houses of Congress"; "by a two-thirds majority of either House if approved in two (or perhaps three) consecutive sessions"; "by a majority of the State legislatures if within a period of five years, they approve the identical proposal"; "by a convention to be convened by Congress either on its own initiative or if requested within a period of five years by a majority of the State legislatures"; or, in a proposal reminiscent of Thomas Jefferson, "by a Convention to be convened regularly every thirty years upon the call of the President" (Hehmeyer 1943, 163–167). Such amendments would be ratified "(a) By two-thirds of the State legislatures acting within four years or (b) By a majority of the voters in two-thirds of the States and a majority of all those voting in the nation at a special election held within two years from the date of the proposal or at the next succeeding election for Representatives" (Hehmeyer 1943, 169).

Hehmeyer admired the role of the Supreme Court in applying constitutional guarantees to modern times and suggested that it might render advisory opinions. He also wanted to fix the number of Supreme Court justices at nine and eliminate federal jurisdiction in diversity of citizenship cases. Under miscellaneous reforms, Hehmeyer included such proposals as having ex-presidents serve for life in the Senate, giving the president an item veto, allowing for the postponing of national elections in times of emergency, abolishing the electoral college and the vice presidency, and abolishing state residency requirements for members of Congress.

For Further Reading:
Hehmeyer, Alexander. 1943. *Time for Change: A Proposal for a Second Constitutional Convention.* New York: Farrar and Rinehart.

❖ HENDERSON, YANDELL (1873–1974) ❖

Yandell Henderson was a professor of physiology at Yale University and an active member of the newly formed Progressive Party, under whose banner he ran unsuccessfully for Congress (Vile 1991c, 54–55). He advocated three major reforms in an article in the *Yale Review* (Henderson 1913).

First, Henderson favored either fusing or otherwise bringing the legislative and executive branches into closer cooperation. He even suggested that, at the state level, legislators might be replaced by a board of directors presided over by the governor. Second, Henderson proposed that the people should be able to "recall" judicial decisions by voting on whether to give sanction to laws that the courts invalidated. Henderson suggested that this would be "a far more sensible method of amending the old and of gradually building up a new set of principles and institutions than the present method of effecting constitutional amendments" (Henderson 1913, 89). Third, Henderson believed that the time had come for the United States to "establish a real nation and a real national government instead of a Union of States and a Federal Government" (Henderson 1913, 89). Henderson favored calling a national constitutional convention to achieve these goals.

For Further Reading:

Henderson, Yandell. 1913. "The Progressive Movement and Constitutional Reform." *Yale Review* n.s. 3: 78–90.

❖ HIGHWAYS ❖

Few states are more closely associated with the automobile than California. The state's clogged freeways are daily reminders of the importance of the car to the state's lifestyle. In 1952 the California legislature petitioned Congress to call a convention relative to the use of federal highway taxes. The proposed amendment specified that:

all money, collected from any taxes now or hereafter imposed by the United States upon motor vehicles or the operation thereof, and upon the manufacture, sale, distribution, or use of motor vehicle fuels, supplies and equipment . . . shall be apportioned by the Congress to the several States and shall be used by the States exclusively for the construction and maintenance of highways in the manner prescribed by Congress. ("Assembly Joint Resolution 8" 1952, 4003)

In 1956, the national government created the Highway Trust Fund, which earmarked moneys from user taxes for highway construction, including the interstate highway system. The fund succeeded in insulating expenditures on highways from competition with projects in the general budget (I. Rubin 1990, 131–141).

For Further Reading:

"Assembly Joint Resolution 8." 1952. *Congressional Record*, 82nd Cong., 2d sess. 1952, Vol. 98, pt. 3: 4003–4004.

Rubin, Irene S. 1990. *The Politics of Public Budgeting: Getting and Spending, Borrowing and Balancing*. Chatham, NJ: Chatham House.

❖ HISTORY OF CONSTITUTIONAL AMENDMENTS IN THE UNITED STATES ❖

Since the U.S. Constitution was ratified in 1789, only twenty-seven amendments have been proposed and ratified by the necessary majorities, and ten of these (known collectively as the Bill of Rights) were adopted practically contemporaneously with the U.S. Constitution. The process is difficult but not impossible, and, although each amendment is treated individually in this volume, a historical overview of all the amendments helps illumine some points that might not be obvious by reviewing each amendment individually.

The Ideas behind Amending Provisions

The idea of balancing constitutional stability with the need for change is obviously an old one. It was put into relief both when the British system proved unresponsive to the demands that led to the Revolutionary War and when the American founders decided to abandon the idea of parliamentary sovereignty for a written Constitution that would delineate governmental powers and limits and that would be unchangeable by ordinary legislative means. The prototype for such mechanisms had already been established in a number of colonial charters that provided that basic freedoms could only be altered, if at all, by extraordinary majorities, as well as in state constitutions that states began writing at the time of the American Revolution. Most states had designed mechanisms, most notably the constitutional convention and subsequent popular ratification mechanisms, to assure that their constitutions had firmer foundations, and were less subject to change, than ordinary legislation. In this manner, such constitutions could serve as fundamental or "higher law."

Under the Articles of Confederation, the government adopted in 1782 that emphasized state sovereignty, the principle of constitutional stability was taken to extremes. The adoption of most legislation required the consent of nine or more states. The Articles had provided that amendments would have to be proposed by Congress and be unanimously ratified by the states. A number of proposals had strong support, but none was ever able to achieve the unanimous consensus required for an amendment. Frustration with this mechanism undoubtedly contributed to the push for a Constitutional Convention. Initially called together to rewrite the Articles, delegates ultimately decided instead to consider a whole new scheme of government that substituted a system of separation of powers and checks and balances. The system that emerged established a bicameral legislature, a president, and a system of courts in place of the single unicameral Congress that was in control under the Articles. Legislation required the consent of both houses of Congress and the president, subject to a two-thirds congressional override or a presidential veto.

The U.S. Constitutional Convention

At the Constitutional Convention, the framers designed a two-step process of proposal and ratification of amendments that they incorporated in Article V. It specified that two-thirds majorities of both houses of Congress would propose amendments, which would then have to be ratified by three-fourths of the states; an alternative mechanism allowing for two-thirds of the state legislatures to propose amendments through a constitutional convention has often been discussed but never used. Highlighting the importance of the Great Compromise whereby states were represented according to population in the House of Representation and equally in the Senate, the framers further provided that no state could be deprived of its equal suffrage in the latter house without its own consent; delegates also agreed that no amendment could prohibit slave importation for the succeeding twenty years. The framers of the new Constitution bypassed the amending provision in the Articles of Confederation, as well as existing state legislatures (which stood to lose some power under the new government), by providing in Article VII that the Constitution would go into effect when ratified by special conventions in nine or more of the states.

The Constitutional Convention of 1787 had barely adjourned before the nation was split into rival Federalist and Anti-Federalist factions, the former supporting, and the latter opposing, ratification of the new document. Anti-Federalists were particularly fearful that the new national government would threaten the rights of the states and of individuals. They increasingly focused in debates on the need for a bill of rights, such as was found in many state constitutions of the day (where they were sometimes called declarations of rights). Initially, most Federalists argued that such a bill of rights was unnecessary because the national government would be able to exercise only a limited set of powers. Federalists further argued that such a list might even prove dangerous if the authors of a bill of rights inadvertently omitted an important right. In time, however, many Federalists were persuaded that a bill of rights could do no harm and might even help. They also decided that such a bill was needed if the possibility of a second convention, which might reverse the gains made at the first, were to be avoided. Thomas Jefferson, then a U.S. ambassador to France, was among those who helped persuade James Madison (often identified as the father of the U.S. Constitution and the Bill of Rights) of the desirability of such a bill of rights.

Proposal and Ratification of the Bill of Rights

Federalists succeeded in getting the Constitution adopted, but state adoption came with the understanding that Federalists would work for adoption of a bill of rights. In the first Congress, Virginia Representative James Madison led the way in crafting a bill of rights from provisions within existing state constitutions and from the many proposals that states had submitted for constitutional change, often along with their ratifications. Fortunately, no states had approved the Constitution contingent upon the adoption of a single provision or set of provisions or the convening of a second convention. Despite arguments from his congressional colleagues that the matter could wait, Madison persuasively argued that the credibility of the new government rested in large part on its ability to carry out the promise to adopt a bill of rights in an expeditious fashion. Madison was unable to get one of his favorite proposals included—a provision providing for the rights of conscience that would have limited both state *and* national governments—but he did succeed ultimately in getting Congress to propose twelve amendments, ten of which were ratified in 1791 as the Bill of Rights. Despite Madison's hope that new amendments could be embedded within the text of the existing document, these rights, like subsequent amendments, were added to the end of the document, where they have come to have increasing importance (see Placement of Constitutional Amendments).

Unlike many rights incorporated in prior state declarations of rights, those in the Bill of Rights were listed as judicially enforceable provisions rather than as mere aspirations. The amendments did not prove particularly important during the first century of the nation's existence for two reasons. First, the national government was relatively small and did not have much occasion to regulate daily life, and, second, as the Supreme Court indicated in *Barron v. Baltimore* (1833), the provisions in the Bill of Rights were understood as limits only on the national government and not the states. Nonetheless, these amendments remained a vital symbol of some of the nation's highest ideals.

The First Amendment provided for freedom of religion; prohibited the establishment of a national religion; and provided for freedom of speech, freedom of the press, and the right of peaceable assembly and petition. The Second Amendment provided for the right to bear arms and is still the object of fierce debate. (Was it primarily intended to identify an individual or a collective right?) The Third Amendment, responding to a grievance that the colonists had against the British, limited the quartering of troops within individual homes without the consent of the owners.

The Fourth Amendment also responded to the system of general warrants, or writs of assistance, that the British had used to search colonial houses and businesses. This amendment limited unreasonable searches and seizures. It further provided that warrants would not issue except upon probable cause and unless they described with particularity the person, place, or thing intended to be searched and/or seized.

The Fifth Amendment followed with a series of rights for those accused of crimes or on trial for such crimes. These included a provision for grand jury indictment, a prohibition against double jeopardy or compulsory self-incrimination, and a provision specifying that individuals could not be deprived of their "life, liberty, or property, without due process of law." The Fifth Amendment further forbade the government from taking private property for public use without "just compensation."

The Sixth Amendment delineated additional rights for the accused, adding the right "to a speedy and public trial, by an impartial jury," the right of defendants to be informed of charges against them, and the right to confront adversary witnesses and compel witnesses to come to court, as well as the right to counsel. The Seventh Amendment extended the right of jury trials to civil cases. The Eighth Amendment prohibited excessive bail, excessive fines, and cruel and unusual punishments.

The Ninth and Tenth Amendments are a bit more elusive. The Ninth Amendment was an apparent response to Anti-Federalist arguments that listing rights could prove to be dangerous. It indicated that the listing of rights did not "deny or disparage others retained by the people." Addressing a somewhat different concern, the Tenth Amendment further specified that powers not delegated to the national government remained with the states or the people.

The Eleventh and Twelfth Amendments and the Quiet Interlude that Followed

During debates over ratification of the Constitution, some Federalists had given assurances that, in accord with the generally accepted doctrine of sovereign immunity then current, states would not be able to be sued without their consent. Consequently, there was a strong outcry when the U.S. Supreme Court upheld such a suit against a state in the case of *Chisholm v. Georgia* (1793). States fairly quickly adopted the Eleventh Amendment, which overturned this decision, arguably returning to the original understanding of most of the framers. Although fairly narrowly worded, this amendment has been further expanded by Supreme Court decisions, including those of recent years.

The complicated electoral college mechanism that had been designed to elect a president who would be independent of the other two branches of government encountered trouble with the development of the two-party system. Under the original electoral college system, each elector cast two votes for president, with the individual receiving the highest number of votes becoming the president and the individual with the second highest becoming the vice president. Not only did this system sometimes result in a president from one party and a vice president from another (as in the election of 1796 when the electors selected Federalist John Adams as president and the Democratic-Republican Thomas Jefferson as

vice president), but in the election of 1800 all the Democratic-Republican electors who voted for Jefferson also voted for Aaron Burr, leading to a tie in the electoral college that had to be resolved in the U.S. House of Representatives, where outgoing Federalists still had a vote. The Twelfth Amendment was accordingly ratified in 1804. It provided that electors would in the future cast separate ballots for the president and vice president, with the House of Representatives choosing from among the top three candidates in cases (like the election of 1824) when no individual received a majority.

The period from 1804 to 1865 was a period of great constitutional struggles over tariffs, slavery, and the relationship between the national government and the states, but no successful amendments were ratified during this time period. In 1819 Congress did propose an amendment that would have stripped individuals who accepted foreign titles of nobility of their citizenship, but, despite some confusion, the requisite number of states never ratified this amendment. Similarly, Congress proposed the Corwin Amendment in 1861 as a means of averting the Civil War. It would essentially have guaranteed the continuing existence of slavery in states where it was already established. This proposal became more and more irrelevant with the beginning of war and Abraham Lincoln's eventual issuance of the Emancipation Proclamation.

Three Post–Civil War Amendments

At war's end, a consensus emerged that the issues that had led to the Civil War were serious enough to be addressed in the Constitution. Three amendments were proposed and ratified from 1865 to 1870. The Thirteenth Amendment attempted to moderate future North/South controversies by eliminating the institution of slavery and giving Congress appropriate enforcement authority. This did not prevent a number of Southern states from enacting restrictive Black Codes regulating the freedom of former slaves.

The Fourteenth Amendment was much more extensive, containing a total of five sections. Most important was the first sentence. It overturned the Supreme Court decision in

[Dred] Scott v. Sandford (1857), which had ruled that blacks were not and could not be American citizens. By contrast, the Fourteenth Amendment declared that all persons who were born or naturalized in the United States were citizens. Section 1 further went on to reaffirm early principles articulated in the Declaration of Independence by guaranteeing that all citizens would be entitled to the privileges and immunities of U.S. citizens, that none would be deprived of life, liberty, or property without due process of law (a provision modeled on that in the Fifth Amendment), and that all would be accorded equal protection of the laws. The due process clause later served as the constitutional basis for the doctrine that key provisions in the Bill of Rights that once limited only the national government would also be applicable to the states. Section 2 of the amendment effectively overturned the three-fifths clause, which had provided that slaves would be counted as "three-fifths of a person" for purposes of taxation and representation, and, in a provision that was never enforced, allowed for diminished representation for states that did not extend the vote to male voters over the age of twenty-one; this was a serious disappointment to women's rights advocates, many of whom had also worked hard for the rights of African Americans. Section 3 disqualified Confederate supporters from office, subject to requalification by a congressional supermajority. Section 4 repudiated Confederate debts, and Section 5 provided for congressional enforcement of the amendment. Congress refused to recognize Southern governments until they adopted this amendment, assuring its passage but also leaving some states feeling that they had been blackmailed and possibly encouraging future evasion of the amendment's provisions. Initial Supreme Court interpretations of this amendment were quite restrictive. The *Slaughterhouse Cases* (1873) gave a narrow reading to the privileges and immunities clause; the *Civil Rights Cases* of 1883 limited governmental intervention to cases involving state, rather than private, action, and *Plessy v. Ferguson* (1896) eventually sanctioned the system of Jim Crow laws under the doctrine of "separate but equal" (a decision later reversed by the Supreme Court's

1954 decision in *Brown v. Board of Education*). Ironically, while the application of the Fourteenth Amendment was being narrowed in the field of civil rights, its provisions were increasingly used to strike down economic legislation that the Supreme Court believed to be in violation of the rights of due process. In *Santa Clara County v. Southern Pacific Railroad* (1886), the Court specifically recognized corporations as legal "persons" entitled to protection under this amendment.

The last of the trio of amendments adopted after the Civil War, the Fifteenth, was initially the least effective. It prevented states from denying the vote to individuals on the basis of race. States evaded the amendment by numerous ploys including poll taxes, literary tests, grandfather clauses, registration requirements, all-white primaries, and even physical violence. Over time, the U.S. Supreme Court struck down many of these mechanisms, and in 1965, Congress used the enforcement mechanism in Section 2 of this amendment to enact a tough Voting Rights Act, which has subsequently been extended in a number of other acts, and which have been approved by the U.S. Supreme Court.

The Progressive Era Amendments
Although constitutional disputes continued, Congress did not propose any new constitutional amendments by the necessary majorities for the next forty years. However, the states ratified four such amendments from 1913 to 1920, a period generally known as the Progressive Era and dominated by movements for direct democracy and other reforms.

The Sixteenth Amendment, adopted in 1913, overturned a Supreme Court decision in *Pollock v. Farmers' Loan & Trust Co. (II)* (1895), in which the Supreme Court had declared that the income tax was unconstitutional. The new amendment provided revenues for an expanding national government that would soon be involved in a world war and also offered a means of equalizing wealth. The Seventeenth Amendment further democratized the Constitution by providing that members of the U.S. Senate would now be selected by direct popular vote rather than being chosen by their state legislatures, some of which had already begun appointing popular vote winners. Most controversial was the Eighteenth Amendment, which provided for national alcoholic prohibition. Partly fueled by the obvious harms of excessive alcohol consumption, which were somehow associated in the popular imagination with immigrants (often Roman Catholics from Eastern and Southern European nations), and partly as a patriotic way of saving foodstuffs in a time of war, the Amendment was interpreted not only to outlaw hard liquors but also beers and wines that were much lower in alcoholic content. This attempt to use the Constitution to enact social policy was widely evaded and led to a significant increase in organized crime. It remains the only amendment ever to have been specifically repealed, with the adoption of the Twenty-first Amendment in 1933, shortly after the election of Franklin D. Roosevelt, who had opposed prohibition in his party's platform.

The last, and arguably most important, of the Progressive Era Amendments was the Nineteenth Amendment, which brought to fruition hopes of women's suffrage that dated at least as far back as the Seneca Falls Convention of 1848. Numerous women's organizations had fought for this amendment in the interim, and President Wilson had eventually supported it in part to achieve unity during World War I. A proposed amendment by Congress in 1924 that would have overturned Supreme Court decisions by allowing Congress to prohibit child labor was never ratified by the required majority of the states, although changes in judicial outlook eventually made such an amendment unnecessary by recognizing the exercise of such powers under the interstate commerce clause.

The New Deal and Thereafter

Although the New Deal is associated with many changes in the role and function of government, the only amendments that it left in its wake were the previously mentioned amendments repealing alcoholic prohibition and an earlier amendment (the Twentieth, also adopted in 1933) moving up the times that newly elected presidents and members of Congress assumed office. This reduced the time period during which so-called lame-duck representatives, who had not been reelected to office, could propose and adopt legislation. The amendment also provided for cases in which a president or vice president died between election and inauguration. Franklin Roosevelt's threat to "pack" the Supreme Court in 1937 was followed by a turnaround in judicial doctrine—"the switch in time that saved nine"—that made many proposed amendments approving the increased national powers associated with the New Deal unnecessary.

Democrat Franklin D. Roosevelt was the first president to break the tradition that limited a president to two terms, and Republicans were especially frustrated and outraged by the long period of Democratic dominance. In a move that some later regretted in the aftermath of the popular presidencies of Republicans Dwight D. Eisenhower and Ronald Reagan, Republicans succeeded in getting the Twenty-second Amendment ratified in 1951. It limited future presidents to two full terms or no more than ten years in office.

Ever since the adoption of the Fourteenth Amendment, there had been questions about which provisions of the Bill of Rights were intended to apply to the states. During the 1960s the Supreme Court nearly completed the job of applying all these provisions (especially those related to the rights of individuals accused of crimes) to the state governments. In addition, three amendments were ratified in the 1960s. The Twenty-third Amendment, adopted in 1961, allowed the District of Columbia to be represented in the electoral college, giving it a number of votes equivalent to that of the smallest states and raising the total number of electoral votes to 538. The Twenty-fourth Amendment, ratified in 1964, abolished the poll tax in national elections. With increased concern over dangers to presidential life and health at a time when presidents could have to decide whether to respond to attacks through use of nuclear weapons, the Twenty-fifth Amendment, ratified in 1967, further provided for cases of presidential disability and for the replacement of vice presidents who died in office.

The Twenty-sixth Amendment, given impetus by the war in Vietnam where many American young people were serving and dying, was adopted in 1972. It lowered the voting age to eighteen. In a previous decision in *Oregon v. Mitchell* (1970), the U.S. Supreme Court had decided that the portion of a congressional law seeking to lower the voting age in state as well as in federal elections was unconstitutional. If uniformity were to be attained, this amendment thus became a virtual necessity.

The requisite number of states did not ratify amendments proposed from this time period to provide equal rights for women (1972) or to grant the District of Columbia voting representation in Congress (1978). In the former case, the proposal failed even after Congress extended its original seven-year deadline. Women proceeded to make dramatic legal gains through the adoption of other legislation at both the state and national levels and through more generous judicial constructions of their rights under the equal protection clause of the Fourteenth Amendment.

No deadline had accompanied one of the twelve amendments originally proposed as the bill of rights (the other, which dealt with the size of Congress, has never been adopted). Largely through the efforts of a Texas student named Gregory Watson, this amendment was resurrected and ratified in 1992 as the Twenty-seventh Amendment in a time of growing distrust of Congress. Dispute continues as to whether it was appropriate for states to add their ratifications to an amendment that many had assumed to have been dead, but the case for the amendment was somewhat bolstered by the fact that no states appear to have attempted to rescind their ratifications during the long period throughout which it was subject to ratification. This amendment provided that laws varying the compensation of members of Congress could not go into effect without an intervening election.

Individual members of Congress have proposed more than 11,000 amendments since the writing of the U.S. Constitution. The states have never succeeded in calling a constitutional convention to propose amendments, and Congress has proposed only thirty-three amendments by the requisite two-thirds majorities of both houses. The twenty-seven amendments

that have been adopted stand as testimony to the fact that amendments are difficult but not impossible to enact. The difficulty of this mechanism arguably cautions against incorporating unduly prescriptive provisions with short-lived goals within the Constitution. This difficulty has also undoubtedly encouraged other branches, particularly the courts, to interpret the Constitution as a broad charter of government that gives adequate powers to Congress and to other branches of the government, while still recognizing the existence and importance of key individual rights.

See also names of individual amendments, for example, First Amendment and Second Amendment.

❖ *HOLLINGSWORTH V. VIRGINIA* (1798) ❖

The Supreme Court heard the case of *Hollingsworth v. Virginia* after ratification of the Eleventh Amendment. The Court was asked to declare that the amendment had not been properly ratified. Opponents argued that Article I, Section 7 required that "every order, resolution, or vote to which the concurrence of the Senate and House of Representatives may be necessary (except on a question of adjournment) shall be presented to the President of the United States," and the president had not signed this measure. The Court was also asked to rule that, if the amendment had been ratified, it should have only a prospective effect, not applying to cases that had been brought before its adoption.

The Court unanimously rejected both arguments, with Justice Samuel Chase responding to attorneys' arguments by saying that the presidential veto applied "only to the ordinary cases of legislation" and that the president "has nothing to do with the proposition, or adoption, of amendments to the Constitution" (*Hollingsworth* 1798, 382).

Professor David Currie noted that, in dismissing a suit seemingly still authorized by Section 13 of the Judiciary Act of 1789 (now thought to be superseded by the Eleventh

Amendment), the Court anticipated the exercise of judicial review of federal legislation that is more commonly traced to the Supreme Court's 1803 decision in *Marbury v. Madison* (Currie 1985, 22). In arguing that an extension of the Equal Rights Amendment ratification deadline required a two-thirds vote of Congress and presidential approval, Yale's Charles Black (1978) warned against any further extension of the *Hollingsworth* precedent regarding the need for presidential signatures.

Although his signature was not required, President James Buchanan signed the proposed (but ultimately unsuccessful) Corwin Amendment, which was designed to head off civil war by guaranteeing the continuing existence of slavery in those states that still wanted it. This may have been the reason that Abraham Lincoln later added his signature to the Thirteenth Amendment abolishing slavery, even though it was not required. Complaining that it had not been submitted to him for signature, President Andrew Johnson proclaimed the validity of the Fourteenth Amendment (Ishikawa 1997, 590). President Lyndon Johnson later had a special ceremony in which he signed as a witness that the Twenty–fifth Amendment, relating to presidential disability and vice-presidential succession, had been ratified, and President Jimmy Carter signed the resolution extending the ratification deadline for the Equal Rights Amendment (Ishikawa 1997, 590). Other presidents who did not formally sign documents have, of course, worked for the adoption of amendments that have been proposed and/or ratified. In one such dramatic act, President Woodrow Wilson addressed Congress on behalf of the adoption of the Nineteenth Amendment.

For Further Reading:

Hollingsworth v. Virginia, 3 U.S. (3 Dall.) 379 (1798).

Ishikawa, Brendon T. 1997. "Everything You Always Wanted to Know about How Amendments Are Made, but Were Afraid to Ask." *Hastings Constitutional Law Quarterly* 24 (Winter): 545–597.

❖ HOPKINS, CASPAR (1826–1893) ❖

Caspar Hopkins was a "pioneer, businessman, author, and former president of the California Immigration Union" (Vile 1991c, 38). He published an article in 1885 advocating a series of ten constitutional amendments (Hopkins 1885). Some of the proposals were unique to Hopkins, but others reflected themes common to his era.

In Hopkins's first two proposals, he called for authorizing Congress to legislate on civil matters such as "marriage, divorce, inheritance, probate proceedings, modes and subjects of taxation, education, the tenure of real estate, and the collection of debts" (Hopkins 1885, 388). He also proposed to clarify congressional jurisdiction "over interstate commerce and communication, and the exclusive regulation of banks, insurance companies, and all other corporations which transact business in more than one State or Territory" (Hopkins 1885, 388). Similarly, state powers would be curtailed in these areas.

Hopkins's third proposal called for increasing federal judicial jurisdiction over all claims against the United States. He would also have invested courts with the power to settle contested elections or cases involving the qualifications of legislators. His fourth proposal called for restricting congressional authority to the adoption of general or public measures, thus eliminating private bills.

Like Woodrow Wilson, Hopkins favored a system whereby the president could appoint cabinet members from the majority party in Congress. This was his fifth proposal. His sixth would have required legislators to undergo special education in colleges specifically designed for the purpose.

Although sentiment was already growing for a system of direct election of senators (which would eventually result in the adoption of the Seventeenth Amendment), in his seventh proposal, Hopkins took a different approach. He advocated recognizing the inevitable influence of wealth by limiting the right to vote for senators to those who had paid taxes on $100,000 or more of their incomes.

Hopkins's eighth and ninth proposals dealt with immigrants and Native Americans. He favored limiting immigration to foreigners with a certain level of education, skills, or property and limiting voting to natural-born citizens. Hopkins wanted to abolish programs that treated American Indians differently from other groups.

Finally, Hopkins proposed a number of changes relative to terms of office. Under his scheme, senators would serve for ten years, the president for eight, and members of the House for six. No executive officers—presumably including the president—with the power of patronage would be eligible for reelection. Hopkins would further eliminate the electoral college and establish two or three vice presidents in case both the president and the first vice president were disabled.

Hopkins believed that the weight of inertia was working against his proposals. He feared that a convention would be "full of peril and probabilities of failure," in part because "the country is full of communists, socialists, advocates of woman suffrage, agrarians, and cranks, whose every effort would be concentrated upon such an opportunity to realize their peculiar views in the fundamental law" (Hopkins 1885, 898).

For Further Reading:
Hopkins, Caspar T. 1885. "Thoughts toward Revising the Federal Constitution." *Overland Monthly* n.s. 6 (October): 388–398.

Vile, John R. 1991c. *Rewriting the United States Constitution: An Examination of Proposals from Reconstruction to the Present.* New York: Praeger.

❖ HOUSING ❖

Unlike many constitutions that were formulated in the two centuries that followed its adoption, the U.S. Constitution confines itself to the protection of political rights and leaves economic and social rights largely to the political process. Although both state and national governments have made periodic attempts to provide housing for those in need, the right to housing has never been considered to be an entitlement (Salins 1987, 176).

In July 1993 Democratic Representative Charles Rangel of New York introduced an amendment designed to guarantee "that all U.S. citizens shall have a right to decent and affordable housing, which shall not be denied or abridged by the United States or any State" (H.J. Res. 64). Representative Jesse Jackson Jr. has since supported a similar proposal. Given the failure of the Constitution to recognize other economic rights, the short-term prospect for such an amendment appears dim.

See also Social and Economic Rights.

For Further Reading:
Salins, Peter D., ed. 1987. *Housing America's Poor.* Chapel Hill, NC: University of North Carolina Press.

❖ HUBBELL, JANETTE ❖

See Dolbeare, Kenneth, and Janette Hubbell.

I

❖ *IDAHO V. FREEMAN* (1981) ❖

One of the most fascinating cases involving the constitutional amending process emerged from the controversy over the proposed Equal Rights Amendment (ERA). Judge Marion Callister from the U.S. District Court in Idaho delivered the verdict in *Idaho v. Freeman.*

A number of Idaho and other state legislators argued that Idaho's rescission of its prior ratification of the ERA was constitutional, that Congress had no right to extend the ERA deadline, and that, in any case, such an extension would have required a two-thirds rather than a simple majority vote. Callister agreed with all three contentions. His ruling was, however, stayed by the U.S. Supreme Court and eventually mooted by the failure of the necessary number of states to ratify the ERA, despite the deadline extension.

The most extended portion of Callister's decision, which relied heavily on the district court decision written by John Paul Stevens in *Dyer v. Blair* (1975), had to do with whether the questions the legislators raised were political questions and therefore inappropriate for judicial resolution. In *Coleman v. Miller* (1939), the Supreme Court had suggested that many amending issues, and specifically the matter of whether amendment ratifications were made contemporaneously, were committed to congressional, rather than judicial, resolution. After reviewing the criteria established in *Baker v. Carr* (1962) for deciding whether issues were political questions, Callister decided that they were not present in this case. He argued

that the Constitution had divided amending powers between Congress and the states rather than granting them exclusively to the former. Moreover, he decided that precedents surrounding the adoption of the Fourteenth Amendment had not yet established the right of a state to rescind ratifications. Callister believed that such issues "must be interpreted with the kind of consistency that is characteristic of a judicial, as opposed to political [congressional] decision making" (*Idaho* 1981, 1139).

Callister settled on a contemporary consensus model similar to the one the Court had articulated in *Dillon v. Gloss* (1921), but arguably since called somewhat into question by the belated ratification of the Twenty-seventh Amendment. Under this contemporary consensus model, he decided that, prior to ratification by three-fourths of the states, a state's last action—whether ratification or rescission—should prevail. Callister further ruled that although Congress was not required to set a ratification deadline, once it did so, it would have to abide by it, because states may have ratified an amendment contingent on their understanding that other states would have to ratify within that limit. In any case, Callister believed that the congressional extension of the ERA deadline had been unconstitutional because Congress could act in such circumstances only in its Article V rather than its Article I capacity, and Article V referred only to actions by two-thirds of that body.

Although this decision hardly settles the issues addressed, *Idaho v. Freeman*, like *Dyer v. Blair,* could undercut *Coleman v. Miller* by providing precedents for judicial resolution of amending issues.

See also *Coleman v. Miller; Dyer v. Blair;* Equal Rights Amendment.

For Further Reading:

Carroll, John. 1982. "Constitutional Law: Constitutional Amendment. Rescission of Ratification. Extension of Ratification Period. *State of Idaho v. Freeman.*" *Akron Law Review* 14 (Summer): 151–161.

Idaho v. Freeman, 529 F. Supp. 1107 (1981).

❖ IMPEACHMENT ❖

Article I, Section 2 of the U.S. Constitution vests the House of Representatives with the power of impeachment, or the power to bring charges against appointed governmental officials. Article II, Section 4 specifies "Treason, Bribery, or other high Crimes and Misdemeanors" as the exclusive grounds for impeachment. Article I, Section 3 further provides that trials of impeachment take place before the Senate; if the president is on trial, the chief justice presides. Conviction of any officer requires a two-thirds vote and results in removal from office. As of 2000, seventeen persons, including twelve lower federal judges, one Supreme Court justice, one cabinet member, one senator (whom the Senate decided not to try), and two presidents have been impeached (Grossman and Yalof 2000, 7); obviously, not all have been convicted.

The meaning of the term "high Crimes and Misdemeanors" remains the subject of popular and scholarly discussion, with most scholars believing that the term refers either to illegal or quasi-illegal acts, typically involving abuse of power. A number of amendments have attempted to alter or clarify this process. Two proposals were introduced in 1913 by Ohio congressmen. One, offered by Democrat Atlee Pomerene, would have provided for a method other than impeachment for removing civil officers other than the president, the vice president, and members of the Supreme Court. A second, proposed by Republican Leonard

Howland, would have allowed for trials of all except top officials by twelve senators. In 1945 Republican Senator William Langer of North Dakota proposed that a vote by a majority of senators present should be sufficient for an impeachment conviction.

Former Democratic Senator Howell Heflin of Alabama introduced a number of amendments on the subject. One would have allowed Congress to remove judges from office for inability to perform their duties, as well as for infractions of the law; this proposal would also have suspended officers indicted for felony offenses. A more detailed proposal offered by Heflin would have provided for a seven-member judicial inquiry commission to discipline judges guilty of violating canons of judicial ethics and to suspend or place on senior status judges unable to perform their duties. A number of recent proposals have also provided that judges would lose their offices immediately upon conviction of a crime.

Such proposals may have been prompted in part by late-twentieth-century cases of impeachment involving U.S. District Judges Harry E. Claiborne, Alcee L. Hastings, and Walter L. Nixon (Abraham 1998, 48–49; Volcansek 1993). Claiborne refused to resign after being convicted of felonies and imprisoned. Hastings was elected to the House of Representatives after being impeached and convicted. Like Claiborne, Nixon refused to resign from office after being convicted, in his case, of perjury. Nixon objected to the procedure by which a committee of the Senate heard his case in 1989 before the full Senate voted to convict him. In *Nixon v. United States* (1993), the Supreme Court upheld the Senate conviction on the basis that Article I, Section 3 of the Constitution vested the Senate with "the sole Power to try all Impeachments," thus implying that matters of procedure were "political questions" for the Senate to resolve.

Although President Richard M. Nixon resigned from the presidency after it became clear that the House of Representatives was likely to accept charges of obstruction of justice, abuse of powers, and failure to turn over papers to investigators that would lead to his conviction in the Senate, only two presidents, Andrew Johnson and Bill Clinton, have actually been impeached. It is generally agreed that the impeachment of Johnson was largely partisan and that the charges against him (falling a single vote shy of the necessary two-thirds needed to convict in the U.S. Senate) did not rise to the level of "high crimes and misdemeanors."

Because the event is so contemporary, debate continues to swirl around the appropriateness of the charges that were brought against President Clinton, but for which he was not convicted and removed from office. The president's defenders claim that he was targeted by right-wing opponents simply for improper sexual behavior with a White House intern. Opponents claimed that this offense against propriety had been compounded by attempts to cover the matter up (thus obstructing justice) and lying to a grand jury. One contemporary author has suggested that future impeachment prosecutions for sexual matters might be avoided if the Constitution were to be amended so as to include the four words in the original draft of the Constitution—"against the United States"—after the words "high crimes and misdemeanors" (Germond and Witcover 1999, 296).

Two other authors, concerned about ambiguities and problems that appeared during the Clinton impeachment, have proposed a far more complex amendment divided into seven sections, some of which incorporate existing language and others of which plough new ground (Grossman and Yalof 2000). The first section would exempt members of Congress, who may already be removed from office by a two-thirds vote of their colleagues, from impeachment and would limit charges to "serious abuses of official power that undermine their conduct of office and threaten the integrity and legitimacy of the government. Such abuses include treason, bribery, and other serious crimes, as well as actions that are not criminal in nature" (Grossman and Yalof 2000, 17). The second section, which would continue to require the chief justice to preside in the case of a trial of the president (but would, by omission, apparently leave open the possibility that a vice president could continue to preside over his or her own trial) would require conviction of two-thirds of the entire Senate membership and would limit impeachments to a biennial Congress and prevent them from taking place "between a general election and the convening of a new Congress" (*Id.*). Section three, reacting to the Supreme Court's decision in *Clinton v. Jones* (1997) permitting the president to be sued in office for alleged sexual harassment he had committed as a state governor, would further prohibit the president from being the subject of a civil suit while in office but would allow Congress to lengthen the statute of limitations in such cases. Section four would allow Congress power "[t]o censure, rebuke, or otherwise publicly condemn official misconduct" and would further allow it to "devise alternative means, other than impeachment, for dealing with the disability, misconduct, or failure to maintain good behaviour, of federal judges other than justices of the Supreme Court" (*id.*). Section five would prevent the president from issuing a self-pardon. Section 6 would somewhat modify the decision in *Nixon v. United States* by allowing the Supreme Court to exercise its original jurisdiction to review, prior to a Senate trial, "a petition submitted by an impeached president, the procedures employed in, and the constitutional basis of, articles of impeachment voted against the president by the House of Representatives" (*Id.*). Section 7 would extend power to Congress to enforce this provision.

See also Judiciary, Removal of Members.

For Further Reading:

Abraham, Henry J. 1998. *The Judicial Process: An Introductory Analysis of the Courts of the United States, England, and France.* 7th ed. New York: Oxford University Press.

Berger, Raoul. 1973. *Impeachment: The Constitutional Problems.* Cambridge, MA: Harvard University Press.

Committee on Federal Legislation of the Bar Association of the City of New York. n.d. *The Law of Presidential Impeachment.* New York: Harrow Books.

Germond, Jack W., and Jules Witcover. 1999. "After the Trial, Revisions Are in Order," *National Journal* 31 (January 30): 296.

Grossman, Joel B., and David A. Yalof. 2000. "The Day After: Do We Need a 'Twenty-Eighth' Amendment?" *Constitutional Commentary* 17 (Spring): 7–17.

Posner, Richard A. 1999. *An Affair of State: The Investigation, Impeachment, and Trial of President Clinton.* Cambridge, MA: Harvard University Press.

Volcansek, Mary L. 1993. *Judicial Impeachment: None Called for Justice.* Urbana, IL: University of Illinois Press.

❖ IMPLEMENTATION DATES OF AMENDMENTS ❖

Amendments are generally forward-looking, applying to the future rather than the past, but some amendments, like the Thirteenth Amendment and the Eighteenth Amendment, which respectively make slavery and the sale or consumption of alcohol illegal, prohibited widespread conduct that was previously considered legal, if not always acceptable. The Articles of Confederation, which required unanimous consent, was proposed in 1777 but did not go into effect until Maryland ratified in 1781. Although they did not designate a specific date, the writers of the U.S. Constitution specified in Article VII that it would go into effect when ratified by nine of the states. Article V now specifies that amendments proposed by two-thirds majorities in Congress or by conventions do not become law until ratified by three-fourths of the states. With problems of implementation in view, the authors of a number of amendments have gone further by designating the time period when they would go into effect.

Although when adopted the Thirteenth Amendment did not provide for a phase-in period for the elimination of slavery, many of the framers of the Constitution appeared to hope that the institution would die out on its own, and a number of previous writers on the subject of slavery had specified a period, often a generation or two in the future, when abolition might go into effect. The Seventeenth Amendment, which provided for the direct election of U.S. Senators, specified that it "shall not be so construed as to affect the election or term of any Senator chosen before it becomes valid as part of the Constitution." The Eighteenth Amendment, providing for national alcoholic prohibition, specified that it would take effect "[a]fter one year from the ratification of this article . . ." (by contrast the Twenty-first Amendment, which repealed the Eighteenth, apparently went into effect immediately). The Twentieth Amendment, relating to terms of Congress, specified that those provisions would "take effect on the 15th day of October following the ratification of this article." The Twenty-second Amendment, which limited presidential terms, provided that it would not "apply to any person holding the office of President when this Article was proposed by the Congress" (at that time Harry Truman was president) and that it would "not prevent any person who may be holding the office of President, or acting as President, during the term within which this Article becomes operative from holding the office of President or acting as President during the remainder of such term." Perhaps anticipating that the amendment might require fairly significant changes in legislation, the proposed Equal Rights Amendment had a provision specifying that it "shall take effect two years after the date of ratification." Many versions of the Balanced Budget Amendment that were proposed in the 1990s provided that it would go fully into effect either two years after ratification or after 2002, whichever came later. Similarly, the proposed Victims' Rights Amendment provides that it would take effect "on the 180th day after the ratification of this article," presumably to give the national government and the states, as well as prosecutors' offices, time to take appropriate implementing actions.

❖ IMPLIED POWERS ❖

See *McCulloch v. Maryland.*

❖ INCORPORATION ❖

Of all the twentieth-century developments in constitutional interpretation, none has been more important than the "incorporation" of prominent provisions of the Bill of Rights into the due process clause of the Fourteenth Amendment. Through this process, such rights now apply to the states as well as to the national government. Prior to the Civil War, Chief Justice John Marshall ruled in *Barron v. Baltimore* (1833) that the provisions in the Bill of Rights were intended to limit only the national government.

The language of the Fourteenth Amendment, however, was directed to the states, which were now prohibited from denying the privileges and immunities or the due process rights of their citizens. Most prominently in the *Slaughterhouse Cases* (1873), the Supreme Court initially gave a narrow reading to these clauses, especially the privileges and immunities provision. In 1884, however, Justice John Marshall Harlan wrote a dissent in *Hurtado v. California* (1884), arguing that the due process guarantees in the Fourteenth Amendment were intended to apply provisions of the Bill of Rights—in this case, the provision for indictment by grand jury—to the states. With the possible exception of Fifth Amendment property rights (*Missouri Pacific Railway Co. v. Nebraska* (1896) and *Chicago, Burlington & Quincy Railway Co. v. Chicago* (1897)), the Court majority rejected Justice Harlan's stand. In 1925, however, the Court declared in *Gitlow v. New York* that freedom of speech did apply to the states, and it recognized several other exceptions in subsequent years.

In *Palko v. Connecticut* (1937), Justice Benjamin Cardozo attempted to provide some organizing principle to distinguish those guarantees in the Bill of Rights that were applicable to the states from those—like the Fifth Amendment guarantee against double jeopardy at issue in this case—that were not. He articulated the idea of selective incorporation, by which he suggested that those guarantees in the Bill of Rights that were "implicit in the concept of ordered liberty" would apply to the states, but others would not.

Few cases better exemplify the varied views on incorporation than the case of *Adamson v. California* (1947). At least four different views were articulated there. In refusing to overrule a decision on a case in which a prosecutor had commented on a defendant's failure to testify in his own defense (forbidden in federal cases by the self-incrimination provision of the Fifth Amendment), Justice Stanley Reed restated the view of selective incorporation for the Supreme Court majority. In a concurring opinion, Justice Felix Frankfurter articulated the view that the due process clause required "fundamental fairness" and that such fairness could not be mechanically ascertained simply by determining whether a provision was or was not in the Bill of Rights. Justice Hugo Black, like Justice Harlan before him, argued for total incorporation. As a former U.S. senator, he based his conclusion on his own reexamination of the debates over the Fourteenth Amendment—an argument that Charles Fairman (1949) and other scholars have since disputed, albeit not without generating questions about their own scholarship. Justices Frank Murphy and Wiley Rutledge articulated the view of total incorporation plus—that is, the idea that there may be rights in addition to those in the first ten amendments that apply to the states. This view became even more prominent in the Connecticut birth-control case, *Griswold v. Connecticut* (1965). Rounding out the picture is the position of "selective incorporation plus" (Abraham and Perry 1994, 87).

Although the view of selective incorporation has dominated most Supreme Court decision making, over the course of time the Supreme Court has incorporated more and more guarantees from the Bill of Rights into the due process clause. Today, only five guarantees have not yet specifically been given judicial protection. They are the Second Amendment right to bear arms, the Third Amendment's guarantee on quartering troops, the Fifth Amendment's guarantee of a grand jury indictment, the Seventh Amendment's right to a jury trial in a civil case, and the Eighth Amendment's guarantee against excessive fines and bail (D. O'Brien 2000a, 311). The last case to incorporate a new provision in the Bill of Rights was the decision to apply the protection against double jeopardy in *Benton v. Maryland* (1968).

See also *Adamson v. California; Barron v. Baltimore;* Fourteenth Amendment; *Palko v. Connecticut.*

For Further Reading:

Abraham, Henry J., and Barbara Perry. 1994. *Freedom and the Court: Civil Rights and Liberties in the United States.* 6th ed. New York: Oxford University Press.

Fairman, Charles. 1949. "Does the Fourteenth Amendment Incorporate the Bill of Rights? The Original Understanding." *Stanford Law Review* 2 (December): 5–139.

O'Brien, David M. 2000a. *Civil Rights and Civil Liberties.* Vol. 2 of *Constitutional Law and Politics.* 4th ed. New York: W. W. Norton.

❖ INDIANS ❖

See Native Americans.

❖ INITIATIVE AND REFERENDUM ❖

In *Federalist No. 10* James Madison distinguished a direct, or pure, democracy from an indirect, or representative, democracy (Hamilton, Madison, and Jay 1961, 81–82). Although he defended the latter, there have been many subsequent advocates of more direct democracy. Among their favorite mechanisms are the initiative and referendum. The former mechanism allows citizens to initiate legislation through petitions, and the latter permits citizens to approve or disapprove legislation; sometimes both mechanisms are classified under the single term "referendum" (Schmidt 1989, 3). Such mechanisms are often linked to the recall, by which voters may petition to remove officeholders with whom they are dissatisfied.

Types of Referendums

Referendums can be limited either to legislative or constitutional change. The first American referendum was the 1788 Massachusetts referendum on the state constitution, and although the U.S. constitution makes no such provision, many American states and foreign nations have subsequently adopted a requirement for popular approval of constitutions or of amendments to them. In early 1861 the Senate apparently came but one vote shy of accepting a proposal for a national plebiscite on a series of compromises offered by Senator John J. Crittenden of Kentucky to avoid the Civil War (Shermer 1969, vii). Historically, initiatives and referendums have often been tied to the recall, a mechanism by which voters can demand the ouster of a sitting officeholder.

Direct Democracy's Three Periods of Popularity

A student of direct democracy has identified three periods during which direct democracy was particularly popular at the national level. These are "the populist and progressive movements (1890–1912); . . . the isolationist and peace movements (1914–1940); and . . . the issue activism both of the left and the right (1970–1988)" (Cronin 1989, 164).

The Populist and Progressive Eras

The movement for the initiative and referendum in the Populist and Progressive Eras began in the states, with South Dakota's adoption of this mechanism in 1898 and adoptions in seventeen other states by 1917 (Musmanno 1929, 173). Perhaps because other representative institutions were less developed, this movement was successful primarily in the West and Midwest—a breeding ground for other Progressive Era amendments (Grimes 1978, 65–100). Four-fifths of the states adopting the mechanism were west of the Mississippi River (Schmidt 1989, 10).

As early as 1895, Populist Kansas Senator William Peffer introduced a national amendment to allow submission of important matters to the people upon petition by one-fifth of the voters or one-fourth of the state legislatures (Musmanno 1929, 173). Other contemporary proposals varied the number of voters required to initiate such a petition—a proposal by Wisconsin Democratic Representative Lucas Miller permitted such action by as few as 1,000 inhabitants. Republican Senator Joseph Bristow of Kansas introduced a proposal allowing the president to go over the head of Congress by placing measures that he favored, but that Congress failed to enact, on the ballot (Musmanno 1929, 175).

The National Direct Legislative League was

formed in the 1890s to push for a national referendum. This idea was often favored by Prohibitionists and other third-party representatives. Theodore Roosevelt and Woodrow Wilson both indicated support for such measures (Cronin 1989, 50).

The Isolationist and Peace Movements

The most popular referendum proposal from 1914 to 1940 was the war referendum, or the Ludlow Amendment (after Democratic Representative Louis Ludlow of Indiana), as it was frequently called. The idea actually appears to have originated during the Civil War in a book by Robert E. Beasley (1864) in which he advocated taking a vote on whether the war should be continued. The idea was subsequently stimulated by hopes of keeping the United States out of World War I and by disillusionment with that war and suspicions that it had been engineered by arms dealers.

Such proposed amendments usually specified that, except in cases of invasion, Congress could not declare war or draft citizens until such a proposal was submitted to the people for approval. Influential supporters included Democratic and Populist presidential candidate and Secretary of State William Jennings Bryan and Republican Senator Robert La Follette of Wisconsin. Both, however, subsequently supported Wilson's decision to enter World War I without such a vote (Cronin 1989, 165). In the 1930s the movement for a war referendum received support from sixty-five college and university presidents, the National Education Association, historian Charles Beard, and even Republican Congressman Everett Dirksen of Illinois (Cronin 1989, 169–170).

In 1938 the House of Representatives voted 209 to 188 not to discharge this amendment from committee. Opposition by Franklin D. Roosevelt and the approach of World War II pretty much brought an end to this proposal, although Oregon Republican Senator Mark Hatfield introduced a variant during the Vietnam War.

Issue Activism of the Right and Left

The 1960s and 1970s witnessed renewed support for the idea of a national initiative and referendum from representatives of both the political right and the political left. The movement received support in 1977 when Roger Telschow and John Forster, who had worked with such measures at the state level, founded a lobby group called Initiative America. Democratic Senator James Abourezk of South Dakota and Democratic Representative James Jones of Oklahoma introduced an amendment supported by at least fifty members of Congress. It would have permitted 3 percent of citizens (including at least 3 percent of the voters in ten or more states) to initiate a referendum that would take effect when subsequently ratified by a majority (Cronin 1989, 159). Supporters included consumer advocate Ralph Nader, New York Republican Representative Jack Kemp, columnist Patrick Buchanan, then Democratic (later Republican) Texas Congressman Phil Gramm, California Republican Congressman Barry Goldwater Jr., Oregon Republican Senator Mark Hatfield, economist Arthur Laffer, and a majority of the American people as measured in public opinion polls (Cronin 1989, 173–175). A fair number of scholars also favored this proposal (Berg, Hahn, and Schmidhauser 1976, 190–201; B. Barber 1984, 281–289). As in the past, there was wide variation as to what percentage or regional representation would be needed to propose or approve referendums, 3 and 8 percent being the most common numbers suggested for proposing a referendum.

Most referendum proposals would have exempted issues of constitutional reform or war-making matters, thus somewhat distancing advocates of this period from those of the preceding one. Many proposals would have prevented Congress from modifying laws adopted by referendum for two years, except by an extraordinary majority of two-thirds or three-fourths. Congress held hearings on the subject in 1977.

National Initiative for Democracy

A more recent attempt at national initiative, the National Initiative for Democracy, which is led by a nonprofit organization, Philadelphia II, is designed to allow the public to propose both laws and constitutional amendments. This movement is predicated on the assumption that the American people are already sovereign and that they have the right to bypass both the regularized processes of adopting legislation and amendments. The amendment of eleven sections that the National Initiative supports would eliminate political parties, reduce most electoral terms to one year, allow for initiatives, referendums, and recalls, and abolish the electoral college system and the income tax.

Concerns of Initiative and Referendum Supporters

Advocates of the initiative and referendum often see these mechanisms as a means of bypassing politicians who have lost touch with the people. The same concern has been shared by advocates of congressional term limits. Perhaps illustrating this tie, in 1993 and 1994 Republican Representative Peter Hoekstra of Michigan offered a bill to provide for a national advisory referendum on term limits for members of Congress.

States continue to experiment with initiative and referendum measures. Such state experiences—for example, the successful movement led by Howard Jarvis in 1978 to adopt Proposition 13 to limit California state property taxes and Coloradans' more recent vote (voided in *Romer v. Evans* (1996)) to prohibit all state and local legislation that protects homosexuals (T. Baker 1995a)—have led to speculation about whether conservatives or liberals would be most likely to gain if such mechanisms were adopted. One student of the subject found that the advantage tends to shift from one side to the other, depending on the issue. He therefore concluded that "the referendum is neither an unfailing friend nor an implacable enemy of either left or right" (Ranney 1978, 85).

See also Congress, Recall of Members; Judiciary entries; National Initiative for Democracy, Removal of Members; President, Vote of No Confidence.

For Further Reading:

Barber, Benjamin. 1984. *Strong Democracy.* Berkeley, CA: University of California Press.

Beasley, Robert. 1864. *A Plan to Stop the Present and Prevent Future Wars: Containing a Proposed Constitution for the General Government of the Sovereign States of North and South America.* Rio Vista, CA: Robert Beasley.

Berg, Larry L., Harlan Hahn, and John R. Schmidhauser. 1976. *Corruption in the American Political System.* Morristown, NJ: General Learning Press.

Cronin, Thomas E. 1989. *Direct Democracy: The Politics of Initiative, Referendum, and Recall.* Cambridge, MA: Harvard University Press.

Grimes, Alan P. 1978. *Democracy and the Amendments to the Constitution.* Lexington, MA: Lexington Books.

Ku, Raymond. 1995. "Consensus of the Governed: The Legitimacy of Constitutional Change." *Fordham Law Review* 64 (November): 535–586.

Musmanno, M. A. 1929. *Proposed Amendments to the Constitution.* Washington, DC: U.S. Government Printing Office.

Ranney, Austin. 1978. "The United States of America." In *Referendums: A Comparative Study of Practice and Theory,* ed. David Butler and Austin Ranney. Washington, DC: American Enterprise Institute for Public Policy Research.

Schmidt, David D. 1989. *Citizen Law Makers: The Ballot Initiative Revolution.* Philadelphia: Temple University Press.

Sullivan, J. W. 1893. *Direct Legislation by the Citizenship.* New York: Nationalist Publishing Company.

❖ INSURANCE ❖

From 1905 through 1933 a number of proposals were introduced in Congress either to allow that body to insure the lives of U.S. citizens or to regulate the insurance industry. The latter proposals were undoubtedly stimulated by the unique position that insurance has had in relation to other industries.

Because of the nation's commitment to free enterprise, most life insurance and many other types of insurance are handled by private companies. Initially, states were responsible for most regulation of the insurance industry, and states often discriminated against companies whose headquarters were located in other states. Such regulations were challenged as a violation of the federal commerce power in *Paul v. Virginia*

(1869), but the U.S. Supreme Court rejected this challenge, deciding that insurance policies were not interstate transactions, and state regulation continued until 1944.

In *United States v. South-Eastern Underwriters Association* (1944), in a close four-to-three decision written by Justice Hugo Black, the Supreme Court reversed course and applied the Sherman Antitrust Act (a federal law) to insurance companies that operated across state lines. The following year, Congress responded by passing the McCarran Act. This law left insurance regulation to the states, absent adoption of congressional laws specifically addressed to the insurance industry. The insurance industry thus rather anomalously continues to be exempt from most of the regulations affecting other industries that operate across state lines.

❖ INTERMARRIAGE ❖

Although amendments have been introduced periodically to vest the national government with the power to regulate marriage and divorce (especially to prohibit polygamy and, more recently, to limit recognition of gay marriages), such laws have been almost exclusively left to state regulation. Through most of U.S. history, many states have passed miscegenation laws limiting or prohibiting interracial marriages, especially between whites and blacks.

There have been at least three proposed amendments (1871, 1912, and 1928) to prohibit interracial marriage. The first was introduced by Missouri Democratic Representative Andrew King. The other two were introduced by Democratic Representatives Seaborn Roddenbery and Coleman Blease of South Carolina.

The issue of state miscegenation laws did not reach the U.S. Supreme Court until 1967. The case was called *Loving v. Virginia* and involved Virginia's attempt to punish a white man and a black woman who had married. In its decision, the Supreme Court decided that prohibitions against interracial marriage violated the equal protection clause of the Fourteenth Amendment and were therefore unconstitutional.

See also Marriage, Divorce, and Parenting.

❖ INTERNAL IMPROVEMENTS ❖

Under the general welfare clause in Article I, Section 8 of the Constitution, Congress may tax and spend for the general welfare. In early American history, Republicans often interpreted this provision quite restrictively. Their reading led many to question the legitimacy of federal expenditures on projects such as roads or canals. Presidents Thomas Jefferson, James Madison, James Monroe, Andrew Jackson, and James Polk all either recommended an amendment specifically to authorize federal expenditures of this nature or vetoed congressional laws for such improvements that they thought were directed chiefly to state rather than national interests (Ames 1896, 260–263). On occasion, as in Jackson's veto of the Maysville Road bill (extending a road from Maysville, Kentucky, to Henry Clay's hometown of Lexington), such concerns may also have been tied to partisan considerations (Urofsky 1988, 280). However, few early presidents took the position of John Quincy Adams, who argued for an expansive list of federal domestic expenditures (McDonald 1982, 71).

In the first half of the nineteenth century, a number of congressmen, including future president Martin Van Buren, introduced constitutional amendments to legitimize federal expenditures on internal improvements; others, including Henry Clay and Abraham Lincoln, took the position that such an amendment was unnecessary because the existing Constitution already permitted such expenditures. With the expansion of federal powers over the last century and a half, the issue of federal aid to the states appears to have become chiefly a prudential rather than a constitutional issue.

See also General Welfare.

For Further Reading:

Ames, Herman. 1896. *The Proposed Amendments to the Constitution of the United States during the First Century of Its History.* Reprint, New York: Burt Franklin, 1970.

McDonald, Forrest. 1982. *A Constitutional History of the United States.* New York: Franklin Watts.

Urofsky, Melvin I. 1988. *A March of Liberty: A Constitutional History of the United States.* New York: Alfred A. Knopf.

❖ INTERNET ❖

Recent years have witnessed increased use of, and reliance upon, communications through the Internet. Courts have had to decide the extent to which their jurisdiction extends under this new medium, whose reach often extends across state, and even national, divisions. Indeed, Internet jurisdiction has been likened to that of admiralty law (Ban 1998). In *Reno v. American Civil Liberties Union* (1997), the Supreme Court struck down an attempt to regulate children's access to obscenity under the Communications Decency Act of 1996 as being so broad as to interfere with the legitimate rights of adults.

In addition to the possibility of disseminating pornographic materials, the Internet may present unique opportunities for fraud and for copyright infringements. An author addressing these and related matters has suggested that while Congress can currently exercise regulations under its power to control interstate commerce, such control could be eroded "if future technological breakthroughs make it possible to distinguish between interstate Internet transmissions and purely intrastate Internet transmissions" (Ban 1998, 539). He has proposed that the adoption of an amendment "may be the most impregnable basis upon which to establish such a jurisdiction" (*Id.,* 540).

The advent of the Internet has provided a new forum for individuals to publicize proposals to either amend or rewrite the U.S. Constitution. A number of these proposals are included in this volume.

See also Alternative U.S. Constitutions, Proposed; Obscenity and Pornography.

For Further Reading:

Ban, Kevin K. 1998. "Does the Internet Warrant a Twenty-Seventh Amendment *[sic.]* to the United States Constitution?" *The Journal of Corporation Law* 23 (Spring): 521–540.

Reno v. American Civil Liberties Union, 521 U.S. 844 (1997).

❖ ITEM VETO ❖

See Presidency, Veto Power of.

J

❖ JACKSON, JESSE L., JR. (1965–) ❖

Representative Jesse L. Jackson Jr., son of civil rights leader Jesse Jackson who heads the Rainbow Coalition and Project PUSH and who twice ran unsuccessfully for the Democratic nomination for president, was elected from the Second Congressional District of Chicago, Illinois, in 1995. Jackson graduated from North Carolina A & T State University and earned a degree from the Chicago Theological Seminary and from the Illinois College of Law at Champaign-Urbana.

In a recent book, written with the help of his press secretary, Frank Watkins, Jackson comments on American history from the dual perspectives of race and federalism—the relation between the national government and the states. Jackson further proposes eight constitutional amendments, which he has introduced in Congress. In contrast to existing constitutional provisions, most of Jackson's proposals center on economic and social, rather than purely political rights.

Jackson regards his proposal for a full-employment amendment to be his "most controversial" and "the most important" (Jackson 2001, 253). It is based on the twenty-third article of the United Nations Universal Declaration of Human Rights and would likely require considerable governmental expenditures. The amendment contains five sections. The first provides that "Every citizen has the right to work, to free choice of employment, to just and favorable conditions of work, and to protection against unemployment" (Jackson 2001, 252). The second section focuses on nondiscrimination and on "equal pay for equal work." Section 3 is designed to see that each citizen receives fair remuneration that provides for that worker and the worker's family; commentary explains that Jackson believes this would require raising the minimum wage. Section 4 provides for an explicit right to form and join trade unions (Jackson opposes "right to work" laws that enable individuals not to join unions at their places of employment, thus permitting individuals who are not members to get benefits that the unions have won). Section 5 is a congressional enforcement mechanism that is added to each of Jackson's proposals (Jackson 2001, 252).

Jackson's second proposal calls for provision of "health care of equal high quality" for all American citizens (Jackson 2001, 285). Again, Jackson believes the government should be willing to commit substantially more resources to health care than it currently does. Jackson believes the details of this and other amendments would have to be left to political processes, but his next proposal for "decent, safe, sanitary, and affordable housing without discrimination" does not contain a similar equality clause (*Id.*, 300). The proposal for a "right to a public education" does specify that it should be "of equal high quality" (*Id.*, 330), although by way of explanation Jackson suggests that the amendment would provide for "a high minimum state floor" rather than a ceiling (*Id.*, 348).

Jackson also proposes an Equal Rights Amendment, to go into effect two years after being ratified (Jackson 2001, 350), but he does not engage in this chapter in the current discussion as to whether the original proposal could be ratified without being reintroduced in Congress. Jackson proposes an environmental amendment that would guarantee each citizen the right to enjoy "a clean, safe, and sustainable environment" (*Id.,* 371), and he includes a copy of The People's Earth Charter as an appendix to his book.

The Sixteenth Amendment to the U.S. Constitution permits an income tax, but does not require that it be progressive, taxing incomes of individuals with higher incomes at higher percentages. Jackson's next proposal would change this. It provides that, "The Congress of the United States shall tax all persons progressively in proportion to the income which they respectively enjoy under the protection of the United States" (Jackson 2001, 385). Jackson is very concerned about current disparities in income and wealth in the United States, and he believes this amendment is part of the remedy. Despite the wording of the amendment, Jackson's commentary suggests that the amendment would also apply to state taxation, which he regards as more regressive than that at the federal level (*Id.,* 403).

Although a number of constitutional amendments relate to voting rights, Jackson would state such provisions affirmatively rather than negatively. His longest amendment, with five sections is called the Proposed Voting Rights Amendment. The first section guarantees the right to vote in public elections to all who are eighteen years of age or older. The second section provides that Congress will establish electoral standards to be reviewed each year. Section 3 would provide for "the opportunity to register and vote on the day of any public election." Section 4 provides for election by majority vote within each state or district, and Section 5 is the familiar enforcement provision (Jackson 2001, 425). Jackson uses the 2000 presidential election as an example of what can happen when votes are cast and counted without adequate federal safeguards and supervision, although he does not appear to be calling for an outright rejection of the current electoral college system. Jackson does think that a system of proportional representation, which would give representation to minor parties, would be preferable to a system like that utilized in the current U.S. House of Representatives, which is composed of single-member districts. He also favors instant runoff voting (IRV), in which individuals indicate their second and third choices for office, allowing votes cast for third-party candidates to be aggregated with those at the top of the ticket in the major parties. Jackson is also concerned about the large number of ex-felons who are currently excluded from voting in many of the states and thinks the Democratic Party would profit from running an African American candidate for vice president.

Jackson appears to favor aspirational amendments that would give increased power to federal courts to intervene on behalf of those who are not currently treated equally. He is often vague about the specific repercussions of his amendments, believing that over time they could result in increased standards. His proposals are among the most comprehensive set of social and political rights to be offered by any modern American writer and are especially relevant given Jackson's seat in Congress and his ties to his father.

See also Social and Economic Rights.

For Further Reading:

Jackson, Jesse L., Jr., with Frank E. Watkins. 2001. *A More Perfect Union: Advancing New American Rights.* New York: Welcome Rain Publishers.

❖ JAMESON, JOHN A. (1824–1890) ❖

John Jameson practiced law in Chicago and served for eighteen years as a judge in the chancery division of Cook County (Malone 1961, 5:601). In 1867 he published the first edition of a work on constitutional conventions, released in a number of subsequent editions (Jameson 1887), that proved to be extremely influential. Stimulated in part by the movement for Southern secession and in part by claims by leaders of state conventions that such bodies were sovereign, Jameson was intent on establishing that a constitutional convention was subject to legal restraints.

Jameson identified four types of conventions: "the spontaneous convention, or public meeting"; "the ordinary legislative convention, or general assembly"; "the revolutionary convention"; and the "constitutional convention" (Jameson 1887, 3–4). Jameson was especially concerned with distinguishing the revolutionary convention, or the provisional government that bridges the gap from one form of government to another, from the constitutional convention, which, he argued, was "subaltern" and "never governs" (*Id.*, 10). Thus domesticated, a constitutional convention was unlikely to pose a threat to existing governments.

Jameson's treatment of more general amending controversies repeated familiar themes. Arguing that amending mechanisms were "in the nature of safety valves," he argued that such provisions needed "to reconcile the requisites for progress with the requisites for safety" (Jameson 1887, 549). Jameson believed that the methods of proposing amendments by conventions and by general assemblies were "of about equal authority," although he speculated that "as our Constitutions become riper and more perfect with time and experience, the necessity of employing the more expensive mode by Conventions will be found to be less and less" (*Id.*, 551–552). Jameson also suggested that the convention method was more suitable for major revisions and the method of legislative proposal more appropriate for less drastic alterations. He further argued that Sidney George Fisher had been mistaken in believing that a system of legislative sovereignty would have prevented the Civil War (*Id.*, 567).

In addressing specific amending issues, Jameson suggested that states had the power to ratify amendments they had previously rejected but not to rescind ratifications once given. He doubted, however, that such ratifications were perpetually valid. Arguing that "an alteration of the Constitution has relation to the sentiments of to-day," he said that, if not ratified in a timely fashion, an amendment "ought to be regarded as waived, and not again to be voted upon, unless a second time proposed by Congress" (Jameson 1887, 634). On this basis, Jameson questioned Ohio's 1873 ratification of what in 1993 putatively became the Twenty-seventh Amendment.

For Further Reading:

Jameson, John A. 1887. *A Treatise on Constitutional Conventions: Their History, Powers, and Modes of Proceeding.* 4th ed. Chicago: Callaghan and Company.

Malone, Dumas, ed. 1961. *Dictionary of American Biography.* 10 vols. New York: Charles Scribner's Sons.

❖ JEFFERSON, THOMAS (1743–1826) ❖

Born in Albemarle County, Virginia, in 1743, Thomas Jefferson was more receptive to the idea of change than most Americans and did much to bring it about. Jefferson was the chief author of the Declaration of Independence, the nation's first secretary of state, its second vice president, and third president. Some of Jefferson's most important pronouncements are found in letters to friends, especially his Virginia neighbor and political ally James Madison. Jefferson was more democratic and far bolder than Madison, and his thoughts generally ranged over much wider territory; Madison's thoughts were arguably both more cautious and deeper.

The view of revolution that Jefferson set forth in the Declaration of Independence was, however, moderate. Jefferson argued not for revolution upon slight provocation but for revolution after "a long train of abuses and usurpations." He noted that "governments long established should not be changed for light and transient causes" (Vile 2001, 272–273). However, at a later time, when leading Americans nearly panicked over Shay's Rebellion, Jefferson—then in France—took a more positive view. He argued that "a little rebellion now and then is a good thing, and as necessary in the political world as storms in the physical" (Jefferson 1905, 5:256). Moreover, he said that "the tree of liberty must be re-

freshed from time to time with the blood of patriots and tyrants. It is its natural manure" (*Id.*,
5:362). Faced with a more serious revolution in
France, Jefferson was, however, more cautious.
Writing to Lafayette in 1814, he urged the revolutionaries to "be contented with a certain
portion of power, secured by formal compact
with the nation, rather than grasping at more,
hazard all upon uncertainty, and risk meeting
the fate of their predecessor" (*Id.*, 11:456).

Jefferson at once expressed faith in the people's ability to make constitutional changes and
a belief, perhaps best articulated in the Declaration of Independence, that there were certain
natural rights that were morally beyond majority control. In authoring his Bill for Establishing Religious Freedom, one of three accomplishments that he asked be recorded on his
gravestone at Monticello (the other two were
his writing of the Declaration of Independence
and the founding of the University of Virginia),
Jefferson noted that a declaration of irrevoca-
bility would not be legally binding. He
nonetheless went on to declare that "the rights
hereby asserted are of the natural rights of
mankind, and . . . if any act shall be hereafter
passed to repeal the present or to narrow its operations, such act will be an infringement of
natural rights" (Jefferson 1905, 2:441). In addition to his other writings, Jefferson wrote the
initial draft for governing the Northwest Territory, including a provision that would ban slavery there after 1800 (Foner and Garraty 1991,
796). As is now well known, Jefferson was himself a slaveholder who died without having the
financial means to free his own slaves and
whose behavior on the subject is often difficult,
if not impossible, to reconcile with his words.

Jefferson was serving as a diplomat in France
when the Constitutional Convention of 1787
was meeting. Although he subsequently favored the Constitution as a whole, he strongly
believed that a bill of rights was needed to
complete the framers' work. His correspondence with Madison on the subject is often
credited with helping to persuade the latter of
the advisability of such protections. Madison
later repeated some of Jefferson's arguments
when advocating the Bill of Rights on the floor
of the House of Representatives (Mason and

Stephenson 2002, 421–423). Ironically, one of
Jefferson's arguments for such a bill of rights
was that, by being placed in the Constitution,
such rights would be enforced by the judiciary.
Later, however, Jefferson became concerned
that John Marshall and his Federalist allies on
the Supreme Court were using such power to
sap democratic institutions. When the Federalists adopted the Alien and Sedition Acts of
1798, the latter of which restricted freedom of
speech, Jefferson took action. Together with
James Madison, the other acknowledged leader
of the opposition Democratic-Republic Party,
Jefferson helped author the Kentucky Resolution (Madison had authored a corresponding
Virginia Resolution) in which he urged states
to "interpose" themselves against unconstitutional federal legislation, and arguably helped
pave the way for the more extreme views of
states' rights that would follow.

Jefferson respected those who had authored
his state's constitution during the Revolution,
but he warned against looking at this or any
other such constitutions "with sanctimonious
reverence" or deeming them to be "too sacred
to be touched" (Jefferson 1905, 12:11). Perhaps because of both his negative experiences
at the hands of the Federalist-dominated Marshall Court and his recognition of how difficult
it was to channel power within constitutional
guidelines, Jefferson feared that the Constitution could be modified by liberal construction
rather than by appeals directly to the people.

In the controversy over the constitutionality
of the national bank, which had been advocated by Treasury Secretary Alexander Hamilton, approved by George Washington, and
later confirmed by the U.S. Supreme Court decision in *McCulloch v. Maryland* (1819), Jefferson relied heavily on the as yet unratified Tenth
Amendment, which spoke of powers reserved
to the states. He took the view that because
such a power was not listed among the powers
of Congress it could not be created under the
existing Constitution.

The election of 1800 helped trigger the
Twelfth Amendment, which modified the electoral college. Because presidential electors did
not initially distinguish between their choices
for president and vice president, Jefferson and

his running mate Aaron Burr ended up in an electoral tie in the presidential election of 1800 (Vile 2002b, 30). This tie was not resolved until thirty-six ballots in the lame-duck Congress, and not until his longtime adversary Hamilton had supported Jefferson over Burr—who later killed Hamilton in a duel. The Twelfth Amendment, adopted during Jefferson's first term, provided that electors would subsequently cast separate ballots for president and vice president, with the House of Representatives choosing from the top three candidates in case no candidate received a majority.

Because of his stance against broad constructions of national powers, Jefferson's opponents chastised him for the most daring and far-sighted act of his administration—namely the purchase of the Louisiana Territory, which also required deficit spending (H. Adams 1974, 1:165–172). This purchase was not directly sanctioned in the Constitution, and Jefferson would have preferred to get approval from an amendment for his action, but he feared that the delay might scuttle the deal, and he proceeded without such specific constitutional authorization. Similarly, Jefferson exercised broad powers later in his second administration when he authorized an embargo against England in the ultimately fruitless hope of avoiding war, which occurred during the administration of his immediate successor, James Madison. Jefferson followed and further entrenched George Washington's practice of not running for a third presidential term, a practice that continued until the administration of Franklin D. Roosevelt and that has subsequently been embodied in the Constitution through passage of the Twenty-second Amendment.

Of all of Jefferson's writings, perhaps none has provided more support for would-be constitutional reformers than a phrase he coined in a letter to James Madison in 1789. There, Jefferson introduced the principle "'*that the earth belongs in usufruct to the living*'; that the dead have neither powers nor rights over it" (Jefferson 1905, 6:3–4). From this principle, Jefferson suggested that every debt and, indeed, every constitution should be renewed every nineteen years.

The more sober-minded Madison, ever concerned about the effect that frequent changes might have on popular appreciation for the Constitution, subjected this proposal to withering criticism, some of which found its way into *Federalist No. 49*. Despite this critique, Jefferson continued to advocate his view. In a letter in 1813, Jefferson repeated his idea that each generation "has . . . a right to choose for itself the form of government it believes most promotive of its own happiness" and that, accordingly, "for the peace and good of mankind . . . a solemn opportunity of doing this every nineteen or twenty years should be provided by the constitution" (Jefferson 1905, 12:13). In this letter, Jefferson noted that "we might as well require a man to wear still the coat which fitted him when a boy, as civilized society to remain ever under the regimen of their barbarous ancestors" (*Id.*, 12:12).

At the national level, Madison's view of cautious constitutional change has dominated. Purposely or otherwise, many states have come closer to the idea that each generation should be able to incorporate its own views into or indeed rewrite its own constitution (Vile 1992, 72–74).

Jefferson died at Monticello on 4 July 1826, fifty years to the day after the adoption of the Declaration of Independence. In a development that convinced many people that divine providence was at work, Jefferson's co-revolutionary, John Adams, with whom Jefferson had had a strained relationship through their two presidencies, but with whom correspondence and friendship had later been resumed, died on the same day.

See also Declaration of Independence; Louisiana Purchase; Madison, James; Virginia and Kentucky Resolutions.

For Further Reading:

Adams, Henry. 1974. *The Formative Years*, ed. Herbert Agar. 2 vols. Westport, CT: Greenwood Press.

Cunningham, Noble E. 1987. *The Pursuit of Reason: The Life of Thomas Jefferson*. Baton Rouge: Louisiana State University Press.

Foner, Eric, and John A. Garraty, eds. 1991. *The Reader's Companion to American History*. Boston: Houghton Mifflin Company.

Jefferson, Thomas. 1905. *The Works of Thomas Jefferson,* ed. Paul Leicester Ford. 12 vols. New York: G. P. Putnam's Sons, Knickerbocker Press.

Mason, Alpheus T., and Donald G. Stephenson Jr. 2002. *American Constitutional Law: Introductory Essays and Selected Cases.* 13th ed. Englewood Cliffs, NJ: Prentice-Hall.

Mayer, David N. 1994. *The Constitutional Thought of Thomas Jefferson.* Charlottesville: University Press of Virginia.

Vile, John R. 2002a. *A Companion to the United States Constitution and Its Amendments.* 3d ed. Westport, CT: Praeger.

———. 2002b. *Presidential Winners and Losers: Words of Victory and Concession.* Washington, DC: Congressional Quarterly.

———. 1992. *The Constitutional Amending Process in American Political Thought.* New York: Praeger.

❖ JEFFS, DANIEL B. ❖

Daniel B. Jeffs has outlined his view on direct democracy and direct education in a book entitled *America's Crisis,* which chiefly outlines what he regards as the flaw of existing American governments. Jeffs portrays himself as a modern-day Thomas Paine, and his book is a follow-up to an earlier pamphlet, "The Truth; the 28th Amendment," published under the name "John Citizen" and advocating interactive television ties to voters homes (see Jeffs 2000, 36–37 for further description). The back cover of *America's Crisis,* which chiefly focuses on problems in contemporary American government, identifies Jeffs as the founder of The Direct Democracy Center with "an extensive investigative background in the criminal justice system" who has run for local office and "holds a law degree and teaching credentials." The text of the book itself indicates that Jeffs "was a career cop" and that, although "I worked with prosecutors, and then defense attorneys, . . . I simply could not be one of them" (Jeffs 2000, 35).

Jeffs has created a website, *www.realdemocracy.com,* in which he has proposed both a twelve-section amendment to implement his plans and a petition whereby individuals "peti-

tion" and "demand" that their representatives work toward this plan. On his website, Jeffs notes that, "In the tradition of the simplicity of the U.S. Constitution, it would be simple to amend a constitution by just writing: 'The government of the United States, and the several states, shall be a nonpartisan direct democracy through established voting networks connected to voters' homes.'" He immediately adds however, that "Unfortunately, if left to the Congress, the Presidency and the Supreme Court, they would soon dilute it out of existence in the same ways they have perverted the U.S. Constitution." Jeffs's amendment is labeled the "Nonpartisan Direct Representative Democracy Government Electorate Voting Networks and Education Networks." The first section of the amendment specifies that the national government and that of the states should be "nonpartisan direct representative democracy government" embodied "through the equality of citizenship." The section states Jeffs's intention "for the electorate to have and maintain absolute control of government and education" and to require "truth and accountability to the electorate from all elected representatives and all government employees."

Section 2 provides that, within four years after ratification, a system of "direct representative democracy" will be established using "electorate voting networks of interactive electronic devices between elected representatives of all levels of government and the homes of the electorate." This section further specifies that "all elected representatives shall be nonpartisan," and it provides for annual confirmation or rejection "by majority vote of the electorate."

Section 3 would further enhance direct democracy by allowing the electorate "to instruct, direct and control all levels of government through their elected representatives by majority vote," with "all elections, recall elections, initiatives and referendums" to "be conducted by means of the electorate voting network."

Section 4 extends direct democracy to members of all U.S. courts and to all cabinet posts and agency heads at both state and national levels. Section 5 repeals the Twelfth Amendment (and presumably other provisions of the Constitution that helped establish the electoral college) and provides for annual direct confirmation or rejection of the president and vice president. Section 6 further repeals the Sixteenth Amendment and the national income tax, which his book identifies as "the gravest mistake the American people ever made" (Jeffs 2000, x).

In a provision that might lead to gridlock, Section 7 provides that "All matters of public policy and taxation shall require a two-thirds majority of the electorate voting." The electorate would also be vested with amending both state and national constitutions by a two-thirds majority vote. Judges would also be subject to electoral recall.

Section 8 moves to Jeffs's second emphasis, namely education. All citizens will be provided with "direct education by interactive electronic devices" in their homes. Section 9 further provides that this education, initially conducted by the government, will subsequently be contracted out to private institutions. It also provides that "quality choice in education shall be provided to all citizen students through means tested vouchers," and that "no student shall be excluded for lack of funds" from education to include the first four years of college. Section 10 further provides that the federal Department of Education "under the direction and control of the electorate" shall set minimum national standards, which states will be free to raise if they choose. The Federal Communications Commission would be entrusted with "the public communication function of direct education."

Section 11 provides that the provisions of the amendment will supersede any conflicting provisions of the Constitution. Section 12 further provides that within four years of establishing voting networks, the people will be given the opportunity of either confirming or repealing "each law, or group of laws, by majority vote." (This section is missing from Jeffs's book, where the text of the amendment is found on pp. 304–307.)

The themes of this amendment harken back to state practices prior to the adoption of the U.S. Constitution for annual elections, to the reservations that many of the American founders had about political parties, through the increasing emphasis on direct democracy of the Jacksonian era, and the provisions of direct democracy (the initiative, referendum, and recall) advocated by the populists and the progressives. Overlaying all these ideas is the idea that direct democracy may be inaugurated through forms of communication that were not previously available. Jeffs's proposal is clearly a departure from the vision of representative democracy advocated by James Madison and the other founders. If adopted, this set of amendments would be likely to obliterate the current distinctions between U.S. representatives and senators and would undoubtedly affect the independence of members of all three branches of government, including the president and members of the judiciary, and it could have similar consequences at the state level.

Jeffs's educational proposals are somewhat more difficult to assess. They would embody education as a constitutional right, but such a right might be meaningless if the necessary two-thirds of the voters failed to adopt taxes necessary to support it or if judges felt too beholden to popular wishes to support the right. Jeffs's is one of a number of new voices calling for more direct democracy in the United States; significantly, his website contains links to "Philadelphia II" and its plans for "Direct Democracy" as well as to other sites advocating the initiative and fair taxation.

See also Education, Right to; Initiative and Referendum; Madison, James.

For Further Reading:

Jeffs, Daniel B. 2000. *America's Crisis: The Direct Democracy and Direct Education Solution*. Amherst Junction, WI: The Hard Shell Word Factory.

"The Direct Democracy Center." At *www.realdemocracy.com*. Accessed 11/26/02.

❖ JOINT RESOLUTION ❖

Although members of Congress occasionally introduce amendments in the form of simple resolutions in a single house, the great majority of amendments in both houses are introduced as joint resolutions. This joint resolution mechanism appears to be dictated by the fact that amendments require approval by a two-thirds vote of both houses of Congress before they are sent to the states, three-fourths of which are required for ratification.

Although it often deals with somewhat narrower matters, a joint resolution has been described as "for all intents and purposes the same as a bill" (Schneier and Gross 1993, 125). Unlike other joint resolutions, resolutions proposing amendments do not require the president's signature (*Hollingsworth v. Virginia* (1798)). Joint resolutions are designated as H.J. Res. or S.J. Res. and are numbered consecutively in each house in the order they are introduced within each two-year congressional session (Kravitz 1993, 139).

For Further Reading:
Kravitz, Walter. 1993. *American Congressional Dictionary.* Washington, DC: Congressional Quarterly.

Schneier, Edward V., and Bertram Gross. 1993. *Legislative Strategy.* New York: St. Martin's Press.

❖ JUDICIAL INTERPRETATION ❖

See Constitutional Interpretation.

❖ JUDICIARY, ADVISORY OPINIONS BY ❖

Ever since the first Supreme Court headed by John Jay declined President Washington's request to define rights under a U.S. treaty, U.S. constitutional courts have declined to issue such advisory opinions. Early in the New Deal, the Supreme Court exercised a fairly obstructionist role, voiding a number of Franklin D. Roosevelt's major programs. Two members of Congress introduced resolutions in 1935, one of which was reintroduced in 1937, that would have required the Supreme Court, when so requested by the president or a set majority of Congress, to issue such an opinion.

In 1934 Congress had already adopted the Federal Declaratory Judgment Act, permitting the Court to issue declaratory judgments in some cases. Like advisory opinions, such judgments are nonbinding, but unlike advisory opinions, they involve real disputes between specific individuals. Professor Henry J. Abraham observed that "the line between advisory opinions and declaratory judgments is a thin one" (1998, 393).

For Further Reading:
Abraham, Henry J. 1998. *The Judicial Process: An Introductory Analysis of the Courts of the United States, England, and France.* 7th ed. New York: Oxford University Press.

❖ JUDICIARY, AGE LIMITS FOR MEMBERS ❖

The judicial branch is the only one for which the U.S. Constitution makes no provision for a minimum age (Vile and Perez-Reilly 1991). Moreover, because federal judges are appointed "during good behavior," they may serve until they are quite old without ever facing voters' judgment of their competency for continued service.

A few proposals have been introduced in Congress that would have required a minimum age for judges and justices (often from thirty to forty). Others would have required that judges have a minimum number of years of legal practice or experience in other courts. Such provisions have typically been introduced as parts of amendments designed to change the current method of judicial selection.

There have been many more proposals (often as part of amendments that also would have applied to members of Congress and other officeholders) to limit the age of sitting judges or require a mandatory retirement age. This practice is followed in many states, and has been upheld against equal protection claims by the U.S. Supreme Court in *Gregory v. Ashcroft* (1991). The most frequently proposed ages range from sixty-five to seventy-five. A proposal advanced in 1937 to require retirement of Supreme Court justices at the age of seventy-five had scholarly and congressional support and might have been adopted had it not been opposed by President Franklin D. Roosevelt, who was concerned with more immediate problems and was pushing for his own "court-packing" plan. This plan, designed to get the Supreme Court to line up behind the New Deal, called for adding one new justice (up to fifteen) for every justice over the age of seventy who remained on the Court (Garrow 2000, 1019–1026). Congress rejected this plan, which would also have enabled the president to appoint additional judges to the lower courts, but it did provide a fairly generous retirement package so that judges would not be forced to continue in office simply for financial reasons.

The American Bar Association, supported by former Supreme Court Justice Owen J. Roberts, launched another such proposal designed to insulate the Supreme Court from future political conflicts (including congressional attempts to trim its appellate jurisdiction) from 1946 to 1955. The U.S. Senate voted positively on this proposal by a vote of fifty-eight to nineteen in 1954. However, this effort was stymied by intense opposition among some members of Congress to the Supreme Court's decision in *Brown v. Board of Education* (1954) mandating desegregation in the field of education (Garrow 2000, 1028–1043). Yet another campaign for an amendment or bill that would have provided for judicial removal or impeachment in cases of mental incapacity was launched, with support from Georgia Democratic Senator Sam Nunn, from 1974 to 1980, but it too proved unsuccessful (Garrow 2000, 1057–1065).

There is reason to believe that mandatory retirement limits might have a significant impact on the composition of the courts, many of whose members continue to serve until reaching an advanced age. Thus, of the 100 Supreme Court vacancies from 1789 to 1994, 48 were created by death in office (Abraham 1998, 44). Moreover, other justices have retired from the Court only after extensive periods of disability (Cooper and Ball 1996, 354–368). Modern commentators are divided as to whether a constitutional amendment is needed, with David Garrow favoring an amendment and pointing to numerous cases throughout American history where he believes justices have served

while they were mentally impaired, and David Atkinson believing that stories of judicial impairment have been exaggerated and that this is a problem that justices can handle on their own (Atkinson 1999).

See also Court-Packing Plan.

For Further Reading:

Abraham, Henry J. 1998. *The Judicial Process: An Introductory Analysis of the Courts of the United States, England, and France.* 7th ed. New York: Oxford University Press.

Atkinson, David N., 1999. *Leaving the Bench: Supreme Court Justices at the End.* Lawrence, KS: University Press of Kansas.

Cooper, Phillip, and Howard Ball. 1996. *The United States Supreme Court from the Inside Out.* Upper Saddle River, NJ: Prentice Hall.

Garrow, David J. 2000. "Mental Decrepitude on the U.S. Supreme Court: The Historical Case for a 28th Amendment." *University of Chicago Law Review* 67: 995–1087.

Gregory v. Ashcroft, 501 U.S. 452 (1991).

Mauro, Tony. 2001. "The Age of Justice." *American Lawyer* 23 (March): 67.

Vile, John R., and Mario Perez-Reilly. 1991. "The U.S. Constitution and Judicial Qualifications: A Curious Omission." *Judicature* 74 (December-January): 198–202.

❖ JUDICIARY, COMPENSATION OF MEMBERS ❖

In an attempt to preserve executive independence, Article II, Section 1 of the Constitution prevents Congress from increasing or diminishing a president's pay during his or her term of office. The Twenty-seventh Amendment now prevents congressional salaries from being raised or lowered prior to an intervening election.

Because judges serve "during good behavior," which effectively means until they die, retire, or are impeached and convicted, their salaries could be eroded by inflation during their service. Article III, Section 1 of the Constitution thus allows Congress to raise, but not to lower, the salaries of judges during their terms of office. In the process of ratifying the Constitution, Virginia and North Carolina proposed that periodic increases or decreases in judicial salaries be enacted as part of more general salary regulations (Ames 1896, 153). No subsequent proposals have addressed this topic, although the subject of judicial raises is periodically the focus of political disputes. In *Atkins v. United States* (1976), the Supreme Court denied review of a lower court decision that had dismissed a claim that the salaries of judges had been unconstitutionally reduced because salaries had not kept up with inflation, but it subsequently ruled in *United States v. Will* (1980) that, while Congress could withhold promised pay raises, it could not roll back such raises that had already been given.

For Further Reading:

Ames, Herman. 1896. *The Proposed Amendments to the Constitution of the United States during the First Century of Its History*. Reprint, New York: Burt Franklin, 1970.

❖ JUDICIARY, COURT OF THE UNION ❖

Although the issue of judicial review of congressional legislation receives the majority of scholarly attention, the Supreme Court's exercise of judicial review of state laws might be just as important, if not more so. The Supreme Court exercised this power as early as 1810 *(Fletcher v. Peck)*, and it often met with stiff resistance from proponents of states' rights.

One of the problems, particularly during the Marshall Court, was that proponents of states' rights thought that the Supreme Court was biased toward federal powers, just as state courts might be biased toward their own. There were a handful of proposals in the nineteenth century, at least two during the period of Reconstruction, to create a special tribunal to resolve questions of conflict between state and national powers. A proposal introduced in 1821, apparently stimulated by the Supreme Court's nationalistic opinion in *Cohens v. Virginia* of that year (Levy 1995, 435), would have had the Senate, whose members were then appointed by state legislatures, serve as the appellate review body for such cases. A proposal submitted in 1867 would have vested this power in a court consisting of one member from each state (Ames 1896, 163).

Reaction to decisions by the Warren Court—especially regarding state legislative apportionment—stimulated renewed attention to this issue in the early 1960s. Among three proposals introduced and adopted at the December 1962 meeting of the General Assembly of States, sponsored by the Council of State Governments, was a resolution to create a Court of the Union composed of the chief justices of each state's highest court. This court would hear appeals when requested to do so by five noncontiguous states and would be authorized by majority vote to reverse Supreme Court decisions relative to the rights reserved to the states under the Tenth Amendment.

Alabama, Arkansas, Florida, South Carolina, and Wyoming subsequently requested a constitutional convention to deal with the topic, and at least fifteen proposals for an amendment were introduced in Congress from 1963 to 1981. South Carolina Senator Strom Thurmond appears to have been the first to introduce this proposal. This, and other proposals by the Council of State Governments, encountered considerable scholarly opposition, one scholar referring to calls for a Court of the Union as "patently absurd" (C. Black 1963, 957).

See also Council of State Governments.

For Further Reading:

Ames, Herman. 1896. *The Proposed Amendments to the Constitution of the United States during the First Century of Its History*. Reprint, New York: Burt Franklin, 1970.

Black, Charles L., Jr. 1963. "The Proposed Amendment of Article V: A Threatened Disaster." *Yale Law Journal* 72 (April): 957–966.

Levy, Leonard W. 1995. *Seasoned Judgments: The American Constitution, Rights, and History*. New Brunswick, NJ: Transaction Publishers.

❖ JUDICIARY, EMERGENCY REPLACEMENT OF MEMBERS ❖

All federal judges and justices are nominated by the president and confirmed or rejected by the U.S. Senate. Although there was an apparent attempt against the life of Justice Stephen Field in the nineteenth century, to date Supreme Court justices have been relatively unknown to the general public and no Supreme Court justice has ever been assassinated (John Grisham's novel *The Pelican Brief* is based around such an event), but, as in the case of Congress, the threat of terrorism always poses the possibility that multiple members could be killed or disabled simultaneously. Recent confirmations of Supreme Court justices, which now regularly involve televised congressional hearings, have sometimes been highly partisan, and they can be lengthy and contentious. A blue-ribbon panel being formed in 2002 by the American Enterprise Institute and the Brookings Institution, two Washington think tanks, for the purpose of holding hearings to examine the replacement of multiple members of Congress in such an emergency also has plans to address this issue as well (personal e-mail correspondence with John C. Fortier, of the American Enterprise Institute, dated 11 June 2002). It is quite possible that a constitutional amendment addressing one or the other or both such issues could be the result.

See also Congress, Emergency Functioning.

❖ JUDICIARY, EXERCISE OF JUDICIAL REVIEW BY ❖

Of all the powers exercised by U.S. courts, none is more important than their exercise of judicial review. This power enables them to declare laws passed by the state legislatures or by Congress, or actions taken by the executive or governmental agencies, to be unconstitutional and hence void. The power of judicial review is not specifically stated in the Constitution, but it was forcefully asserted by Chief Justice John Marshall in *Marbury v. Madison* (1803), who

defended it as a way of ensuring the supremacy of the written constitution over popular willfulness. Such review distinguishes the U.S. system from systems of parliamentary sovereignty, under which decisions of the legislative branch are final.

Although the power of judicial review is consistent with a system providing for checks and balances, it pits the judgment of the only unelected branch of the government against the judgment of the people's elected representatives. This presents what one prominent scholar described as "the counter-majoritarian difficulty" (Bickel 1986, 16–22). Judicial review also continues to spark controversy over the appropriate level of judicial activism or restraint—generally interpreted to mean deference to legislative judgments (Halpern and Lamb 1982; Wolfe 1991)—and helps fuel continuing controversies over questions of constitutional interpretation.

Many of the amending proposals that were introduced in the nineteenth century relative to the judiciary dealt with judicial jurisdiction. The Eleventh Amendment was the most visible and, to date, the only successful proposal designed specifically to limit judicial jurisdiction. A member of Congress introduced a proposal in the December–January session of the 1846–1847 Congress to take away the courts' power to declare laws unconstitutional, but proposals aimed specifically at judicial review are more characteristic of the twentieth century. The Progressive Era, the years surrounding the Court's historic "switch in time that saved nine" in 1937, and the 1960s and 1970s mark the greatest activity in this area. Most proposals did not call for the complete elimination of judicial review but would have limited its exercise by requiring supermajorities of the Supreme Court to act before it invalidated laws. In 1912 Republican Representative Fred Jackson of Kansas thus proposed that when any U.S. court declared a law to be invalid, three-fourths of the state legislatures should then decide on the law's validity (H.J. Res. 351). Numerous proposals have also been introduced to allow Congress to override judicial exercises of its review power.

At least three proposals introduced during the Progressive Era would have required the concurrence of all but two of the Supreme Court justices to declare laws to be unconstitutional. Another proposal from this period would simply have invested Congress with the power to specify the majority on the Court that would be necessary to invalidate such legislation. Republican Senator Joseph Bristow of Kansas introduced another proposal that would have submitted exercises of judicial review to voters, who would be able to reverse such decisions by a majority referendum.

A far greater number of proposals emerged during the New Deal, especially around the time of Franklin D. Roosevelt's court-packing plan. These ranged from giving explicit constitutional recognition to the right to judicial review, to eliminating the power altogether, to providing (as in proposals from the Progressive Era) for supermajority votes, most commonly set at two-thirds.

Beginning in 1958 and reaching a peak in the late 1960s, members of Congress again began introducing amendments to limit judicial review. Louisiana Democratic Representative John Rarick introduced a proposal in 1967 (H.J. Res. 384) that would have limited the power of judicial review to the Supreme Court. It would further have required a unanimous verdict in cases in which the Court decided to void a law. Far more common were proposals to require a two-thirds vote either of the Supreme Court's entire membership or of those voting in a given case. A variation introduced by Republican Representative Jesse Younger of California (H.J. Res. 173) in 1967 would have allowed a two-thirds majority of Congress to limit the power of judicial review. More recently, professor John Kincaid has proposed that the Supreme Court should have to muster a three-fourths vote to "void a state law or local ordinance" (Kincaid 1989, 36). Kincaid believed that such a change—it is not altogether clear whether he thought this would or would not require a constitutional amendment—was necessary to preserve federalism against erosion. He noted that state powers could not currently be taken away by amendment without a similar consent of three-fourths of the states themselves. Although such proposals helped register dissatisfaction with the scope of Supreme Court decision making, particularly during the New Deal and the Warren Court years, to date, none has proved successful.

See also Congress, Overriding Judicial Decisions; Constitutional Interpretation; Court-Packing Plan.

For Further Reading:

Bickel, Alexander. 1986. *The Least Dangerous Branch: The Supreme Court at the Bar of Politics*. 2d ed. New Haven, CT: Yale University Press.

Halpern, Stephen C., and Charles M. Lamb, eds. 1982. *Supreme Court Activism and Restraint*. Lexington, MA: Lexington Books.

Kincaid, John. 1989. "A Proposal to Strengthen Federalism." *The Journal of State Government* 62 (January/February): 36–45.

Wolfe, Christopher. 1991. *Judicial Activism: Bulwark of Freedom or Precarious Security?* Pacific Grove, CA: Brooks/Cole.

❖ JUDICIARY, JURISDICTION OF ❖

Article III, Section 2 of the Constitution outlines the jurisdiction of—that is, the types of cases to be heard by—the federal courts. In a few cases, the Supreme Court exercises original jurisdiction and hears cases for the first time, but in most instances, its jurisdiction is appellate. In such cases, it reviews the judgments of lower federal courts or decisions reaching a state's highest court that involve questions of federal law or constitutional interpretation (Abraham 1998, 189–192).

From the beginning, many advocates of states' rights feared the exercise of federal judicial power and sought to curb it. After the Supreme Court's decision in *Chisholm v. Georgia* (1793), the states succeeded in adopting the Eleventh Amendment, which modified Article III so as to preclude the Court from accepting cases brought against a state by citizens of another state without the defendant state's consent. A number of other proposals designed to clip federal jurisdiction were introduced from 1800 to 1810, but apart from a few proposals designed to provide for an alternative tribunal to adjudicate cases between the states and the national government, the remaining amending proposals—including one that would have repealed the Eleventh Amendment—actually sought to expand federal jurisdiction.

Twentieth-century proposals to alter judicial jurisdiction have varied. They include an attempt in 1901 to extend such jurisdiction to matters involving the use of water, attempts in the second decade to limit federal jurisdiction over matters involving corporations (considered to be citizens under the terms of the Fourteenth Amendment), and limits on the Court's exercise of judicial review of state and federal legislation.

From a somewhat different perspective, individuals who fear that congressional power might be used to undermine individual rights have proposed to limit congressional authority under Article III to make exceptions to and provide regulations for the Supreme Court's appellate jurisdiction. One proponent of the latter amendment was onetime Supreme Court Justice Owen Roberts (R. Smith 1987, 268).

Democratic Representative Robert Sikes of Florida introduced a resolution in 1959 (H.J. Res. 201) prohibiting the Supreme Court from being able to "overrule, modify, or change any prior decision of that Court construing the Constitution or Acts of Congress promulgated pursuant thereto." Given the many times that the Court has made such reversals, often in important cases (Ernst 1973), such an amendment could have a major impact on judicial decision making and might well prompt state legislators and members of Congress to introduce more changes through the amending mechanism.

See also Eleventh Amendment; Judiciary, Court of the Union; Judiciary, Exercise of Judicial Review by.

For Further Reading:
Abraham, Henry J. 1998. *The Judicial Process: An Introductory Analysis of the Courts of the United States, England, and France.* 7th ed. New York: Oxford University Press.

Ernst, Morris L. 1973. *The Great Reversals: Tales of the Supreme Court.* New York: Weybright and Talley.

Smith, Rodney K. 1987. *Public Prayer and the Constitution: A Case Study in Constitutional Interpretation.* Wilmington, DE: Scholarly Resources.

❖ JUDICIARY, LIMITS ON TAXING POWER ❖

On 20 April 1990, Missouri Republican Senator John Danforth introduced an amendment (S.J. Res. 295) with more than twenty-five cosponsors. It was designed to prohibit federal courts from ordering the laying or increasing of taxes. The Senate conducted hearings on the subject in June 1990, and the amending proposal was reintroduced in 1991 and 1992.

Senator Danforth and others were apparently prompted by a Supreme Court decision rendered on 18 April 1990 in *Missouri v. Jenkins,* a desegregation case. The supervisory U.S. district court had initially ordered the Kansas City, Missouri, school district to double property taxes to pay for the construction of magnet schools designed to hasten desegregation. The U.S. Court of Appeals subsequently ruled that, rather than ordering this levy itself, the court could simply order a lifting of state restrictions on such taxes and let the Kansas City school district come up with its own funding.

In upholding this less intrusive approach, the Supreme Court rested its decision on the principle of comity, or respect for state and local initiatives, rather than on constitutional grounds. Writing for the five-person Court majority, Justice Byron White asserted, however, that "a court order directing a local government body to levy its own taxes is plainly a judicial act within the power of a federal court" (*Missouri* 1990, 55). In a vigorous opinion concurring in the result, Justice Anthony Kennedy disagreed. He argued that "today's casual embrace of taxation imposed by the unelected, life-tenured Federal Judiciary disregards fundamental precepts for the democratic control of public institutions" (*Missouri* 1990, 58–59).

One of the last-minute modifications to the Senate version of the balanced budget amendment that came but a single vote shy of adoption in March 1995 was a provision by Democratic Senator Sam Nunn of Georgia that would have provided that "the judicial power of the United States shall not extend to any case or controversy arising under this Article except as may be specifically authorized by legislation adopted pursuant to this section." Nunn's concern suggests that the issue raised by *Missouri v. Jenkins* is still viable.

For Further Reading:
Missouri v. Jenkins, 495 U.S. 33 (1990).

❖ JUDICIARY, NUMBER OF SUPREME COURT JUSTICES ❖

Article III of the U.S. Constitution mentions the Supreme Court but does not specify how many justices it should have. In the Judiciary Act of 1789, Congress set this number at six, but the number alternated between five and ten before Congress settled on nine justices in 1869 (Barnum 1993, 202). In his court-packing plan of 1937, Franklin Roosevelt proposed adding one justice (up to fifteen) for each justice who remained on the Court over the age of seventy. Ultimately defeated in Congress, this plan prompted a score of proposals from 1937 through the 1950s to set the number of justices permanently at nine.

Such proposals sometimes contained other provisions for mandatory retirement of justices at a certain age or specifying that an extraordinary majority would be needed to declare laws unconstitutional. In the Eighty-Third Congress (1953–1954), the Senate voted fifty-eight to nineteen to accept a proposal sponsored by Republican Senator John Marshall Butler of Maryland (S.J. Res. 44) designed to safeguard judicial independence by fixing the number of justices at nine and adopting a number of other reforms. These included setting a compulsory retirement age of seventy-five, making justices ineligible to run for president or vice president, and preventing Congress from being able to alter the appellate jurisdiction of the Supreme Court ("Composition and Jurisdiction" 1953, 1106).

See also Court-Packing Plan.

For Further Reading:
Barnum, David G. 1993. *The Supreme Court and American Democracy.* New York: St. Martin's Press.
"Composition and Jurisdiction of the Supreme Court—Proposed Constitutional Amendment." 1953. In *Congressional Record.* U.S. Senate, 16 February, 1106–1108.

❖ JUDICIARY, OFFICEHOLDING BY MEMBERS ❖

There is some evidence that the framers of the Constitution may have anticipated fairly close ties between the executive and judicial branches of government. Thus, although Article I, Section 6 prohibits members of Congress from holding other offices, it contains no such prohibition for judges and justices (Scigliano 1994, 278).

Especially in early American history, members of the judiciary were sometimes appointed to serve on diplomatic missions or asked to perform other public duties. Even into the twentieth century, Justice Robert Jackson served as the chief U.S. prosecutor at the Nazi war crime trials in Nuremberg, and Chief Justice Earl Warren headed the commission that bore his name and that investigated the assassination of President John F. Kennedy. Justice Abe Fortas's continuing service as an adviser to President Lyndon Johnson was, however, one of the factors that ultimately led to his resignation from the Court (B. Murphy 1988, 114–140), and experience suggests that modern justices are likely to keep informal contacts with the executive at arm's length.

In addition to serving in executive offices, some justices have harbored presidential aspirations. John McLean, who served on the Supreme Court from 1830 to 1861, was called the "politician on the Supreme Court" and was mentioned as a possible presidential candidate for more than thirty years (Gatell 1969, 535). Charles Evans Hughes, who served as an associate Supreme Court justice from 1910 to 1916 and as chief justice from 1930 to 1941, resigned as an associate justice in 1916 to challenge Woodrow Wilson for the presidency. William Howard Taft was appointed chief justice of the Supreme Court after having served a term as president—the only individual to serve in both positions. More recently, in a letter released to the public, Franklin D. Roosevelt listed Justice William O. Douglas as a possible vice presidential running mate in 1944 (McCullough 1992, 304–307).

After President Washington appointed Chief Justice Oliver Ellsworth as a commissioner to France, two proposals were introduced in 1800 to restrict judges from serving in dual offices. In the 1870s and again in 1916—the year Justice Hughes ran unsuccessfully for president—proposals were made that would prevent justices from running for president. In the 1950s the Senate voted positively on an amendment that would have included a prohibition on justices' running for president or vice president, among other provisions designed to guarantee judicial independence.

See also Congress, Members' Eligibility for Other Offices.

For Further Reading:

Gatell, Frank O. 1969. "John McLean." In *The Justices of the United States Supreme Court, 1789–1969: Their Lives and Major Opinions.* Vol. 1, ed. Leon Friedman and Fred L. Israel. New York: R. R. Bowker.

McCullough, David. 1992. *Truman.* New York: Simon and Schuster.

Murphy, Bruce A. 1988. *Fortas: The Rise and Ruin of a Supreme Court Justice.* New York: William Morrow.

Scigliano, Robert. 1994. "The Two Executives: The President and the Supreme Court." In *The American Experiment: Essays on the Theory and Practice of Liberty,* ed. Peter A. Lawler and Robert M. Schoefar. Lanham, MD: Rowman and Littlefield.

❖ JUDICIARY, ORGANIZATION OF ❖

On a few occasions, members of Congress have introduced amendments to reorganize the federal judiciary. However, short of abolishing the Supreme Court, an institution for which the Constitution makes explicit provision, there are few alterations in the judicial system that cannot be made by ordinary acts of legislation. Article III, which describes the judiciary, is the briefest of the three distributing articles; the only court it mentions by name is the Supreme Court; and it does not even specify the number of Supreme Court justices.

Much of the current structure of the federal judicial system was established in a series of judiciary acts that were adopted from 1789 to 1925 (Hall 1992, 172–177). President Franklin D. Roosevelt's court-packing plan was a good example of a proposal to alter the judiciary that failed. Proposals for a Court of the Union fall into a similar category.

See also Court-Packing Plan.

For Further Reading:

Hall, Kermit L., ed. 1992. *The Oxford Companion to the Supreme Court of the United States.* New York: Oxford University Press.

❖ JUDICIARY, QUALIFICATIONS OF MEMBERS ❖

Although possession of the LLB or JD degree is "neither a constitutional nor a statutory requirement for appointment" to the federal bench, "custom would automatically exclude from consideration anyone who did not have them" (Abraham 1998, 55). At least one modern scholar has suggested that individuals with other types of professional training should be considered for the Supreme Court (A. Miller 1982, 286). Moreover, there is considerable scholarly debate as to whether prior judicial experience ought to be required of federal judges or Supreme Court justices. Of the first 110 justices, 42, including such luminaries as John Marshall, Joseph Story, Louis Brandeis, and Felix Frankfurter, had no prior judicial experience at all (Abraham 1998, 56–61). The latter justice was a particularly vocal advocate of the view that such previous experience should not be a prerequisite.

In addition to periodic proposals to require that judges be elected, serve for fixed terms, be subject to Senate reconfirmation, or retire at a certain age, the 1960s and 1970s witnessed a number of proposals that would have mandated judicial qualifications. Some such proposals would have required a specified minimum number of years of prior judicial experience; at least one would have required that judges be natural-born citizens thirty years of age or older with a law degree (see, for example, H.J. Res. 325, 1973); and another attempted to guarantee partisan balance on the Supreme Court.

In 1971 Democratic Representative Charles Griffin of Mississippi reintroduced a proposal (H.J. Res. 95) that he had also advocated in 1968 and 1969 prohibiting two justices from the same state from serving on the Supreme Court. Griffin may have been responding in part to President Nixon's 1970 appointment of Harry Blackmun, who, like Chief Justice Warren Burger (whom Nixon had appointed the previous year), was from Minnesota. Nixon nominated Blackmun after failing to get two southerners, Clement F. Haynesworth Jr. and Harold Carswell, confirmed.

For Further Reading:

Abraham, Henry J. 1998. *The Judicial Process: An Introductory Analysis of the Courts of the United States, England, and France.* 7th ed. New York: Oxford University Press.

Miller, Arthur S. 1982. *Toward Increased Judicial Activism: The Political Role of the Supreme Court.* Westport, CT: Greenwood Press.

❖ JUDICIARY, RECALL OF MEMBERS ❖

One of the mechanisms associated with the Progressive Era was that of the recall, by which voters could remove an official by popular vote. Although recalls are more common for elected officials, several members of Congress have introduced amendments providing for the recall of federal judges—as has Daniel B. Jeffs, the author of a recent book proposing to make the United States government more accountable to the electorate. All federal judges are currently appointed and serve "during good behavior," or for life, but since the Jacksonian era, many states' judges have been elected to fixed terms and subject to reelection or rejection. Plans for judicial recall would be likely to increase popular accountability of judges still further but would also likely erode their independence and possibly their willingness to uphold unpopular constitutional provisions.

See also Jeffs, Daniel B; Judiciary, Removal of Members.

❖ JUDICIARY, REMOVAL OF MEMBERS ❖

Currently, the only legal mechanism that is available for removing sitting federal judges is that of impeachment by the House of Representatives and conviction by a two-thirds vote of the Senate. Article II, Section 4 of the Constitution limits impeachable offenses to "Treason, Bribery, or other high Crimes or Misdemeanors." Although this provision guards judges against being removed for political reasons, it leaves no legal means to remove judges who are incompetent.

Throughout U.S. history, members of Congress have introduced proposals to liberalize this process. The first such plan was introduced by Virginia's flamboyant Representative John Randolph, who had helped lead the unsuccessful impeachment effort against Justice Samuel Chase. Randolph's proposal would have enabled the president to remove judges, provided he gave a joint address to both houses of Congress to justify his actions. Members of Congress introduced several other proposals in the next thirty years, with others following in 1850 and 1867.

At least three proposals for removing judges were introduced in 1912. Democratic Senator Henry Ashurst of Arizona appeared to be influenced by contemporary interest in the recall. Tennessee Democratic Representative Cordell Hull introduced the other two resolutions, providing for the removal of inferior court judges by concurrent resolution in Congress.

Proposals for removing judges have been introduced at a fairly steady pace since 1941. Some such proposals would apply only to lower court judges, and others have been directed specifically to members of the Supreme Court. Louisiana Democratic Representative John Rarick introduced a proposal in 1968 (H.J. Res. 1094) that would allow 1 percent or more of the voters of two-thirds of the states to petition for the removal of a Supreme Court justice, which action would be effected by a majority vote at the next congressional election. Florida Republican Louis Frey introduced a resolution in 1976 (H.J. Res. 912) that would have allowed the Senate, with House concurrence, to remove a justice who was unable to perform his or her duties "by reason of a personal mental or physical disability," including "habitual intemperance." This proposal came within a year of the retirement of Justice William O. Douglas, who had remained on the Supreme Court after suffering a debilitating stroke.

Other proposals from this period would have delegated removal powers to the courts themselves, usually subject to review by the U.S. Supreme Court. Still others would have vested this power directly in the High Court.

Many states now provide for disciplinary commissions, often consisting of fellow judges and laypersons, as well as recall elections for judges thought to be incompetent or out of touch (H. Jacob 1995, 195–196). In 1980 Congress adopted the Judicial Councils Reform and Judicial Conduct and Disability Act. It permits judicial councils in the thirteen federal circuits to discipline, but not to remove, lower court judges (Abraham 1998, 44–45).

For Further Reading:

Abraham, Henry J. 1998. *The Judicial Process: An Introductory Analysis of the Courts of the United States, England, and France.* 7th ed. New York: Oxford University Press.

Jacob, Herbert. 1995. *Law and Politics in the United States.* 2d ed. New York: HarperCollins College Publishers.

❖ JUDICIARY, SELECTION OF MEMBERS ❖

The judicial branch is the only branch of the national government whose members are not elected. Instead, under the terms of Article II,

Section 2 of the Constitution, the president appoints judges with the advice and consent, or approval, of the Senate. Although the framers designed this mechanism in large part to insulate judges from the political process, judicial selection and confirmation can be an extremely political process (Massaro 1990), and nomination is certainly no guarantee of confirmation. Thus, as of the end of the Clinton administration, 30 of 144 nominees to the Supreme Court had failed to be confirmed by the Senate (Abraham 1999, 28).

In contrast to the national government, many states either elect judges or use a mechanism, such as the Missouri and California plans, that combines a system of appointment and electoral confirmation (Abraham 1999, 35–39). The movement for judicial accountability was especially prominent in the Jacksonian period and again in the Progressive Era (Tarr 1994, 69). Despite the former movement, there were only four proposed changes in the method of selecting federal judges in the nation's first ninety years (Ames 1896, 146). Since then there have been more than sixty-five such proposals; many seem to coincide with periods in which there was intense opposition to the Court as an institution or strong concern over controversial rulings (Nagel 1965).

The most common proposal calls simply for the election of federal judges and other appointed officeholders, for example, district attorneys, clerks, marshals, revenue collectors, and postmasters. Such elections may be proposed only for members of the Supreme Court, only for members of lower U.S. district and circuit courts, or for both the Supreme Court and the lower courts. Such proposed elections are also frequently tied to judicial terms of from four to twelve years and are sometimes phrased in terms of a recall.

Most proposals calling for the election of Supreme Court justices appear to foresee the creation of nine electoral districts in the United States for such elections. This might increase the role that geographic representation now plays in such appointments, although it might also reduce minority representation on that body. Some proposals also call for changing the current practice by which the president designates the chief justice (Vile 1994b), specifying instead that the justices would choose their own chief (as is the case in many states).

Other proposals, especially prominent in the 1950s and 1960s, would have allowed the president to appoint Supreme Court justices from a list of five nominees selected by the chief justices of state supreme courts. Some other proposals have called for including members of the House of Representatives in the confirmation process. One of the most innovative such proposals, a kind of congressional court-packing plan, was introduced in 1946 by Democratic Senator James Eastland of Mississippi. It would have provided that no president could appoint more than three justices to the Supreme Court and would have required the retirement of any beyond three that had been so appointed. Such vacancies would have been filled by the U.S. House of Representatives, with the representatives of each state having a single vote.

Recent controversies over nominees to the Supreme Court (and long delays in considering nominees to lower federal court positions in both the Bill Clinton and George W. Bush administrations) have rekindled controversies about possible changes in Senate rules, many of which have grown informally over the course of time (Denning 2001), or constitutional alternatives to the current process. Among proposals that would require an amendment are those providing for judicial term limits, for judicial elections, or for raising the current requirement for Senate confirmation to a two-thirds majority of that body (S. Carter 1994, 195–203).

For Further Reading:

Abraham, Henry J. 1999. *Justices, Presidents, and Senators: A History of the U.S. Supreme Court Appointments from Washington to Clinton.* Lanham, MD: Rowman & Littlefield Publishers, Inc.

Ames, Herman. 1896. *The Proposed Amendments to the Constitution of the United States during the First Century of Its History.* Reprint, New York: Burt Franklin, 1970.

Carter, Stephen L. 1994. *The Confirmation Mess: Cleaning Up the Federal Appointments Process.* New York: Basic Books.

Denning, Brannon P. 2001. "Reforming the New Confirmation Process: Replacing 'Despise and Re-

sent' with 'Advice and Consent.'" *Administrative Law Review* 53 (Winter): 1–44.

Massaro, John. 1990. *Supremely Political: The Role of Ideology and Presidential Management in Unsuccessful Supreme Court Nominations.* Albany, NY: State University of New York Press.

Nagel, Stuart S. 1965. "Court-Curbing Proposals in American History." *Vanderbilt Law Review* 18: 925–944.

Tarr, G. Alan. 1994. *Judicial Process and Judicial Policymaking.* St. Paul, MN: West.

Vile, John R. 1994b. "The Selection and Tenure of Chief Justices." *Judicature* 78 (September-October): 96–100.

❖ JUDICIARY, TERMS OF OFFICE ❖

The president appoints federal judges and justices with the "advice and consent," or approval, of the Senate. Such judges and justices serve "during good behavior," which means that they continue in office until they die or resign or until the House of Representatives impeaches and the Senate convicts them of an impeachable offense. By contrast, many state judges are elected by the people or serve fixed terms of office (Glick 1988, 86–98).

Proposals to limit the terms of federal judges date back to 1808 and have been introduced in almost every subsequent decade. Such proposals are often tied to mandatory retirement ages, typically somewhere between sixty-five and seventy-five. In the 1850s and 1860s Andrew Johnson was a prominent proponent of a twelve-year judicial term (Ames 1896, 152).

Proposals for fixed judicial terms have been especially popular from the late 1960s to the present (with close to 200 proposals introduced in this period), but their specific provisions have varied substantially. Some such proposals would apply only to Supreme Court justices, others only to lower federal judges, and still others to both. Although some call for a one-term limit, the overwhelming majority would allow judges to be reappointed or reelected to office. The process of presidential renomination and Senate reconfirmation appears to be the most popular.

As in recent controversies on congressional term limits, no consensus has emerged as to how long such terms should be. Proposals have varied from four to eighteen years (Ross 1990; Levinson 1992). As part of a package of term limits for members of the House and Senate, Democratic Representative Andrew Jacobs Jr. of Indiana introduced a proposal in 1967 that would have prohibited federal judges from serving more than ten out of any twelve years (H.J. Res. 868).

Senate confirmations of Supreme Court justices have become increasingly public affairs (S. Carter 1994), and at least one recent nominee, Justice Clarence Thomas, is reported to have likened his own confirmation to a type of death (Danforth 1994). In such circumstances, there is likely to be substantial opposition to the idea of Senate reconfirmation of sitting judges and justices.

See also Judiciary, Age Limits for Members.

For Further Reading:

Ames, Herman. 1896. *The Proposed Amendments to the Constitution of the United States during the First Century of Its History.* Reprint, New York: Burt Franklin, 1970.

Carter, Stephen L. 1994. *The Confirmation Mess: Cleaning Up the Federal Appointments Process.* New York: Basic Books.

Danforth, John C. 1994. *Resurrection: The Confirmation of Clarence Thomas.* New York: Viking.

Glick, Henry R. 1988. *Courts, Politics, and Justice?* 2d ed. New York: McGraw-Hill.

Levinson, Sanford. 1992. "Contempt of Court: The Most Important 'Contemporary Challenge to Judging.'" *Washington and Lee Law Review* 49 (Spring): 339–343.

Ross, William G. 1990. "The Hazards of Proposals to Limit the Tenure of Federal Judges and to Permit Judicial Removal without Impediment." *Villanova Law Review* 35 (November): 1063–1138.

❖ JURY TRIALS ❖

Article III of the Constitution provides that "the trial of all crimes, except in cases of impeachment; shall be by jury." The Sixth Amendment also guarantees "an impartial jury" in federal criminal cases, and the Seventh Amendment extends this right to federal civil cases involving more than $20. Applying its incorporation doctrine, the Supreme Court has ruled that the Sixth Amendment right to a jury trial in criminal cases applies to the states via the due process clause of the Fourteenth Amendment (*Duncan v. Louisiana*, 391 U.S. 145 (1968)), but it has not extended the Seventh Amendment right in civil trials. With roots deep in English common law, the jury is thought to guarantee fairness; commentators have also long argued that service on a jury provides an education in citizenship (Tocqueville 1969, 270–276; Abramson 1994).

The fact that only a few amending proposals have been introduced relative to the jury system probably indicates that, despite periodic scholarly criticism (Frank 1969, 108–125), the system continues to be held in general favor. Several proposals introduced around the time of the Civil War would have provided jury trials for escaped slaves. In 1948 a proposal was introduced to permit juries of fewer than twelve members in certain cases.

The Constitution does not specify the number of individuals who must sit on a jury, and the Supreme Court has upheld the use of six-member juries in noncapital cases (*Williams v. Florida*, 399 U.S. 78 (1970)). In *Ballew v. Georgia* (1978), however, the Supreme Court struck down the use of a five-person jury. In *Johnson v. Louisiana* (1972) and *Apodaco v. Oregon* (1972), it upheld nonunanimous jury verdicts in noncapital criminal cases, and in *Burch v. Louisiana* (1979), it ruled that six-member juries must vote unanimously to convict (D. O'Brien 2000a, 1069–1074). The judiciary has thus arguably adapted, or en-abled the jury mechanism to adapt, to modern exigencies.

See also Seventh Amendment; Sixth Amendment.

For Further Reading:

Abramson, Jeffrey. 1994. *We the Jury: The Jury System and the Ideal of Democracy.* New York: Basic Books.

Frank, Jerome. 1969. *Courts on Trial: Myth and Reality in American Justice*. New York: Atheneum.

O'Brien, David M. 2000a. *Civil Rights and Civil Liberties*. Vol. 2 of *Constitutional Law and Politics*. 5th ed. New York: W. W. Norton.

Tocqueville, Alexis de. 1835, 1840. *Democracy in America*, ed. J. P. Mayer. Reprint, Garden City, NY: Anchor Books, 1969.

K

❖

❖ KIMBLE V. SWACKHAMER (1978) ❖

Acting as a circuit justice, Chief Justice Rehnquist upheld a four-to-one Nevada Supreme Court decision by refusing to enjoin the placement of an advisory referendum concerning the Equal Rights Amendment on the upcoming Nevada ballot. Rehnquist said that *Leser v. Garnett* (1922) and *Hawke v. Smith (I)* (1920) "stand for the proposition that the two methods for state ratification of proposed constitutional amendments set forth in Art. V of the United States Constitution are exclusive" (*Kimble* 1978, 1387). Rehnquist noted, however, that this referendum was advisory only and thus was little different from a representative seeking advice from his constituents. By contrast, in *Cook v. Gralike* (2001), a majority of the U.S. Supreme Court led by Justice John Paul Stevens decided that a state did not have authority to "instruct" its representatives in the House of Representatives as to how to vote on an amendment or to put a notation on the ballot as to which representatives had followed such instructions.

For Further Reading:
Kimble v. Swackhamer, 439 U.S. 385 (1978).

❖ KIRSTEIN, HERBERT C. ❖

Herbert Kirstein, identified as a former employee of the Central Intelligence Agency, a staff member of the U.S. Senate, and an employee of the U.S. Department of Health and Human Services, has published his proposal for a new constitution in his book *U.S. Constitution for 21st Century and Beyond*. He also maintains a website where this book and various other proposals are available. [Page numbers cited in this essay are taken from the more accessible website rather than from the printed text, from which it now diverges at some points.]

Kirstein's website lists ten objectives of his government. These include a "stronger 'voice' for citizens; knowledgeable national-global leadership; effective management of government; futurized Congress for the 21st Century; law enforcement, security, and justice; tax laws to accelerate economic progress; monetary policy to finance future; stewardship of national resources; accelerated science and technology; and [a] new "Voice of USAMERICA" (italics and capital letters have been omitted). Each of these objectives is described and explained on the website in detail, often accompanied by sharp criticisms of elements of corruption and inefficiency that Kirstein believes pervade the current system.

Kirstein's constitution is divided into eight articles and is considerably more complex than the Constitution of 1787. Article I describes the "Powers of the Citizens." To existing rights of election, Kirstein adds the right of the voters to "enact laws by a national referendum" and "to instruct, remove, or impeach" elected officials" (Kirstein 1994, 14). Citizenship requires an oath or affirmation to abide by the Constitution. Voting is considered to be a duty as well as a right, and citizens can be fined up to $10 an election for not voting. Although Kirstein is interested in giving increased powers to the people, here, as elsewhere in his proposal, he believes that the people need to be better educated. Article I thus includes a proposed "Universal Academy for Freedom and Democracy," which will educate candidates.

Article II deals with legislative powers. In addition to the existing two houses of Congress, Kirstein wants to create what he calls the "Office of the Premiere Legislative Coordinator of Congress" (Kirstein 1994, 16). Elected to office by a plurality of the people from among those who have attained "one (1) of the four (4) highest scores in the National Knowledge Examination for Premiere Legislative Coordinator of Congress," this individual would establish legislative goals and priorities, enhance legislative management, and exercise veto powers over legislation that are currently exercised by the president. The coordinator would serve for renewable six-year terms (*Id.*, 17–18). Senators and members of the House of Representatives would, under Kirstein's system, be expected to pass national examinations, and the length of House terms would be raised to four years (*Id.*, 21). Kirstein further specifies that "[a]ll proposed amendments or other modifications of legislative proposals shall be required to be germane to the subject matter" (*Id.*, 22). Kirstein lists forty-three separate powers that Congress would be able to exercise (*Id.*, 24–28).

Article III describes executive and administrative powers. The president would become the "Chief Executive Officer of the National Executive and Administrative Service" (Kirstein 1994, 28). Like members of Congress, the president would have to qualify by attaining a certain score on the National Knowledge Examination. Once presidents and vice presidents are so qualified, their terms would be raised to six years, but they would remain limited to two terms. The president would direct the National Council for Progress and Security, which is divided into a number of departments, many of which are renamed cabinet departments (*Id.*, 31). These would include a Department for Legislative Affairs; a Department of National Economic Develop-

ment and Progress (along with a Directorate for [the] National Monetary System, which Kirstein believes needs serious reform, a Directorate for [the] National Banking System, a Directorate for National Value and Pricing Systems, a Directorate for National Investment Policy and Systems, and a Directorate for Market Economy and Enterprise Systems); a Department for National Human Work Force and Automated and Robotic Systems (the former Department of Labor, which will in turn be divided into a number of directorates); a Department for Agriculture, Aquaculture, and other Food-production Systems; a Department for Natural Resources; a Department for Environmental Protection, Preservation, and Enhancement; a Department for Advancing Science and Technology; a Department for International Policy and Global Affairs; a Department for Extraterrestrial and Outer Universe Exploration and Developments Programs (formerly NASA); a Department for Advancing the Status of Citizens (with Directorates for profiling population, providing food and nutrition, furnishing health and medical care, and for Education and Enlightenment—providing among other things for tuition-free education); a Department for National Intelligence and Citizen-Information Systems; a Department for Natural Disaster-Recovery Systems; as well as a number of existing departments, for a total of twenty main departments with many subdirectorates. These departments and directorates are described in great detail; in addition, Kirstein indicates his view that the provision of governmental services will often require the use of "quasi-governmental enterprises" (*Id.*, 38).

Article IV describes judicial powers. It would create a National Judicial System for Law and Justice that would be headed by a Supreme Judicial Minister, qualified like other officeholders by examination, and winning a plurality of votes in a national election (Kirstein 1994, 52–53). This minister would serve renewable six-year terms. The minister, rather than the president, would be responsible for nominating members of the judiciary, but they would continue to be subject to Senate confirmation. The judicial branch would include a Ministry for Law Enforcement and Citizen Security that would replace the current Department of Justice. The minister of this Department would be nominated by the Supreme Judicial Minister and confirmed by a majority of Supreme Court justices with the aim of making this individual less political than the current attorney general. The minister "shall be a permanent, career appointment" (*Id.*, 55).

Kirstein would also establish a "National Societal-Clone Prison System," which, except for its population, would mirror the institutions of the large society and would be expected to be self-supporting. The judicial branch would also include a Ministry of Justice to be composed of members of the U.S. Supreme Court and other courts. The minister of justice would be nominated by the supreme judicial minister for law and justice and confirmed by majority vote of U.S. Supreme Court Justices (Kirstein 1994, 57). In addition to passing tests establishing their knowledge, most judges would be required to have at least "10 years of experience in the U.S. judicial system" (*Id.*). U.S. Supreme Court justices would be nominated by the supreme judicial officer of the National Judicial System for Law and Justice and be confirmed by the Senate. Their terms would be limited to thirty years (*Id.*, 58). Standards would be established for individuals who serve as jurors, with special exams, as for other officeholders. Whereas the current Constitution limits determinations of constitutionality to cases and controversies involving laws that are already in effect, Kirstein would provide for a National Council for Constitutionality of Law (*Id.*, 59). This council would review congressional laws "prior to implementation" (*Id.*, 60). If the council decided that such laws were unconstitutional, Congress would have to reconsider them, the Supreme Court would have to review and approve them, or, if the Supreme Court came to a contrary verdict, they would "remain inoperable" (*Id.*, 60).

Article V of Kirstein's constitution deals with general provisions and includes a phrase making the new Constitution the "supreme law of the land" (Kirstein 1994, 61). Article VI deals with ratification of the constitution. Kirstein proposes that this be done by a national referendum approved by two-thirds or more of the voters. This article includes a provision, presumably to give the new system a chance to show itself in operation, prohibiting amendments during the first three years that the new constitution is in operation.

Article VII provides a right of citizens to alter their government. Amendments may be proposed by congressional legislation or by legislation or referendum in two-thirds of the states. Amendments would be ratified, like the constitution, "by 2/3 or more of citizens voting in a national referendum" (Kirstein 1994, 62).

Article VIII is labeled "Citizen Rights, Obligation, and Rewards" (Kirstein 1994, 63). It contains the previously mentioned citizen oath of allegiance. Among other things, it pledges citizens to obey the law, to vote, to respect the rights of others, and to serve their nation for one or two years upon reaching the age of eighteen. This article also includes what Kirstein calls the "Golden Chronicle of Citizen Rights" (*Id.*), which includes many provisions in the existing U.S. Constitution as well as some that are not. The rights in Kirstein's constitution include freedom; democracy; entitlements to basic needs like "food, housing, health and medical care, education, and acceptable standards of living" (*Id.*, 64); the right to own property, including firearms; freedom to communicate; freedom of assembly; equal status under law "without regard to race, creed, nationality, ethnic origin, gender, ideology, religion, economic status, or other factor or value" (*Id.*, 64); equal status under law; due process of law; protections for private life; protections against exploitation and economic servitude by persons, organizations, and governments; protection against discrimination; the right to worship; the right to present grievances to government without the improper use of money to influence politicians; the sharing of resources; separation of religion and government (with provisions to tax religious groups that use more than 10 percent of their income for nonreligious purposes); human rights; "truth in public communications"; and a provision guaranteeing "general rights and privileges" (*Id.* 65).

Few proposed new U.S. constitutions have rivaled Kirstein's in their complexity. At times his plan appears closer to a blueprint for government than to the general outline that Americans have come to expect from such documents—in this respect, his plan is more like many existing state constitutions than like the U.S. Constitution. Kirstein's plan is unique in its attempt to combine both elements of increased popular participation with increased education of individuals who hold office. If adopted, Kirstein's plan would also appear to have the effect of reducing the power of the presidency by taking away the president's current veto and by effectively giving each of the other two branches a single head. It is difficult to know with certainty the overall effect that many of his other proposals would have.

In 1992 Kirstein published the *Ideology of Freedom and Democracy,* which is described as a "Master Plan for FREEDOM, DEMOCRACY, HUMAN RIGHTS, PROGRESS, SECURITY, and PEACE on Planet EARTH." There he advocated supplanting the United Nations with a more effective world organization and in promoting democracy throughout the world.

For Further Reading:

Kirstein, Herbert C. 1994. *U.S. Constitution for 21st Century and Beyond.* Alexandria, VA: Realistic IDEALIST Enterprise.

———. 1992. *Ideology of Freedom and Democracy.* Alexandria, VA: Realistic IDEALIST Enterprise.

"U.S. Constitution for the 21st Century and Beyond." At *http://www.newusconstitution.org/usc21a. html.* Accessed 6/28/00.

❖ KRUSCH, BARRY (1958–) ❖

In 1992 Barry Krusch of New York offered one of the most ambitious plans for a new U.S. constitution in a book entitled *The 21st Century Constitution* (1992). An extensive opening chapter detailed current faults in the U.S. system. Krusch attributed most of these to separation of powers, to the fact that the Constitution was written prior to the modern information age, and to the fact that actual practices (what he calls the empirical constitution) no longer match the written document. In the rest of his book, Krusch outlined an alternative constitution. His alternative was, however, built around the current constitutional outline. Krusch wanted to make the constitution more responsive to public wishes and more adaptable to modern technologies, but he also expressed great faith in the power of experts to guide legislative decision making and identify national interests.

Under Krusch's plan, Congress would continue to consist of two branches, but with somewhat different functions. Members of both branches would be prohibited from being members of political parties and would be limited to eight years of service. Members of the new House of Representatives, consisting of a minimum of 1,000 members, would serve one-year terms and would be required to be graduates of a federal academy (also responsible for proposing congressional rules). Each state would continue to have two senators, but they would serve two-year terms. The Senate's primary function would be governmental oversight. A federal committee of fifty senators would administer "the National Database, the National Poll, the National Objectives, the National Initiative, the National Referendum, and the National Recall" (Krusch 1992, 128). The committee would also nominate candidates for the House of Representatives and the presidency, making sure that their nominees were "representative of the population . . . with regard to sex, race, national origin and other factors" (Krusch 1992, 129). The Senate would be responsible for setting up a legislative review board of nine members, serving for a single three-year term, that would compile "performance ratings" for representatives according to the degree to which they voted for bills that served the national interest. The Senate would also commission polls to ascertain the public will.

The majority necessary to pass bills—and the determination of whether a bill would need to pass one or both houses and/or be signed by the president—would be based on the evaluation that the bills received from the legislative review board. Any income taxes would have to apply to at least three-fourths of the population, with the highest tax bracket limited to fifty percent and the lowest at least half that amount (Krusch 1992, 158). Borrowing would require a sanction by a two-thirds vote of both houses and the voters. The legislative veto, declared unconstitutional in *Immigration and Naturalization Service v. Chadha* (1983), would be permitted (Krusch 1992, 165). Congress would create and regulate a national academy, a department of rights enforcement, and a federal election commission, with all electoral campaigns to be publicly financed.

The right to an education would be granted, a national database would be created to disseminate information to the citizens, and a national television channel would educate people, with "one-half of the programming" to "reflect the Will of the People as determined by the June National Poll" (Krusch 1992, 179). Current principles regarding freedom of speech, religion, and other rights in the Bill of Rights would be set forth in greater detail that better reflects current case law. One fascinating provision allows for penalties for those distorting "those aspects of reality which have been or can be objectively verified as true" (Krusch 1992, 183).

The president and vice president would be selected by majority vote, with the national recall taking the place of presidential impeachment. Presidential powers to commit troops without congressional authorization would be clipped.

Nine nonpartisan judges representative of the population would serve staggered nine-year terms. Although judges would no longer have the power of judicial review, they would have no obligation to enforce laws that they considered to be unconstitutional.

The current federal arrangement of the government would undergo few changes, but amendments could be proposed by a majority of both houses or two-thirds of the people. Two-thirds of the people or state legislatures could also call for a convention. Amendments would be ratified by two-thirds of the state legislatures or conventions or by three-fifths of the electorate. In a provision similar to one that Thomas Jefferson made, every twenty-five years the people would be asked whether they wanted another convention (Krusch 1992, 236).

The main articles of the new constitution would be augmented by supplements that could be altered more easily. Krusch would also include a rule of constitutional construction that "strict terms such as 'no' or 'all' shall be strictly construed, and broad terms such as 'liberty' and 'justice' shall be broadly construed" (Krusch 1992, 247).

A Second Federal Convention Act would provide the rules for constitutional ratification. Krusch anticipated a convention of 1,200 delegates to write or affirm the constitution, with members of no single profession to compose more than 5 percent of its members (Krusch 1992, 249). The people would choose from among three to six such documents.

Krusch, whose occupation was not specified, was president of Americans for a Constitutional Convention, Inc. His book included an address for people who are interested in serving as delegates to a mock constitutional convention.

For Further Reading:
Krusch, Barry. 1992. *The 21st Century Constitution: A New America for a New Millennium.* New York: Stanhope Press.

L

❖

❖ LABOR, CONVICT ❖

At least one proposal was introduced in 1883 and two in 1886 that would prohibit states from contracting out convict labor. This practice, almost exclusively applied to African Americans (and often involving slavelike conditions that frequently led to loss of health and life), was especially widespread at the time in the South. Although no such amendment was adopted, fears by free laborers of unfair competition continue to limit the tasks that states feel that they can assign to convicts. In the 1990s, however, Alabama and Arizona reinstituted the chain gang as a way of saving state money and deterring crime (Gavzer 1995, 6).

For Further Reading:
Gavzer, Bernard. 1995. "Life behind Bars." *Parade Magazine* 13 August, 4–7.

❖ LABOR, HOURS OF ❖

From 1884 to 1937, members of Congress introduced more than thirty proposals to give that body power to regulate the hours of labor. Some such resolutions applied specifically to factories; some proposed "uniform" hours of labor; and some combined a proposal about hours of labor with power over minimum wages, the prevention of unfair labor practices, child labor, or other aspects of working life.

Proposals for reform coincided with a period during which the federal courts often struck down state and federal regulatory legislation that they perceived to have a class bias (Gillman 1993). The due process clause of the Fourteenth Amendment—which the Supreme Court interpreted as embodying "freedom of contract"—was the tool that the courts used most frequently to accomplish this objective. The best known of these decisions was *Lochner v. New York* (1905), in which the Supreme Court struck down a New York state law regulating the hours of bakers (Kens 1990). Decisions in which the Court upheld such laws usually involved industries considered to be particularly dangerous, such as mining in *Holden v. Hardy* (1898), or individuals whom the Court thought were in need of special state protection, such as women in *Muller v. Oregon* (1908).

Although the analysis has arguably been overdrawn, *West Coast Hotel v. Parrish* (1937) and *National Labor Relations Board v. Jones & Laughlin Steel Corp.* (1937) are often cited as the cases in which the Supreme Court made a historic "switch in time that saved nine" in response to Franklin D. Roosevelt's court-packing plan and began interpreting existing congressional powers under the commerce and taxing provisions generously enough to uphold most labor-related legislation. Such interpretations negated the need for a constitutional amendment, and members of Congress ceased introducing them.

See also Court-packing Plan; *Lochner v. New York*.

For Further Reading:
Gillman, Howard. 1993. *The Constitution Besieged: The Rise and Demise of Lochner Era Police*

Powers Jurisprudence. Durham, NC: Duke University Press.

Kens, Paul. 1990. *Judicial Power and Reform Politics: The Anatomy of* Lochner v. New York. *Lawrence, KS: University Press of Kansas.*

❖ LABUNSKI, RICHARD ❖

Richard Labunski, a journalism professor at the University of Kentucky with both a Ph.D. and J.D., has recently written a book entitled *The Second Constitutional Convention* (2000). Labunski begins his introduction by noting that "Disappointment, disillusionment, and distrust" are shared by many contemporary Americans. His book is divided into four parts. The first discusses the current Constitution and recent perceived abuses, particularly in the areas of campaign financing and congressional resistance to term limits and other proposed changes, as well as judicial limitations in bringing about wholesale reform, that he thinks make a second convention necessary.

The second section of his book discusses how meetings leading to a national "preconvention," and precipitating states to call a real convention, can be organized. The third describes ten amendments that he thinks a constitutional convention should consider, while the fourth attempts to square his proposals with the eight guidelines for amendments advanced by the Citizens for the Constitution. This essay examines the second and third of Labunski's objectives.

Drawing in part from the unsuccessful Peace Convention that preceded the U.S. Civil War, as well as from a National Issues Convention held in 1996 in Austin, Texas, that was designed to educate a group of more than 900 participants on contemporary political issues, Labunski outlines a plan that he hopes will eventually result in sufficient petitions from the states to call a second constitutional convention. Labunski envisions meetings beginning at the county or congressional district level, perhaps attended by no more than two or three dozen people. They would in turn generate publicity about the possibility of another convention, seek to inform and engage the public

(using state-of-the-art interactive Internet technology), discuss key constitutional issues and possible solutions, and elect representatives to state conventions, to be composed of fifty-two or fewer delegates (Labunski 2000, 199). Ideally, all state conventions would take place on the same day, but Labunski thinks that at the least they should take place within a thirty-to-sixty-day period. Each convention would select two delegates to a national preconvention in Washington, D.C. This preconvention would identify "the *problems* that will be addressed by constitutional amendments"; identify "the specific *sections* of the Constitution that will be considered for revisions"; and suggest "in *general terms* language that may be appropriate for the new amendments" (*Id.,* 220–221).

After this preconvention, the work would begin attempting to convince state legislatures to petition Congress for a second constitutional convention. Labunski thinks that the Internet can be used to generate enthusiasm for this project and devotes an entire chapter to this subject. Noting that no previous amendment "has been designed to limit congressional power" (Labunski 2000, 273), Labunski further explores previous attempts by Congress to legislate on the subject of conventions, as well as the fairly limited role that courts have played in overseeing this process in recent years.

Labunski labels his ten amending proposals from "A" to "J." Each proposed amendment is phrased in terms of a legislative petition; each further specifies how long after ratification it would go into effect; contains a built-in seven-year deadline for ratification; and requires ratification by state conventions.

Consistent with his critique of current American government, Amendment "A" deals with campaign finance reform and would overturn parts of the U.S. Supreme Court decision in *Buckley v. Valeo* (1976). Labunski would permit regulations of both campaign contributions and expenditures. He would also require that candidates for Congress raise at least half their funds from within their respective district or state. Congress and state legislatures would be granted power to limit expenditures per voters within districts, limits that would apply both to direct candidate expenditures and to less direct "soft money" expenditures. Provision would be made for "comprehensive disclosure of campaign contributions and expenditures," and Congress and the states would be authorized to "study a plan by which elections are publicly financed" (Labunski 2000, 294).

Amendment "B" is an expanded version of the Equal Rights Amendment. Addressing one of the issues that originally divided supporters of women's rights, Labunski specifically provides that "This amendment shall not be construed to invalidate legislation, administrative regulations, or other acts of Congress or the states that have benign effects on the economic or political status of women" (Labunski 2000, 315), but he does not specifically address the equally provocative issue of women in the military. Undoubtedly with the precedent of *United States v. Morrison* (2000) in view, Labunski further provides that "[t]he interstate commerce clause of Article I, Section 8, shall not be construed by any federal or state court as inhibiting congressional authority to enact laws related to gender-motivated violence" (*Id.*, 316).

Amendment "C" advances the cause of victims' rights. These would include "the right to be present in all public proceedings to determine release from custody, acceptance of a plea agreement, or a sentence; the right to be informed of and to offer written or oral testimony at parole hearings; the right to reasonable notice of release or escape from custody of the defendant; and the right to compensation for crimes in amounts fixed by federal and state law" (Labunski 2000, 338). Labunski's proposal would extend a "civil right of action" against crime perpetrators and waive state immunity (thus presumably modifying existing interpretations of the Eleventh Amendment) in cases in which the conduct of public officials resulted "in gratuitous harm to the crime victim, and where the conduct of such officials is reckless or malicious" (*Id.*, 338).

Labunski groups Amendments "D," "E," and "F" together. Amendment "D" addresses the issue of congressional term limits. Members of the House would be limited to four two-year terms and senators to two six-year terms, with similar overall limits in effect if the term of senators were reduced to four years, as Amendment "E" proposes. On a related noted, Amendment "F" provides for allowing the Senate to ratify treaties by majority vote rather than by the current two-thirds majority.

Amendment "G" is devoted to eliminating the electoral college and replacing it with a system of direct election. Labunski further specifies in this amendment that voters would designate their first, second, and third choices for president. If, when adding second and third choice votes, no candidate gets 40 percent or more of the electoral vote, the electoral outcome would then be resolved by an assembly of both houses of Congress, with each member having a single vote (the Twelfth Amendment currently provides for resolving presidential contests by giving each state a single vote in the House).

Amendment "H" is designed to protect the judiciary. It does so by specifying that Congress "shall not have the power to alter, modify, restrict, or enhance the appellate jurisdiction of the federal courts" (Labunski 2000, 377).

Amendment "I" is designed to alter the amending process by providing for three methods. First, amendments could be proposed and ratified by 60 percent majorities of Congress and of the states. Second, Congress would be obligated to call a constitutional convention within ninety days of receiving "petitions from 50 percent of state legislatures requesting that Congress call a constitutional convention" (Labunski 2000, 388). Third, Congress would be obligated to call such a convention after receiving petitions from 50 percent of state secretaries of states who had in turn received petitions from 10 percent or more of those voting in the last general election (*Id.*). Convention delegates would be elected by the people, and once states had ratified an amendment, such ratifications could not be rescinded.

Labunski's final proposal, Amendment "J," calls for the repeal of the Second Amendment. Noting current controversies over whether this amendment protects individual or group rights (Labunski leans to the latter view), he thinks the best thing to do would be simply to repeal the amendment and allow for state and national gun control laws. To date the only amendment to be so repealed was the Twenty-first Amendment repealing national alcoholic prohibition as established by the Eighteenth Amendment.

Labunski's proposal provides one of the most elaborate mechanisms for building the momentum that might be required to get states to petition Congress to call another constitutional convention, and his proposal for a preconvention is especially fascinating. His proposals are not easily classified under a single rubric but appear to mix concerns expressed by a number of contemporary groups. There might be great difficulty in getting groups to coalesce around proposals as diverse as protecting victims' rights, allowing broad gun control, changing the electoral college, and imposing congressional term limits.

See also Peace Convention.

For Further Reading:
Labunski, Richard. 2000. *The Second Constitutional Convention: How the American People Can Take Back Their Government.* Versailles, KY: Marley and Beck Press.

❖ LAME DUCK AMENDMENT ❖

See Twentieth Amendment.

❖ LAND, DIVISION OF ❖

A number of amendments that have been proposed to grant or expand the national government's power over agriculture have included grants of power to tax or otherwise regulate land. Henry George (1839–1897) promoted a single-tax movement on land with the 1871 publication of his essay "Our Land and Land Policy," which subsequently became the basis of his influential *Progress and Poverty* (1938).

Democratic Representative John Randolph Thayer of Massachusetts offered perhaps the most drastic proposal to alter land distribution by amendment in January 1904 (H.J. Res. 83). Thayer would have allowed the national government to take land from anyone with more than twelve acres and redistribute it so that everyone would have at least eight contiguous acres. Similar distributions were to be made after each census (Musmanno 1929, 1903).

See also Agriculture.

For Further Reading:
George, Henry. 1938. *Progress and Poverty: An Inquiry into the Cause of Industrial Depressions and of Increase of Want with Increase of Wealth, the Remedy.* 50th anniversary ed. New York: Robert Schalkenback Foundation.

❖ LAWRENCE, WILLIAM B. (1800–1881) ❖

American diplomat and international law specialist William B. Lawrence published an article in 1880 in which he advocated substantial changes in the U.S. Constitution (Vile 1991c, 32–34). He was especially concerned about the treatment the South had received during Reconstruction and by the irregularities of the disputed presidential election of 1876. He also considered the power of the presidency to be a special threat to republican government.

Lawrence directed the majority of his article to historical critique and review rather than to suggested changes, but the suggestions he did offer were major ones. Lawrence argued that a system in which Congress selected the president would be better than the existing system because it would lead to greater legislative-executive harmony and would entrust the decision to those who were most knowledgeable. Lawrence believed that it was "impossible to conceive of any worse political machinery" than the national nominating convention (Lawrence 1880, 407).

Lawrence also called the vice presidency "altogether objectionable," noting that vice presidents were often selected "without regard to the possible succession" and that the office had been largely created so that each member of the electoral college could cast two votes (Lawrence 1880, 406). Lawrence argued that a powerful executive was dangerous in a heterogeneous nation, where he could "influence legislation, as well as the administration of the Government, in favor of his section to the prejudice of others" (*Id.*, 408).

Lawrence favored the establishment of a parliamentary system. Passing over more familiar models, Lawrence commended the Swiss form. As he described it, this system vested executive authority in a federal council of seven members from different geographic areas who were selected by the legislature for three-year terms. This legislature chose the president and vice president annually, but neither officer had substantially more powers than members of the council, a majority of which was necessary "to sanction every deliberation" (Lawrence 1880, 408–409).

For Further Reading:

Lawrence, William B. 1880. "The Monarchical Principle in Our Constitution." *North American Review* 288 (November): 385–409.

❖ LAWYERS ❖

Lawyers have long been critical to the implementation of American laws, and judges, as well as many legislators at both the state and national level, are drawn from their ranks (Vile 2001). Although most individuals profess confidence in their own lawyers, as a class lawyers are often blamed for injustices, or perceived injustices, in the legal system. One contemporary, albeit far-fetched, interpretation of the titles of nobility, or the Reed Amendment proposed by Congress in 1812—which, had it been adopted, would have been the Thirteenth—is that it would bar attorneys from holding public office.

Gosta H. Lovgren on a website titled "A Constitutional Amendment Banning Lawyers from Public Office" at *http://www.spectacle. org/797lgosta.html* and who is not otherwise identified, has suggested an amendment providing that "No Person who holds, or has held, a license to practice law; nor any person who has represented any entity (other than himself) in a court of law in these United States, may be elected to any public office." Lovgren's proposal is based on the idea that lawyers already

control two of the three branches of government, that they are "amoral by definition," that they try to complicate matters, that criminal law "has become more of an auction block than a system of justice," and that lawyers help their clients evade personal responsibility. It is not altogether clear how Lovgren believes that an amendment is likely to be proposed and adopted by legislative bodies that have such a high concentration of lawyers.

See also Titles of Nobility.

For Further Reading:

Lovgren, G. H. "A Constitutional Amendment Banning Lawyers from Public Office." At *http:// www. pectacle.org1797/gosta.html*. Accessed 11/25/02.

Vile, John R. 2001. *Great American Lawyers: An Encyclopedia*. 2 vols. Santa Barbara: ABC-CLIO.

❖ LAZARE, DANIEL (1950–) ❖

Lazare, a freelance journalist, has authored a stinging critique of modern American government, *The Frozen Republic: How the Constitution Is Paralyzing Democracy* (1996), in which he argues that most American social problems are the result of an antiquated constitution that stresses checks and balances and separation of powers and produces gridlock rather than governmental accountability. In almost every area he examines, Lazare finds European parliamentary systems to be better, and he condemns what he regards as American worship of a written constitution. He even compares those who admire the American founders, the Constitution, and Federalist justifications of it to "Iranian mullahs waving copies of the Koran" (Lazare 1996, 284).

Lazare argues that Article V is the "dangling thread" (Lazare 1996, 297) that could eventually unravel the existing system that he so criticizes. Lazare imagines a situation in which California threatens to secede unless the current system of equal state apportionment in the Senate is ended. In arguments similar to those raised elsewhere by Akhil Reed Amar, Lazare suggests that the House of Representatives could respond in an extraconstitutional manner by voting by a simple majority to abolish equal representation in the Senate and then allowing the American people to ratify its decision in a referendum.

Although he does not go into detail about the new system this would initiate, he does say that it would not only embody the principle of legislative sovereignty but also "reduce the president to semi-figurehead status" and "effectively rob the judiciary of much of its power" (Lazare 1996, 293–94). Lazare further notes that "not just the Constitution would be toppled, but so would checks and balances, separation of powers, and the deeply inculcated habit of deferring to the authority of a group of eighteenth-century Country gentlemen. Instead of relying on previous generations' judgment and analysis, the people would have no choice than to rely on their own" (Id., 295).

That deference to the current Constitution to which Lazare makes continual reference would appear to present a major obstacle to his plans.

See also Reverence for the Constitution.

For Further Reading:

Lazare, Daniel. 1996. *The Frozen Republic: How the Constitution Is Paralyzing Democracy.* New York: Harcourt Brace & Company.

❖ LEGISLATION PROPOSED ON CONSTITUTIONAL CONVENTIONS ❖

To date, Congress has not adopted legislation to guide a possible convention requested by the states under Article V of the Constitution to propose amendments to the Constitution. One prominent and active supporter of such legislation was Democratic Senator Sam Ervin of North Carolina, who introduced the Federal Constitutional Convention Act in 1967. At that time, he and Republican Senator Everett Dirksen of Illinois were working for a convention to repeal the Supreme Court's reapportionment decisions. The other most prominent supporter of such legislation has been Republican Senator

Orrin Hatch of Utah, who first presented his Constitutional Implementation Act in 1979 and has been advocating it ever since. The Ervin bill passed the Senate in 1971 and 1973 but was never acted on in the House of Representatives. Hatch's bill has been approved by the Senate Judiciary Committee but not by either house of Congress (Caplan 1988, 77).

Both Ervin and Hatch believed that Congress has the power to adopt such legislation under the necessary and proper clause. Both also argued that neutral legislation should be passed that could apply to any issue rather than being tailor-made to specific conventions. Interestingly, both senators took the position that states can call either a limited or an open convention, but their legislation would apply only to the former.

The Ervin and Hatch bills were surprisingly similar. The Ervin bill originally proposed that applications for a convention would be valid for seven years, but Ervin subsequently reduced this period to four years (Ervin 1968, 891). The Hatch bill provides a period of no longer than seven years but allows state applications to specify a shorter period (Hatch 1991, S561). Because no such deadline is now specified, the Hatch bill would give an additional two-year life (absent state rescission) to proposals introduced in the last sixteen years (Hatch 1991, S561). The Hatch bill also encourages, but does not require, states to list other state applications that they believe cover the same topic.

Both the Ervin and the Hatch legislation would permit Congress to specify the time, place, and (consistent with state petitions) the general subject matter of the convention. The original Ervin bill gave each state a number of delegates equal to its representation in the House but required that state delegates vote as a bloc ("Proposed Legislation" 1972, 1625). The revised bill followed the model of the electoral college in giving each state a number of votes equal to its total number of U.S. senators and representatives and allowed for majority rule. The Ervin bill provided that such delegates would be elected in the states. Hatch apparently favors such popular election but would not require it (Hatch 1991, S562). Like the Ervin bill, the Hatch bill would apportion delegates in the same manner as does the electoral college.

The Ervin bill explicitly provided that the convention could propose amendments by a majority rather than by a two-thirds vote; the Hatch bill appears to contemplate this but does not explicitly say so. Although Hatch opposed the amendment designed to treat the District of Columbia as a state for purposes of representation in Congress, his proposal explicitly provides that "the people of the District of Columbia shall elect as many delegates as the whole number of Senators and Representatives to which said District would be entitled in the Congress if it were a State" (Hatch 1991, S564).

Both Ervin and Hatch accepted the doctrine of contemporary consensus as articulated in *Dillon v. Gloss* (1921). Accordingly, in addition to limiting the time span during which convention petitions were valid, both would permit states to rescind petitions for a convention or to rescind ratification of a proposed amendment up to the point where two-thirds of the states had ratified it. If adopted as legislation, such a rule might well apply to all amendments and not simply to those that were proposed by a convention.

Although both Ervin and Hatch believed that Congress was obligated to call a convention when it received the necessary number of applications, both sought to guard against a so-called runaway convention by allowing Congress to refuse to report amendments to the states that were proposed by a convention that exceeded its mandate. The Ervin bill was criticized for attempting to preclude judicial review of important questions related to this legislation ("Proposed Legislation" 1972, 1635–1644). In contrast, the Hatch legislation specifically recognizes such judicial authority. Hatch thus rejects the notion that such matters are political questions beyond judicial cognizance.

If adopted, legislation on the constitutional convention would, like constitutional statutes in England, be considered "quasi-organic" legislation (Ervin 1968, 880). Even if never adopted by Congress, such proposals might be consulted in the event that states muster suffi-cient petitions to call a convention. Absent adoption of such legislation, such decisions will likely be made on an ad hoc political basis.

For Further Reading:
Caplan, Russell L. 1988. *Constitutional Brinkmanship: Amending the Constitution by National Convention*. New York: Oxford University Press.

Ervin, Sam J., Jr. 1968. "Proposed Legislation to Implement the Convention Method of Amending the Constitution." *Michigan Law Review* 66 (March): 875–902.

Hatch, Orrin. 1991. "Constitutional Convention Implementation Act." *Congressional Record*, U.S. Senate, 15 January, S559–S565.

"Proposed Legislation on the Convention Method of Amending the United States Constitution." 1972. *Harvard Law Review* 85: 1612–1648.

❖ LEISURE, RIGHT TO ❖

In contrast to some constitutions (those of Bangladesh and the Peoples' Republic of China, for example), the text of the U.S. Constitution does not guarantee social and economic rights. At least one writer, after first exploring the possibility that a right to leisure might be discovered in the penumbras of the Thirteenth and/or Fourteenth Amendments, has toyed with the idea of adding a constitutional amendment to guarantee a right to leisure. He ultimately concluded both that the amending process was too difficult to accomplish this objective and that such an amendment would face the further obstacles posed by "the American worship of work and the power of large corporations, most of which would probably lobby as hard as they could to sink this proposed addendum" (Kramer 2001, 67).

See also Social and Economic Rights.

For Further Reading:
Kramer, Daniel C. 2001. "The Constitution and the Right to Leisure." *The Good Society* 10: 64–67.

❖ *LESER V. GARNETT* (1922) ❖

In a test of contemporary arguments that there were limits on the amending process, Oscar Leser and other Maryland voters brought suit to strike the names of women from the voting list in Baltimore despite the adoption of the Nineteenth Amendment. In rejecting this attempt, the Supreme Court addressed three arguments.

The first argument was that the Nineteenth Amendment exceeded implicit constitutional limitations by altering the electorates of even those states that had not ratified the amendment, such as Maryland. Justice Louis Brandeis responded by noting the similarities in the language of the Fifteenth and Nineteenth Amendments. He argued that the former could not be valid and the latter invalid. In so ruling, Brandeis rejected the contention that the former amendment was a war measure "validated by acquiescence" (*Leser* 1922, 136) rather than through legitimate amending procedures.

A second argument was that some of the states included in the secretary of state's compilation of ratifying states should not have been counted because of provisions in their constitutions preventing such ratification. Brandeis responded by noting that "the function of a state legislature in ratifying a proposed amendment to the Federal Constitution, like the function of Congress in proposing the amendment, is a federal function derived from the Federal Constitution; and it transcends any limitations sought to be imposed by the people of a State" (*Leser* 1922, 137). Brandeis cited both *Hawke v. Smith* cases (1920) and the *National Prohibition Cases* (1920) to buttress this argument.

The third argument was that ratifications by Tennessee and West Virginia were illegal because they violated the states' own rules of legislative procedure. In responding, Brandeis further ruled that "official notice to the Secretary, duly authenticated," that they had ratified "was conclusive upon him, and, being certified by his proclamation, is conclusive upon the courts" (*Leser* 1922, 137).

See also Constitutional Amendments, Limits on.

For Further Reading:
Leser v. Garnett, 258 U.S. 130 (1922).

❖ LIEBER, FRANCIS (1800–1872) ❖

Lieber was a German-born immigrant who came to the United States after obtaining his doctorate in Germany, fighting as a volunteer in the Greek revolt against Turkey, visiting Rome and being befriended by the scholar and diplomat Barhhold Niebuhr, and being imprisoned in Prussia for his political writings and republican sympathies. Arriving in the United States in 1827, after a brief stint in England (whose legal system he especially admired), he began working on editing the thirteen-volume *Encyclopedia Americana*, which appeared from 1829 to 1833. He also became a citizen; and took a post as professor of history and political economy at South Carolina College (now the University of South Carolina) where he served from 1832 to 1856. Lieber took a similar post in 1857 at Columbia College in New York where he taught—transferring to the law school in 1865—until his death in 1872 (see Lieber 1881, 144).

Lieber was a prolific scholar whose works included the widely read and respected two-volume *Manual of Political Ethics* (1838), *Legal and Political Hermeneutics* (1839), and *Civil Liberty and Self-Government,* published in two volumes in 1853. Lieber also wrote the *Instructions for the Government of the Armies of the United States,* issued by the army secretary in 1863 and later embodied into international law. Despite having taught for so long in South Carolina, Lieber was a longtime defender of the Union against radical theories of states' rights and secession. He served as president of the Loyal Publication Society of New York, for which he wrote in 1865 a pamphlet proposing a series of constitutional amendments, some ideas of which paralleled provisions in the forthcoming Thirteenth, Fourteenth, and Fifteenth Amendments of the U.S. Constitution.

In offering his proposals, Lieber included a long justification for amendments in which he stressed that, however wise the American founders had been, laws and constitutions are organic and need to change in order to preserve themselves. The Civil War had brought certain problems into relief that required resolution, especially the matters of slavery and states' rights. Lieber thought the idea of the nation should be paramount to that of state sovereignty, and his proposals reflected this idea. Interestingly, Lieber did not regard the time in which he was writing as propitious for a constitutional convention (Lieber 1865, 35), preferring to "build additions to the mansion we dwell in" rather than demolishing the edifice and beginning anew. Moreover, although he indicated that he favored a six-year term for the president, an item veto, changes in the constitutional provisions related to "direct" taxes, laws against polygamy, and consideration of an amendment allowing cabinet officers to appear in Congress—a provision whose actual necessity he doubted (Lieber 1865, 31–33)—he decided to limit his own proposals to more urgent concerns for which he proposed seven amendments.

First, Lieber proposed an amendment requiring allegiance from each American native-born and naturalized citizen and guaranteeing to each citizen the government's "full protection" (Lieber 1865, 36). Second, Lieber proposed extending the definition of treason to include attempts to separate any state from the union. His third proposal would have made armed resistance to the United States a "high crime," and his fourth would have permitted trials for treason outside a state or a district during times of war or rebellion. His fifth and most critical amendment would (like the eventual Thirteenth Amendment ratified the same year as his proposal) have abolished slavery forever. Interestingly, in similarly proposing to eliminate the three-fifths clause, Lieber based the number of representatives, as would Section 2 of the Fourteenth Amendment, on the "respective number of male citizens of age" rather than on the number of all adults (Lieber 1865, 38). Lieber's sixth proposed amendment provided that participation in the slave trade would be classified as piracy, while his seventh was designed to provide for the "privileges" of all citizens, including those recently freed (*Id.*, 39). His commentary on the last proposal indicated that he was especially concerned to see

that the courtroom testimony of whites and blacks was treated equally, a comment that could possibly shed light on the use of the "privileges and immunities" clause that found its way into the Fourteenth Amendment.

Lieber was quite articulate in defending the need for amendments, and his proposals make for interesting comparison to those that were actually ratified from 1865 to 1870. In 1867 Lieber published an additional essay on changes he thought were needed in the New York State Constitution of 1846 (Lieber 1888, 183–219).

For Further Reading:
Lieber, Francis. 1888. *Manual of Political Ethics, Designed Chiefly for the Use of Colleges and Students at Law.* 2d ed. Philadelphia: Lippincott.
———. 1881. *Reminiscences, Addresses, and Essays.* Ed. Daniel G. Gilman. 2 vols. Philadelphia: J. B. Lippincott & Co.
———. 1865. *Amendments of the Constitution Submitted to the Consideration of the American People.* New York: Loyal Publication Society.
Vile, John R. 1998a. "Francis Lieber and the Constitutional Amending Process." *The Review of Politics* 60 (Summer): 524–543.

❖ LIMITS ON CONSTITUTIONAL AMENDMENTS ❖

See Constitutional Amendments, Limits on.

❖ LIMITS ON WEALTH AND INCOME ❖

Early in the twentieth century and again during the Great Depression, a number of members of Congress proposed amendments to limit personal wealth or income. In 1933 Washington Democratic Congressman Wesley Lloyd introduced an amendment to limit annual incomes to $1 million (Pizzigati 1992, 55), and Pennsylvania Democrat John Synder introduced an amendment to limit the amount of income derived from capital. The idea was especially appealing among those who considered themselves to be socialists, as well as among those who could be classified as utopian thinkers. Edward Bellamy's widely read novel *Looking Backward* (1968), first published in 1888, foresaw a world in the year 2000 in which there was a relative equality of wealth. Some proponents of the progressive income tax were as motivated by the redistributive possibilities of such a tax as by its potential to raise revenue.

Once the Sixteenth Amendment was adopted, it was more common to propose use of the tax code to effect equalization of wealth or income than to propose amendments to this end. Thus, in his book *My First Days in the White House*, Louisiana's flamboyant Senator Huey P. Long speculated that his own Share the Wealth Program would be upheld by the Supreme Court (Long 1935, 134–135). Although Long's plans went through several alterations, he proposed limiting individual fortunes to $5 million and annual income or inheritance to $1 million. Long also proposed a guaranteed national income of $2,000 to $3,000 a year, "homesteads" for all Americans, and free college education for deserving youth (Williams 1970, 693). Share the Wealth Clubs advocating Long's ideas were quite popular for a time, although they were largely concentrated in the South (Williams 1970, 701). Pressure from Long's followers is believed to have pushed Franklin Roosevelt's own ideas on progressive taxation leftward (Christman 1985, xiv).

In recent years, the gap between the rich and the poor in the United States appears to have widened (Bradsher 1995, 1). Labor journalist Sam Pizzigati, concerned about this increasing gap, has advanced a "10 times rule," or maximum wage. Under such a system, individuals would be limited to earning ten times the minimum wage, with incomes above that amount being paid in taxes. Pizzigati believes that, in such circumstances, people would find it advantageous to donate or distribute assets above that needed to generate the maximum income and that such redistribution would result in a number of societal advantages. Pizzigati advocated beginning a campaign for such a program at the state level and then using those states as a base to call for a constitutional amendment to that end (Pizzigati 1992, 134–136).

For Further Reading:

Bellamy, Edward. 1888. *Looking Backward.* Reprint, New York: Magnum Books, 1968.

Bradsher, Keith. 1995. "Gap in Wealth in U.S. Called Widest in West." *New York Times,* 17 April, 1, C4.

Christman, Henry M., ed. 1985. *Kingfish to America: Share Our Wealth: Selected Senatorial Papers of Huey P. Long.* New York: Shocken Books.

Long, Huey P. 1935. *My First Days in the White House.* Harrisburg, PA: Telegraph Press.

Pizzigati, Sam. 1994. "Salary Caps for Everyone!" *New York Times,* 28 August, 15.

———. 1992. *The Maximum Wage: A Common-Sense Prescription for Revitalizing America—By Taxing the Very Rich.* New York: Appex Press.

Williams, T. Harry. 1970. *Huey Long.* New York: Alfred A. Knopf.

❖ LINCOLN, ABRAHAM (1809–1865) ❖

The election in 1860 of Abraham Lincoln as the United States' sixteenth president helped precipitate the Civil War. The Republican platform of that year, which was committed to the view that slavery was immoral and should not be permitted to expand, convinced Southern states that their cherished institution of slavery would be jeopardized if they remained in the Union.

In the Lincoln-Douglas debates, Lincoln had questioned the finality of the Supreme Court's decision in *Scott v. Sandford* (1857), which had ruled that the Missouri Compromise was illegal and thus allowed for the expansion of slavery into the territories (Johannsen 1965, 64–66). Prior to his inauguration, Lincoln worked behind the scenes with congressional Republicans to oppose the Crittenden Compromise, which would have given some recognition to slavery in the territories. Lincoln did, however, support the Corwin Amendment, which would have guaranteed Southern states that slavery would not be abolished there without their consent.

In his first inaugural address, Lincoln distinguished between the "constitutional" right of amending the Constitution and the "revolutionary" right of dismembering it (J. Richardson 1908, 6:10). He further expressed support both for the Corwin Amendment and for the possibility of a constitutional convention that might propose amendments to the Constitution.

On 1 January 1863, Lincoln issued the Emancipation Proclamation, freeing slaves in states that remained loyal to the Confederacy. Lincoln had announced his intention to issue this proclamation in September, after the Union victory at Antietam Creek in Maryland. In his annual message of 1862, Lincoln also proposed three amendments. They would have compensated slave owners in states abolishing the institution before 1900, given perpetual freedom to all slaves freed by the war and compensated owners loyal to the Union, and provided for voluntary slave colonization abroad (J. Richardson 1908, 6:136). Congress largely ignored these plans (Paludan 1994, 164).

The changes wrought by the Emancipation Proclamation made such gradualism impossible. In January 1864 Democratic Senator John Henderson of Missouri offered the first amendment in Congress to abolish slavery. Soon a passage from the Northwest Ordinance of 1787 had been formulated into the Thirteenth Amendment (Paludan 1994, 300). Lincoln strongly supported this amendment (Donald 1995, 553–554). Contrary to the custom that had been followed with all amendments other than the Corwin Amendment, this amendment was sent to him for his signature before being sent to the states for their eventual ratification. It has been suggested that Lincoln may have signed partly "to wipe out the memory of the Corwin Amendment" (Bernstein with Agel 1993, 100), which President Buchanan had signed.

Lincoln did not live to see the intense controversy generated by the Reconstruction of the South (1865–1877) and the proposal and ratification of the Fourteenth and Fifteenth Amendments, which grew, like the Thirteenth, out of the Civil War. It would appear that Lincoln might have particularly favored the provision in the Fourteenth Amendment reversing the *[Dred] Scott* decision and providing for equal protection of the laws; Lincoln had often argued that the Constitution needed to be un-

derstood and interpreted in light of the Declaration of Independence, which had announced the proposition that "all men are created equal."

After Lincoln's assassination by John Wilkes Booth at Ford's Theater in April 1865, the presidency fell into the far less capable hands of his vice president, Andrew Johnson, one of only two presidents to have been impeached.

See also Emancipation Proclamation; Thirteenth Amendment.

For Further Reading:

Bernstein, Richard B., with Jerome Agel. 1993. *Amending America: If We Love the Constitution So Much, Why Do We Keep Trying to Change It?* New York: Random House.

Donald, David H. 1995. *Lincoln*. New York: Simon & Schuster.

Johannsen, Robert W., ed. 1965. *The Lincoln-Douglas Debates of 1858*. New York: Oxford University Press.

Paludan, Phillip S. 1994. *The Presidency of Abraham Lincoln*. Lawrence, KS: University Press of Kansas.

Richardson, James E., ed. 1908. *A Compilation of the Messages and Papers of the Presidents, 1789–1908*. 11 vols. n.p.: Bureau of National Literature and Art.

❖ *LIVERMORE V. WAITE* (1894) ❖

Developments in state law sometimes influence federal law. *Livermore v. Waite* is a California case that is frequently cited in discussions of the amending process. It is especially relevant to the issue of whether a constitution can be changed other than by its own procedures, as well as to possible limits on the amending process. The case involved an amendment ratified by the California state legislature for approval by state voters to transfer the state capital from Sacramento to San Jose. Adoption was to be contingent upon receipt of a donation of a minimum of ten acres (of a site approved by the governor, secretary of state, and attorney general) and $1 million.

The California Supreme Court distinguished the two methods of amendment provided in the California constitution. The power of a constitutional convention to offer amendments was declared to be limited only by the U.S. Constitution. By contrast, the procedure by which amendments were proposed by two-thirds majorities of both houses of the state legislature and subsequently sent to the people for ratification was declared to be a delegated power "to be strictly construed under the limitations by which it has been conferred" (*Livermore* 1894, 117–118). The court observed that the state's constitution "can be neither revised nor amended except in the manner prescribed by itself, and the power which it has conferred upon the legislature in reference to proposed amendments, as well as to calling a convention, must be strictly pursued" (*Id.*, 117).

In this case, the court struck down the proposed amendment because it did not become operational, as the California constitution appeared to require, upon popular approval but upon considerations not specified there. The court concluded that "the amendment proposed substitutes for, or rather superadds to, the will of the people another will or judgment, without which its own will can have no effect" (*Livermore* 1894, 123).

See also Constitutional Amendments, Limits on.

For Further Reading:
Livermore v. Waite, 102 Cal. 113 (1894).

❖ LIVING CONSTITUTION ❖

It is a rare judge or scholar who would not agree that the U.S. Constitution is a living document, but such individuals may mean quite different things by such a statement. For some, the very presence of an amending process that can and has been utilized is testimony to the fact that the Constitution is a "living" document that can be adapted to changing circumstances. Such individuals are likely to believe that the Constitution should be adapted to technologies unknown to the framers (railroads, steamships, and airplanes, for example) but that major constitutional principles remain the same

and that constitutional innovations should await the proposal and ratification of formal amendments. For others, the idea of a "living" Constitution requires that legislators and/or judges apply and interpret the Constitution expansively and/or attempt to adapt it to the times.

Although the debate has been renewed in modern exchanges between those who advocate concentrating on the framers' intent and those who point either to the elusiveness of this quest or the need to take modern developments into consideration, this debate is hardly new. A recent analyst of the New Deal period (White 2000) notes that debates over the living Constitution were prominent in the period immediately before this time and were reflected in works on the Constitution written by James M. Beck (1922) and Howard Lee McBain (1927). Beck stressed the idea, consistent with earlier views, that "constitutional adaptivity involved the restatement of universal first principles in new contexts" (White 2000, 206). By contrast, McBain and other commentators were

> beginning to treat constitutional adaptivity as signifying something quite different: that constitutional principles themselves could be modified in response to the demands of modern American life. The latter conception of adaptivity illustrated a radically different set of assumptions about the nature of constitutional interpretation. (White 2000, 206)

To the degree that such actors alter what were once considered to be fixed constitutional meanings, formal amendments might be far less necessary. By the same token, overly expansive judicial and political interpretations might erode the value of a fixed text and might well lead to calls for amendments to reverse decisions that are thought to lack adequate constitutional foundation or that conflict with what are considered to be original fundamental principles.

Some constitutional provisions are fairly specific and appear to leave little room for judicial interpretation. By contrast, provisions calling for the prohibition of "cruel and unusual punishments" (the Eighth Amendment), for "due process of law" (the Fifth and Fourteenth

Amendments), or for "equal protection of the law" (the Fourteenth Amendment) require considerable more leeway. Makers and proponents of constitutions and amendments must be cognizant of the possibility, if not the likelihood, that broadly stated principles might be more expansively interpreted than more narrowly specified procedures. Sometimes a hope, and at others a fear, such concerns can impact popular willingness to ratify new amendments, especially those that appear to be broadly or vaguely worded, for example, the Equal Rights Amendment or broad pronouncements about social and economic rights.

See also Constitutional Interpretation.

For Further Reading:

Beck, James M. 1922. *The Constitution of the United States.* New York: G. H. Doran Co.

Friedman, Barry, and Scott B. Smith. 1998. "The Sedimentary Constitution." *University of Pennsylvania Law Review* 147 (November): 1–90.

Gillman, Howard. 1997. "The Collapse of Constitutional Originalism and the Rise of the Notion of the 'Living Constitution' in the Course of American State-Building." *Studies in American Political Development* 11 (Fall): 191–247.

McBain, Howard Lee. 1927. *The Living Constitution: A Consideration of the Realities and Legends of Our Fundamental Law.* New York: Macmillan.

Rehnquist, William H. 1976. "The Notion of a Living Constitution," *Texas Law Review* 54: 693–706.

White, G. Edward. 2000. *The Constitution and the New Deal.* Cambridge, MA: Harvard University Press.

❖ *LOCHNER V. NEW YORK* (1905) ❖

Few cases have more epitomized an era of Supreme Court decision making or indicated the potential scope of Supreme Court decisions in interpreting (and thus effectively amending) the written Constitution than did this 1905 decision. At issue was a New York law limiting the work hours of bakers to ten hours a day and six days a week.

Lochner, who operated a bakery, argued that the law violated his liberty of contract as protected by the due process clause of the Fourteenth Amendment. Writing for a five-to-four majority, Justice Rufus Peckham upheld this idea of substantive due process. Rejecting arguments that the baking industry was unhealthy and thus in need of special legislative solicitude, Peckham found that the state had exceeded its police powers in legislating for adults who were capable of protecting their own interests. He referred to New York's laws as "mere meddlesome interferences with the rights of the individual" (*Lochner* 1905, 61).

Justice John Marshall Harlan wrote a dissenting opinion in which he argued that courts should defer to legislative judgments in cases in which policy makers might disagree and that the Court's interpretations unduly widened the scope of the Fourteenth Amendment. Referring to a notable contemporary proponent of laissez-faire economics, Justice Oliver Wendell Holmes Jr. wrote a dissenting opinion in which he observed that "the Fourteenth Amendment does not enact Mr. Herbert Spencer's Social Statics" (*Lochner* 1905, 75).

In subsequent cases, the Supreme Court expanded on the idea of substantive due process to strike down laws providing for minimum wages and prohibiting child labor. These rulings prompted numerous proposals to amend the Constitution, but after Franklin Roosevelt introduced his court-packing plan in 1937, the Court shifted course and allowed such legislation to be adopted through ordinary legislative means.

See also Court-Packing Plan; Substantive Due Process.

For Further Reading:

Gillman, Howard. 1993. *The Constitution Besieged: The Rise and Demise of Lochner Era Police Powers Jurisprudence.* Durham, NC: Duke University Press.

Kens, Paul. 1990. *Judicial Power and Reform Politics: The Anatomy of* Lochner v. New York. Lawrence, KS: University Press of Kansas.

Lochner v. New York, 198 U.S. 45 (1905).

❖ LOCKWOOD, HENRY C. (1839–1902) ❖

Henry Lockwood wrote a book in 1884 that has been described as "a bestseller and an essential reference work for publicists of his time" (Pious 1978, 4). Although the title of the book, *The Abolition of the Presidency*, focused on the institution that Lockwood believed was most in need of reform, Lockwood also proposed sweeping reforms of the Senate and of state governments. Like other prominent would-be reformers of his day, Lockwood's model was the English constitution, the workings of whose executive Lockwood described as "nearer to the ideal of a representative government than any upon the face of the earth" (Lockwood 1884, 278).

Lockwood devoted much of his book to noting the flaws in the presidency and in those who had been elected to that office. Essentially, Lockwood believed that the presidency was an unwelcome vestige of monarchy. Lockwood outlined his proposals in his last three chapters. Opposed to the idea of state sovereignty, Lockwood placed himself squarely on the side of nationalism. As such, he suggested that the Senate should be abolished, both because it was "the strongest fulcrum of the 'residuary sovereignty' of the States" (Lockwood 1884, 283) and because he did not think that the advantages of a bicameral system outweighed its disadvantages. Moreover, Lockwood saw no need for the existence of states from which the senators were chosen. He thus cited with approval the proposal that David Brearly had made at the Constitutional Convention of 1787 to abolish the existing states and to divide the country into thirteen equal parts (Lockwood 1884, 282–283).

In his last chapter, Lockwood advanced plans for abolishing the presidency, adding the Articles of Confederation to Great Britain as a model. Under Lockwood's plan, the presidency would be replaced by an executive council chosen by Congress and headed by the secretary of state. Members would have seats in Congress, where they would be entitled to debate and to initiate legislation. The council could also dissolve Congress and appeal to the people when the government was deadlocked on an important issue. Congress would, in turn, have the right to remove cabinet members. Lockwood's anticipated result would be "responsible Council Government" (Lockwood 1884, 305).

In such a system, Congress would be sovereign. Lockwood therefore favored eliminating judicial review. The power of the courts would be limited to expounding and interpreting the laws (Lockwood 1884, 308).

Although he did not elaborate at great length, Lockwood clearly thought that other reforms were also desirable. Thus, in critiquing the current system, Lockwood noted that "church property is not taxed, [and] religious laws deface the statute-books" (Lockwood 1884, 313). Similarly, he noted the "tendency towards moneyed aristocracy" and the fact that the secret ballot "opens the door to stupendous frauds." Lockwood specifically pointed to the virtual disenfranchisement of African Americans in the South (Lockwood 1884, 313–314).

However popular it was in its day, Lockwood's book appears to have had little permanent impact. Rather than abolition of the presidency, the institution has arguably been strengthened in the twentieth century. Moreover, the states, the Senate, and judicial review all remain vital parts of the present system.

For Further Reading:

Lockwood, Henry C. 1884. *The Abolition of the Presidency*. New York: R. Worthington. Reprint, Farmingdale, NY: Darbor Social Science Publications, 1978.

Pious, Richard M. 1978. "Introduction." In *The Abolition of the Presidency*. Farmingdale, NY: Darbor Social Science Publications.

❖ LOTTERIES ❖

One senator and two members of the House of Representatives introduced proposals from May 1890 to January 1892 for a constitutional amendment to prohibit lotteries. State-sponsored lotteries have been prominent during three periods in U.S. history—the colonial period to the early nineteenth century, after the Civil War, and from 1964 to the present (Clotfetter and Cook 1989, 42).

Apart from a lottery in 1776 to support the Continental Army and lotteries operated to finance projects in Washington, D.C., from 1792 to 1842, such activity has been sponsored by the states rather than by the national government (Clotfetter and Cook 1989, 36). The 1890s marked a period of revulsion against lotteries that was stimulated by abuses associated with the Louisiana Lottery Company, which had been established in 1868.

Although Congress never adopted an amendment, in 1890 it prohibited use of the mails to promote lotteries, and in 1895 it outlawed interstate transportation of lottery tickets. The Supreme Court upheld the latter law in *Champion v. Ames* (1903). Recent years have witnessed a rebirth of numerous state-sponsored lotteries and privately established casinos, with the desire for state revenues (sometimes specifically designated for education or other desirable social programs) and employment opportunities often overcoming objections based on morals and concerns about the creation by the states of social problems like gambling addiction and poverty.

For Further Reading:
Clotfetter, Charles T., and Phillip Cook. 1989. *Selling Hope: State Lotteries in America*. Cambridge, MA: Harvard University Press.

Mason, John Lyman, and Michael Nelson. 2001. *Governing Gambling*. New York: The Century Foundation Press.

❖ LOUISIANA PURCHASE ❖

One of the most important events in early American history was the purchase in 1803 of the Louisiana Territory, an area of nearly a million square miles that lay from the Mississippi River to the Rocky Mountains. Ironically, the purchase took place during the first-term presidency of Democratic-Republican Thomas Jefferson who, while favoring the growth of an agricultural republic, was a strict constitutional constructionist. As secretary of state in George Washington's administration, Jefferson had opposed the creation of the national bank. Because of his view of the Constitution, Jefferson initially favored adoption of a constitutional amendment that would grant the national government the right to purchase such new territory rather than simply relying on his unspecified executive authority.

Americans in the West relied heavily on the Mississippi River for navigation, and they were concerned about the occupation of the port of New Orleans, first by Spain and then by France. Jefferson had sent James Monroe (a future president) and Robert Livingston to negotiate the purchase of this port. In the meantime, faced with slave revolts in Santo Domingo and the possibility of joint United States–British action against him in the New World, Napoleon had decided to offer the Louisiana Territory to the U.S. negotiators, who eventually settled on a price of $15 million.

Spain was not pleased that France had sold the territory that Spain had only recently ceded to it, and Jefferson feared that if he awaited ratification of an amendment, the French might back out of the deal and jeopardize American interests. United States expansion to the West Coast appears to have vindicated Jefferson's decision to act in the absence of explicit constitutional authorization, but his action has been variously interpreted as wise statesmanship or as an abandonment of his own principles. During the War of 1812, New Orleans became the site of an important victory against the British. Although it would be possible to do so, the United States has never adopted an amendment to acquire any of its additional territories. The Twenty-third Amendment did grant electoral votes to the District of Columbia, but a later amendment proposed by Congress to grant voting representation to the District failed to be ratified by the requisite number of states.

See also Jefferson, Thomas.

For Further Reading:
Hitchcock, Ripley. 1903. *The Louisiana Purchase, and the Exploration, Early History and Building of the West*. Boston: Ginn & Company, Publishers.

❖ LUDLOW AMENDMENT ❖

See Initiative and Referendum.

❖ *LUTHER V. BORDEN* (1849) ❖

Luther v. Borden was an important Supreme Court case, both in addressing the relationship between constitutional and revolutionary change and in developing the political question doctrine. Chief Justice Roger B. Taney wrote the majority decision. The case arose when Martin Luther brought a suit against Luther Martin for trespassing. Luther Martin had entered Martin Luther's house under authority of a declaration of martial law issued by the original charter government of Rhode Island. This declaration had been prompted by the establishment of a new government, under the direction of Thomas W. Dorr, which Martin Luther supported.

The problem arose largely from the fact that the Rhode Island charter, which the colonists had decided to continue with only minor modifications at the time of the American Revolution, did not specify any means of constitutional change. Although the charter government had severely limited the franchise, and Dorr's government may well have had the support of a majority of the citizens of Rhode Island, the Dorr government had come into being through extralegal means, and the charter government did not recognize its legitimacy. Thus, Daniel Webster argued on Luther Martin's behalf that although American government was built upon the consent of the people, such government also secured itself "against sudden changes by mere majorities," and such government "does not draw any power from tumultuous assemblages" (*Luther* 1849, 31).

In deciding the case, Taney focused on the guarantee clause in Article IV, Section 4 of the Constitution. He ruled that this clause delegated to Congress the power to determine whether a state government was republican and whether to render military assistance to a state government. Congress, in turn, had delegated the latter power to the president. In this case, although the president (John Tyler) had not

actually rendered aid, his declaration of support for the charter government had caused the Dorr government to fold. Taney thus decided that some matters "turned upon political rights and political questions," and it was the Court's duty "not to pass beyond its appropriate sphere of action, and to take care not to involve itself in discussions which properly belong to other forums" (*Luther* 1849, 47).

In *Coleman v. Miller* (1939), the Supreme Court decided that certain questions surrounding the amending process were political questions, but the current status of this opinion is in some doubt. In *Baker v. Carr* (1962), the Supreme Court agreed that the issue of whether a government was or was not republican continued to be a political question. It also ruled that the issue of a state's legislative apportionment could be decided on the basis of the equal protection clause of the Fourteenth Amendment.

The Dorr Rebellion stands as a warning both of the ways that constitutions without amending processes can become fossilized and of the kinds of revolutionary actions that they can precipitate. Its development of the political questions doctrine provides a hedge against inappropriate exercises of judicial review, but its subsequent application to questions raised under Article V of the Constitution remains disputed.

See also *Coleman v. Miller*; Political Questions.

For Further Reading:
Dennison, George M. 1976. *The Dorr War: Republicanism on Trial, 1831–1861.* Lexington: University Press of Kentucky.
Luther v. Borden, 48 U.S. (7 How.) 1 (1849).

❖ LYNCHING ❖

Over 5,000 people, most of whom were black, were lynched from the 1890s through the 1950s, often with the complicity of state and local officials (Ferrell 1986, 1). The U.S. House of Representatives spent substantial time debating antilynching legislation from

1918 to 1921, and it adopted an antilynching law in 1921 that died the following year in the Senate (Ferrell 1986, 110–300).

A key objection to such legislation centered on the issue of whether Congress had sufficient authority under the Thirteenth and Fourteenth Amendments to adopt such legislation or whether such laws interfered with state police powers under the Tenth Amendment. Republican Representative Henry Emerson of Ohio introduced an amendment in March 1919 that would have given explicit recognition to federal power in this area. Courts have subsequently recognized substantially broader congressional powers over a variety of subjects. Even in the absence of federal legislation, in cases such as *Moore v. Dempsey* (1923) they were able to rule that mob-dominated trials violated the due process clause of the Fourteenth Amendment.

In recent years, Courts have applied most of the provisions in the Bill of Rights relative to criminal procedures, once applied solely to the national government, to the states via the due process clause of the Fourteenth Amendment through the doctrine of incorporation. There has, however, been renewed attention as to whether it would be desirable to pass national legislation aggravating penalties for so-called hate crimes that are motivated by the race, gender, sexual orientation, or the like, of victims. Once again, conflict has emerged between those who believe that this kind of legislation should be left to the states and those who believe that national legislation is warranted.

For Further Reading:

Curriden, Mark, and Leroy Phillips Jr. 1999. *Contempt of Court: The Turn-of-the-Century Lynching That Launched 100 Years of Federalism.* New York: Faber and Faber.

M

❖ MACDONALD, DWIGHT (1906–1982) ❖

On the magazine's thirty-fifth anniversary in 1968, the editors of *Esquire* magazine asked journalist Dwight Macdonald to draw up a set of proposals to bring the Constitution up to date. His article was a mix of serious proposals and hyperbole.

Macdonald began by proposing that the presidency should be abolished in favor of a chair to be chosen, as in a parliamentary system, by the majority party in Congress. This chairman would serve for six years or until the chair's party lost a major vote in Congress. This proposal also would have eliminated the electoral college, the vice presidency, and the system of primaries. Macdonald also hoped that it would serve to clip the power and pretensions of the chief executive—and also the temptation to assassinate him. Macdonald proposed that terms of members of the House of Representatives should be lengthened to five years and that members of neither the House nor the Senate should be required to be residents of the states that elected them.

Macdonald proposed a number of social reforms. All males between the ages of eighteen and thirty would be conscripted to two years' service either in the military or in "nonmilitary Work of Social Value"—the draftees' choice (Macdonald 1968, 145). The government would establish a negative income tax to bring all citizens up to a "minimum Health & Decency Standard"; this tax would be paid "without regard to Work, Moral Character or any other Consideration except Need" (*Id.*, 146). Macdonald would establish tribunes, or ombudsmen, in each congressional district. He would also set up history preservation and nature preservation commissions to protect historical and environmental sites, limit the number of U.S. soldiers overseas to one-fourth of 1 percent of the population (except by a four-fifths vote of both houses of Congress), and limit military expenditures to 3 percent of the gross national product. Macdonald also wanted to abolish the space program and reconfigure cities and states into more functional units.

An accompanying piece on the Bill of Rights by Karl E. Meyer was an eclectic mix of reforms that would not, like Macdonald's, require changes in governmental structure. He thought that the government should be responsible for providing a number of social and economic rights, such as access to dramatic performances, public parks, meals, and public transit. He also favored eliminating electronic eavesdropping and supersonic aircraft and curtailing the right to bear arms.

For Further Reading:

Macdonald, Dwight. 1968. "The Constitution of the United States Needs to Be Fixed." *Esquire* 70 (October): 143–146, 238, 240, 243–244, 246, 252.

Meyer, Karl E. 1968. "So Does the Bill of Rights." *Esquire* 70 (October): 147–148.

❖ MACDONALD, WILLIAM (1863–1938) ❖

Journalist and college professor William Mac-Donald offered his proposals for constitutional reform shortly after the Wilson administration (MacDonald 1921, 1922). His central objective was the establishment of responsible parliamentary government, and toward this end, he offered a critique and a comprehensive plan of reform intended to reconfigure the federal system and all three branches of the federal government (Vile 1991c, 57–59).

Under MacDonald's scheme, the presidency would be significantly altered, with the president responsible for designating a member of Congress to form a cabinet and, if successful, to be premier. The premier and the premiere's cabinet would exercise most governmental powers, and they would resign when they lost congressional support. In cases in which a new cabinet could not be formed, the president would dissolve Congress and call for new elections.

MacDonald proposed to delete the current requirement that the president be natural born, to replace the electoral college with a system of direct election, to transfer the directorship of the military forces and the negotiation of treaties to the cabinet, to eliminate the president's power of appointment and removal, and to take away the president's power to recommend legislation. MacDonald's plan would also vest the power to execute laws in the cabinet, eliminate the presidential veto, provide for new elections in cases of presidential vacancy, and formulate a provision to deal with presidential disability (MacDonald 1922, 69–89).

MacDonald proposed maintaining a bicameral Congress but would fix uniform four-year terms and a minimum age of twenty-five years for members of both houses. He would eliminate the custom whereby representatives must be residents of their districts, abolish secret congressional sessions, allow both the Senate and the House to ratify treaties, and create a more structured budget system in which both bills raising revenue and those appropriating money would originate in the House. Congress would be given expanded powers over corpora-tions, immigration and naturalization, education, marriage and divorce, the budget, economic control (including possible nationalizations), and internal improvements, and members would be subject to recall (MacDonald 1922, 90–116). MacDonald also favored a system of uniform requirements for voting in federal elections and wanted the House to represent both population and occupations and professions. MacDonald also favored the proliferation of political parties.

MacDonald wanted the Constitution to delineate more clearly the respective roles of the state and national governments. He thought that Congress should be able to ascertain whether a state government is republican and deny it representation, and he thought that state citizens should have a right to petition Congress on the subject (MacDonald 1922, 155). He wanted to guarantee protections for freedom of religion, assembly, and petition, and for the right to bear arms against abridgments by the states as well as by the national government. He also thought that state militias were anachronisms that needed to be eliminated. Interestingly, MacDonald believed that the Eighteenth Amendment (prohibition) was an undue infringement on state police powers.

Under MacDonald's scheme, judges would be appointed by the premier and the cabinet and would be subject to removal not only by impeachment but also at the request of both houses (MacDonald 1922, 181). He wanted to create a system of administrative courts. He also wanted to control the exercise of judicial power over receiverships, cut back on the use of injunctions, and officially recognize the rights of the courts to declare a law to be unconstitutional.

MacDonald proposed that Congress should pass a resolution putting itself on record as favoring a constitutional convention and inviting states to send petitions to this end (MacDonald 1922, 224). Alternatively, arguing that the provisions in Article V might "properly be viewed as permissive and selective, not as exclusive" (MacDonald 1922, 227), he suggested that Congress could call a constitutional convention on its own.

For Further Reading:

MacDonald, William. 1922. *A New Constitution for a New America*. New York: B. W. Heubsch.

Vile, John R. 1991c. *Rewriting the United States Constitution: An Examination of Proposals from Reconstruction to the Present*. New York: Praeger.

❖ MADISON, JAMES (1751–1836) ❖

Few individuals have had as profound an influence on the formation and understanding of the U.S. Constitution and the Bill of Rights as James Madison, the nation's fourth president. Madison also wrote and thought profoundly about the constitutional amending process.

In addition to taking the most complete notes of the proceedings of the Constitutional Convention of 1787, the physically diminutive Madison, who received his education at Princeton, was one of the guiding forces behind the Virginia Plan, the first major plan to be proposed there. This plan, which differed significantly from the existing Articles of Confederation, proposed three branches of government and a bicameral legislature representing states according to their population and exercising significantly wider powers. This plan indicated that provision should be made for "amendment of the Articles of Union whensoever it shall seem necessary." It further specified that the consent of Congress should not be necessary, but it was otherwise nonspecific (Vile 1992, 27). Madison subsequently supported a proposal, however, that would funnel amendments through the national legislature, apparently opposing the state-requested convention mechanism largely on the basis of practical considerations (Weber 1989, 36).

Although Madison had failed in achieving a number of his goals (for, example, he had favored representation by population in both houses of Congress and a Council of Revision with power to void state laws that conflicted with the Constitution, neither of which the Convention had adopted), at the convention's end Madison was one of the Constitution's most outspoken and articulate defenders. When Patrick Henry argued at the Virginia state ratifying convention that the amending process in Article V was too difficult, Madison pointed out that the mechanism was much easier than the one under the Articles of Confederation.

Madison's most memorable defense of the new Constitution, however, came in his role as one of the three authors of the *Federalist Papers*, who wrote under the name of Publius. In his landmark essay in *Federalist No. 10*, Madison disputed the notion (which Anti-Federalist opponents of the new Constitution had borrowed from the Baron de Montesquieu) that it was impossible to establish a republican, or representative, government over a large land area like that in the United States. Madison argued that the size of the nation, and the system of representative democracy that it utilized, would, in fact, serve as a cure for the "mischiefs" of "faction," or private interests as expressed in interest groups and political parties; he thus opposed direct, or pure, democracy where he thought factions were often magnified. In *Federalist No. 38*, although acknowledging that it was not perfect, Madison defended the new Constitution as being infinitely better than the Articles of Confederation. In *Federalist No. 43*, Madison argued that the amending process "guards equally against that extreme facility, which would render the Constitution too mutable; and that extreme difficulty, which might perpetuate its discovered faults" (Hamilton, Madison, and Jay 1961, 278).

Federalist Nos. 49 and *50* may well constitute Madison's deepest and most original thinking on the idea of constitutional change. His reasoning there is especially interesting, because it was designed in part as a response to a proposal made by Madison's close friend, fellow Virginian and later fellow Democratic-Republican Party leader Thomas Jefferson. In *Federalist No. 49*, Madison opposed Jefferson's suggested plan that would enable two of three branches of the government to call a convention for altering the Constitution. Focusing on the advantages of stability, Madison honed in on the stabilizing advantages of inculcating "veneration" for the Constitution (Levinson 1990b). Madison noted that "as every appeal to the people would carry an implication of some defect in the government, frequent appeals would, in great measure, deprive the government of that veneration which time bestows on everything, and without which perhaps the wisest and freest governments would not possess the requisite stability" (Hamilton et al. 1961, 314). Madison offered similar arguments in private correspondence in regard to Jefferson's idea that the Constitution should be rewritten each generation (Vile 1992, 64–65). Similarly rejecting periodic appeals to the people in *Federalist No. 50*, Madison drew largely from the negative experiences that Pennsylvania had encountered with the Council of Censors. Madison went on in *Federalist No. 51* to explain and praise the system of checks and balances established under the new Constitution.

The most persistent criticism of the new Constitution was that it lacked a bill of rights. Initially little concerned about this omission, Madison appears to have been persuaded in part by arguments from Thomas Jefferson and in part by his fear that if Federalist supporters of the Constitution did not make such a promise to the Anti-Federalists, these opponents would call a second convention before the work of the first one was ratified (Weber 1989; Finkelman 1991). Subsequently elected to the House of Representatives, Madison took the lead in formulating, advocating, and shepherding the Bill of Rights through the First Congress. He thought that adoption of such a bill was essential to securing popular approval of the Constitution. Madison structured the Bill of Rights so that it would focus primarily on individual rights rather than on possible structural changes to the yet untried national government. The Bill of Rights limited the national government; Madison did not succeed in getting an amendment adopted that would have limited the states, which at the time he thought were more likely to abuse civil liberties.

As power shifted in the new government to political opponents in the Federalist Party, who were not always sensitive to the protection of individual rights (the party adopted the Sedition Act, limiting speech, in 1798), Madison often joined with Jefferson and other Democratic-Republicans in defending states' rights and opposing broad interpretations of federal

powers like those announced in *McCulloch v. Maryland* (1819). Madison helped author the Virginia Resolution that suggested (along with Jefferson's Kentucky Resolution) that states might "interpose" themselves against unconstitutional legislation like the Sedition Act. Madison also served as Thomas Jefferson's secretary of state and was one of the parties in *Marbury v. Madison* (1803), in which Chief Justice John Marshall asserted the courts' power of judicial review.

As president, Madison recommended an amendment designed to permit the national government to undertake internal improvements. When no such amendment was adopted, he vetoed such legislation. By the same token, during his term, Madison approved the reestablishment of the national bank that he had previously argued was unconstitutional; in this case, he argued that established precedents, as well as necessities demonstrated during the War of 1812, were more important here than his own initial judgment. Significantly, Madison saw that his notes of the Constitutional Convention of 1787 would not be published until after his death, when most precedents would already be established.

In 1829–1830 Madison participated in the convention that met to redraw the Virginia state constitution. His final words to his country were an appeal that "the Union of States be cherished and perpetual" (Meyers 1973, 576). At his death in 1836, Madison was the only surviving member of the Constitutional Convention of 1787.

See also Bill of Rights; Constitutional Convention of 1787; Federalists.

For Further Reading:

Banning, Lance. 1995. *The Sacred Fire of Liberty: James Madison and the Founding of the Federal Republic*. Ithaca, NY: Cornell University Press.

Finkelman, Paul. 1991. "James Madison and the Bill of Rights: A Reluctant Paternity." In *The Supreme Court Review, 1990*. Chicago: University of Chicago Press.

Hamilton, Alexander, James Madison, and John Jay. 1787–1788. *The Federalist Papers*. Reprint, New York: New American Library, 1961.

Levinson, Sanford. 1990b. "'Veneration' and Constitutional Change: James Madison Confronts the Possibility of Constitutional Amendment." *Texas Tech Law Review* 21: 2443–2461.

Matthews, Richard K. 1995. *If Men Were Angels: James Madison and the Heartless Empire of Reason.* Lawrence: University Press of Kansas.

Meyers, Marvin, ed. 1973. *The Mind of the Founder: Sources of the Political Thought of James Madison.* Indianapolis, IN: Bobbs-Merrill.

Miller, William Lee. 1992. *The Business of May Next: James Madison and the Founding.* Charlottesville: University Press of Virginia.

Morgan, Robert J. 1988. *James Madison on the Constitution and the Bill of Rights.* New York: Greenwood Press.

Rutland, Robert A. 1987. *James Madison: The Founding Father.* New York: Macmillan.

Vile, John R. 1992. *The Constitutional Amending Process in American Political Thought.* New York: Praeger.

Weber, Paul. 1989. "Madison's Opposition to a Second Convention." *Polity* 20 (Spring): 498–517.

❖ MAGNA CARTA ❖

Although the "unwritten" English Constitution is often contrasted to the written Constitution of the United States, this contrast is not completely accurate. Not only does the English constitution rest in part on written documents, but the United States has also adopted many extraconstitutional customs and usages that influence how the document is applied and interpreted.

The Magna Carta is one of the most significant milestones in the history of English liberty. Extracted by the English barons from King John at Runnymede in 1215 (and later reaffirmed by a number of subsequent monarchs), the document, consisting of a preamble and sixty-three clauses, was designed to limit perceived abuses of the barons and their subjects on the part of the king. The document provided for the writ of habeas corpus and for a variety of procedural rights that Americans today associate with the Bill of Rights, and, more particularly, with the due process clauses of the Fifth and Fourteenth Amendments. By

creating a council to assure that the document would be followed, the Magna Carta also marked one of the steps in the development of parliament, which became the prototype for legislative bodies that were later adopted in the United States.

The English jurist and commentator Edward Coke used the Magna Carta to argue against royal prerogatives. In their dispute with Great Britain that led up to the Revolutionary War, the American colonists who initially considered themselves to be English citizens with accompanying rights, in turn, utilized Coke's arguments to strike out against the doctrine of parliamentary sovereignty, which most British legal commentators were then embracing. The colonial rejection of parliamentary sovereignty led in turn to their espousal of the doctrine of "no taxation without representation."

The example of the Magna Carta serves both as a foundation for the idea of a written constitution and for the idea that such constitutions should be designed to protect individual rights. The document also serves as an example of the continuing power that written words can have in rallying individuals to protect their liberties.

For Further Reading:
Walker, David M. 1980. "Magna Carta." In *The Oxford Companion to Law.* Oxford, UK: Clarenden Press, pp. 795–797.

❖ MARBURY, WILLIAM ❖

During the Progressive Era, Maryland attorney William Marbury was one of the most prominent proponents of the argument that there were inherent limits on the power to amend the U.S. Constitution (Vile 1992, 157–171). Marbury presented his arguments in at least two law review articles questioning the legitimacy of the Eighteenth and Nineteenth Amendments (Marbury 1919, 1920; for response, see Frierson 1920). He also served as an attorney for the state of Maryland in *Myers v. Anderson* (1915)—unsuccessfully seeking to uphold the constitutionality of the state's grandfather clause against provisions of the Fifteenth Amendment, which denied discrimination in voting on the basis of race—and *Leser v. Garnett* (1922), also unsuccessfully questioning the legitimacy of the Nineteenth Amendment, denying discrimination on the basis of sex.

Marbury's arguments, like those of contemporary Selden Bacon, were built partly on views of state sovereignty that have received increased attention before the U.S. Supreme Court during the administration of Chief Justice Rehnquist. In recent years, the idea that there might be judicially enforceable inherent limitations on the amending process has been revived by individuals such as Walter Murphy, who are more concerned about the protection of individual rights than with state sovereignty.

See also Bacon, Selden.

For Further Reading:

Frierson, William. 1920. "Amending the Constitution of the United States: A Reply to Mr. Marbury." *Harvard Law Review* 33 (March): 659–666.

Marbury, William L. 1920. "The Nineteenth Amendment and After." *Virginia Law Review* 7 (October): 1–29.

———. 1919. "The Limitations upon the Amending Power." *Harvard Law Review* 33 (December): 223–235.

❖ *MARBURY V. MADISON* (1803) ❖

In Britain, Parliament is considered to be supreme. Because it exercises such legislative sovereignty and because the country has no single written constitution, a formal amendment process is not necessary. By contrast, in the United States, the Constitution is supreme over ordinary acts of legislation. If Congress wishes to alter the Constitution, it must proceed via the Article V amending processes.

In large part, this system emerged because of the extraordinarily important decision that Chief Justice John Marshall authored in *Marbury v. Madison* (1803). Marbury brought his case to the Supreme Court after Thomas Jefferson's new secretary of state, James Madison, refused to deliver a commission to Marbury, who had been appointed a justice of the peace

by the outgoing administration of John Adams.

Marshall agreed that Marbury was entitled to his commission and that laws provide a remedy in such circumstances. Marshall decided, however, that the remedy was not a writ of mandamus, a judicial order issued to an executive official issuing from the Court. He reasoned that the provision of the Judiciary Act of 1789 that appeared to grant this power to the Court was flawed because Article III of the Constitution clearly limited the original jurisdiction of the Supreme Court to certain circumstances, of which this was not one. In deciding that the Court had the responsibility of exercising judicial review and of striking down this provision of the law, Marshall, a Federalist appointee, thus avoided a direct confrontation with the new Democratic-Republican administration.

In outlining his case for judicial construction of the Constitution, Marshall noted that the creation of a constitution was "a very great exertion," not "to be frequently repeated" (*Marbury* 1803, 176). He further said that the Constitution was "either a superior paramount law, unchangeable by ordinary means, or it is on a level with ordinary legislative acts, and like other acts, is alterable when the legislature shall please to alter it" (*Marbury* 1803, 177). Arguing that it was "emphatically the province and duty of the judicial department to say what the law is" (*Marbury* 1803, 177), Marshall thus ruled that he must be bound by the Constitution rather than by the Judiciary Act.

In assuming a power not directly stated in, but arguably implied by, the Constitution, Marshall at once limited changes that Congress could make in constitutional understandings and ensured that the judicial branch would play a big role in interpreting that document. If some institution in government did not have this power of interpretation, it might be necessary to resort to the constitutional amending process far more frequently.

See also Madison, James; Marshall, John; Judiciary entries.

For Further Reading:

Alfange, Dean, Jr. 1994. "*Marbury v. Madison* and Original Understandings of Judicial Review: In

Defense of Traditional Wisdom." In *The Supreme Court Review, 1993*. Chicago: University of Chicago Press.

Clinton, Robert L. 1989. *Marbury v. Madison and Judicial Review*. Lawrence: University Press of Kansas.

Marbury v. Madison, 5 U.S. (1 Cranch.) 137 (1803).

❖ MARDUKE, P. G. ❖

In 1970 P. G. Marduke (otherwise unidentified) published a hand-typed brochure entitled *The CASCOT System for Social Control of Technology*. Marduke's premise was that although many individuals feared technology, it could actually be a potent force for change at a time when the world was in crisis and greater democratic participation was desirable. Marduke devoted separate chapters to different areas of concern.

Marduke proposed that the political system be changed from a "system of 'power politics' to a system of 'people politics'" (Marduke 1970, 37). One specific proposal was the initiation of a system of Touch-Tone voting whereby citizens could vote on pending legislation. Marduke also advocated abolishing the Senate, with its malapportionment, and granting public officials "a life-time salary" while prohibiting all other income and investment (Marduke 1970, 43). Marduke proposed conducting nominations by telephone computer system, requiring that the media give candidates opportunity to talk to the public, and limiting campaign spending to a fixed amount of money. Marduke also favored the elimination of independent regulatory agencies and an expansion of the congressional representative's role as ombudsman. Marduke would replace the presidency with an elected National Council of five officials, each heading an agency (international affairs, environment, commerce, public welfare, and administration) consisting of five persons, each, in turn, responsible for a single technical area.

Considering the existing economic system to be seriously flawed, Marduke proposed a number of far-reaching changes also based on the application of modern technology, including replacing the system of currency with electronic transactions, recording all capital assets over $25 in value, imposing limits on individual net worth as well as a minimum below which no one should be permitted to fall, and redistributing wealth according to public vote. The system would also be designed to provide "whatever amount of credit the people wanted" (Marduke 1970, 70–71).

In the area of health care, Marduke favored establishing parallel public and private health systems. In defense matters, Marduke advocated hiring a network of foreign agents pledged to stop their nations from "the first use of atomic, biochemical or other mass-murder weaponry" (Marduke 1970, 94). The ultimate goal was a "cosmopolitan system where people, not nations or institutions, are the essential ingredients" (Marduke 1970, 95). In a chapter on international relations, Marduke thus proposed opening the doors "to any and every other nation that cares to enter the system" (Marduke 1970, 98). This would involve sharing economic resources as well as political ideals and would begin with pressure exerted by refusing to import goods from foreign nations.

In analyzing sex and morals, Marduke worked from the premise that "sex is fun" (Marduke 1970, 105) and argued that technological advances made traditional prohibitions against premarital sex outdated. Marduke favored the establishment of a fairly permissive "code for what is legally and morally prohibited," as well as a nonbinding code for "what is socially encouraged and discouraged" (Marduke 1970, 110). The latter would involve polling the public on attitudes about "dating, drinking and drugs; fashion, fads and fornication" (Marduke 1970, 111). Marduke further suggested a "random-sample-censorship" for media productions (Marduke 1970, 112) and the establishment of social centers to distribute drugs to addicts.

In order to deal with environmental problems, Marduke advocated the creation of mass-transit systems. Marduke also advocated banning all chemicals "applied to soil or vegetation for any purpose" (Marduke 1970, 126), creating sewage treatment plants in every city, ending offshore oil drilling, declaring minerals to be the property of all people, and making birth control available on a voluntary basis, with the possibility of a compulsory system if this did not work.

Marduke wanted to replace the existing welfare system with social centers for mass feeding and care. Marduke also advocated the establishment of more extensive consumer education and examinations for people in the repair business. Marduke favored extensive educational reform. Education would be divided into four levels, with the first levels oriented toward practical training and consumer education.

Marduke criticized the legal system for preoccupation with money and favored devising a legal system with three levels consisting of a public arbitrator, three-person investigatory boards, and an appeals investigatory board. Criminal sanctions would be designed not to punish but to motivate better behavior or to isolate the criminal from society.

Clearly, Marduke's proposals called for extensive change involving not only the Constitution but the entire social structure. Accordingly, Marduke recognized that "the most difficult problem will be to keep the change on an evolutionary, rather than a revolutionary scale" (Marduke 1970, 163). Marduke hoped to run CASCOT candidates in the 1972 elections. Senatorial candidates would be pledged to abolish that institution. Marduke also favored modifying the amending process sometime before 1980 so that a majority of the House could propose amendments to be approved by popular majorities. That change would be followed by "the chain of amendments necessary to establish the popular voting system and the economic system and the form of government that can effectively deal with the world's crisis" (Marduke 1970, 170). Despite such hopes, Marduke's proposals appear to have had little impact.

For Further Reading:

Marduke, P. G. 1970. *The CASCOT System for Social Control of Technology.* Silver Spring, MD: Citizens' Association for Social Control of Technology.

❖ MARRIAGE, DIVORCE, AND PARENTING ❖

States are responsible for enacting most laws involving domestic relations, including marriage and divorce, matters that are considered among the "police powers" reserved to the states by the Tenth Amendment. Article IV, Section 1 provides, however, that states shall give "Full Faith and Credit . . . to the public Acts, Records, and judicial Proceedings of every other State." Moreover, Article IV, Section 3 of the Constitution entrusts Congress with the power to "make all needful Rules and Regulations respecting the Territory or other Property belonging to the United States."

In exercise of this power, Congress adopted several laws in the nineteenth century aimed at the practice of polygamy, which since 1852 had been sanctioned by the Mormon Church and practiced by church leaders (G. Larson 1971, 37). Congressional laws included the Morrill Act of 1862 restricting polygamy; a bill sponsored by Vermont Republican Luke Porter Poland in 1874 strengthening federal judicial power in the Utah Territory; and the Edmunds bill of 1874 (strengthened by the Tucker amendment in 1887), which was especially hard on polygamists and restricted their political participation (G. Larson 1971, 58–59; Peterson 1977, 102).

The U.S. Supreme Court unanimously upheld the constitutionality of such laws in *Reynolds v. United States* (1879), the first case in which it ever ruled on the First Amendment. In upholding Reynolds's conviction for polygamy, the Court said that although the federal government could not legislate belief, it could regulate conduct. This distinction has subsequently been applied in numerous cases involving interpretation of the religion clauses in the First Amendment.

Judging from the number of amending proposals that were introduced in Congress, as well as by the fact that Utah was not admitted into the Union as a state until January 1896, after Mormon Church leaders had renounced polygamy (Lyman 1986), polygamy stirred substantial national concern. In part, that concern was motivated by the belief that polygamy, like slavery, was a relic of barbarism. President Ulysses S. Grant thus noted in his seventh annual message in 1875:

> That polygamy should exist in a free, enlightened, and Christian country, without the power to punish so flagrant a crime against decency and morality seems preposterous. True there is no law to sustain this unnatural vice; but what is needed is a law to punish it as a crime, and at the same time to fix the status of the innocent children, the offspring of this system, and of the possibly innocent plural wives. But as an institution polygamy should be banished from the land. (J. Richardson 1908, 7:355)

Republican Representative Julius Caesar Burrows of Michigan introduced the first amendment designed to restrict polygamy in 1879, with more than twenty such proposals following in each successive decade through the 1920s. From 1906 to 1913, sixteen states applied for a convention to deal with this issue. Most amendments introduced in Congress specifically sought to outlaw polygamy, but some were phrased in terms of allowing Congress to make uniform rules on marriage and divorce (see Godkin 1864) or of prohibiting polygamists from assuming public office. From the 1930s on, the introduction of such proposals slowed but did not end completely.

Absent such an amendment, states continue to regulate most family matters within their jurisdictions, with none now sanctioning polygamy. A number of federal court decisions have, however, somewhat limited state regulation of domestic matters. The most notable cases have been *Griswold v. Connecticut* (1965), which recognized a right of marital privacy and provided access to contraceptives; *Loving v. Virginia* (1967), which struck down state restrictions on interracial marriage; *Roe v. Wade* (1973), which struck down most laws restricting access to abortion; and *Zablocki v. Redhail* (1978), which struck down a state law forbidding a noncustodial parent who was delinquent in child support from remarrying. Similarly, in *Romer v. Evans* (1996), the

Supreme Court used the equal protection clause of the Fourteenth Amendment to overturn Colorado's Amendment 2, a provision Colorado voters had accepted in a referendum that would have prohibited the government from taking action to protect individuals based on their sexual orientation or lifestyle. Also, since passage of the Mann Act (also known as the White Slave Act) in 1910, the national government has selectively prosecuted individuals who have transported women across state lines for immoral purposes (Langum 1994).

Fearing that Hawaii courts might extend marriage rights to homosexuals, Congress adopted the Defense of Marriage Act in 1996. Defining marriage under federal law as the union of a male and a female, the law, adopted under a perceived congressional authority to make exceptions under the full faith and credit clause, prevents states from having to recognize same-sex marriages performed in other states. Responding to a state supreme court decision, Vermont adopted a law that went into effect in July 2000 giving same-sex couples the same benefits, albeit not marriage licenses, accorded to different-sex couples. However, this decision has led to a political backlash against legislators who supported the amendment in Vermont, and at least thirty-four states have adopted laws rejecting recognition of gay marriages. Hawaii was one of a number of states that foreclosed state judicial action by adopting a constitutional amendment limiting marriages to those between a man and a woman (George 2001, 33). Some social conservatives, concerned about preserving the institution of the family, which they believe is closely tied to keeping traditional marriage arrangements distinctive, are now advocating a federal constitutional amendment that would provide:

> Marriage in the United States shall consist only of the union of a man and a woman. Neither this constitution or the constitution of any state, nor state or federal law, shall be construed to require that marital status or the legal incidents thereof be conferred upon unmarried couples or groups. (George 2001, 34)

Supported by a broadly based group known as the Alliance for Marriage that is headed by

Matt Daniels, three Democrats and three Republicans introduced this amendment in Congress on 15 May 2002, along with a provision opposed by a group known as the Family Research Council (Gallagher, 2002), allowing states to decide whether to permit domestic partnerships or civil unions (Henneberg 2002). Some proponents of the amendment have regarded it as doing little more than stating the obvious, asserting something "like the sky is blue or cows make milk" (Graham 2002, 14), but supporters think that stating the obvious may be a valid mechanism for precluding judicial decisions employing equal protection analysis to mandate such marriages (Budziszewski 2002).

According to one scholarly proponent, the amendment introduced in Congress would not forbid corporations from giving health-care benefits or hospitals from giving visitation rights to same-sex couples, but would prevent "the automatic, across-the-board qualification of same-sex partners for whatever marital benefits happen to exist" (George 2001, 34). Matt Daniels, an executive director of the Alliance for Marriage, notes that "Gays and lesbians have a right to live as they choose, but they don't have a right to redefine marriage for our entire country" (Henneberg 2002). The Alliance for Marriage has a website labeled *allianceformarriage.org.*

Other defenders of traditional marriage fear that concessions of any kind might undermine the institution: "They argue that if you preserve the word *marriage* for its traditional definition, but allow 'civil unions' that accomplish a similar objective, what have you won?" As Ken Connor of the Family Research Council has asked, "If you back a counterfeit solution, it depreciates the value of the real thing" (Graham 2002, 17).

By contrast to proponents of traditional marriage who fear that the amendment does not go far enough, defenders of gay rights are quite concerned that the amendment goes too far. Chris Anders of the American Civil Liberties Union claims that the amendment "would wipe out every last protection there is for gay and lesbian families and other unmarried couples" (Henneberg 2002), and Kim Gandy, president of the National Organization for Women, has described the amendment as "a vicious attempt to make the U.S. Constitution explicitly anti-lesbian and gay rights" (quoted in Gallagher 2002).

On another family issue, proponents of parental rights, including Republican Senator Charles Grassley of Iowa and Republican Representative Steve Largent of Oklahoma, have proposed a Parental Rights and Responsibility Act to limit governmental regulation of family life absent a "compelling state interest." The bill focuses on four main areas—education, health care, discipline, and religious training (Lawton 1996, 57). Since 1995 "parental rights amendments" have been introduced both in Congress and in a majority of states, where most attention appears to have been directed. Such amendments would alter state constitutions to provide that "the rights of parents to direct the upbringing and education of their children shall not be infringed" (Lawton 1996, 57). The Court has recognized related rights in *Meyer v. Nebraska* (1923), in *Pierce v. Society of Sisters* (1925), and in *Wisconsin v. Yoder* (1972). The first struck down a state law prohibiting the teaching of modern foreign languages in school, the second permitted parents to send their children to parochial rather than to public schools, and the third allowed Amish parents to withdraw their children, who were in Amish-directed apprenticeship programs, from school after the eighth grade. A still more recent decision in *Troxel v. Granville* (2000) has asserted parental control over visits by third parties (in that case, grandparents) with their children. Still, some critics fear that the new parental rights amendments might increase parental rights at the expense of those of children and spawn unnecessary litigation that might give parents too much control of school curricula (Sabourin 1999; Ross 2000).

For Further Reading:

Budziszewski, J. 2002. "Judicial Restraints." *World* 17 (June 8): 16–18.

Gallagher, Maggie. 2002. "Live Your Life, but Marriage Is for Men and Women." *The Tennessean,* 30 May, 9A.

George, Robert P. 2001. "The 28th Amendment:

It Is Time to Protect Marriage, and Democracy, in America." *National Review* 53 (July 23): 32–34.

Godkin, E. L. 1864. "The Constitution and Its Defects." *North American Review* 99 (July): 117–143.

Gordon, Sarah Barringer. 2002. *The Mormon Question: Polygamy and Constitutional Conflict in Nineteenth-Century America.* Chapel Hill, NC: University of North Carolina Press.

Graham, Tim. 2002. "Prenuptial Disagreement." *World* 17 (June 8): 14–18.

Henneberg, Molly. 2002. "Marriage Amendment Preserves Male-Female Union." *http://www.foxnews. com/story/0,2933,52891,00.html.* Accessed 5/16/02.

Langum, David J. 1994. *Crossing Over the Line: Legislating Morality and the Mann Act.* Chicago: University of Chicago Press.

Larson, Gustave O. 1971. *The "Americanization" of Utah for Statehood.* San Marino, CA: Huntington Library.

Lyman, Edward L. 1986. *Political Deliverance: The Mormon Quest for Utah Statehood.* Urbana, IL: University of Illinois Press.

Richardson, James E., ed. 1908. *A Compilation of the Messages and Papers of the Presidents, 1789–1908.* 11 vols. n.p.: Bureau of National Literature and Art.

Ross, William G. 2000. "The Contemporary Significance of *Meyer* and *Pierce* for Parental Rights Issues Involving Education." *Akron Law Review* 34: 177–207.

Sabourin, Jennifer L. 1999. "Note: Parental Rights Amendments: Will a Statutory Right to Parent Force Children to 'Shed Their Constitutional Rights' at the Schoolhouse Door?" *Wayne State University Law Review* 44 (Winter): 1899–1926.

❖ MARSHALL, JOHN (1755–1835) ❖

No one has had a greater impact on the interpretation of the U.S. Constitution than John Marshall. Marshall fought during the Revolutionary War and, although he did not attend the Constitutional Convention of 1787, served as a delegate to the Virginia ratifying convention. As a prominent Federalist, Marshall served as John Adams's secretary of state and was subsequently appointed to the Supreme Court, where he was chief justice from 1801 to 1835.

Marshall significantly enhanced the prestige of the Supreme Court. During his long tenure, it became customary for the Court to issue majority opinions (most of which he authored) rather than, as previously, for each justice to write separately. Much to the frustration of the Democratic-Republicans, Marshall was generally able to mass even their appointees behind his decisions supporting strong national powers—for example, *Cohens v. Virginia* (1821)—and establishing the authority of the Court.

There are few areas of constitutional law on which Marshall did not have an impact. One of his most important contributions was in the area of judicial review. By asserting the right of the judiciary "to say what the law is" and to invalidate federal laws in *Marbury v. Madison* (1803), Marshall made it possible on many occasions for the Court to initiate changes in constitutional interpretation and to apply the Constitution to new circumstances without the need for constitutional amendments (Cahn 1954, 19). Indeed, in *Marbury*, Marshall specifically noted that the creation of a new government "is a very great exertion, nor can it, nor ought it, to be frequently repeated." His justification for judicial review in this case rested largely on the proposition that, in invalidating a law, the Supreme Court was not exerting its own will but simply enforcing written agreements already embodied within the Constitution. In *Cohens v. Virginia,* Marshall noted that "The people made the constitution, and the people can unmake it. It is the creature of their own will, and lives only by their will" (quoted in Kyvig 1996a, 486).

Still, Marshall believed that the Constitution should be interpreted expansively. In upholding the constitutionality of the national bank in *McCulloch v. Maryland* (1819), Marshall used the necessary and proper clause in Article I, Section 8 to argue for a broad interpretation of the Constitution. In so doing, he distinguished such a broad charter intended to endure for generations from more prolix legal codes that should be interpreted more strictly. Without such an interpretation, the Constitution would have required many more amendments than it has received for Congress to exercise its current powers.

Marshall was a strong proponent of vested rights, most notably in cases such as *Fletcher v. Peck* (1810) and *Dartmouth College v. Woodward* (1819), in which he gave a broad reading to the contract clause. Similarly, Marshall upheld broad national authority over interstate commerce, especially in *Gibbons v. Ogden* (1824), where he used the grant of a federal license to a steamship to strike down a conflicting state monopoly over navigation in its waters.

Although Marshall generally chartered a bold course in constitutional interpretation, his decision in *Barron v. Baltimore* (1833) limited the application of the Bill of Rights to the national government. This interpretation stood until 1868, when the adoption of the Fourteenth Amendment led to renewed questions about the scope of such rights, most of which have subsequently been applied to the states via the due process clause of this amendment.

Marshall's vigorous tenure on the Court prompted numerous amending proposals to clip the federal judiciary, but like the efforts to convict Marshall's colleague Justice Samuel Chase on charges of impeachment, they came to nothing. When Marshall left the Court, it was well situated as a coordinate branch of the national government, with power to interpret the law and even to strike down laws it judged to be in conflict with the Constitution.

See also *Marbury v. Madison; McCulloch v. Maryland.*

For Further Reading:

Baker, Leonard. 1974. *John Marshall: A Life in Law.* New York: Macmillan Publishing Company.

Beveridge, Albert J. 1916. *The Life of John Marshall.* 4 vols. Boston: Houghton Mifflin.

Cahn, Edmond. 1954. "An American Contribution." In *Supreme Court and Supreme Law.* Bloomington, IN: Indiana University Press.

Kyvig, David E. 1996a. *Explicit and Authentic Acts: Amending the Constitution, 1776–1995.* Lawrence, KS: University Press of Kansas.

Newmyer, R. Kent. 1968. *The Supreme Court Under Marshall and Taney.* New York: Thomas Y. Crowell.

Smith, Jean Edward. 1996. *John Marshall: Definer of a Nation.* New York: Henry Holt and Company.

White, G. Edward. 1991. *The Marshall Court and Cultural Change 1815–1835.* New York: Oxford University Press.

❖ MASON, GEORGE (1725–1792) ❖

This Virginia planter, often incorrectly thought to be a lawyer, perhaps because of his role as a commissioner of the peace in Fairfax County, Virginia, played an important part in the development of American constitutionalism. A longtime neighbor and friend of George Washington, Mason was the chief author of the Virginia Declaration of Rights, which later served as a model of other bills of rights, and Virginia's revolutionary constitution. Although, largely for reasons of poor health and impatient temperament, Mason refused most public offices, he did attend the Constitutional Convention of 1787 as a delegate from Virginia. He was a strong advocate of an amending provision. Early in the convention, just after the Virginia Plan had been introduced, Mason noted that:

> The plan now to be formed will certainly be defective, as the Confederation has been found on trial to be. Amendments therefore will be necessary, and it will be better to provide for them, in an easy, regular and Constitutional way than to trust to chance and violence. It would be improper to require the consent of the Natl. Legislature, because they may abuse their power, and refuse their consent on that very account. (Farrand 1966, 1:202–203)

Two days before the Constitution was signed, Mason objected to the amending mechanism that then relied solely on congressional proposal and state ratification. Arguing that "no amendment of the proper kind would ever be obtained by the people, if the Government should become oppressive, as he verily believed would be the case" (Farrand 1966, 2:629), Mason's objection became the basis for the addition of the still unused provision that enables two-thirds of the states to petition Congress to call a constitutional convention to propose amendments.

Although he was himself a slaveholder, Mason believed that slavery was morally wrong, he expressed this opinion at the Constitutional Convention, and he was disappointed that the new Constitution did nothing to address the problem. Concerned that the Constitution "had been formed without the knowledge of the idea of the people," Mason suggested toward the end of the Constitutional Convention that "[a] second Convention will know more of the sense of the people, and be able to provide a system more consonant to it" (Farrand 1996, 2:632). As one who had authored the Virginia Declaration of Rights, Mason also argued that the Constitution should contain a similar provision. Because it did not, he was one of three remaining delegates to the Constitutional Convention (the others were Elbridge Gerry and Edmund Randolph) who refused to sign the document and continued his opposition to the point of alienating himself from George Washington. Eventually, Federalist supporters of the Constitution relented on one key point, and the first ten amendments (the Bill of Rights) were proposed and ratified in 1791.

See also Virginia Declaration of Rights.

For Further Reading:

Farrand, Max, ed. 1966. *The Records of the Federal Convention*. 4 vols. New Haven, CT: Yale University Press.

Senese, Donald J. 1989. *George Mason and the Legacy of Constitutional Liberty: An Examination of the Influence of George Mason on the American Bill of Rights*. Fairfax County, VA: Fairfax County Historical Commission.

❖ *MCCULLOCH V. MARYLAND* (1819) ❖

McCulloch v. Maryland remains one of the most important decisions written by Chief Justice John Marshall and, in fact, by any justice. By establishing the doctrine of implied powers and the principle of broad constitutional construction, this decision did much to obviate the need for many amendments that have been introduced to expand congressional powers. By

the same token, by recognizing the broad reach of such powers, the decision has arguably enhanced the importance of explicit restraints on such powers, such as those found in the Bill of Rights and elsewhere in the Constitution.

McCulloch arose when the state of Maryland attempted to levy a tax on a branch of the national bank established in Baltimore, which the teller McCulloch refused to pay. The Supreme Court had to decide whether the bank, which was first established after vigorous debate between Alexander Hamilton and Thomas Jefferson in the George Washington administration and subsequently reestablished during James Madison's presidency, was constitutional. The second issue centered on the legitimacy of Maryland's attempt to tax the bank.

In sanctioning the bank, Marshall developed the idea of implied powers. Although the power to incorporate a bank was not specifically granted in the Constitution, neither was it prohibited. In reserving powers to the states, the Tenth Amendment omitted the word "expressly," thus specifying that the powers "not delegated to the United States, nor prohibited to the States, are reserved to the States or to the people," and thus not precluding the idea of implied powers. Moreover, the right to create a corporation such as a bank was not an end in itself but a means to other ends, or powers, that were designated in the Constitution.

Specifying that under Article I, Section 8 of the Constitution Congress could exercise all powers that were "necessary and proper," Marshall argued that the framers had intended to expand rather than restrict such authority. In context, the word "necessary" neither denoted absolute necessity nor limited Congress to the most restrictive means. As Marshall observed, "The provision is made in a constitution intended to endure for ages to come, and, consequently, to be adapted to the various *crises* of human affairs (*McCulloch* 1819, 415). In justifying the creation of the bank, Marshall wrote, "Let the end be legitimate, let it be within the scope of the constitution, and all means which are appropriate, which are plainly adapted to that end, which are not prohibited, but consist with the letter and spirit of the constitution, are constitutional" (*McCulloch* 1819, 421).

In upholding national sovereignty over state sovereignty, Marshall ruled that Maryland had no right to tax the bank. Such a power would inappropriately give parts of the Union, the states, the power to destroy the whole, the Union.

Virginia's John Taylor of Caroline and Judge Spencer Roane severely criticized *McCulloch,* and the state proposed an amendment to create an institution other than the Supreme Court for resolving conflicts between the national government and the states (Levy 1995, 428). Long after this proposal has been largely forgotten, the Court continues to interpret constitutional powers broadly enough that the most important restrictions on such powers continue to be explicit constitutional restrictions rather than the lack of explicit constitutional grants of power.

See also Marshall, John; Necessary and Proper Clause; Tenth Amendment.

For Further Reading:

Levy, Leonard W. 1995. *Seasoned Judgments: The American Constitution, Rights, and History.* New Brunswick, NJ: Transaction Publishers.

McCulloch v. Maryland, 17 U.S. (4 Wheat.) 316 (1819).

❖ MCKEE, HENRY S. (1868–1956) ❖

California businessman Henry McKee presented his plans for political, economic, and educational reform in a book published in 1933. Like Karl Marx, with whom he otherwise shared little in common, McKee predicted that without reform, the next economic depression was likely to lead to complete political breakdown. Perhaps because he was a businessman, most of McKee's political solutions were borrowed from earlier thinkers such as Woodrow Wilson and Gamaliel Bradford.

McKee was an opponent of government by committee and a proponent of strong executive power. Like Wilson, McKee believed that by forcing individuals to articulate and defend their views publicly, a parliamentary system would attract men of greater talents. Accompanying a strengthened cabinet would be a type of "question hour," during which members of the cabinet would have to defend their views before Congress. McKee believed that such debates would expose demagogic appeals and flawed programs, in which category he placed the progressive income tax and inheritance taxes.

McKee favored more centralized governmental control over economic problems, subject again to the increased scrutiny and accountability that a parliamentary system would bring. McKee favored creating a single national bank in place of the system of twelve federal reserve institutions. The central bank should, in turn, be headed by a governor, "not by a Board or Committee" (McKee 1933, 91). McKee also favored the establishment of a cabinet department to head transportation and a similar cabinet office to deal with retailing and extractive industries. He believed that businesses would welcome such control, as long as it was accountable.

Although it would not have required a constitutional amendment, McKee's solution to the problems of poverty and unemployment was perhaps his most novel. He viewed both problems as essentially moral problems, resulting from poor personal finance. He therefore proposed that public schools should teach children to keep expenditures within income and to save at least 10 percent of their income a year. As has been observed elsewhere (Vile 1991c, 72), however modern his views of increased governmental control might seem, McKee took a dim view of the values of modern consumer society, stressing instead more traditional values of saving and thrift.

For Further Reading:

McKee, Henry S. 1933. *Degenerate Democracy.* New York: Thomas Y. Crowell.

Vile, John R. 1991c. *Rewriting the United States Constitution: An Examination of Proposals from Reconstruction to the Present.* New York: Praeger.

❖ MEDICAL CARE ❖

Among advanced industrial nations, the United States is one of the few that relies primarily on private medical insurance rather than on government-financed health care. Moreover, although the Constitution guarantees many political rights, it makes no explicit provision for social and economic rights.

The 1940s, the 1970s, and the early 1990s all witnessed attempts to adopt national health insurance, but each effort failed (Laham 1993, 1–6). President Lyndon Johnson did succeed in 1965 in getting Congress to adopt programs for the poor (Medicaid) and the elderly (Medicare).

In October 1991 and again in February 1993, Democratic Representative Pete Stark of California, chair of the Health Subcommittee of the Ways and Means Committee, introduced an amendment that would have granted U.S. citizens a right to health care and granted Congress power to enforce this right. Although health care has not been so established as a constitutional right, current obstacles to national health insurance are political rather than legal. Major health care reform was among the significant accomplishments that President Bill Clinton (aided by his wife Hillary) was unable to achieve. Such barriers have not stopped Representative Jesse Jackson Jr. (D-IL) from proposing a constitutional amendment specifying that "[a]ll citizens of the United States shall enjoy the right to health care of equal high quality" (Jackson with Watkins 2001, 285).

See also Social and Economic Rights.

For Further Reading:

Jackson, Jesse L., Jr., with Frank E. Watkins. 2001. *A More Perfect Union: Advancing New American Rights.* New York: Welcome Rain Publishers.

❖ MERRIAM, CHARLES (1874–1953) ❖

Charles Merriam was a political science professor at the University of Chicago who served from 1924 to 1925 as president of the American Political Science Association. In 1931 he published a book entitled *The Written Constitution and the Unwritten Attitude.* In this book, he discussed the process of constitutional change as well as several concrete contemporary proposals for such alterations (Vile 1991c, 65–66).

Merriam's main thesis was that provisions in constitutions were often ineffective if not supported by public opinion. The chief threat to modern government was not in "*lack of stability, but lack of mobility,* failure to make prompt adjustments to the new era in industry and science" (Merriam 1931, 25). Merriam was particularly impressed by the growth of cities, whose increases in population often were not reflected in state apportionment schemes. He also thought that states had lost significant power to the national government and suggested the feasibility of recognizing certain large cities as states.

Generally, Merriam seemed receptive to the idea of further alterations in the relation between the nation and the states. In addition, although he thought that there was little chance that the United States would adopt a parliamentary system, he did suggest that there were no obstacles to allowing members of the cabinet to appear before, or participate in debates within, Congress (Merriam 1931, 74). At a time prior to *United States v. Classic* (1941), when the Supreme Court limited federal oversight over primary elections (*Newberry v. United States* (1921)), Merriam suggested that an amendment might be adopted to provide greater uniformity in such elections (Merriam 1931, 81). In a theme prominent in the wake of the Senate rejection of U.S. participation in the League of Nations, Merriam also favored altering the requirement that treaties be adopted by two-thirds votes of the Senate.

For Further Reading:

Merriam, Charles E. 1931. *The Written Constitution and the Unwritten Attitude.* New York: Richard R. Smith.

❖ MERTENS, JOHN ❖

John Mertens, the author of *The Second Constitution for the United States of America,* first printed in 1990 and subsequently reissued in 1991 and 1997, is otherwise unidentified, but also appears to have been the author of a 1998 novel entitled *The Fall of America.* Mertens described his Constitution as "a fantasy of which some should not be taken too seriously" (title page), but the publishers noted that they were releasing the volume because "we believe that some of the propositions and ideas put forth in the *Second Constitution* will become realities at some time in the future." What seems to distinguish the *Second Constitution* from fantasy (although the author of this essay does not believe this to be the case, there is an outside chance that some or all sections are intended to be ironic or satiric) is the fact that it takes the form of a written constitution, containing six articles and multiple sections, much like the U.S. Constitution of today. Considerably longer, the *Second Constitution* is remarkable for combining such diverse ideas as population limitation, concern about the environment and dependence on foreign resources, a desire to limit government to those of European dissent, sexual equality, limitations on wealth, and massive governmental involvement and intrusion in many issues currently left to private enterprise. The *Second Constitution,* consisting of fifty-seven printed pages, includes no commentary but, at least initially, follows the general outline of the current document.

Article I would establish a legislative department consisting of an altered House and Senate. Nominees for members of both houses would initially be selected at random from among previous state legislators and would have to be "third-generation citizens" (Mertens 1997, 2–3). Elections would be radically shortened, and all campaign contributions would be forbidden, with states reimbursing candidates for "reasonable travel expenses incurred during the campaign" (*Id.,* 2). The House would consist of 300 members and the Senate of one from each state; House members would serve four-year terms and senators for three years. While serving in office, members would be considered on leave from their regular jobs and receive similar compensation (*Id.,* 5). Perhaps in an effort to undercut the influence of the Senate, all bills would be voted on in joint session. Budgets would be strictly limited, and a onetime tax on assets and incomes would be used to pay off the national debt within three years (*Id.,* 7). Congressional powers would be similar to those of today, with some novel provisions—allowing, for example, for use of the armed forces in eradicating "the drug traffic and organized crime worldwide" (*Id.,* 9). State officers would be selected much like federal officials with state legislatures nominating candidates for governor (*Id.,* 13).

Article II proposed to divide the presidency into three parts. The executive president would command the military, with copresidents supervising foreign and domestic affairs. Presidents would serve six-year terms and would rotate offices every two years. All three would have adjoining offices and live within a short distance of the White House.

Like other branches, the judiciary would be split equally between men and women. Supreme Court justices would serve for ten-year terms. Each of six identified regions would have an appellate court. The Supreme Court would have the power to grant pardons (a power transferred from the president) by a unanimous vote. The Court would also appoint an ad hoc commission to create a uniform code of laws, "which the Supreme Court shall review, amend, or change as they deem proper" (Mertens 1997, 19). Provisions related to the rights of criminal defendants in the U.S. Bill of Rights are moved to this section of the Constitution. Mertens provides that prisoners "shall work for their keep, at hard labor, and be incarcerated in remote areas at minimum comfort" with more serious offenders being sterilized (*Id.,* 21).

Section IV provides for states, which would, however, be grouped into six designated regions. U.S. territories would become independent nations. No new states could be admitted to the Union, although Mertens later indicates that there would be a total of fifty-eight of them.

Section V combines the treatment of rights,

privileges, and responsibilities. The voting age would apparently be set at twenty-one (thus overturning the Twenty-sixth Amendment), and voting and "equality of rights" would not be abridged "on account of race, color, or sex" (Mertens 1997, 23). Indeed, "Men and women shall be equal in all respects." Citizens would be guaranteed free health care as well as a right of privacy. Duties would include giving at least one year in the National Labor Service and one in the military, limiting offspring to no more than two per family (unmarried couples would be forbidden from reproducing), and maintaining "personal and family health."

Section VI of the *Second Constitution* is the most complex and different. It sets forth seventeen "critical goals" for the United States, including reducing the population to 200 million and distributing it equally among fifty-eight states (Mertens does not appear to identify the source of the additional eight states), "eliminating the causes of inflation," "reducing oil consumption to three million barrels a day," building "a national electrified rail transport system," eliminating welfare, establishing national health care and "an effective national education system," preserving the environment, and the like (Mertens 1997, 26–27). These tasks would be effected by councils and subcouncils.

Attempts to control and relocate populations would include compulsory sterilizations and the provision of "minimal health care for illness caused by consumption of tobacco, drugs, alcohol, and overeating" (Mertons 1997, 28). Population density would be limited to "two hundred persons per square mile" (*Id.*, 30), with citizens of cities and states larger than this encouraged or forced to relocate. The Council for an Integrated Economy would limit an individual's accumulation of wealth to $5 million, although a subsequent amendment appears to raise this amount to $750 million for those engaged in production. Corporate bonds would be exchanged for U.S. stocks, with the national government either taking over or directing most major industries. The Council for the Conservation, Generation, and Consumption of Energy would abolish busing in favor of neighborhood schools of no more than 300 students, build windmills for the milling of

grain, and replace fossil fuel plants with nuclear reactors. The Council for Transport would plan and build electrified mass-transit systems and consolidate and operate airlines "as a single national fleet" (*Id.*, 37). The Council for Education would limit or reduce college enrollment to no more than 5,000 students while increasing the number of doctors. A Council for Production and Distribution of Food would have power to forbid the service of fast foods that were found to "lack nutritional and health benefits" (*Id.*, 41). A Council for Healthcare and Care for Senior Americans would take control of all hospitals and nursing homes and create orphanages. The Council for the Protection of the Environment would establish a 200-mile off-shore fishing limit, abolish clearcutting of forests, phase out "internal combustion engines running on fossil fuels or their derivatives," and see that half of the U.S. land area was devoted to national parks, on which environmentally friendly farming could be conducted (*Id.*, 49). A Council for Racial Affairs would offer "immigrants of Non-European origin who have entered the United States of American since 1945" incentives to "return to the country of their origin with their descendants" (*Id.*, 54). The United States would further engage in an exchange with South Africa whereby the United States would buy property from whites there, and American blacks would migrate there and South African whites would migrate here (*Id.*, 55).

A Council for Religious Affairs would guarantee that churches were independent of foreign control. They would also monitor church affairs "for deliberate acts of mismanagement, embezzlement or fraud involving their organization's assets" (Mertens 1997, 55).

Three amendments (second thoughts?) round out the document. One is the previously mentioned $750 million limit on individual accumulations. The second would provide for distributing $50 million each year to 100 of the nation's best scientists and teachers. The third would establish two juries, the first of which would monitor television advertising and the second of which would monitor other types.

There is no implementing article for the *Second Constitution* and thus no discussion of how it might be adopted (the Preamble, at p.1, does refer to "We, the majority of the people of the United States"). And, as indicated above, there is no indication of its provenance and even some question about its complete seriousness. Apart from the provision allowing the Supreme Court to amend the code of laws, the document appears to have no formal amending process. The *Second Constitution* appears to contain provisions that would be bound both to anger and to please just about everyone. Many provisions are aspirational in quality, and those provisions that state specific goals give little indication about how they would be implemented, other than through massive new assumptions of governmental powers. Although many provisions are unique, and arguably outrageous, they are presented in a conventional format that resembles, borrows from, and, in many instances, follows the form of the existing U.S. Constitution.

For Further Reading:

Mertens, John. 1997. *The Second Constitution for the United States of America.* Cottonwood, CA: Gazelle Books.

❖ MIGRATORY BIRDS ❖

In June 1911 Republican Senator George McLean of Connecticut introduced an amendment to give Congress power to protect migratory birds. Even without such explicit constitutional authority, in March 1913 Congress adopted legislation that McLean sponsored to regulate migratory birds (Lofgren 1975, 79). U.S. district court decisions in *United States v. Shauver* (1914) and *United States v. McCullagh* (1915) found that such legislation infringed on powers reserved to the states by the Tenth Amendment, and the federal government decided not to appeal to the Supreme Court.

Congress then entered into a treaty with Great Britain in 1916, providing for the protection of birds flying between the United States and Canada, and adopted legislation implementing this treaty in 1918. In a decision written by Justice Oliver Wendell Holmes Jr., the Court upheld the constitutionality of this

treaty and accompanying legislation in *Missouri v. Holland* (1920). This decision, based in part on a distinction (probably initially inserted to guarantee that the new government would continue to honor its treaties) in Article V between laws "made in Pursuance" of the Constitution and treaties "under the Authority of the United States," contributed to concerns, reflected in many versions of the Bricker Amendment, that Congress might by treaty deny or abridge rights that it would be unable to deny or abridge under ordinary laws.

Although the Supreme Court has subsequently qualified the treaty-making power in cases such as *Reid v. Covert* (1957), it has generally given more expansive readings to congressional authority under the commerce clause. Such readings suggest that no amendment is needed for Congress to continue its regulation of migratory birds.

See also Bricker Amendment; *Missouri v. Holland;* Tenth Amendment.

❖ MILITIA ❖

When they ratified the Constitution, a number of states proposed amendments calling for the prohibition of standing armies or for state regulation of the militia. Despite such pleas, the only mention of militias in the Bill of Rights is contained in the Second Amendment in connection with the right to bear arms.

After some New England states declined to allow their militias to participate in the War of 1812, Ohio Representative (and later President) William Henry Harrison introduced amendments to give Congress power concurrent with the states to provide militia training (Ames 1896, 270–271). In 1864 Democratic Senator Willard Saulsburg of Delaware introduced a series of proposals that would have permitted slavery to continue in the South. One provision stated that the people should have certain rights against the militia.

Today the central arguments around a militia continue to center on the meaning of the word in the context of the Second Amendment. Does the reference to the militia provide a rationale for restricting gun ownership only to those officially registered in such bodies, or their equivalents, or may all citizens, or at least all who are law abiding, be regarded as constituting this body and thus be considered entitled to their firearms?

See also Second Amendment.

❖ MILLER, ARTHUR S. (1917–1988) ❖

Arthur Miller, while a professor emeritus at George Washington University, presented his ideas for major constitutional change in a book published in the year of the bicentennial of the U.S. Constitution (A. Miller 1987). This book reflected views presented in an earlier article (A. Miller 1984). Miller wrote out of the conviction that there was an increasing disjunction between the United States' formal written constitution and the "secret" constitution by which it was actually governed. Much like critics from the Progressive Era, Miller believed that propertied elites wielded true power in American society (Vile 1991c, 143–145).

Miller began his chapter on proposed reforms by listing five major proposals. First, he wanted Congress to have the power to make all laws needed "to provide for and maintain an environment conducive to the attainment of a sustainable society." This would include the power "to achieve an optimum population, to control and diffuse the threat of nuclear war, and to control environmental degradation" (A. Miller 1987, 105). Second, Congress should have authority "to provide for and maintain the reasonable satisfaction of human needs and fulfillment of human desires." Specifically, Miller wanted Congress to be responsible for providing "sufficient meaningful job opportunities for all who are able to work" (*Id.*). Third, Congress should be able to check excessive presidential and bureaucratic power. To this end, Miller wanted to establish a council of state with which the president would have to discuss his decisions; Miller also advocated increased use of the legislative veto. Fourth, Miller wanted to expand the Supreme Court's origi-

nal jurisdiction so that any voter could bring a suit to "determine the validity of allegations that Congress had failed in any of its duties" (*Id.*). Fifth, Miller proposed rewriting the Constitution so that it applied not only to the government but also "to any societal group that exercises substantial power over individuals." Such groups would include "the supercorporations, the major trade unions, churches, farmers' leagues, [and] professional associations" (*Id.*, 106). Miller, who was highly critical of nationalism, also wanted the Constitution altered so as to recognize the United States' close relations with other nations.

Believing that the idea of a parliamentary system was meritorious, Miller made six additional proposals. He proposed making Congress a unicameral body of 100 members; dividing the presidency into a separate head of government and head of state; strengthening political parties so that they would have greater control over members of Congress; substituting ten or twelve regional governments for the existing fifty states; recognizing "supercorporations" in the Constitution and bringing greater power to bear against them; and, consistent with his earlier pleas for judicial activism (A. Miller 1982), expanding the role of the Supreme Court to take cases against both the two political branches and "private governments" (A. Miller 1987, 123). Miller hoped to transform the Constitution from a collection of negative prohibitions into a set of more affirmative guarantees.

There have been few proposals that are more far-reaching, or more politically unlikely, than Miller's.

For Further Reading:

Miller, Arthur S. 1987. *The Secret Constitution and the Need for Constitutional Change*. Westport, CT: Greenwood Press.

———. 1984. "The Annual John Randolph Tucker Lecture: Taking Needs Seriously: Observations on the Necessity for Constitutional Change." *Washington and Lee Law Review* 41 (Fall): 1243–1306.

———. 1982. *Toward Increased Judicial Activism: The Political Role of the Supreme Court*. Westport, CT: Greenwood Press.

❖ MILLER, JEREMY M. (1954–) ❖

In the year the nation celebrated the bicentennial of the U.S. Constitution, Jeremy M. Miller, a professor at Western State University College of Law, wrote an article offering a new constitution for consideration (J. Miller 1987). In the essay accompanying this proposal, Miller argued that the Constitution should embody natural law and that, consistent with libertarian principles, it should avoid "paternalistic legislation" (J. Miller 1987, 221). Miller also argued that the Constitution should further the values of truth, dignity, equality, and fundamental fairness.

Such values were incorporated into Miller's expanded preamble, which explicitly included a number of the principles of the Declaration of Independence and specifically invoked "the Supreme Judge of the World" (J. Miller 1987, 226). Article I of Miller's constitution was an expanded version of the Bill of Rights that applied limits to "federal, state, and municipal governments" (*Id.*). Much more detailed than the current Bill of Rights, the provisions for religious freedom would specifically prohibit either the use of "government monies for" or "government endorsement of any religion" (*Id.*, 227). It also distinguished between religious belief and religious conduct and specified that "a short prayer to God, as 'God,' is not a government endorsement of religion" (*Id.*, 227). Similarly, provisions for freedom of speech prohibited "prior licensing" but allowed reasonable "time, place, and manner restrictions" (*Id.*, 227). The right to bear arms included the right to own and carry "non-automatic pistols and non-automatic rifles" (*Id.*, 228). Traffic regulations were to be entrusted to unarmed personnel; most abortions, dissections of the dead, and mechanical organ transplants were to be limited; judicial procedures and warrant requirements were to be made much more detailed; and juries were to be composed of seven persons.

Article II outlined citizen duties. These included the duty of males aged seventeen and older to be subject to the military draft, the duty of families to find "gainful employment" (J. Miller 1987, 232), and the duty of losing

plaintiffs to pay double a defendant's attorney's fees. Amendment procedures were also included in this section. All laws were to be open to such alterations. The exclusive method of change was to be for two-thirds of the states to call conventions (each state supplying a single delegate), proposals from which would subsequently become part of the Constitution when ratified by a majority of those voting in two-thirds of the states—a provision that appears to allow amendments to be adopted by less than a majority.

Article III outlined the three branches of government, "executive, parliamentary, and judicial" (J. Miller 1987, 233). The president would serve a three-year term, to be followed by possible reelection to a six-year term and subsequent two-year terms. The president would be elected by popular vote (with a runoff required when no one received a majority) and would share the power to nominate federal judges with the two houses of Congress and the Constitutional Court. Given increased powers over the budget, the president would have an item veto, power to hold a national lottery when bankruptcy threatened, and instructions to keep income taxes from 2 to 15 percent of individual income.

The parliament, like today's Congress, would consist of a House and a Senate, each state to have one senator and from one to three representatives, depending on its population. Members of the House would serve a maximum of two three-year terms. A four-fifths vote of both houses would be required to overturn decisions by the Constitutional Court on matters of constitutional interpretation, and majorities of both houses would ratify treaties.

The judicial system would be organized like the current one, with membership on the Constitutional Court specifically set at nine members, and judges serving twelve-year terms. Given power to interpret the Constitution, the Constitutional Court was to be "bound by its letter and by its spirit" (J. Miller 1987, 237).

Miller included neither federal protections for voting rights nor an equal protection clause, and he has been criticized for writing a constitution that, because of "the undue specificity of some sections," was too much like a legal code (Knipprath 1987, 253–254). By the same token, his proposal omits a number of powers (for example, over the post office and copyrights) currently entrusted to Congress. Noting this, a critic said that Miller's plan "looks like a patchwork quilt, not a balanced, patterned tapestry" (*Id.,* 256). Another critic suggested that part of the problem is that because Miller presented his ideas in an article rather than a book, he did not, like authors of numerous other proposed constitutions, have adequate space both to outline and to justify his numerous additions to and departures from the current Constitution (Vile 1991c, 148).

For Further Reading:

Knipprath, Joerg W. 1987. "To See the Trees, but Not the Forest in Constitution Making: A Commentary on Professor Miller's Proposed Constitution." *Southwestern University Law Review* 17: 239–256.

Miller, Jeremy. 1987. "It's Time for a New Constitution." *Southwestern University Law Review* 17: 207–237.

Vile, John R. 1991c. *Rewriting the United States Constitution: An Examination of Proposals from Reconstruction to the Present.* New York: Praeger.

❖ MINIMUM WAGES ❖

Like the related problem of child labor, minimum wages were often associated with the so-called sweating system, under which laborers were employed for subsistence wages in large factories or unsanitary conditions. Such issues came into prominence with the rise of U.S. industrialization. Because of their position in the economy, women were inordinately affected by such conditions (Hart 1994, 64).

The first attempts to remedy the evils of the sweating system centered on limiting the number of hours that individuals could be asked to work. This movement faced a setback with the Supreme Court's decision in *Lochner v. New York* (1905), which declared that New York's regulation of bakers' work hours was in violation of the bakers' freedom of contract. In *Muller v. Oregon* (1908), however, future Supreme Court Justice Louis Brandeis—who

had been hired by the National Consumers League (NCL)—successfully argued on behalf of a Washington state law that limited women's work to ten hours a day. Brandeis relied chiefly on evidence, presented in his historic "Brandeis brief," showing that women were especially vulnerable to such exploitation, and the Supreme Court responded with a unanimous decision upholding the legislation.

A number of states, often prodded by the Women's Trade Union League, subsequently adopted legislation providing minimum wages for women and children. Such a policy sometimes split feminist ranks, however. It pitted those who argued that half a loaf was better than none against those who disfavored any gender-specific legislation—an issue that would also emerge with the first introduction of the Equal Rights Amendment in Congress in 1923 (Hart 1994, 111).

In the same year that the Equal Rights Amendment was first introduced, the Supreme Court issued a decision in *Adkins v. Children's Hospital* (1923). Justice George Sutherland authored this five-to-three decision for a divided Court. The Court struck down a minimum-wage law for women on the basis that although the Constitution permitted regulation of "incidents of employment" such as hours and working conditions, the due process clause mitigated against interferences with the "heart of the contract," that is, with wages. Interestingly, Sutherland relied in part on the equalizing effect that the ratification of the Nineteenth Amendment was alleged to have had on women's ability to enter into their own contracts.

Even prior to the decision, at least one amendment had been introduced in Congress to establish governmental powers to set minimum wages. However, most such amendments—some seeking to vest such powers in the states, some in Congress, and some in both—were introduced between 1925 and 1937, when Supreme Court decisions based on substantive due process were at their peak. As late as 1936, in *Morehead v. New York ex rel. Tipaldo,* the Court continued to strike down minimum-wage legislation.

In *West Coast Hotel v. Parrish* (1937), a narrow Court majority led by Chief Justice

Charles Evans Hughes overturned *Adkins* and upheld a Washington state minimum-wage law for women. This case is often called the "switch in time that saved nine," because many believe that it was a political reaction to Franklin D. Roosevelt's court-packing plan introduced earlier in the year.

Congress subsequently adopted the Fair Labor Standards Act in 1938, providing for minimum wages and maximum hours for both men and women in industries affecting interstate commerce. The Supreme Court upheld this law in *United States v. Darby* (1941), thus overturning its earlier decision in *Hammer v. Dagenhart* (1918) and sanctioning the regulation of this issue by the national government.

Calls for amendments on the subject have subsequently ceased, although renewed attention was spurred by the decision in *Garcia v. San Antonio Metropolitan Transit Authority* (1985), in which such minimum-wage laws were applied to state governments. In the United States, minimum-wage laws now apply to most industries. By contrast, in Britain, the minimum wage never applied beyond a few basic industries and was eliminated altogether in 1993. A student of the subject recently concluded that, despite claims for the flexibility of the British constitution, written constitutional guarantees ultimately strengthened U.S. minimum-wage policies in a positive direction (Hart 1994, 182). Debates periodically erupt about how high the minimum wage should be and whether it is adequate to support a family. Conservative economists have argued that higher minimum wages are generally believed to contribute to higher unemployment rates, but other students of the subject believe that higher wages actually pump more money into local economies (because the recipients of the higher wages now have some discretionary income) and thus result in more employment.

See also Child Labor Amendment; Court-Packing Plan; Labor, Hours of.

For Further Reading:
Hart, Vivien. 1994. *Bound by Our Constitution: Women, Workers, and the Minimum Wage.* Princeton, NJ: Princeton University Press.

❖ MINNESOTA BOUNDARY ❖

Amendments are sometimes proposed not so much to get a policy adopted as to draw attention to a problem. There are few better illustrations of this than an amendment introduced in Congress by Minnesota Democrat Collin C. Peterson in March 1998. Peterson proposed that Congress should relinquish claims to that portion of Minnesota above the forty-ninth parallel. At issue was the small Northwest Angle of Minnesota, a peninsula north of the forty-ninth parallel that belongs to the United States and is considered a part of Minnesota, even though it borders completely on Canada and juts into the Lake of the Woods. Under a fishing treaty being worked out between the United States and Canada, individuals who camped on fishing resorts on the American land were to be given the right to keep fewer fish from the Lake of the Woods than those who camped on Canadian resorts that bordered the Lake. Peterson, who had no desire to part with territory belonging either to his state or his nation, introduced his proposal to gain the attention of the U.S. trade representative negotiating for America. He apparently succeeded in getting enough attention to gain more favorable treatment than under the original terms of the agreement. (Telephone interview by John R. Vile with Bill Black, Legislative Assistant for Congressman Collin C. Peterson of Minnesota, conducted 04/29/02). This amendment appears to be unique in being the only one ever introduced specifically to protect the rights of American fishermen.

❖ MINOR V. HAPPERSETT (1875) ❖

Despite the expanded recognition of rights in the Thirteenth through Fifteenth Amendments and extensions of the right to vote in the Wyoming and Utah territories, the nineteenth century did not prove to be a good time for advocates of women's rights at the national level. Declaring in *Bradwell v. Illinois* that "the law of the Creator" mandated that "the paramount destiny and mission of woman are to fulfill the noble and benign offices of wife and mother"

(1873, 141), the Supreme Court refused to overturn the decision of the Illinois bar to exclude Myra Bradwell from the practice of law simply because she was a woman. Similarly, speaking through Chief Justice Waite in *Minor v. Happersett* (1875), the Court unanimously upheld a registrar's refusal to allow Virginia Minor to vote in the presidential election of 1872. Susan B. Anthony had asserted a similar privilege, but her case had not made it to the Supreme Court (Basch 1992, 57).

Minor and her husband cited a number of constitutional arguments, all of which the Court rejected. It recognized that women were citizens of the United States both before and after adoption of the Fourteenth Amendment. However, in an interpretation similar to that advanced in the *Slaughterhouse Cases* (1873), it rejected the argument that the right to vote was among the privileges and immunities guaranteed to all citizens by the Fourteenth Amendment. The Court noted that voting qualifications had been set, up to that point, by individual states. No state that had refused to grant suffrage to women had been considered to lack a "republican" government because of this omission. The Court further noted that Section 2 of the Fourteenth Amendment specifically mentioned males and that the Fifteenth Amendment did not extend the right to vote to females. Moreover, if that right had been included among the privileges and immunities protected by the Fourteenth Amendment, then the Fifteenth Amendment would have been unnecessary.

The reference to males in the Fourteenth Amendment, as well as the effect of *Minor v. Happersett,* was overturned with the adoption of the Nineteenth Amendment in 1920.

See also Nineteenth Amendment.

For Further Reading:
Basch, Norma. 1992. "Reconstructing Female Citizenship: *Minor v. Happersett.*" In *The Constitution, Law, and American Life: Critical Aspects of the Nineteenth Century Experience,* ed. Donald G. Nieman. Athens, GA: University of Georgia Press.

Minor v. Happersett, 88 U.S. (21 Wall.) 162 (1875).

❖ *MISSOURI V. HOLLAND* (1920) ❖

Political scientist Louis Henkin called this case "perhaps the most famous and most discussed case in the constitutional law of foreign affairs" (1972, 144). At issue was the constitutionality of a law passed under authority of a treaty with Great Britain whereby the U.S. government set rules for the protection of migratory birds between the United States and Canada. U.S. district courts had previously voided legislation adopted in the absence of such a treaty on the basis that such laws were a federal invasion of powers reserved to the states by the Tenth Amendment.

Writing on behalf of the Court, Justice Oliver Wendell Holmes Jr. upheld the legislation. He said that "there may be matters of the sharpest exigency for the national well-being that an act of Congress could not deal with but that a treaty followed by such an act could" (*Missouri* 1920, 433). Holmes further advanced the view that the Constitution was "an organism" whose life "could not have been foreseen completely by the most gifted of its begetters" (*Missouri* 1920, 322). Although Holmes cautioned that treaties could not "contravene any prohibitory words to be found in the Constitution" (*Missouri* 1920, 433), his opinion raised fears that the Constitution might be effectively amended by treaty rather than by constitutional amendment (Lofgren 1975, 93).

In the 1950s such fears helped fuel support for the Bricker Amendment, a proposal designed in part to limit the reach of federal treaties. Ironically, after 1937 the Supreme Court had already given a broad reading to other constitutional sources of federal power—especially the commerce clause and the taxing and spending clause—that seems to have undermined the importance of *Missouri v. Holland* as a source of federal authority (Lofgren 1975, 122). The Court qualified *Missouri v. Holland* in *Reid v. Covert* (1957). American commitments to international trade organizations like the World Trade Organization (WTO) and the ratification of the North American Free Trade Agreement (NAFTA) through expedited "fast track" congressional votes could renew questions about the possible effects of international agreements on matters of domestic policy (see Thomas 2000).

See also Bricker Amendment; Migratory Birds; Tenth Amendment.

For Further Reading:
Henkin, Louis. 1972. *Foreign Affairs and the Constitution*. Mineola, NY: Foundation Press.

Lofgren, Charles A. 1975. "*Missouri v. Holland* in Historical Perspective." In *The Supreme Court Review*. Chicago: University of Chicago Press.

Missouri v. Holland, 252 U.S. 416 (1920).

Thomas, Chantal. 2000. "Constitutional Change and International Government." *Hastings Law Journal* 52 (November): 1–46.

❖ MOMENT OF SILENCE ❖

See Prayer in Public Schools.

❖ MONEY ❖

See Currency.

❖ MONOPOLIES AND TRUSTS ❖

Among the restrictions that Thomas Jefferson wanted to include in a national bill of rights was a "restriction against monopolies" (Mason and Baker 1985, 285). Such a resolution was introduced in the Senate in March 1793 but was subsequently tabled, possibly in the belief that such matters were more appropriate for state control. One of the Marshall Court's most popular decisions was in *Gibbons v. Ogden* (1824) when it utilized congressional authority over interstate commerce to strike down New York's grant of a steamboat monopoly.

Concern over monopolies was renewed as the United States industrialized and industries began to combine into giant trusts. At least eighteen amendments were introduced from 1889 to 1913 to give Congress power to regulate such combinations. In 1890 Congress adopted the Sherman Antitrust Act, which was followed by the Clayton Act of 1914 and the Federal Trade Commission Act of the same year (J. May 1992, 34). Initially, however, the Supreme Court interpreted the Sherman Antitrust Act narrowly. Thus, in *United States v. E.C. Knight Co.* (1895), the Court ruled that Congress could not control the acquisition of sugar refineries that led to a near monopoly because the acquisitions took place within a state and were a matter for state control.

In 1900 the House of Representatives debated an amendment submitted by Republican George Washington Ray of New York. It provided that "Congress shall have power to define, regulate, prohibit, or dissolve trusts, monopolies, or combinations, whether existing in the form of a corporation or otherwise." The unsuccessful House vote of 154 to 132 in favor of the measure has been attributed to the Republicans' inclusion of a provision, of great concern to states' rights advocates, that "the several States may continue to exercise such power in any manner not in conflict with the laws of the United States" (Musmanno 1929, 116–119). Also, many members of Congress believed that existing laws could be written and additional laws adopted to address the problem. Today, few doubt that congressional powers extend to this domain.

For Further Reading:
Mason, Alpheus T., and Gordon E. Baker. 1985. *Free Government in the Making: Readings in American Political Thought*. 4th ed. New York: Oxford University Press.

May, James. 1992. "Antitrust." In *The Oxford Companion to the Supreme Court of the United States*, ed. Kermit L. Hall. New York: Oxford University Press.

Musmanno, M. A. 1929. *Proposed Amendments to the Constitution*. Washington, DC: U.S. Government Printing Office.

❖ MORRIS, GOUVERNEUR (1752–1816) ❖

Gouverneur Morris, originally a New Yorker, was a delegate to the Constitutional Convention from Pennsylvania, where he had established his law practice. A large man with a wooden leg (he had lost his in an accident in his twenties), Morris was an advocate of a strong national government and he spoke more frequently than any other delegate to the convention. He is perhaps best known for being the individual who is believed to have given the final "polish" to the wording of the Constitution that the convention proposed. Although he was largely an advocate of the interests of the large states at the convention, Morris was the individual who proposed on 15 September 1787 that no state could be deprived of its equal suffrage in the Senate without its consent (Farrand 1966, 2:631). This proposal was unanimously adopted, perhaps in recognition of the importance that the Connecticut Compromise (providing for this equal Senate representation) had contributed to consensus at the convention. Many critics of the modern U.S. Constitution regard this compromise as an unfortunate concession that will forever stand in the way of more democratic alternatives.

For Further Reading:

Bradford, M. E. 1994. *Founding Fathers: Brief Lives of the Framers of the United States Constitution.* 2d ed. Lawrence, KS: University Press of Kansas.

Farrand, Max, ed. 1966. *The Records of the Federal Convention.* 4 vols. New Haven, CT: Yale University Press.

❖ MORRIS, HENRY O. ❖

Little is known about Henry Morris other than his authorship of the novel *Waiting for the Signal* (1897) and its publication by a socialist-leaning press (Boyd 1992, 106–109). The novel's main characters, Wesley Stearns and John McDermott, are reporters for the Chicago *Biograph,* owned by Adam Short. Short is sympathetic to the woes of the working class and gives his reporters the opportunity to report on the increasing gap between rich and poor and on the moral degradation of the plutocrats, especially those who live in New York City.

During the course of the novel, set shortly after the election of William McKinley in 1896

(Morris appears to have detested Cleveland and McKinley—and Mark Hanna—about equally but supported William Jennings Bryan's advocacy of a silver standard), a working-class revolution is initiated. The revolution results in little bloodshed except in New York City, which is almost completely burned by those trying to take advantage of the chaos.

A convention is subsequently held in Chicago, where Ignatius Donnelly heads a committee that writes a new declaration of independence. The convention also writes a new constitution, and William J. Lyon of Nebraska is nominated and subsequently elected president, replacing the military leader who oversaw the revolution. Adoption of the constitution leads to a new era of national peace and prosperity that haunts European plutocrats, who have reason to fear that their own revolutions will come with greater loss of life.

In his draft of a new constitution, Morris largely keeps the structure of the existing government in place, although he does propose some changes. Each state would be guaranteed at least three members in the House of Representatives, and the Speaker—Morris had particular disdain for Speaker Thomas B. Reed—would lose power to retard the progress of legislation (H. Morris 1897, 338). Members of Congress would be limited to twelve years in office. Although the president would continue to have a veto power, both houses of Congress would be able to override this veto by majority vote. In anticipation of the Sixteenth Amendment, Congress would have the power to levy income and other taxes, and, in anticipation of the Seventeenth Amendment, senators would be elected by popular vote. The president, also elected by popular vote, would serve a single eight-year term.

Morris's constitution embodied a number of socialist elements. The national government would take over most means of production, destroy monopolies and trusts, and (in the novel) limit individual wealth.

Congress would establish uniform codes of civil and criminal procedure. Indians would be treated like other citizens, and foreign immigration would be restricted to "the healthy, moral, intelligent and self-supporting" (Morris

1897, 344). Morris's novel indicates that he was generally suspicious of both Jews and foreigners. The people would vote on whether they wanted an initiative and referendum.

Morris would expand most constitutional rights, and his constitution devotes special attention to freedom of speech and of the press. Judicial powers to issue injunctions would be limited, and no one could be imprisoned for violating a court order except after a jury trial.

In Morris's scheme, a majority of both houses of Congress would be able to propose amendments or call a constitutional convention. Amendments would be ratified by a majority of the state legislatures.

In a preface to the third edition, Morris notes that he had been "deluged with letters" asking when the revolution would occur. He answered that he did not know the date but that "the revolution is sure to come—it is on the way. I leave the reader to guess when the storm will burst" (Morris 1897, ix).

For Further Reading:

Boyd, Steven R., ed. 1992. *Alternative Constitutions for the United States: A Documentary History.* Westport, CT: Greenwood Press.

Morris, Henry O. 1897. *Waiting for the Signal, a Novel.* Chicago: Schulte.

❖ MOTT, LUCRETIA COFFIN (1793–1880) ❖

Lucretia Coffin Mott was a Quaker minister and political reformer. She provided leadership in the movement for the abolition of slavery that eventually led to the Thirteenth Amendment and in the movement for women's rights that eventually resulted in the Nineteenth Amendment.

Mott, the mother of six children, helped found the Philadelphia Female Anti-Slavery Society in the 1830s and helped establish Swarthmore College in 1864. With Elizabeth Cady Stanton, Mott helped organize the Seneca Falls Convention of 1848, where the idea of women's suffrage first emerged as an important concern. The proposed Equal Rights Amendment was often called the Lucretia Mott amendment in her honor.

See also Equal Rights Amendment; Nineteenth Amendment; Seneca Falls Convention; Thirteenth Amendment.

❖ MURDER AND KIDNAPPING ❖

In the U.S. federal system, most matters of criminal law are handled by the states. A number of members of Congress have proposed amendments to give Congress power to punish criminals for felonies such as murder, kidnapping, lynching, or polygamy or to invest the trials for such offenses in federal courts.

The most notorious kidnapping of the last century, that of Charles Lindbergh's baby, occurred in March 1932. The baby's body was found on 12 May 1932 (Knappman 1994, 386), and a week later, Illinois Democratic Representative Charles Karch introduced a resolution to give Congress power to punish murder and kidnapping. Although states retain primary jurisdiction over these offenses, Congress has exercised its power under the commerce clause to adopt the Lindbergh Act, making it a crime to transport a victim across state or national lines and creating a presumption that such transit has occurred when a victim is not released within twenty-four hours (*Black's Law Dictionary* 1969, 837).

See also Marriage, Divorce, and Parenting.

For Further Reading:

Knappman, Edward W., ed. 1994. *Great American Trials.* Detroit, MI: Visible Ink Press.

❖ MURPHY, CORNELIUS F., JR. (1933–) ❖

In a chapter of a book published a year after the bicentennial of the Constitution, *Philosophical Dimensions of the Constitution,* Duquesne law professor Cornelius Murphy recommended the convening of a constitutional convention. More concerned about the positive implications that such a convention would have for democratic theory than about advocating a specific agenda, Murphy sketched four areas for possible reform.

He suggested, somewhat vaguely, that a convention might seek to "delineate the boundaries between personal freedom and social order." He favored adding "economic, social and cultural entitlements," like those recognized in the Universal Declaration of Human Rights, to the Constitution. He wanted to combine states into more functional regional units. He also thought that problems created by the separation of the legislative and executive branches and the "fractionation of power" needed to be addressed. Murphy did not believe that the reforms he proposed could be adequately addressed "within the inherited constitutional structure" or by "piecemeal amendment" (C. Murphy 1988, 70).

For Further Reading:
Murphy, Cornelius F., Jr. 1988. "Constitutional Revision." In *Philosophical Dimensions of the Constitution,* ed. Diana T. Meyers and Kenneth Kipnis. Boulder, CO: Westview Press.

❖ MURPHY, WALTER F. (1929–) ❖

Walter F. Murphy is a retired Edward S. Corwin professor of politics at Princeton University. Murphy, who is known for his wide-ranging scholarship on matters related to the judicial process and constitutional interpretation, is also one of the most articulate and persistent modern defenders of the view that there may be implicit and judicially enforceable limits on constitutional amendments within a true constitutional democracy. Murphy has defended his view in numerous essays over an extended time (W. Murphy 1978, 1980, 1987, 1990, 1992a, 1992b, 1995).

Drawing in part from judicial decisions in other constitutional governments, Murphy argues that the very notion of a constitutional democracy committed to principles of justice and the preservation of human dignity serves to limit the scope of change permitted within such a system. In a system that consists of a hierarchy of values, more important values must necessarily predominate over those with which they are in conflict. Moreover, the U.S. Constitution is informed by and based on the values of the Declaration of Independence, and the natural rights articulated there serve to limit what the Constitution can permit. The whole notion of amendments refers to those types of alterations that are consistent with the instrument being amended, not simply to changes that follow procedural guidelines.

Although Murphy's writings have not convinced all observers (Vile 1995), his work continues to provoke reflection about the scope and nature of constitutional change.

See also Constitutional Amendments, Limits on.

For Further Reading:
Murphy, Walter F. 1995. "Merlin's Memory: The Past and Future Imperfect of the Once and Future Polity." In *Responding to Imperfection,* ed. Sanford Levinson. Princeton, NJ: Princeton University Press.
———. 1992a. "Consent and Constitutional Change." In *Human Rights and Constitutional Law: Essays in Honour of Brian Walsh,* ed. James O'Reilly. Dublin, Ireland: Found Hall Press.
———. 1992b. "Staggering Toward the New Jerusalem of Constitutional Theory: A Response to Ralph F. Graebler." *American Journal of Jurisprudence* 37: 337–357.
———. 1990. "The Right to Privacy and Legitimate Constitutional Change." In *Constitutional Bases of Political and Social Change in the United States,* ed. Shlomo Slonin. New York: Praeger.
———. 1987. "*Slaughterhouse, Civil Rights,* and Limits on Constitutional Change." *American Journal of Jurisprudence* 23: 1–22.
———. 1980. "An Ordering of Constitutional Values." *Southern California Law Review* 53: 703–760.
———. 1978. "The Art of Constitutional Interpretation: A Preliminary Showing." In *Essays on the Constitution of the United States,* ed. M. Harmon. Port Washington, NY: Kennikat Press.
———. 1962. *Congress and the Court.* Chicago: University of Chicago Press.

❖ *MYERS V. ANDERSON* (1915) ❖

In this case, a companion to *Guinn v. United States* (1915), the Supreme Court struck down provisions of a Maryland law regulating voting in Annapolis. This law, like the Oklahoma law at issue in *Guinn,* contained a grandfather clause that imposed a literacy test only on those—namely, African Americans—whose ancestors were not entitled to vote prior to 1 January 1868, that is, prior to ratification of the Fourteenth and Fifteenth Amendments.

Chief Justice Edward White struck the law down as a violation of the Fifteenth Amendment. In so doing, he implicitly rejected arguments for limits on the amending process that had been offered by William Marbury and other attorneys for the state. They had argued that "if construed to have reference to voting at state or municipal elections, the Fifteenth Amendment would be beyond the amending power conferred upon three-fourths of the States by Art V. of the Constitution" (*Myers* 1915, 373).

See also Constitutional Amendments, Limits on.

For Further Reading:
Myers v. Anderson, 238 U.S. 368 (1915).

N

❖ NASHVILLE CONVENTION ❖

The June 1850 convention of nine Southern states that met in Nashville, Tennessee, appears to have been an extralegal (albeit far from secret) affair, rather than one called under provisions of Article V of the U.S. Constitution. In this it resembled the earlier Hartford Convention of Northern States and the later Peace Convention of 1861. Attended by more than 175 delegates, the majority from Tennessee, the Nashville Convention was concerned about many of the issues that would be soon resolved, at least in the short term, by the Compromise of 1850. Altogether, the convention made twenty-eight proposals, one of which would have extended the Missouri Compromise line dividing slave and free states all the way to the Pacific Coast. It also adopted Robert Barnwell Rhett's radical "Address to the People of the South" before more moderate voices prevailed. A follow-up meeting attended by far fewer delegates in November 1850 affirmed the right of secession, but the two conventions are collectively better known for averting this contingency, at least in the short term, than for their contributions to eventual disunion.

See also Hartford Convention; Peace Convention.

For Further Reading:
Jennings, Thelma. 1998. "Nashville Convention." In *The Tennessee Encyclopedia of History & Culture,* ed. Carroll Van West. Nashville, TN: Rutledge Hill Press, pp. 674–675.

———. 1980. *The Nashville Convention: Southern Movement for Unity, 1848–1851.* Memphis, TN: Memphis State University Press.

❖ NATIONAL ASSOCIATION FOR THE ADVANCEMENT OF COLORED PEOPLE (NAACP) ❖

Few issues have had more impact on the United States than has the issue of race, and few organizations have been as important in addressing this issue as the National Association for the Advancement of Colored People (NAACP). The NAACP was founded in New York City in 1909–1910, at a time when the rights guaranteed to all Americans under the Fourteenth and Fifteenth Amendments (respectively providing for equal rights for all Americans and prohibiting voting discrimination on the basis of race) had been eroded by narrow constructions of these amendments and by practices like Jim Crow segregation laws that the U.S. Supreme Court had approved in *Plessy v. Ferguson* (1896). The NAACP utilized a variety of mechanisms to fight for the rights of African Americans. These included lobbying; the publication of *The Crisis* (a magazine long edited by W. E. B. DuBois); successful legal challenges to grandfather clauses and the all-white primaries, both of which had been designed to deprive blacks of the right to vote; and efforts to adopt antilynching legislation.

The NAACP's most important legal efforts came with the establishment of the Legal Defense Fund, long directed by Charles Houston and Thurgood Marshall, who would later serve as the first African American U.S. Supreme Court Justice. Initially bringing cases involving law and graduate schools that required states to adhere to the "equal" provision of the "separate but equal" doctrine announced in *Plessy v. Ferguson,* the NAACP eventually challenged the doctrine head on, representing individuals in a number of states and the District of Columbia. It achieved success in *Brown v. Board of Education* (1954), when, in a unanimous decision authored by Chief Justice Earl Warren, the U.S. Supreme Court declared that separate educational facilities were inherently unequal. Uncertain whether the Fourteenth Amendment had been specifically adopted with the intention of outlawing racial discrimination, Warren argued that education was so important in the modern context and the effects of segregation were so inimical to the self-image of minority students and so negatively impacted their ability to learn, that segregation could no longer be tolerated.

This decision was the first of many Court decisions on the subject and was, along with actions led by the NAACP and other civil rights organizations, the catalyst for congressional legislation like the Civil Rights Act of 1964 (outlawing discrimination in places of public accommodation) and the Voting Rights Act of 1965, which has been subsequently extended a number of times. Although the Supreme Court has continued consistently to rule against *de jure* segregation, it has had greater difficulty in addressing *de facto* racial segregation and in settling issues like affirmative action and school busing, both of which have been the subject of proposed constitutional amendments and continuing court actions.

Pressures exerted by NAACP-sponsored boycotts and marches undoubtedly influenced the adoption of the Twenty-fourth Amendment outlawing poll taxes, as well as the less successful attempt to provide voting representation in Congress for the District of Columbia. However, the NAACP is not so much known for contributing to the adoption of new amendments as it is for insisting that the nation recognize, and its courts enforce, amendments already on the books. The NAACP strategy of

utilizing courts to ensure the enforcement of constitutional norms has subsequently been utilized by a variety of other interest groups from those favoring and opposing abortion rights, to those concerned about religious freedoms, to those favoring and disfavoring the death penalty, and so forth.

See also *Brown v. Board of Education;* Fourteenth Amendment; Fifteenth Amendment.

❖ NATIONAL INITIATIVE FOR DEMOCRACY ❖

The National Initiative for Democracy is a plan, sponsored in part by former Alaskan Senator Mike Gravel, that is designed to adopt legislation and constitutional amendments through initiative and referendum mechanisms. The Initiative is associated with a nonprofit corporation designated "Philadelphia II" and has an extensive website on the Internet. The Initiative sponsored a conference in February 2002 in Williamsburg, Virginia, that included presentations by a number of scholars, including Akhil Reed Amar, who are convinced that "We the People" can exercise sovereignty by amending the U.S. Constitution outside of the formal constitutional-amending mechanism.

The amendment proposed by the National Initiative for Democracy includes eleven sections (at present, no amendment to the U.S. Constitution has more than six sections), many of which would bring about significant alterations to American government. Collectively, these proposals would bring the government far closer to the idea of a direct, rather than a representative, democracy.

Section 1 calls for establishing a "nonpartisan direct representative democracy" in which "all political and sovereign power and public policy shall be vested in the electorate." Section 2 specifies the creation of "electoral voting networks of interactive electronic devices between elected representatives of all levels of government and the homes of the electorate." All representatives will be "nonpartisan," and all will be subject to annual elections. Section 3 furthers this ideal by allowing the electorate "to instruct, direct and control all levels of government through their elected representatives by majority vote." Section 4 further extends the idea of annual elections to include all members of the judicial branch. Section 5 repeals the Twelfth Amendment and provides direct annual elections of the president and vice president. Section 6 repeals the Sixteenth Amendment, which currently provides for a national income tax, while Section 7 provides that "all matters of public policy and taxation shall require a two-thirds majority of the electorate voting." This section also provides that the electorate shall have the right to amend the U.S. Constitution (thus attempting to confirm in writing the very premise on which the amendment is itself predicated), and allows for the recall of the president and members of the judiciary. Section 8 relates to educating the citizenry and for providing "interactive electronic devices" in the homes of all voters. Section 9 relates to funding; Section 10 returns to the subject of increasing minimum educational levels in the population; and Section 11 provides that this amendment "shall supersede all provisions of this Constitution and laws enacted thereunder in conflict therewith" (http:// www. realdemocracy.com/art28.txt).

Perhaps because of the unlikelihood that members of Congress or the state legislatures would agree to such a diminution of their own powers in favor of the people, the National Initiative for Democracy has also proposed the Democracy Act. This law, intended to be enacted directly "By the People Of the United States," is designed to establish a "Legislature of the People" and allow for initiatives of 5,000 words or less, which could be proposed by a legislative body, by citizen petition, or by public opinion polls. Citizen petitions would put initiatives on the ballot when proposed "by a number of registered voters within the relevant jurisdiction equal to at least 2 percent of those voting in the presidential election occurring immediately prior to the collection of the first signature." Initiatives for constitutional amendments would require a minimum of 5 percent. The law would also provide that initiatives shall qualify for votes "if at least 50 percent of the respondents in a public opinion poll express their desire that the initiative qualify for election." The law goes on to provide for public hearings and the creation of a deliberative committee (that could alter the initiative by a two-thirds vote). It specifies that "No local, state or federal court shall have the power to enjoin any initiative election, except on grounds of fraud." The law limits contributions to initiatives to "natural persons" (thus excluding corporations and unions), and provides mechanisms for financial disclosure and for informing the public about initiatives. The program would be administered by an Electoral Trust, the first director of which would be appointed by the Board of Directors of Philadelphia II for a six-year term, with subsequent directors to be appointed by the U.S. president. Most novel is Section 5 of the law, which is designed to provide for its own self-enactment. Under this provision:

> When the number of ballots reflecting a "Yes" vote executed by a registered voter and received by Philadelphia II is greater than 50 percent of the total number of ballots cast in the presidential election occurring immediately prior to certification, the accompanying Amendment shall be ratified and this Act shall become federal law effective on the date of certification by the President of Philadelphia II to the President of the United States . . . provided that the number of ballots reflecting a "Yes" vote exceeds the number of "No" votes received by Philadelphia II at that time. (http://p2dd.org/nationalinitiative/act.htm)

Taken singly or together, if enacted, these provisions would significantly alter representative government as it is now practiced in the United States and could arguably prepare the way for a multitude of new laws and/or amendments enacted directly by the people.

See also Amar, Akhil Reed; Initiative and Referendum.

For Further Reading:
Gravel, Mike. 1995. "Philadelphia II: National Initiatives." *Campaigns and Elections* 16 (December): 25.

"Proposed Article of Amendment XXVIII (28) to the United States Constitution." At *http://www.re-aldemocracy.com/art28.txt.* Accessed 11/15/02.

❖ *NATIONAL PROHIBITION CASES* (1920) ❖

Seven cases challenging the constitutionality of the Eighteenth Amendment and the Volstead Act, the lead being *Rhode Island v. Palmer,* were grouped together and brought before the Supreme Court in 1920. Justice Willis Van Devanter delivered the Court's opinion. Judging from the arguments that accompanied the cases, the challengers' primary hope was to convince the Court that the Eighteenth Amendment exceeded certain limits on the constitutional amending process as well as fell short of a number of procedural qualifications.

Rather than grapple directly with these arguments, Van Devanter basically stated conclusions. Thus, he simply stated that the power to regulate alcohol "is within the power to amend reserved by Article V of the Constitution" (*National Prohibition Cases* 1920, 386). This prompted Justice Joseph McKenna to note in dissent that such a policy, if established, "will undoubtedly decrease the literature of the court if it does not increase lucidity" (*Id.,* 393). However, in their dissenting opinions, McKenna and John Clarke likewise focused primarily on the meaning of "concurrent powers" in Section 2 of the Eighteenth Amendment rather than providing any in-depth discussion of possible limits on the amending process.

Van Devanter decided that Congress's vote, rather than an explicit statement, was enough to show that it considered the Eighteenth Amendment to be necessary. He also noted that the two-thirds majority required by Article V was two-thirds of a quorum rather than of the entire membership. Van Devanter cited *Hawke v. Smith* (1920) as authority for excluding any state requirements that amendments also be confirmed or rejected by referendum.

On the matter of concurrent powers, which so distressed the dissenters, Van Devanter argued that the clause granting such powers to the nation and the states was intended to allow neither government "to defeat or thwart the prohibition, but only to enforce it by appropriate legislation" (*National Prohibition Cases* 1920, 387). Moreover, he decided that the Eighteenth Amendment, and the accompanying Volstead Act (which applied to all beverages with 0.5 percent or more alcohol content), could be applied both to preexisting alcohol and to that manufactured or imported after its passage.

Opposition to the Eighteenth Amendment was intense, but its opponents ultimately succeeded in the court of public opinion rather than at the bar of the Supreme Court, which rejected another legal challenge in *United States v. Sprague* (1931). Eventually, the Twenty-first Amendment, ratified shortly after the first election of President Franklin D. Roosevelt, repealed the Eighteenth.

See also Constitutional Amendments, Limits on.

For Further Reading:
National Prohibition Cases, 253 U.S. 350 (1920).

❖ NATIVE AMERICANS ❖

The U.S. Constitution mentions Native Americans in few places, yet their treatment and status have been a perpetual source of shame and controversy throughout American history. Both Article I, Section 2 of the Constitution and Section 2 of the Fourteenth Amendment exclude "Indians not taxed" from the numbers used to calculate representation in the House. Article I, Section 8 further extended congressional power over commerce "with the Indian tribes."

The earliest proposed amendment related to Native Americans was introduced in 1832 when the state of Georgia petitioned Congress for a convention to clarify the rights of Indians. The state had been stung by John Marshall's opinion in *Worcester v. Georgia* (1832). In that case, the Supreme Court had invalidated a Georgia statute requiring a minister to obtain a license to live in Cherokee country and enlarged the right of Indian sovereignty. With

President Andrew Jackson (who upheld strong national powers in the Nullification Controversy) unwilling to enforce this judgment holding Georgia to treaties it had made, the state proceeded to remove the Cherokees in the historic evacuation known as the "Trail of Tears."

There appears to have been at least one attempt to include Indians within the citizenship guarantee of the Fourteenth Amendment, but in cases such as *Elk v. Wilkins* (1884), the Supreme Court did not interpret the amendment to confer citizenship on Indians. Congress finally took this action in 1924 (Wunder 1994, 50; Maltz 2002, 572).

In 1937 a South Dakota representative proposed including Indians in apportioning the House of Representatives, and in 1940 a North Dakota representative voted to deprive Congress of the power to regulate intrastate commerce with them. When they were charged with one of a number of major crimes defined by Congress or when they were off reservations, Native Americans were governed by federal constitutional guarantees, but on the reservations, tribal courts were not bound by the Bill of Rights (Wunder 1994, 132–133). At least four proposals from 1939 through 1953 were introduced—three by Democratic Senator Patrick McCarran of Nevada—to restore the same rights to American Indians as were enjoyed by other American citizens. In 1968 Congress adopted legislation known as the Indian Bill of Rights. It applied most, but not all, provisions of the Bill of Rights to proceedings on Indian reservations (Wunder 1994, 135–144).

For Further Reading:

Maltz, Earl M. 2002. "The Fourteenth Amendment and Native American Citizenship." *Constitutional Commentary* 17 (Winter): 555–573.

Wunder, John R. 1994. *"Retained by the People": A History of American Indians and the Bill of Rights*. New York: Oxford University Press.

❖ NATURAL LAW ❖

Many of the American founders believed strongly in the idea of natural law. This idea, traceable back to ancient Greek and Roman as well as to medieval Christian philosophers, posits the existence of an unwritten set of unchanging moral principles that can be ascertained through human reason (Sigmund 1971). In the eighteenth century, such ideas were transfigured into the idea of natural rights.

Thomas Jefferson premised the Declaration of Independence on this latter doctrine, which he linked to the "unalienable rights" of "life, liberty, and the pursuit of happiness." Pointing to the fact that the Declaration is included at the beginning of the U.S. Code, some have argued that it is part of the organic law of the land (Jaffa 1994, 4–5) and that judges should enforce this part of the nation's "unwritten constitution" (Grey 1975). Others prefer to maintain the distinction between natural law and positive law (O'Neil 1995) and think that judges should enforce only those natural-law principles that are embodied in such parts of the Constitution as the Bill of Rights, the Fourteenth Amendment, and other specific provisions.

It appears that prior to 1787 American courts frequently resorted to natural-law concepts in justifying their decisions and that they later devoted greater attention to specific phrases and more general principles of the written Constitution (L. Goldstein 1991, 15). In *Calder v. Bull* (1798), a decision about the scope of the ex post facto provision, Justice Samuel Chase argued for judicial enforcement of such natural-law principles, whereas Justice James Iredell thought that courts should base their judgments only on specific constitutional provisions. From the late nineteenth century through 1937, the Supreme Court's focus on substantive due process appeared to embody a type of natural-law reasoning that some scholars believe served to usurp the people's role in amending the Constitution. Arguably, modern opinions on the right to privacy have a similar natural-law foundation—as do some of the opposition arguments against abortion. Some advocates of limits on the amending process have based their argument on natural-law principles said to be implicit in the Constitution (Rosen 1991, 1086).

Principles of natural law are generally thought to be unalterable. To the extent that the Constitution is regarded as embodying such natural-law principles, judicial interpretations are likely to be considered largely unalterable. This idea is in tension with some versions of "the living Constitution," whereby judges are expected to adapt constitutional provisions not simply to new developments in technology but also to contemporary changes in thinking.

See also Declaration of Independence; Jefferson, Thomas; Living Constitution.

For Further Reading:
Corwin, Edward S. 1955. *The "Higher Law" Background of American Constitutional Law.* Ithaca, NY: Cornell University Press.
Goldstein, Leslie F. 1991. *In Defense of the Text: Democracy and Constitutional Theory.* Savage, MD: Rowman and Littlefield.
Grey, Thomas C. 1975. "Do We Have an Unwritten Constitution?" *Stanford Law Review* 27 (February): 703–718.
Hamburger, Philip A. 1993. "Natural Rights, Natural Law, and American Constitutionalism." *Yale Law Journal* 102 (January): 907–960.
Jaffa, Harry V. 1994. *Original Intent and the Framers of the Constitution: A Disputed Question.* Washington, DC: Regnery Gateway.
O'Neil, Patrick M. 1995. "The Declaration as Un-Constitution: The Bizarre Jurisprudential Philosophy of Professor Harry V. Jaffa." *Akron Law Review* 28 (Fall/Winter): 237–252.
Rosen, Jeff. 1991. "Was the Flag Burning Amendment Unconstitutional?" *Yale Law Review* 100: 1073–1092.
Sigmund, Paul E. 1971. *Natural Law in Political Thought.* Cambridge, MA: Winthrop Publishers.

❖ NAYLOR, THOMAS H. (1936–), AND WILLIAM H. WILLIMON (1946–) ❖

Since the end of the U.S. Civil War, there have been relatively few advocates of secession, but the fear that James Madison battled in arguing in *Federalist No. 10* for an extended republic continues to be raised by those who fear bigness in all its forms. Thomas Naylor, a professor emeritus of economics from Duke University, and William H. Willimon, then dean of the chapel and professor of Christian Ministry at the same institution, combine both themes in a book, *Downsizing the U.S.A.,* which they published in 1997.

The authors are advocates of the thesis that "small is beautiful," and their primary example is the state of Vermont. Surveying the ills of modern America, they attribute almost all of them to bigness. Corporations are too large; cities are too large; schools and universities are too large; the United States is too large; and even many of the fifty states are too large.

For each large institution, there is a set of strategies. Corporations can be brought down to size by "abolishing the U.S. Departments of Commerce and Labor"; encouraging "corporate downsizing"; buying locally; avoiding large chain stores; and attempting to spend money at home (Naylor and Willimon 1997, 77). Cities can be downsized by abolishing the U.S. Department of Housing and Urban Development; eliminating "most federal subsidies"; allowing cities to limit their growth; and permitting "cities to secede from the state in which they are located and form independent city-states" (*Id.,* 75). Rural America can be revitalized by abolishing the U.S. Department of Agriculture; subsidizing "family farms, not large corporate farms"; revoking federal aid for interstate highways; and patronizing local merchants (*Id.,* 93). Education can be downsized by abolishing the U.S. Department of Education; using educational vouchers; limiting schools to 300 students (*Id.,* 121); dividing universities with more than 10,000 students into colleges of 3,000, with residential colleges of about 300 students; reducing federal aid to colleges and universities; and replacing tenure with long-term contracts (*Id.,* 135). Religious organizations should "decentralize decision-making power" to "the local congregation," reduce denominational central offices, and cultivate small groups within congregations (*Id.,* 154). Cures for the welfare state include the abolition of Medicare and Medicaid; closing the U.S. Department of Health and Human Services; practicing holistic medicine; and using more resources to teach people "how to live healthy, meaningful lives and how to die happy" (*Id.*, 171). Superpowers like the United States can be brought to heel by substituting "constructive engagement, tension reduction, and power sharing for military confrontation"; reducing troop commitments abroad; resigning from the United Nations and the World Bank; and substituting voluntary for compulsory alliances (*Id.*, 202). States may be empowered and downsized by reducing federal regulations; allowing large states to split; and allowing large cities to "become separate states" (*Id.*, 236).

Drawing from a law review article, Naylor and Willimon proceed to make four arguments for the legitimacy of secession. They believe that states should be permitted to call conventions at which secession is the only issue on the agenda (Naylor and Willimon 1997, 250). Naylor and Willimon believe the central issues that would emerge would be economic, namely:

(1) compensation for U.S. government-owned property within the state, (2) payment of relocation costs for citizens who want to leave the state but remain in the United States, (3) disposition of the state's share of the federal debt, and (4) settlement of the state's pro rata claim on the total net worth of the United States taken as a whole. (Naylor and Willimon 1997, 256)

Fairly conveniently perhaps, Naylor and Willimon believe that the states' share of national wealth will more than compensate for their share of the national debt.

Naylor and Willimon describe their view as "a form of anarchism" (Naylor and Willimon 1997, 259). Once two-thirds of a state's conventional delegates agree to secede, a state would present its petition to the U.S. secretary of state and follow with "a strategy of constructive engagement with the U.S. government" (*Id.*, 276). Naylor and Willimon further envision a system of "free trade and free travel among states having a single currency and a common economic system. Member states might form a mutual defense alliance" (*Id.*, 278). States would, in turn, "have complete responsibility for and total control for and total

control of their own taxes, schools, social welfare, health care, law enforcement, highways, airports, housing, and physical environment" (*Id.*, 278).

Naylor and Willimon suggest various regional state groupings including a black nation in the Mississippi Delta. They note, however, that they have "no grand scheme for downsizing America, for such a plan would be antithetical to what we are trying to accomplish" (Naylor and Willimon 1997, 284). Although full of suggestions for downsizing governments, this book is less likely to serve as a model for specific amendments than as a possible catalyst to thinking, and rethinking, the advantages and disadvantages of institutions of increasing size and complexity.

See also Cummings, Richard.

For Further Reading:
Naylor, Thomas H., and William H. Willimon. 1997. *Downsizing the U.S.A.* Grand Rapids, MI: William B. Eerdmans Publishing Company.

❖ NECESSARY AND PROPER CLAUSE ❖

The last clause in Article I, Section 8 of the Constitution grants Congress power "to make all laws which shall be necessary and proper for carrying into Execution the foregoing Powers." Often called the "elastic" or "sweeping" clause, this clause serves as the textual basis for the notion that Congress can exercise certain implied powers. It served as one of the central constitutional supports by which John Marshall justified the constitutionality of the national bank in *McCulloch v. Maryland* (1819). Marshall argued that the national bank was not an end in and of itself but was a means for effecting ends, or powers (like raising revenue), that were specified within the Constitution. Contrary to the arguments that Thomas Jefferson had made in opposing the establishment of a national bank, Marshall argued that the word "necessary" did not mean "absolutely necessary" but permitted Congress to exercise some choice of means. Without such a provision, many more amendments would undoubtedly have been necessary in order to expand congressional powers.

If not tied specifically to constitutional ends, however, the clause could undermine the whole notion of a constitution of enumerated powers (Engdahl 1994, 13). In 1806 John Clopton, a Democratic representative from Virginia, introduced an amendment to construe the clause so as "to comprehend only such laws as shall have a natural connection with and immediate relation to the powers enumerated in the said section, or such other powers as are expressly vested by the Constitution in the Government of the United States" (Ames 1896, 168). Democratic-Republicans were quite concerned that Marshall's decision in *McCulloch v. Maryland* was so broad that it undermined the idea of a government of limited powers. More recently, a participant in a law review symposium cited the ambiguity of the necessary and proper clause as a reason for nominating it as the most "stupid" provision in the current document (Eskridge and Levinson 1998, 43–50).

For Further Reading:

Ames, Herman. 1896. *The Proposed Amendments to the Constitution of the United States during the First Century of Its History.* Reprint, New York: Burt Franklin, 1970.

Engdahl, David E. 1994. "The Spending Power." *Duke Law Journal* 44 (October): 1–109.

Eskridge, William N., Jr., and Sanford Levinson. 1998. *Constitutional Stupidities, Constitutional Tragedies.* New York: New York University Press.

❖ NEW DEAL ❖

See Court-packing Plan.

❖ NINETEENTH AMENDMENT ❖

Although they proclaimed human equality, the American founding fathers did little to heed Abigail Adams's plea to "remember the Ladies, and be more generous and favourable to them than your ancestors" (letter to John Adams dated 31 March 1776, quoted in Mason and Baker 1985, 119). Only in New Jersey were women permitted to vote, and there the doctrine of coverture, by which a married couple constituted a single entity, essentially limited this right to unmarried women (Bernstein with Agel 1993, 129). Moreover, throughout most of the eighteenth and nineteenth centuries, women were subjected to a number of legal disabilities that affected their title to land, custody of their children in the case of divorce, and access to occupations (Van Burkleo 1990, 10).

Origins of the Suffrage Movement

The movement for women's suffrage is usually dated to the Seneca Falls Convention of 1848, where Elizabeth Cady Stanton drew up the Seneca Falls Declaration of Rights and Sentiments that she patterned after the Declaration of Independence. The convention's support for women's suffrage was considered to be one of its more radical stances and was widely ridiculed in the press of the day. Many of the early leaders of the women's suffrage movement were also active in the abolition movement and in the movement for national alcoholic prohibition. These women were understandably upset when the Fourteenth and Fifteenth Amendments made no specific provisions for women. Indeed, the Fourteenth Amendment was the first to introduce the term "male" into the Constitution. Largely because of disputes arising over the proper stance for women to take toward these amendments, women's suffrage proponents split into two main groups. Elizabeth Cady Stanton and Susan B. Anthony, who opposed adoption of the Fourteenth Amendment, formed the National Woman Suffrage Association; Henry Ward Beecher and Lucy Stone, who favored the amendment, formed the American Woman Suffrage Association (Kraditor 1981, 3–4). This rivalry continued until the two groups joined in 1890 to become the National American Woman Suffrage Association (NAWSA).

Democratic Representative James Brooks of New York was the first to offer a women's suffrage amendment in Congress. He introduced his proposal in 1866 as an amendment to Section 2 of the Fourteenth Amendment and again in 1869 as an addition to the Fifteenth Amendment. Although Brooks was not successful, the Fifteenth Amendment subsequently became the model for the women's suffrage amendment (also called the Susan B. Anthony amendment), which was introduced regularly in Congress from 1880 until it was proposed by the necessary majorities in 1919. Few observers could have been surprised when in *Minor v. Happersett* (1875) the Supreme Court rejected the argument that the Fourteenth Amendment extended the right to vote to women.

Much of the pressure for women's suffrage came from the western states. They were motivated partly by their desire to get enough voters to qualify for statehood. The Wyoming Territory granted suffrage to women in 1869, and other states and territories followed. Some allowed women to vote in all elections, and others limited such voting to school board elections or elections for the president (Bernstein with Agel 1993, 132).

Debates over Women's Suffrage

As in other amending controversies, most notably the later disputes over the Equal Rights Amendment, both sides of the women's suffrage debate claimed more radical consequences for the amendment than it would eventually generate. Opponents feared that women would be sullied by their participation in politics and forecast dire changes in family and social structures. Whereas some proponents of suffrage argued that it simply recognized women's equality under the law, others anticipated that women would have an ennobling influence on political life that would inaugurate major political reforms. The argument was also advanced from time to time that the votes of educated women might help counteract the votes of African Americans and immigrants (Kraditor 1981, 14–74).

The tie between women's suffrage and other issues was sometimes a disability. Women (especially those in the Women's Christian Temperance Union) had taken such an active part in the movement for national alcoholic prohibition that those opposed to Prohibition feared that women's suffrage would lead to adoption

of the Prohibition Amendment. Especially in the South, fears were raised that an amendment granting women the right to vote might renew federal efforts to enforce the Fifteenth Amendment, prohibiting discrimination in voting on the basis of race. Southerners were a major source of support for the Shafroth-Palmer Amendment of 1914, which would have allowed each state to have a referendum (if so requested by 8 percent or more of the voters) on the women's suffrage issue rather than setting a single national standard (for Southern views, see Wheeler 1993). Some supporters of women's suffrage wanted it limited to white women (Grimes 1978, 91).

Growing Support for the Amendment

As increasing numbers of states began to extend the right to vote in whole or in part to women, pressures for a federal amendment increased. In 1914 the Senate voted 35 to 34 for the amendment, with the House falling far shorter in 1915 with a vote of 174 to 204. That same year, under the leadership of Alice Paul, the Congressional Union for Woman Suffrage (CU)—later the Woman's Party (WP)—broke with NAWSA and advocated more militant measures, including campaigns against all Democrats, who were generally less supportive of the amendment than Republicans. The CU also led a series of parades and controversial pickets outside the White House.

The adoption of the Eighteenth Amendment probably aided the Nineteenth Amendment, in that some of those who had opposed women's suffrage for fear that it would lead to Prohibition now had nothing more to lose. World War I also mobilized increasing numbers of women into the workforce and led some to believe that their sacrifices should be acknowledged. Initially a tepid supporter of the amendment, President Woodrow Wilson addressed the Senate in 1918 in support of it (Flexnor 1974, 307–309), but it again fell short of the necessary votes, as it would in early 1919 as well. Wilson subsequently called a special session of Congress in May 1919, and the amendment finally succeeded, with the final Senate vote coming on 28 May 1919. Proposals to limit the vote to white women, to ratify the amendment by convention rather than by state legislatures, and to entrust states with primary enforcement powers were all rejected at this time (U.S. Senate Committee on the Judiciary, Subcommittee on the Constitution 1985, 56).

Ratification of the Amendment
The amendment was ratified in just over a year, with most opposition coming, as expected, in the South. The thirty-sixth state to ratify was Tennessee. Several prominent leaders of the women's movement, including Carrie Chapman Catt, president of the National Woman Suffrage Association, came to Nashville to lobby and were met by almost equally well-organized opponents. The Tennessee constitution contained a provision that the state legislature could not vote for a proposed amendment until after an intervening election (A. Taylor 1957, 104), but both the U.S. solicitor general and Tennessee's attorney general declared this provision invalid after the Supreme Court's two decisions in *Hawke v. Smith* (1920). The Tennessee Senate subsequently adopted the resolution by a vote of twenty-four to four and sent it to the House, where a motion to table the resolution failed by a vote of forty-eight to forty-eight. When the measure came up for a vote, a twenty-four-year-old state representative named Harry Burn switched votes because of his mother's request to adopt the amendment, and another member did the same in order to call the vote up for reconsideration. The "Red Rose Brigade," consisting of opponents of the amendment (supporters wore yellow roses), subsequently left the state for Alabama to prevent a quorum on reconsideration, but after a series of complicated maneuvers, they proved unsuccessful. The U.S. secretary of state apparently ignored a later House resolution of nonconcurrence (A. Taylor 1957, 122–124).

Subsequent Developments
The amendment was quickly implemented. In *Leser v. Garnett* (1922), the Supreme Court rejected a challenge to this amendment, and in *Adkins v. Children's Hospital* (1923), the Court cited the amendment in striking down a minimum-wage law for women in the District of Columbia. Partly on the basis of this precedent

and on the basis of the long debates on this amendment, some recent authors have argued that the Nineteenth Amendment might be interpreted, particularly in conjunction with the Fourteenth Amendment, as a broader guarantee of women's rights than has so far been the case (J. Brown 1993; Siegel 2002).

Celebrations in Tennessee and throughout the nation marked the seventy-fifth anniversary of the Nineteenth Amendment in 1995. Events in Washington, D.C., were held in the basement of the Capitol near a statue of Susan B. Anthony, Elizabeth Cady Stanton, and Lucretia Mott, because the House had failed to vote on an earlier Senate resolution to move the monument—donated by the National Woman's Party in 1921—to the main rotunda. Among the dozens of statues of American forefathers there, none depicted American women ("A Celebration" 1995, 9).

See also Anthony, Susan Brownell; Catt, Carrie Lane Chapman; Paul, Alice; Seneca Falls Convention; Shafroth-Palmer Amendment; Stanton, Elizabeth Cady; Willard, Frances.

For Further Reading:
Bernstein, Richard B., with Jerome Agel. 1993. *Amending America: If We Love the Constitution So Much, Why Do We Keep Trying to Change It?* New York: Random House.
Brown, Jennifer K. 1993. "The Nineteenth Amendment and Women's Equality." *Yale Law Journal* 102 (June): 2174–2204.
"A Celebration of Women's Right to Vote." 1995. *New York Times,* 27 August, 9.
Flexnor, Eleanor. 1974. *Century of Struggle: The Woman's Rights Movement in the United States.* New York: Atheneum.
Grimes, Alan P. 1978. *Democracy and the Amendments to the Constitution.* Lexington, MA: Lexington Books.
Kraditor, Aileen S. 1981. *The Idea of the Woman's Suffrage Movement, 1890–1920.* New York: W. W. Norton.
Siegel, Reva B. 2002. "She the People: The Nineteenth Amendment, Sex Equality, Federalism, and the Family." *Harvard Law Review* 115 (February): 947–1046.
Stevens, Doris. 1995. *Jailed for Freedom: Ameri-*

can Women Win the Vote. Troutdale, OR: New Sage.

Taylor, A. Elizabeth. 1957. *The Woman Suffrage Movement in Tennessee*. New York: Bookman Associates.

U.S. Senate Committee on the Judiciary, Subcommittee on the Constitution, *Amendments to the Constitution: A Brief Legislative History*. 1985. Washington, DC: U.S. Government Printing Office.

Van Burkleo, Sandra F. 1990. "No Rights but Human Rights." *Constitution* 2 (Spring-Summer): 4–19.

Wheeler, Marjorie S. 1995b. *Votes for Women! The Woman Suffrage Movement in Tennessee, the South, and the Nation*. Knoxville, TN: University of Tennessee Press.

Wheeler, Marjorie S., ed. 1995. *One Woman, One Vote: Rediscovering the Woman Suffrage Movement*. Troutdale, OR: New Sage.

❖ NINTH AMENDMENT ❖

One of the most elusive and controversial amendments to the Constitution is the Ninth Amendment. It was ratified in 1791 as part of the Bill of Rights. This amendment provides that "the enumeration in the Constitution of certain rights, shall not be construed to deny or disparage others retained by the people."

Arguably a reflection of the natural-rights philosophy of the founding fathers, this provision appears to have originated in a proposed amendment to the Virginia constitution. A similar provision had been proposed by both the Virginia and the North Carolina ratifying conventions (Lutz 1992, 53, 57, 63) before being incorporated in the Bill of Rights that James Madison proposed in the First Congress. Madison's original provision actually incorporated the ideas that would later appear in both the Ninth and the Tenth Amendments: "The exceptions here or elsewhere in the Constitution, made in favor of particular rights, shall not be so construed as to diminish the just importance of other rights retained by the people, or to enlarge the powers delegated by the Constitution; but either as actual limitations of such powers, or as inserted merely for greater caution" (Kurland and Lerner 1987, 5:25).

One of the Federalists' original objections to the inclusion of a bill of rights was that it would be impossible to make a complete list of human rights. Such a bill might prove dangerous if observers concluded that because a right was not enumerated it had therefore been forfeited. The Ninth Amendment appears to have been introduced with this problem in mind. Speaking before the House of Representatives, Madison thus noted:

> It has been objected also against a bill of rights, that, by enumerating particular exceptions to the grant of power, it would disparage those rights which were not placed in that enumeration; and it might follow by implication, that those rights which were not singled out, were intended to be assigned into the hands of the General Government, and were consequently insecure. This is one of the most plausible arguments I have ever heard urged against the admission of a bill of rights into this system; but, I conceive, that it may be guarded against. I have attempted it [in the Ninth Amendment]. (Kurland and Lerner 1987, 5:399)

The only recorded debate on the subject in the First Congress centered on Elbridge Gerry's unsuccessful motion to substitute the word "impair" for "disparage" (Kurland and Lerner 1987, 5:400); other modifications were insignificant (Caplan 1983, 258).

For most of its first 150 years, the Ninth Amendment lacked the judicial gloss so typical of other provisions in the Bill of Rights. What judicial interpretations there were suggested what a leading student of the Ninth Amendment called a "rights-powers" approach to the amendment. Under this approach, courts considered unenumerated rights under the amendment to consist only of those rights that remained because the government was granted no power over them (Barnette 1989, 14). An alternative approach would be to conceive of the protections for unenumerated rights in the Ninth Amendment, like other protections in the first ten amendments, as "power-constraints" on government (Barnette 1989, 14).

This interpretation received some backing with the Supreme Court's decision invalidating Connecticut's birth-control law in *Griswold v. Connecticut* (1965). Although mentioned in Douglas's majority opinion, it was given considerably more emphasis in Justice Arthur Goldberg's concurring opinion.

The main obstacles to this "power-constraints" approach appear to be twofold. First is the difficulty of deciding precisely what unenumerated rights would be protected by the Ninth Amendment. Second is the related concern that expansive interpretation of such unenumerated rights might upset the scheme of separation of powers or federalism by unduly empowering the judiciary (DeRosa 1996).

Another way of interpreting the Ninth Amendment is to view it simply as a recognition that rights protected under state constitutions when it was adopted would continue in force "until modified or eliminated by state enactment, by federal preemption, or by a judicial determination of unconstitutionality" (Caplan 1983, 228).

With such wide disparities of interpretation, the Ninth Amendment is likely to continue to be the focus of intense scholarly debate.

For Further Reading:

Barnette, Randy E., ed. 1989. *The Rights Retained by the People: The History and Meaning of the Ninth Amendment.* Fairfax, VA: George Mason University Press.

Caplan, Russell L. 1983. "The History and Meaning of the Ninth Amendment." *Virginia Law Review* 69 (March): 223–268.

DeRosa, Marshall L. 1996. *The Ninth Amendment and the Politics of Creative Jurisprudence: Disparaging the Fundamental Right of Popular Control.* New Brunswick, NJ: Transaction Publishers.

Kurland, Philip B., and Ralph Lerner, eds. 1987. *The Founders' Constitution.* 5 vols. Chicago: University of Chicago Press.

Lutz, Donald S. 1992. *A Preface to American Political Theory.* Lawrence, KS: University Press of Kansas.

Massey, Calvin R. 1995. *Silent Rights: The Ninth Amendment and the Constitution's Unenumerated Rights.* Philadelphia: Temple University Press.

Patterson, Bennett B. 1955. *The Forgotten Ninth Amendment.* Indianapolis, IN: Bobbs-Merrill.

❖ NORDEEN, ROSS ❖

Ross Nordeen, a Floridian who identifies himself as a an engineer and an amateur economist, has joined those who have used the Internet to reprint the Constitution along with changes that he thinks should be added or deleted. His site *(www.amatecon.com)*, which the author of this book first visited in June 2000, is still available and does not appear to have changed in significant measure. Nordeen indicates that he became interested in the idea of constitutional reform because of Florida's recent look at its own constitution, and cites a number of conservative and libertarian individuals and groups that have influenced his thinking.

In revising Article I, Nordeen proposes to eliminate all indirect references to slavery. He would also limit members of the House of Representatives to three terms and members of the U.S. Senate to two. Both houses would be limited to meeting no more than sixty days per year, except by a two-thirds vote permitting an additional sixty-day term. Nordeen proposes a number of alterations in the list of congressional powers in Article I, Section 8. He would require a two-thirds vote for levying any new taxes; would delete the provision giving Congress power to establish post offices and post roads; would alter the necessary and proper clause by giving Congress power "to make only those laws which shall be necessary and proper" and by further providing that all congressional laws shall expire after ten years. Additionally, he would prohibit taxes with retroactive effect and would prohibit deficit spending unless such spending were approved by three-fourths majorities of both houses.

Nordeen would leave Articles II and III relatively untouched, but he would also add a provision to Article IV specifying that "[a] state may secede from the union by a two-thirds vote of its citizens. Congress may levy additional requirements on the secession of a state with a two-thirds vote of both houses." Nordeen adds, by way of explanation that:

> Giving the states an explicit method of secession might have prevented the bloodshed of the Civil War. If the southern states were allowed to peacefully secede,

the remaining states could have easily passed an amendment barring slavery and acted as a safe haven for runaway slaves.

Nordeen would further provide in Article V "nor shall a state's method of electing Senators be changed without its consent," apparently in the hopes of allowing states who choose to do so to revert to the method of selecting Senators prior to the introduction of the Seventeenth Amendment, which, however, remains unchanged in his document.

Nordeen advocates a number of changes in the Bill of Rights. The word "abridging" in the First Amendment would be changed to "infringing." He further adds a provision, which appears largely to codify existing case law, stating that:

> The rights of electoral participation and political association are fundamental; any law burdening their exercise is subject to strict judicial scrutiny for legitimacy regarding ends and means, and must be supported by clear and convincing evidence. Political choices and competition are primary interests of the citizenry.

Nordeen would eliminate the preface to the Second Amendment, thus simply providing that "Congress shall make no law infringing on the right of the people to keep and bear arms." He also adds a provision to the Third Amendment requiring that "Congress shall make no law requiring service in the army, navy, the militia or any civil service." The Fourth Amendment is prefaced with a provision stating that "Congress shall make no law infringing on the right of the people to privacy." Nordeen would further strengthen the takings clause of the Fifth Amendment by providing that private property shall not be taken "except for a substantial, explicit public use and with full compensation therefore paid to each owner." Nordeen adds a provision to the Sixth Amendment providing that "The jury shall have the power to judge the law in all instances in which the government or any of its agencies is an opposing party." Nordeen proposes fairly extensive changes to the Eighth Amendment. It would, like the First Amendment, now begin

with the words, "Congress shall make no law," and would add the following provisions designed to strengthen property rights:

> Forfeiture of estate, indefinite imprisonment, and unreasonable detention of witnesses are forbidden. There shall be proportionality between magnitude of felony and the severity of forfeiture of property. No person charged with a crime shall be compelled to pay costs before a judgment of conviction has become final. A person not found guilty of a crime shall not be assessed fees or costs to recover property seized as evidence or otherwise held, impounded, or stored by the government.

Nordeen also adds new language to the Tenth Amendment designed to rein in federal powers. Nordeen's new language would specify that:

> Relative to the people, no branch of government has inherent or reserved powers, implicit or assumed prerogatives, or presupposed attributes of sovereignty. Powers must be expressly granted to government by the people, and the extent and range of such powers shall be strictly, narrowly construed.

Nordeen does not propose any alterations in the other seventeen amendments that have been ratified.

Nordeen's suggestions are clearly influenced by concerns of other conservatives and libertarians and would push the Constitution further in these directions. His plan of indicating how his proposals would fit into the existing Constitution, although not unique, adds to the clarity of his amendments. The concern by an admitted "novice" about constitutional issues is another indication of the importance that private citizens in the United States often place on the written constitution.

For Further Reading:

Nordeen, Ross. "Home Page." *www.amatecon. com*. Accessed 6/30/00. Reaccessed for updates on 5/17/02. There are few significant changes in the two documents. Quotations are taken from the first.

❖ NORRIS, GEORGE (1861–1944) ❖

Although the Sixteenth through Nineteenth Amendments were the ones actually adopted during the Progressive Era, the Twentieth, or Lame Duck, Amendment ratified in 1933 is also consistent with the Progressives' desire for greater electoral accountability. Perhaps more than any single amendment, the Twentieth is largely attributable to the work of a single individual, namely Nebraska Senator George W. Norris.

Born in Ohio in 1861, Norris graduated from what is now Baldwin-Wallace College and began teaching school before studying law at what is today Valparaiso University in Indiana. After teaching a while longer, Norris went to Nebraska where, in addition to practicing law (the Burlington and Missouri Railroad was among his clients), he became engaged in the milling and mortgage loan businesses. Initially successful, his businesses fell prey to a depression in the state in the 1890s. At that time, Norris was employed as a prosecutor and served from 1885 to 1902 as a state circuit judge before running for Congress as a Republican.

Initially beholden to some of the interests that he had represented as an attorney, Norris became increasingly independent of these interests and of the Republican Party that had nominated him. In 1910 Norris had a major impact in lessening the role of U.S. House Speaker Joseph Cannon when Norris successfully introduced and helped pass a motion expanding membership on the powerful House Rules Committee and excluding the Speaker from this group.

In 1912 Norris ran for the U.S. Senate where he served for five terms. Often in the political wilderness, Norris ended up supporting Franklin D. Roosevelt in his presidential bid of 1932 and subsequently won reelection to the U.S. Senate as an independent. He was finally defeated when he ran for his sixth term in 1942.

Norris lobbied for the Twentieth Amend-

ment for close to a decade. Norris supported many other Progressive causes, among them conservation, rural electrification, labor reform, and the establishment of the Tennessee Valley Authority. Norris favored the direct election of the president and proposed a nine-year nonrenewable term for federal judges and a requirement that the Supreme Court not be permitted to invalidate an act of Congress without a two-thirds vote (Norris perceived these as alternatives to Franklin Roosevelt's court-packing plan). Perhaps more importantly, Norris was a driving force behind the adoption of a constitutional amendment in Nebraska providing for a unicameral legislature, which continues to be the only one of its kind in the nation.

In 1932 Franklin Roosevelt referred to Norris "as the very perfect gentle knight of American progressive ideals" (Lowitt 1973). A seemingly fearless orator, Norris was also adept at behind-the-scenes political maneuvering.

See also Court-packing Plan; Progressive Era; Twentieth Amendment.

For Further Reading:

Lowitt, Richard. 1973. "George William Norris." *Dictionary of American Biography:* Supplement 3: 1941–1945. American Council of Learned Societies. At *http://www.galenet.com/servlet/BioRC*. Accessed 11/26/02.

"George William Norris." 1998. *American Decades CD-ROM*. Gale Research. Last accessed at *http://www.galenet.com/servlet/BioRC*.

❖ NUMBER OF PROPOSED AMENDMENTS ❖

When historian Herman Ames surveyed the amendments that had been proposed during the nation's first 100 years, he counted 1,736 proposals. He noted, however, that "it is scarcely possible that all the proposed amendments presented to Congress have been included" (Ames 1896, 11). The precision of his count is further undercut by the fact that he included some state petitions and proposals for amendments that presidents made in speeches but that were not necessarily introduced as amendments in Congress. Also, Ames some-times split a single proposal into several components, each of which he numbered separately. Notwithstanding such limitations, his count still remains the best approximation for the nation's first 100 years.

In the next published list of amendments, the Library of Congress counted 1,316 amendments that had been introduced in Congress from 1890 through 1926 (Tansill 1926). Clearly, the rate at which amendments were being introduced was increasing. It has continued to do so.

When the last list of proposed amendments was published in 1992, the author counted 10,431 proposals. These included the 3,000-plus amendments counted by Ames and Tansill, as well as 2,340 amendments introduced from 1926 to 1962 (*Proposed Amendments* 1963; this study duplicates parts of *Proposed Amendments* 1957), 1,548 from 1963 to 1968 (*Proposed Amendments* 1969), 3,054 from 1969 to 1984 (Davis 1985), and 437 from 1985 to 1990 (D. Harris 1992, CRS-8).

The best count available for the Congresses since 1990 are as follows: 152 proposals for the 102nd Congress (1991–1992); 156 for the 103rd Congress; 287 for the 104th Congress; 110 for the 105th Congress; and 69 for the 106th Congress (1999–2000). The 107th Congress proposed 52 amendments in 2001 (Vile 2003). If it proposes an equal number in 2002, this would bring the total number to 11,309, with proposals in 2003 likely to bring the number fairly close to 11,500. This number does not include all the petitions that have been made to Congress by private groups and by governments for particular amendments. The most complete list of state applications for a constitutional convention, which was published in 1993, lists 399 such proposals, some of which were included in Ames's count of the first 100 years (Paulsen 1993). It should be noted that a number of states have recently rescinded their calls for a convention either for a specific issue, like balanced budgets, or for a convention in general.

Counting the total number of amendments proposed in Congress is somewhat deceptive, because most such proposals are repetitive.

An author writing in 1964 noted the "recent trend toward the introduction, all at once, of dozens of identically worded proposals . . . boosts the total far out of any meaningful relation to the number of topics under consideration (Leedham 1964, 264). The author thus noted that of 328 proposals introduced in the Eighty-eighth Congress, there were only "37 distinct propositions in the House and 13 in the Senate." He further observed that:

> The Senate manages to keep the total number of proposals rather low by listing each resolution only once and noting that it may have more than one sponsor. The House clutters up the record with dozens of individually entered "Joint Resolutions," each one commemorating no more than the fact that an individual representative likes the idea. (Leedham 1964, 264)

There are thus literally hundreds of proposals to introduce an Equal Rights Amendment, to restore public prayer in schools, to provide for a balanced budget amendment, and the like.

Of the thousands of proposed amendments, only thirty-four have been proposed by the requisite congressional majorities. Of these, six remain failed amendments, and only twenty-seven have been adopted by the states. One such amendment (the Twenty-first) repealed another (the Eighteenth), and doubts continue as to the legitimacy of the Twenty-seventh Amendment, which was ratified in 1993, more than 200 years after first being proposed by Congress.

For Further Reading:

Ames, Herman. 1896. *The Proposed Amendments to the Constitution of the United States during the First Century of Its History.* Reprint, New York: Burt Franklin, 1970.

Davis, Richard. 1985. *Proposed Amendments to the Constitution of the United States of America Introduced in Congress from the 91st Congress, 1st Session, through the 98th Congress, 2d Session, January 1969–December 1984.* Washington, DC: Congressional Research Service Report no. 85–36 GOV.

Harris, Daryl B. 1992. *Proposed Amendments to*

the U.S. Constitution: 99th–101st Congresses (1985–1990). Washington, DC: Congressional Research Service, Library of Congress.

Leedham, Charles. 1964. *Our Changing Constitution: The Story behind the Amendments.* New York: Dodd, Mead & Company.

Paulsen, Michael S. 1993. "A General Theory of Article V: The Constitutional Issues of the Twenty-seventh Amendment." *Yale Law Journal* 103: 677–789.

Proposed Amendments to the Constitution of the United States, Introduced in Congress from the 69th Congress, 2d Session through the 84th Congress, 2d Session, December 6, 1926, to January 3, 1957. 1957. Washington, DC: U.S. Government Printing Office.

Proposed Amendments to the Constitution of the United States of America Introduced in Congress from the 69th Congress, 2d Session through the 87th Congress, 2d Session, December 6, 1926, to January 3, 1963. 1963. Washington, DC: U.S. Government Printing Office.

Proposed Amendments to the Constitution of the United States of America Introduced in Congress from the 88th Congress, 1st Session through the 90th Congress, 2d Session, January 9, 1963, to January 3, 1969. 1969. Washington, DC: U.S. Government Printing Office.

Tansill, Charles C. 1926. *Proposed Amendments of the Constitution of the United States Introduced in Congress from December 4, 1889, to July 2, 1926.* Washington, DC: U.S. Government Printing Office.

Vile, John R., ed. 2003. *Proposed Amendments to the U.S. Constitution, 1787–2001.* 3 vols. Union, NJ: Law Book Exchange.

O

See Ellis, Frederick, and Carl Frederick.

❖ OBSCENITY AND PORNOGRAPHY ❖

Laws directed toward the regulation of obscenity and pornography arouse intense emotions. Those favoring such laws believe that they help promote morality and protect minors; those opposed to such laws believe that they infringe on the freedoms of speech and the press guaranteed by the First and Fourteenth Amendments. At least half a dozen proposals were introduced in Congress from 1959 to 1970 to grant that body or the states the power to enact legislation regulating obscenity. During this same period, U.S. court decisions were often criticized for being too tolerant of obscenity.

In the nineteenth century, U.S. courts gave fairly wide range to state antiobscenity statutes under the so-called Hicklin test. Under this formula, obscenity was judged according to "whether the tendency of the matter charged as obscenity is to deprave and corrupt those whose minds are open to such immoral influence and into whose hands a publication of this sort may fall" (quoted in Abraham and Perry 1994, 206). As the Supreme Court began to give increasing scrutiny to such legislation in the 1950s, it liberalized its standards in cases such as *Roth v. United States* and *Alberts v. California* (1957) but still denied that the First Amendment protected obscenity.

Since then, the Court's most difficult problem has been that of identifying obscenity. Some justices, such as William Brennan, eventually concluded that it was impossible to regulate obscenity without infringing on other First Amendment rights. But in *Miller v. California* (1973), Chief Justice Warren Burger formulated a three-part test that, with minor modifications, is still in force today. This test provided that a work is obscene if "(a) the average person, applying contemporary community standards, would find that the work, taken as a whole, appeals to the prurient; (b) the work depicts or describes, in a patently offensive way, sexual conduct specifically defined by the applicable state law; and (c) the work, taken as a whole, lacks serious literary, artistic, political, or scientific value" (*Miller* 1973, 25).

Since then, the Supreme Court has permitted governments to tighten the regulation of pornography involving juveniles (see especially *New York v. Ferber* [1982]) or directed to juveniles or nonconsenting adults. It has also allowed local governments to use zoning ordinances to regulate pornography in towns and cities. Regulation of obscenity on the Internet has proven to be more difficult. Thus, in *Reno v. American Civil Liberties Union* (1997), the Court invalidated provisions of the Communications Decency Act of 1996 that it thought, in protecting children, also unduly restricted access by adults to chat rooms with mature content that fell short of being defined as obscene. Similarly, in *Ashcroft v. Free Speech Coalition* (2002), the Court struck down part of the Child Pornography Prevention Act of 1996 regulating computer-generated depictions of minors engaged in sexual activities; here the Court thought that depictions of actual children engaged in sexual behavior generated concrete harms that depictions of computer-generated images of children did not. George W. Bush's attorney general, John Ashcroft, expressed fears that this decision would make it more difficult to prosecute child pornographers, and it certainly would not be surprising to see additional legislation, and/or amendments, proposed on the subject.

See First Amendment.

For Further Reading:

Abraham, Henry J., and Barbara Perry. 1994. *Freedom and the Court: Civil Rights and Liberties in the United States.* 6th ed. New York: Oxford University Press.

Miller v. California, 413 U.S. 15 (1973).

❖ OCEANIA ❖

See Davidson, Jim.

❖ O'CONOR, CHARLES (1804–1888) ❖

Charles O'Conor was a successful New York attorney who put forward proposals for constitutional reforms in the 1870s and 1880s. Like his contemporaries who were concerned with political corruption, O'Conor hoped to eliminate private legislation at both state and national levels (O'Conor 1877, 29). He also hoped to cut off the source of government graft by eliminating duties and tariffs, limiting government revenues to what could be raised by "immediate taxation," and prohibiting governments from borrowing or coining money (*Id.,* 1314–1316). O'Conor also proposed to reduce the number of laws by adopting general statutes that would be suitable for each kind of political subdivision, and he thought that the invention of the telegraph made it possible to eliminate the diplomatic corps (*Id.,* 1316). He favored shortening the ballot and reducing the number of elected offices, but, convinced that

voting was a duty rather than a right, he also favored limiting the franchise and eliminating the secret ballot (*Id.,* 6).

As a Catholic, O'Conor wanted to exclude public schools from teaching religion or other sectarian ideals. O'Conor wanted to outlaw polygamy, and he opposed liberal divorce laws. He also suggested that state autonomy could be preserved and greater uniformity could be achieved if a "court of ultimate appeal" was created to hear cases coming from both state and federal courts. It would be composed of judges selected by the states to deal with "conflicting laws" and "jarring jurisprudence" (O'Conor 1881, 1317).

O'Conor favored making both Congress and state legislatures unicameral, but his most radical proposal related to the presidency. O'Conor proposed that the office be filled each month by lot from the legislature, in his own words, "thus substantially extinguishing the great office of President" (O'Conor 1877, 35). He predicted that efforts expended on competition for this office could then be diverted to more productive private enterprises.

Largely as a result of the novelty of O'Conor's ideas and their failure "to form a coherent whole" (Vile 1991c, 27), they do not appear to have been very influential.

For Further Reading:

O'Conor, Charles. 1881. "Democracy." In *Johnson's New Universal Cyclopaedia: A Treasury of Scientific and Popular Treasure of Useful Knowledge.* Vol. 1, Part 2. New York: A. J. Johnson.

———. 1877. Address by Charles O'Conor Delivered before the New York Historical Society at the Academy of Music. 8 May. New York: Anson D. F. Randolph.

Vile, John R. 1991c. *Rewriting the United States Constitution: An Examination of Proposals from Reconstruction to the Present.* New York: Praeger.

❖ OFFICE OF THE FEDERAL REGISTER ❖

Although the national archivist of the United States is currently entrusted with the official duty of certifying and publishing the state ratification of proposed amendments, the archivist has delegated some of these duties to the director of the federal register. This individual examines ratifications for "facial legal sufficiency and an authenticating signature," and, if a sufficient number of states ratify, subsequently "drafts a formal proclamation for the Archivist to certify that the amendment is valid and has become part of the Constitution." If so, the amendment is then "published in the *Federal Register* and U.S. Statutes at Large and serves as official notice to the Congress and to the Nation that the amendment process has been completed" ("The Constitutional Amendment Process" Archives website).

See also Archivist of the United States.

For Further Reading:
"The Constitutional Amendment Process." *http://www.archives.gov/federal_register/constitution/amendment_process.html.*

❖ OFFICES, FORFEITURE OF, OR INELIGIBILITY FOR ❖

The Constitution does not prohibit individuals who are convicted of crimes from serving in office, but it does provide some mechanisms for removing such individuals. Thus, Article I, Section 2 of the Constitution gives the House of Representatives the sole power of impeachment, and the subsequent section provides that the Senate shall try impeachments. Article I, Section 4 extends the prospect of impeachment to the president, vice president, "and all civil Officers of the United States" but limits the grounds of such impeachment to conviction of "Treason, Bribery, or other high Crimes and Misdemeanors." Article I, Section 3 specifies that conviction requires a two-thirds vote. Conviction is to extend no further "than to removal from Office, and disqualification to hold and enjoy any Office of honor, Trust or Profit under the United States." Of the seven impeachment convictions the Senate has rendered (all of federal judges), it has voted for disqualification to future offices in only two cases (Peltason 1994, 53).

According to Article I, Section 5, each house of Congress may "punish its Members for disorderly Behavior, and, with the Concurrence of two thirds, expel a Member." It was under such a threat that Oregon Republican Bob Packwood resigned from the Senate in 1995 after a Senate committee unanimously voted to recommend such a penalty for sexual harassment and other wrongdoing.

Congress may further exclude members by a majority vote. According to the Supreme Court's decision in *Powell v. McCormack* (1969), it can do so only when members fail to meet the constitutionally specified age, citizenship, or residence requirements. If Congress wants to expel a member, it must do so by the two-thirds vote cited above.

As the framers undoubtedly intended, neither the procedure for impeaching and convicting governmental officials nor that for expelling members of Congress is simple. Moreover, unless the Senate so specifies when it convicts an individual of an impeachable offense, even a person removed from one office may be eligible for another. Two proposals were offered in the nineteenth century, one in 1838 and the other in 1876, to prohibit individuals convicted of embezzlement or bribery from holding office. Some of the contemporary proposals to outlaw polygamy also contained provisions designed to exclude polygamists from holding office.

Since 1985 there have been about twenty more proposals directed at prohibiting convicted felons from serving as federal officials, as members of Congress, or as judges. These proposals may have been stimulated by the conduct of Harry E. Claiborne, a U.S. district court judge in Nevada, who continued to draw his salary after being convicted and imprisoned and subsequently became the fifth federal judge in history to be impeached and convicted (Abraham 1998, 45). In 1992 Florida judge Alcee Hastings was elected to Congress after having been successfully removed from office by a Senate vote of impeachment (Peltason 1994, 53). Ironically, as a congressman, he cast one of the votes against the impeachment of President Bill Clinton.

See also Marriage, Divorce, and Parenting.

For Further Reading:
Abraham, Henry J. 1998. *The Judicial Process: An Introductory Analysis of the Courts of the United States, England, and France.* 7th ed. New York: Oxford University Press.
Peltason, Jack W. 1994. *Corwin and Peltason's Understanding the Constitution.* 13th ed. Fort Worth, TX: Harcourt Brace College Publishers.

❖ *OREGON V. MITCHELL* (1970) ❖

The decision for the Supreme Court in *Oregon v. Mitchell* (consolidated with two other cases, *Texas v. Mitchell* and *United States v. Arizona*) precipitated the proposal and ratification of the Twenty-sixth Amendment. The cases also serve as classic examples of differences among the justices as to the meaning of the post–Civil War amendments and the degree to which these amendments permit legislative and judicial extensions of constitutional rights.

The Court considered three questions involving congressional authority exercised in the 1970 amendments to the 1965 Voting Rights Act. These questions involved congressional authority to lower the voting age to eighteen in state and federal elections, bar the use of literacy tests, and eliminate state residency requirements in presidential elections.

Justice Hugo Black's opinion, which garnered four votes from the two major divisions of the Court, recognized congressional authority under Article I, Section 4; Article II, Section 1; and the necessary and proper clause to lower the voting age for federal elections. Black also stated that Article I, Section 2 limited federal power to lower the voting age in state and local elections. He further denied that the equal protection clause of the Fourteenth Amendment, which was directed primarily to discrimination on the basis of race, provided such authority. Black accepted the literacy test ban on the basis of the enforcement clauses of the Fourteenth and Fifteenth Amendments,

and elimination of residency requirements on the basis of congressional authority over federal elections.

Justice William O. Douglas would have relied on the authority of the equal protection and privileges and immunities clauses of the Fourteenth Amendment to lower the voting age in both state and federal elections. He would also have upheld the other provisions of the law.

Justice John Marshall Harlan accepted the congressionally imposed literacy ban on the basis of the Fifteenth Amendment. However, he used exhaustive analysis of the framing of the Fourteenth Amendment to deny that the amendment had been intended to provide authority for other federal measures at issue. Citing powers reserved to the states by the Tenth Amendment, Harlan suggested that federal authority over these other voting matters would require amendments similar to the Fifteenth, Nineteenth, and Twenty-fourth Amendments. Harlan also rejected Black's analysis of Article I, Sections 2 and 4.

Justices William Brennan, Byron White, and Thurgood Marshall disputed Harlan's narrow reading of the Fourteenth Amendment. They would have upheld all aspects of the law under the equal protection clause and congressional enforcement powers under the Civil War amendments.

Justices Potter Stewart, Warren Burger, and Harry Blackmun accepted Black's distinction between congressional power over federal elections and that over state and local elections. However, they grounded congressional power over residency requirements on the privileges and immunities of American citizens, including the right to travel.

See also Black, Hugo Lafayette; Supreme Court Decisions Reversed by Constitutional Amendments; Twenty-sixth Amendment.

For Further Reading:
Oregon v. Mitchell, 400 U.S. 112 (1970).

P

❖ PACE, JAMES O. (1954–) ❖

New York attorney James Pace advanced one of the most novel and racist contemporary proposals for constitutional amendment in a book entitled *Amendment to the Constitution: Averting the Decline and Fall of America* (Pace 1986). Addressing a variety of concerns related to the decline of the family, permissive sexual relations, crime, disrespect for religion, poverty, and declining educational standards, Pace's primary concern was the nation's increasing racial diversity. He was also troubled by the way that the Fourteenth Amendment had enabled the federal courts to oversee traditional state and local controls in areas such as pornography and crime.

Pace called for the adoption of an amendment that would repeal the Fourteenth and Fifteenth Amendments and alter the Tenth Amendment by adding the word "expressly" before the word "delegated." This would thereby foreclose the possibility of implied congressional powers that Chief Justice Marshall recognized in *McCulloch v. Maryland* (1819). Pace would further limit citizenship to "non-Hispanic white [people] of the European race, in whom there is no ascertainable trace of Negro blood, nor more than one-eighth Mongolian, Asian, Asia Minor, Middle Eastern, Semitic, Near Eastern, American Indian, Malay or other non-European or nonwhite blood" (Pace 1986, 140). Pace would restrict the right to reside permanently in the United States to citizens. He advocated programs for resettling noncitizens in other nations while allowing those who were needed—for example, blacks, who, "because of their physical abilities," might be employed as police officers to enforce the amendment—to get temporary work permits (Pace 1986, 118). Pace favored calling a constitutional convention to inaugurate his plans.

For Further Reading:

Pace, James O. 1986. *Amendment to the Constitution: Averting the Decline and Fall of America.* Los Angeles, CA: Johnson, Pace, Simmons and Fennell.

❖ *PALKO V. CONNECTICUT* (1937) ❖

Palko v. Connecticut remains one of the leading cases dealing with the incorporation controversy (Abraham and Perry 1994, 56–59). At issue was a Connecticut law that permitted the state to retry an individual if there had been errors in that individual's first trial. Here, the state retried a case in which Palka (his name was misspelled in the official case reporter) had been sentenced to life in prison for second-degree murder. On retrial, the state won a conviction of murder in the first degree, carrying the death penalty. If that had occurred in a federal court, it would have been considered to be double jeopardy, in violation of the Fifth Amendment. Palka argued for the view that all the prohibitions in the Bill of Rights that applied to the federal government should also apply to the states through the due process clause of the Fourteenth Amendment.

In an eight-to-one decision for the Court, Justice Benjamin Cardozo rejected this contention. His task was complicated by the fact that, by 1937, the Court had accepted the idea that some provisions of the Bill of Rights—for example, protections for freedom of speech and the press—did apply to the states through the Fourteenth Amendment, although it had rejected the application of other rights. Cardozo attempted to reconcile these cases by articulating the doctrine of selective incorporation, or fundamental rights. According to this view, the due process clause of the Fourteenth Amendment incorporated only those provisions that are "of the very essence of a scheme of ordered liberty" or that are based on principles of justice "so rooted in the traditions and conscience of our people as to be ranked as fundamental" (*Palko* 1937, 325). Seeing this case as a legitimate state attempt to remedy past errors rather than as an attempt to wear the defendant down, Cardozo decided that no violation of due process had taken place.

The arguments in *Palko* would later be repeated in *Adamson v. California* (1947), where Justice Hugo Black advanced his support for the doctrine of total incorporation and Justice Felix Frankfurter advocated a view akin to Cardozo's. Although continuing to profess adherence to the doctrine of selective incorporation or fundamental fairness, over time, the Court ruled that most provisions in the Bill of Rights were fundamental and should be applied to the states. In *Benton v. Maryland* (1969), the Court finally applied the double-jeopardy provision to the states, thus overruling the specific decision in *Palko*.

See also *Adamson v. California;* Fourteenth Amendment; Incorporation.

For Further Reading:
Abraham, Henry J., and Barbara Perry. 1994. *Freedom and the Court: Civil Rights and Liberties in the United States.* 6th ed. New York: Oxford University Press.
Palko v. Connecticut, 302 U.S. 319 (1937).

❖ PARDON POWER ❖

See Presidency, Pardon Power.

❖ PARLIAMENTARY SOVEREIGNTY ❖

In Great Britain the struggle for liberty centered on the struggle for power between the Crown and Parliament. Because the Crown was a hereditary office and Parliament was an elected body, the idea of democracy came to be identified with the latter body. Over time, the British accepted the notion that democratic rule required that Parliament be sovereign.

By contrast, in America, the struggle for independence began with the rejection of parliamentary sovereignty, especially as it related to taxation (Reid 1993). Moreover, as American constitutional theory developed, it put increasing emphasis on the idea that all three branches of the new government were limited by the written Constitution.

In consequence of these developments, Americans had to formulate a different theory of constitutional amendment than did the British. When the British refer to their constitution, they do not refer to a single document but to a host of documents, practices, and understandings that have developed over a long period. In practice, this system has adopted constitutional change fairly cautiously (Vile 1993c), but in theory, constitutional changes can be effected simply by parliamentary action. By contrast, the U.S. system is based on a written constitution that is not changeable by ordinary acts of legislation but requires extraordinary majorities at both state and national levels. Thus it is not surprising that characterizations of the U.S. Constitution as "rigid" appear to have been initiated by James Bryce, an English observer (Bryce 1905, 1906; Vile 1992, 137–138). Because the United States' written constitution is a brief outline that leaves many matters to legislative majorities, many policy changes can be initiated short of constitutional amendment.

Although the U.S. Constitution does not use the term "sovereignty," the reference in the preamble to "We the People" is often cited as an indication that the people are the ultimate sovereigns in the United States. The constitutionally designated method for exercising this sovereignty to pass laws is through procedures designated within the document. Article V further designates a method for supermajorities of the people to alter that document. Many contemporary proposals for initiatives and referendums would shift this sovereignty more directly to popular majorities.

See also Rigid Constitution; Sovereignty.

For Further Reading:

Bryce, James. 1905. "Flexible and Rigid Constitutions." In *Constitutions*. Germany: Scientia Verlag Aalen. Reprint of New York and London edition, 1980.

Reid, John P. 1993. *Constitutional History of the American Revolution. The Authority of Law.* Madison, WI: University of Wisconsin Press.

Vile, John R. 1993c. "Three Kinds of Constitutional Founding and Change: The Convention Model and Its Alternatives." *Political Research Quarterly* 46: 881–895.

———. 1992. *The Constitutional Amending Process in American Political Thought.* New York: Praeger.

❖ PARLIAMENTARY SYSTEM ❖

Among those who have proposed major constitutional changes, few alterations have been more popular than those designed to incorporate one or another aspect of parliamentary systems, especially as this system is practiced in Great Britain. This system generally avoids the problem of divided government, wherein the legislative majority and the chief executive are from different parties. It does so by allowing the majority party or majority coalition within the legislative branch, generally designated as the parliament, to choose the chief executive, who is usually called a prime minister.

In contrast to the U.S. system, in which members of Congress are forbidden to hold executive office, members of the British cabinet are chosen from and continue to serve in the Parliament. Fairly strict party discipline is the norm, and if Parliament rejects one of the prime minister's major bills or gives a vote of "no confidence" in the existing administration,

the monarch dissolves the Parliament and calls new parliamentary elections, in which all members of the House of Commons are up for election. The parliamentary system also stresses norms of collective decision making and ministerial responsibility, and it requires the prime minister to appear before Parliament on a regular basis to answer questions—the so-called question hour. In this system, the lower house, designated as the House of Commons, has substantially greater powers than does the upper house, the House of Lords.

Although some individuals have advocated an entirely new U.S. Constitution along British lines, many members of Congress have introduced amendments to adopt one or more parts of this system. Such proposals have included plans allowing members of Congress to serve in the cabinet or permitting Congress to take a vote of "no confidence" in the president.

Proponents of the parliamentary model defend it as a way of making government more responsive to the people and of overcoming problems of stalemate and inaction attributed in the U.S. system to the separation of powers. One recent study, however, suggested that the problems of divided government in the United States may be exaggerated (Mayhew 1991); another study denies that separation of powers is responsible for many of the problems that have been attributed to it (Sargentich 1993). Others suggest that systems that appear from a distance to have advantages may, on closer inspection, demonstrate weaknesses. Moreover, the strengths of some such systems may result in part from greater social homogeneity and from factors other than constitutional structures (Ceaser 1986).

Yale's Bruce Ackerman has recently argued that nations considering new constitutional systems might consider adopting a model of what he describes as "constrained parliamentarianism" like governments in Germany, Japan, Canada, and other nations, rather than the pure parliamentary model in Britain. Such a system seeks "to check the power of the cabinet and the chamber [parliament] . . . by giving independence to a variety of other checking institutions, including a constitutional court" (Ackerman 2000, 634).

See also Ackerman, Bruce; Divided Government; Presidency, Vote of No Confidence.

For Further Reading:
Ackerman, Bruce. 2000. "The New Separation of Powers." *The Harvard Law Review* 113 (January): 633–728.
Ceaser, James W. 1986. "In Defense of Separation of Powers." In *Separation of Powers—Does It Still Work?* Ed. Robert A. Goldwin and Art Kaufman. Washington, DC: American Enterprise Institute.
Mayhew, David R. 1991. *Divided We Govern: Party Control, Lawmaking, and Investigations, 1946–1990.* New Haven, CT: Yale University Press.
Sargentich, Thomas O. 1993. "The Limits of the Parliamentary Critique of the Separation of Powers." *William and Mary Law Review* 34 (Spring): 679–739.

❖ PAROCHIAL SCHOOLS, AID TO ❖

Long before provisions of the First Amendment's establishment clause were applied to the states through the due process clause of the Fourteenth Amendment, proponents of the Blaine Amendment sought to restrict state governmental funding of parochial schools. This issue reemerged when at least four proposals were introduced from 1973 to 1975 to allow tax credits or other types of state financial assistance to parochial schools.

In several cases, most notably *Lemon v. Kurtzman* (1971), the Supreme Court has invalidated most forms of direct aid to parochial schools, claiming that they either favor religion over irreligion or that they lead to excessive entanglement between church and state. The Supreme Court has, however, upheld the constitutionality of state payments to parents for bus fares to parochial schools (*Everson v. Board of Education* (1947)) and the provision of secular textbooks for such schools (*Meek v. Pittenger* (1973)). In *Mueller v. Allen* (1983), the Court upheld a state law that permitted tax deductions for all parents for school expenses, including tuition for parochial schools. After ruling in *Witters v. Washington Department of*

Services for the Blind (1986) that a blind student at a Christian college could use a vocational tuition grant and deciding in *Zobrest v. Catalina Foothills School District* (1993) that a deaf student could bring a state-employed sign language teacher to a parochial school, in *Agostini v. Felton* (1997) the Court reversed an earlier ruling that had barred the state from sending public school teachers into parochial schools in order to provide remedial education. Recent debates have shifted attention to the constitutionality of voucher systems that would allow parents to use such state-provided vouchers for publicly or privately administered schools of the parents' own choosing (Skillen 1993). A narrowly divided Supreme Court recently upheld the constitutionality of such a voucher system in Cleveland, Ohio, in the case of *Zelman v. Simmons-Harris* (2002), in which it ruled that the state was pursuing a secular legislative purpose that furthered parental, rather than governmental, choices. The constitutionality of such plans might be on firmer footing if the proposed Religious Equality Amendment is adopted.

See also Blaine Amendment; Religious Equality Amendment.

For Further Reading:
Skillen, James W., ed. 1993. *The School Choice Controversy: What Is Constitutional?* Grand Rapids, MI: Baker Books.
Zelman v. Simmons-Harris, 122 S. Ct. 2460 (2002).

❖ PATENTS AND COPYRIGHTS ❖

Article I, Section 8 of the Constitution grants Congress power "to promote the Progress of Science and useful Arts, by securing for limited Times to Authors and Inventors the exclusive Right to their respective Writings and Discoveries." The 1952 Patent Act grants inventors a seventeen-year monopoly over their inventions (Lieberman 1992, 371). Copyrights now extend fifty years beyond an author's death (*Information Please Almanac* 1993, 594–595).

In 1953 New Jersey Democratic Representative Hugh Addonizio introduced an amendment to grant copyrights and patents "in perpetuity." Although such an amendment might increase rewards for authors and inventors, it might also slow progress by retarding the free flow of ideas.

In early 2003 the U.S. Supreme Court, in *Eldred v. Ashcroft*, No. 01–618, upheld the constitutionality of the Copyright Term Extension Act of 1998. This act extended copyrights for an additional ten years and protected, among other properties, the copyright that the Disney Company owns in Mickey Mouse, which was otherwise scheduled to expire in 2003 (Hudson 2002, 1).

See also Progress and the Amending Process.

For Further Reading:

Hudson, David L, Jr. 2002. "Top Court Docket: Copyright to Cross Burning." *Chicago Daily Law Bulletin,* 16 September, 1.

Information Please Almanac: Atlas and Yearbook. 1993. 43d ed. Boston: Houghton Mifflin.

Lieberman, Jethro K. 1992. *The Evolving Constitution: How the Supreme Court Has Ruled on Issues from Abortion to Zoning.* New York: Random House.

❖ PAUL, ALICE (1885–1947) ❖

Alice Paul is often identified as one of the "new suffragists" (Lunardini 1986, 17) Paul, who never married, earned a Ph.D. in political science from the University of Pennsylvania and law degrees from the Washington College of Law and American University. After taking part in suffragist demonstrations in England—where she met fellow American Lucy Burns, with whom she would subsequently work quite closely—Paul was appointed chair of the Congressional Committee of the National American Woman Suffrage Association (NAWSA) in 1912. Paul subsequently founded the Congressional Union for Woman Suffrage, which became independent in 1914 and firmly opposed the Shafroth-Palmer Amendment (which would have left women's suffrage to be determined by individual state referendums), which NAWSA representatives had initially approved.

Paul was a persistent organizer who sponsored a suffragist parade the day before Woodrow Wilson's inaugurations in 1913 and 1917 and founded the National Woman's Party in 1916. This organization, which was regarded as more radical than the NAWSA, worked to oppose candidates who did not support the Anthony Amendment. It also sponsored a series of pickets in front of the Wilson White House for eighteen months beginning in January 1917, the same year that the Congressional Union merged with the National Woman's Party (NWP). Picketers, including Paul, were jailed; Paul was force-fed after she declared a hunger strike. Unlike the NAWSA, the NWP refused to support Wilson's war efforts. Still, the combined pressures from the NAWSA and the NWP, along with Wilson's hopes that such a measure would help boost war morale, convinced him to endorse the Anthony Amendment, which became the Nineteenth Amendment in 1920.

Thereafter, the NWP continued its push for women's rights. Initially, it was the only such women's organization to support the Lucretia Mott, or Equal Rights, Amendment. The amendment was written and first proposed by Paul at the seventy-fifth anniversary of the Seneca Falls Convention and subsequently was introduced in Congress in December 1923 by Republican Senator Charles Curtis (S.J. 21) and Republican Representative Daniel Anthony, both of Kansas.

Paul crusaded for the League of Nations in the 1920s and 1930s. She was also instrumental in getting recognition of equal gender rights in the preamble to the United Nations Charter (McHenry 1980, 320). Paul opposed the seven-year deadline for ratification of the Equal Rights Amendment, as well as the deletion of concurrent enforcement power in the states (Fry 1986, 21).

See also Equal Rights Amendment; Nineteenth Amendment; Shafroth-Palmer Amendment.

For Further Reading:

Flexnor, Eleanor. 1974. *Century of Struggle: The*

Woman's Rights Movement in the United States. New York: Atheneum.

Fry, Amelia R. 1986. "Alice Paul and the ERA." In *Rights of Passage: The Past and Future of the ERA,* ed. Joan Hoff-Wilson. Bloomington, IN: Indiana University Press.

Lunardini, Christine A. 1986. *From Equal Suffrage to Equal Rights: Alice Paul and the National Woman's Party, 1910–1928.* New York: New York University Press.

❖ PEACE CONVENTION ❖

In February 1861, the same month that the states of the Deep South were meeting in Montgomery, Alabama, to draw up a new Confederate constitution, the governor of Virginia called for a convention of the states to devise a plan of reconciliation. Such a call deviated from the convention procedure specified in Article V of the Constitution but was especially popular in border states that were still undecided as to how to respond to Abraham Lincoln's election and were interested in averting civil war.

Twenty-one of the thirty-four states responded by sending 132 delegates to the Willard Hotel in Washington, D.C. (Dumond 1973, 241). Because Virginia did not specify how states would be represented, states sent anywhere from five to eleven delegates, and the convention ended up voting, as at the U.S. Constitutional Convention of 1787, by state (Dumond 1973, 244). Although the proceedings were secret, an account was later published by L. E. Chittenden (1864), one of the delegates. The convention commenced on 4 February 1861. The delegates selected former President John Tyler of Virginia as president, and many other notables attended. Indeed, at the time, the qualifications of the convention's members were favorably compared to those of the members of the U.S. Constitutional Convention of 1787. A scholar has noted that:

> Included on the roll were a former president of the United States [John Tyler], six former cabinet members, nineteen former governors, fourteen former United States senators, fifty former congressmen, five former ministers or ambas-

sadors, ten circuit judges, and twelve state supreme court justices. One hundred and three were lawyers; sixty-one had once served in their respective state legislatures; many were prominent old-line Whigs. (Gunderson 1961, 10)

Delegates were selected by state legislatures, some of which simply authorized their congressional representatives to serve.

The convention ended up creating a committee of one delegate from each state, headed by former Secretary of the Treasury James Guthrie of Kentucky. This committee reported seven proposals to the full convention on 15 February; these were in turn modified and proposed collectively to Congress as what would have been the Thirteenth Amendment. Many of the provisions resembled those of the Crittenden Compromise being hammered out in Congress.

Section 1 of the amendment proposed reinstating the 36 degrees 30 minutes line of latitude created under the Missouri Compromise of 1820. Thus proposing to reverse that portion of the *[Dred] Scott* decision (1857) declaring such legislation invalid, this section would have permitted slavery south of the line and prevented it north of the line in all existing territories, with new states in each area permitted to join the Union when they had sufficient populations to do so.

Section 2 would have prohibited the acquisition of new territory except by a majority vote of both free and slave states in the Senate and agreement by the requisite two-thirds majority required to approve a treaty. Section 3 of the amendment would have prohibited Congress from interfering with slavery in those states where it existed or abridging slavery in the nation's capital without the consent of Maryland (from which what remained of the District had been originally carved) without giving compensation to slave owners. This section would also have permitted the continuing transit of slaves between slave states, albeit not through states that disapproved of that institution. This section did prohibit the transit of slaves to the capital for transfer to other states.

Section 4 was designed to enforce the fugitive slave law. Similarly, Section 5 prohibited the "foreign slave trade." Section 6 would have added an entrenchment clause to the Constitution by providing that Sections 1, 3, and 5 of the amendment, as well as other constitutional provisions relating to slavery, "shall not be amended or abolished without the consent of all the States." Section 7 further provided that the national government would compensate owners who lost their slaves as a result of "violence or intimidation from mobs or riotous assemblages," but such compensation would not preclude further attempts to secure such individuals. Finally, Congress was authorized to "provide by law for securing to the citizens of each State the privileges and immunities of citizens of the several States" (Gunderson 1961, 62, 86, 107–109). Majorities of states at the convention favoring these proposals varied from as low as nine to eight (Section 1) to sixteen to five (Section 5).

Although the Peace Convention had no specific constitutional authorization (Congress calls an Article V Convention after receiving petitions from two-thirds of the states), the convention arguably kept border states within the Union long enough for Lincoln to be inaugurated as president. Apparently, the convention hoped that its proposed amendments would be submitted by Congress directly to the states for their approval. This would have bypassed the requirement in Article V for a prior congressional sanction by a two-thirds vote of both houses. The convention further proposed ratification, as in the case of the original Constitution, by state conventions (Keogh 1987, 291). Never considered by the full House, which failed to muster the necessary two-thirds majority to consider the proposals, the convention proposals (substituted for the Crittenden Compromise) were defeated on the closing day of the lame-duck Senate by a vote of seven to twenty-eight. The House and Senate did adopt the Corwin Amendment, which would have protected slave states from amendments interfering with that institution, but like the Peace Convention's proposals, this failed to avert civil war.

Richard Labunski has recently cited the Peace Convention as a kind of precedent, or prototype, for his own proposed preconvention.

Labunski envisions such a preconvention meeting in Washington, D.C., and growing out of a series of meetings and conventions at the state and local level. Labunski further anticipates that his national preconvention would recommend petitions to the states for subjects on which they might petition Congress to call a second convention (Labunski 2000, 181–185).

See also Crittenden Compromise; Labunski, Richard; Nashville Convention.

For Further Reading:
Gunderson, Robert Gray. 1961. *Old Gentleman's Convention: The Washington Peace Conference of 1861.* Madison, WI: University of Wisconsin Press.
Labunski, Richard. 2000. *The Second Constitutional Convention: How the American People Can Take Back Their Government.* Versailles, KY: Marley and Beck Press.

❖ PEI, MARIO (1901–1978) ❖

Mario Pei, a professor of Romance languages at Columbia University, called for a constitutional convention in an article published in the late 1960s (Pei 1967–1968; Vile 1991c, 100–101). He argued that such a convention would be a better way of revising and clarifying ambiguous sections of the current document than would more piecemeal reform.

Pei presented his own agenda for reform as more of a set of suggestions than a settled scheme. His proposals included four-year terms for the members of the House of Representatives; clarification of constitutional provisions relative to declarations of war; reform of the electoral college system; and the popular election and/or confirmation of Supreme Court justices, with the possibility of limited terms of office. Other ideas included having the president run on a ticket with members of the cabinet and reconsidering Supreme Court rulings relative to the establishment clause of the First Amendment and the right of peaceable assembly. Pei would also examine existing interpretations of the Second Amendment and the relation between the nation and the states. Among his proposed tax reforms was a plan to repeal the Sixteenth Amendment and to allocate different kinds of taxes among the different levels of government.

Pei envisioned a convention that would meet for a year or two. He thought that the voters of each state should choose delegates on nonpartisan ballots, with elected delegates to resign from any other offices. He also thought that proposed reforms should require the approval of two-thirds of the delegates.

Pei argued that the convention mechanism was democratic. He suggested that one of the major parties should propose such a convention as part of its platform.

For Further Reading:

Pei, Mario. 1967–1968. "The Case for a Constitutional Convention." *Modern Age* 12 (Winter): 8–13.

Vile, John R. 1991c. *Rewriting the United States Constitution: An Examination of Proposals from Reconstruction to the Present.* New York: Praeger.

❖ PENN, WILLIAM (1644–1718) ❖

William Penn was an English Quaker. Along with parishioner William Mead, Penn had been arrested and tried in 1670 for preaching to his congregation, and he was subjected to a kangaroo judicial proceeding that led to his popular vindication (Peck 1992, 85–87). He later received a land grant in America from the king. Penn's Frame of Government for Pennsylvania (1682–1683) was the first such document to contain an amending mechanism (Beatty 1975, 61).

In the preamble to this document, Penn observed, "I do not find a model in the world that time, place, and some singular emergences have not necessarily altered" (Thorpe 1909, 5:3053–3054). Here and in subsequent charters that he drew up for Delaware and Pennsylvania, Penn allowed for future charter alterations with the consent of the governor and six-sevenths of the assembly. Drawing on his view that freedom of conscience was especially fundamental, however, Penn provided that protections for this right should never be altered (*Id.*, 5:3079–3080). Both the required super-

majorities to initiate change and the presence of entrenchment mechanisms find echoes in the amending article of the U.S. Constitution.

For Further Reading:

Beatty, Edward C. 1975. *William Penn as Social Philosopher.* New York: Octagon Books.

Peck, Robert S. 1992. *The Bill of Rights and the Politics of Interpretation.* St. Paul, MN: West.

Thorpe, Francis N. 1909. *The Federal and State Constitutions, Colonial Charters and Other Organic Laws of the States, Territories, and Colonies Now or Heretofore Forming the United States of America.* 7 vols. Washington, DC: U.S. Government Printing Office.

❖ PENSIONS ❖

The Constitution makes no explicit mention of pensions. There was no general scheme of government pensions in the nation's early history, but controversy periodically surfaced with respect to military pensions, bonuses, and land grants. These were given to compensate those who had served in the military, to provide care to those wounded in the service, or as support for the widows and children of such veterans (Glasson and Kinley 1918). In the 1880s and 1890s, members of Congress introduced amending resolutions to prevent the decrease or repeal of promised pensions, to limit pensions to those provided under law at the time an individual enlisted, or to restrict pensions to individuals or to the families of individuals actually wounded in service (Musmanno 1929, 129–131).

Although there are still occasional disputes about veterans' benefits, today primary attention has shifted from military pensions to old-age and disability pensions provided under the Social Security system established in 1935 (Myles 1989). At least one amendment proposed in 1935 attempted to give Congress power to establish this program. Despite Supreme Court decisions upholding the taxation provisions of the act in *Steward Machine Co. v. Davis* (1937) and *Helvering v. Davis* (1937), several amendments were introduced from 1939 to 1941 to formalize this power. A handful of subsequent proposals have attempted to place limits on the extent to which Social Security and other related taxes can be raised.

There are continuing concerns that the Social Security program might become bankrupt as the number of senior citizens and the ratio of nonworking to working individuals increase. In 1964 Massachusetts submitted a petition for a constitutional convention to deal with this issue, but no other state joined in this call. In recent years, some members of Congress have added provisions to calls for a Balanced Budget Amendment that would require that current Social Security surpluses could not be used in such budget calculations.

See also Balanced Budget Amendment; Social Security.

For Further Reading:
Glasson, William H., and David Kinley. 1918. *Federal Military Pensions in the United States.* New York: Oxford University Press.
Musmanno, M. A. 1929. *Proposed Amendments to the Constitution.* Washington, DC: U.S. Government Printing Office.
Myles, John. 1989. *Old Age in the Welfare State: The Political Economy of Public Pensions.* Lawrence, KS: University Press of Kansas.

❖ PETITIONS FOR AMENDMENTS ❖

Before they become law, amendments must be proposed by sufficient majorities in Congress (or by a Constitutional convention called at the behest of the states) and ratified by three-fourths of the states. Members of Congress generally introduce amendments as joint resolutions. In addition, the Congress frequently receives petitions from a variety of private groups and state and local governmental entities on behalf of various causes, including adoption of constitutional amendments. These petitions are not nearly as well publicized as are those that are introduced by individual members (and are not included in the lists of proposed amendments that have been published

from time to time), but they reflect a basic American right to petition the government that has been advocated since the Declaration of Independence, that is incorporated into the First Amendment, and that has been recognized by U.S. Supreme Court Justice Anthony Kennedy in a concurring opinion (see *Cook v. Gralike* 2001, 60). There does not appear to be any systematic study of petitions to Congress specifically on the subject of constitutional amendments.

See also Joint Resolution.

For Further Reading:
Cook v. Gralike, 531 U.S. 510 (2001).

❖ PHILADELPHIA II ❖

See National Initiative for Democracy.

❖ PHILIPPINE INDEPENDENCE ❖

In July 1930 Democratic Senator Royal Copeland of New York introduced an amending resolution to grant independence to the Philippines, an objective subsequently accomplished by ordinary legislation. After defeating the Spanish in the Spanish-American War of 1898, the United States purchased these Pacific islands from Spain and, much to the chagrin of American anti-imperialists, forcefully overwhelmed the independence movement there.

Subsequently, the Jones Act of 1916 promised eventual independence ("Philippines" 1994). After the Filipinos rejected the provisions for independence in the 1933 Hawes-Cutting-Hare bill, Congress adopted the Tydings McDuffie Act of 1934 (Grunder and Livezey 1973, 220–223). It provided for an interim commonwealth to be followed by complete independence in 1946 ("Philippines" 1994).

This timetable was followed despite the disruptions caused by the Japanese seizure of the islands in World War II. The United States, however, continued to view the Philippines as a special area of responsibility and influence

(Shalom 1981), and it maintained military bases there until quite recently. After the terrorist attacks on the United States of 11 September 2001, and the capture of a number of Americans by Muslim extremists, the U.S. government again sent troops to the Philippines to help the government there combat terrorism.

For Further Reading:

Grunder, Garel A., and William E. Livezey. 1973. *The Philippines and the United States.* Westport, CT: Greenwood Press.

"Philippines, Republic of the." 1994. *Microsoft Encarta Multimedia Encyclopedia.*

Shalom, Stephen R. 1981. *The United States and the Philippines: A Study of Neocolonialism.* Philadelphia: Institute for the Study of Human Issues.

❖ PIBURN, JOHN L. (1872–?) ❖

John Piburn was a medical doctor and author of a book published in 1932 proposing the text of a new U.S. Constitution and a revised code suitable for California and other states. Although much of his proposed constitution simply rearranged the provisions in the existing document, it also contained a number of innovative ideas.

Most prominent was the creation of the Educational Department and Educational College, the organization of which led off the document. Consisting of five recent graduates elected by each college and initially governed by the first member to be selected from the University of Missouri (Piburn 1932, 12), the department was to have extensive powers to promote and oversee education, including power to specify how grading would be done (*Id.,* 20–24), designate what size diplomas should be (*Id.,* 24), and set tax rates for education (*Id.,* 14). "Religious," "denominational," and "sectarian" schools were to be prohibited, as would night classes, the use of initials on diplomas (*Id.,*16), and the issuance of any doctoral degrees other than in medicine (*Id.,* 27). B.S. and M.S. degrees were to be designated as outranking B.A.s or M.A.s (*Id.,* 27).

In Piburn's scheme, the House of Representatives would be designated as the House of Solons (Piburn 1932, 32). Piburn would prohibit laws from being rewritten; any changes would have to be adopted as new laws and their predecessors repealed (*Id.,* 39). Piburn's prohibition against "sumptuary laws" (*Id.,* 46) was apparently designed to abolish the Eighteenth Amendment, which he described in his introduction as "a crime"—an introduction in which he likewise saw the only good in the Nineteenth Amendment as the fact that "it will help to un-Christianize women." Piburn would replace the congressional power to declare war with the power to call an election for declaring war, which election would require a majority of males under age forty—presumably those most likely to serve—to approve (*Id.,* 41). Piburn applied the restraints in the Bill of Rights directly to Congress, although he extended the establishment clause to both the nation and the states and specified that "all the promoters of religion, and their followers, are jointly and severally liable for damages, libel, and slander for their utterances and practices" (*Id.,* 49–50). Piburn further modified what is now the First Amendment by explicitly providing for civil and criminal libel (*Id.,* 46–47). On another matter, he would have prohibited miscegenation laws "restricting the amalgamation of the races; or the mating of the sexes" (*Id.,* 50), a move that the U.S. Supreme Court did not make until its 1967 decision in *Loving v. Virginia.*

Piburn would have eliminated the office of vice president and provided that presidential vacancies be filled by the oldest senator from the president's party (Piburn 1932, 55). Piburn also included a provision for presidential disability similar to that now found in the Twenty-fifth Amendment (*Id.,* 55). Piburn would have explicitly provided for the exercise of judicial review (*Id.,* 59) and would have imposed a one-term limit on all offices (*Id.,* 66).

Piburn's constitution was to be ratified by the people in three-fourths of the states, and the amending process now in Article V would have been altered so that amendments could be ratified in the same fashion. In a scheme somewhat reminiscent of Thomas Jefferson, a nine-member committee appointed by the Educational College, the Senate, and the House of Solons was to consider revising the document in the year 2000 and "once every fifty years thereafter" (Piburn 1932, 71).

A peculiar blend of the farsighted and the eccentric, of prejudice and enlightenment, Piburn's proposal does not appear to have sparked significant popular or scholarly interest.

For Further Reading:

Piburn, John L. 1932. *A Constitution and a Code.* San Diego: Bowman Printing Company.

❖ PLACEMENT OF CONSTITUTIONAL AMENDMENTS ❖

Today all twenty-seven amendments that have been adopted are found at the end of the constitutional text that was written in 1787, but it was not initially clear that they would be so. Indeed, Virginia's James Madison, the individual most responsible for compilation of the first ten amendments, originally proposed that new amendments should be integrated into the constitutional text, giving the amended document greater coherence than if amendments trailed behind in a postscript. Connecticut's Roger Sherman, initially an opponent of the Bill of Rights, argued instead that new amendments should be listed separately, so, among other reasons, it would not appear as though George Washington and other framers had signed on to provisions that they had not contemplated. Congress initially voted to accept Madison's plan but changed its mind a week later and adopted Sherman's. There is some evidence that "Madison compromised on form to secure the substance of the larger project of amendments" (Marshall 1998, 110).

Because Sherman's view was victorious, it is much easier to trace American constitutional history than if amendments were scattered within the text and earlier conflicting provisions had been deleted. Moreover, some scholars have argued that the Bill of Rights has achieved more prominence as a separate section of the Constitution than had these provisions been incorporated into the text. However, one prominent scholar has also argued

that "The decision to make amendments supplementary increased the need for an arbiter of disputes over constitutional interpretation," thereby increasing the power of U.S. courts (Kyvig 1996a, 102).

Similarly, in a recent article, Professor Edward Hartnett of Seton Hall University has argued that incorporating new amendments within the text would have made the Constitution more comprehensible and would have forced Congress to give greater consideration as to how new amendments are designed to relate to existing constitutional provisions. In surveying how the current Constitution would be different, Hartnett begins by showing where Madison would have placed the provisions of the Bill of Rights, and then surmises where subsequent amendments would have been placed. He notes that some provisions in the current Bill of Rights would have ended up by Madison's specification in Article I, Section 9, which limits Congress, whereas other provisions (including provisions for a grand jury indictment and jury trials in civil cases, neither of which has been applied as most other provisions in the Bill of Rights to limit the states as well as the national government) would have been moved to Article III, the judicial article. The Tenth Amendment would have become a separate article. Hartnett believes that had Madison's suggestion been heeded, the current Constitution would be shorter and more coherent. Superseded provisions would have been eliminated from the document, and one would not have to depend on notes or italics within the text to identify provisions, like some related to the electoral college, for example, that have been subsequently altered. Hartnett argues that the purpose of some amendments, for example, the Eleventh, which he believes would have been incorporated into the judicial article (Article III), would have been clearer, whereas the array of amendments that remove barriers to voting rights would be grouped together, probably after the provision in Article IV granting each state a "republican" form of government. Hartnett includes a copy of the Constitution as he believes it would be had Madison's ideas been followed (Hartnett 1998, 284–299).

Some state and foreign constitutions do incorporate constitutional changes into the text much as Madison had recommended, with attendant advantages and disadvantages similar to those discussed above.

For Further Reading:

Hartnett, Edward. 1998. "A 'Uniform and Entire' Constitution: Or, What if Madison Had Won?" *Constitutional Commentary* 15 (Summer): 251–297.

Kyvig, David E. 1996a. *Explicit and Authentic Acts: Amending the Constitution, 1776–1995.* Lawrence, KS: University Press of Kansas.

Marshall, Price. 1998. "'A Careless Written Letter'—Situating Amendments to the Federal Constitution." *Arkansas Law Review* 51: 95–115.

❖ PLEDGE OF ALLEGIANCE ❖

See Flag Salute.

❖ *PLESSY V. FERGUSON* (1896) ❖

Plessy v. Ferguson was one of the most important decisions about the meaning of the Thirteenth and Fourteenth Amendments to be handed down in the nineteenth century (Lofgren 1987). In the *Slaughterhouse Cases* (1873), the Supreme Court had given a restrictive reading to the privileges and immunities clause. In the *Civil Rights Cases* (1883), the Supreme Court had further ruled that Congress did not have the power to remedy individual acts of racial discrimination that were not the result of state action. By contrast, in *Plessy v. Ferguson,* the Court upheld a Louisiana Jim Crow law requiring that white and black passengers be seated in separate train cars. This law was challenged by Homer Plessy, an individual who was seven-eighths white and one-eighth black, after he was denied seating on a car reserved for whites.

In rejecting Plessy's Thirteenth Amendment claim, Justice Henry Brown, writing the Court's seven-to-one majority decision, cited the *Civil Rights Cases* as evidence that the Thirteenth Amendment had the limited purpose of freeing the slaves. In interpreting the Fourteenth Amendment, Brown distinguished between legal and social rights and concluded that "it could not have been intended to abolish distinctions based on color, or to enforce social, as distinguished from political, equality, or a commingling of the two races upon terms unsatisfactory to either" (*Plessy* 1896, 544). In response to John Marshall Harlan's dissenting opinion suggesting that racial discrimination was as arbitrary as requiring members of different races to walk on different sides of the street or to live in houses of different colors, Brown upheld Jim Crow laws as reasonable. He ascertained such reasonableness by deferring to the state's "liberty to act with reference to the established usages, customs, and traditions of the people, and with a view to the promotion of their comfort, and the preservation of the public peace and good order" (*Id.,* 550). Brown further denied that segregation was a badge of inferiority: "If this be so, it is not by reason of anything found in the act, but solely because the colored race choses [sic] to put that construction upon it" (*Id.,* 551).

John Marshall Harlan's dissent took a broad view of both the Thirteenth and the Fourteenth Amendments, with his invocation of the former amendment suggesting that, for at least some contemporaries, it was thought to have done more than simply providing freedom for former slaves. Harlan is best known for articulating his vision of a color-blind Constitution: "But in view of the Constitution, in the eye of the law, there is in this country no superior, dominant, ruling class of citizens. Our Constitution is color-blind, and neither knows nor tolerates classes among citizens. In respect of civil rights, all citizens are equal before the law" (*Plessy* 1896, 559).

Plessy v. Ferguson remained the law of the land until it was reversed by the Supreme Court's decision in *Brown v. Board of Education* (1954). Contemporary affirmative action programs, often designed to make up for past inequalities in the areas of race or sex, continue to raise questions as to whether the Fourteenth Amendment was designed to eliminate all considerations of race (and thus provide for a color-blind Constitution) or simply those that invidiously discriminated against minority groups.

See also Affirmative Action; *Brown v. Board of Education.*

For Further Reading:
Plessy v. Ferguson, 163 U.S. 537 (1896).

❖ POLITICAL QUESTIONS ❖

The political questions doctrine has proved to be one of the most elusive doctrines of U.S. constitutional law. Basically, the doctrine is designed to allow courts to defer judgments on issues that they think are, for one reason or another, best left to the "political," that is, the elected, branches of government. However, the Supreme Court has sometimes equivocated as to whether this doctrine is motivated by constitutional or practical concerns. Moreover, some issues that courts once considered to be political are no longer considered to be so (Scharpf 1966).

As early as *Marbury v. Madison* (1803), Chief Justice John Marshall had asserted that the Supreme Court dealt with individual rights and that "questions in their nature political . . . can never be made in this Court" (*Marbury* 1803, 168). The major nineteenth-century case involving the political questions doctrine, however, was *Luther v. Borden* (1849). Asked to determine which of two rival Rhode Island governments was "republican" under the guarantee clause in Article IV, Section 4 of the Constitution (an issue precipitated by the fact that Rhode Island had made no provision for formal constitutional changes), the Court deferred to the decisions already made by the president and Congress.

Although it had previously answered a number of important amending issues, in *Coleman v. Miller* (1939) the Supreme Court applied the political questions doctrine to the amending process. It proclaimed itself "equally divided" on the issue of whether a state's lieutenant governor could break a tie on a state's ratification of an amendment. On the issue of whether a state could ratify an amendment it had previ-

ously rejected, however, the Court decided that this question, as well as the related question of whether a state could rescind a ratification once it was given, was a political question for Congress to decide. Similarly, it decided that Congress had the responsibility for ascertaining whether amendments were ratified in a timely fashion (Vile 1993b, 24–35).

A number of developments have affected the political questions doctrine since *Coleman.* Most significantly, in *Baker v. Carr* (1962), the Supreme Court reversed course on the justiciability of state legislative apportionment. Whereas in *Colegrove v. Green* (1946) it had decided that such issues fell under the guarantee clause and were nonjusticiable, in *Baker v. Carr* it decided that such issues could be reached under the equal protection clause of the Fourteenth Amendment. In *Powell v. McCormack* (1969), the Court subsequently decided that the question of qualifications of a member of Congress was not a political question but was one that the Court could decide. By contrast, in *Nixon v. United States* (1993), the Court decided that the Constitution vested the issue of impeachment proceedings exclusively in Congress.

In *Dyer v. Blair* (1975), a U.S. district court decided that it was not precluded under the political questions doctrine from deciding that a state legislature (albeit not a state constitution) had the right to set an extraordinary majority requirement for ratification of an amendment. Similarly, in *Idaho v. Freeman* (1981), another district court called into question the application of the political questions doctrine as it related to a number of issues surrounding ratification of the Equal Rights Amendment.

Justice William Brennan offered the most complete catalog of questions that are considered political in *Baker v. Carr,* where he cited six:

> [1] a textually demonstrable constitutional commitment of the issue to a coordinate political department; [2] or a lack of judicially discoverable and manageable standards for resolving it; [3] or the impossibility of deciding without an initial policy determination of a kind clearly for nonjudicial discretion; [4] or the impossibility of a court's undertaking indepen-

dent resolution without expressing lack of the respect due coordinate branches of government; [5] or an unusual need for unquestioning adherence to a political decision already made; [6] or the potentiality of embarrassment from multifarious pronouncements by various departments on one question. (*Baker* 1962, 217)

Applying these principles, especially in light of precedents that have been written since *Coleman v. Miller,* a number of scholars have argued that the Supreme Court has considerable leeway in deciding modern amending controversies (Dellinger 1983; Rees 1986; Vile 1993a). In *Bush v. Gore* (2000), the Supreme Court took jurisdiction of an issue, namely vote counting in a presidential election, that many thought should have been left to the political branches. Some scholars think that this decision signals a shift away from traditional understandings of the political questions doctrine.

See also *Baker v. Carr; Coleman v. Miller; Dyer v. Blair;* Guarantee Clause; *Idaho v. Freeman; Luther v. Borden.*

For Further Reading:

Baker v. Carr, 369 U.S. 186 (1962).

Barkow, Rachel E. 2000. "More Supreme Than Court? The Fall of the Political Question Doctrine and the Rise of Judicial Supremacy." *Columbia Law Review* 102 (March): 237–336.

Dellinger, Walter. 1983. "The Legitimacy of Constitutional Change: Rethinking the Amending Process." *Harvard Law Review* 97 (December): 380–432.

Marbury v. Madison, 5 U.S. (1 Cranch.) 137 (1803).

Rees, Grover, III. 1986. "The Amendment Process and Limited Constitutional Conventions." *Benchmark* 2: 67–108.

Scharpf, Fritz W. 1966. "Judicial Review and the Political Question: A Functional Analysis." *Yale Law Journal* 75 (March): 517–597.

Vile, John R. 1993a. *Contemporary Questions Surrounding the Constitutional Amending Process.* Westport, CT: Praeger.

❖ POLL TAXES ❖

See Twenty-fourth Amendment.

❖ *POLLOCK V. FARMERS' LOAN & TRUST CO.* (1895) ❖

In one of the most controversial rulings in its day, the Supreme Court first invalidated taxes on income from state and municipal bonds and on income from property (*Pollock (I)* (1895)); on reargument, it invalidated the federal tax on personal and corporate income (*Pollock (II)* (1895)). Although the decisions appeared to conflict with earlier rulings, including dicta in *Hylton v. United States* (1796) and a decision upholding a Civil War income tax in *Springer v. United States* (1881), in the second *Pollock* decision, Chief Justice Melville Fuller stated that the Court was doing no more than reading the constitutional language about direct taxes in its "obvious sense" (1895, 618). He further noted that if the people desired to change this language, "the ultimate sovereignty may be . . . called into play by a slow and deliberate [constitutional amending] process, which gives time for mere hypothesis and opinion to exhaust themselves, and for the sober second thought of every part of the country to be asserted" (1895, 635).

In one of four dissenting opinions, Justice John Marshall Harlan criticized the majority for departing from precedents. He stated, "If this new theory of the Constitution . . . is justified by the fundamental law, the American people cannot too soon amend their Constitution" (1895, 674).

Harlan's advice was heeded when the Sixteenth Amendment was ratified in 1913, effectively overturning the *Pollock* decision. This was only the third such amendment in U.S. history to have such an effect.

See also Sixteenth Amendment; Supreme Court Decisions Reversed by Constitutional Amendments.

For Further Reading:

Pollock v. Farmers' Loan & Trust Co. (I), 157 U.S. 429 (1895).

Pollock v. Farmers' Loan & Trust Co. (II), 158 U.S. 601 (1895).

❖ POLYGAMY ❖

See Marriage, Divorce, and Parenting.

❖ POPULIS ❖

See Vanguard, Virginia.

❖ PORNOGRAPHY ❖

See Obscenity and Pornography.

❖ POST OFFICE ❖

Throughout much of U.S. history, the post office has been a major source of political patronage. In 1829 President Andrew Jackson made the postmaster general a cabinet official, albeit "not so much to honor the Post Office as to control it" (Cullinan 1968, 44). The president subsequently exercised the right both to appoint (subject to Senate confirmation) and fire first-, second-, and third-class postmasters (Cullinan 1968, 221). The president's power to fire such officials without Senate approval was confirmed in *Myers v. United States* (1926).

There have been a number of proposals throughout U.S. history to make the positions of postmasters and other presidential appointees (for example, revenue assessors) elective. Although most such proposals came in the nineteenth century, Democratic Texas Representative Olin Teague offered several such proposals in the 1960s. The Postal Reorganization Act of 1970 removed the postmaster general from the cabinet and made the U.S. Postal Service into a public corporation with its own civil service system. It thus dried up what has been called the "last great pool of patronage" (M. Nelson 1989, 854). Calls to make postmasters' positions elective appear to have ceased, but some libertarians have proposed constitutions under which tasks currently performed by the post office would be turned over to private enterprise.

In 1973 Democratic Representative Tom Bevill of Alabama proposed an amendment prohibiting the use of U.S. mails for "the transmission, carriage, or delivery of communications hostile to or subversive of this Constitution and the laws and form of government of the U.S. or of any State" (H.J. Res. 131). This proposal could be in conflict with the free speech provision of the First Amendment.

For Further Reading:
Cullinan, Gerald. 1968. *The Post Office Department*. New York: Praeger.
Nelson, Michael, ed. 1989. *Guide to the Presidency*. Washington, DC: Congressional Quarterly.

❖ PRAYER IN PUBLIC SCHOOLS ❖

Since 1962 several hundred amendments have been introduced to allow spoken prayer in public schools and/or public buildings, making this one of the most frequently offered proposals in U.S. history.

Catalysts for the Prayer Amendment
The proposals began in the aftermath of the Supreme Court's decision in *Engel v. Vitale* (1962), which struck down a nondenominational prayer composed by the New York State Board of Regents for public schools. In an eight-to-one decision written by Justice Hugo Black, the Court found that the prayer constituted an impermissible establishment of religion in violation of the First Amendment. In *Abington v. Schempp* (1963), in an eight-to-one decision written by Justice Tom Clark, the Court subsequently extended its ruling to prohibit devotional readings from the Bible and recitation of the Lord's Prayer.

These two cases, especially the first, hit like bombshells and provoked numerous cries of outrage. One congressman noted that "we ought to impeach these men in robes who put themselves up above God," and another commented that "they put the Negroes in the schools and now they've driven God out" (cited in Laubach 1969, 2). Although Congress did not act on one member's proposal to buy a Bible "for the personal use of each justice," the House voted, in September 1962, to put the words "In God We Trust" behind the Speaker's desk (Laubach 1969, 3).

Congressional Amending Efforts

Early efforts to overturn the Supreme Court's decisions centered on a proposal offered by New York Democratic Representative Frank J. Becker of New York. A devout Roman Catholic who was not running for reelection, Becker devoted much of his effort toward getting a majority of his colleagues in the House to vote for a discharge petition to pry the amendment from the House Judiciary Committee, where fellow New York Democrat Emanuel Celler was trying to keep it bottled up.

Becker's proposal, as modified in conjunction with other House sponsors, had four sections, the last of which contained a seven-year ratification deadline. The other three sections were as follows:

Sec. 1: Nothing in this Constitution shall be deemed to prohibit the offering, reading from, or listening to prayers or Biblical scriptures, if participation therein is on a voluntary basis, in any governmental or public school, institution or place.
Sec. 2: Nothing in this Constitution shall be deemed to prohibit making reference to, belief in, reliance upon, or invoking the aid of God or a Supreme Being in any governmental or public document, proceeding, activity, ceremony, school, institution, or place, or upon any coinage, currency, or obligation of the United States.
Sec. 3: Nothing in this article shall constitute an establishment of religion.
(Beaney and Beiser 1973, 32)

Celler reluctantly called for hearings, but an increasing number of scholars and religious leaders began to raise questions about the implications of this amendment—for example, which version of the Bible would be used—and others questioned the wisdom of altering the Bill of Rights. Becker's discharge petition failed.

In 1964 the Republican platform called for an amendment to permit prayer and Bible reading in schools. In 1966 Illinois Republican Senator Everett Dirksen (who had also been active in trying to repeal the Supreme Court's reapportionment decisions) introduced such an amendment, the heart of which provided that "nothing contained in this Constitution shall prohibit the authority administering any school, school system, educational institution or other public building supported in whole or in part through the expenditure of public funds from providing for or permitting the voluntary participation by students or others in prayer" (Laubach 1969, 142).

Indiana Democratic Senator Birch Bayh subsequently presided over hearings on this amendment. Again, scholars and religious leaders raised questions. Dirksen subsequently brought his amendment to the floor without the support of the Senate Judiciary Committee. The vote of forty-nine to thirty-seven fell short of the required two-thirds (Laubach 1969, 149).

In 1967 Dirksen revised his amendment to provide that "nothing in this Constitution shall abridge the rights of persons lawfully assembled, in any public building that is supported in whole or in part through the expenditure of public funds, to participate in non-denominational prayer" (Laubach 1969, 149). Again the amendment proved unsuccessful, as did a similar amendment sponsored in 1970 by Tennessee Republican Senator Howard Baker. A 1971 vote in the House of Representatives on a similar measure garnered 240 votes to 163, again falling short of the necessary two-thirds (Keynes with Miller 1989, 194).

In 1979 Ronald Reagan made prayer in school part of his platform for the presidency. The year before, hearings had been held on a proposal by North Carolina Republican Senator Jesse Helms to curb the jurisdiction of the Supreme Court over such issues. Helms's proposal was eventually stopped by a filibuster (R. Smith 1987, 276).

Congress subsequently considered Reagan's amendment. It provided that "nothing in this Constitution shall be construed to prohibit individual or group prayer in public schools or other public institutions. No person shall be required by the United States or by any state to participate in such prayer" (R. Smith 1987, 276). In March 1984 the amendment received a vote of fifty-six to forty-four in the Senate, again falling short of the required two-thirds majority (R. Smith 1987, 278). However, that same year, Congress adopted the Equal Access Act, designed to allow religious groups to meet on public school property if noncurricular nonreligious groups were also permitted to meet there.

In *Wallace v. Jaffree* (1985), the Supreme Court struck down an Alabama law that specifically allowed students to use a moment of silence for the purpose of prayer. The Court decided that, because the law had been altered specifically to mention prayer, it did not have a "secular legislative purpose," the first of three requirements that the Supreme Court generally applies under the so-called *Lemon* test. This test, named after the case in which it was announced *(Lemon v. Kurtzman* (1971)), also requires that laws neither "advance nor inhibit" religion and that they avoid "excessive entanglement" between church and state. *Wallace v. Jaffree,* however, did not resolve the issue of whether a moment of silence that does not specifically endorse prayer might be valid. Utah Republican Senator Orrin Hatch subsequently introduced an amendment providing that "nothing in this Constitution shall be construed to prohibit individual or group silent prayer or reflection in public schools. Neither the United States nor any state shall require any person to participate in such prayer or reflection, nor shall they encourage any particular form of prayer or reflection" (R. Smith 1987, 188). Again, hearings were held, with the Judiciary Committee favorably reporting out the amendment.

Current Developments

To date, no such amendment has been adopted. Doubts remain as to both the proper wording of such an amendment and the wisdom of modifying any part of the Bill of Rights. Some proponents of greater religious freedom retain the hope that the Supreme Court will eventually ease the tension by officially sanctioning some existing moment-of-silence laws. In 1995 President Clinton attempted to fend off a prayer amendment by stressing religious rights that schoolchildren already have under the Equal Access Act and other judicial decisions. A majority of the House of Representatives adopted a prayer amendment in 1998, but it did not muster the two-thirds vote required of amendments (Marshall 2001, 5). Although in *Sante Fe Independent School District v. Doe* (2000) the U.S. Supreme Court struck down a provision whereby a student council chaplain offered a prayer broadcast over the public address systems prior to football games, more recently it declined to review a U.S. Fourth Circuit Court of Appeals decision allowing Virginia's moment of silence law (Masters 2001, B01).

The proposed Religious Equality Amendment is chiefly designed to protect the free exercise rights of religious believers in the wake of U.S. Supreme Court decisions in *Employment Division v. Smith* (1990) and *City of Boerne v. Flores* (1997). These decisions did not require states to show a "compelling interest" when applying generally applicable laws that fall more heavily on religious believers than on others. Some versions of this amendment specifically provide for reinstitution of public prayer in schools. Largely because of past difficulties in adopting a prayer in school amendment, the versions without a provision calling for the restoration of school prayer as an objective appear to have garnered wider support.

See also *Abington v. Schempp; Engel v. Vitale;* Religious Equality Amendment.

For Further Reading:

Beaney, William M., and Edward N. Beiser. 1973. "Prayer and Politics: The Impact of *Engel* and *Schempp* on the Political Process." In *The Impact of Supreme Court Decisions: Empirical Studies.* 2d ed. Eds. Theodore L. Becker and Malcolm M. Feeley. New York: Oxford University Press.

Keynes, Edward, with Randall K. Miller. 1989. *The Court vs. Congress: Prayer, Busing, and Abortion.* Durham, NC: Duke University Press.

Laubach, John H. 1969. *School Prayers: Congress, the Courts and the Public.* Washington, DC: Public Affairs Press.

Marshall, Patrick. 2001. "Religion in Schools." *CQ Researcher,* 12 January, *http://library.cqpress. com/cqres/1pext.dll/cqpres/print/print20010112.* Accessed 3/18/02.

Masters, Brooke A. 2001. "Va. Minute of Silence Survives Test in High Court: 4th Circuit Ruling Allowed to Stand Without Comment." *The Washington Post,* 30 October, B01.

Schotten, Peter, and Dennis Stevens. 1996. *Religion, Politics and the Law: Commentaries and Controversies.* Belmont, CA: Wadsworth.

Smith, Rodney K. 1987. *Public Prayer and the Constitution: A Case Study in Constitutional Interpretation.* Wilmington, DE: Scholarly Resources.

❖ PREAMBLE TO THE CONSTITUTION ❖

The first paragraph of the Constitution is called the preamble. In elegant language, it delineates the primary purposes of the document. The preamble has an "aspirational tone" (S. Barber 1984, 34). However, a scholar of the Constitution has observed that "[t]he Preamble does not confer any power upon any branch or agency of the national government. A person cannot go into a federal court and claim any right under the Preamble" (Cooke 1984, 26).

There have been at least four proposals to alter the preamble, one in 1869 and three in the 1960s. At least one wanted to incorporate the principles of the Declaration of Independence there. Many of those who have proposed texts of new constitutions have also altered the preamble to reflect new or widened purposes for government to achieve. The Confederate constitution altered the preamble to reinforce Southern claims of state sovereignty (a matter that the opening words of the preamble, "We the people of the United States," arguably left ambiguous). In a move later advocated by proponents of the Christian Amendment, the Confederate constitution preamble also mentioned "Almighty God" (DeRosa 1991, 135).

Most proposals for a new constitution include a new preamble, often designating contemporary problems that their authors believe they are needed to solve. In proposing a "Court of Generations," futurist Bruce E. Tonn suggested an amendment that would incorporate some of the language in the existing preamble by specifying that "[t]he power to judge threats to the security of the blessings of liberty to our posterity shall be vested in the Court of Generations" (Tonn 1991, 483). In suggesting that the U.S. Constitution should be rewritten, Joseph Church proposed adding many additional provisions to the existing preamble.

See also Church, Joseph; Tonn, Bruce E.

For Further Reading:

Barber, Sotirios A. 1984. *On What the Constitution Means.* Baltimore: Johns Hopkins University Press.

Cooke, Edward F. 1984. *A Detailed Analysis of the Constitution.* 5th ed. Savage, MO: Littlefield Adams Quality Paperbacks.

DeRosa, Marshall L. 1991. *The Confederate Constitution of 1861: An Inquiry into American Constitutionalism.* Columbia, MO: University of Missouri Press.

Tonn, Bruce E. 1991. "A Court of Generations: A Proposed Amendment to the U.S. Constitution." *Futures* 21: 413–431.

❖ PRESIDENCY, AGE LIMITS FOR ❖

The Constitution sets a minimum age of thirty-five for the president but does not specify a maximum age. When Ronald Reagan was inaugurated for his first term in 1981, he was just shy of his seventieth birthday, and the "age issue" had already emerged when he first sought the Republican nomination five years earlier (Ceaser 1988, 183). Republican Bob Dole of Kansas began his third attempt for the Republican nomination for president in 1995 at the age of 72.

A number of amending proposals introduced in the 1970s would have made Reagan ineligible for a second term or Dole ineligible for a first because they would have denied eligibility to presidential or vice presidential candidates who had reached the age of seventy. Most would have provided that the president serve for a single six-year term.

The Twenty-fifth Amendment limits a president to two full terms, but the amendment is not specifically tied to age and applies equally to a relatively young individual like Bill Clinton who leaves the presidency after two full terms as well as to an older one like Ronald Reagan.

For Further Reading:

Ceaser, James W. 1988. "The Reagan Presidency and American Public Opinion." In *The Reagan Legacy: Promise and Performance*, ed. Charles O. Jones. Chatham, NJ: Chatham House.

❖ PRESIDENCY, APPOINTMENT AND REMOVAL POWERS OF ❖

Article II, Section 2 of the Constitution outlines the power to appoint executive officials and vests this power largely in the president, who must operate with the "Advice and Consent of the Senate." The Constitution does not specify who has the power to remove executive officials. This issue was an especially controversial one in the nineteenth century and was a major bone of contention between President Andrew Johnson and the Reconstruction Congress. Johnson's secretary of war, Edwin M. Stanton, refused to accept Johnson's authority to fire him until the impeachment effort against Johnson failed in the Senate.

In *Myers v. United States* (1926), Chief Justice (and ex-president) William Howard Taft authored a decision upholding President Wilson's authority to fire a first-class postmaster without Senate concurrence. Taft argued that the framers intended to vest this power in the president, who would best be able to ascertain the capabilities and performance of his subordinates. Taft further argued that "the power to remove inferior executive officers, like that to remove superior officers, is an incident of the power to appoint them, and is in its nature an executive power" (*Myers* 1926, 161).

Two subsequent cases have somewhat qualified this power. In *Humphrey's Executor v. United States* (1935), the Supreme Court unanimously ruled that a president could not fire a member of the Federal Trade Commission—considered a quasi-legislative and quasi-judicial body. Similarly, in *Wiener v. United States* (1958), the Court denied that President Eisenhower could remove without cause a member of the War Claims Commission, also described by the Court as a quasi-judicial body.

Most proposals for altering or clarifying presidential appointment and removal powers came in the nineteenth century. Some were designed to give Congress the power to appoint and remove the secretary of the Treasury Department, members of the Post Office Department, or various other members of the cabinet; some proposed including the House of Representatives in the advice and consent function and in removals; some would have permitted cabinet officers (rather than the president) to select officers under them; others attempted to set specific terms for executive officials; and still others attempted to exclude various individuals—members of Congress, for example—from executive offices (Ames 1896, 134–138). The nineteenth century also witnessed the development of the civil service system.

Judicial decisions have clarified the appointment and removal power in the twentieth century, and the executive's power to remove members of his or her administration is generally accepted. Periodically, members of Congress have introduced proposals to provide a means, in addition to impeachment and conviction, to remove judicial officers. Members of Congress have also periodically called for the people's right to recall elected or appointed officials.

See also Civil Service Reform.

For Further Reading:

Ames, Herman. 1896. *The Proposed Amendments to the Constitution of the United States during the First Century of Its History.* Reprint, New York: Burt Franklin, 1970.

Myers v. United States, 272 U.S. 52 (1926).

❖ PRESIDENCY, COMPENSATION FOR ❖

Article II, Section 1 of the Constitution provides that "the President shall, at stated Times, receive for his Services, a Compensation, which shall neither be increased nor diminished during the period for which he shall be elected, and he shall not receive within that Period any other Emolument from the United States, or any of them."

The first Congress set the president's salary at $25,000 a year (although Washington, and later Kennedy, refused such compensation), a figure that was doubled in 1873. As of 2001, the president's pay was raised from $200,000 to $400,000 annually, but there are other perquisites, such as travel, expense accounts, use of the White House, and the like (Bledsoe 1989, 830).

In 1808 Federalist Senator James Hillhouse of Connecticut introduced an amendment to cut the president's salary to $15,000 a year, and in 1822 Democrat Timothy Fuller of Massachusetts proposed that such compensation be fixed—along with that of members of Congress—every ten years. Amendments introduced in 1882 and 1884 to limit the president to one term also had a provision to grant him a pension (Ames 1896, 129). The United States did not provide such pensions until 1958. Today, ex-presidents receive a salary equal to that of a cabinet secretary (Bledsoe 1989, 839), but some have made millions of dollars in writing, speaking, and consulting fees. After 200 years it appears that further adjustments in presidential compensation or perquisites are likely to continue to be resolved by ordinary legislation rather than by constitutional amendment.

For Further Reading:
Bledsoe, Craig W. 1989. "Executive Pay and Perquisites." In *Guide to the Presidency,* ed. Michael Nelson. Washington, DC: Congressional Quarterly Press.

❖ PRESIDENCY, CREATION OF A SEPARATE CHIEF OF STATE ❖

In Great Britain, the prime minister serves as chief of government, and the monarch serves as ceremonial chief of state. In the United States, by contrast, the president carries out both sets of responsibilities. Although ceremonial tasks can be wearisome, a president can also manip-

ulate them to increase his or her visibility and prestige. President Richard M. Nixon was especially fond of the ceremonial aspects of his office.

In 1975, after the collapse of Nixon's presidency, Democratic Representative Henry Reuss of Wisconsin proposed a constitutional amendment to create a ceremonial chief of state who would be confirmed by a majority vote of both houses of Congress. The chief of state could serve an unlimited number of four-year terms and would receive the same salary as the president. Terms of the chief of state would overlap with those of presidents, the first to be appointed two years into the president's term. Reuss's proposal generated little support (Diller 1989, 594). A number of proposed new constitutions have, however, called for making a similar distinction between the head of the U.S. government and its head of state.

For Further Reading:
Diller, Daniel C. 1989. "Chief of State." In *Guide to the Presidency,* ed. Michael Nelson. Washington, DC: Congressional Quarterly.

❖ PRESIDENCY, MEMBERSHIP IN SENATE FOR EX-PRESIDENTS ❖

In a parliamentary system, unsuccessful candidates for prime minister generally continue to lead their party in that body, assuming that they are reelected to the parliament. In contrast, once U.S. presidents leave office, they have no official governmental post, although the visibility and government-provided financial support for such individuals have grown fairly dramatically in recent years. As early as 1875, proposals were introduced to make ex-presidents lifetime at-large or ex officio nonvoting members of the U.S. Senate (M. Nelson 1989, 1079–1080), a proposal apparently later supported by perpetual presidential candidate William Jennings Bryan (William Howard Taft, who humorously proposed that ex-presidents, like himself, be chloroformed, noted that Bryan seemed to prefer that such individuals "should expire under the anaesthetic effect of the debates of the Senate") (Vile 2002b, 188).

A resolution introduced in 1917 would have given ex–vice presidents at-large membership in the House of Representatives. The period from 1960 to 1963 witnessed at least seven proposals to give ex-presidents ex officio status in the Senate. At least one of these proposals, offered by Democratic Representative Morris Udall of Arizona, would apply to all unsuccessful candidates for president.

In 1963 the Senate altered its rules to provide that "former presidents of the United States shall be entitled to address the Senate upon appropriate notice to the presiding officer who shall thereupon make the necessary arrangements." The next year, Truman made some remarks to the Senate, but to date, no ex-president has delivered a formal address there (M. Nelson 1989, 1080).

For Further Reading:

Clark, James C. 1985. *Faded Glory: Presidents out of Power.* New York: Praeger.

Nelson, Michael, ed. 1989. *Guide to the Presidency.* Washington, DC: Congressional Quarterly.

Vile, John R. 2002b. *Presidential Winners and Losers: Words of Victory and Concession.* Washington, DC: Congressional Quarterly.

❖ PRESIDENCY, OATH OF ❖

The only oath specifically included in the U.S. Constitution is the oath of the president. He or she swears or affirms faithfully to "execute the office of President . . . and . . . preserve, protect, and defend the Constitution of the United States."

A number of the practices currently associated with the oath—for example, swearing on a Bible and having the oath administered by the chief justice of the United States—are not specified in the Constitution (Euchner and Maltese 1989, 262). The words "so help me God" are not included in the Constitution either, although President Washington began the practice of adding them. Several proposals—the most persistent being that of Democrat John Rarick of Louisiana—have called for these words to be added to the text of the Constitution. If they were so added, it would be the first

explicit mention of God in the document, a longtime objective of supporters of the Christian Amendment.

See also Christian Amendment.

For Further Reading:

Euchner, Charles C., and John A. Maltese. 1989. "The Electoral Process." In *Guide to the Presidency,* ed. Michael Nelson. Washington, DC: Congressional Quarterly.

❖ PRESIDENCY, PARDON POWER ❖

Since 1974 more than twenty-five amending proposals have been introduced in Congress to modify the president's pardon power. This power is delineated in Article II, Section 2 of the Constitution, which grants him or her "Power to grant Reprieves and Pardons for Offenses against the United States, except in Cases of Impeachment."

In *Federalist No. 74*, Alexander Hamilton defended this provision not simply as a way of mitigating individual injustices but also as a means of restoring domestic peace. Hamilton noted that "in seasons of insurrection or rebellion, there are often critical moments when a well-timed offer of pardon to the insurgents or rebels may restore the tranquillity of the commonwealth: and which if suffered to pass unimproved, it may never be possible afterwards to recall" (Hamilton, Madison, and Jay 1961, 449).

The Supreme Court has interpreted the pardon power broadly. In *Ex parte Garland* (1867), upholding a pardon to a former Confederate issued by President Andrew Johnson, the Court said that the executive pardon "extends to every offense known to the law, and may be exercised at any time after its commission, either before legal proceedings are taken, or during their pendency, or after conviction and judgment" (380). Similarly, in *Schick v. Reed* (1974), upholding a condition to a pardon issued by President Eisenhower, the Court said that the purpose of the power was "to allow plenary authority in the President to 'forgive' the convicted person in part or entirely, to reduce a penalty in terms of a specified number of years, or to alter it with conditions which are themselves constitutionally unobjectionable" (266). The pardon power includes the authority to issue general amnesties, which several presidents have granted. President Carter made such provision for Vietnam-era draft evaders.

President Ford issued the most controversial pardon in U.S. history in 1974 when he extended a "full, free, and absolute pardon" to former President Nixon "for all offenses against the United States which he had committed or may have committed or taken part in" (McDonald 1992, 620). This pardon appears to have been the catalyst for most amendment proposals that followed. Most such proposals, including one introduced by Minnesota Democratic Senator (later Vice President) Walter Mondale, would have allowed Congress to disapprove such pardons by a two-thirds vote within 180 days (Duker 1977, 537). Other proposals would have limited the president to pardoning only those convicted of crimes or, like a proposal offered by California's Democratic Senator Barbara Boxer, would have prohibited the president from pardoning individuals employed in his own administration. As he left office President George Bush Sr. pardoned a number of former members of his administration including former Secretary of Defense Caspar Weinberger, who had been implicated in the Iran-Contra Scandal involving the illegal sale of arms to Iran to raise money to fight communism in Nicaragua.

Questions about presidential pardons were renewed at the end of President Bill Clinton's administration. Although he had not previously issued many pardons, at the end of his administration he made a flurry of last-minute pardons that some thought were influenced either by campaign contributions to his party (Clinton was prohibited by the Twenty-second Amendment from running for a third term), by attempts to influence his wife's election to the U.S. Senate seat in the state of New York, or by undue pressure on the part of the president's brother-in-law on behalf of some of his clients. Clinton issued pardons to fugitive Marc Rich for tax fraud, to his brother, Roger Clinton, for conspiring to distribute cocaine, and to Susan McDougal (who had stayed in jail rather than testify in the Whitewater land deal investigation) for bank fraud. This was the impetus for a proposal by Massachusetts Democrat Representative Barney Frank in February 2001 that would have prohibited presidential pardons and reprieves between 1 October of an election year and the inauguration of a new president. Although presidents presumably still care about how they are treated by future historians, it can certainly be argued that outgoing presidents have fewer political constraints on issuing pardons during such time periods than they might if they planned to serve another term in office (Sisk 2000).

For Further Reading:

Duker, William F. 1977. "The President's Power to Pardon: A Constitutional History." *William and Mary Law Review* 18 (Spring): 475–538.

Ex parte Garland, 71 U.S. 333 (1867).

Hamilton, Alexander, James Madison, and John Jay. 1787–1788. *The Federalist Papers.* Reprint, New York: New American Library, 1961.

McDonald, Forrest. 1992. "Pardon Power." In *The Oxford Companion to the Supreme Court of the United States,* ed. Kermit L. Hall. New York: Oxford University Press.

Schick v. Reed, 419 U.S. 256 (1974).

Sisk, Gregory C. 2002. "Suspending the Pardon Power During the Twilight of a Presidential Term." *Missouri Law Review* 67 (Winter): 13–27.

❖ PRESIDENCY, PLURAL EXECUTIVE ❖

One of the most important decisions that the delegates to the Constitutional Convention made was to fashion the presidency as a singular office rather than to entrust such powers in a dual executive or executive council. Pennsylvania's James Wilson defended a singular executive to those who feared that it would assume monarchical powers. He argued that a single individual would be better able to assume responsibility for executive tasks (M. Nelson 1989, 23). In *Federalist No. 70,* Alexander Hamilton further defended a singular executive as a means of achieving "energy" and "unity" in government (Hamilton, Madison, and Jay 1961, 423–434).

As the slavery controversy grew, however, some began to fear that a single president might tilt the resolution of this issue toward the interest of a single section of the nation. Indeed, the election of Abraham Lincoln eventually prompted the Southern secession movement. Picking up on an earlier idea of John C. Calhoun's, Virginia Democratic Representative Albert Jenkins introduced a resolution in 1860 to create a dual executive; that same year, Democratic Representative John Noell of Missouri proposed replacing the president with a three-person executive council. In 1878 Ohio Democratic Representative Milton Southard, who feared that the presidency was becoming too monarchical, proposed creating a presidency of three men representing the western, eastern and middle, and southern states (Ames 1896, 69–70). In 1975 Democratic Representative Henry Reuss of Wisconsin introduced proposals for the creation of a separate chief of state to perform ceremonial functions now assumed by the president.

From a somewhat different perspective, political scientist Matthew Holden Jr. advocated an amendment to create a plural executive, with the prospect of guaranteeing that at least one of the vice presidents forming the resulting executive would be an African American (Holden 1973b, 252–253). Herman Finer proposed adding eleven vice presidents, who, with the president, would exercise collective responsibility in much the same way as the cabinet in Great Britain (Finer 1960, 304). Some proponents of new constitutions have proposed either eliminating the presidency or making the president, as in parliamentary systems, a spokesperson for Congress.

For Further Reading:

Ames, Herman. 1896. *The Proposed Amendments to the Constitution of the United States during the First Century of Its History*. Reprint, New York: Burt Franklin, 1970.

Finer, Herman. 1960. *The Presidency, Crisis and Regeneration: An Essay in Possibilities*. Chicago: University of Chicago Press.

Hamilton, Alexander, James Madison, and John Jay. 1787–1788. *The Federalist Papers*. Reprint, New York: New American Library, 1961.

Holden, Matthew, Jr. 1973b. *The White Man's Burden*. New York: Chandler.

Nelson, Michael, ed. 1989. *Guide to the Presidency*. Washington, DC: Congressional Quarterly.

❖ PRESIDENCY, PROPERTY SEIZURE POWERS OF ❖

In April 1952 President Harry Truman issued Executive Order 10340, which directed the secretary of commerce to seize and operate U.S. steel mills. Truman took this action, which he immediately reported to Congress, to avert a threatened strike that might interfere with U.S. war efforts in Korea (Westin 1990). In so acting, Truman decided against simply delaying the strike by calling for a cooling-off period under the Taft-Hartley Act of 1947. Instead, he relied on the broad grants of executive power within the Constitution itself. As a consequence, at least three resolutions were introduced that April and May in the House of Representatives calling for a constitutional amendment to limit executive seizure powers.

Such an amendment proved to be unnecessary. On 2 June 1952, the Supreme Court ruled in *Youngstown Sheet & Tube Co. v. Sawyer* (often known simply as the *Steel Seizure Case*) that the president had exceeded his constitutional powers. Justice Hugo Black authored the six-to-three decision, which was especially skeptical of the president's broad claim of inherent executive authority. The equally celebrated concurring opinion of Justice Robert Jackson, however, suggested that the president's actions might have been constitutional if Congress had authorized them.

For Further Reading:

Westin, Alan. 1990. *The Anatomy of a Constitutional Law Case:* Youngstown Sheet and Tube Co. v. Sawyer; *the Steel Seizure Decision*. New York: Columbia University Press.

❖ PRESIDENCY, QUALIFICATIONS FOR ❖

The Constitution requires that the president be at least thirty-five years old and have resided in the United States for fourteen years or more. Article II, Section 1 of the U.S. Constitution further specifies that the president must be "a natural born Citizen" or citizen when the Constitution was adopted, a provision that appears to have been inserted in part at the insistence of Pennsylvania delegate James Wilson, who had been born in Scotland (Miller 2001, 23). The provision forbidding other immigrants from becoming president was apparently designed to ease fears that the delegates to the Constitutional Convention of 1787 might be planning to invite a European monarch to serve as chief executive (M. Nelson 1987, 395).

The term "natural born citizen" has been subject to some dispute and could one day be clarified by an amendment. Meanwhile, it probably already includes individuals—such as George Romney, who ran unsuccessfully for the 1968 Republican nomination—born overseas to parents who were American citizens (Gordon 1968).

Members of Congress have proposed a number of amendments to alter presidential qualifications, many in the first 100 years of the nation's history. These included proposals to raise the age of eligibility from thirty-five to forty-five, to exclude former secessionists from the office (a qualified version of which appeared in Section 3 of the Fourteenth Amendment), and to bar members of Congress or those who are holding office or have held office within two or four years of a presidential election from the job (Ames 1896, 74–75).

In 1976 House Minority Leader John Rhodes and Senator Barry Goldwater, both Arizona Republicans, sponsored a version of this last proposal that would have barred members of Congress from the presidency for two years after they left office. Their primary intention was to avoid excessive absences by members of Congress running for chief executive. As the 1964 Republican presidential candidate, Goldwater could testify from personal experi-ence to the difficulty of pursuing both tasks. Their proposal would not have affected the provisions for appointing vice presidents under the Twenty-fifth Amendment.

The most popular proposal affecting presidential qualifications, first offered in the 1860s and periodically introduced from the 1940s to the present, would alter the requirement that a president be a natural-born citizen. This would allow foreign-born citizens to be eligible after being American citizens and residents for a certain number of years (Massachusetts Congressman Barney Frank has suggested twenty). Although sponsors of this proposal have included Missouri Senator Thomas Eagleton (S.J. Res. 72, 1983), who was George McGovern's initial Democratic nominee for vice president in 1972, the idea has not received much attention (Gordon 1968, 27). One writer of an article in a conservative magazine has suggested that such an amendment would be a way for President George W. Bush to increase his popularity among immigrants (Miller 2001). Another writer, who also favors eliminating the disability on foreign birth, suggests that foreign-born citizens could, if congressionally authorized to do so, serve as an "acting president" in cases under the Twenty-fifth Amendment, where a president—and possibly a vice president—is temporarily incapacitated (Ho 2000).

For Further Reading:

Ames, Herman. 1896. *The Proposed Amendments to the Constitution of the United States during the First Century of Its History.* Reprint, New York: Burt Franklin, 1970.

Gordon, Charles. 1968. "Who Can Be President of the United States: The Unresolved Enigma." *Maryland Law Review* 28 (Winter): 1–32.

Ho, James C. 2000. "Unnatural-Born Citizens and Acting Presidents," *Constitutional Commentary* 17: 575–585.

Miller, John C. 2001. "Immigrants for President: Why the Foreign-born Should Be Allowed to Compete for the Big Job." *National Review* 53 (6 August): 22–24.

Nelson, Michael. 1987. "Constitutional Qualifications for President." *Presidential Studies Quarterly* 17 (Spring): 383–399.

❖ PRESIDENCY, ROLE IN THE AMENDING PROCESS ❖

Article V of the Constitution does not designate a role for the president in the amending process. However, Article I, Section 7 specifies that "every order, resolution, or vote to which the concurrence of the Senate and the House of Representatives may be necessary (except on the question of adjournment) shall be presented to the President of the United States" for his or her approval or veto. This clause has led to questions as to whether the president's signature is needed for an amendment to be valid.

Historically, the answer has been negative. A review of the deliberations of the Constitutional Convention of 1787 indicates that the veto power was discussed in the context of legislation rather than with respect to constitutional amendments (Edel 1981, 33–38). Because amendments must already have been proposed by the same majority needed to override a presidential veto, it is not likely that presidential vetoes would have any significant effect. Moreover, in an early decision in *Hollingsworth v. Virginia* (1798), the U.S. Supreme Court declared that the president's signature was not necessary. Even a critic of this decision, who wants it confined as narrowly as possible, does not appear to advocate reversal of the ruling (C. Black 1978).

On two occasions, presidents have signed amendments before they were sent to the states for approval. The first such signature occurred in 1861, when outgoing President James Buchanan signed the Corwin Amendment (which was not subsequently ratified), designed to prevent any congressional interference with the institution of slavery; the second occurred in 1865, when President Abraham Lincoln signed the Thirteenth Amendment abolishing slavery (Bernstein with Agel 1993, 91, 100). President Lyndon Johnson also insisted on having a ceremony in which he signed as a witness to ratification of the Twenty-fifth Amendment, which provided for presidential disability and, in cases where the need arose, for the replacement of vice presidents.

Although their signatures are not required, presidents frequently take positions on constitutional amendments. Article II, Section 3 of the Constitution grants the president power to "recommend" to Congress "such Measures as he shall judge necessary and expedient." Presidents from George Washington to the present have recognized that this right encompasses power to recommend constitutional amendments (Sidak 1989, 2085).

See also *Hollingsworth v. Virginia.*

For Further Reading:

Bernstein, Richard B., with Jerome Agel. 1993. *Amending America: If We Love the Constitution So Much, Why Do We Keep Trying to Change It?* New York: Random House.

Black, Charles L., Jr. 1978. "Correspondence: On Article I, Section 7, Clause 3—and the Amendment of the Constitution." *Yale Law Journal* 87: 896–900.

Edel, Wilbur. 1981. *A Constitutional Convention: Threat or Challenge?* New York: Praeger.

Sidak, J. Gregory. 1989. "The Recommendation Clause." *Georgetown Law Journal* 77 (August): 2070–2135.

❖ PRESIDENCY, SUCCESSION ❖

See Twenty-fifth Amendment.

❖ PRESIDENCY, TERM LIMITS ❖

See Twenty-second Amendment.

❖ PRESIDENCY, VETO POWER OF ❖

Of all the domestic powers exercised by the president, few are as formidable as the veto, which is outlined in Article I, Section 7 of the Constitution. Qualified rather than absolute, the presidential veto can be overridden by a two-thirds vote of both houses of Congress. The veto's placement within Article I of the Constitution indicates that the framers understood it to be a legislative power and that it therefore represents a departure from strict separation of powers (Spitzer 1988, 18). The threat of such a veto can give a president considerable influence over the formulation of pending legislation. Although presidents may use the veto to void laws they consider to be unconstitutional, the Constitution did not limit use of the mechanism to such circumstances.

President Andrew Jackson reflected his view of the presidency as an embodiment of popular will by exercising the veto twelve times, more than all his predecessors combined (Spitzer 1988, 33). Jackson's administration also marked the introduction of the first of at least eleven proposals introduced in the nineteenth century that would have allowed Congress to override such vetoes by a simple majority vote (Spitzer 1988, 38). Former president John Quincy Adams and perpetual presidential candidate Henry Clay both offered such proposals during the administration of John Tyler, who was especially criticized for his use of the veto power. The House of Representatives voted ninety-nine to ninety in favor of one such bill in 1842, thus falling substantially below the two-thirds majority required (Ames 1896, 132). Proposals to override presidential vetoes by majority vote were reintroduced in Congress in 1912 and 1913 and from 1943 to 1945.

There were two proposals in the first half of the nineteenth century to eliminate the presidential veto. A number of other proposals later in the century would have required vetoes to be overridden by two-thirds of the members elected in each house rather than by two-thirds of a quorum. The latter was a long-standing practice that was eventually legitimated in *Missouri Pacific Railway Co. v. Kansas* (1919).

New York Democratic Representative Jonathan Bingham introduced an amendment resolution in the House in 1975 that would have allowed Congress to override a veto by a three-fifths vote of both houses, but it applied only in the case of an unelected president (such as Gerald Ford, who was then serving) appointed under the Twenty-fifth Amendment (H.J. Res. 529). After the Supreme Court's opinion in *Immigration and Naturalization Service v. Chadha* (1983), in which it declared the so-called legislative veto to be unconstitutional, at least two resolutions were introduced to restore this mechanism, one coming a week after the decision. Such a veto, a part of about 200 laws, allowed Congress to delegate to the president certain powers, with the understanding that one or both houses could later veto his or her action. The Court found that such legislative vetoes violated the presentment clause (requiring bills to be presented to the president for a possible veto) and, in some cases, the requirement that legislation be passed by both houses of Congress.

A president exercises a pocket veto by deciding not to sign a bill presented to him or her within ten days of a congressional adjournment. In early American history, questions were raised as to whether a president could sign a bill once Congress had adjourned. President Ulysses S. Grant accordingly proposed an amendment that would have forbidden Congress to pass any laws in its final twenty-four hours (Spitzer 1988, 110).

By far the most popular proposed reform of the veto power has been the proposal to give the president a so-called line-item veto, similar to that exercised by many state governors. Such a power was entrusted to, but never exercised by, the president of the Confederate States of America (Spitzer 1988, 126) and has been advocated by members of Congress from both parties and from both ends of the political spectrum. Georgia's Republican Senator Mack Mattingly introduced a bill that received substantial support in the Senate in 1985. It provided that all major spending proposals would be divided into separate bills before being presented to the president (Cronin and Weill 1985, 127).

Most proposed amendments dealing with item vetoes have been limited specifically to appropriations bills. The 1880s witnessed the introduction of at least two such item-veto proposals for rivers and harbors bills. A number of nineteenth-century presidents, including James Madison, vetoed legislation on the basis that Congress had no constitutional authority to pass legislation for internal improvements.

President Grant asked for an item veto in his annual message of 1873, and the first such proposal was introduced in Congress three years later by West Virginia Congressman James Faulkner. Since then, more than 150 item-veto amendments have been introduced, but only once—in 1884—has such an amendment been favorably reported out of committee, and this was not acted on by the Senate (Spitzer 1988, 127). Modern advocates of the item veto have included Presidents Harry S. Truman, Dwight D. Eisenhower, Gerald Ford, Ronald Reagan, George Bush, and Bill Clinton. Indeed, all three presidential candidates in the 1992 election endorsed this proposal. The only presidents on record against such an item veto are William Howard Taft (Ross and Schwengel 1982, 72), who later served as chief justice of the United States, and Jimmy Carter, who initially supported the proposal but later changed his mind (Cronin and Weill 1985, 130).

Advocates of the item veto believe that it represents a return to the founders' original intention, which has been subverted by the increased use of "riders," or nongermane amendments, that Congress often adds to appropriations bills (Best 1984a). There have been at least half a dozen proposals in U.S. history to prevent such riders or to limit each bill to a single subject as well as a recent law review article on the subject (Denning and Smith 1999). Proponents also see the item veto as a way of trimming the federal budget, which has itself been the subject of numerous proposed amendments. Critics of the item veto doubt that it would have a significant effect on the budget and fear that it might unduly increase presidential powers. Some critics even suggest that it might ultimately result in greater spending, as members of Congress add items in the expectation of some presidential vetoes and as presidents accept such items in exchange for support of other bills.

The item veto was one of the proposals in the Republicans' Contract with America. In March 1996 Republicans agreed on a "functional equivalent of the line-item veto" by means of legislation rather than amendment (Taylor 1996b, 637). Incorporated into the Line Item Veto Act that went into effect in January 1997, this law allowed presidential rescissions of individual budget items to stand unless Congress disapproved within thirty days. It also contained a "lockbox mechanism" designed to dedicate any savings from the item veto to a reduction of the national debt (Taylor 1996b, 866). The U.S. Supreme Court struck the Line Item Veto Act down in *Clinton v. City of New York* (1998), indicating that if a line-item veto were to be enacted, it would have to be adopted by constitutional amendment. Declines in annual deficits during the Clinton administration may have eroded some of the sentiment on behalf of an item veto amendment, which might, however, be reawakened if deficit spending again becomes common.

See also Congress, Legislative Veto; *Clinton v. City of New York.*

For Further Reading:

Ames, Herman. 1896. *The Proposed Amendments to the Constitution of the United States during the First Century of Its History.* Reprint, New York: Burt Franklin, 1970.

Best, Judith. 1984a. "The Item Veto: Would the Founders Approve?" *Presidential Studies Quarterly* 14 (Spring): 183–188.

Clinton v. City of New York, 524 U.S. 417 (1998).

Cronin, Thomas E., and Jeffrey J. Weill. 1985. "An Item Veto for the President?" *Congress & the Presidency* 12 (Autumn): 127–151.

Denning, Brannon P., and Brooks R. Smith. 1999. "Uneasy Riders: The Case for a Truth-in-Legislation Amendment." *Utah Law Review:* 957–1025.

Ross, Russell M., and Fred Schwengel. 1982. "An Item Veto for the President?" *Presidential Studies Quarterly* 12 (Winter): 66–79.

Sidak, J. Gregory. 1995. "The Line-Item Veto Amendment." *Cornell Law Review* 80 (July): 1498–1505.

Spitzer, Robert J. 1988. *The Presidential Veto: Touchstone of the American Presidency.* Albany: State University of New York Press.

Taylor, Andrew. 1996b. "Republicans Break Logjam on Line-Item Veto Bill." *Congressional Quarterly Weekly Report* 54 (16 March): 687.

❖ PRESIDENCY, VOTE OF NO CONFIDENCE ❖

Unless they are impeached and convicted for constitutionally designated offenses, U.S. presidents serve for fixed terms of office. In American history, only President Richard Nixon has resigned under the threat of impeachment, while Presidents Andrew Johnson and Bill Clinton, although impeached in the House of Representatives, failed to be convicted by the necessary two-thirds majority in the Senate. By contrast, new elections are called in parliamentary systems when parliament votes "no confidence" in the prime minister. Commended for making government responsive to the people, such a mechanism has been proposed as part of a number of plans to rewrite the Constitution. Although his attorney general eventually convinced him that the idea was not feasible, during debates over the League of Nations, Democratic President Woodrow Wilson proposed that senators opposing the plan resign and put themselves up for reelection, with the understanding that if a majority were reelected, Wilson would resign and allow a Republican to assume office (Link 1963, 70–71).

Congressional amending proposals for a vote of "no confidence" in the president have been clustered in two periods—the early 1950s and the early 1970s. Republican Representatives Frederick R. Coudert Jr. of New York and Charles Kersten of Wisconsin and Republican Senator Robert Hendrickson of New Jersey offered the first set of proposals, perhaps in reaction to the fact that the presidency had been occupied by Democrats from 1933 to 1953. Democrat Edith Green of Oregon introduced a resolution in July 1973 (H.J. Res. 666) tied to concerns over President Nixon's abuse of office. It provided that Congress could, by a two-thirds vote of both houses, adopt a resolution stating that the president had failed to execute the laws, had willfully exceeded his powers, or had violated individual rights. In such a case, Congress could call for a new publicly funded election to be held within ninety days. With a view to the situation at hand, Green further specified that such an election would not preclude use of the impeachment procedure.

Democratic Representative Henry Reuss of Wisconsin, who also advocated creation of a separate chief of state and a number of other reforms (Vile 1991c, 119–121), was another supporter of such a mechanism. In 1974 he proposed that a three-fifths vote of both houses of Congress should be able to declare "no confidence" in the president and institute an election within 90 to 110 days. His initial proposal contemplated that the vice president would serve during the interim period, but a subsequent proposal left the president in office during this time and required that all members of Congress also stand for reelection. Reuss's resolution was the subject of deliberation, both in a special law review symposium ("Symposium on the Reuss Resolution" 1975) and in subsequent congressional hearings (*Political Economy and Constitutional Reform* 1982).

Interest in the "no confidence" vote appears to have waned with Nixon's resignation.

For Further Reading:

Link, Arthur S. 1963. *Woodrow Wilson: A Brief Biography*. Cleveland: World.

Political Economy and Constitutional Reform. 1982. Hearings before the Joint Economic Committee of the Congress of the United States. 97th Cong., 2d Sess.

"Symposium on the Reuss Resolution: A Vote of No Confidence in the President." 1975. *George Washington Law Review* 43 (January): 328–500.

Vile, John R. 1991c. *Rewriting the United States Constitution: An Examination of Proposals from Reconstruction to the Present*. New York: Praeger.

❖ PRICE CONTROLS ❖

In 1932 and 1933 at least four amendments were proposed to allow Congress to control prices and prevent profiteering during war. Especially during wartime, power to control prices already appears to have been well established when these amendments were introduced. During World War I, over a dozen federal agencies regulated prices, with the Food and Fuel Administrations having primary control over consumer prices (C. May 1989, 95).

During World War II, the Supreme Court also upheld the Emergency Price Control Act of 1942 in *Yakus v. United States* (1944). At the state level, the Court had already sanctioned New York's regulation of milk prices in *Nebbia v. New York* (1934).

For Further Reading:

May, Christopher N. 1989. *In the Name of War.* Cambridge, MA.: Harvard University Press.

❖ PRIOR STATE REJECTION OF AMENDMENTS ❖

Article V of the Constitution does not specifically address whether a state legislature or convention can ratify an amendment that it has previously rejected. Precedents indicate that this practice is on far firmer ground than a state's power to rescind its ratification of a pending amendment (Edel 1981, 47–48).

One basis on which Kansas's ratification of the proposed child labor amendment was challenged in *Coleman v. Miller* (1939) was that the legislature had previously rejected the amendment. In that decision, although acknowledging "that Article V says nothing of rejection but speaks only of ratifications," the Supreme Court ultimately grounded its refusal to intervene in the matter on the idea that the issue was a political question for Congress to resolve (*Coleman* 1939, 447–450).

Although subsequent cases have called into question the application of the political questions doctrine to some amending issues, it seems doubtful that the Supreme Court would deny a state the right to ratify an amendment it has previously rejected. Without such authority, the Fourteenth Amendment would probably not have been ratified, and the amending process would be even more difficult than it is now. Although never adopted, most proposed legislation on the subject has recognized such a right.

See also *Coleman v. Miller;* Legislation Proposed on Constitutional Conventions; Rescission of Ratification of Pending Amendments.

For Further Reading:

Coleman v. Miller, 307 U.S. 433 (1939).

Edel, Wilbur. 1981. *A Constitutional Convention: Threat or Challenge?* New York: Praeger.

❖ PRIVACY, RIGHT TO ❖

Although the U.S. Constitution does not specifically list a right to privacy, modern Supreme Court decisions have carved out such a right, most notably in *Griswold v. Connecticut* (1965) and in *Roe v. Wade* (1973). Faced in the first decision with a long-standing state law that banned the use or prescription of contraceptives, even for married couples, a court majority led by Justice William O. Douglas decided that the law was an unconstitutional infringement on the right to privacy that, although not directly stated in the Constitution, could be ascertained by the "penumbras," or shadows, cast by provisions of the First Amendment (with its presumption of a right of association), the Third Amendment (limiting the quartering of troops in private residences), the Fourth Amendment (with its protections against "unreasonable searches and seizures"), the Fifth Amendment (with its prohibition against self-incrimination), the Ninth Amendment (with its reference to unspecified rights), and the Fourteenth Amendment (with its reference to due process). Justice Hugo Black registered a strong dissent in this case, acknowledging that, while he enjoyed his own privacy, he did not find a sufficient constitutional basis for the judicial construction of such a right and thought the Court was effectively amending the constitution by relying on such a right.

Griswold v. Connecticut was extended in *Roe v. Wade* when the Supreme Court ruled that the right of privacy was extensive enough to permit a woman and her doctor to choose to terminate her pregnancy, especially during the first two trimesters, or six months. Numerous subsequent decisions have allowed for some state regulations of abortion procedures that do not constitute an "undue burden" on a woman's right to choose this procedure.

In related Fourth Amendment developments that were highlighted in the U.S. Supreme

Court decision in *Katz v. United States* (1967) outlawing warrantless electronic surveillance, Justice John Marshall Harlan articulated a two-part standard that continues to be applied. The test specified that, when ascertaining whether an individual had a right to privacy, the Court would ask whether such an individual had an expectation of privacy and whether that expectation was reasonable.

Although recognizing rights to control over reproduction, the Supreme Court has been hesitant to expand such rights in the absence of firmer constitutional foundations. Thus, in *Bowers v. Hardwick* (1986), the Supreme Court refused in a five-to-four vote to outlaw a Georgia sodomy law that had been applied to two consenting adults engaged in homosexual conduct. However, this decision has arguably been undercut by another opinion in *Romer v. Evans* (1996) in which a Colorado state amendment prohibiting laws protecting homosexuals was voided. In *Cruzan v. Missouri Department of Health* (1990) and companion cases in *Washington v. Glucksberg* and *Vacco v. Quill* (1997), the Supreme Court has refused to recognize a "constitutional right to die," especially when such a "right" would imply an "obligation" on the part of medical personnel to prescribe lethal doses of medication.

A number of state constitutions have specific provisions that acknowledge a right to privacy and a number of proposed new constitutions for the United States contain similar provisions. These often include specific language regarding abortion, the right to die, or private sexual conduct between consenting adults (in addition, in recent years, many state courts and legislatures have voided or repealed laws on the subject). Issues of privacy are likely to remain subjects for proposed amendments not only as disputes continue between prolife and prochoice forces but also as medical and other forms of technology lead into new frontiers.

See also Abortion; Black, Hugo Lafayette; *Griswold v. Connecticut;* Right to Life; *Roe v. Wade.*

❖ PROGRESS AND THE AMENDING PROCESS ❖

The constitutional amending process is a means of correcting errors in the existing constitutional structure and of adapting to new and unforeseen circumstances. However, it also presents the possibility of incorporating new ideas and even new rights into the Constitution. Throughout much of human history, the emphasis within law has been on stability rather than progress. A historian has noted that "[d]uring most of history, people were more impressed by the destructive effects of time than by the good things it held in store" (Lasch 1995, 546). Many early notions of history were cyclical. Periods of progress would be followed by periods of decline, and the cycle would repeat itself again.

Although not completely unique, the Christian perspective tends to view time in a more linear fashion. In particular, Christians believe that God revealed himself more clearly in the New Testament than he had in the Old, and there was a still better world to follow. Although most Christians understand that ultimate progress awaits another world, the idea of such progress has taken on secular (and sometimes even utopian) overtones, especially during the Enlightenment period during which the U.S. Constitution was written. This notion was further secularized when ideas of Darwinian biological evolution were applied to political and social structures. Progress was especially associated with the idea of increased human freedom (Nisbet 1980, 179–236), although it was often balanced with a darker view linking it to increased power to bring about totalitarian visions of new societies (Nisbet 1980, 237–296).

In allowing Congress to provide for copyright and patent protection, Article I, Section 8 of the Constitution refers specifically to "the Progress of Science and useful Arts." Although this is the only specific reference to progress in the document, the constitutional amending process provides a means through which progress may be incorporated into the Constitution. In recognition that majorities in favor of a particular constitutional reform could prove to be mistaken or ephemeral, this process requires supermajorities at both the proposal and ratification stages. Although making such written reforms difficult to initiate, the amending mechanism also assures that, once incorporated into the text, they will also be quite difficult to repeal.

Thomas Jefferson was among those who argued that, with increased knowledge and experience, it was foolish to be permanently bound by ancient constitutions, so much so that his friend James Madison had to temper Jefferson's view that each generation should write its own constitution. Many proposals for new constitutions have similarly been predicated on the idea that new forms of government are needed either to respond to, or to initiate, greater progress. The idea of progress is often tied to economic growth, and constitutions predicated on releasing new human energies are often based on ideas of removing governmental regulations that are viewed as obstacles to further economic development. Similarly, many proposals for more direct forms of democracy are based either on the assumption that more widespread education, or more modern forms of communication and other forms of technology, have made such direct citizen participation more feasible and less dangerous than in the past.

It is not uncommon to describe the history of the constitutional amending process in America in progressive terms. Alan Grimes's *Democracy and the Amendments to the Constitution* (1978) is a good example. Certainly, the amending process has allowed for the wide expansion of suffrage and democracy as well as for increased guarantees of civil liberties, especially in the Bill of Rights (and its subsequent application to state governments) and the adoption of the Thirteenth Amendment eliminating slavery and the Fourteenth Amendment expanding the rights of citizenship. It is not surprising that a number of democratizing amendments were specifically associated with the Progressive Era in American history and that other mechanisms from this period like the initiative, referendum, and recall continue to be proposed. To date, the only serious restriction on civil liberties to be added to the U.S. Constitution by amendment,

namely national alcoholic prohibition, has been repealed (see the Eighteenth and Twenty-first Amendments).

This rosy view of constitutional progress may mask less savory extraconstitutional developments like increases in wars and other forms of violence, increased overcrowding, environmental degradation, family disintegration, moral degeneration, or even increased feelings of spiritual emptiness. Although many of these problems may not be amenable to constitutional solution, the constitutional amending process remains a viable mechanism for incorporating newly discovered or better appreciated rights and advanced procedural mechanisms into the constitutional text.

See also Amendment, Definition; Democracy and Constitutional Amendments.

For Further Reading:
Grimes, Alan P. 1978. *Democracy and the Amendments to the Constitution.* Lexington, MA: Lexington Books.

Lasch, Christopher. 1995. "Progress." *A Companion to American Thought,* eds. Richard Wightman Fox and James T. Kloppenberg. Malden, MA: Blackwell Publishers.

Nisbet, Robert. 1980. *The Idea of Progress.* New York: Basic Books.

❖ PROGRESSIVE ERA ❖

Amendments have not been adopted at a uniform pace in U.S. history but have tended to be adopted in clusters. The Bill of Rights was adopted as a unit, three amendments were ratified in the five years that followed the end of the Civil War, and four more were adopted from 1913 to 1920.

This latter period corresponds roughly with the end of the Progressive Era, a time during which reformist sentiments were strong and reformers were optimistic about their ability to solve social problems (Ekirch 1974; Gould 1974; Link and McCormick 1983). Prominent Progressives included Herbert Croly, Theodore Roosevelt, and—to a lesser degree—Woodrow Wilson.

Many Progressives, undoubtedly influenced by the long hiatus of the amending process, started out with fairly critical views of the U.S. Constitution and its possibility for change. Progressives were also especially critical of the political party system—with its bosses, patronage, and vote buying—that had developed in the wake of Jacksonian politics. Progressives wanted to transfer power from the parties to the people, but this desire was combined with the desire to elevate and reform individuals as well.

The four amendments ratified from 1913 to 1920 illumine different aspects of Progressive thought. The Sixteenth Amendment, which legalized the income tax, is, in a sense, the foundation of the powers of the modern national government. Without this or an equivalent revenue source, the national government simply could not take on all its modern functions. The fact that this tax can also be made progressive, so that it takes a higher percentage of the income of the rich than of the poor, means that it has the ability to redistribute income, the disparities of which concerned Progressive reformers.

The Seventeenth Amendment, providing for the direct election of senators, was a strike at the party politics that had dominated senatorial selection in the state legislatures, as well as a more direct expression of the voice of the people. The Eighteenth Amendment, providing for national alcoholic prohibition, seems more problematic, especially in retrospect, but it was tied to Progressive strands of Protestant moralism (often directed against Catholic immigrants, who generally had more tolerant attitudes toward alcohol consumption) and to a desire to combat a genuine social evil. Finally, the Nineteenth Amendment capped more than half a century of reform efforts on behalf of women's suffrage, which many believed would not only promote fairness but also serve to bring women's elevated moral sensibilities to bear at the ballot box.

In addition to these amendments, Progressive leaders advocated numerous other reforms, many of which still influence U.S. politics. These include the direct primary; the initiative, referendum, and recall (also closely associated with midwestern Populism, with at least indi-

rect ties to Progressivism); compulsory schooling; and such economic reforms as antitrust measures, protections against child labor, maximum-hours legislation, and minimum wages (Eisenach 1994, 8–9). Although it was adopted later, the Twentieth Amendment, limiting the terms of "lame-duck" representatives and presidents, and introduced by Progressive Senator George Norris, was also a product of sentiments that grew out of the Progressive Era.

For Further Reading:

Eisenach, Eldon J. 1994. *The Lost Promise of Progressivism.* Lawrence, KS: University Press of Kansas.

Ekirch, Arthur A., Jr. 1974. *Progressivism in America: A Study of the Era from Theodore Roosevelt to Woodrow Wilson.* New York: New Viewpoints.

Gould, Lewis L., ed. 1974. *The Progressive Era.* Syracuse, NY: Syracuse University Press.

Link, Arthur S., and Richard L. McCormick. 1983. *Progressivism.* Arlington Heights, IL: Harlan Davidson.

❖ PROMULGATION OF AMENDMENTS ❖

In *Coleman v. Miller* (1939) the Supreme Court indicated that most issues surrounding the constitutional amending process were "political questions" for Congress to resolve. In so ruling, the Court appears to have been influenced in large part by the actions of the Reconstruction Congress regarding the dispute as to whether the Fourteenth Amendment had been ratified. The situation was a messy one, but on that occasion, faced with attempts by Ohio and New Jersey to rescind their ratifications of the amendment, Congress adopted a joint resolution counting those states in the final total and stating that the Fourteenth Amendment was "hereby declared to be a part of the Constitution of the United States, and it shall be duly promulgated by the Secretary of State" (quoted in Dellinger 1983, 397). More recently, Congress adopted a similar resolution declaring that the Twenty-seventh Amendment had been ratified. There was good reason for taking such action as the amendment, which had originally been proposed as part of the Bill of Rights, was not ratified by the requisite number of states until 1992.

Article V of the Constitution makes no mention of the need for congressional promulgation of amendments. Moreover, the Supreme Court's decision in *Dillon v. Gloss* (1921) indicated that amendments become part of the law of the land when ratified by the necessary number of states rather than when acknowledged, or promulgated, by the secretary of state, or, in later practice, the administrator of the General Services Administration or the archivist of the Library of Congress.

Law professor Walter Dellinger has argued that congressional promulgation can neither add to nor detract from the legitimacy of an amendment. Believing that such a mechanism is likely to be "an unwieldy, uncertain and unpredictable mechanism for resolving amendment disputes" (Dellinger 1983, 392), he thinks that such matters can better be resolved through the exercise of judicial review.

For Further Reading:

Dellinger, Walter. 1983. "The Legitimacy of Constitutional Change: Rethinking the Amending Process." *Harvard Law Review* 97 (December): 380–432.

❖ PROPER GOVERNMENT ❖

Proposals for constitutional change often come from unexpected places. Increasingly, the Internet is one source of proposals. In 1998 a site was established under the title of "Proper Government," with four proposals (although recent updates suggest that the project was first constructed in 1981 or 1982), and it has continued to grow into a site of well over 100 pages (see *http://www.ebtx.com*). The author was not identified on the original site and remains anonymous. Self-described as "an intellectual pig," who "will investigate anything no matter how common, bizarre or crude," he (deprecatory remarks about women on the site indicate that the author is a man) lists his "immediate goals" as attempting to "figure out the universe; fix the world, conquer life; and think & do & run & jump & play." The site contin-

ues to change and includes e-mail messages, many of which appear to question the sanity of the author of the site.

The four central reform proposals offered by the author of "Proper Government" appear under the title of "The New Proposed Constitution" and are, to say the least, unusual. The first proposal is likely to be the most unpopular. It calls for limiting the right to vote (or at least the right to votes that count; he seems to have no problem with advisory votes) to men and would therefore reverse the Nineteenth Amendment. Perhaps to counter problems with representative government, the author's second main proposal would require that each individual would have to vote for a "personal acquaintance." Votes would be cast by computer and aggregated with individuals getting the highest votes, and in any event no "less than twice the votes of any of his electors," selected as representatives. The third plank of this plan calls for paying representatives on the basis of how many votes they captured. A president winning 100 million votes could thus earn $2 billion, thus presumably shielding him from the possibility of bribery. The fourth plank of the plan would allow votes collectively to decide by what percentage taxes would go up or down each year. Through a point system, voters would also determine how tax dollars would be distributed.

Guided largely by libertarian ideals, the author believes that "[t]he goal of law must be to preserve the autonomy of the individual" and that "no individual can be punished for NOT performing an action." This would exempt individuals from being required to file tax returns, serve in the military, or buy insurance. The author expresses disdain for the income tax and for welfare programs. Although advocating the formation of an online "American Party," he favors nonparticipation and disrespect for existing governmental officials in the meantime. Believing that a second civil war is inevitable, his advice to "[a]rm yourselves as heavily as possible" is qualified: citizens should be armed "with a purpose and a plan."

The plan for "Proper Government" demonstrates both the strength and weakness of the Internet in advancing ideas for constitutional change. The Internet serves as a platform for points of view that might not otherwise be aired, but it can also serve to insulate anonymous authors from scholarly reviews and criticisms that they might receive were their views to be published in more traditional printed forms.

For Further Reading:
"Proper Government," *http://www.ebtx.com.* Last accessed 5/17/02.

Vile, John R. 2003b. "Proposals for a New Constitution: The Last Decade of the Twentieth Century." Forthcoming in Vol. 13, *Journal of Contemporary Thought.*

❖ PROPOSAL OF AMENDMENTS ❖

Article V of the Constitution divides the amending process into two steps, proposal and ratification. Although more controversies have arisen with regard to the ratification of amendments than their proposal, both areas have been fields for controversy.

Whereas ratification requires approval by three-fourths of the states, the Constitution requires that amendments be proposed by two-thirds majorities of both houses of Congress or by a convention called by Congress when it receives petitions from two-thirds of the states. However, perhaps because American parties are relatively decentralized and there is relatively little party discipline by comparison to the legislative bodies in other democratic nations, the mechanisms for proposing amendments have been greater obstacles to the adoption of new amendments than have the proposals for ratification (Ferreres-Comella 2000, 48). Thus, states have ratified twenty-seven of thirty-three amendments proposed by Congress.

In the *National Prohibition Cases* (1920), the Supreme Court declared that when Congress proposed an amendment by the requisite two-thirds majorities, there was no need for it to adopt a separate resolution stating its judgment that such an amendment was necessary. In the same decision, the Court decided that the required two-thirds majority vote "is a vote of two-thirds of the members present—assum-

ing the presence of a quorum—and not a vote of two-thirds of the entire membership, present and absent" (1920, 386). On at least some occasions, such majorities have been ascertained by voice vote rather than by roll call.

The most controversial issue involving the proposal of amendments centers on the still untried Article V mechanism for a convention to propose amendments, which Congress is supposed to call after two-thirds of the state legislatures petition it to do so. As is the case with the ratification of amendments, the Constitution does not specify how contemporaneous such applications must be; it also does not specify whether such calls have to center on the same topic.

Some scholars argue that the states can call for only a general convention and that other calls are invalid (C. Black 1979; Dellinger 1979). Others scholars believe that states may call a convention on a single topic or subject area (Rees 1986; Van Alstyne 1978; for discussion of this issue, see Vile 1993a, 54–73). Some scholars argue that, based on the nature of petitions it has received, Congress is already bound to call such a convention (Paulsen 1993, 1995; Van Sickle and Boughey 1990). Absent some catalytic event, it seems unlikely that this view will prevail.

See also Constitutional Conventions; *National Prohibition Cases.*

For Further Reading:
Black, Charles L., Jr. 1979. "Amendment by a National Constitutional Convention: A Letter to a Senator." *Oklahoma Law Review* 32: 626–644.

Dellinger, Walter. 1979. "The Recurring Question of the 'Limited' Constitutional Convention." *Yale Law Journal* 88: 1623–1640.

Ferreres-Comella, Victor. 2000. "A Defense of Constitutional Rigidity." In *Analysis and Right,* ed. Paul Comanducci and Riccardo Guastine. Turin, Italy: G. Biappichelli Publisher.

Paulsen, Michael S. 1995. "The Case for a Constitutional Convention." *Wall Street Journal* 3, May, A-15.

———. 1993. "A General Theory of Article V: The Constitutional Issues of the Twenty-seventh Amendment." *Yale Law Journal* 103: 677–789.

National Prohibition Cases, 253 U.S. 350 (1920).

Rees, Grover, III. 1986. "The Amendment Process and Limited Constitutional Conventions." *Benchmark* 2: 67–108.

Van Alstyne, William. 1978. "Does Article V Restrict the States to Calling Unlimited Conventions Only?—A Letter to a Colleague." *Duke Law Journal* 1978 (January): 1295–1306.

Van Sickle, Bruce M., and Lynn M. Boughey. 1990. "Lawful and Peaceful Revolution: Article V and Congress' Present Duty to Call a Convention for Proposing Amendments." *Hamline Law Review* 14 (Fall): 1–115.

Vile, John R. 1993b. *Contemporary Questions Surrounding the Constitutional Amending Process.* Westport, CT: Praeger.

❖ PROPOSED AMENDMENTS THAT FAILED ❖

See Failed Amendments.

❖ PUBLIC OPINION AND THE AMENDING PROCESS ❖

The preamble to the U.S. Constitution begins with the words "We the People," and Americans pride themselves on living in a democracy. However, as James Madison argued in *Federalist No. 10,* the system created by the Constitution is a system of republican, or representative, rather than direct democracy, and it falls short of true democracy in many respects. Although it is difficult to gauge public opinion at the time with any precision, the U.S. Constitution did not go into effect in any state until it was approved by a popular convention there, and subsequent states cast similar votes before deciding whether to join the Union. Article VII specified that the Constitution would not go into effect until ratified by nine or more of the thirteen states, and subsequent amendments have all been adopted by two-thirds majorities in both houses of Congress and three-fourths of the states. Amendments have been ratified as early as 1791 (the Bill of Rights) and as late as 1992 (the Twenty-seventh Amendment).

As in the case of the original Constitution, new amendments call for supermajorities rather than for mere majorities, although because of differential state populations and federalism, it is possible to imagine scenarios both in which amendments favored by majorities are not adopted and scenarios in which amendments are proposed and/or ratified with less than majority support. The fact that the Eighteenth Amendment providing for national alcoholic prohibition is the only one specifically to have been repealed (by the Twenty-first Amendment) is probably testimony not only to the difficulty of the amending process, but also to the fact that, hypotheticals aside, few amendments can pass through the current amending gauntlet without a solid majority of the people supporting them.

Unlike a number of its states, the United States has not adopted a mechanism whereby the people can propose or ratify constitutional amendments directly. Some scholars have proposed altering the Constitution so as to allow for national initiatives and referendums. Akhil Reed Amar (1994) has argued that such a power exists even without direct constitutional language providing for its support. Moreover, Bruce Ackerman (1991) argues that public opinion might be expressed in certain "constitutional moments" (as, for example, during the New Deal period) that are incorporated into constitutional understandings without necessarily being incorporated into the constitutional text. Such understandings would appear to be less stable than those that are incorporated specifically into constitutional language.

The current amending process is designed to promote deliberation and stability. At least during certain periods, large majorities of the people have clearly supported proposals—like prayer in schools, electoral college reform, or an amendment to prohibit flag desecration—that were not adopted as national amendments. In some cases, reforms can be carried out within individual states that do not require amendments of the national constitution. Still, most amendments that have been ratified have promoted greater democracy and an expansion of civil rights and liberties, and it would be difficult to identify a constitutional amendment that has been adopted and that remains in effect that would currently be disfavored by a majority of the people.

As fundamental law, most Americans probably understand that the Constitution is not intended to embody the latest public sentiment on every issue. The government takes no official notice of public opinion polls as such, and even elections are imperfect measures of public opinion. The First Amendment does guarantee that individuals can express their views on the desirability or undesirability of constitutional amendments, just as they can on other matters. If the system is properly functioning, existing constitutional amending mechanisms should, at least over time, reflect consistent thoughtful majority opinion with nationwide support as to what the Constitution should include and what it should not.

See also Deliberation and the Amending Process; Democracy and Constitutional Amendments; Federalism and the Amending Process; Initiative and Referendum; Supermajorities.

For Further Reading:
Ackerman, Bruce. 1991. *We the People: Foundations.* Cambridge, MA: Belknap.

Amar, Akhil Reed. 1994. "The Consent of the Governed: Constitutional Amendment outside Article V." *Columbia Law Review* 94 (March): 457–508.

Cushman, Barry. 2002. "Mr. Dooley and Mr. Gallup: Public Opinion and Constitutional Change in the 1930s." *Buffalo Law Review* 50 (Winter): 7–101.

❖ PUERTO RICO, REPRESENTATION IN ELECTORAL COLLEGE ❖

In 1961 the states ratified the Twenty-third Amendment granting the District of Columbia representation in the electoral college equivalent to that of the least populous state—presently three votes. In the two years that followed, representatives from New York, Texas, and New Mexico, all states with sizable Hispanic populations, introduced amendments to grant similar representation for Puerto Rico, a U.S. commonwealth acquired from Spain in the Spanish-American War of 1898.

The commonwealth now holds presidential primaries and sends delegates to both major party conventions. It remains unrepresented, however, in the electoral college. Either the adoption of a constitutional amendment like the Twenty-third giving electoral votes to the District of Columbia, or Puerto Rico's admission as a state, a long-discussed option (Melendez 1988), appears to be a prerequisite to such representation. However, the allocation of electoral votes under the Twenty-third Amendment for the District of Columbia (that of the smallest state, or three votes) would arguably be inadequate for a jurisdiction with more than six times its population. With or without such representation in the electoral college for Puerto Rico, American Hispanics are exerting increased influence on American politics. Hispanic support appears to have been one of the reasons for George Bush's ultimate success in the state of Florida, and, consequently, in the electoral college, in the presidential election of 2000.

See Voting Rights, Constitutional Amendments Relating to.

For Further Reading:
Melendez, Edgardo. 1988. *Puerto Rico's Statehood Movement.* New York: Greenwood Press.

R

❖

❖ RATIFICATION OF AMENDMENTS ❖

Article V of the Constitution specifies the manner in which amendments are proposed and ratified. After being proposed either by the necessary congressional majorities or by a special convention, they become part of the Constitution "when ratified by the Legislatures of three fourths of the several States, or by Conventions in three fourths thereof, as the one or the other Mode of Ratification may be proposed by the Congress." Acknowledging the difficulty of amendment, one author noted that "ratification isn't beanbag" (Vose 1979, 113). Yet to date the states have failed to ratify only six of thirty-three amendments that Congress has submitted to them. State legislatures ratified twenty-six amendments; special state conventions ratified the Twenty-first Amendment. Congress specified this form of ratification within the Twenty-first Amendment; in the other three times that Congress has specified the mode of ratification within an amendment (the Eighteenth, Twentieth, and Twenty-second Amendments) rather than in accompanying legislation, it provided for state legislative ratification.

Although ratification by state constitutional conventions would appear to be more democratic than ratification by state legislative delegations (whose members are often chosen for their positions on issues other than their approval or disapproval of pending amendments), a recent study has pointed to serious flaws in the ratification of the Twenty-first Amend-

ment, which repealed national alcoholic prohibition. This study notes that the off-year elections had low voter turnouts; selection by at-large, rather than single-member, districts greatly exaggerated popular approval of the amendment; and the conventions engaged in little deliberation. Only in Indiana does there appear to have been any real deliberation at the convention, and in New Hampshire, delegates voted for repeal and adjourned within seventeen minutes (Schaller 1998)!

A number of legal questions have arisen concerning the process of ratification. In an early case, *Hollingsworth v. Virginia* (1798), the Supreme Court decided that the president's signature was not required for amendment ratifications. In *Hawke v. Smith* (1920), it subsequently decided that a state could not require such amendments to be approved by referendum. Although the Supreme Court later ruled in *Kimble v. Swackhamer* (1978) that a nonbinding referendum to ascertain state sentiment was not unconstitutional, in *Cook v. Gralike* (2001) it prohibited states from instructing legislators as to how they should vote on amendments or making negative notations on ballots of those who did not follow the state's will. In *Dillon v. Gloss* (1921), the Court declared that ratification must be soon enough after Congress has proposed an amendment to reflect a contemporary consensus of the states; it also held that such ratification was complete on the date that the last of the necessary number of states approved rather than on the date that the secretary of state declared such ratification complete. In *United States v. Sprague* (1931), the Supreme Court affirmed that Congress had the responsibility of designating which of the two modes specified in the Constitution the states would follow when ratifying an amendment.

Coleman v. Miller (1939) subsequently raised additional issues, including whether prior rejection of an amendment precluded subsequent ratification, whether a state's lieutenant governor could cast a tie-breaking vote in the state legislature in favor of an amendment, and whether a state's ratification had been made within a reasonable length of time. In this case, the Court declared that it was "equally divided" on the issue of the lieutenant governor's veto and decided that the other issues were "political questions" for Congress to resolve.

The Equal Rights Amendment subsequently brought renewed attention to ratification issues. A lower court case, *Dyer v. Blair* (1975), raised the issue of whether a state could require the ratification of amendments by supermajority—in this case, a three-fifths vote. Future Supreme Court Justice John Paul Stevens ruled that this issue was justiciable and that the state ratifying bodies should ascertain the majority that would be required; he did, however, rule that any requirements found in a state's constitution on the subject were invalid.

Another district court decision in *Idaho v. Freeman* (1981) also focused on the proposed Equal Rights Amendment. At issue was a state's right to rescind ratification of an amendment that had not yet been ratified by the necessary three-fourths of the states. Also at issue was the right of Congress to extend the ratification deadline. Like the issues that Stevens had examined, these issues were deemed justiciable by the district judge. Working from the principle of contemporary consensus, the judge declared that a state should be able to rescind ratification of a pending amendment. He further argued that Congress had no power to extend the original deadline for the Equal Rights Amendment, and even if it did, such action would require a two-thirds vote of both houses (Vile 1993b, 49–51). This decision became moot when the Equal Rights Amendment failed to be adopted. A seemingly surefire way to avoid future controversies over ratification

deadlines is to include them within the text of proposed amendments (as was done in the case of the Eighteenth, Twentieth, Twenty-first, and Twenty-second Amendments), where they will be self-executing (Dellinger 1983, 409).

The proposal that putatively became the Twenty-seventh Amendment did not have such a deadline. Considerable controversy was generated by the decision of the national archivist—subsequently affirmed by Congress—to accept this amendment that was originally proposed in 1789 but not ratified by the necessary majority of states until 1992. The Twenty-seventh Amendment, like the previous ones, had to be ratified by three-fourths of the states in existence at the time of ratification, rather than at the time the amendment was proposed (see Silversmith 1999, 595–597).

For Further Reading:

Dellinger, Walter. 1983. "The Legitimacy of Constitutional Change: Rethinking the Amending Process." *Harvard Law Review* 97 (December): 380–432.

Schaller, Thomas F. 1998. "Democracy at Rest: Strategic Ratification of the Twenty-First Amendment," *Publius: The Journal of Federalism* 28 (Spring): 81–97.

Silversmith, Jol A. 1999. "The 'Missing Thirteenth Amendment': Constitutional Nonsense and Titles of Nobility." *Southern California Interdisciplinary Law Journal* 8 (Spring): 577–611.

Vile, John R. 1993b. *The Theory and Practice of Constitutional Change in America: A Collection of Original Source Materials.* New York: Peter Lang.

Vose, Clement E. 1979. "When District of Columbia Representation Collides with the Constitutional Amendment Institution." *Publius: The Journal of Federalism* 9 (Winter): 105–125.

❖ RATIFICATION OF THE EXISTING U.S. AND/OR FUTURE U.S. CONSTITUTIONS ❖

The Articles of Confederation provided that Congress would propose amendments and that they would have to be unanimously ratified by the state legislatures. This process was so difficult that no amendments were adopted during the duration of the Articles. Moreover, the process would presumably have become even more difficult had other states joined. When the delegates gathered at the U.S. Constitutional Convention in Philadelphia, they ultimately decided to pursue a new form of government rather than attempting to build on existing foundations. The result was a Congress with substantially greater powers, as well as a government of three coordinate branches that embodied checks and balances that were missing under the Articles.

The state of Rhode Island never sent delegates to the Constitutional Convention, making the prospect of immediate ratification of the new document quite unlikely indeed; moreover, there was intense opposition to the new Constitution by Anti-Federalists in many states. Not only did delegates to the convention reasonably fear that existing state legislators might be reluctant to give up powers to the new national government, but they also hoped that the new Constitution purporting to represent "We the People" might be put on firmer ground than would likely be provided by mere legislative ratification. The delegates addressed both concerns by providing in Article VII of the new document that it would go into effect with "the Ratification of the Conventions of nine States."

The ninth state to ratify was New Hampshire, which did so on 21 June 1788. But, because of the size and population of Virginia and New York, the fate of the new Union was still not secure until these states joined somewhat later. The first Congress under the new system did not meet until 4 March 1789, and the president was not sworn in until 30 April 1789. In *Owings v. Speed* (1820), Chief Justice John Marshall ruled that the Constitution did not become effective until the first Congress met, but two recent scholars have suggested that some provisions of the new document were self-executing and should be considered to have gone into effect on 21 June 1788, with others going into effect at various subsequent dates (Lawson and Seidman 2001).

Debates over the U.S. Constitution produced *The Federalist Papers,* which are still considered to be among the best sources for understanding that document; they were written by Alexander Hamilton, James Madison, and John Jay. Anti-Federalists also produced notable tracts. One of the results of the intense debate surrounding the document was that key Federalists (most notably James Madison) understood that a bill of rights would have to be adopted to ease public fears about the power of the new central government. The first ten amendments were subsequently composed and proposed in the first Congress by Madison and his colleagues. Had there been no process for introducing such amendments, the fate of the new constitution might have been very much at risk.

Although the contest between Federalists and Anti-Federalists was often bitter at the state conventions (see Gillespie and Lienesch 1989), fortunately for the new Constitution, the states that initially ratified included large states like Virginia, New York, and Massachusetts, and others (like North Carolina and Rhode Island) joined relatively quickly after the new government was established. In any event, although the Articles of Confederation had been effectively dissolved, states were not bound to the new government until they consented to it.

Were a new constitution to be formulated today, it is possible that it might also seek to bypass existing requirements in Article V for constitutional amendment. If Article V were followed, amendments proposed through the unused Article V convention mechanism would continue to require ratification of three-fourths of the state legislatures or of specially called state conventions (as happened in the case of the Twenty-first Amendment repealing national alcoholic prohibition), but fears continue to linger about what a "runaway" convention might propose and, perhaps, about how it might seek to have its proposals ratified. Given advances in technology and increased clamor for forms of direct democracy like the initiative and referendum, it is quite possible that proponents of a new constitution might well seek to have it affirmed either by a majority, or perhaps a supermajority, of the voters. Despite the failure of the current Constitution to specify any such mechanism, a number of scholars are currently on record as believing that popular electoral majorities already have the inherent authority both to initiate and ratify amendments in this manner.

See also Articles of Confederation; Constitutional Convention of 1787; Ratification of Amendments.

For Further Reading:
Gillespie, Michael L., and Michael Lienesch, eds. 1989. *Ratifying the Constitution*. Lawrence, KS: University Press of Kansas.

Lawson, Gary, and Guy Seidman. 2001. "When Did the Constitution Become Law?" *Notre Dame Law Review* 77 (November): 1–37.

Utley, Robert L., Jr., and Patricia B. Gray. 1989. *Principles of the Constitutional Order: The Ratification Debates*. Lanham, MD: University Press of America.

❖ RECALL ❖

See Congress, Recall of Members; Judiciary, Removal of Members; Presidency, Vote of No Confidence.

❖ REFERENDUM ❖

See Initiative and Referendum.

❖ REID V. COVERT (1957) ❖

This case set aside the convictions by courts-martial of Clarice Covert and Dorothy Smith, wives of U.S. military personnel stationed overseas who had killed their husbands. The courts-martial had been held under putative authority of executive agreements that had been reached with the nations involved.

Writing for Chief Justice Earl Warren and for Justices William O. Douglas, William Brennan, and himself, Justice Hugo Black ruled that provisions of the Bill of Rights—including Fifth and Sixth Amendment guarantees of grand jury indictment and trial by a petit jury—applied to U.S. citizens abroad. Black argued that "no

agreement with a foreign nation can confer power on Congress, or on any other branch of Government, which is free from the restraints of the Constitution" and that allowing agreements with foreign governments to override the Constitution would be to "permit amendment of that document in a manner not sanctioned by Article V" (*Reid* 1957, 16–17).

Although Black denied that his decision was in conflict with *Missouri v. Holland* (1920), his opinion helped ease fears that that case had raised. In easing such fears, the *Reid* decision may well have undercut support for the Bricker Amendment, designed to limit the scope of federal treaties.

More recent attention appears to have shifted to whether the United States has ceded some of its sovereignty to international trade organizations, membership in which is sometimes approved by majority vote in both houses of Congress rather than by the two-thirds majority required in the Senate under the Constitution for approval of treaties.

See also Bricker Amendment; *Missouri v. Holland*.

For Further Reading:
Reid v. Covert, 354 U.S. 1 (1957).

❖ RELEVANCE OF CONSTITUTIONAL AMENDMENTS ❖

Although amendments are the constitutionally prescribed means for adding language to the written Constitution, changes in understanding of that document may also be brought about through judicial interpretations, through changes in social customs, through the development of extraconstitutional institutions like presidential nominating conventions and political parties (somewhat recognized by the changes the Twelfth Amendment made in the electoral college), and through presidential and congressional practices. Although this has long been known, if not always celebrated, most scholars of the subject have still understood constitutional amendments to be a dynamic part, if not the driving force, in this mix.

By contrast, Davis A. Strauss, a Chicago law professor, has recently advanced the provocative thesis that constitutional amendments are essentially irrelevant, at least in what he calls "a mature democratic society," like the United States is today (Strauss 2001, 1460). This reservation may be significant in that it essentially allows Strauss to exclude the effect of the Bill of Rights (the first ten amendments, which were adopted just as the nation was getting established) from his analysis, as well as any effect that the presence of an amending process may have initially had in leading to acceptance of that document. Still, Strauss's thesis is bold, and it certainly poses a challenge to those who consider the process to be important.

Strauss advances four main arguments:

> First . . . sometimes matters addressed by the Constitution change even though the text of the Constitution is unchanged. Second, and more dramatically, some constitutional changes occur even though amendments that would have brought about those very changes are explicitly rejected. Third, when amendments are adopted, they often do no more than ratify changes that have already taken place in society without the help of an amendment. The changes produce the amendment, rather than the other way around. Fourth, when amendments are adopted even though society has not changed, the amendments are systematically evaded. They end up having little effect until society catches up with the ambitions of the amendment. (Strauss 2001, 1459)

Strauss acknowledges that amendments serve "certain ancillary functions," among which he lists the role of "establishing 'rules of the road'" by "settling matters that are not themselves controversial but that must be settled clearly, one way or another" (Strauss 2001, 1461). He also believes that amendments serve "the distinct function of suppressing outliers," often turning "all-but-unanimity into unanimity" (*Id.*, 1461).

Professors Brannon Denning and John Vile have acknowledged some of the points that Strauss has made, while arguing that he has dramatically overstated his argument. They believe that Strauss has minimized the "settling function" that amendments perform as well as the role of amendments in suppressing outliers—it is important (especially to the women involved) that all states, and not simply 90 percent, allow women to vote. Denning and Vile argue that some changes that have been brought about in the absence of amendments that were not adopted may nonetheless have been hastened by such proposals, if not directly attributable to them. Moreover, even "premature" amendments (like the Fifteenth Amendment, which sought to deny discrimination against voters on the basis of race) may ultimately succeed in a way that they would not have been able to do in the absence of a specific text.

Denning and Vile further argue that amendments serve several discrete functions that Strauss does not adequately appreciate. These include the "corrective function" in remedying constitutional defects that become apparent over time; a "checking function" allowing for checks on U.S. Supreme Court decisions (at least four amendments have overturned such decisions); the function of providing an alternative to violence and thus "domesticating revolution"; the function of "legitimization" of changes that are incorporated into formal amendments; and the function of giving "publicity" to those changes that are so incorporated (Denning and Vile 2002–2003). Denning and Vile are further concerned that dismissing the importance of the written guarantees in formal amendments could lead to the erosion of constitutional guarantees found in parts of the original written text.

In another recent article, Yale law professor Reva B. Siegel has argued that Strauss's argument underestimates the role that the movement for women's rights, and the accompanying Nineteenth Amendment prohibiting discrimination in voting on the basis of gender, has had on American constitutional understandings (Siegel 2001).

For Further Reading:

Denning, Brannon P., and John R. Vile. 2002. "The Relevance of Constitutional Amendments: A

Response to David Strauss." *Tulane Law Review* 77 (November): 247–282.

Siegel, Reva B. 2001. "Gender and the Constitution from a Social Movement Perspective," *University of Pennsylvania Law Review* 150 (November): 297–351.

Strauss, David A. 2001. "Commentary: The Irrelevance of Constitutional Amendments," *Harvard Law Review* 114: (March): 1457–1505.

❖ RELIGIOUS EQUALITY AMENDMENT ❖

For decades, members of some religious groups have complained that they have been treated unfairly. They believe that, in attempting to enforce the First Amendment's prohibition against an establishment of religion, courts and other governmental agencies have often denied the legitimate free exercise and free speech rights of those with strong religious beliefs (Reed 1995, 1–12; but see Folton 1996).

In *Employment Division v. Smith* (1990), the Supreme Court denied unemployment compensation to state employees who had been fired from their jobs for ingesting peyote as part of their Native American religious practice. In so doing, the Court apparently abandoned the strict scrutiny it had previously extended to laws impinging on free exercise rights. Although this decision was blunted by subsequent adoption of the Religious Freedom Restoration Act (Vile 1994a, 61), concerns were renewed with the federal court of appeals decision in *Rosenberger v. Rector and Visitors of the University of Virginia* (1994). This ruling upheld the University of Virginia's decision to deny expenditure of student activity fee funds to an evangelical Christian publication while funding similar publications that did not have such an evangelical orientation. Although the Supreme Court overturned this ruling in 1995 and decided that the university could not deny funding to a group simply because it was religious, concerns remained that the free exercise clause of the First Amendment was not being fully honored. These concerns led to a number of individuals to advocate a Religious Equality Amendment (Casey 1995; Goodstein 1995).

In November 1995 two Republicans introduced separate amending resolutions in Congress. Representative Henry Hyde of Illinois proposed in H.J. Res. 121 that

> neither the United states nor any state shall deny benefits to or otherwise discriminate against any private person or group on account of religious expression, belief, or identity; nor shall the prohibition on laws respecting an establishment of religion be construed to require such discrimination.

In contrast to Hyde's proposal, the proposal introduced by Representative Ernest Istook Jr. of Oklahoma (H.J. Res. 127) specifically mentioned prayer in the public schools:

> To secure the people's right to acknowledge God according to the dictates of conscience: Nothing in this Constitution shall prohibit the acknowledgements of the religious heritage, beliefs, or traditions of the people, or prohibit student-sponsored prayer in public schools. Neither the United States nor any State shall compose any official prayer or compel joining in prayer, or discriminate against religious expression or belief.

Although Istook's proposal specifically permits student-sponsored prayer in schools, advocates of a religious equality amendment generally note that it differs from earlier proposals to permit public prayer in schools or to acknowledge God in the Constitution. One advocate specifically asserts that the proposal "is not a 'school prayer' amendment (as that term is commonly understood) because it does not permit state-sponsored teacher-led prayer." He further notes, however, that "if a school board sets aside a time for a student message at a graduation ceremony, the student speaker would have the right to say a prayer under the proposed amendment." Moreover, although the amendment would not permit "special funding of religious schools and social service providers," under such an amendment, "the Constitution would no longer prohibit religious entities from participating in neutrally available government funding programs" including a school voucher system (Baylor 1995, 4–5).

The Religious Equality Amendment was the first of ten proposals included in the Christian Coalition's Contract with the American Family—a take-off of the earlier Republican Contract with America (Reed 1995, 1–12).

In a related vein, in 1995 Republican Senator Thad Cochrane of Mississippi introduced an amendment prohibiting the state or national governments from abridging the free exercise of religion and granting Congress power to enforce this amendment. Cochrane noted on the Senate floor that the First Amendment already contained a free exercise clause, but he feared that the adoption of the Religious Freedom Restoration Act of 1993 might have shifted the protection of religious liberty from the Constitution, where it had been secure, to Congress, where it might be more vulnerable (Cochrane 1994, S6867).

With the Court's decision in *City of Boerne v. Flores* (1997) that the Religious Freedom Restoration Act was an unconstitutional attempt by Congress to interpret (rather than simply to enforce) the provisions of the Fourteenth Amendment, there have been renewed calls for a constitutional amendment to provide broader protection for religious liberty. In the meantime, Congress adopted the Religious Liberty Protection Act of 1999, providing more partial coverage than the earlier Religious Freedom Restoration Act by limiting its effect to cases that substantially affect interstate commerce or cases arising from federal programs (Farris 1999, 703). Review of this law, which many defenders of religious liberty consider to be too limited, might give the Supreme Court a second chance to reconsider its rulings in *Smith* and *Boerne*. State courts are also free to interpret religious freedoms more broadly under their state constitutions than the U.S. Supreme Court currently does under the First Amendment.

See also *Boerne, City of v. Flores;* Christian Amendment; Prayer in Public Schools.

For Further Reading:
Baylor, Gregory S. 1995. "The Religious Equality Amendment." *Christian Legal Society Quarterly* 16 (Summer): 4–5.

Casey, Samuel B. 1995. "Religious Freedom Makes Good Neighbors." *Christian Legal Society Quarterly* 16 (Summer): 3.

Cochrane, Thad. 1994. "Constitutional Amendment Restoring the Right to the Free Exercise of Religion." *Congressional Record,* U.S. Senate, 14 June, 103rd Cong., 2d sess., 1994, Vol. 140, pt. 9.

Farris, Michael P. 1999. "Only a Constitutional Amendment Can Guarantee Religious Freedom for All," *Cardozo Law Review* 21 (December): 689–706.

Folton, Richard T. 1996. "Horror Stories." *Liberty* (March/April): 6–8.

Goodstein, Laurie. 1995. "Religious Freedom Amendment Passed." *Washington Post,* 9 June, A-12.

Greenawalt, Kent. 1998a. "Introduction: Should the Religion Clauses of the Constitution Be Amended?" *Loyola of Los Angeles Law Review* 32 (November): 9–25.

Reed, Ralph. 1995. *Contract with the American Family: A Bold Plan by Christian Coalition to Strengthen the Family and Restore Common-Sense Values.* Nashville, TN: Moorings.

"Symposium: A Religious Equality Amendment?" 1996. *Brigham Young University Law Review* 561–688.

Vile, John R. 1994a. *Constitutional Change in the United States: A Comparative Study of the Role of Constitutional Amendments, Judicial Interpretations, and Legislative and Executive Actions.* Westport, CT: Praeger.

❖ REPRODUCTIVE RIGHTS ❖

Since the Supreme Court's decision in *Roe v. Wade* (1973), American women have had the legal right to obtain abortions, especially during the first two trimesters of pregnancy. Abortion opponents have introduced numerous calls for a right-to-life amendment to overturn this decision. Although such an amendment has not been adopted, in cases such as *Webster v. Reproductive Health Services* (1989) and *Planned Parenthood of Southeastern Pennsylvania v. Casey* (1992), the Supreme Court has permitted states to impose greater restrictions on this procedure.

Perhaps with a view to such restrictions, in April 1993 Democratic Representative Patsy Mink of Hawaii introduced an amendment to protect the rights of individuals "to have full control over reproductive decisions affecting their own bodies" (H.J. Res. 176). If the Supreme Court ever reversed its decision in *Roe v. Wade,* there might be considerable support for such an amendment.

See also Abortion; Right to Life.

❖ RESCISSION OF RATIFICATION OF PENDING AMENDMENTS ❖

Periodically, questions have arisen about the states' power to rescind their ratifications of pending constitutional amendments. The Constitution is silent on this point. Congress has yet to adopt legislation to deal with the subject, although legislation proposed by North Carolina Democratic Senator Sam Ervin and Utah Republican Senator Orrin Hatch would have accepted the legitimacy of such rescissions.

In dealing with ratification of the Fourteenth Amendment, Congress indicated that it did not accept the legitimacy of two attempted rescissions, but the precedent is a muddy one, and it is not clear whether the congressional judgment was actually essential to the amendment's ratification (Vile 1990, 112). Moreover, when the issue of rescissions reemerged during the controversy over the Equal Rights Amendment, a U.S. district court ruled in *Idaho v. Freeman* (1981) that such rescissions are permissible. This precedent is complicated, however, by the fact that Congress had not only extended the original ratification deadline but had done so by simple majority vote. Also, the decision was eventually mooted when the amendment failed to receive the necessary number of state ratifications.

One argument for permitting states to rescind ratification of pending amendments is an argument from balance, because states have been permitted to ratify amendments that they have previously rejected (Grinnell 1959,

1164). The doctrine of contemporary consensus that the Supreme Court articulated in *Dillon v. Gloss* (1921) also suggests that states should not be included in a consensus they no longer share. It has also been argued that the ability to rescind is a guard against hasty change.

Arguments against rescission include the value of finality (Orfield 1942, 70). Some also fear that if state legislators knew that a vote to ratify an amendment would not be final they might be tempted to treat their votes less seriously (Freedman and Naughton 1978, 11). It can also be argued that the process of amendment is difficult enough without allowing states additional leeway in rejecting amendments.

In the absence of clear precedents, it appears likely that Congress will resolve this issue on a case-by-case basis. Although this is consistent with the Supreme Court's decision in *Coleman v. Miller* (1939) that amending issues are "political questions," such discretion continues the uncertainty about a matter that should arguably be covered by preordained rules (Dellinger 1983, 395–396).

See also *Idaho v. Freeman.*

For Further Reading:

Baker, A. Diane. 1979. "ERA: The Effect of Extending the Time for Ratification on Attempts to Rescind Prior Ratifications." *Emory Law Journal* 28: 71–110.

Burke, Yvonne B. 1976. "Validity of Attempts to Rescind Ratification of the Equal Rights Amendment." *University of Los Angeles Law Review* 8: 1–22.

Dellinger, Walter. 1983. "The Legitimacy of Constitutional Change: Rethinking the Amending Process." *Harvard Law Review* 97 (December): 380–432.

Freedman, Samuel S., and Pamela J. Naughton. 1978. *ERA: May a State Change Its Vote?* Detroit, MI: Wayne State University Press.

Ginsburg, Ruth B. 1969. "Ratification of the Equal Rights Amendment: A Question of Time." *Texas Law Review* 57: 919–945.

Grinnell, Frank W. 1959. "Petitioning Congress for a Convention: Cannot a State Change Its

Mind?" *American Bar Association Journal* 45: 1164–1165.

Kanowitz, Leo, and Marilyn Klinger. 1978. "Can a State Rescind Its Equal Rights Amendment Ratification: Who Decides and How?" *Hastings Law Journal* 28 (March): 969–1009.

Orfield, Lester B. 1942. *The Amending of the Federal Constitution*. Ann Arbor, MI: University of Michigan Press.

Planell, Raymond M. 1974. "The Equal Rights Amendment: Will States Be Allowed to Change Their Minds?" *Notre Dame Lawyer* 49 (February): 657–670.

Vierra, Norman. 1981. "The Equal Rights Amendment: Rescission, Extension and Justiciability." *Southern Illinois Law Journal* 1981: 1–29.

Vile, John R. 1990. "Permitting States to Rescind Ratifications of Pending Amendments to the U.S. Constitution." *Publius: The Journal of Federalism* 20 (Spring): 109–122.

❖ RESPONSIBILITIES ❖

See Bill of Responsibilities.

❖ REVENUE SHARING ❖

In the early 1960s the national government appeared to have a much stronger and fairer revenue base than did the states. Between 1965 and 1971, fourteen states petitioned Congress to call a constitutional convention to amend the Constitution to provide for federal revenue sharing.

In contrast to more traditional categorical grant-in-aid programs and block grants, revenue sharing was designed to give maximum leeway to state funding decisions. Georgia Republican Representative Standish Thompson introduced amendments providing for revenue sharing in 1967 and 1969. Under his plan, the national government would eventually have provided 10 percent of the money it collected through income taxes to the states, based on their populations and with no strings other than an antidiscrimination provision.

Although little progress was made on proposed amendments, in 1972 the Nixon admin-

istration successfully launched revenue sharing for state and local governments. State governments were dropped from the program in 1980, and the entire program—under which some $85 billion had been funneled to states and localities—was terminated in 1986 during the Reagan administration (Harrigan 1994, 41).

For Further Reading:

Harrigan, John J. 1994. *Politics and Policy in States and Communities.* 5th ed. New York: HarperCollins College Publishers.

❖ REVERENCE FOR THE CONSTITUTION ❖

As of 2003 members of Congress have introduced about 11,500 proposals (most redundant) to amend the U.S. Constitution, but it has only been successfully amended twenty-seven times. In more than 210 years, neither has it been completely revised nor have a sufficient majority of states called on Congress to call a new convention to do so. Moreover, there have been two fairly long periods in American history—one from 1804 through 1865 and the second from 1870 through 1913—when no amendments were added to the document.

James Madison defended the amending mechanisms as guarding "equally against that extreme facility, which would render the Constitution too mutable; and that extreme difficulty, which might perpetuate its discovered faults" (Hamilton et al. 1961, 278). However, by comparison to mechanisms in other nations and in the states, the processes for formal change of the Constitution that Article V outlines are fairly onerous (Lutz 1994). The difficulty of these procedures lends stability to the document.

An additional obstacle to constitutional amendment is the feeling of reverence, or veneration, that the existing written document has often generated in the past and that it continues to generate into the present. The reputations and achievements of many of its authors (including George Washington and James Madison) as well as its relatively early successes in alleviating many of the more obvious problems under the Articles of Confederation have contributed to the document's permanence. These factors have been further enhanced by the age of the document and remain as continuing barriers to major or precipitous changes.

In the United States, the written Constitution arguably plays the role in unifying the nation that monarchs play in other nations, and critics of existing policy, for example, gun control, often take the position that it is not the Constitution, or, in the case of gun control, the Second Amendment, that needs amending so much as current misunderstandings of that document. Especially for Christians, Jews, Muslims, and other groups who guide their lives by a set of written scriptures, and especially to the extent that the Constitution is treated as a form of sacred scripture (as it often is), it may sometimes seem sacrilegious to add to or alter it (see Levinson 1990b). A historian who has examined the role of the U.S. Constitution in U.S. history has observed that it has often been an item of near worship and that early schoolbooks often "stated that the Constitution had been divinely inspired" (Kammen 1987, 3). He further quotes Harvard's A. Lawrence Lowell in 1889:

> For a long time the Constitution of the United States was the object of what has been called a fetish worship; that is, it was regarded as something peculiarly sacred, and received an unquestioned homage for reasons quite apart from any virtues of its own. The Constitution was to us what a king has often been to other nations. It was the symbol and pledge of our national existence, and the only object on which the people could expend their new-born loyalty. Let us hope that such a feeling will never die out, for it is a purifying and ennobling one; but to-day our national union is so fully accomplished, that we need no symbol or pledge to assure us of the fact. (Quoted in Kammen 1987, 22–23)

The fact that the framers of the Constitution recognized the need to include a formal amending process within the document, and engaged in some early alterations of their own—including the addition of the Bill of Rights—make it clear that they did not regard the document as perfect when written. They recognized that it embodied many compromises, some of which helped initially perpetuate slavery and others of which sometimes distorted representative institutions, and they recognized that alterations would be required as circumstances changed. Framers like Thomas Jefferson would undoubtedly have created a more flexible instrument than was adopted. Although he accepted the idea of some unalterable natural rights, Jefferson was also known for his view that the dead should not bind the living and that each generation had the right to rewrite a constitution. The more predominate view appears to have been shared by Jefferson's friend James Madison, who opposed frequent constitutional conventions and other alterations on the basis, which he explained in *Federalist No. 49,* that "as every appeal to the people would carry an implication of some defect in the government, frequent appeals would, in great measure, deprive the government of that veneration which time bestows on everything, and without which perhaps the wisest and freest governments would not possess the requisite stability" (Hamilton et al. 1961, 314). The framers thus rejected a mechanism like that found within the Pennsylvania Constitution for a Council of Censors that would periodically review the Constitution and propose changes.

There are times in American history when Madison may have succeeded too well. Particularly prior to the Civil War, the Constitution often seemed to assume so much of the character of a sacred text and the founders the character of demigods, that reformers were reluctant to seek constitutional changes, even when it was clear that they were needed (Vorenberg 2001, 192–193); up until late 1863, many of the individuals advocating constitutional reforms in the United States were "radical, foreign-born reformers who were not burdened by the illusion that amending the Constitution necessarily jeopardized American democracy" (*Id.,* 14). By contrast, some abolitionists, like William Lloyd Garrison, clearly put the blame on the Constitution, calling it a "Covenant with Death, an agreement with Hell" (Pease and Pease 1965, lx). Although this was clearly a minority view, to some extent the outbreak of the Civil War helped individuals to see that the framers and their solutions to the nation's problems had not been perfect. Still, as late as 1864 journalist E. L. Godkin found himself having to argue—much as Jefferson had done in an earlier day and as a contemporary, Francis Lieber, also had to do—for some of the alterations that would soon be made in that document:

> But where they [the founders] saw as in a glass darkly, we see face to face; where they struggled through mire, we stand on firm ground. To abandon our right to amend it, or to reason for ourselves on the altered state of facts which surrounds us, in deference to their authority, would be as degrading and as extraordinary a confession of degeneracy as has ever been made by any body of civilized men. (Godkin 1864, 127)

Many of today's fears of a possible "runaway" convention appear to stem from concerns that excessive "tinkering" could destroy the existing Constitution. To some extent the Bill of Rights appears to have assumed a quasi-constitutional status of its own, with opponents of amendments prohibiting flag desecration or other alterations in rights currently guaranteed in the first ten amendments often citing the fact that no amendments (the Eighteenth Amendment providing for national alcoholic prohibition, which has since been repealed, is a possible exception) have ever restricted existing rights. Noting that the Bill of Rights has never been amended, one recent commentator observed that "[i]ts symbolic strength is tied to its constancy" (Greenawalt 1998b, 11). In another article, he observed that "[a]ny amendment to overturn an unpopular decision will make subsequent amendments of that kind easier to adopt. If the first such amendment overturns a decision someone does not like, then the next two or three may overturn decisions the same person favors" (Greenawalt 1998b, 697). Reverence for the existing Constitution has not, of course, prevented many alterations in constitutional understandings that have been brought about through judicial interpretations and through congressional and presidential practices. Although changes in the constitutional text do not always prove to be immediately effective (the Fifteenth Amendment, prohibiting discrimination in voting on the basis of race, was largely moribund for almost a hundred years), changes effected through constitutional interpretation, like broader interpretations of congressional powers that followed Franklin D. Roosevelt's court-packing plan, could prove to be even less permanent. However much the Constitution continues to be venerated, ultimately the amending process continues to lie "at the very center of American constitutionalism" (Kyvig 1996a, xvii).

See also Constitutional Conventions; Jefferson, Thomas; Lieber, Francis; Madison, James; Rigid Constitution

For Further Reading:

Godkin, E. L. 1864. "The Constitution and Its Defects." *North American Review* 99 (July): 117–143.

Greenawalt, Kent. 1998b. "Symposium: Reflections of *City of Boerne v. Flores:* Why Now Is Not the Time for Constitutional Amendment: The Limited Reach of *City of Boerne v. Flores.*" *William & Mary Law Review* 39 (February): 689–698.

Hamilton, Alexander, James Madison, and John Jay. 1787–1788. *The Federalist Papers.* Reprint, New York: New American Library, 1961.

Kammen, Michael. 1987. *A Machine That Would Go of Itself: The Constitution in American Culture.* New York: Alfred A. Knopf.

Kyvig, David E. 1996a. *Explicit and Authentic Acts: Amending the Constitution, 1776–1995.* Lawrence, KS: University Press of Kansas.

Levinson, Sanford. 1990b. "'Veneration' and Constitutional Change: James Madison Confronts the Possibility of Constitutional Amendment." *Texas Tech Law Review* 21: 2443–2461.

Lutz, Donald S. 1994. "Toward a Theory of Constitutional Amendment." *American Political Science Review* 88 (June): 355–370.

Pease, William H., and June H. Pease, eds. 1965. *The Antislavery Argument.* Indianapolis, IN: Bobbs-Merrill.

Vorenberg, Michael. 2001. *Final Freedom: The Civil War, the Abolition of Slavery, and the Thirteenth Amendment.* Cambridge, UK: Cambridge University Press.

❖ REVOLUTION ❖

In modern times the term *revolution* has been used to denote violent political changes, such as those associated with the French Revolution of 1789 or the Russian Revolution of 1917. Originally, however, the term appears to have derived from astronomy, where it referred to the more orderly processes that could be observed in the heavens (Wills 1978, 51). Moreover, although they were not bloodless, it can be argued that revolutions like those in Great Britain in 1688 and America in 1776 were qualitatively different from those that followed (Diamond 1976).

Whatever distinctions there might be among different types of revolutions, they all resort to change from outside the existing legal framework. By contrast, formal amending processes are designed as means of effecting change within the system. Although the Declaration of Independence proclaimed that the people had a right to revolution, such revolution, as Thomas Jefferson described it in the Declaration, was a last resort, not to be undertaken "for light and transient Causes."

The seeming inability of the British constitution to accommodate change was doubtless on the minds of delegates at the Constitutional Convention of 1787. Thus, Virginia's George Mason noted that change was inevitable and that it would be better to provide for amendments "in an easy, regular and Constitutional way than to trust to chance and violence" (Farrand 1966, 1:203).

Although he stated a moderate view of revolution in the Declaration of Independence, Thomas Jefferson elsewhere blurred the lines between constitutional and revolutionary change. At a time when many countrymen were horrified by Shays's Rebellion, Jefferson calculated that, with thirteen colonies that had been independent for eleven years each, Shays's Rebellion amounted to but one revolution in a century and a half. He further asked, "What signify a few lives lost in a century or two? The tree of liberty must be refreshed from time to time with the blood of patriots & tyrants. It is its natural manure" (Jefferson 1905, 5:362).

The tie between amendment and revolution was forcefully demonstrated during the Dorr War in Rhode Island. The forceful attempt to replace Rhode Island's charter government with a more democratic scheme arose largely from the charter government's failure to provide a means of peaceful change. Defending the charter government as the legitimate government in the case of *Luther v. Borden*, Daniel Webster argued that "our American mode of government does not draw any power from tumultuous assemblages" and that "when it is necessary to ascertain the will of the people, the legislature must provide the means of ascertaining it" (*Luther* 1849, 31). A political opponent on many other subjects, South Carolina Senator John C. Calhoun agreed. He said, "It would be the death-blow of constitutional democracy to admit the right of the numerical majority, to alter or abolish constitutions at pleasure—regardless of the consent of the Government, or the forms prescribed for their amendment" (Calhoun 1851–1856, 6: 229–230).

The safety-valve analogy, often used to describe a formal amending process, also highlights the manner in which peaceful mechanisms for change help avert the need for violence. This analogy has increasingly given way to more organic analogies, which also suggest that the capability for constitutional growth by interpretation, as well as by amendment, helps avoid the need for violent revolution.

See also *Luther v. Borden;* Safety-valve Analogy.

For Further Reading:

Calhoun, John C. 1851–1856. *The Works of John C. Calhoun.* 6 vols. Ed. Richard K. Crallé. Reprint, New York: Russell and Russell, 1968.

Diamond, Martin. 1976. "The Revolution of Sober Expectations." In *America's Continuing Revolution.* Garden City, NY: Anchor Press.

Farrand, Max, ed. 1966. *The Records of the Federal Convention.* 4 vols. New Haven, CT: Yale University Press.

Jefferson, Thomas. 1905. *The Works of Thomas Jefferson,* ed. Paul Leicester Ford. 12 vols. New York: G. P. Putnam's Sons, Knickerbocker Press.

Luther v. Borden, 48 U.S. (7 How.) 1 (1849).

Wills, Gary. 1978. *Inventing America: Jefferson's Declaration of Independence.* New York: Doubleday.

❖ REYNOLDS, EUSTACE ❖

In 1915 a New Yorker named Eustace Reynolds published a modified constitution for consideration. Aside from the fact that a number of his ideas were similar to those advocated by William Jennings Bryan, who was then secretary of state (Boyd 1992, 129), and that Reynolds promised to use any money from reprints of his constitution for the cause of international peace (Reynolds 1915, 18), no biographical information is available. Most of Reynolds's plan is simply a reprint of the existing Constitution with proposed changes highlighted in bold type. Although most changes involved the conduct of foreign affairs, some other alterations were also proposed.

"Sex qualifications" for voting were to be eliminated (as they soon would be in the Nineteenth Amendment), but the voting age was to be raised to twenty-five and limited to those who could read and write (Reynolds 1915, 1–2). The vice president, who would serve with the president in a single six-year term, was assigned to represent the United States in a council of other viceroys and vice presidents. With approval of another body consisting of "under-secretaries of state and deputy-ministers for foreign affairs," this council would have power to "make and promulgate decrees in all matters affecting international intercourse, commerce, affairs, or relations"; to "regulate commerce with foreign nations"; and to punish "offenses against the law of nations" (*Id.,* 2–3). Such regulations would be recognized in Article VI as the supreme law of the land (*Id.,* 13). Congress would, in turn, lose its power to "enter into any agreement or contract with another state, or with a foreign power, to engage in war," except in cases of "invasion" or "imminent danger" (*Id.,* 7).

The judicial power would have been altered in Reynolds's scheme so as to require the chief justice to appoint another Supreme Court justice to sit en banc with members of judiciaries from other nations "and pass upon international questions as they come properly before the court for adjudication" (Reynolds 1915, 10–11). This international court would have appellate jurisdiction in cases involving controversies between American states or their citizens and foreign citizens, and it would have original jurisdiction when the United States and foreign governments were involved. United States courts would be given explicit authority to disregard unconstitutional laws and decrees.

Reynolds would have maintained the guarantees in the Bill of Rights, but he would have permitted a prosecutor to comment, and a jury to weigh this fact, when a defendant chose to exercise the right against self-incrimination. He would also have restricted the national government's right to collect income tax on state securities. The impact of Reynolds's work, if any, on the public is unknown (Boyd 1992, 131).

For Further Reading:
Boyd, Steven R., ed. 1992. *Alternative Constitutions for the United States: A Documentary History.* Westport, CT: Greenwood Press.

Reynolds, Eustace. 1915. *A New Constitution: A Suggested Form of Modified Constitution.* New York: Nation Press.

❖ *REYNOLDS V. SIMS* (1964) ❖

This case was one of the most important and controversial cases decided by the Warren Court. It established that the equal protection clause of the Fourteenth Amendment required that both houses of a state legislature—in this case, Alabama's—need to be apportioned according to the "one person, one vote" standard.

In so ruling, Chief Justice Earl Warren extended the earlier decision in *Baker v. Carr* (1962), which had established that state legislative apportionment schemes were justiciable under the equal protection clause but had not specified the standard to be utilized. Over the objections of dissenting Justice John Marshall Harlan that the Court was misinterpreting the Fourteenth Amendment, Warren argued that "the right of suffrage can be denied by a debasement or dilution of the weight of a citizen's vote just as effectively as by wholly prohibiting the free exercise of the franchise" (*Reynolds* 1964, 555).

Together, *Baker v. Carr* and *Reynolds v. Sims* provoked numerous calls for an amendment to give states greater leeway. Illinois Republican Senator Everett Dirksen led the call for a constitutional convention on the subject. These efforts failed, and both decisions remain in effect. As the Court indicated in the *Reynolds* case, however (1964, 578), it is willing to accept somewhat greater population disparities among state legislative districts than it permits with respect to state-drawn congressional districts.

See also *Baker v. Carr*; States, Legislative Apportionment.

For Further Reading:
Reynolds v. Sims, 377 U.S. 533 (1964).

❖ *RHODE ISLAND V. PALMER* ❖

See *National Prohibition Cases.*

❖ RICE, ISAAC L. (1850–1915) ❖

Isaac Rice was a gifted man who was born in Bavaria and educated at Columbia Law School, where he stayed an additional six years to study and teach before going into the practice of law (Malone 1961, 3:541). In 1884 Rice published an article in which he advocated calling a constitutional convention to address a number of problems, most of which he attributed to the U.S. system of separation of powers and checks and balances. Rice believed that this system was "both weak and irresponsible" (Rice 1884, 534) and that it led to political corruption. In its place, he hoped to establish a parliamentary system (Vile 1991c, 37–38).

Rice proposed three major reforms. The first was to expand the powers of Congress to enable it "to settle all questions of national concern" (Rice 1884, 540). Specifically, he wanted to institute "a uniform code of commerce for the whole country" so that "powerful combinations" would be unable to hide behind artificial state boundaries (*Id.*). Second, Rice proposed ending the separation of legislative and executive powers. In his words, "the executive must be entitled to propose laws necessary for the preservation of the public welfare, and the legislative must be enabled to control the execution of all laws passed" (*Id.*). As in a parliamentary system, Rice wanted the heads of executive agencies to serve in Congress; although he did not use the term, he also appears to have contemplated the creation of a prime minister. Third, Rice proposed making the legislature "the sole and responsible judge of the constitutionality of its acts," leaving the judiciary to "interpret" congressional will rather than "to control it" (*Id.*).

One of numerous reformers who have looked to parliamentary systems for guidance, Rice does not appear to have stirred much contemporary interest with his proposal for a convention.

For Further Reading:
Malone, Dumas, ed. 1961. *Dictionary of American Biography.* 10 vols. New York: Charles Scribner's Sons.
Rice, Isaac. 1884. "Work for a Constitutional Convention." *Century Magazine* 28 (August): 534–540.
Vile, John R. 1991c. *Rewriting the United States Constitution: An Examination of Proposals from Reconstruction to the Present.* New York: Praeger.

❖ RIGHT TO LIFE ❖

Few issues have proved to be more emotionally wrenching or politically divisive than the issue of abortion. From the time shortly after *Roe v. Wade* was first argued in 1971 to the present, more than 325 proposals have been introduced in Congress to restrict abortions, and at least 19 states have called for a constitutional convention to address this issue. The fact that most such proposals have been made by those opposed to abortion is not a sign that congressional opinion on the subject is uniform but rather an indication that, throughout this period, those who accept a woman's right to choose an abortion have had the weight of the courts on their side and thus had no need to introduce such amendments.

Background to *Roe v. Wade*

Prior to 1973 the issue of abortion was largely a state matter. Most states had adopted laws restricting abortions in the second half of the nineteenth century, at which time abortions were often medically dangerous for women. By 1972 nineteen states had liberalized their laws to permit therapeutic abortions, but this meant that, in most states, such procedures were still illegal (Keynes with Miller 1989, 249).

In 1965 the Supreme Court ruled in *Griswold v. Connecticut* that there was a constitutional right to privacy granted by various penumbras of the Bill of Rights and the Fourteenth Amendment. This decision, in turn, served as the basis for the Court's decision in *Roe v. Wade* (1973), which overturned a Texas abortion law. Written by Justice Harry Blackmun for a seven-to-two majority of the Court, the opinion stated that the constitutional right to privacy was sufficient to permit a woman to choose to have an abortion without state interference, at least through the first two trimesters (the first six months) of pregnancy. Thereafter, a state could legislate on behalf of the fetus, except in cases in which the life or health of the mother was threatened (see Garrow 1994).

Reactions to *Roe v. Wade*

Perhaps because *Roe v. Wade* was thrust so suddenly into the public consciousness (Glendon 1987), it engendered strong responses from both supporters and opponents. Undoubtedly, the decision galvanized public opinion in a way that would not have occurred in the face of state liberalization of abortion laws and the ever-increasing number of legal abortions that were being performed in the years leading up to the decision (Rosenberg 1991, 178–180). Subsequent developments have proceeded on a number of different fronts.

Legislatively, opponents of abortion have followed four distinct strategies: (1) adopting amendments; (2) limiting judicial jurisdiction over the subject of abortion; (3) restricting abortion funding; and (4) passing other laws, including those defining the moment that human life begins as being before birth, requiring informed consent prior to an abortion, establishing waiting periods, regulating clinics, or

otherwise restricting abortion access without outlawing it completely (Keynes with Miller 1989, 247). Such strategies are sometimes pursued independently and sometimes in tandem.

It should be noted that the idea of restricting judicial jurisdiction has also been advocated by opponents of prayer in school and school busing. Republican Representative Philip Crane of Illinois introduced such a proposal relative to abortion in 1979. It provided that:

> [T]he Supreme Court shall not have jurisdiction to review, by appeal, writs of certiorari, or otherwise, any case arising out of any State statute, ordinance, rule, regulation or any part thereof, or arising out of any Act interpreting, applying, or enforcing a State statute, ordinance, rule or regulation, which relates to abortion. The district courts shall not have jurisdiction of any case or question which the Supreme Court does not have jurisdiction to review. (Keynes with Miller 1989, 292)

Much of the controversy over attempts to restrict abortion funding have focused on the Hyde amendment, named after its sponsor, Republican Representative Henry Hyde of Illinois. The Supreme Court upheld this law, which limits federal funding for nontherapeutic abortions, in *Harris v. McRae* (1980). It decided that the right to an abortion did not include the right to government funding for such an abortion. In *Beal v. Doe* (1977), the Court had previously decided that states did not have to provide such funding either.

Judicial Responses to Legislation

The Supreme Court's reactions to other legislative attempts to regulate abortions have arguably zigged and zagged with the mood of the nation, the nature of the specific controversy, and the individuals who have occupied the judiciary. For example, the Court struck down laws that require spousal consent for abortions or that absolutely mandate parental consent for minors to obtain abortions. It has been more sympathetic, however, to laws providing for parental consent when such laws permit some form of judicial bypass. In *Webster v.*

Reproductive Health Services (1989) and in *Planned Parenthood of Southeastern Pennsylvania v. Casey* (1992), the Court accepted various other state-imposed restrictions on abortion. The latter case is especially significant; the majority, although arguing that such restrictions should not impose an "undue burden" on a woman's right to choose an abortion, appeared largely to scuttle the trimester analysis that was a significant part of the Court's decision in *Roe v. Wade* (for short summaries of cases since *Roe v. Wade*, see D. O'Brien 2000a, 2:1215–1219).

Amendments Designed to Overturn *Roe v. Wade*

Amendments on abortion have been divided into four categories:

> Those amendments [that] would (1) restore the states' authority to restore the status quo ante, (2) authorize Congress and the states to protect human life at every stage of biological development, (3) prohibit Congress and the states from interfering with human life at every stage of development, or (4) define the fetus as a person within the meaning of the Fifth and Fourteenth amendment's due process clauses and extend due process rights to the unborn child. (Keynes with Miller 1989, 280)

It should be noted that North Carolina Republican Senator Jesse Helms pushed for legislation in 1982 that would accomplish the last of these four objectives. The law was based on the premise that, since the Court had stated in *Roe v. Wade* that it did not know when human life began, it might defer to congressional judgments and congressional enforcement powers under Section 5 of the Fourteenth Amendment. His attempt was unsuccessful.

At times, abortion opponents have been split between those who want to use the amending process to restrict or prohibit abortion throughout the nation and those who are willing to settle for returning this matter to the states. In 1981 Utah Republican Senator Orrin Hatch sponsored legislation that would give both Congress and the states concurrent authority to restrict abortions. The Senate subse-

quently voted forty-nine to fifty against a substitute amendment offered by Missouri Democratic Senator Thomas Eagleton that provided simply that "a right to abortion is not secured by the Constitution." Most recent proposals to restrict abortion have mandated exceptions in cases when a woman's life is at stake. Rather than focusing on a constitutional amendment, the Christian Coalition's recent Contract with the American Family advocates legislation protecting states that do not choose to fund abortion, limiting late-term abortions, and eliminating federal funding of groups that support abortion (Reed 1995, 63–84).

Other Consequences of *Roe v. Wade*

The abortion controversy has been a major bone of contention in a number of congressional confirmation hearings, including the unsuccessful confirmations of Judge Robert Bork (who was thought to be unsympathetic to a constitutional right to privacy) to the Supreme Court in the Reagan administration, and of Dr. Henry Foster (who had performed abortions) to be surgeon general in the Clinton administration. Presidents have also used executive orders to permit or restrict fetal tissue research and abortion counseling (Vile 1994a, 58). Although more than thirty years have elapsed since the Court's historic attempt to resolve the abortion issue in *Roe v. Wade*, emotional debates continue in Congress and elsewhere (Fraley 1995).

See also Abortion; Privacy, Right to; Reproductive Rights; *Roe v. Wade*.

For Further Reading:

Fraley, Colette. 1995. "House Opponents Savor Gains; Senate Outlook Is Unclear." *Congressional Quarterly Weekly Report* 53 (29 July): 2276–2277.

Garrow, David J. 1994. *Liberty and Sexuality: The Right to Privacy and the Making of* Roe v. Wade. New York: Macmillan.

Glendon, Mary A. 1987. *Abortion and Divorce in Western Law.* Cambridge, MA: Harvard University Press.

Keynes, Edward, with Randall K. Miller. 1989. *The Court vs. Congress: Prayer, Busing, and Abortion.* Durham, NC: Duke University Press.

O'Brien, David M. 2000a. *Civil Rights and Civil Liberties*. Vol. 2 of *Constitutional Law and Politics*. 5th ed. New York: W. W. Norton.

O'Connor, Karen. 1996. *No Neutral Ground? Abortion Politics in an Age of Absolutes*. Boulder, CO: Westview.

Rosenberg, Gerald N. 1991. *The Hollow Hope: Can Courts Bring about Social Change?* Chicago: University of Chicago Press.

❖ RIGHT TO WORK ❖

A major piece of legislation that covers U.S. labor relations is the Taft-Hartley Act of 1947. This law permits states to adopt a so-called closed, or union, shop requiring all workers to belong to unions that a majority has selected (Tomlins 1985, 282–316). It also permits states to adopt open shops, or right-to-work laws, allowing individuals to choose whether to belong to such unions. Union advocates argue that the open shop is unfair because it allows nonmembers to benefit from contract negotiations made by an organization to which they did not contribute. Some civil libertarians respond that a closed shop violates individual freedom of association.

In the years immediately prior to the Taft-Hartley Act, a number of amendments were proposed that would guarantee an open shop. The most persistent supporter of such an amendment was Democratic Representative Wilbert O'Daniel of Texas. In July 1955 Indiana Representative William Jenner introduced another resolution that would guarantee the rights of workers for hire "to receive their earnings in full"; Jenner probably thereby intended also to prohibit a union shop under which workers must pay dues to the union.

Representative Jesse Jackson Jr. has recently proposed a "Full-Employment Amendment" to the U.S. Constitution. Although he writes about what he considers to be the baneful influence of "right to work" laws, his specific proposal, which is also designed to guarantee "equal pay for equal work" and a decent minimum wage, does not appear specifically to abolish such laws. It does, however, provide that "every citizen who works has the right to form and join trade unions for the protection of their interests" (Jackson with Watkins 2001, 252).

See also Jackson, Jesse L., Jr.

For Further Reading:

Jackson, Jesse L., Jr., with Frank E. Watkins. 2001. *A More Perfect Union: Advancing New American Rights*. New York: Welcome Rain Publishers.

Tomlins, Christopher L. 1985. *The State and the Unions: Labor Relations, Law, and the Organized Labor Movement in America, 1880–1960*. Cambridge, UK: Cambridge University Press.

❖ RIGID CONSTITUTION ❖

In his acclaimed book on American politics (1906, 1:370), as well as in an essay (1905), Lord James Bryce of England developed a distinction between flexible and rigid constitutions. This distinction was a frequent point of reference in the early years of the twentieth century and a basis for many of the criticisms of the amending process that were made by reformers of the Progressive Era.

Bryce offered his classification as an alternative to early distinctions between written and unwritten constitutions. Like those earlier schemes, however, Bryce's distinguished between constitutions that had developed by customs and usages, like that of Great Britain, and constitutions that were considered to be paramount law unchangeable by ordinary legislative means, like the United States'.

Although Bryce noted that rigid constitutions "mark a comparatively advanced stage in political development, when the idea of separating fundamental laws from other laws has grown familiar, and when considerable experience in the business of government and in political affairs generally has been accumulated" (Bryce 1905, 46), the designation of such a constitution as "rigid" may not have been an altogether impartial designation (Vile 1992, 138). At one point likening a rigid constitution to an iron bridge, Bryce noted that "the fact that it is very strong and all knit tightly into one fabric, while enabling it to stand firm under small oscillations or disturbances, may aggravate small ones" (Bryce 1905, 68), and he cited the U.S. Civil War as an example. Moreover, writing in the time between the post–Civil War amendments and the Progressive Era amendments, Bryce identified the U.S. Constitution as "the most difficult to change" (Bryce 1905, 61).

Today, the older distinction between written and unwritten constitutions is more common than Bryce's distinction between flexible and rigid constitutions. One writer has suggested a classification of constitutions into those formulated by a single lawgiver, those based on immemorial customs and usages, and those formulated by a constitutional convention (Vile 1993c). A more recent article notes that constitutions vary in rigidity according to "the number of political institutions that are legally required to participate in the amending process," "the size of the majorities that are needed to approve an amendment," and "whether the participation of the people is required" either directly or indirectly (Ferreres-Comella 2000, 46–47). This same author believes that moderate, albeit not absolute, rigidity can be justified as a means of protecting fundamental rights within political systems that utilize judicial review.

Whatever classification is used, it is important not to let labels obscure complexities and to recognize that most systems blend characteristics of more than one ideal type. Also, a constitution that may seem relatively rigid in one period might prove quite susceptible to change in other circumstances.

For Further Reading:
Bryce, James. 1906. *The American Commonwealth.* 3d ed. 2 vols. New York: Macmillan.

———. 1905. "Flexible and Rigid Constitutions." In *Constitutions.* Germany: Scientia Verlag Aalen. Reprint of New York and London edition, 1980.

Ferreres-Comella, Victor. 2000. "A Defense of Constitutional Rigidity." In *Analysis and Right,* ed. Paul Comanducci and Riccardo Guastini. Turin, Italy: G. Giappichelli Publisher.

Vile, John R. 1993c. "Three Kinds of Constitutional Founding and Change: The Convention Model and Its Alternatives." *Political Research Quarterly* 46: 881–895.

———. 1992. *The Constitutional Amending Process in American Political Thought.* New York: Praeger.

❖ ROBINSON, DONALD L. (1936–) ❖

Donald Robinson, a professor of political science at Smith College, has been closely associated with the Committee on the Constitutional System (CCS). Robinson has published two books designed to elicit discussion about reforms considered and proposed by this committee (Robinson 1985, 1989; for discussion, see Vile 1991c, 129–131).

In an article reflecting his own views, Robinson advocated three constitutional reforms: lengthening the terms of members of the House of Representatives to four years and those of senators to eight, allowing members of Congress to head executive agencies, and allowing the president and one-third of both houses of Congress or a majority of either house to call an election (Robinson 1987).

For Further Reading:
Robinson, Donald. 1989. *Government for the Third American Century.* Boulder, CO: Westview Press.

———. 1985. *Reforming American Government: The Bicentennial Papers of the Committee on the Constitutional System.* Boulder, CO: Westview Press.

Vile, John R. 1991c. *Rewriting the United States Constitution: An Examination of Proposals from Reconstruction to the Present.* New York: Praeger.

❖ ROE V. WADE (1973) ❖

Roe v. Wade is one of the most controversial and far-reaching decisions of the twentieth century, and it stimulated numerous efforts to adopt a "right to life" amendment. In *Roe,* a seven-to-two majority of the Supreme Court, led by Justice Harry Blackmun, struck down state abortion laws for the first time. The Court based its decision on the constitutional right of privacy, which it had recognized in *Griswold v. Connecticut* (1965) and other cases.

Blackmun argued that most U.S. abortion laws had been enacted in the second half of the nineteenth century. He traced the origins of such laws to three causes: the desire to discourage illicit sexual activity, protect women's health, and guard prenatal life. In this case, the state did not assert the first interest. Blackmun further found that the state's interest in prohibiting abortion to protect women's health was not as pressing as it had been before the discovery of antiseptics, when abortion was a far riskier procedure. As to the protection of prenatal life, Blackmun argued that no consensus had emerged as to when human life begins. However, the common law generally did not punish abortions that were performed prior to "quickening," and even then, the offense was not generally regarded as murder.

In an attempt to balance the state's concern with the potential life of the fetus and the health of the mother, Blackmun formulated different rules for each of the three trimesters of pregnancy. During the first, the decision of the woman and her doctor was to be decisive. In the second trimester, the state could set forth requirements as to the licensing and qualifications of doctors, types of facilities, and the like, which were designed to ensure that the abortion procedure was safe for the woman. In the third trimester, the outset of which generally marked the period of "viability," that is, the point at which a fetus could survive outside its mother's womb, Blackmun said that the state could pass laws protecting the fetus. He made an exception, however, when abortion might be "necessary to preserve the life or health of the mother" (*Roe* 1973, 164).

In addition to stimulating calls for an amendment, *Roe v. Wade* has stirred considerable controversy. The Supreme Court has subsequently faced numerous issues related to its first decision (D. O'Brien 2000a, 1215–1219).

Prominent cases have included *Harris v. McRae* (1980), upholding the constitutionality of the Hyde amendment, which prohibits federal funding of nontherapeutic abortions; *Webster v. Reproductive Health Services* (1989), upholding a number of restrictions imposed by the state of Missouri; and *Planned Parenthood of Southeastern Pennsylvania v. Casey* (1992), upholding several state-imposed restrictions on abortion—including a twenty-four-hour waiting period and a requirement for a parent's or judge's consent for a minor to obtain an abortion—that it claimed were not substantial enough to impose an "undue burden." In the *Planned Parenthood* opinion written by Justices Sandra Day O'Connor, Anthony Kennedy, and David Souter, the Court professed to be upholding the central holding of *Roe* even while rejecting much of its rigid trimester analysis.

Roe v. Wade continues to be a controversial decision. It is always possible that new appointments to the Court, most likely by a Republican president, could tilt the balance in a prolife, or profederalism, direction (leaving the matter to be resolved by the states). Just as *Roe v. Wade* has led to proposals for a prolife amendment, so, too, an amendment reversing or significantly restricting *Roe* would likely lead not only to a renewed round of state legislation but also to the introduction of prochoice amendments in Congress.

See also *Griswold v. Connecticut;* Right to Life.

For Further Reading:

Garrow, David J. 1994. *Liberty and Sexuality: The Right to Privacy and the Making of* Roe v. Wade. New York: Macmillan.

O'Brien, David M. 2000a. *Civil Rights and Civil Liberties.* Vol. 2 of *Constitutional Law and Politics.* 5th ed. New York: W. W. Norton.

Roe v. Wade, 410 U.S. 113 (1973).

S

❖ SAFETY-VALVE ANALOGY ❖

Consistent with the parallels that were often drawn in early American history between the Constitution and a machine (Kammen 1987), one of the most frequently repeated analogies used in early U.S. history for the amending process was that of a safety valve. It is possible that the specific analogy was coined by Justice Joseph Story when he wrote that the amending process was "the safety valve to let off all temporary effervescences and excitements; and the real effective instrument to control and adjust the movements of the machinery, when out of order, or in danger of self-destruction" (Story 1987, 680).

In critiquing this analogy, Sidney George Fisher later claimed that Article V had been more like an "iron fetter" than a safety valve; "the efficacy of a safety-valve depends on the promptness with which it can be opened and the width of the throttle. If defective in either of these, when the pressure of steam is too high the boiler will burst" (S. Fisher 1862, 33). Attorney Frederic B. Johnstone later criticized the amending process during the Progressive Era by noting that the difficulty of constitutional amendment made the Constitution like a dangerous boiler that "becomes a source of danger under pressure in the absence of a safety valve" (1912, 282).

However mechanical, the safety-valve analogy highlights the way in which a method for peaceful and legal change helps alleviate pressures that might otherwise be channeled into violence and revolution. In modern discourse that goes at least as far back as Woodrow Wilson, the Constitution is less frequently referred to as a Newtonian "mechanism" than as a Darwinian "organism," and as prominent scholars and judges have adopted the analogy of a "living Constitution" that they can adapt through constitutional interpretation, the safety-valve analogy has accordingly been used less frequently (Gillman 1997, 215).

See also Living Constitution; Story, Joseph.

For Further Reading:
Fisher, Sidney G. 1862. *The Trial of the Constitution*. Reprint, New York: Da Capo Press, 1972.
Gillman, Howard. 1997. "The Collapse of Constitutional Originalism and the Rise of the Notion of the 'Living Constitution' in the Course of American State-Building." *Studies in American Political Development* 11 (Fall): 191–247.
Story, Joseph. 1987. *Commentaries on the Constitution of the United States*. Durham, NC: Carolina Academic Press.

❖ SCHLAFLY, PHYLLIS (1924–) ❖

Phyllis Schlafly is the individual most frequently associated with the defeat of the Equal Rights Amendment. As the 1972 founder and current president of the conservative Eagle Forum, Schlafly continues to take credit for leading "the pro-family movement to victory over the principal legislative goal of the radical feminists, called the Equal Rights Amendment" (1995 biographical data sheet provided by the Eagle Forum). Her views on the subject are more thoroughly explained in an Eagle Forum video entitled "What's Wrong with ERA?"

Schlafly has a master's degree in political science from Harvard University as well as undergraduate and law degrees from Washington University. She continues to be a prominent conservative spokesperson on college campuses, writes a widely distributed syndicated column, publishes the *Phyllis Schlafly Report,* and has authored or edited sixteen books. These include *A Choice Not an Echo* (1964), which supported Republican Senator Barry Goldwater's bid for the presidency in 1964, and books on U.S. foreign policy, illiteracy, and education.

Schlafly is a strong believer in the U.S. Constitution and in Article V, which outlines the amending process. She opposed plans by the Council of States for a conference of the states, fearing that it might develop into an open-ended convention to rewrite the U.S. Constitution (*Phyllis Schlafly Report* April 1995, May 1995). She also opposes an amendment to make the District of Columbia a state. The mother of six children, Schlafly was named 1992 Illinois Mother of the Year.

See also Equal Rights Amendment.

For Further Reading:
Phyllis Schlafly Report, April 1995, May 1995.

❖ SCHOOL BUSING ❖

In the wake of the Supreme Court's decision in *Brown v. Board of Education* (1954), which called for an end to school segregation, a number of congressmen from the South proposed amendments that would give states exclusive administrative control over public schools. Over time, most proposed amendments came to focus specifically on the assignment of students to schools on the basis of race and the use of busing to achieve racial balance.

On this issue, individuals who supported the decision in *Brown* were divided. Praise for the effectiveness of busing as a means of promoting desegregation was balanced by concerns about the associated costs, the impact of busing on the quality of education and the idea of com-

munity schools, and the resulting creation of private one-race schools and the "white flight" that sometimes resulted from forced busing.

There were about twenty-five amending proposals introduced in Congress dealing with busing in the 1960s, over 225 in the 1970s, and more than twenty in the 1980s. Congressional sponsors from outside the South increased in the late 1970s and the 1980s. Ten states, including Michigan (1971) and Massachusetts (1974, 1976), also petitioned Congress for a convention on this issue during the 1960s and 1970s.

Contrary to the hopes of President Richard Nixon, the Burger Court unanimously upheld the use of busing as a tool to remedy past cases of *de jure* (legalized) segregation in *Swann v. Charlotte-Mecklenburg Board of Education* (1971). The Court's decision indicated that there were limits to the use of busing, however, and in *Milliken v. Bradley* (1974), in a five-to-four decision also written by Chief Justice Burger, the Supreme Court refused to uphold a district court mandate providing for an interdistrict remedy for an intradistrict case of *de jure* segregation. This and subsequent decisions appeared to limit the scope of busing in cases of *de facto* segregation that resulted from voluntarily chosen housing patterns rather than from discriminatory governmental actions.

A summary of amending proposals has divided them into five categories:

[those] that would prohibit: (1) the federal courts from assigning students to public schools on the basis of their race; (2) *any* governmental authority from assigning students to public schools on the basis of their race; (3) governmental authorities from assigning students on the basis of their race to any public school other than the one closest to their residence; (4) governmental authority from assigning students to schools other than the one closest to their residence, without exception; and (5) governmental interference with parents' or guardians' rights to choose a public school for their children. (Keynes with Miller 1989, 225)

In the 1970s, both the House and Senate Judiciary Committees held hearings on antibusing amendments. A proposed amendment by Democratic Representative Ronald M. Mottl of Ohio was discharged from committee, but it was defeated in 1979 by a vote of 209 to 206 in the House of Representatives (Keynes with Miller 1989, 226). There were other attempts to limit busing through restrictions on the Department of Health, Education, and Welfare; through restrictions on the Justice Department; and through controversial and unsuccessful congressional attempts to restrict judicial jurisdiction over this issue (Keynes with Miller 1989, 219).

See also *Brown v. Board of Education.*

For Further Reading:

Keynes, Edward, with Randall K. Miller. 1989. *The Court vs. Congress: Prayer, Busing, and Abortion.* Durham, NC: Duke University Press.

Schwartz, Bernard. 1986. *Swann's Way: The School Busing Case and the Supreme Court.* New York: Oxford University Press.

Wilkinson, J. Harvie, III. 1979. *From* Brown *to* Bakke: *The Supreme Court and School Integration: 1954–1978.* New York: Oxford University Press.

❖ SCHOOLS, PUBLIC ❖

The U.S. Constitution does not say anything directly about education. Many states provided for public education in constitutional reforms made in the 1840s and 1850s (Butts 1978, 81). Others, especially in the South, lagged behind in establishing public school systems. In the decades immediately following the Civil War, several members of Congress introduced national amendments calling on states to provide public education for their citizens. In his annual message of December 1875, President Ulysses S. Grant tied this proposed amendment to a restriction on aid to parochial schools (J. Richardson 1908, 8:334), which resulted in the proposal of the unsuccessful Blaine Amendment.

All states eventually established public schools. The Supreme Court endorsed racial segregation in *Plessy v. Ferguson* (1896), and this policy extended to schools and did not change until the Court's decision in *Brown v. Board of Education* (1954). Modern amending proposals have attempted to limit the use of school busing and to permit prayer and Bible reading in public schools.

See also Blaine Amendment; Education, Right to; Prayer in Public Schools; School Busing.

For Further Reading:

Butts, R. Freeman. 1978. *Public Education in the United States: From Revolution to Reform.* New York: Holt, Rinehart, and Winston.

Richardson, James E., ed. 1908. *A Compilation of the Messages and Papers of the Presidents, 1789–1908.* 11 vols. n.p.: Bureau of National Literature and Art.

❖ SCOTT V. SANDFORD (1857) ❖

Few cases in American history have stirred more controversy that did the majority opinion in this case. It was written by Chief Justice Roger B. Taney—a Jackson appointee from Maryland who served on the Court from 1836 to 1864 and had succeeded Chief Justice John Marshall. Dred Scott, a slave, had been taken by his master Dr. Emerson, an army surgeon, to a free state and a free territory and back to Missouri, which was a slave state. Scott and his wife Harriet sued Sanford (incorrectly spelled by the Court reporter as Sandford), the executor of Emerson's estate, for their freedom on the basis of their residence on free soil.

Taney ruled against the Scotts. He declared that however states might choose to define state citizenship, the Constitution limited national citizenship to whites. He interpreted the Declaration of Independence and other founding documents as applying only to whites. Taney cited both the slave importation clause and the fugitive slave clause (omitting the three-fifths clause from his discussion) to indicate that the American framers had regarded African Americans as an inferior class not entitled to the privileges of citizenship. Taney further held it to be the Court's duty to interpret the Constitution with the same words and meaning it had when it was adopted. In a reference to the amending provisions, Taney noted that if parts of the Constitution were thought to be unjust, "there is a mode prescribed in the instrument itself by which it may be amended, but while it remains unaltered, it must be construed now as it was understood at the time of its adoption" (*Scott* 1857, 426). As a noncitizen, Scott therefore had no right to appear in a federal court.

Taney went on, however, to examine the Missouri Compromise of 1820, by which slavery had been excluded from much of the Louisiana Territory. Again, Taney gave a narrow construction to the Constitution. He claimed that the provision related to the governance of territories referred only to territories in possession of the government in 1789 and not to territory that was subsequently purchased. People in such territory were guaranteed the same constitutional protections as other citizens, including the Fifth Amendment right not to be deprived of their property (slaves) without their consent. This interpretation served as the basis for the notion of substantive due process that would so affect constitutional interpretation during the next seventy-five years of Court history.

As to Scott's claim to have become free by reason of his residence in a free state, Taney ruled that such matters were governed by state law. He thus accepted the judgment of the Missouri Supreme Court that such residence in Illinois had not given Scott his freedom.

This case served as a catalyst to civil war rather than, as Taney had hoped, providing a solution to a vexing national problem. *Scott* was subsequently overturned by the Thirteenth and Fourteenth Amendments. The former abolished slavery, and the latter defined citizenship to apply to all persons born in the United States. Ironically, however, in the *Slaughterhouse Cases* (1873), the first Supreme Court decision to interpret the Fourteenth Amendment, the Court continued to rely on the distinction between state and federal citizenship that Taney had developed in *Scott* to give a restrictive reading of the amendment.

See also Fourteenth Amendment; Substantive Due Process; Supreme Court Decisions Reversed by Constitutional Amendments.

For Further Reading:
Scott v. Sandford, 60 U.S. (19 How.) 393 (1857).

❖ SECESSIONISTS, LIMITING THE RIGHTS OF ❖

After the Civil War, numerous attempts were made to exclude individuals who had been active in or had given support to the Confederate States of America from holding office, voting, or participating in certain professions. Some of these attempts took the form of legislation, and some were proposed as amendments.

In *Cummings v. Missouri* (1867), the Supreme Court invalidated a Missouri law requiring individuals in certain professions to swear that they had never supported the Confederacy. Similarly, in a companion case, *Ex parte Garland* (1867), it struck down a similar oath required of attorneys practicing in federal courts. In both cases, the Court decided that such laws were unconstitutional ex post facto laws (retroactive criminal laws) and bills of attainder (legislative punishments without benefit of a trial).

Numerous amendment proposals were introduced in Congress to exclude former members of the Confederacy from civil office or from voting. Republican Senator Jacob Howard of Michigan eventually introduced the resolution that became Section 3 of the Fourteenth Amendment. This section provided:

No person shall be a Senator or Representative in Congress, or elector of President and Vice President, or hold any office, civil or military, under the United States, or under any State, who, having previously taken an oath, as a member of Congress, or as an officer of the United States, or as a member of any State legislature, or as an executive or judicial officer of any State, shall have engaged in insurrection or rebellion against the same, or given aid or comfort to the enemies thereof.

This section also gave Congress the power to remove this disability by a two-thirds vote, and it did so on behalf of most Southerners in a vote in 1872 (Grimes 1978, 55).

See also Fourteenth Amendment.

For Further Reading:
Grimes, Alan P. 1978. *Democracy and the Amendments to the Constitution.* Lexington, MA: Lexington Books.

❖ SECOND AMENDMENT ❖

Few, if any, provisions of the Constitution are more controversial than the Second Amendment. It was ratified in 1791 as part of the Bill of Rights. It provides that "a well regulated Militia, being necessary to the security of a free State, the right of the people to keep and bear Arms, shall not be infringed."

Several states that had ratified the Constitution proposed such an amendment (Vandercoy 1994, 1029–1032), and such a proposal was among those that James Madison proposed in the First Congress in 1789. His original proposal contained a related provision that would have established a right of conscientious objection for religious reasons (see Kurland and Lerner 1987, 5:25), but the Senate deleted it.

In recent years, the Second Amendment has drawn renewed scholarly attention (S. Heller 1995) and has even prompted a full-page advertisement signed by scholars who believe that the amendment has been too narrowly interpreted (Academics for the Second Amendment 1995, A23). Interpretations of the Second Amendment differ radically. The National Rifle Association (NRA) has argued for an absolutist view of this amendment as guaranteeing individual rights and it has opposed legislation that would ban certain types of guns, including handguns and assault rifles. By contrast, the American Civil Liberties Union has supported gun regulations and has interpreted the amendment to refer to the protection of collective state militia rather than of individual rights (for contrasting positions, see Levinson 1989). This debate has encompassed both his-

torians and political scientists, with great attention being given to a Bancroft Prize–winning book by Michael A. Bellesiles entitled *Arming America: The Origins of a National Gun Culture* (2000). Bellesiles had argued that the modern pervasiveness of guns did not arise from the early republic but from the period after the Civil War. Now generally discredited, the book continues to be the center of academic debate including a forum in the January 2002 issue of *The William and Mary Quarterly.*

The difficulty of interpreting the Second Amendment centers on its statement of purpose. Interpreters have to decide whether the purpose limits the meaning of the entire amendment or whether the right to "keep and bear Arms" that follows has independent meaning.

Even a resolution of this issue does not necessarily solve the interpretive problems, because it can and has been argued that the framers interpreted the idea of the militia quite broadly, believing that an armed citizenry was a guard against tyranny. Thus, during debates in the First Congress, Elbridge Gerry noted that the proposal that became the Second Amendment "is intended to secure the people against the mal-administration of the Government." He further connected the militia with the desire "to prevent the establishment of a standing army" (Kurland and Lerner 1987, 5:210). Thus, some proponents of original intent argue that the amendment should be interpreted quite expansively (see Halbrook 1994; Cramer 1994).

By contrast, others argue that the basic thrust of the amendment was simply to ensure "that citizens have a constitutionally protected right to serve in militia in defense of state and country" (Spitzer 1995, 35). Under this interpretation, "the Second Amendment is founded on *federalism,* balancing powers between the federal government and the states; and *military necessity,* developing a political compromise between politically popular militias and a politically unpopular but militarily necessary national professional army." Such a view would denigrate arguments on behalf of "hunting, sporting, recreation, or even personal protection" (*Id.,* 35–36). Because state militias have for all practical purposes ceased, those who hold this view also hold that "the Second Amendment has been rendered essentially irrelevant to modern American life" (*Id.,* 38). Moreover, under such an interpretation, both state and federal governments have the power to regulate gun ownership, which is blamed by many for the rising tide of violence in the nation.

To date, the Supreme Court has rarely ventured into the gun-control controversy. In *United States v. Miller* (1939), the Supreme Court unanimously upheld a federal law against the use of sawed-off shotguns by ruling that the Second Amendment protected only weapons that could be used as part of a militia. Ironically, this principle would make regulation of assault weapons quite difficult. In *Quilici v. Village of Morton Grove* (1983), the Court refused to review a lower court decision upholding a ban on the ownership of handguns. To date, the Second Amendment remains one of the few guarantees in the Bill of Rights that has not been applied to the states via the due process clause of the Fourteenth Amendment and has been described as an "underenforced constitutional norm" (Denning 1998).

This situation may soon be changing. On 6 May 2002, U.S. Solicitor General Theodore B. Olson filed briefs in two gun-control cases that the U.S. Supreme Court later rejected for review *(Emerson v. United States* and *Haney v. United States)* arguing for the first time on behalf of the national government that the Second Amendment is a grant of a personal right to bear arms (Walsh 2002, A01). The cases at hand involved an indictment against a man who owned a Beretta pistol while subject to a restraining order for domestic violence against his wife and the other involved a man convicted for possessing an illegal machine gun. Although arguing that gun ownership was an individual rather than a purely collective right limited to members of the militia, Olson agrees that the right is "subject to reasonable restrictions designed to prevent possession by unfit persons or to restrict the possession of firearms that are particularly suited to criminal misuse" (Walsh 2002, A01). Thus, in the cases at hand, Olson supports the gun regulations as appropriate.

Two proposed amendments were introduced in 1913 to authorize Congress to regulate the carrying of concealed weapons in the District of Columbia and the territories. The next proposal appears to have been the one that New York Democratic Representative Major Owens introduced in 1992. He made another appeal for an amendment designed to clarify the Second Amendment in June 1995, calls that have been subsequently repeated.

The paucity of proposed amendments certainly does not stem from disinterest in the Second Amendment. The likely explanation is that most proponents and opponents of gun control have preferred to battle over the meaning of the existing constitutional provision rather than to introduce a new one.

For Further Reading:

Academics for the Second Amendment. 1995. "An Open Letter on the Second Amendment." *Chronicle of Higher Education* 41 (11 August): A23.

Belleisles, Michael A. 2000. *Arming America: The Origins of a National Gun Culture.* New York: Alfred A. Knopf.

Cottrol, Robert J., ed. 1994. *Gun Control and the Constitution: Sources and Explorations of the Second Amendment.* 3 vols. New York: Garland.

Cramer, Clayton E. 1994. *For the Defense of Themselves and the State: The Original Intent and Judicial Interpretation of the Right to Keep and Bear Arms.* Westport, CT: Praeger.

Denning, Brannon P. 1998. "Gun Shy: The Second Amendment as an 'Underenforced Constitutional Norm.'" *Harvard Journal of Law & Public Policy* 21 (Summer): 719–791.

Emerson v. United States, 122 S. Ct. 2362 (2002).

"Forum: Historians and Guns." 2002. *William and Mary Quarterly* 59, 3d Series (January): 203–268.

Halbrook, Stephen D. 1994. *That Every Man Be Armed: The Evolution of a Constitutional Right.* Oakland, CA: Independent Institute.

Haney v. United States, 122 S. Ct. 2362 (2002).

Heller, Scott. 1995. "The Right to Bear Arms." *Chronicle of Higher Education* 41 (21 July): A8, A12.

Kurland, Philip B., and Ralph Lerner, eds. 1987. *The Founders' Constitution.* 5 vols. Chicago: University of Chicago Press.

Levinson, Sanford. 1989. "The Embarrassing Second Amendment." *Yale Law Journal* 99 (December): 637–660.

McClurg, Andrew J., David B. Kopel, and Brannon P. Denning, eds. 2002. *Gun Control & Gun Rights: A Reader and Guide*. New York: New York University Press.

"Second Amendment Symposium." 1995. *Tennessee Law Review* 62 (Spring): 443–821.

Spitzer, Robert J. 1995. *The Politics of Gun Control*. Chatham, NJ: Chatham House Publishers.

Vandercoy, David E. 1994. "The History of the Second Amendment." *Valparaiso University Law Review* 28 (Spring): 1007–1039.

Walsh, Edward. 2002. "U.S. Argues for Wider Gun Rights: Supreme Court Filing Reverses Past Policy," *The Washington Post*, 8 May, A01.

❖ SECRETARY OF STATE ❖

The secretary of state served until 1818 by custom, and from then until 1951 by statute, as the person responsible for certifying and proclaiming the ratification of constitutional amendments. Congress transferred this function to the administrator of the General Services Administration in 1951 and to the archivist of the Library of Congress in 1984 (Bernstein with Agel 1993, 246).

The action of certifying amendments is generally routine, but Secretary William Seward faced anything but a routine situation when deciding what to do about the Fourteenth Amendment. Although one more than the necessary twenty-eight states had ratified, North and South Carolina had done so in the face of prior rejections of the amendment, and Ohio and New Jersey had subsequently voted rescissions (Dellinger 1983, 389). Seward reported these facts to Congress, directing particular attention to the attempted rescissions. Congress subsequently voted to promulgate the amendment, which Seward then did (James 1984, 289–304). The issue is further confused, however, by the fact that a telegram had been introduced in congressional debates indicating that Georgia had also ratified. This provided the necessary three-fourths majority whether the two rescissions were counted or not (A. Baker 1979, 79–80).

Walter Dellinger has argued that the congressional promulgation of the Fourteenth Amendment was unique, unwarranted, and unnecessary. In his view, an amendment becomes effective the moment it is ratified by the necessary states, whether it is so noted at the time by the official responsible or not (Dellinger 1983, 402).

The controversial ratification of the Twenty-seventh Amendment brought renewed attention to the role of the official responsible for certifying amendments. In that case, the decision by the archivist of the Library of Congress to certify the amendment was confirmed by an overwhelming vote in Congress, whose members were feeling heat from their constituents for being unresponsive to public sentiments. In the minds of critics concerned about the possible absence of a contemporary consensus, however, this did little to justify the ratification of an amendment more than 200 years after it had been proposed.

For Further Reading:

Baker, A. Diane. 1979. "ERA: The Effect of Extending the Time for Ratification on Attempts to Rescind Prior Ratifications." *Emory Law Journal* 28: 71–110.

Bernstein, Richard B., with Jerome Agel. 1993. *Amending America: If We Love the Constitution So Much, Why Do We Keep Trying to Change It?* New York: Random House.

Dellinger, Walter. 1983. "The Legitimacy of Constitutional Change: Rethinking the Amending Process." *Harvard Law Review* 97 (December): 380–432.

❖ SEGREGATION ❖

One of the Supreme Court's most important decisions of the twentieth century was its ruling in *Brown v. Board of Education* (1954). In this decision, the Court unanimously declared an end to the system of state-mandated segregation that it had previously sanctioned in *Plessy v. Ferguson* (1896).

In 1948, even before the *Brown* decision, Democratic Representative Oren Harris of Arkansas had introduced an amendment designed to allow individuals to segregate themselves from others voluntarily. He reintroduced this amendment in 1958 and 1961. Three days after the *Brown* decision, Democratic Representative John Bell Williams of Mississippi introduced an amendment designed to allow states to maintain racial segregation in schools. Other proposals with a similar aim were introduced to limit federal interference with state police powers. Numerous other proposals have been introduced specifically to limit the use of school busing to achieve racial balance. Supreme Court decisions often distinguish *de jure* from *de facto* segregation as well as between state and private action. Racially discriminatory laws are almost always subjected to "strict scrutiny" and declared unconstitutional; discrimination by individuals that does not have state sanction or segregation that results from personal choice is far less likely to be invalidated.

See also *Brown v. Board of Education; Plessy v. Ferguson;* School Busing; States, Police Powers.

❖ SELF-INCRIMINATION ❖

The Fifth Amendment provides that no person "shall be compelled in any criminal case to be a witness against himself." In *Malloy v. Hogan* (1964) the Supreme Court reversed earlier rulings and decided that this guarantee applied to state as well as federal trials. The right was further expanded by the Warren Court in *Miranda v. Arizona* (1966) to preclude the use of confessions made in the absence of warnings about self-incrimination and the right to an attorney. Although *Miranda* significantly expanded the right against self-incrimination, this right has deep roots in English common law and has variously been defended as a way of promoting fairness in an accusatorial legal system, as a way to prevent cruel and inhumane treatment of defendants, and as a way of protecting personal privacy (D. O'Brien 2000a, 974–977).

A number of congressmen have proposed modifications of the Fifth Amendment. Among the most prominent advocates of a modification from 1968 to the present has been Democratic Representative Andrew Jacobs Jr. of Indiana, who worked as a police officer while in law school (Barone and Ujifusa 1994, 464). His proposal has three parts: it would stipulate that individuals could not be compelled to incriminate themselves "except in open court"; it would prevent the introduction of prior criminal convictions, "except where they are an element of the crime charged"; and it would alter the Sixth Amendment so that defendants would be informed not only of the nature and cause of the accusations against them but also of the evidence (H.J. Res. 314, 1979). In 1971 Republican Representative Carleton King of New York introduced a proposal (H.J. Res. 903) prohibiting the use of physical or mental torture to extract confessions, but permitting inferences that might be made from failure to testify. King would also have permitted "the reasonable in-custody questioning of suspects by police."

For Further Reading:

Barone, Michael, and Grant Ujifusa. 1994. *The Almanac of American Politics 1994.* Washington, DC: National Journal.

O'Brien, David M. 2000a. *Civil Rights and Civil Liberties.* Vol. 2 of *Constitutional Law and Politics.* 5th ed. New York: W. W. Norton.

❖ SENECA FALLS CONVENTION (1848) ❖

Although the Nineteenth Amendment prohibiting discrimination against women in voting was not ratified until 1920, the movement for women's suffrage is often traced to the Seneca Falls Convention. It met at the Wesleyan Chapel (now a national historic site) in Seneca Falls, New York, on 19 and 20 July 1848. Largely organized by Elizabeth Cady Stanton and Lucretia Mott, who literally called it just days before it was held, and attended by about 300 men and women, the convention adopted a "Declaration of Sentiments."

Patterned after the U.S. Declaration of Independence, it declared that "all men and women are created equal," and listed numerous deprivations that women faced. These included the denial of the right to vote, the requirement that women submit to laws that they had no part in making, the moribund legal status of married women, the subjection of women to physical punishment by their husbands, the denial of the guardianship of children to women who were divorced, the exclusion of women from key professions, and the like (see Wheeler 1995a, 40–42). In one passage that is sometimes regarded as racist but which may have resonated with many contemporaries and became a renewed matter of controversy when the Fourteenth and Fifteenth Amendments later (at least on paper) guaranteed rights to African American men that were denied to either white or black women, the Declaration noted that "He [mankind] has withheld from her [women] rights which are given to the most ignorant and degraded men—both natives and foreigners" (Wheeler 1995a, 40).

Although the Convention was the brainchild of Stanton and Mott, Mott's husband, as well as the husband of another participant, presided over the meeting so as to prevent undue offense to public sensibilities, at a time when women did not speak in public unless it was to a group of other women. One hundred delegates, both men and women, subsequently signed a set of resolutions designed to provide for women's equality. Although the Nineteenth Amendment (as well as future calls for an Equal Rights Amendment) can be traced to these resolutions, they did not specifically call for a constitutional amendment or set of amendments. Interestingly, the provision for "the elective franchise" was considered to be the most controversial (so much so, that it was the only provision not to be adopted unanimously, and many who signed the resolutions later renounced them). It probably would not have been included but for the insistence of Elizabeth Cady Stanton and Frederick Douglass that this right was a key to others. Stanton's own husband absented himself from the convention; her father reportedly "rushed to Seneca Falls fearing for his daughter's sanity," and her older sister "wept over . . . her involvement in such a radical cause" (Bernard and Fox-Gen-

ovese 1995, 11). Not surprisingly, the resolution for women's suffrage was long subject of journalistic ridicule, and the task of obtaining suffrage proved to be far more extended than many probably would have anticipated. Only one young woman who was present at the Seneca Falls Convention, Charlotte Woodward, survived long enough to cast her vote in a presidential election seventy-two years later (Palmer 2000, 433).

In the meantime, the Seneca Falls Convention sparked other conventions, including one that was held two weeks later in Rochester, New York, and the first of many subsequent national women's rights conventions, which was held in Worcester, Massachusetts, in 1850. During the next seven decades, Carrie Chapman Catt noted that women participated in a total of:

> 56 campaigns of state referenda, 480 campaigns to convince state legislatures to submit suffrage amendments to voters, 47 campaigns attempting to get state constitutional conventions to write woman suffrage into state constitutions, and 19 campaigns with 19 successive Congresses. (Summarized in Palmer 2000, 429)

See also Declaration of Independence; Douglass, Frederick; Equal Rights Amendment; Mott, Lucretia Coffin; Nineteenth Amendment; Stanton, Elizabeth Cady.

For Further Reading:
Bernhard, Virginia, and Elizabeth Fox-Genovese, eds. 1995. *The Birth of American Feminism: The Seneca Falls Woman's Convention of 1848.* St. James, NY: Brandywine Press.

Palmer, Kris E. 2000. *Constitutional Amendments: 1789 to the Present.* Detroit, MI: Gale Group.

Wheeler, Marjorie S., ed. 1995a. *One Woman, One Vote: Rediscovering the Woman Suffrage Movement.* Troutdale, OR: New Sage.

❖ SEPARATION OF POWERS AND THE AMENDING PROCESS ❖

One of the unstated innovations of the U.S. Constitution was its creation of a system of separation of powers. This principle was reflected in the division of its first three articles of the document—the first outlining the legislative, the second the executive, and the third the judicial branches. Under this plan, although it was generally understood that the legislative branch would, as an elective body, be the one closest to the people, it was not, like the British Parliament, entrusted with complete sovereignty, which the American framers equated with tyranny. Instead, congressional powers were shared with an independently elected executive branch and a judicial branch appointed by the executive with the advice and consent of the Senate.

Separation of powers was based on the framers' belief that men were not "angels" and their fear that individuals with power would seek to abuse it. As James Madison explained in *Federalist No. 51*, the framers thought that the presence of three branches, the concurrence of at least two of which would be needed for the adoption of legislation, would result in a system of checks and balances in which each branch would protect liberty by resisting encroachments on their own power by the other two:

> But the great security against a gradual concentration of the several powers in the same department consists in giving to those who administer each department the necessary constitutional means and personal motives to resist encroachments of the others. The provision for defense must in this, as in all other cases, be made commensurate to the danger of attack. Ambition must be made to counteract ambition. The interest of the man must be connected with the constitutional rights of the place. (Ford 1898, 345)

Although separation of powers was adopted as a method of keeping the three branches of the national government in check, the division of power between the national government and the states, or federalism, was thought to create additional security for liberty. Provisions for federalism are included in Article IV of the Constitution and reflected in a number of subsequent amendments, most notably the Tenth and Fourteenth, in the latter of which state powers were somewhat reduced in order to provide for greater federal protections of individual rights.

Curiously, separation of powers appears to play relatively little role in the constitutional amending process. Given that all the branches were the creation of a constitutional convention consisting of delegates from the states called with the acquiescence of the existing Congress under the Articles of Confederation, perhaps the delegates thought that federalism was a more relevant consideration in the adoption of amendments. Moreover, it was logical for the delegates at the Constitutional Convention to follow the model of the Articles of Confederation under which amendments were proposed by Congress and ratified by state legislatures.

Of the three branches of the existing national government, Congress has had the central role in the amending process. This role might be curtailed, but not eliminated, if the Article V provision granting two-thirds of the states the power to petition Congress to call a special convention to propose amendments were utilized. However, to date this provision has not been directly exercised, although it has sometimes prompted Congress to take preemptive action by proposing amendments that the states favored. Instead, to date, two-thirds majorities of both houses of Congress have proposed all existing amendments.

Article V makes no mention of a role for the president in the amending process. In *Hollingsworth v. Virginia* (1798), the Supreme Court decided that the president's signature was not required for amendments to become the law of the land. When presidents lobby for, or (as on occasion) sign, amendments, they do so in an extra-constitutional capacity.

The role of the judiciary in the amending process is more complex and debatable. Until its decision in *Coleman v. Miller* (1939), the Supreme Court fairly regularly resolved amending issues—as, for example, in the case of *Hollingsworth v. Virginia* cited above. In *Coleman,* the Court indicated that most amending issues (and particularly the issue of whether amendments had been ratified within an appropriate time period) were "political questions" for Congress to resolve. In the case of extending the deadline for the Equal Rights Amendment and affirming the belated ratification of the Twenty-seventh Amendment related to the timing of congressional pay raises, the Congress has made important decisions in this area. However, the Court has occasionally patrolled the boundaries of the process since *Coleman,* and the status of that decision remains in some doubt after significant changes in the political questions doctrine. Moreover, there is something of a dialectical relationship between courts and constitutional amendments. Decisions of the courts can be, and sometimes have been, reversed by constitutional amendments, but courts, in turn, must interpret amendments that are adopted, and their interpretations, particularly of the post–Civil War Amendments, have sometimes been more restrictive than they might have been.

To date, amendments have done far more to address issues of federalism than to adjust mechanisms connected with the doctrine of separation of powers. Although the First Amendment is stated as a limitation on Congress, it, like most of the rest of the Bill of Rights, has in fact been applied to all branches of the national government and, since the adoption of the Fourteenth Amendment and the incorporation doctrine, has also been applied to state governments. The Tenth Amendment is a specific recognition of powers reserved to the states, and the Eleventh is designed to provide state immunity against certain lawsuits. The Twelfth Amendment probably undercut congressional power just a bit by making it less likely that Congress would have to resolve future presidential elections, but it was chiefly designed to remedy what was regarded as a flaw in the original electoral college mechanism. The post–Civil War amendments, and others with enforcement clauses, increased

congressional powers, but chiefly served to limit the states. The Sixteenth Amendment (providing for a national income tax) increased congressional powers but had the same effect on other branches of the national government. In providing for direct election of senators, the Seventeenth Amendment did more to decrease state legislative control of senators than to increase federal powers. The Eighteenth Amendment, providing for national alcoholic prohibition, increased powers of both state and national governments, but its repeal limited the powers of the latter.

The Twenty-second Amendment, limiting a president to two full terms in office, arguably decreased the power of second-term presidents (by making them "lame ducks" vis-à-vis the Congress), but this result seems largely to have been an unintended consequence of a more important objective. Amendments (the Fifteenth, Nineteenth, and Twenty-sixth) denying voting discrimination again appear to have largely affected state powers rather than the allocation of national ones. The Twentieth Amendment, relating to lame-duck terms of both Congress and the president, was not aimed at lessening the power of these institutions per se, but only in assuring their accountability. Amendments like the Twenty-fifth, providing for presidential disability and succession, have arguably protected the executive branch against future dangers without significantly altering its relation to the other two branches.

In some ways, it is curious to see how little connection the amending process has toward what is generally considered to be a major principle of American government, but the process continues to shape judicial interpretations of the Constitution, as in its decisions to reject the so-called "legislative veto" or the "item veto." Similarly, the amending process could still alter the relation among the three branches of the national government either by approving one of these mechanisms that the Court has struck down, by otherwise investing one of the existing branches of government with increased power, or by divesting one of them of powers they now wield. Similarly, proposals for replacing the current Constitution with one that would be based on parliamentary principles could have a major effect on current national institutions and the relationships among them.

See also *Coleman v. Miller;* Federalism and the Amending Process; *Hollingsworth v. Virginia;* Parliamentary Sovereignty; Supreme Court Decisions Reversed by Constitutional Amendments.

For Further Reading:
Ford, Paul L., ed. 1898. *The Federalist.* New York: Henry Holt.

❖ SEVENTEENTH AMENDMENT ❖

The American framers considered bicameralism, the division of Congress into two branches, to be quite important. Anticipating that the legislative body would be the most powerful in a republic, the framers hoped that the Senate would be a somewhat smaller, wiser body capable of tempering "the sudden and violent passions" thought to be more characteristic of larger legislative chambers (Hamilton, Madison, and Jay 1961, 379). This was one reason that the term of senators was set at six years rather than two, as in the case of members of the House of Representatives. Consistent with a federal system of government balancing the national government with state governments, the framers also thought that a group of appointed senators might represent states better than senators with an independent electoral base.

The Framers' Scheme
Whereas members of the House of Representatives were apportioned according to population, each state was guaranteed two senators. This provision, part of the Great Compromise that was necessary at the Constitutional Convention of 1787 to reconcile the interests of the large and small states (Vile 2001, 16–17), was further entrenched by a provision in Article V providing that no state shall be deprived of its equal Senate representation without its consent. In an attempt to give the Senate a different electoral base than the House, the framers specified in Article I, Section 3 that it would be composed of "two Senators from each State, chosen by the Legislature thereof, for six Years." Although senators were permitted to cast separate votes (thus potentially representing differing political bases within their states), on key issues, including the proposal of constitutional amendments, state legislatures sometimes attempted to "instruct" their senators. Senators did not always comply and could not, under the Constitution, be recalled when they failed to do so, but a number of senators resigned when they found that their consciences required a vote other than the one that their state legislature had mandated (Bybee 1997, 526).

Calls for Change
Beginning in 1826, calls increased to change this method of selection to popular election, a movement notably supported by Tennessee Senator and later President Andrew Johnson. This movement hit full stride at the end of the nineteenth century. By the time the amendment was ratified in 1913, there had been close to 200 proposals introduced in Congress to this effect, including over 50 petitions (some redundant) from 31 states. The threat of a convention appears to have been a strong motive that finally prompted the Senate to act.

Early in American constitutional history, there had been considerable controversy about how state legislatures were to make their choices. Congress adopted legislation on the subject on 25 July 1866, but the legislation proved singularly ineffective in solving many of the problems (Haynes 1960, 85), and may even have complicated them by requiring that state legislatures had to select senators by majority vote, thus increasing the possibility of deadlocks (Bybee 1997, 536–537). Many thought that the system allowed money and influence to control the political system (Grimes 1978, 79).

A close scholar of the subject identified the following problems: deadlocks, stampeded elections, bribery and corruption, unfilled vacancies depriving states of their constitutionally entitled equal representation, misrepresentation of popular wishes, interference with the states' regular legislative business, and confusion and corruption of state politics (Haynes

1960, 86–95). In one notorious example in Missouri in 1904, representatives attempted to stop the legislative clock to give time for a senatorial election. Tactics included hoisting a ladder, fistfighting, and throwing books. It was reported that "the glass of the clock front was broken, but the pendulum still persisted in swinging until, in the midst of a yelling mob, one member began throwing ink bottles at the clock, and finally succeeded in breaking the pendulum" (Haynes 1960, 90).

Action by the States

After the Senate's repeated refusal to act, a number of states began to take matters into their own hands. Most popular was a method, initially adopted in Oregon by popular referendum, and thereby usually referred to as the "Oregon Model," whereby candidates for the state legislature were asked to pledge their votes for the candidate who won the party primary (Haynes 1960, 101–104). Senators so selected naturally felt obligated to support an amendment for popular election. As Idaho Senator Borah remarked, "I should not be here if it [election by the legislature under direct instructions of a popular vote] had not been practiced, and I have great affection for the bridge which carried me over" (Haynes 1960, 108).

Proposal and Ratification

An amendment providing for the direct election of senators was first adopted in the House on 21 July 1894. The House was also successful in votes taken in 1898, 1900, and 1902. The Senate's first vote in 1911 proved unsuccessful, and there was considerable friction between the two houses about the so-called race rider, introduced by Republican Representative Horace Young of Michigan and largely supported by Southern Democrats. Although accepting the direct election of senators, this rider would have removed such elections from federal supervision, including protections offered to black voters by the Fifteenth Amendment. Eventually, Republican Senator Francis Bristow of Kentucky succeeded in invalidating the race rider by adding an amendment to the resolution that became the Seventeenth Amendment (Grimes 1978, 79–81). On 11

April 1911, Socialist Representative Victor Berger of Wisconsin introduced a resolution for abolition of the Senate (H.J. Res. 79). Like petitions for a convention, it seems likely that this proposal was designed to pressure senators. Both houses finally agreed on the Seventeenth Amendment in May 1912.

The amendment was ratified by the necessary number of states on 8 April 1913, Massachusetts being the first and Connecticut the thirty-sixth to ratify (U.S. Senate 1985, 46). As ratified, the amendment calls for the direct election of senators by state voters with the qualifications "requisite for electors of the most numerous branch of the State legislatures." These were the same qualifications previously introduced in Article I, Section 2 of the Constitution for voting for members of the House of Representatives. The amendment also provides that state executives may temporarily fill vacancies until the people vote. Thus, when Democratic Senator Al Gore Jr. of Tennessee became vice president in 1993, Democratic Governor McWherter appointed Democrat Harlan Matthews until state voters chose Republican Fred Thompson in the next regular congressional election in 1994.

Critiques and Implications of the Amendment

The Seventeenth Amendment has been called "the most drastic alteration in the system of federalism since the Civil War Amendments" (Bernstein with Agel 1993, 122). The amendment appears to have had the effect of leading to the election of more people on the basis of their governmental experience than on the basis of their wealth or family connections. As a result of the amendment, the Senate also appears to have become more responsive to fluctuations in popular party preferences (Crook and Hibbing 1997, 352). One result, however, is that, since adoption of the Seventeenth Amendment, the senators of a state often represent a different party than the one that dominates the state legislature (Bybee 1997, 553–554).

Although it is difficult to imagine its repeal, one such proposal was introduced in June 1939 by a Montana representative. The amendment is occasionally criticized for weakening political parties and for reducing the proper influence of the states in the federal system. With the increasingly high costs of political campaigns and the lack of any limits on what an individual can contribute to his or her own efforts, the goal of seeing that the Senate is not a "millionaires club" may also have been thwarted (R. Peters 1990).

In her dissenting opinion in *Garcia v. San Antonio Metropolitan Transit Authority,* a case involving congressional authority to set wage regulations for state and local governments, Justice Sandra Day O'Connor, a former Arizona legislator, referred to the direct election of senators as one factor that may have "lessened the weight Congress gives to the legitimate interests of States as States" (1985, 584). It is possible that increased concerns about federalism could eventually result in another constitutional amendment to redress a perceived imbalance.

Citing the implications of the Seventeenth Amendment as "unchartered waters," one author criticized a U.S. circuit court opinion in *Trinsey v. Pennsylvania* (1991). This case dealt with the procedures used to select party nominees for the election of a successor to Republican Senator John Heinz of Pennsylvania, who died in a plane crash. The author of the article argued that the amendment should be interpreted to prohibit a state from selecting candidates for senatorial vacancies without following normal primary election procedures (Little 1991).

For Further Reading:

Bernstein, Richard B., with Jerome Agel. 1993. *Amending America: If We Love the Constitution So Much, Why Do We Keep Trying to Change It?* New York: Random House.

Bybee, Jay S. 1997. "Ulysses at the Mast: Democracy, Federalism, and the Sirens' Song of the Seventeenth Amendment." *Northwestern University Law Review* 91 (Winter): 500–569.

Crook, Sara Brandes, and John R. Hibbing. 1997. "A Not-So-Distant Mirror: the 17th Amendment and Congressional Change." *American Political Science Review* 91 (December): 845–853.

Garcia v. San Antonio Metropolitan Transit Authority, 469 U.S. 528 (1985).

Grimes, Alan P. 1978. *Democracy and the Amendments to the Constitution.* Lexington, MA: Lexington Books.

Hamilton, Alexander, James Madison, and John Jay. 1787–1788. *The Federalist Papers.* Reprint, New York: New American Library, 1961.

Haynes, George H. 1960. *The Senate of the United States, Its History and Practice.* New York: Russell and Russell.

Hoebeke, C. H. 1995. *The Road to Mass Democracy: Original Intent and the Seventeenth Amendment.* New Brunswick, NJ: Transaction.

Little, Laura E. 1991. "An Excursion into the Uncharted Waters of the Seventeenth Amendment." *Temple Law Review* 674 (Fall): 629–658.

Peters, Ronald M., Jr. 1990. "Repeal the Seventeenth!" *Extensions* 2 (Spring): 16–17.

Rossum, Ralph A. 2001. *Federalism, the Supreme Court, and the Seventeenth Amendment: The Irony of Constitutional Democracy.* Lanham, MD: Lexington Books.

U.S. Senate, Subcommittee on the Constitution, Committee on the Judiciary. 1985. *Amendments to the Constitution: A Brief Legislative History.* Washington, DC: U.S. Government Printing Office.

Vile, John R. 2001. *A Companion to the United States Constitution and Its Amendments.* Westport, CT: Praeger.

❖ SEVENTH AMENDMENT ❖

The Seventh Amendment was proposed by the First Congress and ratified as part of the Bill of Rights in 1791. The amendment provides that "in suits at common law, when the value in controversy shall exceed twenty dollars, the right of trial by jury shall be preserved, and no fact tried by a jury, shall be otherwise re-examined in any Court of the United States, than according to the rules of common law." The Seventh Amendment thus complements the Sixth, which provides for jury trials in criminal cases.

The absence of a guarantee of juries in civil cases was a prominent Anti-Federalist criticism of the new document, and the ratifying conventions of Massachusetts, Maryland, Virginia, and North Carolina all called for guarantees of juries in civil cases (Lutz 1992, 57). Accordingly, when James Madison offered his proposal for a bill of rights, he included a provision that "in suits at common law, between man and man, the trial by jury as one of the best securities to the rights of the people, ought to remain inviolate" (Kurland and Lerner 1987, 5:26).

Supreme Court decisions have extended guarantees for jury trials to federal statutory law, as well as to common, or judge-made, law cases. However, courts have limited civil juries in four types of cases: those in which individuals sue the government; cases involving congressionally created rights; maritime cases; and equity cases that do not involve money (Pendergast, Pendergast, and Sousanis 2001, 1:142). Moreover, as in the case of the Sixth Amendment, the Supreme Court has not required that such juries consist of the traditional twelve members. Whereas the Sixth Amendment provision for a jury trial in criminal cases has been applied to the states via the due process clause of the Fourteenth Amendment, the provision in the Seventh Amendment has not been so applied. States are therefore free to dispense with such requirements in their civil proceedings.

In the past dozen years, at least two individuals have advocated repeal of the Seventh Amendment (Antieau 1995; Kennedy 1991).

See also Sixth Amendment.

For Further Reading:

Antieau, Chester J. 1995. *A U.S. Constitution for the Year 2000.* Chicago: Loyola University Press.

Kennedy, Devin C. 1991. "We Need a Fresh Start; Repeal the Seventh Amendment." *Detroit College of Law Review* (Winter): 1289–1301.

Kurland, Philip B., and Ralph Lerner, eds. 1987. *The Founders' Constitution.* 5 vols. Chicago: University of Chicago Press.

Lutz, Donald S. 1992. *A Preface to American Political Theory.* Lawrence, KS: University Press of Kansas.

Pendergast, Tom, Sara Pendergast, and John Sousanis, with Elizabeth Shaw Grunow, eds., 2001. *Constitutional Amendments: From Freedom of Speech to Flag Burning.* 3 vols. Detroit, MI: U.X.L. imprint of Gale Group.

❖ SHAFROTH-PALMER AMENDMENT ❖

Sometimes simply referred to as the Shafroth Amendment, this proposal was introduced in Congress in March 1914 and was sponsored by Democratic Senator John F. Shafroth of Colorado and Democratic Representative Mitchell Palmer of Pennsylvania (Kraditor 1981, 204–209). Initially, the amendment also had the support of Ruth Hanna McCormick of the National American Woman Suffrage Association (NAWSA).

The amendment proposed allowing 8 percent of a state's voters to petition to place women's suffrage on the state ballot, the issue subsequently to be decided by a state referendum. This would have left the issue of women's suffrage a matter for state rather than for federal action (Lunardini 1986, 55). NAWSA's endorsement of the proposal was dropped in 1915 when Carrie Chapman Catt was elected its president, and the organization directed renewed attention to the alternative Anthony Amendment, which became the Nineteenth Amendment in 1920 (Lunardini 1986, 182).

See also Initiative and Referendum; Nineteenth Amendment.

For Further Reading:

Kraditor, Aileen S. 1981. *The Idea of the Woman's Suffrage Movement, 1890–1920.* New York: W. W. Norton.

Lunardini, Christine A. 1986. *From Equal Suffrage to Equal Rights: Alice Paul and the National Woman's Party, 1910–1928.* New York: New York University Press.

❖ SHERMAN, ROGER (1721–1793) ❖

Roger Sherman was an American founding father from Connecticut who served on the committee that drafted the Declaration of Independence; he also signed the Articles of Confederation and attended the Constitutional Convention of 1787 (M. Bradford 1994,

21–28). Sherman was an active member of the convention who helped formulate the Connecticut Compromise, providing that states would be represented by population in the House of Representatives (as the Virginia Plan had proposed) and equally in the Senate (as the New Jersey Plan had advocated). At the convention, Sherman suggested inclusion of the provision in Article V that the states could not be deprived of their equal representation in the Senate without their consent, a provision initially rejected but later adopted after being reintroduced by Pennsylvania's Gouverneur Morris. Sherman did not succeed in adding a provision that would have prevented a state from being affected "in its internal police" without its consent (Farrand 1966, 2:630).

Although he eventually gave his support, Sherman initially opposed the Bill of Rights on the theory that such a bill would allow the national government to control the acts of individuals within the states (M. Bradford 1994, 26). As a member of the first House of Representatives, Sherman raised the initial objection to James Madison's plan to incorporate new amendments within the text of the document rather than adding such amendments, as Congress eventually decided to do, at the end of the document. Sherman observed, "We ought not to interweave our propositions into the work itself, because it will be destructive of the whole fabric. We might as well endeavor to mix brass, iron, and clay, as to incorporate such heterogeneous articles; the one contradictory to the other" (Kurland and Lerner 1987, 5:34).

See also Placement of Constitutional Amendments.

For Further Reading:

Bradford, M. E. 1994. *Founding Fathers: Brief Lives of the Framers of the United States Constitution.* 2d ed. Lawrence, KS: University Press of Kansas.

Kurland, Philip B., and Ralph Lerner, eds. 1987. *The Founders' Constitution.* 5 vols. Chicago: University of Chicago Press.

❖ SIXTEENTH AMENDMENT ❖

The Sixteenth Amendment provides that "the Congress shall have power to lay and collect taxes on incomes, from whatever source derived, without apportionment among the several States, or without regard to any census or enumeration." By giving sanction to the income tax, this amendment has had a profound effect on everyday life (Carson 1973). Coming forty-three years after the adoption of the Fifteenth Amendment, the Sixteenth Amendment also restored faith in the efficacy of the constitutional amending process and initiated a seven-year period in which three additional amendments were proposed and ratified (Kyvig 1988).

Although the U.S. Supreme Court narrowly decided to void the income tax law of 1894 in *Pollock v. Farmers' Loan & Trust Co.* (1895), it had previously accepted a wartime income tax in *Springer v. United States* (1881). Not only had war ceased in the interim, but the rhetoric had also been raised by those who argued against the income tax in *Pollock,* including New York attorneys Joseph H. Choate and William D. Guthrie. They charged that the tax, with its potential for redistributing income by charging higher rates on higher incomes, smacked of populism and socialism (Kyvig 1988, 187).

In addition to Populists, Democrats generally favored the income tax, as did the Theodore Roosevelt–William Howard Taft wing of the Republican Party. Support was especially strong in the South, Midwest, and West, with greater opposition in the northeast industrial states, which could be expected to bear a greater percentage of the tax. When the Payne-Aldrich Tariff Bill was debated in Congress in 1909, a number of individuals, including Tennessee's Democratic Representative Cordell Hull, wanted to include an income tax provision in the hope that the Supreme Court would reconsider its decision in *Pollock.* Others, including President (and future chief justice) William Howard Taft, feared the impact that a judicial turnabout might have on the prestige of the Supreme Court (Kyvig 1988, 191–192).

The leader of the Senate Republicans, Conservative Rhode Island millionaire Nelson Aldrich, sought to stymie the so-called Bailey-Cummins income tax addition by proposing an income tax amendment in its place. It seems clear that Aldrich's proposal was a tactical maneuver based on the premise, supported by more than forty years of Article V quiescence, that such an amendment would never be adopted. Voting 77 to 0, however, the Senate approved the amendment in July 1909, and the House followed by a 318 to 14 majority that same month. The necessary number of states ratified the amendment in 1913. Ironically, such ratification closely followed a unanimous Supreme Court decision that upheld a corporate tax adopted in 1909 (*Flint v. Stone Tracy Co.* (1911)).

Relying on arguments from the Tenth Amendment similar to those advanced by Selden Bacon and others that the Court would soon dismiss, at least one commentator argued that the Sixteenth Amendment was the type of amendment that only the people of a state—as opposed to its legislature—could ratify (R. Brown 1920). In more recent years, a number of individuals on the far right, who have received almost no scholarly notice, have attempted to challenge the validity of the ratification of the Sixteenth Amendment largely on the basis of minute differences in wording between various ratifications that were sent to Congress (Benson and Beckman, 1985). This claim has been rejected in a U.S. appellate court decision (*United States v. Benson,* 941 F.2d 598 (1991)).

In the 1930s, opponents of big government often focused their wrath on the income tax, and the American Taxpayers Association and the Committee for Constitutional Government both proposed to repeal the amendment or provide for a maximum limit of 25 percent. Although this proposal got some support in Congress (see *Hearings* 1954, 1956), where it was introduced by, among others, Democratic Representative Emanuel Celler of New York, its proponents were far more successful in mobilizing calls from the states for a convention. Apparently, thirty-four states filed such petitions, although twelve of these also appear to have rescinded their calls (Caplan 1988, 69). In recent years, Republican Representative Ron Paul of Texas has proposed an amendment abolishing the personal income tax as well as estate and gift taxes; his proposal would also prohibit the U.S. government from competing with private businesses.

The income tax is often favored, especially by political liberals, over other taxes because it is thought to be progressive, taking a higher percentage of income from those who earn more, as opposed to regressive taxes, like sales or property taxes, which are more frequently used at the state level and that sometimes fall more harshly on the poor. Illinois Democrat Representative Jesse Jackson Jr. has proposed an amendment that would require that Congress "tax all persons progressively in proportion to the income which they respectively enjoy under the protection of the United States" (Jackson with Watkins, 2001, 385). Jackson apparently intends for this proposal to apply to state taxation as well (Jackson with Watkins, 2001, 403). There is currently no constitutional provision that either provides for, or prohibits, such redistributive uses of the amendment. Much of the initial opposition to the income tax stemmed from those who feared that it might have such "socialistic" tendencies.

See also Jackson, Jesse L., Jr.; *Pollock v. Farmers' Loan & Trust Co.*

For Further Reading:

Benson, Ben, and M. J. "Red" Beckman. 1985. *The Law That Never Was—The Fraud of the 16th Amendment and Personal Income Tax.* South Holland, IL: Constitutional Research Association.

Brown, Raymond G. 1920. "The Sixteenth Amendment to the United States Constitution." *American Law Review* 54: 843–854.

Caplan, Russell L. 1988. *Constitutional Brinkmanship: Amending the Constitution by National Convention.* New York: Oxford University Press.

Carson, Gerald. 1973. "The Income Tax and How It Grew." *American Heritage* 25 (December): 5–9, 79–88.

Jackson, Jesse L., Jr., with Frank E. Watkins. 2001. *A More Perfect Union: Advancing New American Rights.* New York: Welcome Rain Publishers.

Kyvig, David E. 1988. "Can the Constitution Be Amended? The Battle over the Income Tax, 1895–1913." *Prologue* 20 (Fall): 181–200.

Schrader, George D. 1970. "Constitutional History of the Income Tax." *Georgia State Bar Journal* 7 (August): 39–55.

❖ SIXTH AMENDMENT ❖

The Sixth Amendment was proposed by the First Congress as part of the Bill of Rights and ratified in 1791. It contains multiple guarantees, all of which relate to the rights of an accused in criminal proceedings:

> In all criminal prosecutions, the accused shall enjoy the right to a speedy and public trial, by an impartial jury of the State and district wherein the crime shall have been committed; which district shall have been previously ascertained by law, and to be informed of the nature and cause of the accusation; to be confronted with the witnesses against him; to have compulsory process for obtaining witnesses in his favor, and to have the assistance of counsel for his defense.

Most of the provisions of the Sixth Amendment were found in the Bill of Rights that James Madison presented to the First Congress (Kurland and Lerner 1987, 5:25). He, in turn, drew from provisions in existing state constitutions and proposals made by the state conventions that ratified the Constitution.

Each of the provisions of the Sixth Amendment has been fleshed out in judicial decisions. Although the guarantees in the Bill of Rights applied initially only to the national government, all the provisions of the Sixth Amendment have subsequently been made applicable to the states via the due process clause of the Fourteenth Amendment. The provisions of the Sixth Amendment that have evoked the most attention and controversy in recent years are those related to jury trials and the right to counsel.

The jury specified in the Sixth Amendment is known as a petit jury. Unlike the grand jury required by the Fifth Amendment, a petit jury in a criminal case (the Seventh Amendment deals with juries in civil cases) is one that determines guilt or innocence and, in some instances, decides on an appropriate penalty. In recent years, the issues of jury size and unanimity have dominated discussion of this institution. In *Williams v. Florida* (1970), the Supreme Court ruled that juries of six persons were appropriate in noncapital criminal cases. Similarly, in *Johnson v. Louisiana* (1972) and *Apodaco v. Oregon* (1972), the Court upheld the use of nonunanimous juries, although it decided in *Burch v. Louisiana* that juries of six did have to be unanimous.

The right to counsel has also undergone substantial reevaluation in recent years. Originally, it was interpreted merely to guarantee that an individual had the right to employ an attorney. However, in the famous trial of the Scottsboro Boys, a group of black youths arrested in Alabama and charged with the rape of two white girls, the Court decided that certain extraordinary situations called for state-appointed counsel when individuals could not afford to defend themselves (*Powell v. Alabama* (1932); D. Carter 1964). Then, in *Gideon v. Wainwright* (1963), the Supreme Court extended the right to court-appointed counsel to indigents in all felony cases (see Lewis 1974). *Argersinger v. Hamlin* (1972) extended the guarantee to all cases in which imprisonment was possible. More recently the Court has begun to pay some attention to the quality of representation, especially in death-row cases. In refusing to hear an appeal of a Texas case in 2002, the Court left standing a decision that had invalidated a death penalty conviction in a case where a defendant alleged that his attorney had fallen asleep during the proceedings (Lane 2002). In *Miranda v. Arizona* (1966) the Supreme Court required police officers to inform suspects being interrogated of this right. The Court recently reaffirmed this right in *Dickerson v. United States* (2000).

As concerns about law enforcement have increased in recent years, some scholars have expressed concern that Supreme Court decisions have eroded some of the guarantees in the Sixth Amendment (Garcia 1992), but this very debate may reflect the continuing relevance of the rights of criminal defendants (Bodenhamer 1992, 138). Although members of Congress have often reacted angrily to Supreme Court decisions expounding the rights of criminal defendants, they have offered no provisions to repeal this amendment.

Some scholars have expressed concern about the effect of the USA Patriot Act of 2001, passed in the aftermath of the September 11 terrorist attacks on the United States, on the Sixth Amendment. Not only does the law appear to allow for possible military trials of noncitizens engaged in terrorist activities, but it also allows for detaining "enemy combatants" (even those who are not citizens) without giving them access to their attorneys (Whitehead 2002, 1118–1127).

See also Seventh Amendment; Terrorism.

For Further Reading:

Bodenhamer, David J. 1992. *Fair Trial: Rights of the Accused in American History.* New York: Oxford University Press.

Carter. Dan T. 1964. *Scottsboro: A Tragedy of the American South.* New York: Oxford University Press.

Garcia, Alfredo. 1992. *The Sixth Amendment in Modern American Jurisprudence: A Critical Perspective.* New York: Greenwood Press.

Kurland, Philip B., and Ralph Lerner, eds. 1987. *The Founders' Constitution.* 5 vols. Chicago: University of Chicago Press.

Lane, Charles. 2002. "High Court Denies Texas Death Appeal: Court Declines to Intervene in 'Sleeping Lawyer Case,'" *The Washington Post,* 3 June, at *washingtonpost.com.*

Lewis, Anthony. 1974. *Gideon's Trumpet.* New York: Vintage Books.

Whitehead, John W. 2002. "Forfeiting 'Enduring Freedom' for 'Homeland Security': A Constitutional Analysis of the USA Patriot Act and the Justice Department's Anti-Terrorism Initiatives." *American University Law Review* 51 (August): 1081–1133.

❖ *SLAUGHTERHOUSE CASES* (1873) ❖

A group of Supreme Court decisions known collectively as the *Slaughterhouse Cases* were the first adjudicated under the Thirteenth and Fourteenth Amendments. They had a profound impact on the interpretation of these amendments and their subsequent legal evolution. At issue was a series of regulations that the state of Louisiana had imposed on those who butchered animals in New Orleans and surrounding parishes. Apparently motivated by a combination of noble concerns about health and crass political considerations (Labbe 1983), the law limited butchering to the facilities of a single privately owned company; these facilities were to be open to all, with both price and safety regulations.

Butchers with their own facilities sued and challenged this law as a violation of the Thirteenth and Fourteenth Amendments, with special emphasis on the privileges and immunities clause of the latter. Writing for a majority of five, Justice Samuel Miller rejected these claims. In looking at the postwar amendments, Miller stated that "the one pervading purpose found in them all" was "the freedom of the slave race." Although acknowledging that the amendments might also forbid "Mexican peonage or the Chinese coolie labor system," he found that their central purpose needed to be kept in view.

Miller interpreted the privileges and immunities clause as requiring states to extend the same rights to citizens of other states within their jurisdiction as they extended to their own citizens. Noting that the Fourteenth Amendment distinguished between state and national citizenship, Miller argued that it intended to leave the protection of most citizen privileges and immunities where it had always been, that is, at the state level. In rejecting the idea of broad nationally based rights, Miller stated that this would make courts "a perpetual censor upon all legislation of the States" and would be inconsistent with American notions of federalism:

> The argument, we admit, is not always the most conclusive which is drawn from the consequences urged against the adoption of a particular construction of an instrument. But when, as in the case before us, these consequences are so serious, so far-reaching and pervading, so great a departure from the structure and spirit of

our institutions; when the effect is to fetter and degrade the State governments by subjecting them to the control of Congress, in the exercise of powers hitherto-fore universally conceded to them of the most ordinary and fundamental character; when in fact it radically changes the whole theory of the relations of the State and Federal Governments to each other and of both these governments to the people; the argument has a force that is irresistible, in the absence of language which expresses such a purpose too closely to admit of doubt. (*Slaughterhouse Cases* 1873, 78)

Miller also rejected pleas based on the Thirteenth Amendment and on the due process and equal protection clauses of the Fourteenth Amendment.

In dismissing Miller's narrow reading of the Fourteenth Amendment, Justice Stephen Field said in his dissent that if the privileges and immunities guaranteed by the amendment were so limited, the Fourteenth Amendment "was a vain and idle enactment, which accomplished nothing, and most unnecessarily excited Congress and the people on its passing" (*Slaughterhouse Cases* 1873, 96). Similarly, in his dissent, Justice Noah Swayne said that the post–Civil War amendments had been designed "to rise to the dignity of a new Magna Charta." He further noted that the Fourteenth Amendment was designed to "embrace equally all races, classes and condition of men" and that, however novel such power might seem, "the novelty was known and the measure deliberately adopted" (*Id.,* 125, 129).

The due process and equal protection clauses of the Fourteenth Amendment have subsequently been interpreted quite broadly, but the privileges and immunities clause has never rebounded from the narrow reading it received in this case. Scholars are still divided as to whether the decision appropriately recognized necessary state police powers and the continuity with the federal system that the authors of the postwar amendments intended, or whether the decision represented a judicial "amendment" of these additions in the guise of interpretation.

For Further Reading:
Agnes, Richard L. 1994. "Constricting the Law of Freedom: Justice Miller, the Fourteenth Amendment, and the *Slaughter-House Cases.*" *Chicago-Kent Law Review* 70: 627–688.
Labbe, Donald M. 1983. "New Light on the Slaughterhouse Monopoly of 1869." In *Louisiana's Legal Heritage,* ed. Edward F. Haas. Pensacola, FL: Peridido Bay Press.
Slaughterhouse Cases 83 U.S. (16 Wall.) 36 (1873).

❖ SLAVEHOLDERS, COMPENSATION TO ❖

A critical obstacle to slave emancipation was the financial loss that such emancipation represented to the owners. William Lloyd Garrison was among abolitionists who were adamantly opposed to any compensation for owners, but, in his annual message of 1862, President Abraham Lincoln proposed a scheme of compensation for states that abolished slavery by January 1900 (J. Richardson 1908, 6:136).

Instead, Lincoln later issued the Emancipation Proclamation freeing slaves behind enemy lines, and the Thirteenth Amendment abolished the remnants of this institution in 1865. Fearful that slaveholders might later press their claims for compensation, a number of congressmen introduced resolutions to prohibit such compensation. Section 4 of the Fourteenth Amendment subsequently incorporated a provision prohibiting the United States from assuming any debts incurred by those in rebellion "or any claim for the loss or emancipation of any slave."

See also Garrison, William Lloyd; Lincoln, Abraham; Thirteenth Amendment.

For Further Reading:
Richardson, James E., ed. 1908. *A Compilation of the Messages and Papers of the Presidents, 1789–1908.* 11 vols. n.p.: Bureau of National Literature and Art.

❖ SLAVERY AND COLONIZATION ❖

One of the obstacles to slave emancipation was the fear that the white and black races would find it difficult to live together. Thus, in favorably reporting a proposed plan in Virginia to alter the laws so as to free slaves born after the act and to colonize them "to such place as the circumstances of the time should render most proper," Thomas Jefferson noted the problem with allowing them to stay:

> Deep-rooted prejudices entertained by whites; ten thousand recollections, by the blacks, of the injuries they have sustained; new provocations; the real distinctions which nature has made; and many other circumstances, will divide us into parties and produce convulsions, which will probably never end but in the extermination of the one or the other race. (Jefferson 1964, 132–133)

An American Colonization Society was founded in December 1816–January 1817, with the hope that the colonization of free blacks might eventually be followed by complete emancipation (see letter of Robert G. Harper in Pease and Pease 1965, 18–59). In 1832 Whig Representative William Archer of Virginia introduced an amendment calling on Congress to aid the colonization movement from the sale of public lands, a resolution seconded that same congressional session by the Maryland state legislature.

A number of similar plans were introduced in the early 1860s, one of which was part of a series of proposals by Democratic Senator Stephen A. Douglas of Illinois in 1860. In his annual message of 1862, President Abraham Lincoln recommended three amendments, one of which called on Congress to provide money for the recolonization of free blacks who were willing to relocate (J. Richardson 1908, 6:136). With the final emancipation of all African Americans by the Thirteenth Amendment, the financial and other practical obstacles to such a plan became overwhelming, and calls for such an amendment ceased.

For Further Reading:

Jefferson, Thomas. 1785. *Notes on the State of Virginia*. New York: Harper and Row, 1964.

Pease, William H., and June H. Pease, eds. 1965. *The Antislavery Argument*. Indianapolis, IN: Bobbs-Merrill.

Richardson, James E., ed. 1908. *A Compilation of the Messages and Papers of the Presidents, 1789–1908*. 11 vols. n.p.: Bureau of National Literature and Art.

❖ SLAVERY, DISTRICT OF COLUMBIA ❖

The existence of slavery in the District of Columbia caused special consternation among representatives of the free states. In 1839 former President John Quincy Adams, then serving as a Whig representative from Massachusetts, proposed the abolition of slavery and the slave trade in the nation's capital after 1845. The Compromise of 1850 subsequently abolished the slave trade in that city.

A number of proposals relating to slavery in the District of Columbia were among the wave of amendments introduced in Congress beginning in 1860. Some sought to guarantee the continuing legality of slavery in the District, and some attempted to abolish it. Others sought to have the question determined by practices in nearby Virginia and Maryland or in the latter state alone, and still others proposed to guarantee the right of federal officers who owned slaves to bring them into the District with them. Congress abolished slavery in the District in April 1862 (prior to the Thirteenth Amendment) and provided for the compensation of owners who were loyal to the Union (Urofsky 1988, 419).

For Further Reading:

Urofsky, Melvin I. 1988. *A March of Liberty: A Constitutional History of the United States*. New York: Alfred A. Knopf.

❖ SLAVERY, FOREIGN COMMERCE ❖

Even many slave owners who attended the Constitutional Convention of 1787 appear to have had antipathy for the slave trade. Largely at the insistence of the South Carolina delegation, however, Article I, Section 9 of the Constitution withheld power over this trade from Congress until 1808.

In the years immediately preceding this date, seven state legislatures, the first of which was North Carolina's, petitioned for amendments to end the slave trade. In 1807, during Thomas Jefferson's administration, Congress adopted legislation outlawing American participation in the slave trade beginning the following January. This legislation was later strengthened in 1818 (Finkelman 1992, 792).

United States law did not, of course, apply internationally. Thus, the Supreme Court had to deal with a number of subsequent cases, most notably *The Antelope* (1825), involving slaves who had come ashore from other nations. It generally took the position that the slave trade, although contrary to natural law, was not contrary to international law but was rather subject to the rules adopted by individual nations. Moreover, the continuing submission of amendments to end the slave trade right up to the Civil War was an indication that existing laws on the subject were not always effective.

It is fascinating that although the constitution of the Confederate States of America was in many ways a slave document, it banned the importation of additional slaves, thus effectively reaching beyond the U.S. Constitution on this point. The adoption of the Thirteenth Amendment ended any incentive to bring slave ships to the United States.

For Further Reading:

Finkelman, Paul. 1992. "Slavery." In *The Oxford Companion to the Supreme Court of the United States,* ed. Kermit L. Hall. New York: Oxford University Press.

Rawley, James A. 1981. *The Transatlantic Slave Trade: A History.* New York: W. W. Norton.

Reynolds, Edward. 1985. *Stand the Storm: A History of the Atlantic Slave Trade.* London: Allison & Busby.

❖ SLAVERY, INSURRECTIONS ❖

One of the catalysts to the Civil War was the raid that John Brown led on Harpers Ferry in 1859. He hoped that this action would trigger a general slave revolt. Although his hope was not realized, his raid renewed fears among Southern slaveholders.

Three proposals were offered in 1861 to give Congress power to pass penal laws to punish individuals who incited or aided such insurrections or conspiracies, and another was proposed in 1864 as a substitute for the Thirteenth Amendment (Ames 1896, 206). Ironically, federal powers under the Fourteenth Amendment would later be evoked in cases such as *United States v. Guest* (1966) and *United States v. Price* (1966) to punish conspiracies against the rights of African Americans.

See also Brown, John.

For Further Reading:

Ames, Herman. 1896. *The Proposed Amendments to the Constitution of the United States during the First Century of Its History.* Reprint, New York: Burt Franklin, 1970.

❖ SLAVERY, INTERSTATE COMMERCE ❖

Article I, Section 9 granted Congress the power to limit the foreign slave trade after 1808, but it did not directly address congressional control of the interstate slave trade. Although Congress never attempted to restrict slavery through use of this mechanism, Southerners appeared to regard such a use as a real possibility. Several amendments proposed on the eve of the Civil War, including those by Tennessee's Democratic Representative (and future president) Andrew Johnson, Kentucky's Unionist Representative John Crittenden, and Illinois' Democratic Senator Stephen Douglas, attempted expressly to guarantee the right to engage in such interstate trade.

Long before, in 1823, Georgia had proposed an amendment supported by three other states that had been designed to keep any part of the

Constitution from being interpreted "to authorize the importation or ingress of any person of color into any one of the United States contrary to the law of such State" (quoted in Ames 1896, 210). This proposal was prompted by the South Carolina Seaman Act of 1822. The original law, later modified, had provided for the jailing and possible enslavement of free blacks who left their ships for shore. In his role as a circuit court judge, Associate Supreme Court Justice William Johnson described the law as being in conflict with both federal commerce power and a treaty with Great Britain. William Wirt, President John Quincy Adams's attorney general, subsequently reaffirmed Johnson's opinion. President Andrew Jackson's attorney generals, John Macpherson Berrien and future Chief Justice Roger B. Taney, later reversed Wirt's opinion, and the issue continued to be contested until the Thirteenth Amendment abolished slavery (Wiecek 1977, 133–139).

For Further Reading:

Ames, Herman. 1896. *The Proposed Amendments to the Constitution of the United States during the First Century of Its History*. Reprint, New York: Burt Franklin, 1970.

Wiecek, William. 1977. *The Sources of Antislavery Constitutionalism in America, 1760–1848*. Ithaca, NY: Cornell University Press.

❖ SLAVERY, PROTECTION FOR ❖

Slavery was an issue long before the Civil War (Lively 1992, 11–37). One of the South's greatest fears, a fear that eventually led to secession, was that the more populous Northern states might one day use the law or the constitutional amending process to abolish slavery.

In 1850 Democratic Representative John Daniels of North Carolina introduced an amendment to prevent such abolition. Beginning in 1860, there were a number of similar proposals (one introduced by Mississippi Democratic Representative Jefferson Davis, future president of the Confederacy) designed to protect slavery by specifically recognizing the institution or prohibiting any federal interference with it.

The best known of these proposals, designed to be unalterable, was the Corwin Amendment, which had the support of President Abraham Lincoln, at least for a time. Southern secession marked the failure of this proposal and prepared the way for the very thing that the Southerners had feared. In 1865 the Thirteenth Amendment abolished slavery.

See also Corwin Amendment.

For Further Reading:

Lively, Donald E. 1992. *The Constitution and Race*. New York: Praeger.

❖ SLAVERY, RETURN OF FUGITIVES ❖

One of the most persistent problems engendering controversy between Northern and Southern states prior to the Civil War concerned the pursuit and capture of slaves who fled north to obtain their freedom.

Article IV, Section 2 of the Constitution provided that "no Person held to Service or Labour in one State, under the Laws thereof, escaping into another, shall, in Consequence of any Law or Regulation therein, be discharged from such Service or Labour, but shall be delivered upon Claim of the Party to whom such Service or Labour shall be due." This provision did not, however, explicitly designate whose obligation it was to return fugitives. Highhanded actions by some Southern slave catchers—who tended to presume that all blacks were escaped slaves—led many Northern states to adopt personal liberty laws designed to provide legal protections against false kidnappings.

Congress adopted a fugitive slave law in 1793, which it later strengthened in 1850 as part of the compromise adopted that year, but as abolitionist sentiment grew, Northern states became increasingly uncooperative. Court decisions written by Joseph Story (a Northerner) in *Prigg v. Pennsylvania* (1842) and by Chief Justice Roger Taney (a Southerner) in *Abelman v. Booth* (1859) attempted to uphold the rights of slaveholders, but sentiment in some Northern states remained hostile, and Southerners were unsatisfied. In his annual message of 1860, President James Buchanan proposed what he termed an "explanatory amendment" recognizing "the right of property in slaves." He further proposed "a like recognition of the right of the master to have his slave who has escaped from one State to another restored and 'delivered up' to him, and the validity of the fugitive-slave law enacted for this purpose, together with a declaration that all State laws impairing or defeating this right are violations of the Constitution, and are consequently null and void" (J. Richardson 198, 5:638).

For his part, incoming President Abraham Lincoln was willing to enforce the fugitive slave law against any conflicting state legislation, but he did not think that a constitutional amendment was necessary (T. Morris 1974, 205).

About thirty amending resolutions followed in the year after Buchanan's speech. Most would have affirmed or strengthened the fugitive slave law. Some would have struck down conflicting state legislation. Some, like a proposal by Tennessee's Andrew Johnson (who would later become president), would have had the government provide compensation for fugitive slaves who were not returned. A few, reflecting the sentiments that had led to the personal liberty laws, provided that fugitive slaves would be entitled to a jury or to other procedural protections of regular criminal trials.

In June 1864 Congress repealed the fugitive slave law, and subsequent adoption of the Thirteenth Amendment ended this controversy. One writer believes that the Thirteenth and Fourteenth Amendments "carried forward the commitment that had been embodied in the Personal Liberty Laws" (T. Morris 1974, 218).

For Further Reading:

Morris, Thomas D. 1974. *Free Men All: The Personal Liberty Laws of the North, 1780–1861.* Baltimore, MD: Johns Hopkins University Press.

Richardson, James E., ed. 1908. *A Compilation of the Messages and Papers of the Presidents, 1789–1908.* 11 vols. n.p.: Bureau of National Literature and Art.

❖ SLAVERY, RIGHT TO TRAVEL WITH SLAVES ❖

In the early years of the Republic, Northern free states generally made provision for slave owners to travel there with their slaves. By 1860, however, most Northern states explicitly denied this right (Finkelman 1981, 340).

A notorious case was initiated in 1852 when a Virginia slave owner, Jonathan Lemmon, came by ship to New York with his slaves, intending to take a steamboat to New Orleans. When Lemmon came ashore with his slaves, New York courts, including New York's highest tribunal, held that the slaves had become free (*Lemmon* (1860)). Many slavery opponents subsequently feared, however, that *Scott v. Sandford* (1857) signaled an increased willingness on the part of the U.S. Supreme Court to protect slavery, even in the Northern states (Finkelman 1981, 313–338).

In attempts to reduce the friction that this issue was causing, four amendments were introduced on 12 December 1860 with provisions that would have protected the rights of slave owners to travel with their slaves. A substitute for the Thirteenth Amendment, which was introduced in 1864, would have limited the right to such travel to other slave states. For its part, the Constitution of the Confederate States of America granted citizens "the right to travel and sojourn in any State of this Confederacy, with their slaves and other property," thus attempting to guarantee the kind of comity that had ended in the North (Finkelman 1981, 21).

For Further Reading:

Finkelman, Paul. 1981. *An Imperfect Union: Slavery, Federalism and Comity.* Chapel Hill, NC: University of North Carolina Press.

❖ SLAVERY, THE TERRITORIES AND ❖

Numerous amending proposals were introduced just before the outbreak of the Civil War to resolve the issue of slavery in the territories.

This issue was important because these territories were the breeding ground for new states and because such states threatened the precarious balance that had been established in the early years of the Republic between free states and slave states, which eventually ended with the admission of California.

The Northwest Ordinance of 1787, adopted under the Articles of Confederation and reauthorized by the new government in 1789, had prohibited slavery in that area. Subsequent congressional legislation regarding the Southwest Territory and the Louisiana and Missouri Territories had prohibited the federal government from interfering with the institution there. Slavery was, however, later forbidden in the Illinois, Indiana, and Michigan Territories (Lively 1992, 12).

The divergent policy for northern and southern territories was formalized with the Missouri Compromise of 1820. Under this plan, Missouri was admitted as a slave state, Maine was admitted as a free state, and slavery was forbidden in the Louisiana Territory north of a line at 36 degrees 30 minutes of latitude. The failed Wilmot Proviso, which was introduced during the Mexican-American War, subsequently stirred passions by proposing to abolish slavery in any territories acquired from Mexico. Moreover, the Kansas-Nebraska Act of 1854 effectively repealed the Missouri Compromise line between free and slave states by specifying that Kansas and Nebraska, both north of the line, would decide for themselves whether they wanted to be slave or free. This law embodied the principle of popular sovereignty championed by Illinois Democratic Senator Stephen Douglas. Similarly, in 1857 Chief Justice Roger Taney decided in *Scott v. Sandford* that the provisions of the Missouri Compromise that restricted slavery in the northern territories were unconstitutional.

Members of the newly formed Republican Party were especially concerned about the Kansas-Nebraska Act and the *Scott* decision. Both actions appeared to open the prospect for the expansion of slavery, and Republicans were committed to the principle that slavery could be tolerated only if it were placed on a course of ultimate extinction (Foner 1970). Many

Southern Democrats were just as concerned that, as the balance of the Union tipped toward the free states, their peculiar institution would be jeopardized.

Proposed constitutional amendments reflected national divisions. In an apparent attempt to reaffirm the much-criticized *Scott* decision, President James Buchanan called for federal protection of slavery in the territories in his 1860 annual message. Other proposals repeated Buchanan's call for federal protection of slavery in the territories, called for resurrection of the 36 degrees 30 minutes line drawn by the Missouri Compromise, proposed to take away any authority of the federal government or the territorial legislatures regarding slavery, or called for states to decide whether they wanted to have slaves at the time they joined the Union.

Ultimately, no compromises proved successful, and the nation plunged into the Civil War. The Thirteenth Amendment subsequently prohibited slavery not only in the northern territories but also in those Southern states where the institution had been so entrenched.

See also *Scott v. Sandford;* Thirteenth Amendment.

For Further Reading:

Foner, Eric. 1970. *Free Soil, Free Labor, Free Men: The Ideology of the Republican Party before the Civil War.* New York: Oxford University Press.

Lively, Donald E. 1992. *The Constitution and Race.* New York: Praeger.

❖ SMITH, GOLDWIN (1823–1910) ❖

British-born Goldwin Smith, a barrister and professor who eventually settled in Canada, presented his views on the need for American constitutional reform in an article published in 1898. His thoughts appear to have been largely stimulated by the threat of "Bryanism" in the previous presidential contest, and like others of his day, his solution was that of a cabinet, or parliamentary, government (Vile 1991c, 40–42).

Smith favored reducing the power of the Senate; he thought that some states, such as Nevada, had been introduced prematurely into the Union, and he thought that small states had inordinate influence. He also considered the two-year term for members of the House of Representatives to be too short to allow members to gain the requisite knowledge or perform as statesmen. In Smith's judgment, however, the most urgent weakness in U.S. government was "the want of initiative and control in legislation and, still more palpably, in finance, arising from the exclusion of the responsible ministers of state from the assembly which makes the laws, regulates the expenditure, and imposes the taxes" (G. Smith 1898, 262).

Smith also believed that the change of administration every four years needlessly destroyed continuity in the State Department. Because he was especially concerned about the Supreme Court's acceptance of inconvertible paper money, Smith thought that the Court should be limited to interpreting, rather than modifying, the Constitution. Pointing to the sectional strife that disputes over tariff policy had spawned throughout American history, Smith advocated "an equal *ad valorem* duty on all imports, variable in amount with the necessities of the treasury" (G. Smith 1898, 266).

Believing that the Fifteenth Amendment had become a dead letter, Smith favorably cited a petition by Louisiana and two other states for a convention to repeal it. He also believed that immigration (and possibly suffrage) restrictions were needed, especially in the case of "the Russian or Hungarian Jew" (G. Smith 1898, 267). Anticipating that Cuba might be annexed to the United States, he also favored an amendment to regulate the governing of such dependencies.

Elsewhere, Smith speculated that "a union of this Northern Continent" might be an appropriate occasion for revising the Constitution (G. Smith 1906, 851). Sharing the common belief of his day that it was extremely difficult to change the U.S. Constitution, Smith did not, however, hold out much prospect for the reforms he advocated.

For Further Reading:

Smith, Goldwin. 1906. "Chief Justice Clark on the Defects of the American Constitution." *North American Review* 183 (1 November): 845–851.

———. 1898. "Is the Constitution Outworn?" *North American Review* 166 (March): 257–267.

Vile, John R. 1991c. *Rewriting the United States Constitution: An Examination of Proposals from Reconstruction to the Present*. New York: Praeger.

❖ *SMITH V. UNION BANK* (1831) ❖

Smith v. Union Bank involved the disposition of an estate. The specific question was whether debts should be paid according to the laws where the decedent had been domiciled or according to the laws of the state where he held his property. The Supreme Court decided that the latter rule should govern.

In so ruling, Justice William Johnson noted, "Whether it would or would not be politic to establish a different rule by a convention of the States, under constitutional sanction, is not a question for our consideration" (*Smith* 1831, 528). A modern scholar who believes that constitutional conventions may be limited to a single subject has cited this decision as support for his view (Caplan 1988, 45–46).

For Further Reading:

Caplan, Russell L. 1988. *Constitutional Brinkmanship: Amending the Constitution by National Convention*. New York: Oxford University Press.

Smith v. Union Bank, 30 U.S. (5 Pet.) 518 (1831).

❖ SOCIAL AND ECONOMIC RIGHTS ❖

By contrast to many twentieth-century constitutions, the eighteenth-century authors of the U.S. Constitution, who were alive before the birth of the modern welfare state, were more concerned about protecting citizens from government (so-called "negative rights") than they were for guaranteeing that government would provide certain social, economic, and welfare-related rights (so-called "positive rights"). From time to time, individuals, U.S. Representative Jesse Jackson Jr. among them, have proposed amendments, similar to those in some Western European nations, that would guarantee education, housing, vacations, welfare, work, or the like. However, to date no such amendments have been adopted. Even the prohibition against child labor (which was still phrased as a negative rather than as a positive right) was eventually enacted through legislation, and confirmed by judicial acquiescence, rather than through constitutional amendment. Similarly, although the U.S. Supreme Court agreed that the right to an education was an important right in *Brown v. Board of Education* (1954), it subsequently refused in *San Antonio Independent School District v. Rodriguez* (1973) to declare that the right to a particular level of education was a fundamental right or to require that states fund all schools equally.

Harvard Law Professor Mary Ann Glendon has observed that those nations that do include social and economic rights within their constitutions usually list them as aspirations rather than as judicially enforceable guarantees, such as those with which Americans accustomed to fairly broad exercises of judicial review are familiar (Glendon 1992, 528). She believes that the consequence of adding such rights as amendments to the U.S. Constitution might be to increase litigation without necessarily resulting in higher levels of welfare-related benefits.

See also Housing; Jackson, Jesse L., Jr.; Welfare Payments, Right to.

For Further Reading:

Glendon, Mary Ann. 1992. "Rights in Twentieth-Century Constitutions," *University of Chicago Law Review* 59 (Winter): 519–538.

San Antonio Independent School District v. Rodriguez, 411 U.S. 1 (1973).

❖ SOCIAL SECURITY ❖

Introduced during the administration of Franklin D. Roosevelt, Social Security has become one of the largest entitlement programs in America today. It provides both for the children of working individuals who die and retirement pensions for individuals who have paid into the program. Partly because of this program, poverty, once pervasive in this age group, has significantly decreased among retired individuals in the United States. The program, which is financed by mandatory payments from most American workers and their employers, has been generally understood to be a supplement to savings and other retirement pensions rather than as an exclusive means of support for senior citizens. Highly controversial when Roosevelt first proposed it, the program is now supported by leaders of both major political parties.

Some recent projections have indicated that the program could run out of money during the time when the large number of "baby boom" children, born in the relatively prosperous years directly following the soldiers' return home from World War II, retire. Largely as a result, there has been increased political concern about the continuing viability of this program. It was a fairly significant issue in the presidential election campaign of 2000, with both leading candidates addressing the issue and Republican George Bush proposing that young individuals be permitted to divert some of their Social Security contributions into private investment programs.

A number of proposals in recent years that have called for balanced budgets have included provisions that Social Security funds (which are currently in the black) not be used in computing the budget. Republican backers of the Balanced Budget Amendment sometimes charged that Democratic opponents were using the highly emotional Social Security issue as a smokescreen for more deep-seated opposition to the amendment.

For Further Reading:

Livingston, Steven G. 2002. *Student's Guide to Landmark Congressional Legislation on Social Security and Welfare.* Westport, CT: Greenwood Press.

❖ SOCIALIST PARTY OF AMERICA ❖

Although Socialist candidates for president such as Eugene Debs and Norman Thomas have occasionally attracted national attention, unlike many Western European democracies, the United States has never had a strong Socialist Party (Shannon 1967). This may reflect the comparative weakness of organized labor in the United States, but it may also stem from the fact that Americans have often associated the agenda of the Socialists with that of the Communists. Although both parties are traditionally committed to governmental ownership of major industries, Socialists favor reform through the ballot box and are committed to other democratic methods. By contrast, Communists are traditionally committed to revolutionary violence and show little respect for democracy.

Of all their platforms, the Socialist platform of 1932 focused the most on constitutional reforms. Many of these reforms showed clear consistency with those of earlier progressivists (Vile 1991c, 67–68) and included provisions for "proportional representation" (presumably in Congress), "direct election of the President and Vice President," and adoption of "the initiative and referendum" (Porter and Johnson 1966, 353). The platform also called for the elimination of the Supreme Court's power to declare laws unconstitutional and liberalization of the amending process. In addition, the platform proposed repeal of the Eighteenth Amendment and national alcoholic prohibition.

For Further Reading:

Porter, Kirk H., and Donald B. Johnson. 1966. *National Party Platforms, 1840–1964*. Urbana, IL: University of Illinois Press.

Shannon, David A. 1967. *The Socialist Party of America: A History*. Chicago: Quadrangle Books.

Vile, John R. 1991c. *Rewriting the United States Constitution: An Examination of Proposals from Reconstruction to the Present*. New York: Praeger.

❖ *SOUTH CAROLINA V. BAKER* (1988) ❖

This case involved a section of the Tax Equity and Fiscal Responsibility Act of 1982, which had removed the federal tax exemption for interest earned on unregistered state bonds. South Carolina argued that this provision violated both the Tenth Amendment and the doctrine of intergovernmental tax immunities.

Writing for a seven-to-one majority of the Court, Justice William Brennan upheld the law. Working from the precedent in *Garcia v. San Antonio Metropolitan Transit Authority* (1985), Brennan dealt with the Tenth Amendment argument by ruling that states "must find their protection from congressional regulation through the national political process, not through judicially defined spheres of unregulated state activity" (*South Carolina* 1988, 512). On the related matter of the national government's authority to force states to adopt regulations on behalf of federal interests (an issue also raised by the amendment to prohibit unfunded federal mandates), Brennan found that the law in question did not significantly differ from other such laws that the Court had upheld.

The issue of intergovernmental tax immunity dated back to the decision in *Pollock v. Farmers' Loan & Trust Co.* (1895), which immunized interest earned on state bonds from federal taxation. Even after the adoption of the Sixteenth Amendment, the Court had upheld this exemption, prompting numerous amending proposals to permit the taxation of state securities. Noting that the *Pollock* decision regarding state bonds represented but one of a number of intergovernmental tax immunities that were recognized at that time, Brennan pointed out that most such immunities had since been abandoned. He therefore decided that the *Pollock* decision was no longer valid on this point, and he overturned it.

Justices John Paul Stevens, Antonin Scalia, and William Rehnquist each wrote concurring opinions. Justice Sandra Day O'Connor dissented. She believed that the existing tax immunity doctrine, which accepted taxes that were not directly imposed on—or discriminatory with regard to—state governments, was inadequate to protect state sovereignty.

Delaware Republican Senator William Roth has since proposed an amendment to limit federal taxation of state and local obligations issued to finance governmental activities or public purposes. Cosponsors included South Carolina Republican Senator Strom Thurmond, South Carolina Democratic Senator Ernest Hollings, and Kansas Republican Senator Bob Dole.

See also *Garcia v. San Antonio Metropolitan Transit Authority;* Tenth Amendment.

For Further Reading:
South Carolina v. Baker, 485 U.S. 505 (1988).

❖ SOVEREIGNTY ❖

Once at the center of much of the discussion of law and politics, the idea of sovereignty is often traced back to the French philosopher Jean Bodin and the English philosophers Thomas Hobbes and John Austin. A modern writer noted that "sovereignty was an attribute of a determinate person or body to whom the generality of the society gave habitual obedience and who or which was not itself habitually obedient to any other person or body. Within that society the sovereign had ultimate power to lay down the law" (Walker 1980, 1163).

It is difficult to identify the sovereign in a system like that of the United States, in which state and national powers are divided in a federal system and in which the powers of both sets of governments are further divided into three major branches. There is, however, considerable warrant for suggesting that the ultimate sovereign—what one writer called the "pro-sovereign" (Radin 1930) to distinguish it from the regularly functioning government—is the amending mechanism. Lester B. Orfield noted that "in the last analysis, one is brought to the conclusion that sovereignty in the United States, if it can be said to exist at all, is located in the amending body" (1942, 154). Orfield further noted that "the sovereign is a

real sovereign, though one fluctuating in its composition" (1942, 159).

The idea that the amending process is sovereign is sometimes called into question by the entrenchment provision providing for equal state representation in the Senate. However, since this limit can be overridden with the states' consent, it is not absolute, and in any case, it has little "practical significance" (Orfield 1942, 162).

The idea advanced by some writers that there are implicit limits on the amending process suggests that sovereignty rests elsewhere, namely, in whatever body or bodies—perhaps the courts—have responsibility for ascertaining or enforcing such limits. Some such authors may, however, simply be making a claim that Thomas Jefferson, Abraham Lincoln, and others have often made, that popular sovereignty needs to be in accord with natural justice in order to be right. It might also be argued on the basis of the preamble and the Ninth and Tenth Amendments that "the people" are the sovereign. It is largely on this basis that Akhil Reed Amar has argued that the people have the power to amend the Constitution outside of the specific procedures designated by Article V. Proposals to amend Article V to provide for greater popular participation are often based on theories of popular sovereignty.

See also Initiative and Referendum.

For Further Reading:
Orfield, Lester B. 1942. *The Amending of the Federal Constitution.* Ann Arbor, MI: University of Michigan Press.

Radin, Max. 1930. "The Intermittent Sovereign." *Yale Law Journal* 30: 514–531.

Walker, David M. 1980. *The Oxford Companion to Law.* Oxford: Clarenden Press.

❖ SPECIAL PROSECUTOR ❖

Although the Watergate scandal did not mark the first use of a special prosecutor, this position has assumed increased visibility and was more frequently utilized since this historic event. Great concern was raised over the independence of this office on 20 October 1973 when, in the so-called Saturday Night Massacre, President Richard Nixon fired Watergate special prosecutor Archibald Cox. After the consequent public uproar, Nixon appointed Leon Jaworski to this post on 1 November 1973.

Shortly thereafter, Missouri Democrat William Randall offered what he called "the Executive Investigation and Prosecution Amendment." Randall wanted to alleviate questions—later largely resolved in favor of the arrangement in *United States v. Nixon* (1974)—about the propriety of one executive official, namely, the president, appointing another officer to investigate other executive officials. Randall therefore proposed giving this authority to Congress.

The Ethics in Government Act of 1978—subsequently revised and reauthorized in 1982, 1987, and 1992—provided that a special court could appoint such prosecutors at the request of the attorney general, who could remove them only for cause. The Supreme Court upheld this arrangement in *Morrison v. Olson* (1988), a decision notable for a strong dissent by Justice Antonin Scalia, who thought the special prosecutor was too independent of executive authority and thus in violation of separation of powers. After costly investigations of the Iran-Contra Affair in the Reagan Administration (involving the sale of weapons to Iran in exchange for money to fight against communism in Nicaragua) and then first of President Bill Clinton's Whitewater land deal and then of his truthfulness about sexual affairs that led to his impeachment by the U.S. House of Representatives, even Special Prosecutor Kenneth Starr was among those who questioned the efficacy of the mechanism. The special prosecutor law has accordingly been allowed to lapse.

❖ STABILITY AND THE AMENDING PROCESS ❖

One typically associates the constitutional amending process with change and progress, but the fact that it is more difficult than that for adopting ordinary legislation indicates that the process is also designed to assure stability. Without any process of constitutional change, progress would be difficult, and individuals might be tempted to follow the example of the American revolutionaries and seek to overthrow the government by force. Once established, however, constitutions are designed to be fundamental law. It is important that this law be protected against unnecessary upheavals that could prove to be more disquieting than changes in ordinary legal statutes.

A recent article has pointed both to the increased range and velocity of legal change in recent years and to the fact that all changes in law involve costs (Van Alstine 2002). Although the author of the article does not specifically focus on changes in constitutional law, such changes would undoubtedly involve similar, if not greater, costs. In early discussions between Thomas Jefferson and James Madison, after Jefferson suggested that constitutions should be rewritten every generation, Madison pointed out that such continual change could create instability and other unwanted consequences, and he defended the mechanism in Article V as guarding against either too much or too little change. The U.S. Constitution has been identified as a "rigid" constitution in that the framers rejected the idea of parliamentary sovereignty whereby fundamental law could be initiated through ordinary legislation.

Although some constitutional amendments have brought about and/or ratified significant changes (consider the Thirteenth Amendment abolishing slavery or the Nineteenth Amendment guaranteeing that women would not be denied the right to vote on the basis of their sex) in American history, the nation continues to operate under the document written in 1787, as amended. To date the only convention that has met to formulate a completely new Constitution was that held by the seceding Confederate States of America. With a few key differences (most tied to the institution of slavery), it continued to be patterned on the Constitution for the United States that was already in existence.

Article VII specified that the Constitution of 1787 would not go into effect until ratified by nine states. So too, modern amendments do not go into effect until they are adopted by the requisite number of states. Such amendments sometimes provide for a stated implementation period—the Eighteenth Amendment, for example, specified that it would no go into effect until one year after it was ratified.

The primary way that the constitutional amending process attempts to provide for stability in the fundamental law is through the use of supermajority requirements that are designed to assure deliberation and consensus. Article V of the Constitution requires two-thirds majorities to propose amendments and three-fourths majorities to ratify them. To date, only twenty-seven such amendments have been adopted. At least one such amendment, the Eighteenth (imposing national alcoholic prohibition), proved so costly that it was later repealed by the Twenty-first. The Eighteenth Amendment serves as a good example of the unintended consequences that an unwise or unenforceable amendment can impose.

Because amendments are so difficult to adopt, many changes in constitutional understandings are brought about through judicial interpretations and changing customs and practices. These can bring their own costs and generate their own instability (especially if they are not stated in clear language), although they may typically be altered more easily than changes incorporated into the constitutional text.

See also Confederate States of America, Constitution of; Implementation Dates of Amendments; Jefferson, Thomas; Madison, James; Progress and the Amending Process; Rigid Constitution; Unintended Consequences of Constitutional Amendments.

For Further Reading:

Van Alstine, Michael P. 2002. "The Costs of Legal Change." *UCLA Law Review* 49 (February): 789–870.

❖ STANTON, ELIZABETH CADY (1815–1902) ❖

Elizabeth Cady Stanton was one of the nation's foremost proponents of women's rights and women's suffrage. Her husband, Henry Brew-

ster Stanton, whom she married in 1840, was then an executive of the abolitionist American Anti-Slavery Society. Elizabeth was a proponent of abolition and temperance when she met Lucretia Mott at the London Anti-Slavery Convention in 1840 and became more active in feminist issues.

In 1848 Stanton and Mott helped organize the historic Seneca Falls Women's Rights Convention in New York. In what has been described as "a brilliant propagandistic stroke" (Banner 1980, 41), delegates chose to pattern their plea for women's equality on the language of the Declaration of Independence. At the time, many citizens regarded Stanton's call for women's suffrage as radical. This label often stuck with her, despite the fact that she was married and raised seven children.

Stanton is often associated with Susan B. Anthony. Stanton made Anthony's acquaintance in 1851, and she worked with her (sometimes envying the unmarried Anthony's greater mobility) for much of her remaining life. In 1863 Stanton and Anthony helped gather 300,000 petitions for the emancipation of slaves, an objective accomplished with the Thirteenth Amendment. In 1866 Stanton became the first woman to run for the U.S. House of Representatives. In 1868 Stanton and Anthony founded the Workingwoman's Association, and in 1869 they founded the National Woman Suffrage Association. They did so after having opposed women who had supported the Fourteenth and Fifteenth Amendments despite the failure of these amendments to extend legal protections to women. When Stanton and Anthony's group merged with the rival American Woman Suffrage Association to form the National American Woman Suffrage Association (NAWSA) in 1890 and to push for what was to become the Nineteenth Amendment, Stanton became the first president. She served until Anthony became president in 1892.

Stanton generally kept little distance between herself and those espousing radical causes. Stanton's *Woman's Bible*, which she published in 1895 and which reflected her own religious skepticism, provoked considerable controversy, and NAWSA disavowed any tie with the work the following year. A list of causes Stanton supported in addition to suffrage includes "coeducation, girls' sports, job training, equal wages, labor unions, birth control, cooperative nurseries and kitchens, property rights for wives, child custody rights for mothers, and reform of divorce laws" (Griffith 1984, xiv). The decision to acknowledge Anthony rather than Stanton as the mother of the Nineteenth Amendment appears to have been part of a conscious strategy to avoid what was perceived to be Stanton's more radical stigma (Griffith 1984, xv).

See also Anthony, Susan Brownell; Nineteenth Amendment; Seneca Falls Convention.

For Further Reading:
Banner, Lois W. 1980. *Elizabeth Cady Stanton: A Radical for Women's Rights.* Boston: Little, Brown.

Griffith, Elisabeth. 1984. *In Her Own Right: The Life of Elizabeth Cady Stanton.* New York: Oxford University Press.

❖ STARE DECISIS ❖

One element that contributes to the stability of interpretations of the U.S. Constitution is the legal doctrine of *stare decisis.* Under this generally accepted doctrine, which is nowhere stated in the Constitution, courts generally adhere to the rulings in prior cases and constitutional interpretations without examining the document *de novo,* or "anew," each time they have to make a decision.

If the principle were absolute, unwise or mistaken judicial interpretations like those upholding the doctrine of "separate but equal" in *Plessy v. Ferguson* (1896) or mandating compulsory flag salutes in *Minersville School District v. Gobitis* (1940) could never be reversed other than by the difficult process of constitutional amendment. Although courts thus pay great deference to the principle, it is not absolute. Lower federal courts, which are understood to be subservient to the Supreme Court, are generally less likely to depart from established U.S. Supreme Court decisions than is the Supreme Court itself.

The result complicates constitutional changes in the United States. Individuals who might otherwise push for the proposal and rat-

ification of constitutional amendments might simply vote for the election of presidents and senators who they think will appoint and confirm Supreme Court justices who will reverse existing decisions with which they disagree. In *Planned Parenthood of Southeastern Pennsylvania v. Casey* (1992), Justices Sandra Day O'Connor, Anthony Kennedy, and David Souter put particular emphasis on the doctrine in upholding the central ruling in the Supreme Court's decision in *Roe v. Wade* (1973) recognizing the right to obtain legal abortions. These three justices were particularly concerned that if the Supreme Court reversed course, it might look as though it were caving in to popular pressure.

The Child Labor Amendment is an example of a proposal whose need was undercut by judicial decisions that reversed earlier rulings and accepted regulation of this subject. Arguably too, the Equal Rights Amendment may have lost momentum in part due to Supreme Court decisions expanding its interpretations of women's rights under the equal protection clause of the Fourteenth Amendment and to related fears that expansive new constitutional language might give the Court greater leeway in interpreting women's rights than the public actually desired.

One advantage of precisely drawn amendments is that they are unlikely to be altered or reversed through judicial interpretation. Broadly worded provisions like "due process" or "equal protection of the laws" (both found in the Fourteenth Amendment) clearly give greater leeway for judicial decision making than do more narrowly worded provisions.

See also Child Labor Amendment; Equal Rights Amendment; Stability and the Amending Process; Supreme Court Decisions Reversed by Constitutional Amendments.

❖ STATE-FEDERAL RELATIONS ❖

Political scientists recognize three basic forms of government: confederal, federal, and unitary. In confederal governments, such as the Articles of Confederation, power is divided between the states and a national government, but because the latter must operate through the former—in raising taxes and armies, for example—the former is more powerful. In a unitary government, like that in Great Britain, there are no permanent state governments. By contrast, a federal government retains states but allows both state and national governments to operate directly upon individuals. In both confederal and federal governments, written constitutions are necessary. Otherwise, there would be no clear way to allocate power between the two levels of government (Vile 2002a, 104).

By its very nature, a federal government is complex. Even with a written constitution, there are likely to be disputes about the appropriate allocation of authority between the nation and the states, and adjustments may be needed. A number of constitutional amendments have addressed federal concerns. These include the Bill of Rights, especially the Tenth Amendment; the Eleventh, Fourteenth, and Seventeenth Amendments; and amendments (for example, the Fifteenth, Nineteenth, and Twenty-sixth) that have set national standards for voting rights.

Of all the conflicts over federalism in the United States, none proved more irreconcilable than the one that led to the Civil War. This conflict, in turn, reflected tensions in the original debates between the Federalists and the Anti-Federalists (Mason 1964) and had roots in the conflict from 1828 to 1832 over federal tariff policies. This tariff controversy led to a number of proposals, some for a constitutional convention, to deal with the situation.

The period from 1860 to 1861, just before the outbreak of the Civil War, led to a virtual avalanche of proposals. Many were designed to deal specifically with the issue of slavery and its many ramifications, but others were directed more generally to state-federal relations. Proposals included defining those powers that were reserved to the states or denied to the national government, guaranteeing state equality, providing that states should be permitted to appoint federal officers within their boundaries, creating a plural executive or otherwise guaranteeing that legislation could not be adopted without the concurrence of each section of the

nation, providing a legal means for states to secede, prohibiting such secession, or recognizing federal law as supreme.

Within five years of the end of the Civil War, the nation had adopted three amendments (the Thirteenth, Fourteenth, and Fifteenth Amendments), and in *Texas v. White* (1869), the Supreme Court declared that the Constitution had created "an indestructible Union of indestructible States" (725). The vigorous debates reflected in the *Slaughterhouse Cases* (1873), however, indicated that even the postwar amendments had not resolved federalism issues. State-federal conflict was especially prominent in the wake of the Supreme Court's ruling in *Brown v. Board of Education* (1954), which declared *de jure* segregation to be illegal. This decision subsequently led to calls for protection of state police powers. More recently, the belief that federal regulations have become stifling has led to renewed attention to the Tenth and Eleventh Amendments and to calls for adjusting state-federal relations by amendment ("Conference of the States" 1995).

See also Federalism and the Amending Process.

For Further Reading:

"Conference of the States: An Action Plan to Restore Balance in the Federal System." 1995. Concept paper adopted by the Council of State Governments, the National Governors' Association, and the National Conference of State Legislatures. 1 February.

Mason, Alpheus T. 1964. *The States' Rights Debate: Antifederalism and the Constitution.* Englewood Cliffs, NJ: Prentice-Hall.

Vile, John R. 2001a. *A Companion to the United States Constitution and Its Amendments.* 3d ed. Westport, CT: Praeger.

❖ STATES, ADMISSION OF NEW ❖

The framers of the Constitution were farsighted enough to provide in Article IV, Section 3 that "new states may be admitted by Congress into the Union." This was subject to the reservation that new states would be formed neither within existing states nor by joining two or more states or parts of states without their consent. In cases such as *Coyle v. Smith* (1911), involving Oklahoma's authority to move its capital after it became a state, the Supreme Court has established that new states enter on an equal basis with older ones.

The admission of new states was especially controversial in the nation's early history, when both North and South examined each new candidate for statehood with a view to its impact on the respective balance that free and slave states would have in the Senate. Apparently with this issue in mind, in 1815 Senator Joseph Varnum of Massachusetts introduced a resolution to prevent the admission of new states except by a two-thirds vote. In 1839, former President John Quincy Adams, then serving as a Whig in the House of Representatives, sought an amendment to impose a flat ban on the admission of new slave states.

Controversy shifted but continued after the Civil War, when the admission of Utah, where polygamy was then practiced, became especially controversial. In 1871 Democratic Representative Abram Comingo of Missouri introduced an amendment requiring that a new state have at least enough population to entitle it to one member in the House of Representatives under the ratio for representation then in use.

In 1896 Ohio Republican Representative Lucien Fenton introduced an amendment to prohibit the admission of states from any territories south of 30 degrees north latitude, thus excluding Hawaii from future statehood. Several other proposed amendments sought either to prevent the acquisition of any noncontiguous territories, several of which the United States acquired as a result of the Spanish-American War, or to require the admission of such territories by approval of two-thirds votes of both houses of Congress and three-fourths of the state legislatures.

Close to thirty amending resolutions were introduced in Congress from 1953 to 1961 regarding the admission of new states. These amendments were apparently aimed at Alaska and Hawaii. Concerns were raised about the nation's ability to defend these areas and, especially in the case of Hawaii, about the Americanization of an area with such a large Asian population (Bell 1984).

Most of the proposals introduced in the 1950s resurrected the idea that new states should be admitted only by the procedures and majorities needed to amend the federal Constitution. Almost as if their sponsors feared that such a policy might be applied retroactively, a number of such resolutions specifically exempted the procedure under which the Republic of Texas (which joined as a republic rather than as a prior territory) had been admitted as a state. Perhaps as a way of highlighting population disparities, especially in the case of Alaska, some resolutions in the 1950s would have allowed Congress to limit the representation of new states in the U.S. Senate.

See also Marriage, Divorce, and Parenting.

For Further Reading:

Bell, Roger. 1984. *Last Among Equals: Hawaii Statehood and American Politics*. Honolulu: University of Hawaii Press.

Onuf, Peter. 1984. "Territories and Statehood." In *Encyclopedia of American Political History: Studies of Principal Movements and Ideas*, ed. Jack P. Greene, 3: 1283–1304. New York: Charles Scribner's Sons.

❖ STATES, BOUNDARIES OF ❖

Numerous proponents of a new constitution for the United States have suggested that state boundaries need to be redrawn along more functional lines. Political scientist Rexford Tugwell, for example, wanted to divide existing states into approximately twenty "newstates" (Tugwell 1974); historian Leland Baldwin (1972) called for approximately fifteen states, with Alaska being permitted to join Oregon or become a commonwealth. Political scientist Charles Merriam also thought that state boundaries needed to be redrawn, with some large cities being given status as states. He noted that the *Chicago Tribune* received some 3,000 proposed maps when it held a contest for redrawing the boundaries of existing states (Merriam 1931, 58).

More recently, political scientist Matthew Holden Jr. suggested giving statehood to the nineteen cities with populations over 500,000, thereby ensuring greater representation to African Americans and urban interests (Holden 1973b, 245–252). In a related vein, radical African Americans such as Detroit's Brother Imari (formerly Richard B. Henry) have argued for setting aside five Gulf Coast states to create a special black nation (Holden 1973a, 69; Imari 1968, 30–31).

The fact that members of Congress are elected from states may account for the paucity of proposals that have been introduced there for redrawing state boundaries. Several proposals introduced before the Civil War attempted to ensure that legislation would require the consent of the nation's major regions, and others called for a plural executive representing the nation's major sections.

Whig Senator Garrett Davis of Kentucky also introduced two proposals in 1864 for a new division of New England. One such proposal would have combined Maine and Massachusetts into East New England and the other states in the region into West New England, leaving the latter state composed of two noncontiguous parts. Apparently, Davis's proposal was designed to express his disdain for Massachusetts; he believed that its leaders' rhetoric had been largely responsible for the Civil War (Ames 1896, 215–16).

For Further Reading:

Ames, Herman. 1896. *The Proposed Amendments to the Constitution of the United States during the First Century of Its History.* Reprint, New York: Burt Franklin, 1970.

Baldwin, Leland. 1972. *Reframing the Constitution: An Imperative for Modern America.* Santa Barbara, CA: ABC-CLIO.

Holden, Matthew, Jr. 1973a. *The Politics of the Black Nation.* New York: Chandler.

———. 1973b. *The White Man's Burden.* New York: Chandler.

Imari, Brother (Richard B. Henry). 1968. *War in America: The Malcolm X Doctrine.* Detroit, MI: Malcolm X Doctrine.

Merriam, Charles E. 1931. *The Written Constitution and the Unwritten Attitude.* New York: Richard R. Smith.

Tugwell, Rexford. 1974. *The Emerging Constitution.* New York: Harper and Row.

❖ STATES, CONSTITUTIONAL REVISION ❖

The federal amending mechanism developed in large part from the experience with such provisions in state constitutions and charters, but the traditions of state and federal reform now differ significantly.

The federal Constitution is a brief document that has been in force since 1789 and has been formally amended only twenty-seven times. By contrast, state constitutions are often codelike documents and are much more frequently amended and revised. The constitutions of the southern states have been revised and replaced particularly frequently. This difference between federal and state constitutions has led one observer to comment on what he calls "the Dual American Constitutional Tradition" (Cornwell 1981, 9). The fact that the guarantee clause in Article IV of the U.S. Constitution provides only that a state have a "republican" form of government gives states considerable leeway in initiating constitutional reforms.

State constitutions may be altered in one of three ways. Like the national Constitution, they may be altered by interpretation, especially by the judicial branch. They may also be altered by piecemeal amendments or through wholesale constitutional reform (Cornwell, Goodman, and Swanson 1975, 8–9). Such reforms are often initiated by either constitutional conventions or constitutional commissions, although the former are becoming less common, as fears of "runaway" conventions become more widespread (see Benjamin and Gais 1996).

Piecemeal amendments usually follow two stages—initiation and ratification. Unlike the national government, where this reform has been the subject of amending proposals, a number of states permit amendments to be introduced by popular initiatives (J. May 1987, 158–160). More commonly, however, amendments to state constitutions are introduced by constitutional conventions, by constitutional commissions, or by the state legislatures (Cornwell et al. 1975, 8–9). Most states require that the state legislature propose amendments by extraordinary majorities; some require votes in successive sessions of the legislature. All states except Delaware require ratification of amendments by popular vote. Most states require ratification by a simple majority, but at least two require extraordinary majorities *(Id.)*.

Constitutional conventions are the most frequent vehicle for complete state constitutional overhauls, and most state constitutions explicitly provide for them. Although the topic is one over which there has been considerable disagreement (compare Jameson 1887 and Dodd 1910), in most states, such conventions are subject to at least some legislative control. Like regular amendments proposed at the state level, most new constitutions must be approved by the voters. In a proposal reminiscent of one made by Thomas Jefferson that was rejected at the national level, a number of states require the people to vote periodically on constitutional revision (Sturm and May 1982, 122).

See also Initiative and Referendum.

For Further Reading:

Benjamin, Gerald, and Thomas Gais. 1996. "Constitutional Conventionphobia." *Hofstra Law and Policy Symposium* 1: 53–77.

Cornwell, Elmer E., Jr. 1981. "The American Constitutional Tradition: Its Impact and Development." In *The Constitutional Convention as an Amending Device*, ed. Kermit L. Hall, Harold M. Hyman, and Leon V. Sigal. Washington, DC: American Historical Association.

Cornwell, Elmer E., Jr., Jay S. Goodman, and Wayne R. Swanson. 1975. *State Constitutional Conventions: The Politics of the Revision Process in Seven States.* New York: Praeger.

May, Janice C. 1987. "Constitutional Amendment and Revision Revisited." *Publius: The Journal of Federalism* 17 (Winter): 153–179.

Sturm, Albert L., and Janice May. 1982. "State Constitutions and Constitutional Revision: 1980–81 and the Past 50 Years." In *The Book of the States: 1982–1983.* Lexington, KY: Council of State Governments.

❖ STATES, CONTROL OVER NATURAL RESOURCES ❖

In *United States v. California* (1947) and related cases, the U.S. Supreme Court decided that offshore oil was the property of the national government. In 1953 Congress enacted the Submerged Lands Act to vest ownership of lands within three miles of the coast in the states.

Beginning in the 1950s, the national government has become increasingly active in environmental regulation, an area previously left largely to state control. In March 1956, even before the adoption of much federal legislation on the subject, Democratic Representative Walter Rogers of Texas introduced an amendment to allow states "to conserve and regulate the exploration, production, and distribution of their petroleum products, water, sulfur, and all other minerals and natural resources" (H.J. Res. 588). Although no subsequent amendments on the topic have been introduced, controversy continues over the extent to which federal regulation is appropriate in this area.

See also Environmental Protection.

❖ STATES, LEGISLATIVE APPORTIONMENT ❖

One of the most influential and disputed areas in which the Warren Court intervened was the area of state legislative apportionment; it also issued decisions on the apportionment of congressional districts. The Constitution provides for reapportionment of House seats after each census. From 1842 to 1929 Congress required states to establish "contiguous equal districts," a requirement that it omitted in its 1929 and subsequent apportionment laws (D. O'Brien 2000b, 1:790).

Throughout most of the nineteenth century, states entering the Union were also required to guarantee representation in their state legislatures based on population. At the turn of the century, however, states began to react to the flood of new immigrants and the rise of large cities by refusing to reapportion their legislatures (D. O'Brien 2000b, 670). The result was that thinly populated rural areas often had the same representation within states as did urban areas with many times the population.

In *Colegrove v. Green* (1946), the Supreme Court refused to accept a challenge brought under the guarantee clause of the Constitution and overturn an Illinois legislative apportionment scheme in which population discrepancies were fairly large. Pointing to *Luther v. Borden* (1849), the Court decided that such matters were political questions, more appropriate for resolution by other branches of government. In *Gomillion v. Lightfoot* (1960), the Court seemed to open the door when it struck down a clear scheme of racial gerrymandering in Tuskegee, Alabama, but the case in which the Court truly reversed the course it had proclaimed in *Colegrove* was *Baker v. Carr* (1962). This case challenged the system of representation in Tennessee, which had last reapportioned itself in 1902. In a decision authored by Justice William Brennan, the Court decided that the matter of state legislative apportionment was justiciable under the equal protection clause of the Fourteenth Amendment.

In *Gray v. Sanders* (1963), the Court invalidated Georgia's system of primary elections, and Justice William O. Douglas articulated the principle of "one person one vote" that would be evoked in future cases. Most notably, in *Reynolds v. Sims* (1964), the Court applied this standard to both houses of a state legislature, and in *Wesberry v. Sanders* (1964), it applied it to House congressional districts. The principles of both decisions were reiterated in a series of related rulings (D. O'Brien 1991, 674–677).

Few decisions have led to sharper criticisms than those dealing with the apportionment question. Senate Minority Leader Everett Dirksen led a personal crusade to overturn *Reynolds v. Sims,* and more than 200 proposals were introduced in Congress on the subject from the decision in *Baker v. Carr* through the 1960s. The Council of State Governments pushed for amendments to overturn the reapportionment decisions, make the amending process easier, and clip the power of the Supreme Court. Twice failing to win a Senate vote for an amendment to permit states to apportion at least one house on

a basis other than population (Urofsky 1988, 835), proponents of such an amendment pushed for a constitutional convention. By 1969, thirty-three states had applied for such a convention ("33 States Ask Congress" 1969).

As more and more states were being reapportioned, however, and previously neglected urban and suburban areas were beginning to receive fairer representation, there was increasing support for the Court's rulings. A few more proposals were introduced in the 1970s, but the issue now appears largely to have faded from public consciousness.

Even while equalizing district populations, many states continue to show themselves adept at gerrymandering, that is, at configuring district boundaries to advantage particular parties or candidates. In recent cases such as *Shaw v. Reno* (1993) and *Miller v. Johnson* (1995), attention has gradually shifted to this issue, with special focus on whether districts can be gerrymandered in ways designed to increase representation for racial minorities. To date the U.S. Supreme Court has overturned extreme examples of racial gerrymandering without making altogether clear the extent to which racial considerations may influence district line-drawing.

See also *Baker v. Carr;* Council of State Governments; Dirksen, Everett McKinley; Political Questions; *Reynolds v. Sims.*

For Further Reading:

O'Brien, David M. 2000b. *Struggles for Power and Governmental Accountability.* 5th ed., Vol. 1 of *Constitutional Law and Politics.* New York: W. W. Norton.

"33 States Ask Congress for Constitutional Convention." 1969. *Congressional Quarterly Weekly Report* 27 (1 August): 1372–1373.

Urofsky, Melvin I. 1988. *A March of Liberty: A Constitutional History of the United States.* New York: Alfred A. Knopf.

❖ STATES, POLICE POWERS ❖

Throughout U.S. history, scholars and politicians have argued about the proper allocation of power between the state and national governments. Powers reserved to the states by the Tenth Amendment are often referred to as state police powers. Such powers typically involve regulation of morality, of marriage and family matters, of health and safety, and of property, but the term *police powers* is amorphous and clearly resists easy definition (Scheiber 1992, 639).

Although the national government does not have direct constitutional authority over most such matters, it may affect them in the course of exercising its powers over interstate commerce, taxation, and the like (Curry, Riley, and Battistoni 1989, 250–252). Thus, in *Champion v. Ames* (1903), the Supreme Court upheld the federal government's prohibition of the interstate sale of lottery tickets, and other cases upheld congressional regulation of "white slavery," or prostitution.

Beginning with a resolution introduced on 24 May 1954 by Democratic Senator James Eastland and continuing through 1973, about twenty-five proposals were introduced in Congress to limit interference with state powers over health, morals, education, marriage, and good order; to give states the right to manage their own internal affairs; or to protect the reserved rights of the states. Almost without exception, the sponsors of these amendments were southerners, most from the Deep South. This suggests that most of these proposals were in response to the Supreme Court's decision in *Brown v. Board of Education*, issued on 17 May 1954, and subsequent cases that called for an end to racial segregation. Interestingly, a key rationale for *Plessy v. Ferguson* (1896)—the Supreme Court decision mandating the doctrine of "separate but equal" that *Brown* overturned—had been the states' right to follow local custom and preserve public order.

See also Tenth Amendment.

For Further Reading:

Curry, James A., Richard B. Riley, and Richard M. Battistoni. 1989. *Constitutional Government: The American Experience.* St. Paul, MN: West.

Scheiber, Harry N. 1992. "Police Power." In *The Oxford Companion to the Supreme Court of the United States,* ed. Kermit L. Hall. New York: Oxford University Press.

❖ STICKNEY, ALBERT (1839–1908) ❖

Albert Stickney was a New York lawyer who published a book in 1879 advocating major constitutional changes (Vile 1991c, 27–29). Stickney's central objective was to create a system that would secure in each governmental department the "best men" and see that they gave "their best work" (Stickney 1879, 15). In Stickney's view, the primary obstacle to such objectives was the political party system, which he linked to a system of limited terms in office. He associated both parties and fixed terms with political corruption. In contrast to those who advocated a pure parliamentary system, however, Stickney favored neither the fusion of the legislative and executive branches nor the system of calling for a vote of no confidence by the majority.

Stickney began his description of proposed reforms by focusing on the judiciary. In a sense, this branch of government provided a model for the other branches in that its members already serve during good behavior. Believing that such tenure provided security against abuse, Stickney thought that judges, even at the federal level, could be elected rather than appointed. Stickney believed that voters would take their cues from the legal profession in making their selections.

Stickney advocated lodging executive power in one man with the power to appoint all heads of departments. These heads would, in turn, have authority over their subordinates. The president would serve during good behavior and would be responsible to the legislature, which could remove him only by a two-thirds vote. Stickney proposed to revive the electoral college as a deliberative body, free of partisanship, that would choose the president.

Initially, Stickney indicated that the real work of the legislature should not be making and revising laws—a task for judges—but rather "supervision and control" (Stickney 1879, 214). Specialists within departments would submit spending plans, and then the legislature would look them over, approve, authorize, and supervise them. Stickney favored a legislature (presumably unicameral) of 500 men who would devote their full time to their duties and would not have fixed terms. The legislature would have "absolute control of the money," power of "making *all necessary laws,*" power to remove any governmental official by a two-thirds vote, but no power over appointments (*Id.,* 218). Stickney clearly believed that there were many areas of legislation, including the laws of marriage and divorce, where Congress should have greater authority. Believing that there must be a supreme power within the state, Stickney proposed eliminating the executive veto, but in its place, he proposed that all legislation would have to be adopted by a two-thirds majority—a majority that would presumably be easier to obtain.

Stickney thought that the vice presidency should be eliminated. In cases of presidential vacancies, he would allow the senior cabinet officer to serve until the electoral college could choose a new president. Believing that only men with established reputations would be selected to legislative office, Stickney thought that the average member would serve about twelve years. Moreover, freed from party influence, such legislators would be able to serve the public. Legislatures would exercise greater wisdom than the people could exercise on their own behalf.

Stickney acknowledged that his plan would establish an aristocracy, but it would be an aristocracy of talent rather than of heredity. Whereas the American founders had sought the solution to government in institutions, Stickney professed to find the key in selecting men of good character to govern (Stickney 1879, 258). Perhaps because his plan was so novel, it appears to have had little contemporary influence, but Woodrow Wilson did cite Stickney's criticism of political parties in arguing for responsible cabinet government (Wilson 1882, 208–210).

For Further Reading:

Stickney, Albert. 1879. *A True Republic.* New York: Harper and Brothers.

Vile, John R. 1991c. *Rewriting the United States Constitution: An Examination of Proposals from Reconstruction to the Present.* New York: Praeger.

Wilson, (Thomas) Woodrow. 1882. "Government by Debate: Being a Short View of Our National Government as It Is and as It Might Be." In *The Papers of Woodrow Wilson,* Vol. 2, ed. Arthur S. Link. Reprint, Princeton, NJ: Princeton University Press, 1967.

❖ STORY, JOSEPH (1779–1845) ❖

In addition to serving as an associate justice of the U.S. Supreme Court from 1811 to 1845, Joseph Story was one of the most influential legal commentators of the nineteenth century. His analysis of the amending process reflected the general esteem with which the process was held, at least until the criticisms initiated by Sidney George Fisher at the time of the Civil War and the later criticisms that were raised during the Progressive Era.

Story commended the founders for recognizing the need for an amending process while also recognizing that "a government forever changing and changeable, is, indeed, in a state bordering upon anarchy and confusion" (Story 1987, 678–679). Summarizing his view, Story observed that "the great principle to be sought is to make the changes practicable, but not too easy; to secure due deliberation, and caution; and to follow experience, rather than to open a way for experiments, suggested by mere speculation or theory" (*Id.,* 679).

Story went on to describe the amending process as "the safety valve to let off all temporary effervescences and excitements; and the real effective instrument to control and adjust the movements of the machinery, when out of order, or in danger of self-destruction" (Story 1987, 680). Although the analogy of the Constitution to a machine was frequently evoked in the nineteenth century (Kammen 1987), Story appears to have been the first to use the "safety-valve" analogy in reference to the amending process.

For Further Reading:

Kammen, Michael. 1987. *A Machine That Would Go of Itself: The Constitution in American Culture.* New York: Alfred A. Knopf.

Story, Joseph. 1833. *Commentaries on the Constitution of the United States.* Boston: Hilliard, Gray. Reprint New York: Da Capo Press, 1970.

❖ STRITTMATTER, BILL ❖

One of the more novel, and far-reaching, attempts to rewrite the U.S. Constitution was composed by Bill Strittmatter, who was identified in the pamphlet only as the Pastor of the Church of Jesus Christ in Lakemore, Ohio, a group with possible ties to the Ku Klux Klan. The document is titled "A Christian Constitution and Civil Law for the Kingdom of Heaven on Earth," with the cover picturing an early American flag and identifying America with the words "Ameri meaning heavenly and rica (reich) meaning kingdom."

The pamphlet was not dated but contained a cartoon on p. 12 featuring presidential appointees Dr. [Henry] Kissinger and Dr. [Arthur] Burns, thus probably dating it to the early 1970s. The introduction noted that:

1. The United States was founded as a Christian Nation.
2. Article 1 of the Constitution of The United States of America DOES NOT SAY "separation of Church and State." Read it for yourself.
3. The Supreme Court of the United States has declared that America is a Christian Nation (Holy Trinity Church vs. United States, 143 U.S.471). (Strittmatter, unnumbered introduction)

This section further indicated that "civil Rulers are God's Ministers," and showed a diagram of an open Bible in which 71 percent of the material there is identified as relating to government and 29 percent as relating to that which is "personal" (Strittmatter 1).

Whereas there is considerable recent sentiment for posting the Ten Commandments in public buildings, Strittmatter composed his entire constitution around these commandments, with scripture citations to each section. Most of the passages were from that part of Hebrew Scriptures that Christians refer to as the Old Testament, but some are entwined with passages from the New Testament as well.

Like the Ten Commandments, the first articles of Strittmatter's constitution dealt with individuals' relations with God. Article One thus began with the declaration, "I AM THE

LORD THY GOD, THOU SHALT HAVE NO OTHER GODS BEFORE ME" (Strittmatter, 4). God was identified early in this article as Jesus Christ, with the penalty of stoning provided for those who worship others. Christ was further identified as the nation's Commander and Chief, and all citizens were invested with the responsibility of receiving military training. Under specified "rules of war," all enemies who did not surrender as tributaries should be slaughtered, and covenants were forbidden with "heathen people" (Strittmatter, 6). This Article contained admonitions to cleanliness, and it limited citizenship to "the Christian Race," with persons of "mixed race" being denied citizenship, and "hyphenated citizens such as German-Americans, Mexican-Americans or Italian-Americans" being prohibited (Id., 7). Generally, Strittmatter had little to say about rights, and the "Christian religion" and only that religion was to be accorded "freedom of religion," with only citizen members of the "Christian Race" permitted to hold office in the church; the writings and other productions of "the children of Belial" were to be burned (Id., 7).

Article Two of the Constitution prohibited the worship of "graven images," and Article Three prohibited the taking of God's name in vain. The penalty for blasphemy against Jesus Christ was specified as death (Strittmatter, 9).

Article Four provided for the keeping of the Sabbath, with "those rendering essential services" on the Sabbath taking off Wednesdays. As in other articles, death was prescribed as a punishment for noncompliance. Specific feast days and holidays were also specified, including Pentecost and Thanksgiving. This section also recognized the Passover and the year of Jubile[e] in which every man's land would be returned to him.

The second part of the constitution dealt with individuals' relations with their neighbors, again following the structure of the Ten Commandments. Article Five focused on honoring one's parents, with penalties of death for those who smite or curse their parents. Civil power was to be committed to "a[n] elder . . . whom Jesus Christ your King shall choose" (Strittmatter, 13), and who shall take his judgments from the Bible. "Judges, elders and officers" were also cited, with people further divided into tens, fifties, hundreds, and thousands, and "priests" making final judgments in difficult cases (*Id.*, 16). Punishment by "stripes" was specified. This Article further specified that "Once elected, selected or appointed, elders officers and ministers have absolute authority under and within law, likewise the principle of absolute responsibility" (*Id.*, 17). Church and state would both be supported by tithes.

Article Six dealt with murder. As in the Old Testament, cities of refuge were to be provided for those who commit involuntary manslaughter. The inclusion of matters of criminal law in this national constitution would tend to indicate that Strittmatter was not (like previous defenders of racial segregation) particularly committed to a division of power between state and federal authorities. Strittmatter also included a section on liability, most provisions taken from Old Testament passages relating to damage done by animals belonging to others.

Article Seven, prohibiting adultery, defined the practice to include "inter-racial marriage and miscegenation" (Strittmatter, 19). The penalty for such miscegenation was to be stoning to death. Rules were also specified indicating which plants, animals, and foods were to be considered unclean. One fairly antiquated prohibition included that of plowing "with an ox and an ass together" (*Id.*, 20).

Article Eight prohibited theft, and dealt with weights and measures, restitution, lost and found articles, confessions of guilt, usury, and wages. Usury (excessive interest) was permitted to strangers but not to fellow citizens. The spoils of war were to be divided between Jesus and those who fought in a war, with "the five hundreth part" going to the "National Cathedral" (Strittmatter, 23).

Article Nine dealt with bearing false witness. It also committed individuals to the keeping of vows.

Article Ten dealt with coveting. This included explicit instructions about the obligations of husbands and wives and sexual relations. It permitted divorce in certain cases but prohibited incest. It also related to inheritance. A welfare provision was included for "the

stranger, the fatherless, [and] the widow." A provision was also made for gleaning, whereby individuals in need are permitted to follow behind harvesters and appropriate any remaining food (Strittmatter, 28).

Article Ten was followed with a specific prohibition against adding amendments to the Constitution: "Ye shall not add unto the word which I command you, neither shall ye diminish ought from it" (Strittmatter, 28). Although officials were permitted to settle controversies under the law, their decisions "shall not become case law to base further decisions thereon" (*Id.*, 28). This section further specified that "The rest of the Bible not mentioned herein is made a part hereof" (*Id.*, 18).

The middle two pages of the pamphlet explained a number of American symbols designed to show that "America has scores of the marks of Israel upon her" (Strittmatter, 14). America was identified as "the 'New Order of the Ages' as prophesied by Daniel" (*Id.*, 15). The last page of the pamphlet, which included a picture of the great seal of America with the all-seeing eye of God shedding a tear, similarly identified America as "the apple" of Christ's eye.

This author has been unable to find any secondary literature on this constitution, but it seems clearly tied to the modern Christian identity movement and other movements motivated by ideals of racial purity and the hope of governing America under a system of divine law. It is the only document that this author has found that tries to write a new American constitution using scripture.

See also Christian Reconstructionism.

For Further Reading:
Strittmatter, Bill. n.d. "A Christian Constitution and Civil Law for the Kingdom of Heaven on Earth." Lakemore, OH: 28 pp.

❖ STRUBLE, ROBERT, JR. ❖

The Internet has opened up the possibility for individuals to communicate who may not otherwise be able to do so, but it sometimes presents problems for scholars, who would desire more permanent records of proposals that are posted there. One such proposal for constitutional reform that printed out to well over 200 pages was posted by Robert Struble Jr. under the title of "Redeeming U.S. Democracy," and was introduced by former Senator, and one-time presidential contender, Minnesota's Eugene McCarthy. Struble identified himself as a Republican Party official living in Bremerton, Washington, and apparently hoped to solicit comments with the view of publishing a book, which apparently never materialized.

Unfortunately, Struble's website, which the author of this book accessed in July 1997, is no longer available. The most important part of the site was the introduction of a Twelve Code, which Struble hoped to propose through constitutional convention. It consisted of a unique blend of proposals, some of which would likely be favored by cultural conservatives who were chiefly concerned about perceived cultural decay, and others of which would be more likely favored by liberals concerned about unemployment.

Struble dedicated his work to Mary, the mother of Jesus, and began his preface by asking that God "forgive us the offenses and help us to turn, individually and socially, from license to liberty." In the preamble to his Twelve Code, Struble further noted that "[t]he authority of government is the people's from God," but most of his proposals dealt with quite practical matters.

The first section of Struble's proposal called for limiting members of the U.S. House of Representatives to one term, with the hope of making that body more democratic. Struble thought that the Senate should have more "expertise and institutional memory," and he therefore did not favor imposing limits on this body, although he was willing to allow states to set such limits on their own.

The second section of Struble's Twelve Code clarified the first by indicating that members of the House would begin their first two years of service as tribunates, during which time they would perform functions as ombudsmen, investigators, and assistants to the vice president. The vice president, in turn, would be granted power to veto existing regulations sub-

ject to veto by either the U.S. president, both houses of congress, or the Committee of Cuts. After the Representatives served as tribunates for two years, and were given two months to make a transition, they would in turn become regular House members for their single term. Their income would be set at "twice the median income of the American household." Representatives would be subject to recall. Ex-representatives would serve as a local advisory body to the president and could "propose nominees for the office of Tenth Justice," described later in Struble's proposals.

The third section of the Twelve Code was directed to "Checks against Judicial Usurpation." Concerned chiefly with Congress's power to strip the Supreme Court of its appellate jurisdiction, Struble proposed that whenever jurisdiction was so clipped, "the court of last resort for cases of that class becomes the respective state supreme court." He also suggested that Congress might specify a date, for example ten years after the decision in *Brown v. Board of Education* (1954) declaring racial segregation in schools to be unconstitutional, as a time before which precedents would remain in force. Struble further provided for automatic "sunset provisions" for limitations of judicial jurisdiction. When jurisdiction is stripped from the Supreme Court, Struble specified that lower courts should abide by six considerations "in order of priority." They are:

> First, the written Constitution; second, the intent of the Framers, as best verifiable; third, the federal precedent deriving from decisions rendered since the jurisdiction's restoration; fourth, federal precedent prior to the congressionally specified date . . . ; fifth, federal precedent antedating Appomattox; and sixth, statute law which is not inconsistent with the U.S. Constitution.

Struble devoted sections four and five of the Twelve Code to congressional procedures. His proposals would limit the influence of congressional committees by subordinating their deliberations to the will of the majority and by permitting majority rule on the floor. Committees would be divided into fortnight committees (in which members could serve for a maximum of two weeks), half tribute committees (where tributes or volunteers would make up at least half of the membership), and joint Senate-House Committees. Members would have greater choice over the selection and removal of committee chairs.

Before dealing in sections six through eight of the Twelve Code with problems of unemployment and underemployment, Struble included a preface in which he specified that "we the people require of the American economy that it afford able-bodied citizens the opportunity to make a living by working. We enforce this earning opportunity not by legislating job security or guaranteeing anyone a place, but by making jobs plentiful enough to match the will to work."

Section six would allow Congress to equalize work by "reducing the duration of the workweek, workmonth, or workyear." He also favored "expanding the labor market structurally." To this end, Struble would grant Congress power in section seven to generate jobs by working with private businesses to create Private Enterprise Projects (PEP). Section eight would further use taxation of from 0 percent of those businesses that were most labor intensive to 10 percent for those that used the least.

Sections nine through twelve of Struble's proposals dealt with cultural and religious issues and also came with a preamble in which he noted that "Civil rights and liberties necessitate a sense of community, duty and responsibility." Section nine was designed "to counter the commerce in lewdness which undermines human dignity and degrades the culture in which we must live." To this end, Struble would create a Tenth Justice of the U.S. Supreme Court, elected by the voters from among five women, and with power to issue injunctions against the importation, exportation, dissemination, or broadcast of "sexually licentious or pornographic phenomena," abbreviated as SLOPP. Struble would provide for "subsequent punishment" of enjoined materials rather than for "prior restraint." Work consisting of "only the written word shall never qualify as SLOPP."

Section ten would provide for a place for scripture in schools. Teachers could read such passages in public schools for up to twelve minutes a day. Similarly, contrary to existing judicial precedents, teachers would be permitted to post the Ten Commandments and up to ten other scripture verses.

Section eleven provided that pupils who dissented from such readings should "practice silent [and inconspicuous] non-participation." States would also be permitted to give money to religious schools or to parents paying tuition to the same, but never in a way so as to "undermine or modify a school's moral and religious character, or to change its religious exercises."

Section twelve explicitly provided for prayers, including the Lord's Prayer, in public schools, as long as they were "initiated in the classroom by the respective teacher." Struble ended with a benediction that included a number of scriptures. Further commenting in an appendix on his Twelve Code, Struble indicated that his amendments were only 20 percent shorter than the Constitution they were amending, but noted that "A few brief sentences will not suffice to streamline today's Capitol City apparatus."

It is a shame that Struble's extensive Internet posting is apparently not available in book form. His proposals remain a peculiar amalgam of traditionally conservative and liberal concerns and an example of the concern that an individual citizen can have over the refining of the nation's basic document.

For Further Reading:

Struble, Robert, Jr., "Redeeming U.S. Democracy," *http://tcmnet.com/~rusd/*. Accessed on 7/11/97. No longer appears to be available.

❖ SUBSTANTIVE DUE PROCESS ❖

Both the Fifth Amendment and the Fourteenth Amendment contain clauses prohibiting deprivation of "life, liberty, or property, without due process of law." The guarantee in the Fifth Amendment applies to the national government, and the guarantee in the Fourteenth Amendment applies to the states. Through the latter clause, the courts have applied most of the guarantees in the Bill of Rights to state governments.

Although the language of the clauses in both the Fifth and the Fourteenth Amendments focuses on *process*, at various times the Court has also given them a substantive meaning (Abraham and Perry 1994, 92–153). Indeed, the courts have interpreted these clauses so flexibly that their decisions have approached the kinds of changes usually reserved for constitutional amendments.

The Supreme Court's first use of substantive due process appears to have been in *Scott v. Sandford* (1857) and the *Slaughterhouse Cases* (1873). Especially from the end of the nineteenth century until the shift in judicial emphasis and philosophy in 1937, the Supreme Court used the idea of substantive due process to strike down state and federal regulations believed to interfere unreasonably with liberty of contract. *Lochner v. New York* (1905), striking down hours regulations for bakers, and *Adkins v. Children's Hospital* (1923), voiding federal minimum-wage laws for women in the District of Columbia, epitomized this judicial philosophy. More recently, critics have alleged that the Court's decisions in *Griswold v. Connecticut* (1965), striking down Connecticut's prohibition of birth-control devices, and in *Roe v. Wade* (1973), legalizing abortion, were based primarily on substantive ideas of justice not found within the constitutional text.

Numerous amendments, including those attempting to regulate child labor, provide minimum wages, limit workers' hours, and the like, were proposed to overturn decisions by the Court when it was using the due process clause to strike at such economic regulations. More recently, the Right-to-Life Amendment has been intended to strike down the Court's decisions on abortion.

See also *Lochner v. New York; Scott v. Sandford.*

For Further Reading:

Abraham, Henry J., and Barbara Perry. 1994. *Freedom and the Court: Civil Rights and Liberties in the United States.* 6th ed. New York: Oxford University Press.

❖ SUBVERSION ❖

The fear of subversion dates at least as far back as the Alien and Sedition Laws of 1798. Such fear was heightened by suspicions directed at the Communist Party during the Cold War, which followed World War II.

Initially, federal courts proved fairly deferential to legislation designed to register and control communists. Focusing specifically on decisions in *Dennis v. United States* (1951) and *Communist Party v. Subversive Activities Control Board* (1961), one observer said that such decisions demonstrated "deference to legislative judgments about the existence of a subversive conspiracy, minimal rationality standards for review of the means chosen to suppress subversion, and a balancing of the rights of individuals to freedom of political expression versus the state's interest in maintaining its power" (Wiecek 1992, 847).

As it began to give greater attention to individual rights, however, the Warren Court began to examine such legislation more closely for possible conflicts with the First Amendment and other constitutional protections. Thus, in *United States v. Robel* (1967), the Supreme Court struck down a provision of the Subversive Activities Control Act of 1950 that prohibited members of the Communist Party from working at defense facilities.

This decision prompted a bevy of amending proposals, most from southern representatives, to allow Congress to exclude from employment at defense facilities individuals who knowingly became or remained a member of any organization committed to overthrowing the government by force. Even before *Robel*, an Alabama representative had introduced an amendment designed to allow public schools to exclude subversives from the classroom. Subsequent proposals also sought to extend federal power to control the transmission of subversive materials through the U.S. mails.

For Further Reading:

Wiecek, William. 1992. "Subversion." In *The Oxford Companion to the Supreme Court of the United States,* ed. Kermit L. Hall. New York: Oxford University Press.

❖ SUNDQUIST, JAMES (1915–) ❖

Political scientist James Sundquist has authored one of the most historically informed surveys of constitutional reforms in the United States (1986). He was at once aware of the reasons that the American founders settled on a system of checks and balances and convinced that the framers may have solved the problem of tyranny by creating a system that results in excessive deadlock and stalemate (Vile 1991c, 131–133).

As a scholar, Sundquist devoted most of his attention to a discussion of past reform proposals, but he concluded by advocating consideration of nine constitutional amendments. Many overlap with proposals offered by the Committee on the Constitutional System, for which one edition of his book was published.

Sundquist's recommendations were as follows: combine the president and the president's running mate on a team ticket with members of the House and Senate, so voters would be unable to split their votes; raise terms of members of the House of Representatives to four years and terms of senators to eight; allow either the president or a majority of either house of Congress to call special elections in which all members of the legislative and executive branches would be up for election; remove the constitutional prohibition that prevents members of Congress from serving in the executive branch; create a limited presidential item veto, subject to an override by a majority of both houses of Congress; restore the legislative veto, albeit only when both houses of Congress concur; add an amendment effectively incorporating the provisions of the War Powers Resolution of 1973 into the Constitution; allow majorities of both houses of Congress (rather than two-thirds of the Senate) to approve treaties; and provide for a national referendum to break legislative-executive deadlocks (Sundquist 1986, 241–242).

See also Committee on the Constitutional System.

For Further Reading:

Sundquist, James L. 1986. *Constitutional Reform* *and Effective Government.* Washington, DC: Brookings Institution.

Vile, John R. 1991c. *Rewriting the United States Constitution: An Examination of Proposals from Reconstruction to the Present.* New York: Praeger.

❖ SUPERMAJORITIES ❖

Although the United States government is often described as a democracy and criticized for not fully embodying democratic ideals (see Dahl 2001), James Madison, writing in *Federalist No. 10,* as well as other framers of the Constitution, specifically distinguished the "republican" form of government that they favored from other forms of "direct democracy" that they thought led to faction and injustice. In a recent article, two law professors, John O. McGinnis and Michael B. Rappaport, have argued that "the central principle underlying the Constitution is governance through supermajority rules" (McGinnis and Rappaport 2002, 705). There are seven direct constitutional provisions in the original constitution requiring supermajority approval—for example, it takes two-thirds of the Senate to ratify a treaty and two-thirds of both houses of Congress to override a presidential veto. McGinnis and Rappaport believe that other requirements, like bicameralism and the requirement that all laws be presented to the president for a signature, have a similar impact.

Among the provisions for supermajorities are those in Article V providing that two-thirds of both houses of Congress may propose constitutional amendments or must call a convention for this purpose when petitioned by two-thirds of the states, and that three-fourths of the states must subsequently ratify them. Such requirements clearly pose obstacles to many constitutional changes that may be favored by temporary majorities, or by majorities that are concentrated unduly in one or another region of the nation. Although McGinnis and Rappaport believe that the idea of supermajorities was a unique contribution of the New World to political theory, the U.S. Constitution is not unique in this respect. Thus, the supermajority requirements in the Articles of Confederation, including a provision for unanimous state consent to amendments, were even more onerous than those in the current Constitution (McGinnis and Rappaport 2002, 717).

McGinnis and Rappaport identify the rules "that govern the adoption and amendment of the Constitution" as "the most important supermajority rules in the Constitution" (McGinnis and Rappaport 2002, 780). They believe that the supermajority requirement in Article V is one way to answer the question, often associated with Thomas Jefferson, as to why people of today should be bound by decisions made by previous generations (sometimes referred to as "the dead hand of the past") and embodied within the constitutional text (*Id.*, 796). Considering that the initial Constitution was written by delegates from twelve of the existing states, was approved by Congress, and subsequently required ratification of nine or more of the thirteen states, McGinnis and Rappaport point out that (with the possible exception of the entrenchment clause forbidding states from being deprived of their equal suffrage in the U.S. Senate without their consent) existing generations face no greater barrier to changing the Constitution than did the original framers (*Id.*, 796–800).

The Fourteenth Amendment contained a provision requiring that individuals who had served in the Confederacy could not accept public offices without approval by a two-thirds vote of Congress; the Twenty-fifth Amendment further provides for a two-thirds supermajority to certify that a president who says otherwise is not capable of serving (McGinnis and Rappaport 2002, 724). Other supermajority requirements have been suggested in proposed amendments relating to governmental spending and other matters (McGinnis and Rappaport 1999). At other times, amendments have been proposed that would eliminate existing supermajority requirements, thus, for example, allowing the Senate to approve of treaties by majority vote.

See also Article V of the U.S. Constitution; Articles of Confederation; Entrenchment Clauses; Ratification of the Existing U.S. and/or Future U.S. Constitutions.

For Further Reading:
Dahl, Robert. 2001. *How Democratic Is the American Constitution?* New Haven, CT: Yale University Press.

McGinnis, John O. and Michael B. Rappaport. 2002. "Our Supermajoritarian Constitution." *Texas Law Review* 80 (March): 703–805.

———. 1999. "Supermajority Rules as a Constitutional Solution." *William and Mary Law Review* 40 (February): 365–470.

❖ SUPREME COURT DECISIONS REVERSED BY CONSTITUTIONAL AMENDMENTS ❖

At least since John Marshall's decision in *Marbury v. Madison* (1803), the U.S. Supreme Court has asserted its power to interpret both state and federal laws and the Constitution and to interpret laws and to strike down those that it believes to be in contravention of this document. When the Supreme Court exercises its power (known as statutory interpretation) to interpret a law in a way that Congress thinks is unjustified, Congress can adopt another law, making its intentions clearer, and the Court will generally accept this new interpretation. When the Supreme Court exercises its power to strike down a law that it believes to be unconstitutional (known as judicial review), however, the effects are more profound. In debates with Stephen Douglas, Abraham Lincoln pointed out that the people would no longer be sovereign if all such decisions by unelected judges were considered to be the final word on the subject. Over the course of time, the constitutional amending process has been recognized as one such check on judicial excess or misinterpretation of the document. One of the ironies of this process, which can sometimes look like a dog chasing its tail, is that the courts, in turn, end up interpreting any new amendments.

This power to overturn a Supreme Court interpretation of the U.S. Constitution was actually exercised even before *Marbury*. Thus, in 1795 the Eleventh Amendment reversed a

Court decision in *Chisholm v. Georgia* (1793) by limiting suits that individuals could bring against individual states without their consent. When the Supreme Court decided in *[Dred] Scott v. Sandford* (1857) that blacks were not and could not be citizens, this decision was in turn overturned by the Fourteenth Amendment (1868) that declared that all persons born or naturalized within the United States were citizens thereof and were entitled to certain basic rights like due process and equal protection of the laws. The Thirteenth Amendment had already eliminated slavery, and the Fifteenth would go on to prohibit discrimination against voting on the basis of race. Supreme Court decisions in the years immediately after the adoption of the Fourteenth Amendment may have shown some of the limits of the amending process (as well as ambiguity about the amendment's meaning), by interpreting the amendment fairly restrictively. Eventually, however, the Fourteenth Amendment became the vehicle by which the Court reversed the course it had set in *Barron v Baltimore* (1833), where it had declared that the Bill of Rights only limited the national government; subsequent decisions, especially during the Warren Court, would also extend almost all of these limitations to the states.

The Sixteenth Amendment (1913) overturned the Supreme Court's controversial decision in *Pollock v. Farmers' Loan & Trust Co.* (1895) by establishing the constitutionality of the income tax. Similarly, the Twenty-sixth Amendment (1971) responded to the Supreme Court's decision of the previous year in *Oregon v. Mitchell* in which the Court had held that Congress could lower the age of voting in federal, but not in state, elections, by lowering this age in both types of electoral contests.

Some scholars (for example, Kyvig 1996b, 112) would also include the Nineteenth Amendment, or woman's suffrage amendment, as an example of an amendment that overturned a Court decision because it effectively overturned the Court's ruling in *Minor v. Happersett* (1875) that had declared that the federal constitution did not prevent discrimination against women voters on the basis of their gender. This writer believes instead that *Minor*

was, and remains, a proper interpretation of the Fourteenth Amendment that has been subsequently and positively modified by the Nineteenth, but such differences in interpretation demonstrate that amendments may often be interpreted in conflicting fashions.

Scores of amendments have been proposed to overturn Supreme Court decisions throughout American history. In some cases—for example, child labor—the Court has reversed itself before an amendment was ratified. In recent years, there have been proposals to reverse Court decisions relative to prayer and Bible reading in schools, state legislative apportionment, abortion, the rights of criminal defendants, the legitimacy of campaign financing laws, the standard of review to be applied in cases related to the free exercise of religion, flag desecration, and so forth. Other amendments have proposed limiting the exercise of judicial review or requiring supermajorities before the Court can overturn legislation. It is not uncommon for members of Congress to propose such amendments within days of controversial decisions. To date, all such proposals have proven unsuccessful.

The line between constitutional amendment and constitutional interpretation is often a fine one—justices not uncommonly accuse one another of attempting to "amend" the Constitution under the guise of interpretation (Vile 1980). Still the amending process makes it clear that ultimate power over the Constitution rests with the people, or at least a people who can muster the supermajorities necessary for an amendment. Because of the difficulty of this process, the Court has reversed far more of its own decisions than have been reversed by amendments. To cite but a few examples, the Supreme Court's decision outlawing racial segregation in *Brown v. Board of Education* (1954) overturned a previous ruling in *Plessy v. Ferguson* (1896); similarly, in *West Virginia Board of Education v. Barnette* (1943), the Court overturned *Minersville School District v. Gobitis* (1940), which had declared that public school students had to salute the American flag. Although the story is often told simplistically, the Supreme Court's historic "switch in time that saved nine," reversing course on some key New

Deal programs in 1937, is often attributed to Roosevelt's court-packing plan and has been cited by Bruce Ackerman as one of three important "constitutional moments" in American history.

The fact that the Supreme Court can reverse its own decisions, combined with the difficulty of the constitutional amending process, often leads advocates of reform to argue that the problem with a given ruling is not a problem with the constitution itself but simply with its interpretation. This, in turn, often diverts attention away from amendments and toward the election of presidents that reformers believe will introduce new personnel on the Supreme Court who might be willing to reconsider earlier opinions. One of the reasons that Senate confirmation hearings for Supreme Court justices, and indeed for judges in general, have become intense is the belief that new appointees might very well change existing constitutional interpretations.

One reason for declaring issues involving the amending process to be "political questions" for the political branches to resolve is the fact that such issues sometimes arise in cases involving amendments designed to overturn Supreme Court decisions. Although it is diffi-cult to point to provisions since those in the Bill of Rights that have specifically curtailed congressional powers (the Twenty-seventh Amendment made a minor alteration in the timing of congressional pay raises), numerous amendments, including amendments for balanced budgets and term limits, have also been directed at Congress, hardly leaving it as a neutral observer. Questions therefore continue about the validity of the Supreme Court decision in *Coleman v. Miller* (1939) declaring that most amending issues are political questions.

See also *Chisholm v. Georgia;* Court-Packing Plan; Eleventh Amendment; Fourteenth Amendment; *Marbury v. Madison; Oregon v. Mitchell;* Political Questions; *Pollack v. Farmers' Loan & Trust Co.; Scott v. Sandford;* Sixteenth Amendment; Twenty-sixth Amendment.

For Further Reading:

Kyvig, David E. 1996b. "Appealing Supreme Court Decisions: Constitutional Amendments as Checks on Judicial Review." *Journal of Supreme Court History* 2: 111–119.

Vile, John R. 1980. "The Supreme Court and the Amending Process." *Georgia Political Science Association Journal* 8 (Fall): 33–66.

T

❖ TARIFFS ❖

In a book first published in 1903, a scholar identified the tariff as "the most persistent issue in American politics" (Stanwood 1903, 1:1). Yet during the first hundred years of the nation's history, only three amending proposals dealt with this issue. After the Nullification Crisis of 1828–1832, which largely centered on Southern objections to the sectional character of existing tariff policies that tended—as John C. Calhoun and other Southern statesmen argued—to benefit Northern industrial states at the expense of the more agrarian South, Georgia and Alabama petitioned for a constitutional convention to resolve the issue. An 1864 substitute for the Thirteenth Amendment would have permitted the use of tariffs for raising revenue as long as they were not excessive. A third proposal, offered in 1871, would have substituted direct taxes for tariffs (Ames 1896, 252).

The Payne-Aldrich Tariff Bill of 1907 gave Congress the power to establish a tariff board to give advice on tariff rates, but by the language of Article I, Section 8 of the Constitution, Congress continues to have the duty to set tariff rates. From 1916 to 1922, three proposals were introduced to transfer the power of setting tariff rates to a nonpartisan board or tariff commission. Recent debates over the North American Free Trade Agreement (NAFTA) and whether to extend so-called favorite nation trade status to nations like the People's Republic of China indicate that trade and tariff issues can still stir considerable political controversy.

See also Calhoun, John C.

For Further Reading:
Ames, Herman. 1896. *The Proposed Amendments to the Constitution of the United States during the First Century of Its History.* Reprint, New York: Burt Franklin, 1970.
Stanwood, Edward. 1903. *American Tariff Controversies in the Nineteenth Century.* 2 vols. Reprint, New York: Russell and Russell, 1967.
Taylor, George R., ed. 1993. *The Great Tariff Debate, 1820–1830.* Boston: D. C. Heath.

❖ TAXATION, DIRECT ❖

In an attempt to protect the least populous states, Article I, Section 9 of the Constitution specifies that "no Capitation, or other direct, Tax shall be laid, unless in Proportion to the Census." However, the document does not define what direct taxes are.

In 1793 an amending resolution was introduced to define direct taxes, and three years later, in upholding a federal tax on carriages as an indirect tax, the Supreme Court indicated in *Hylton v. United States* that only taxes on persons and land fell into the direct tax category. *Pollock v. Farmers' Loan & Trust Co.* (1895) subsequently included income taxes in this category but was overturned by the Sixteenth Amendment.

Eighteen provisions were introduced in the nation's first century relative to the apportionment of direct taxes. Some would have overturned the three-fifths clause (as the Fourteenth Amendment eventually did) to require that only free individuals be counted in such apportionment. Others would have apportioned direct taxes according to property values (Ames 1896, 143–144).

Today the issue is moot because the national government relies on the income tax that was sanctioned by the Sixteenth Amendment and on various other excise taxes that are considered to be indirect.

See also *Pollock v. Farmers' Loan & Trust Co;* Sixteenth Amendment; Three-fifths Clause.

For Further Reading:
Ames, Herman. 1896. *The Proposed Amendments to the Constitution of the United States during the First Century of Its History.* Reprint, New York: Burt Franklin, 1970.

❖ TAXATION, EXPORT ❖

In a provision meant to protect the agricultural states, Article I, Section 9 of the Constitution prohibits Congress from levying a tax "on Articles exported from any State." In addition, Article I, Section 10 specifies that "no State shall, without the Consent of Congress, lay any Imposts or Duties on Imports or Exports, except what may be absolutely necessary for executing its inspection Laws."

From 1812 to 1914, twelve attempts were made to repeal the ban on congressional export levies. Most grouped around three periods—the War of 1812, the Civil War, and World War I—when governmental resources were down (Musmanno 1929, 112). Two proposals introduced in 1866 and one in 1884 would have applied specifically to exports of cotton, suggesting a possible intent to retaliate against the South.

In 1974 Michigan Republican Representative Robert Huber renewed the call to grant Congress power to levy export fees. It is difficult to imagine such a proposal, adverse to the interests of so many states, gaining the necessary majorities.

For Further Reading:
Musmanno, M. A. 1929. *Proposed Amendments to*

the Constitution. Washington, DC: U.S. Government Printing Office.

❖ TAXATION, INCOME ❖

See Sixteenth Amendment.

❖ TAXATION, INHERITANCE ❖

The Supreme Court upheld the constitutionality of a federal inheritance tax in *New York Trust Co. v. Eisner* (1916). Still, at least ten amendment proposals have contained provisions designed explicitly to recognize such a power in the Constitution, with at least two such proposals declaring that such taxes could be levied only on estates valued at $50,000 or $100,000 or more (Musmanno 1929, 164). Some of the proposals to repeal the Sixteenth Amendment have also called for limits on, or abolition of, inheritance taxes.

In 2001 Congress adopted and President George W. Bush signed the Economic Growth and Tax Relief Reconciliation Act of 2001. Under this legislation, the tax rate on estate taxes will be lowered from the 60 percent in effect in 2001 to 45 percent by 2009; during this same time exclusions from this tax would be raised from $675,000 to $3.5 million. Under the current law, estate taxes would be ended altogether in 2010, but the following year, it would go back to the 60 percent rate with a $1 million exclusion (O'Connell 2001, 588). It seems quite likely that this legislation will undergo further refinement before 2010, but this legislation would certainly appear to indicate that estate taxes can be taken care of through ordinary legislation rather than requiring a constitutional amendment.

For Further Reading:
O'Connell, Frank J., Jr. 2001. "Estate Tax Repeal: What Now?" *The Tax Adviser* 32 (September): 588.

❖ TAXATION, LAND ❖

At least two proposals have been introduced, one by Democratic Representative Horace Voorhis of California in 1942 and the other by Democratic Representative Herman Eberharter of Pennsylvania in 1944, to allow Congress to tax land values. From a somewhat different perspective, Democratic Senator Morris Sheppard of Texas introduced three resolutions from 1937 to 1941 that would provide for a homestead exemption of up to $5,000 for a head of a household. Since Sheppard's proposal, an increasing number of states have exempted such property from taxes (Roemer 1983, 110); it is unclear whether Sheppard intended to universalize such exceptions against state taxation or whether he intended to guard against a future federal tax on land.

For Further Reading:

Roemer, Arthur C. 1983. "Classification of Property." In *The Property Tax and Local Finance,* ed. C. Lowell Harris. New York: Proceedings of the Academy of Political Science.

❖ TAXATION, MAJORITIES NEEDED TO INCREASE ❖

Some proponents of a balanced budget amendment foresee reaching the balanced budget goal by cuts in spending, but others anticipate that federal taxes will also need to be raised to accomplish this. Opponents of such taxes believe that they simply encourage the government to increase spending.

The Constitution does not set any special majorities for the passage of tax legislation. In the last two decades, several members of Congress have proposed a constitutional amendment that would require a two-thirds vote of both Houses to raise taxes, the same vote now required to override a presidential veto. In December 1994 Republican members of the House of Representatives proposed a change in House rules that would require a three-fifths vote of the House to enact tax increases. Although the constitutionality of this measure has been questioned (Ackerman et al. 1995;

Soller 1995; but see McGinnis and Rappaport 1995), the House adopted it as Rule XXI, Section 5 (b) in January 1995 by a 279-to-152 vote, and courts have rejected a challenge to the act (see Leach 1997).

See also Balanced Budget Amendment; Supermajorities.

For Further Reading:

Ackerman, Bruce, et al. 1995. "An Open Letter to Congressman Gingrich." *Yale Law Journal* 104 (April): 1539–1544.

Leach, Robert S. 1997. "House Rule XXI and an Argument against a Constitutional Requirement for Majority Rule in Congress." *UCLA Law Review* 44 (April): 1253–1288.

McGinnis, John O., and Michael B. Rappaport. 1995. "The Constitutionality of Legislative Supermajority Requirements: A Defense." *Yale Law Journal* 105 (November): 483–511.

Soller, Christopher J. 1995. "Newtonian Government: Is the Contract with America Unconstitutional?" *Duquesne Law Review* 33 (Summer): 959–984.

❖ TAXATION, RETROACTIVE ❖

As part of the Revenue Reconciliation Act of 1993, Congress retroactively raised taxes on high incomes and estates. The Supreme Court has subsequently upheld the constitutionality of such provisions ("Retroactive Tax Increases" 1994, 1588). Since the adoption of the 1993 law, however, numerous members of Congress—mostly Republicans—have sponsored what they call a "Citizens Tax Protection Amendment" designed to make such retroactive taxes illegal. Since *Calder v. Bull* (1798), courts have interpreted the current sections of Article I, Sections 9 and 10, which prohibit ex post facto laws, to apply only to criminal laws. Martin J. Bailey is among those who have included provisions against retroactive taxes in his *Constitution for a Future Country* (2001). Under House Rule XXI 5 (c), which could be altered more easily than could a direct constitutional prohibition, the U.S. House of Representatives currently has a prohibition against considering retroactive income tax increases.

For Further Reading:
Bailey, Martin J. 2001. *Constitution for a Future Country.* New York: Palgrave.
"Retroactive Tax Increases: No Problem, Say Justices." 1994. *Congressional Quarterly Weekly Report* 52 (18 June): 1588.

❖ TAXATION, STATE AND FEDERAL EMPLOYEES ❖

The Constitution does not specifically prohibit the national government from taxing the states or the states from taxing the federal government, but limitations can easily be surmised based on considerations of federalism. As early as *McCulloch v. Maryland* (1819), Chief Justice John Marshall ruled that the states could not tax a branch of the national bank.

In *Dobbins v. Commissioners of Erie County* (1842), the Court extended this rather sensible prohibition to the more problematic cases of states taxing the salaries of federal officials. In *Collector v. Day* (1871), the prohibition was made reciprocal, and it stayed so until *Graves v. New York ex rel. O'Keefe* (1939). There, the Supreme Court repudiated its earlier prohibitions on the taxation of the salaries of governmental officials, now insisting only that such salaries not be singled out for special taxation.

From 1932 to two weeks prior to the *Graves* decision, at least four proposals were introduced in Congress that would have permitted state and federal taxation of governmental officials' incomes. *Graves* made such an amendment unnecessary, and Congress subsequently amended its tax laws in accord with this new precedent.

❖ TAXATION, STATE INCOME TAX OF NONRESIDENTS ❖

From 1953 to 1965, about fifty proposals were introduced in Congress to prohibit states or localities from taxing the income of nonresidents or from discriminating against nonresidents. In

1958 Connecticut also submitted a request to Congress for a convention to deal with this issue.

Most of the resolutions introduced in Congress were introduced by representatives of states surrounding New York. New York is one of those states that taxes all income earned within the state as well as income that its residents earn in other states (Penniman 1980, 13). Thirteen states permit local governments to levy income or payroll taxes on all who work there, and Philadelphia even applies this law to visiting athletes (Christensen 1995, 273).

For Further Reading:
Christensen, Terry. 1995. *Local Politics: Governing at the Grassroots.* Belmont, CA: Wadsworth.
Penniman, Clara. 1980. *State Income Taxation.* Baltimore, MD: Johns Hopkins University Press.

❖ TAXATION, STATE SECURITIES ❖

Throughout most of American history, the U.S. Supreme Court has upheld a doctrine of intergovernmental tax immunity that prevented both state and national governments from taxing the interest on bonds issued by one another. This prohibition was articulated, among other places, in *Pollock v. Farmers' Loan & Trust Co.* (1895).

From 1920 to 1943, more than 100 amendments were introduced that would either allow Congress to tax the interest on state securities or allow both state and national governments to tax interest on bonds issued by one another. Some such proposals were linked to proposals for the taxation of state and federal employees' income. Others would apply only when such income exceeded a set amount, such as $12,500.

Although Congress still does not tax revenues from registered state securities, its decision in *South Carolina v. Baker* (1988) indicated that the Supreme Court did not see any constitutional barriers preventing it from doing so.

See also Taxation, State and Federal Employees.

❖ TENTH AMENDMENT ❖

The Tenth Amendment was ratified in 1792 as the last provision of the Bill of Rights. The amendment provides that "the powers not delegated to the United States by the Constitution, nor prohibited by it to the states, are reserved to the States respectively or to the people."

One of the major concerns of Anti-Federalist opponents of the new Constitution centered on the scope of powers of the new central government. Five of the seven states that proposed amendments in the process of ratifying the Constitution suggested an amendment to protect the rights of the states under the new system. James Madison made such a provision part of the Bill of Rights that he offered in the First Congress. His first version of this provision mixed guarantees that are now found in the Ninth and Tenth Amendments.

The primary debate over the Tenth Amendment in the First Congress centered on whether to include the word "expressly" before the word "delegated" (Kurland and Lerner 1987, 5:403–404). Had Congress done so, the provision would have closely resembled Article 2 of the Articles of Confederation, which had provided that "every state retains its sovereignty, freedom, and independence, and every Power, Jurisdiction and right, which is not by this confederation expressly delegated to the United States, in Congress assembled" (*Id.*, 5:400). James Madison opposed this emendation, believing that "there must necessarily be admitted powers by implication, unless the Constitution descended to recount every minutia" (*Id.*, 5:403). His view was eventually validated by a vote of thirty-two to seventeen.

Even before the Tenth Amendment was ratified, Thomas Jefferson, who would soon be allied with James Madison in the Democratic-Republican Party, used it as part of his "strict construction" argument against the constitutionality of the national bank. The rival view of Alexander Hamilton was eventually vindicated in *McCulloch v. Maryland* (1819), in which Chief Justice John Marshall cited the omission of the word "expressly" as a justification for the doctrine of implied powers.

The great difficulty in interpreting the Tenth Amendment stems from the fact that it does not specify precisely what powers are delegated to the national government. Moreover, those parts of the Constitution that do enumerate such powers—most notably, Article I, Section 10—allow for implied powers.

Early Supreme Court decisions referred to state "police powers" over such matters as education, health, welfare, land management, and the policing of its citizens' activities. However, after the Civil War, the national government asserted full control over most such functions in the states of the former Confederacy, and the Fourteenth Amendment subsequently raised the possibility that the old relationship between the states and the national government had been drastically altered (McDonald 1992, 863).

Initially reluctant to interpret the Fourteenth Amendment so expansively, the Supreme Court adopted somewhat contradictory lines of opinion on the matter from roughly the turn of the century until 1937. In some notable cases, particularly those involving the regulation of activities such as gambling, prostitution, and the consumption of alcoholic beverages, which the Court regarded as moral evils, it generally recognized broad federal authority under the commerce clause and other federal powers. On other occasions, the Court invalidated legislation. Most notably, in *Hammer v. Dagenhart* (1918), the Court invalidated a federal child labor law adopted under putative authority of the commerce clause; it thought that the law invaded state police powers or interfered with free market forces. In a classic error that showed seeming ignorance of the decision at the Constitutional Convention of 1787 to omit the word "expressly" from the amendment, Justice William Day declared that "to them [the states] and to the people the powers not expressly delegated to the national government are reserved" (*Hammer* 1918, 275).

In 1937, shortly after Franklin D. Roosevelt's court-packing plan, the Supreme Court reversed course in this second area of cases and began interpreting the commerce clause and other grants of federal powers more liberally. In *United States v. Darby* (1941), Justice Harlan Fiske Stone pronounced that the Tenth Amendment "states but a truism that all is retained which has not been surrendered" (124). Until recent years, the amendment laid relatively dormant but this now appears to be changing.

In *National League of Cities v. Usery* (1976), the Supreme Court relied on the Tenth Amendment to overturn the application of federal minimum-wage laws to certain state employees, but this decision was subsequently overturned in *Garcia v. San Antonio Metropolitan Transit Authority* (1985), in which the Court indicated that the states should look to their representatives in Congress rather than to the courts for protection. The Supreme Court's decision in *United States v. Lopez* (1995), declaring that the federal law prohibiting the carrying of guns within 1,000 feet of a school zone exceeded federal authority under the commerce clause, suggests, however, that the idea of states' rights articulated in the Tenth Amendment continues to be a concern. In a similar decision in *United States v. Morrison* (2000), the U.S. Supreme Court struck down a section of the Violence Against Women Act of 1994 on the basis that it exceeded congressional authority by infringing on state criminal laws. And in *Jones v. United States* (2000) it limited the reach of the interstate commerce clause in a case involving prosecution for throwing a Molotov cocktail at a private residence. Recent decisions relative to the Eleventh Amendment have further reinforced judicial concerns for the rights traditionally exercised by the states.

Concern for such rights was reflected in reactions to the Supreme Court's reapportionment decisions in the 1960s, in recent proposals for an amendment to forbid unfunded federal mandates, and in increased references to the Tenth Amendment, especially among Republican officeholders. Kansas Senator Bob Dole, for example, made the Tenth Amendment an issue in his 1996 presidential campaign. Many believe that the national government has gone too far in the direction of consolidation and has paid too little attention to the powers reserved to the states. Worldwide, there appears to be increased attention to principles of "devolution" to state and local entities.

See also Eleventh Amendment; *Garcia v.*

San Antonio Metropolitan Transit Authority; McCulloch v. Maryland; States, Police Powers; *United States v. Morrison.*

For Further Reading:

Killenback, Mark R. ed. 2002. *The Tenth Amendment and State Sovereignty: Constitutional History and Contemporary Issues.* Lanham, MD: Rowman & Littlefield.

Kurland, Philip B., and Ralph Lerner, eds. 1987. *The Founders' Constitution.* 5 vols. Chicago: University of Chicago Press.

Jones v. United States, 529 U.S. 848 (2000).

McDonald, Forrest. 1992. "Tenth Amendment." In *The Oxford Companion to the Supreme Court of the United States,* ed. Kermit L. Hall. New York: Oxford University Press.

United States v. Morrison, 529 U.S. 528 (2000).

❖ TERM LIMITS ❖

See Congress, Term Limits; Judiciary, Terms of Office; Twenty-second Amendment.

❖ TERRITORIES ❖

Article IV, Section 3 grants Congress power to "make all needful Rules and Regulations respecting the Territory or other Property belonging to the United States." Surprisingly, it makes no specific provision for the acquisition of new territories.

This omission presented a dilemma for President Thomas Jefferson in 1803. Although he favored a strict construction of the Constitution, and therefore wanted a constitutional amendment to legitimize his purchase of Louisiana, he eventually acquiesced with congressional leaders of his party who thought that such an amendment was unnecessary and feared that it might complicate the diplomatic situation (Vile 1992, 70–71).

In the early years of the Republic, most issues relating to the territories centered on the issue of slavery. Ironically, at least one amendment introduced in 1866 sought to reduce the states that had participated in the rebellion to territories. Although this did not happen,

Southern states were divided into military districts during the period of Reconstruction (1865–1877), with the national government exercising a relatively strong hand, including the demand that the states ratify the Fourteenth Amendment before their representatives were fully accepted into Congress.

Issues involving territories often centered on the admission of new states, requiring a certain population before this occurred, or seeking to prevent certain territories (especially those that were not contiguous with existing states) from being admitted into statehood. A resolution introduced by a California representative in 1872 sought to provide that public lands in the territories be given only to those who actually settled there. At least three resolutions introduced from 1875 to 1880 proposed that territories should have at least one member in the House of Representatives and one vote in the electoral college. In an idea more fully implemented with the adoption of the Twenty-third Amendment in 1961, at least one such proposal would also have given one electoral vote to the District of Columbia. Since 1975 there have been a number of proposals to provide representation in the electoral college for U.S. territories. Puerto Rico is currently among the territories whose residents are U.S. citizens but who have no right to vote in presidential elections.

See also Louisiana Purchase; Puerto Rico, Representation in Electoral College; Slavery, the Territories and.

For Further Reading:

Onuf, Peter. 1984. "Territories and Statehood." In *Encyclopedia of American Political History: Studies of Principal Movements and Ideas,* ed. Jack P. Greene. Vol. 3: 1283–1304. New York: Charles Scribner's Sons.

Vile, John R. 1992. *The Constitutional Amending Process in American Political Thought.* New York: Praeger.

❖ TERRORISM ❖

To date, the United States has not, like Israel and other nations, faced widespread weekly acts of terrorism, but Timothy McVeigh's bombing of the Murrah Federal Building in Oklahoma City on 19 April 1995, as well as the more recent and even deadlier airplane attacks on the World Trade Center in New York and the Pentagon outside Washington, D.C., on 11 September 2001, have led not only to American intervention in Afghanistan in an attempt to destroy the Taliban, but also to renewed questions about whether civil liberties might need to be curtailed in order to combat terrorism. As of this writing (mid-2002), there is also ongoing discussion about the possibility that terrorists, especially those of foreign nationalities who are now being detained in a U.S. naval base in Cuba, might be tried by military courts.

In what appears to have been designed simply as a teaching exercise to help students think through the implications of this problem, the Constitutional Rights Foundation has designed and posted a "Safe America" Amendment that would begin by providing that U.S. citizens "shall enjoy the right of safety from terrorist attack," and that proceeds to authorize Congress to establish special military courts that could ignore key provisions for individual rights in the Bill of Rights and to ban "the manufacture, sale and possession of all handguns and concealable weapons within the territorial boundaries of the United States" (Constitutional Rights Foundation, 2002), the second issue being one currently addressed by the Second Amendment. A U.S. Supreme Court decision in *Ex parte Milligan* (1866) currently appears to limit military trials of U.S. civilians when regular courts are open, but this decision might or might not be considered to apply to foreign nationals, especially those who have never actually landed in American territory. In *Ex Parte Quirin* (1942), the U.S. Supreme Court upheld military trials of German saboteurs who had landed in the United States.

As of November 2002 the U.S. government was holding two American citizens, Yaser Hamdi and Jose Padilla, in military brigs as "enemy combatants," and refusing to give them access to attorneys. The former was a Baton Rouge–born American citizen captured in Afghanistan; the second was arrested in the United States on suspicion of attempting to manufacture a "dirty bomb." The government's action has come under fire from a task force on the "Treatment of Enemy Combatants" sponsored by the American Bar Association (Kay 2002, A10).

Most American responses to the threat of terror have centered on constitutional alterations have focused on how the nation might better prepare to meet the emergency that could be caused by widespread losses of members of the House of Representatives (the Constitution currently provides that such members must be replaced by elections, which take time, whereas state governors are now free to make temporary replacements of members of the U.S. Senate).

See also Congress, Emergency Functioning

For Further Reading:

Constitutional Rights Foundation. "America Responds to Terrorism." *http://www.crf-usa/terror/ America.* Accessed 5/18/02.

Kay, Julie. 2002. "War of, for Words: South Florida Lawyers on ABA Task Force Lead Fight For Right of Enemy Combatants to Counsel." *Broward Daily Business Review* 43 (21 October): A10.

❖ *TEXAS V. JOHNSON* (1989) ❖

Texas v. Johnson was one of the Supreme Court's most controversial decisions in recent years. It prompted numerous calls for a constitutional amendment to prohibit flag desecration.

The case involved the actions of Gregory Johnson, who took part in a "Political War Chest Tour" at the Republican National Convention of 1984. At one point in this demonstration, he publicly burned an American flag and was subsequently arrested and convicted under a Texas statute prohibiting desecration of a venerated object. Prior to being appealed to the U.S. Supreme Court, one Texas court of appeals upheld his conviction and another struck it down.

In this case, Justice William Brennan led a five-to-four majority affirming that Johnson's conduct was a form of symbolic speech pro-

tected by the First and Fourteenth Amendments. The Court ruled that the value of such speech outweighed the two interests advanced by Texas.

The majority rejected Texas's argument that prosecution was needed to prevent a breach of the peace, since no such breach occurred or appeared imminent. Along these lines, the majority further rejected the idea that Johnson's words fell into the small class of "fighting words" that it had recognized in prior cases could be restricted, most notably in *Chaplinsky v. New Hampshire* (1942).

As to Texas's desire to preserve the flag as a symbol of national unity, Brennan noted that the law in question did not prohibit all types of destruction of the flag but only that which would be offensive to others. As such, the restriction on speech was "content based" and subject to special scrutiny (*Texas* 1989, 412). Brennan argued that "government may not prohibit the expression of an idea simply because society finds the idea itself offensive or disagreeable" (*Texas* 1989, 414). Government could adopt precatory, or recommendatory, regulations, but it must use persuasion rather than force when attempting to curb symbolic speech.

Chief Justice William Rehnquist and Justice John Paul Stevens wrote dissenting opinions focusing on the uniqueness of the flag as a national symbol. They argued that Johnson was not being prosecuted for what he said but rather for what he did.

Congress responded to the decision by adopting the Flag Protection Act of 1989 rather than by proposing a constitutional amendment. The Court subsequently struck down this new law in *United States v. Eichman* (1990), and debate over the wisdom of a flag desecration amendment continues.

See also Flag Desecration; *United States v. Eichman.*

❖ THEONOMY ❖

See Christian Reconstructionism.

❖ THIRD AMENDMENT ❖

The Third Amendment is part of the Bill of Rights and is among the least controversial amendments to the U.S. Constitution. The amendment, which has deep roots in English prohibitions against billeting troops that go back to a charter that Henry I granted to London in 1131 (Bell 1993, 118), grew more immediately out of some of the abuses by Great Britain under its Quartering Acts that led, in part, to the Boston Massacre, and later to the Revolutionary War. The amendment provides that "no Soldier shall, in time of peace be quartered in any house, without the consent of the Owner, nor in time of war but in a manner to be prescribed by law."

A similar provision was contained in the English Petition of Rights of 1628. In addition, at the time the U.S. Constitution was written, four state constitutions had such a provision, and three state ratifying conventions proposed such a guarantee before James Madison incorporated it in the list of rights he presented to the First Congress (Lutz 1992, 52, 56, 64).

The amendment was little debated in the House of Representatives and was unaltered by either it or the Senate. Although the amendment appears to have been violated during both the War of 1812 and the U.S. Civil War (Bell 1993, 136–137), it has neither been the subject of more than a passing reference by the U.S. Supreme Court nor the subject of a proposed constitutional amendment. Although the Third Amendment remains one of the few provisions of the Bill of Rights that the Supreme Court has not applied to the states via the due process clause of the Fourteenth Amendment, the U.S. Second Court of Appeals ruled in *Engblom v. Carey* (1982)—a case involving whether the state of New York could quarter National Guard troops at a correctional residence it owned whose members were on strike—that the amendment was so incorporated. Moreover, Justice William O. Douglas cited this amendment in *Griswold v. Connecticut* (1965) as one of a number of amendments that serve as a foundation for a right to privacy.

For Further Reading:

Bell, Tom W. 1993. "The Third Amendment: Forgotten but Not Gone." *William & Mary Bill of Rights Journal* 2: 117–150.

Lutz, Donald S. 1992. *A Preface to American Political Theory*. Lawrence, KS: University Press of Kansas.

❖ THIRTEENTH AMENDMENT ❖

The Constitution of 1787 circumspectly omitted direct mention of slavery. Still, a number of clauses—most notably the three-fifths clause (Article I, Section 2), the migration and importation clause (Article IV, Section 9), and the fugitive from labor clause (Article IV, Section 2)—gave implicit sanction to the institution in states where it already existed. The predominant attitude about slavery even in the South was that it was at best a necessary evil, and a number of prominent Southerners were among those who supported the idea of freeing slaves and colonizing them in Liberia.

No constitutional amendments were both proposed and ratified from 1804 to 1865. Indeed, prior to 1860, few proposals were introduced in Congress to eliminate slavery by constitutional amendment. Arthur Livermore, a Democratic representative from New Hampshire, introduced one such proposal in 1818; another was introduced by Whig Representative (and former president) John Quincy Adams of Massachusetts in 1839, who had become an increasingly vocal foe of slavery. The latter amendment would have abolished hereditary slavery after 1842, prohibited the admission of further slave states into the Union, and abolished slavery and the slave trade in the District of Columbia after 1845.

Just prior to the Civil War, there were more proposals—including the Corwin Amendment and the Crittenden Compromise—relative to slavery, but most sought to reassure the Southern states that were about to secede by guaranteeing that slavery would be perpetual. In 1861 and 1862, Congress adopted confiscation laws relating to slaves who had been used in the rebellion or those who had escaped to or been captured by the Union armies. In 1862 Congress provided for compensated emancipation in the District of Columbia and—despite the 1857 decision in *Scott v. Sandford*—outlawed slavery in the federal territories (Maltz 1990, 13). In September 1862 President Abraham Lincoln issued his preliminary Emancipation Proclamation. Officially proclaimed on 1 January 1863, it freed all slaves held in areas of rebellion and was justified as a war measure (*Id.*, 14).

Although there was some sentiment to abolish slavery by statute, there was general agreement that Congress lacked such power. In December 1863 Republican Representatives James M. Ashley of Ohio and James F. Wilson of Iowa introduced emancipation amendments. Senator John B. Henderson, a Missouri Democrat, introduced a similar amendment in the Senate in January 1864, with Republican Charles Sumner of Massachusetts offering a somewhat different version the next month (Maltz 1990, 15). Such amendments were justified both on the grounds of morality and as a means of securing future peace by eliminating the situation of the nation being half slave and half free (*Id.*, 15–16).

Although the amendment had broad Republican support, some of the congressional Democrats who were left after the secession of the Southern states argued that Article V could not legally be used to effect such a major change. Although the amendment passed the Senate by a vote of thirty-eight to six in August 1864, the ninety-three-to-sixty-five vote it received in the House in June fell thirteen votes shy of the required two-thirds majority (Maltz 1990, 19). Republican James Ashley of Ohio then switched his vote—in a maneuver mimicked by Kansas Republican Senator Bob Dole after the 1995 Senate defeat of the Balanced Budget Amendment—to allow him room to reintroduce the amendment in the second session of the Thirty-eighth Congress (*Id.*).

The Republicans won substantial victories in the election of 1864. This election and Abraham Lincoln's endorsement of the amendment in his annual message, along with fears that Democrats might forever be saddled with the onus of slavery, led to another vote in January 1865, when the House adopted the amendment by a vote of 119 to 56 (Maltz 1990, 20).

Significantly, abolitionist William Lloyd Garrison, who had once described the Constitution as "a covenant with death," now proclaimed that it had been replaced by "a covenant with life" (quoted in Vorenberg 2001, 208). The states ratified the amendment this same year, and, Lincoln, whose signature was not needed, signed the amendment, perhaps in response to Buchanan's earlier signature on the Corwin Amendment (*Id.*, 210). Lincoln was assassinated before the amendment was ratified.

The Thirteenth Amendment is divided into two parts. The first section prohibits "slavery" and "involuntary servitude, except as a punishment for crime." This language was taken almost directly from the Northwest Ordinance of 1787, but by distinguishing slavery and involuntary servitude appears to indicate (and courts have so interpreted the provision) that the amendment would outlaw practices like peonage as well as the kinds of practices extant before the U.S. Civil War. Section 1 is fairly unique in that it "covers private conduct as well as state action" (Kares 1995, 375). Section 2 grants Congress power to enforce the amendment. Questions would subsequently be raised as to whether Section 1 was intended to grant any rights other than freedom from bondage (see, for example, *The Civil Rights Cases* of 1883) and precisely what powers Congress was intended to have under Section 2. A recent treatment of the Thirteenth Amendment has suggested that subsequent interpreters "failed to remember that the amendment was once seen as the pinnacle of freedom instead of a mere precursor to the Fourteenth and Fifteenth Amendments" (Vorenberg 2001, 239). Still, the precise scope of the Thirteenth Amendment is difficult to resolve on the basis of contemporary debates (Maltz 1990, 21–28), and, at least to some extent, such issues have been mooted by the more explicit and expansive language that was adopted in the Fourteenth Amendment, and by subsequent legislative reliance on provisions in this and the Fifteenth Amendment.

In *Jones v. Alfred H. Mayer Co.* (1968), the Supreme Court upheld a ban on racial discrimination in housing on the basis of a law adopted under authority of the Thirteenth Amendment.

A recent commentator has suggested that the Thirteenth Amendment could serve as the basis of regulating abusive treatment of "mail-order brides," who are brought to the United States from foreign countries (Vergara 2000).

See also *Civil Rights Cases;* Corwin Amendment; Crittenden Compromise; Emancipation Proclamation; Lieber, Francis.

For Further Reading:

Kares, Lauren. 1995. "Note: The Unlucky Thirteenth: A Constitutional Amendment in Search of a Doctrine." *Cornell Law Review* 80 (January): 372–412.

Maltz, Earl M. 1990. *Civil Rights, the Constitution, and Congress, 1863–1869.* Lawrence, KS: University Press of Kansas.

Vergara, Vanessa B. M. 2000. "Comment: Abusive Mail-Order Bride Marriage and the Thirteenth Amendments." *Northwestern University Law Review* 94 (Summer): 1547–1599.

Vorenberg, Michael. 2001. *Final Freedom: The Civil War, the Abolition of Slavery, and the Thirteenth Amendment.* Cambridge, UK: Cambridge University Press.

❖ THREE-FIFTHS CLAUSE ❖

At the Constitutional Convention of 1787, representatives of Northern and Southern states had different interests with respect to taxation and representation. Northerners wanted any direct taxes to be apportioned to include the slave population, but they did not want slaves to figure in the formula for apportioning seats in the U.S. House of Representatives. By contrast, southern representatives did not want their slaves to be taxed, but they did want them counted for representation purposes (Vile 2002a, 29–30).

The delegates settled on an expedient compromise. It was based on a formula used under the Articles of Confederation and was incorporated in Article I, Section 2 of the Constitution. This compromise provided that both taxation and representation would be based on the "whole Number of free Persons" and "three fifths of all other Persons."

The three-fifths clause is arguably one of the most foul compromises adopted by the Constitutional Convention, but it cut both ways. Although it allowed for blacks to count as less than full persons, the term "persons" did implicitly recognize their humanity. It may be significant that Chief Justice Roger Taney ignored the three-fifths clause when arguing in the *[Dred] Scott* decision (1857) that blacks were not, and could not be, American citizens and must therefore be considered as chattel property.

Prior to the Civil War, a number of congressmen, including former President John Quincy Adams, proposed modifying the Constitution so that both taxes and representation would be based solely on the number of free persons. With the adoption of the Thirteenth Amendment, slavery was eliminated. This meant that Southern states, and the Democratic Party, might actually gain representation in the House of Representatives. Section 2 of the Fourteenth Amendment subsequently specified that representation would now be apportioned "counting the whole number of persons in each State, excluding Indians not taxed." In an ultimately futile attempt to prevent Southern states from disenfranchising the newly freed slaves, this amendment further provided that if states denied such voting rights, "the basis of representation therein shall be reduced in the proportion which the number of such [disenfranchised] male citizens shall bear to the whole number of male citizens twenty-one years of age in such State."

See also Fourteenth Amendment; *Scott v. Sandford.*

For Further Reading:

Vile, John R. 2001a. *A Companion to the United States Constitution and Its Amendments.* 3d ed. Westport, CT: Praeger.

❖ THREE-FOURTHS MAJORITY TO RATIFY AMENDMENTS ❖

Article V of the U.S. Constitution proposes that amendments must be proposed by a convention called by Congress at the request of two-thirds of the states or (as has been the practice) by two-thirds majorities in both houses of Congress. These amendments must then be approved, at congressional specification, either by three-fourths of the state legislatures or—as in the solitary case of the Twenty-first Amendment repealing national alcoholic prohibition—by special conventions called within the states.

The supermajority requirement for ratification by the states, like the supermajority requirement for proposing amendments, appears designed to assure that amendments are not adopted unless they have widespread geographical support. Curiously, the Constitution does not specify a time limit during which amendments must be adopted. In *Dillon v. Gloss* (1921), the U.S. Supreme Court agreed that ratification should reflect a contemporary consensus of the states, but in *Coleman v. Miller* (1939), the Court subsequently decided that it was up to Congress to decide whether amendments reflected such a consensus. In the case of the Twenty-seventh Amendment (relating to the timing of congressional pay raises), the requisite number of states did not ratify the amendment until more than 200 years after it was proposed (a time, however, during which no states attempted to rescind their ratifications). Some proposed amendments have contained self-enforcing provisions stating that they will not go into effect unless ratified within a seven-year period. When such a provision was included in the authorizing resolution, rather than in the text, of the proposed Equal Rights Amendment, Congress subsequently extended the deadline, but the amendment still failed.

Especially considering that Rhode Island had not attended the Constitutional Convention, the three-fourths requirement for ratification is close to the requirement that the Constitution of 1787 would not go into effect unless and until ratified by nine of the states. Two modern authors have suggested that this parallel is purposeful and helps explain why today's generation continues to be bound to a Constitution made before its members were born. If today's generation wants to alter the Constitution, it must muster majorities similar to those of the founding generation (see McGinnis and Rappaport 2002).

See also Consensus and the Amending Process; Deliberation and the Amending Process; Ratification of Amendments; Supermajorities.

For Further Reading:

McGinnis, John O., and Michael B. Rappaport. 2002. "Our Supermajoritarian Constitution." *Texas Law Review* 80 (March): 703–805.

❖ TIEDEMAN, CHRISTOPHER (1857–1904) ❖

It is common to distinguish the written Constitution of the United States from the unwritten constitution of Great Britain. However, law professor Christopher Tiedeman wrote a book in 1890 that pointed to the similarities of the two constitutions and the way that they change. He argued that law necessarily arose from the legal and moral habits of a people and what he called the "prevalent sense of right" (Tiedeman 1890, 7).

Tiedeman argued that regardless of what the written words of a constitution appear to say, courts use interpretation and construction to see that laws comport with popular understandings. Moreover, in the United States, the written Constitution provides only a skeleton, with most governmental operations less determined by what is written than by what is unwritten. Tiedeman argued that the flesh and blood of a constitution is "not to be found in the instrument promulgated by a constitutional convention, but in the decisions of the courts and acts of the legislature, which are published and enacted in the enforcement of the written Constitution" (Tiedeman 1890, 43).

Much of Tiedeman's book was devoted to a development of this thesis. Changes in the operation of the electoral college, the understanding by which presidents served no more than two terms, and changing interpretations of the contracts clause and of the doctrine of natural rights provided some of his illustrations. Whereas some scholars would criticize judges for going against the original intent of those who wrote the Constitution, Tiedeman praised them for interpreting law in accord with the needs and desires of the present generation.

Nowhere was this clearer than in Tiedeman's discussion of the Fourteenth Amendment. Tiedeman agreed with those who thought that this amendment was intended to have a broad scope. Still, Tiedeman praised the Court for "keeping the operation of this amendment within the limits which they felt assured would have been imposed by the people, if their judgment had not been blinded with passion, and which in their cooler moments they would ratify" (Tiedeman 1890, 108).

Because the unwritten constitution so frequently limits the written words, Tiedeman was led to inquire into the value of a written constitution. His response was that the Constitution enabled judges with power "to serve as a check upon the popular will in the interest of the minority" (Tiedeman 1890, 163).

For Further Reading:

Halper, Louise A. 1990. "Christopher G. Tiedeman, 'Laissez-Faire Constitutionalism' and the Dilemma of Small-Scale Property in the Gilded Age." *Ohio State Law Journal* 51: 1349–1384.

Mayer, David N. 1990. "The Jurisprudence of Christopher G. Tiedeman: A Study in the Failure of Laissez-Faire Constitutionalism." *Missouri Law Review* 55 (Winter): 93–161.

Tiedeman, Christopher G. 1890. *The Unwritten Constitution of the United States.* New York: G. P. Putnam's Sons.

Vile, John R. 1992. *The Constitutional Amending Process in American Political Thought.* New York: Praeger.

❖ TIME LIMITS ON AMENDMENTS ❖

The Constitution does not specify the length of time during which a proposed amendment can be ratified. When the Eighteenth Amendment was being debated in 1917, however, Republican Senator (later president) Warren G. Harding of Ohio proposed that a deadline for ratification be set at 1 January 1923, apparently in the unrealized hope of putting an effective obstacle in the amendment's path (Bernstein with Agel 1993, 173–174). Similar deadlines were included in the Twentieth Amendment, the Twenty-first Amendment, and the Twenty-second Amendment. Deadlines were also included in the amendment proposed in 1978 to treat the District of Columbia as a state for purposes of representation in Congress, presidential elections, and the amending process.

In *Dillon v. Gloss,* the Supreme Court ruled that the Constitution implied that ratification must "reflect the will of the people in all sections at relatively the same period" (1921, 375). It thus upheld the constitutionality of the seven-year deadline in the Eighteenth Amendment.

The amendment proposed in 1924 that would have given Congress the power to regulate child labor did not contain such a time limit. In *Coleman v. Miller* (1939), the Court examined Kansas's attempt to ratify the amendment thirteen years after it was proposed and ruled that the determination of the contemporaneousness of such a ratification was a "political question" for Congress to resolve.

When Congress proposed the Equal Rights Amendment in 1972, it included a seven-year deadline. Largely to keep the Constitution from being cluttered with ratification deadlines, this deadline was not included in the text of the proposed amendment itself, where it would presumably be self-enforcing, but in an accompanying resolution. In 1978 Congress extended the ratification deadline of the Equal Rights Amendment to 1982. This action was successfully challenged in a U.S. district court in *Idaho v. Freeman* (1981), but the issue became moot when the amendment failed to meet even this new deadline—a failure that has not silenced voices of those who still believe that states may ratify the amendment.

The amendment that has done the most to stretch the idea of contemporary consensus expressed in *Dillon v. Gloss* is the putative ratification of the Twenty-seventh Amendment relative to congressional pay raises. Despite concerns raised by scholars (Vile 1991a), both the National Archivist and a majority of Congress accepted the legitimacy of this amendment, first proposed as part of the Bill of Rights in 1789, even though the necessary number of states did not ratify until 1992.

The last two controversies make it a virtual certainty that Congress will place ratification deadlines within the texts of future proposals. Still, there is no apparent legal barrier to keep Congress from departing from the seven-year formula. The author of a recent law review article has argued that time limits on constitutional amendments are an unconstitutional attempt to alter the specific amending guidelines established in Article V (Kalfus 1999). According to this view, once proposed by Congress, amendments always remain subject to state ratification. Yet another author believes that the omission of a ratification deadline within Article V was a serious omission that should be cured by the adoption of a constitutional amendment (Hanlon 2000). That author, who believes that the decision in *Dillon v. Gloss* calling for a contemporary consensus represented wise social policy but lacked specific constitutional support, believes that an amendment providing for a seven-year deadline would be reasonable.

See also *Coleman v. Miller; Dillon v. Gloss;* Equal Rights Amendment; Failed Amendments; Implementation Dates of Amendments; Twenty-Seventh Amendment.

For Further Reading:
Bernstein, Richard B., with Jerome Agel. 1993. *Amending America: If We Love the Constitution So Much, Why Do We Keep Trying to Change It?* New York: Random House.
Dillon v. Gloss, 256 U.S. 368 (1921).
Hanlon, Michael C. 2000. "Note: The Need for a General Time Limit on Ratification of Proposed Constitutional Amendments." *Journal of Law & Politics* 16 (Summer): 663–698.
Kalfus, Mason. 1999. "Why Time Limits on the Ratification of Constitutional Amendments Violate Article V." *University of Chicago Law Review* 66 (Spring): 437–467.
Vile, John R. 1991a. "Just Say No to 'Stealth' Amendment." *National Law Journal* 14 (22 June): 15–16.

❖ TITLES OF NOBILITY ❖

Article I, Section 9 currently contains a provision that

> [n]o Title of Nobility shall be granted by the United States: And no Person holding any Office of Profit or Trust under them, shall, without the Consent of the Congress, accept of any present, Emolument, Office, or Title, of any kind whatever, from any King, Prince, or foreign State.

One of the earliest proposed amendments prescribing loss of citizenship would have supplemented these restrictions by further proposing that

> [i]f any citizen of the United States shall accept, claim, receive or retain any title of nobility or honour or shall, without the consent of Congress, accept and retain any present, pension, office or emolument of any kind whatever, from any emperor, king, prince or foreign power, such person shall cease to be a citizen of the United States, and shall be incapable of holding any office of trust or profit under them, or either of them. (Bernstein with Agel 1993, 178)

Republican Senator Philip Reed of Maryland introduced this amendment in January 1810, and it was ratified by 1 May by a vote of eighty-seven to three in the House and nineteen to five in the Senate.

Sometimes called the Reed Amendment, or the "Phantom Amendment," this proposal was included in a congressionally authorized printing of the Constitution made in 1815 (known as the "Bioren edition") (Silversmith 1999, 586) and later copied by other publishers, including a number of states. In 1817, following an inquiry from then President James Monroe, Secretary of State John Quincy Adams found that the Titles of Nobility Amendment had not been ratified. With seventeen states in the Union at the time the amendment was submitted, thirteen states would have been required for ratification, and twelve, and only twelve, apparently ratified. However, new states were admitted during the ratification period, thus apparently never putting the amendment any closer than two states away from ratification (Silversmith 1999, 596–599). Moreover, there is nothing in the act of "publishing" an amendment—especially if done mistakenly—that would give it the force of law.

Long a mystery to historians, who found a lack of contemporary debate on the topic, the amendment might have been motivated by what one author has described as "general animosity to foreigners evident in the United States before the War of 1812" (Silversmith 1999, 583). It might also have been motivated by fears that the son of Jerome Bonaparte (brother to Napoleon) and his onetime Baltimore wife, Elizabeth Patterson, might one day try to claim an American throne. Apparently, Republicans—who were closer on foreign policy matters to France than to England—introduced the measure to defuse criticisms raised by Patterson's pretensions and her associations with top party officials. Federalists had little choice but to concur or face charges that they were hoping to get titles from England (Earle 1987, 37). One historian noted that, with Napoleon's defeat in Europe, "by the time of the amendment's bizarre reappearance in the House of Representatives [in the form of the printed Constitution that included it], it was an anachronism" *(Id.)*. However, Congress apparently applied most provisions of this proposed amendment to American diplomats in 1874 (Pendergast, Pendergast, and Sousanis 2001, 511).

In recent years, David Dodge, the publisher of an extremist magazine called *AntiShyster*, has raised the claim (largely based on the publication of the amendment in the Bioren and other editions of the Constitution) that the Titles of Nobility Amendment was legitimately ratified and is part of the U.S. Constitution (Silversmith 1999, 580). Dodge and his followers, who have also posted their views on the Internet, believe that the amendment might be a vehicle for excluding lawyers, who are sometimes called "esquire," from holding office. Even had the amendment been ratified, this interpretation of the amendment is fairly fanciful, since such a title is not "conferred" by any foreign government, and the title when used in the

United States seems to be "nothing more than a custom" (Silversmith 1999, 602).

One scholar of this amendment notes that the proposed amendment carries two important messages:

> That concern about divisions in society in the United States is an historic problem, and that the legal community, both in the nineteenth and the twentieth centuries has not invested sufficient effort into accurately communicating the law to the profession, as well as to the public. (Silversmith 1999, 610)

The Phantom Amendment remains one of six amendments proposed by Congress but never ratified by the requisite number of states.

For Further Reading:

Bernstein, Richard B., with Jerome Agel. 1993. *Amending America: If We Love the Constitution So Much, Why Do We Keep Trying to Change It?* New York: Random House.

Conklin, Curt E. 1996. "The Case of the Phantom Thirteenth Amendment: A Historical and Bibliographic Nightmare." *Law Library Journal* 88 (Winter): 121–127.

Earle, W. H. 1987. "The Phantom Amendment and the Duchess of Baltimore." *American History Illustrated* 22 (November): 32–39.

Pendergast, Tom, Sara Pendergast, and John Sousanis, with Elizabeth Shaw Grunow, ed., 2001. *Constitutional Amendments: From Freedom of Speech to Flag Burning*. 3 vols. Detroit, MI: U.X.L. imprint of Gale Group.

Silversmith, Jol A. 1999. "The 'Missing Thirteenth Amendment': Constitutional Nonsense and Titles of Nobility. *Southern California Interdisciplinary Law Journal* 8 (Spring): 577–611.

❖ TOFFLER, ALVIN AND HEIDI (1928– , 1929–) ❖

Alvin and Heidi Toffler are known as futurists, whose primary influence has been through the publication of the books *Future Shock* and *The Third Wave*. Taking a broad view of history, the Tofflers argue that civilization has been hit by three primary waves, the first being the conversion from nomadic existence to agriculture; the second being industrialization; and the third the development and distribution of information. Like the first and second waves, the third wave will involve massive reconfigurations of existing institutions that were designed for earlier forms of organization, according to the Tofflers. In a book introduced by then Speaker of the House Georgia Republican Newt Gingrich (a friend of the Tofflers), the Tofflers discuss some of these implications.

The Tofflers begin the final chapter of this book with a letter to the founding fathers in which they extol what the framers did, especially the creation of the Bill of Rights, but indicated that:

> You would have understood why even the Constitution of the United States needs to be reconsidered and altered—not to cut the federal budget or embody this or that narrow principle, but to expand its Bill of Rights, taking account of threats to freedom unimagined in the past, and to create a whole new structure of government capable of making intelligent, democratic decisions necessary for our survival in a Third Wave, twenty-first century America. (Toffler and Toffler 1995, 90)

Rather than outlining a whole new plan of government, the Tofflers sketch three key principles that they believe should guide such reconfiguration.

The first is that of "minority power" (Toffler and Toffler 1995, 92). Believing that the "massified" society of the Second Wave is giving way to more tailored forms of production, the Tofflers note that "we have a configurative society—one in which thousands of minorities, many of them temporary, swirl and form highly novel, transient patterns, seldom coalescing into a consensus on major issues" *(Id.)*. The Tofflers express concern that existing mechanisms for measuring opinion do not always measure the depth of such an opinion, signaling "when a minority feels so threatened or attaches such life-and-death significance to a single issue that its views should perhaps receive more than ordinary weight" (*Id.*, 95). It is not altogether clear

how the principle of "minority power" differs from the classic American principle of "majority rule, and minority rights," but this was the first principle the Tofflers articulated.

Their second principle may provide part of the key. Here the Tofflers advance "the principle of 'semidirect democracy'—a shift from depending on representatives to representing ourselves" (Toffler and Toffler 1995, 96). Acknowledging that the constitutional framers thought that representative democracy would be "less emotional and more deliberative" (*Id.*, 97), the Tofflers believe these problems could be handled through mechanisms "requiring a cooling-off period or second vote before implementation of major decisions taken via referendum or other forms of direct democracy" (*Id.*, 98). Moreover, they foresee the possibility of developing arrangements that "*combine* direct and indirect democracy" (*Id.*, 98–99). Noting that legislatures have not always been responsive to popular concerns, the Tofflers suggest that voters might petition legislative bodies "to set up committees on topics the public—not the lawmakers—deem appropriate" (*Id.*, 99).

The Tofflers call their third principle "decision division" (Toffler and Toffler 1995, 99), and it appears aimed in two directions. The Tofflers believe that some decisions that are now being made by governments need to be made transnationally. By the same token, they believe that modern central governments, like second-wave industries, are often so top-heavy that they fail from information overload. They think it is necessary "to move a vast amount of decision making downward from the center" (*Id.*, 100), and they argue that "there is no possibility of restoring sense, order and management 'efficiency' to many governments without a substantial devolution of central power. We need to divide the decision load and shift a significant part of it downward" (*Id.*, 101). They note that "the need for new political institutions exactly parallels our need for new family, educational and corporate institutions as well" (*Id.*, 103). They further observe that "we should think not of a single massive reorganization or of a single revolutionary, cataclysmic change imposed from the top, but of thousands of conscious, decentralized experiments that permit us to test new models of political decision making at local and regional levels in advance of their application to the national and transnational levels" (*Id.*, 107).

There is an element of utopianism in the Tofflers' thinking—with practically unlimited opportunities stemming from what they consider to be the "the inexhaustibility of knowledge" (Toffler and Toffler 1995, 76). The Tofflers' principles are relatively vague, but their plan is unique in attempting not simply to respond to existing problems, but also to anticipate future changes. Bruce E. Tonn is among other futurists who have given some attention to the problem of how modern governmental forms might be adopted to emerging changes.

See also Tonn, Bruce E.

For Further Reading:

Toffler, Alvin, and Heidi Toffler. 1995. *Creating a New Civilization: The Politics of the Third Wave.* Atlanta: Turner Publishing, Inc.

❖ TONN, BRUCE E. (1955–) ❖

The Constitution was designed for posterity, and it is not therefore surprising that futurists are among those who have attempted to consider how the Constitution might be adapted to future needs. Bruce E. Tonn, a researcher at the Oak Ridge National Laboratory in Oak Ridge, Tennessee, has written two articles in which he addresses the futurist audience, although he notes in a subsequent interview that his ideas appear to have generated little attention outside this community and will require either extraordinary leadership or a possible crisis before they are likely to get such scrutiny (Pollard and Tonn 1998).

Tonn's first article proposed and described a specific constitutional amendment, which he dubbed the "Court of Generations" Amendment. The amendment, which was divided into four sections, appeared to share characteristics of the Council of Revision that was rejected at the Constitutional Convention, of Thomas Jefferson's idea of periodic revision of

constitutions, and the Council of Censors mechanism that was once employed in the State of Pennsylvania.

Section I of the proposed amendments created a "Court of Generations, which shall be an adjunct of the judicial department of the national government" (Tonn 1991, 483). This section specifically employed the language of the U.S. Constitution's preamble in securing "the blessings of liberty to our posterity." Sections II and III indicated that the Court of Generations would consist of a grand jury composed of the Supreme Court and one representative from each of the U.S. states and territories. Its function would be to "return a bill of indictment to the members of the Supreme Court if evidence suggests an intolerable threat to the security of the blessings of liberty to our posterity" (*Id.*). Interestingly, the Court of Generations would have no authority to do anything about the problems it diagnosed, but "[t]he members of the Supreme Court shall decide whether we and/or our ancestors are in contempt of intolerably threatening the security of the blessings of liberty to our posterity" (*Id.*). Finally, Section IV provided that the first Court of Generations would meet within five years after the adoption of the amendment and "every subsequently term of five years." Congress would be responsible for assuring that the Court had "reasonable resources at its disposal to assist its deliberations (*Id.*).

Tonn's proposal was especially motivated by his concerns over long-term environmental issues like "species extinction, deforestation and desertification, soil erosion, air and water pollution, toxic waste and radioactive waste" but also about issues like "drug abuse, sexually transmitted diseases (e.g., AIDS), abortion, housing, education and local and national transportation" (Tonn 1991, 484). He was quite concerned with creating a mechanism that was outside of existing partisan structures and wanted to associate the new court with the U.S. Supreme Court so that it would have "the same stature and visibility" (*Id.*, 490). As a grand jury, the Court of Generations would have subpoena power and would meet in secret. States and territories would select members through special processes that they would themselves create. Tonn regarded his proposal not as a substitute for, but rather as a "complement" to the existing document that he hoped would "create a dialogue between living generations" (*Id.* 496).

Tonn subsequently elaborated his ideas in a later article that, while not, like the first, proposing specific constitutional language, was far more detailed in the kinds of institutions that Tonn thought would be required for "future-oriented government" (Tonn 1996). Tonn began by listing nine criteria by which he thought a future-oriented government could be judged. These included:

(1) Explicit recognition of future generations and future-oriented issues. [Italics and intervening language here and throughout the rest of this paragraph are omitted.]
(2) Explicit implementation of a structured decision-making process.
(3) Bias toward consensual decision making.
(4) Incentives to include people of wisdom.
(5) Effective and broad-based citizen participation.
(6) Prevention of special-interest lobbying.
(7) Ability to balance long-term and short-term interests.
(8) Ability to make stable commitments to long-term plans and actions [and]
(9) Ability to foster learning. (Tonn 1996, 414–416)

Like many other individuals who have examined modern politics, Tonn was especially concerned that the qualities that make for good legislators may not make for individuals with long-term vision. He noted that:

People of wisdom are not self-selected or self-centered. That is, they do not normally declare to the world that they are the wisest, because that would violate their values. Wisdom cannot be conveyed via 20-second commercials. It can be recognized by others only through close association in various difficult and trying contests. Current processes tend to drive people of wisdom away from the fray, do not hold wisdom as a central characteristic for political office, and are, in any case,

incapable of identifying people of wisdom and nurturing their growth over the years. (Tonn 1996, 415)

Tonn proceeded to supplement his earlier proposal for a Court of Generations with a proposal for a "Futures Congress" and a "Futures Administration" that would "build and administer (1) a Diagnostic and Decision Support System; (2) the Futures Congress Management System; and (3) systems that integrate with other national and global information systems" (Tonn 1996, 424). His proposal for the Futures Congress was his most elaborate and would consist of four chambers composed (from top to bottom) of Elders, Visionaries, Realists, and Decision Makers (*Id.*, 418–419). Citizens, hypothetically specified at 200 million, would choose 2 million Decision Makers, each of whom would have to be 30 years or older, would have to have the support of from 100 to 200 individuals, and would use "moral and ethical judgment" to "choose among future-oriented decision alternatives." The Decision Makers would also choose approximately 20,000 Realists (with a minimum age of 40) whose function would be to evaluate "future-oriented decision alternatives." Realists would choose 200 Visionaries (50 years of age or older) who would create "future-oriented decision alternatives." Finally, a group of 20 elders (60 years of age or older) would set "criteria to guide the creation and evaluation of future-oriented decisions" (*Id.*, 420).

At times Tonn appeared to get bogged down in the complexities of his own proposals. He recognized that he was not completely sure how the structures he was proposing would relate to structures already in existence, but the basic distinction focused on allowing institutions to handle short-term problems and the new institutions to look toward long-term ones. He also recognized that his new proposals could result in some instability, as individuals in the Futures Congress gain and lose support, but he stressed that, in current circumstances, "the best one can hope for is a retrofit to existing institutions, which this design represents" (Tonn 1996, 430).

See also Council of Censors; Environmental

Protection; Jefferson, Thomas; Toffler, Alvin and Heidi.

For Further Reading:

Pollard, Vincent Kelly, and Bruce E. Tonn. 1998. "Revisiting the 'Court of Generations' Amendment." *Futures* 30: 345–352.

Tonn, Bruce E. 1991. 1996. "A Design for Future-Oriented Government." *Futures* 28 (June): 413–431.

———. 1991. "The Court of Generations: A Proposed Amendment to the U.S. Constitution." *Futures* 21 (June): 482–498.

❖ TRADEMARKS ❖

Article I, Section 8 of the Constitution grants Congress power "to promote the Progress of Science and useful Arts, by securing for limited Times to Authors and Inventors the exclusive Right to their respective Writings and Discoveries." In the *Trade Mark Cases* (1879), however, the Supreme Court unanimously ruled that this provision did not grant Congress power over trademarks. The Court ruled that the exercise of any such congressional power would have to be restricted to transactions in interstate or foreign commerce.

Almost immediately, Iowa Republican Representative Moses McCoid introduced an amendment to grant Congress power to regulate trademarks. Similar proposals were introduced in 1911 and 1913 and in the late 1940s and early 1950s. As early as 1881, however, Congress had adopted new legislation on trademarks under the authority of its commerce powers, and since 1937, the Supreme Court has interpreted such powers broadly.

Congress has exercised such powers over trademarks in the U.S. Trademark Act of 1946, generally known as the Lanham Act, as well as in the Trademark Counterfeiting Act of 1984. Trademarks are registered with the U.S. Trademarks Office.

❖ TREASON ❖

Article III, Section 3 of the Constitution specifies that "treason against the United States, shall consist only in levying War against them, or in adhering to their Enemies, giving them Aid and Comfort." It further specifies that conviction of treason requires either a confession in open court or the testimony of two or more witnesses to an overt act. Although entrusting Congress with the power "to declare the punishment of Treason," the Constitution prevents such penalties from being passed from one generation to another.

In addition to the grounds for treason listed in the U.S. Constitution, the British permitted conviction for "compassing or imagining the death of the king (Chapin 1964, 3). Clearly, the framers feared the impact that such a broad definition might have on freedom of expression. With this in mind, the courts have construed the treason clause strictly throughout most of U.S. history (Hurst 1971, 192).

There have been about twenty-five proposals introduced in Congress relative to treason. Two such proposals, both introduced in 1901 after the assassination of President William McKinley, would have broadened the definition of treason to include such assassination attempts.

In 1924 Missouri Democratic Representative Joseph Wolff introduced a measure, later reflected in concerns raised by the Nye Commission investigating war-profiteering during World War I, that would make it treason to defraud the government with respect to war materials and equipment. That same year, Pennsylvania Republican George Washington Edmonds would have extended the definition of treason to include any efforts to establish a new form of government except by constitutional amendment.

Most proposals that have been introduced since the end of World War II have attempted to expand the definition of treason to include adherence to or support of groups advocating the overthrow of the government by force; some have specifically mentioned the Communist Party. A 1968 proposal by Louisiana Democratic Representative John Rarick would have defined treason against the United States to include "levying war against them or in adhering to their enemies, giving them aid or comfort, or engaging in acts of subversion." Reflecting his distrust of the courts, Rarick further specified "that the judicial power shall not extend to limit, transfer or negate the powers granted herein, exclusively to the Congress or to alter or amend by interpretation or otherwise the commonly accepted meaning of the language imployed [sic] by Congress in laws enacted pursuant to such powers" (H.J. Res. 1213).

The presence of American John Walker Lindh among those captured while fighting with the Taliban against U.S. forces in Afghanistan in the wake of the terrorist attack against the World Trade Center and the Pentagon on 11 September 2001 raised the issue as to whether he should be charged with treason. Ultimately, the government decided to prosecute him for other crimes.

For Further Reading:

Chapin, Bradley. 1964. *The American Law of Treason: Revolutionary and Early National Origins.* Seattle: University of Washington Press.

Hurst, James W. 1971. *The Law of Treason in the United States: Collected Essays.* Westport, CT: Greenwood Press.

❖ TREASURY, DEPARTMENT OF ❖

Congress is the branch of government most frequently associated with the power of the purse. Under the Constitution, however, the president appoints all cabinet members, including the secretary of the treasury.

Although the Constitution does not specify who has the power to remove such officials, court decisions, most notably that in *Myers v. United States* (1926), have confirmed that this power is vested in the president. The Supreme Court noted that the president was responsible for enforcing the laws and would presumably be best informed about the performance of his subordinates.

Chief Justice (and former president) William Howard Taft, who wrote the decision in *Myers,* relied heavily on debates in the First Congress, where James Madison had been a strong advocate of the president's removal power. During these debates, however, Madison had sug-

gested that because of the secretary's tie to the power of the purse there might be a reason to treat the secretary of the treasury differently from other officials (D. O'Brien 2000b, 1:316). In the nation's early years, at least three members of Congress—States' Rights Democratic Representative John Barbour of Virginia (1828) and Whig Representatives John Underwood (1836, 1838), and Henry Clay (1841) of Kentucky—proposed amendments to vest either the appointment or the appointment and removal of the treasury secretary in Congress.

In *Bowsher v. Synar* (1986), the Supreme Court reaffirmed presidential authority over budget cuts when it struck down a provision of the Balanced Budget and Emergency Deficit Control Act of 1985. That provision had entrusted the specification of such cuts to the comptroller general, who was subject to removal by Congress rather than by the president.

For Further Reading:

O'Brien, David M. 2000b. *Struggles for Power and Governmental Accountability.* 5th ed., Vol. 1 of *Constitutional Law and Politics.* New York: W. W. Norton.

❖ TREATIES, RATIFICATION OF ❖

As disputes about the Bricker Amendment demonstrate, the treaty-making power has been a subject of intense debate. Article II, Section 2 of the Constitution provides that the president "shall have Power, by and with the Advice and Consent of the Senate, to make Treaties, provided two-thirds of the Senators present concur."

Early in American history, the House of Representatives threatened to annul this constitutional provision by failing to appropriate funds needed to carry out the Jay Treaty. The Virginia legislature subsequently proposed that the House of Representatives share in approving treaties, a proposal that was not introduced again until 1884. In 1899 there were two proposals, probably stimulated by the Spanish-American War, to provide for treaty ratification by a majority vote of the Senate.

The two world wars both provoked proposals to alter the treaty power. President Woodrow Wilson's failure to get the Treaty of Versailles ratified by the necessary two-thirds of the Senate (the vote was forty-nine to thirty-five) appears to have triggered several proposals that were introduced from 1919 to 1925. Some proposed that such treaties should become effective by a majority vote in the Senate, some wanted treaties to be ratified by a majority vote in both the House and the Senate, and at least one representative wanted treaties to be ratified by a national referendum.

Such proposals took on a new urgency with U.S. entry into World War II. In May 1945 the House of Representatives voted 288 to 88 (with 56 members abstaining) for an amendment to enable a majority of both houses to ratify treaties, but the Senate was not keen on giving up its prerogative (Ackerman and Golove 1995, 865, 889). In the meantime, the lines between treaties ratified by the Senate, executive agreements entered into by the president, and other international agreements negotiated by the president with the approval of both houses of Congress were being obscured. The Senate appears to have accepted this situation in part as an alternative to formal constitutional change.

By 1954 the agreement between the United States and Canada regarding the St. Lawrence Seaway, which had previously been sent to the Senate for approval as a treaty, was adopted by a simple majority of both houses of Congress (Ackerman and Golove 1995, 893). In 1993 a similar procedure, negotiated under the Trade Act of 1974, was used to ratify the North American Free Trade Agreement (NAFTA). This bill was put on a legislative "fast track" in exchange for constant presidential-legislative collaboration during the negotiating process. Bruce Ackerman, a prominent theorist on the amending process, has cited this development as an example of constitutional innovation outside the Article V amending process and praised it for its "efficacy, democracy [and] legitimacy" (Ackerman and Golove 1995, 916).

Proposals to alter the formal treaty-making process continued throughout the 1950s, 1960s, and 1970s. A number of the later proposals, undoubtedly stimulated by the United

States' experience in Vietnam, would have required the involvement of both houses of Congress in any treaty committing U.S. forces abroad.

Although the Constitution specifies that the Senate must approve treaties by a two-thirds vote, it does not specify how treaties are terminated. In *Goldwater v. Carter* (1979), the Court refused to invalidate a challenge by some senators to President Carter's termination of a treaty with Taiwan that conflicted with U.S. recognition of the People's Republic of China. The justices split as to whether the case was "ripe" for adjudication (the senators who challenged the treaty termination did not constitute a majority of that body), whether the issue was "political" and should be left to the elected branches to solve on their own, or whether the president possessed the power the annul treaties.

See also Bricker Amendment.

For Further Reading:
Ackerman, Bruce, and David Golove. 1995. "Is NAFTA Constitutional?" *Harvard Law Review* 108 (February): 799–929.
Goldwater v. Carter, 444 U.S. 996 (1979).

❖ TRUTH-IN-LEGISLATION AMENDMENT ❖

Two authors of a recent law review article have called for a "Truth-in-Legislation Amendment" (Denning and Smith 1999). Such an amendment is based on a provision of the Tennessee Constitution, which is similar to provisions also adopted in other states. The proposed amendment would require that "Congress shall pass no bill, and no bill shall become law, which embraces more than one subject, that subject being clearly expressed in the title" (*Id.,* 962). This amendment is designed to address the problem of legislative "riders." Members of Congress often insert such provisions (frequently during last-minute, behind-the-scenes committee negotiations over pieces of legislation) bearing little relation to the title or central purpose of bills in so-called omnibus legislation on behalf of special interests within their districts. If the truth-in-legislation amendment proved effective, whether in influencing the legislative and executive branches or through judicial enforcement, the amendment might serve (much like the proposed item veto, balanced budget, or term limit amending proposals) to limit congressional spending. It might also increase the accountability of Congress to constituents and watchdog groups who are attempting to follow and influence the course of legislation in the public interest.

See also Presidency, Veto Power of.

For Further Reading:
Denning, Brannon P., and Brooks R. Smith. 1999. "Uneasy Riders: The Case for a Truth-in-Legislation Amendment." *Utah Law Review* (1999): 957–1025.

❖ TUGWELL, REXFORD (1891–1979) ❖

No modern would-be constitutional reformer has worked longer or more diligently on a new United States constitution than Rexford Tugwell. One of the three members of Franklin Roosevelt's original "brain trust" who had once worked with other scholars on a preliminary draft of a World Constitution, Tugwell had an active life as both a college professor and a public servant before joining the Center for the Study of Democratic Institutions (headed by Robert Hutchins) as a senior fellow (Ashmore 1970).

In his first six years there, Tugwell initiated discussions that led him to draft thirty-seven successive versions of a proposed constitution. This draft was published in a special issue of the center's magazine in 1970. Tugwell continued his revisions and offered his fortieth version in a book published in 1974 (for analysis, see Vile 1991c, 106–110).

Tugwell's proposals were quite complex, and they were such a departure from the existing constitutional scheme that they are not easily summarized. Certainly, Tugwell put great emphasis on governmental planning, adding numerous new boards, commissions, and positions. He also believed that existing state governments were antiquated and needed to be altered radically. Unlike many twentieth-century reformers, however, Tugwell would have maintained the system of separated powers and did not advocate a parliamentary system.

Tugwell's fortieth constitution differed significantly in organization from his thirty-seventh and consisted of twelve articles. Article I dealt with rights and responsibilities. In addition to most guarantees now found in the Bill of Rights and various amendments, this section contained protections for individual privacy; guarantees against discrimination based on "race, creed, color, origin, or sex"; prohibitions against any public support for religion; a guarantee that those unable to "contribute to productivity shall be entitled to a share of the national product"; and a guarantee of education "at public expense" for those establishing eligibility (Tugwell 1974, 595–596). Citizen responsibilities included respecting the rights of others, participating in democratic processes, and avoiding violence. To promote the latter goal, and in contrast to the Second Amendment of the existing Constitution, Tugwell would reserve the bearing of arms to "the police, members of the armed forces, and those licensed under law" (*Id.*, 597).

Tugwell designated the government under his fortieth constitution the "Newstates of America" (the thirty-seventh version referred instead to the "United Republic of America"). Article II dealt with these newstates, none of which was to contain less than 5 percent of the existing population. Each would have its own constitution as well as its own "governors, legislatures, and planning, administrative, and judicial systems" (Tugwell 1974, 598). Like present states, they would exercise "police powers"; all rights and responsibilities applied at the national level would also apply to the states.

Article III established an "electoral branch" of government supervised by an "overseer" selected by the Senate. The overseer would "supervise the organization of national and district parties, arrange for discussion among them, and provide for the nomination and election of candidates for public office" (Tugwell 1974,

599). Duties would include assisting in the nomination of candidates and in arranging and supervising elections. All costs would be paid from public funds, and all private personal expenditures would be prohibited.

Article IV delineated a planning branch headed by a national planning board of fifteen members. It would be responsible for submitting six- and twelve-year plans.

Article V described the president, who was designated as "the head of government, shaper of its commitments, expositor of its policies, and supreme commander of its protective forces" (Tugwell 1974, 604). The president would serve a nine-year term subject to recall by 60 percent of the voters after three years. The president would be served by two vice presidents, one for internal affairs and the other for general affairs. The latter would supervise "Chancellors of External, Financial, Legal, and Military Affairs" (*Id.*, 604). Treaties negotiated by the president would go into effect unless rejected by a majority of the Senate. The president would appoint a public custodian in charge of governmental property and an intendant to supervise intelligence and investigation offices.

Article VI described a drastically altered Congress. A Senate of seventy to eighty members would be appointed by various groups and individuals, and members would serve for life terms. The Senate's main function would be to consider, and at times delay, but not initiate legislation. It would also select a three-person national security council to consult with the president about the deployment of American troops abroad. The Senate would also select the national watchkeeper, a type of ombudsman. Members of the House of Representatives would be selected from 100 districts, each of which would select three members for three-year terms; to give the body a more national orientation, there would be another 100 at-large members. The House would be "the original lawmaking body of the Newstates of America" (Tugwell 1974, 609). In contrast to the current Constitution, which is silent on such matters, Tugwell's document outlined the selection of committees and their chairs and included a much longer list of congressional powers, including powers over banking, insurance, communications, transportation, space exploration, welfare, education, libraries, the conservation of natural resources, and civil service.

Article VII established a regulatory branch headed by a national regulator to be selected by the Senate and to serve as head of a regulatory board of seventeen members. The regulator would charter corporations, regulate industrial mergers, and supervise the marketplace.

The judicial branch was delineated in Article VIII in considerable more complexity than the current Constitution. Section 1 of this article began as follows: "There shall be a Principal Justice of the Newstates of America; a Judicial Council; and a Judicial Assembly. There shall also be a Supreme Court and a High Court of Appeals; also Courts of Claims, Rights and Duties, Administrative Review, Arbitration Settlements, Tax Appeals, and Appeals from Watchkeeper's Findings" (Tugwell 1974, 614). The principal justice would preside over the system and appoint all members of the national courts; the justice would serve an eleven-year term and would share with the president the power to grant reprieves and pardons. Although Tugwell criticized the extent of judicial review as currently exercised, the Supreme Court would continue to exercise such power under his plan.

Article IX dealt with general provisions, Article X with governmental arrangements, and Article XII with transition to the new government. Article XI dealt with the amending process. The judicial council would have the power to formulate amendments to be approved by the Senate and president and submitted to the people and adopted by majority vote. Every twenty-five years the overseer would conduct a referendum on whether a new constitution was needed. If approval was given, the judicial council would draw up a constitution to go into effect if not disapproved by a majority.

Tugwell's various proposals were the topic of considerable discussion and criticism (Kelly 1981, 650), some of it quite fanatical (Preston 1972), but they generated little in the way of practical results.

See also World Government.

For Further Reading:

Ashmore, Harry S. 1970. "Rexford Guy Tugwell: Man of Thought, Man of Action." *Center Magazine* 3 (September/October): 2–7.

Kelly, Frank K. 1981. *Court of Reason: Robert Hutchins and the Fund for the Republic*. New York: Free Press.

Preston, Robert L. 1972. *The Plot to Replace the Constitution*. Salt Lake City, Utah: Hawkes Publications.

Tugwell, Rexford. 1974. *The Emerging Constitution*. New York: Harper and Row.

Vile, John R. 1991c. *Rewriting the United States Constitution: An Examination of Proposals from Reconstruction to the Present*. New York: Praeger.

❖ TULLER, WALTER (1886–1939) ❖

California attorney Walter Tuller wrote an article in 1911 that advocated the calling of a constitutional convention to propose an amendment for the direct election of U.S. senators. Although he devoted most of the article to showing that Congress was obligated to call such a convention when requested to do so by two-thirds of the states and that the Court could enforce such a responsibility (see Vile 1991c, 53–54), Tuller also advanced two subjects that he wanted a convention to handle.

First, Tuller wanted to reduce the number of states required to call such a convention from two-thirds to one-half. At a time when many regarded the amending process as too rigid, Tuller saw such a reduction as a way of keeping the Constitution from becoming "too far removed from the people." Second, Tuller wanted an amendment granting the national government power "to regulate corporations or monopolies in any form" (Tuller 1911, 385).

Tuller anticipated a convention of "the strongest and ablest men in the nation" (Tuller 1911, 386). Contrary to most modern convention proposals, Tuller anticipated that each state would be represented equally, but he was willing to let the convention decide whether members would vote individually or by state.

See also Seventeenth Amendment.

For Further Reading:

Tuller, Walter K. 1911. "A Convention to Amend the Constitution—Why Needed—How It May Be Obtained." *North American Review* 193: 369–387.

Vile, John R. 1991c. *Rewriting the United States Constitution: An Examination of Proposals from Reconstruction to the Present*. New York: Praeger.

❖ TWELFTH AMENDMENT ❖

There have been hundreds of proposals to alter the process of presidential and vice presidential selection, but the Twelfth Amendment is the only substantial change that has been made in this procedure. This amendment grew out of America's early experience that the original manner of selecting the executive as specified in Article II of the Constitution had some unintended consequences. Many of these were hastened and exaggerated by a development that most of the framers neither anticipated nor easily welcomed, namely, the development of political parties (Turner 1973; Bernstein 1993).

Operation of the Electoral College

The electoral college is a system of indirect election whereby state-designated electors choose the president and vice president. The design of this mechanism was a major development at the Constitutional Convention of 1787, because the electoral college provided a way for the executive to act independently of Congress and thus furthered the idea of a system of separated powers.

Alan Grimes identified six defining features of the electoral college system: (1) it allowed states to determine whether electors would be chosen by the people or by the state legislatures; (2) it gave each state a number of electors equal to its total representation in the House and Senate, thus somewhat advantaging both large states (with the greatest number of representatives) and small states (guaranteed at least three votes); (3) electors met within each state and cast two ballots for president; (4) members of Congress were prohibited from serving as electors; (5) other federal officeholders were also excluded from the job; and (6) electors had to cast at least one of their two votes for someone from another state (Grimes 1978, 20).

The framers thought that such a procedure would avoid the tumult and possible uncertainties of popular election at a time when technology was more primitive. The framers also anticipated that electors would have a better knowledge of candidates from other states than would the populace as a whole.

Early Presidential Elections

Although it is sometimes asserted that the framers anticipated that electors would perform a deliberative function, from the very first election in 1788, electors came ready to cast predetermined votes (Kuroda 1994, 31). Some states selected delegates by direct election (now the universal procedure) and others by legislative appointment; similarly, some used an at-large system of election, and others chose electors by district. In the first election, all sixty-nine delegates who participated (New York was unable to settle on the method of selecting electors and did not cast ballots) each cast one of their two votes for George Washington. The second votes were split among eleven other men, with John Adams's thirty-four votes putting him in second place and earning him the vice presidency, a position that one representative, knowing Adams's penchant for titles, called "His Superfluous Excellency" (*Id.*, 24).

By the election of 1792, the Federalist and Democratic-Republican Parties had begun to emerge. Once again, however, Washington was selected unanimously, this time with 132 votes. Adams came in second. The fact that Adams had only seventy-seven votes indicated that the party "ticket" had not yet completely emerged.

Washington decided to retire after his second term, so the election of 1796 was the first without his candidacy. This election saw a closer contest between the top two party candidates and greater cohesion in voting combinations. Because some Federalists who voted for Adams did not vote for Thomas Pinckney, however, the person with the second highest number of votes was Thomas Jefferson, head of the emerging Democratic-Republican Party. This meant that the president and vice president would be from different parties.

The Election of 1800

Although having a president and vice president from different parties was far from a desirable situation, the election of 1800 was the one that finally galvanized action by revealing yet another flaw in the original electoral system. In this election, all seventy-three electors who cast a vote for Jefferson also voted for Aaron Burr, in an attempt to avoid the different-party problem of the previous election. Because the Constitution did not provide separate designations for presidential and vice presidential candidates, the result was a tie in the electoral college, which threw the election into the House of Representatives, where each state had one vote and where the outgoing Federalists effectively had the ability to make the choice. In the initial ballot, Jefferson got the votes of eight states and Burr of six, with two states divided. Because the Constitution required a president to get a majority, more ballots had to be taken. It took about a week of balloting, and thirty-six ballots, before enough Federalists abstained (in part at the urging of Alexander Hamilton, who distrusted Burr even more than he distrusted Jefferson and would eventually forfeit his life in a duel with Burr, largely over publication of negative assessments of Burr's character) to give the election to Jefferson.

Proposal and Ratification of the Twelfth Amendment

The years immediately following produced scores of proposals, including an automatic plan (supported for a time by Thomas Jefferson) whereby the office of electors would be eliminated and the person receiving the plurality of a state's votes would get all its electoral votes. Other plans proposed eliminating the vice presidency and reconsidering the three-fifths compromise under which electors were allocated to Southern states; specifically designating votes for president and vice president; and requiring district elections both for electors and for members of Congress (Kuroda 1994, 107–126).

The election of 1802 brought substantial gains to the Democratic-Republicans in Congress and renewed pressure for a constitutional amendment. In October 1803 the House voted eighty-eight to thirty-nine for an amendment that would have had electors designate which ballot they were casting for president and which for vice president and would have reduced from five to three the number of candidates the House would choose among if no candidate received a majority.

The Senate then began its own debate, which resulted in the current language of the Twelfth Amendment. Like the version accepted in the House, this proposal specified that when no one received a majority, the House of Representatives would choose from among the top three candidates, rather than the top five. It also provided that if the House did not choose a candidate by 4 March (subsequently changed by the Twentieth Amendment to 20 January), the vice president would act as president. The amendment stirred highly partisan debate. Federalists, who purported to represent the interests of the small states, fought the reduction from five candidates to three. Others felt that any constitutional changes might dangerously lower the floodgates to reform (Kuroda 1994, 141).

There was also debate whether amendments required a two-thirds vote of all members or only of those members present. On 2 December 1803, the amendment was narrowly carried by a vote of twenty-two to ten—although this was short of two-thirds of the entire membership of thirty-four (Kuroda 1994, 142–143).

The new Senate version then went back to the House, where, on 8 December 1803, after an initial count of eighty-three to forty-one, Speaker Nathaniel Macon cast his vote with the majority to give it precisely the two-thirds majority needed. New Hampshire attempted to become the necessary thirteenth state to ratify in June 1804, but the governor created a state of confusion with a veto, and the honor apparently went to Tennessee in late July. The new amendment set the framework for the 1804 presidential election. In this contest, Jefferson was elected on a ticket that included New York's George Clinton.

Consequences and Implications of the Twelfth Amendment

Although it did not specifically mention them, the amendment affirmed the role that political parties had come to play in designating candidates. It also arguably denigrated the vice presidency. The individual in this position was now clearly recognized as second fiddle; subsequently, he would often be chosen more for regional or ideological balance than for his qualifications to be president (Kuroda 1994, 172).

The political parties subsequently acquired a share in the system that was reaffirmed as large and small states both continued their overrepresentation under the new plan. Despite numerous subsequent proposals, including many calls for complete abolition of the electoral system, it has not been substantially altered by constitutional amendment since 1804. The Twenty-third Amendment did extend some representation in the electoral college to the District of Columbia.

See also Electoral College Reform; Twenty-third Amendment.

For Further Reading:

Bernstein, Richard B. 1993. "Fixing the Electoral College." *Constitution* 5 (Winter): 42–48.

Grimes, Alan P. 1978. *Democracy and the Amendments to the Constitution.* Lexington, MA: Lexington Books.

Kuroda, Tadahisa. 1994. *The Origins of the Twelfth Amendment: The Electoral College in the Early Republic, 1878–1804.* Westport, CT: Greenwood Press.

Turner, John J., Jr. 1973. "The Twelfth Amendment and the First American Party System." *Historian* 35: 221–237.

❖ TWELVE SOUTHERNERS ❖

Especially since the Civil War, the United States has become an increasingly urban and increasingly industrialized nation. Although the idea of a huge commercial republic was certainly a dream of many of the founding fathers, most notably Alexander Hamilton, the nation's first secretary of the treasury, others, most notably

Thomas Jefferson, the nation's first secretary of state, long held a view of a nation of independent-minded citizen-farmers. There has been tension between these two ideals ever since. Initially, this tension was reflected in the differing economies of the North and South, but the later development of the Populist Movement in the Midwest also demonstrated that other parts of the nation were affected as well.

Especially after the Civil War, there were many who saw the solution to many problems in the South as increased industrialization. Fearing that this approach was undercutting values that Southerners long held dear, a group of twelve scholars (many who would establish themselves in the field of literature) from Vanderbilt University in Nashville, Tennessee, drafted a book containing a series of essays in which they argued for agrarian and individualistic values. The authors were Donald Davidson, John Gould Fletcher, Henry Blue Kline, Lyle H. Lanier, Andrew Nelson Lytle, Herman Clarence Nixon, Frank Lawrence Owsley, John Crowe Ransom, Allen Tate, John Donald Wade, Robert Penn Warren, and Stark Young.

The joint introduction questioned the value of industrialization for its own sake, the modern near worship of science, the idea that every labor-saving device was a positive good, and consumerism, with its handmaidens of advertising and salesmanship. The Twelve Southerners argued that such ideas had corrupted religion, labor, art, leisure, and the deeper values of life in general. The authors were uncertain as to how the South, or indeed any area of the nation, might resist such forces or whether agrarians should attempt to capture the Democratic Party—at the time the South was solidly Democrat—or create a new one (Twelve Southerners 1930, xivii). Their work thus serves less as a guide to specific political or constitutional amendments than as an alternate vision of a direction that America might have taken. Thomas H. Naylor and William H. Willimon, who are familiar with the Twelve Southerners, have championed some similar values in their book *Downsizing the U.S.A.* (1997).

See also Naylor, Thomas H., and William H. Willimon.

For Further Reading:

Naylor, Thomas H. and William H. Willimon. 1997. *Downsizing the U.S.A.* Grand Rapids, MI: William B. Eerdmans Publishing Company.

Twelve Southerners. 1930. *I'll Take My Stand: The South and the Agrarian Tradition.* Reprint, Baton Rouge: Louisiana State University Press, 1977.

❖ TWENTIETH AMENDMENT ❖

Although it is separated by more than a dozen years from its four immediate predecessors, like them the Twentieth Amendment grew from the democratic sentiment spawned by the Progressive Era. Progressive Republican Senator George Norris of Nebraska was a key architect of the amendment that altered the dates that members of the national legislative and executive branches took office (Grimes 1978, 104–105). Adoption followed about thirty proposals made prior to 1900 and about ninety more in the early twentieth century. The first two proposals were introduced by famous New Yorkers, Aaron Burr (1795) and Millard Fillmore (1840). These and other proposals suggested that the inauguration date be set as early as December and as late as May.

The Congress under the Articles of Confederation set things in motion when it provided that the first Congress under the new Constitution would begin on 4 March. Although this date was not specified in the Constitution, it was perpetuated both by custom and by concern that moving it forward would unconstitutionally shorten terms (Bernstein with Agel 1993, 154). Prior to the adoption of the Seventeenth Amendment, the 4 March date also gave time to state legislatures, which typically did not begin sessions until January, to make their selections (Grimes 1978, 105). Article I, Section 4 of the Constitution, however, specified that the annual meeting of Congress should begin on the first Monday in December. This meant that a new Congress would not come into regular session until thirteen months after it was elected in November. In the meantime, the outgoing lame-duck legislature (some of whose members had been electorally wounded but not killed—hence the term "lame duck") could adopt legislation without being accountable to the voters. Thus, in a series of events that eventually led to the Supreme Court's historic decision in *Marbury v. Madison* (1803), an outgoing Federalist Congress adopted the Judiciary Act of 1801, adding fellow Federalists to the judiciary, much to the consternation of the newly elected Republican administration. Similarly, President Warren G. Harding used his influence with outgoing members of Congress to enact a ship subsidy bill in 1922. This action enraged Nebraska Senator George W. Norris, who sponsored a constitutional amendment in 1922 to reduce lame-duck terms and persisted in supporting this amendment over the next decade.

Whereas progressives like Norris viewed the situation as undemocratic, many congressional conservatives, including Republican House Speaker Nicholas Longworth, actually "preferred a cooling-off period before the new Congress came into session" (Grimes 1978, 106). Some also liked the short congressional session (from December through March) in alternate years. Thus, although the amendment passed the Senate in 1923, 1924, and 1926, it failed to receive the necessary majority of votes when first voted on in the House in 1928. In 1929 a conference committee failed to resolve differences between the two houses. A 1930 Democratic landslide broke the deadlock and resulted in the elevation of Democrat John N. Garner of Texas, who favored the amendment, as House Speaker. Although the House of Representatives initially adopted a provision that would have required at least one house of the ratifying state legislatures to be elected before ratifying the amendment, this provision was dropped in conference committee (Grimes 1978, 108). The Senate subsequently voted for the amendment by a vote of 63 to 7 (with 25 abstaining) on 6 January 1932; the House followed with a 336 to 56 vote (1 answering present and 38 not voting) on 16 February 1932. Virginia was the first state to ratify on 4 March 1932; Utah put the amendment over the top on 23 January 1933, and the last of the existing 48 states (Florida) ratified on 26 April of that year (U.S. Senate 1985, 62).

The Twentieth Amendment has six sections. The first, and most important, sets the beginning of congressional terms on 3 January and those of the president and vice president on 20 January. Section 2 provides that the annual session of Congress begins on 3 January. Anticipating some of the problems later addressed in the Twenty-fifth Amendment, Section 3 specifies that if the president-elect dies prior to inauguration, the vice president–elect becomes president. It also allows the vice president–elect to serve if no one has received a majority of the electoral college and the House of Representatives has not yet chosen among the finalists. It further allows Congress to provide by law for an interim in cases in which neither officer has been selected. Section 4 grants the same power in the case of the death of a candidate during congressional deliberations. Section 5 provides that the amendment would become effective on 15 October after its ratification, and Section 6 makes the Twentieth Amendment the second to contain a seven-year ratification deadline.

A number of subsequent proposals have been introduced to modify the Twentieth Amendment. In a sense, however, they are in the same spirit, because they are designed to move inauguration dates even further back to November or December (see Levinson 1995, 185). It is not altogether clear that the authors of the Twentieth Amendment anticipated that Congress would meet from the period from current November congressional elections to the January installation of new members (Nagle 1997), thus allowing the perpetuation of lame-duck sessions, albeit shorter ones. Some scholars thus questioned whether the impeachment of President Bill Clinton by the outgoing House of Representatives of 1998 should be valid when reported to the incoming Senate of 1999, but, although it did not result in a conviction, the trial proceeded ahead.

Several other amending proposals have been made to end congressional sessions in July, probably with a view to shortening the period in which Congress can legislate. In a less hurried time (1878), an amendment was even offered to provide for biennial congressional sessions. Five years earlier, in a speech on 2 December 1873, President Ulysses S. Grant had proposed that when the president called special sessions of Congress (as permitted in Article II, Section 3), such sessions should be limited to subjects the president proposed (J. Richardson 1908, 7:242–243). A number of subsequent proposals would have enabled Congress to call itself into special session. Proposals introduced in 1920 and 1923 by House Republican Edward Browne of Wisconsin, precipitated by President Woodrow Wilson's debilitating stroke, would have enabled Congress to provide for cases of such presidential disability, an issue later addressed in the Twenty-fifth Amendment.

For Further Reading:

Bernstein, Richard B., with Jerome Agel. 1993. *Amending America: If We Love the Constitution So Much, Why Do We Keep Trying to Change It?* New York: Random House.

Grimes, Alan P. 1978. *Democracy and the Amendments to the Constitution.* Lexington, MA: Lexington Books.

Levinson, Sanford. 1995. "Presidential Elections and Constitutional Stupidities." *Constitutional Commentary* 12 (Summer): 183–186.

Nagle, John Copeland. 1997. "Essay: A Twentieth Amendment Parable." *New York University Law Review* 72 (May): 470–494.

Richardson, James E., ed. 1908. *A Compilation of the Messages and Papers of the Presidents, 1789–1908.* 11 vols. n.p.: Bureau of National Literature and Art.

U.S. Senate, Subcommittee on the Constitution, Committee on the Judiciary. 1985. *Amendments to the Constitution: A Brief Legislative History.* Washington, DC: U.S. Government Printing Office.

❖ TWENTY-FIFTH AMENDMENT ❖

Amendments have been introduced throughout American history to deal with presidential disability and with vacancies in the office of vice president.

Although a number of early vice presidents died in office and one, John C. Calhoun, resigned to become a senator, no president died until 1841, when the elderly William Henry Harrison passed away shortly after his inauguration. His successor, John Tyler, made it clear that he considered himself to be the president and not simply an "acting" president until a re-election could be called. Despite ambiguity about the framers' intentions on this matter, this precedent became standard practice for other vice presidents who replaced chief executives. Tyler's precedent, however, neither addressed the issue of what would happen in cases of presidential disability nor made provision for filling vice presidential vacancies.

Laws Dealing with Presidential Succession

Congress addressed the issue of vice presidential vacancies in a number of laws, but their diversity demonstrated the lack of consensus on how the issue was best resolved. In 1792 Congress adopted legislation putting the president pro tempore of the Senate and the Speaker of the House of Representatives behind the vice president in the line of succession, but this arrangement made it possible that, in cases of a double vacancy, the presidency might change political parties without an intervening election. After a period during which both the president pro tempore and the Speaker positions were vacant, Congress revised the law in 1886 to provide that the heads of the executive departments, beginning with the secretary of state and the secretary of the treasury, would be in the line of succession. Because it is possible that such officials may never have held elective office (a particular concern of President Harry S. Truman), however, this law was altered in 1947 to place the Speaker and the president pro tempore ahead of cabinet officers in the line of succession (Feerick 1992, 37–47). Scholar Norman Ornstein, writing in light of the terrorist attack on the World Trade Center and the Pentagon of 11 September 2001 has suggested that this law of presidential succession needs to be revisited. He pointed specifically to the possibility that, under existing legislation, succession could be passed from one party to another and to the fact that the president pro tempore of the Senate is usually chosen because he or she is the oldest (but not necessarily the fittest) member. He also noted the possibility that some governors, outside the Washington, D.C., area, should be included on the list of presidential successors (Ornstein 2002).

Presidential Disability

In the meantime, the issue of presidential disability remained. In 1881 President James A. Garfield lingered for eighty days before dying from an assassin's bullet. President William McKinley also lived several days before dying of another assassin's bullet in 1901, and President Woodrow Wilson suffered a debilitating stroke in 1919. The problem of such disabilities became especially acute with the invention of nuclear weapons. President Dwight D. Eisenhower suffered a number of health problems during his tenure, and he eventually drew up a letter of understanding allowing Vice President Richard Nixon to assume his duties during such times as President Eisenhower might be disabled.

Adoption of the Twenty-fifth Amendment

Following President John F. Kennedy's assassination, calls increased to transform informal arrangements into a viable constitutional procedure. Shortly after the assassination, Indiana Democratic Senator Birch Bayh, who chaired the Senate Judiciary Committee's Subcommittee on Constitutional Amendments, held hearings on the subject. The Senate subsequently approved a proposed amendment in 1964 by a vote of 64 to 0. In 1965 it again approved an amendment by a 72 to 0 vote, with the House concurring by a vote of 368 to 29. A conference committee version was subsequently adopted by voice vote in the House and by a vote of 68 to 5 in the Senate, with the latter vote occurring on 6 July 1965. Ratification by the necessary number of states was completed on 10 February 1967 (Feerick 1992, 95–111). Informed that he had no official role in the ratification of amendments, President Lyndon Johnson insisted on holding a televised ceremony in the White House Rose Garden when he signed a proclamation indicating that he had received official notice of state ratification of the Amendment (Kyvig 1996a, 362).

Provisions of the Twenty-fifth Amendment

The Twenty-fifth Amendment has four sections. An observer noted that it "rivals the Fourteenth in length, and surpasses all other amendments in wordage" (Young 1974, 395). The first section officially confirms John Tyler's 1841 precedent by specifying that when the president dies or resigns, "the Vice President shall become president."

Section 2 provides for filling vice presidential vacancies. It rejected earlier proposals that had been introduced to provide for multiple vice presidents (New York Senator Kenneth Keating wanted to create separate executive and legislative vice presidents) or to provide that vice presidential vacancies be filled by a vote of the last electoral college (a position advocated for a time by Richard Nixon). Instead, this section provides that the president shall nominate a replacement when the vice presidency is vacant. Such nominations are confirmed by a majority vote of both houses of Congress.

Although they do not specifically define it, Sections 3 and 4 of the Twenty-fifth Amendment deal with the problem of presidential disability. Section 3 provides that when the president informs the president pro tempore of the Senate and the Speaker of the House that he or she is unable to perform his or her duties, "such powers and duties" shall be performed by the vice president until such time as the president sends a letter stating that his or her disability is over.

Section 3 handles an ideal case, but what happens if the president fails to recognize or acknowledge that he or she has a disability? Section 4 sets up a complicated system of checks and balances. Rejecting earlier proposals to require a special commission to deal with such matters or to entrust such decisions to the Supreme Court, Section 4 outlines another route. Under this provision, the vice president assumes the president's duties if the vice president and a majority "of the principal officers of the executive departments or such other body as Congress may by law provide" transmit a written declaration to the president pro tempore of the Senate and the Speaker of the House that the president is unable to carry out his or her duties. The president may subsequently submit his or her own written declaration that the disability has ended and resume his or her duties, assuming that the vice president and members of the cabinet or other congressionally designated body do not disagree within four days. If there is such a disagreement, the vice president continues to exercise presidential duties. Congress, in turn, assembles within forty-eight hours. If, within twenty-one days, two-thirds of both houses of Congress affirm that the president is disabled, the vice president continues in office. If Congress reaches no such agreement, the president resumes his or her duties.

Operation of the Twenty-fifth Amendment

After being wounded in an attempted assassination by John Hinckley in 1981, President Ronald Reagan was reluctant to invoke the disability provisions of the Twenty-fifth Amendment, apparently fearing that it would cause popular alarm (Feerick 1992, xiii–xiv; also see Abrams 1994). Although he later declared that he was not invoking provisions of this amendment when he underwent cancer surgery, he appears to have adhered fairly closely to the amendment's procedures (Feerick 1992, xvi–xvii). Citing the fact that the nation was "at war" [with terrorists], President George Bush Jr. did specifically follow the guideline of the Twenty-fifth Amendment when he was under brief sedation for a colonoscopy (a procedure designed to detect polyps or cancer of the lower intestine) on 29 June 2002 (Bumiller 2002, A1).

The provision of the Twenty-fifth Amendment that has been most frequently exercised is the section dealing with filling vice presidential vacancies. President Nixon nominated, and Congress subsequently confirmed, Gerald Ford when Vice President Spiro Agnew resigned in 1973 after being charged with accepting bribes while in the Maryland government. When Ford was subsequently elevated to the presidency after Nixon resigned in the wake of the Watergate scandal, he selected, and Congress confirmed, former New York governor Nelson Rockefeller as vice president. The Twenty-fifth Amendment took on new importance during the electoral controversy and first term of George W. Bush when Vice President Dick Cheney, who had a past history of heart attacks, was twice admitted to the hospital for chest pains.

Proposals to Alter the Twenty-fifth Amendment

There have been several proposals to repeal either Section 2 (dealing with filling vice presidential vacancies) or the entire Twenty-fifth Amendment. Some such proposals appear to stem from concerns that the existing disability provision is too complex and might be abused by an overly ambitious vice president. Other proposals stem from concern that the Twenty-fifth Amendment allows the office of both president and vice president to be filled by individuals who have not been popularly elected.

Focusing in part on the latter concern and in part on the putative failure of the office to attract strong characters from the adoption of the Twelfth Amendment through the Nixon administration, historian Arthur M. Schlesinger Jr. (1974) has advocated eliminating the vice presidency. He proposes allowing the secretary of state or another eligible cabinet officer to serve in cases of a presidential vacancy (assuming there is more than a year until the next regularly scheduled election) until a new election can be held. A Twentieth Century Fund Task Force Report on the Vice Presidency (1988) opposed this recommendation.

Another scholar has recently suggested that Congress should act under Section 4 of the Amendment (with its reference to "such other body as Congress may by law provide") to provide for a medical advisory committee that would, with the president's personal physician, review the results of the president's annual physical and assemble at times when there were serious questions about the president's health. The advocate of this committee, which he believes should include internists, neurologists, a surgeon, and a psychiatrist, believes that it would be more likely to provide objective information than would the president's personal physician, who might have a conflict of interest in the case of his patient being removed because of disability (Abrams 1999).

See also Congress, Emergency Functioning.

For Further Reading:
Abrams, Herbert L. 1999. "Can the Twenty-Fifth Amendment Deal with a Disabled President? Pre-

venting Future White House Cover–Ups." *Presidential Studies Quarterly 29* (March): 115–133.

Bumiller, Elisabeth. 2002. "Bush to Undergo Colon Procedure: President Will Transfer Power to Cheney before Sedation." *The New York Times,* 29 June, A1, A11.

Feerick, John D. 1992. *The Twenty-fifth Amendment: Its Complete History and Applications.* New York: Fordham University Press.

Kyvig, David E. 1996a. *Explicit and Authentic Acts: Amending the Constitution, 1776–1995.* Lawrence, KS: University Press of Kansas.

Ornstein, Norman J. 2002. "Preparing for the Unthinkable: Bush's 'Shadow Government' Plan Is a Start—But Only a Start." *The Wall Street Journal,* 11 March, A18.

Schlesinger, Arthur M., Jr. 1974. "On the Presidential Succession." *Political Science Quarterly* 89 (Fall): 475–505.

Twentieth Century Fund Task Force on the Vice Presidency. 1988. *A Heartbeat Away.* New York: Printing Press Publications.

"The Twenty-fifth Amendment: Preparing for Presidential Disability." 1995. *Wake Forest Law Review* 30 (Fall): 427–648.

Young, Donald. 1974. *American Roulette: The History and Dilemma of the Vice Presidency.* New York: Viking Press.

❖ TWENTY-FIRST AMENDMENT ❖

The Twenty-first Amendment is distinctive in at least two ways. It is the only amendment ever to have repealed another, and to date, it is the only amendment ever to be ratified by state conventions rather than by state legislatures.

The Eighteenth Amendment, ratified in 1919, represented a great social experiment in its attempt to outlaw the consumption of alcoholic beverages. Although the amendment appears to have cut the consumption of alcohol, it was far from successful in eliminating it. Organized crime and its accompanying violence received a major boost, providing a product that so many wanted and were willing to break the law to get. Speakeasies, where one could drink in social settings, flourished. Many feared that true temperance was less likely to be achieved by the flouting of such complete prohibition than by less invasive governmental regulations.

Moreover, almost from the time that the Eighteenth Amendment was adopted, it was challenged as an unconstitutional interference with state police powers. Although the Supreme Court rejected this argument in the *National Prohibition Cases* (1920), critics continued to believe that the amendment represented an unwarranted federal intrusion into an area of personal relations best left to state control.

Supporters of the Eighteenth Amendment included Democratic Senator Morris Sheppard of Texas, who boasted that "there is as much chance of repealing the Eighteenth Amendment as there is for a hummingbird to fly to the planet Mars with the Washington Monument tied to its tail" (Kyvig 1985, 14). Despite such predictions, the year that the Eighteenth Amendment was ratified, Captain William H. Slayton founded the Association Against the Prohibition Amendment (AAPA), which lobbied throughout the next decade for repeal of the Eighteenth Amendment (Kyvig 1979, 39–52). A prominent supporter was New York Republican Senator James W. Wadsworth. In the mid-1920s the organization also received important support from the Du Pont family, especially Pierre. He enlisted the aid of John J. Raskob, who would later exert considerable influence for the repeal amendment after being appointed by Al Smith—the Democratic candidate for president in 1928—to chair the Democratic National Committee (Kyvig 1979, 101). Also important was the foundation in 1929 of the Women's Organization for National Prohibition Reform (WONPR). It provided something of a counterweight to the Women's Christian Temperance Union, which had been so influential in mustering support for the Eighteenth Amendment.

Almost from the adoption of the Eighteenth Amendment until its repeal, proposals were periodically introduced to modify it. Proposals included plans to repeal the amendment, hold a referendum on the question of repeal of the amendment, permit beverages with alcohol below a certain percentage (the Volstead Act, which enforced the Eighteenth Amendment, had applied even to beer with 3.2 percent alcohol content), or allow the federal government to tax and license alcoholic beverages.

Two events—the Great Depression, which began in 1929, and the election of 1932—eventually gave impetus to adoption of the Twenty-first Amendment. The first event encouraged the government to look at alcohol as a potential source of revenue as well as a source of employment. The second brought the Democratic Party into power. Whereas the Republican Convention of 1932 merely proposed allowing voters to consider repeal of the Eighteenth Amendment, the Democrats took a clear stand against Prohibition.

The vote for Democrats was so overwhelming that the lame-duck Congress ended up repealing the amendment even before the new one came into office. Initially, the Senate version contained four sections: Section 1 would have repealed the Eighteenth Amendment; Section 2 reserved to the states and territories powers to regulate alcohol; Section 3 granted Congress concurrent power to regulate the consumption of alcohol at places of sale (an antisaloon provision); and Section 4 set a seven-year ratification deadline. Section 3 was subsequently deleted, and Section 4 was modified to provide for ratification by state conventions rather than state legislatures. This move may have been stimulated in part by discussion generated by the decision in *Hawke v. Smith* (1920), in which the Supreme Court had struck down Ohio's attempt to decide on the ratification of the Eighteenth Amendment by a state referendum; the convention mechanism also helped bypass state legislatures that were believed to be dominated by dry forces.

The Senate voted 63 to 23 (10 not voting) for this amendment on 16 February 1933, and the House followed with a vote of 289 to 121 (with 16 not voting) on 20 February (U.S. Senate 1985, 67–68). In the absence of federal guidelines, states set up their own ratifying conventions (see E. Brown 1935, 1938). These bodies served more as referendums on Prohibition than deliberative assemblies, and the amendment was ratified in a record (for then) of 10 months. Of some 21 million Americans who voted on the subject, 72.9 percent expressed support of repeal (Kyvig 1979, 178).

Ironically, it was predominantly Mormon Utah that jockeyed its deliberations to provide the thirty-sixth ratification needed to put the amendment over the top (Kyvig 1979, 182).

On at least five occasions from 1935 to 1939, Texas Democratic Senator Morris Sheppard, author of the Eighteenth Amendment, introduced resolutions to repeal the Twenty-first Amendment, thereby reinstating national alcoholic prohibition. In 1938 Democratic Representative Gomer Smith of Oklahoma introduced an amendment prohibiting drunkenness in the United States and its territories.

It should be noted that the Twenty-first Amendment recognizes that states have explicit power over alcohol. Many states use a local option system that gives individual cities and counties considerable autonomy to decide what regulation of alcohol is appropriate. In her dissenting opinion in *South Dakota v. Dole* (1987), Justice Sandra Day O'Connor argued that the amendment gave states authority to set their own minimum drinking age free of federal threats to cut state highway budgets. In 1996 the U.S. Supreme Court decided in *44 Liquormart v. Rhode Island* that the Twenty-first Amendment does not negate First Amendment free speech rights; the Court thus voided a state law prohibiting the advertisement of liquor prices in newspapers or on billboards.

See also Eighteenth Amendment; Ratification of Amendments.

For Further Reading:

Kyvig, David E. 1979. *Repealing National Prohibition*. Chicago: University of Chicago Press.

Kyvig, David E., ed. 1985. *Alcohol and Order: Perspectives on National Prohibition*. Westport, CT: Greenwood Press.

❖ TWENTY-FOURTH AMENDMENT ❖

Initially intended to serve as a means of ascertaining that voters had a financial stake in the community, the poll tax was increasingly used after the Civil War as a means of keeping African Americans from voting. In *Breedlove v.*

Suttles (1937), the Supreme Court unanimously upheld such a state law against a challenge under the equal protection clause of the Fourteenth Amendment.

In 1941 Democratic Representative Lee Geyer of California introduced legislation to repeal state poll taxes; Geyer also founded the short-lived National Committee to Abolish the Poll Tax (Lawson 1976, 61). The next year, the House of Representatives voted favorably on the bill, but it was killed in the Senate by a filibuster. By the late 1950s, the House had voted favorably on such legislation on five occasions, but the Senate had never approved it (Ogden 1958, 243).

In part because of continuing questions about the constitutionality of such legislation, opponents of the poll tax increasingly began to focus on proposals for a constitutional amendment that had first been introduced in 1941. Florida Democratic Senator Spessard Holland was a persistent and forceful advocate of this amendment. By June 1961, his proposal (S.J. Res. 58) had sixty-seven cosponsors, but it was tied up in the Senate Judiciary Committee by the committee chair, Democrat James O. Eastland of Mississippi. In order to break this logjam, the Committee on Interior and Insular Affairs subsequently introduced a resolution (S.J. Res. 29) to make Alexander Hamilton's house a national monument. By prearrangement, this resolution instead became the focus of the poll tax issue. After ten days, debate was cut off, and thereafter, the Holland amendment was successfully offered as a substitute and approved by a vote of 77 to 16 on 27 March 1961. Leaders of the House suspended the rules to limit debate, and it approved the amendment 294 to 86 (with 54 not voting and 1 voting present) on 27 August 1961 (U.S. Senate 1985, 75–76). The necessary number of states ratified by February 1964, but by then, only five states still retained such a tax (Bernstein with Agel 1993, 138). In a telling demonstration of the symbolic power of amendments, a group of high school students subsequently organized a successful effort to add North Carolina's ratification during the celebration of the bicentennial of the U.S. Constitution ("North Carolina Ratifies the 24th Amendment" 1989).

The Twenty-fourth Amendment provides that "the right of citizens of the United States to vote in any primary or other election for President or Vice President, or for Senator or Representative in Congress, shall not be denied or abridged by the United States or any State by reason of failure to pay any poll tax or other tax." Section 2 vests enforcement authority in Congress.

The language of the amendment covers only federal elections, but in *Harper v. Virginia State Board of Elections* (1966), the Supreme Court overturned *Breedlove v. Suttles* (1937) and held that such a tax violated the equal protection clause of the Fourteenth Amendment. At least in retrospect, this decision suggests that the Supreme Court might have accepted a legislative rather than a constitutional solution to the poll tax problem. Such a judicial decision might not, however, have had either the same symbolic importance or the same staying power of a constitutional amendment.

For Further Reading:

Bernstein, Richard B., with Jerome Agel. 1993. *Amending America: If We Love the Constitution So Much, Why Do We Keep Trying to Change It?* New York: Random House.

Lawson, Steven F. 1976. *Black Ballots: Voting Rights in the South, 1944–1969.* New York: Columbia University Press.

"North Carolina Ratifies the 24th Amendment." 1989. *We the People: A Newsletter of the Commission on the Bicentennial of the United States Constitution* 5 (July): 10.

Ogden, Frederic D. 1958. *The Poll Tax in the South.* University: University of Alabama Press.

U.S. Senate, Subcommittee on the Constitution, Committee on the Judiciary. 1985. *Amendments to the Constitution: A Brief Legislative History.* Washington, DC: U.S. Government Printing Office.

❖ TWENTY-SECOND AMENDMENT ❖

One of the most persistent proposals for reform in U.S. history was the one that ultimately resulted in the Twenty-second Amendment. Exempting the current presidential officeholder (President Harry S. Truman) from its provisions, this amendment limited all subsequent persons from being elected as president more than twice or, in the case of a vice president who succeeded to the presidency, from serving a total of more than ten years.

Proposals for Reform
At least 270 proposals for term limits were introduced in Congress from 1789 to 1947, with the average frequency increasing from just over one per session in the first 100 years, to two from 1890 to 1928, and to three thereafter (Willis and Willis 1952, 469). Although it is probably true that the American people "show little sign of wanting to abandon the Twenty-second Amendment" (M. Nelson 1989, 48), numerous proposals have been introduced in Congress both to lift the two-term limit and to substitute a single six-year presidential term.

The Constitutional Convention and Early Practices
At the Constitutional Convention of 1787, the original Virginia plan, which contemplated that Congress would select the president, proposed a single term of unspecified length (Padover 1962, 53). Delegates apparently feared that separation of powers might be undermined if a president attempted to bargain with legislators to gain reelection. With the invention of the electoral college mechanism—in which members would meet only once within individual states and then dissolve—this fear largely evaporated, and the delegates decided not to impose any term limits. Indeed, Alexander Hamilton defended the president's "duration in office" as a key to executive energy and firmness. Writing in *Federalist No. 72* Hamilton noted that "nothing appears more plausible at first sight, nor more ill founded upon close inspection, than a scheme . . . of continuing the Chief Magistrate in office for a certain time, and then excluding him from it, either for a limited period, or forever after" (Hamilton, Madison, and Jay 1961, 437).

President George Washington decided to retire after two terms, and President John Adams was defeated in his bid for a second term. In responding to a request from the Vermont state legislature encouraging him to run for a third term, President Thomas Jefferson, who appears to have left open the possibility of running for a third term if it were necessary to exclude a "monarchist" from gaining the presidency (Peabody and Gant 1999, 579), elevated Washington's prudent decision not to run for a third term into a political principle (M. Nelson 1989, 46–47). President Andrew Jackson later urged Congress to propose an amendment limiting the president to a single four- or six-year term (J. Richardson 1908, 2:519, 3:117). The Senate approved two term limits in 1824 and 1826, but both died in the House; the constitution of the Confederate States of America provided for a single six-year term (Stathis 1990, 63). Presidents Ulysses S. Grant and Woodrow Wilson were tempted to run for third terms. The House dampened Grant's hopes when, in December 1875, it passed a resolution, known as the "Springer Resolution," stating that the "precedent established by Washington and other presidents of the United States, in retiring from the presidential office after their second term, has become, by universal concurrence, a part of our republican scheme of government" (quoted in Stathis 1990, 64), but this did not keep Grant, four years after the end of his second term, from leading on the first thirty-five ballots at the Republican Party Convention before James A. Garfield was eventually selected (Peabody and Gant 1999, 581). Theodore Roosevelt, who had served a full second term and all but six months of his first term when he took office after William McKinley's assassination, ran as a Progressive, or "Bull-Moose," candidate for president in 1912, after waiting out four years and failing to secure the nomination from his own Republican Party. The election of 1912 led to a favorable Senate vote on a single six-year term, but the measure died after incoming President Woodrow Wilson (who appears, prior to his own serious health problems, to have considered the possibility of a third term) announced his opposition to it (Sundquist 1986, 46). The two-term tradition seemed so well fixed by 1925 that Herbert Horwill cited it as part of the United States' customs and usages that rose to the level of constitutional principles.

Adoption of the Twenty-second Amendment

Faced with the outbreak of World War II in Europe, President Franklin D. Roosevelt consented to renomination in 1940 (he sent signals that he would accept a party draft without actively "running" for the renomination) and was eventually elected to four terms, his last being cut short by his death. The fact that he had broken with the two-term tradition was an issue that was especially hotly discussed in the 1940 election. Republican frustrations with his multiple terms appear to have accounted in large part for adoption of the Twenty-second Amendment (Stathis 1990). The Twenty-second Amendment passed the House by a vote of 285 to 121 in February 1947 and the Senate by a vote of 59 to 23 the following month. By a vote of 82 to 1, the Senate rejected a substitute amendment that would have fixed the terms of all federal officeholders at six years (Willis and Willis 1952, 478). The partisan aspects of support for the amendment were demonstrated by the fact that Republicans supported the amendment unanimously in both the House (238 to 0) and the Senate (46 to 0), whereas Democrats opposed it by respective votes of 121 to 47 and 23 to 13. President Harry S. Truman, who later criticized the amendment after it had been adopted, basically stayed on the sidelines, and the amendment took almost four full years to be ratified, a record prior to the putative ratification of the Twenty-seventh Amendment in 1993 (M. Nelson 1989, 47–48). Of thousands of Republican state legislators whose votes were recorded, only 83 voted against the amendment (Stathis 1990, 70).

Issues and Consequences

Some of the debates over presidential term limits were surprisingly similar to more modern debates over congressional term limits, with which such proposals were often conjoined. Proponents argued that long terms threaten a system of separated powers and checks and balances. Perhaps remembering that Franklin Roosevelt's decision to seek a third term had been a prominent campaign issue, opponents said that the people decided whether to impose

term limits when they voted (Willis and Willis 1952, 476–478).

Prior to the adoption of the Twenty-second Amendment, there were actually more proposals for a single presidential term—ranging from four to eight years, with four- and six-year proposals being most common—than there were for a two-term limit. A two-term limit appears to have tilted some power away from the president and toward Congress, but a one-term limit would arguably have had a much greater impact, effectively making every elected president a lame duck and thereby increasing congressional control over lawmaking (Willis and Willis 1952, 480). The one-term proposal continues to be introduced, sometimes along with proposals for direct popular election or proposals for limiting other officeholders. Supporters of a single six-year presidential term have included Republican Senator Jesse Helms of North Carolina (1977), Democratic Representative John Conyers of Michigan (1980), Democratic Senator Lloyd Bentsen of Texas (1981), and Republican Senator Strom Thurmond of South Carolina (1981).

Despite the Republican role in ratification of the amendment, to date, its effects have been felt primarily by two Republican presidents, Dwight D. Eisenhower and Ronald Reagan (although there had been some indication prior to the Watergate controversy that Richard Nixon might also be interested in running for a third term, and, despite his impeachment, Bill Clinton continued to be popular enough that a run for a third term could have been a possibility). Interestingly, twenty-four of twenty-nine scholars who responded to a survey in 1957 indicated their belief that the amendment ought to be repealed (Stathis 1990, 73). While in office, Reagan lobbied for repeal of the amendment, and resolutions to this effect continue to be introduced in Congress. In the lead essay in a book published after he left office, Reagan described the Twenty-second Amendment as "a perversion of the Constitution's sound design for a limited but energetic government" (Reagan et al. 1990, 1). He was particularly concerned about the effect the amendment had on a president's effectiveness during his second term.

Parsing the language and examining the history of the Twenty-second Amendment, two recent scholars have argued that there are at least six circumstances under which it might be possible for an individual who has already served two terms to serve for a period as president or acting president, as long as such service did not involve another *election* to the *presidential* office. Their examples include the case of an individual who had served for two terms as president, was then elected as *vice president,* and either succeeded a president who had died, stepped aside in the ex-presidents's favor, or served as "acting president" during the newly elected president's illness. These authors succeed in demonstrating that the language of the amendment, the result of apparent compromise between those in Congress who wanted an absolute two-term limit and those who were willing to allow individuals who had succeeded another president in the second half of that president's term to serve two addition terms, is not as clear as it could be. They ultimately conclude, however, that officeholding in the circumstances that they outline, if not absolutely unconstitutional, "would seemingly amount to 'constitutional improprieties'" (Peabody and Gant 1999, 632 citing a term apparently coined by Stephen L. Carter).

See also Congress, Term Limits; Electoral College Reform.

For Further Reading:
Hamilton, Alexander, James Madison, and John Jay. 1787–1788. *The Federalist Papers.* Reprint, New York: New American Library, 1961.
Nelson, Michael, ed. 1989. *Guide to the Presidency.* Washington, DC: Congressional Quarterly.
Padover, Saul K. 1962. *To Secure These Blessings.* New York: Washington Square Press/Ridge Press.
Peabody, Bruce G., and Scott E. Gant. 1999. "The Twice and Future President: Constitutional Interstices and the Twenty-second Amendment." *Minnesota Law Review* 83 (February): 565–635.
Reagan, Ronald, et al. 1990. *Restoring the Presidency: Reconsidering the Twenty-second Amendment.* Washington, DC: National Legal Center for Public Interest.
Richardson, James E., ed. 1908. *A Compilation of the Messages and Papers of the Presidents, 1789–1908.* 11 vols. n.p.: Bureau of National Literature and Art.
Stathis, Stephen. 1990. "The Twenty-second Amendment: A Practical Remedy or Partisan Maneuver?" *Constitutional Commentary* 7 (Winter): 61–88.
Sundquist, James L. 1986. *Constitutional Reform and Effective Government.* Washington, DC: Brookings Institution.
Willis, Paul G., and George L. Willis. 1952. "The Politics of the Twenty-second Amendment." *Western Political Quarterly* 5 (September): 469–482.

❖ TWENTY-SEVENTH AMENDMENT ❖

Article I, Section 6 of the U.S. Constitution provides that "the Senators and Representatives shall receive a Compensation for their Services, to be ascertained by Law, and paid out of the Treasury of the United States." The latter part of this clause is especially important because it enabled legislators to gain an independence that they might not have had if their salaries had been dependent on the states (Bernstein 1992, 502).

The fact that members of Congress are elected could be a plausible argument for protection against congressional aggrandizement, but when the Constitution was being debated, three states sensed enough danger that they proposed amendments to limit congressional pay raises. In compiling a bill of rights in the First Congress in 1789, James Madison proposed an amendment specifying that "no law, varying the compensation for the services of the Senators and Representatives, shall take effect, until an election of Representatives shall have intervened." This was originally the second of twelve amendments submitted to the states, but as only six states ratified it, it did not become part of the Bill of Rights.

In the nineteenth century, congressional pay increases twice provoked renewed pleas for ratification of the congressional pay-raise amendment. In 1817 Congress passed a compensation bill switching its salary from $6 a day to $1,500 a year and provoking such controversy that the bill was repealed—albeit not retroactively. Many members, including Daniel Webster (then representing New Hampshire), were voted out of office (Miller and Dewey 1991, 98). Similarly, in 1873 Congress adopted what became known as the Salary Grab Act, retroactively increasing salaries by $2,500 a year and provoking such outrage that it was repealed (Bernstein 1992, 534). The original second amendment was reintroduced in Congress, and Ohio ratified it eighty-two years after the last ratification (Strickland 1993, 716).

Congress twice voted to cut its salary during the Great Depression, but the twentieth century otherwise witnessed a steady progression of congressional salary increases. Salaries went from $10,000 a year in 1935 to $125,100 in August 1991 (Bernstein 1992, 535). Moreover, Congress invented a number of mechanisms by which pay raises could be recommended by special commissions and go into effect without a direct vote. In 1978, 105 years after Ohio's ratification, Wyoming became the eighth state to ratify the pay-raise amendment. During this same period, faith in Congress appeared to decline, as members were caught in check-kiting controversies involving the congressional credit union and in questions of undue influence in the failure of prominent savings and loan institutions (Vile 1992, 15–16).

In 1982 Gregory Watson, a student at the University of Texas at Austin, wrote a term paper for a government course in which he examined the congressional pay-raise amendment and concluded that it could still be ratified. Although he received a "C" from his skeptical instructor (Bernstein 1992, 537), he launched a one-man effort and spent over $5,000 of his own money to persuade additional state legislatures to ratify. The effort was not a very public one, but from 1983 to 1992, an additional thirty-two states ratified. On 14 May 1992, Don Wilson, the national archivist, certified the amendment as part of the Constitution, a decision that was approved shortly thereafter by votes of 99 to 0 in the Senate and 414 to 3 in the House (Bernstein 1992, 542).

Wilson's certification and the congressional votes have not necessarily settled the legitimacy issue. In *Dillon v. Gloss* (1921), the Supreme Court indicated that, to be valid, ratifications of amendments should be contemporaneous with their proposal. In *Coleman v. Miller* (1939), the Court later ruled that the issue of contemporaneousness was a political question for Congress to solve, but subsequent cases appear to have eroded this precedent. Not surprisingly, the putative ratification of the Twenty-seventh Amendment has stirred considerable rethinking of the amending process (Dalzell and Beste 1994; Paulsen 1993; Levinson 1994; Spotts 1994; Van Alstyne 1993).

A U.S. district court decision in *Boehner v. Anderson* (1992) ruled that automatic cost-of-living adjustments for members of Congress that were provided in the Ethics Reform Act of 1989 were not prohibited by the Twenty-seventh Amendment, and this decision was subsequently affirmed by the U.S. Court of Appeals for the District of Columbia. This and other developments have led at least some observers to believe that the late ratification of the Twenty-seventh Amendment may have made courts more reticent to enforce its provisions than had the amendment been ratified in a more regularized fashion.

See also Watson, Gregory.

For Further Reading:

Bernstein, Richard B. 1992. "The Sleeper Wakes: The History and Legacy of the Twenty-seventh Amendment." *Fordham Law Review* 56 (December): 497–557.

Boehner v. Anderson, 1809 F. Supp. 138 (1992), aff'd 30 F.3d 156 (1994).

Dalzell, Stewart, and Eric J. Beste. 1994. "Is the Twenty-seventh Amendment 200 Years Too Late?" *George Washington Law Review* 62 (April): 501–545.

Levinson, Sanford. 1994. "Authorizing Constitutional Text: On the Purported Twenty-seventh Amendment." *Constitutional Commentary* 11 (Winter): 101–113.

Paulsen, Michael S. 1993. "A General Theory of Article V: The Constitutional Issues of the Twenty-seventh Amendment." *Yale Law Journal* 103: 677–789.

Spotts, JoAnne D. 1994. "The Twenty-seventh Amendment: A Late Bloomer or a Dead Horse?"

Georgia State University Law Review 10 (January): 337–365.

Strickland, Ruth A. 1993. "The Twenty-seventh Amendment and Constitutional Change by Stealth." *P.S. Political Science and Politics* 26 (December): 716–722.

Van Alstine, William. 1993. "What Do You Think about the Twenty-seventh Amendment?" *Constitutional Commentary* 10 (Winter): 9–18.

Vile, John R. 1992. *The Constitutional Amending Process in American Political Thought.* New York: Praeger.

❖ TWENTY-SIXTH AMENDMENT ❖

Under the Constitution, voting qualifications are set by the states, subject to any restrictions incorporated in constitutional amendments. Prior to 1971 there were no constitutional age restrictions for voting, although Section 2 of the Fourteenth Amendment had implicitly sanctioned the widespread twenty-one-year minimum (as well as all-male suffrage, which was not eliminated until adoption of the Nineteenth Amendment in 1920) by specifying that state representation in Congress could be reduced only when states denied the vote to men twenty-one years of age or older.

World War II marks the beginning of interest in reducing the voting age to eighteen. This reduction was tied to the fact that many men were being drafted for military service at that age, and it seemed ironic that one could be called upon to defend a nation in which one could not vote. In 1942 at least four members of Congress introduced resolutions to reduce the voting age to eighteen. They were Republican Senator Arthur Vanderberg of Michigan and Democratic Representatives Jennings Randolph of West Virginia and Jed Johnson and Victor Wickersham of Oklahoma. More than 150 proposals were subsequently introduced between 1942 and 1971, with an occasional proposal to set the age at nineteen rather than eighteen, and with New York Democratic Representative Emanuel Celler of New York introducing at least one proposal in 1954 to freeze the age at twenty-one. In 1953 the Senate debated a resolution to lower the voting age to eighteen, but it failed by a vote of thirty-four to twenty-four (U.S. Senate 1985, 89).

Support for the amendment increased during the Vietnam War, and Congress held hearings on the subject in 1968 and 1970. The public and some members of Congress—a number of whom had proposed extending the vote to active-duty military personnel regardless of age—may have been focusing on the link between military service and voting. The hearings, however, tended to put greater emphasis on the increased educational levels of modern youth (perhaps in recognition that only men could be drafted). The hearings also cited other responsibilities and privileges that eighteen-to-twenty-one-year-olds were exercising—including driving automobiles, drinking alcohol (an age that most states have subsequently raised), holding jobs, having families, being tried as adults in court, and attending college. Although some witnesses pointed to antiwar demonstrations as evidence that eighteen-to-twenty-one-year-olds were immature, others, including future Republican Senator Samuel I. Hayakawa, joined those who attributed such demonstrations to a small group of radicals rather than to the age group as a whole (*Hearings* 1970, 36–43).

After the hearings, Massachusetts Democratic Senator Edward Kennedy focused on the Supreme Court's decision in *Katzenbach v. Morgan* (1966) upholding federal suspension of state literacy tests. He suggested bypassing the amending process and lowering the voting age by statute, and such a provision was subsequently added to the Voting Rights Act of 1970. The testimony of Assistant Attorney General (later chief justice) William Rehnquist that this could be accomplished only through amendment (Hearings 1970, 233–249) proved prescient. In *Oregon v. Mitchell* (1970), a narrow Court majority, with Justice Hugo Black holding the balance, decided that Congress could lower the voting age in federal but not in state elections.

Only three states had voting ages of eighteen (Georgia was the first to lower the age to eighteen in 1943), with three others setting the age at nineteen, three at twenty, and the rest at twenty-one (Grimes 1978, 142–143). This meant that absent repeal of the Voting Rights provision or adoption of an amendment, most states would have to create a dual voting system. This created the impetus for Jennings Randolph, then a West Virginia senator, to reintroduce the eighteen-year-old vote as an amendment. Accepted on 10 March 1971 by a vote of 94 to 7 in the Senate and on 23 March by a vote of 401 to 19 (with 12 not voting) in the House (U.S. Senate 1985, 90), the amendment was ratified within three months, the fastest ratification in U.S. history. Altogether, forty-two states ratified. Ironically, the eighteen-to-twenty-one age group has subsequently had one of the lowest voting rates in the general population.

In 1992 Minnesota Democratic Farm-Labor Representative Timothy Penny introduced a proposal to repeal the Twenty-sixth Amendment and lower the voting age to sixteen, but this proposal did not garner significant support. The eighteen-year age requirement seems unlikely to be changed in the near future.

See also *Oregon v. Mitchell.*

For Further Reading:

Grimes, Alan P. 1978. *Democracy and the Amendments to the Constitution.* Lexington, MA: Lexington Books.

Hearings before the Subcommittee on Constitutional Amendments of the Committee on the Judiciary: *Lowering the Voting Age to 18.* 1968. U.S. Senate, 90th Cong., 2d Sess., 14, 15, 16 May.

U.S. Senate, Subcommittee on the Constitution, Committee on the Judiciary. 1985. *Amendments to the Constitution: A Brief Legislative History.* Washington, DC: U.S. Government Printing Office.

Uradnik, Kathleen. 2002. *Student's Guide to Landmark Congressional Laws on Youth.* Westport, CT: Greenwood Press.

❖ TWENTY-THIRD AMENDMENT ❖

Because Article II, Section 1 of the Constitution limited the selection of presidential electors to states, Washington, D.C., had no input in presidential elections up to 1961. At that time, its population exceeded that of the thirteen least populous states (U.S. Senate 1985, 75). As early as 1883, Republican Representative Henry Blair of New Hampshire introduced an amendment to remedy this situation by granting the District representation in the electoral college. More than a dozen such proposals were introduced in Congress between 1915 and 1923, with others following from 1945 and thereafter.

In 1959 Tennessee Democratic Senator Estes Kefauver introduced S.J. Res. 39 to provide for the emergency functioning of Congress by granting state governors the right to fill mass vacancies. When the Senate Committee on the Judiciary reported this amendment favorably to the Senate floor, Florida Democrat Spessard Holland proposed an amendment to abolish the poll tax (a proposal that later became the Twenty-fourth Amendment), and New York Republican Kenneth B. Keating introduced an amendment to grant the District of Columbia both the right to select presidential electors and the right to representation in the House of Representatives (Grimes 1978, 127; U.S. Senate 1985, 76–77). The Senate voted favorably on all three proposals and sent them to the House.

The House decided to concentrate on H.J. Res. 757, a proposal introduced by Democrat Emanuel Celler of New York containing the current language of the Twenty-third Amendment. It grants the District "a number of electors of President and Vice President equal to the whole number of Senators and Representatives in Congress to which the District would be entitled if it were a State, but in no event more than the least populous state [which is entitled to three]." Although this proposal was criticized for being too narrow, Celler argued that his proposal was more likely to be ratified and indicated that he had agreed to support Holland's poll tax amendment separately (Grimes 1978, 129).

The House approved the Celler amendment by voice vote on 14 June 1960, and the Senate concurred, also by voice, on 16 June 1960. The amendment was ratified in nine months, with New Hampshire rescinding its 29 March ratification and readopting it the next day to become the thirty-eighth state to approve, providing the necessary three-fourths (U.S. Senate 1985, 77).

The Twenty-third Amendment did not completely equalize the District of Columbia's weight in the electoral college, because the District still has no role in the event that the House or Senate has to decide an electoral deadlock. Rhode Island Democrat Claiborne Pell introduced amendments in 1963 and 1967 to remedy this situation. The unratified amendment that Congress proposed in 1978 to treat the District of Columbia as a state for purposes of representation in Congress, presidential and vice presidential electors, and the amending process contained an explicit repeal of the Twenty-third Amendment, and at least one scholar has argued that the adoption of the Twenty-third Amendment "had the effect of thwarting a full, not to mention more equitable, resolution of the District of Columbia problem, which, as a result, is ongoing" (Kyvig 2000, 244). In 1990 Virginia Republican Representative Stanford Parris introduced an amendment to remove electors for the District of Columbia from the electoral college.

For Further Reading:

Grimes, Alan P. 1978. *Democracy and the Amendments to the Constitution.* Lexington, MA: Lexington Books.

Kyvig, David E. 2000. *Unintended Consequences of Constitutional Amendments.* Athens: The University of Georgia Press.

U.S. Senate, Subcommittee on the Constitution, Committee on the Judiciary. 1985. *Amendments to the Constitution: A Brief Legislative History.* Washington, DC: U.S. Government Printing Office.

❖ TWO-THIRDS MAJORITY TO PROPOSE AMENDMENTS ❖

Article V of the Constitution specifies that two-thirds majorities are required in both houses of Congress to propose constitutional amendments. Alternatively, in a still unused provision, Article V provides that two-thirds of the states may petition Congress for a constitutional convention. In the *National Prohibition Cases* (1920), the Supreme Court ruled that the two-thirds majority of Congress that is specified in Article V "is a vote of two-thirds of the members present—assuming the presence of a quorum—and not a vote of two-thirds of the entire membership, present and absent" (386). The Citizens for the Constitution authoring the Constitutional Amendment Initiative (who fear that future amendments might be proposed without adequate deliberation) have recently suggested that the two-thirds requirement should be of the entire house. Gregory Watson, the individual primarily responsible for ratification of the Twenty-seventh Amendment (related to the timing of congressional pay raises), has taken a similar position (Watson 2000, 16). The Citizens for the Constitution have also suggested that amendments should not be reported to the floor of Congress unless they have two-thirds support from the committee from which they originated.

In 1798 the U.S. Supreme Court decided in *Hollingsworth v. Virginia* (1798) that constitutional amendments did not require a president's signature. This decision may have been predicated in part on the fact that amendments are already proposed by the same majority required to overrule a presidential veto.

The two-thirds requirement for proposing amendments, like the three-fourths requirement for ratifying them, indicates that the amending process was not designed to incorporate all changes favored by the majority but only those with an unusually strong consensus behind them. In effect, the requirement for such majorities gives a veto to strong minority interests. The requirement for proposal would appear to have been a greater obstacle than the requirement for ratification by three-fourths of the states. To date states have ratified twenty-seven of the thirty-three amendments that Congress has proposed.

See also Citizens for the Constitution, the Constitutional Amendment Initiative; *Hollingsworth v. Virginia; National Prohibition Cases;* Watson, Gregory.

For Further Reading:

Watson, Gregory. 2000. "I Have a Better Way." *Insights on Law & Society* 1 (Fall): 16.

National Prohibition Cases, 253 U.S. 350 (1920).

U

❖

❖ UNFUNDED FEDERAL MANDATES ❖

The relation between the nation and the states was a concern even before the adoption of the U.S. Constitution, and it has continued to be so ever since. As the Supreme Court has recognized increasingly broad congressional powers under the provisions in Article I, Section 8 related to federal taxation and regulation of commerce between the states (see, for example, the analysis under Child Labor Amendment), some advocates of states' rights have argued that state powers have been unduly eroded in violation of the language and spirit of the Tenth Amendment.

The Supreme Court registered this concern when, in *National League of Cities v. Usery* (1976), it decided by a five-to-four vote that the wage and hour provisions of the Fair Labor Standards Act that applied to private industries should not apply to traditional state functions. In 1985, however, in another five-to-four decision, the Court reversed course in *Garcia v. San Antonio Metropolitan Transit Authority* and decided that the line between traditional and nontraditional state functions was too difficult for the Court to draw. It further decided that the Constitution gave states adequate representation within Congress and other parts of the national government to protect their own interests.

States have subsequently complained not only about such wage and hour regulations (indeed, states have actually succeeded in having some such regulations repealed) but also about unfunded congressional mandates that pass costs on to states and localities without providing federal funding for such requirements. The U.S. Conference of Mayors even sponsored a National Unfunded Mandate Day to protest what the mayors regarded as the unfair burden and the displacement of local choices that such mandates were imposing on states and localities (Gillmor and Eames 1994, 397).

Ohio Republican Congressman Paul Gillmor has proposed an amendment that would prohibit Congress from enacting unfunded mandates but would not prohibit states from voluntarily spending their own funds as a condition to receiving federal funds. Gillmor is especially concerned that the adoption of a balanced budget amendment "could increase the pressure for Congress to impose unfunded mandates" (Gillmor and Eames 1994, 410). Estimates of the cost of such mandates run up to $11 billion a year (Pear 1994, 20).

In March 1995 President Bill Clinton signed the Unfunded Mandate Reform Act, which had received a boost from the Republican congressional elections of 1994 (Hosanky 1995, 40). This act, which appears to undercut the need for a constitutional amendment, makes it more difficult for Congress to adopt unfunded mandates, requires more information about the projected costs of federal regulations, and restricts unfunded or underfunded federal mandates (Conlan, Riggle, and Schwartz 1995, 23). Members of Congress have continued, however, to propose an amendment that would give greater security to the provisions of this legislation.

See also Balanced Budget Amendment; Child Labor Amendment.

483

For Further Reading:

Conlan, Timothy J., James D. Riggle, and Donna E. Schwartz. 1995. "Deregulating Federalism? The Politics of Mandate Reform in the 104th Congress." *Publius: The Journal of Federalism* 25 (Summer): 23–40.

Gillmor, Paul, and Fred Eames. 1994. "Reconstruction of Federalism: A Constitutional Amendment to Prohibit Unfunded Mandates." *Harvard Journal on Legislation* 31 (Summer): 395–413.

Hosanky, David. 1995. "Mandate Bill Is More Moderate Than Proposed in 'Contract.'" *Congressional Quarterly Weekly Report* 53 (7 January): 40.

Pear, Robert. 1994. "State Officials Worry That a Federal Budget Will Be Balanced on Their Books." *New York Times,* 11 December, 34.

❖ UNINTENDED CONSEQUENCES OF CONSTITUTIONAL AMENDMENTS ❖

Once incorporated into the U.S. Constitution, constitutional amendments become the supreme law of the law. Scholars have long known that laws, court decisions, and constitutional amendments may all have unintended consequences. Although such consequences are therefore not unique to amendments, they can be more substantial in the case of amendments precisely because amendments are so difficult both to enact and repeal. The Twenty-first Amendment (repealing national alcoholic prohibition as established in the Eighteenth Amendment) remains the only example of an amendment that has specifically repealed another.

The consideration of unintended consequences thus becomes important when proposing amendments, especially amendments that appear to be politically popular, such as attempting to mandate balanced budgets or term limits, but whose full consequences may not be perceived until they are enacted. To take one of the most obvious examples, few people who proposed the Eighteenth Amendment favored the rise in organized crime that it appeared to spawn, as gangsters supplied the alcohol that individuals could not legally obtain. Similarly,

many believe that the Twenty-second Amendment, limiting American presidents to two full terms (or a total of ten years) in office, has had the effect of making presidents "lame ducks" during their second terms and thus enhancing congressional powers, while the Twenty-third amendment providing representation in the electoral college to the District of Columbia might have served to dissuade Congress from proposing a more comprehensive solution to this problem. Many scholars believe that expansive interpretations of the equal protection clause of the Fourteenth Amendment to include rights for women led many individuals to conclude that ratification of the Equal Rights Amendment was unnecessary. One substantial objection to the proposed Equal Rights Amendment for women was that, while expressing a noble aspiration, the language of the proposed amendment was so general that it left too much leeway to judicial interpretations, and, perhaps again, to unintended consequences.

For Further Reading:

Kyvig, David E., ed. 2000. *Unintended Consequences of Constitutional Amendments.* Athens: The University of Georgia Press.

❖ UNITED NATIONS ❖

The United Nations was created at the end of World War II in the hope of promoting international cooperation. Some individuals feared that such an organization might undermine the sovereignty of individual nations. This appears to have been the concern of Republican Representative Stephen Day of Illinois, who introduced an amending resolution in May 1944 intended to preserve "the independence and sovereignty of the United States" (H.J. Res 277). Similarly, a proposal introduced by North Dakota Democratic Representative Quentin Burdick in 1957 to prohibit the service of United States citizens under any banner other than the stars and stripes (H.J. Res 20) may have been aimed at U.S. participation in U.N. peacekeeping missions.

A key component of the organization is the Security Council. Originally composed of eleven members, five of which (including the United States) were permanent, the council has subsequently expanded to fifteen members. The five permanent members each have a veto, which was frequently wielded by both the United States and the Soviet Union during the Cold War period. Had Russia not been boycotting at the time of the Korean conflict, it is unlikely that actions could have been taken, as they were, to repel North Korea's invasion of the South.

The U.S. president appoints the U.S. ambassador to the United Nations with the advice and consent of the Senate. The year after the United Nations was established, Connecticut Republican Congresswoman Clare Boothe Luce introduced a resolution relative to the election of U.S. representatives to the Security Council. The proposal is otherwise obscure and does not appear to have elicited further congressional debate or support.

See also World Government.

For Further Reading:
Claude, Inis L., Jr. 1971. *Swords into Plowshares: The Problems and Progress of International Organization*. 4th ed. New York: Random House.

❖ UNITED STATES OF AMERICA, PROPOSED NAME CHANGES ❖

Simon Willard Jr. authored a proposed new Constitution for the United States in 1816 (treated in greater detail elsewhere in this volume) that gave great attention to the idea of renaming the United States Columbia, in honor of Christopher Columbus. It appears that there were others at the time who also believed the nation should be named in Columbus's honor. Radical Republican Representative George Washington Anderson of Missouri proposed an amendment shortening the nation's name to America in 1866 (H.R. 61). Similarly, Wisconsin Democratic Representative Lucas Miller introduced an amendment in 1893 to rename the nation the United States of the World (H.J. Res. 208). This latter name corresponded with that proposed by Victoria Claflin Woodhull in 1870 (Stern 1974). After first suggesting that it be called "the United Republic of America," Rexford Tugwell wrote a proposed constitution for what he designated the "Newstates of America."

See also Willard, Simon, Jr.; Woodhull, Victoria Claflin.

For Further Reading:
Stern, Madeline B., ed. 1974. *The Victoria Woodhull Reader*. Weston, MA: M & S Press.

❖ *UNITED STATES V. EICHMAN* (1990) ❖

After the U.S. Supreme Court invalidated a Texas statute preventing flag desecration in *Texas v. Johnson* (1989), members of Congress who opposed the decision had to decide whether to respond with a flag-burning amendment or with legislation. A majority adopted the latter course, passing the Flag Protection Act of 1989. Protesters in Seattle and Washington, D.C., immediately challenged this law.

The Flag Protection Act asserted an interest in preserving the nation's flag without making reference to explicit content-based limitations on speech. Still, the Supreme Court found that "it is nevertheless clear that the Government's asserted *interest* is 'related "to the suppression of free expression"' . . . and concerned with the content of such expression" (*Eichman* 1990, 315). As in *Texas v. Johnson*, the Court found that the law "suppresses expression out of concern for its likely communicative impact" (*Id.*, 317) and must be subject to strict scrutiny under the First Amendment. In exercising such scrutiny, a majority of five justices led by Justice William Brennan refused to overrule its earlier decision and thus struck down the new law. Justice John Paul Stevens authored the dissenting opinion, restating his stance in the earlier case. The push for a flag desecration amendment gained renewed momentum after the historic elections of 1994.

See also Flag Desecration; *Texas v. Johnson*.

For Further Reading:
United States v. Eichman, 496 U.S. 310 (1990).

❖ *UNITED STATES V. MORRISON* (2000) ❖

This recent Supreme Court decision is helpful in understanding the current Court's posture in interpreting congressional powers under its enforcement powers in Section 5 of the Fourteenth Amendment; toward federalism; and, by implication, toward the Tenth Amendment, which reserves certain unspecified powers to the states. At issue in *Morrison* was a provision of the Violence Against Women Act of 1994 that allowed citizens to bring federal civil suits against perpetrators of crimes motivated by a victim's gender (prior to this time, an individual would have to bring any such claims under state law). In this case, a former student of Virginia Tech had brought a civil suit against two football players for rape after the university ultimately failed to discipline either player.

In a narrow five-to-four majority decision written by Chief Justice William Rehnquist and joined by Justices O'Connor, Scalia, Kennedy, and Thomas, the Supreme Court built on an earlier opinion in *United States v. Lopez* (1995)—a case that had invalidated a federal gun law punishing individuals who brought a gun within a specified distance from a school. Here, as in that case, the Court decided that Congress had exceeded its authority both under Article I, Section 8, which grants specific powers to Congress as well as the power to make all laws "necessary and proper" to carrying out those listed, and under Section 5 of the Fourteenth Amendment, which provides power to enforce other provisions of that amendment. As in *Lopez,* the Court decided that there was an inadequate showing that the law in question was related to congressional control either of the channels or instrumentalities of interstate commerce or of a matter that had a "substantial relation" to such commerce (*Morrison,* 609). Although Congress had demonstrated the pervasiveness and widespread impact of violence against women, the Court thought that the tie to economic damages, and hence to interstate *commerce,* was weak.

The Court majority further expressed concern that, if such an impact were accepted here, in a matter previously understood to be governed by criminal law or state tort law (both traditional areas for the exercise of state police powers), there would be literally little or nothing left for state control. In interpreting federal authority under Section 5 of the Fourteenth Amendment, the Court noted that previous interpretations of this amendment had limited congressional remedies to violations of individual rights that were the result of state action rather than to control over the actions of private individuals.

Justices Souter, Stevens, Ginsburg, and Breyer all dissented, believing that Congress had demonstrated adequate connection between the Violence Against Women Act and its power to regulate commerce. This narrow division has long characterized Supreme Court decision making relative to federalism. Such jurisprudence could be readily influenced either by future appointments to the Court or by the adoption of future amendments.

See also Fourteenth Amendment; Tenth Amendment.

For Further Reading:
United States v. Lopez, 514 U.S. 549 (1995).
United States v. Morrison, 529 U.S. 528 (2000).

❖ *UNITED STATES V. SPRAGUE* (1931) ❖

This case, like the *National Prohibition Cases* (1920), arose from a challenge to the Eighteenth Amendment. Although citing its own rationale, the U.S. district court accepted the conclusion of Seldon Bacon and other opponents of the Prohibition Amendment, who argued that no matter what Congress specified, such an amendment restricting the rights of the people could not be appropriately ratified by state legislatures. Instead, it required ratification by state conventions.

In writing the unanimous opinion for the Court, in which Chief Justice Charles Evans Hughes did not participate, Justice Owen

Roberts argued that the "plain language of Article V" should take priority over any hypothesized "intent of its framers" (*Sprague* 1931, 729). Citing the language of Article V of the Constitution, Roberts argued that the choice between the two means of ratification "rests solely in the discretion of Congress" (*Id.*, 732). Because Congress in making this selection acts "as the delegated agent of the people in the choice of the method of ratification," it is not limited (as Bacon had argued) by the Tenth Amendment, which refers to powers "not delegated to the United States" rather than to powers specifically delegated to Congress (*Id.*, 733).

Roberts further argued that, contrary to Bacon's argument, a number of prior amendments—most notably "the Thirteenth, Fourteenth, Sixteenth, and Nineteenth," all of which the Court had accepted—also touched on the rights of individual citizens (*Sprague* 1931, 734). The Court's acceptance of the lawfulness of their ratifications was an additional argument for accepting the lawfulness of the Eighteenth Amendment.

Ironically, the Eighteenth Amendment would be repealed within two years of the decision in *United States v. Sprague* by the Twenty-first Amendment in the very manner—namely, by state conventions—by which its opponents said that it should have been ratified.

See also Eighteenth Amendment; Twenty-first Amendment.

For Further Reading:
United States v. Sprague, 282 U.S. 716 (1931).

❖ UNRATIFIED AMENDMENTS ❖

See Failed Amendments.

❖ UNWRITTEN CONSTITUTION ❖

See Customs and Usages; Relevance of Constitutional Amendments.

❖ UPHAM, THOMAS CARLTON (1894–?) ❖

About the only biographical information that is known about Thomas C. Upham is the proposal for a new constitution that he apparently composed in large part in 1937 and 1938 and offered in a book published in 1941 (Boyd 1992, 176). In this proposal, Upham provided a bit of biographical insight when he noted that part of his antipathy to charity derived from the fact that "I have had to take charity myself a few times" (Upham 1941, 56).

Upham aimed to "retain much of the framework, some of the contents, and all of the spirit—plus—of the old constitution" (Upham 1941, 32). While building on the existing document, Upham proposed a number of utopian and socialistic features, and he was particularly concerned about promoting greater equality. His preamble lists, among other objectives, that of forming a society "of mutual co-operation, human brotherhood, general kindliness, common welfare, equal rights, economic security, material prosperity, and universal peace" (*Id.*, 67).

Upham's constitution begins with the executive branch, consisting of a president nominated by petition and elected by a plurality of voters for a single six-year term. A senator would succeed the president in case of vacancy or incapacity. The president's power as commander in chief would be subject to override by a three-fourths vote of Congress. The president would have the right to submit legislation directly to Congress or to the people for approval and would be subject to recall by petition and a vote of two-thirds of the population.

The Senate would consist of seventeen nonpartisan citizens elected for a maximum of two six-year terms. Each would also head one of seventeen departments, including one dealing with "cultural security" and another with "private relations" (Upham 1941, 77). Members of the House would be chosen from twenty-four newly created districts that would take the place of the existing state and local governments, which Upham would eliminate. Congressional laws would be subject to an item veto. The people would have the right of petition, referendum, and recall.

The Supreme Court would be maintained, with justices retiring at age seventy-five. There would also be district courts and criminal boards. Petit juries would consist of six local citizens and six citizens from another part of the country, with a guarantee that at least one juror would be "of the same race, color, sex, and religious persuasion as the accused" (Upham 1941, 91). Government attorneys would serve both as defense counsel and as prosecutors.

At age eighteen every citizen would have the obligation to register for citizenship. Citizens would be required to work from age twenty-one to seventy. They could not be required to work more than five days and thirty-five hours a week and would be guaranteed a two-week vacation. All would be paid on a standard wage scale ranging (for those aged twenty-four to sixty) from $1,000 a year to $10,000 a year so that the maximum wage would be no more than ten times the minimum. Although individuals would be permitted to own small businesses, the government would own major industries, and individuals would be limited to owning $100,000 of private property. Strikes would be outlawed, medical care and education would be guaranteed to all, charity would be forbidden, and all citizens would be required to learn English. A "work and wages" standard would replace the gold standard (Upham 1941, 113). Rights would be protected against both governmental and private action, with existing rights preserved and occasionally expanded.

Wars would be outlawed, some exception apparently being made for defense and for actions within the Western Hemisphere (Upham 1941, 61). The United States would seek to form an international union that would work for "the attainment of Christian or other good ideals in the world" (*Id.,* 115).

Upham favored calling a convention of eighty-four individuals to write the constitution, its work to become effective when ratified by the people. Future amendments would be instituted by two-thirds of both houses of Congress and ratified by two-thirds of those voting.

The president would also have the right to take proposed changes to the people.

For Further Reading:
Upham, Thomas C. 1941. *Total Democracy: A New Constitution for the United States. A Democratic Ideal for the World.* New York: Carlyle House.

❖ *U.S. TERM LIMITS, INC. V. THORNTON* (1995) ❖

In this case, the U.S. Supreme Court struck down a term-limit provision in the Arkansas state constitution. By implication, the Court also voided laws and constitutional provisions limiting the terms of national legislators that had been adopted in twenty-two other states.

Thornton centered on the provisions of Article I, Sections 2 and 3 of the U.S. Constitution setting forth age, citizenship, and residency requirements for members of the U.S. House and Senate. Arkansas had attempted to keep candidates off the ballot when they had served three terms in the House or two terms in the Senate.

Relying in large part on the decision in *Powell v. McCormack* (1969), the Court majority of five, led by Justice John Paul Stevens, held that the qualifications established in Article I were designed to be exclusive and that the Arkansas constitution added another qualification. Stevens argued that such additional state-imposed qualifications were "inconsistent with the Framers' vision of a uniform national legislature, representing the people of the United States" (*U.S. Term Limits* 1995, 783). He further opined that if states wanted to add to constitutionally specified qualifications, such a change, like other alterations in electoral processes, would have to be adopted "through the amendment procedures set forth in Article V" (*Id.,* 837).

By contrast, Justice Clarence Thomas, who wrote the dissenting opinion, said that although the Constitution established minimum qualifications for legislators, it was silent about additional qualifications. In Thomas's view, such restrictions were thus reserved, under provisions of the Tenth Amendment, to the people of the states. Noting that "the Constitution simply does not recognize the mechanism for action by the undifferentiated people of the Nation," Thomas observed that the amending process "calls for amendments to be ratified not by a convention of the national people, but by conventions in each state or by the state legislatures elected by these people" (*U.S. Term Limits* 1995, 928).

At least one senator, Republican Hank Brown of Colorado, announced a plan to get around this decision by passing legislation defining the term "inhabitant" to exclude members of Congress who had been gone from their districts for more than half a year for twelve consecutive years (Seelye 1995, A11). Other supporters of term limits renewed calls for a constitutional amendment on the subject. Some versions of this plan would impose a single nationwide standard while others would specifically reverse *U.S. Term Limits v. Thornton* (1995) by allowing states to set their own limits.

The state of Missouri attempted to evade the decision in *U.S. Term Limits* by including a ballot notation indicating whether representatives had supported term limits or not. The U.S. Supreme Court struck down this provision in *Cook v. Gralike* (2001).

See also Congress, Term Limits; *Cook v. Gralike.*

For Further Reading:
   U.S. Term Limits, Inc. v. Thornton, 514 U.S. 779 (1995).

V

❖ VANGUARD, VIRGINIA ❖

Virginia Vanguard is the pseudonym under which a book entitled *The Populis: A Draft Constitution for a New Political Age* was published in 1995. The author, who was influenced by futuristic plans for greater voter participation in politics, says that he/she was using the pseudonym not to conceal identity but "rather to focus attention on arguments versus personalities." The author began with a preface describing a voter calling in to a National Decision Center, entering a voting code, and registering her opinion on a matter of public importance. The author then proceeded to describe how the concept of democracy could be enhanced by such forms of direct democracy. The book consisted of the draft of a proposed constitution of a preamble and twelve articles followed by a brief description of how the new constitution would work. The Preamble is almost identical to that of the current constitution except for the fact that it omits the words "of the United States"; the proposal was relatively vague as to what role such states, if they remain at all, will play in the new system.

Article I described five elements of the new national government. They were the Populis, responsible for determining basic policies and selecting office holders; the Caucis, which would select and present policy issues and candidates to the voters; the Legis, which would translate public decisions into law; the Executis, which would implement and enforce such laws; and the Judicis, which would interpret the laws and attempt to assure fair treatment for all.

Article II defined citizenship, which was to be limited to individuals born to a citizen parent or naturalized. Citizenship could be forfeited upon "accepting the citizenship of another nation, upon conviction of a serious criminal act, or upon death" (Vanguard 1995, 19). Citizens were charged with gaining adequate education and training and would be required to "possess sufficient financial insurance against personal calamity" (*Id.*, 19). Citizenship carried with it, as a birthright, "all freedoms," and these may only be abridged "with the explicit consent of the Populis" (*Id.*, 20). The right of the Populis "to directly and collectively determine all national policy" was described as "indelible" (*Id.*, 20).

Citizens eighteen years and older "may choose to join the Populis" (Vanguard 1995, 20). Only such individuals could hold office or participate in national elections and referenda. Such citizens would be required to perform at least four years of military and civilian service. Individuals who failed to join the Populis within four years would permanently lose this opportunity, although, if they continued on the nation's soil, they continued to be bound by its laws.

The provision for the Causis was fairly unique. Patterned after a grand jury, this caucis consisted of "seven willing persons selected randomly and secretly from the rolls of the Populis" (Vanguard 1995, 22). Selected every two months, members "will be sequestered at a central location, along with their immediate families, to allow full concentration on their tasks" (*Id.*, 22). The Caucis would be responsible for identifying issues of national importance, framing issues for the National Policy

Referendum, and presenting candidates for high offices. It would also oversee the Civis, or National Service Board.

Article V described the single-house Legis, which might actually be less democratically accountable than the current Congress, although this arguably matters far less because the new body would basically be simply incorporating the will of the Populis. The next lower governmental entities, whether "state, province, or territory" (Vanguard 1995, 24), would select two representatives to the Legis who would each serve one three-year term. The Legis would "formulate national laws that faithfully implement the policies of the Populis, as reflected in the results of National Policy Referenda" (*Id.*, 25). These would be known as "the National Code of Justice" (*Id.*, 25). The Legis would have some additional powers in times of national emergency. Each year the Legis would select a chief legislator.

Article VI outlined the duties of the Executis, who was given the duty "to faithfully and efficiently implement, administer, and enforce the laws as codified by the Legis" (Vanguard 1995, 27). It would consist of a Chief Executive, a Deputy Executive, and administrators of civilian and military programs. Much like the current president, the chief executive would sign treaties, appoint ambassadors, and serve as commander in chief of the armed forces. The chief and deputy would serve for a single five-year term, with the chief legislator designated as following next in succession. No mention is made of a veto power.

Article VII outlined the Judicis. It would "rule on the correctness of conflicting interpretations of the law, develop consistent guidelines for punishments and awards, and render timely judgments" (Vanguard 1995, 29). However, the Populis could overrule it. The Populis would elect a High Court, consisting of seven judges, serving seven-year single terms, and defining its own jurisdiction. The High Court would also set standards for criminal penalties. The chief justice would be elected annually, with no individual serving for more than a single year.

Article VIII outlined the Civis. It consisted of "all persons employed by the Legis, the Judicis, the various civilian and military agencies of the Executis and the National Service Board." All would be compensated on a consistent scale, with the chief executive being paid the most, albeit no more than "twenty times that of the lowest full-time employee of the national government" (Vanguard 1995, 32). All new members of the Populis would serve in the Civis for at least four years. Boards of Inquiry would hear charges against members of the Civis accused of not doing their duties.

Article IX dealt with making, amending, and repealing laws. The Caucis presented such laws after each meeting, initiating a two-month referendum, during which each member of the Populis was expected to vote. Each action selected by a majority would become law and would have to be implemented by the Legis within 120 days. Laws and policies would be guided by ten principles. These included the requirement that such laws shall "perpetually strive for Justice, by ensuring equal protection under the law and equal application of the law"; "be applied universally"; be national in scope; not address "infrequent events"; not be ex post facto; not include unrelated clauses; have benefits that outweigh their costs; only regulate personal behavior "where significant harm or risk to self or a fellow Citizen is inevitable"; and expire within twenty-five years (Vanguard 1995, 36–37). The Legis would review existing laws and would assure that "the nation's Code of Justice will be subjected to a general revalidation at least once per century" (*Id.*, 37).

Article X provided for the election of national representatives. The Caucis was charged with a screening function for all such candidates and would be responsible for presenting from two to five candidates to the Populis for each. To obtain office, an individual must receive "at least 3 percent more of the vote than the next most popular candidate" (Vanguard 1995, 39). Otherwise, the Caucis would make the choice.

Article XI provided for governmental financing. All revenues would be raised by a personal income tax. It would not include any "deduction, allowance, or exemption" (Vanguard 1995, 40). The government would be forbidden from "incurring any long-term indebtedness or credits." Likewise, it "may neither borrow money from nor lend money to another government, organization, financial institution, or person without the consent of the Populis" (*Id.*, 40–41). The Executis, with Legis approval, would determine the amount of money in circulation but could not artificially manipulate its value without consent of the Populis.

Article XII described other governmental entities. The national government was to be carefully circumscribed: "It shall provide no service that can reasonably and more efficiently be made available through a non-government entity or a lower government entity" (Vanguard 1995, 42). The Populis might create "the permanent or temporary formation of such states, regions, provinces, territories, etc., as may be necessary" (*Id.*, 42). The structure of subgovernments would complement those of the national government and could be dissolved. All policies of subgovernments would have to conform to those of the national government. Governments would practice reciprocity. Although the nation was encouraged to join "benevolent international organizations," Virginia Vanguard specified that "any surrender of national prerogatives to such an organization must be explicitly approved by the Populis" (*Id.*, 43).

Designed both to enshrine popular sovereignty and to end the "paternal relationship" between government and the people" (Vanguard 1995, 45), the Populis contained a number of unique features. Based on the notion that governmental powers would be significantly limited, few rights were listed. This was because, "In the POPULIS, Citizens will conditionally relinquish to government only those powers they deem absolutely necessary and retain the right to reclaim even those" (*Id.*, 56). This proposal would require a high degree of citizen education and participation and might be hindered by the relatively short terms in office, especially those applied to member of the Caucis.

For Further Reading:

Vanguard, Virginia. 1995. *The Populis: A Draft Constitution for a Political New Age.* Brentsville, VA: The Wingspread Enterprise.

❖ VANSICKLE, JOHN (1965–) ❖

John VanSickle identifies himself as an individual who has spent fourteen years in military service. As of 2002 he was working on a bachelor's degree in computer and information sciences (personal e-mail correspondence with author, 10 June 2002). His website, which includes information on his family, science fiction pages, political pages, and raytracing pages (these have to do with computer simulations), includes proposals for a twenty-eighth, twenty-ninth, thirtieth, thirty-first, and thirty-second amendment, each followed by brief commentary. Most of the amendments are quite complex, and many are fairly novel. Most of VanSickle's ideas could be classified as conservative; he says that his "political leanings are the result of reading most of Ayn Rand's works that are presently in print (although I do not agree with everything she says, and with even less of what is said in her name by her followers)" (personal e-mail correspondence, 10 June 2002). VanSickle further indicates that he believes he began posting his proposals in 1998 (*Id.*, 11 June 2002).

VanSickle's proposed twenty-eighth amendment, the language of which is modeled after the First Amendment, would prohibit Congress or the states from making laws "respecting an establishment of production, trade, employment, education, medicine, culture, or charity, or restricting the free exercise thereof." The amendment would further repeal the Sixteenth Amendment (which legitimized the national income tax), and congressional power "to borrow or lend money" or "consider any bill to reverse any part of this amendment."

VanSickle's twenty-ninth amendment is composed of eighteen sections, which deal chiefly with the criminal justice system. It would prohibit fines or forfeitures except for a crime of which an individual has been convicted (Section 1); compensate individuals for property damaged during governmental seizures (Section 2); require unanimous jury verdicts and limit their application to crimes involving an "identifiable harm to a specific person or party of persons (Section 3); eliminate "peculiar courts" (Section 4); provide for the selection of jurors by lottery with exclusions for individuals in law enforcement or with personal interests in the case (Section 5); allow jurors to judge matters of both law and fact "independent of the instructions of the court" (Section 6); prohibit convictions based simply on the testimony of governmental officials or from individuals engaged in plea-bargaining (Section 7); prohibit the use of testimony "obtained by coercion or fraud" (Section 8); separate individuals whose crimes involved bodily harm to others from being incarcerated with those who committed such violent offenses (Section 9); reserve the death penalty for specified crimes (Section 10); limit the definition of cruel and unusual punishment of prisoners to the infliction of "injury or illness" (Section 11); make it an abuse for governmental officials to abridge the "rights, privileges, or immunities" of persons under guise of their authority and make them liable for the same (Sections 12 and 13); prohibit punitive damages (Section 14); specify the presumption of innocence and sanity and provide that the "beyond a reasonable doubt" standard be applied in both criminal and civil cases (Section 15); distribute fines to individuals harmed or, if no such individuals can be identified, to taxpayers (Section 16); make it a crime for governmental officials to cover up evidence tending to exonerate a defendant (Section 17); and make "entrapment" by law enforcement officials a crime (Section 18).

VanSickle's proposed thirtieth amendment deals with what he perceives to be governmental abuses. Section 1 would apply all laws passed by Congress to itself. Section 2 would limit regulations to those that are "expressly worded." Section 3 would require all governmental representatives and appointees to divest themselves of "commercial interests" and prohibit pensions to the same. Section 4 would require elected officials to take an oath to tell the truth and make them impeachable for violating this oath. Section 5 would enable each individual to place bills before Congress. Sections 6 and 7 would permit the nomination of presidents and vice presidents by petitions of 1 percent or more of the voters. Section 8 would prohibit monies from the treasury from being spent on petitions, and Section 9 would pro-

hibit felons or ex-felons from serving in office. Section 10 would specify that any crime for which an individual could be incarcerated would be considered to be an impeachable offense. Section 11 would prohibit the use of federal expenditures to induce state behavior. Section 12 would limit congressional powers to regulate trade only when such trade "transacts state borders," and Section 13 would provide an automatic sunset for any law on its tenth anniversary, with the understanding that Congress could adopt new laws to replace them.

VanSickle's proposed thirty-first amendment relates to the military. Section 1 would eliminate the draft. Section 2 would limit the stationing of troops abroad "except in prosecution of a war declared by Congress." Sections 3 and 4, much like some earlier versions of the Bricker Amendment, would prohibit the United States from entering into treaties abridging citizen "rights, privileges, or immunities."

VanSickle's proposed thirty-second amendment largely limits both state and federal powers. Section 1 limits the power of licensing and keeps any such fees to a minimum. Section 2 reaffirms the Second Amendment right to "keep and bear arms" without being "subject to any system of governmental consent or license" except for limitations on the ownership of individuals who had used weapons to cause or threaten harm. Section 3 limits legislation designed to preserve endangered species. Section 4 provides that child welfare shall be the basis of "all custody decisions." Section 5 allows states to prohibit governments within their jurisdiction from exercising jurisdiction over matters the states have reserved to themselves. Section 6 limits restrictions on individual rights "only to those restrictions that are enumerated in this constitution." Section 7 limits the information that governments may collect on private individuals. Section 8 provides for a referendum initiated by 1 percent or more of the voters of any state and enacted into law when favored by "a majority of votes." The amendment further provides that "[a] referendum may repeal any law passed by the legislature of that state, remove from office any appointed official of that State, amend the Constitution of that State, ratify a pending amendment to the Constitution of the United States, or withdraw that State's ratification of a pending amendment to the Constitution of the United States."

The final section limits U.S. governmental ownership to "only those lands used in the exercise of the powers reserved to it in this constitution."

VanSickle's site includes other reflections on government, most notably a copy of "The No Bill of Rights," borrowed from another website, which basically lets individuals know, in a structure similar to that of the original bill of rights, that individuals are entitled to opportunities but not to government largesse in such areas as food, housing, health care, or the like.

For Further Reading:

http://enphilistor.users4.50megs.com/index.htm Accessed 8 June 2002.

❖ VENERATION FOR THE CONSTITUTION ❖

See Reverence for the Constitution.

❖ VETO ❖

See *Clinton v. City of New York;* Presidency, Veto Power of.

❖ VICE PRESIDENT ❖

There is no other U.S. constitutional office that has been subjected to greater scorn than that of the vice presidency (Twentieth Century Fund Task Force 1988, 21; also see Young 1974). Especially in recent years, however, this office has increased in power and visibility and has become a major springboard to the presidency, much as the position of secretary of state did in early American history. Vice presidents who have run for president since 1960 have included Richard Nixon, Hubert Humphrey, Gerald Ford (who had become president after Nixon's resignation), Walter Mondale, George Bush Sr., and Al Gore Jr.

The Constitution of 1787 assigns only two functions to the vice president. One is to be available in case the president dies. The second, mixing executive and legislative powers, is to preside over and break tie votes in the U.S. Senate.

In large part, the vice presidency appears to have been created as a concomitant of the electoral college (Schlesinger 1974, 490). Under the original electoral scheme, each elector was to cast two votes. The person with the greatest number would become president, and the runner-up would become vice president. With the emergence of political parties, this scheme hit two major snags. First, it permitted a president and vice president to be elected from different parties; Federalist John Adams thus had a Democratic-Republican vice president, Thomas Jefferson. Second, there was the possibility of a tie in the electoral college. Such a tie occurred in the election of 1800, when all the Democratic-Republican electors for Thomas Jefferson also cast their votes for fellow party member Aaron Burr, and the election had to be resolved by the U.S. House of Representatives. The Twelfth Amendment was subsequently adopted and specified that electors would cast separate votes for the two offices.

After adoption of this amendment, the vice presidency declined in stature, and some members of Congress began to introduce resolutions to abolish the institution. Alternatively, there were proposals to establish multiple vice presidencies or to permit Congress to fill vice presidential vacancies.

Although the institution was generally weak, in 1841 John Tyler established an important precedent. In succeeding William Henry Harrison, who died in office, Tyler insisted that he was the real and not simply an "acting" president. Subsequent vice presidents who have fallen heir to the presidency have taken similar positions, without which their hands would undoubtedly have been weakened.

The Twentieth Amendment settled one issue

surrounding the vice presidency when it specified that if a president is not chosen in time for his or her term, the vice president–elect should be president. The amendment simply allowed Congress to legislate in cases in which neither the president nor the vice president had been so selected, but to date, Congress has yet to adopt such legislation.

The two greatest problems with the vice presidency were that the Constitution did not establish a procedure whereby a vice president could take over in cases of presidential disability, and it made no provision for filling vice presidential vacancies. The Twenty-fifth Amendment addressed both problems; it permitted the president temporarily to transfer power to the vice president (during medical operations, times of ill health, and the like) and established a complex procedure whereby the vice president and cabinet could declare a president disabled. It also allowed a president to nominate, and a majority of Congress to confirm, vice presidential replacements. This second procedure for nominating vice presidents essentially confirmed a practice, first established when Franklin D. Roosevelt was president, of allowing the candidate to pick his running mate, in a choice almost always subsequently confirmed by the party nominating convention; prior to that time, conventions typically made their selections primarily on their own.

Adoption of the Twenty-fifth Amendment has not ended calls to abolish the vice presidency or for further clarification of procedures to be followed in cases of presidential disability. Some questions also remain about how presidents choose their vice presidents, with concerns being expressed that considerations of ticket balancing sometimes outweigh fitness to assume the presidency. Perhaps with such problems in mind, proposals were introduced in 1956 and 1957 to elect the vice president separately from the president. Since adoption of the Twenty-fifth Amendment, there have also been occasional calls to fill vice presidential vacancies by special elections rather than by presidential appointment and congressional confirmation. Health problems of George W. Bush's vice president, Dick Cheney (who has had a long history of heart ailments), some of which

emerged in the thirty-six-day period during which the presidential election of 2000 was being resolved, have further highlighted concerns about the current method of vice presidential selection.

See also Twelfth Amendment; Twentieth Amendment; Twenty-fifth Amendment.

For Further Reading:
Schlesinger, Arthur M., Jr. 1974. "On the Presidential Succession." *Political Science Quarterly* 89 (Fall): 475–505.

Twentieth Century Fund Task Force on the Vice Presidency. 1988. *A Heartbeat Away.* New York: Printing Press Publications.

Young, Donald. 1974. *American Roulette: The History and Dilemma of the Vice Presidency.* New York: Viking Press.

❖ VICTIMS' RIGHTS ❖

As courts have widened their understanding of the provisions of the Bill of Rights and the Fourteenth Amendment to extend broader protection to the rights of criminal defendants (most of the provisions related to the rights of criminal defendants in the Bill of Rights were applied to the states during the years of the Warren Court), attention has begun to focus as well on the rights of victims. Thus, in *Payne v. Tennessee* (1991), the Supreme Court overturned two earlier decisions and upheld the use of victim impact statements, allowing victims to testify as to the effect of crimes on their lives, in the penalty phase of capital trials. Despite this decision, some observers still believe that prosecutors often ignore the interests of victims at other stages of the trial, denying them the psychological sense of closure that they might feel if they were otherwise consulted during judicial proceedings.

Florida Republican Representative Ileana Ros-Lehtinen, the first Cuban-born American to serve in such a capacity, introduced amending resolutions in 1990 and 1991 to guarantee victims' rights, and many proposals have been introduced since. A recent proposal introduced on 15 April 2002 by California Senator Diane

Feinstein and Arizona Republican Senator Jon Kyl, and supported by President George W. Bush, is a revision of earlier proposals designed, according to Feinstein, so as not "to abridge the rights of defendants or offenders, or otherwise disrupt the delicate balance of our Constitution." It has four sections. The first applies to both state and national governments and provides that:

> The rights of victims of violent crime, being capable of protection without denying the constitutional rights of those accused of victimizing them, are hereby established and shall not be denied by any State or the United States and may be restricted only as provided in this article.

The commentary in the first part of this section is somewhat unique, although it bears some resemblances to statements that begin the Second and Fourth Amendments.

Section 2 of the proposed Victims' Rights Amendment attempts to flesh out such rights by making them more specific:

> A victim of violent crime shall have the right to reasonable and timely notice of any public proceeding involving the crime and of any release or escape of the accused; the rights not to be excluded from such public proceeding and reasonably to be heard at public release, plea, sentencing, reprieve, and pardon proceedings; and the right to adjudicative decisions that duly consider the victim's safety, interest in avoiding unreasonable delay, and just and timely claims to restitution from the offender. These rights shall not be restricted except when and to the degree dictated by a substantial interest in public safety or the administration of criminal justice, or by compelling necessity.

The provisions for "reasonable and timely notice" and for judgments of "a substantial interest" in public safety or "compelling necessity" would obviously be subject to judicial construction.

Section 3 is designed to thwart the use of the amendment to "provide [for defendants'] grounds for a new trial or to authorize any claim for damages." Similarly, it declares that "[o]nly the victim or the victim's lawful representative may assert the rights established by this article, and no person accused of the crime may obtain any form of relief hereunder." Section 4 provides Congress with appropriate enforcement authority and further specifies that "[n]othing in this article shall affect the President's authority to grant reprieves or pardons" (quoted in "New Proposal for Constitutionalizing Victims' Rights" 2002, 2679).

Congress has in part responded to concerns for victims' rights by adopting the Victims' Bill of Rights in 1994 and the Victims' Rights Clarification Act of 1997 (Cassell 1999, 520). This legislation demonstrates that at least some of the goals that proponents of the victims' rights amendment favor can currently be enacted through state and/or federal legislation. However, state legislation currently varies widely from one jurisdiction to another and does not always appear to be effective (*Id.*, 515–522). Victims' rights advocates believe that, if incorporated into an amendment, such rights would be more secure. Opponents fear that such requirements could prove to be burdensome and inflexible. One opponent of the amendment has thus argued that, "although well-intentioned," the proposed amendment is "unnecessary, undemocratic [because it would leave an unelected judiciary to decide who the victims were and what measures were "reasonable"], and at odds with principles of federalism" (Taylor 2000).

For Further Reading:
Cassell, Paul G. 1999. "Barbarians at the Gates? A Reply to the Critics of the Victims' Rights Amendment," *Utah Law Review* 1999: 479–537.

Cassell, Paul G., and Steven J. Twist. 1996. "A Bill of Rights for Crime Victims." 127 *Wall Street Journal* (24 April): A15.

Kyl, John. 1996. "Why Victims Need a Bill of Rights." *Washington Times* (22 April): A21.

"New Proposal for Constitutionalizing Victims' Rights Introduced in Congress." 2002. *U.S. Law Week* 70 (30 April): 2679.

Taylor, Stuart, Jr. 2000. "Victim's Rights: Leave the Constitution Alone." *National Journal* 32 (April 22): 1254.

❖ VIRGINIA AND KENTUCKY RESOLUTIONS ❖

Although it is common to refer collectively to the American framers and their intent when interpreting the U.S. Constitution, the Virginia and Kentucky Resolutions illustrate that even these framers had different understandings of the document they had created. The documents are also important in that they give a glimpse of the early effectiveness, or perhaps more accurately, the ineffectiveness, of the Bill of Rights.

During the presidency of John Adams when the nation was close to going to war against France, the Federalists became increasingly concerned about the growing opposition of the Democratic-Republican Party led by Thomas Jefferson and James Madison. They accordingly adopted laws known as the Alien and Sedition Acts. The first made it more difficult for immigrants, many of whom favored the Democratic-Republicans, to become citizens, while the second made it a federal crime to criticize the government or the president of the United States. Contemporary scholars generally agree with Democratic-Republicans of the day that the Sedition Act was in violation of the U.S. Constitution.

Today, courts would almost certainly invalidate the Sedition Act, but in Adams's administration Federalist nominees unlikely to be sympathetic to such pleas dominated the courts. Moreover, there was continuing concern on the part of the Democratic-Republicans, who had opposed the establishment of the national bank, that Federalists were interpreting the Constitution, not as a limited compact among the states that had ratified it, but as a document giving the national government virtually unlimited power—a charge that would later lead some of Jefferson's opponents to charge him with hypocrisy when he exercised federal powers to purchase the Louisiana Territory and to declare an embargo against Great Britain.

Democratic-Republicans chose to respond to the Alien and Sedition Acts by adopting the Virginia and Kentucky Resolutions, the first largely authored by James Madison and the second by Thomas Jefferson (secretly, because he was vice president at the time). These resolutions, adopted by the respective state legislatures, were designed to encourage other states to "interpose" themselves against the Alien and Sedition Acts on the basis that these laws exceeded federal delegated powers, that they violated various guarantees of due process guaranteed within the Bill of Rights, and that they violated the Tenth Amendment, reserving powers to the states. In the Kentucky Resolution, Jefferson expressed sentiments that had led him to advocate the Bill of Rights. He thus noted that "free government is founded in jealousy and not in confidence" and that "in questions of power, then, let no more be heard of confidence in man, but bind him down from mischief, by the chains of the Constitution" (Ford 1898, 683). Although others undoubtedly shared Jefferson's sentiments, other states did not at the time respond positively to these resolutions, but had they done so, this method might have been resorted to far more frequently.

In 1801 Thomas Jefferson was elected to the presidency and members of his party gained control of Congress. The Alien and Sedition Acts all either lapsed or were repealed (Willis 2002, 9). Jefferson pardoned individuals who had been convicted under the sedition law. States' rights sentiment subsequently shifted from the South to the North with the Hartford Convention of 1815, and then back to the South with controversies over tariffs and slavery that ultimately produced the now discredited doctrines of nullification and secession.

See also First Amendment; Hartford Convention; Jefferson, Thomas; Madison, James; Tenth Amendment.

For Further Reading:
Ford, Paul L., ed. 1898. *The Federalist.* New York: Henry Holt.
Willis, Clyde E. 2002. *Student's Guide to Landmark Congressional Laws on the First Amendment.* Westport, CT: Greenwood Press.

❖ VIRGINIA DECLARATION OF RIGHTS ❖

Largely drafted by George Mason and adopted by state convention in June 1776, prior to the time that the rest of the colonies had declared their independence, the Virginia Declaration of Rights is believed to have influenced both the writing of the Declaration of Independence and the wording of the Bill of Rights to the U.S. Constitution. The Virginia Declaration started from the premise that "all men are by nature equally free and independent, and have certain inherent rights, of which, when they enter into a state of society, they cannot, by any compact, deprive or divest their posterity." The document went on to proclaim that "whenever any Government shall be found inadequate or contrary to these purposes, a majority of the community hath an indubitable, unalienable, and indefeasible right, to reform, alter, or abolish it, in such manner as shall be judged most conducive to the publick weal" (quoted in Kurland and Lerner 1987, 5:3).

In addition to announcing the doctrine of separation of powers, the Virginia Declaration proceeded to enumerate a number of important rights, some of which later found their way into other state declarations of rights and, eventually, into the U.S. Bill of Rights—Mason, who had served as a Virginia representative to the U.S. Constitutional Convention of 1787, had vigorously opposed the adoption of the U.S. Constitution on the basis that it did not contain such a Bill. The rights listed in the Virginia Declaration of Rights included the right to confrontation in capital cases; the right "to a speedy trial"; a provision against self-incrimination and against deprivation of liberty "except by the law of the land" (a phrase similar to that later incorporated into the due process clauses of the Fifth and Fourteenth Amendments); a prohibition against "excessive bail" and "cruel and unusual punishments"; a prohibition against general warrants or seizures of persons "whose offense is not particularly described and supported by evidence" (this has a parallel in the Fourth Amendment of the U.S. Constitution); a provision for trial by jury; a provision for freedom of the press; and a provision for "the free exercise of religion." The Virginia Declaration's proclamation, similar to language later used in the Second Amendment to the U.S. Constitution, "that a well-regulated Militia, composed of the body of the people, trained to arms, is the proper, natural, and safe defense of a free State" was specifically tied to the principles that "Standing Armies, in time of peace, should be avoided as dangerous to liberty" and that "the military should be under strict subordination to, and governed by, the civil power." The Declaration also refers to the necessity of "frequent recurrence to fundamental principles" (quoted in Kurland and Lerner 1987, 5:3–4).

See also Bill of Rights; Declaration of Independence; Mason, George.

For Further Reading:

Kurland, Philip B., and Ralph Lerner, eds. 1987. *The Founders' Constitution*. 5 vols. Chicago: University of Chicago Press.

❖ VOTING RIGHTS, CONSTITUTIONAL AMENDMENTS RELATING TO ❖

By comparison to other areas of the world, voting in the American colonies was fairly widespread, but many of the colonies essentially limited the franchise to white male property owners, sometimes also requiring that they be church members or that they affirm basic tenets of Protestant Christianity. Delegates to the U.S. Constitutional Convention debated whether voting rights should extend to all males or be limited to those who owned a specified amount of property. Many framers believed that a modicum of property was necessary both to secure a degree of independence—at a time when many elections were public—and to prevent the poor from using their votes to despoil the rich. Others expressed greater faith in the "common man" and believed that individuals without large amounts of property had demonstrated their commitment to the nation during the Revolutionary War.

Ultimately, the delegates to the Constitutional Convention of 1787 did not provide a universal standard for voting in the United States. Instead, Article I, Section 2 specified that electors for the U.S. House of Representatives "in each State shall have the Qualifications requisite for Electors of the most numerous Branch of the State Legislature," thus allowing qualifications to vary from one state to another. The Constitution also specified that individuals who were held in slavery—the specific term was not used—would be counted as three-fifths of a person for purposes of taxation and representation.

Although voting rights have waxed and waned within various time periods in American history (Keyssar 2000), constitutional amendments have gradually eliminated barriers to voting so that the right now applies fairly universally to adults eighteen years of age and older who have met minimal residency requirements. Many states do limit the right to vote of incarcerated felons, or ex-felons (a particularly questionable practice that has fallen particularly hard on some African American and lower-income communities and that arguably continues to depress political participation), or to individuals with mental illnesses. In addition, partly through the development of more democratic selection processes and partly through formal amendments, the electoral college, while not always guaranteeing that the winner of the electoral vote will also be the winner of the popular vote (witness the presidential election of 2000), has also become more democratic. Citizens generally cast their votes for presidential electors not in the belief that such individuals will exercise independent judgment but because these electors are pledged to vote for candidates whom the majority favors.

Thus, the Twelfth Amendment accommodated the development of political parties by specifying that presidential electors should cast separate votes for president and vice president, generally assuring that the two candidates would be from the same political party and could not tie as Thomas Jefferson and Aaron Burr had done in the presidential election of 1800. Similarly, the Twenty-third Amendment now provides for representation in the electoral college for citizens of the District of Columbia.

On a related matter, the Seventeenth Amendment, ratified in 1913, provides for direct popular election of U.S. Senators, who had previously been selected by state legislatures. According to the operative language of this amendment, however, state voters continued to be designated as those with "the qualifications requisite for electors of the most numerous branch of the State legislatures." The Seventeenth Amendment clearly increased direct popular power over the Senate, but may also have undermined federalism.

Qualifications based on property and religious affiliation had largely faded at the state level by the time Andrew Jackson was elected president. In addition, more offices, including many state judgeships, were made elective during this time. Still, many states continued to restrict the rights of African Americans, and none yet extended the right to vote to women. The Fourteenth Amendment eliminated the three-fifths clause and provided, in Section 2, that state representation could be reduced in states that abridged the rights of males over the age of twenty-one, but this provision was never enforced, actually leading to increased representation of some of the Southern states in the U.S. House of Representatives after the emancipation of the slaves. The corresponding provision in Section 3 limiting the right of individuals who had engaged in rebellion against the United States to serve as presidential electors or hold office (the only limitation of voting rights ever adopted by constitutional amendment) allowed Congress to remove this "disability" by a two-thirds vote.

At least on paper, the Fifteenth Amendment (1870) was designed to remedy the states' exclusion of blacks from their electorates, but states widely evaded this amendment during the first 100 years of its history through mechanisms as diverse as all-white primaries, grandfather clauses, poll taxes, unequal application of literacy tests, and voter intimidation, and not until 1965 did Congress adopt effective legislation on its behalf. Three years earlier, the states had ratified the Twenty-fourth Amendment, outlawing use of the poll tax in federal elections, a prohibition that the Supreme Court extended to the states in *Harper v. Virginia State Board of Elections* (1966).

Women, many of whom had been disappointed that their efforts on behalf of abolitionism did not result in voting rights for themselves when the Fourteenth and Fifteenth Amendments were adopted, waged a long campaign for suffrage that won some early successes in the territories and the western states (Wyoming was the first to extend the vote to women). This movement did not finally succeed at the national level until the adoption of the Nineteenth Amendment in 1920. In contrast to the Fifteenth Amendment, once this amendment was adopted, it was quickly implemented. Similarly, the Australian, or secret, ballot (named after its nation of origin), which is regarded as a mainstay of modern democracy, was first introduced in the United States in 1888 and quickly spread throughout the nation without a constitutional amendment (Keyssar 2000, 143).

The Supreme Court has often announced that it considers voting to be a "fundamental right" that is subject to "strict scrutiny," but it stated in *Bush v. Gore* (2000) that there was "no federal constitutional right to vote" (cited in Raskin 2001). Accordingly, although individuals born in Puerto Rico have been declared to be U.S. citizens since 1917, as long as they reside in Puerto Rico, which is currently a commonwealth but not a state, they have no right to vote in U.S. presidential elections (Roman 2002). This could possibly be remedied by an amendment like the Twenty-third Amendment that gave the District of Columbia representation in the electoral college, but the formula used there (the equivalent electoral votes of the smallest state) would arguably be unfair for a jurisdiction with over six times the population (Roman 2002, 1713). The most obvious way for the residents of Puerto Rico to obtain voting rights would be for Puerto Rico to become a state.

The fact that there remains no federal constitutional right to vote was demonstrated when the U.S. Supreme Court partially rebuffed Congress in *Oregon v. Mitchell* (1970) when it decided that Congress had power to lower voting ages to eighteenth (they had generally been set at twenty-one) in federal, but not state, elections. Congress subsequently proposed and the states ratified the Twenty-sixth Amendment (1971), equalizing the lower qualification for both jurisdictions.

Most battles for national amendments relating to voting rights have been preceded by victories in individual states. The roles of amendments as both instruments of effecting policies relative to voting and as symbols of national aspirations to equality are difficult to separate; thus the Fifteenth and Nineteenth Amendments both serve as benchmarks in the progress of African Americans and American women.

Although the Constitution has successfully extended the vote to most citizens, many remain apathetic, and low American electoral turnouts, especially among the young, the poor, and the uneducated, remain a frequent subject of popular and scholarly commentary. Particularly during the populist and progressive eras, many states, especially in the West, developed mechanisms for voter initiatives and referendums on items of legislation and amendments and recalls of elected officials. Similarly, in a move referred to, but not specifically endorsed by the Twenty-fourth Amendment, many states adopted direct primaries as the chief mechanism by which to select electoral candidates. Although the initiative and referendum have been frequent subjects of proposed amendments at the national level, they have not been embodied into amendments. Similarly, parties continue to select their nominees for national offices largely on the basis of a patchwork of state legislation.

Despite all the constitutional amendments that have been adopted preventing various forms of discrimination related to voting, the Constitution still does not provide an affirmative guarantee of the "right to vote." Professor Jamin B. Raskin, of the Washington College of Law at American University, has pointed out that 135 national constitutions do guarantee such an affirmative right. Raskin advocates a twentieth-eighth, or right-to-vote, amendment consisting of four sections. The first would affirmatively specify the right of citizens to vote in local, state, and national elections. The second would prevent such voting from being denied on the basis of "political party affiliation or prior condition of incarceration." Section three would resurrect an amendment that was proposed by Congress but failed to receive the necessary number of state ratifications by providing that residents of the District of Columbia would have the same congressional representation to which the District would be entitled "if it were a State," and section four would provide enforcement power to Congress. Although Raskin also favors abolition of the electoral college, he omitted that suggestion from his proposal for fear that opposition to that particular measure would jeopardize the entire amendment (Raskin 2001).

Other reformers, especially those who have actually proposed new constitutional systems, have suggested that voting reforms are needed to enable voters to indicate their second and third choices in elections and/or to change the method whereby members of the U.S. House of Representatives are currently chosen from single-member, winner-take-all districts to a system in which they are selected through a system of proportional representation. Political scientists generally believe that the current system of single-member districts (in combination with a presidential rather than a parliamentary system) supports the existing two-party system by making it unlikely that a party with some support throughout the entire nation, but no majority within a single district or set of districts, will be at all represented in Congress or the presidency. By contrast to the United States, many European democracies use systems of proportional representation.

See also Democracy and Constitutional Amendments; Fifteenth Amendment; Initiative and Referendum; Nineteenth Amendment; Seventeenth Amendment; Twelfth Amendment; Twenty–fourth Amendment; Twenty-sixth Amendment; Twenty-third Amendment; other Voting Rights entries.

For Further Reading:
Keyssar, Alexander. 2000. *The Right to Vote: The Constitutional History of Democracy in the United States.* New York: Basic Books.
Raskin, Jamin B. 2001. "A Right to Vote." *The American Prospect* 12 (27 August): 10–12.
Roman, Jose D. 2002. "Trying to Fit an Oval Shaped Island into a Square Constitution: Arguments for Puerto Rican Statehood." *Fordham Urban Law Journal* 29 (April): 1681–1713.

❖ VOTING RIGHTS, LITERACY TESTS ❖

Literacy tests were among the tools used by whites in Southern states to discriminate against African Americans. Although the idea that voters should be able to read and write can be justified under democratic theory, literacy and "understanding" tests were frequently administered in a way that permitted illiterate whites to vote but excluded highly educated blacks (Lawson 1976, 86–88).

In *Lassiter v. North Hampton County Board of Elections* (1959), the Supreme Court ruled that state power over suffrage included the right to set literacy requirements. That same year, at least two amendments were introduced to limit state voting restrictions to those concerned with age, residence, or imprisonment. From 1961 through 1963, several amendments were introduced either to establish free and universal suffrage throughout the United States or specifically to abolish the use of literacy tests in federal elections.

In the Voting Rights Act of 1965, Congress decided to address this issue through legislation instead. In *South Carolina v. Katzenbach* (1966), the Court held that congressional power under Section 2 of the Fifteenth Amendment was sufficient to uphold a literacy test ban in states identified as having low registration and voting rates. Similarly, in *Katzenbach v. Morgan* (1966), the Court upheld a provision of the law granting the right to vote to anyone who had completed a sixth-grade education in an accredited Puerto Rican school. In 1970, in the first of a number of extensions of the 1965 Act that are still in effect, Congress banned literacy tests completely. Relying on the enforcement provisions of the Fourteenth and Fifteenth Amendments, the Court upheld this ban in *Oregon v. Mitchell* (1970).

See also Enforcement Clauses in Amendments; Fifteenth Amendment.

❖ VOTING RIGHTS, RESIDENCY REQUIREMENTS ❖

More than thirty proposals were introduced from 1959 to 1971 seeking to address state residency requirements for voting. None were adopted.

In *Oregon v. Mitchell* (1970), however, the Supreme Court upheld a provision in the 1970 revision of the Voting Rights Act of 1965 that standardized such requirements for federal elections at thirty days. Similarly, in *Dunn v. Blumstein* (1972), the Court struck down a Tennessee residency requirement of one year in the state and three months in the county as a violation of the equal protection clause of the Fourteenth Amendment and impairment of the right to travel. The Court was not opposed to the state desire to avoid fraud but thought there were less intrusive measures to combat it. It also noted that extended periods of residence were no guarantees of voter competence or familiarity with the issues. In *Marston v. Lewis* (1973), the Supreme Court upheld a fifty-day requirement designed to allow states to prepare accurate voting lists.

For Further Reading:
   Dunn v. Blumstein, 405 U.S. 330 (1972).

W

❖

❖ WADE, EDWIN LEE (1932–) ❖

Described on the flyleaf of his book *Constitution 2000: A Federalist Proposal for the Next Century* (published in 1995) as "a businessman, lawyer, writer, lecturer, and former public official" who worked as a foreign service officer and who holds a number of degrees including a law degree from Georgetown University, Edwin Wade used his book to call for ten new amendments, most of which were designed to strengthen the national government. His first amendment, the twenty-eighth, was for congressional reform. It proposed cutting the size of the House essentially in half, that is, to 225 members, apportioned as now according to population. Wade further hoped to cut the total number of House committees to twelve and to limit the number of subcommittees on any committee to five. Total House employees would be restricted to no more than twenty times its membership, and expenditures for "partisan or religious" activities would be curtailed (Wade 1995, 292). This, like the rest of the proposed amendments, was to be inoperative unless ratified by conventions in three-fourths of the states by 31 December 2001.

Wade's next proposal would apply a similar remedy to the U.S. Senate. Cutting the number of senators in half, Wade proposed limiting its total number of committees to eight and the number of employees to 2,500. A provision to subject Senate debate to "reasonable limitations" was apparently designed to limit filibusters.

Wade's third proposal complemented the previous two by specifying that House members would serve four-year terms and be selected in presidential election years, with senators also serving four-year terms but being elected in off-year elections, beginning in 2006.

Wade's next three proposals were directed to the executive branch, which he believed has been severely weakened. Wade proposed allowing presidential and vice presidential tickets to be placed on the ballot if they got petitions "equal to or greater than two percent of the total popular vote cast in the immediately preceding [presidential] election" (Wade 1995, 294). These officeholders would be selected directly by "either a plurality or a majority of the national popular vote" (*Id.,* 295). The president would select a cabinet officer to serve as a personal chief of staff, thus helping to assure their direct access to the president. Wade would have further limited the presidential staff to no more than twice the size of Congress. A separate amendment would repeal the Twenty-second Amendment, so that presidents would no longer be limited to serving two full terms. Interestingly, Wade did not favor a presidential item veto, fearing that with such power the president "will have become the 536th member of Congress" (*Id.,* 145).

Wade next turned his attention to matters involving justice in the courts. He was particularly concerned about pretrial discovery procedures, which be believed were often used more to embarrass litigants than to get to the truth. He accordingly provided in his next amendment that no persons in civil cases should be compelled to give testimony "except before or under the supervision of a judge or other officer or officers of the United States as provided by law" (Wade 1995, 296–297). Wade further proposed establishing and maintaining "a system of pretrial court-annexed mandatory arbitration" to most civil cases (*Id.*, 297). Fearing that judges were leaving the judiciary to take jobs with some of the interests in whose behalf they had previously ruled, Wade further provided that every judicial official must accept the limitation that:

> He or she will not represent, acquire an interest in, become employed by, or otherwise become associated or affiliated with any person, partnership, corporation, or other enterprise or organization which appeared before such officer in any case or proceeding or as the legal representative of any such party, at any time within five years of such resignation. (Wade 1995, 298)

Individuals serving as judges at the time of this amendment's adoption would be expected to take a similar oath as a condition of keeping their jobs.

Believing that the Federal Reserve System was exercising inordinate power that belonged only to Congress, Wade's next proposal was aimed at that institution. It provided that:

> Congress shall make no law which delegates any power it possesses pursuant to Article I, Section 8 for the purpose of regulating banks and the banking system or credit and money in its several forms to any department or agency of the government of the United States unless such delegation is based on a clear statement of legislative policy and contains a system of precise, objective standards for application to specific cases, and in no case shall such delegation be made to any private persons, firms, partnerships, corporations, or to any other private enterprises or privately owned organizations. (Wade 1995, 299)

Although citing Supreme Court decisions restricting the regulation of vulgar words and flag burning (232), Wade focuses his last proposed amendment on campaign financing. Specifi-

cally, he would allow Congress to limit expenditures for elections and forbid "federal general revenue of any nature or description" from being "used to finance or otherwise assist any political campaign for any elective office anywhere in the United States of America" (Wade 1995, 300).

Although he proposed ten amendments, Wade also made it clear that he thought there were a number of proposed amendments that should not be adopted. He believed that the existing Second Amendment was directly tied to the maintenance of a militia and that it was thus not designed to create an individual personal right to own guns. On this basis, he proposed maintaining the Second Amendment as he believed it already was meant to be. Believing that the U.S. Supreme Court had usurped power when it upheld the right to abortion in *Roe v. Wade* (1973), Wade argued that this issue should be left to the states. Wade was as adamant against a human life amendment as against Supreme Court action, believing that "neither the decision nor the Amendment belong in the Constitution. Our Constitution again is about the way our federal government is *constituted*. It is not about social policy" (Wade 1995, 259). Finding a number of flaws in proposed balanced budget amendments, Wade also argued that the solution to annual budget deficits lies "in Congress, not in the Constitution" (*Id.*, 267).

In an appendix to his book, Wade included a "Proposed Uniform Application From the Several States to Congress Requesting and Requiring That a Constitutional Convention Be Called" (Wade 1995, 287). Scheduled to meet in Philadelphia no later than 6 January 1999, the convention was to consist of "no more than two hundred twenty-five delegates, to be apportioned among the several states in proportion to the total number of Representatives and Senators possessed by each state" (*Id.*, 287). The convention was to be limited to the matters addressed in his book, with the results to be ratified by conventions within the states. No federal officeholders were to be permitted to serve as delegates. The convention was mandated to establish a nine-member Committee on Consolidation and Restatement, which would "prepare a Consolidation and Restatement of the Constitution as then in effect" (*Id.,* 290).

Although Wade's deadline for both his proposed convention and amendments has passed, his proposals make an interesting contrast to a number of others that are designed to return more power to states and localities. By contrast, Wade believed the current central government suffered not from too much power but from too little. His rejection of a number of other popular proposals as inappropriate constitutional additions is also fascinating.

For Further Reading:

Wade, Edwin L. 1995. *Constitution 2000: A Federalist Proposal for the Next Century.* Chicago, Illinois: Let's Talk Sense.

❖ WALLACE, WILLIAM KAY (1886–?) ❖

American diplomat William Kay Wallace offered his critique of the U.S. Constitution and proposals for reform during the Great Depression (see Vile 1991c, 68–70). Wallace believed that the Constitution had been built on such ideas as individualism, natural rights, the social contract, and a geographically based state that were now seriously outdated. He further believed that economic reorganization was as important as political change.

Wallace advocated what he identified as "scientific capitalism" and declared it to be "the one best way, or the method of efficiency" (Wallace 1932, 104). Here, as elsewhere, Wallace seemed to assume that readers had as clear a view of what was required as he did. His initial description of the state as "the directive agency of social control, a clearing-house that will expedite and adjust public affairs" (*Id.,* 137), also seemed vague, although he did articulate his belief that a new government should outlaw war. Initially, he indicated that the form, but not the substance, of the existing three branches of government could be maintained.

Wallace presented his specific proposals, which he hoped to initiate through a constitutional convention, in a chapter near the end of his book. There he outlined five broad guarantees that the new government should assume. The first was a guarantee of economic liberty. He included specific rights "to the full fruits of one's labor," "to economic security," "to education," and "to leisure" (Wallace 1932, 182).

The second was a guarantee of social security designed to cover "all of the contingencies and possible caprices of fortune in the life of the individual." More specific guarantees included "social insurance" covering old age and unemployment, "child welfare and training," adjusted work schedules, and "adult education" (Wallace 1932, 183).

Wallace's third guarantee was that of a "more effective government." To this end, he proposed replacing the current states with nine regional states, each with four to six representatives. These representatives would form a national board of directors (presumably unicameral) that would select from its members a president, appoint all governmental officials from the civil service, and exercise legislative functions.

To implement his fourth guarantee of "personal liberty and property," Wallace advocated transferring all corporate enterprises from private to public ownership and paying current holders of such property in governmental bonds. The new industries would be "scientifically regulated," with the profit motive being replaced; individuals would, however, still be able to own other forms of private property "in order to stimulate the creative ingenuity of all the citizens" (Wallace 1932, 188).

Wallace's fifth guarantee was for a "planned national economy" (Wallace 1932, 189). To this end, the state would become the "supreme economic arbiter," with power to conscript citizens in war and peace. The state would further coordinate economic activities and organize credit "as a public not a private function" (*Id.,* 191).

Wallace's proposal was unique in its rejection of natural rights and in its almost complete embrace of a planned socialistic economy. Perhaps for this reason, his calls for a constitutional convention had no significant impact, and his proposals have been largely unknown to or ignored by subsequent reformers.

For Further Reading:

Wallace, William Kay. 1932. *Our Obsolete Constitution*. New York: John Day.

Vile, John R. 1991c. *Rewriting the United States Constitution: An Examination of Proposals from Reconstruction to the Present*. New York: Praeger.

❖ WAR, DECLARATION OF ❖

When New York and Rhode Island ratified the U.S. Constitution, they proposed that Congress should not be able to declare war except by a two-thirds vote. This proposal was reintroduced at the Hartford Convention of 1815. Beginning about the time of World War I, a number of proposals were introduced either to require supermajorities of two-thirds or three-fourths or to prohibit Congress from declaring war except in cases of invasion. Some proposals for a national initiative and referendum would also have required voter initiation or approval of such declarations.

World War II marks the last occasion that the United States officially declared war, yet the nation has subsequently been involved in costly conflicts in Korea and Vietnam as well as in a host of other minor engagements for which congressional approval was either tepid or lacking. Congress attempted to rein in presidential powers in the War Powers Resolution of 1973, but the law has not proved altogether successful (J. H. Ely 1993). Perhaps in part because of this resolution, President George Bush did get prior congressional consent for what proved to be a successful repulsion of Iraq in 1991 after its invasion of Kuwait.

Beginning in 1986, Democratic Representative Andy Jacobs Jr. of Indiana, a veteran of the Korean War, introduced several proposals to repeal the provision in Article I, Section 8 that grants Congress the power to declare war. According to one of his legislative aides, Jacobs's proposals were designed to call attention to the manner in which presidential foreign policy decisions have encroached on congressional powers (Tom Runge, telephone conversation with author, 15 June 1995).

An author concerned with distortions of the U.S. Constitution by members of the press has proposed an amendment to "clarify the war powers of both Congress and the president" (Bonsell 1995, 345). He would require a three-fourths majority of Congress to declare war, a declaration that would result in the automatic suspension of "the privilege of the Writ of Habeas Corpus and the Thirteenth Amendment [presumably to allow for a draft]." Congress would be permitted to declare war, without the accompanying power to suspend the writ of habeas corpus or the Thirteenth Amendment, by a two-thirds vote. Interestingly, the proposal also called for a provision, relating to the First Amendment, specifying that "[t]he right of the people to peacefully protest or legally resist any military action under this article shall be protected by all governments within the United States" (*Id.*, 345).

See also Hartford Convention; Initiative and Referendum.

For Further Reading:

Bonsell, Thomas. 1995. *The Un-Americans: Trashing of the United States Constitution in the American Press*. Wauna, WA: Country Cottage Publishing.

Ely, John Hart. 1993. *War and Responsibility: Constitutional Lessons of Vietnam and Its Aftermath*. Princeton, NJ: Princeton University Press.

❖ WAR, OPPOSITION TO GOVERNMENT DURING ❖

The U.S. Constitution protects dissent even in times of war. The Supreme Court has ruled, however, that speech that is normally permissible might be suppressed during wartime when such speech creates a "clear and present danger" that Congress has a right to prevent (*Schenck v. United States* 1919, 52).

Public opposition to U.S. participation in the Vietnam War was particularly intense. Although the Supreme Court upheld a federal law prohibiting the destruction of draft cards (*United States v. O'Brien* (1968)), it was otherwise fairly protective of political protesters during this period.

Between 1966 and 1969, Democratic Representative Olin (Tiger) Teague of Texas, a World War II veteran who chaired the Veterans' Affairs Committee, introduced at least three resolutions that would have made it unlawful to aid or encourage the United States' enemies during a war. His proposal, in obvious tension with the free speech and press guarantees of the First Amendment, would have included restrictions on "public demonstrations, public writings, [and] public speeches" (H.J. Res. 102, 1967).

For Further Reading:
Schenck v. United States, 249 U.S. 47 (1919).

❖ WAR, POWER DURING ❖

Constitutional provisions have afforded legal authority for extensive expansion of federal war powers, especially in this century. During World War I, such powers were utilized as a basis for seizing the nation's railroads and telephone and telegraph systems. Concern with winning the war also fueled the drive for national alcoholic prohibition (C. May 1989, 26, 60–93).

From 1922 to 1939, at least twenty-five amendments sought to grant the government power not only to conscript soldiers but also to conscript property during times of war (sponsors included Indiana Democratic Representative Louis Ludlow and North Dakota Republican Senator Gerald Nye). At least some of these proposals were motivated by a desire to take any profits out of war. Some proposals specifically sought to exempt governmental takings in wartime from the Fifth Amendment requirement that the government provide just compensation.

Short of this requirement, there appear to be few constitutional obstacles to governmental seizures and operation of industries during times of war. In *Youngstown Sheet & Tube Co. v. Sawyer* (1952), however, the Supreme Court invalidated President Harry S. Truman's seizure of the steel mills during the Korean War, but the justices focused on the lack of congressional authority for such a seizure (Congress had decided against such authority

when it adopted the Taft-Hartley Act of 1947) rather than on any inherent constitutional limitations on the subject.

The "war" on terrorism poses special problems because part of it takes place on American soil. In the aftermath of the terrorist attacks against the United States of 11 September 2001, many questions remain about the appropriateness of military trials, of the detention of suspects, and related issues.

See also War, Declaration of.

For Further Reading:
May, Christopher N. 1989. *In the Name of War.* Cambridge, MA.: Harvard University Press.

❖ WAR, PROHIBITION OF ❖

Republican Senator Lynn Frazier of North Dakota consistently introduced amending proposals from 1926 to 1939 to prohibit war by declaring it to be illegal. New York Republican (and later American Laborite) Representative Vito Marcantonio also submitted such a proposal in 1936.

Although the scope of these proposals was unusual and arguably utopian, the 1920s and 1930s saw substantial growth in antiwar sentiment and an American Committee for the Outlawry of War was established in December 1921. In August 1928 representatives of the United States and fourteen other nations signed the Kellogg-Briand Pact renouncing the use of war, but the Senate's eighty-five-to-one ratification of this treaty in January 1929 was predicated on reserving the nation's right to self-defense (Ellis 1961, 212). Not surprisingly, the treaty proved ineffective in preventing World War II and subsequent conflicts.

For Further Reading:
Ellis, L. Ethan. 1961. *Frank B. Kellogg and American Foreign Relations, 1925–1929.* New Brunswick, NJ: Rutgers University Press.

Morrison, Charles C. 1972. *The Outlawry of War: A Constructive Policy for World Peace.* New York: Garland Publishing.

❖ WARREN COURT ❖

Earl Warren served as chief justice of the United States Supreme Court from 1953 to 1969, and the Court during this period is generally referred to as the Warren Court. A former district attorney, attorney general, three-term California governor, and Republican vice presidential candidate, Warren proved to be a far more liberal and activist justice than President Eisenhower, who appointed him to the position, had anticipated. Moreover, although not nearly as intellectual as his strong-minded colleagues Hugo Black, William O. Douglas, Felix Frankfurter, John Marshall Harlan, and William Brennan (another liberal appointment that Eisenhower grew to regret), Warren proved to be an effective leader who could often achieve a greater degree of consensus than might otherwise have been expected.

Shortly after Warren assumed the reins of the Court, it issued its unanimous decision in *Brown v. Board of Education* (1954), overturning *Plessy v. Ferguson* (1896) and declaring an end to long-standing *de jure* racial segregation in the United States. In numerous subsequent decisions, the Court showed some flexibility in the implementation of desegregation decisions but never deviated from the central principle articulated in *Brown*. Significantly, in *Bolling v. Sharpe* (1954), the Court held that the due process clause of the Fifth Amendment could be used to strike down egregious forms of discrimination at the federal level, just like the equal protection clause of the Fourteenth Amendment was being used to strike down state segregation laws.

In 1962 the Court issued its decision in *Baker v. Carr*, declaring that state legislative apportionment was not a political question but was justiciable under the equal protection clause of the Fourteenth Amendment. In a follow-up case, *Reynolds v. Sims* (1964), the Court applied the "one person one vote" standard to both houses of state legislatures. These decisions stirred considerable sentiment for a constitutional amendment to give states greater leeway. Focusing on the apportionment decisions and other liberal rulings, the conservative John Birch Society launched an effort to impeach Earl Warren. Such attempts had little apparent effect on the Supreme Court's liberal decisions related to the First Amendment and in other areas of the law.

The Warren Court's rulings on the Fourteenth Amendment contained some of its most influential constitutional interpretations. Before Warren came to the Court, it had already begun the process of selectively incorporating some of the important limitations on the national government that were found in the Bill of Rights and applying them to the states—see *Palko v. Connecticut* (1937) and *Adamson v. California* (1947). The Warren Court rapidly accelerated this process, especially with respect to the rights of criminal defendants. Thus, in *Mapp v. Ohio* (1961), it applied the exclusionary rule to the states; in *Gideon v. Wainwright* (1963), it extended the right to appointed counsel for indigents; and in *Miranda v. Arizona* (1966), it extended a whole panoply of rights previously required only at the federal level. In *Griswold v. Connecticut* (1965), the Court struck down a Connecticut law proscribing birth control by holding that the provisions in the Bill of Rights had penumbras that encompassed the right to privacy, thus laying a foundation for the Court's liberal abortion decision in *Roe v. Wade* (1973) in the following decade. The Court also broadened protection under the Fourth Amendment, specifically outlawing warrantless eavesdropping in *Katz v. United States* (1967). In his last major decision from the bench, *Powell v. McCormack* (1969), Warren further narrowed the political questions doctrine (overturning an attempt by the House of Representatives by majority vote to preclude the seating of a member who met the age, residency, and citizenship requirements spelled out in the Constitution), with possible implications for future amending cases.

Many of the Warren Court's decisions led to proposed amendments, but none proved successful. The Court did, however, encounter considerable political opposition. When Warren first expressed his desire to resign, many of the criticisms of the Court as being too liberal and too activist fell on President Lyndon Johnson's choice of Justice Abe Fortas, who withdrew from consideration for chief justice and later resigned from the Court. President Richard Nixon subsequently had the chance to appoint Warren Burger to this position. Both Burger and his successor, William Rehnquist, have issued more conservative decisions, in many cases not so much reversing as slowing earlier trends (Funston 1977). The Courts headed by Warren Burger and William Rehnquist have been considerably more sympathetic to states' interests than was the Warren Court. The Warren Court stands as one of the clearest examples of the way the Supreme Court can inaugurate a constitutional revolution without the adoption of new amendments.

For Further Reading:

Funston, Richard Y. 1977. *Constitution Counterrevolution? The Warren Court and the Burger Court: Judicial Policy Making in Modern America*. New York: Schenkman.

Schwartz, Bernard. 1988. *Super Chief: Earl Warren and His Supreme Court—A Judicial Biography*. New York: New York University Press.

❖ WASHINGTON, GEORGE (1732–1799) ❖

George Washington fought for the colonists and British in the French and Indian War, served as leader of American forces during the Revolutionary War, presided over the Constitutional Convention of 1787, and served as the nation's first president. Washington set a noble example for the nation, later incorporated into the presidency, in submitting to civilian authority as commander in chief during the Revolutionary War and in subsequently renouncing the use of force against Congress to gain legitimate demands of members of the military. Although he was not as intellectually gifted as John Adams, Thomas Jefferson, or James Madison, he articulated a vision of America's destiny that was remarkably prescient (Bradley 1945). At the Constitutional Convention, over which he presided, Washington did not speak frequently. However, he appears to have contributed to the Virginia Plan; his regal bearing lent a solemnity to the occasion; and the delegates' conviction that he would serve as the na-

tion's first president led them to create a stronger executive than they probably otherwise would have done. Washington's subsequent whole-hearted support of the new Constitution, and his service as first president (he remains the only president who received the unanimous votes of all the presidential electors), were critical to the forging of the Union. He was supremely conscious that his actions as president would set important precedents, and he acted accordingly. His farewell address, in which he warned about the dangers of encroachments by one governmental branch over others; about what he considered to be the baneful role of political parties (although often identified as a Federalist, Washington had both Federalists and Democratic-Republicans in his cabinet and tried to project the image that he was above parties); and of the danger of entangling foreign alliances, is an important state paper. Washington's precedent of stepping down from the presidency after two terms was not broken until the twentieth century administration of President Franklin D. Roosevelt, after which it was formally reestablished by adoption of the Twenty-second Amendment.

The Bill of Rights, consisting of the first ten amendments, was proposed and ratified during Washington's first term, as was the Eleventh Amendment. Much like James Madison, Washington appears to have believed that although not all the amendments in the Bill of Rights were absolutely necessary, they could do no harm and would help quiet the fears that opponents of the new Constitution had stirred (Vile 1992, 50). As President, Washington agreed to the plan by Alexander Hamilton, his secretary of the treasury, for the establishment of a national bank, even though the creation of such a bank rested on implied, rather than specifically enumerated, constitutional powers and thus had been opposed by Secretary of State Thomas Jefferson, who also thought that the bank interfered with powers reserved to the states under the Tenth Amendment. Without Washington's and Hamilton's broad interpretation of the Constitution, later ratified by the U.S. Supreme Court in *McCullock v. Maryland* (1819), the Constitution would have required considerably more amendments.

In his farewell address and elsewhere, Washington drew the obligation to obedience to government from the presence of a means of peaceful change:

> The Government . . . containing within itself a provision for its own amendment, has a just claim to your confidence and support. Respect for its authority, compliance with its laws, acquiescence in its measures, are duties enjoined by the fundamental maximums of true liberty. The basis of our political system is the right of the people to make and to alter their constitution of government. But the constitution which at any time exists till changed by an explicit and authentic act of the whole people is sacredly obligatory upon all. (quoted in Kaufman 1969, 21)

The author of one of the most comprehensive books on the history of the amending process has used Washington's reference to "explicit and authentic acts" in the above quotation for the title of his volume (Kyvig 1996a). On many other occasions, Washington referred to the amending process as a "constitutional door" (Norham 1988). Thus, in arguing that the new Constitution was not perfect but was a distinct improvement over the Articles of Confederation, Washington noted that it was one in which "a Constitutional door is left open for its amelioration" (Fitzpatrick 1931–1944, 29:411).

See also Constitutional Convention of 1787; Hamilton, Alexander; Jefferson, Thomas; Twenty-second Amendment.

For Further Reading:

Bradley, Harold W. 1945. "The Political Thinking of George Washington." *Journal of Southern History* 11 (November): 469–486.

Fitzpatrick, John C. 1931–1944. *The Writings of George Washington.* 39 vols. Washington, DC: U.S. Government Printing Office.

Kaufman, Burton I. 1969. *Washington's Farewell Address: The View from the 20th Century.* Chicago: Quadrangle Books.

Kyvig, David E. 1996a. *Explicit and Authentic Acts: Amending the Constitution, 1776–1995.* Lawrence, KS: University Press of Kansas.

Norham, George W. 1988. "A Constitutional Door Is Opened for Amendment." *Texas Bar Journal* 51 (September): 804–806.

Rhodehamel, John. 1998. *The Great Experiment: George Washington and the American Republic.* New Haven, CT: Yale University Press.

Vile, John R. 1992. *The Constitutional Amending Process in American Political Thought.* New York: Praeger.

❖ WATSON, GREGORY (1960–) ❖

Gregory Watson served as an aide to Texas state senator Ric Williamson. As a sophomore economics major at the University of Texas at Austin, Watson wrote a paper for a government class in which he examined the amendment to delay congressional pay raises until an election intervened, which had been introduced in 1789 as part of the original Bill of Rights. He concluded that this proposal was still a viable subject for state ratification.

Despite receiving a "C" on this paper, Watson launched a one-man campaign, financed with his own funds, for ratification of this amendment (Bernstein 1992, 537). Watson's efforts were rewarded in 1992 (Watson was then thirty years old) with the putative ratification of the Twenty-seventh Amendment.

Today Watson, who continues to be a legislative assistant in the Texas House of Representatives, advocates "updating" the constitutional amending process, presumably by constitutional amendment. Watson favors requiring that amendments be proposed by a two-thirds vote of the entire congressional membership (rather than, as at present, by those in attendance), and eliminating state legislative ratification. He advocates ratification by national referendum in an election year, with amendments requiring ratification by "a simple majority of all votes cast in not less than two-thirds of the geographical districts that comprise the U.S. House of Representatives" (G. Watson 2000, 16). Watson would permit only one such amendment to be offered in any given election, and it would have to be proposed "no later than a full calendar year prior to the election date so that there can be public discussion and debate on the matter" (*Id.*, 16).

See also Twenty-seventh Amendment.

For Further Reading:

"The Man Who Would Not Quit." 1992. *People* 37 (1 April): 72.

Watson, Gregory. 2000. "I Have a Better Way." *Insights on Law & Society* 1 (Fall) 16.

❖ WEDGWOOD, WILLIAM B. (?–1883) ❖

William B. Wedgwood was a Maine native who moved to New York, where he joined the bar in 1841. He favored numerous reforms during his life, including civil service reform and the emancipation and recolonization of the slaves and the compensation of their owners (Boyd 1992, 22). An author and educator as well as a lawyer, Wedgwood wrote books on New York law and the U.S. Constitution and helped found the City University of New York School of Law (Boyd 1992, 29). Wedgwood's most novel contribution to thinking about constitutional change was a new constitution included in his 1861 book entitled *The Reconstruction of the Government of the United States of America*.

Wedgwood's immediate aim was to halt the progression of the Civil War, and his solution was to allow North and South to form two republics, joined together as the "Democratic Empire." Believing that the United States was heir to the blessings that had once been bestowed on ancient Israel, Wedgwood described his proposed plan as a "theocratic Democracy" (Wedgwood 1861, 15). As did the future constitution for the Confederate states, Wedgwood's contained an acknowledgment of God in the preamble. He also stated that the primary purpose of government was to "develop and arrange" natural law principles into "a written code, under the sanction of legislative enactment" (Wedgwood 1861, 17). Early articles of Wedgwood's constitution elaborately described the flag and seal of the Democratic Empire, the former to contain seven colors and thirteen stripes in a double rainbow containing, among other things, the otherwise unexplained symbolical letters W.C.P.P.

Wedgwood's constitution contained a number of novel features. In several places it went into detail about the relationship between natural rights and political rights. It guaranteed a good education to all and required that all citizens labor (Wedgwood 1861, 16). Although protecting the right to worship, it prohibited "the worship of idols and the sacrifice of human beings" (*Id.*, 17). Several times it sanctioned the government's right to exercise eminent domain.

Wedgwood would have set up three degrees, or levels, of government—state, national, and imperial. Each would comprise officeholders "of high moral and religious character" (Wedgwood 1861, 18). States would fall naturally into "Labor States" and "Capital States," with Wedgwood advocating extension of the Missouri Compromise line "west until it reaches the Atlantic [*sic*] Ocean" (*Id.*, 19). Each of the three levels of government would be divided into legislative, executive, and judicial branches, with terms in the respective Houses of Representatives being one, two, and four years and those in the respective Senates being two, four, and six years. Similarly, state governors would serve for two years, the president for four years, and the emperor for six years.

Wedgwood went into surprising detail in describing the powers of state governments. State powers would include regulation of property, education, and highways; providing employment for the needy; and enacting laws for domestic relations. National powers seemed to be designed to handle problems between and among the states. The imperial government (headquartered in New York) would deal with matters of defense and diplomacy, with the emperor serving as commander in chief of the army and navy.

Wedgwood believed that the impending Civil War had been brought on in large part by those who had spoken contemptuously, sometimes from the pulpit, of the old Constitution and of those who owned slaves. In a provision that appears to have been in serious tension with the First Amendment, Wedgwood accordingly proposed that "slanderous words, coming from whatever source they may come, must be suppressed and punished. All unkind language, by which the feelings of a fellow-citizen may be injured, should be carefully avoided" (Wedgwood 1861, 26).

Wedgwood hoped that Canada, Mexico, and other Central and South American republics would eventually join the new empire, "triumphantly" vindicating the Monroe Doctrine (Wedgwood 1861, 27). Wedgwood ended his discourse with reference to the four horses of the biblical book of Revelation. Clearly, Wedgwood's primary, and unsuccessful, hope was to avoid the impending conflict.

For Further Reading:

Boyd, Steven R., ed. 1992. *Alternative Constitutions for the United States: A Documentary History.* Westport, CT: Greenwood Press.

Wedgwood, William B. 1861. *The Reconstruction of the Government of the United States of America: A Democratic Empire Advocated and an Imperial Constitution Proposed.* New York: John H. Tingley.

❖ WELFARE PAYMENTS, RIGHT TO ❖

Although it is generally accurate to say that "welfare benefits are legislative choices, not constitutional commands" (Lieberman 1992, 574), courts have surrounded welfare recipients with certain constitutional protections. Thus, in *Shapiro v. Thompson* (1969), the Supreme Court ruled that a Connecticut one-year residency requirement for welfare recipients violated the right to travel, and in *Saenz v. Roe* (1999) the Court struck down differential welfare benefits for new state residents. Similarly, in *Goldberg v. Kelly* (1970), the Court ruled that a New York law that did not provide welfare recipients with a hearing before terminating benefits was unconstitutional.

In 1971 Republican Representative Edwin Eshleman of Pennsylvania introduced an amendment related to welfare rights. It declared that welfare was "not a right, but is to be determined in accordance with the specific provisions of . . . laws, duly enacted by the Congress of the United States or by the State or political subdivision involved" (H.J. Res. 206). On a related topic, a proposal by Rhode Island's ratifying convention in 1790 would have

specified "that Congress should have power to establish a uniform rule of inhabitancy and settlement of the poor of the different States throughout the United States" (Ames 1896, 189).

In recent years, Congress has largely attempted to deal with the issue of welfare through legislative action. This legislation has allowed states to require that those on welfare seek employment. It has also limited the number of years that recipients can remain on welfare. Despite some attempts to embody such social and economic rights into the Constitution, this would generally appear to be a matter that can better be addressed by legislation, which is subject to repeal and modification through regular legislative processes, than through the more cumbersome amending process.

For Further Reading:

Ames, Herman. 1896. *The Proposed Amendments to the Constitution of the United States during the First Century of Its History.* Reprint, New York: Burt Franklin, 1970.

Lieberman, Jethro K. 1992. *The Evolving Constitution: How the Supreme Court Has Ruled on Issues from Abortion to Zoning.* New York: Random House.

❖ WEST, JAMES C. (?–1946) ❖

One of the least accessible proposals for a new constitution was contained in a book published by James C. West in Springfield, Missouri, in 1890. The only known copy is now a fragile document in the Library of Congress, but fortunately, the proposal has recently been reprinted (Boyd 1992).

West served as a clerk, a newspaper editor, and a prosecuting attorney, and although he was a Democrat, his ideology was close to that of the Populists (Boyd 1992, 68–69). The historian who reprinted West's constitution noted that it reflected "the limited horizon of a midwestern small town political observer" (*Id.*, 70). Although most of West's proposals followed the outline of the Constitution of 1787, he added several features that made his proposal unique.

Congress remained fairly similar, but West added a requirement that members be natural born and sought to guarantee one representative for every 175,000 persons. He also would have excluded individuals from the House who were worth more than $25,000 and senators who were worth more than $50,000. The terms of senators would be reduced to four years, and no person would be eligible to either house who had "not labored five years, after he had attained the age of ten years, at either agricultural or some mechanical arts" (Boyd 1992, 74). Members would have to attend all congressional sessions except in cases of sickness. Their oath would obligate them to seek "the greatest good of the greatest number," and they would swear not to "approve of anything contrary to the spirit of the Constitution, either express or implied" or risk "the vengeance of God . . . and the universal detestation of mankind" (*Id.,* 74). The wages of members of Congress were not to exceed fifteen times the wage of laboring farmhands. West attempted to guard against committee changes in a bill contrary to its sponsor's intentions and appeared to make provision for the House of Representatives to act alone to override a presidential veto of a finance bill.

In listing the powers of Congress, West attempted to prevent the government from collecting surplus revenue. However, he favored introduction of "a tax on the sumptuousness of the people" as well as taxes on land and income. He also sought to limit borrowing except in cases of war and not until "the circulating medium has been increased to $60 sixty dollars per capita" (Boyd 1992, 78). Generally, he wanted the circulating capital to be maintained at $40 per person. West wanted to make it a crime for persons or corporations to "engage in any pool, combine, trust or rebate system," and he hoped to prevent the immigration of persons who "Congress thinks are detrimental" (*Id.,* 78, 81).

West wanted the president to be elected by popular vote. The president's salary could not exceed 125 times the average wage for a laboring farmhand. The president's powers, like those of the judiciary, remained unchanged.

After repeating the core of the current amending process, West went on to suggest that amendments "which will render null and void any provision of this Constitution" would require consent by three-fourths of the House and a majority of voters, whereas amendments adding to the Constitution would require only the former. West proposed that his constitution would go into effect when ratified by two-thirds of the states. His document included all fifteen amendments that were then part of the Constitution, except for the Twelfth, which he omitted in recognition that the president would, under his system, be elected by popular vote.

For Further Reading:
Boyd, Steven R., ed. 1992. *Alternative Constitutions for the United States: A Documentary History.* Westport, CT: Greenwood Press.

❖ WILLARD, FRANCES (1839–1898) ❖

Descended from a prominent New England family, Frances Willard was one of the driving forces both for national alcoholic prohibition (for which she is better known) and for women's suffrage. Both movements began as state-based movements, the first being embodied for a time after her death in the Eighteenth Amendment before being repealed by the Twenty-First, and the second coming to fruition with the ratification of the Nineteenth Amendment in 1920.

Born in new Rochester, New York, but largely raised on a farm in the Wisconsin Territory, Frances Willard, who preferred to be called "Frank," attended college in Milwaukee and at the Northwestern Female College in Evanston, Illinois. While in college, Willard had a conversion experience, later joining the Methodist Church. Subsequently serving in a number of teaching and educational administration positions, which included the presidency of the Evanston College of Ladies and, when it was made part of Northwestern University, as dean of women, Willard became actively involved in the temperance movement in Chicago. She rapidly rose from serving as president of the Chicago Woman's Christian Temperance Union to the corresponding secretaryship of the National Women's Temperance Convention, to the presidency of the Woman's Christian Temperance Union, where she served from 1879 until her death, and of the World's Woman's Christian Temperance Union ("Francis Willard," 1928–1936).

Although she would have preferred to be self-supporting, Willard, who remained unmarried, accepted a salary with the organization so that she could devote all her efforts to the cause. At least initially, the organization flourished under her leadership. Rather than focusing on economic arguments, she emphasized protecting the values of home and hearth, and was willing to advocate women's suffrage and other reform issues. Her later conversion to the ideas of Fabian socialism did not prove particularly popular in America. She traveled and lectured widely for the WCTU and spent considerable time in England in her later years.

See also Eighteenth Amendment; Nineteenth Amendment; Women's Christian Temperance Union.

For Further Reading:

Dubois, Ellen Carol. 1991. "Frances Willard. *The Reader's Companion to American History.* P. 1151. Accessed through *www.galenet.com.*

"Francis Elizabeth Caroline Willard." 1928–1936. *Dictionary of American Biography* Base Set. American Council of Learned Societies. Accessed through *www.galenet.com.*

❖ WILLARD, SIMON, JR. (1795–1874) ❖

One of the most elaborate plans to rewrite the U.S. Constitution was also one of the earliest, but it slipped quickly into obscurity and does not appear to have been the subject of any commentary prior to this encyclopedia entry. Written by Simon Willard Jr., the 195-page proposal was printed in New York in 1815. It has the prolix title *The Columbian Union, Containing General and Particular Explanations of Government, and the Columbian Constitution,*

Being an Amendment to the Constitution of the United States: Providing a Yearly Revenue to Government of About Forty Millions of Dollars, and the Inevitable Union of the People by a Rule of Voting, and Exemption from Unnecessary Taxation, Consequently Their Permanent and Perpetual Freedom (Willard 1815).

The author was the descendant of a well-known Indian fighter and colonist also named Simon Willard, the son of a notable Massachusetts clockmaker (to whom the "banjo clock" is attributed) and the father of another. Born in Roxbury, Massachusetts, in 1795, Willard apparently had a hard childhood, was apprenticed to another watchmaker, and then entered the West Point Military Academy in 1813 at the age of eighteen. He graduated in 1815, and resigned from the military a year later (Willard 1968, 68). Failing at a crockery-making business, Simon went into clock making with his father, later specializing in chronometers and other nautical devices. He was the oldest living graduate of West Point when he died in 1874 (Robinson and Burt 1996, 13). Biographical information about Willard is sketchy, but none appears to refer to his proposal for a new Union, which, given its date of publication, was probably written while he was at West Point. By contrast, Willard Sr.'s correspondence with Thomas Jefferson about a clock purchased for the Rotunda at the University of Virginia is well known.

As the title of his proposal suggests, Willard was especially interested in renaming the nation. Willard used lots of religious language, with a fairly strong emphasis on the doctrine of original sin, which he associated in politics largely with what he considered to be the baneful influence of political parties, monarchy, and aristocratic privilege. Apart from his religious language, Willard's sentiments were for the most part strongly republican, resembling ideas current not only during the French Revolution in France of 1789 but also ideas espoused in America by such writers as Joel Barlow and Thomas Jefferson. Thus, reflecting a Jeffersonian emphasis on farmers, early in his book Willard noted that:

The tiller's soul, forms the patriot of nature, but the civil minds of commodities

invites the foreigner of wrong; the move-
ables of traffic, foreign to the fixidity of
the soil.

The fixed agriculturalists, are manufacturers most humble servants, and only
guardian parent of all commerce.
(Willard 1815, 12)

Unlike Jefferson and other contemporary
American republicans (as well as New England
Federalists of the day), however, Willard had
little interest in federalism, believing that rival
governments disrupt civic unity. By contrast:

A general constitution is an agreement,
by which not a part, but all the people
can understand each other, so as not only
to keep out of war, but to direct each
other in that kind of pursuit, the most
common in society for the general happiness of all. (Willard 1815, 15)

Willard further observed that:

The Columbian Constitution, amendatory to that of the United States, only
takes from it partial power, but adds to
me more general energy, more liberty,
and more unity of general government.
(Willard 1815, 23)

In the preamble to the Columbian Constitution that he proposed, Willard noted "the overthrow of the world's maritime equilibrium"
(Willard 1815, 25), an apparent reference to the
War of 1812. He also cites the need "for our ref-
ormation and the preservation of all that country, that unity of government, and that liberty for
which our fathers fought" (*Id.*, 26). The text of
the proposed printed Constitution was followed
by long explanations that took up almost the last
half of the Willard's book. Willard's constitution
was divided into twenty-seven articles.

Article I of the Columbian Constitution proposed renaming the nation the "Columbian
Union" (after Christopher Columbus, who,
along with George Washington, was associated
with divine providence) and dividing it into
geometrical units. Initially, Columbia would
have thirty-four such districts, populated
roughly equally. Many would have been named
after existing states, but Willard also hoped to

include Canada in the new Union. Districts
would be divided into counties, each with its
own capitol, its own towns and town houses,
called "Temples" (Willard 1815, 30). Each
county with 3,125 or more voters should in
turn select a representative to the Columbian
Congress, with one representative in the upper
house for each five in the lower.

Article II provided for nine annual meetings
of states, designated as the May Election, the
July Election, the September Election, the Ver-
nal Council, the Summer Council, the Autum-
nal Council, the August Assembly, the New
Year Assembly and the Columbian Congress,
the latter to meet from November through
March (Willard 1815, 32–33).

Article III proposed annual elections for the
legislative and executive divisions. Six classes of
legislators were designated—"actors, directors,
commissioners, representers, legislators, and mediators," with the executive being divided into
minor presidents, major presidents, special presidents, and the general president (Willard 1815,
34). The Columbian Congress would be bicameral with mediators serving in the higher branch
and general legislators in the lower. Suffrage
would extent "to every free male person of the
Columbian Union, having attained to the age of
twenty-one years" (*Id.*, 36). Stockholders (perhaps derived from opposition to a national
bank?), members of a "partial body politic"
(presumably, political parties), and, as of the end
of the nineteenth century, slaveholders, would
be prevented from holding office (*Id.*, 37).

Article IV provided for other governmental
offices. One fascinating proposal would limit the
kinds of information that could be published in
campaign materials (Willard 1815, 43).

Article V contained eleven sections and specified how and when various representatives
would be elected. Similarly, Article VI dealt
with the elections of presidents, who were por-
trayed—much as in contemporary parliamentary systems—as heads of the respective legislative bodies.

Article VII specified the pay scale for public
officials, which was to be paid in "talents," each
worth thirteen and one-third cents. The general president would receive 150,000 talents.
The Columbian Congress would allocate

monies from general revenues to the states to pay for the salaries of county officials.

Article VIII limited the authorization of public monies except through sovereign officials. Article IX extended the privilege against arrest to such officials. Article X gave equivalences of officers under the old and new constitutions, with, for example, the U.S. Senate to be called the Mediation, the House of Representatives designated as the Grand Council, governors now being called special presidents, and so on. Willard did specify that "For the unity of general government all inferior legislative bodies shall be subservient to those of higher legislative powers" (Willard 1815, 59–60). Similarly, Section 3 voided all conflicting provisions of the current Constitution. Section 4 of this article allowed slavery to continue in states where it then existed with the slave trade and further growth of slavery to be discouraged. A slave line, similar to that later enacted in the Missouri Compromise, was also proposed, north of which slavery would have been prohibited.

Article XI allowed Congress to "make all laws necessary for carrying into effect the powers contained in this constitution" (Willard 1815, 52), but it is not clear whether the word "proper" was purposely omitted or not. Congress was given power to encourage internal improvements.

Article XII authorized the production of Columbian maps with "an accurate projection of uniform points, relatively denoting the places of all capitols, and degree lines describing of Columbia the parallels of latitude, and meridians of longitude, representing oblong squares, in imitation of and equal to all the degrees of Columbia" (Willard 1815, 63). Article XIII further provided for subservient "military, judiciary and other necessary officers" (*Id.*, 64).

Article XIII dealt with Columbian courts, dividing them into four parts. In part tracking and in part elaborating on the language of the Second Amendment, Article XV specified that "A well-regulated militia under the general subordination and enfranchisement of all the people being required for their common freedom, the Columbian Congress . . . shall establish . . . a uniform military system of general order throughout the Columbian Union, for training, equipping, instructing, directing and governing the militia" (Willard 1815, 65–66). This article was extensive, specifying military organization, and introducing the general president's executive council, perhaps similar to the modern cabinet.

Article XVI was an extensive article outlining plans for a general currency, protecting against counterfeiting and specifying the denominations of bills (to include bills of $3, $30, $200, and $300). This Article also set interest rates at 6 percent per year (Willard 1815, 78). Article XVII further specified the coins that would be used in the improved union.

The title of Willard's book focused in part on revenue, and revenue and taxation are the subject of Article XVIII. This article distinguished between "ratemen," who are taxable, and "freeman," who would not be (Willard 1815, 84). To be considered a freeman, an individual:

shall not be a member privileged, or stockholder of any incorporated company, or partial body politic, or of any pursuit pernicious to the general obedience and welfare of the Columbian Union, who shall be the owner of and not exceeding the quantity of land of either of the following description, viz: an improved farm of one hundred acres of good feasible land. (Willard 1815, 85)

Different standards were set for those pursuing "a necessary mechanical pursuit" (Willard 1815, 85). Taxation would be extended to those who owned or hired slaves, and imported luxuries, as well as gambling, would be taxed.

Article XIX provided for clarity in the conveyance of land titles and mortgages. All freemen "shall have an equal right to the common forest of Columbia," with protections provided for "obedient" Indian tribes (Willard 1815, 91). Article XX further provided for uniform weights and measures, while Article XXI provided for copyrights and patents.

Whereas the U.S. Constitution does not specifically mention schools, Willard provided in Article XXII that:

The Columbian Congress shall establish and make all needful rules and regulations expedient for free schools throughout the Columbian Union under the direction of a general school office, to be kept in the vicinity of the Columbian Capitol: and which shall provide that the attention of orphans, and minors of poor parents (slaves excepted) shall be as constant and faithful at school, in acquiring a knowledge of government, and other essential advantages of society as those of the rich. (Willard 1815, 93)

Article XXIII further provided for "a general benevolent office" to provide for "the support of the needy" (Willard 1815, 93). Again, because the proposed Columbian constitution would blend responsibilities then exercised by state governments, in Article XXIV its Congress was granted full power to regulate marriages and divorces, estates, criminal procedures, bankruptcies, and so forth.

Article XXV provided for the continuing validity of acts of the prior Constitution. Article XXVI permitted inducements to be given to English and Canadian officers who shall cease war against the United States (with an apparent view of uniting the United States and Canada). This novel provision further stated that:

The Columbian Union shall never assume the superior power and dominion of the seas, but the Columbian Congress shall cause to be kept dismantled, the guns of their vectored ships, so that Columbia shall never excel any combination of naval power. (Willard 1815, 96)

Article XXVII, the final article, provided that the Columbian constitution shall go into effect when ratified in conventions "of three fourths of the compacts of the United States called towns in this constitution, or of two thirds of the legislatures of the several states" (Willard 1815, 96).

After completing the outline of his proposed Columbian Constitution, Willard provided for the adoption of either of two additional provisions (both designated as Article I). The first appeared designed to repeal the three-fifths clause in 1830. The second would have prohibited individuals with direct financial interests in foreign trade from passing laws dealing

with the same. Willard further printed the existing U.S. Constitution and specified that the existing Constitution "will remain in full force, and so far constitute a part of the Columbian Constitution" (Willard 1815, 97).

Willard's proposed constitution remains one of the most detailed and enigmatic on record. Reflecting a mixture of ideas from a variety of sources, as well as an excessive attention to precision and detail that one might expect from an individual who would distinguish himself as a clockmaker, the proposal does not appear to have served as a model for others, although in its detail and originality, it arguably foreshadows the constitutions later proposed by Rexford Tugwell, and its method of taxation might foreshadow the later proposal by Henry George for a single tax on land. Given the breadth of Willard's proposals, there is a clear need for additional research that will situate this proposal within its historical context.

For Further Reading:

Robinson, Roger W., and Herschel B. Burt, ed. by Robert Edwards. 1996. *The Willard House and Clock Museum and the Willard Family Clockmakers.* Columbia, PA: National Association of Watch and Clock Collectors, Inc.

Willard, John Ware. 1911. *Simon Willard and His Clocks.* Reprint, New York: Dover Publications, 1968. Unabridged and corrected version of 1911, *A History of Simon Willard, Inventor and Clockmaker.*

Willard, Simon, Jr. 1815. *The Columbian Union, Containing General and Particular Explanations of Government, and the Columbian Constitution, Being an Amendment to the Constitution of the United States: Providing a Yearly Revenue to Government of About Forty Millions of Dollars, and the Inevitable Union of the People by a Rule of Voting, and Exemption from Unnecessary Taxation, Consequently Their Permanent and Perpetual Freedom.* Albany, NY: printed for the author.

❖ WILSON, THOMAS WOODROW (1856–1924) ❖

In addition to serving as the twenty-eighth president of the United States, Thomas Woodrow Wilson was an influential critic of the constitutional amending process and the U.S. system of checks and balances. He was also a strong advocate of the British parliamentary system and was more influential than many merely academic critics of the U.S. system.

In an early work, *Congressional Government,* Wilson noted that "it would seem that no impulse short of the impulse of self-preservation, no force less than the force of revolution, can nowadays be expected to move the cumbrous machinery of formal amendment erected in Article V" (Wilson 1885, 242). Similarly, in a later work, Wilson contrasted the Newtonian system outlined in the U.S. Constitution with the Darwinian system of the natural world: "The trouble with the [Newtonian] theory is that government is not a machine, but a living thing. It falls, not under the theory of the universe, but under the theory of organic life. It is accountable to Darwin, not to Newton" (Wilson 1908, 56).

Wilson was a strong admirer of the English governmental system and of responsible cabinet government. He believed that parliamentary debates refined and enlarged public views and attracted gifted and principled men to involvement in politics. In a work that was not published in his lifetime, Wilson advocated two constitutional changes to advance the nation closer to such a system. One would allow the president to choose members of Congress for his cabinet. They would, in turn, be permitted to initiate legislation and lead debate (Wilson 1882, 202). Elsewhere, Wilson indicated that such a system would also require "ministerial responsibility," under which the cabinet would resign if Congress rejected "any important part of their plans" (Wilson 1879, 498). Wilson's second proposal called for lengthening the terms of both the president and members of Congress (Wilson 1882, 202). When he feared loss of the presidency in his 1916 contest with Charles Evans Hughes, Wilson apparently considered appointing Hughes as secretary of state and then having him and his vice president resign so that Hughes could assume office early.

Although Wilson's early focus was on congressional government, he increasingly advocated presidential leadership. Competently leading the nation through World War I, Wil-

son was unable to get the nation to join the League of Nations after the war, and he ruined his health in the process of trying.

The Progressive Era, during which Wilson served as president, witnessed the addition of four constitutional amendments, somewhat undermining Wilson's own observations about constitutional inflexibility. The Sixteenth and Seventeenth Amendments were ratified almost simultaneously with Wilson's inauguration. Wilson opposed the Eighteenth Amendment but, faced with constant demonstrations in front of the White House, was eventually persuaded to support the Nineteenth Amendment in part as a way of unifying the nation during a time of war. Both amendments were ratified toward the end of his second term.

For Further Reading:

Wilson, (Thomas) Woodrow. 1908. *Constitutional Government in the United States.* Reprint, New York: Columbia University Press, 1961.

———. 1885. *Congressional Government: A Study in American Politics.* Boston: Houghton Mifflin.

———. 1882. "Government by Debate: Being a Short View of Our National Government as It Is and as It Might Be." In *The Papers of Woodrow Wilson,* vol. 2, ed. Arthur S. Link. Reprint, Princeton, NJ: Princeton University Press, 1967.

———. 1879. *Cabinet Government in the United States.* In *The Papers of Woodrow Wilson,* vol. 1, ed. Arthur S. Link. Reprint, Princeton, NJ: Princeton University Press, 1966.

❖ WOMEN'S CHRISTIAN TEMPERANCE UNION ❖

Like the struggle for women's suffrage that culminated in the adoption of the Nineteenth Amendment, the movement that led to national alcoholic prohibition and the ratification of the Eighteenth Amendment was decades in the making. The Women's Christian Temperance Union (WCTU) was among the most important groups in the early struggle for Prohibition. The WCTU was founded in Lake Chautauqua, New York, in August 1874, the year after lectures in Ohio by Dr. Diocletion Lewis sparked the women's crusade to force the closure of saloons.

By the 1880s the WCTU was "the largest organization of women the United States had yet known" (Bordin 1981, xvi). Indeed, the WCTU has been described as "unquestionably the first mass movement of American women" (*Id.*, 156). At its first national convention held in Cleveland, Ohio, in 1874, the WCTU elected Annie Wittmyer, founder of the Methodist Home Missionary Society and editor of the *Christian Woman,* as its first president. The WCTU selected Frances Willard of Illinois, a college educator, as corresponding secretary. Willard would head the WCTU in its glory days from 1879 until her death in 1898. She was succeeded by Lillian M. Stevens, who served as president from 1898 to 1914.

The WCTU succeeded in mobilizing large numbers of women—mostly, but not exclusively, middle- and upper-class white evangelical Protestants—under the banner of "home protection." Such women were able to engage in political action in defense of what had traditionally been regarded as women's chief sphere—a sphere often threatened when the male breadwinner became an alcoholic. Moreover, following Willard's "do everything" philosophy, the organization sponsored a variety of political programs, with state and local chapters being given considerable discretion in choosing where they would focus their energies. Concerns of the WCTU included women's suffrage, prison reform, the establishment of kindergartens and Sunday schools, Sabbath observance, temperance education, proposals for moral purity and the elevation of prostitutes, labor reforms, eugenics, and antismoking. For a time during the 1880s, the WCTU was closely allied with the National Prohibition Party. Some, but by no means all, members embraced contemporary antinativist and anti–Roman Catholic sentiments. The *Union Signal* was the main WCTU newspaper.

Most WCTU members did not join in Willard's espousal of Christian socialism in the 1890s. By the time of her death, the organization had begun a slow decline as women increasingly joined the National Federation of Women's Clubs, the National American Woman Suffrage Association, and other such organizations (Bordin 1981, 149–159). During Lillian Stevens's presidency, the WCTU's earlier broad agenda gradually narrowed. An analyst noted that the WCTU's image changed from that of containing "the best, most respected, most forward-looking women in town to narrow-minded antilibertarians riding a hobbyhorse" (*Id.*, 155).

See also Eighteenth Amendment.

For Further Reading:
Bordin, Ruth. 1981. *Women and Temperance: The Quest for Power and Liberty, 1873–1900.* Philadelphia: Temple University Press.
Epstein, Barbara L. 1981. *The Politics of Domesticity: Women, Evangelism, and Temperance in Nineteenth-Century America.* Middletown, CT: Wesleyan University Press.

❖ WOODHULL, VICTORIA CLAFLIN (1838–1927) ❖

Victoria Claflin Woodhull led an active life. She was a stockbroker and onetime protégé of Cornelius Vanderbilt; a reformer, lecturer, spiritualist, and sometime advocate of free love; a proponent of woman's suffrage who split with Susan B. Anthony's National Woman Suffrage Association; and an editor of *Woodhull and Claflin's Weekly* and later the *Humanitarian.* Woodhull was also a thrice-married member of an eccentric family; her sister was the vivacious Tennessee Celeste Claflin. Victoria Woodhull was the primary catalyst for charges of adultery against popular preacher Henry Ward Beecher (see McHenry 1980, 451–52; Marberry 1967; Arling 1972). Woodhull proposed a Constitution of the United States of the World in a speech in 1870, two years before her first of five bids for the presidency.

Her proposed constitution was a unique blend of old and new provisions. Congress would continue to be bicameral, with senators serving terms of ten years and members of the House serving for five years; all bills would originate in the House (Stern 1974, 6), with the possibility of abolishing the Senate if three-fifths of the House and the American people concurred (*Id.*, 22). Moreover, the House could override presidential vetoes by a simple majority vote (*Id.*, 6). Congress would prescribe a common form of constitution for each state (*Id.*, 7); exercise expanded powers to guarantee equal rights; establish a uniform criminal code, a common law, a system of welfare-workfare, prison discipline, inheritance and other progressive taxes, and a system of national railroads; and propose a world tribunal (*Id.*, 8–11).

The president and the president's ministerial cabinet of sixteen designated officers would be selected by an electoral college and serve ten-year nonrenewable terms (Stern 1974, 12–16). Judges would also be selected by the electoral college, with a judicial system consisting of district courts, a three-judge Supreme Court of the States, and a five-person Supreme Court of the United States (*Id.*, 18).

The franchise would extend to all eighteen-year-old citizens other than "idiots and the insane" (Stern 1974, 19), thus anticipating both the Nineteenth and the Twenty-sixth Amendments. Woodhull's constitution further provided for the recall, the initiative, and the referendum, with amendments to be adopted by three-fifths of the voters either on their own or in response to proposals made by a three-fifths vote of the House of Representatives (*Id.*, 22–23).

Although there were a number of provisions for equality, no bill of rights was included. Woodhull's proposal received little publicity and "had little discernible impact on the American political process or the condition of women in American life" (Boyd 1992, 43).

In 1893, Congressman Lucas Miller of Wisconsin offered a resolution to change the name of the United States to the United States of the World (H.J. Res. 208). This proposal, which he presented by request, contained a number of whimsical features (Musmanno 1929, 185–186), some of which resembled features of the Woodhull plan.

See also Anthony, Susan Brownell; Nineteenth Amendment.

For Further Reading:

Arling, Emanie. 1972. *The Terrible Siren: Victoria Woodhull.* New York: Arno Press.

Boyd, Steven R., ed. 1992. *Alternative Constitutions for the United States: A Documentary History.* Westport, CT: Greenwood Press.

Gabriel, Mary. 1998. *Notorious Victoria: The Life of Victoria Woodhull,* uncensored. Chapel Hill: Algonquin Books.

Goldsmith, Barbara. 1998. *Other Powers: The Age of Suffrage, Spiritualism, and the Scandalous Victoria Woodhull.* New York: Alfred A. Knopf.

Marberry, M. M. 1967. *Vicky: A Biography of Victoria C. Woodhull.* New York: Funk and Wagnalls.

McHenry, Robert, ed. 1980. *Liberty's Women.* Springfield, MA: G. and C. Merriam.

Musmanno, M. A. 1929. *Proposed Amendments to the Constitution.* Washington, DC: U.S. Government Printing Office.

Stern, Madeline B., ed. 1974. *The Victoria Woodhull Reader.* Weston, MA: M & S Press.

❖ WOODWARD, AUGUSTUS B. (1775?–1827) ❖

Augustus Woodward provided one of the earliest comprehensive analyses of the U.S. Constitution and its operation in an 1825 publication called *The Presidency of the United States.* Woodward concentrated a great deal of attention on the emerging cabinet system, whose history he described before he enumerated twenty "evils" that needed solutions.

The problems Woodward identified were as follows (Woodward 1825, 43–67):

1. The exclusion of the vice president from cabinet councils that would better familiarize him with the job to which he might succeed;
2. The conflict among cabinet members for the presidential post;
3. The difficulty that noncabinet officers had in becoming presidential candidates;
4. The misuse of patronage;
5. The problems caused by party opposition that was often fueled by sectional jealousies;
6. Variations in the methods of selecting presidential electors;
7. Problems arising when the House of Representatives had to choose among the top candidates for the presidency;
8. Problems arising when presidential electors were not chosen on the same day as the general election;

9. The need for a presidential secretary;

10. The failure of Washington, D.C., to have representatives either in the electoral college [a problem not addressed until 1961 by adoption of the Twenty-third Amendment] or in Congress;

11. Corruption of Congress brought about by inadequate attention to the doctrine of separation of powers;

12. Providing the president with a furnished residence without explicit constitutional sanction and despite the constitutional provision preventing additional emoluments for that office;

13. The need for a mechanism whereby the president could establish a committee of investigators;

14. The failure to standardize rules of presidential etiquette;

15. The need for a method whereby various regions of the country would be granted an opportunity to fill the presidency;

16. The need to acquaint the vice president with presidential duties and relieve him of responsibility for presiding over the Senate;

17. The lack of a cabinet office relating to domestic affairs;

18. Concern that cabinet meetings might detract from cabinet officers' attention to their respective departments;

19. Concern that cabinet officers, fearful of losing their jobs, might fail to provide the president with independent counsel; and

20. Concern that the cabinet system lacked adequate constitutional sanction.

Woodward did not elaborate on how all these problems should be solved or provide specific language for constitutional amendments. He did provide an outline for a Department of Domestic Affairs that would include branches for advancing sciences and the arts; for agriculture, commerce, and internal improvements; for preservation of public documents; and so forth. Woodward also proposed dividing the Department of Foreign Affairs into eight bureaus, each to deal with a different area of the world.

Many of the problems Woodward addressed are dated. Other concerns—representation for the District of Columbia, the electoral college, and the role of the president in a republican system—remain.

For Further Reading:
Woodward, Augustus B. 1825. *The Presidency of the United States*. New York: J. & J. Harper.

❖ WORKERS' COMPENSATION LAWS ❖

In the nineteenth century several common-law principles limited employer liability for on-the-job accidents. The fellow-servant rule allowed employers to evade responsibility when other employees were negligent; contributory negligence exempted employers when the injured person shared in the fault; and the assumption-of-risk doctrine presumed that employees who knew of workplace dangers assumed the risks (Urofsky 1988, 558).

At the turn of the century, states began creating insurance pools and requiring employees either to participate or to secure private insurance coverage for on-the-job injuries. Beginning in 1906 the national government adopted legislation to cover industries engaged in interstate commerce. In 1908 the Supreme Court struck down the federal law as overly broad, and in *Ives v. South Buffalo Railway Co.* (1911), the New York Court of Appeals invalidated a state law granting compensation for injured workers (Urofsky 1988, 560–561).

That year, Illinois Democratic Representative Frank Buchanan introduced an amendment giving Congress the power to pass laws granting compensation to injured workers. Within months of the *Ives* decision, however, state courts began ruling favorably on other state laws (Hall 1989, 244), and the Supreme Court upheld a revised Federal Employers' Liability Act of 1908 in the *Second Employers' Liability Case* of 1912. Amending proposals on the topic subsequently ceased.

For Further Reading:
Hall, Kermit L. 1989. *The Magic Mirror: Law in American History*. New York: Oxford University Press.

Urofsky, Melvin I. 1988. *A March of Liberty: A Constitutional History of the United States.* New York: Alfred A. Knopf.

❖ WORLD GOVERNMENT ❖

One proposed solution to the problem of international conflict is the establishment of international organizations or a world government. Colorado Democratic Senator John Safroth offered an amendment in 1916 to authorize the creation of an international peace tribunal. Despite the intense efforts of Woodrow Wilson, the United States never joined the League of Nations, which was established at the end of World War I. The United States was, however, a founding member of the United Nations, which emerged at the end of World War II.

Allowing each nation-state to preserve its sovereignty and independence, the United Nations fell far short of the world government that many thought was necessary to preserve peace and halt the spread of nuclear weapons. This idea appears to have had special support in the 1940s and early 1950s (see Johnsen 1947; Mangone 1951), with prominent advocates including President Harry Truman, General Douglas MacArthur, and Supreme Court Justice Owen Roberts (Johnsen 1948, 65).

In 1949 Democratic Representative Charles Bennett of Florida introduced an amendment to permit U.S. participation in a limited world government. That same year, five states (California, Connecticut, Maine, New Jersey, and North Carolina) petitioned for a convention to propose amendments authorizing U.S. participation in such a body.

Just prior to this, eleven scholars including Robert M. Hutchins and Mortimer Adler of the University of Chicago and Rexford Tugwell, who would go on to be the most prolific source of proposed new constitutions for the United States, issued a *Preliminary Draft of a World Constitution* (1948). The proposal grew out of thirteen meetings they had held between 1945 and 1947.

The document began with a "Declaration of Rights and Duties," based on "the law of Nature" and the rights of man. The most controversial proposal in this section, which attempted to work in both socialistic and capitalistic economic systems, provided that:

> The four elements of life—earth, water, air, energy—are the common property of the human race. The management and use of such portions thereof as are vested in or assigned to particular ownership, private or corporate or national or regional, of definite or indefinite tenure, of individualistic or collective economy, shall be subordinated in each and all cases to the interest of the common good. (Committee 1948, 6)

The first section of the proposed constitution focused on "grants of power." It hoped to solve the problem of war by creating a "Federal World Republic," which would be indivisible and one" (Committee 1948, 7). The Federal Republic would be responsible for maintaining peace, settling conflicts, settling boundary disputes, sending troops, and the like. A provision, similar to the Tenth Amendment of the U.S. Constitution, would have reserved nondelegated rights to composite nations and states.

The Federal Republic would vest primary powers in five bodies: the Federal Convention; the President; the Council and Special Bodies; the Grand Tribunal, the Supreme Court, and the Tribune of the People; and the Chamber of Guardians. The Federal Convention, in which states would have one delegate for each one million people, would meet every three years, and would divide into nine electoral colleges from Europa, Atlantis (including the United States and Britain), Eurasia, Afrasia, Africa, India (and maybe Pakistan), Asia Major, Austrasia, and Columbia (South America). This convention would select a president who would serve for six years.

The World Council of twenty-seven members, drawn from these nine electoral colleges and serving for three-year terms, would "initiate and enact legislation" (Committee 1948, 13). In conjunction with the president, the Council would select a House of Nationalities and States to safeguard "local institutions and autonomies and the protection of minorities *(Id.).* A "Syndical or functional Senate" *(Id.)*

would protect both union and corporate interests. The Council would also create an Institute of Science, Education and Culture (*Id.*, 14). An additional planning agency would prepare budgets and plan for "improvement of the world's physical facilities" (*Id.*, 14).

The president would appoint a chancellor who would form a cabinet. The president would have veto power over council legislation and would be subject to impeachment (Committee 1948, 17). The president would also serve as chief justice of the Supreme Court. Sixty justices, a Grand Tribunal, would serve on five branches dealing with different subjects and subject to review by the seven-member Supreme Court. Other lower courts would also be established.

A Tribune of the People, serving for a three-year term, would protect minority rights. Discrimination would be outlawed on the basis of "race or nation or sex or caste or creed or doctrine" (Committee 1948, 25). Protections would also be established for "the freedom of communication and information, of speech, of the press, and of expression by whatever means, of peaceful assembly, [and] of travel" (*Id.*, 26). Federal (albeit not state) capital punishment statutes would be banned. Balancing political rights with economic and social rights, provisions were also to be made for "old age pensions, unemployment relief, insurance against sickness and accident, just terms of leisure, and protection to maternity and infancy," as well as a right to publicly funded education (*Id.*, 27).

A Chamber of Guardians would provide for the "control and use" of armed forces, as well as for regulating the size of domestic militias.

Further provision was to be made for a Federal Capital and for the designation of a single official language "which shall be standard for the formulation and interpretation of the federal law" (Committee 1948, 33). Amendments would be recommended by concurrent two-thirds majorities of the Council and the Grand Tribunal and by approval by a two-thirds majority of the Federal Convention (*Id.*, 34).

An accompanying "Summary Report" indicated that the authors of the constitution believed that world government was "the only alternative to world destruction" (Committee 1948, 41).

The proposed constitution was described as being the "maximal" feasible one that could be made but as not being "utopian." World federalism was presented as a scheme for working within existing national boundaries, which most countries would be reluctant to abrogate. A subsequent section of the report notes that this plan was not necessarily a substitute for the United Nations and might even be adopted as "an all-round amendment to the U.N. Charter" (*Id.*, 82).

Despite its authors' efforts, this document appears to have been largely the product of Western, and specifically American, ideals of governance. Whatever chances this proposal may have had when it was made, it appears to have been a casualty of the continuing Cold War between East and West.

Although international organizations have been strengthened in recent years and regions like Europe and the Americas have increased economic and trade ties, the idea of a world government is still a distant dream, unlikely to be adopted absent some kind of worldwide calamity.

In recent years, Herbert C. Kirstein, the author of the *U.S. Constitution for the 21st Century and Beyond*, has also published a book, *Ideology of Freedom and Democracy*, which was subtitled, "Master Plan for FREEDOM, DEMOCRACY, HUMAN RIGHTS, PROGRESS, SECURITY, and PEACE on Planet EARTH." It proposed a world forum of nation-states that would take the place of the current United Nations.

See also Kirstein, Herbert C.; Tugwell, Rexford.

For Further Reading:

The Committee to Frame a World Constitution. 1948. *Preliminary Draft of a World Constitution.* Chicago: The University of Chicago Press.

Johnsen, Julia E., ed. 1948. *Federal World Government.* Vol. 19, no. 5 of the Reference Shelf. New York: H. W. Wilson.

Kirstein, Herbert C. 1994. *U.S. Constitution for 21st Century and Beyond.* Alexandria, Virginia: Realistic IDEALIST Enterprise.

Mangone, Gerald J. 1951. *The Idea and Practice of World Government.* New York: Columbia University Press.

APPENDIX A

The Constitution of the United States

Preamble

We the People of the United States, in Order to form a more perfect Union, establish Justice, insure domestic Tranquility, provide for the common defence, promote the general Welfare, and secure the Blessings of Liberty to ourselves and our Posterity, do ordain and establish this Constitution for the United States of America.

Article I

Section 1. All legislative Powers herein granted shall be vested in a Congress of the United States, which shall consist of a Senate and House of Representatives.

Section 2. The House of Representatives shall be composed of Members chosen every second Year by the People of the several States, and the Electors in each State shall have the Qualifications requisite for Electors of the most numerous Branch of the State Legislature.

No Person shall be a Representative who shall not have attained to the age of twenty five Years, and been seven Years a Citizen of the United States, and who shall not, when elected, be an Inhabitant of that State in which he shall be chosen.

Representatives and direct Taxes shall be apportioned among the several States which may be included within this Union, according to their respective Numbers, which shall be determined by adding to the whole Number of free Persons, including those bound to Service for a Term of Years, and excluding Indians not taxed, three fifths of all other Persons [changed by Section 2 of the Fourteenth Amendment]. The actual Enumeration shall be made within three Years after the first Meeting of the Congress of the United States, and within every subsequent Term of ten Years, in such Manner as they shall by Law direct. The Number of Representatives shall not exceed one for every thirty Thousand, but each State shall have at Least one Representative; and until such enumeration shall be made, the State of New Hampshire shall be entitled to choose three, Massachusetts eight, Rhode-Island and Providence Plantations one, Connecticut five, New-York six, New Jersey four, Pennsylvania eight, Delaware one, Maryland six, Virginia ten, North Carolina five, South Carolina five, and Georgia three.

When vacancies happen in the Representation from any State, the Executive Authority thereof shall issue Writs of Election to fill such Vacancies.

The House of Representatives shall choose their Speaker and other Officers; and shall have the sole Power of Impeachment.

Section 3. The Senate of the United States shall be composed of two Senators from each State, *chosen by the Legislature thereof* [changed by the Seventeenth Amendment], for six Years; and each Senator shall have one Vote.

Immediately after they shall be assembled in Consequence of the first Election, they shall be divided as equally as may be into three Classes. The seats of the Senators of the first Class shall be vacated at the Expiration of the second Year, of the second Class at the Expiration of the fourth Year, and of the third Class at the Expiration of the sixth Year, so that one third may be chosen every second Year; *and if Vacancies happen by Resignation, or otherwise, during the Recess of the Legislature of any State, the Executive thereof may make temporary Appointments until the next Meeting of the Legislature, which shall then fill such Vacancies* [changed by Section 2 of the Twentieth Amendment].

No Person shall be a Senator who shall not have attained to the Age of thirty Years, and been nine Years a Citizen of the United States, and who shall not, when elected, be an Inhabitant of that State for which he shall be chosen.

The Vice President of the United States shall be President of the Senate, but shall have no Vote, unless they be equally divided.

The Senate shall choose their other Officers, and also a President pro tempore, in the Absence of the Vice President, or when he shall exercise the Office of President of the United States.

The Senate shall have the sole Power to try all Impeachments. When sitting for that Purpose, they shall be on Oath or Affirmation. When the President of the United States is tried the Chief Justice shall preside: And no Person shall be convicted without the Concurrence of two thirds of the Members present.

Judgment in Cases of Impeachment shall not extend further than to removal from Office, and disqualification to hold and enjoy any Office of honor, Trust or Profit under the United States: but the Party convicted shall nevertheless be liable and subject to Indictment, Trial, Judgment and Punishment, according to Law.

Section 4. The Times, Places and Manner of holding Elections for Senators and Representatives, shall be prescribed in each State by the Legislature thereof; but the Congress may at any time by Law make or alter such Regulations, except as to the Places of choosing Senators.

The Congress shall assemble at least once in every Year, and such Meeting shall be *on the first Monday in December* [changed by Section 2 of the Twentieth Amendment], unless they shall by Law appoint a different Day.

Section 5. Each House shall be the Judge of the Elections, Returns and Qualifications of its own Members, and a Majority of each shall constitute a Quorum to do Business; but a smaller Number may adjourn from day to day, and may be authorized to compel the Attendance of absent Members, in such Manner, and under such Penalties as each House may provide.

Each House may determine the Rules of its Proceedings, punish its Members for disorderly Behaviour, and, with the Concurrence of two thirds, expel a Member.

Each House shall keep a Journal of its Proceedings, and from time to time publish the same, excepting such Parts as may in their Judgment require Secrecy; and the Yeas and Nays of the Members of either House on any question shall, at the Desire of one fifth of those Present, be entered on the Journal.

Neither House, during the Session of Congress, shall, without the Consent of the other, adjourn for more than three days, nor to any other Place than that in which the two Houses shall be sitting.

Section 6. The Senators and Representatives shall receive a Compensation for their Services, to be ascertained by Law, and paid out of the Treasury of the United States. They shall in all Cases, except Treason, Felony and Breach of the Peace, be privileged from Arrest during their Attendance at the Session of their respective Houses, and in going to and returning from the same; and for any Speech or Debate in either House, they shall not be questioned in any other Place.

No Senator or Representative shall, during the Time for which he was elected, be appointed to any civil Office under the Authority of the United States, which shall have been created, or the Emoluments whereof shall have been increased during such time; and no Person holding any Office under the United States, shall be a Member of either House during his Continuance in Office.

Section 7. All Bills for raising Revenue shall originate in the House of Representatives; but the Senate may propose or concur with amendments as on other Bills.

Every Bill which shall have passed the House of Representatives and the Senate, shall, before it become a Law, be presented to the President of the United States; If he approve he shall sign it, but if not he shall return it, with his Objections to that House in which it shall have originated, who shall enter the Objections at large on their Journal, and proceed to reconsider it. If after such Reconsideration two thirds of that House shall agree to pass the Bill, it shall be sent, together with the Objections, to the other House, by which it shall likewise be reconsidered, and if approved by two thirds of that House, it shall become a Law. But in all such Cases the Votes of both Houses shall be determined by Yeas and Nays, and the Names of the Persons voting for and against the Bill shall be entered on the Journal of each House respectively. If any Bill shall not be returned by the President within ten Days (Sunday excepted) after it shall have been presented to him, the Same shall be a Law, in like Manner as if he had signed it, unless the Congress by their Adjournment prevent its Return, in which Case it shall not be a Law.

Every Order, Resolution, or Vote to which the Concurrence of the Senate and House of Representatives may be necessary (except on a question of Adjournment) shall be presented to the President of the United States; and before the Same shall take Effect, shall be approved by him, or being disapproved by him, shall be repassed by two thirds of the Senate and House of Representatives, according to the Rules and Limitations prescribed in the Case of a Bill.

Section 8. The Congress shall have Power To lay and collect Taxes, Duties, Imposts and Excises, to pay the Debts and provide for the common Defence and general Welfare of the United States; but all Duties, Imposts and Excises shall be uniform throughout the United States;

To borrow Money on the credit of the United States;

To regulate Commerce with foreign Nations, and among the several States, and with the Indian Tribes;

To establish a uniform Rule of Naturalization, and uniform Laws on the subject of Bankruptcies throughout the United States;

To coin Money, regulate the Value thereof, and of foreign Coin, and fix the Standard of Weights and Measures;

To provide for the Punishment of counterfeiting the Securities and current Coin of the United States;

To establish Post Offices and post Roads;

To promote the Progress of Science and useful Arts, by securing for limited Times to Authors and Inventors the exclusive Right to their respective Writings and Discoveries;

To constitute Tribunals inferior to the Supreme Court;

To define and punish Piracies and Felonies committed on the high Seas, and Offences against the Law of Nations;

To declare War, grant Letters of Marque and Reprisal, and make Rules concerning Captures on Land and Water;

To raise and support Armies, but no Appropriation of Money to that Use shall be for a longer Term than two Years;

To provide and maintain a Navy;

To make Rules for the Government and Regulation of the land and naval Forces;

To provide for calling forth the Militia to execute the Laws of the Union, suppress Insurrections and repel Invasions;

To provide for organizing, arming, and disciplining the Militia, and for governing such Part of them as may be employed in the Service of the United States, reserving to the States respectively, the Appointment of the Officers, and the Authority of training the Militia according to the discipline prescribed by Congress;

To exercise exclusive Legislation in all Cases whatsoever, over such District (not exceeding ten Miles square) as may, by Cession of Particular States,

and the Acceptance of Congress, become the Seat of the Government of the United States, and to exercise like Authority over all Places purchased by the Consent of the Legislature of the State in which the Same shall be, for the Erection of Forts, Magazines, Arsenals, dock-Yards, and other needful Buildings; And

To make all Laws which shall be necessary and proper for carrying into Execution the foregoing Powers, and all other Powers vested by this Constitution in the Government of the United States, or in any Department or Officer thereof.

Section 9. The Migration or Importation of such Persons as any of the States now existing shall think proper to admit, shall not be prohibited by the Congress prior to the Year one thousand eight hundred and eight, but a Tax or duty may be imposed on such Importation, not exceeding ten dollars for each Person.

The Privilege of the Writ of Habeas Corpus shall not be suspended, unless when in Cases of Rebellion or Invasion the public Safety may require it.

No Bill of Attainder or ex post facto Law shall be passed.

No capitation, or other direct, Tax shall be laid, unless in Proportion to the Census of Enumeration herein before directed to be taken [changed by the Sixteenth Amendment].

No Tax or Duty shall be laid on Articles exported from any State.

No Preference shall be given by any Regulation of Commerce or Revenue to the Ports of one State over those of another; nor shall Vessels bound to, or from, one State, be obliged to enter, clear or pay Duties in another.

No Money shall be drawn from the Treasury, but in Consequence of Appropriations made by Law; and a regular Statement and Account of the Receipts and Expenditures of all public Money shall be published from time to time.

No Title of Nobility shall be granted by the United States: And no Person holding any Office of Profit or Trust under them, shall, without the Consent of the Congress, accept of any present, Emolument, Office, or Title, of any kind whatever, from any King, Prince or foreign State.

Section 10. No State shall enter into any Treaty, Alliance, or Confederation; grant Letters of Marque and Reprisal; coin Money; emit Bills of Credit; make any Thing but gold and silver Coin a Tender in Payment of Debts; pass any Bill of Attainder, ex post facto Law, or Law impairing the Obligation of Contracts, or grant any Title of Nobility.

No State shall, without the Consent of the Congress, lay any Imposts or Duties on Imports or Exports, except what may be absolutely necessary for executing it's inspection Laws: and the net Produce of all Duties and Imposts, laid by any State on Imports or Exports, shall be for the Use of the Treasury of the United States; and all such Laws shall be subject to the Revision and Control of the Congress.

No State shall, without the Consent of Congress, lay any Duty of Tonnage, keep Troops, or Ships of War in time of Peace, enter into any Agreement or Compact with another State, or with a foreign Power, or engage in War, unless actually invaded, or in such imminent Danger as will not admit of delay.

Article II

Section 1. The executive Power shall be vested in a President of the United States of America. He shall hold his Office during the Term of four Years, and, together with the Vice President, chosen for the same Term, be elected, as follows.

Each State shall appoint, in such Manner as the Legislature thereof may direct, a Number of Electors, equal to the whole Number of Senators and Representatives to which the State may be entitled in the Congress: but no Senator or Representative, or Person holding an Office of Trust or Profit under the United States, shall be appointed an Elector.

The Electors shall meet in their respective States, and vote by Ballot for two Persons, of whom one at least shall not be an Inhabitant of the same State with themselves. And they shall make a List of all the Persons voted for, and of the Number of Votes for each; which List they shall sign and certify, and transmit sealed to the Seat of the Government of the United States, directed to the President of the Senate. The President of the Senate shall, in the Presence of the Senate and House of Representatives, open all the Certificates, and the Votes shall then be counted. The Person having the greatest Number of Votes shall be the President, if such Number be a Majority of the whole Number of Electors appointed; and if there be more than one who have such Majority, and have an equal Number of Votes, then the House of Representatives shall immediately choose by Ballot one of them for President; and if

no Person have a Majority, then from the five highest on the list the said House shall in like Manner choose the President. But in choosing the President, the Votes shall be taken by States, the Representation from each State having one Vote; a quorum for this Purpose shall consist of a Member or Members from two thirds of the States, and a Majority of all the States shall be necessary to a Choice. In every Case, after the Choice of the President, the Person having the greatest Number of Votes of the Electors shall be the Vice President. But if there should remain two or more who have equal Votes, the Senate shall choose from them by Ballot the Vice President [changed by the Twelfth Amendment].

The Congress may determine the Time of choosing the Electors, and the Day on which they shall give their Votes; which Day shall be the same throughout the United States.

No Person except a natural born Citizen, or a Citizen of the United States, at the time of the Adoption of this Constitution, shall be eligible to the Office of President; neither shall any Person be eligible to that Office who shall not have attained to the Age of thirty five Years, and been fourteen Years a Resident within the United States.

In Case of the Removal of the President from Office, or of his Death, Resignation, or Inability to discharge the Powers and Duties of the said Office, the Same shall devolve on the Vice President, and the Congress may by Law provide for the Case of Removal, Death, Resignation or Inability, both of the President and Vice President, declaring what Officer shall then act as President, and such Officer shall act accordingly, until the Disability be removed, or a President shall be elected [changed by the Twenty-fifth Amendment].

The President shall, at stated Times, receive for his Services, a Compensation, which shall neither be increased nor diminished during the Period for which he shall have been elected, and he shall not receive within that Period any other Emolument from the United States, or any of them.

Before he enter on the Execution of his Office, he shall take the following Oath or Affirmation: "I do solemnly swear (or affirm) that I will faithfully execute the Office of President of the United States, and will to the best of my Ability, preserve, protect and defend the Constitution of the United States."

Section 2. The President shall be Commander in Chief of the Army and Navy of the United States, and of the Militia of the several States, when called into the actual Service of the United States; he may require the Opinion, in writing, of the principal Officer in each of the executive Departments, upon any Subject relating to the Duties of their respective Offices, and he shall have Power to grant Reprieves and Pardons for Offenses against the United States, except in Cases of Impeachment.

He shall have Power, by and with the Advice and Consent of the Senate, to make Treaties, provided two thirds of the Senators present concur; and he shall nominate, and by and with the Advice and Consent of the Senate, shall appoint Ambassadors, other public Ministers and Consuls, Judges of the Supreme Court, and all other Officers of the United States, whose Appointments are not herein otherwise provided for, and which shall be established by Law: but the Congress may by Law vest the Appointment of such inferior Officers, as they think proper, in the President alone, in the Courts of Law, or in the Heads of Departments.

The President shall have Power to fill up all Vacancies that may happen during the Recess of the Senate, by granting Commissions which shall expire at the End of their next Session.

Section 3. He shall from time to time give to the Congress Information of the State of the Union, and recommend to their Consideration such Measures as he shall judge necessary and expedient; he may, on extraordinary Occasions, convene both Houses, or either of them, and in Case of Disagreement between them, with Respect to the Time of Adjournment, he may adjourn them to such Time as he shall think proper; he shall receive Ambassadors and other public Ministers; he shall take Care that the Laws be faithfully executed, and shall Commission all the Officers of the United States.

Section 4. The President, Vice President and all Civil Officers of the United States, shall be removed from office on Impeachment for, and Conviction of, Treason, Bribery, or other high Crimes and Misdemeanors.

Article III

Section 1. The judicial Power of the United States shall be vested in one Supreme Court, and in such inferior Courts as the Congress may from time to time ordain and establish. The Judges, both of the supreme and inferior Courts, shall hold their Offices during good Behaviour, and shall, at stated Times, receive for their Services, a Compensation, which shall not be diminished during their Continuance in Office.

Section 2. The judicial Power shall extend to all Cases, in Law and Equity, arising under this Constitution, the Laws of the United States, and Treaties made, or which shall be made, under their Authority; to all Cases affecting Ambassadors, other public Ministers and Consuls; to all Cases of admiralty and maritime Jurisdiction; to Controversies to which the United States shall be a Party; to Controversies between two or more States; *between a State and Citizens of another State* [changed by the Eleventh Amendment]; between Citizens of different States; between Citizens of the same State claiming Lands under Grants of different States, *and between a State, or the Citizens thereof, and foreign States, Citizens or Subjects* [changed by the Eleventh Amendment].

In all Cases affecting Ambassadors, other public Ministers and Consuls, and those in which a State shall be Party, the Supreme Court shall have original Jurisdiction. In all the other Cases before mentioned, the Supreme Court shall have appellate Jurisdiction, both as to Law and Fact, with such Exceptions, and under such Regulations as the Congress shall make.

The Trial of all Crimes, except in cases of Impeachment, shall be by Jury; and such Trial shall be held in the State where the said Crimes shall have been committed; but when not committed within any State, the Trial shall be at such Place or Places as the Congress may by Law have directed.

Section 3. Treason against the United States shall consist only in levying War against them, or in adhering to their Enemies, giving them Aid and Comfort. No Person shall be convicted of Treason unless on the Testimony of two Witnesses to the same overt Act, or on Confession in open Court.

The Congress shall have Power to declare the Punishment of Treason, but no Attainder of Treason shall work Corruption of Blood, or Forfeiture except during the Life of the Person attainted.

Article IV

Section 1. Full Faith and Credit shall be given in each State to the public Acts, Records, and judicial

Proceedings of all other States. And the Congress may by general Laws prescribe the Manner in which such Acts, Records and Proceedings shall be proved, and the Effect thereof.

Section 2. The Citizens of each State shall be entitled to all Privileges and Immunities of Citizens in the several States.

A Person charged in any State with Treason, Felony, or other Crime, who shall flee from Justice, and be found in another State, shall on Demand of the executive Authority of the State from which he fled, be delivered up, to be removed to the State having Jurisdiction of the Crime.

No Person held to Service or Labour in one State, under the Laws thereof, escaping into another, shall, in Consequence of any Law or Regulation therein, be discharged from such Service or Labour, but shall be delivered up on Claim of the Party to whom such Service or Labour may be due [changed by the Thirteenth Amendment].

Section 3. New States may be admitted by the Congress into this Union; but no new State shall be formed or erected within the Jurisdiction of any other State; nor any State be formed by the Junction of two or more States, or Parts of States, without the Consent of the Legislatures of the States concerned as well as of the Congress.

The Congress shall have Power to dispose of and make all needful Rules and Regulations respecting the Territory or other Property belonging to the United States; and nothing in this Constitution shall be so construed as to Prejudice any Claims of the United States, or of any particular State.

Section 4. The United States shall guarantee to every State in this Union a Republican Form of Government, and shall protect each of them against Invasion; and on Application of the Legislature, or of the Executive (when the Legislature cannot be convened) against domestic Violence.

Article V

The Congress, whenever two thirds of both Houses shall deem it necessary, shall propose Amendments to this Constitution, or, on the Application of the Legislatures of two thirds of the several States, shall call a Convention for proposing Amendments,

which, in either Case, shall be valid to all Intents and Purposes, as Part of this Constitution, when ratified by the Legislatures of three fourths of the several States, or by Conventions in three fourths thereof, as the one or the other Mode of Ratification may be proposed by the Congress; Provided that no Amendment which may be made prior to the Year One thousand eight hundred and eight shall in any Manner affect the first and fourth Clauses in the Ninth Section of the first Article; and that no State, without its Consent, shall be deprived of its equal Suffrage in the Senate.

Article VI

All Debts contracted and Engagements entered into, before the Adoption of this Constitution, shall be as valid against the United States under this Constitution, as under the Confederation.

This Constitution, and the Laws of the United States which shall be made in Pursuance thereof; and all Treaties made, or which shall be made, under the Authority of the United States, shall be the supreme Law of the Land; and the Judges in every State shall be the supreme Law of the Land; and the Judges in every State shall be bound thereby, any Thing in the Constitution or Laws or any State to the Contrary notwithstanding.

The Senators and Representatives before mentioned, and the Members of the several State Legislatures, and all executive and judicial Officers, both of the United States and of the several States, shall be bound by Oath or Affirmation, to support this Constitution; but no religious Test shall ever be required as a Qualification to any Office or public Trust under the United States.

Article VII

The Ratification of the Conventions of nine States, shall be sufficient for the Establishment of this Constitution between the States so ratifying the Same.

❖ AMENDMENTS ❖

Amendment I

[First ten amendments ratified 15 December 1791]
Congress shall make no law respecting an establishment of religion, or prohibiting the free exercise thereof; or abridging the freedom of speech, or of

the press; or the right of the people peaceably to as-semble, and to petition the Government for a re-dress of grievances.

Amendment II

A well regulated Militia, being necessary to the se-curity of a free State, the right of the people to keep and bear Arms, shall not be infringed.

Amendment III

No Soldier shall, in time of peace be quartered in any house, without the consent of the Owner, nor in time of war, but in a manner to be prescribed by law.

Amendment IV

The right of the people to be secure in their persons, houses, papers, and effects, against unreasonable searches and seizures, shall not be violated, and no Warrants shall issue, but upon probable cause, sup-ported by Oath or affirmation, and particularly de-scribing the place to be searched, and the persons or things to be seized.

Amendment V

No person shall be held to answer for a capital, or otherwise infamous crime, unless on a presentment or indictment of a Grand Jury, except in cases arising in the land or naval forces, or in the Militia, when in actual service in time of War or public danger; nor shall any person be subject for the same offence to be twice put in jeopardy of life or limb; nor shall be compelled in any criminal case to be a witness against himself, nor be deprived of life, liberty, or property, without due process of law; nor shall private property be taken for public use, without just compensation.

Amendment VI

In all criminal prosecutions, the accused shall enjoy the right to a speedy and public trial, by an impartial jury of the State and district wherein the crime shall have been committed, which district shall have been previously ascertained by law, and to be informed of the nature and cause of the accusation; to be con-fronted with the witnesses against him; to have com-pulsory process for obtaining witnesses in his favor, and to have the Assistance of Counsel for his defence.

Amendment VII

In Suits at common law, where the value in contro-versy shall exceed twenty dollars, the right of trial by jury shall be preserved, and no fact tried by a jury, shall be otherwise re-examined in any Court of the United States, than according to the rules of the common law.

Amendment VIII

Excessive bail shall not be required, nor excessive fines imposed, nor cruel and unusual punishments inflicted.

Amendment IX

The enumeration in the Constitution, of certain rights, shall not be construed to deny or disparage others retained by the people.

Amendment X

The powers not delegated to the United States by the Constitution, nor prohibited by it to the States, are reserved to the States respectively, or to the peo-ple.

Amendment XI

[Ratified 7 February 1795]

The Judicial power of the United States shall not be construed to extend to any suit in law or equity, commenced or prosecuted against one of the United States by Citizens of another State, or by Citizens or Subjects of any Foreign State.

Amendment XII

[Ratified 15 June 1804]

The Electors shall meet in their respective states and vote by ballot for President and Vice-President, one of whom, at least, shall not be an inhabitant of the same state with themselves; they shall name in their ballots the person voted for as President, and in dis-tinct ballots the person voted for as Vice-President, and they shall make distinct lists of all persons voted for as President, and of all persons voted for as Vice-President, and of the number of votes for each, which lists they shall sign and certify, and transmit sealed to the seat of the government of the United States, directed to the President of the Senate; The President of the Senate shall, in the presence of the Senate and House of Representatives, open all the certificates and the votes shall then be counted; The person having the greatest number of votes for Pres-ident, shall be the President, if such number be a majority of the whole number of Electors appointed; and if no person have such majority, then from the persons having the highest numbers not exceeding three on the list of those voted for as President, the House of Representatives shall choose immediately, by ballot, the President. But in choosing the President, the votes shall be taken by states, the representation from each state having one vote; a quorum for this purpose shall consist of a member or members from two-thirds of the states, and a majority of all the states shall be necessary to a choice. *And if the House of Representatives shall not choose a President whenever the right of choice shall devolve upon them, before the fourth day of March next following, then the Vice-President shall act as President, as in the case of the death or other constitutional disability of the President* [superseded by Section 3 of the Twentieth Amendment]. The person having the greatest number of votes as Vice-President, shall be the Vice-President, if such number be a majority of the whole number of Electors appointed, and if no person have a majority, then from the two highest numbers on the list, the Senate shall choose the Vice-President; a quorum for the purpose shall consist of two-thirds of the whole number of Senators, and a majority of the whole number shall be necessary to a choice. But no person constitutionally ineligible to the office of President shall be eligible to that of Vice-President of the United States.

Amendment XIII

[Ratified 6 December 1865]
Section 1. Neither slavery nor involuntary servitude, except as a punishment for crime whereof the party shall have been duly convicted, shall exist within the United States, or any place subject to their jurisdiction.
Section 2. Congress shall have power to enforce this article by appropriate legislation.

Amendment XIV

[Ratified 9 July 1868]
Section 1. All persons born or naturalized in the United States and subject to the jurisdiction thereof, are citizens of the United States and of the State wherein they reside. No State shall make or enforce any law which shall abridge the privileges or immunities of citizens of the United States; nor shall any State deprive any person of life, liberty, or property, without due process of law; nor deny to any person within its jurisdiction the equal protection of the laws.

Section 2. Representatives shall be apportioned among the several States according to their respective numbers, counting the whole number of persons in each State, excluding Indians not taxed. But when the right to vote at any election for the choice of electors for President and Vice President of the United States, Representatives in Congress, the Executive and Judicial officers of a State, or the members of the Legislature thereof, is denied to any of the male inhabitants of such State, being twenty-one years of age, and citizens of the United States, or in any way abridged, except for participation in rebellion, or other crime, the basis of representation therein shall be reduced in the proportion which the number of such male citizens shall bear to the whole number of male citizens twenty-one years of age in such State.

Section 3. No person shall be a Senator or Representative in Congress, or elector of President and Vice President, or hold any office, civil or military, under the United States, or under any State, who, having previously taken an oath, as a member of Congress, or as an officer of the United States, or as a member of any State legislature, or as an executive or judicial officer of any State, to support the Constitution of the United States, shall have engaged in insurrection or rebellion against the same, or given aid or comfort to the enemies thereof. But Congress may by a vote of two-thirds of each House, remove such disability.

Section 4. The validity of the public debt of the United States, authorized by law, including debts incurred for payment of pensions and bounties for services in suppressing insurrection or rebellion, shall not be questioned. But neither the United States nor any State shall assume or pay any debt or obligation incurred in aid of insurrection or rebellion against the United States, or any claim for the loss or emancipation of any slave; but all such debts, obligations and claims shall be held illegal and void.

Section 5. The Congress shall have power to enforce, by appropriate legislation, the provisions of this article.

Amendment XV

[Ratified 3 February 1870]
Section 1. The right of citizens of the United States to vote shall not be denied or abridged by the

United States or by any State on account of race, color, or previous condition of servitude.

Section 2. The Congress shall have power to enforce this article by appropriate legislation.

Amendment XVI
[Ratified 3 February 1913]
The Congress shall have power to lay and collect taxes on incomes, from whatever source derived, without apportionment among the several States, and without regard to any census or enumeration.

Amendment XVII
[Ratified 8 April 1913]
The Senate of the United States shall be composed of two Senators from each State, elected by the people thereof, for six years; and each Senator shall have one vote. The electors in each State shall have the qualifications requisite for electors of the most numerous branch of the State legislatures.

When vacancies happen in the representation of any State in the Senate, the executive authority of such State shall issue writs of election to fill such vacancies: Provided, That the legislature of any State may empower the executive thereof to make temporary appointments until the people fill the vacancies by election as the legislature may direct.

This amendment shall not be so construed as to affect the election or term of any Senator chosen before it becomes valid as part of the Constitution.

Amendment XVIII
[Ratified 16 January 1919; repealed by the Twenty-first Amendment]
Section 1. After one year from the ratification of this article the manufacture, sale, or transportation of intoxicating liquors within, the importation thereof into, or the exportation thereof from the United States and all territory subject to the jurisdiction thereof for beverage purposes is hereby prohibited.

Section 2. The Congress and the several States shall have concurrent power to enforce this article by appropriate legislation.

Section 3. This article shall be inoperative unless it shall have been ratified as an amendment to the Constitution by the legislatures of the several States, as provided in the Constitution, within seven years from the date of the submission hereof to the States by the Congress.

Amendment XIX
[Ratified 18 August 1920]
The right of citizens of the United States to vote shall not be denied or abridged by the United States or by any State on account of sex.

Congress shall have power to enforce this article by appropriate legislation.

Amendment XX
[Ratified 23 January 1933]
Section 1. The terms of the President and Vice President shall end at noon on the 20th day of January, and the terms of Senators and Representatives at noon on the 3rd day of January, of the years in which such terms would have ended if this article had not been ratified; and the terms of their successors shall then begin.

Section 2. The Congress shall assemble at least once in every year, and such meeting shall begin at noon on the 3d day of January, unless they shall by law appoint a different day.

Section 3. If, at the time fixed for the beginning of the term of the President, the President elect shall have died, the Vice President elect shall become President. If a President shall not have been chosen before the time fixed for the beginning of his term, or if the President elect shall have failed to qualify, then the Vice President elect shall act as President until a President shall have qualified; and the Congress may by law provide for the case wherein neither a President elect nor a Vice President elect shall have qualified, declaring who shall then act as President, or the manner in which one who is to act shall be selected, and such person shall act accordingly until a President or Vice President shall have qualified.

Section 4. The Congress may by law provide for the case of the death of any of the persons from whom the House of Representatives may choose a President whenever the right of choice shall have devolved upon them, and for the case of the death of any of the persons from whom the Senate may choose a Vice President whenever the right of choice shall have devolved upon them.

Section 5. Sections 1 and 2 shall take effect on the 15th day of October following the ratification of this article.

Section 6. This article shall be inoperative unless it shall have been ratified as an amendment to the Constitution by the legislatures of three-fourths of the several States within seven years from the date of its submission.

Amendment XXI
[Ratified 5 December 1933]
Section 1. The eighteenth article of amendment to the Constitution of the United States is hereby repealed.

Section 2. The transportation or importation into any State, Territory or possession of the United States for delivery or use therein of intoxicating liquors, in violation of the laws thereof, is hereby prohibited.

Section 3. This article shall be inoperative unless it shall have been ratified as an amendment to the Constitution by conventions in the several States, as provided in the Constitution, within seven years from the date of the submission hereof to the States by the Congress.

Amendment XXII
[Ratified 27 February 1951]
Section 1. No person shall be elected to the office of the President more than twice, and no person who has held the office of President, or acted as President, for more than two years of a term to which some other person was elected President shall be elected to the office of the President more than once. But this Article shall not apply to any person holding the office of President when this Article was proposed by the Congress, and shall not prevent any person who may be holding the office of President, or acting as President, during the term within which this Article becomes operative from holding the office of President or acting as President during the remainder of such term.

Section 2. This Article shall be inoperative unless it shall have been ratified as an amendment to the Constitution by the legislatures of three-fourths of the several States within seven years from the date of its submission to the States by the Congress.

Amendment XXIII
[Ratified 29 March 1961]
Section 1. The District constituting the seat of Government of the United States shall appoint in such manner as the Congress may direct:

A number of electors of President and Vice President equal to the whole number of Senators and Representatives in Congress to which the District would be entitled if it were a State, but in no event more than the least populous State; they shall be in addition to those appointed by the States, but they shall be considered, for the purposes of the election of President and Vice President, to be electors appointed by a State; and they shall meet in the District and perform such duties as provided by the twelfth article of amendment.

Section 2. The Congress shall have power to enforce this article by appropriate legislation.

Amendment XXIV
[Ratified 23 January 1964]
Section 1. The right of citizens of the United States to vote in any primary or other election for President or Vice President, for electors for President or Vice President, or for Senator or Representative in Congress, shall not be denied or abridged by the United States or any State by reason of failure to pay any poll tax or other tax.

Section 2. The Congress shall have power to enforce this article by appropriate legislation.

Amendment XXV
[Ratified 10 February 1967]
Section 1. In case of the removal of the President from office or of his death or resignation, the Vice President shall become President.

Section 2. Whenever there is a vacancy in the office of the Vice President, the President shall nominate a Vice President who shall take office upon confirmation by a majority vote of both Houses of Congress.

Section 3. Whenever the President transmits to the President pro tempore of the Senate and the Speaker of the House of Representatives his written declaration that he is unable to discharge the powers and duties of his office, and until he transmits to them a written declaration to the contrary, such powers and duties shall be discharged by the Vice President as Acting President.

Section 4. Whenever the Vice President and a majority of either the principal officers of the executive departments or of such other body as Congress may by law provide, transmit to the President pro tempore of the Senate and the Speaker of the House of Representatives their written declaration that the President is unable to discharge the powers and duties of his office, the Vice President shall immediately assume the powers and duties of the office as Acting President.

Thereafter, when the President transmits to the President pro tempore of the Senate and the Speaker of the House of Representatives his written declaration that no inability exists, he shall resume the powers and duties of his office unless the Vice President and a majority of either the principal officers of the executive department or of such other body as Congress may by law provide, transmit within four days to the President pro tempore of the Senate and the Speaker of the House of Representatives their written declaration that the President is unable to discharge the powers and duties of his office. Thereupon Congress shall decide the issue, assembling within forty-eight hours for that purpose if not in session. If the Congress, within twenty-one days after receipt of the latter written declaration, or, if Congress is not in session, within twenty-one days after Congress is required to assemble, determines by two-thirds vote of both houses that the President is unable to discharge the powers and duties of his office, the Vice President shall continue to discharge the same as Acting President; otherwise, the President shall resume the powers and duties of his office.

Amendment XXVI
[Ratified 1 July 1971]
Section 1. The right of citizens of the United States, who are eighteen years of age or older, to vote shall not be denied or abridged by the United States or by any State on account of age.

Section 2. The Congress shall have power to enforce this article by appropriate legislation.

Amendment XXVII
[Ratified 8 May 1992]
No law, varying the compensation for the services of the Senators and Representatives, shall take effect, until an election of Representatives shall have intervened.

APPENDIX B

Dates Amendments Were Proposed and Ratified

Amendment Number	Date Congress Proposed	Date Ratified
1–10	26 September 1789	15 December 1791
11	Senate: 4 March 1794	7 February 1795
	House: 4 March 1794	
12	Senate: 3 December 1803	15 June 1804
	House: 9 December 1803	
13	Senate: 8 April 1864	6 December 1865
	House: 31 January 1865	
14	Senate: 8 June 1866	9 July 1868
	House: 13 June 1866	
15	Senate: 26 February 1869	3 February 1870
	House: 25 February 1869	
16	Senate: 5 July 1909	3 February 1913
	House: 12 July 1909	
17	Senate: 9 June 1911	8 April 1913
	House: 13 April 1911	
18	Senate: 18 December 1917	16 January 1919
	House: 17 December 1917	
19	Senate: 4 June 1919	18 August 1920
	House: 21 May 1919	
20	Senate: 6 January 1932	23 January 1933
	House: 16 February 1932	
21	Senate: 16 February 1933	5 December 1933
	House: 20 February 1933	
22	Senate: 12 March 1947	27 February 1951
	House: 6 February 1947	
23	Senate: 2 February 1960	29 March 1961
	House: 14 June 1960	
24	Senate: 27 March 1962	23 January 1964
	House: 27 August 1962	
25	Senate: 19 February 1965	10 February 1967
	House: 13 April 1965	
26	Senate: 10 March 1971	1 July 1971
	House: 23 March 1971	
27	26 September 1787	8 May 1992

Most of this information was adapted from information found in an appendix entitled "Congressional Votes on Amendments" in U.S. Senate, Subcommittee on the Constitution, Committee on the Judiciary. *Amendments to the Constitution: A Brief Legislative History* (Washington D.C.: U.S. Government Printing Office, 1985), pp. 99–133.

APPENDIX C

Number of Amendments by Decade

Decade	Amendments Proposed (Approximate)	Amendments Adopted
1780s	196	0
1790s	42	1
1800s	65	1
1810s	93	0
1820s	111	0
1830s	102	0
1840s	59	0
1850s	22	0
1860s	518	3
1870s	177	0
1880s	264	0
1890s	265	0
1900s	269	0
1910s	467	3
1920s	393	1
1930s	646	2
1940s	404	0
1950s	793	1
1960s	2,598	3
1970s	2,019	1
1980s	827	0
1990s	774	1

APPENDIX D

Most Popular Amending Proposals by Year &
Key Events and Publications Related to Constitutional Amendments

Year	Number of Proposals[1]	Key Events[2]	Most Frequent Proposals Introduced in Congress[3]
1683		William Penn includes amending provision in charter	
1775		American Revolution begins	
1776		Declaration of Independence written defending Revolution States begin writing constitutions	
1777		Continental Congress proposes Articles of Confederation	
1781		Articles of Confederation ratified Battle of Yorktown marks defeat of British forces	
1786		Annapolis Convention meets to discuss commercial problems Shays's Rebellion stirs fear of governmental collapse	
1787		Continental Congress adopts Northwest Ordinance regulating settlement in the territories Constitutional Convention meets in Philadelphia	
1788	124	Federalists and Anti-Federalists debate merits of new Constitution	Bill of Rights
1789	173	George Washington assumes presidency Congress decides to add new amendments to the end of the Constitution rather than incorporating them in the text After an effort led by James Madison, Congress proposes 12 amendments, 10 of which will become the Bill of Rights and 1 of which will be putatively ratified in 1992	Bill of Rights
1791	15	States ratify Bill of Rights Washington accepts Hamilton's proposal for national bank	The judiciary
1793	8	*Chisholm v. Georgia* allows states to be sued by out-of-state citizens	Judiciary (suits against the states)
1794	6	Congress proposes Eleventh Amendment limiting suits against states	Judicial jurisdiction
1795	4	States ratify Eleventh Amendment	Legislative terms

540

Year	Number of Proposals[1]	Key Events[2]	Most Frequent Proposals Introduced in Congress[3]
1797	1		Selection of executive
1798	5	*Hollingsworth v. Virginia* decides that president's signature not needed for amendment Federalist-dominated Congress passes Alien and Sedition Acts Madison and Jefferson write Virginia and Kentucky Resolutions	Officeholding restricted to native-born
1799	2		Electors to designate choice of president
1800	7	Realigning presidential election passes control from Federalists to Democratic-Republicans and results in Jefferson-Burr tie	Selection of president
1801	1	John Marshall becomes chief justice of United States	Uniform method of selecting president
1802	12		Choice of executive
1803	7	John Marshall issues decision in *Marbury v. Madison* establishing judicial review Congress proposes Twelfth Amendment altering electoral college Louisiana is purchased without adoption of constitutional amendment	Choice of executive
1804	4	States ratify the Twelfth Amendment	Slave importation
1805	4	Samuel Chase brought to trial before Senate on impeachment charges but not convicted	Judicial jurisdiction and removal of judges
1806	10		Slave importation
1807	2	Jefferson imposes embargo in attempt to avert war with European powers	Judicial jurisdiction and compensation
1808	16	American participation in slave trade ended	Judicial, legislative, executive reforms
1809	2		Duration of embargoes
1810	3	Congress proposes amendment limiting titles of nobility; never ratified	Titles of nobility Exclusion of congressmen from executive offices
1811	2		Removal of judges Executive appointments

Year	Number of Proposals[1]	Key Events[2]	Most Frequent Proposals Introduced in Congress[3]
1812	2	U.S. and Britain engage in War of 1812	Export duties Removal of judges Legislative terms
1813	9		Choice of executive and legislators by districts
1814	9		Internal improvements National bank Legislative terms
1815	8	Hartford Convention meets Americans hear of end of war of 1812 after Jackson routs British troops at New Orleans Simon Willard Jr. publishes *The Columbian Union*	Slavery War-power issues
1816	30	American Colonization Society founded with intention of settling African Americans abroad	War and embargo powers Choice of executive and legislators by districts
1817	8		Choice of executive and legislators by districts
1818	19		Choice of executive and legislators by districts
1819	3	*McCulloch v. Maryland* upholds constitutionality of U.S. bank	Choice of executive and legislators by districts
1820	10	Congress adopts Missouri Compromise, limiting slavery in the territories	National bank prohibited
1821	8		Choice of executive and legislators by districts
1822	9		Choice of executive Compensation of Congress Internal improvements
1823	18	President James Monroe announces the Monroe Doctrine to deter European expansion in Western Hemisphere	Choice of executive and legislators
1824	5	Election of 1824 results in no winner; contest goes to U.S. House of Representatives, where John Quincy Adams is selected	Choice of executive by districts No third term

Year	Number of Proposals[1]	Key Events[2]	Most Frequent Proposals Introduced in Congress[3]
1825	9	Augustus B. Woodward publishes *The Presidency of the United States*	Choice of executive by districts
1826	30	Thomas Jefferson and John Adams both die on the fiftieth anniversary of the Declaration of Independence	Choice of executive
1827	5		Choice of executive
1828	6	Andrew Jackson elected president Next four years mark controversy over national tariffs	Choice of executive
1829	11		Choice of executive
1830	5		Choice of executive
1831		Anti-Mason Party holds first national nominating convention; other parties follow, replacing "King Caucus" in Congress	Choice of executive
1832	19		Choice of executive Division of state and federal powers
1833	4	*Barron v. Baltimore* says that Bill of Rights limits only the national government	Choice of executive
1834	6		Choice of executive
1835	12	Roger B. Taney is appointed chief justice of United States	Choice of executive Terms and removal of judges
1836	18		Choice of executive
1837	7		Choice of executive
1838	16		Choice of executive
1839	12		Executive powers
1840	5		One term for executive
1841	12	William Henry Harrison dies in office and is succeeded by Vice President John Tyler	One term for executive
1842	14		Executive powers
1843	3		Executive choice and term
1844	8		Choice of executive

Year	Number of Proposals[1]	Key Events[2]	Most Frequent Proposals Introduced in Congress[3]
1845	1		Choice of executive
1846	6	U.S. enters two-year war with Mexico	Executive selection and term
1847	1		Limit judicial review of state legislation
1848	4	Seneca Falls Convention calls for women's suffrage	Executive powers
1849	5	*Luther v. Borden* clarifies political questions doctrine	Executive offices
1850	9	Congress adopts Compromise of 1850 in unsuccessful attempt to heal growing sectional divisions	Executive powers and offices
1851	4		Assorted
1852	4		Direct election of senators
1853	1		Choice of executive by districts
1854	3	Kansas-Nebraska Act opens decision about slavery in the territories to "popular sovereignty" Republican Party is founded in Ripon, Wisconsin	Executive and legislative branches
1857	0	*Scott v. Sandford* invalidates Missouri Compromise and declares that African Americans cannot become citizens	
1858	1	John Brown and his followers adopt a new provisional constitution	Qualification to vote for Congress
1859	0	John Brown and his followers launch unsuccessful raid at Harper's Ferry	
1860	74	Abraham Lincoln becomes first Republican elected president	Slavery-related issues
1861	121	Congress proposes Corwin Amendment, which is never ratified by the states Unsuccessful "Peace Convention" is convened The Civil War starts The Southern states draw up their own constitution William B. Wedgwood publishes *The Reconstruction of the Government of the United States of America*	Slavery-related issues
1862	8	Sidney George Fisher publishes *Trial of the Constitution*, commending British model of constitutional change Congress abolishes slavery in District of Columbia	Slavery and chief executive

Year	Number of Proposals[1]	Key Events[2]	Most Frequent Proposals Introduced in Congress[3]
1863	2	Emancipation Proclamation goes into effect but applies only behind enemy lines	Slavery prohibited
1864	57	Senate proposes Thirteenth Amendment abolishing slavery Robert Beasley publishes *A Plan to Stop the Present and Prevent Future Wars*, proposing new constitution	Slavery prohibited
1865	26	House proposes and states ratify Thirteenth Amendment Civil War ends Lincoln is assassinated	Slavery Representation Suffrage
1866	129	Congress proposes Fourteenth Amendment extending rights of citizenship Southern Reconstruction begins John A. Jameson publishes first edition of *Treatise on Constitutional Conventions* denying that such conventions are sovereign	Apportionment of representatives Suffrage Equal rights
1867	29		Citizenship Executive term and selection
1868	25	U.S. Senate impeaches President Andrew Johnson; House falls a single vote short of majority needed to convict him	Executive choice and qualifications Suffrage
1869	76	Congress proposes Fifteenth Amendment extending suffrage to blacks Susan B. Anthony and Elizabeth Cady Stanton found the National Woman Suffrage Association; their rivals found the American Woman Suffrage Association The Anti-Prohibition Party is founded Congress establishes number of Supreme Court justices at nine	Suffrage
1870	6	States ratify Fifteenth Amendment Victoria C. Woodhull proposes a Constitution of the United States of the World	Suffrage
1871	13		Executive eligibility and terms
1872	16		Executive choice, eligibility, term
1873	19	*Slaughterhouse Cases* restrict privileges and immunities clause of the Fourteenth Amendment	Executive choice and term Legislative compensation
1874	10	Women's Christian Temperance Union is founded	Direct election of senators

Year	Number of Proposals[1]	Key Events[2]	Most Frequent Proposals Introduced in Congress[3]
1875	11	Decision in *Minor v. Happersett* declares that women are not entitled to vote under the Fourteenth Amendment	Single six-year executive term
1876	34	Disputed election of 1876 goes to U.S. House of Representatives Centennial of the Declaration of Independence	No establishment of religion Executive choice and terms
1877	22	End of congressional Reconstruction; federal troops leave the South	Choice of executive
1878	20		War claims prohibited
1879	26	Centennial of George Washington's inauguration Albert Stickney publishes *A True Republic*	War claims Item veto
1880	13		Choice of executive
1881		Supreme Court upholds constitutionality of income tax in *Springer v. United States*	Alcoholic prohibition
1882	35		Item veto
1883	29	*Civil Rights Cases* of 1883 restrict Fourteenth Amendment by focusing on distinction between state and federal action Pendleton Act establishes civil service system	Item veto
1884	33	Henry C. Lockwood publishes *The Abolition of the Presidency*	Congressional powers
1885	14		Direct election of senators
1886	35		Prohibition of polygamy
1887	12	Centennial of U.S. Constitution	Dates of congressional sessions
1888	42		Regulation of polygamy
1889	30		Uniform laws on marriage and divorce Beginning of sessions of Congress and president

Year	Number of Proposals[1]	Key Events[2]	Most Frequent Proposals Introduced in Congress[3]
1890	19	Christopher Tiedeman publishes *The Unwritten Constitution of the United States* Rival women's suffrage associations merge into the National American Woman Suffrage Association (NAWSA) *Hans v. Louisiana* effectively interprets the Eleventh Amendment as a restatement rather than an amendment of the Constitution	Popular election of senators
1891	7		Popular election of senators
1892	57	Columbian Exposition in Chicago marks 400th anniversary of Columbus's discovery of the New World	Popular election of senators
1893	27		Popular election of senators
1894	18		Limit president to one term
1895	23	*Pollock v. Farmers' Loan & Trust* outlaws income tax	Direct election of senators
1896	26	*Plessy v. Ferguson* endorses "separate but equal" Herman Ames publishes first list and analysis of constitutional amendments in nation's first century Frederick Upham Adams publishes *President John Smith* with proposed text of new constitution Utah is admitted to the Union after extensive debates about the need for an amendment outlawing polygamy William McKinley defeats William Jennings Bryan in critical presidential election	Direct election of senators Women's suffrage
1897	31	Henry O. Morris publishes *Waiting for the Signal: A Novel*	Income tax
1898	14	U.S. fights Spain in a war that leads to acquisition of overseas territories	Income tax
1899	43		Uniform marriage and divorce laws; prohibit polygamy
1900	27		Uniform marriage and divorce laws Income tax
1901	42		Direct election of senators

Year	Number of Proposals[1]	Key Events[2]	Most Frequent Proposals Introduced in Congress[3]
1902	20		Income tax Regulation of trusts
1903	25		Direct election of senators Income tax
1904	9		Assorted proposals
1905	25	*Lochner v. New York* invalidates New York's limits on the hours of bakers and highlights growth of substantive due process	Direct election of senators
1906	18		Direct election of senators Six-year presidential term
1907	45		Direct election of senators Election of federal judges
1908	20	Woodrow Wilson publishes *Constitutional Government in the United States*	Direct election of senators
1909	38	Congress proposes Sixteenth Amendment legitimizing income tax	Direct election of senators
1910	25	Walter Dodd publishes *The Revision and Amendment of State Constitutions*	Change date that Congress convenes
1911	47	Congress proposes Seventeenth Amendment providing for direct election of senators The size of the U.S. House of Representatives is capped at 435	Direct election of senators
1912	42		Change presidential term length and limit terms Election and terms for judges
1913	74	States ratify Sixteenth Amendment States ratify Seventeenth Amendment	Change presidential term length and limit terms Popular election of president Prohibition of alcohol
1914	38	World War I begins in Europe Alice Paul forms the Congressional Union for Woman Suffrage	Prohibition of alcohol

Year	Number of Proposals[1]	Key Events[2]	Most Frequent Proposals Introduced in Congress[3]
1915	39	Eustace Reynolds publishes *A New Constitution: A Suggested Form of Modified Government*	Women's suffrage
1916	48	Jones Act promises eventual independence to Philippines	Election of president by popular vote
1917	75	U.S. enters World War I Congress proposes Eighteenth Amendment providing for national alcoholic prohibition	Women's suffrage
1918	23	*Hammer v. Dagenhart* invalidates use of federal commerce power to regulate child labor	Restricting voting to citizens
1919	56	States ratify Eighteenth Amendment Congress proposes Nineteenth Amendment extending suffrage to women President Wilson suffers stroke during unsuccessful attempt to secure U.S. participation in League of Nations "Red scare" reflects fear of communism in aftermath of the Russian Revolution of 1917 Roger Hoar publishes *Constitutional Conventions: Their Nature, Powers and Limitations*	Women's suffrage
1920	20	States ratify Nineteenth Amendment *National Prohibition Cases* declare that "two-thirds" means two-thirds of a quorum *Hawke v. Smith* overturns state requirement that amendments be ratified by state referendum *Missouri v. Holland* raises fears that treaties might take away individual rights	Treaty ratification Presidential disability Amendment ratification
1921	61	*Dillon v. Gloss* expresses need for amendments to reflect contemporary consensus U.S. House of Representatives adopts anti-lynching law that is subsequently defeated in the Senate	Changes in amending procedure
1922	39	*Bailey v. Drexel Furniture Company* invalidates use of federal taxing power to regulate child labor William MacDonald publishes *A New Constitution for a New America*	Child labor amendment
1923	86		Child labor
1924	30	Congress proposes child labor amendment; never ratified	Child labor Income tax
1925	31	Herbert Horwill publishes *The Usages of the American Constitution*, stressing role of customs and usages	Dates of terms for president and Congress
1926	20	*Myers v. United States* upholds broad presidential removal powers	Dates of terms for president and Congress

Year	Number of Proposals[1]	Key Events[2]	Most Frequent Proposals Introduced in Congress[3]
1926 (cont.)			Repeal Eighteenth Amendment
1927	42	Charles Lindbergh crosses the Atlantic in *Spirit of St. Louis*	Repeal or modify Eighteenth Amendment
1928	30		Amending procedures
1929	34	Stock market crash leads to Great Depression M. A. Musmanno publishes second analysis of amendments	Modify Eighteenth Amendment
1930	31		Modify or repeal Eighteenth Amendment
1931	61	*United States v. Sprague* says Congress has choice of how amendments are ratified and refuses to accept implicit limits on the amending process	Modify or repeal Eighteenth Amendment
1932	100	Franklin D. Roosevelt is elected president William Kay Wallace publishes *Our Obsolete Constitution*	Repeal Eighteenth Amendment
1933	62	FDR launches his ambitious New Deal programs	Provide for taxation of income from securities
1934	28		Provide for taxation of income from securities
1935	69	William Yandell Elliott publishes *The Need for Constitutional Reform*, advocating parliamentary mechanisms *Schechter Poultry Corp. v. United States* invalidates FDR's National Industrial Recovery Act; other decisions invalidate other New Deal programs U.S. Supreme Court moves into its own building, across from the Capitol	Provide for taxation of income from securities
1936	29		Minimum wage Regulation of agriculture
1937	154	U.S. Constitution has its sesquicentennial FDR introduces "court-packing" plan Court inaugurates historic "switch in time that saves nine" in *West Coast Hotel v. Parrish* and *N.L.R.B. v. Jones & Laughlin Steel Corp.* *Palko v. Connecticut* articulates "selective incorporation" of the Bill of Rights to the states	Reform of judiciary Taxation of securities War-related issues

Year	Number of Proposals[1]	Key Events[2]	Most Frequent Proposals Introduced in Congress[3]
1937 (cont.)		Ralph Cram publishes *The End of Democracy*, advocating an iconoclastic scheme of constitutional reform	
1938	24	Justice Stone authors famous footnote in *Carolene Products* case Hugh Hamilton publishes *A Second Constitution for the United States of America*	War-related issues
1939	88	*Coleman v. Miller* declares that most amending issues are "political questions" World War II begins in Europe	War-related issues Old-age assistance
1940	4	FDR runs for unprecedented third term	Two-term presidential limit
1941	45	Japanese attack Pearl Harbor; U.S. enters World War II Thomas Upham publishes *Total Democracy: A New Constitution for the United States, a Democratic Ideal for the World*	Limit terms of president
1942	12	Henry Hazlitt advocates a parliamentary system in *A New Constitution Now* Lester Orfield publishes *The Amending of the Federal Constitution*	Suffrage for 18-year-olds
1943	46	Alexander Hehmeyer publishes *Time for Change: A Proposal for a Second Constitutional Convention*	Ratification of amendments 18-year-old vote Presidential term limits
1944	22	FDR successfully runs for unprecedented fourth term	Limit presidential terms
1945	116	Thomas Finletter publishes *Can Representative Government Do the Job?* FDR dies and Harry Truman assumes presidency World War II ends after U.S. drops two atomic bombs on Japan; Cold War follows	Presidential terms Treaty ratification Equal rights amendment
1946	10		Organization of judiciary
1947	78	Congress proposes Twenty-second Amendment, limiting president to two terms *Adamson v. California* reveals diverse judicial views on incorporation controversy	Limit presidential terms
1948	7		Assorted
1949	64		Change or abolish electoral college Equal rights amendment

Year	Number of Proposals[1]	Key Events[2]	Most Frequent Proposals Introduced in Congress[3]
1950	11	U.S. comes to aid of South Korea under UN flag	Electors for District of Columbia
1951	73	States ratify Twenty-second Amendment	Change or abolish electoral college Equal rights amendment Limit treaties
1952	31	*Steel Seizure* cases invalidate Truman's takeover of steel industry	Treaties in conflict with Constitution
1953	120	President Eisenhower appoints Earl Warren as chief justice	Limit treaties and executive agreements Reform electoral college Equal rights amendment
1954	43	*Brown v. Board of Education* calls for desegregation and overturns *Plessy v. Ferguson* U.S. Senate narrowly defeats a version of the Bricker amendment designed to limit scope of treaties	Amending procedures
1955	115	Dr. Martin Luther King Jr. leads Montgomery bus boycott after Rosa Parks refuses to give up her seat	Change electoral college Scope of treaties Equal rights amendment
1956	27		Electoral college reform
1957	141		Electoral college reform Treaties Equal rights amendment Admission of new states Tax limits
1958	38	President Eisenhower sends troops to Little Rock, Arkansas, to uphold authority of federal law against Southern defiance	Limit state collection of taxes on nonresidents Presidential disability
1959	194	Alaska and Hawaii become 49th and 50th states admitted to the Union	Equal rights amendment
1960	28	Congress proposes Twenty-third Amendment granting electors to District of Columbia	Alter electoral college
1961	291	States ratify Twenty-third Amendment	Equal rights amendment

Year	Number of Proposals[1]	Key Events[2]	Most Frequent Proposals Introduced in Congress[3]
1961 (cont.)			Direct election of president
1962	105	Congress proposes Twenty-fourth Amendment abolishing use of poll tax in federal elections *Engel v. Vitale* outlaws public prayer in public schools *Baker v. Carr* decides that state legislative apportionment is a justiciable issue Council of State Governments calls for liberalization of the amending process Cuban missile crisis stimulates fears about the emergency functioning of the government	Prayer in schools
1963	395	Dr. Martin Luther King Jr. delivers famous "I Have a Dream" speech at March on Washington, D.C. President John F. Kennedy is assassinated	Prayer in schools Equal rights amendment Electoral college reform
1964	130	Civil Rights Act of 1964 outlaws racial discrimination in places of public accommodation States ratify Twenty-fourth Amendment *Reynolds v. Sims* extends one-person, one-vote principle to both houses of state legislatures; *Wesberry v. Sanders* applies standard to House congressional districts	State legislative apportionment
1965	411	Congress proposes Twenty-fifth Amendment on presidential disability Congress adopts Voting Rights Act of 1965 *Griswold v. Connecticut* establishes a constitutional right to privacy and strikes down Connecticut birth-control law	State legislative apportionment Equal rights amendment Presidential disability Prayer in schools
1966	88	*Harper v. Virginia State Board of Elections* strikes down use of poll tax in state elections *Miranda v. Arizona* expands rights of criminal defendants and stirs criticisms of the Supreme Court	Equal rights amendment Prayer in schools
1967	403	States ratify Twenty-fifth Amendment Senator Sam Ervin introduces the Federal Constitutional Convention Act, but it is not adopted President Johnson appoints Thurgood Marshall, the first African American to serve on the U.S. Supreme Court	Equal rights amendment Right to vote Prayer in schools Electoral college
1968	122	States appear on verge of calling a constitutional convention on state legislative apportionment Martin Luther King Jr. and Robert Kennedy are assassinated	Appointment, tenure, removal of judges Equal rights amendment

Year	Number of Proposals[1]	Key Events[2]	Most Frequent Proposals Introduced in Congress[3]
1968 (cont.)		George Wallace makes impressive showing in three-way race for president that Richard Nixon wins	Electoral college
1969	625	Nixon appoints Warren Burger as chief justice to replace retiring Earl Warren American astronauts take first walk on the moon Number of amendments proposed in Congress is the most in any year since the nation's founding	Equal rights amendment Direct election of president Prayer in public places
1970	149	*Oregon v. Mitchell* rules that Congress can lower voting ages for federal but not for state elections Black Panthers meet in Philadelphia in a "Revolutionary People's Convention"	Equal rights amendment Voting rights School busing
1971	453	Congress proposes Twenty-sixth Amendment extending vote to 18-year-olds; states ratify amendment Supreme Court upholds limited use of school busing in *Swann v. Charlotte-Mecklenburg Board of Education*	Equal rights amendment School busing Prayer in schools Electoral college
1972	73	Congress proposes equal rights amendment; states do not ratify Leland Baldwin publishes *Reframing the Constitution: An Imperative for Modern America* *Furman v. Georgia* outlaws death penalty as then administered	Nomination and election of president School busing
1973	326	Decision in *Roe v. Wade* extends privacy rights to protect most cases of abortion *Miller v. California* sets standards for regulation of pornography *Frontiero v. Richardson* indicates increasing judicial sensitivity to women's rights Congress adopts war powers resolution to limit future overseas involvements without congressional support Last U.S. troops withdrawn from South Vietnam; it falls to North Vietnamese two years later	School busing Prayer in schools Electoral college Right to life
1974	56	Supreme Court rejects claim of executive privilege in *U.S. v. Nixon* President Nixon resigns from office after Watergate scandal and is pardoned by incoming President Ford Charles Hardin publishes *Presidential Power and Accountability: Toward a New Constitution* Rexford Tugwell publishes *The Emerging Constitution*, advancing the most complete scheme of constitutional reform ever offered in the U.S.	State jurisdiction over abortion Pardon power Balanced budget
1975	273	Lower court decision in *Dyer v. Blair* upholds Illinois' requirement for amendment ratification by a three-fifths majority	Right to life Balanced budget Electoral college

Year	Number of Proposals[1]	Key Events[2]	Most Frequent Proposals Introduced in Congress[3]
1976	58	Bicentennial of Declaration of Independence celebrated	Right to life Congressional tenure
1977	300		Right to life Balanced budget Electoral college
1978	70	Congress proposes amendment to treat District of Columbia as state in Congress; states do not ratify Justice Rehnquist upholds a Nevada advisory referendum on the equal rights amendment in *Kimble v. Swackhamer* Supreme Court rules on affirmative action in Bakke case Alan P. Grimes publishes *Democracy and the Amendments to the Constitution*	Balanced budget Right to life
1979	261	Congress extends seven-year deadline on equal rights amendment for an additional three years	Balanced budget Right to life Direct election of president
1980	29		Right to life
1981	186	Lower court decision in *Idaho v. Freeman* calls into question extension of equal rights amendment and raises possibility of state rescissions President Reagan appoints Sandra Day O'Connor as the first woman to serve on the U.S. Supreme Court	Balanced budget Right to life
1982	35		Balanced budget Equal rights amendment
1983	148	*Immigration and Naturalization Service v. Chadha* strikes down the legislative veto Walter Dellinger publishes influential article in *Harvard Law Review* entitled "The Legitimacy of Constitutional Change: Rethinking the Amending Process"	Balanced budget Right to life Prayer in schools
1984	13	Congress designates the administrator of the General Services Administration to certify the ratification of amendments, a task previously entrusted to the secretary of state and the archivist of the United States	Item veto Prayer in public places
1985	113	*Garcia v. San Antonio Metropolitan Transit Authority* appears to withdraw judiciary from most federalism issues	Balanced budget
1986	17	James Sundquist publishes *Constitutional Reform and Effective Government* President Reagan appoints William Rehnquist to replace retiring Chief Justice Warren Burger	Assorted issues

Year	Number of Proposals[1]	Key Events[2]	Most Frequent Proposals Introduced in Congress[3]
1986 (cont.)		*Challenger* space shuttle explodes, killing its crew and temporarily halting further shuttle flights	
1987	108	Bicentennial celebrations of U.S. Constitution Committee on the Constitutional System issues proposals for constitutional reform Reagan's nomination of Robert Bork to Supreme Court is rejected but initiates renewed debate about role of the Court	Balanced budget Right to life
1988	10	Russell Caplan publishes *Constitutional Brinkmanship,* a book on the constitutional convention option	Assorted issues
1989	168	*Texas v. Johnson* upholds constitutional right of flag burning Congress adopts the Flag Protection Act	Flag desecration Balanced budget
1990	16	*United States v. Eichman* reaffirms constitutional right of flag burning and overturns Flag Protection Act *Missouri v. Jenkins* stimulates fears that courts might order tax increases	Assorted issues
1991	115	American Operation "Desert Storm" forces Iraqi troops from Kuwait, where they had positioned themselves in a surprise invasion the previous year Bicentennial of the ratification of the Bill of Rights Bruce Ackerman publishes *We the People: Foundations,* stressing unofficial amending mechanisms John Vile publishes *Rewriting the United States, Constitution* the first of a number of books on proposed new constitutions and the amending process	Balanced budget Term limits Item veto
1992	55	States ratify putative Twenty-seventh Amendment limiting timing of congressional pay raises Barry Krusch publishes *The 21st Century Constitution* Steven Boyd publishes *Alternative Constitutions for the United States* In *Planned Parenthood v. Casey,* the Supreme Court modifies but does not overturn abortion decision in *Roe v. Wade*	Electoral college Balanced budget
1993	144	Richard Bernstein and Jerome Agel publish *Amending America,* a comprehensive history of the amending process in the U.S.	Congressional term limits
1994	14	House Republicans agree to Contract with America, including a number of proposed amendments Midterm elections end 50-year domination of Congress by Democrats	Congressional tenure
1995	121	*U.S. Term Limits, Inc. v. Thornton* indicates that states cannot limit terms of members of Congress	Congressional term limits Budget-related matters

Year	Number of Proposals[1]	Key Events[2]	Most Frequent Proposals Introduced in Congress[3]
1995 (cont.)		*U.S. v. Lopez* recognizes limits on congressional powers under the commerce clause Senate narrowly rejects flag desecration amendment after House approves it Sanford Levinson publishes book of essays on the amending process entitled *Responding to Imperfection* Chester J. Antieau publishes *A U.S. Constitution for the Year 2000*	
1996	26	Presidential election highlights many of the issues in the Contract with America, especially a balanced federal budget Kenneth Dolbeare and Janette Hubbell publish *USA 2012: After the Middle-Class Revolution* David Kyvig publishes *Explicit and Authentic Acts: Amending the U.S. Constitution, 1776–1995* John R. Vile publishes first edition of *Encyclopedia of Constitutional Amendments, Proposed Amendments, and Amending Issues, 1789–1995*	Victims' rights
1997	93	*Boerne v. Flores* limits congressional enforcement powers under the Fourteenth Amendment	Budget issues Term limits
1998	17	Bruce Ackerman publishes *We the People: Transformations,* second of three volumes U.S. House of Representatives impeaches President Bill Clinton for trying to cover up extramarital affairs U.S. Supreme Court decision in *Clinton v. City of New York* outlaws congressionally enacted item veto	Budget and tax issues
1999	54	U.S. Senate acquits President Clinton on impeachment charges	Budget related issues
2000	15	George Bush gets narrow win in the electoral college after U.S. Supreme Court decision in *Bush v. Gore* brings Florida vote-counting to an end U.S. Supreme Court decision in *Cook v. Gralike* prohibits states from "instructing" members of Congress on how to vote on constitutional amendments Palmer publishes *Constitutional Amendments: 1789 to the Present* Richard Labunski publishes *The Second Constitutional Convention*	Electoral College reform Balanced budget
2001	57	Terrorist attacks against the U.S. raise concern about national security and possible mass losses in Congress *Cook v. Gralike* voids Mo's attempt to note on ballot the candidates who support term limits *Santa Fe Independent School District v. Doe* extends ban on prayer in public schools to high school football games Kris Palmer, ed., publishes *Constitutional Amendments: 1789 to the Present* Shaw Grunow, ed., publishes *Constitutional Amendments: From Freedom of Speech to Flag Burning,* 3 vols.	Balanced budget Electoral College

Year	Number of Proposals[1]	Key Events[2]	Most Frequent Proposals Introduced in Congress[3]
2002	16 (list incomplete)	John R. Vile, ed., publishes *Proposed Amendments to the U.S. Constitution, 1787–2001*, 3 vols. U.S. Ninth Circuit Court of Appeals decision prohibiting public school recitations of the words "under God" in the pledge of allegiance stir controversy Republicans recapture U.S. Senate U.S. contemplates war with Iraq	Victims' rights Balanced budget/ "Under God" in flag salute

[1]These numbers were compiled from the following lists of amendments:

For the years 1787 through 1889, Herman Ames, *The Proposed Amendments to the Constitution of the United States During the First Century of Its History* (New York: Burt Franklin, 1970; reprint of 1896 edition). (Numbers in 1788–1789 reflect proposals of state ratifying conventions.)

For the years 1889 through 1926, *Proposed Amendments of the Constitution of the United States Introduced in Congress from December 4, 1889, to July 2, 1926,* arranged by Charles C. Tansil (Washington, DC: U.S. Government Printing Office, 1926).

For the years 1927 through 1962, *Proposed Amendments to the Constitution of the United States of America Introduced in Congress from the 69th Congress, 2d Session Through the 87th Congress, 2d Session, December 6, 1926, to January 3, 1963* (Washington, DC: U.S. Government Printing Office, 1963).

For the years 1963 through 1968, *Proposed Amendments to the Constitution of the United States of America Introduced in Congress from the 88th Congress, 1st Session Through the 90th Congress, 2d Session, January 9, 1963, to January 3, 1969* (Washington, DC: U.S. Government Printing Office, 1969).

For the years 1969 through 1984, Richard Davis, *Proposed Amendments to the Constitution of the United States of America Introduced in Congress from the 91st Congress, 1st Session, Through the 98th Congress, 2d Session, January 1969–December 1984,* Congressional Research Service Report No. 85-36 GOV (Washington, DC: Congressional Research Service, 1985).

For the years 1985 through 1990, Daryl B. Harris, *Proposed Amendments to the U.S. Constitution: 99th–101st Congresses (1985–1990)* (Washington, DC: Congressional Research Service, Library of Congress, 1992).

For the years from 1990 to the present, lists taken from the author's compilation as found on pp. 1663–1709, vol. 3 of 3 vols. of John R. Vile, ed. *Proposed Amendments to the U.S. Constitution, 1787–2001* (Union, New Jersey: The Lawbook Exchange, 2002). This set reprints all the sources above providing a "one-stop" source for topics of all amendments proposed through 2001.

The list used for the first 100 years includes some proposals that were introduced in state legislatures. Petitions for conventions that occurred in the second 100 years are not included in this survey. Any mistakes made in counting the proposals from each year are mine.

[2]Most events were chosen because of their relation to the amending process, but some are presented merely as markers of contemporaneous events.

[3]I read through each list of amendments and prepared this survey with as much completeness as possible, but with no pretense to absolute accuracy. In a few years marked "assorted," no amendment proposal predominated. In years in which numerous amendments were proposed, the proposals are listed according to their frequency. The number of times that amendments were offered does not necessarily indicate which ones had the most support, since a single amendment might have had multiple cosponsors.

APPENDIX E

Chronological List of Proposals by Individuals outside Congress Significantly to Revise or to Rewrite the U.S. Constitution

1789–1865

1815, Willard, Jr., Simon
1825, Woodward, Augustus
1858, Brown, John
1861, Confederate States of America
1861, Wedgwood, William B.
1864, Beasley, Robert

1866–1900

1870, Woodhull, Victoria Chaflin
1879, Stickney, Albert
1880, Lawrence, William B.
1884, Lockwood, Henry C.
1884, Rice, Isaac
1885, Hopkins, Caspar
1887, O'Connor, Charles
1890, West, James C.
1896, Adams, Frederick Upham
1897, Morris, Henry O.
1898, Smith, Goldwin

1900–1929

1906, Clark, Walter
1911, Tuller, Walter
1913, Henderson, Yandell
1915, Reynolds, Eustace
1922, McDonald, William

1930–1945

1931, Merriam, Charles
1932, Piburn, John
1932, Wallace, William K.
1933, McKee, Henry S.
1937, Cram, Ralph
1937, Eiselin, Malcolm
1937, Elliott, William Yandell
1938, Coleman, Charles
1938, Hamilton, Hugh
1941, Upham, Thomas Carlyle
1942, Agar, Herbert
1942, Hazlett, Henry
1943, Hehmeyer, Alexander
1945, Finletter, Thomas

1946–1969

1967–1968, Pei, Mario
1968, MacDonald, Dwight
1969, Finer, Herman

1970–1979

1970, Marduke, P.J.
1972, Baldwin, Leland
1973, Gardiner, William
1970s, Strittmatter, Bill
1974, Dillon, Conley
1974, Hardin, Charles
1974, Tugwell, Rexford
1976, Becker, Theodore

1980–1989

1980, Cummings, Richard
1981, Church, Joseph
1985, 1989, Robinson, Donald
1986, Pace, James O.
1986, Sundquist, James
1987, Miller, Arthur
1987, Miller, Jeffrey
1988, Anonymous (Proper Government)
1988, Murphy, Cornelius

1990–1999

1990, Mertens, John
1991, 1996, Tonn, Bruce E.
1992, Krusch, Barry
1994, Davidson, Jim
1994, Kirstein, Herbert C.
1995, Antieau, Chester
1995, Toffler, Alvin, and Heidi
1995, Vanguard, Virginia
1995, Wade, Edwin Lee
1996, Dolbeare, Kenneth, and Janel Hubbell
1996, Lazare, David
1997, Naylor, Thomas H., and William H.
    Willimon
1997, Struble, Jr., Robert

2000–2002

c2000, Durst, Jack
2000, Ellis, Frederick, and Carl Frederick
2000, Jeffs, David B.
2000, Labunski, Richard
2000, Nordeen, Ross
2000, VanSickle, John
2001, Bailey, Martin I.
2001, Jackson, Jr., Jesse L.

APPENDIX F
Major Proposals by Individuals outside Congress
Seeking Major Constitutional Changes

Name	Occupation	Title	Year	Did they write a new document?
Adams, Frederick Upham	Labor Editor	*President John Smith* (novel)	1896	Yes
Agar, Herbert (1897–1980)	Historian/Editor	Chapter in *A Time for Greatness*	1942	No
Anonymous	Proper Government (Website)		c1988	Yes
Antieau, Chester (1913–)	Professor Emeritus	*A U.S. Constitution for the Year 2000*	1995	No
Bailey, Martin I. (1927–2000?)	Economist	*Constitution for a Future Country*	2001	Yes
Baldwin, Leland (1897–1981)	Retired Historian	*Reframing the Constitution: An Imperative for Modern America*	1972	Yes
Beasley, Robert	Unknown	*A Plan to Stop the Present and Future Wars*	1864	Yes
Becker, Theodore (1932–)	Law & Pol. Sci. Prof	*American Government— Past—Present—Future*	1976	No
Brown, John (1800–1859)	Abolitionist	Provisional Constitution	1858	Yes
Church, Joseph (1918–)	Psychologist	*America the Possible: Why and How the Constitution Should Be Rewritten*	1982	No
Clark, Walter (1846–1942)	Judge	Speech	1906	No
Coleman, Charles (1900–)	Education	*The Constitution Up to Date*	1938	Yes
Confederate States of America		The Confederate Constitution	1861	Yes
Cram, Ralph (1863–1942)	Architect	*The End of Democracy*	1937	No
Cummings, Richard (1938–)	Attorney, Professor	*Proposition Fourteen: A Secessionist Remedy*	1980	No
Davidson, Jim, et al.		*The Atlantis Papers* & Website	c2000	Yes
Dillon, Conley (1906–1987)	Political Scientist	Public Administration Report	1974	No
Dolbeare, Kenneth (1930–) Hubbell, Janette (1948–)	College Professor Businessperson	*USA 2012: After the Middle Class Revolution*	1996	No
Durst, Jack (1980–)	College student	Constitution of the Republic (Website)	c2000	Yes
Eiselin, Malcolm (1902–1965)	Historian	Journal article	1937	No
Elliott William Yandell (1896–1979)	Political Scientist	*The Need for Constitutional Reform*	1937	No
Ellis, Frederick Frederick Carl	Political Activist	*The Oakland Statement* (novel)	2000	28th and 29th Amendments
Finer, Herman (1898–1969)	Political Scientist	*The Presidency: Crisis and Regeneration*	1969	No
Finletter, Thomas (1893–1980)	Attorney	*Can Representative Government Do the Job?*	1945	No
Gardiner, William (1885–)	Educator	*A Proposed Constitution for the United States of America*	1973	Yes
Hamilton, Hugh	Unknown	*A Second Constitution for the United States of America*	1938	Yes
Hardin, Charles (1908–)	Political Scientist	*Presidential Power and Accountability*	1974	No
Hazlitt, Henry (1894–1993)	Journalist	*A New Constitution Now*	1942	No
Hehmeyer, Alexander (1910–1993)	Attorney	*Time for Change: A Proposal for a Second Constitutional Convention*	1943	No

Name	Occupation	Title	Year	Did they write a new document?
Henderson, Yandell (1873–1974)	Physiologist	Article	1913	No
Hopkins, Caspar (1826–1893)	Businessman	Article	1885	Series of 10 Amendments
Jackson, Jesse L., Jr. (1965–)	Legislator	*A More Perfect Union: Advancing New American Rights*	2001	Series of Amendments
Jeffs, David B.	Police Officer	*America's Crisis* (Website)	2000	Multifaceted Amendment
Kirstein, Herbert C.	Government Employee	*U.S. Constitution for the 21st Century and Beyond*	1994	Yes
Krusch, Barry (1958–)		*The 21st Century Constitution*	1992	Yes
Labunski, Richard	Journalism Professor	*The Second Constitutional Convention*	2000	10 Proposed Amendments
Lawrence, William B.	Diplomat	Article	1880	No
Lazare, David	Journalist	*The Frozen Republic and How the Constitution Is Paralyzing Democracy*	1996	No
Lockwood, Henry C.	Historian	*The Abolition of the Presidency*	1884	Series of Proposals
MacDonald, Dwight (1906–1982)	Journalist	Article	1968	No
MacDonald, William (1863–1938)	Journalist/Professor	*A New Constitution for a New America*	1922	
McKee, Henry S. (1868–1956)	Businessman	*Degenerate Democracy*	1933	No
Marduke, P.J.		*The CASCOT System for Social Control of Technology* (Internet)	1970	No
Merriam, Charles (1874–1953)	Political Scientist	*The Written Constitution and the Unwritten Attitude*	1931	No
Mertens, John	Novelist	*The Second Constitution for the United States of America*	1990	Yes
Miller, Arthur (1917–1988)	Law Professor	*The Secret Constitution and the Need for Constitutional Change*	1987	No
Miller, Jeremy M. (1954)	Law Professor	Article	1987	Yes
Morris, Henry O.	Novelist	*Waiting for the Signal* (novel)	1897	Yes
Murphy, Cornelius F., Jr. (1933–)	Law Professor	Article	1988	No
Naylor, Thomas H.	Economics Professor	*Downsizing the U.S.A.*	1997	No
Willimon, William H.	Dean of Chapel			
Nordeen, Ross	Engineer	Website	c2000	Yes
O'Conor, Charles	Attorney	Articles	1887	No
			1881	No
Pace, James O.	Attorney	*Amendment to the Constitution: Averting the Decline and Fall of America*	1986	No
Pei, Mario	Linguist	Article	1967–68	No
Piburn, John (1872–)	Medical Doctor	*A Constitution and a Code*	1932	Yes
Reynolds, Eustace	Unknown	*A New Constitution: A Suggested Form of Modified Constitution*	1915	Yes
Rice, Isaac L. (1815–1915)	Attorney	Article	1884	3 major reforms
Robinson, Donald L. (1936–)	Political Scientist	2 books on reform	1985	No
			1989	No
Scott, Rodney D. (1949–)	Social Worker	*The Great Debate: The Need for Constitutional Reform*	1999	Yes
Smith, Goldwin (1823–1920)	Lawyer/Professor	Article	1898	No
Stickney, Albert (1839–1908)	Lawyer	*A True Republic*	1879	No
Strittmatter, Bill	Preacher	*A Christian Constitution and Civil Law for the Kingdom on Earth*	1970s	Yes

Name	Occupation	Title	Year	Did they write a new document?
Struble, Robert, Jr. (1915–)	Republican Official	*"Redeeming U.S. Democracy"* (Website)	c1997	A Twelve Code
Sundquist, James (1915–)	Political Scientist	*Constitutional Reform and Effective Government*	1986	No
Toffler, Alvin and Heidi (1928– , 1929–)	Journalist/Futurists	*Creating a New Civilization*	1995	No
Tonn, Bruce E.	Researcher	Articles	1991	No
			1996	No
Tugwell, Rexford (1891–1969)	Professor & Official	*The Emerging Constitution*	1974	Yes, many versions.
Tuller, Walter (1886–1939)	Attorney	Article	1911	No
Upham, Thomas Carlyle		*Total Democracy: A New Constitution for the United States*	1941	Yes
Vanguard, Virginia	Unknown	*The Populis: A Draft Constitution for a New Political Age*	1995	Yes
Vansickle, John	Soldier	Website	c2000	28th–32nd Amendments
Wade, Edwin Lee (1932–)	Businessman/Lawyer	*Constitution 2000: A Federalist Proposal for the Next Century*	1995	10 proposed amendments
Wallace, William K. (1886–)	Diplomat	*Our Obsolete Constitution*	1932	No
Wedgwood, William B. (–1883)	Attorney	*The Reconstruction of the Government of the United States*	1861	Yes
West, James C. (–1946)	Educator/Attorney	*A Proposed New Constitution for the United States*	1890	Yes
Willard, Simon, Jr. (1795–1874)	West Point Cadet	*The Columbian Union*	1815	Yes
Woodhull, Victoria Chaflin (1838–1927)	Activist	Speech	1870	Yes
Woodward, Augustus (1775–1827)		*The Presidency of the United States*	1825	No

BIBLIOGRAPHY

Abraham, Henry J. 1999. *Justices, Presidents, and Senators: A History of the U.S. Supreme Court Appointments from Washington to Clinton*. Lanham, MD: Rowman & Littlefield Publishers, Inc.

———. 1998. *The Judicial Process: An Introductory Analysis of the Courts of the United States, England, and France*. 7th ed. New York: Oxford University Press.

Abraham, Henry J., and Barbara Perry. 1994. *Freedom and the Court: Civil Rights and Liberties in the United States*. 6th ed. New York: Oxford University Press.

Abrams, Herbert L. 1999. "Can the Twenty-Fifth Amendment Deal with a Disabled President? Preventing Future White House Cover-ups." *Presidential Studies Quarterly* 29 (March): 115–133.

———. 1994. *The President Has Been Shot: Confusion, Disability and the Twenty-fifth Amendment*. Stanford, CA: Stanford University Press.

Abramson, Jeffrey. 1994. *We the Jury: The Jury System and the Ideal of Democracy*. New York: Basic Books.

Academics for the Second Amendment. 1995. "An Open Letter on the Second Amendment." *Chronicle of Higher Education* 41 (11 August): A23.

Ackerman, Bruce. 2000. "The New Separation of Powers." *The Harvard Law Review* 113 (January): 633–729.

———. 1996. *We the People: Transformation*. Cambridge, MA: Harvard University Press.

———. 1991. *We the People: Foundations*. Cambridge, MA: Belknap.

———. 1989. "Constitutional Politics/Constitutional Law." *Yale Law Journal* 99 (December): 453–547.

———. 1988. "Transformative Appointments." *Harvard Law Review* 101: 1164–1184.

———. 1984. "The Storrs Lectures: Discovering the Constitution." *Yale Law Journal* 93: 1013–1072.

———. 1979. "Unconstitutional Convention." *New Republic* 180 (3 March): 8–9.

Ackerman, Bruce, et al. 1995. "An Open Letter to Congressman Gingrich." *Yale Law Journal* 104 (April): 1539–1544.

Ackerman, Bruce, and David Golove. 1995. "Is NAFTA Constitutional?" *Harvard Law Review* 108 (February): 801–929.

Ackerman, Bruce, and Ned Katyal. 1991. "Our Unconventional Founding." *University of Chicago Law Review* 62 (Spring): 475–573.

Adams, Frederick U. 1896. *President John Smith: The Story of a Peaceful Revolution*. Chicago: Charles H. Kerr & Company; reprint, New York: Arno Press, 1970.

Adams, Henry. 1974. *The Formative Years*, ed. Herbert Agar. 2 vols. Westport, CT: Greenwood Press.

Adler, Mortimer J. 1987. *We Hold These Truths: Understanding the Ideas and the Ideals of the Constitution*. New York: Macmillan.

Advisory Commission on Intergovernmental Relations. 1987. *Is Constitutional Reform Necessary to Reinvigorate Federalism? A Roundtable Discussion*. November. Washington, DC: ACIR.

———. 1986. *Reflections on Garcia and Its Implications for Federalism*. February. Washington, DC: ACIR.

Agar, Herbert. 1942. *A Time for Greatness*. Boston: Little, Brown.

Agnes, Richard L. 1994. "Constricting the Law of Freedom: Justice Miller, the Fourteenth Amendment, and the *Slaughter-House Cases*." *Chicago-Kent Law Review* 70: 627–688.

"Albany Plan of Union." *http://www.constitution. org/bcp/albany.htm*. Accessed 27 April 2002.

Alderman, Ellen, and Caroline Kennedy. 1991. *In Our Defense: The Bill of Rights in Action*. New York: William Morrow.

Aldous, Joan. 1997. "The Political Process and the Failure of the Child Labor Amendment." *Journal of Family Issues* 18 (January): 71–92.

Alexander, Herbert E. 1992. *Financing Politics: Money, Elections and Political Reform*. 4th ed. Washington, DC: Congressional Quarterly Press.

Alfange, Dean, Jr. 1994. "*Marbury v. Madison* and Original Understandings of Judicial Review: In Defense of Traditional Wisdom." In *Supreme Court Review, 1993*. Chicago: University of Chicago Press.

Amar, Akhil R. 1998. *The Bill of Rights: Creation and Reconstruction*. New Haven, CT: Yale University Press.

———. 1997. *The Constitution and Criminal Procedure: First Principles*. New Haven, CT: Yale University Press.

———. 1994. "The Consent of the Governed: Constitutional Amendment outside Article V." *Columbia Law Review* 94 (March): 457–508.

———. 1992. "The Bill of Rights as a Constitution." *Yale Law Journal* 100 (Winter): 1131–1210.

———. 1988. "Philadelphia Revisited: Amending the Constitution outside Article V." *University of Chicago Law Review* 55 (Fall): 1043–1104.

Amar, Vikram David. 2000. "The People Made Me Do It: Can the People of the States Instruct and Coerce Their State Legislatures in the Article V Convention Amendment Process?" *William and Mary Law Review* 41 (March): 1037–1092.

Ambrose, Stephen E. 1966. *Duty, Honor, Country: A History of West Point.* Baltimore, MD: Johns Hopkins University Press.

American Political Science Association, Committee on Political Parties. 1950. *Toward a More Responsible Two-Party System.* New York: Rinehart.

Ames, Herman. 1896. *The Proposed Amendments to the Constitution of the United States during the First Century of Its History.* Reprint, New York: Burt Franklin, 1970.

Anastaplo, George. 1995. *The Amendments to the Constitution: A Commentary.* Baltimore, MD: Johns Hopkins University Press.

———. 1989. *The Constitution of 1787: A Commentary.* Baltimore, MD: Johns Hopkins University Press.

Antieau, Chester J. 1995. *A U.S. Constitution for the Year 2000.* Chicago: Loyola University Press.

Arling, Emanie. 1972. *The Terrible Siren: Victoria Woodhull.* New York: Arno Press.

Ashmore, Harry S. 1970. "Rexford Guy Tugwell: Man of Thought, Man of Action." *Center Magazine* 3 (September/October): 2–7.

"Assembly Joint Resolution 8." 1952. *Congressional Record,* 82nd Cong., 2d sess. 1952, Vol. 98, pt. 3: 4003–4004.

Atkinson, David N. 1999. *Leaving the Bench: Supreme Court Justices at the End.* Lawrence, KS: University Press of Kansas.

Ayers, Ian, and Bruce A. Ackerman. 2002. *Voting with Dollars: A New Paradigm for Campaign Finance.* New Haven, CT: Yale University Press.

Babson, Jennifer. 1995. "House Rejects Term Limits: GOP Blames Democrats." *Congressional Quarterly Weekly Reports* 53 (1 April): 918–919.

Bacon, Margaret H. 1980. *Valiant Friend: The Life of Lucretia Mott.* New York: Walker and Company.

Bacon, Selden. 1930. "How the Tenth Amendment Affected the Fifth Article of the Constitution." *Virginia Law Review* 16 (June): 771–791.

Bailey, Martin J. 2001. *Constitution for a Future Country.* New York: Palgrave.

Baker, A. Diane. 1979. "ERA: The Effect of Extending the Time for Ratification on Attempts to Rescind Prior Ratifications." *Emory Law Journal* 28: 71–110.

Baker, Deborah. 1999. "The Fight Ain't Over."

American Bar Association Journal 85 (August): 52.

Baker, Leonard. 1974. *John Marshall: A Life in Law.* New York: Macmillan.

Baker, Lynn A., and Samuel H. Dinkin. 1997. "The Senate: An Institution Whose Time Has Gone?" *Journal of Law & Politics* 13 (Winter): 21–95.

Baker, Richard A. 1992. "Congress, Arrest and Immunity of Members Of." In *The Oxford Companion to the Supreme Court of the United States,* ed. Kermit L. Hall. New York: Oxford University Press.

Baker, Thomas E. 2000. "Towards a 'More Perfect Union.'" *Insights on Law & Society* 1 (Fall): 4–7.

———. 1995a. "Can Voters Exclude Homosexuals and Their Interests from the Legislative Process?" *Preview of United States Court Cases* (20 September): 11–18.

———. 1995b. "Exercising the Amendment Power to Disapprove of Supreme Court Decisions: A Proposal for a 'Republican Veto.'" *Hastings Constitutional Law Quarterly* 22 (Winter): 325–357.

"The Balanced Budget Amendment: An Inquiry into Appropriateness." 1983. *Harvard Law Review* 96 (May): 1600–1620.

Baldwin, Leland. 1972. *Reframing the Constitution: An Imperative for Modern America.* Santa Barbara, CA: ABC-CLIO.

Ban, Kevin K. 1998. "Does the Internet Warrant a Twenty-Seventh Amendment *[sic]* to the United States Constitution?" *The Journal of Comparative Law* 23 (Spring): 521–540.

Banner, Lois W. 1980. *Elizabeth Cady Stanton: A Radical for Women's Rights.* Boston: Little, Brown.

Banning, Lance. 1995. *The Sacred Fire of Liberty: James Madison and the Founding of the Federal Republic.* Ithaca, NY: Cornell University Press.

Barber, Benjamin. 1984. *Strong Democracy.* Berkeley, CA: University of California Press.

Barber, Sotirios A. 1984. *On What the Constitution Means.* Baltimore, MD: Johns Hopkins University Press.

Barkow, Rachel E. 2000. "More Supreme Than Court? The Fall of the Political Question Doctrine and the Rise of Judicial Supremacy." *Columbia Law Review* 102 (March): 237–336.

Barnette, Randy E., ed. 1989. *The Rights Retained by the People: The History and Meaning of the Ninth Amendment.* Fairfax, VA: George Mason University Press.

Barnum, David G. 1993. *The Supreme Court and American Democracy.* New York: St. Martin's Press.

Baron, Dennis. 1990. *The English-Only Question: An*

Official Language for America? New Haven, CT: Yale University Press.

Barone, Michael, and Grant Ujifusa. 1994. *The Almanac of American Politics 1994.* Washington, DC: National Journal.

Basch, Norma. 1992. "Reconstructing Female Citizenship: *Minor v. Happersett.*" In *The Constitution, Law, and American Life: Critical Aspects of the Nineteenth-Century Experience,* ed. Donald G. Nieman. Athens, GA: University of Georgia Press.

Bates, Stephen. 1991. "Deconstructing the Flag-Burning Debate." *This World & I* 7 (July): 523–529.

Baumer, Donald C., and Carl E. Van Horn. 1985. *The Politics of Employment.* Washington, DC: Congressional Quarterly Press.

Bayh, Birch. 1968. *One Heartbeat Away: Presidential Disability and Succession.* Indianapolis, IN: Bobbs-Merrill.

———. 1966. *The Making of an Amendment.* Indianapolis, IN: Bobbs-Merrill.

Baylor, Gregory S. 1995. "The Religious Equality Amendment." *Christian Legal Society Quarterly* 16 (Summer): 4–5.

Beaney, William M., and Edward N. Beiser. 1973. "Prayer and Politics: The Impact of *Engel* and *Schempp* on the Political Process." In *The Impact of Supreme Court Decisions: Empirical Studies.* 2d ed. Eds. Theodore L. Becker and Malcolm M. Feeley. New York: Oxford University Press.

Beasley, Robert. 1864. *A Plan to Stop the Present and Prevent Future Wars: Containing a Proposed Constitution for the General Government of the Sovereign States of North and South America.* Rio Vista, CA: Robert Beasley.

Beatty, Edward C. 1975. *William Penn as Social Philosopher.* New York: Octagon Books.

Beauregard, Erving E. 1989. *Bingham of the Hills: Politician and Diplomat Extraordinary.* New York: Peter Lang.

Beck, James M. 1922. *The Constitution of the United States.* New York: G. H. Doran Co.

Becker, Carl L. 1970. *The Declaration of Independence: A Study in the History of Political Ideas.* New York: Vintage Books.

Becker, Theodore L. 1976. *American Government: Past—Present—Future.* Boston: Allyn and Bacon.

Becker, Theodore L., and Crista Daryl Slaton. 2000. *The Future of Teledemocracy.* Westport, CT: Praeger.

Becker, Theodore L., and Malcolm M. Feeley, eds. 1973. *The Impact of Supreme Court Decisions: Empirical Studies.* 2d ed. New York: Oxford University Press.

Belknap, Michael R. 1992. "Communism and the Cold War." In *The Oxford Companion to the Supreme Court of the United States,* ed. Kermit L. Hall. New York: Oxford University Press.

Bell, Roger. 1984. *Last Among Equals: Hawaii Statehood and American Politics.* Honolulu, HI: University of Hawaii Press.

Bell, Tom W. 1993. "The Third Amendment: Forgotten but Not Gone." *William & Mary Bill of Rights Journal* 2: 117–150.

Bellamy, Edward. 1888. *Looking Backward.* Reprint, New York: Magnum Books, 1968.

Bellesiles, Michael A. 2000. *Arming America: The Origins of a National Gun Culture.* New York: Alfred A. Knopf.

Benjamin, Gerald, and Thomas Gais. 1996. "Constitutional Conventionphobia." *Hofstra Law and Policy Symposium* 1: 53–77.

Benjamin, Gerald, and Michael J. Malbin, eds. 1992. *Limiting Legislative Terms.* Washington, DC: Congressional Quarterly Press.

Bennett, Robert W. 2001. "Popular Election of the President without a Constitutional Amendment." *Green Bag* 2d 4 (Spring): 241–246.

Benson, Ben, and M. J. "Red" Beckman. 1985. *The Law That Never Was—The Fraud of the 16th Amendment and Personal Income Tax.* South Holland, IL: Constitutional Research Association.

Benson, Paul R., Jr. 1970. *The Supreme Court and the Commerce Clause, 1937–1970.* New York: Denellen.

Berg, Larry L., Harlan Hahn, and John R. Schmidhauser. 1976. *Corruption in the American Political System.* Morristown, NJ: General Learning Press.

Berger, Raoul. 1973. *Impeachment: The Constitutional Problems.* Cambridge, MA: Harvard University Press.

Berke, Richard L. 1995. "Epic Political Realignments Often Aren't." *New York Times,* 1 January, E-3.

Bernhard, Virginia, and Elizabeth Fox-Genovese, eds. 1995. *The Birth of American Feminism: The Seneca Falls Woman's Convention of 1848.* St. James, NY: Brandywine Press.

Berns, Walter., ed. 1992. *After the People Vote: A Guide to the Electoral College.* Rev. ed. Washington, DC: AEI Press.

Bernstein, Richard B. 1993. "Fixing the Electoral College." *Constitution* 5 (Winter): 42–48.

———. 1992. "The Sleeper Wakes: The History and Legacy of the Twenty-seventh Amendment." *Fordham Law Review* 56 (December): 497–557.

Bernstein, Richard B., with Jerome Agel. 1993. *Amending America: If We Love the Constitution So Much, Why Do We Keep Trying to Change It?* New York: Random House.

Berry, Mary F. 1987. "How Hard It Is to Change."

New York Times Magazine, 13 September, 93–98.

———. 1986. *Why ERA Failed: Politics, Women's Rights, and the Amending Process of the Constitution.* Bloomington, IN: Indiana University Press.

Best, Judith. 1984a. "The Item Veto: Would the Founders Approve?" *Presidential Studies Quarterly* 14 (Spring): 183–188.

———. 1984b. *National Representation for the District of Columbia.* Frederick, MD: University Publications of America.

———. 1971. *The Case against Direct Election of the President: A Defense of the Electoral College.* Ithaca, NY: Cornell University Press.

Betts, James T. 1967. "The Scope of Immunity for Legislators and Their Employees." *Yale Law Journal* 77 (December): 366–389.

Beveridge, Albert J. 1916. *The Life of John Marshall.* 4 vols. Boston: Houghton Mifflin.

The Bible in the Public Schools. 1870. Cincinnati, OH: Robert Clarke & Co. Reprint, New York: Da Capo Press, introduction by Robert G. McCloskey, 1967.

"A Bicentennial Analysis of the American Political Structure." 1987. Washington, DC: Report and Recommendations of the Committee on the Constitutional System. January.

Bickel, Alexander. 1986. *The Least Dangerous Branch: The Supreme Court at the Bar of Politics.* 2d ed. New Haven, CT: Yale University Press.

"The Bill of Rights." 1991. Bicentennial issue of *Life* (Fall).

"Birch E(vans) Bayh, Jr." 2001. In *Contemporary Authors Online.* The Gale Group. Accessed 7 August 2001.

Birkby, Robert H. 1973. "The Supreme Court and the Bible Belt: Tennessee Reaction to the 'Schempp' Decision." In *The Impact of Supreme Court Decisions: Empirical Studies.* 2d ed. Ed. Theodore L. Becker and Malcolm M. Feeley. New York: Oxford University Press.

"The Birthright Citizenship Amendment: A Threat to Equality." 1994. *Harvard Law Review* 107: 1026–1043.

Biskupic, Joan. 1990. "Critics of Measure Win Fight, but Battle Scars Run Deep." *Congressional Quarterly Weekly Report* 48 (30 June): 2063–2064.

Bittker, Boris I. 1999. *Bittker on the Regulation of Interstate and Foreign Commerce.* Gaithersburg, MD: Aspen Law & Business.

Black, Charles L., Jr. 1979. "Amendment by a National Constitutional Convention: A Letter to a Senator." *Oklahoma Law Review* 32: 626–644.

———. 1978. "Correspondence: On Article I, Section 7, Clause 3—and the Amendment of the Constitution." *Yale Law Journal* 87: 896–900.

———. 1963. "The Proposed Amendment of Article V: A Threatened Disaster." *Yale Law Journal* 72 (April): 957–966.

Black, Hugo L. 1969. *A Constitutional Faith.* New York: Alfred A. Knopf.

Black's Law Dictionary. 1969. 5th ed. St. Paul, MN: West.

Bledsoe, Craig W. 1989. "Executive Pay and Perquisites." In *Guide to the Presidency,* ed. Michael Nelson. Washington, DC: Congressional Quarterly Press.

Blocker, Jack S., Jr. 1976. *Retreat from Reform: The Prohibition Movement in the United States, 1890–1916.* Westport, CT: Greenwood Press.

Bloom, Joshua. 2000. "Black Panther Party." In *Civil Rights in the United States.* 2 vols. Edited by Waldo E. Maqrtin Jr. and Patricia Sullivan. New York: Macmillan Reference USA.

Bloomfield, Maxwell. 2000. *Peaceful Revolution: Constitutional Change and American Culture from Progressivism to the New Deal.* Cambridge, MA: Harvard University Press.

Bobbitt, Philip. 1992. "Constitutional Interpretation." In *The Oxford Companion to the Supreme Court of the United States,* ed. Kermit L. Hall. New York: Oxford University Press.

Bodenhamer, David J. 1992. *Fair Trial: Rights of the Accused in American History.* New York: Oxford University Press.

Bodenhamer, David J., and James W. Ely Jr., eds. 1993. *The Bill of Rights in Modern America after 200 Years.* Bloomington, IN: Indiana University Press.

Boles, Janet K. 1979. *The Politics of the Equal Rights Amendment: Conflict and the Decision Process.* New York: Longman.

Boller, Paul E., Jr. 1984. *Presidential Campaigns.* New York: Oxford University Press.

Bonfield, Arthur E. 1968. "The Dirksen Amendment and the Article V Convention Process." *Michigan Law Review* 66 (March): 949–1000.

Bonsell, Thomas. 1995. *The Un-Americans: Trashing of the United States Constitution in the American Press.* Wauna, WA: Country Cottage Publishing.

Borden, Morton. 1979. "The Christian Amendment." *Civil War History* 25 (June): 156–167.

Bordin, Ruth. 1981. *Women and Temperance: The Quest for Power and Liberty, 1873–1900.* Philadelphia: Temple University Press.

Bork, Robert H. 1990. *The Tempting of America: The Political Seduction of the Law.* New York: Free Press.

Bowen, Catherine Drinker. 1966. *Miracle at Philadelphia: The Story of the Constitutional Convention May to September 1787.* Boston: Little, Brown.

Bowen, James W. 1994. "Enforcing the Balanced Budget Amendment." *Constitutional Law Journal* 4 (Spring): 565–620.

Bowling, Kenneth R. 1991. *The Creation of Washington, D.C.: The Idea and Location of the American Capital.* Fairfax, VA: George Mason University Press.

Boyd, Steven R., ed. 1992. *Alternative Constitutions for the United States: A Documentary History.* Westport, CT: Greenwood Press.

Bradford, Gamaliel. 1893. "Congress and the Cabinet—II." *Annals of the American Academy of Political and Social Sciences* 4 (November): 289–299.

———. 1891. "Congress and the Cabinet." *Annals of the American Academy of Political and Social Sciences* 4 (November): 404–424.

Bradford, M. E. 1994. *Founding Fathers: Brief Lives of the Framers of the United States Constitution.* 2d ed. Lawrence, KS: University Press of Kansas.

Bradley, Harold W. 1945. "The Political Thinking of George Washington." *Journal of Southern History* 11 (November): 469–486.

Bradsher, Keith. 1995. "Gap in Wealth in U.S. Called Widest in West." *New York Times,* 17 April, 1, C4.

Brandon, Mark E. 1995. "The 'Original' Thirteenth Amendment and the Limits to Formal Constitutional Change." In *Responding to Imperfection: The Theory and Practice of Constitutional Amendment,* ed. Sanford Levinson. Princeton, NJ: Princeton University Press.

Brasseau, Carl A. 1989. "Four Hundred Years of Acadian Life in North America." *Journal of Popular Culture* 23 (Summer): 3–22.

Bridwell, R. Randall, and William J. Quirk. *Judicial Dictatorship.* New Brunswick, NJ: Transaction Publishers.

Brown, Everett S. 1938. *Ratification of the Twenty-first Amendment to the Constitution of the United States; State Convention Records and Laws.* Ann Arbor, MI: University of Michigan Press.

———. 1935. "The Ratification of the Twenty-first Amendment." *American Political Science Review* 29 (December): 1005–1017.

Brown, Jennifer K. 1993. "The Nineteenth Amendment and Women's Equality." *Yale Law Journal* 102 (June): 2174–2204.

Brown, Raymond G. 1920. "The Sixteenth Amendment to the United States Constitution." *American Law Review* 54: 843–854.

Bryant, Douglas H. 2002. "Unorthodox and Paradox: Revisiting the Ratification of the Fourteenth Amendment." *Alabama Law Review* 53: 555–581.

Bryant, Irving. 1965. *The Bill of Rights: Its Origin and Meaning.* Indianapolis, IN: Bobbs-Merrill.

Bryce, James. 1906. *The American Commonwealth.* 3d ed. 2 vols. New York: Macmillan.

———. 1905. "Flexible and Rigid Constitutions." In *Constitutions.* Germany: Scientia Verlag Aalen. Reprint of New York and London edition, 1980.

Budziszewski, J. 2002. "Judicial Restraints." *World* 17 (June 8): 16–18.

Bumiller, Elisabeth. 2002. "Bush to Undergo Colon Procedure: President Will Transfer Power to Cheney before Sedation." *The New York Times,* 29 June, A1 and A11.

Burke, Yvonne B. 1976. "Validity of Attempts to Rescind Ratification of the Equal Rights Amendment." *University of Los Angeles Law Review* 8: 1–22.

Burnham, Walter D. 1995. "Realignment Lives: The 1994 Earthquake and Its Implications." In *The Clinton Presidency: First Appraisals,* ed. Colin Campbell and Bert Rockman. Chatham, NJ: Chatham House.

———. 1970. *Critical Elections and the Mainsprings of American Politics.* New York: W. W. Norton.

Butler, David, and Bruce Cain. 1992. *Congressional Redistricting: Comparative and Theoretical Perspectives.* New York: Macmillan.

Butts, R. Freeman. 1978. *Public Education in the United States: From Revolution to Reform.* New York: Holt, Rinehart, and Winston.

Butzner, Jane, comp. 1941. *Constitutional Chaff—Rejected Suggestions of the Constitutional Convention of 1787 with Explanatory Argument.* New York: Columbia University Press.

Bybee, Jay S. 1997. "Ulysses at the Mast: Democracy, Federalism, and the Sirens' Song of the Seventeenth Amendment." *Northwestern University Law Review* 91 (Winter): 500–569.

Cahn, Edmond. 1954. "An American Contribution." In *Supreme Court and Supreme Law.* Bloomington, IN: Indiana University Press.

Calhoun, John C. 1953. *A Disquisition on Government and Selections from the Discourse.* Edited by C. Gordon Post. Indianapolis, IN: Bobbs-Merrill. [Originally published as part of *The Works of John C. Calhoun.* Edited by Richard K. Crallé. New York: D. Appleton and Company, 1851–1856.] Reprint, New York: Russell and Russell, 1968.

———. 1851–1856. *The Works of John C. Calhoun,* ed. Richard K. Crallé. Reprint, New York: Russell and Russell, 1968.

Calmes, Jackie. 1996. "In Symbolical Gesture, House Is to Vote Today on Amendment Making It Harder to Boost Taxes." *Wall Street Journal* 127 (April 15): A20.

Caplan, Russell L. 1988. *Constitutional Brinkmanship: Amending the Constitution by National Convention.* New York: Oxford University Press.

———. 1983. "The History and Meaning of the Ninth Amendment." *Virginia Law Review* 69 (March): 223–268.

Carleton, David. 2002. *Student's Guide to Landmark Congressional Laws on Education.* Westport, CT: Greenwood Press.

Carroll, John. 1982. "Constitutional Law: Constitutional Amendment. Rescission of Ratification. Extension of Ratification Period. *State of Idaho v. Freeman.*" *Akron Law Review* 14 (Summer): 151–161.

Carson, Gerald. 1973. "The Income Tax and How It Grew." *American Heritage* 25 (December): 5–9, 79–88.

Carter. Dan T. 1964. *Scottsboro: A Tragedy of the American South.* New York: Oxford University Press.

Carter, Stephen L. 1994. *The Confirmation Mess: Cleaning Up the Federal Appointments Process.* New York: Basic Books.

Casey, Samuel B. 1995. "Religious Freedom Makes Good Neighbors." *Christian Legal Society Quarterly* 16 (Summer): 3.

Cassell, Paul G. 1999. "Barbarians at the Gates? A Reply to the Critics of the Victims' Rights Amendment." *Utah Law Review* 1999: 479–537.

Cassell, Paul G., and Steven J. Twist. 1996. "A Bill of Rights for Crime Victims." 127 *Wall Street Journal* (24 April): A15.

Ceaser, James W. 1988. "The Reagan Presidency and American Public Opinion." In *The Reagan Legacy: Promise and Performance,* ed. Charles O. Jones. Chatham, NJ: Chatham House.

———. 1986. "In Defense of Separation of Powers." In *Separation of Powers—Does It Still Work?* Ed. Robert A. Goldwin and Art Kaufman. Washington, DC: American Enterprise Institute.

Ceaser, James W., and Andrew W. Busch. 2001. *The Perfect Tie: The True Story of the 2000 Presidential Election.* Lanham, MD: Rowman & Littlefield.

"A Celebration of Women's Right to Vote." 1995. *New York Times,* 27 August, 9.

Chapin, Bradley. 1964. *The American Law of Treason: Revolutionary and Early National Origins.* Seattle, WA: University of Washington Press.

Chemerinsky, Erwin. 2000. "Citizens for the Constitution." *Insights on Law & Society* 1 (Fall): 14–15.

"Children Adopted Abroad Win Automatic Citizenship." 2001. *Migration World Magazine* 19 (March): 12.

Chittenden, Lucius E. 1864. *A Report of the Debates and Proceedings in the Secret Sessions of the Conference Convention for Proposing Amendments to the Constitution of the United States.* New York: D. Appleton & Company. Reprint, New York: Da Capo Press, 1971.

Christensen, Terry. 1995. *Local Politics: Governing at the Grassroots.* Belmont, CA: Wadsworth.

Christman, Henry M., ed. 1985. *Kingfish to America: Share Our Wealth: Selected Senatorial Papers of Huey P. Long.* New York: Shocken Books.

Church, Joseph. 1982. *America the Possible: Why and How the Constitution Should Be Rewritten.* New York: Macmillan.

Citizens for the Constitution. 1999. *Great and Extraordinary Occasions.* New York: Century Foundation, Inc.

Clapp, Rodney. 1990. *The Reconstructionists.* Downers Grove, IL: Intervarsity Press.

Clark, James C. 1985. *Faded Glory: Presidents out of Power.* New York: Praeger.

Clark, Walter. 1906. "Some Defects of the Constitution of the United States." In *The Papers of Walter Clark.* Vol. 2, 1902–1924, ed. Aubrey L. Brooks and Hugh T. Lefler. Reprint, Chapel Hill, NC: University of North Carolina Press, 1950.

Claude, Inis L., Jr. 1971. *Swords into Plowshares: The Problems and Progress of International Organization.* 4th ed. New York: Random House.

Clem, Alan L. 1989. *Congress: Powers, Processes, and Politics.* Pacific Grove, CA: Brooks/Cole.

Clinton, Robert L. 1989. Marbury v. Madison *and Judicial Review.* Lawrence: University Press of Kansas.

Clotfetter, Charles T., and Phillip Cook. 1989. *Selling Hope: State Lotteries in America.* Cambridge, MA: Harvard University Press.

Clymer, Adam. 1996. "Senator Still Plans to Push Amendment on Tax Increase." *New York Times* 145 (April 17): A12.

Cobb, Frank. 1924. "A Twentieth Amendment." In *Cobb of "The World": A Leader in Liberalism,* ed. John L. Heaton. New York: E. P. Dutton.

Cochrane, Thad. 1994. "Constitutional Amendment Restoring the Right to the Free Exercise of Religion." *Congressional Record,* U.S. Senate, 14 June, 103rd Cong., 2d sess., 1994, Vol. 140, pt. 9.

Cogan, Neil H. ed. 1997. *The Complete Bill of Rights: The Drafts, Debates, Sources, and Origins.* New York: Oxford University Press.

Cohen, Patricia. 2002. "9/11 Law Means More Snooping? Or Maybe Less?" *The New York Times,* 7 September, B9.

Coit, Margaret L. 1961. *John C. Calhoun: American Portrait.* Boston: Houghton Mifflin.

Cole, Wayne S. 1962. *Senator Gerald P. Nye and American Foreign Relations.* Minneapolis, MN: University of Minnesota Press.

Coleman, Charles. 1938. *The Constitution up to Date.* Bulletin no. 10. Cambridge, MA: National Council for Social Studies.

Coleman, Peter J. 1992. "Bankruptcy and Insolvency Legislation." In *The Oxford Companion to the Supreme Court of the United States,* ed. Kermit L. Hall. New York: Oxford University Press.

———. 1974. *Debtors and Creditors in America: Insolvency, Imprisonment for Debt, and Bankruptcy, 1607–1900.* Madison, WI: State Historical Society of Wisconsin.

Committee on Federal Legislation of the Bar Association of the City of New York. n.d. *The Law of Presidential Impeachment.* New York: Harrow Books.

Committee on Federal State Relations. 1963. "Amending the Constitution to Strengthen the States in the Federal System." *State Government* 10 (Winter): 10–15.

The Committee to Frame a World Constitution. 1948. *Preliminary Draft of a World Constitution.* Chicago: The University of Chicago Press.

"Composition and Jurisdiction of the Supreme Court—Proposed Constitutional Amendment." 1953. In *Congressional Record.* U.S. Senate, 16 February, 1106–1108.

"Conference of the States: An Action Plan to Restore Balance in the Federal System." 1995. Concept paper adopted by the Council of State Governments, the National Governors' Association, and the National Conference of State Legislatures. 1 February.

"Congressional Bomb Shelter Revealed." 1992. *Facts on File* 52: 681.

Congressional Quarterly. 2000. *American Political Leaders, 1789–2000.* Washington, DC: Congressional Quarterly.

———. 1991. *Guide to Congress.* 4th ed. Washington, DC: Congressional Quarterly.

Conklin, Curt E. 1996. "The Case of the Phantom Thirteenth Amendment: A Historical and Bibliographic Nightmare." *Law Library Journal* 88 (Winter): 121–127.

Conlan, Timothy J., James D. Riggle, and Donna E. Schwartz. 1995. "Deregulating Federalism? The Politics of Mandate Reform in the 104th Congress." *Publius: The Journal of Federalism* 25 (Summer): 23–40.

Conley, Patrick T., and John P. Kaminski, eds. 1992. *The Bill of Rights and the States: The Colonial and Revolutionary Origins of American Liberties.* Madison, WI: Madison House.

"The Conservation Bill of Rights." *Congressional Record*, 90th Cong., 2d sess., 13 June 1968, Vol. 114, pt. 13: 17116–17117.

"Constitution for a United Republic of America, Followed by an Index." 1970. *Center Magazine* 3 (September/October): 24–49.

"Constitution Party 2000 National Platform." *http://www.constitutionparty.com/ustp–99p1. html.* Accessed 29 May 2002.

"The Constitutional Amendment Process." *http://www.archives.gov/federal_register/constitution/amendment_process.html.* Accessed 11/26/02.

Constitutional Rights Foundation. "America Responds to Terrorism." *http://www.crf-usa/terror/America.* Accessed 18 May 2002.

Contemporary Authors Online. 2001. The Gale Group.

"Continuity of Congress." *http://www.aeipolitical-corner.org/continuity.htm.* Accessed 20 May 2002.

Cooke, Edward F. 1984. *A Detailed Analysis of the Constitution.* 5th ed. Savage, MO: Littlefield Adams Quality Paperbacks.

Cooper, Phillip, and Howard Ball. 1996. *The United States Supreme Court from the Inside Out.* Upper Saddle River, NJ: Prentice Hall.

Cornwell, Elmer E., Jr. 1981. "The American Constitutional Tradition: Its Impact and Development." In *The Constitutional Convention as an Amending Device,* ed. Kermit L. Hall, Harold M. Hyman, and Leon V. Sigal. Washington, DC: American Historical Association.

Cornwell, Elmer E., Jr., Jay S. Goodman, and Wayne R. Swanson. 1975. *State Constitutional Conventions: The Politics of the Revision Process in Seven States.* New York: Praeger.

Correspondents of *The New York Times.* 2001. *36 Days: The Complete Chronicle of the 2000 Presidential Election Crisis.* New York: Henry Holt.

Cortner, Richard C. 1993. *The Iron Horse and the Constitution: The Railroads and the Transformation of the Fourteenth Amendment.* Westport, CT: Greenwood Press.

Corwin, Edward S. 1981. "The Constitution as Instrument and as Symbol." In *Corwin on the Constitution,* vol. 1, ed. Richard Loss. Ithaca, NY: Cornell University Press.

———. 1955. *The "Higher Law" Background of American Constitutional Law.* Ithaca, NY: Cornell University Press.

Cottrol, Robert J., ed. 1993. *Gun Control and the Constitution: Sources and Explorations of the Second Amendment.* 3 vols. New York: Garland.

"Covenant, Polity, and Constitutionalism." 1980. Special issue of *Publius: The Journal of Federalism* (Fall).

Craig, Barbara H. 1988. *Chadha: The Story of an Epic Constitutional Struggle.* New York: Oxford University Press.

Craig, Barbara H., and David M. O'Brien. 1993. *Abortion and American Politics*. Chatham, NJ: Chatham House.

Cram, Ralph. 1937. *The End of Democracy*. Boston: Marshall Jones Company.

———. 1935. *Convictions and Controversies*. Reprint, Freeport, NY: Books for Libraries Press, 1970.

Cramer, Clayton E. 1994. *For the Defense of Themselves and the State: The Original Intent and Judicial Interpretation of the Right to Keep and Bear Arms*. Westport, CT: Praeger.

Croly, Herbert. 1914. *Progressive Democracy*. New York: Macmillan. Reprint, New Brunswick, NJ: Transaction Publishers, 1998.

———. 1909. *The Promise of American Life*. New York: Macmillan Company. Reprint, Indianapolis: Bobbs-Merrill, 1965.

Cronin, Thomas E. 1989. *Direct Democracy: The Politics of Initiative, Referendum, and Recall*. Cambridge, MA: Harvard University Press.

Cronin, Thomas E., and Jeffrey J. Weill. 1985. "An Item Veto for the President?" *Congress & the Presidency* 12 (Autumn): 127–151.

Crook, Sara Brandes, and John R. Hibbing. 1997. "A Not-So-Distant Mirror: The 17th Amendment and Congressional Change." *American Political Science Review* 91 (December): 845–853.

Cullinan, Gerald. 1968. *The Post Office Department*. New York: Praeger.

Cummings, Richard. 1980. *Proposition Fourteen: A Secessionist Remedy*. Sagaponack, NY: The Permanent Press.

Cunningham, Noble E. 1987. *The Pursuit of Reason: The Life of Thomas Jefferson*. Baton Rouge, LA: Louisiana State University Press.

Curriden, Mark, and Leroy Phillips Jr. 1999. *Contempt of Court: The Turn-of-the-Century Lynching That Launched 100 Years of Federalism*. New York: Faber and Faber, Inc.

Currie, David P. 1985. *The Constitution in the Supreme Court: The First One Hundred Years, 1789–1888*. Chicago: University of Chicago Press.

Curry, James A., Richard B. Riley, and Richard M. Battistoni. 1989. *Constitutional Government: The American Experience*. St. Paul, MN: West.

Curtis, Michael K. 1986. *No State Shall Abridge: The Fourteenth Amendment and the Bill of Rights*. Durham, NC: Duke University Press.

Curtis, Michael K., ed. 1993. *The Constitution and the Flag*. Vol. 2 of *The Flag Burning Cases*. New York: Garland.

Cushman, Barry. 2002. "Mr. Dooley and Mr. Gallop: Public Opinion and Constitutional Change in the 1930s." *Buffalo Law Review* 50 (Winter): 7–101.

Dahl, Robert. 2001. *How Democratic Is the American Constitution?* New Haven, CT: Yale University Press.

Dalzell, Stewart, and Eric J. Beste. 1994. "Is the Twenty-seventh Amendment 200 Years Too Late?" *George Washington Law Review* 62 (April): 501–545.

D'Amato, A. D. 1995. "Conflict of Laws Rules and the Interstate Recognition of Same-Sex Marriages." *University of Illinois Law Review* 1995: 911–943.

Danforth, John C. 1994. *Resurrection: The Confirmation of Clarence Thomas*. New York: Viking.

Daniels, Roger. 1968. *The Politics of Prejudice*. New York: Antheneum.

Davidson, Elizabeth H. 1939. *Child Labor Legislation in the Southern Textile States*. Chapel Hill, NC: University of North Carolina Press.

Davidson, James D. 1992. "Yes, to Save Congress from Itself." *The World & I* 7 (August): 110, 112–115.

Davidson, Jim, with Eric Klien, Norm Doering, and Lee Crocker. 1994. *The Atlantis Papers*. Houston, TX: Interglobal Paratronics, Inc.

Davidson, Michael. 2002. "Notes on Proposed Constitutional Amendments on Temporary Appointments of Members of the House." 20 January. *www.aeipoliticalcorner.org/continuity.htm*. Accessed 16 May 2002.

Davidson, Roger H., and Walter J. Oleszek. 1994. *Congress and Its Members*. 4th ed. Washington, DC: Congressional Quarterly.

Davis, Richard. 1985. *Proposed Amendments to the Constitution of the United States of America Introduced in Congress from the 91st Congress, 1st Session, through the 98th Congress, 2d Session, January 1969–December 1984*. Washington, DC: Congressional Research Service Report no. 85–36 GOV.

Davis, William C. 1994. *"A Government of Our Own": The Making of the Confederacy*. New York: Free Press.

DeConde, Alexander. 1971. *A History of American Foreign Policy*. 2d ed. New York: Charles Scribner's Sons.

Dellinger, Walter. 1983. "The Legitimacy of Constitutional Change: Rethinking the Amending Process." *Harvard Law Review* 97 (December): 380–432.

———. 1979. "The Recurring Question of the 'Limited' Constitutional Convention." *Yale Law Journal* 88: 1623–1640.

Denning, Brannon P. 2001. "Reforming the New Confirmation Process: Replacing 'Despise and Resent' with 'Advice and Consent'" *Administrative Law Review* 53 (Winter): 1–44.

———. 1998. "Gun Shy: The Second Amendment as an 'Underenforced Constitutional Norm.'" *Harvard Journal of Law & Public Policy* 21 (Summer): 719–791.

Denning, Brannon P., and Brooks R. Smith. 1999. "Uneasy Riders: The Case for a Truth-in-Legislation Amendment." *Utah Law Review* (1999): 957–1025.

Denning, Brannon P., and John R. Vile. 2002. "The Relevance of Constitutional Amendments: A Response to David Strauss." *Tulane Law Review* 77 (November): 247–282.

———. 2000. "Necromancing the Equal Rights Amendment." *Constitutional Commentary* 17 (Winter): 593–602.

Dennison, George M. 1976. *The Dorr War: Republicanism on Trial, 1831–1861.* Lexington, KY: University Press of Kentucky.

DeRosa, Marshall L. 1996. *The Ninth Amendment and the Politics of Creative Jurisprudence: Disparaging the Fundamental Right of Popular Control.* New Brunswick, NJ: Transaction Publishers.

———. 1991. *The Confederate Constitution of 1861: An Inquiry into American Constitutionalism.* Columbia, MO: University of Missouri Press.

Dershowitz, Alan M. 2001. *Supreme Injustice: How the High Court Hijacked Election 2000.* New York: Oxford University Press.

Diamond, Martin. 1976. "The Revolution of Sober Expectations." In *America's Continuing Revolution.* Garden City, NY: Anchor Press.

Diller, Daniel C. 1989. "Chief of State." In *Guide to the Presidency*, ed. Michael Nelson. Washington, DC: Congressional Quarterly.

Dillon, Conley. 1977. "American Constitutional Review: Are We Preparing for the 21st Century?" *World Affairs* 140 (Summer): 5–24.

———. 1974. "Recommendation for the Establishment of a Permanent Commission of Constitutional Review." *Bureaucrat* 3 (July): 211–224.

Dillon, Merton L. 1974. *The Abolitionists: The Growth of a Dissenting Minority.* De Kalb, IL: Northern Illinois University Press.

Dionne, E. J., and William Kristol, eds. 2001. *Bush v. Gore: The Court Cases and the Commentary.* Washington, DC: The Brookings Institution.

Dirksen, Everett M. 1968. "The Supreme Court and the People." *Michigan Law Review* 66 (March): 837–874.

Dodd, Walter F. 1921. "Amending the Federal Constitution." *Yale Law Journal* 30 (February): 321–354.

———. 1910. *The Revision and Amendment of State Constitutions.* Baltimore, MD: Johns Hopkins University Press.

Dolbeare, Kenneth M., and Janette K. Hubbell. 1996. *USA 2012: After the Middle-Class Revolution.* Chatham, NJ: Chatham House Publishers.

Donald, David H. 1995. *Lincoln.* New York: Simon & Schuster.

Dorsen, Norman. 2000. "Flag Desecration in Courts, Congress, and Country." *Thomas M. Cooley Law Review* 17 (Michaelmas Term): 417–442.

Douglass, Frederick. 1845. *Narrative of the Life of Frederick Douglass: An American Slave.* Boston: Anti-Slavery Office. Reprint, New York: Signet Books, 1968.

Dow, David R. 1990. "When Words Mean What We Believe They Say: The Case of Article V." *Iowa Law Review* 76 (October): 1–66.

Dreisbach, Daniel L. 1996. "In Search of a Christian Commonwealth: An Examination of Selected Nineteenth-Century Commentaries on References to God and the Christian Religion in the United States Constitution." *Baylor Law Review* 48: 928–1000.

Dry, Murray. 1991. "Flag Burning and the Constitution." In *The Supreme Court Review, 1990*, ed. Gerhard Casper et al. Chicago: University of Chicago Press.

Dubois, Ellen Carol. 1991. "Frances Willard. *The Reader's Companion to American History.* P. 1151. Accessed through *http://www.galenet.com.*

———. 1978. *Feminism and Suffrage: The Emergence of an Independent Women's Movement in America, 1848–1869.* Ithaca, NY: Cornell University Press.

Du Bois, W. E. Burghardt. 1928–1936. "Frederick Douglass." *Dictionary of American Biography.* American Council of Learned Societies. Accessed through *http://www.galenet.com.*

Duker, William F. 1977. "The President's Power to Pardon: A Constitutional History." *William and Mary Law Review* 18 (Spring): 475–538.

Dumond, Dwight L. 1973. *The Secession Movement, 1860–1861.* New York: Octagon Books.

Dunne, Gerald T. 1977. *Hugo Black and the Judicial Revolution.* New York: Simon & Schuster.

Durst, Jack. 2000. "Constitution of the Republic." *http://synx_jd.tripod.com.* Accessed 18 May 2002.

Earle, W. H. 1987. "The Phantom Amendment and the Duchess of Baltimore." *American History Illustrated* 22 (November): 32–39.

Eastland, Terry. 1996. *Ending Affirmative Action: The Case for Colorblind Justice.* New York: Basic Books.

Eastland, Terry, and William J. Bennett. 1979. *Counting by Race.* New York: Basic Books.

Edel, Wilbur. 1981. *A Constitutional Convention: Threat or Challenge?* New York: Praeger.

Edgar, William. 2001. "The Passing of R. J. Rushdonny." *First Things: A Monthly Journal of Religion and Public Life* (August): 24.

Ehrlich, Walter. 1965. *They Have No Rights: Dred Scott's Struggle for Freedom.* Westport, CT: Greenwood Press.

Eidelberg, Paul. 1968. *The Philosophy of the American Constitution: A Reinterpretation of the Intentions of the Founding Fathers.* New York: Free Press.

Eiselen, Malcolm R. 1941. "Can We Amend the Constitution?" *South Atlantic Quarterly* 40 (October): 333–341.

———. 1937. "Dare We Call a Federal Convention?" *North American Review* 244 (Autumn): 27–28.

Eisenach, Eldon J. 1994. *The Lost Promise of Progressivism.* Lawrence, KS: University Press of Kansas.

Ekirch, Arthur A., Jr. 1974. *Progressivism in America: A Study of the Era from Theodore Roosevelt to Woodrow Wilson.* New York: New Viewpoints.

Elliott, Ward. 1974. *The Rise of Guardian Democracy.* Cambridge, MA: Harvard University Press.

Elliott, William Y. 1935. *The Need for Constitutional Reform: A Program for National Security.* New York: Whittlesey House.

Ellis, Frederick, with Carl Frederick. 2000. *The Oakland Statement: A Political Adventure Novel.* Miami, FL: Synergy International of the Americas.

Ellis, L. Ethan. 1961. *Frank B. Kellogg and American Foreign Relations, 1925–1929.* New Brunswick, NJ: Rutgers University Press.

Ely, James W. 1992. *The Guardian of Every Other Right: A Constitutional History of Property Rights.* New York: Oxford University Press.

Ely, John Hart. 1993. *War and Responsibility: Constitutional Lessons of Vietnam and Its Aftermath.* Princeton, NJ: Princeton University Press.

———. 1980. *Democracy and Distrust.* Cambridge, MA: Harvard University Press.

Engdahl, David E. 1994. "The Spending Power." *Duke Law Journal* 44 (October): 1–109.

The English Language Amendment. 1985. Hearings before the Subcommittee on the Constitution of the Committee on the Judiciary, U.S. Senate. Washington, DC: U.S. Government Printing Office.

English Language Constitutional Amendments. 1989. Hearings before the Subcommittee on the Judiciary, House of Representatives. Washington, DC: U.S. Government Printing Office.

Epstein, Barbara L. 1981. *The Politics of Domesticity: Women, Evangelism, and Temperance in Nineteenth-Century America.* Middletown, CT: Wesleyan University Press.

Epstein, Lee, and Joseph F. Kobylka. 1992. *The Supreme Court and Legal Change: Abortion and the Death Penalty.* Chapel Hill, NC: University of North Carolina Press.

Erdman, Sol, and Lawrence Susskind. 1995. *Reinventing Congress for the 21st Century: Toward a Politics of Accountability, Participation and Consensus.* New York: Frontier Press.

Ernst, Morris L. 1973. *The Great Reversals: Tales of the Supreme Court.* New York: Weybright and Talley.

Ervin, Sam J., Jr. 1984. *Preserving the Constitution: The Autobiography of Sam J. Ervin Jr.* Charlottesville, VA: Michie.

———. 1968. "Proposed Legislation to Implement the Convention Method of Amending the Constitution." *Michigan Law Review* 66 (March): 875–902.

Eskridge, William N., Jr. 1991. "Overriding Supreme Court Statutory Interpretations Decisions." *Yale Law Journal* 101 (November): 331–455.

Eskridge, William N., Jr., and Sanford Levinson. 1998. *Constitutional Stupidities, Constitutional Tragedies.* New York: New York University Press.

Estaville, Lawrence E. 1990. "The Louisiana French Language in the Nineteenth Century." *Southeastern Geographer* 30 (November): 107–120.

Euchner, Charles C., and John A. Maltese. 1989. "The Electoral Process." In *Guide to the Presidency,* ed. Michael Nelson. Washington, DC: Congressional Quarterly.

Fairman, Charles. 1949. "Does the Fourteenth Amendment Incorporate the Bill of Rights? The Original Understanding." *Stanford Law Review* 2 (December): 5–139.

Fallon, Richard H., Jr. 2001. *Implementing the Constitution.* Cambridge, MA: Harvard University Press.

Farnsworth, Ward. 2000. "Women under Reconstruction: The Congressional Understanding." *Northwestern University Law Review* 94 (Summer): 1229–1295.

Farrand, Max, ed. 1966. *The Records of the Federal Convention.* 4 vols. New Haven, CT: Yale University Press.

Farris, Michael P. 1999. "Only a Constitutional Amendment Can Guarantee Religious Freedom for All." *Cardozo Law Review* 21 (December): 689–706.

Feerick, John D. 1992. *The Twenty-fifth Amendment: Its Complete History and Applications.* New York: Fordham University Press.

Fehrenbacher, Don E. 1978. *The Dred Scott Case: Its Significance for American Law and Politics.* New York: Oxford University Press.

Fernandez, Ferdinand F. 1966. "The Constitution-ality of the Fourteenth Amendment." *Southern California Law Review* 39: 378–407.

Ferrell, Claudine L. 1986. *Nightmare and Dream: Anti-Lynching in Congress 1917–1922.* New York: Garland.

Ferreres-Comella, Victor. 2000. "A Defense of Con-stitutional Rigidity." In *Analysis and Right,* ed. Paul Comanducci and Riccardo Guastini. Turin, Italy: G. Giappichelli Publisher.

Fineman, Howard. 2002. "One Nation, Under . . . Who?" *Newsweek* 140 (July 8): 20–25.

Finer, Herman. 1960. *The Presidency, Crisis and Re-generation: An Essay in Possibilities.* Chicago: Uni-versity of Chicago Press.

Fink, Richard H., and Jack C. High, eds. 1987. *A Nation in Debt: Economists Debate the Federal Budget Deficit.* Frederick, MD: University Publi-cations of America.

Finkelman, Paul. 2000. "'A Well Regulated Militia': The Second Amendment in Historical Perspec-tive. *Chicago-Kent Law Review* 76: 195–236.

———. 1992. "Slavery." In *The Oxford Companion to the Supreme Court of the United States,* ed. Ker-mit L. Hall. New York: Oxford Universisty Press.

———. 1991. "James Madison and the Bill of Rights: A Reluctant Paternity." In *The Supreme Court Re-view, 1990.* Chicago: University of Chicago Press.

———. 1981. *An Imperfect Union: Slavery, Federal-ism and Comity.* Chapel Hill, NC: University of North Carolina Press.

Finletter, Thomas K. 1945. *Can Representative Government Do the Job?* New York: Reynal and Hitchcock.

Fiscus, Ron. 1992. *The Constitutional Logic of Affir-mative Action.* Durham, NC: Duke University Press.

Fisher, Louis. 1993. "The Legislative Veto: Invali-dated, It Survives." *Law and Contemporary Prob-lems* 56 (Autumn): 273–292.

———. 1991. *Constitutional Conflicts between Con-gress and the President.* 3d ed. Lawrence, KS: Uni-versity Press of Kansas.

Fisher, Sidney G. 1862. *A Philadelphia Perspective: The Diary of Sidney George Fisher Covering the Years 1834–1871.* Reprint, Philadelphia: Historical Society of Pennsylvania, 1967.

———. 1862. *The Trial of the Constitution.* Reprint, New York: Da Capo Press, 1972.

Fitzpatrick, John C. 1931–1944. *The Writings of George Washington.* 39 vols. Washington, DC: U.S. Government Printing Office.

Flack, Horace E. 1908. *The Adoption of the Four-teenth Amendment.* Baltimore, MD: Johns Hop-kins. Reprint, Gloucester, MA: Peter Smith, 1965.

Flexnor, Eleanor. 1974. *Century of Struggle: The Woman's Rights Movement in the United States.* New York: Atheneum.

Fogleson, Robert M., and Richard E. Rubenstein. 1969. *Mass Violence in America: Invasion at Harper's Ferry.* New York: Arno Press.

Foley, Michael. 1989. *The Silence of Constitutions: Gaps, "Abeyances" and Political Temperament in the Maintenance of Government.* London: Rout-ledge.

Folton, Richard T. 1996. "Horror Stories." *Liberty* (March/April): 6–8.

Foner, Eric. 1970. *Free Soil, Free Labor, Free Men: The Ideology of the Republican Party before the Civil War.* New York: Oxford University Press.

Foner, Eric, and John A. Garraty, eds. 1991. *The Reader's Companion to American History.* Boston: Houghton Mifflin.

Ford, Paul L., ed. 1898. *The Federalist.* New York: Henry Holt. [Originally published as series of newspaper articles from 1787–1788.]

"Forum: Historians and Guns." 2002. *William and Mary Quarterly* 59, 3d Series (January): 203–268.

Fowler, Robert B. 1986. *Carrie Catt: Feminist Politician.* Boston: Northeastern University Press.

Fraley, Colette. 1995. "House Opponents Savor Gains; Senate Outlook Is Unclear." *Congressional Quarterly Weekly Report* 53 (29 July): 2276–2277.

"Francis Elizabeth Caroline Willard." 1928–1936. *Dictionary of American Biography* Base Set. Amer-ican Council of Learned Societies. Accessed through *http://www.galenet.com.*

Frank, Jerome. 1969. *Courts on Trial: Myth and Re-ality in American Justice.* New York: Atheneum.

Frankfurter, Felix. 1974. *The Commerce Clause un-der Marshall, Taney and Waite.* Chicago: Quad-rangle Books.

Freedman, Russell. 1994. *Lewis Hine and the Cru-sade against Child Labor.* New York: Clarion Books.

Freedman, Samuel S., and Pamela J. Naughton. 1978. *ERA: May a State Change Its Vote?* Detroit, MI: Wayne State University Press.

Freedoms Foundation. 1985. "Bill of Responsibili-ties." Valley Forge: Freedom Foundation.

Frenzel, Bill. 1992. "Term Limits and the Immortal Congress." *Brookings Review* 10 (Spring): 18–22.

Freyer, Tony. 1990. *Hugo L. Black and the Dilemma of American Liberalism.* Glenville, IL: Scott Foresman.

Friedman, Barry, and Scott B. Smith. 1998. "The Sedimentary Constitution." *University of Pennsyl-vania Law Review* 147 (November):1–90.

Friendly, Henry J. 1968. "The Fifth Amendment

Tomorrow: The Case for Constitutional Change." *University of Cincinnati Law Review* 37 (Fall): 671–726.

Frierson, William. 1920. "Amending the Constitution of the United States: A Reply to Mr. Marbury." *Harvard Law Review* 33 (March): 659–666.

Fry, Amelia R. 1986. "Alice Paul and the ERA." In *Rights of Passage: The Past and Future of the ERA,* ed. Joan Hoff-Wilson. Bloomington, IN: Indiana University Press.

Fuess, Calude Moore. 1928–1936. "William Lloyd Garrison." *Dictionary of American Biography,* Base Set. American Council of Learned Societies. Accessed through *http://www.galenet.com.*

Funston, Richard Y. 1977. *Constitution Counterrevolution? The Warren Court and the Burger Court: Judicial Policy Making in Modern America.* New York: Schenkman.

Gabriel, Mary. 1998. *Notorious Victoria: The Life of Victoria Woodhull,* uncensored. Chapel Hill, NC: Algonquin Books.

Gallagher, Maggie. 2002. "Live Your Life, but Marriage Is for Men and Women." *The Tennessean,* 30 May, 9A.

Gammie, Beth. 1989. "State ERA's: Problems and Possibilities." *University of Illinois Law Review* 1989: 1123–1159.

Garcia, Alfredo. 1992. *The Sixth Amendment in Modern American Jurisprudence: A Critical Perspective.* New York: Greenwood Press.

Gardiner, William. 1973. *A Proposed Constitution for the United States of America.* Summerfield, FL: William Gardiner.

Garrett, Stephen A. 1972. "Foreign Policy and the American Constitution: The Bricker Amendment in Contemporary Perspective." *International Studies Quarterly* 16 (June): 187–220.

Garrow, David J. 2000. "Mental Decrepitude on the U.S. Supreme Court: The Historical Case for a 28th Amendment." *University of Chicago Law Review* 67: 995–1087.

———. 1994. *Liberty and Sexuality: The Right to Privacy and the Making of* Roe v. Wade. New York: Macmillan.

Gatell, Frank O. 1969. "John McLean." In *The Justices of the United States Supreme Court, 1789–1969: Their Lives and Major Opinions.* Vol. 1, ed. Leon Friedman and Fred L. Israel. New York: R. R. Bowker.

Gavzer, Bernard. 1995. "Life behind Bars." *Parade Magazine* 13 August, 4–7.

Geiger, Virginia, and Jeanne H. Stevenson. 1989. *The Living Constitution, 1787, 1987, 2187.* Lanham, MD: University Press of America.

George, Henry. 1938. *Progress and Poverty: An Inquiry into the Cause of Industrial Depressions and of Increase of Want with Increase of Wealth, the Remedy.* 50th anniversary ed. New York: Robert Schalkenback Foundation.

George, Robert P. 2001. "The 28th Amendment: It Is Time to Protect Marriage, and Democracy, in America." *National Review* 53 (July 23): 32–34.

Gerber, Scott D. 1995. *To Secure These Rights: The Declaration of Independence and Constitutional Interpretation.* New York: New York University Press.

Germond, Jack W., and Jules Witcover. 1999. "After the Trial, Revisions Are in Order." *National Journal* 31 (January 30): 296.

Gettlinger, Stephen. 1994. "New Filibuster Tactics Imperil Next Senate." *Congressional Quarterly* 52 (5 November): 3198.

Gillespie, Ed, and Bob Schellhas, eds. 1994. *Contract with America: The Bold Plan by Rep. Newt Gingrich, Rep. Dick Armey, and the House Republicans to Change the Nation.* New York: Random House.

Gillespie, Michael L., and Michael Lienesch, eds. 1989. *Ratifying the Constitution.* Lawrence, KS: University Press of Kansas.

Gillman, Howard. 2001. *The Votes That Counted: How the Court Decided the 2000 Presidential Election.* Chicago: University of Chicago Press.

———. 1997. "The Collapse of Constitutional Originalism and the Rise of the Notion of the 'Living Constitution' in the Course of American State-Building." *Studies in American Political Development* 11 (Fall): 191–247.

———. 1993. *The Constitution Besieged: The Rise and Demise of Lochner Era Police Powers Jurisprudence.* Durham, NC: Duke University Press.

Gillmor, Paul, and Fred Eames. 1994. "Reconstruction of Federalism: A Constitutional Amendment to Prohibit Unfunded Mandates." *Harvard Journal on Legislation* 31 (Summer): 395–413.

Ginsburg, Ruth B. 1989–1990. "On Amending the Constitution: A Plea for Patience." *University of Arkansas at Little Rock Law Journal* 12: 677–694.

———. 1969. "Ratification of the Equal Rights Amendment: A Question of Time." *Texas Law Review* 57: 919–945.

Glasson, William H., and David Kinley. 1918. *Federal Military Pensions in the United States.* New York: Oxford University Press.

Glendon, Mary Ann. 1992. "Rights in Twentieth-Century Constitutions." *University of Chicago Law Review* 59 (Winter): 519–538.

———. 1991. *Rights Talk: The Impoverishment of Political Discourse.* New York: Free Press.

———. 1987. *Abortion and Divorce in Western Law.* Cambridge, MA: Harvard University Press.

Glick, Henry R. 1988. *Courts, Politics, and Justice?* 2d ed. New York: McGraw-Hill.

Godkin, E. L. 1864. "The Constitution and Its Defects." *North American Review* 99 (July): 117–143.

Goldsmith, Barbara. 1998. *Other Powers: The Age of Suffrage, Spiritualism, and the Scandalous Victoria Woodhull.* New York: Alfred A. Knopf.

Goldstein, Leslie F. 1991. *In Defense of the Text: Democracy and Constitutional Theory.* Savage, MD: Rowman and Littlefield.

———. 1987. "The ERA and the U.S. Supreme Court." In *Research in Law and Policy Studies,* ed. Stuart S. Nagel. Greenwich, CT: JAI.

Goldstein, Robert J. 2000. *Flag Burning and Free Speech.* Lawrence, KS: University Press of Kansas.

———. 1996. *The American Flag Desecration Controversy: A Collection of Documents from the Civil War to 1990.* Kent, OH: Kent State University Press.

———. 1995. *Burning the Flag: The Great 1989–1990 American Flag Desecration Controversy.* Kent, OH. Kent State University Press.

———. 1994. *Saving "Old Glory": The History of the American Flag Desecration Controversy.* Boulder, CO: Westview.

———. 1990. "The Great 1989–1990 Flag Flap: A Historical, Political, and Legal Analysis." *University of Miami Law Review* 45 (September): 19–106.

Goodnow, Frank J. 1911. *Social Reform and the Constitution.* New York: The Macmillan Co. Reprint, New York: Burt Franklin, 1970.

Goodstein, Laurie. 1995. "Religious Freedom Amendment Passed." *Washington Post,* 9 June, A12.

Gordon, Charles. 1982. "The Power of Congress to Terminate United States Citizenship." *Connecticut Law Review* 4 (Spring): 611–632.

———. 1968. "Who Can Be President of the United States: The Unresolved Enigma." *Maryland Law Review* 28 (Winter): 1–32.

Gordon, Sarah Barringer. 2002. *The Mormon Question: Polygamy and Constitutional Conflict in Nineteenth-Century America.* Chapel Hill, NC: University of North Carolina Press.

Gould, Lewis L., ed. 1974. *The Progressive Era.* Syracuse, NY: Syracuse University Press.

Graber, Mark A. 1995. "Unnecessary and Unintelligible." *Constitutional Commentary* 12 (Summer): 167–170.

Graham, Tim. 2002. "Prenuptial Disagreement." *World* 17 (June 8): 14–18.

Gravel, Mike. 1995. "Philadelphia II: National Initiatives." *Campaigns and Elections* 16 (December): 25.

Green, Steven K. 1992. "The Blaine Amendment Reconsidered." *American Journal of Legal History* 36 (January): 38–69.

Greenawalt, Kent. 1998a. "Introduction: Should the Religion Clauses of the Constitution Be Amended?" *Loyola of Los Angeles Law Review* 32 (November): 9–25.

———. 1998b. "Symposium: Reflections of *City of Boerne v. Flores:* Why Now Is Not the Time for Constitutional Amendment: The Limited Reach of *City of Boerne v. Flores.*" *William and Mary Law Review* 39 (February): 689–698.

Greenhouse, Linda. 1996. "Justices Curb Federal Power to Subject States to Lawsuits." *New York Times,* 28 March, A1, A12.

Gregg, Gary L., II, ed. 2001. *Securing Democracy: Why We Have an Electoral College.* Wilmington, DE: ISI Books.

Grey, Thomas C. 1975. "Do We Have an Unwritten Constitution?" *Stanford Law Review* 27 (February): 703–718.

Griffin, Stephen M. 1996. *American Constitutionalism: From Theory to Practice.* Princeton, NJ: Princeton University Press.

Griffith, Elisabeth. 1984. *In Her Own Right: The Life of Elizabeth Cady Stanton.* New York: Oxford University Press.

Grimes, Alan P. 1978. *Democracy and the Amendments to the Constitution.* Lexington, MA: Lexington Books.

Grinnell, F. W. 1925. "Finality of State's Ratification of a Constitutional Amendment." *American Bar Association Journal* 11 (March): 192–193.

Grinnell, Frank W. 1959. "Petitioning Congress for a Convention: Cannot a State Change Its Mind?" *American Bar Association Journal* 45: 1164–1165.

Grodzins, Morton. 1966. *The American System: A New View of the Government in the United States.* Chicago: Rand McNally.

Grossman, Joel B., and David A. Yalof. 2000. "The Day After: Do We Need a 'Twenty-Eighth' Amendment?" *Constitutional Commentary* 17 (Spring): 7–17.

Grunder, Garel A., and William E. Livezey. 1973. *The Philippines and the United States.* Westport, CT: Greenwood Press.

Gulliuzza, Frank, III. 2000. *Over the Wall: Protecting Religious Expression in the Public Square.* Albany, NY: State University of New York Press.

Gunderson, Robert Gray. 1961. *Old Gentleman's Convention: The Washington Peace Conference of 1861.* Madison, WI: The University of Wisconsin Press.

Hahn, Jeanne. 1987. "Neo-Hamiltonianism: A Democratic Critique." In *The Case against the*

Constitution from Anti-Federalists to the Present, ed. John F. Manley and Kenneth M. Dolbeare. New York: M. E. Sharpe.

Halbrook, Stephen D. 1994. *That Every Man Be Armed: The Evolution of a Constitutional Right.* Oakland, CA: Independent Institute.

Hall, Kermit L. 1989. *The Magic Mirror: Law in American History.* New York: Oxford University Press.

Hall, Kermit L., ed. 1992. *The Oxford Companion to the Supreme Court of the United States.* New York: Oxford University Press.

———, ed. 1991. *By and for the People: Constitutional Rights in American History.* Arlington Heights, IL: Harlan Davidson.

Halper, Louise A. 1990. "Christopher G. Tiedeman, 'Laissez-Faire Constitutionalism' and the Dilemma of Small-Scale Property in the Gilded Age." *Ohio State Law Journal* 51: 1349–1384.

Halpern, Stephen C., and Charles M. Lamb, eds. 1982. *Supreme Court Activism and Restraint.* Lexington, MA: Lexington Books.

Hamburger, Philip A. 2002. *Separation of Church and State.* Cambridge, MA: Harvard University Press.

———. 1993. "Natural Rights, Natural Law, and American Constitutionalism." *Yale Law Journal* 102 (January): 907–960.

Hamilton, Alexander, James Madison, and John Jay. 1787–1788. *The Federalist Papers.* Reprint, New York: New American Library, 1961.

Hamilton, Hugh L. 1938. *A Second Constitution for the United States of America.* Richmond, VA: Garrett and Massie.

Hamilton, Robert W. 1987. *The Law of Corporations.* St. Paul, MN: West.

Hamm, Richard F. 1995. *Shaping the 18th Amendment: Temperance Reform, Legal Culture and the Polity, 1880–1920.* Chapel Hill, NC: University of North Carolina Press.

Handy, Robert T. 1971. *A Christian America: Protestant Hopes and Historical Realities.* New York: Oxford University Press.

Hanlon, Michael C. 2000. "Note: The Need for a General Time Limit on Ratification of Proposed Constitutional Amendments." *Journal of Law & Politics* 16 (Summer): 663–698.

Hardaway, Robert M. 1994. *The Electoral College and the Constitution: The Case for Preserving Federalism.* Westport, CT: Praeger.

Hardin, Charles M. 1989. *Constitutional Reform in America: Essays on the Separation of Powers.* Ames, IA: Iowa State University Press.

———. 1974. *Presidential Power and Accountability: Toward a New Constitution.* Chicago: University of Chicago Press.

Hare, Lloyd C. 1970. *The Greatest American Woman: Lucretia Mott.* New York: Negro Universities Press.

Harrigan, John J. 1994. *Politics and Policy in States and Communities.* 5th ed. New York: HarperCollins College Publishers.

Harriger, Katy J. 1992. *Independent Justice: The Federal Special Prosecutor in American Politics.* Lawrence, KS: University Press of Kansas.

Harris, Daryl B. 1992. *Proposed Amendments to the U.S. Constitution: 99th–101st Congresses (1985–1990).* Washington, DC: Congressional Research Service, Library of Congress.

Harris, William F., II. 1993. *The Interpretable Constitution.* Baltimore, MD: Johns Hopkins University Press.

Hart, Vivien. 1994. *Bound by Our Constitution: Women, Workers, and the Minimum Wage.* Princeton, NJ: Princeton University Press.

Hartnett, Edward. 1998. "A 'Uniform and Entire' Constitution: Or, What if Madison Had Won?" *Constitutional Commentary* 15 (Summer): 251–297.

Hatch, Orrin. 1991. "Constitutional Convention Implementation Act." *Congressional Record,* U.S. Senate, 15 January, S559–S565.

———. 1979. "Should the Capital Vote in Congress? A Critical Analysis of the Proposed D.C. Representation Amendment." *Fordham Urban Law Journal* 7: 479–539.

Haynes, George H. 1960. *The Senate of the United States, Its History and Practice.* New York: Russell and Russell.

Hazlitt, Henry. 1987. "A Proposal for Two Constitutional Amendments." In *A Nation in Debt: Economists Debate the Federal Budget Deficit,* ed. Richard H. Fink and Jack H. High. Frederick, MD: University Publications of America.

———. 1974. *A New Constitution Now.* New Rochelle, NY: Arlington House.

———. 1942. *A New Constitution Now.* New York: Whittlesey House.

———. 1931. "Our Obsolete Constitution." *Nation* 132 (4 February): 124–125.

Hehmeyer, Alexander. 1943. *Time for Change: A Proposal for a Second Constitutional Convention.* New York: Farrar and Rinehart.

Held, Allison L., Sheryl L. Herndon, and Danielle M. Stager. 1997. "The Equal Rights Amendment: Why the ERA Remains Legally Viable and Properly before the States." *William and Mary Journal of Women and Law* 3: 113.

Heller, Francis H. 1982. "Limiting a Constitutional Convention: The State Precedents." *Cardozo Law Review* 3: 563–579.

Heller, Scott. 1995. "The Right to Bear Arms." *Chronicle of Higher Education* 41 (21 July): A8, A12.

Henderson, Yandell. 1913. "The Progressive Movement and Constitutional Reform." *Yale Review* n.s. 3: 78–90.

Henkin, Louis. 1972. *Foreign Affairs and the Constitution*. Mineola, NY: Foundation Press.

Henneberg, Molly. 2002. "Marriage Amendment Preserves Male-Female Union." 16 May. *http://www.foxnews.com*. Accessed 16 May 2002.

Hitchcock, Ripley. 1903. *The Louisiana Purchase, and the Exploration, Early History and Building of the West*. Boston: Ginn & Company.

Ho, James C. 2000. "Unnatural-Born Citizens and Acting Presidents." *Constitutional Commentary* 17: 575–585.

Hoban, Thomas M., and Richard O. Brooks. 1987. *Green Justice: The Environment and the Courts*. Boulder, CO: Westview Press.

Hoebeke, C. H. 1995. *The Road to Mass Democracy: Original Intent and the Seventeenth Amendment*. New Brunswick, NJ: Transaction

Hoffman, Joseph L., and William J. Stuntz. 1994. "Habeas after the Revolution." In *Supreme Court Review*. Chicago: University of Chicago Press.

Hoffman, Ronald, and Peter J. Albert, eds. 1997. *The Bill of Rights: Government Proscribed*. Charlottesville, VA: University Press of Virginia.

Hoff-Wilson, Joan, ed. 1986. *Rights of Passage: The Past and Future of ERA*. Bloomington, IN: Indiana University Press.

Holden, Matthew, Jr. 1973a. *The Politics of the Black Nation*. New York: Chandler.

———. 1973b. *The White Man's Burden*. New York: Chandler.

Holmes, Stephen. 1995. *Passions and Constraint: On the Theory of Liberal Democracy*. Chicago: University of Chicago Press.

Hook, Janet, and Donna Cassata. 1995. "Low-Key Revolt May Spur Thurmond to Give Colleagues Freer Hand." *Congressional Quarterly Weekly Report* 53 (11 February): 466.

Hopkins, Caspar T. 1885. "Thoughts toward Revising the Federal Constitution." *Overland Monthly* n.s. 6 (October): 388–398.

Horn, Dottie. 1990. "Another Star for the Stripes?" *Endeavors* 8 (Fall): 4–6.

Horwill, Herbert W. 1925. *The Usages of the American Constitution*. Reprint, Port Washington, NY: Kennikat Press, 1969.

Hosanky, David. 1995. "Mandate Bill Is More Moderate Than Proposed in 'Contract.'" *Congressional Quarterly Weekly Report* 53 (7 January): 40.

"House Resolution 14." *Congressional Record* 89th Cong., 1st sess., 1965, Vol. 111, pt. 12: 15770.

Hsieh, Christine J. 1998. "Note: American Born Legal Permanent Residents? A Constitutional Amendment Proposal." *Georgetown Immigration Law Journal* 12 (Spring): 511–529.

Hudson, David L, Jr. 2002. "Top Court Docket: Copyright to Cross Burning." *Chicago Daily Law Bulletin*, 16 September, 1.

Hunter, James D. 1994. *Before the Shooting Begins: Searching for Democracy in America's Culture War*. New York: Free Press.

Hurst, James W. 1971. *The Law of Treason in the United States: Collected Essays*. Westport, CT: Greenwood Press.

Imari, Brother (Richard B. Henry). 1968. *War in America: The Malcolm X Doctrine*. Detroit, MI: Malcolm X Doctrine.

Information Please Almanac: Atlas and Yearbook. 1993. 43d ed. Boston: Houghton Mifflin.

Irons, Peter. 1989. *Justice Delayed: The Record of the Japanese Internment Cases*. Middletown, CT: Wesleyan University Press.

———. 1983. *Justice at War*. New York: Oxford University Press.

Irons, Peter, and Stephanie Guitton, eds. 1993. *May It Please the Court*. New York: New Press.

Isaacson, Eric A. 2000. "The Stealth Amendment: The Impending Ratification and Repeal of a Federal Budget Amendment." *Tulsa Law Journal* 35 (Winter): 353–382.

———. 1990. "The Flag-Burning Issue: A Legal Analysis and Comment." *Loyola of Los Angeles Law Review* 23 (January): 535–600.

Ishikawa, Brendon T. 2000. "The Stealth Amendment: The Impending Ratification and Repeal of a Federal Budget Amendment." *Tulsa Law Journal* 33 (Winter): 353–381.

———. 1997. "Everything You Always Wanted to Know about How Amendments Are Made, but Were Afraid to Ask." *Hastings Constitutional Law Quarterly* 24 (Winter): 545–597.

———. 1996a. "Amending the Constitution: Just Not Every November." *Cleveland State Law Review* 44: 303–343.

———. 1996b. "Toward a More Perfect Union: The Role of Amending Formulae in the United States, Canadian, and German Constitutional Experiences." *Journal of International Law & Policy* 2 (Spring): 267–294.

Jackson, Donald W. 1992. *Even the Children of Strangers: Equality under the U.S. Constitution*. Lawrence, KS: University Press of Kansas.

Jackson, Jesse L., Jr., with Frank E. Watkins. 2001.

A More Perfect Union: Advancing New American Rights. New York: Welcome Rain Publishers.

Jackson, Robert H. 1941. *The Struggle for Judicial Supremacy*. New York: Vintage Books.

Jacob, Clyde E. 1972. *The Eleventh Amendment and Sovereign Immunity*. Westport, CT: Greenwood Press.

Jacob, Herbert. 1995. *Law and Politics in the United States*. 2d ed. New York: HarperCollins College Publishers.

Jacoby, Steward O. 1984. *The Religious Amendment Movement: God, People and Nation in the Gilded Age*. 2 vols. Ph.D. dissertation, University of Michigan.

Jaffa, Harry V. 1994. *Original Intent and the Framers of the Constitution: A Disputed Question*. Washington, DC: Regnery Gateway.

James, Joseph B. 1984. *The Ratification of the Fourteenth Amendment*. Macon, GA: Mercer University Press.

———. 1956. *The Framing of the Fourteenth Amendment*. Urbana, IL: University of Illinois Press.

Jameson, John A. 1887. *A Treatise on Constitutional Conventions: Their History, Powers, and Modes of Proceeding*. 4th ed. Chicago: Callaghan and Company.

Jaschik, Scott, and Douglas Lederman. 1996. "Appeals Court Bars Racial Preference in College Admissions." *Chronicle of Higher Education* 43 (29 March): A26–A27.

Jefferson, Thomas. 1964. *Notes on the State of Virginia*. New York: Harper and Row. [Originally published as part of Vol. VIII of *The Writings of Thomas Jefferson*, ed. by H. A. Washington. New York: H. W. Darby, 1861.]

———. 1905. *The Works of Thomas Jefferson*, ed. Paul Leicester Ford. 12 vols. New York: G. P. Putnam's Sons, Knickerbocker Press.

———. 1902. *The Jefferson Bible: The Life and Morals of Jesus of Nazareth*. St. Louis, MO: N. D. Thompson. Reprint, Introduction by F. Forrester Church. Boston: Beacon Press, 1989.

———. 1791. "Opinion of the Constitutionality of a National Bank." In *Documents of American Constitutional and Legal History*, ed. Melvin I. Urofsky. New York: Alfred A. Knopf, 1989.

Jeffries, Judson L. 1998. "Black Panther Party." In *The Encyclopedia of Civil Rights in America*. Edited by David Bradley and Shelley Fisher Fishkin. Armond, NY: M. E. Sharpe, Inc.

Jeffs, Daniel B. 2000. *America's Crisis: The Direct Democracy and Direct Education Solution*. Amherst Junction, WI: Hard Shell Word Factory.

Jennings, Thelma. 1998. "Nashville Convention." In *The Tennessee Encyclopedia of History and Culture*, ed. Carroll Van West. Nashville, TN: Rutledge Hill Press.

———. 1980. *The Nashville Convention: Southern Movement for Unity, 1848–1851*. Memphis, TN: Memphis State University Press.

Jensen, Merrill. 1966. *The Articles of Confederation*. Madison: University of Wisconsin Press.

Johannsen, Robert W., ed. 1965. *The Lincoln-Douglas Debates of 1858*. New York: Oxford University Press.

Johnsen, Julia E., ed. 1948. *Federal World Government*. Vol. 19, no. 5 of the Reference Shelf. New York: H. W. Wilson.

———. 1947. *United Nations or World Government*. Vol. 20, no. 5 of the Reference Shelf. New York: H. W. Wilson.

Johnstone, Frederic B. 1912. "An Eighteenth-Century Constitution." *Illinois Law Review* 7 (December): 265–290.

Kalfus, Mason. 1999. "Why Time Limits on the Ratification of Constitutional Amendments Violate Article V." *University of Chicago Law Review* 66 (Spring): 437–467.

Kammen, Michael. 1987. *A Machine That Would Go of Itself: The Constitution in American Culture*. New York: Alfred A. Knopf.

Kanowitz, Leo, and Marilyn Klinger. 1978. "Can a State Rescind Its Equal Rights Amendment Ratification: Who Decides and How?" *Hastings Law Journal* 28 (March): 969–1009.

Kaplan, Morton A. 1991. "Freedom of Speech: Its Constitutional Scope and Function." *This World & I* 7 (July): 531–541.

Kares, Lauren. 1995. "Note: The Unlucky Thirteenth: A Constitutional Amendment in Search of a Doctrine." *Cornell Law Review* 80 (January): 372–412.

Katz, Elai. 1996. "On Amending Constitutions: The Legality and Legitimacy of Constitutional Entrenchment." *Columbia Journal of Law and Social Problems* 29 (Winter): 251–292.

Kaufman, Burton I. 1969. *Washington's Farewell Address: The View from the 20th Century*. Chicago: Quadrangle Books.

Kauper, Paul G. 1968. "The Alternate Amending Process: Some Observations." *Michigan Law Review* 66 (March): 903–920.

Kay, Julie. 2002. "War of, for Words: South Florida Lawyers on ABA Task Force Lead Fight for Right of Enemy Combatants to Counsel." *Broward Daily Business Review* 43 (21 October): A10.

Kay, Richard S. 1987. "The Illegality of the Constitution." *Constitutional Commentary* 4 (Winter): 57–80.

Keller, Morton. 1987. "Failed Amendments to the

Constitution." *The World & I* 9 (September): 87–97.

Kelly, Frank K. 1981. *Court of Reason: Robert Hutchins and the Fund for the Republic.* New York: Free Press.

Kennedy, Devin C. 1991. "We Need a Fresh Start; Repeal the Seventh Amendment." *Detroit College of Law Review* (Winter): 1289–1301.

Kens, Paul. 1990. *Judicial Power and Reform Politics: The Anatomy of* Lochner v. New York. Lawrence, KS: University Press of Kansas.

Kenyon, Cecelia, ed. 1985. *The Antifederalists.* Boston: Northeastern University Press.

Keogh, Stephen. 1987. "Formal and Informal Constitutional Lawmaking in the United States in the Winter of 1860–1861." *Journal of Legal History* 8 (December): 275–299.

Kerber, Linda K. 1998. *No Constitutional Right to Be Ladies: Women and the Obligations of Citizenship.* New York: Hill and Wang.

Kerr, K. Austin. 1985. *Organized for Prohibition: A New History of the Anti-Saloon League.* New Haven, CT: Yale University Press.

Kershen, Drew L. 1992. "Agriculture." In *The Oxford Companion to the Supreme Court of the United States,* ed. Kermit L. Hall. New York: Oxford University Press.

Kesler, Charles R. 1990. "Bad Housekeeping: The Case against Congressional Term Limits." *Policy Review* 53 (Summer): 20–25.

Keynes, Edward, with Randall K. Miller. 1989. *The Court vs. Congress: Prayer, Busing, and Abortion.* Durham, NC: Duke University Press.

Keyssar, Alexander. 2000. *The Right to Vote: The Constitutional History of Democracy in the United States.* New York: Basic Books.

Killenback, Mark R., ed. 2002. *The Tenth Amendment and State Sovereignty: Constitutional History and Contemporary Issues.* Lanham, MD: Rowman & Littlefield.

Kincaid, John. 2000. "Constitutional Proposals from the States." *Insights on Law & Society* 1 (Fall): 15.

———. 1989. "A Proposal to Strengthen Federalism." *The Journal of State Government* 62 (January/February): 36–45.

Kirstein, Herbert C. 1994. *U.S. Constitution for 21st Century and Beyond.* Alexandria, VA: Realistic IDEALIST Enterprise.

———. 1992. *Ideology of Freedom and Democracy.* Alexandria, VA: Realistic IDEALIST Enterprise.

Kirwan, Albert D. 1962. *John J. Crittenden: The Struggle for the Union.* n.p.: University of Kentucky Press.

Klinkhammer, Marie C. 1965. "The Blaine Amend-

ment of 1875." *Catholic Historical Review* 21: 15–49.

Kluger, Richard. 1975. *Simple Justice: The History of* Brown v. Board of Education *and Black America's Struggle for Equality.* 2 vols. New York: Alfred A. Knopf.

Knappman, Edward W., ed. 1994. *Great American Trials.* Detroit, MI: Visible Ink Press.

Knipprath, Joerg W. 1987. "To See the Trees, but Not the Forest in Constitution Making: A Commentary on Professor Miller's Proposed Constitution." *Southwestern University Law Review* 17: 239–256.

Kobach, Kris W. 1999. "May 'We the People' Speak? The Forgotten Role of Constituent Instructions in Amending the Constitution." *University of California Davis Law Review* 33 (Fall): 1–94.

Kraditor, Aileen S. 1981. *The Idea of the Woman's Suffrage Movement, 1890–1920.* New York: W. W. Norton.

Kramer, Daniel C. 2001. "The Constitution and the Right to Leisure." *The Good Society* 10: 64–67.

Kramnick, Isaac, and R. Laurence Moore. 1996. *The Godless Constitution: The Case against Religious Correctness.* New York: W. W. Norton.

Kravitz, Walter. 1993. *American Congressional Dictionary.* Washington, DC: Congressional Quarterly.

Krusch, Barry. 1992. *The 21st Century Constitution: A New America for a New Millennium.* New York: Stanhope Press.

Ku, Raymond. 1995. "Consensus of the Governed: The Legitimacy of Constitutional Change." *Fordham Law Review* 64 (November): 535–586.

Kuic, Vukan. 1983. "John C. Calhoun's Theory of the 'Concurrent Majority.'" *American Bar Association* 69: 482–486.

Kurland, Philip B., and Ralph Lerner, eds. 1987. *The Founders' Constitution.* 5 vols. Chicago: University of Chicago Press.

Kuroda, Tadahisa. 1994. *The Origins of the Twelfth Amendment: The Electoral College in the Early Republic, 1878–1804.* Westport, CT: Greenwood Press.

Kyl, John. 1996. "Why Victims Need a Bill of Rights." *Washington Times* (22 April): A21.

Kyvig, David E. 2000. *Unintended Consequences of Constitutional Amendments.* Athens, GA: The University of Georgia Press.

———. 1996a. *Explicit and Authentic Acts: Amending the Constitution, 1776–1995.* Lawrence, KS: University Press of Kansas.

———. 1996b. "Appealing Supreme Court Decisions: Constitutional Amendments as Checks on Judicial Review." *Journal of Supreme Court History* 2: 105–119.

————. 1995. "Reforming or Resisting Modern Government? The Balanced Budget Amendment to the U.S. Constitution." *Akron Law Review* 28 (Fall/Winter): 97–124.

————. 1989. "The Road Not Taken: FDR, the Supreme Court and Constitutional Amendment." *Political Science Quarterly* 104 (Fall): 463–481.

————. 1988. "Can the Constitution Be Amended? The Battle over the Income Tax, 1895–1913." *Prologue* 20 (Fall): 181–200.

————. 1979. *Repealing National Prohibition.* Chicago: University of Chicago Press.

Kyvig, David E., ed. 1985. *Alcohol and Order: Perspectives on National Prohibition.* Westport, CT: Greenwood Press.

Labbe, Donald M. 1983. "New Light on the Slaughterhouse Monopoly of 1869." In *Louisiana's Legal Heritage,* ed. Edward F. Haas. Pensacola, FL: Peridido Bay Press.

Labunski, Richard. 2000. *The Second Constitutional Convention: How the American People Can Take Back Their Government.* Versailles, KY: Marley and Beck Press.

Laham, Nicholas. 1993. *Why the United States Lacks a National Health Insurance Program.* Westport, CT: Greenwood Press.

Landry, Thomas K. 1993. "Constitutional Invention: A Patent Perspective." *Rutgers Law Journal* 25 (Autumn): 67–104.

Lane, Charles. 2002. "High Court Denies Texas Death Appeal: Court Declines to Intervene in 'Sleeping Lawyer Case,'" *The Washington Post,* 3 June, at *washingtonpost.com.*

Langum, David J. 1994. *Crossing Over the Line: Legislating Morality and the Mann Act.* Chicago: University of Chicago Press.

Larson, Edward J. 1993. "The 'Blaine Amendment' in State Constitutions." In *The School-Choice Controversy: What Is Constitutional?* Ed. James W. Skillen. Grand Rapids, MI: Baker Books.

Larson, Gustave O. 1971. *The "Americanization" of Utah for Statehood.* San Marino, CA: Huntington Library.

Lasch, Christopher. 1995. "Progress." In *A Companion to American Thought,* eds. Richard Wightman Fox and James T. Kloppenberg. Malden, MA: Blackwell Publishers.

Lash, Kurt T. 1994. "Rejecting Conventional Wisdom: Federalist Ambivalence in the Framing and Implementation of Article V." *American Journal of Legal History* 38 (April): 197–231.

Laubach, John H. 1969. *School Prayers: Congress, the Courts and the Public.* Washington, DC: Public Affairs Press.

Lawrence, William B. 1880. "The Monarchical Principle in Our Constitution." *North American Review* 288 (November): 385–409.

Lawson, Gary, and Guy Seidman. 2001. "When Did the Constitution Become Law?" *Notre Dame Law Review* 77 (November): 1–37.

Lawson, Steven F. 1976. *Black Ballots: Voting Rights in the South, 1944–1969.* New York: Columbia University Press.

Lawton, Kim A. 1996. "'The Right to Parent': Should It Be Fundamental?" *Christianity Today* 40 (29 April): 57.

Lazare, Daniel. 1996. *The Frozen Republic: How the Constitution Is Paralyzing Democracy.* New York: Harcourt Brace & Company.

Leach, Robert S. "House Rule XXI and an Argument against a Constitutional Requirement for Majority Rule in Congress." *UCLA Law Review* 44 (April): 1253–1288.

Lee, Calvin B. T. 1967. *One Man One Vote: WMCA and the Struggle for Equal Representation.* New York: Charles Scribner's Sons.

Lee, Charles Robert, Jr. 1963. *The Confederate Constitutions.* Chapel Hill, NC: University of North Carolina Press.

Lee, R. Alton. 1961. "The Corwin Amendment in the Secession Crisis." *Ohio Historical Quarterly* 70 (January): 1–26.

Lee, Robert W. 1999. "Battling for the Constitution." *The New American* 15 (26 April), at *http://www.thenewamerican.com/tna/1999/04/vol5no09_constitution.htm.* Accessed 24 April 2002.

Leedham, Charles. 1964. *Our Changing Constitution: The Story behind the Amendments.* New York: Dodd, Mead & Company.

Legislative Reference Service of the Library of Congress. 1936–1996. *Digest of Public General Bills and Resolutions.* Washington, DC: Library of Congress.

Leish, Kenneth W., ed. 1968. *The American Heritage Pictorial History of the Presidents of the United States.* 2 vols. n.p.: American Heritage.

Leuchtenburg, William E. 1995. *The Supreme Court Reborn: The Constitutional Revolution in the Age of Roosevelt.* New York: Oxford University Press.

Levinson, Sanford. 1996a. "Constitutional Imperfection, Judicial Misinterpretation, and the Politics of Constitutional Amendment: Thoughts Generated by Some Current Proposals to Amend the Constitution." *Brigham Young University Law Review* (1996): 611–626.

————. 1996b. "The Political Implications of Amending Clauses," *Constitutional Commentary* 13 (Spring): 107–123.

————. 1995. "Presidential Elections and Constitutional Stupidities." *Constitutional Commentary* 12 (Summer): 183–186.

———. 1994. "Authorizing Constitutional Text: On the Purported Twenty-seventh Amendment." *Constitutional Commentary* 11 (Winter): 101–113.

———. 1992. "Contempt of Court: The Most Important 'Contemporary Challenge to Judging.'" *Washington and Lee Law Review* 49 (Spring): 339–343.

———. 1990a. "On the Notion of Amendment: Reflections on David Daube's 'Jehovah the Good.'" *S'vara: A Journal of Philosophy and Judaism* 1 (Winter): 25–31.

———. 1990b. "'Veneration' and Constitutional Change: James Madison Confronts the Possibility of Constitutional Amendment." *Texas Tech Law Review* 21: 2443–2461.

———. 1989. "The Embarrassing Second Amendment." *Yale Law Journal* 99 (December): 637–660.

Levinson, Sanford, ed. 1995. *Responding to Imperfection: The Theory and Practice of Constitutional Amendment.* Princeton, NJ: Princeton University Press.

Levy, Leonard W. 1995. *Seasoned Judgments: The American Constitution, Rights, and History.* New Brunswick, NJ: Transaction Publishers.

———. 1988. *Original Intent and the Framers' Constitution.* New York: Macmillan.

———. 1986. *The Establishment Clause and the First Amendment.* New York: Macmillan.

———. 1968. *Origins of the Fifth Amendment: The Right against Self-Incrimination.* New York: Oxford University Press.

Lewis, Anthony. 1991. *Make No Law: The Sullivan Case and the First Amendment.* New York: Random House.

———. 1974. *Gideon's Trumpet.* New York: Vintage Books.

Lieber, Francis. 1888. *Manual of Political Ethics, Designed Chiefly for the Use of Colleges and Students at Law.* 2d ed. Philadelphia: Lippincott.

———. 1881. *Reminiscences, Addresses, and Essays.* Ed. Daniel G. Bilman. 2 vols. Philadelphia: J. B. Lippincott.

———. 1865. *Amendments of the Constitution Submitted to the Consideration of the American People.* New York: Loyal Publication Society.

Lieberman, Jethro K. 1992. *The Evolving Constitution: How the Supreme Court Has Ruled on Issues from Abortion to Zoning.* New York: Random House.

Lind, Michael. 1966. "Pat Answers." *New Republic* 214 (February 19): 13–14.

Linder, Douglas. 1981. "What in the Constitution Cannot Be Amended?" *Arizona Law Review* 23: 717–731.

Link, Arthur S. 1963. *Woodrow Wilson: A Brief Biography.* Cleveland, OH: World.

Link, Arthur S., and Richard L. McCormick. 1983. *Progressivism.* Arlington Heights, IL: Harlan Davidson.

Little, Laura E. 1991. "An Excursion into the Uncharted Waters of the Seventeenth Amendment." *Temple Law Review* 674 (Fall): 629–658.

Lively, Donald E. 1992. *The Constitution and Race.* New York: Praeger.

Livingston, Steven G. 2002. *Student's Guide to Landmark Congressional Legislation on Social Security and Welfare.* Westport, CT: Greenwood Press.

Livingston, William S. 1956. *Federalism and Constitutional Change.* Oxford, UK: Clarendon Press.

Lockwood, Henry C. 1884. *The Abolition of the Presidency.* New York: R. Worthington. Reprint, Farmingdale, NY: Darbor Social Science Publications, 1978.

Lofgren, Charles A. 1987. *The Plessy Case: A Legal-Historical Interpretation.* New York: Oxford University Press.

———. 1975. "*Missouri v. Holland* in Historical Perspective." In *The Supreme Court Review.* Chicago: University of Chicago Press.

Long, Huey P. 1935. *My First Days in the White House.* Harrisburg, PA: Telegraph Press.

Longley, Lawrence D., and Alan G. Braun. 1972. *The Politics of Electoral College Reform.* New Haven, CT: Yale University Press.

Lunardini, Christine A. 1986. *From Equal Suffrage to Equal Rights: Alice Paul and the National Woman's Party, 1910–1928.* New York: New York University Press.

Lutz, Donald S. 1994. "Toward a Theory of Constitutional Amendment." *American Political Science Review* 88 (June): 355–370.

———. 1992. *A Preface to American Political Theory.* Lawrence, KS: University Press of Kansas.

———. 1988. *The Origins of American Constitutionalism.* Baton Rouge, LA: Louisiana State University Press.

Lyman, Edward L. 1986. *Political Deliverance: The Mormon Quest for Utah Statehood.* Urbana, IL: University of Illinois Press.

Lynch, Michael J. 2001. "The Other Amendments: Constitutional Amendments That Failed." *Law Library Journal* 92 (Spring): 303–310.

Macdonald, Dwight. 1968. "The Constitution of the United States Needs to Be Fixed." *Esquire* 70 (October): 143–146, 238, 240, 243–244, 246, 252.

MacDonald, William. 1922. *A New Constitution for a New America*. New York: B. W. Heubsch.

———. 1921. "A New American Constitution." *Proceedings of the American Antiquarian Society* 2 (October): 439–447.

Machen, Arthur W., Jr. 1910. "Is the Fifteenth Amendment Void?" *Harvard Law Review* 23 (January): 169–193.

MacPherson, Peter. 1995. "Contested Winners Seated; Challengers in Pursuit." *Congressional Quarterly Weekly Report* 53 (7 January): 28.

Maier, Pauline. 1997. *American Scripture: Making the Declaration of Independence*. New York: Alfred A. Knopf.

Main, Jackson T. 1961. *The Antifederalists: Critics of the Constitution, 1781–1788*. Chicago: Quadrangle Books.

Malone, Dumas, ed. 1961. *Dictionary of American Biography*. 10 vols. New York: Charles Scribner's Sons.

Maltz, Earl M. 2002. "The Fourteenth Amendment and Native American Citizenship." *Constitutional Commentary* 17 (Winter): 555–573.

———. 1995. "The Impact of the Constitutional Revolution of 1937 on the Dormant Commerce Clause—A Case Study in the Decline of State Autonomy." *Harvard Journal of Law & Public Policy* 19 (Fall): 121–145.

———. 1990. *Civil Rights, the Constitution, and Congress, 1863–1869*. Lawrence, KS: University Press of Kansas.

"The Man Who Would Not Quit." 1992. *People* 37 (April 1): 72.

Mangone, Gerald J. 1951. *The Idea and Practice of World Government*. New York: Columbia University Press.

Mann, Thomas E. 1992. "The Wrong Medicine." *Brookings Review* 10 (Spring): 23–25.

Mansbridge, Jane J. 1986. *Why We Lost the ERA*. Chicago: University of Chicago Press.

Marberry, M. M. 1967. *Vicky: A Biography of Victoria C. Woodhull*. New York: Funk and Wagnalls.

Marbury, William L. 1920. "The Nineteenth Amendment and After." *Virginia Law Review* 7 (October): 1–29.

———. 1919. "The Limitations upon the Amending Power." *Harvard Law Review* 33 (December): 223–235.

Marduke, P. G. 1970. *The CASCOT System for Social Control of Technology*. Silver Spring, MD: Citizens' Association for Social Control of Technology.

Marshall, Patrick. 2001. "Religion in Schools." *CQ Researcher*. 12 January. *http://library.cqpress.com/cqres/lpext.dll/cqpres/print/print20010112?*.

Marshall, Price. 1998. "'A Careless Written Letter'—Situating Amendments to the Federal Constitution." *Arkansas Law Review* 51: 95–115.

Masei, David. 1995. "Flag Resolution's Future Murky in More Divided Senate." *Congressional Quarterly Weekly Report* 53 (22 July): 2195.

Mason, Alpheus T. 1964. *The States' Rights Debate: Antifederalism and the Constitution*. Englewood Cliffs, NJ: Prentice-Hall.

Mason, Alpheus T., and Gordon E. Baker. 1985. *Free Government in the Making: Readings in American Political Thought*. 4th ed. New York: Oxford University Press.

Mason, Alpheus T., and Donald G. Stephenson Jr. 2002. *American Constitutional Law: Introductory Essays and Selected Cases*. 13th ed. Englewood Cliffs, NJ: Prentice-Hall.

Mason, John Lyman, and Michael Nelson. 2001. *Governing Gambling*. New York: The Century Foundation Press.

Massaro, John. 1990. *Supremely Political: The Role of Ideology and Presidential Management in Unsuccessful Supreme Court Nominations*. Albany, NY: State University of New York Press.

Massey, Calvin R. 1995. *Silent Rights: The Ninth Amendment and the Constitution's Unenumerated Rights*. Philadelphia: Temple University Press.

Masters, Brooke A. 2001. "Va. Minute of Silence Survives Test in High Court: 4th Circuit Ruling Allowed to Stand Without Comment." *The Washington Post*, 30 October, B01.

Mathews, John M. 1908. *Legislative and Judicial History of the Fifteenth Amendment*. Reprint, New York: Da Capo Press, 1971.

Mathis, Doyle. 1967. "*Chisholm v. Georgia:* Background and Settlement." *Journal of American History* 54: 19–29.

Matthews, Richard K. 1995. *If Men Were Angels: James Madison and the Heartless Empire of Reason*. Lawrence, KS: University Press of Kansas.

Mauro, Tony. 2001. "The Age of Justice." *American Lawyer* 23 (March): 67.

May, Christopher N. 1989. *In the Name of War*. Cambridge, MA.: Harvard University Press.

May, James. 1992. "Antitrust." In *The Oxford Companion to the Supreme Court of the United States*, ed. Kermit L. Hall. New York: Oxford University Press.

May, Janice C. 1987. "Constitutional Amendment and Revision Revisited." *Publius: The Journal of Federalism* 17 (Winter): 153–179.

Mayer, Carl J. 1990. "Personalizing the Impersonal: Corporations and the Bill of Rights." *Hastings Law Journal* 41 (March): 577–667.

Mayer, David N. 1994. *The Constitutional Thought of Thomas Jefferson*. Charlottesville, VA: University Press of Virginia.

———. 1990. "The Jurisprudence of Christopher G. Tiedeman: A Study in the Failure of Laissez-Faire Constitutionalism." *Missouri Law Review* 55 (Winter): 93–161.

Mayers, Lewis. 1959. *Shall We Amend the Fifth Amendment?* New York: Harper and Brothers.

Mayhew, David R. 1991. *Divided We Govern: Party Control, Lawmaking, and Investigations, 1946–1990.* New Haven, CT: Yale University Press.

McBain, Howard Lee. 1927. *The Living Constitution: a Consideration of the Realities and Legends of Our Fundamental Law.* New York: Macmillian.

McBride, James. 1991. "'Is Nothing Sacred?' Flag Desecration, the Constitution and the Establishment of Religion." *St. John's Law Review* 65: 297–324.

McClurg, Andrew J., David B. Kopel, and Brannon P. Denning, eds. 2002. *Gun Control & Gun Rights: A Reader & Guide.* New York: New York University Press.

McConnell, Michael W. 1995. "Originalism and the Desegregation Decisions." *Virginia Law Review* 81 (May): 947–1140.

McCullough, David. 1992. *Truman.* New York: Simon and Schuster.

McDonald, Forrest. 1992. "Pardon Power." In *The Oxford Companion to the Supreme Court of the United States,* ed. Kermit L. Hall. New York: Oxford University Press.

———. 1982. *A Constitutional History of the United States.* New York: Franklin Watts.

———. 1979. *Alexander Hamilton: A Biography.* New York: Norton.

McFeely, William S. 1991. *Frederick Douglass.* New York: W. W. Norton.

McGinnis, John O., and Michael B. Rappaport. 2002. "Our Supermajoritarian Constitution." *Texas Law Review* 80 (March): 703–805.

———. 1999. "Supermajority Rules as a Constitutional Solution." *William and Mary Law Review* 40 (February): 365–470.

———. 1995. "The Constitutionality of Legislative Supermajority Requirements: A Defense." *Yale Law Journal* 105 (November): 483–511.

McHenry, Robert, ed. 1980. *Liberty's Women.* Springfield, MA: G. and C. Merriam.

McIntyre, Robert S. 1992. "No, It Would Wreck the Economy." *The World & I* 7 (August): 111, 116–117, 119.

McKee, Henry S. 1933. *Degenerate Democracy.* New York: Thomas Y. Crowell.

Meador, Lewis H. 1898. "The Council of Censors." *Pennsylvania Magazine of History and Biography* 22: 265–300.

Melendez, Edgardo. 1988. *Puerto Rico's Statehood Movement.* New York: Greenwood Press.

Meltsner, Michael. 1974. *Cruel and Unusual: The Supreme Court and Capital Punishment.* New York: William Morrow.

Merriam, Charles E. 1931. *The Written Constitution and the Unwritten Attitude.* New York: Richard R. Smith.

Mertens, John. 1997. *The Second Constitution for the United States of America.* Cottonwood, CA: Gazelle Books.

Meyer, Alfred W. 1951. "The Blaine Amendment and the Bill of Rights." *Harvard Law Review* 64: 939–945.

Meyer, Karl E. 1968. "So Does the Bill of Rights." *Esquire* 70 (October): 147–148.

Meyers, Marvin, ed. 1973. *The Mind of the Founder: Sources of the Political Thought of James Madison.* Indianapolis, IN: Bobbs-Merrill.

Miller, Arthur S. 1987. *The Secret Constitution and the Need for Constitutional Change.* Westport, CT: Greenwood Press.

———. 1984. "The Annual John Randolph Tucker Lecture: Taking Needs Seriously: Observations on the Necessity for Constitutional Change." *Washington and Lee Law Review* 41 (Fall): 1243–1306.

———. 1982. *Toward Increased Judicial Activism: The Political Role of the Supreme Court.* Westport, CT: Greenwood Press.

Miller, Jeremy. 1987. "It's Time for a New Constitution." *Southwestern University Law Review* 17: 207–237.

Miller, John C. 2001. "Immigrants for President: Why the Foreign-born Should Be Allowed to Compete for the Big Job." *National Review* 53 (6 August): 22–24.

Miller, Robert S., and Donald O. Dewey. 1991. "The Congressional Salary Amendment: 200 Years Later." *Glendale Law Review* 10: 92–109.

Miller, William L. 1992. *The Business of May Next: James Madison and the Founding.* Charlottesville, VA: University Press of Virginia.

Monaghan, Henry P. 1996. "We the People[s], Original Understanding, and Constitutional Amendment." *Columbia Law Review* 96 (January): 121–177.

Monsma, Stephen V. 1993. *Positive Neutrality: Letting Religious Freedom Ring.* Westport, CT: Greenwood Press.

Moore, Charles Forrest. 1925. *The Challenge of Life.* New York: William Edwin Rudge.

Moore, John. 1995. "Pleading the 10th." *National Journal* 28 (29 July): 1940–1944.

Moore, Trevor W. 1970. "A Rumbling in Babylon:

Panthers Host a Parley." *Christian Century* 87 (28 October): 1296–1300.

Moore, W. S., and Rudolph G. Penner, eds. 1980. *The Constitution and the Budget: Are Constitutional Limits on Tax, Spending and Budget Powers Desirable at the Federal Level?* Washington, DC: American Enterprise Institute for Public Policy Research.

Morehead, Joe. 1985. "Private Bills and Private Laws: A Guide to the Legislative Process." *Serials Librarian* 9 (Spring): 115–125.

Morgan, Robert J. 1988. *James Madison on the Constitution and the Bill of Rights.* New York: Greenwood Press.

Morgan, Thomas J. 1963. "Seventeen States Vote to Destroy Democracy as We Know It." *Look* 27 (3 December): 76–88.

Morin, Isobel V. 1998. *Our Changing Constitution: How and Why We Have Amended It.* Brookfield, CT: Millbook Press.

Morris, Henry O. 1897. *Waiting for the Signal, a Novel.* Chicago: Schulte.

Morris, Thomas D. 1974. *Free Men All: The Personal Liberty Laws of the North, 1780–1861.* Baltimore, MD: Johns Hopkins University Press.

Morrison, Charles C. 1972. *The Outlawry of War: A Constructive Policy for World Peace.* New York: Garland Publishing.

Morrison, Stanley. 1949. "Does the Fourteenth Amendment Incorporate the Bill of Rights? The Judicial Interpretation." *Stanford Law Review* 2 (December): 140–173.

Morton, Robert K. 1933. *God in the Constitution.* Nashville, TN: Cokesbury Press.

Murphy, Bruce A. 1988. *Fortas: The Rise and Ruin of a Supreme Court Justice.* New York: William Morrow.

Murphy, Cornelius F., Jr. 1988. "Constitutional Revision." In *Philosophical Dimensions of the Constitution,* ed. Diana T. Meyers and Kenneth Kipnis. Boulder, CO: Westview Press.

Murphy, Walter F. 1995. "Merlin's Memory: The Past and Future Imperfect of the Once and Future Polity." In *Responding to Imperfection,* ed. Sanford Levinson. Princeton, NJ: Princeton University Press.

——. 1992a. "Consent and Constitutional Change." In *Human Rights and Constitutional Law: Essays in Honour of Brian Walsh,* ed. James O'Reilly. Dublin, Ireland: Found Hall Press.

——. 1992b. "Staggering Toward the New Jerusalem of Constitutional Theory: A Response to Ralph F. Graebler." *American Journal of Jurisprudence* 37: 337–357.

——. 1990. "The Right to Privacy and Legitimate Constitutional Change." In *Constitutional Bases of Political and Social Change in the United States,* ed. Shlomo Slonin. New York: Praeger.

——. 1987. "*Slaughterhouse, Civil Rights,* and Limits on Constitutional Change." *American Journal of Jurisprudence* 23: 1–22.

——. 1980. "An Ordering of Constitutional Values." *Southern California Law Review* 53: 703–760.

——. 1978. "The Art of Constitutional Interpretation: A Preliminary Showing." In *Essays on the Constitution of the United States,* ed. M. Harmon. Port Washington, NY: Kennikat Press.

——. 1962. *Congress and the Court.* Chicago: University of Chicago Press.

Murphy, Walter F., James E. Fleming, and Sotirios Barber. 1995. *American Constitutional Interpretation,* 2d ed. Westbury, NY: Foundation Press.

Musmanno, M. A. 1929. *Proposed Amendments to the Constitution.* Washington, DC: U.S. Government Printing Office.

Myles, John. 1989. *Old Age in the Welfare State: The Political Economy of Public Pensions.* Lawrence, KS: University Press of Kansas.

Nader, Ralph, and Carl J. Mayer. 1988. "Corporations Are Not Persons." *The New York Times* (9 April), sect. 1, p. 31.

Nagel, Stuart S. 1965. "Court-Curbing Proposals in American History." *Vanderbilt Law Review* 18: 925–944.

Nagle, John Copeland. 1997. "Essay: A Twentieth Amendment Parable." *New York University Law Review* 72 (May): 470–494.

Natelson, Robert G. 2002. "A Republic, Not a Democracy? Initiative, Referendum, and the Constitution's Guarantee Clause." *Texas Law Review* 80 (March): 807–857.

Naylor, Thomas H., and William H. Willimon. 1997. *Downsizing the U.S.A.* Grand Rapids, MI: William B. Eerdmans.

Nelson, Michael. 1987. "Constitutional Qualifications for President." *Presidential Studies Quarterly* 17 (Spring): 383–399.

Nelson, Michael, ed. 1989. *Guide to the Presidency.* Washington, DC: Congressional Quarterly.

Nelson, William E. 1988. *The Fourteenth Amendment: From Political Principle to Judicial Doctrine.* Cambridge, MA: Harvard University Press.

Newman, Roger K. 1994. *Hugo Black: A Biography.* New York: Pantheon Books.

Newmyer, R. Kent. 1968. *The Supreme Court Under Marshall and Taney.* New York: Thomas Y. Crowell.

"New Proposal for Constitutionalizing Victims' Rights Introduced in Congress." 2002. *U.S. Law Week* 70 (30 April): 2679.

Nisbet, Robert. 1980. *The Idea of Progress.* New York: Basic Books.

Niven, John. 1988. *John C. Calhoun and the Price of Union: A Biography.* Baton Rouge, LA: Louisiana State University Press.

Nordeen, Ross. "Home Page." *http://www.amatec on.com.* Accessed 5/7/02.

Norham, George W. 1988. "A Constitutional Door Is Opened for Amendment." *Texas Bar Journal* 51 (September): 804–806.

"North Carolina Ratifies the 24th Amendment." 1989. *We the People: A Newsletter of the Commission on the Bicentennial of the United States Constitution* 5 (July): 10.

Oates, Stephen B. 1970. *To Purge This Land with Blood: A Biography of John Brown.* New York: Harper and Row.

O'Brien, David M. 2000a. *Civil Rights and Civil Liberties.* Vol. 2 of *Constitutional Law and Politics.* 5th ed. New York: W. W. Norton.

———. 2000b. *Struggles for Power and Governmental Accountability.* 5th ed., Vol. 1 of *Constitutional Law and Politics.* New York: W. W. Norton.

O'Brien, F. William. 1965. "The States and 'No Establishment': Proposed Amendments to the Constitution since 1798." *Washburn Law Journal* 4: 183–210.

———. 1963. "The Blaine Amendment, 1875–1876." *University of Detroit Law Journal* 41 (December): 137–205.

O'Connell, Frank J., Jr. 2001. "Estate Tax Repeal: What Now?" *The Tax Adviser* 32 (September): 588.

O'Connor, Karen. 1996. *No Neutral Ground? Abortion Politics in an Age of Absolutes.* Boulder, CO: Westview.

O'Conor, Charles. 1881. "Democracy." In *Johnson's New Universal Cyclopaedia: A Treasury of Scientific and Popular Treasure of Useful Knowledge.* Vol. 1, Part 2. New York: A. J. Johnson.

———. 1877. Address by Charles O'Conor Delivered before the New York Historical Society at the Academy of Music. 8 May. New York: Anson D. F. Randolph.

Ogden, Frederic D. 1958. *The Poll Tax in the South.* University, AL: University of Alabama Press.

O'Neil, Patrick M. 1995. "The Declaration as Un-Constitution: The Bizarre Jurisprudential Philosophy of Professor Harry V. Jaffa." *Akron Law Review* 28 (Fall/Winter): 237–252.

Onuf, Peter. 1984. "Territories and Statehood." In *Encyclopedia of American Political History: Studies of Principal Movements and Ideas,* ed. Jack P. Greene. Vol. 3. New York: Charles Scribner's Sons.

Orfield, Lester B. 1942. *The Amending of the Federal Constitution.* Ann Arbor, MI: University of Michigan Press.

Ornstein, Norman J. 2002. "Preparing for the Unthinkable: Bush's 'Shadow Government' Plan Is a Start—But Only a Start." *Wall Street Journal,* 11 March, A18.

———. 1994. "Congress Inside Out." *Roll Call* 39 (10 March): 5–6.

Ornstein, Norman J., and Amy L. Schenhenberg. 1995. "The 1995 Congress: The First Hundred Days and Beyond." *Political Science Quarterly* 110 (Summer): 183–206.

Orth, John V. 1992. "Eleventh Amendment." In *The Oxford Companion to the Supreme Court of the United States,* ed. Kermit L. Hall. New York: Oxford University Press.

———. 1987. *The Judicial Power of the United States: The Eleventh Amendment in American History.* New York: Oxford University Press.

O'Toole, Lawrence J., Jr., ed. 1985. *American Intergovernmental Relations: Foundations, Perspectives, and Issues.* Washington, DC: Congressional Quarterly.

Pace, James O. 1986. *Amendment to the Constitution: Averting the Decline and Fall of America.* Los Angeles, CA: Johnson, Pace, Simmons and Fennell.

Padover, Saul K. 1962. *To Secure These Blessings.* New York: Washington Square Press/Ridge Press.

Palmer, Kris E. 2000. *Constitutional Amendments: 1789 to the Present.* Detroit, MI: Gale Group.

Paludan, Phillip S. 1994. *The Presidency of Abraham Lincoln.* Lawrence, KS: University Press of Kansas.

"Panthers Plan New Convention." 1971. In *Facts on File Yearbook, 1970.* Vol. 30. New York: Facts on File.

Paschal, Richard A. 1991. "The Continuing Colloquy: Congress and the Finality of the Supreme Court." *Journal of Law and Politics* 8 (Fall): 143–226.

Patrick, John J. 1994. *The Young Oxford Companion to the Supreme Court of the United States.* New York: Oxford University Press.

Patterson, Bennett B. 1955. *The Forgotten Ninth Amendment.* Indianapolis, IN: Bobbs-Merrill.

Paulsen, Michael S. 1995. "The Case for a Constitutional Convention." *Wall Street Journal,* 3 May, A-15.

———. 1994. "Is Lloyd Bentsen Unconstitutional?" *Stanford Law Review* 46 (April): 907–918.

———. 1993. "A General Theory of Article V: The Constitutional Issues of the Twenty-seventh Amendment." *Yale Law Journal* 103: 677–789.

Peabody, Bruce G., and Scott E. Gant. 1999. "The Twice and Future President: Constitutional Interstices and the Twenty-second Amendment." *Minnesota Law Review* 83 (February): 565–635.

Pear, Robert. 1994. "State Officials Worry That a Federal Budget Will Be Balanced on Their Books." *New York Times,* 11 December, 34.

Pearson, Hugh. 1994. *The Shadow of the Panther: Huey Newton and the Price of Black Power in America.* Reading, MA: Addison-Wesley.

Pease, William H., and June H. Pease, eds. 1965. *The Antislavery Argument.* Indianapolis, IN: Bobbs-Merrill.

Peck, Robert S. 1992. *The Bill of Rights and the Politics of Interpretation.* St. Paul, MN: West.

Pei, Mario. 1967–1968. "The Case for a Constitutional Convention." *Modern Age* 12 (Winter): 8–13.

Peirce, Neal R. 1968. *The People's President: The Electoral College in American History and the Direct-Vote Alternative.* New York: Simon and Schuster.

Peltason, Jack W. 1994. *Corwin and Peltason's Understanding the Constitution.* 13th ed. Fort Worth, TX: Harcourt Brace College Publishers.

Pendergast, Tom, Sara Pendergast, and John Sousanis, with Elizabeth Shaw Grunow, ed., 2001. *Constitutional Amendments: From Freedom of Speech to Flag Burning.* 3 vols. Detroit, MI: U.X.L. imprint of Gale Group.

Penney, Annette C. 1968. *The Golden Voice of the Senate.* Washington, DC: American Enterprise Institute for Public Policy Research.

Penniman, Clara. 1980. *State Income Taxation.* Baltimore, MD: Johns Hopkins University Press.

Perry, Michael J. 1999. *We the People: The Fourteenth Amendment and the Supreme Court.* Oxford, UK: Oxford University Press.

Peters, Ronald M., Jr. 1990. "Repeal the Seventeenth!" *Extensions* 2 (Spring): 16–17.

Peters, William. 1987. *A More Perfect Union: The Making of the United States Constitution.* New York: Crown.

Peterson, Charles S. 1977. *Utah: A Bicentennial History.* New York: W. W. Norton.

"Philippines, Republic of the." 1994. *Microsoft Encarta Multimedia Encyclopedia.*

Piburn, John L. 1932. *A Constitution and a Code.* San Diego, CA: Bowman Printing Company.

Pious, Richard M. 1978. "Introduction." In *The Abolition of the Presidency.* Farmingdale, NY: Darbor Social Science Publications.

Pizzigati, Sam. 1994. "Salary Caps for Everyone!" *New York Times,* 28 August, 15.

———. 1992. *The Maximum Wage: A Common-Sense Prescription for Revitalizing America—By Taxing the Very Rich.* New York: Appex Press.

Planell, Raymond M. 1974. "The Equal Rights Amendment: Will States Be Allowed to Change Their Minds?" *Notre Dame Lawyer* 49 (February): 657–670.

Political Economy and Constitutional Reform. 1982. Hearings before the Joint Economic Committee of the Congress of the United States. 97th Cong., 2nd Sess.

Political Staff of *The Washington Post.* 2001. *Deadlock: The Inside Story of America's Closest Election.* New York: Public Affairs.

Pollard, Vincent Kelly, and Bruce E. Tonn. 1998. "Revisiting the 'Court of Generations' Amendment." *Futures* 30: 345–352.

Porter, Kirk H., and Donald B. Johnson. 1966. *National Party Platforms, 1840–1964.* Urbana, IL: University of Illinois Press.

Posner, Richard A. 1999. *An Affair of State: The Investigation, Impeachment, and Trial of President Clinton.* Cambridge, MA: Harvard University Press.

Powe, Lucas A., Jr. 1991. *The Fourth Estate and the Constitution: Freedom of Press in America.* Berkeley, CA: University of California Press.

Preston, Robert L. 1972. *The Plot to Replace the Constitution.* Salt Lake City, UT: Hawkes Publications.

Prinz, Timothy S. 1992. "Term Limitation: A Perilous Panacea." *The World & I* 7 (January): 143–153.

Proceedings of the National Convention to Secure the Religious Amendment of the Constitution of the United States Held in Pittsburgh, February 4, 5, 1874, with an Account of the Origin and Progress of the Movement. 1874. Philadelphia: Christian Statesman Association.

"Proper Government." *http://www.ebtx.com.* Accessed 5/17/02.

Proposals for a Constitutional Convention to Require a Balanced Federal Budget. 1979. Washington, DC: American Enterprise Institute for Public Policy Research.

Proposed Amendments to the Constitution of the United States of America Introduced in Congress from the 69th Congress, 2d Session through the 87th Congress, 2d Session, December 6, 1926, to January 3, 1963. 1963. Washington, DC: U.S. Government Printing Office.

Proposed Amendments to the Constitution of the United States of America Introduced in Congress from the 88th Congress, 1st Session through the 90th Congress, 2d Session, January 9, 1963, to January 3, 1969. 1969. Washington, DC: U.S. Government Printing Office.

Proposed Amendments to the Constitution of the United States, Introduced in Congress from the 69th Congress, 2d Session through the 84th Congress,

2d Session, December 6, 1926, to January 3, 1957. 1957. Washington, DC: U.S. Government Printing Office.

"Proposed Legislation on the Convention Method of Amending the United States Constitution." 1972. *Harvard Law Review* 85: 1612–1648.

Pullen, William R. 1948. *Applications of State Legislatures to Congress for the Call of a National Constitutional Convention, 1788–1867.* Master's thesis, University of North Carolina at Chapel Hill.

Radin, Max. 1930. "The Intermittent Sovereign." *Yale Law Journal* 30: 514–531.

Rakove, Jack N., ed. 1990. *Interpreting the Constitution: The Debate over Original Intent.* Boston: Northeastern University Press.

Ranney, Austin. 1978. "The United States of America." In *Referendums: A Comparative Study of Practice and Theory,* ed. David Butler and Austin Ranney. Washington, DC: American Enterprise Institute for Public Policy Research.

Raskin, Jamin B. 2001. "A Right to Vote." *The American Prospect* 12 (27 August): 10–12.

Rasmussen, Jorgen S., and Joel C. Moses. 1995. *Major European Governments.* 9th ed. Belmont, CA: Wadsworth.

Raven-Hansen, Peter. 1975. "Congressional Representation for the District of Columbia: A Constitutional Analysis." *Harvard Journal of Legislation* 12: 167–192.

Rawley, James A. 1981. *The Transatlantic Slave Trade: A History.* New York: W. W. Norton.

Reagan, Ronald, et al. 1990. *Restoring the Presidency: Reconsidering the Twenty-second Amendment.* Washington, DC: National Legal Center for Public Interest.

Records of the Council of Censors. 1783–1784. Journal vols. 1–3. Division of Archives and Manuscripts, Pennsylvania Historical and Museum Commission.

Redinger, Paul. 1996. "The Faltering Revolution." *ABA Journal* 82 (February): 56–59.

Reed, Ralph. 1995. *Contract with the American Family: A Bold Plan by Christian Coalition to Strengthen the Family and Restore Common-Sense Values.* Nashville, TN: Moorings.

Rees, Grover, III. 1986. "The Amendment Process and Limited Constitutional Conventions." *Benchmark* 2: 67–108.

Rehnquist, William H. 1976. "The Notion of the Living Constitution." *Texas Law Review* 54: 693–706.

Reid, John P. 1993. *Constitutional History of the American Revolution. The Authority of Law.* Madison, WI: University of Wisconsin Press.

Reidinger, Paul. 1996. "The Faltering Revolution." *ABA Journal* 82 (February): 56–59.

Renehan, Edward J., Jr. 1995. *The Secret Six: The True Tale of the Men Who Conspired with John Brown.* New York: Crown.

"The Report of the National Symposium on Presidential Selection." 2001. The Center for Governmental Studies at the University of Virginia. *http://www.goodpolitics.org/reform/report/electoral.htm.* Accessed 11/29/02.

Report on the Condition of Women and Children as Wage Earners. 1910–1913. U.S. Department of Labor. 19 vols. Washington, DC: U.S. Government Printing Office.

Report to the Attorney General. 1987. *The Question of Statehood for the District of Columbia.* 3 April. Washington, DC: U.S. Government Printing Office.

"Rethinking the Electoral College Debate: The Framers, Federalism, and One Person, One Vote." 2001. *Harvard Law Review* 114 (June): 2526–2549.

"Retroactive Tax Increases: No Problem, Say Justices." 1994. *Congressional Quarterly Weekly Report* 52 (18 June): 1588.

Reynolds, Edward. 1985. *Stand the Storm: A History of the Atlantic Slave Trade.* London: Allison and Busby.

Reynolds, Eustace. 1915. *A New Constitution: A Suggested Form of Modified Government.* New York: Nation Press.

Rhodehamel, John. 1998. *The Great Experiment: George Washington and the American Republic.* New Haven, CT: Yale University Press.

Rice, Isaac. 1884. "Work for a Constitutional Convention." *Century Magazine* 28 (August): 534–540.

Rich, Bennett M. 1960. *Major Problems in State Constitutional Revision,* ed. W. Brooke Groves. Chicago: Public Administration Service.

Richards, David A. J. 1993. *Conscience and the Constitution: History, Theory, and Law of the Reconstruction Amendments.* Princeton, NJ: Princeton University Press.

Richardson, James E., ed. 1908. *A Compilation of the Messages and Papers of the Presidents, 1789–1908.* 11 vols. n.p.: Bureau of National Literature and Art.

Richardson, Sula. 1991. *Congressional Terms of Office and Tenure: Historical Background and Contemporary Issues.* Washington, DC: Congressional Research Service, Library of Congress.

———. 1989. *Congressional Tenure: A Review of Efforts to Limit House and Senate Service.* Washington, DC: Congressional Research Service, Library of Congress.

Richie, Robert. 1995. "Democracy and Majority Preference Voting." *Rainbow* 3, no. 30 (27 July).

Riker, William H. 1954. "Sidney George Fisher and the Separation of Powers during the Civil War." *Journal of the History of Ideas* 15 (June): 397–412.

"Rising Clamor for Black Separatism." 1970. *U.S. News and World Report* 69 (21 September): 82.

Robinson, Donald. 1989. *Government for the Third American Century*. Boulder, CO: Westview Press.

———. 1987. "Adjustments Are Needed in the System of Checks and Balances." *Polity* 19: 660–666.

———. 1985. *Reforming American Government: The Bicentennial Papers of the Committee on the Constitutional System*. Boulder, CO: Westview Press.

Robinson, Lloyd. 1996. *The Stolen Election, Hayes versus Tilden—1876*. New York: Forge.

Robinson, Roger W., and Herschel B. Burt., ed. by Robert Edwards. 1996. *The Willard House and Clock Museum and the Willard Family Clockmakers*. Columbia, PA: National Association of Watch and Clock Collectors, Inc.

Rodick, Burleigh C. 1953. *American Constitutional Custom: A Forgotten Factor in the Founding*. New York: Philosophical Library.

Roemer, Arthur C. 1983. "Classification of Property." In *The Property Tax and Local Finance,* ed. C. Lowell Harris. New York: Proceedings of the Academy of Political Science.

Rohde, David W. 1994. "The Fall Elections: Realignment or Dealignment." *Chronicle of Higher Education* 41 (14 December): B1–B2.

Roman, Jose D. 2002. "Trying to Fit an Oval Shaped Island into a Square Constitution: Arguments for Puerto Rican Statehood." *Fordham Urban Law Journal* 29 (April): 1681–1713.

Rosen, Jeffrey. 1996. "Just a Quirk." *New Republic* 214 (March 18): 16–17.

———. 1991. "Was the Flag Burning Amendment Unconstitutional?" *Yale Law Review* 100: 1073–1092.

Rosenberg, Gerald N. 1991. *The Hollow Hope: Can Courts Bring about Social Change?* Chicago: University of Chicago Press.

Rosenbloom, David H. 1971. *Federal Service and the Constitution: The Development of the Public Employment Relationship*. Ithaca, NY: Cornell University Press.

Ross, Russell M., and Fred Schwengel. 1982. "An Item Veto for the President?" *Presidential Studies Quarterly* 12 (Winter): 66–79.

Ross, William G. 2000. "The Contemporary Significance of *Meyer* and *Pierce* for Parental Rights Issues Involving Education." *Akron Law Review* 34: 177–207.

———. 1990. "The Hazards of Proposals to Limit the Tenure of Federal Judges and to Permit Judicial Removal without Impediment." *Villanova Law Review* 35 (November): 1063–1138.

Rossiter, Clinton. 1987. *1787: The Grand Convention*. New York: W. W. Norton.

Rossum, Ralph A. 2001. *Federalism, the Supreme Court, and the Seventeenth Amendment: The Irony of Constitutional Democracy*. Lanham, MD: Lexington Books.

Rossum, Ralph A., and G. Alan Tarr. 1999. *American Constitutional Law: The Structure of Government*. 5th ed. New York: St. Martin's Press.

Rothwax, Harold J. 1996. *Guilty: The Collapse of Criminal Justice*. New York: Random House.

Rousseau, Jean-Jacques. 1762. *On the Social Contract with Geneva Manuscript and Political Economy*. Reprint, ed. Roger D. Masters. New York: St. Martin's Press, 1978.

Rubenfeld, Jed. 2001. "The New Unwritten Constitution." *Duke Law Journal* 51 (October): 289–305.

Rubin, Alissa J. 1995. "Democrats Hope Tax-Raising Rule Will Come Back to Haunt GOP." *Congressional Quarterly Weekly Report* 53 (15 July): 2045–2046.

Rubin, Irene S. 1990. *The Politics of Public Budgeting: Getting and Spending, Borrowing and Balancing*. Chatham, NJ: Chatham House.

Ruhl, J. B. 1999. "The Metrics of Constitutional Amendments: Why Proposed Environmental Quality Amendments Don't Measure Up." *Notre Dame Law Review* 74 (January): 245–281.

Rushdoony, Rousas J. 1973. *The Institutes of Biblical Law*. Phillipsburg, NJ: Presbyterian and Reformed Publishing Co.

Rutland, Robert A. 1987. *James Madison: The Founding Father*. New York: Macmillan.

Sabourin, Jennifer L. 1999. "Note: Parental Rights Amendments: Will a Statutory Right to Parent Force Children to 'Shed Their Constitutional Rights' at the Schoolhouse Door?" *Wayne State University Law Review* 44 (Winter): 1899–1926.

Sager, Lawrence Gene. 1978. "Fair Measure: The Legal Status of Underenforced Connstitutional Norms." *Harvard Law Review* 92: 1212–1264.

Salins, Peter D., ed. 1987. *Housing America's Poor*. Chapel Hill, NC: University of North Carolina Press.

Sargentich, Thomas O. 1993. "The Limits of the Parliamentary Critique of the Separation of Powers." *William and Mary Law Review* 34 (Spring): 679–739.

Sartori, Giovanni. 1994. *Comparative Constitutional Engineering: An Inquiry into Structures, In-*

centives and Outcomes. New York: New York University Press.

Savage, James D. 1988. *Balanced Budgets and American Politics.* Ithaca, NY: Cornell University Press.

"Sawing a Justice in Half." 1939. *Yale Law Journal* 48: 1455–1458.

Schaller, Thomas F. 1998. "Democracy at Rest: Strategic Ratification of the Twenty-First Amendment." *Publius: The Journal of Federalism* 28 (Spring): 81–97.

Schapsmeier, Edward L., and Frederick H. Schapsmeier. 1985. *Dirksen of Illinois: Senatorial Statesman.* Urbana, IL: University of Illinois Press.

Scharpf, Fritz W. 1966. "Judicial Review and the Political Question: A Functional Analysis." *Yale Law Journal* 75 (March): 517–597.

Schechter, Stephen L. 2000. "Amending the Constitution: Current Proposals." *Insights on Law & Society* 1 (Fall): 11–13.

Scheef, Robert W. 2001. "'Public Citizens' and the Constitution: Bridging the Gap between Popular Sovereignty and Original Intent." *Fordham Law Review* 69 (April): 2201–2251.

Scheiber, Harry N. 1992. "Police Power." In *The Oxford Companion to the Supreme Court of the United States,* ed. Kermit L. Hall. New York: Oxford University Press.

Schlesinger, Arthur M., Jr. 1974. "On the Presidential Succession." *Political Science Quarterly* 89 (Fall): 475–505.

Schlickeisen, Rodger. 1994. "Protecting Biodiversity for Future Generations: An Argument for a Constitutional Amendment." *Tulane Environmental Law Journal* 8 (Winter): 181–221.

Schmidt, David D. 1989. *Citizen Law Makers: The Ballot Initiative Revolution.* Philadelphia: Temple University Press.

Schmidt, Peter. 2002. "Next Stop, Supreme Court? Appeals Court Upholds Affirmative Action at University of Michigan Law School." *Chronicle of Higher Education* 48 (24 May): A24–26.

Schneier, Edward V., and Bertram Gross. 1993. *Legislative Strategy.* New York: St. Martin's Press.

Schotten, Peter, and Dennis Stevens. 1996. *Religion, Politics, and the Law: Commentaries and Controversies.* Belmont, CA: Wadsworth.

Schouler, James. 1908. "A New Federal Constitution." In *Ideals of the Republic,* ed. James Schouler. Boston: Little, Brown.

Schrader, George D. 1970. "Constitutional History of the Income Tax." *Georgia State Bar Journal* 7 (August): 39–55.

Schrag, Philip G. 1985. *Behind the Scenes: The Politics of a Constitutional Convention.* Washington, DC: Georgetown University Press.

Schubert, Glendon. 1954. "Politics and the Constitution: The Bricker Amendment during 1953." *Journal of Politics* 16 (May): 257–298.

Schuck, Peter H., and Rogers M. Smith. 1985. *Citizenship without Consent: Illegal Aliens in the American Polity.* New Haven, CT: Yale University Press.

Schwartz, Bernard. 1992. *The Great Rights of Mankind: A History of the American Bill of Rights.* Madison, WI: Madison House.

———. 1988. *Super Chief: Earl Warren and His Supreme Court—A Judicial Biography.* New York: New York University Press.

———. 1986. *Swann's Way: The School Busing Case and the Supreme Court.* New York: Oxford University Press.

Schwartz, Bernard, ed. 1980. *The Roots of the Bill of Rights.* 5 vols. New York: Chelsea House.

Scigliano, Robert. 1994. "The Two Executives: The President and the Supreme Court." In *The American Experiment: Essays on the Theory and Practice of Liberty,* ed. Peter A. Lawler and Robert M. Schoefar. Lanham, MD: Rowman and Littlefield.

Scott, Rodney. 1999. *The Great Debate: The Need for Constitutional Reform.* Chicago: Rampant Lion Press.

"Second Amendment Symposium." 1995. *Tennessee Law Review* 62 (Spring): 443–821.

Seelye, Katharine Q. 1995. "Congress Members off Hook on Re-election, but Not Issue." *New York Times,* 23 May, A-1, A-11.

Seitz, Don C. 1929. *Famous American Duels: With Some Account of the Causes That Led up to Them and the Men Engaged.* Reprint, Freeport, NY: Books for Libraries Press, 1966.

Senese, Donald J. 1989. *George Mason and the Legacy of Constitutional Liberty: An Examination of the Influence of George Mason on the American Bill of Rights.* Fairfax County, VA: Fairfax County Historical Commission.

Shalom, Stephen R. 1981. *The United States and the Philippines: A Study of Neocolonialism.* Philadelphia: Institute for the Study of Human Issues.

Shand-Tucci, Douglass. 1995. *Ralph Adams Cram: Life and Architecture.* Vol. 1. Amherst, MA: University of Massachusetts Press.

———. 1975. *Ralph Adams Cram: American Medievalist.* Boston: Boston Public Library.

Shannon, David A. 1967. *The Socialist Party of America: A History.* Chicago: Quadrangle Books.

Shermer, Matt. 1969. *"The Sense of the People" or the Next Development in American Democracy.* New York: American Referendum Association.

Sidak, J. Gregory. 1995. "The Line-Item Veto

Amendment." *Cornell Law Review* 80 (July): 1498–1505.

———. 1989. "The Recommendation Clause." *Georgetown Law Journal* 77 (August): 2070–2135.

Siegel, Reva B. 2002. "She the People: The Nineteenth Amendment, Sex Equality, Federalism, and the Family." *Harvard Law Review* 115 (February): 947–1046.

———. 2001. "Gender and the Constitution From a Social Movement Perspective." *University of Pennsylvania Law Review* 150 (November): 297–351.

Sigler, Jay A. 1969. *Double Jeopardy: The Development of a Legal and Social Policy.* Ithaca, NY: Cornell University Press.

Sigmund, Paul E. 1971. *Natural Law in Political Thought.* Cambridge, MA: Winthrop Publishers.

Silva, Edward J. 1970. "State Cohorts and Amendment Clusters in the Process of Federal Constitutional Amendments in the United States, 1869–1931." *Law and Society Review* 4 (February): 445–466.

Silversmith, Jol A. 1999. "The 'Missing Thirteenth Amendment': Constitutional Nonsense and Titles of Nobility." *Southern California Interdisciplinary Law Journal* 8 (Spring): 577–611.

Sisk, Gregory C. 2002. "Suspending the Pardon Power during the Twilight of a Presidential Term." *Missouri Law Review* 67 (Winter): 13–27.

Skillen, James W., ed. 1993. *The School Choice Controversy: What Is Constitutional?* Grand Rapids, MI: Baker Books.

Smith, Goldwin. 1906. "Chief Justice Clark on the Defects of the American Constitution." *North American Review* 183 (1 November): 845–851.

———. 1898. "Is the Constitution Outworn?" *North American Review* 166 (March): 257–267.

Smith, Jean Edward. 1996. *John Marshall: Definer of a Nation.* New York: Henry Holt and Company.

Smith, Page. 1995. *Democracy on Trial: The Japanese American Evacuation and Relocation in World War II.* New York: Simon and Schuster.

Smith, Rodney K. 1987. *Public Prayer and the Constitution: A Case Study in Constitutional Interpretation.* Wilmington, DE: Scholarly Resources.

Smith, Steven. 1989. "Taking It to the Floor." In *Congress Reconsidered,* ed. Lawrence C. Dodd and Bruce I. Oppenheimer. Washington, DC: Congressional Quarterly.

Solberg, Winton, ed. 1958. *The Federal Convention and the Formation of the Union.* Indianapolis, IN: Bobbs-Merrill.

Soller, Christopher J. 1995. "Newtonian Government: Is the Contract with America Unconstitu-

tional?" *Duquesne Law Review* 33 (Summer): 959–984.

Sorauf, Frank J. 1988. *Money in American Elections.* Glenview, IL: Scott, Foresman.

Spitzer, Robert J. 1995. *The Politics of Gun Control.* Chatham, NJ: Chatham House Publishers.

———. 1988. *The Presidential Veto: Touchstone of the American Presidency.* Albany, NY: State University of New York Press.

Spotts, JoAnne D. 1994. "The Twenty-seventh Amendment: A Late Bloomer or a Dead Horse?" *Georgia State University Law Review* 10 (January): 337–365.

Stanwood, Edward. 1903. *American Tariff Controversies in the Nineteenth Century.* 2 vols. Reprint, New York: Russell and Russell, 1967.

Stathis, Stephen. 1990. "The Twenty-second Amendment: A Practical Remedy or Partisan Maneuver?" *Constitutional Commentary* 7 (Winter): 61–88.

Steamer, Robert J. 1992. "Commerce Power." In *The Oxford Companion to the Supreme Court of the United States,* ed. Kermit L. Hall. New York: Oxford University Press.

Stern, Madeline B., ed. 1974. *The Victoria Woodhull Reader.* Weston, MA: M & S Press.

Stevens, Doris. 1995. *Jailed for Freedom: American Women Win the Vote.* Troutdale, OR: New Sage.

Stickney, Albert. 1879. *A True Republic.* New York: Harper and Brothers.

Stone, Geoffrey R., Richard A. Epstein, and Cass R. Sunstein, eds. 1992. *The Bill of Rights in the Modern State.* Chicago: University of Chicago Press.

Stoner, James R., Jr. 1995. "Amending the School Prayer Amendment." *First Things* 51 (May): 16–18.

Storing, Herbert, ed. 1981. *The Complete Anti-Federalist.* 7 vols. Chicago: University of Chicago Press.

———, ed. 1970. *What Country Have I? Political Writings by Black Americans.* New York: St. Martin's Press.

Story, Joseph. 1987. *Commentaries on the Constitution of the United States.* Durham, NC: Carolina Academic Press.

———. 1833. *Commentaries on the Constitution of the United States.* Boston: Hilliard, Gray. Reprint, New York: Da Capo Press, 1970.

Stowe, Steven M. 1987. *Intimacy and Power in the Old South: Ritual in the Lives of the Planters.* Baltimore, MD: Johns Hopkins University Press.

Strauss, David A. 2001. "Commentary: The Irrelevance of Constitutional Amendments." *Harvard Law Review* 114 (March): 1457–1505.

Strickland, Ruth A. 1993. "The Twenty-seventh Amendment and Constitutional Change by

Stealth." *P.S. Political Science and Politics* 26 (December): 716–722.

———. 1989. *The Ratification Process of U.S. Constitutional Amendments: Each State Having One Vote as a Form of Malapportionment.* Ph.D. dissertation, University of South Carolina.

Strittmatter, Bill. n.d. "A Christian Constitution and Civil Law for the Kingdom of Heaven on Earth." Lakemore, OH: 28 pp.

Struble, Robert, Jr. "Redeeming U.S. Democracy." *http://temnet.com/~rusd.* Accessed 11 July 1997. No longer available on the Internet.

Sturm, Albert L., and Janice May. 1982. "State Constitutions and Constitutional Revision: 1980–81 and the Past 50 Years." In *The Book of the States: 1982–1983.* Lexington, KY: Council of State Governments.

Suber, Peter. 1990. *The Paradox of Self-Amendment: A Study of Logic, Law, Omnipotence, and Change.* New York: Peter Lang.

———. 1987. "Population Changes and Constitutional Amendments: Federalism versus Democracy." *Journal of Law Reform* 20 (Winter): 409–490.

Sullivan, J. W. 1893. *Direct Legislation by the Citizenship.* New York: Nationalist Publishing Company.

Sullivan, Kathleen M. 1995. "Constitutional Constancy: Why Congress Should Cure Itself of Amendment Fever." *Record of the Bar of the City of New York* 50 (November): 724–735.

Sundquist, James L. 1986. *Constitutional Reform and Effective Government.* Washington, DC: Brookings Institution.

Suthon, Walter J., Jr. 1953. "The Dubious Origin of the Fourteenth Amendment." *Tulane Law Review* 28: 22–44.

Swanson, Wayne R. 1990. *The Christ Child Goes to Court.* Philadelphia: Temple University Press.

Swindler, William. 1963. "The Current Challenge to Federalism: The Confederating Proposals." *Georgetown Law Review* 52 (Fall): 1–41.

"Symposium: A Religious Equality Amendment?" 1996. *Brigham Young University Law Review* 1996: 561–688.

"Symposium on the Reuss Resolution: A Vote of No Confidence in the President." 1975. *George Washington Law Review* 43 (January): 328–500.

Taft, Henry. 1930. "Amendment of the Federal Constitution: Is the Power Conferred by Article V Limited by the Tenth Amendment?" *Virginia Law Review* 16 (May): 647–658.

Tananbaum, Duane. 1988. *The Bricker Amendment Controversy: A Test of Eisenhower's Political Leadership.* Ithaca, NY: Cornell University Press.

Tansill, Charles C. 1926. *Proposed Amendments of the Constitution of the United States Introduced in Congress from December 4, 1889, to July 2, 1926.* Washington, DC: U.S. Government Printing Office.

Tarr, G. Alan. 1994. *Judicial Process and Judicial Policymaking.* St. Paul, MN: West.

Tatalovich, Raymond. 1995. *Nativism Reborn? The Official English Language Movement and the American States.* Lexington, KY: University Press of Kentucky.

Taylor, A. Elizabeth. 1957. *The Woman Suffrage Movement in Tennessee.* New York: Bookman Associates.

Taylor, Andrew. 1997. "Senate Again One Vote Short: GOP Says House Will Act." *Congressional Quarterly* 55 (8 March): 577–578.

———. 1996a. "Congress Hands Presidency a Budgetary Scalpel." *Congressional Quarterly Weekly Report* 54 (30 March): 864–867.

———. 1996b. "Republicans Break Logjam on Line-Item Veto Bill." *Congressional Quarterly Weekly Report* 54 (16 March): 687.

Taylor, George R., ed. 1993. *The Great Tariff Debate, 1820–1830.* Boston: D. C. Heath.

Taylor, Joe Gray. 1976. *Louisiana: A Bicentennial History.* New York: W. W. Norton.

Taylor, Stuart, Jr. 2000. "Victims' Rights: Leave the Constitution Alone." *National Journal* 32 (22 April): 1254.

TenBroek, Jacobus. 1951. *The Antislavery Origins of the Fourteenth Amendment.* Berkeley, CA: University of California Press.

"Text of Amendment." 1995. *Congressional Quarterly Weekly Report* 53 (4 March): 673.

Thierer, Adam D. 1999. "The Bliley 'States' Initiative': Empowering States and Protecting Federalism." 2 March. No. 576. The Heritage Foundation Executive Memorandum.

"33 States Ask Congress for Constitutional Convention." 1969. *Congressional Quarterly Weekly Report* 27 (1 August): 1372–1373.

Thomas, Chantal. 2000. "Constitutional Change and International Government." *Hastings Law Journal* 52 (November): 1–46.

Thorpe, Francis N. 1909. *The Federal and State Constitutions, Colonial Charters and Other Organic Laws of the States, Territories, and Colonies Now or Heretofore Forming the United States of America.* 7 vols. Washington, DC: U.S. Government Printing Office.

Tiedeman, Christopher G. 1890. *The Unwritten Constitution of the United States.* New York: G. P. Putnam's Sons.

Timberlake, James H. 1970. *Prohibition and the Progressive Movement, 1900–1920.* New York: Atheneum.

Tocqueville, Alexis de. 1835, 1840. *Democracy in America*. 2 vols. Reprint, ed. J. P. Mayer. Garden City, NY: Anchor Books, 1969.

Toffler, Alvin, and Heidi Toffler. 1995. *Creating a New Civilization: The Politics of the Third Wave*. Atlanta: Turner Publishing.

Tolchin, Mark. 1990. "Fifteen States Rally behind Calls for Amendment to Gain More Powers." *New York Times*, 26 June, A-12, col. 3–6.

Tomlins, Christopher L. 1985. *The State and the Unions: Labor Relations, Law, and the Organized Labor Movement in America, 1880–1960*. Cambridge, UK: Cambridge University Press.

Toner, Robin. 1995. "Flag Burning Amendment Fails in Senate, but Margin Narrows." *New York Times*, 13 December, 1.

Tonn, Bruce E. 1996. "A Design for Future-Oriented Government." *Futures* 28 (June): 413–431.

———. 1991. "The Court of Generations: A Proposed Amendment to the U.S. Constitution." *Futures* 21: 482–498.

Toole, James F., Robert J. Joynt, and Arthur S. Link, eds. 2001. *Presidential Disability: Papers, Discussions, and Recommendations on the Twenty-Fifth Amendment and Issues of Inability and Disability among Presidents*. Rochester, NY: University of Rochester,

Torke, James W. 1994. "Assessing the Ackerman and Amar Theses: Notes on Extratextual Constitutional Change." *Widener Journal of Public Law* 4: 229–271.

Trattner, Walter I. 1970. *Crusade for the Children: A History of the National Child Labor Committee and Child Labor Reform in America*. Chicago: Quadrangle Books.

Traynor, Roger J. 1927. *The Amending System of the United States Constitution, a Historical and Legal Analysis*. Ph.D. dissertation, University of California.

Tribe, Laurence H. 1990. *Abortion: The Clash of Absolutes*. New York: W. W. Norton.

———. 1983. "A *Constitution* We Are Amending: In Defense of a Restrained Judicial Role." *Harvard Law Review* 97 (December): 433–445.

Tribe, Laurence H., and Michael C. Dorf. 1991. *On Reading the Constitution*. Cambridge, MA: Harvard University Press.

Tugwell, Rexford. 1974. *The Emerging Constitution*. New York: Harper and Row.

Tuller, Walter K. 1911. "A Convention to Amend the Constitution—Why Needed—How It May Be Obtained." *North American Review* 193: 369–387.

Turner, John J., Jr. 1973. "The Twelfth Amendment and the First American Party System." *Historian* 35: 221–237.

Tushnet, Mark. 1990. "The Flag-Burning Episode: An Essay on the Constitution." *University of Colorado Law Review* 61: 39–53.

Twelve Southerners. 1930. *I'll Take My Stand: The South and the Agrarian Tradition*. Introduction by Louis D. Rubin Jr. Reprint, Baton Rouge, LA: Louisiana State University Press, 1977.

Twentieth Century Fund Task Force on the Vice Presidency. 1988. *A Heartbeat Away*. New York: Printing Press Publications.

"The Twenty-fifth Amendment: Preparing for Presidental Disability." 1995. *Wake Forest Law Review* 30 (Fall): 427–648.

Unger, Sanford J. 1972. *The Paper and the Papers*. New York: E. P. Dutton.

Upham, Thomas C. 1941. *Total Democracy: A New Constitution for the United States. A Democratic Ideal for the World*. New York: Carlyle House.

Uradnik, Kathleen. 2002. *Student's Guide to Landmark Congressional Laws on Youth*. Westport, CT: Greenwood Press.

Urofsky, Melvin I. 1988. *A March of Liberty: A Constitutional History of the United States*. New York: Alfred A. Knopf.

U.S. Senate Committee on the Judiciary, *Proposing an Amendment to the Constitution of the United States Relative to Taxes on Incomes, Inheritance, and Gifts: Hearings on S.J. Res. 23*, 83rd Cong., 2d sess., 1954.

U.S. Senate Committee on the Judiciary, *Proposing an Amendment to the Constitution of the United States Relative to Taxes on Incomes, Inheritance, and Gifts: Hearings on S.J. Res. 23*, 84th Cong., 2d sess., 1956.

U.S. Senate Committee on the Judiciary, Subcommittee on Constitutional Amendments, *Lowering the Voting Age to 18*, 90th Cong., 2d sess., 14, 15, 16 May 1968.

U.S. Senate Committee on the Judiciary, Subcommittee on Constitutional Amendments, *Lowering the Voting Age to 18*, 91st Cong., 2d sess., 16, 17 February, 9, 10 March 1970.

U.S. Senate Committee on the Judiciary, Subcommittee on the Constitution, *Affirmative Action and Equal Protection: Hearings on S.J. 41*, 97th Cong., 1st sess., 11 May, 18 June, and 16 July 1981.

U.S. Senate Committee on the Judiciary, Subcommittee on the Constitution, *Amendments to the Constitution: A Brief Legislative History*. 1985. Washington, DC: U.S. Government Printing Office.

Utley, Robert L., Jr., and Patricia B. Gray. 1989. *Principles of the Constitutional Order: The Ratification Debates*. Lanham, MD: University Press of America.

Van Alstine, Michael P. 2002. "The Costs of Legal

Change." *UCLA Law Review* 49 (February): 789–870.

Van Alstyne, William. 1993. "What Do You Think About the Twenty-seventh Amendment?" *Constitutional Commentary* 10 (Winter): 9–18.

———. 1979. "The Limited Constitutional Convention—The Recurring Answer." *Duke Law Journal* 1979 (September): 985–1001.

———. 1978. "Does Article V Restrict the States to Calling Unlimited Conventions Only?—A Letter to a Colleague." *Duke Law Journal* 1978 (January): 1295–1306.

Van Burkleo, Sandra F. 1990. "No Rights but Human Rights." *Constitution* 2 (Spring-Summer): 4–19.

Van Deusen, Glyndon. 1937. *The Life of Henry Clay.* Boston: Little, Brown.

Van Doren, Carl. 1948. *The Great Rehearsal: The Story of the Making and Ratifying of the Constitution of the United States.* New York: Viking Press.

Van Riper, Paul P. 1958. *History of the United States Civil Service.* Evanston, IL: Row, Peterson.

Van Sickle, Bruce M., and Lynn M. Boughey. 1990. "Lawful and Peaceful Revolution: Article V and Congress' Present Duty to Call a Convention for Proposing Amendments." *Hamline Law Review* 14 (Fall): 1–115.

Vandercoy, David E. 1994. "The History of the Second Amendment." *Valparaiso University Law Review* 28 (Spring): 1007–1039.

Vanguard, Virginia. 1995. *The Populis: A Draft Constitution for a New Political Age.* Brentsville, VA: The Wingspread Enterprise.

Vergara, Vanessa B. M. 2000. "Comment: Abusive Mail-Order Bride Marriage and the Thirteenth Amendment." *Northwestern University Law Review* 94 (Summer): 1547–1599.

Vermeule, Adrian. 2001. "The Facts about Unwritten Constitutionalism: A Response to Professor Rubenfeld." *Duke Law Journal* 51 (October): 473–476.

Vidal, Gore. 1997. "Time for a People's Convention." *The Nation* 254 (27 January): 73.

Vierra, Norman. 1981. "The Equal Rights Amendment: Rescission, Extension and Justiciability." *Southern Illinois Law Journal* 1981: 1–29.

Vile, John R. 2003a. *Great American Judges: An Encyclopedia.* 2 vols. Santa Barbara: ABC-CLIO.

———. 2003b. "Proposals for a New Constitution: The Last Decade of the Twentieth Century." *Journal of Contemporary Thought.* Forthcoming in Vol. 13.

———. 2001a. *A Companion to the United States Constitution and Its Amendments.* 3d ed. Westport, CT: Praeger.

———. 2002. *Presidential Winners and Losers: Words of Victory and Concession.* Washington, DC: Congressional Quarterly.

———. 2001. *Great American Lawyers: An Encyclopedia.* 2 vols. Santa Barbara: ABC-CLIO.

———. 2000. "Up Close: Three Recent Amendments." *Insights on Law & Society* 1 (Fall): 8–11.

———. 1998a. "Francis Lieber and the Constitutional Amending Process." *The Review of Politics* 60 (Summer): 524–543.

———. 1998b. *The United States Constitution: Questions and Answers.* Westport, CT: Greenwood Press.

———. 1995. "The Case against Implicit Limits on the Constitutional Amending Process." In *Responding to Imperfection,* ed. Sanford Levinson. Princeton, NJ: Princeton University Press.

———. 1994a. *Constitutional Change in the United States: A Comparative Study of the Role of Constitutional Amendments, Judicial Interpretations, and Legislative and Executive Actions.* Westport, CT: Praeger.

———. 1994b. "The Selection and Tenure of Chief Justices." *Judicature* 78 (September-October): 96–100.

———. 1993a. *Contemporary Questions Surrounding the Constitutional Amending Process.* Westport, CT: Praeger.

———. 1993b. *The Theory and Practice of Constitutional Change in America: A Collection of Original Source Materials.* New York: Peter Lang.

———. 1993c. "Three Kinds of Constitutional Founding and Change: The Convention Model and Its Alternatives." *Political Research Quarterly* 46: 881–895.

———. 1992. *The Constitutional Amending Process in American Political Thought.* New York: Praeger.

———. 1991a. "Just Say No to 'Stealth' Amendment." *National Law Journal* 14 (22 June): 15–16.

———. 1991b. "Proposals to Amend the Bill of Rights: Are Fundamental Rights in Jeopardy?" *Judicature* 75 (August-September): 62–67.

———. 1991c. *Rewriting the United States Constitution: An Examination of Proposals from Reconstruction to the Present.* New York: Praeger.

———. 1990–1991. "Legally Amending the United States Constitution: The Exclusivity of Article V's Mechanisms." *Cumberland Law Review* 21: 271–307.

———. 1990. "Permitting States to Rescind Ratifications of Pending Amendments to the U.S. Constitution." *Publius: The Journal of Federalism* 20 (Spring): 109–122.

———. 1989. "How a Constitutional Amendment Protecting the Flag Might Widen Protection of

Symbolic Expression." *Louisiana Bar Journal* 37 (October): 169–172.

———. 1985. "Limitations on the Constitutional Amending Process." *Constitutional Commentary* 2 (Summer): 373–388.

———. 1980. "The Supreme Court and the Amending Process." *Georgia Political Science Association Journal* 8 (Fall): 33–66.

Vile, John R., and Mario Perez-Reilly. 1991. "The U.S. Constitution and Judicial Qualifications: A Curious Omission." *Judicature* 74 (December-January): 198–202.

Vile, John R., ed. 2002. *Proposed Amendments to the U.S. Constitution, 1787–2001.* 3 Vols. Union, NJ: Law Book Exchange.

Virginia Commission on Constitutional Government. 1967. *The Reconstruction Amendments Debates.* Richmond, VA: Virginia Commission on Constitutional Government.

Volcansek, Mary L. 1993. *Judicial Impeachment: None Called for Justice.* Urbana, IL: University of Illinois Press.

Voorhis, Jerry. 1947. *Confessions of a Congressman.* Reprint, Westport, CT: Greenwood Press, 1970.

Vorenberg, Michael. 2001. *Final Freedom: The Civil War, the Abolition of Slavery, and the Thirteenth Amendment.* Cambridge, UK: Cambridge University Press.

———. 2000. "Bringing the Constitution Back In: Amendment, Innovation, and Popular Democracy during the Civil War Era." Paper presented at the "Democracy in America" Conference, M.I.T., Cambridge, Massacnusetts, September 21–23.

Vose, Clement E. 1979. "When District of Columbia Representation Collides with the Constitutional Amendment Institution." *Publius: The Journal of Federalism* 9 (Winter): 105–125.

———. 1972. *Constitutional Change: Amendment Politics and Supreme Court Litigation since 1900.* Lexington, MA: D. C. Heath.

Wade, Edwin. 1995. *Constitution 2000: A Federalist Proposal for the Next Century.* Chicago: Let's Talk Sense.

Walker, David M. 1980. *The Oxford Companion to Law.* Oxford, UK: Clarenden Press.

Wallace, William Kay. 1932. *Our Obsolete Constitution.* New York: John Day.

Walroff, Jonathan L. 1985. "The Unconstitutionality of Voter Initiative Applications for Federal Constitutional Conventions." *Colorado Law Review* 85: 1525–1545.

Walsh, Edward. 2002. "U.S. Argues for Wider Gun Rights: Supreme Court Filing Reverses Past Policy," *Washington Post,* 8 May, A01.

Watson, Gregory. 2000. "I Have a Better Way." *Insights on Law & Society* 1 (Fall): 16.

Watson, Richard A. 1985. *Promise and Performance of American Democracy.* 5th ed. New York: John Wiley & Sons.

Weber, Paul. 1989. "Madison's Opposition to a Second Convention." *Polity* 20 (Spring): 498–517.

Weber, Paul J., and Barbara A. Perry. 1989. *Unfounded Fears: Myths and Realities of a Constitutional Convention.* New York: Praeger.

Wedgwood, William B. 1861. *The Reconstruction of the Government of the United States of America: A Democratic Empire Advocated and an Imperial Constitution Proposed.* New York: John H. Tingley.

Weeks, Kent M. 1971. *Adam Clayton Powell and the Supreme Court.* New York: Dunellen.

Weiser, Philip J. 1993. "Ackerman's Proposal for Popular Constitutional Lawmaking: Can It Realize His Aspirations for Dualist Democracy?" *New York University Law Review* 68 (October): 907–959.

Welch, Susan, et al. 1993. *Understanding American Government.* 2d ed. Minneapolis–St. Paul, MN: West.

Wenner, Lettie M. 1982. *The Environmental Decade in Court.* Bloomington, IN: Indiana University Press.

Westin, Alan. 1990. *The Anatomy of a Constitutional Law Case:* Youngstown Sheet & Tube Co. v. Sawyer; *the Steel Seizure Decision.* New York: Columbia University Press.

Wheeler, Marjorie S. 1993. *New Women of the New South: The Leaders of the Woman Suffrage Movement in the Southern States.* New York: Oxford University Press.

Wheeler, Marjorie S., ed. 1995a. *One Woman, One Vote: Rediscovering the Woman Suffrage Movement.* Troutdale, OR: New Sage.

———. 1995b. *Votes for Women! The Woman Suffrage Movement in Tennessee, the South, and the Nation.* Knoxville, TN: University of Tennessee Press.

Whitaker, L. Paige. 1992. *The Constitutionality of States Limiting Congressional Terms.* Washington, DC: Congressional Research Service, Library of Congress.

White, G. Edward. 2000. *The Constitution and the New Deal.* Cambridge, MA: Harvard University Press.

———. 1991. *The Marshall Court and Cultural Change 1815–1835.* New York: Oxford University Press.

White, Welsh S. 1991. *The Death Penalty in the Nineties: An Examination of the Modern System of Capital Punishment.* Ann Arbor, MI: University of Michigan Press.

Whitehead, John W. 2002. "Forefeiting 'Enduring Freedom' for 'Homeland Security': A Constitutional Analysis of the USA Patriot Act and the Justice Department's Anti-Terrorism Initiatives." *American University Law Review* 51 (August): 1081–1133.

Whitman, Alden, ed. 1985. *American Reformers.* New York: H. W. Wilson.

Whittington, Keith E. 1999. *Constitutional Construction: Divided Powers and Constitutional Meaning.* Cambridge, MA: Harvard University Press.

Wiecek, William. 1992. "Subversion." In *The Oxford Companion to the Supreme Court of the United States,* ed. Kermit L. Hall. New York: Oxford University Press.

———. 1977. *The Sources of Antislavery Constitutionalism in America, 1760–1848.* Ithaca, NY: Cornell University Press.

———. 1972. *The Guarantee Clause of the U.S. Constitution.* Ithaca, NY: Cornell University Press.

Wiggins, Charles. 1973. "A Constitutional Amendment Concerning Information Proceedings and Grand Jury Indictments." *Congressional Record.* 93rd Cong. 1st sess., 1973, Vol. 119, pt. 25: 32911–32912.

Wilcox, Clyde. 1995. *The Latest American Revolution? The 1994 Elections and Their Implications for Governance.* New York: St. Martin's Press.

Wilkinson, J. Harvie, III. 1979. *From* Brown *to* Bakke: *The Supreme Court and School Integration: 1954–1978.* New York: Oxford University Press.

Willard, John Ware. 1968. *Simon Willard and His Clocks.* New York: Dover Publications, Inc., Unabridged and corrected version of 1911, *A History of Simon Willard, Invention and Clockmaker.*

Willard, Simon, Jr., 1815. *The Columbian Union, Containing General and Particular Explanations of Government, and the Columbian Constitution, Being an Amendment to the Constitution of the United States: Providing a Yearly Revenue to Government of About Forty Millions of Dollars, and the Inevitable Union of the People by a Rule of Voting, and Exemption from Unnecessary Taxation, Consequently Their Permanent and Perpetual Freedom.* Albany, NY: printed for the author.

Williams, T. Harry. 1970. *Huey Long.* New York: Alfred A. Knopf.

Willis, Clyde E. 2002. *Student's Guide to Landmark Congressional Laws on the First Amendment.* Westport, CT: Greenwood Press.

Willis, Paul G., and George L. Willis. 1952. "The Politics of the Twenty-second Amendment." *Western Political Quarterly* 5 (September): 469–482.

Wills, Garry. 1981. *Explaining America: The Federalist.* Garden City, NY: Doubleday.

———. 1978. *Inventing America: Jefferson's Declaration of Independence.* New York: Doubleday.

Wilson, James G. 1992. "American Constitutional Conventions: The Judicially Unenforceable Rules That Combine with Judicial Doctrine and Public Opinion to Regulate Political Behavior." *Buffalo Law Review* 40 (Fall): 645–738.

Wilson, (Thomas) Woodrow. 1908. *Constitutional Government in the United States.* Reprint, New York: Columbia University Press, 1961.

———. 1885. *Congressional Government: A Study in American Politics.* Boston: Houghton Mifflin.

———. 1882. "Government by Debate: Being a Short View of Our National Government as It Is and as It Might Be." In *The Papers of Woodrow Wilson,* Vol. 2, ed. Arthur S. Link. Reprint, Princeton, NJ: Princeton University Press, 1967.

———. 1879. *Cabinet Government in the United States.* In *The Papers of Woodrow Wilson,* Vol. 1, ed. Arthur S. Link. Reprint, Princeton, NJ: Princeton University Press, 1966.

Wirenius, John F. 1994. "The Road to *Brandenburg:* A Look at the Evolving Understanding of the First Amendment." *Drake Law Review* 43: 1–49.

Wolfe, Christopher. 1991. *Judicial Activism: Bulwark of Freedom or Precarious Security?* Pacific Grove, CA: Brooks/Cole.

Wood, Charles. 1999. "Losing Control of America's Future: The Census, Birthright Citizenship, and Illegal Aliens." *Harvard Journal of Law and Public Policy* 22 (Spring): 465–522.

Wood, Gordon S. 1969. *The Creation of the American Republic, 1776–1787.* New York: W. W. Norton.

Wood, Stephen B. 1968. *Constitutional Politics in the Progressive Era: Child Labor and the Law.* Chicago: University of Chicago Press.

Woodward, Augustus B. 1825. *The Presidency of the United States.* New York: J. & J. Harper.

Wright, Benjamin F. 1938. *The Contract Clause of the Constitution.* Cambridge, MA: Harvard University Press.

Wright, R. George. 1991. "Could a Constitutional Amendment Be Unconstitutional?" *Loyola University of Chicago Law Review* 22: 741–764.

Wunder, John R. 1994. *"Retained by the People": A History of American Indians and the Bill of Rights.* New York: Oxford University Press.

Wyatt-Brown, Bertram. 1948. *Southern Honor: Ethics and Behavior in the Old South.* New York: Oxford University Press.

Yandle, Bruce. 1995. *Land Rights: The 1990s' Property Tax Rebellion.* Lanham, MD: Rowman & Littlefield.

Yarbrough, Tinsley E. 1988. *Mr. Justice Black and His Critics.* Durham, NC: Duke University Press.

Young, Donald. 1974. *American Roulette: The History and Dilemma of the Vice Presidency.* New York: Viking Press.

Zuckerman, Edward. 1984. *The Day after World War III.* New York: Viking Press.

LIST OF CASES

Ex parte Milligan, 71 U.S. 2 (1866)
Ex parte New York, 256 U.S. 490 (1921)
Ex parte Quirin, 317 U.S. 1 (1942)
Ex parte Young, 209 U.S. 123 (1908)
Fairchild v. Hughes, 258 U.S. 126 (1922)
Federal Maritime Commission v. South Carolina State Ports Authority, 535 U.S. 743 (2002)
Fletcher v. Peck, 10 U.S. (6 Cranch) 87 (1810)
Flint v. Stone Tracy Co., 220 U.S. 107 (1911)
44 Liquormart v. Rhode Island, 517 U.S. 484 (1996)
Frontiero v. Richardson, 411 U.S. 677 (1973)
Fujii v. California, 217 P.2d 481 (1950)
Furman v. Georgia, 408 U.S. 238 (1972)
Garcia v. San Antonio Metropolitan Transit Authority, 469 U.S. 528 (1985)
Gertz v. Robert Welch, Inc., 418 U.S. 323 (1974)
Gibbons v. Ogden, 22 U.S. 1 (1824)
Gideon v. Wainwright, 372 U.S. 335 (1963)
Gitlow v. New York, 268 U.S. 652 (1925)
Goesaert v. Cleary, 335 U.S. 464 (1948)
Goldberg v. Kelly, 397 U.S. 254 (1970)
Goldwater v. Carter, 444 U.S. 996 (1979)
Gomillion v. Lightfoot, 364 U.S. 339 (1960)
Gravel v. United States, 408 U.S. 606 (1972)
Graves v. New York ex rel. O'Keefe, 306 U.S. 466 (1939)
Gray v. Sanders, 372 U.S. 368 (1963)
Green v. United States, 355 U.S. 184 (1957)
Gregg v. Georgia, 428 U.S. 153 (1976)
Gregory v. Ashcroft, 501 U.S. 452 (1991)
Griffin v. California, 380 U.S. 609 (1965)
Griswold v. Connecticut, 381 U.S. 479 (1965)
Grutter v. Bollinger, 288 F.3d 732 (2002)
Guinn v. United States, 238 U.S. 347 (1915)
Gyuro v. Connecticut, 393 U.S. 937 (1968)
Halter v. Nebraska, 205 U.S. 34 (1907)
Hammer v. Dagenhart, 247 U.S. 251 (1918)
Haney v. United States, 122 S. Ct. 2362 (2002)
Hans v. Louisiana, 134 U.S. 1 (1890)
Harmelin v. Michigan, 501 U.S. 294 (1991)
Harper v. Virginia State Board of Elections, 383 U.S. 663 (1966)
Harris v. McRae, 448 U.S. 297 (1980)
Hawke v. Smith (I), 253 U.S. 221 (1920)
Hawke v. Smith (II), 253 U.S. 231 (1920)
Heart of Atlanta Motel v. United States, 379 U.S. 241 (1964)
Helvering v. Davis, 301 U.S. 619 (1937)
Hepburn v. Griswold, 75 U.S. 603 (1870)
Hirabayashi v. United States, 320 U.S. 81 (1943)
Holden v. Hardy, 169 U.S. 366 (1898)
Hollingsworth v. Virginia, 3 U.S. (3 Dall.) 379 (1798)
Home Building and Loan Association v. Blaisdell, 290 U.S. 398 (1934)

Hopwood v. Texas, 78 F.3d 932 (1996)
Humphrey's Executor v. United States, 295 U.S. 602 (1935)
Hurtado v. California, 110 U.S. 516 (1884)
Hutchinson v. Proxmire, 443 U.S. 111 (1979)
Hylton v. United States, 3 U.S. (3 Dall.) 171 (1796)
Idaho v. Freeman, 529 F. Supp. 1107 (1981)
Immigration and Naturalization Service v. Chadha, 462 U.S. 919 (1983)
Ives v. South Buffalo Railway Co., 201 N.Y. 271 (1911)
Jacobson v. Massachusetts, 197 U.S. 11 (1905)
Johnson v. Board of Regents of the University of Georgia, 263 F.3d 1234 (11th Cir. 2001)
Johnson v. Louisiana, 406 U.S. 356 (1972)
Jones v. Alfred H. Mayer Co., 392 U.S. 409 (1968)
Jones v. United States, 529 U.S. 848 (2000)
Katz v. United States, 389 U.S. 346 (1967)
Katzenbach v. McClung, 379 U.S. 294 (1964)
Katzenbach v. Morgan, 384 U.S. 641 (1966)
Kimble v. Swackhamer, 439 U.S. 385 (1978)
Kimel v. Florida Board of Regents, 528 U.S. 62 (2000)
Knox v. Lee, 79 U.S. 457 (1871)
Korematsu v. United States, 323 U.S. 214 (1944)
Lassiter v. North Hampton County Board of Elections, 360 U.S. 45 (1959)
Lau v. Nichols, 414 U.S. 563 (1974)
Lee v. Weisman, 505 U.S. 577 (1992)
Leisy v. Hardin, 135 U.S. 100 (1890)
Lemon v. Kurtzman, 403 U.S. 602 (1971)
Lemmon v. People, 20 N.Y. 562 (1860)
Leser v. Garnett, 258 U.S. 130 (1922)
Lincoln County v. Luning, 133 U.S. 529 (1890)
Livermore v. Waite, 102 Cal. 113 (1894)
Lochner v. New York, 198 U.S. 45 (1905)
Louisiana ex rel. Elliott v. Jamel, 107 U.S. 711 (1883)
Louisville Joint Stock Land Bank v. Radford, 295 U.S. 555 (1935)
Loving v. Virginia, 388 U.S. 1 (1967)
Luther v. Borden, 48 U.S. (7 How.) 1 (1849)
Lynch v. Donnelly, 465 U.S. 688 (1984)
Maher v. Roe, 432 U.S. 464 (1977)
Malloy v. Hogan, 378 U.S. 1 (1964)
Mapp v. Ohio, 367 U.S. 643 (1961)
Marbury v. Madison, 5 U.S. (1 Cranch.) 137 (1803)
Marsh v. Chambers, 463 U.S. 783 (1983)
Marston v. Lewis, 410 U.S. 679 (1973)
McCulloch v. Maryland, 17 U.S. (4 Wheat.) 316 (1819)
Meek v. Pittenger, 413 U.S. 349 (1973)
Meyer v. Nebraska, 262 U.S. 390 (1923)
Miller v. California, 413 U.S. 15 (1973)
Miller v. Johnson, 515 U.S. 900 (1995)
Milliken v. Bradley, 418 U.S. 717 (1974)

ligence Surveillance Court of Review. Decided November 18, 2002. *http://www.fas.org/irp/agency/doj/fisa/fiscr111802.html*. Accessed 11/29/02.

Second Employers' Liability Case, 223 U.S. 1 (1912)

Seminole Tribe v. Florida, 517 U.S. 44 (1996)

Shapiro v. Thompson, 394 U.S. 618 (1969)

Shaw v. Hunt, 517 U.S. 899 (1996)

Shaw v. Reno, 509 U.S. 630 (1993)

Skinner v. Railway Labor Executives' Ass'n, 489 U.S. 602 (1989)

Slaughterhouse Cases, 83 U.S. (16 Wall.) 36 (1873)

Smith v. Allwright, 321 U.S. 649 (1944)

Smith v. Goguen, 415 U.S. 566 (1974)

Smith v. Union Bank, 30 U.S. (5 Pet.) 518 (1831)

South Carolina v. Baker, 485 U.S. 505 (1988)

South Carolina v. Katzenbach, 383 U.S. 301 (1966)

South Dakota v. Dole, 483 U.S. 203 (1987)

Spence v. Washington, 418 U.S. 405 (1974)

Springer v. United States, 102 U.S. 586 (1881)

Steward Machine Co. v. Davis, 301 U.S. 548 (1937)

Stone v. Graham, 449 U.S. 41 (1980)

Stone v. Powell, 428 U.S. 465 (1976)

Street v. New York, 394 U.S. 576 (1969)

Stromberg v. California, 283 U.S. 359 (1931)

Sturges v. Crowinshield, 17 U.S. (4 Wheat.) 122 (1819)

Swann v. Charlotte-Mecklenburg Board of Education, 402 U.S. 1 (1971)

Terry v. Ohio, 392 U.S. 1 (1968)

Texas v. Johnson, 491 U.S. 397 (1989)

Texas v. White, 74 U.S. 700 (1869)

Tinker v. Des Moines Independent Community School District, 393 U.S. 503 (1969)

Trade Mark Cases, 100 U.S. 82 (1879)

Trinsey v. Pennsylvania, 766 F. Supp. 1338 (E.D. Pa 1991), *rev'd* 941 F. 2d 224 (3d Cir. 1991)

Trono v. United States, 199 U.S. 521 (1905)

Trop v. Dulles, 356 U.S. 86 (1958)

Troxel v. Granville, 530 U.S. 57 (2000)

Twining v. New Jersey, 211 U.S. 78 (1908)

U.S. Department of Commerce v. Montana, 503 U.S. 442 (1992)

U.S. Term Limits, Inc. v. Thornton, 514 U.S. 779 (1995)

United States v. Anthony, 24 F. Cas. 829 (N.D.N.Y. 1873)

United States v. Benson, 941 F.2d 598 (1991)

United States v. Brewster, 408 U.S. 501 (1972)

United States v. Butler, 297 U.S. 1 (1936)

United States v. California, 332 U.S. 19 (1947)

United States v. Carolene Products Co., 304 U.S. 144 (1938)

United States v. Classic, 313 U.S. 299 (1941)

United States v. Darby Lumber Co., 312 U.S. 100 (1941)

United States v. E.C. Knight Co., 156 U.S. 1 (1895)

United States v. Eichman, 496 U.S. 310 (1990)

United States v. Guest, 383 U.S. 745 (1966)

United States v. Leon, 468 U.S. 897 (1984)

United States v. Lopez, 514 U.S. 549 (1995)

United States v. McCullagh, 221 F. 228 (C.D. Kan. 1915)

United States v. Miller, 307 U.S. 174 (1939)

United States v. Morrison, 529 U.S. 598 (2000)

United States v. Nixon, 418 U.S. 683 (1974)

United States v. O'Brien, 391 U.S. 367 (1968)

United States v. Pink, 315 U.S. 204 (1942)

United States v. Price, 383 U.S. 787 (1966)

United States v. Robel, 389 U.S. 258 (1967)

United States v. Shauver, 214 F. 154 (E.D. Ark. 1914)

United States v. South-Eastern Underwriters Ass'n, 322 U.S. 533 (1944)

United States v. Sprague, 282 U.S. 716 (1931)

United States v. Virginia, 518 U.S. 515 (1996)

United States v. Will, 499 U.S. 200 (1980)

United States v. Wong Kim Ark, 169 U.S. 649 (1898)

Utah v. Evans, 122 S. Ct. 2191 (2002)

Vacco v. Quill, 521 U.S. 793 (1997)

Vernonia School District 47J v. Acton, 515 U.S. 646 (1995)

Wallace v. Jaffree, 472 U.S. 38 (1985)

Walter L. Nixon v. United States, 506 U.S. 224 (1993)

Washington v. Glucksberg, 521 U.S. 702 (1957)

Watkins v. United States, 354 U.S. 178 (1957)

Webster v. Reproductive Health Services, 492 U.S. 490 (1989)

Weeks v. United States, 232 U.S. 383 (1914)

Wesberry v. Sanders, 376 U.S. 1 (1964)

West Coast Hotel v. Parrish, 300 U.S. 379 (1937)

West Virginia State Board of Education v. Barnette, 319 U.S. 624 (1943)

Wickard v. Filburn, 317 U.S. 111 (1942)

Wiener v. United States, 357 U.S. 349 (1958)

Williams v. Florida, 399 U.S. 78 (1970)

Wisconsin v. Yoder, 406 U.S. 205 (1972)

Witters v. Catalina Foothills School District, 474 U.S. 481 (1993)

Witters v. Washington Department of Services for the Blind, 474 U.S. 481 (1986)

Woodson v. North Carolina, 428 U.S. 280 (1976)

Worcester v. Georgia, 31 U.S. (6 Pet.) 515 (1832)

Yakus v. United States, 321 U.S. 414 (1944)

Youngstown Sheet & Tube Co. v. Sawyer, 343 U.S. 579 (1952)

Zablocki v. Redhail, 434 U.S. 374 (1978)

Zelman v. Simmons-Harris, 122 S. Ct. 2460 (2002)

Zobrest v. Catalina Foothills School District, 509 U.S. 1 (1993)

❖ INDEX ❖

Douglas, William O., *continued*
elections, opinion regarding, 336
incorporation, dissenting opinion regarding, 6
poll tax, opinions regarding, 221
as potential Roosevelt running mate, 259
prayer in public schools, concurring opinion regarding, 172
privacy, opinions regarding right to, 196, 207, 214, 328, 365, 449
ratification, opinion regarding, 61
retirement of, 261
Warren Court, member of, 510
Douglass, Frederick, 2–3, 19, **145–147**, 211, 401
Dow, David R., 14
Downsizing the U.S.A., 322–323, 467
Drake, Charles, 145
Dred Scott decision. *See Scott v. Sandford*
Drinan, Robert, 86
Du Pont, Pierre, 472
Dual citizenship, **73**
DuBois, W. E. B., 317
Due process, 190–191. *See also* Substantive due process
Dueling, **147**
Duncan v. Louisiana, 263
Dunn v. Blumstein, 503
Durst, Jack, **147–150**
Duties. *See* Tariffs
Dyer v. Blair, **150–151**, 179, 235, 349, 374

Eagle Forum, 178, 393–394
Eagleton, Thomas, 360, 388
Eastland, James O., 262, 430, 474
Eberharter, Herman, 443
Economic Growth and Tax Relief Reconciliation Act of 2001, 442
Edmonds, George Washington, 459
Edmunds Bill of 1874, 296
Education
Brown v. Board of Education, 53–54. *See also Brown v. Board of Education*
busing, **394–395**

national university, establishment of, **153**
parochial schools, aid to, 340
prayer in schools. *See* Prayer in public schools
right to, **153–154**
schools, public, **395**
Edwards, Mickey, 70
Eighteenth Amendment, xxix, **154–156**, 231
concurrent powers enforcing, 83
democracy and, 136–137
Dirksen's support for repeal of, 139
effective date of, 238
enforcement clause of, 171–172
National Reform Association, support of, 65
as progressive amendment, 368
public opinion and, 371
ratification of, 222–223, 453
separation of powers and, 403
unintended consequences, example of, 423
validity of challenged, 106
War Time Prohibition Act and, 9
See also Anti-Saloon League; *National Prohibition Cases; Twenty-first Amendment; United States v. Sprague;* Women's Christian Temperance Union
Eighth Amendment, **156–157**, 229
capital punishment, implications for, 59
English Bill of Rights, influence of, 173
incorporation, exception to, 239
proposals for changing the, 20
selective incorporation and, 6
Eiselen, Malcolm R., **157–158**
Eisenhower, Dwight D.
health problems of, 470
line-item veto, advocacy of, 363
pardon issued by, 357
treaty-making power, opposition to limitations on, 52
Twenty-second Amendment,

impact on, 231, 476
Warren, appointment of, 510
Eldred v. Ashcroft, 341
Elections
campaign finance, 4–5, 57–58, 272–273
citizenship status and voting, 72
critical, **124–125**
dates of, **158**
disputed, **158–159**
early presidential, 465–466
the electoral college, 159–163, 464–466
Jackson's proposals for, 246
low turnouts at, 501
poll taxes, 221, 473–474. *See also* Twenty-fourth Amendment
primary, **159**
secret ballot, 501
single-member districts and the party system, 502
state legislative apportionment, 31–32, 140, 385–386, 428–429
voting age, 479–480. *See also* Twenty-sixth Amendment
voting rights, state establishment of, 136
See also Democracy; Fifteenth Amendment; Representation; Seventeenth Amendment; Twelfth Amendment; Voting rights
Electoral college
operation and alteration of, 464–466
Puerto Rico, representation for, **372**
reform of, **159–163**
See also Twelfth Amendment
Electronic Privacy Information Center, 206
Eleventh Amendment, xxviii, **164–165**, 229
democracy and, 136–137
federalism, impact on, 185
Hans v. Louisiana and interpretation of, 219–220
in Supreme Court decision-making, 64
judicial jurisdiction, limiting of, 255–256
separation of powers and, 403
See also Chisholm v. Georgia

ABOUT THE AUTHOR

Dr. John R. Vile is professor and chair of the Department of Political Science at Middle Tennessee State University. He has written and edited more than a dozen books including *Great American Lawyers: An Encyclopedia*. 2 vols. (2001); *A Companion to the United States Constitution and Its Amendments*. 3d ed. (2002); *Presidential Winners and Losers: Words of Victory and Concession* (2002); *Proposed Amendments to the U.S. Constitution, 1787–2002*. 3 vols. (2002); and *Great American Judges: An Encyclopedia*. 2 vols. (2003); as well as the first edition of the *Encyclopedia of Constitutional Amendments, Proposed Amendments, and Amending Issues* (1996). That work received a starred review in *The Library Journal,* and was selected by the *Journal*'s editors as one of the best reference books of 1996. The Reference and User's Association of the American Library Association listed it as one of the thirty best reference books of 1996. The *Law Library Journal* listed the first edition as one of the best legal reference books of the year, and the Society of School Librarians International selected it as an honor book in 7–12 Social Studies. This revised second edition builds on the edifice of the first edition, with over 100 new entries and rich new insights into existing entries. See About This Edition for a detailed discussion.